D1605522

Psychopathology

Psychopathology
History, Diagnosis, and Empirical Foundations

EDITED BY

W. EDWARD CRAIGHEAD

and

David J. Miklowitz
Linda W. Craighead

WILEY

JOHN WILEY & SONS, INC.

Library of Congress Cataloging-in-Publication Data:

Psychopathology: history, theory, and diagnosis for clinicians / edited by W. Edward Craighead, David J. Miklowitz, Linda W. Craighead.
    p.; cm.
Includes bibliographical references and index.
ISBN 978-0-471-76861-6 (cloth: alk. paper) 1. Psychology, Pathological. I. Craighead, W. Edward. II. Miklowitz, David Jay, 1957- III. Craighead, Linda W.
[DNLM: 1. Mental Disorders–diagnosis. 2. Mental Disorders–classification. 3. Mental Disorders–therapy. 4. Psychiatry–methods.
WM 141 P9749 2008]
  RC454. P7865 2008
  616.89'075–dc22   2007047636

Printed in the United States of America

10 9 8 7 6 5 4 3

Contributors

Jonathan S. Abramowitz, PhD
Department of Psychology
University of North Carolina at
  Chapel Hill
Chapel Hill, North Carolina

Martin M. Antony, PhD
Department of Psychology
Ryerson University
Toronto, Ontario

Joanna Arch
Department of Psychology
UCLA
Los Angeles, California

Eirikur O. Arnarson, PhD
Landspitali and University Hospital
Reykjavik, Iceland

W. Edward Craighead, PhD
Department of Psychology
Emory University
Atlanta, Georgia

Linda W. Craighead, PhD
Department of Psychology
Emory University
Atlanta, Georgia

Michelle G. Craske, PhD
Department of Psychology
UCLA
Los Angeles, California

Polina Eidelman
Department of Psychology
University of California
Berkeley, California

Brigette A. Erwin
Department of Psychology
Temple University
Philadelphia, Pennsylvania

Charles F. Gillespie, MD, PhD
Department of Psychiatry and Behavioral
  Sciences
Emory University School of Medicine
Atlanta, Georgia

Allison G. Harvey, PhD
Department of Psychology
University of California
Berkeley, California

Monika Hauser, PhD
Department of Psychology
University of Colorado
Boulder, Colorado

Richard G. Heimberg, PhD
Department of Psychology
Temple University
Philadelphia, Pennsylvania

Jill M. Hooley
Department of Psychology
Harvard University
Cambridge, Massachusetts

Kent E. Hutchison, PhD
Department of Psychology
University of New Mexico
Albuquerque, New Mexico

Sheri L. Johnson, PhD
Department of Psychology
University of Miami
Coral Gables, Florida

Nina Kirz, MD
Clinical Instructor
Stanford University School of Medicine
Stanford, California

Daniel N. Klein
Department of Psychology
Stony Brook University
Stony Brook, New York

Kristin Landfield
Department of Psychology
Emory University
Atlanta, Georgia

Deborah Roth Ledley
Department of Psychology
Temple University
Philadelphia, Pennsylvania

Scott O. Lilienfeld, PhD
Department of Psychology
Emory University
Atlanta, Georgia

James Lock, MD, PhD
Professor of Psychiatry and Behavioral
   Sciences
Stanford University School of Medicine
Stanford, California

Cindy M. Meston, PhD
Department of Psychology
University of Texas at Austin
Austin, Texas

David J. Miklowitz, PhD
Department of Psychology
University of Colorado
Boulder, Colorado

Vijay Mittal, MA
Department of Psychology
Emory University
Atlanta, Georgia

Candice M. Monson, PhD
National Center for PTSD
VA Boston Healthcare
Boston University
Boston, Massachusetts

Joseph P. Newman, PhD
Department of Psychology
University of Wisconsin-Madison
Madison, Wisconsin

Lara A. Ray, PhD
Center for Alcohol and Addiction Studies
Brown Medical School
Providence, Rhode Island

Alessandra Rellini, PhD
Department of Psychology
University of Texas at Austin
Austin, Texas

Patricia A. Resick, PhD
National Center for PTSD
VA Boston Healthcare
Boston University
Boston Massachusetts

Lorie A. Ritschel
Department of Psychiatry and Behavioral
   Sciences
Emory University School of Medicine
Atlanta, Georgia

Shireen L. Rizvi, PhD
New School for Social Research
New York, New York

Lucy T. Smith
Department of Psychology
University of Colorado
Boulder, Colorado

Karen Rowa, PhD
Department of Psychiatry and Behavioral
   Neurosciences
McMaster University
Hamilton, Ontario

Sarah St. Germain
Department of Psychology
Harvard University
Cambridge, Massachusetts

Lisa S. Talbot
Department of Psychology
University of California
Berkeley, California

Kevin Tessner, MA
Department of Psychology
Emory University
Atlanta, Georgia

Hanan Trotman, MA
Department of Psychology
Emory University
Atlanta, Georgia

Jennifer E. Vitale, PhD
Department of Psychology
Hampden-Sydney College
Hampden-Sydney, Virginia

Elaine Walker, PhD
Department of Psychology
Emory University
Atlanta, Georgia

Eric Youngstrom, PhD
Department of Psychology
University of North Carolina
Chapel Hill, North Carolina

Contents

Preface

This book provides a basic description and evaluation of clinical theory and research regarding psychopathology. It is intended primarily as an advanced text for psychopathology courses taught to graduate students in clinical, counseling, and school psychology, as well as neuroscience, psychiatry, and social work. Some instructors may find it appropriate for an upper level undergraduate course in abnormal psychology or psychopathology. It can also provide updated and refresher materials for mental health professionals engaged in assessment, diagnosis, and treatment of psychological disorders.

The book emerged from our many discussions regarding how best to provide reading materials for the graduate psychopathology course at the University of Colorado. From time to time different faculty members had been called upon to teach this course, and each time this occurred we had lengthy discussions about the most appropriate reading lists and books. In addition to the standard materials regarding psychopathology, we wanted to include clinically relevant materials that focused on vulnerability and stress, human development, affective neuroscience, translational research, empirically supported treatments, and efficacy and effectiveness outcomes. We faced repeated difficulties in assembling such materials and requesting readings from colleagues around the world. We concluded that it was an appropriate time to ask several of our colleagues who are clinical scientists to help us create a resource that would incorporate these current and critical areas of interest. We asked them to provide a broad range of information drawn from psychopathology and related basic research for each disorder, so the reader would have a comprehensive view of each of the topics in 30 to 40 pages.

Historical Perspective

Though the description of psychopathological disorders, at least on a nonscientific basis, has occurred for hundreds of years, the first modern attempts to classify behaviors, thoughts, biology, and feelings within a formal classification system are usually attributed to the prominent German psychiatrist, Emil Kraepelin, who did most of his work at the end of the nineteenth century. Psychology emerged as a discipline at about that same time, but was largely unconcerned with psychopathology, with the possible exception of learning disabilities and a few of the childhood disorders. Although it occurred half a century later, psychiatry (via the American Psychiatric Association) offered the first full-scale and systematic modern classification manual—the *Diagnostic and Statistical Manual of Mental Disorders*—in 1952. As Lilienfeld and Landfield note in the first chapter in this book, this manual has undergone extensive revisions and reorganizations over the past half-century. The fifth edition is currently being prepared.

In order to understand the slow development of psychology's role in the evolution of theories and research in psychopathology, it is important to have at least a glimpse of the history of professional developments within psychology. By the time of WWI (ca. 1914–1918), psychologists had emerged on mental health teams as professionals who primarily conducted formal clinical assessments. Psychologists' activities proliferated during WWI, though the emphasis remained on assessment. Psychologists focused primarily on intellectual assessment, but this focus shifted to include assessment of personality, largely in order to assess and predict what is now known as Posttraumatic Stress Disorder. Between WWI and WWII clinical psychology continued to emphasize the development of intelligence tests and assessment of intelligence, but the discipline also began in earnest to develop instruments and methods to assess personality. It was only during WWII and subsequent years that psychology began conducting psychotherapy, initially under the supervision of psychiatrists and only later, during the 1960–1970 era, as independent professionals. This movement toward broader involvement in clinical, counseling, and school intervention brought with it an interest in psychopathology as well as psychotherapy. A number of theoretical and practical developments (ranging from insurance reimbursement for clinical practice to National Institute of Health funding for research) contributed to fairly wide-scale acceptance of the *DSM* classification system, even though this framework has been associated with much controversy, as will be evident throughout this book.

During the preceding professional developments, it was psychiatry that first led most mental health teams in child hygiene clinics and community mental health centers. Psychologists became genuinely concerned with more broadly defined psychopathology and its assessment only as they became involved in the delivery of therapeutic services. The field of psychopathology has thus emerged over the past three to four decades to reflect advances in psychology, psychiatry, and neuroscience. There have been very few books since Maher's (1968) that have provided extensive, comprehensive, and scientifically based overviews of theories and empirical foundations of psychopathology at the graduate level. It is our hope that this tightly coordinated book will be a step toward filling that vacuum.

This book begins with a chapter that picks up where the preceding brief historical review leaves off. Lilienfeld and Landfield have presented an overview of the major issues that arise in the study of psychopathology at an advanced level. This chapter is followed by Youngstrom's advanced summary of the major issues associated with assessment of various forms of psychopathology. Both of these chapters are very timely and introduce the student or professional to the complex issues one encounters in studying psychopathology.

These introductory chapters are followed by overviews of most of the major clinical disorders. In order to assure consistency in the material presented in each chapter, we asked authors to follow a specific format, though some chapter topics and the associated research fit more easily within that format than others. The general outline for each chapter is as follows: (1) description of the disorder, including a brief history, a case example, and epidemiological findings; (2) empirical foundations of the disorder, including findings regarding neurobiology, behavioral, cognitive, and emotion factors; (3) assessment of the disorder, including interviews, self-reports, neurobiological assessment, and clinical rating scales; (4) a brief description and evaluation of current interventions for each disorder; and (5) a summary and future directions. We greatly appreciate the willingness of our authors to adhere to this suggested uniform outline. This approach improved our ability to provide consistent coverage across disorders, which makes this volume particularly suitable for coursework. It also makes it easier for readers to find the needed information if the volume is used as a reference or resource book.

Following a long tradition that dates back to Freud's view of the centrality of anxiety in psychopathology, the *DSM* anxiety disorders are presented first. The anxiety disorders include Generalized Anxiety Disorder (Rowa & Antony), Panic Disorder (Arch & Craske), Obsessive-Compulsive Disorder (Abramowitz), Social Anxiety Disorder. including Avoidant Personality Disorder (Ledley, Erwin, & Heimberg), and Posttraumatic Stress Disorder (Resick, Monson, & Rizvi). The book continues with three chapters related to the various mood disorders, including Major Depressive Disorder (W. E. Craighead, Ritschel, Arnarson, & Gillespie), Dysthymia and Chronic Depression (Klein), and bipolar disorders (Miklowitz & Johnson). The next chapter, by Walker, Mittal, Tessner, and Trotman provides a thorough discussion of Schizophrenia and the psychotic spectrum disorders. This is followed by two chapters regarding eating disorders: Bulimia Nervosa and binge eating (L. W. Craighead & Smith) and Anorexia Nervosa (Lock & Kirz). Alcohol use disorders, by Ray, Hutchison, and Hauser, sleep disorders, by Harvey, Eidelman, and Talbot, and sexual dysfunction, by Meston and Rellini comprise the next three chapters. The remainder of the book includes chapters on psychopathy (Vitale & Newman) and Borderline Personality Disorder (Hooley & St. Germain). As is apparent from the list, the authors were chosen because of their and their students' major contributions to our knowledge of psychopathology, which is apparent in the materials included in each chapter.

ACKNOWLEDGMENTS

A very large number of people have contributed to the development and publication of this book. First, we acknowledge our own mentors: Leonard Ullmann, Gordon Paul, Alan Kazdin, Carolyn Sherif, and Michael Goldstein are greatly appreciated. Colleagues, students, and friends who have contributed to our understanding of psychopathology, assessment, and interventions are just too numerous to mention, but they and we know who they are. We are especially appreciative to the Craighead and Miklowitz families for their support and caring while we completed this project. Specifically, we thank Ben, Wade, Margaret, and Daniel Craighead, and Mary Yaeger and Ariana Miklowitz.

We have been fortunate to have the assistance of our staff in the completion of this project. We would like to thank Beth Smith and Tara Dempsey at the University of Colorado, who were very helpful in the earlier phases of the planning of the book. Since the Craigheads moved to Emory University, Jennifer D. Moore has been responsible for coordinating the activities associated with completion of the book. She has kept the flow of materials between authors and editors on track, and she has coordinated our submissions of the manuscripts back and forth with Wiley.

We cannot imagine a better editor than Patricia Rossi at Wiley, who has been of great help from our very earliest conceptualization of this book. She has been involved in every phase of its production, and in this process we have come to appreciate her insights and professional expertise in every phase of the editing process. It is a pleasure to work with such a talented person and genuinely fine human being. We also appreciate the help of her assistant, Kathleen DeChants, and the other fine people at John Wiley & Sons, including Linda Witzling and Heather Dunphy.

Finally, we would like to express our gratitude to the authors of the various chapters in this book. Each chapter's author team includes at least one of the established international leaders studying the topic. Coauthors were carefully chosen in their areas of expertise. As planned, the chapters reflect not only the contributions of the authors but also detailed reviews of the larger literature pertinent to each disorder. Thus, the reader can enjoy the detailed review of the psychopathology of the disorder in each chapter as well as the interesting commentary and thoughts about future directions for research and clinical issues from the perspective of individuals who are intimately involved in ongoing clinical psychopathology research. Our hope is that this will inform readers and also stimulate the thinking of developing research investigators and students to inspire them to ask important questions regarding psychopathology. These outstanding scholars, in the composite, have done what no one individual (or even three) can do today—namely, provide a thorough and comprehensive summary of the current state of knowledge regarding psychopathology.

References

American Psychiatric Association. (1952). *Diagnostic and statistical manual of mental disorders* (1st ed.). Washington, D.C.: Author.

Maher, B. (1968). *Principles of psychopathology: An experimental approach*. New York: McGraw-Hill.

Chapter 1

Issues in Diagnosis: Categorical vs. Dimensional

Scott O. Lilienfeld and Kristin Landfield

Psychiatric diagnosis is fundamental to the understanding of mental illness. Without it, the study, assessment, and treatment of psychopathology would be in disarray. In this chapter, we examine: (1) the raison d'etre underlying psychiatric diagnosis; (2) widespread misconceptions regarding psychiatric diagnosis; (3) the present system of psychiatric diagnosis and its strengths and weaknesses; and (4) and fruitful directions for improving this system.

There are a myriad of forms of abnormality housed under the exceedingly broad umbrella of mental disorders. Indeed, the current psychiatric classification system contains well over 350 diagnoses (American Psychiatric Association [APA], (2000)). The enormous heterogeneity of psychopathology makes a formal system of organization imperative. Just as in the biological sciences where Linnaeus' hierarchical taxonomy categorizes fauna and flora and in chemistry where Mendeleev's periodic table orders the elements, a psychiatric classification system helps to organize the bewildering subforms of abnormality. Such a system, if effective, permits us to parse the variegated universe of psychological disorders into more homogeneous, and ideally more clinically meaningful, subtypes.

From the practitioner's initial inchoate impression that a patient's behavior is aberrant to later and better elaborated case conceptualization, diagnosis plays an integral role in the clinical process. Indeed, the essential reason for initiating assessment and treatment is often the observer's sense that "something is just not quite right" about that person. Meehl (1973) commented that the mental health professional's core task is to answer the question, "what does this person have, or what befell him, that makes him different

1

from those who have not developed clinical psychopathology" (p. 248). Therein lies the basis for psychiatric diagnosis.

General Terminological Issues

Before proceeding, a bit of terminology is in order. It's crucial at the outset to distinguish two frequently confused terms: classification and diagnosis. A system of *classification* is an overarching taxonomy of mental illness, whereas *diagnosis* is the act of placing an individual, based on a constellation of *signs* (observable indicators, like crying in a depressed patient), *symptoms* (subjective indicators, like feelings of guilt in a depressed patient), or both, into a category within that taxonomy. Classification is a prerequisite for diagnosis.

Another key set of terminological issues concerns the distinctions among *syndrome*, *disorder*, and *disease*. As Kazdin (1983) observed, we can differentiate among these three concepts based on our levels of understanding of their *pathology*—the physiological changes that may accompany the condition—and *etiology*, that is, causation (Gough, 1971; Lilienfeld, Waldman, & Israel, 1994).

At the lowest rung of the hierarchy of understanding lie *syndromes*, which are typically constellations of signs and symptoms that co-occur across individuals (syndrome means *running together* in Greek). In syndromes, neither pathology nor etiology is well understood, nor is their causal relation to other conditions established. Antisocial Personality Disorder is a relatively clear example of a syndrome because its signs (e.g., the use of alias) and symptoms (e.g., lack of remorse) tend to covary across individuals. Nevertheless, its pathology and etiology are largely unknown, and its causal relation to other conditions poorly understood (Lykken, 1995).

In rare cases, syndromes may also constitute groupings of signs and symptoms that exhibit minimal covariation across individuals but that point to an underlying etiology (Lilienfeld, Waldman, & Israel, 1994). For example, Gerstmann's syndrome in neurology (Benton, 1992) is marked by four major symptoms: agraphia (inability to write), acalculia (inability to perform mental computation), finger agnosia (inability to differentiate among fingers on the hand), and left-right disorientation. Although these symptoms are negligibly correlated across individuals in the general population, they co-occur dependably following certain instances of parietal lobe damage.

At the second rung of the hierarchy of understanding lie *disorders*, which are syndromes that cannot be readily explained by other conditions. For example, in the present diagnostic system, Obsessive-Compulsive Disorder (OCD) can be diagnosed only if its symptoms (e.g., recurrent fears of contamination) and signs (e.g., recurrent hand washing) cannot be accounted for by a specific phobia (e.g., irrational fear of dirt). Once we rule out other potential causes of OCD symptoms, such as specific phobia, anorexia nervosa, trichotillomania (compulsive hair-pulling), and hypochondriasis, we can be reasonably certain that an individual exhibiting marked obsessions, compulsions, or both, suffers from a well-defined disorder (APA, 2000, p. 463).

At the third and highest rung of the hierarchy of understanding lie *diseases*, which are disorders in which pathology and etiology are reasonably well understood (Kazdin, 1983; McHugh & Slavey, 1998). Sickle-cell anemia is a prototypical disease because its pathology (crescent-shaped erythrocytes containing hemoglobin S) and etiology (two autosomal recessive alleles) have been conclusively identified (Sutton, 1980). For other conditions that approach the status of bona fide diseases, such as Alzheimer's disease, the primary pathology (senile plaques, neurofibrillary tangles, and granulovacuolar degeneration) has been identified, while their etiology is evolving but incomplete (Selkoe, 1992).

With the possible exception of Alzheimer's disease and a handful of other organic conditions, the diagnoses in our present system of psychiatric classifications are almost exclusively syndromes or, in rare cases, disorders (Kendell & Jablensky, 2003). This fact is a sobering reminder that the pathology in most cases of psycho*pathology* is largely unknown, and their etiology poorly understood. Therefore, although we genuflect to hallowed tradition in this chapter by referring to the major entities within the current psychiatric classification system as mental disorders, readers should bear in mind that few are disorders in the strict sense of the term.

Functions of Psychiatric Diagnosis

Diagnosis serves three principal functions for practitioners and researchers alike. We discuss each in turn.

DIAGNOSIS AS COMMUNICATION

Diagnosis furnishes a convenient vehicle for communication about an individual's condition. It allows professionals to be reasonably confident that when they use a diagnosis (such as Dysthymic Disorder) to describe a patient, other professionals will recognize it as referring to the same condition. Moreover, a diagnosis (such as Borderline Personality Disorder) distills relevant information, such as frantic efforts to avoid abandonment and chronic feelings of emptiness, in a short-hand form that aids in other professionals understanding of a case. Blashfield and Burgess (2007) described this role as "information retrieval." Just as botanists use the name of a species to summarize distinctive features of a specific plant, psychologists and psychiatrists rely on a diagnosis to summarize distinctive features of a specific mental disorder (Blashfield & Burgess, 2007). Diagnoses succinctly convey important information about a patient to clinicians, investigators, family members, managed care organizations, and others.

LINKAGES TO OTHER DIAGNOSES

Psychiatric diagnoses are organized within the overarching nosological structure of other diagnoses. *Nosology* is the branch of science that deals with the systematic classification of diseases. Within this system, most diagnostic categories are arranged in relation to other conditions; the nearer in the network two conditions are, the more closely related they ostensibly are as disorders. For example, Histrionic Personality Disorder (HPD) and Narcissistic Personality Disorder (NPD)—both classified within Cluster B, the dramatic and emotional group of personality disorders—are presumably more closely linked etiologically than are HPD and schizoid personality disorder, a condition falling into Cluster A, the odd, eccentric group of personality disorders. Thus, diagnoses help to locate the patient's presenting problems with the context of both more and less related diagnostic categories.

SURPLUS INFORMATION

Perhaps most important, a diagnosis helps us to learn new things; it affords us surplus information that we did not have previously. Among other things, a diagnosis allows us to generate predictions regarding case trajectory. As Goodwin and Guze (1996) note, perhaps hyperbolically, "diagnosis is prognosis" (Kendler, 1980). The diagnostic label of Bipolar I Disorder describes a distinctive constellation of indicators (e.g., one or more manic or mixed episodes) that discriminates the course, rate of recovery, and treatment response from such related conditions as Major Depression and Bipolar II Disorder, the latter of which is marked by one or more episodes of hypomania and disabling depression.

But a valid diagnosis does considerably more than predict prognosis. Robins and Guze's (1970) landmark article delineated formal criteria for ascertaining whether a diagnosis is valid. *Validity* refers to the extent to which a diagnosis measures what it purports to measure. More colloquially, validity is truth in advertising: a valid diagnosis is true to its name in that it correlates in expected directions with external criteria. Specifically, Robins and Guze outlined four requirements for the validity of psychiatric diagnoses. According to them, a valid diagnosis offers information regarding:

- *Clinical Description,* including symptomatology, demographics, precipitants, and differences from seemingly related disorders. The lattermost task of distinguishing a diagnosis from similar diagnoses is called *differential diagnosis;*
- *Laboratory Research,* including data from psychological, biological, and laboratory tests;
- *Natural history,* including course and outcome; and
- *Family Studies,* especially studies examining the prevalence of a disorder in the first-degree relatives of *probands,* that is, individuals identified as having the diagnosis in question.

As a further desideratum, some authors have suggested that a valid diagnosis should ideally be able to predict the individual's response to treatment (Waldman, Lilienfeld, & Lahey, 1995). Nevertheless, this criterion should probably not be mandatory given that the treatment of a condition bears no necessary implications for its etiology. For example, although both schizophrenia and nausea induced by food poisoning generally respond to psychopharmacological agents that block the action of the neurotransmitter dopamine, these two conditions spring from entirely distinct causal mechanisms. Some authors (e.g., Ross & Pam, 1996) have invoked the felicitous phrase ex juvantibus reasoning (reasoning backward from what works) to describe the error of inferring a disorder's etiology from its treatment. Headaches, as the hoary example goes, are not caused by a deficiency of aspirin.

There's reasonably strong evidence that many mental disorders fulfill Robins and Guze's (1970) criteria for validity. When these criteria are met, the diagnosis offers additional information about the patient, information that was not available before this diagnosis was made. For example, if we correctly diagnose a patient with schizophrenia, we have learned that this patient:

1. Is likely to exhibit psychotic symptoms that are not solely a consequence of a severe mood disturbance;

2. Has a higher than expected likelihood of exhibiting abnormalities on several laboratory measures, including indices of sustained attention and smooth pursuit eye tracking;

3. Has a higher than average probability of having close biological relatives with schizophrenia and schizophrenia-spectrum disorders, such as schizotypal and paranoid personality disorders;

4. Is likely to exhibit a chronic course, with few or no periods of entirely normal functioning, but approximately a 30 percent chance of overall improvement; and

5. Is likely to respond positively to medications that block the action of dopamine.

Andreasen (1995) extended the Robins and Guze (1970) framework to incorporate indicators from molecular genetics, neurochemistry, and functional and structural brain imaging as additional validating indicators for psychiatric diagnoses (Kendell & Jablensky, 2003). Her friendly amendment to the Robins and Guze criteria allows us to use endophenotypic indicators to assist in the validation of a diagnosis. *Endophenotypes* are biomarkers; that is, "measurable components unseen by the unaided eye along the pathway between disease and distal genotype" (Gottesman & Gould, 2003, p. 636; Waldman, 2005). They are often contrasted with *exophenotypes*, the traditional signs and symptoms of a disorder.

We can view the process of validating psychiatric diagnoses within the overarching framework of *construct validity* (Cronbach & Meehl, 1955; Loevinger, 1957; Messick, 1995), which refers to the extent to which a measure assesses a hypothesized attribute of individuals. As Morey (1991) noted, psychiatric classification systems are collections of hypothetical constructs; thus, the process of validating psychiatric diagnoses is also a process of construct validation. More broadly, we can conceptualize most or even all psychiatric diagnoses as *open concepts* (Meehl, 1977, 1990). Open concepts are marked by (a) fuzzy boundaries, (b) a list of indicators (signs and symptoms) that are indefinitely extendable, and (c) an unclear inner nature.

Recalling that psychiatric diagnoses are open concepts helps us to avoid the perils of premature reification of diagnostic entities (Faust & Miner, 1986). For example, the present diagnostic criteria for schizophrenia are not isomorphic with the latent construct of schizophrenia; they are merely fallible, albeit somewhat valid, indicators of this construct. Yet, the past few decades have occasionally witnessed a troubling tendency to reify and deify the categories within the current classification system, with some authors regarding them as fixed Platonic essences rather than rough approximations to the true state of nature (Ghaemi, 2003; Michels, 1984). This error is manifested, for example, when journal or grant reviewers criticize researchers for examining alternative operationalizations of mental disorders that depart from those in the current diagnostic manual (see section Psychiatric Classification from *DSM-I* to the Present).

In a classic article, Cronbach and Meehl (1955) adopted from neopositivist philosophers of science the term *nomological network* to designate the system of lawful relationships conjectured to hold between theoretical entities (states, structures, events, dispositions) and observable indicators. They selected the network metaphor to emphasize the structure of such systems in which the nodes of the network, representing the postulated theoretical entities, are connected by the strands of the network, representing the lawful relationships hypothesized to hold among the entities (Garber & Strassberg, 1991).

For Cronbach and Meehl (1955), construct validation is a progressive and never ending process of testing the links between hypothesized strands of the nomological network, especially those that connect latent constructs—which include psychiatric diagnoses (e.g., schizophrenia and major depression)—to manifest indicators—which include the external criteria (e.g., laboratory tests and family history) laid out by Robins and Guze (1970). The more such construct-to-manifest indicator links are corroborated, the more certain we can be that our conception of the diagnosis in question is accurate. From this perspective, the approach to diagnostic validation outlined by Robins and Guze is merely one specific instantiation of construct validation.

One shortcoming of the Robins and Guze (1970) approach to construct validation is its exclusive emphasis on *external validation*, that is, the process of ascertaining the construct's associations with correlates that lie outside of the construct itself. As Skinner (1981, 1986; also Loevinger, 1957) observed, *internal validation*, ascertaining the construct's inner structure, is also a key component of construct validation. Internal validation can help investigators to test hypotheses regarding a construct's homogeneity (versus heterogeneity) and factor structure (Waldman et al., 1995). For example, if analyses suggest that a diagnosis consists of multiple and largely independent subtypes, the validity of the diagnosis would be called into question.

In summary, valid psychiatric diagnoses serve three primary functions:

1. They summarize distinctive features of a disorder and thereby allow professionals to communicate clearly with one another;
2. They place each diagnosis under the umbrella structure of other diagnoses. This nosological framework links one diagnosis to both more and less related diagnoses; and
3. They provide practitioners and researchers with surplus information regarding diagnosed patients' clinical profile, laboratory findings, natural history, family history, and possibly response to treatment; they may also offer information regarding endophenotypic indicators.

Misconceptions Regarding Psychiatric Diagnosis

Beginning psychology graduate students and much of the general public hold a plethora of misconceptions regarding psychiatric diagnosis; we examine five such misconceptions here. Doing so will also permit us to introduce a number of key principles of psychiatric diagnosis. As we will discover, refuting each misconception regarding psychiatric diagnosis affirms at least one important principle.

MISCONCEPTION # 1: "MENTAL ILLNESS" IS A MYTH

The person most closely associated with this position is Szasz (1960), who has argued famously for over 40 years that the term mental illness is a false and misleading metaphor (Schaler, 2004). For Szasz, individuals who psychologists and psychiatrists term mentally ill actually suffer from *problems in living* (that is, difficulties in adjusting their behaviors to the demands of society). Moreover, Szasz contended that mental health professionals often apply the mental illness label to nonconformists who jeopardize the status quo (Sarbin, 1969; Szasz, 1960). This label serves as a convenient justification for forcing maladjusted, malcontented, and maverick members of society to comply with prevailing societal norms.

Specifically, Szasz maintained that medical disorders can be clearly recognized by a lesion to the anatomical structure of the body, but that the disorder concept cannot be extended to the mental realm because there is no such lesion to indicate deviation from the norm. According to him only the body can become diseased, so mentally ill people do not suffer from an illness akin to a medical disorder.

It is undeniable that psychiatric diagnoses are sometimes misapplied. Nevertheless, this legitimate pragmatic concern must be logically separated from the question of whether the mental illness concept itself exists (Wakefield, 1992). We should recall the logical principle of *abusus non tollit usum*: historical and sociological misuses of a concept do not negate its validity.

Wakefield (1992) and others (Kendell, 1975) have observed that the Szaszian argument is problematic on several fronts. Among others, it assumes that medical disorders are in every case traceable to discernible lesions in an anatomical structure, and that all lesions give rise to medical disorders. Yet identifiable lesions cannot be found in certain clear-cut medical diseases—such as trigeminal neuralgia and senile pruritis—and certain identifiable lesions, such as albinism, are not regarded as medical disorders (Kendall, 1975; Wakefield, 1992). Szasz's assertion that identifiable lesions are essentially synonymous with medical disorders is false; therefore, his corollary argument that mental disorders cannot exist because they are not invariably associated with identifiable lesions is similarly false.

MISCONCEPTION # 2: PSYCHIATRIC DIAGNOSIS IS MERELY PIGEON-HOLING

According to this criticism, when we diagnose people with a mental disorder, we deprive them of their uniqueness: We imply that all people within the same diagnostic category are alike in all important respects.

To the contrary, a psychiatric diagnosis does nothing of the sort; it implies only that all people with that diagnosis are alike in at least one important way. Psychologists and psychiatrists are well aware that even within a given diagnostic category, such as Schizophrenia or Bipolar Disorder, people differ dramatically in their race and cultural background, personality traits, interests, and cognitive skills (APA, 2000, p. xxxi).

MISCONCEPTION # 3: PSYCHIATRIC DIAGNOSES ARE UNRELIABLE

Reliability refers to the consistency of a diagnosis. As many textbooks in psychometrics remind us, reliability is a prerequisite for validity but not vice versa. Just as a bathroom scale cannot validly measure weight if it yields dramatically different weight estimates for the same person over brief periods of time, a diagnosis cannot validly measure a mental disorder if it yields dramatically different scores on measures of psychopathology across times, situations, and raters.

Because validity is not a prerequisite for reliability, extremely high reliability can exist without validity. A researcher who based his diagnoses of schizophrenia on patients' heights would end up with extremely reliable but entirely invalid diagnoses of schizophrenia.

There are three major subtypes of reliability. Contrary to popular (mis)conception, these subtypes are frequently discrepant with one another, so high levels of reliability for one metric do not necessary imply high levels for the others.

Test-retest reliability refers to the stability of a diagnosis following a relatively brief time interval, typically about a month. In other words, after a short time lapse, will patients receive the same diagnoses? Note that we wrote brief and short in the previous sentences; marked changes following lengthy time lapses, such as several years, may reflect genuine changes in patient status rather than the measurement error associated with test-retest unreliability.

In general, we assess test-retest reliability using either a Pearson correlation coefficient or, more rigorously, an *intraclass correlation* coefficient. Intraclass correlations tend to provide the most stringent estimates of test-retest reliability because, in contrast to Pearson correlations, they are influenced not merely by the rank ordering and differences among people's scores, but by their absolute magnitude.

Our evaluation of a diagnosis' test-retest reliability hinges on our conceptualization of the disorder. We should anticipate high test-reliability only for diagnoses that are trait-like, such as personality disorders, or that tend to be *chronic* (long-lasting), such as schizophrenia. In contrast, we should not necessarily anticipate high levels of test-test reliabilities for diagnoses that tend to be *episodic* (intermittent), such as major depression.

Internal consistency refers to the extent to which the signs and symptoms comprising a diagnosis "hang together," that is, correlate highly with one another. We generally assess internal consistency using such metrics as coefficient alpha (Cronbach, 1951) or the mean interitem correlation. Cronbach's alpha can overestimate the homogeneity of a diagnosis, however, if this diagnosis contains numerous signs and symptoms because this statistic is affected by test length (Schmidt, Le, & Ilies, 2003). We should anticipate high levels of internal consistency for most conditions in the current classification system given that most are syndromes, which are typically constellations of signs and symptoms that covary across people.

Inter-rater reliability is the degree to which two or more observers, such as different psychologists or psychiatrists, agree on the diagnosis of a set of individuals. High inter-rater reliability is a perquisite for all psychiatric diagnoses, because different observers must agree on the presence or absence of a condition before valid research on that condition can proceed.

Many early studies of psychiatric diagnosis operationalized inter-rater reliability in terms of percentage agreement, that is, the proportion of cases on which two or more raters agree on the presence of absence of a given diagnosis. Nevertheless, measures of percentage agreement tend to overestimate inter-rater reliability. Here's why: imagine two diagnosticians working in a setting (e.g., an outpatient phobia clinic) in which the *base rate* (prevalence) of the diagnosis of specific phobia is 95%. The finding that they agree with each other on the diagnosis of specific phobia 95% of the time would hardly be impressive and could readily be attributed to chance. As a consequence, most investigators today operationalize inter-rater reliability in terms of the *kappa coefficient*, which assesses the degree to which raters agree on a diagnosis after correcting for chance, with chance being the base rate of the disorder in question. Nevertheless, the kappa coefficient often provides a conservative estimate of inter-rater reliability, as the correction for chance sometimes penalizes raters for their independent expertise (Meyer, 1997).

Many laypersons and even political pundits believe that psychiatric diagnoses possess low levels of reliability, especially inter-rater reliability. This perception is probably fueled by high-profile media coverage of dueling expert witnesses in criminal trials in which one expert diagnoses a defendant as schizophrenic, for example, and another diagnoses him as normal. After the widely publicized 1982 trial of John Hinckley, who was acquitted on the basis of insanity for his attempted assassination of then-president Ronald Reagan, political commentator George Will maintained (on national television) that the disagreements among expert witnesses regarding Hinckley's diagnosis merely bore out what most people already knew: psychiatric diagnosis is wildly unreliable (Lilienfeld, 1995).

Yet there is a straightforward explanation for such disagreement: Given the adversarial nature of our legal system, the prosecution and defense typically go out of their way to find expert witnesses who will present their point of view. This inherently antagonistic arrangement virtually guarantees that the inter-rater reliabilities of experts in criminal trials will be modest at best.

Certainly, the inter-rater reliability of psychiatric diagnoses is far from perfect. Yet for most major mental disorders, such as schizophrenia, mood disorders, anxiety disorders, and alcohol dependence (alcoholism), inter-rater reliabilities are typically about as high—intraclass correlations between raters of 0.8 or above, out of a maximum of 1.0—as those for most well established medical disorders (Matarazzo, 1983). Still, the picture is not entirely rosy. For most personality disorders in particular, inter-rater reliabilities tend to be considerably lower than for other conditions (Zimmerman, 1994), probably because most of these disorders comprise highly inferential constructs (e.g., lack of empathy) that raters find difficult to assess during the course of brief interviews.

MISCONCEPTION # 4: PSYCHIATRIC DIAGNOSES ARE INVALID

From the standpoint of Szasz (1960) and other critics of psychiatric diagnosis (Eysenck, Wakefield, & Friedman, 1983), psychiatric diagnoses are largely useless because they do not provide us with new information. According to them, diagnoses are merely descriptive labels for behaviors we do not like. Millon (1975) proposed a helpful distinction between psychiatric *labels* and *diagnoses*; a label simply describes behaviors, whereas a diagnosis helps to explain them.

When it comes to a host of informal pop psychology labels, like sexual addiction, Peter Pan syndrome, co-dependency, shopping disorder, and road rage disorder, Szasz and his fellow critics probably have a point. Most of these labels merely describe collections of socially problematic behavior and do not provide us with much, if any, new information (McCann, Shindler, & Hammond, 2003). The same may hold for some personality disorders in the current classification system; for example, the diagnosis of Dependent Personality Disorder appears to do little more than describe ways in which people are pathologically dependent on others, such as relying excessively on others for reassurance and expecting others to make everyday life decisions for them.

Yet, as we have already seen, many psychiatric diagnoses, such as Schizophrenia, Bipolar Disorder, and Panic Disorder, do yield surplus information (Robins & Guze, 1970; Waldman et al., 1995) and, therefore, possess adequate levels of validity. Nevertheless, because construct validation, like all forms of theory testing in science, is a never ending process, the validity of these diagnoses is likely to improve over time with subsequent revisions to the present classification system.

MISCONCEPTION # 5: PSYCHIATRIC DIAGNOSES STIGMATIZE PEOPLE, AND OFTEN RESULT IN SELF-FULFILLING PROPHECIES

According to advocates of labeling theory, including Szasz (1960), Sarbin (1969), and Scheff (1975), psychiatric diagnoses produce adverse effects on labeled individuals. They argue that diagnostic labels not only stigmatize patients, but also frequently become self-fulfilling prophecies, leading observers to interpret ambiguous and relatively mild behaviors (e.g., occasional outbursts of anger) as reflecting serious mental illness.

A sensational 1973 study by Rosenhan appeared to offer impressive support for labeling theory. Rosenhan, along with seven other normal individuals, posed as pseudopatients (fake patients) in 12 U.S. psychiatric hospitals (some of the pseudopatients presented at more than one hospital). They informed the admitting psychiatrist only that they were hearing a voice saying "empty, hollow, and thud." All were promptly admitted to the hospital and remained there for an average of three weeks, despite displaying no further symptoms or signs of psychopathology. In 11 of 12 cases, they were discharged with diagnoses of schizophrenia in remission (the 12th pseudopatient was discharged with a diagnosis of manic depression in remission).

Rosenhan (1973) noted that the hospital staff frequently interpreted pseudopatients' innocuous behaviors, such as note taking, as indicative of abnormality. In case summaries, these staff also construed entirely run of the mill details of pseudopatients' life histories, such as emotional conflicts with parents during adolescence, as consistent with their present illness. These striking results led Rosenhan to conclude that psychiatric labels color observers' perceptions of behavior, often to the point that they can no longer distinguish mental illness from normality.

Even today, some writers interpret Rosenhan's findings as a resounding affirmation of labeling theory (e.g., Slater, 2004). Yet, the evidence for labeling theory is less impressive than it appears. As Spitzer (1975) observed, the fact that all 12 of Rosenhan's pseudopatients were released with diagnoses in remission (meaning showing no indications of illness) demonstrates that the psychiatrists who treated them were in all cases able to distinguish mental illness from normality. Spitzer went further, demonstrating in a survey of psychiatric hospitals that in remission diagnoses of previously psychotic patients are exceedingly infrequent, showing that the psychiatrists in Rosenhan's study successfully made an extremely rare judgment with perfect consensus.

Although incorrect psychiatric diagnoses can engender stigma, at least in the short run (Harris, Milich, Corbett, Hoover, & Brady, 1992; Milich, McAninich, & Harris, 1992) there is scant evidence to support the popular claim that correctly applied psychiatric diagnoses do so. The lion's share of the research suggests that stigma is a consequence not of diagnostic labels, but of disturbed and sometimes disturbing behavior that precedes labeling (Link & Cullen, 1990; Ruscio, 2004). For example, within 30 minutes or less, children begin to react negatively to children with Attention-Deficit/Hyperactivity Disorder (ADHD) who have joined their peer group (Milich et al., 1992; Pelham & Bender, 1982).

Contrary to the tenets of labeling theory, there is evidence that accurate psychiatric diagnoses sometimes reduce stigma, because they provide observers with at least a partial explanation for otherwise inexplicable behaviors (Ruscio, 2004). For example, adults tend to evaluate mentally retarded children more positively when these children are labeled as mentally retarded than when they are not (Seitz & Geske, 1976), and peers rate the essays of children with ADHD more positively when these children are labeled with ADHD than when they are not (Cornez-Ruiz & Hendricks, 1993).

What Is Mental Disorder?

Our discussion up to this point presupposes that the boundaries of the higher-order concept of "disorder," including mental disorder, are clear-cut or at least reasonably well-delineated.[1] To develop a classification system of disorders, one must first be able to ascertain whether a given condition is or is not a disorder. Yet the answer to the question of how best to define disorder, including mental disorder, remains elusive (Gorenstein, 1992). The issues here are of more than academic interest, because each revision of psychiatry's diagnostic manual has been marked by contentious disputes regarding whether such conditions as Attention-Deficit/Hyperactivity Disorder, Posttraumatic Stress Disorder, and Premenstrual Dysphoric Disorder are *really* disorders (Wakefield, 1992). The fact that homosexuality was removed from the formal psychiatric classification system in 1974 by a majority vote of the membership of the American Psychiatric Association (Bayer & Spitzer, 1982) further demonstrates that these debates are frequently resolved more by group consensus than by scientific research.

Here we evaluate several influential attempts to delineate the boundaries of disorder. As we will discover, each approach has its limitations but each captures something important about the concept of disorder. As we will also discover, these approaches differ in the extent to which they embrace an *essentialist* as opposed to a *nominalist* view of disorder (Ghaemi, 2003; Scadding, 1996). Advocates of an essentialist view (Widiger & Trull, 1985) believe that all disorders share some essence or underlying property, whereas advocates of a nominalist view (Lilienfeld & Marino, 1999) believe that the higher-order concept of disorder is a social construction that groups together a variety of largely unrelated conditions for the purposes of social or semantic convenience.

STATISTICAL MODEL

Advocates of a *statistical model*, such as Cohen (1981), equate disorder with statistical rarity. According to this view, disorders are abnormal because they are infrequent in the general population. This definition accords with findings that many mental disorders are indeed rare; schizophrenia, for example, is found in about 1% of the population across much of the world (APA, 2000).

Yet, a purely statistical model falls short on at least three grounds. First, it offers no guidance for where to draw cut-offs between normality and abnormality. In many cases, these cut-offs are scientifically arbitrary. Second, it is silent on the crucial question of which dimensions are relevant to abnormality. As a consequence, a statistical model misclassifies high scores on certain adaptive dimensions (like intelligence, creativity, and altruism) as inherently abnormal. Moreover, it does not explain why high scores on certain dimensions (e.g., anxiety) but not others (e.g., hair length) are pertinent to psychopathology. Third, by definition a statistical model assumes that all common conditions are normal (Wakefield, 1992). Yet the common cold is still an illness despite its essentially 100% lifetime prevalence in the population, and the Black Death (bubonic plague) was still an illness in the mid-1300s despite wiping out approximately one-third of the European population.

---

[1] In our discussion of the definition of disorder, we use the term disorder, including mental disorder, generically to refer to all medical and psychological conditions and do not distinguish disorder from disease (Wakefield, 1992).

Subjective Distress Model

Proponents of a *subjective distress* model maintain that the core feature distinguishing disorder from nondisorder is psychological pain. This model unquestionably contains a large kernel of truth; many serious mental illnesses (such as Major Depression, Obsessive-Compulsive Disorder, Generalized Anxiety Disorder, and Gender Identity Disorder) are marked by considerable distress, even anguish.

The subjective distress model also falls short of an adequate definition of mental illness, because it fails to distinguish *ego-dystonic* conditions—those that conflict with one's self-concept—from *ego-syntonic* conditions—those that are consistent with one's self-concept. Although most mental disorders are ego-dystonic, some (like Antisocial Personality Disorder) are largely or entirely ego-syntonic, because individuals with these conditions frequently see nothing wrong with their behavior. They experience little or no distress in conjunction with their condition, and frequently seek treatment only when demanded by courts or significant others, or when their condition is complicated by a secondary condition that generates interpersonal difficulties (e.g., alcoholism). Moreover, approximately half of patients with schizophrenia and other severe psychotic conditions are afflicted with *anosognosia*, meaning that they are not aware of the fact that they are ill (Amador & Paul-Odouard, 2000).

Biological Model

Proponents of a *biological model* (Kendell, 1975) contend that disorder can be defined in terms of a biological or evolutionary disadvantage to the organism, such as reduced lifespan or fitness (i.e., the ability to pass on genes to subsequent generations). Indeed, some mental disorders are associated with biological disadvantages; for example, major depression is associated with a dramatically increased risk for completed suicide (Joiner, 2006), and between 5 and 10% of patients with anorexia nervosa eventually die from complications due to starvation (Goodwin & Guze, 1996).

A biological model, however, also falls prey to numerous counterexamples. For example, being a soldier in front-line combat is not a disorder despite its average adverse effect on longevity and fitness. Conversely, some relatively mild psychological conditions, such as most specific phobias, are probably not associated with decreased longevity or fitness, yet are still mental disorders.

Need for Treatment

One parsimonious definition is simply that disorders are a heterogeneous class of conditions all characterized by a perceived need for medical intervention on the part of health (including mental health) professionals (Kraupl Taylor, 1971). Like other definitions, this definition captures an important truth: Many or most mental disorders, such as Schizophrenia, Bipolar Disorder, and Obsessive-Compulsive Disorder, are indeed viewed by society as necessitating treatment. Nevertheless, this definition too falls victim to counterexamples. For example, pregnancy clearly is associated with a perceived need for medical intervention, yet it is not regarded as a disorder.

Harmful Dysfunction

In an effort to remedy the shortcomings of extant models of disorder, Wakefield (1992) proposed a hybrid definition that incorporates both essentialist and nominalist features.

According to Wakefield, all disorders, including all mental disorders, are harmful dysfunctions: socially devalued (harmful) breakdowns of evolutionarily selected systems (dysfunctions). For example, according to Wakefield, panic disorder is a mental disorder because it (a) is negatively valued by society and often by the individual afflicted with it, and (b) reflects the activation of the fight-flight system in situations for which it was not evolutionary selected, namely those in which objective danger is absent. In other words, panic attacks are false alarms (Barlow, 2001). Wakefield's operationalization of disorder has its strengths; for example, it acknowledges (correctly) that most and perhaps all disorders are viewed negatively by others. The concept of disorder, including mental disorder, is clearly associated with social values. As Wakefield (1992) noted, however, social devaluation is not sufficient to demarcate disorder from nondisorder, claims by Szasz (1960) to the contrary. For example, rudeness, laziness, slovenliness, and even racism are viewed negatively by society, but are not disorders (for a dissenting view regarding racism, see Poussaint, 2002). Therefore, Wakefield contends something else is necessary to distinguish disorder from nondisorder, namely evolutionary dysfunction.

Nevertheless, the dysfunction component of Wakefield's analysis appears to fall prey to counterexamples. In particular, many medical disorders appear to be adaptive defenses against threat or insult. For instance, the symptoms of influenza (flu), such as vomiting, coughing, sneezing, and fever, are all adaptive efforts to expel an infectious agent rather than failures or breakdowns in an evolutionarily selected system (Lilienfeld & Marino, 1999; Nesse & Williams, 1994). Such counterexamples appear to falsify the harmful dysfunction analysis. Similarly, many psychological conditions appear to be adaptive reactions to perceived threat. For example, in contrast to other specific phobias, blood phobia is marked by a coordinated set of dramatic parasympathetic reactions—especially rapid decreases in heart rate and blood pressure—that were almost surely evolutionarily selected to minimize blood loss (Barlow, 2001). Although these responses may not be especially adaptive in the early 21st century, they were adaptive prior to the advent of Band-Aids, tourniquets, and anticoagulants (Lilienfeld & Marino, 1995).

ROSCHIAN ANALYSIS

An alternative approach to defining disorder is radically different. According to a *Roschian analysis*, the attempt to define disorder explicitly is sure to fail because disorder is intrinsically undefinable (Gorenstein, 1992). Drawing on the work of cognitive psychologist Eleanor Rosch (Rosch, 1973; Rosch & Mervis, 1975), advocates of a Roschian analysis contend that the concept of mental disorder lacks defining (i.e., singly necessary and jointly sufficient) features and possesses intrinsically fuzzy boundaries. In this respect, mental disorder is similar to many other concepts. For example, the concept of a chair lacks strictly defining features (e.g., a human-made object with four legs that someone one can sit on does not succeed as a defining feature, because one can sit on a table and many chairs do not have four legs) and displays unclear boundaries. In addition, the concept of mental disorder, like many other concepts, is organized around a prototype that shares all of the features of the category. Just as certain chairs (e.g., a typical office chair) are more chair-like than others (e.g., a bean-bag), certain mental disorders (e.g., Schizophrenia) are more disorder-like than others (e.g., Hypoactive Sexual Desire Disorder). Not surprisingly, it is at the fuzzy boundaries of disorder where controversies concerning whether a psychological condition is really a disorder most frequently arise. According to the Roschian analysis, these controversies are not only inevitable, but also not resolvable by scientific data.

Even if the Roschian analysis is correct (see Wakefield, 1999, and Widiger, 1997, for criticisms of this approach), it would not imply that specific mental disorders themselves are not amenable to scientific inquiry. As Gorenstein (1992) noted, the concept of a "drug" is inherently undefinable; there are no scientific criteria for deciding whether caffeine, nicotine, or some other widely used but addictive substances are drugs. Yet, this problem has not stopped psychopharmacologists from studying specific drugs' properties, modes of action, or behavioral effects. Nor should the absence of an explicit definition of mental disorder preclude psychopathology researchers from investigating the diagnosis, etiology, treatment, and prevention of Schizophrenia, Major Depression, Panic Disorder, and other conditions.

The recent controversy regarding whether Pluto is a planet is another telling case in point. Following weeks of heated discussion, the International Astronomical Union caused a furor in 2006 by ignominiously demoting Pluto from its lofty planetary status. Yet, as most witnesses to this acrimonious debate acknowledged, the question of whether Pluto is genuinely a planet is largely or entirely arbitrary from a scientific standpoint. One prominent astronomer, Michael Brown (2006), wrote in the *New York Times* that:

The term "planet" is similar to "continent." The word helps us organize our world, but the division between continents and subcontinents is thoroughly arbitrary. Yet no union of geologists has tried to vote on a definition of "continent," and no one is concerned that letting culture determine the difference between Australia, the smallest continent, and Greenland, the largest island, somehow erodes science. (p. 17)

Just as the question of Pluto's planet-hood has had no discernable impact on planetary astronomers' daily activities, the question of whether controversial psychological conditions are mental disorders should have no effect on the day-to-day activities of practitioners or psychopathology researchers.

Psychiatric Classification from *DSM-I* to the Present

Prior to the 1950s, the state of psychiatric classification in the United States was largely disorganized, as no standard system was in place for operationalizing specific mental disorders. Indeed, prior to World War I, there was scant interest in developing a systematic classification of mental disorders (Grob, 1991), and even after World War I no consensual system of classification was in place for over three decades. As a consequence, what one diagnostician meant by major depression might bear minimal correspondence to what another diagnostician meant by the same term.

DSM-I AND *DSM-II*

This situation changed in 1952, when the American Psychiatric Association released the first edition of its *Diagnostic and Statistical Manual of Mental Disorders*, abbreviated as *DSM-I* (APA, 1952). Although *DSM-I* was a slim 132 pages in length, it was a landmark. For the first time, it offered reasonably clear, albeit brief, descriptions of major psychiatric diagnoses, thereby facilitating inter-rater reliability among clinicians and researchers. Here, for example, was the description for "manic depressive action, depressed type" (later to become "major depression") in *DSM-I*:

Here will be classified those cases with outstanding depression of mood and with mental and motor retardation and inhibition; in some cases there is much uneasiness and apprehension. Perplexity, stupor or agitation may be prominent symptoms, and may be added to the diagnosis as manifestations. (APA, 1952, p. 25)

DSM-II appeared 16 years later (APA, 1968) and was similar in approach and scope to *DSM-I*, although it provided somewhat greater detail concerning the signs and symptoms of many diagnoses. Despite their strengths, *DSM-I* and *DSM-II* suffered from several notable weaknesses, three of which we discuss here:

1. The inter-rater reliabilities of many of their diagnoses were still problematic, probably because these manuals consisted of global and often vague descriptions of mental illnesses that necessitated considerable subjective judgment on the part of diagnosticians. For example, returning to the description of manic depressive reaction, depressed type, *DSM-I* is silent on what qualifies as "outstanding depression," and how much motor retardation and inhibition are necessary for the diagnosis.
2. *DSM-I* and *DSM-II* were not theoretically agnostic. In particular, they were influenced by psychoanalytic concepts of mental disorders and often made references to defense mechanisms and other concepts derived from Freudian theory. As a consequence, diagnosticians whose orientation was not psychoanalytic, such as behaviorists, cognitive-behaviorists, or humanistic-existential psychologists, found these classification systems difficult to use. *DSM-I* and *DSM-II* also conceptualized mental disorders largely from the perspective of psychiatrist Adolph Meyer (1866–1950), who regarded most forms of psychopathology as aberrant reactions to life events (Lief, 1948). Hence, the use of the term reaction in the diagnosis of manic depressive reaction, depressed type and many other *DSM-I* and *DSM-II* diagnoses. Nevertheless, this assumption was based more on plausible theoretical conjecture than on evidence.
3. Despite their Meyerian emphasis, *DSM-I* and *DSM-II* focused almost exclusively on patients' mental disorders per se, and largely neglected to consider contextual factors, such as co-occurring medical conditions, life stressors, and adaptive functioning, which can play key roles in the etiology and maintenance of psychopathology.

DSM-III AND BEYOND

Largely in response to these criticisms, the American Psychiatric Association, with psychiatrist Robert Spitzer at the helm, released *DSM-III* in 1980 (APA, 1980). As most historians of psychiatric classification and diagnosis now recognize, *DSM-III* was an important revision of the diagnostic manual; it represented a radical change in thinking and approach from all that came before, and has provided the template for all that has come since (Klerman, 1984; Mayes & Horwitz, 2005). In this respect, it was every bit as much a landmark, if not more, than *DSM-I* was. Coming in at a hefty 494 pages, a nearly four-fold increase from *DSM-II*, *DSM-III* not only dramatically increased the coverage of mental disorders—from 163 to 224—but also presented far more detailed guidelines than its predecessors for establishing diagnoses. The operational and philosophical approach of *DSM-III* is often termed *neo-Kraepelinian* (Compton & Guze, 1995) because it followed in the footsteps of the great German psychiatrist Emil Kraepelin (1856–1926), who grouped and differentiated psychological conditions on the basis on their signs, symptoms, and natural history.

Diagnostic Criteria, Algorithms, and Hierarchical Exclusion Rules

In accord with its neo-Kraepelinian emphasis, *DSM-III* instituted several major changes in psychiatric classification and diagnosis. First and foremost, it standardized: (a) *diagnostic criteria*, and (b) *algorithms*, or decision rules, for each diagnosis. Rather than merely describing each diagnosis as *DSM-I* and *DSM-II* had done, *DSM-III* explicitly delineated the signs and symptoms comprising each diagnosis and the method by which these signs and symptoms needed to be combined to establish each diagnosis. In these respects, it was influenced heavily by the pioneering efforts of the St. Louis group at Washington University (including Robins, Guze, Winokur, and other giants of descriptive psychopathology), who had introduced preliminary diagnostic criteria and algorithms for 14 major mental disorders in the early 1970s (Feighner et al., 1972).

For example, to meet criteria for the diagnosis of major depressive episode, *DSM-III* required that clients: (1) experience "dysphoric mood or loss of interest or pleasure in all or almost all activities" (p. 213; with dysphoric mood described in terms of seven symptoms, including depression, hopelessness, and irritability), and (2) experience at least four of eight symptoms, such as poor appetite, insomnia, loss of energy, difficulty thinking and concentrating, nearly every day for at least a two week period. Compare the specificity of these criteria with the skimpy and highly impressionistic description in *DSM-I* presented earlier.

DSM-III also outlined *hierarchical exclusion rules* for many diagnoses; such rules prevent clinicians and researchers from making these diagnoses if other diagnoses can account for their clinical picture. For example, *DSM-III* forbade clinicians and researchers from making a diagnosis of major depressive episode if the episode was superimposed on Schizophrenia, Schizophreniform Disorder, or a Paranoid Disorder, or if it appeared to be due to either an organic mental disorder (e.g., hypothyroidism) or uncomplicated bereavement (a prolonged grief reaction). Among other things, hierarchical exclusion rules remind diagnosticians to think organic: that is, to rule out potential physical causes of mental disorders before diagnosing them (Morrison, 1997).

DSM-III's use of diagnostic criteria, algorithms, and hierarchical exclusion rules has been criticized by many commentators as the Chinese menu approach to diagnosis (choose three from column A, two from column B, four from column C). Despite these criticisms, there is evidence that this approach has markedly decreased the subjectivity of diagnostic decision-making and increased the inter-rater reliabilities of many diagnoses (Spitzer, Forman, & Nee, 1979). However, some authors argue that these increases are exaggerated by *DSM-III*'s proponents (Kirk & Kutchins, 1992).

The inter-rater reliability of *DSM* diagnoses has also been enhanced by the development of *structured* and *semi-structured diagnostic interviews*, such as the Structured Clinical Interview for *DSM* (SCID; First, Spitzer, Gibbon, & Williams, 2002), which are coordinated explicitly around *DSM* criteria. These interviews consist of standardized questions—to be read verbatim by interviewers—and required and suggested follow-up probes with which to assess specific diagnostic criteria. For example, the SCID provides the following question to assess the criterion of current, unexpected panic attacks in the current *DSM* diagnosis of Panic Disorder: "Have you ever had a panic attack, when you suddenly felt frightened or anxious or suddenly developed a lot of physical symptoms?" If the respondent replies yes, the SCID instructs the interviewer to ask, "Have these attacks ever come on completely out of the blue—in situations where you didn't expect to be nervous or uncomfortable?" (First et al., 2002).

Theoretical Agnosticism

In sharp contrast to its predecessors, *DSM-III* was agnostic with respect to etiology (with the exception of one diagnosis, Posttraumatic Stress Disorder, which required the presence of a traumatic event ostensibly tied to the symptoms of the disorder). In particular, *DSM-III* assiduously shunned concepts, such as defense mechanisms, that were tied to psychoanalysis or other specific theoretical orientations. By doing so, it permitted practitioners and researchers of varying persuasions to use the manual with equal ease and comfort. It also facilitated scientific progress by allowing researchers to pit differing theoretical orientations against each other to determine which offered the most scientifically supported etiological explanations for specific disorders (Wakefield, 1998).

Multiaxial Approach

DSM-III adopted a *multiaxial* approach to diagnosis, in which each client is described along a series of axes (that is, dimensions). A multiaxial approach forces clinicians to adopt a more *holistic* approach to diagnosis by considering variables in addition to the individuals' mental disorders. In *DSM-III* (and its revision), the first two axes are restricted to mental illnesses, and the last three axes assess other dimensions often relevant to psychological functioning.

On Axis I most of the major mental disorders are found, including Schizophrenia and other psychotic disorders, mood disorders, anxiety disorders, impulse control disorders, eating disorders, sleep disorders, and substance-related disorders. On Axis II mental retardation and the *personality disorders* are found, believed to be extremes of personality traits that are inflexible, maladaptive, or both. The Axis I–Axis II distinction, although at times fuzzy, ostensibly reflects the difference between conditions (e.g., Major Depression and Panic Disorder) that tend to be superimposed on the individuals' pre-existing functioning (Axis I) and conditions (e.g., Borderline Personality Disorder), which tend to capture the person's longstanding ways of viewing and relating to the world (Axis II). More colloquially and perhaps less precisely, Axis I is intended to assess what the person *has*, whereas Axis II is intended to assess what the person *is*.

Axis III assesses medical disorders, which again reminds clinicians to consider physical conditions that can mimic or complicate the course of psychological disorders. Axis III is especially important given estimates that 50% of psychiatric patients suffer from at least one major medical condition (Cooper, 2007). Axis IV assesses psychosocial stressors, including recent major life events, and Axis V assesses the individual's overall level of adaptive functioning on a 1–100 Global Assessment of Functioning (GAF) scale, with 100 representing optimal functioning.

DSM-III-R and DSM-IV

DSM-III-Revised (*DSM-III*-R), which appeared in 1987, and *DSM-IV*, which appeared in 1994 (and in a more expanded text revision in 2000), retained all of the major features and innovations of *DSM-III* (APA, 1987, 1994, 2000). Nevertheless, they continued to increase their coverage of psychopathology; *DSM-IV*, now 943 pages long, contains 374 diagnoses (APA, 2000).

Both *DSM-III*-R and *DSM-IV* gradually moved away from a *monothetic approach* to diagnosis, emphasized in much of *DSM-III*, toward a *polythetic approach*. In a monothetic approach, the signs and symptoms are singly necessary and jointly sufficient for a diagnosis. In contrast, in a polythetic approach the signs and symptoms are neither necessary nor sufficient for a diagnosis.

The potential disadvantage of a polythetic approach is extensive heterogeneity at the symptom and (perhaps) etiological levels. In *DSM-IV*, for example, 256 different symptom combinations are compatible with a diagnosis of Borderline Personality Disorder. It is implausible that the etiologies of all of these combinations are similar, let alone identical. It is even possible for two people to meet *DSM-IV* criteria for Obsessive-Compulsive Disorder yet share no diagnostic criteria in common (Widiger, 2007). Nevertheless, most scholars agree that the potential disadvantage of symptomatic heterogeneity is outweighed by the higher inter-reliability of the polythetic approach (Widiger, Frances, Spitzer, & Williams, 1991). In a monothetic approach, a disagreement about the presence or absence of only one criterion necessarily leads to a disagreement about the presence or absence of the diagnosis. In contrast, in a polythetic approach, such disagreement often has no impact on levels of agreement about the presence or absence of the diagnosis, because raters can still agree on the presence or absence of the diagnosis even if they disagree on one or more specific criteria.

The shift toward a polythetic approach is also an implicit nod to the fact that few, if any, signs and symptoms of psychopathology are *pathognomonic*. A pathognomonic indicator is characteristic of a disorder that can be used by itself to establish its diagnosis. For example, Koplik's spots—tiny spots in the mouth that look much like grains of sand surrounded by red rings—are essentially pathognomonic for measles. A sign or symptom can in principle be one-way pathognomonic, meaning that it is a perfect *inclusion test* (the sign or symptom's presence always indicates the presence of the disorder) or two-way pathognomonic, meaning that it is both a perfect inclusion test and *exclusion test* (the sign or symptom's presence always indicates the presence of the disorder, and the sign or symptom's absence always indicates the absence of the disorder). With the possible exception of organic brain disorders, no *DSM* diagnoses boast a one-way pathognomonic indicator.

DSM-III-R and *DSM-IV* also witnessed a relaxation of many, though not all, of *DSM-III*'s hierarchical exclusion rules (Pincus, Tew, & First, 2004). This change largely reflected the paucity of research evidence concerning the causal primacy of certain disorders above others. In addition, many of these exclusion rules proved difficult to apply in practice, because they required subjective and highly inferential judgments of causal primacy on the part of diagnosticians.

Finally, *DSM-IV* added an appendix for *culture-bound syndromes*, recognizing the fact that some conditions vary, or at least vary markedly in their expression, across cultures (Draguns & Tanaka-Matsumi, 2003). Most of these culture-bound syndromes are widely known in non-Western cultures, although their etiology and relation to conditions diagnosed in Western cultures are poorly understood. For example, *koro*, an epidemic condition observed in parts of China and Malaysia, is marked by abrupt and intense fears that the penis (in men) or vulva or breasts (in women) are receding into the body. Still other culture-bound syndromes appear to be variants of diagnoses that we readily recognize in Western culture. For example, *taijin kyofusho*, common in

Japan, refers to a fear of offending others by one's appearance, body odor, nonverbal behavior, and so on. It may be a subspecies of social phobia that is especially prevalent in cultures, especially in Asia, that stress group harmony above individual autonomy (Kleinknecht, Dinnel, Tanouye-Wilson, & Lonner, 1994).

Criticisms of the Current Classification System

Recent versions of the diagnostic manual have helped to place the field of psychopathology on firmer scientific ground, largely because they have established reasonably reliable operationalizations for most mental disorders and furthered the development of standardized instruments, such as structured psychiatric interviews, to assess these disorders. The theoretical agnosticism of recent *DSM*s has also facilitated research comparing the scientific support for competing theoretical conceptualizations of psychopathology (Wakefield, 1998). Despite the undeniable advances of *DSM-III* and its progeny, many critics have charged that these manuals are scientifically problematic in several respects. Here we examine five key criticisms of the current classification system: comorbidity, proliferation of diagnoses, neglect of the attenuation paradox, adoption of a categorical model, and a scientifically unsupported distinction between Axis I and Axis II.[2]

COMORBIDITY

DSM-III and its revisions are marked by high levels of co-occurrence and covariation among many of its diagnostic categories, a phenomenon known, perhaps misleadingly, as *comorbidity* (Caron & Rutter, 1991; Lilienfeld et al., 1994; Pincus et al., 2004). We say misleadingly because it is premature in most cases to assume that comorbidity reflects the overlap among etiologically distinct conditions, as opposed to slightly different variants of the same underlying condition (Drake & Wallach, 2007). Although comorbidity is frequent among Axis I conditions, it is especially rampant among Axis II conditions (Widiger & Rogers, 1989). In one analysis based on multiple sites, patients who met criteria for one personality disorder met criteria for approximately two additional personality disorders, on average—with 10% meeting criteria for four or more personality disorders (Stuart et al., 1998). One patient in a research study met criteria for all ten *DSM* personality disorders (Widiger et al., 1998).

The extent of comorbidity among both Axis I and II disorders is often underestimated in routine clinical practice (Zimmerman & Mattia, 2000), in part because of a phenomenon known as *diagnostic overshadowing*. Diagnostic overshadowing refers to the tendency for a more florid disorder to draw attention away from less florid co-occurring

---

[2] One frequent criticism of the *DSM* revision process (for example, Caplan, 1995) that we do not discuss at length here is the reliance on committee consensus in settling on both the: (a) inclusion and exclusion of specific disorders from the manual, and (b) the diagnostic criteria for specific disorders, largely because we find this criticism to be without substantial merit. Although expert consensus inevitably introduces subjective and political considerations into the diagnostic revision process (Ghaemi, 2003; Kirk & Kutchins, 1992) and has almost certainly resulted in flawed decisions, it is almost surely superior to a system in which one appointed expert adjudicates scientific complex disputes without the benefit of input from other experts. As Widiger and Clark (2000) observed, "no diagnostic manual can be constructed without a group of fallible persons interpreting the results of existing research" (p. 948). To paraphrase Winston Churchill's famous wisecrack about democracy, the *DSM* revision process is probably the worst system possible except for every other system.

disorders, thereby leading diagnosticians to either overlook them or attribute them to the more florid disorder. For example, the dramatic symptoms of Borderline Personality Disorder frequently lead clinicians to under diagnose commonly co-occurring but less salient conditions, such as Narcissistic and Dependent Personality Disorders (Garb, 1998). The genuine extent of comorbidity among personality disorders typically becomes evident only when structured and semistructured diagnostic interviews, which force assessors to inquire about all diagnostic criteria, are administered (Zimmerman & Mattia, 2000).

There are multiple potential explanations for comorbidity—some primarily substantive, others primarily methodological (see Klein & Riso, 1993, and Lilienfeld, 2003, for reviews). On the substantive front, one disorder (e.g., Generalized Anxiety Disorder) may predispose to another disorder (e.g., Dysthymic Disorder), the two disorders may mutually influence each other, or both disorders may be slightly different expressions of the same latent liability (e.g., neuroticism or negative emotionality). On the methodological front, comorbidity may result from overlapping diagnostic criteria, *clinical selection bias* (du Fort, Newman, & Bland, 1993), that is, the tendency for psychiatric patients with one disorder to seek treatment only when they develop a co-occurring disorder. In addition, comorbidity can be produced by *logical errors* (Guilford, 1936), mistakes stemming from the tendency of diagnosticians to assume that two largely unrelated conditions are correlated.

Whatever its causes, extensive comorbidity is potentially problematic for the *DSM*, because an ideal classification system yields largely mutually exclusive categories with few overlapping cases (Lilienfeld, VanValkenberg, Larntz, & Akiskal, 1986; Sullivan & Kendler, 1998). As a consequence, such comorbidity may suggest that the current classification system is attaching multiple labels to differing manifestations of the same underlying condition. Defenders of the current classification system are quick to point out that high levels of comorbidity are also prevalent in organic medicine, and often indicate that certain conditions (e.g., diabetes) increase individuals' risk for other conditions (e.g., blindness), a phenomenon that Kaplan and Feinstein (1974) termed *pathogenetic comorbidity*. Nevertheless, in stark contrast to organic medicine, in which the causal pathways contributing to pathogenetic comorbidity are often well understood, the causal pathways contributing to pathogenetic comorbidity in the domain of psychopathology remain unknown.

Proliferation of Diagnoses

One dramatic change from *DSM-I* to *DSM-IV* has been the massive increase in the sheer number of diagnoses. Some critics have argued that this increase reflects the tendency for successive editions of the *DSM* to expand their range of coverage into new and largely uncharted waters (Houts, 2001). Many of these novel diagnoses may be of dubious validity, often reflecting a tendency to medicalize behaviors previously thought to be merely odd or unusual (Sommers & Satel, 2005). For example, the relatively recent *DSM* diagnosis of Asperger's syndrome, often believed to be a mild form of autism, appears to be applied increasingly to children who are withdrawn, shy, or awkward (Gernsbacher, Dawson, & Goldsmith, 2005).

Nevertheless, as Wakefield (2001) noted, there is little or no evidence that *DSM* has expanded its range of coverage. Instead, the increase in the number of diagnoses across *DSM*s reflects an increased splitting of broader diagnoses into progressively narrower subtypes. The distinction between *splitting* and *lumping* derives from biological taxonomy (Mayr, 1982) and refers to the difference between two classificatory styles: the tendency to subdivide broad and potentially heterogeneous categories into narrower and presumably more homogeneous categories (splitting) or the tendency to combine narrow and presumably more homogeneous categories into broad and potentially heterogeneous categories (lumping). For example, given evidence that Bipolar I Disorder and Bipolar II Disorder are related (although by no means identical) conditions with relatively similar family histories, laboratory correlates, prognoses, and treatment response, should we keep these diagnoses separate or combine them into a more encompassing, albeit more heterogeneous, category?

The splitting preferences of the architects of recent *DSM*s have been widely maligned (Houts, 2001). Herman van Praag (2000) even humorously diagnosed the *DSM*'s predilection for splitting as the disorder of Nosologomania (also see Ghaemi, 2003). A preference for splitting is entirely defensible from the standpoint of research and nosological revision. A key point is that the relation between splitting and lumping is asymmetrical: If we begin by splitting diagnostic categories, we can always lump them later if research demonstrates that they are essentially identical according to the Robins and Guze (1970) criteria for validity. Yet, if we begin by lumping it would be more problematic to split later. As a consequence, we may overlook potentially crucial distinctions among etiologically separable subtypes that bear differing implications for treatment and prevention.

NEGLECT OF THE ATTENUATION PARADOX

Much of the impetus behind *DSM-III* was the laudable attempt to increase the reliability of psychiatric diagnosis and, thereby, place the fields of psychiatry and clinical psychology on firmer scientific footing. Nevertheless, reliability is only a means to an end, namely validity; moreover, as noted earlier, validity is limited not by reliability per se, but by its square root (Meehl, 1986). Therefore, diagnoses of even modest reliability can, in principle, achieve high levels of validity.

Ironically, efforts to achieve higher reliability, especially internal consistency, can sometimes produce decreases in validity, a phenomenon that Loevinger (1957) referred to as the *attenuation paradox* (also see Clark & Watson, 1995). This paradox can result when an investigator uses a narrowly circumscribed pool of items to capture a broad and multifaceted construct. In such a case, the measure of the construct may exhibit high internal consistency yet low validity, because it does not adequately tap the full breadth and richness of the construct.

Some authors have argued that this state of affairs occurred with several *DSM* diagnoses. Putting it a bit differently, they have suggested that *DSM-III* and its descendants sacrificed validity at the altar of reliability (Vailliant, 1984). For example, the current *DSM* diagnosis of Antisocial Personality Disorder (ASPD) is intended to assess the core interpersonal and affective features of psychopathic personality (psychopathy) delineated by Cleckley (1941), Karpman (1948), and others. Indeed, the accompanying text of *DSM-IV* even refers misleadingly to ASPD as synonymous with psychopathy (APA, 2000, p. 702). Because the developers of *DSM-III* (APA, 1980) were concerned that the personality features of psychopathy—such as guiltlessness, callousness, and self-centeredness—were difficult to assess reliably, they opted for a diagnosis emphasizing overt and easily agreed on antisocial behaviors—such as vandalism, stealing, and physical aggression (Lilienfeld, 1994). These changes may have resulted in a diagnosis with greater internal consistency and inter-rater reliability than the more traditional construct of psychopathy (although evidence for this possibility is lacking). Nevertheless, they may have also resulted in a diagnosis with lower validity, because the *DSM* diagnosis of ASPD largely fails to assess the personality features central to psychopathy (Lykken, 1995). Indeed, accumulating evidence suggests that measures of ASPD are less valid for predicting a number of theoretically meaningful variables—including laboratory indicators—than are measures of psychopathy (Hare, 2003; also see Vailliant, 1984, for a discussion of the reliability-tradeoff in the case of the *DSM-III* diagnosis of schizophrenia).

ADOPTION OF A CATEGORICAL MODEL

Technically, the *DSM* is agnostic on the question of whether psychiatric diagnoses are truly categories in nature, or what Meehl (Meehl & Golden, 1982) termed *taxa*, as opposed to continua or dimensions. Taxa differ from normality in kind, whereas dimensions differ in degree. Pregnancy is a taxon, as a woman cannot be slightly pregnant; in contrast, height is a dimension (although certain taxonic conditions, like hormonal abnormalities, can lead to heights that differ qualitatively from the general population). The opening pages of *DSM-IV* state: "There is no assumption that each category of mental disorder is a completely discrete entity with absolute boundaries dividing it from other mental disorders or from no mental disorder" (p. xxxi). Yet at the measurement level, the *DSM* embraces an exclusively categorical model, classifying individuals as either meeting criteria for a disorder or not.

This categorical model is problematic for at least two reasons. First, there is growing evidence from *taxometric analyses* (Meehl & Golden, 1982); namely, those that allow researchers to ascertain whether a single observed distribution is decomposable into multiple independent distributions, that many or even most *DSM* diagnoses are underpinned by dimensions rather than taxa (Kendell & Jablensky, 2003), with schizophrenia and schizophrenia-spectrum disorders being notable probable exceptions (Lenzenweger & Korfine, 1992). This is particularly true for most personality disorders (Cloninger, in press; Trull & Durrett, 2005), including Antisocial Personality Disorder (Marcus, Edens, Lilienfeld, & Poythress, 2006). Even many or most Axis I disorders, such as Major Depression (Slade & Andrews, 2005) and Social Phobia (Kollman, Brown, Liverant, & Hoffman, 2006), appear to be dimensional as opposed to taxonic in structure.

Second, setting aside the ontological issue of taxonicity versus dimensionality, there is good evidence that measuring most disorders (especially personality disorders) dimensionally by using the full range of scores typically results in higher correlations with external validating variables than does measuring them categorically in an all-or-none fashion (Ullrich, Borkenau, & Marneros, 2001). Such findings are not surprising given that artificial dichotomization of variables almost always results in a loss of information and, hence, statistical power (Cohen, 1983; MacCallum, Zhang, Preacher, & Rucker, 2002).

AXIS I –AXIS II DISTINCTION

The rationale for the Axis I-Axis II distinction has never been grounded in high quality scientific evidence (Harkness & Lilienfeld, 1997). As already noted, there is increasing evidence that some Axis I conditions, including mood and anxiety disorders, are under-pinned by dimensions that (e.g., high levels of negative emotionality) may be the same that underpin many Axis II conditions. Moreover, there is no compelling evidence for a qualitative difference between Axis I and Axis II conditions.

DSM-III and its revisions have not been consistent in their handling of some Axis I and Axis II disorders (Frances, 1980). Certain Axis I conditions—such as Schizophrenia, Dysthymic Disorder, or Cyclothymic Disorder—are at least as chronic as most Axis II disorders and arguably belong on Axis II given its emphasis on trait-like stability. The *DSM*'s placement of Axis II disorders has also been inconsistent in many cases. For example, Cyclothymic Disorder appears to be a subsyndromal form of Bipolar Disorder and is placed on Axis I, yet Schizotypal Personality Disorder appears to be a subsyndromal form of Schizophrenia and is placed on Axis II. The reasons for this differential treatment of Cyclothymic Disorder and Schizotypal Personality Disorder are unclear, and they do not appear to be based primarily on scientific considerations.

The DSM: *Quo Vadis?*

In some respects, *DSM-III*-R and *DSM-IV* have been disappointments, as they have not resolved many of serious problems endemic to *DSM-III* (Ghaemi, 2003). Comorbidity in *DSM-III*-R and *DSM-IV* has, if anything, mushroomed since the dismantling of many hierarchical exclusion rules (Lilienfeld & Waldman, 2004). Some diagnostic categories (e.g., Antisocial Personality Disorder) of questionable validity remain, and the Axis I-Axis II distinction remains in place despite a conspicuous lack of compelling scientific evidence. The planning for the next edition of the American Psychiatric Association's diagnostic manual, *DSM-V*, began in 1999, with its projected publication date in 2011. *DSM-V*, to be spearheaded by David Kupfer, presents both challenges and opportunities: challenges because many conceptual and methodological quandaries regarding psychiatric diagnosis remain unresolved, and opportunities because a new manual opens the door for novel approaches to the classification of psychopathology.

With these considerations in mind, we sketch out two promising future directions for *DSM-V*: adoption of a dimensional approach and the incorporation of endophenotypic markers into psychiatric diagnosis (see Widiger & Clark, 2000, for other proposals for *DSM-V*).

A DIMENSIONAL APPROACH

The accumulating evidence for the dimensionality of many psychiatric conditions, particularly personality disorders, has led many authors to suggest replacing or at least supplementing the *DSM*—Axis-II in particular—with a set of dimensions derived from the science of personality (Widiger & Clark, 2000). The leading candidate for a dimensional model is the Five Factor Model (FFM; Goldberg, 1993), which consists of five major dimensions that have emerged repeatedly in factor analyses of omnibus (broad) measures of personality: extraversion, neuroticism, agreeableness, conscientiousness, and openness to experience (the FFM, incidentally, can easily be recalled using the water-logged mnemonics of OCEAN or CANOE). These five dimensions also contain lower-order facets that provide a fine-grained description of personality; for example,

the FFM dimension of extraversion contains facets of warmth, gregariousness, assertiveness, excitement seeking, and so on (Costa & McCrae, 1992).

The FFM may be able to accommodate variations not only in normal but also in
abnormal personality (Costa & Widiger, 2001). For example, within the FFM the prototypical individual with Antisocial Personality Disorder might be described as low in
most facets of agreeableness and conscientiousness, low in some facets of neuroticism
(especially those relevant to anxiety), high in other facets of neuroticism (especially
those relevant to hostility), and high in some facets of extraversion (especially those
relevant to assertiveness and excitement seeking) The FFM has the distinct advantages
of being consistent with emerging data on the dimensionality of most personality disorders, and of being widely replicated in studies using diverse methodologies. In addition,
research suggests that much of the comorbidity among *DSM-IV* personality disorders
can be reproduced by the patterns of correlations among FFM dimensions (Lynam &
Widiger, 2001).

There are, however, at least two major obstacles confronting the implementation of a
dimensional system within *DSM-V*. First, the FFM —although influential and widely
used—is far from universally accepted (Block, 1995). Moreover, a number of authors
have offered plausible and reasonably well supported competing models of the structure
of personality (Cloninger, in press; Eysenck & Eysenck, 1975; Livesley, 2003; Tellegen, 1982). For example, Tellegen (1982) has proposed a three-dimensional model of
personality encompassing *positive emotionality* (the enduring propensity to experience
pleasant affects of many kinds, including cheerfulness, social intimacy, and achievement striving), *negative emotionality* (the enduring propensity to experience unpleasant
affects of many kinds, including anxiety, hostility, and mistrust), and *constraint*
(response inhibition and impulse control). The differences across dimensional systems
may not be an insurmountable problem, however, because some authors have noted significant correspondences among competing models of personality structure (Watson,
Clark, & Harkness, 1994). For example, Tellegen's "Big Three" Model maps nicely
onto much of the FFM, with positive emotionality largely subsuming FFM extraversion,
negative emotionality largely subsuming FFM neuroticism and some features of
reversed agreeableness, and constraint largely subsuming FFM conscientiousness and
reversed openness to experience (Church, 1994).

A second and perhaps more serious objection to a purely dimensional approach
derives from the often neglected distinction between *basic tendencies* and *characteristic
adaptations* in personality psychology (Harkness & Lilienfeld, 1997; McCrae & Costa,
1995). Basic tendencies are core personality traits, whereas characteristic adaptations
are the behavioral manifestations of these traits. A large body of personality research
suggests that basic tendencies can often be expressed in a wide variety of different characteristic adaptations depending on the upbringing, interests, cognitive skills, and other
personality traits of the individual. For example, the scores of firemen on a
well-validated measure of the personality trait of sensation seeking (a construct closely
related to, although broader than, risk-taking) are significantly higher than those of
college students, but comparable to those of incarcerated prisoners (Zuckerman, 1994).
This finding dovetails with the notion that the same basic tendency, in this case sensation seeking, can be expressed in either socially constructive or destructive outlets depending on yet unidentified moderating influences.

The distinction between basic tendencies versus characteristic adaptations implies
that personality dimensions, such as those from the FFM, may never be sufficient to

capture the full variance in personality disorders, because these dimensions (basic tendencies) do not adequately assess many key aspects of psychopathological functioning, many of which can be viewed as maladaptive characteristic adaptations (Sheets & Craighhead, 2007). This theoretical conjecture is corroborated by findings that the FFM dimensions do not account for a sizeable chunk of variance in many *DSM-IV* personality disorders. For example, in one study the correlations between FFM prototype scores of *DSM-IV* personality disorders (derived from expert ratings of the FFM facets most closely associated with each disorder) and structured interview-based measures of these disorders were high for some disorders (e.g., Avoidant Personality Disorder; $r = .67$) and modest and even negligible for others (e.g., Obsessive-Compulsive Disorder; $r = .13$; Miller, Reynolds, & Pilkonis, 2004). The lattermost finding may reflect the fact that some obsessive-compulsive traits—such as perfectionism—may be adaptive in certain settings and, therefore, may not lead inevitably to personality pathology. Moreover, Skodol et al. (2005) reported that the dimensions of the Schedule for Nonadaptive and Adaptive Personality (SNAP; Clark, 1993)—a measure that assesses many pathological behaviors associated with personality disorders—displayed incremental validity above and beyond the FFM dimensions in distinguishing among *DSM-IV* personality disorders (also see Reynolds & Clark, 2001). This finding suggests that the FFM overlooks crucial distinctions captured by the SNAP, perhaps in part because the SNAP assesses not only basic tendencies but also the maladaptive characteristic adaptations of many personality disorders (Lilienfeld, 2005).

The findings reviewed here imply that a dimensional model may be useful in capturing core features of many *DSM* personality disorders. Nevertheless, they raise the possibility that personality dimensions, including the FFM, may not be sufficient by themselves to capture personality pathology, because they cannot tell us whether individuals' behavioral adaptations to these dimensions were adaptive or maladaptive, nor the phenotypic (behavioral) manifestations these adaptations have assumed.

ENDOPHENOTYPIC MARKERS

As noted earlier, considerable recent interest has focused on the use of endophenotypes in the validation of psychiatric diagnoses (Andreasen, 1995; Waldman, 2005). Nevertheless, endophenotypic markers have thus far been excluded from *DSM* diagnostic criterion sets, which consist entirely of the classical signs and symptoms of disorders (exophenotypes). This omission is noteworthy, because endophenotypes may lie closer to the etiology of many disorders than exophenotypes.

This situation may change in coming years with accumulating evidence from studies of biochemistry, brain imaging, and performance on laboratory tasks, which hold the promise of identifying more valid markers of certain mental disorders (Widiger & Clark, 2000). To take just two examples, many impulse control disorders (e.g., Pathological Gambling, Intermittent Explosive Disorder) appear to be associated with low levels of serotonin metabolites (Moeller, Barratt, Dougherty, Schmitz, & Swann, 2001) and major depression is frequently associated with left frontal hypoactivation (Henriques & Davidson, 1991).

Nevertheless, at least two potential obstacles confront the use of endophenotypic markers in psychiatric diagnosis, the first conceptual and the second empirical. First, the widespread assumption, that endophenotypic markers are more closely linked to underlying etiological processes than exophenotypic markers (Kihlstrom, 2002), is just that, an assumption. For example, the well replicated finding that diminished amplitude of the P300 (an brain event-related potential appearing approximately 300 milliseconds following stimulus onset) is dependably associated with externalizing disorders—such as Conduct Disorder and drug dependence (Patrick et al., 2006)—could reflect the fact that P300 is merely a sensitive indicator of attention. As a consequence, diminished P300 amplitude could be a downstream consequence of the inattention and low levels of motivation often associated with externalizing disorders. This possibility would not necessarily negate the incorporation of P300 amplitude into diagnostic criterion sets, although it could raise questions concerning its specificity for externalizing disorders, let alone specific externalizing disorders.

Second, no endophenotypic markers, yet, identified are close to serving as inclusion tests for their respective disorders. Even smooth pursuit eye movement dysfunction, which is perhaps the most dependable biological marker of schizophrenia, is only present in anywhere from 40% to 80% of patients with schizophrenia, so it would miss many individuals with the disorder. It may come closer, however, to serving as a good exclusion test, as it is present in only about 10% of normal individuals (Clementz & Sweeney, 1990; Keri & Janka, 2004). Thus, although endophenotypic markers may eventually add to the predictive efficiency of some diagnostic criteria assets, they are likely to be fallible indicators, just like traditional signs and symptoms. These markers also sustain the hope of assisting in the identification of more etiologically pure subtypes of disorders; for example, schizophrenia patients with abnormal smooth pursuit eye movements may prove to be separable in important ways from other schizophrenia patients.

Summary and Future Directions

We conclude the chapter with ten take-home messages:

1. A systematic system of psychiatric classification is a prerequisite for psychiatric diagnosis.
2. Psychiatric diagnoses serve important, even essential, communicative functions.
3. A valid psychiatric diagnosis gives us new information—for example, it tells about the diagnosed individuals' probable family history, performance on laboratory tests, natural history, and perhaps response to treatment—and it also distinguishes that person's diagnosis from other, related diagnoses.
4. The claim that mental illness is a myth rests on a misunderstanding of the role of lesions in medical disorders.
5. Prevalent claims to the contrary, psychiatric diagnoses often achieve adequate levels of reliability and validity, and do not typically pigeon-hole or stigmatize individuals when correctly applied.
6. There is no clear consensus on the correct definition of mental disorder, and some authors have suggested that the higher-order concept of mental disorder is intrinsically undefinable. Even if true, this should have no effect on the scientific investigation, assessment, or treatment of specific mental disorders (e.g., Schizophrenia, Panic Disorder), which undeniably exist.

7. Early versions of the diagnostic manual (*DSM-I* and *DSM-II*) were problematic because they provided clinicians and researchers with minimal guidance for establishing diagnoses and required high levels of subjective judgment and clinical inference.

8. *DSM-III*, which appeared in 1980, helped to alleviate this problem by providing diagnosticians with explicit diagnostic criteria, algorithms (decision-rules), and hierarchical exclusion criteria, leading to increases in the reliability of many psychiatric diagnoses.

9. The current classification system, *DSM-IV*, is a clear advance over *DSM-I* and *DSM-II*. Nevertheless, *DSM-IV* continues to be plagued by a variety of problems, especially extensive comorbidity, reliable diagnoses that are of questionable validity, adoption of a categorical model in the absence of compelling evidence, and a largely arbitrary distinction between Axis I (major mental disorders) and Axis II (mental retardation and personality disorders).

10. Fruitful potential directions for *DSM-V* include a dimensional model of personality to replace or supplement the existing categorical system of Axis II, and the incorporation of endophenotypic markers into the diagnostic criteria for some disorders.

References

Amador, X. F., & Paul-Odouard, R. (2000). Defending the unabomber: Anosognosia in schizophrenia. *Psychiatric Quarterly, 71,* 363–371.

American Psychiatric Association. (1952). *Diagnostic and statistical manual of mental disorders.* Washington, DC: Author.

American Psychiatric Association. (1968). *Diagnostic and statistical manual of mental disorders* (2nd ed.). Washington, DC: Author.

American Psychiatric Association. (1980). *Diagnostic and tatistical manual of mental disorders* (3rd ed.). Washington, DC: Author.

American Psychiatric Association. (1987). *Diagnostic and statistical manual of mental disorders* (3rd ed., rev). Washington, DC: Author.

American Psychiatric Association. (1994). *Diagnostic and statistical manual of mental disorders* (4th ed.). Washington, DC: Author.

American Psychiatric Association. (2000). *Diagnostic and statistical manual of mental disorders* (Text rev.). Washington, DC: Author.

Andreasen, N. C. (1995). The validation of psychiatric diagnosis: New models and approaches. *American Journal of Psychiatry, 152,* 161–162.

Barlow, D. H. (2001). *Anxiety and its disorders: The nature and treatment of anxiety and panic* (2nd ed.). New York: Guilford.

Bayer R., & Spitzer, R. L. (1982). Edited correspondence on the status of homosexuality in *DSM-III. Journal of the History of the Behavioral Sciences, 18,* 32–52.

Benton, A. L. (1992). Gerstmann's syndrome. *Archives of Neurology, 49,* 445–447.

Blashfield, R., & Burgess, D. (2007). Classification provides an essential basis for organizing mental disorders. In S. O. Lilienfeld & W. T. O'Donohue (Eds.), *The great ideas of clinical science: 17 principles that every mental professional should understand* (pp. 93–118). New York: Routledge.

Block, J. (1995). A contrarian view of the five-factor approach to personality description. *Psychological Bulletin, 117,* 187–215.

Brown, M. (2006, August 16). War of the worlds. *New York Times,* p. 17.

Caron, C., & Rutter, M. (1991). Comorbidity in child psychopathology: Concepts, issues and research strategies. *Journal of Child Psychology and Psychiatry, 32,* 1063–1080.

Clark, L. A. (1993). *Manual for the schedule for nonadaptive and adaptive personality (SNAP).* Minneapolis: University of Minnesota Press.

Clark, L. A., & Watson, D. (1995). Constructing validity: Basic issues in objective scale development. *Psychological Assessment, 7,* 309–319.

Cleckley, H. (1941). *The mask of sanity.* St. Louis, MO: Mosby.

Clementz, B. A., & Sweeney, J. A. (1990). Is eye movement dysfunction a biological marker for schizophrenia? A methodological review. *Psychological Bulletin, 108,* 77–92.

Cloninger, C. R. (2007). Foreward. In W.O'Donohue, K. A. Fowler, & S. O. Lilienfeld, (Eds.), *Personality disorders: Toward the DSM-V* (pp. vii–xvi). Thousand Oaks, CA: Sage.

Cohen, H. (1981). The evolution of the concept of disease. In A. L. Caplan, H. T. Engelhardt, Jr., & J. J. McCartney (Eds.), *Concepts of health and disease: Interdisciplinary perspectives* (pp. 209–220). Reading, MA: Addison-Wesley.

Cohen, J. (1983). The cost of dichotomization. *Applied Psychological Measurement, 7,* 249–253.

Compton, W. M. & Guze, S. B. (1995). The neoKraepelinian revolution in psychiatric diagnosis. *European Archives of Psychiatry and Clinical Neuroscience, 245,* 196–201.

Cooper, G. (2007). Medical errors with psychiatric patients. *Psychotherapy Networker, 31*(3), 17–18.

Cornez-Ruiz, S., & Hendricks, B. (1993). Effects of labeling and ADHD behaviors on peer and teacher judgments. *Journal of Educational Research, 86,* 349–355.

Costa, P. T., Jr., & McCrae, R. R. (1992). Normal personality assessment in clinical practice: The NEO personality inventory. *Psychological Assessment, 4,* 5–13.

Costa, P. T., & Widiger, T. A. (2001). *Personality disorders and the five-factor model of personality* (2nd ed.). Washington, DC: American Psychological Association.

Cronbach, L. J. (1951). Coefficient alpha and the internal structure of tests. *Psychometrika, 16,* 297–335.

Cronbach, L. J., & Meehl, P. E. (1955). Construct validity in psychological tests. *Psychological Bulletin, 52*, 281–302.

Draguns, J. G., & Tanaka-Matsumi, J. (2003). Assessment of psychopathology across and within cultures: Issues and findings. *Behaviour Research and Therapy, 41*, 755–776.

Drake, R. E., & Wallach, M. A. (2007). Is comorbidity a psychological science? *Clinical Psychology: Science and Practice, 14*, 20–22.

Du Fort, G. G., Newman, S. C., & Bland, R. C. (1993). Psychiatric comorbidity and treatment seeking: Sources of selection bias in the study of clinical populations. *Journal of Nervous and Mental Disease, 181*, 467–474.

Eysenck, H. J., & Eysenck, S. B. G. (1975). *Manual of the Eysenck personality questionnaire* (adult and junior). London: Hodder and Stoughton.

Eysenck, H. J., Wakefield, J., & Friedman, A. (1983). Diagnosis and clinical assessment: The *DSM-III*. *Annual Review of Psychology, 34*, 167–193.

Faust, D., & Miner, R. A. (1986). The empiricist in his new clothes: *DSM-III* in perspective. *American Journal of Psychiatry, 143*, 962–967.

Feighner, J., Robins, E., Guze, S., Woodruff, R., Winokur, G., & Munoz, R. (1972). Diagnostic criteria for use in psychiatric research. *Archives of General Psychiatry, 26*, 57–63.

First, M. B., Spitzer, R. L., Gibbon, M., & Williams, J. B. W. (2002). *Structured clinical interview for DSM-IV-TR axis I disorders, research version, patient edition*. New York: Biometrics Research, New York State Psychiatric Institute.

Frances, A. J. (1980). The *DSM-III* personality disorders section: A commentary. *American Journal of Psychiatry, 137*, 1050–1054.

Garb, H. N. (1998). *Studying the clinician: Judgment research and psychological assessment*. Washington, DC: American Psychological Association.

Garber, J., & Strassberg, Z. (1991). Construct validity: History and application to developmental psychopathology. In W. M. Grove & D. Cicchetti (Eds.), *Personality and psychopathology* (pp. 218–258). Minneapolis: University of Minnesota Press.

Gernsbacher, M. A., Dawson, M., & Goldsmith, H. H. (2005). Three reasons not to believe in an autism epidemic. *Current Directions in Psychological Science, 14*, 55–58.

Ghaemi, N. (2003). *The concepts of psychiatry: A pluralistic approach to the mind and mental illness*. Baltimore, MD: Johns Hopkins University Press.

Goldberg, L. R. (1993). The structure of phenotypic personality traits. *American Psychologist, 48*, 266–275.

Goodwin, D. W., & Guze, S. B. (1996). *Psychiatric diagnosis* (5th ed.) New York: Oxford University Press.

Gorenstein, E. E. (1992). *The science of mental illness*. San Diego, CA: Academic Press.

Gottesman, I. I., & Gould, T. D. (2003). The endophenotype concept in psychiatry: Etymology and strategic intentions. *American Journal of Psychiatry, 160*, 636–645.

Gough, H. (1971). Some reflections on the meaning of psychodiagnosis. *American Psychologist, 26*, 160–167.

Grob, G. N. (1991). Origins of *DSM-I*: A study in appearance and reality. *American Journal of Psychiatry, 148*, 421–431.

Guilford, J. P. (1936). *Psychometric methods*. New York: McGraw-Hill.

Harkness, A. R., & Lilienfeld, S. O. (1997). Individual differences science for treatment planning: Personality traits. *Psychological Assessment, 9*, 349–360.

Harris, M. J., Milich, R., Corbitt, E. M., Hoover, D. W., & Brady, M. (1992). Self-fulfilling effects of stigmatizing information on children's social interactions. *Journal of Personality and Social Psychology, 63*, 41–50.

Henriques, J. B., & Davidson, R. J. (1991). Left frontal hypoactivation in depression. *Journal of Abnormal Psychology, 100*, 535–545.

Houts, A. C. (2001). The diagnostic and statistical manual's new white coat and circularity of plausible dysfunctions: Response to Wakefield, part 1. *Behavior Research and Therapy, 39*, 315–345.

Joiner, T. (2006). *Why people die by suicide*. Cambridge, MA: Harvard University Press.

Kaplan, M. H., & Feinstein, A. R. (1974). The importance of classifying initial co-morbidity in evaluating the outcome of diabetes mellitus. *Journal of Chronic Diseases, 27*, 387–404.

Karpman, B. (1948). The myth of the psychopathic personality. *American Journal of Psychiatry, 104*, 523–524.

Kazdin, A. E. (1983). Psychiatric diagnosis, dimensions of dysfunction, and child behavior therapy. *Behavior Therapy, 14*, 73–99.

Kendell, R. E. (1975). The concept of disease and its implications for psychiatry. *British Journal of Psychiatry, 127*, 305–315.

Kendell, R., & Jablensky, A. (2003) Distinguishing between the validity and utility of psychiatric diagnoses. *American Journal of Psychiatry, 160*, 4–12.

Kendler, K. S. (1980). The nosologic validity of para-noia (simple delusional disorder): A review. *Archives of General Psychiatry, 37*, 699–706.

Keri, S., & Janka, Z. (2004). Critical evaluation of cognitive dysfunctions as endophenotypes of schizo-phrenia. *Acta Psychiatrica Scandinavica, 110*, 83–91.

Kihlstrom, J. F. (2002). To honor Kraepelin . . . : From symptoms to pathology in the diagnosis of mental illness. In L. Beutler & M. Malik (Eds.), *Rethinking the* DSM: *A psychological perspective* (pp. 279–303). Washington, DC: American Psychological Association.

Kirk, S. A., & Kutchins, H. (1992). *The selling of DSM: The rhetoric of science in psychiatry.* New York: Aldine de Gruy.

Klein, D., & Riso, L. P. (1993). Psychiatric disorders: Problems of boundaries and comorbidity. In C. G. Costello (Ed.), *Basic issues in psychopathology* (pp. 19–66). New York: Guilford.

Kleinknecht, R. A., Dinnel, D. L., Tanouye-Wilson, S., & Lonner, W. J. (1994). Cultural variation in social anxiety and phobia: A study of *Taijin Kyofusho. The Behavioral Therapist, 17*(8), 175–178.

Klerman, G. (1984). The advantages of DSM-III. *American Journal of Psychiatry, 141*, 539–542.

Kollman, D. M., Brown, T. A., Liverant, G. I., & Hofmann, S. G. (2006). A taxometric investigation of the latent structure of social anxiety disorder in outpatients with anxiety and mood disorders. *Depression and Anxiety, 23*, 190–199.

Kraupl Taylor, F. (1971). A logical analysis of medico-physiological concept of disease. *Psychological Medicine, 1*, 356–364.

Lenzenweger, M. F., & Korfine, L. (1992). Confirming the latent structure and base rate of schizotypy: A taxometric analysis. *Journal of Abnormal Psychology, 101*, 567–571.

Lief, A. A. (Ed.). (1948). *The commonsense psychiatry of Dr. Adolf Meyer: Fifty-two selected papers.* New York: McGraw-Hill.

Lilienfeld, S. O. (1994). Conceptual problems in the assessment of psychopathy. *Clinical Psychology Review, 14*, 17–38.

Lilienfeld, S. O. (1995). *Seeing both sides: Classic controversies in abnormal psychology.* Pacific Grove, CA: Brooks/Cole.

Lilienfeld. S. O. (2003). Comorbidity between and within childhood externalizing and internalizing dis-orders: Reflections and directions. *Journal of Abnor-mal Child Psychology, 31*, 285–291.

Lilienfeld, S. O. (2005). Longitudinal studies of person-ality disorders: Four lessons from personality psy-chology. *Journal of Personality Disorders, 19*, 547–556.

Lilienfeld, S. O., & Marino, L. (1995). Mental disorder as a Rochian concept: A critique of Wakefield's "harmful dysfunction" analysis. *Journal of Abnor-mal Psychology, 104*, 411–420.

Lilienfeld, S. O., & Marino, L. (1999). Essentialism revisited: Evolutionary theory and the concept of a mental disorder. *Journal of Abnormal Psychology, 108*, 400–411.

Lilienfeld, S. O., VanValkenburg, C., Larntz, K., & Akiskal, H. S. (1986). The relationship of histrionic personality to antisocial personality and somatiza-tion disorders. *American Journal of Psychiatry, 143*, 718–722.

Lilienfeld, S. O., Waldman, I. D., & Israel, A. C. (1994). A critical note on the use of the term and concept of "comorbidity" in psychopathology research. *Clinical Psychology: Science and Prac-tice, 1*, 71–83.

Link, B. G., & Cullen, F. T. (1990). The labeling theory of mental disorder: A review of the evidence. *Research in Community and Mental Health, 6*, 75–105.

Livesley, W. J. (2003). Diagnostic dilemmas in the classification of personality disorder. In K. A. Phil-lips, M. B. First, & H. A. Pincus (Eds.), *Advancing the* DSM: *Dilemmas in psychiatric diagnosis* (pp. 153–189). Washington, DC: American Psychiatric Association.

Loevinger, J. (1957). Objective tests as instruments of psychological theory. *Psychological Reports, 3*, 635–694.

Lykken, D. T. (1995). *The antisocial personalities.* Hillsdale, NJ: Erlbaum.

Lynam, D. R., & Widiger, T. A. (2001). Using the five-factor model to represent the *DSM-IV* personality disorders: An expert consensus approach. *Journal of Abnormal Psychology, 110*, 401–412.

MacCallum, R. C., Zhang, S., Preacher, K. J., & Rucker, D. D. (2002). On the practice of dichotomi-zation of quantitative variables. *Psychological Methods, 7*, 19–40.

Marcus, D. K., Lilienfeld, S. O., Edens, J. F., & Poy-thress, N. G. (2006). Is antisocial personality disor-der continuous or categorical? A taxometric analysis. *Psychological Medicine, 36*, 1571–1581.

Matarazzo, J. D. (1983). The reliability of psychiatric and psychological diagnosis. *Clinical Psychology Review, 3*, 103–145.

Mayes, R., & Horwitz, A. V. (2005). *DSM-III* and the revolution in the classification of mental illness.

Journal of the History of the Behavioral Sciences, *41*, 249–267.

Mayr, E. (1982). *The growth of biological thought: Diversity, evolution, and inheritance*. Cambridge, MA: Belknap Press.

McCann, J. T., Shindler, K. L., & Hammond, T. R. (2003). The science and pseudoscience of expert testimony. In S. O. Lilienfeld, J. M. Lohr, & S. J. Lynn (Eds.), *Science and pseudoscience in contemporary clinical psychology* (pp. 77–108). New York: Guilford.

McCrae, R. R., & Costa, P. T. (1995). Trait explanations in personality psychology. *European Journal of Personality*, *9*, 231–252.

McHugh, P. R., & Slavney, P. R. (1998). *The perspectives of psychiatry* (2nd ed.). Baltimore: Johns Hopkins University Press.

Meehl, P. E. (1973). Why I do not attend case conferences. In P. E. Meehl (Ed.), *Psychodiagnosis: Selected papers* (pp. 225–302). Minneapolis: University of Minnesota Press.

Meehl, P. E. (1977). Specific etiology and other forms of strong influence: Some quantitative meanings. *Journal of Medicine and Philosophy*, *2*, 33–53.

Meehl, P. E. (1986). Diagnostic taxa as open concepts: Metatheoretical and statistical questions about reliability and construct validity in the grand strategy of nosological revision. In T. Millon & G. L. Klerman (Eds.), *Contemporary directions in psychopathology: Toward the* DSM-IV (pp. 215–231). New York: Guilford.

Meehl, P. E. (1990). Schizotaxia as an open concept. In A. I. Rabin, R. Zucker, R. Emmons, & S. Frank (Eds.), *Studying persons and lives* (pp. 248–303). New York: Springer.

Meehl, P. E., & Golden, R. (1982). Taxometric methods. In P. C. Kendall & J. N. Butcher (Eds.), *Handbook of research methods in clinical psychology* (pp. 127–181). New York: Wiley.

Messick, S. (1995). Validity of psychological assessment: Validation of inferences from persons' responses and performances as scientific inquiry into score meaning. *American Psychologist*, *50*, 741–749.

Meyer, G. J. (1997). Assessing reliability: Critical corrections for a critical examination of the Rorschach Comprehensive System. *Psychological Assessment*, *9*, 480–489.

Michels, R. (1984). A debate on *DSM-III*: First rebuttal. *American Journal of Psychiatry*, *141*, 548–553.

Milich, R., McAninich, C. B., & Harris, M. J. (1992). Effects of stigmatizing information on children's peer relations: Believing is seeing *School Psychology Review*, *21*, 399–408.

Miller, J. D., Reynolds, S. K., & Pilkonis, P. A. (2004). The validity of the five-factor model prototypes for personality disorders in two clinical samples. *Psychological Assessment*, *16*, 310–322.

Millon, T. (1975). Reflections on Rosenhan's "On being sane in insane places."*Journal of Abnormal Psychology*, *84*, 456–461.

Moeller, F. G., Barratt, E. S., Dougherty, D. M., Schmitz, J. M., & Swann, A. C. (2001.) Psychiatric aspects of impulsivity. *American Journal of Psychiatry*, *158*, 1783–1793.

Morey, L. C. (1991). Classification of mental disorders as a collection of hypothetical constructs. *Journal of Abnormal Psychology*, *100*, 289–293.

Morrison, J. (1997). *When psychological problems mask medical disorders: A guide for psychotherapists*. New York: Guilford.

Neese, R., & Williams, G. (1994). *Why we get sick*. New York: Vintage.

Patrick, C. J., Bernat, E., Malone, S. M., Iacono, W. G., Krueger, R. F., & McGue, M. K. (2006). P300 amplitude as an indicator of externalizing in adolescent males. *Psychophysiology*, *43*, 84–92.

Pelham, W. E., & Bender, M. E. (1982). Peer relationships in hyperactive children: Description and treatment. In K. D. Gadow & I. Bialer (Eds.), *Advances in learning and behavioral disabilities* (Vol. 1, pp. 365–436). Greenwich, CT: JAI Press.

Pincus, H. A., Tew, J. D., & First, M. B. (2004). Psychiatric comorbidity: Is more less? *World Psychiatry*, *3*, 18–23.

Pouissant, A. F. (2002). Is extreme racism a mental illness? Point-counterpoint. *Western Journal of Medicine*, *176*, 4.

Reynolds, S. K., & Clark, L. A. (2001). Predicting personality disorder dimensions from domains and facets of the five-factor model. *Journal of Personality*, *69*, 199–222.

Robins, E., & Guze, S. B. (1970). Establishment of diagnostic validity in psychiatric illness: Its application to schizophrenia. *American Journal of Psychiatry*, *126*, 983–987.

Rosch, E. R. (1973). Natural categories. *Cognitive Psychology*, *4*, 328–350.

Rosch, E. R., & Mervis, C. B. (1975). Family resemblances: Studies in the internal structure of categories. *Cognitive Psychology*, *7*, 573–605.

Rosenhan, D. L. (1973). On being sane in insane places. *Science*, *179*, 250–258.

Ross, C., & Pam, A. (1996). *Pseudoscience in biological psychiatry: Blaming the body*. New York: Wiley.

Ruscio, J. (2004). Diagnoses and the behaviors they denote: A critical evaluation of the labeling theory of mental illness. *Scientific Review of Mental Health Practice, 3*(1), 5–22.

Sarbin, T. R. (1969). On the distinction between social roles and social types, with special reference to the hippie. *American Journal of Psychiatry, 125*, 1024–1031.

Scadding, J. G. (1996). Essentialism and nominalism in medicine: Logic of diagnosis in disease terminology. *Lancet, 348*, 594–596.

Schaler, J. A. (Ed.). (2004). *Szasz under fire: The psychiatric abolitionist faces his critics.* Chicago: Open Court.

Scheff, T. (Ed.). (1975). *Labeling madness.* New Jersey: Prentice Hall.

Schmidt, F. L., Lee, H., & Ilies, R. (2003). Beyond Alpha: An empirical examination of the effects of different sources of measurement error on reliability estimates for measures of individual differences constructs. *Psychological Methods, 8*, 206–224.

Seitz, S., & Geske, D. (1976). Mothers' and graduate trainees' judgments of children: Some effects of labeling. *American Journal of Mental Deficiency, 81*, 362–370.

Selkoe, D. J. (1992). Aging brain, aging mind. *Scientific American, 267*, 134–142.

Sheets, E., & Craighead, W. E. (2007). Toward an empirically based classification of personality pathology. *Clinical Psychology: Science and Practice, 14*, 77–93.

Skinner, H. A. (1981). Toward the integration of classification theory and methods. *Journal of Abnormal Psychology, 90*, 68–87.

Skinner, H. A. (1986). Construct validation approach to psychiatric classification. In T. Millon & G. L. Klerman (Eds.), *Contemporary directions in psychopathology: Toward the* DSM-IV (pp. 307–330). New York: Guilford.

Slade, T., & Andrews, G. (2005). Latent structure of depression in a community sample: A taxometric analysis. *Psychological Medicine, 35*, 489–497.

Slater, L. (2004). *Opening Skinner's box: Great psychological experiments of the 20th century.* New York: W.W. Norton.

Sommers, C. H., & Satel, S. (2005). *One nation under therapy: How the helping culture is eroding self-reliance.* New York: St. Martin's.

Spitzer, R. L. (1975). On pseudoscience, logic in remission, and psychiatric diagnosis: A critique of Rosenhan's "On being sane in insane places."*Journal of Abnormal Psychology, 84*, 442–452.

Spitzer, R. L., Foreman, J. B. W., and Nee, J. (1979). *DSM-III* field trials. *American Journal of Psychiatry, 136*, 815–820.

Stuart, S., Pfohl, B., Battaglia, M., Bellodi, L., Grove, W., & Cadoret, R. (1998). The cooccurrence of *DSM-III-R* personality disorders. *Journal of Personality Disorders, 12*, 302–315.

Sullivan, P. F., & Kendler, K. S. (1998). The genetic epidemiology of smoking. *Nicotine and Tobacco Research, 1*, S51–S57.

Sutton, E. H. (1980). *An introduction to human genetics.* Philadelphia: Saunders College.

Szasz, T. (1960). The myth of mental illness. *American Psychologist, 15*, 113–118.

Tellegen, A. (1982). *Manual for the Multidimensional Personality Questionnaire.* Unpublished manuscript, University of Minnesota.

Trull, T. J., & Durett, C. A. (2005). Categorical and dimensional models of personality disorder. *Annual Review of Clinical Psychology, 1*, 355–380.

Ullrich, S., Borkenau, P., & Marneros, A. (2001). Personality disorders in offenders: Categorical versus dimensional approaches. *Journal of Personality Disorders, 15*, 442–449.

VanPraag, H. M. (2000). Nosologomania: A disorder of psychiatry. *World of Biological Psychiatry, 1*, 151–158.

Wakefield, J. C. (1992). The concept of mental disorder: On the boundary between biological facts and social values. *American Psychologist, 47*, 373–388.

Wakefield, J. C. (1998). The *DSM*'s theory-neutral nosology is scientifically progressive: Response to Follette and Houts. *Journal of Consulting and Clinical Psychology, 66*, 846–852.

Wakefield, J. C. (1999). Evolutionary versus prototype analyses of the concept of disorder. *Journal of Abnormal Psychology, 108*, 374–399.

Wakefield, J. C. (2001). The myth of *DSM*'s invention of new categories of disorder: Houts's diagnostic discontinuity thesis disconfirmed. *Behaviour Research and Therapy, 39*, 575–624.

Waldman, I. D. (2005). Statistical approaches to complex phenotypes: Evaluating neuropsychological endophenotypes of attention-deficit/hyperactivity disorder. *Biological Psychiatry, 57*, 1347–1356.

Waldman, I. D., Lilienfeld, S. O., & Lahey, B. B. (1995). Toward construct validity in the childhood disruptive behavior disorders: Classification and diagnosis in *DSM*-IV and beyond. In T. H.Ollendick & R. J. Prinz (Eds.), *Advances in clinical child psychology* (Vol. 17, pp. 323–363). New York: Plenum.

Watson, D., Clark, L. A., & Harkness, A. R. (1994). Structures of personality and their relevance to psychopathology. *Journal of Abnormal Psychology, 103,* 18–31.

Widiger, T. A. (1997). The construct of mental disorder. *Clinical Psychology: Science and Practice, 4,* 262–266.

Widiger, T. A. (2007). Alternatives to DSM-IV: Axis II. In W. O'Donohue, K. A. Fowler, & S. O. Lilienfeld (Eds.), *Personality disorders: Toward the DSM-V* (pp. 21–40). Thousand Oaks, CA: Sage.

Widiger, T. A., & Clark, L. A. (2000). Toward *DSM-V* and the classification of psychopathology. *Psychological Bulletin, 126,* 946–963.

Widiger, T. A., Frances, A. J., Pincus, H. A., Ross, R., First, M. B., & Davis, W. W. (Eds.). (1998). DSM-IV *sourcebook* (Vol. 4). Washington, DC: American Psychiatric Press.

Widiger, T. A., & Rogers, J. H. (1989). Prevalence and comorbidity of personality disorders. *Psychiatric Annals, 19,* 132–136.

Widiger, T. A., & Trull, T. (1985). The empty debate over the existence of mental illness: Comments on Gorenstein. *American Psychologist, 40,* 468–470.

Widiger, T. A., Frances, A. J., Spitzer, R. L., & Williams, J. B. W. (1991). The *DSM-III-*R personality disorders: An overview. *American Journal of Psychiatry, 145,* 786–795.

Zimmerman, M. (1994). Diagnosing personality disorders. *Archives of General Psychiatry, 51,* 225–245.

Zimmerman, M., & Mattia, J. I. (2000). Principal and additional *DSM-IV* disorders for which outpatients seek treatment. *Psychiatric Services, 51,* 1299–1304.

Zuckerman, M. (1994). *Behavioral expressions and biosocial bases of sensation seeking.* New York: Cambridge University Press.

Chapter 2

Evidence-Based Strategies for the Assessment of Developmental Psychopathology: Measuring Prediction, Prescription, and Process

ERIC YOUNGSTROM

"I often say that when you can measure what you are speaking about and express it in numbers you know something about it; but when you cannot measure it, when you cannot express it in numbers, your knowledge is of a meagre [sic] and unsatisfactory kind: it may be the beginning of knowledge, but you have scarcely, in your thoughts, advanced to the stage of science, whatever the matter may be."

— Lord Kelvin, Sir William Thomson, Electrical Units of Measurement (1883),
Popular Lectures and Addresses (1891), Vol. 1, pp. 80–81.

The goal of this chapter is to critically evaluate psychological assessment as it applies to developmental psychopathology. The litmus test for assessment methods is the extent to which they succeed in answering one of the "Three Ps" of assessment: Do they *predict* important criteria? Do they *prescribe* specific treatments? Do they inform our understanding of *processes* in developmental psychopathology? If they cannot contribute to one of these purposes, then it is not clear why we would add them to a research protocol or a clinical assessment battery. This review also evaluates the practice of assessment through a quantitative lens. One of the central ideas of this chapter is that changes in quantitative methods can contribute much toward bridging the science-practice gap by helping make better use of existing tools.

Background

Assessment represents a paradox in the field of psychology. On the one hand, it has a long history, and is arguably the single activity most germane to the province of psychology. Whereas multiple professional disciplines can offer therapy or counseling, or conduct basic research into social behavior or neuroscience, psychometric and behavioral assessment typically has remained within the guild of professional psychological activities. Measurement of constructs as diverse as personality, cognitive abilities, academic achievement, behavior problems, family functioning, quality of life, and other diverse constructs has been a distinctly psychological enterprise.

The paradox is that graduate training and psychological practice have increasingly become disconnected from this core professional function (Archer & Newsom, 2000; Stedman, Hatch, & Schoenfeld, 2001). There are several forces contributing to a current state of torpor in psychological assessment. One major issue is a lack of clear linkage between measurement tools and clinical practices. Well-developed instruments often have painstakingly honed psychometric properties, yet unclear validity in terms of guiding treatment or improving outcomes. Cognitive ability tests are an excellent case in point. They have the longest pedigree and most extensive corpus of research of any assessment tool, yet many experts question their treatment utility (Flanagan, McGrew, & Ortiz, 2000).

Another factor has to do with the emergence of managed care. The resulting erosion of reimbursement for services and the challenge to demonstrate cost effectiveness of assessment have raised the potential barriers between tool and practice from an intellectual issue to an iceberg against which clinical assessment practices have foundered (Eisman et al., 1998).

The history of psychological assessment has also contributed much inertia to contemporary practices. Our current battery of measures is based more on convention and habit than any clear sense that these are the best tools for specific purposes. Much of the validity evidence for contemporary tests is also recursive: The *Wechsler Intelligence Scales for Children, Fourth Edition* (Wechsler, 2003), was validated against the third edition, which was validated against the WISC-R, which in turn was validated against the WISC, the Binet, and ultimately against the Raven's Progressive Matrices, the Army Alpha, and other primordial ability measures (Sattler, 2001). There are far fewer studies that shine a light forward instead of backward into the prior validating lineage, and show that the test accomplishes some external criterion task better than competing measures. In the cognitive ability literature, there are fewer studies showing predictive or ecological validity than there are other criterion correlations (Neisser et al., 1996), yet cognitive ability probably represents the place where more work has been done than anywhere else in the field of developmental psychopathology assessment.

It is appropriate to have some degree of conservatism and inertia in clinical practice. Well-established measures will connect with the largest portion of the installed base of test users. There are also economies of scale for professionals and institutions when certain tests become industry standards. The most popular tests often (though not always) will have the most research available pertaining to them. However, correlations between popularity and research quantity are imperfect, and the strength of the association becomes even smaller when comparing popularity with the amount of high-quality, clinically relevant research.

The assessment of *developmental psychopathology* faces further obstacles. One is the inheritance of nosological systems that were developed first for adult clinical presentations and then later adapted for use with adolescents or children (Kazdin & Kagan, 1994). Another disconnect between the field of developmental psychopathology and typical clinical assessment is that developmental psychopathology focuses on understanding *processes* and *mechanisms*, whereas adult nosology has consciously adopted a noncausal approach to diagnosis, using phenomenological description instead of mechanisms as a way of organizing observations and classifying presentations (Carson, 1997). Adding further complexity, developmental psychopathology recognizes that people grow and change, and their growth is embedded in the context of other systems such as the family as well as the broader cultural environment. Understanding this growth requires the use of tools that are developmentally appropriate and that can be deployed at multiple levels of analysis in order to form an integrated model of change.

The following sections provide a brief overview of current practices in assessment and training, and then develop the concepts of the "Three Ps" of assessment (*prediction, prescription*, and *process*), and also lay out a framework for evaluating and refining tests to better approach these targets. Subsequent sections examine the added considerations imposed by studying developmental phenomena, including the issues of norms, developmentally appropriate modalities and content, continuity and discontinuity of phenomena, and the concepts of equipotentiality and multifinality (Cicchetti & Cohen, 1995; Kazdin & Kagan, 1994). The chapter concludes with recommendations about priority areas for research and also for technology transfer from existing research into meaningful changes in clinical practice and clinical training.

A Snapshot of Current Assessment Training and Practice

There has been considerable stability in the choice of assessment tools taught in graduate training programs or internships, and also used in clinical practice. Table 2.1 lists tests used for the assessment of personality and psychopathology in both children and adults, in descending order of use by practicing clinical psychologists (Camara, Nathan, & Puente, 1998). The table also reports the rank for usage by practicing neuropsychologists responding to the same survey (Camara et al., 1998), along with a ranking of what percentage of assessment courses cover a particular instrument (based on syllabi and questionnaire responses from 84 doctoral programs; Childs & Eyde, 2002). There is a high degree of consistency in the ranking of different tests across levels of training and across disciplines, with the Wechsler scales, the MMPI, and projective tests all showing high levels of usage. These tests were also the most widely used in prior surveys of practice and training, although there has been a historical trend for the emphasis on projective techniques to decrease at the predoctoral training level (although projectives are alive and well in clinical practice, as evidenced by the rankings in Table 2.1).

One striking feature of the list of instruments is the persistence of established incumbents among the measures. Although many other measures of cognitive ability are available, and many arguably have technical advantages over the Wechslers, the Wechslers remain the industry standard for training and practice (Sattler, 2001). Despite a vigorous debate about the validity and utility of the Rorschach (cf. Meyer & Handler, 1997; Wood, Nezworski, & Stejskal, 1996), it remains near the top of the list as well, as do other projective techniques that have more fundamental questions about the reliability

TABLE 2.1 Commonly Used Assessment Methods for Personality and Psychopathology Assessment

Test	Clinical Psychology Rank (n) (Camara et al., 1998)	Neuropsychology Rank (n) (Camara et al., 1998)	Training Rank (Percentage of Programs Teaching) (Childs & Eyde, 2002)	Rank by Median Number of Reports Written (Median # of Reports)—Clinical Programs (N = 111) (Stedman et al., 2001)
MMPI	1 (n=131)	1 (n=310)	3 (86)	1 (7.5 reports)
Rorschach	2 (n=122)	3 (n=144)	4 (81)	4 (4.3)
TAT	3 (n=100)	5 (n=84)	5 (71)	7 (1.5)
House-Tree-Person	4 (n=60)	6 (n=72)	17 (24)*	9.5 (1.0)*
Bender Gestalt	5 (n=54)	16 (n=27)	7 (46)	12 (0.5)
Beck Depression Inventory	6 (n=52)	2 (n=163)	–	5 (4.0)
Millon Clinical Multiaxial Inventory	7 (n=51)	4 (n=96)	8 (38)	13 (0.3)
WAIS-R/-III	8 (n=48)	9 (n=42)	1 (93)	2 (6.2)
Human Figure Drawing	9 (n=46)	8 (n=47)	17 (24)*	9.5 (1.0)*
Rotter Incomplete Sentences	10 (n=43)	10 (n=36)	–	–
Sentence Completion	11 (n=40)	7 (n=49)	12 (29)	6 (2.0)
MACI	12 (n=38)	11.5 (n=33)	–	–
WISC-III	13 (n=35)	19 (n=23)	2 (88)	3 (6.0)
CBCL	17 (n=22)	11.5 (n=33)	–	–

*Indicates a tie in the ranking—these were lumped together in the studies reported in the last column, and reported separately in the first columns.

of their administration or scoring procedures. Apparently, despite scores of alternate measures being developed and published, there is a substantial amount of inertia in the choice of tests used to assess personality, cognitive ability, and psychopathology.

A second observation is that many other well-validated instruments do not appear to have permeated far into clinical training or practice. In spite of the wealth of research on the "Big Three" or "Big Five" models of personality, for example, none of the instruments available to directly assess these constructs appears in the top dozen assessment tools, despite their demonstrated validity as measures of personality and their clinical relevance (Harkness & Lilienfeld, 1997). Although there is a substantial corpus of research developing both parent report and laboratory measures of temperament (e.g., Carey, 1998; Derryberry & Rothbart, 1997; Kagan, 1997b), none of these tools are reflected in the modal assessment batteries of practitioners. The Child Behavior Checklist (CBCL), which has been used in thousands of research studies and translated into dozens of languages (Achenbach, 1991; Achenbach & Rescorla, 2001), appears at number 17 on the list of assessment devices used by clinical psychologists (Camara et al., 1998), and neither the CBCL nor "behavior checklists" more generally appear in the top 20 tools or techniques covered in graduate assessment courses (Stedman et al., 2001). It is possible that there have been changes in training or usage in the 6 to 10 years since these surveys were conducted, but it is sobering to consider that the CBCL was initially published in 1983 and thus had 15 years of research and dissemination before the survey results that are reflected in Table 2.1. The stability in the ranking of tests when surveys have been repeated (Archer & Newsom, 2000; Stedman et al., 2001) also indicates that there is more reason to expect that there has been inertia rather than innovation in recent years.

A third observation, more subtle yet still discouraging, is that the order of popularity does not appear tightly correlated to evidence of validity. Established measures of psychopathology, such as the CBCL or the Beck Depression Inventory (Beck & Steer, 1987), rank below measures such as the Bender Gestalt Test and the Wechslers. This order ignores not only the validity evidence that has accumulated for the rating scales and checklists (e.g., Achenbach, 1999; Beck, Steer, & Garbin, 1988), but it also fails to take into account the lack of evidence for the validity of the Bender Gestalt as a measure of personality or psychopathology besides visual-motor integration difficulties (Sattler, 2002), or the demonstrated invalidity of subtest analysis from cognitive ability batteries as a measure of personality or psychopathology (Glutting, McDermott, Konold, Snelbaker, & Watkins, 1998; Glutting, Youngstrom, Oakland, & Watkins, 1996; M. W. Watkins, Glutting, & Youngstrom, 2005). Unfortunately, the lack of connection between evidence and practice is a phenomenon that has been observed throughout medicine (Guyatt & Rennie, 2002), and the enduring popularity of tests that are devoid of evidence has been true for decades—causing the editor of the *Mental Measurements Yearbooks* to opine that "bad tests will always be with us" (Buros, 1965).

The First P: Prediction

What assessment tools should be used to measure the development of psychopathology? How can users compare the myriad tests that are available and make an informed choice among them? What evidence would persuade a user to adopt a different test rather than continuing to rely on an entrenched approach to assessment? One of the first heuristics for evaluating an assessment strategy is determining whether it *predicts* criteria of interest. Prediction could mean demonstrating concurrent correlations as well as showing associations with criteria that are separated by time.

CONCURRENT CRITERION VALIDITY

Assessment tools can be useful by virtue of correlating with other meaningful criteria. Screening measures are useful because they correlate with diagnosis. Diagnoses are valuable in part because they correlate with associated features of illness, as well as course and outcomes. A nomothetic network of correlations also helps validate a diagnosis as a construct, by showing associations with family history, biological processes, or experimental psychopathology task performance (Cantwell, 1996; Robins & Guze, 1970).

An important part of the research enterprise is establishing the validity of a construct or diagnosis. This can be thought of as an iterative process that involves both *elaboration* and *consolidation*. Elaboration can involve expanding the network of correlations to include not just validators but also correlates in terms of typical treatment response, outcome, quality of life, and functioning. The *elaborative* process is crucial to contextualizing the construct and understanding its connections to various aspects of development.

The *consolidation* aspect of research involves clarifying when different measures are assessing the same underlying latent variables, and also creating models about the relationships between these underlying processes. The consolidation aspect becomes increasingly valuable as the number of measures proliferate. To what extent are different self-report measures that claim to assess depression really measuring the same thing? Instruments may include scales named "Externalizing" (Achenbach & Rescorla, 2001), "Undercontrolled Behavior" (McDermott, 1994), and "Aggression," but despite the different names, these are likely to be tapping similar phenomena and underlying latent constructs.

The consolidation process can be expanded to include theoretical or conceptual linkages across constructs. For example, Gray has developed a model focusing on three major systems: The Behavioral Inhibition System (BIS; focused on cues of threat or punishment); the Behavioral Activation System (BAS; focused on cues of reward); and the relatively less researched Fight/Flight System (FFS; Gray & McNaughton, 1996). Other scholars have investigated the relationship between these basic motivational systems and either underlying neurophysiological systems (Panksepp, 2000) or markers of temperament, personality, and psychopathology (Depue & Lenzenweger, 2001; Depue, Luciana, Arbisi, Collins, & Leon, 1994; Quay, 1993, 1997). The BIS/BAS example also underscores two other facets along which meaningful consolidation can occur: (1) across systems of functioning, as has been done with the construct of emotions, which in turn organize behavior at a physiological, cognitive, facial, and behavioral level (Lazarus, 1991), and (2) across different informants who are reporting about the same behaviors (Achenbach, McConaughy, & Howell, 1987).

STATISTICAL METHODS

Correlations

The correlation coefficient is probably the most widely reported measure of predictive association in developmental psychopathology. It provides a useful measure of strength of association and it can be compared readily across studies and across measures within studies. Advantages of the correlation coefficient include its familiarity, as well as offering a standardized metric that also can be interpreted as an effect size. The main drawback of the correlation coefficient as an index of prognosis is that it is difficult to apply to individual cases (Wiggins, 1973). A second limitation is that it can only consider one correlate at a time.

Comparing Correlations

It is possible to test formally whether correlation coefficients between the same variables but drawn from different samples are close enough in size to attribute any differences to sampling error. This can be done with a z-test (Cohen & Cohen, 1983). Conceptually, this could be considered a meta-analytic method, and it is also a test of whether differences between the two samples moderate or change the correlation between the variables. An example of this would be to compare the correlation between externalizing and internalizing problem scores in a new sample of data with the correlation published in the standardization sample. If the z-test rejected the null hypothesis that the two coefficients were sampled from the same population, then investigators would be alerted to look for aspects of the sample or design that might have changed the relationship between the two dimensions of behavior problems.

It also is possible to test whether the correlations between two different predictors and the same criterion are different from each other in the same sample. For example, one could test whether parent-report or teacher-report of depressive symptoms shows a stronger correlation with youth self-report within the same sample. The formula for this test is more complicated, as it needs to account for the "nuisance" correlation between the two predictors (in this case, the correlation between parent and teacher report; see Cohen & Cohen, 1983, pp. 56–57; note that this formula is not included in the newer edition). Conceptually, this formal comparison of correlations addresses a pragmatic assessment question: Is one of these scores a significantly better predictor of the criterion than the other? In assessment situations where both tools are available, the one with the higher correlation would typically be the first-choice assessment strategy.

The formal test is also strongly preferable to the more common practice of examining the statistical significance of both correlations. It is possible for both correlations to be significantly different from zero (the null hypothesis), yet still have one be a better predictor than the other. More insidiously, it is possible for one to be statistically significant (i.e., different from zero) and the other not achieve significance, yet for the two coefficients to not differ reliably. For example, with an N of 100, a correlation of .22 would be significant ($p < .05$, two-tailed), but a correlation of .18 would not. However, it would be a mistake to conclude that the predictor yielding a correlation of .22 had reliably outperformed the other predictor. Unfortunately, this is what commonly happens when people focus only on whether particular variables achieve "statistical significance" and tally up "significant" versus "nonsignificant" variables (all compared to the null hypothesis of a zero correlation in the population). The field would benefit from more widespread adoption of this type of direct comparison of validity correlations for different measures, which would help clarify when a particular test outperformed a competitor.

Regression

Regression analyses offer several additional refinements beyond what is possible with simple correlational analyses. These include: (a) preserving the actual units of measurement in the unstandardized regression weights, (b) providing formal tests of whether combinations of predictors provide incremental improvement over a single predictor, (c) making predictions about an individual's score on the criterion variable, and (d) creating a framework where it is possible to test statistical mediation or moderation of relationships.

Raw Is Good

As a field, developmental psychopathology has tended to ignore the unstandardized coefficients and focus instead on standardized correlations. However, there are major advantages to working with the variables in their actual metric when it comes to assessment of an individual, as has long been recognized in industrial-organizational psychology (Guion, 1998; Wiggins, 1973). Working in the raw units brings the focus back to how clinicians would actually use the instrument. Instead of relatively abstract concepts such as the correlation being .3 (or the predictor explaining 9% of the variance in the criterion), the unstandardized regression coefficients would indicate the actual scores that would be predicted on the dependent variable (e.g., every point increase in depression is associated with a third of a point decrement in average scores on the quality of life measure, or a 10-point increase in attention problems is linked with a 25% decrease in grade point average).

Incremental Validity

The test of incremental validity has been widely used in research. If the additional variable can provide a statistically significant improvement in prediction of the criterion (quantified as a significant increase in the R^2 of the regression model, or as a significant regression weight for the new variable entered in the model), then it has demonstrated incremental validity at a statistical level. This would provide statistical justification for exploring a more complex assessment battery that included both sources of information in order to provide a more accurate prediction about the individual.

Observed versus Predicted Performance

A third potential advantage would be that it becomes possible to use regression formulae to compare an individual's observed scores to what would be predicted based on the general relationship of the variables in the population. This technique has been most articulated in the area of comparing cognitive ability with academic achievement, and it has formed the basis for identifying learning disabilities in many states in the United States. Youths whose observed achievement fell below a confidence interval centered around their predicted achievement were identified as potentially having a learning disability—implicitly defined as a latent process that led to academic achievement substantially lower than would be expected based on their cognitive ability (The Psychological Corporation, 1992). Although there has been dissatisfaction with this approach as a way of defining learning disability—largely because it identifies a heterogeneous group of youths who are showing similar discrepancies, but for very different reasons (Fletcher, Francis, Morris, & Lyon, 2005)—this approach could be productively applied to other areas of psychopathology research.

For example, clinicians often are struck by the relatively low levels of concerns reported by teachers or youths when referrals are initiated by parents. Applying the regression framework would remind clinicians that given the typical amount of agreement between parents and youths ($r = .22$ in a meta-analysis; Achenbach et al., 1987), the level of concern we intuitively might expect to see across informants would actually represent an exceptionally high level of agreement (Youngstrom, Meyers, Youngstrom, Calabrese, & Findling, 2006a, 2006b). This method could also identify instances where cross-informant agreement was actually significantly worse than expected based on normative data, leading to detailed examination of the factors contributing to the disagreement in the specific case. This method has been applied to both parent-youth and parent-teacher agreement about mood symptoms, emphasizing that substantial differences in opinion are par for the course given the relatively modest levels of typical agreement across informants (Youngstrom et al., 2006a, 2006b).

Challenges to Using Regression Equations Clinically

Obstacles to applying regression models in clinical practice have included the lack of sufficient published statistics (for example, when researchers publish correlations or regression weights without including the intercept statistic), the increased computational burden on the clinician, and the fact that the regression weights are dependent on the specific combination of instruments used. Some experts also have been concerned about whether the weights are sample specific, or conversely, whether predictions generalize better when weighting is ignored and unit weights are used instead (Perloff & Persons, 1988).

All of these challenges are solvable. Researchers can publish more complete details of the regression results. The computational burden has sometimes been managed by creating tables where clinicians can look up the predicted value (e.g., The Psychological Corporation, 1992), although this usually only works well for simple bivariate models. A more flexible approach that is now feasible would be to have Web-based or personal digital assistant (PDA) applications that could perform the necessary calculations quickly, conveniently, and accurately. The question of sample dependence is an empirical issue that meta-analyses can formally evaluate. If sample characteristics change the performance of the measure, then separate regression models can be used as appropriate (much as separate norms are used for many tests). In short, the technical challenges are no longer a major impediment to applying regression models to individual cases. The benefits could be considerable: Even relatively simple models often provide predictions that are much more accurate than the results achieved via nonactuarial decision making (Grove, Zald, Lebow, Snitz, & Nelson, 2000; Meehl, 1954).

Statistical Methods for Consolidation of Scores

Principal components analysis, exploratory factor analysis, and confirmatory factor analysis are all methods for synthesizing correlations among sets of variables. Within an assessment framework, these techniques have been widely used to test the dimensionality of assessment instruments (i.e., how many factors drive the relationship between the 118 behavior problem items on the Achenbach Child Behavior Checklist?). There are a variety of different methods available for determining the number of dimensions underlying a battery. Three have consistently performed well in simulation studies (Velicer, Eaton, & Fava, 2000; Zwick & Velicer, 1986), yet are rarely used in developmental psychopathology research. These are the Scree Test, Minimum Average Partials

(Velicer, 1976), and Parallel Analysis (Glorfeld, 2008; Horn, 1965). The latter two are not included as options in the most popular statistical packages, but free code is available to run these techniques on many platforms (O'Connor, 2000). All three of these methods tend to converge on more parsimonious factor structures than maximum-likelihood-based techniques identify, which form the basis of confirmatory factor analytic approaches. Parsimony offers considerable advantages. Retaining fewer factors means that there will be fewer scales to interpret, reducing the risk of Type I (false positive) errors in clinical assessment (Silverstein, 1993). The smaller number of factors also tend to include a larger number of items per factor, yielding greater internal consistency reliability, smaller standard errors of measurement, and more accurate description of an individual (Brown, 2006).

Experts who have suggested that overfactoring is preferable to underfactoring (e.g., Fabrigar, Wegener, MacCallum, & Strahan, 1999) view the issue from the perspective of a statistician, not a clinician or researcher who needs to apply measurement to a specific individual. Greater reliance on approaches such as Parallel Analysis would accelerate the consolidation of measures and also promote the development of scales with psychometric properties better suited for making decisions about individuals. By putting factor structures on a firmer footing using exploratory methods early in the cycle of scale development, it is likely that the field will produce more robust scales for validation with confirmatory methods.

An example of this has developed in the cognitive ability assessment literature. Decades of research have failed to demonstrate the clinical utility of interpreting subtest scores (McDermott, Fantuzzo, & Glutting, 1990; Watkins & Kush, 1994), and it has been almost as difficult to demonstrate clinical utility for factor scores when related to academic achievement (Kahana, Youngstrom, & Glutting, 2002; Oh, Glutting, Watkins, Youngstrom, & McDermott, 2004) or behavior problem criteria (Glutting et al., 1996). There has been considerable disagreement about the factor structure underlying widely used tests such as the Wechslers (Kaufman, 1994; Sattler, 2001; Wechsler, 1974, 1991, 2003). Almost all published cognitive ability tests have recommended grouping scales into "factors" that are poorly specified, often with only two or three subtests per factor. The resulting factors fail to satisfy the more accurate and conservative statistical decision rules (Frazier & Youngstrom, 2007). It is likely that the relatively modest specification of factors has led directly to poor measurement of the underlying traits at the clinical or individual level, which in turn has resulted in difficulty demonstrating the clinical utility of factor scores. The clearest evidence for differential validity of constructs is available for the factor scores that have historically been best specified from a psychometric perspective: verbal versus nonverbal cognitive ability (Moffitt & Silva, 1987).

Covariance modeling approaches can also quantify the overlap between related constructs. To what extent are anxiety and depression distinct phenomena, as opposed to sharing a common general internalizing component? Are the more than 200 extant measures of depression and internalizing problems all measuring the same underlying latent variable (Nezu, Ronan, Meadows, & McClure, 2000)? Within a developmental framework, covariance models are also important methods to clarify the points of contact between assessment tools deployed at different ages, such as measures of temperament versus measures of personality (Shiner, 1998). All of these can be viewed as examples of conceptual consolidation, where covariance modeling is used to integrate and synthesize different sources of information, different tests, and different age epochs to identify underlying constructs. However, the same tools can also be helpful in the context of elaboration, as in the case of structural equation models, where path models link latent constructs that are quantified by means of a measurement model that includes a factor analysis for each of the latent variables (Bollen, 1989).

Grouping Individuals Instead of Items or Scales

An alternate approach to descriptive assessment would be to seek to group *individuals* together based on similarity, rather than grouping *variables* together. These have been described as "*q*-methods," as distinct from the "*r*-methods" of describing correlation among variables (Thompson, 2000). One specific statistical method would be to use common factor analysis but to aggregate people with similar profiles of scores across variables, rather than the more widespread approach of grouping variables with similar scores across people. Cluster analysis is another method that has a long history of use to aggregate similar cases in biology as well as the social sciences (Achenbach, 1993; Aldenderfer & Blashfield, 1984). Latent class analysis (McCutcheon, 1987) is a related methodology for clustering similar cases on the basis of observed categorical indicator variables. Latent class analysis has enjoyed a notable resurgence of popularity in clinical psychology and psychiatry, and it has been applied variously to epidemiological twin data as well as clinical samples as a way of identifying cases with similar profiles of problem behaviors (e.g., Hudziak, Althoff, Derks, Faraone, & Boomsma, 2005; Hudziak et al., 1998). A third family of methods is the "coherent cut kinetics" or "taxometric" methods developed by Meehl, Waller, and colleagues (Schmidt, Kotov, & Joiner, 2004; Waller & Meehl, 1998). Taxometric methods are well suited for testing whether data are distributed along a continuum or whether they reflect two naturally occurring underlying categories, but they will not perform well in situations where there are three or more underlying categories. Latent class analysis and cluster analyses, on the other hand, are better suited to applications where there are multiple underlying groups, but will provide inaccurate clustering solutions in situations where the underlying data actually are dimensional. This has led many to suggest that perhaps both methods should be brought to bear on research questions, or perhaps even used to analyze the same samples (Beauchaine & Beauchaine, 2002; Solomon, Haaga, & Arnow, 2001).

Assessment models in developmental psychopathology have often employed *q*-tests. Taxometric methods have been used with child and adolescent depression (Ambrosini, Bennett, Cleland, & Haslam, 2002; Danielson, 2002), and latent class analyses have been applied to attention problems, aggression, and other behavior problems, as mentioned earlier (Hudziak, Wadsworth, Heath, & Achenbach, 1999). There also are intriguing examples of using clustering methods to define normative profiles within standardization samples of measures. These methods were independently applied to both clinical syndrome scales (Achenbach, 1993; Achenbach & Edelbrock, 1983; Kamphaus, Huberty, DiStefano, & Petoskey, 1997; Kamphaus, Petoskey, Cody, Rowe, & Huberty, 1999; McDermott, 1994) and to the standardization samples of cognitive ability tests (Glutting, McDermott, Prifitera, & McGrath, 1994; Glutting, McGrath, Kamphaus, & McDermott, 1992; Konold, Glutting, & McDermott, 1997).

These *q*-methods are intriguing as a way of describing developmental psychopathology. They provide an empirical approach for creating a nosology of common patterns of behavior problems. Clustering methods allow the data to dictate how many core profiles emerge, and their relative prevalence. If the same indicators are used at multiple settings or time points, it then becomes possible to identify secular trends in prevalence and group composition. For example, by clustering the entire standardization sample together (pooling ages, sex groups, and ethnicity), it becomes evident that profiles characterized by elevations in attention problems and aggressive behavior are more common in males but decrease in prevalence with age, whereas anxious and depressed profiles are more common in females, with the depressed scores rising even higher in females after the transition to adolescence (McDermott & Weiss, 1995). *Q*-methods also provide a parsimonious response to the problem of comorbidity: Most core profiles involve elevations on multiple scales, reflecting that symptoms and behaviors described as separate disorders in *DSM* have a strong tendency to co-occur (Caron & Rutter, 1991).

It is also possible to use *q*-methods to classify individual cases, assigning them to group membership based on the similarity of their scores to the average scores for each core profile. In the Achenbach approach, similarity was indexed as a set of *q*-correlations between the individual's profile of scores and the average scores for each of the core profiles, with the individual classified as belonging to the group that showed the highest correlation coefficient (Achenbach, 1993). In another approach, the similarity of an individual to each core profile was quantified using "generalized distance"—the sum of the squared discrepancies between the individual's score and the cluster average on each measure (McDermott, 1998).

An extra fillip offered by McDermott's method was the inclusion of a "maximum distance," after which an individual's scores would be considered unique and not closely matching any of the core profiles from the standardization sample (McDermott, 1998). This threshold was empirically determined by examining the frequency distribution of discrepancy scores and finding what generalized distance score was so extreme that 95% of cases in the standardization sample scored at or below that point. This approach offers a statistically based system for determining when a person shows an unusual multivariate profile. Advantages of this include that the clustering method accommodates the fact that the average profile is not flat (i.e., the average youth does not have all of his or her cognitive abilities equally developed, nor does he or she typically display a wide range of behavior problems to the same degree), and it also avoids making multiple univariate decisions about an individual when looking at correlated measures (McDermott & Weiss, 1995). Thus, these methods would help to cut down on the rate of Type I errors, or false positive inferences, in clinical decision making (Silverstein, 1993).

Another advantage of multivariate profiles is that they can incorporate information from different domains of functioning. To date, this has only been done in a limited way. For example, some investigators have clustered intelligence and academic achievement data at the same time to identify profiles of the functioning, including commonly occurring patterns when academic achievement is markedly different than the level of cognitive abilities (e.g., Konold et al., 1997). An intriguing extension of this methodology would be to cluster behavior problems and positive aspects of social functioning or quality of life at the same time. Epidemiological studies have shown that there are many people who present with symptoms of psychopathology but without impairment or decrement in quality of life (Bird, 1996; Bird et al., 1990). It would be interesting to document how common are these patterns of functioning that show elevated symptom levels without a corresponding deficit in functioning. These individuals have sometimes been described as the "worried well," but an alternate conceptualization might be that these are people who are resilient despite having some symptoms. These individuals also might be important to include in investigations of endophenotypic markers or heritability studies (Gottesman & Gould, 2003; Hasler, Drevets, Gould, Gottesman, & Manji, 2006).

Prognosis: Prediction into the Future

Clinical prognostication has been more obvious in the area of developmental psychopathology than in many other areas of psychology. *Prognosis* is used here to refer to the course of illness or the longitudinal outcomes that are likely for individuals affected by a particular condition or showing a particular marker or trait. Prognostic data provide important information about the validity of diagnoses and also help in making decisions about whether to intervene. Anxiety problems in childhood frequently have been dismissed as simple shyness or as a behavior pattern that youths are likely to outgrow; however, longitudinal data have demonstrated that children meeting criteria for anxiety disorders are at higher risk for a variety of poor outcomes, including higher rates of substance use, depression, peer rejection, and continued dependence on parents or the welfare system as young adults (Silverman & Ollendick, 2005). Thus the prognostic value of a diagnosis of an Anxiety Disorder contributes to the justification for clinical intervention. Similarly, the higher rates of car accidents, substance use, arrest, and other poor outcomes associated with a diagnosis of ADHD provide grounds for initiating treatment (Barkley, 2002). Prognostic value can apply to test results or to clinical signs as well.

Addressing questions of development or change over time are more an issue of research design than analysis, in the sense that the underlying matrix algebra is the same regardless of whether the covariances are drawn from a single panel or multiple time points. Stated differently, all of the analytic methods described in the previous section could be thought of as special cases of more general analytic methods, where both the independent and dependent variables happened to have been gathered at the same time. Thus, correlation, regression, and other covariance structure-based methods continue to be helpful in describing and quantifying longitudinal relationships. The strength of the inference comes from the research design, and having the same participants followed for multiple time points.

Individual Trajectories (Growth on Continuous Measures)

There are a variety of statistical refinements that are available for modeling longitudinal data with even greater sophistication. These include repeated-measures ANOVAs (Tabachnick & Fidell, 2007); mixed-effect models (also referred to as *hierarchical linear models*), when repeated measures are treated as being "nested" within the individual participant and other stable differences between participants (such as sex or ethnicity) are modeled in a second, higher-level regression equation (Raudenbush & Bryk, 2002); and growth curve models, where observed variables are treated as indicators of change for indirectly observed "latent variables" (Duncan, Duncan, Strycker, Li, & Alpert, 1999). All of these techniques are methods for modeling covariance structures over time, but each has specific advantages and disadvantages. A technical treatment of these methods is outside the scope of a single chapter on assessment, and the interested reader is referred to the more comprehensive treatments cited previously or to more conceptual overviews offered elsewhere (Grimm & Yarnold, 1995a, 1996b).

For the purposes of the present chapter, an important generalization to bear in mind is that these techniques concentrate on a change in scores on a continuous dependent measure, such as academic achievement, or level of anxiety symptoms over time. In principle, each of these methods could also be used to generate a predicted score on the dependent measure for an individual, as discussed earlier in the regression section. These predictions could be incorporated into a clinical decision-making framework (Straus, Richardson, Glasziou, & Haynes, 2005), or they could be used to generate more refined hypotheses for future research or policy work (Kaplan & Elliott, 1997). However, there is a trade-off, such that as the models or analytic methods become more complex, the application to an individual case becomes more difficult. With structural equation models or growth curve models, the author is unaware of examples of applying a model to make predictions about individual cases, although such an exercise is technically possible. Some believe that this represents a limitation to the clinical utility of these approaches (Oh et al., 2004).

Time Until an Event Occurs

A second family of methods, less used in developmental psychopathology research to date, is *event history analysis*. This family of techniques includes survival analysis and Cox regression—both methods for looking at the length of time until a particular event of interest happens (Tabachnick & Fidell, 2007). The event is categorical; examples could include pregnancy, dropping out of school, graduation, arrest, relapse of an illness, or any other binary outcome. One of the major strengths of survival analyses or Cox regression is that these methods can model data when the outcome is "censored," or not directly observed in all participants at the time of analysis. For example, when investigating time until arrest, survival analysis can accommodate the fact that many participants have not been arrested at the time of the conclusion of the study, without needing to assume that these people would never get arrested. Instead, the survival analysis weights these censored cases differently than cases where the outcome was directly observed, producing unbiased estimates (Tabachnick & Fidell, 2007). Kaplan-Meier survival analysis can compare times until the event for different categories of participants (e.g., males versus females, or new therapy versus treatment as usual). Cox regression is even more flexible, in that both continuous and categorical predictors can be included in the regression model as covariates that may account for differences in the time until the occurrence of the event (Willett & Singer, 1993).

These event-history methods provide a natural model matched to many developmental psychopathology questions of interest. Event-history methods are uniquely suited to investigations of onset, cessation, relapse, and recovery (Willett & Singer, 1993). There are even models that allow for repeated recurrences of the event of interest (as would happen, for example, with multiple nonfatal heart attacks, or relapses of Mood Disorder). Event-history techniques also produce *hazard ratios* or regression weights that could be applied to an individual case to make predictions about risk or outcome. Although event-history models are beginning to appear in the research literature, particularly in forensic assessment contexts (e.g., Richards, Casey, & Lucente, 2003; Tengstroem, Grann, Langstroem, & Kullgren, 2000), there have been fewer attempts to generate individual prediction models. This has been due to the combination of unfamiliarity with Cox regression in the field of psychopathology assessment and because of the computational burden involved in applying the regression weights (which represent changes in the log odds of the event happening). However, the greater availability of inexpensive computing power in the form of personal digital assistants (PDAs) or Web programs greatly reduces the computational barriers to use. Both Cox regression and survival analysis are now available in popular statistical software packages such as statistical analysis system (SAS) and statistical package for the social sciences (SPSS), and more specialized software such as M-Plus (Muthen & Muthen, 2004) makes it possible to test models that mix together growth curve and event history analyses—enabling the flexible specification of models that closely approximate the developmental processes of interest.

SUMMARY AND FUTURE DIRECTIONS

Prediction is one of the cornerstones of both clinical assessment and developmental psychopathology. There is a wealth of published data containing correlations between published measures of myriad constructs. However, most articles and test manuals have concentrated on the statistical significance of associations, sometimes also reporting the correlation coefficient. The extant literature on almost all measures falls short of its potential to inform choices about test selection or application to decisions about individuals. From a research standpoint, the agenda for improving the predictive value of assessment tools would include: (a) publishing studies that consolidate existing measures into more parsimonious dimensions, (b) conducting studies that elaborate the connections between measures and constructs across development, such as linking measures of temperament to personality, (c) directly comparing the predictive value of multiple tests under the same conditions (versus the current convention of focusing only on null-hypothesis significance testing) so that test selection can be guided by empirical results, and (d) supplementing or supplanting correlational analyses with regression analyses, reported in enough detail to allow application to individual cases (with appropriate confidence bands). More speculative research endeavors could include development of q-method approaches to assessment, creating empirical and multivariate taxonomies of individuals.

The Second P: Prescription

Assessment should inform choices about treatment. Assessment findings can lead to a prescription of a type of treatment, sometimes referred to as treatment matching between a diagnosis and an intervention strategy. Assessment can also guide the decision about whether to initiate treatment at all.

THRESHOLDS FOR ASSESSMENT AND TREATMENT

The likelihood of a person having a particular condition can be thought of as a probability ranging somewhere between 0% (when they definitely do not have the condition) and 100% (when they definitely do have the condition). In clinical practice, we are never absolutely positive about the presence or absence of a condition. Instead, our assessment of the probability will range somewhere in between these two extremes. Within this conceptual framework, assessment is helpful to the extent that it changes our estimate of the probability. Low scores or negative results on a valid test decrease the probability of a condition, and high scores or positive results increase the probability.

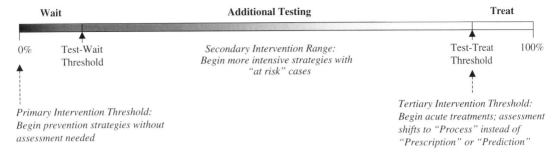

FIGURE 2.1 Decision Thresholds for Assessment and Treatment, Combined with the "Levels of Intervention" Model.

When we become sufficiently confident in a diagnosis or a case formulation, we proceed to initiate treatment. Not all cases receiving treatment actually have the condition—clinical diagnosis is imperfectly reliable (Garb, 1998). Similarly, we cannot be 100% certain that any specific child actually has a given disorder. However, once our estimate of the probability exceeds a certain point, we are confident enough to go ahead and begin treatment. This has been called the *treatment threshold* (Sackett, Straus, Richardson, Rosenberg, & Haynes, 2000). If our estimate of the probability falls below this threshold, then we would conduct additional assessment until either we achieved sufficient confidence that the condition was present to warrant intervention, or else until the probability estimate became so low that we considered the diagnosis ruled out. There is a second threshold, the *assessment threshold*, below which the diagnosis is considered so unlikely that further testing is not needed. The range of probabilities falling between the assessment threshold and the treatment threshold represents the situation when additional assessment is clinically indicated, as we are neither confident enough to begin treatment nor certain that the condition is absent. Figure 2.1 illustrates the threshold concept.

Typically the assessment and treatment thresholds are not explicitly defined by clinicians. Instead, we make intuitive decisions about when testing is needed. Writing down our probability estimate and our thresholds would immediately make the decision-making process more conscious and transparent. This framework also can be empowering for the patient, as it makes it possible to weigh the costs and benefits associated with testing and with treatment, and to negotiate where to set the assessment and treatment thresholds (Sackett et al., 2000).

It is interesting to combine the threshold model of decision making with the idea of levels of intervention that developed independently in the community psychology literature (Mechanic, 1989). *Primary intervention*, or universal prevention, treats everyone, regardless of risk. This approach is rational when treatment costs and risks are low and are decisively outweighed by the benefits. Primary interventions include such techniques as fluoridating drinking supplies to prevent dental problems, mandating a comprehensive vaccination program, or advertising the benefits of exercise as a protective factor against heart disease. In terms of the threshold model of decision making, primary intervention sets the treatment threshold at a probability of zero: Even if it is highly unlikely that a person has the target condition, he or she will still receive the treatment. Assessment is not needed as a gatekeeper to determine eligibility in a primary intervention model; in fact, assessment may add unnecessary expense.

Secondary interventions concentrate on those who are at risk of developing a condition but who have not yet fully manifested the syndrome (Mechanic, 1989). *Risk* could be defined by exposure to a risk factor, such as a traumatic event, or it could be defined as a prodromal expression of the condition. The advantages of secondary intervention include that fewer cases are treated, permitting the dose or expense of the treatment to be greater than in a primary prevention model. Limiting treatment to those at probable risk also avoids the ethical concerns inherent in universal treatment, when informed consent may not exist.

Secondary interventions may be appropriate for cases who are in the midrange of probability of having a diagnosis. In this view, secondary interventions might be deployed for the same people who would also fall between the assessment and treatment thresholds—cases where the probability is high enough to justify taking treatment precautions as well as continuing assessment, but not yet so diagnostically clear as to warrant bringing the heavy artillery of tertiary interventions to bear. For example, after gathering test data and clinical history, a practitioner using an evidence-based assessment approach might conclude that a person has a 60% probability of having schizophrenia. This is above the assessment threshold, so continued evaluation would be indicated. At the same time, the probability is likely below the treatment threshold at which the clinician and patient would be ready to start antipsychotic medication. In addition to recommending continued evaluation, the clinician might also recommend initiating secondary interventions at this point, such as reducing stressors, curtailing substance use, or seeking supportive interactions with friends.

An alternate way of integrating secondary interventions with the assessment threshold model would be to make clear definitions of risk status that are triggers for intervention. In cardiology, elevated blood pressure has become conceptualized as a risk factor or prodrome of heart disease that is sufficient to trigger a variety of interventions, including changes in diet, exercise, or the use of medications specifically intended to regulate blood pressure. Similarly, the schizotaxic construct (or *schizotypy*) appears to be a constellation of behaviors and biological markers that signal a diathesis for developing schizophrenia (Blanchard, Gangestad, Brown, & Horan, 2000). Schizotaxia appears much more common in the general population than fully syndromal schizophrenia (Lenzenweger & Korfine, 1992). It is conceivable that screening or early identification programs could be designed to identify individuals with schizotaxia, and then initiate psychoeducational and prevention programs with them to lessen the risk of progression into schizophrenia. This model could be extended to include a variety of other temperamental or personality dimensions that have become well established as correlates of different forms of pathology. High-trait neuroticism, shyness, or behavioral inhibition are not exactly the same thing as a *DSM*-defined psychiatric disorder of anxiety or Social Phobia, but each of these variables has demonstrated robust associations with anxiety disorders as well as mood disorders (Harkness & Lilienfeld, 1997 Kagan, 1997a; Lonigan, Vasey, Phillips, & Hazen, 2004). Analogous to blood pressure elevation, these factors could be conceptualized as triggers for secondary intervention to prevent exacerbation into an impairing disorder.

Tertiary interventions are the most intense treatments. They also are often the most expensive, and may also have the most serious risks of side effects. The increased costs (both fiscal and risk of harm) militate against deploying tertiary interventions more broadly. Assessment serves as the gatekeeper, determining when to start tertiary interventions. In the evidence-based medicine (EBM) threshold model, the treatment threshold is set based on the costs and benefits associated with treatment; and treatment begins when the diagnostic probability of having the condition rises above the treatment threshold. One of the main sources of dissatisfaction with tertiary intervention models is that the illness is often quite advanced by the time it is recognized and treated. The severe progression of the condition often makes it more difficult to treat, with even greater expense and lower rates of success. At an individual level, it is much less costly to treat high blood pressure than it is to do open heart surgery, and the patient has a higher probability of survival. Assessment also protects people from unnecessary interventions that convey all of the risks associated with the treatment, but few or none of the potential benefits. At the tertiary intervention level, the assessment question is usually not *if* there is a problem, but rather *what* the specific nature of the problem is, so that optimal treatment can be prescribed. Figure 2.1 maps the levels of intervention model onto the Test and Treat threshold model.

DIAGNOSIS AS A SHORTHAND

There have been extensive critiques of the validity of the *DSM* and International Classification of Diseases (ICD) diagnostic systems (e.g., Carson, 1997; Kihlstrom, 2001; Wakefield, 1997). The number of diagnoses has proliferated with each revision of the nosology, with *DSM-IV-TR* containing more than 350 distinct diagnoses. It is unclear whether each of these actually represents a distinct categorical entity, versus being a somewhat arbitrary label that is imposed on extreme levels of an underlying trait. In fact, accumulating evidence suggests that most conditions are more likely to be quantitative traits that vary along a continuum rather than representing distinct categories (Frazier, Youngstrom, & Naugle, 2007; Markon & Krueger, 2005; Ruscio & Ruscio, 2002; Schmidt et al., 2004). The extremely high rate of comorbidity among putative psychiatric diagnoses also strongly suggests that the current classification systems are "splitting" too much—imposing artificial distinctions that do not have an underlying basis (Angold, Costello, & Erkanli, 1999; Caron & Rutter, 1991). For example, the high rates of overlap between ADHD and Bipolar Disorder (Faraone, Biederman, Mennin, Wozniak, & Spencer, 1997) or between generalized anxiety and major depression (Mineka, Watson, & Clark, 1998) suggest that there may be shared mechanisms leading to the apparent comorbidity.

However, there are major advantages to categorical classification. There usually is a dichotomous choice between treating or not treating something, as well as the practical issues of billing and the conceptual advantages of a label as short-hand for a constellation of related variables. One of the important agenda items for developmental psychopathology is determining how to consolidate diagnoses into more parsimonious groupings that could guide treatment. Once these groups are defined, then assessment tools can be reevaluated in terms of how well they help to detect the group and to differentiate it from other groups that would benefit from a different intervention approach. Although the subsequent examples will concentrate on current diagnoses, please bear in mind that: (a) current diagnoses need further validation and will likely be modified during the validation process, (b) the assessment framework being advocated here would still apply to any categorical decision, and (c) it will be incumbent on developmental psychopathology researchers to revisit the validity of extant measures with regard to any new diagnostic definitions.

Assessment as Aid in Diagnosis

Assessment can greatly aid practitioners in their decision about whether to initiate treatment, or which treatment to select. However, this capacity has largely been underutilized in psychology as a field, where interpretation of tests has largely been intuitive and impressionistic (Garb, 1998). There is a highly refined framework for evaluating the contributions of a test to diagnosis, based on signal detection theory or Bayes Theorem (Kraemer, 1992). The performance of a test can be described in terms of its *sensitivity* and *specificity* to a diagnosis, where sensitivity refers to the percentage of cases with the diagnosis that would be classified correctly by the test. Specificity quantifies the percentage of cases without the diagnosis that would be classified correctly by the test. The specificity of a test can always be improved by using a more stringent threshold. However, there is almost always a trade-off between sensitivity and specificity.

Receiver Operating Characteristic (ROC) analysis is a method for quantifying the relationship between the sensitivity and the specificity of an assessment tool for a particular diagnosis. Receiver Operating Characteristic curves plot the sensitivity as a function of the specificity (or the "false alarm rate"—the complement of specificity), moving across the entire range of possible test scores. It is possible to measure the Area Under the Curve (AUC) for the ROC plot of test performance, yielding an index that ranges from 1.00 (for a perfectly discriminating test, achieving 100% sensitivity and 0% false alarms, or 100% specificity) to .50 (reflecting chance performance). Conceptually, the AUC can be thought of as the probability that a randomly selected case with the diagnosis would have a higher score on the test than would a randomly selected case without the disorder (McFall & Treat, 1999). The AUC is helpful in that it provides a single, global index of how well a test can aid in the differentiation of a diagnosis.

There are statistical methods for comparing the AUCs for the same test evaluated in different samples (Hanley & McNeil, 1983). This procedure is helpful because it is possible for the performance of the test to change depending on sample characteristics. A common study design that exaggerates test performance compared to what it would actually deliver under clinically realistic conditions would be to limit the sample to affected versus healthy normal controls (e.g., Steer, Cavalieri, Leonard, & Beck, 1999; Tillman & Geller, 2005). Such designs magnify the apparent discriminating power in two ways: (1) they create groups that differ based on global impairment, as well as specific features of the illness, making the groups easier to tell apart (increasing the sensitivity of the test to the target condition); and (2) the samples exclude other illnesses that might share some of the features of the target condition (decreasing the number of false alarms for the test, and thus raising its apparent specificity). Youngstrom, Meyers, Youngstrom, Calabrese, & Findling, 2006b demonstrated this by analyzing the same mood-rating scales under two different sampling designs.

Figure 2.2 is an ROC plot of different tests measured against the same diagnostic criterion. It is possible to test whether the one instrument is performing significantly better than another in the same sample, adjusting for the correlation between the two assessment measures (Hanley & McNeil, 1983). Because the two tests are being compared in the same study, most of the factors that might differ across studies of diagnosis (such as definitions of the illness, the base rate of the illness, the severity of the presentation, or the amount of comorbidity present in the sample) are held constant while comparing the tests. Such "horse race" designs, which simultaneously evaluate

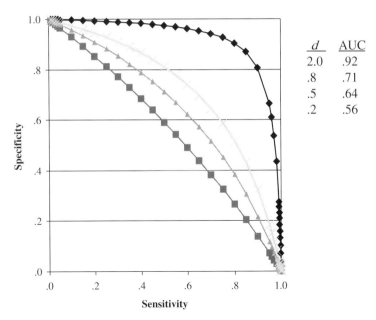

FIGURE 2.2 Plot of Receiver Operator Characteristic (ROC) Curves for Tests with Different Effect Sizes (Cohen's *d*) for Differences Between Target and Comparison Groups.

multiple measures under the same conditions, offer compelling evidence if there are differences between the measures' diagnostic performance.

Clinical Implications

Clinicians should be on the watch for diagnostic horse race papers, and if a measure performs better than the tool they are currently using, then they should change their choice of instrument. These studies also will be greatly helpful in winnowing the field of assessment measures. Consider the example of assessing depression. There are more than 200 published depression measures available (Nezu et al., 2000). It is unlikely they will be equally good at discriminating depression from other presenting problems or diagnoses. The sheer number of published measures creates an obstacle to identifying the instruments with the best validity for the purpose of detecting depression. It would take a prohibitive amount of time for a practitioner to obtain and evaluate all 200 tests, let alone survey all of the published literature on each. As reviewed earlier, neither graduate training nor internship supervision were likely to provide thorough exposure to the different tests available for this purpose (only the Beck Depression Inventory and the Child Behavior Checklist appear in the top 20 frequently taught or administered tests based on multiple surveys). If the clinician consulted a handbook or assessment text, he or she would receive no guidance on the comparison of tests in terms of diagnostic efficiency.

Evidence-based medicine recommends using online search engines to answer clinical questions (Straus et al., 2005). In this case, the question might be formulated as, "What is the best assessment tool to improve diagnosis of depression in children and adolescents?" Searching MedLine using the term "depression" in any field yields an unmanageable number of hits, with 199,652 records (all searches conducted in May 2007).

However, limiting the search to "children and adolescents," and "depression and diagnosis" and "sensitivity and specificity" (which is the recommended Medical Sub-Heading, or MeSH term, to identify studies of diagnostic methods)(Straus et al., 2005) produces 537 hits, of which 15 are reviews. A quick scan of the titles of the reviews eliminates several as being peripherally related (depression as correlate of cancer or recurrent abdominal pain), and finds a review that synthesizes 160 studies covering 33 different diagnostic and symptom assessment measures (Brooks & Kutcher, 2001).

Based on this quick search and review, the list of candidate instruments dropped from several hundred to a half dozen. Having identified these as contenders, the clinician could then concentrate on the more recent studies and attend only to articles reporting AUCs of $\sim$.8 or higher in outpatient samples (i.e., performing as well or better than the tests covered in the Brooks & Kutcher review). If an instrument demonstrated higher diagnostic efficiency, then the article would warrant more careful scrutiny to determine if the results were valid (Bossuyt et al., 2003) and if they were more applicable to the specific patient in question (Jaeschke, Guyatt, & Sackett, 1994). This brief exercise indicates several important general conclusions: (a) both typical clinical training and review materials (textbooks, handbooks) often fail to provide the information necessary to answer clinically relevant questions, (b) relevant information often exists in the published literature, (c) rapid online searches using appropriate keywords can find clinically relevant evidence, and (d) online searches can both identify high-quality reviews and also augment them with more current clinical evidence. With regard to the specific question of assessing depression in youths, the evidence indicates that of the plethora of available tests, only a handful have been investigated in sufficient detail to consider adoption as an evidence-based tool for the purpose of aiding diagnosis. Thus this exercise simultaneously sheds light in both directions, illuminating important next steps to take in research (evaluating the diagnostic efficiency of tests, developing tests that discriminate depression better than a moderate AUC of .80, determining what factors might moderate the ability of a test to identify depression) as well as guiding evidence-based approaches to clinical assessment.

Applying Test Results to Individual Cases

Both clinicians and consumers are primarily concerned with the status of an individual child, not with abstract properties of instruments applied to large groups. It is possible to take information about the probability of a diagnosis and combine it with the test result to estimate a new probability (posterior probability) that the person has the diagnosis in question. The algebra needed to integrate these two pieces of information has been known for several centuries in the form of Bayes' Theorem. However, recent approaches have attempted to simplify the application so that the clinician need not formally do computation to estimate the posterior probability. Figure 2.3 provides a "nomogram" designed to aid the clinical use of test results. The left-hand column charts the prior probability. The middle column contains the likelihood ratio, which is simply the ratio of the percentage of cases with the diagnosis that would exceed the cutoff (i.e., the sensitivity of the test) divided by the percentage of cases without the diagnosis that would also exceed the cutoff (the false alarm rate, or the complement of specificity). A practitioner would simply put a dot on the left-hand line to indicate the prior probability, then put a dot on the middle line corresponding to the likelihood ratio (the

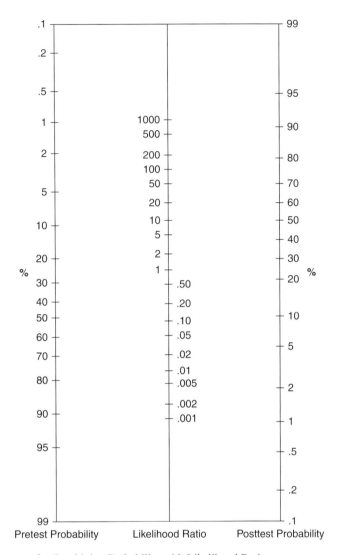

FIGURE 2.3   Nomogram for Combining Probability with Likelihood Ratios.

sensitivity divided by false alarm rate), and finally connect the two dots with a straight line, extending it across the right-hand line to indicate the new, posterior probability.

The starting probability on the left-hand line can be chosen to reflect the "base rate" of the diagnosis in a particular setting based either on local data (such as would be obtained from a record review) or from published estimates drawn from similar settings, such as epidemiological (e.g., Costello et al., 1996) or clinical-epidemiological studies drawn from clinical or forensic settings (e.g., Teplin, Abram, McClelland, Dulcan, & Mericle, 2002). Alternately, the entry point for the nomogram could be an estimate based on the particular risk factors present in the given case, such as family history of the disorder (Youngstrom & Duax, 2005). Most flexibly, the clinician could simply begin by quantifying his or her own clinical impression as a probability (assigning a number from .00 to 1.00) and then use the nomogram to see how the test result is changing that impression. This can include sensitivity analyses, where the clinician examines the impact of "what if" scenarios by bracketing initial estimates with more liberal and more conservative values.

Where does the practitioner find the likelihood ratios to use in the nomogram? Occasionally these are published directly in a table in a test manual or research report (e.g., Youngstrom et al., 2004), but this is not yet common practice. More often, articles will include the sensitivity and specificity values, which provides sufficient information to calculate the likelihood ratios. The likelihood ratio associated with a positive test result is the sensitivity divided by (1−specificity). The likelihood ratio for a negative test result is the false negative rate (1−sensitivity) divided by the true negative rate (i.e., the specificity). It is also possible to estimate likelihood ratios if normative data are given for people with the condition and without the condition (Frazier & Youngstrom, 2006). Once the practitioner identifies the most valid estimates of sensitivity and specificity, it is only necessary to calculate the likelihood ratio once, and then the clinician can use the nomogram with all subsequent evaluations that include the measure in question.

The advantages of using a nomogram to facilitate interpretation of test results are considerable. Foremost among them is that the nomogram makes it possible to apply test results to a specific individual, directly estimating the posterior probability. The posterior probability is what all parties to an assessment find most relevant, but it cannot be estimated by researchers because it varies depending on the base rate, which will change across settings. Additional advantages of the nomogram include: (a) substantial improvements in the accuracy and precision of test interpretation, (b) reducing the influence of cognitive heuristics on the interpretation of test results, (c) flexibility in choice of starting point (i.e., base rate, clinical impression, or the combination of either of those with other quantitative information; Youngstrom & Youngstrom, 2005), (d) elimination of computation, and (e) facilitation of discussion between the practitioner and the family to determine when to initiate treatment versus continuing assessment. The principal drawbacks of the nomogram approach are that it is unfamiliar to most clinicians and training programs and that few researchers are publishing the likelihood ratios directly in their research reports. More technical limitations include that the nomogram involves a loss of precision compared to using Bayes Theorem (which PDA or Web applications could support), and that applications combining multiple sources of information assume that the sources are independent. In practice, so long as the data come from different sources (e.g., parent versus teacher report, or family history versus youth self-report), then the correlations are likely to be only small to moderate, and the effect on the results derived from the nomogram will be minor compared to the increases in accuracy and precision afforded by the nomogram versus typical intuitive test interpretation.

ASSESSMENT AS AID IN TREATMENT SELECTION

A second way that assessment can help guide the prescription of interventions is by providing a mechanism for comparing treatments. Within the evidence-based medicine literature, a variety of different metrics have been developed. These include the *absolute risk reduction* (ARR), which subtracts the rate of a negative categorical event (suicide, relapse, etc.) in the treatment group from the rate in the comparison group, and the *Number Needed to Treat* (NNT), which is equal to 1 divided by the ARR. The NNT has limitations from a statistical standpoint, but it has advantages as a common-sense metric—it indicates the number of people who would need to receive a particular treatment in order for one more case to achieve a desirable outcome (Straus et al., 2005). For example, if a particular therapy achieved a response rate of 70% versus treatment as usual achieving a response rate of 35%, then the ARR would be 35% and the NNT would be about 3, meaning that for every three people receiving the new treatment instead of treatment as usual, one more patient would achieve the desirable outcome.

There is a corollary to the NNT, focused on risk of iatrogenesis—the *Number Needed to Harm* (NNH). The NNH is calculated as 1 divided by the rate of adverse events in the group receiving the treatment versus the rate of the same adverse events in the comparison group. Until recently, there has not been much attention to the fact that psychosocial interventions can produce harmful effects (cf. Lilienfeld, 2007). Estimation of the NNH could remind therapists that some treatments pose significant risks, and it could also provide a common metric that could be used to help families compare the risks associated with psychosocial versus pharmacological or other interventions. If both the NNT and NNH are available, then it is also possible to compute the *Likelihood of Help versus Harm* (LHH; Straus et al., 2005). The LHH is the ratio of NNT to NNH, with both being adjusted for the clinician's judgment of the patient's risk compared to the risk of the average patient in the studies providing the values of NNT and NNH. Straus et al. (2005) present detailed descriptions and examples, including methods for weighting outcomes according to patient preferences. The message to remember from this chapter is that there is a framework for comparing risks and benefits of treatment that can be used to compare treatment options and that can also incorporate clinical impressions and patient values (see also Kraemer, 1992).

Although the NNT, NNH, and LHH derive from outcome data, they are most helpful in terms of guiding treatment selection for an individual (and hence are included in the "Prescription" section instead of the "Process" section of this chapter). A limitation of these parameters is that they assume dichotomous outcomes. In practice, decisions about treatment choice are also typically categorical, and continuous measures can be dichotomized if the practical advantages outweigh the statistical consequences of lost precision and power (Kraemer et al., 1999).

Clinical Implications

The NNT statistics tend to be large, underscoring the need for improved interventions. The NNH statistics are a helpful reminder that treatments almost always involve some risk, offering a nudge toward Hippocratic caution in prescribing interventions. The LHH provides a promising framework for thinking about the trade-off between benefits and risks for competing treatment options. At present, this is a little-used perspective on the evaluation of psychosocial interventions, but the advantages of this view include a clear emphasis on the lower risk of harm associated with most psychosocial interventions compared with pharmacotherapies, and also the promotion of active negotiation about choice of treatment with consumers.

The Third P: Process

A third major way that assessment tools can be informative in a developmental psychopathology framework is by measuring *process*. One significant subcategory would be clinical outcomes, which quantify the degree of change occurring as the result of treatment; but the concept of processes can be used more broadly, to also encompass the measurement of variables that are informative about the mechanisms for growth and change. In statistical terminology, the variables that account for change processes have been described as *mediators* (Baron & Kenny, 1986; Holmbeck, 1997; Kraemer, Wilson, Fairburn, & Agras, 2002). In a clinical context, markers of adherence to treatment or fidelity of delivery represent another class of important process variables to consider. Finally, assessment can be used to detect variables that will change the prognosis or response to treatment. Such variables have been called *moderators*, and their effect on other variables is sometimes termed *interaction* (Baron & Kenny, 1986; Holmbeck, 1997). The following paragraphs elaborate on some issues pertaining to each of these uses of assessments, intended to be informative about process.

Treatment Outcome Evaluation

The measurement of outcomes is an important role for assessment tools in the context of psychopathology. Outcomes most often have been defined as reductions in the severity of symptoms, or alternately, as no longer meeting criteria for a diagnosis of disorder (Jacobson & Truax, 1991). Assessment scales have most commonly been given at the end of treatment, and then either compared to pretest baseline measurement or compared to the mean outcome in a comparison group. There has been movement toward repeating outcome assessments, sometimes using long-term follow-ups to look at the maintenance of gains, and sometimes following people long term to look at relapse prevention (e.g., Multimodal Treatment Study of ADHD (MTA) Cooperative Group, 1999).

Outcome assessment has an inherent tension between the goals of psychometric accuracy versus feasibility. Reliable assessment requires the use of longer scales or the use of shorter skills that are repeated many times. Either of these strategies increases the burden on the respondent. If people rush to fill out a questionnaire, they may respond less thoughtfully and accurately, lowering the reliability and validity of the scale. There also are likely to be much higher rates of skipped items or incomplete scales, creating a missing data problem. In clinical contexts, reliance on too intensive an assessment strategy will result in increased burden, not only for the patient, but also for the practicing clinician, who may not have the time, training, or motivation to pursue such an intensive schedule of evaluation. A practical consequence of this has been a push to develop shorter outcome scales (e.g., Ware, Kosinski, & Keller, 1996). One logical endpoint of this process of adaptation would be to have single-item outcome measures that are repeated multiple times over the course of treatment. Alternately, a well-developed measure of a focal construct could be used as a primary outcome measure, or else included as part of a suite of specialized instruments capturing a broader sense of the person's functioning.

Repeated, Brief Measures

The simplest form of a brief, repeated measure would be when a therapist asks a patient, "How are you doing now?" For research, brief assessments need to be standardized, written down, and quantitative. Using a simple scaling question, such as, "How has your anxiety been this week, on a scale from 1 to 10?" would be an example of the next level of refinement. The Longitudinal Interview Follow-up Evaluation (LIFE; Keller et al., 1987) represents an example of a tool that is designed to make relatively simple ratings on a fixed scale and then repeat them for each week. The reliability of a single-item rating for each week is likely to be low. The strength of the approach comes from amassing ratings about lots of weeks, allowing a clearer picture of the dynamics of functioning and course to emerge. Other versions of the brief, repeated assessment strategy include "life charting" of mood and energy levels (Denicoff et al., 1997), or daily report cards used as a way of monitoring changes in fairly high frequency behaviors in settings such as the classroom or home (Evans & Youngstrom, 2006).

The principal advantages of these sorts of assessment strategies include the relatively low burden placed on the respondent and their sensitivity to trends of change over the course of treatment. A major disadvantage of these tools from a research perspective is that the resulting data are challenging to analyze using conventional statistical methods. Another major drawback is that compliance rates often are low in spite of efforts to minimize burden.

Behavioral Checklists and Questionnaires as Outcome Measures

Behavioral checklists and questionnaires, or interview-based rating scales, have been the most widely used method for evaluating outcomes in both psychotherapy and pharmacotherapy research. Ironically, the proliferation of potential outcome measures has clouded the fundamental questions of how effective a treatment is, or whether one treatment performs significantly better than another. A 10 point reduction in the Internalizing Problems T-score does not indicate the same degree of efficacy as a 10 point reduction in the Child Depression Inventory, due to differences in scaling as well as differences in content validity. Converting outcomes to effect sizes, such as Cohen's d (the mean difference between the treatment and comparison group, divided by the pooled standard deviation), provides only a partial solution. Effect sizes convert the outcomes of different studies (or different measures) into a common metric, but they do not address the possibility of differential validity changing the magnitude of the outcomes. Meta-analytic methods testing the homogeneity of effects provide an indication of when the effect sizes are more discrepant than could be attributed to simple sampling variations (Lipsey & Wilson, 2001); and with large enough numbers of studies, it becomes possible to estimate how much of the variation might be due to choice of outcome measure instead of other sample or treatment characteristics.

Two other limitations of effect sizes, such as d or r, include that they do not yield response rates and that they also are group statistics versus measures of individual outcome status. Rates are more intuitive for many consumers and policymakers, and many of the summary statistics favored in evidence-based medicine (e.g., the ARR, NNT, NNH, LHH) are derived from rates. This is not a major barrier to using effect sizes, however, as effect sizes can be converted into each other (Lipsey & Wilson, 2001), and also into various measures of non-overlap (such as the three Cohen U statistics, representing the percentages of the treatment or comparison group scoring above or below the average score in the other group; Cohen, 1988). This makes it possible to have the best of both approaches. Keeping outcome measures as continuous scores preserves more information and increases statistical power to detect treatment effects (Cohen, 1983); but it also is possible to re-express the outcomes in dichotomous rates when that would be helpful.

The more complicated challenge comes from the goal of defining successful treatment response at the individual level. Many ad hoc definitions have been used, including percentage reductions from the initial symptom level (e.g., 30% reduction in severity of depression counts as a "response," or 50% reduction indicates a different level). Percent-reduction definitions have been used frequently in pharmacotherapy trials and older psychosocial treatment studies. However, they are generally acknowledged to be problematic for various reasons, including that the choice of a threshold percentage is usually arbitrary. Such definitions also ignore the varying degrees of retest stability afforded by different instruments, conflating instability due to poor reliability with treatment response. This artifact has probably inflated the size of the placebo response in many clinical trials.

Clinically Significant Change

One response has been to develop more complicated definitions of treatment response and remission, including algorithms that combine different sources of information or different aspects of functioning, as well as sometimes including durational requirements (Findling et al., 2003; Frank et al., 1991). In the psychosocial literature, the need for a psychometrically sophisticated definition of clinical response that also could be meaningfully applied to individual cases led to the development of the "clinically significant change" model (Jacobson & Truax, 1991). This model focuses on two key components: "Reliable change," and change that moves the patient's score below a predefined threshold set by normative data.

The reliable change portion of the definition focuses on whether the amount of change shown by an individual case is large enough to reflect true change (in the classical test theory sense) rather than possibly being attributable to the unreliability of the measure. Jacobson proposed that the raw change score should be divided by the standard error of the difference for the measure, which takes into account the retest stability of the measure. The reliable change index (RCI) is expressed as a z-score with the standard error of the difference acting as the denominator. The RCI makes it possible to compare individual change across multiple outcome measures because RCIs for each will be in the same z-metric, and all will be adjusted for the amount of stability

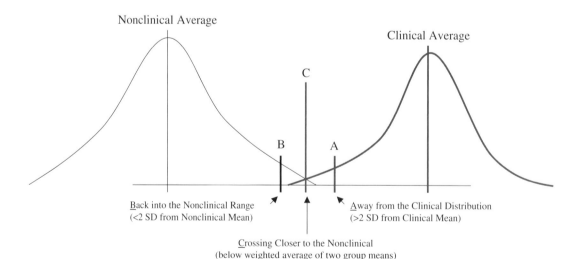

FIGURE 2.4 Thresholds for "Clinically Significant Change" based on Clinical and Nonclinical Distributions of Scores.

inherent in each measure. Jacobson and colleagues suggested interpreting RCIs of 1.96 or larger as reflecting "reliable change" (based on the 95% threshold for the normal distribution, two-tailed), or 1.65 or larger reflecting reliable change with 90% confidence. Jacobson argued that interpretations of reliable change should always be two-tailed, as there was the possibility that treatment might actually harm the individual (cf. Lilienfeld, 2007). If the individual's improvement was smaller than 1.96, then the Jacobsonian approach would declare that their response was inadequate to be considered clinically significant.

A suitably large RCI is a necessary, but not sufficient, condition for clinically significant change in the Jacobsonian model. The second key element is demonstrating that the patient's outcome score had moved past at least one of three potential benchmarks based on normative data. These could be labeled the "ABCs of change:" Moving A̲way from the clinical range (operationally defined as the threshold two standard deviations below the clinical average score on the measure), moving B̲ack into the normal range (operationally defined as being within two standard deviations of the mean for a nonclinical standardization sample), or crossing C̲loser to the nonclinical than the clinical mean (defined by calculating a weighted average of the two means that adjusts for differences in the standard deviations of the clinical versus nonclinical groups). Figure 2.4 presents these three thresholds for a hypothetical measure with a very high degree of separation between the clinical and nonclinical means ($d > 4$). Table 2.2 presents these

TABLE 2.2 **Clinically Significant Change Benchmarks Calculated for the Child Behavior Checklists (Achenbach & Rescorla, 2001)**

Measure	Cut Scores*			Critical Change (Unstandardized Scores)		
	A	B	C	95%	90%	$SE_{difference}$
CBCL T-Scores						
Total	49	70	58	5	4	2.4
Externalizing	49	70	58	7	6	3.4
Internalizing	n/a	70	56	9	7	4.5
Attention Problems	n/a	66	58	8	7	4.2
TRF T-Scores						
Total	n/a	70	57	5	4	2.3
Ext	n/a	70	56	6	5	3.0
Int	n/a	70	55	9	7	4.4
Attention Problems	n/a	66	57	5	4	2.3
YSR T-Scores						
Total	n/a	70	54	7	6	3.3
Ext	n/a	70	54	9	8	4.6
Int	n/a	70	54	9	8	4.8

*"A" = Away from the clinical range, "B" = Back into the nonclinical range, "C" = Closer to the nonclinical than clinical mean.

Note: Benchmarks for YSR Attention Problems are not presented because of consistent findings that self-report is not an effective modality for assessing attention problems.

benchmarks for the broad-band scales for the parent, teacher, and youth-report versions of the Child Behavior Checklist, calculated based on the data in the technical manual (Achenbach & Rescorla, 2001).

Multivariate Outcomes

One of the limitations of the models discussed earlier is that they are univariate. Each outcome measure is considered separately. In clinical trials, this leads to concerns about Type I errors and spurious findings. It also creates the opportunity for ambiguous situations when there is adequate response on one measure but not others (such as a reduction in hyperactivity, but no improvement in attention, social skills, or grades). Clustering methods might offer an attractive, multivariate definition of treatment outcomes. Rather than focusing on changes in a single scale or area of functioning, these approaches would make it possible to evaluate whether multivariate changes in functioning and problems were sufficient to change the person's cluster membership from a more severe or impaired group to a less severe or better-functioning profile. An interesting start in this direction has been supported by the Ohio Department for Mental Health, which sponsored the development of a cluster-based typology of adult consumers using statistical methods, with supplemental qualitative methods being used to refine and validate the cluster descriptions in collaboration with providers and consumers (Rubin & Panzano, 2002). The cluster typologies developed for different behavior checklists (as previously discussed) could similarly be used to define profiles of behavior at treatment endpoints as well as at initial assessment.

Research and Clinical Implications

There is a great deal of work to do in order to realize the potential for evidence-based assessment of outcomes in developmental psychopathology. The research agenda should include: (a) establishing relevant normative data for clinical and nonclinical groups, (b) publishing standard errors of the measure and the difference, (c) using Item Response Theory and other methods to enhance the precision of estimates of individual functioning and to better calibrate comparisons across samples and settings (Embretson, 1996), and (d) comparing different measures and measurement strategies in terms of their sensitivity to treatment effects and their criterion validity in terms of associations with client satisfaction and functioning. Additional contributions could be made by exploring multivariate approaches to defining functioning and outcomes, such as cluster-based methods. The creative tension will involve developing more sophisticated methods that inform treatment without requiring cumbersome procedures that dissuade clinicians or consumers from adopting them.

MEDIATORS

Mediators are the intermediate variables that act as vehicles carrying cause to effect, providing mechanisms of change (Holmbeck, 1997; Kraemer et al., 2002). There has been extensive debate about the conceptual requirements necessary for demonstrating mediation, including temporal sequencing or theoretical explanatory models, and there has also been debate about the statistical models used to test and demonstrate mediation (Baron & Kenny, 1986; Kraemer et al., 2002; MacKinnon, Krull, & Lockwood, 2000). A regression-based approach presented by Baron & Kenny has been highly influential, but it was published before the widespread availability of covariance-modeling statistical software that make it possible to correct for measurement error and to directly estimate indirect efforts through mediational pathways. Measurement error, potential suppression effects (where two or more variables have opposite effects on the outcome), and low statistical power all complicate the assessment of mediational models (MacKinnon et al., 2000).

Despite these difficulties, mediation is a core theme in developmental psychopathology. Mediation tells the story of processes rather than cataloging correlations. Mediational models have the potential to explicate routes of development. Within the context of treatment, mediation examines the "active ingredients" and how they produce therapeutic change. Better understanding of mechanisms offers huge benefits. These include offering strong confirmation of the theoretical models underpinning therapies, as would occur if cognitive-behavioral therapies produced measurable changes in cognitions (the purported mediator) that accounted for the changes in the outcome variables, or if family therapy produced quantifiable improvements in communication and problem solving that in turn explained the reductions in symptoms or gains in functioning. Careful examination of biological variables over the coming decades will also help clarify whether shifts in neurophysiological activity or morphology reflect a mediator or a peripheral outcome of change processes in psychopathology and treatment. Although there is great enthusiasm for the application of imaging techniques to "brain diseases," for example, there are numerous examples in medicine of supposed mechanisms or proxy variables having either no relationship or the opposite of what was believed once clinical trials were performed (Silverman, 1998).

An additional benefit would be conceptual consolidation. On the one hand, it is unlikely that all of the various purported mechanisms of therapeutic change contribute equally to outcome. Mediational analyses provide a framework for identifying the more powerful drivers of change. Conversely, there has been a proliferation of psychotherapies, with reviews finding more than 300 psychosocial interventions that are at least nominally different. It is unlikely that this plethora of treatments involves a similar number of unique mechanisms. In fact, it is more likely that the majority share only nonspecific factors that permeate most interventions and account for a surprisingly large proportion of the outcome variance (Wampold, 2001).

A third potential benefit of elucidating change mechanisms would be that techniques could then be refined to produce larger effects on the intervening variables, and thus potentially better outcomes. For example, if improved emotion recognition were identified as a mediating agent (Izard et al., 2001), then other therapies could add emotion recognition components to the treatment package (Greenberg, Kusche, Cook, & Quamma, 1995), or more powerful methods for improving emotion recognition could be developed and deployed (Duke, Nowicki, & Martin, 1996).

MODERATORS

Moderators are variables that change the relationship between another pair of variables. Statistical moderation has also been termed an *interaction effect*, and discussions of interaction effects in analyses of variance are relevant along with the more regression-oriented discussions of moderation (Aiken & West, 1991; Holmbeck, 1997). Moderator variables qualify the main effects that variables have on development and outcome.

Moderator variables include patient characteristics that change response to risk factors or treatment. The "diathesis-stress" model of developmental psychopathology is an example of an interaction effect: Neither the predisposition (diathesis) nor the stressor is sufficient in itself to produce the poor outcome, whereas the combination is. The 5HTTP short allele of the serotonin transporter gene offers an example of this type of interaction: Individuals with this genetic polymorphism are particularly susceptible to the effects of stress, although they still show good outcomes in the absence of acute stressors (Caspi et al., 2003).

The range of possible moderator variables is broad. Genetic differences will receive a great deal of attention in the next decade, now that the human genome is mapped (e.g., Wellcome Trust Case Control Consortium (WTCCC), (2007)). Genotypic differences will interact with the metabolism of medications, producing changes in efficacy as well as side effects (Mrazek, 2007). However, genes will also be linked with responses to changes in diet, social environment, and other environmental factors. All of these factors will often be moderators of psychological processes in their own right.

Cultural variables are another level of analysis likely to yield fruitful moderator variables. Drawing again on psychotherapy for examples, there is some indication that cognitive therapy may be particularly well-matched to families from European backgrounds, whereas Asians tend to focus more on somatic and less on cognitive features of illness, and Latin American families may be especially receptive to interpersonal approaches to therapy (Mufson, Dorta, Olfson, Weissman, & Hoagwood, 2004). Cultural differences are likely to influence rates of treatment seeking, degree of engagement with different modalities of therapy, extent of social support available, and other factors likely to play key roles in development and outcome.

Patient and therapist characteristics also may serve crucial roles in determining response course. For example, higher cognitive ability appears to be a protective factor that moderates the deleterious effects of many other adverse events and factors (Gottfredson, 1997), is generally associated with more positive response to psychotherapy (Neisser et al., 1996), and probably is linked with the ability to benefit from cognitive-behavior therapy, in particular at younger ages (Garfield, 1994). Personality and temperament are also likely to be important predictors of engagement in therapy, chronicity, and proneness to relapse (Harkness & Lilienfeld, 1997). There have also been multiple recent calls from different quarters to begin serious investigation of therapist characteristics as potential moderators of treatment (Garfield, 1997; Wampold, 2001). The dearth of studies in this area more likely reflects the hesitance of psychologists to publicly examine ourselves rather than the relative contribution of these variables to the outcome.

Adherence and Fidelity

Two additional examples of moderators merit consideration here. One is the degree of client adherence to a regimen of treatment, and the other is therapist fidelity to a prescribed approach to intervention. Both adherence and fidelity influence the effectiveness of an intervention, by determining the degree of engagement (and thus the "dosing" of the therapy) for the two main parties in the treatment endeavor. Some experts have argued that moderators should be variables that are fixed prior to the beginning of treatment (Kraemer et al., 2002). However, fidelity and adherence seem to be important counterexamples. They are not immutable, they can change over the course of treatment, and they certainly can have a substantial impact on the outcome. Measures of adherence can include things such as rate of completion of homework assignments, attendance of scheduled sessions, pill counts, and other markers of activities integral to treatment. Measures of fidelity include therapist progress notes, checklists or rating scales completed by the therapist (or less frequently, by the client) after each session, or ratings of audio- or videotapes of sessions.

Both adherence and fidelity deserve greater attention in developmental psychopathology. Some psychotherapies appear to produce their positive effects by means of improved adherence to other components of a comprehensive treatment package. For example, one of the vectors by which psychoeducation about mood disorders produces better outcomes is probably through improved adherence to adjunctive pharmacotherapy (Fristad, 2006). Cultural factors are also especially likely to influence adherence, by promoting enthusiasm or opposition to particular components of treatment.

Similarly, fidelity is also likely to influence outcome. Lower fidelity implementations would dilute the dosage of any active ingredients specific to a therapy (Crits-Christoph et al., 1991). More controversially, there is debate about whether high degrees of fidelity to manualized treatments undercut the flexibility and interpersonal factors that might be major, nonspecific contributors to the effectiveness of therapy (Wampold, 2001). Thus, there are competing hypotheses with regard to fidelity, where some predict that greater fidelity explains much of the gap between the magnitude of outcomes in efficacy versus effectiveness studies, and others argue that too much fidelity might actually constrain the therapist in a way that handicaps outcome. What the debate makes clear is that this would be a productive area for further inquiry.

Priority Areas for Research, Training, and Practice

The goal of this chapter has been to review the assessment of developmental psychology from the perspective of both practicing clinicians as well as researchers. Evidence-based medicine has provided a lens for evaluating the psychological literature in terms of methodological rigor as well as clinical relevance. At heart, though, this chapter is more intended to provoke reflection and stimulate new research and practice than it is to catalog and organize the existing literature. Consistent with this spirit, the chapter closes with a summary that outlines actions for change.

CRITICAL REAPPRAISAL AGAINST THE "THREE PS" OF ASSESSMENT

The perspective of this chapter is definitely skewed toward the applied and clinical view. This is not intended to slight the contributions of basic science, but it does reflect a pragmatic perspective that psychopathology creates an important set of challenges that need attention. Although literally scores of books, hundreds of instruments, and thousands of articles have been written on psychological assessment, it is a meager portion that have clear significance for clinical work with developmental psychopathology. The "Three Ps" of prediction, prescription, and process are not intended to be exhaustive, but instead provide a core set of heuristics that hopefully will promote reevaluation of existing tools against clear criteria tied to clinical utility. As alluded to earlier, there are more than 300 measures of depression available to clinicians. They cannot all be equally good for each of the distinct purposes for which they might be used.

There are three strategies that will winnow the field and yield swift rewards. One is for the practitioner to critically read the literature and look for new measures to dethrone incumbents. The assessment tools in one's cabinet should be sized up in terms of their ability to predict criteria of interest (e.g., validity correlations), prescribe treatments (by means of diagnostic efficiency or by criterion validity without relying on diagnosis as a proxy, as could happen with predictors of suicide, aggression, recidivism, or other important clinical conditions), or measure process (as quantified by sensitivity to treatment effects, or else providing guidance about treatment course and response via measuring factors that moderate treatment).

A second strategy would be to conduct studies that directly compare assessment methods on these key dimensions. As previously noted, investigations that simultaneously compare multiple measures are extremely informative because they level the playing field. All participating instruments are performing in the same theater, equally susceptible to the vagaries of study design characteristics. Clinicians would be well served by finding and digesting such articles.

Meta-analysis offers a third approach for comparing tests. More recent meta-analyses have become much more sophisticated in terms of testing whether parameters are converging on a single general value versus being moderated by sample or design characteristics, and they are starting to provide useful guidance about patient features that might change the validity of different assessments or treatments. Recent attention to the preparation of meta-analyses and systematic reviews has also led to the promulgation of guidelines to critically evaluate the design characteristics of assessment studies (Bossuyt et al., 2003). Although there are ways that these tools can be formally applied in meta-analyses (Whiting, Rutjes, Reitsma, Bossuyt, & Kleijnen, 2003), the primary intent is for clinicians to have a convenient yet systematic way of critically appraising assessment tools and determining the appropriateness of their use with any given individual client (Straus et al., 2005).

At present, articles and manuals are scant that present such clinically relevant information while also drawing on good research designs. Evidence-based medicine authorities estimate that less than 2% of articles indexed in Medline currently fulfill all of these criteria (Straus et al., 2005). They suggest referring to outlets of systematic reviews, such as "Evidence-Based Mental Health" and the Cochrane Collaborative Systematic Reviews, as ways of finding syntheses of rigorous studies with a clinical focus. They also provide suggestions for search strategies in databases such as MedLine and PsycINFO to increase the chances of finding relevant information, such as incorporating MeSH terms in searches. To identify studies relevant to prediction, consider using MeSH terms such as *prognosis* and *criterion validity*. To identify studies of prescription, use *sensitivity* or *specificity* and *prescription*. To identify studies of process, use *outcome measurement* or *outcome assessment, clinical evaluation*, or perhaps *adherence* or *fidelity* and *assessment* or *measurement*—depending on the purposes of the search.

Once relevant articles are found, it is straightforward to compare studies on the basis of sample composition, design features, and the magnitude of effects. There are helpful checklists to facilitate evaluation of studies against methodological criteria (Bossuyt et al., 2003; Whiting et al., 2003), as well as recommendations about determining the match between features of the patient in question versus the sample composition of the study (Jaeschke et al., 1994). If two or more measures appear to perform similarly, then considerations of cost effectiveness and burden break "ties." All other things being equal, then less expensive and invasive procedures will clearly be preferable. This will be important to keep in mind during the coming wave of enthusiasm for neuroimaging and biomarkers of brain disease: Unless these methods demonstrate substantially improved performance over less expensive methods, there is the risk that their adoption will increase costs without providing commensurate improvements in outcomes. In evaluating assessment tools, it will also be useful to use an analogy to sporting events—few tools will excel across the full range of demands for assessment, much as it is difficult for an athlete to perform exceptionally well at every event in a decathlon. Specialized assessment tools are more likely to perform well in the niches for which they were optimized, but they should not be applied to all cases any more than a single athlete should be entered into all events in a tournament.

Develop New Measures

Other commentators have stated that we have enough assessment tools, and there is not a need for new ones (Kazdin, 2005). Although I agree that there is a surfeit of assessment tools that have failed to distinguish themselves from each other, I also believe that most instruments have not yet been evaluated against the metrics attached to the "Three Ps" of assessment. As these metrics are applied to the portfolio of tools available, not only is it likely that a much smaller number of competitive tools will emerge, but I also expect that the process will reveal many areas where it will be beneficial to refine or develop new measures. The application of more conservative statistical methods (such as the exploratory factor analysis [EFA] decision rules advocated earlier) will expose many examples of mediocre measurement, where tools fail to adequately measure constructs from a rigorous statistical perspective, let alone from the vantages of development, prediction, or high-stakes decisions about individuals. There are considerable costs involved in using poorly validated scales. Among the psychometric deficiencies are poor content coverage, lower reliability (often due to insufficient length), lower validity (limited by reliability and poor content coverage), unnecessary or unsupportable increase in complexity of the overall battery (including Type I errors due to the proliferation of scales; as well as Type II errors due to reduction of power via low reliability or validity), and increased burden and expense (Kraemer, 1992). Not only does each test add to the burden and expense for the clinician and participant, but the addition of lower quality or irrelevant tests can actually lead to degradation of the quality of clinical decision making (Kraemer, 1992).

Another specific need is for tools that produce large effect sizes. Viewed through multiple lenses, most existing measures do not deliver adequate effect sizes to support the intended clinical or research applications. A large effect size is $d \sim .8$, based on Cohen's reviews of typical effect sizes found in top psychology journals (Cohen, 1988, 1944). However, this translates into an AUC of .71, meaning that what the field has accepted as a large difference in group distributions is not adequate when trying to use the instrument to classify individuals. Even d of .8 renders many of the outcome benchmarks implied by the Jacobson and Truax clinical significance model silly or impossible (such as requiring negative raw scores in order to achieve a statistical definition of clinical significance). Meehl has recommended using indicators with $d = 2.0$ or larger for taxometric investigations (although simulations now indicate that the methods may be robust with indicator validities as low as 1.25—still more than 50% larger than what has conventionally been accepted as large; Beauchaine & Beauchaine, 2002; Ruscio & Marcus, 2007).

Adaptive testing, using Item Response Theory to quantify item properties, will make it possible to obtain increased precision and better range of scores without increasing participant burden (but not without increasing expenses, as these approaches typically will require computer-assisted testing). The increases in validity would be worth some added investment, particularly as computing costs continue to fall. Priorities for new measures should include demonstration of more robust factor structures (and more indicators per factor), larger effect sizes than incumbent measures using clinically relevant comparisons, and more evidence of clinical validity (ideally quantified in terms linked to the Three Ps).

FACILITATE EVIDENCE-BASED PRACTICE

There is a great deal that could be done to improve the clinical utility of existing assessment practices without developing new instruments. Much good could be accomplished by presenting additional psychometric information about instruments, especially by adopting the statistics espoused by evidence-based medicine. Table 2.3 presents a "ladder of improvements" that could be used for the validation of assessment tools, organized around the Three Ps. Incorporation of these techniques into the evaluation and packaging of assessment tools would markedly increase their utility for prediction, prescription, and monitoring the processes of development and treatment. Another refinement that could be woven into the developmental psychopathology literature would be to more consistently use MeSH search terms as key words to index articles, making them easier for users to locate in the future.

DO THESE RESULTS APPLY TO MY CLIENT?

Table 2.3 can also be read as a treasure hunt list for practitioners. Each further rung along the ladder provides more directly clinically relevant information, or more nuanced applications of assessment results to an individual. The ideal endpoint would be to have an evidence base that supports the choice of instrument and the customization of interpretation to meet the individual circumstances of the client. The choice of measure is always provisional, to the degree that a better instrument could be published at any time. "Better" within this context is primarily determined by either having demonstrated greater validity (under equal or more challenging conditions), or else by showing more validity for a subgroup to which the patient also belongs.

When the library of assessment tools is rated against these standards, there are many gaps in coverage. The gaps grow geometrically larger when trying to consider potential differences in needs for persons from culturally diverse backgrounds, or with distinct clinical profiles. Does a measure of attention problems still work when translated into Spanish? Does it provide meaningful information when used with a patient who also has a Pervasive Developmental Disorder?

The recommended strategy is to proceed with the best available tools based on the evidence, but to add an element of caution. The gains inherent in shifting to an evidence-based strategy of assessment are profound. The factors that might change the performance of a test in a particular subgroup are instances of moderator effects. These can be empirically tested, and they have proven fairly rare to date. Some of this scarcity is probably due to a lack of systematic investigation, and some is due to the challenges of demonstrating an interaction effect. But from a clinician's or client's perspective, this is still good news: It means that the full armamentarium of assessment tools is available,

TABLE 2.3 Ladder of Improvements for Developmental Psychopathology Assessments

Prediction

Intuitive, impressionistic interpretation

Statistical significance ($p < .05$)

Effect sizes

Confidence intervals

Unstandardized regressions weights (for complete prediction model)

Multivariate regression models with interaction effects

Present NNT, NNH, LHH

Prescription

Intuitive, impressionistic formulation

Statistical significance

Effect size

Sensitivity & specificity for one threshold

Receiver Operating Characteristic (ROC) analyses

Multi-level likelihood ratios

Logistic regressions—testing incremental validity and combinations of variables

Quality ROC and cost-benefit analyses

Differential Item Functioning analyses and other evidence of moderators

Multistage assessment evaluations

Process

Intuitive

Statistical significance

Elaborated tests of significance (e.g., considering positive functioning as well as symptom reduction)

Multivariate models (clusters of functioning)

Clinical significance definitions

Social validation

Mediators of treatment (although these may be more useful in treatment development than in daily clinical practice)

Moderators (such as adherence, fidelity, patient characteristics [including gene x environment interactions], and therapist characteristics)

unless there is a published example that contradicts the validity for a particular characteristic of the patient. Just as we would not withhold an AIDS vaccine from Asian families simply because it had been developed on a European participant pool, we should not refrain from using tests with validity data that imperfectly match the patient. This perspective does not undercut the importance of research to examine potential moderators. Quite the opposite: Until the appropriate large-group studies can be performed, the clinician should adopt a "single subject study" mentality and cautiously proceed with the best available assessments and treatments, while carefully attending to the possibility that the individual outcome might diverge from the published tendency. There are definitely risks in using assessment tools developed on one group and applying them to patients from other populations. The risks are far greater for denying the use of an assessment instrument until it can be validated via a rigorous, large group design.

Implications for Training: Using the Evidence Base as Occam's Razor

This chapter began with a review of the content of assessment training in both graduate programs and predoctoral internships. It concludes with recommendations about training, but it extends to include continuing education and other forms of self-improvement.

The first challenge is to reevaluate the core of one's clinical battery, whether in private practice or teaching an assessment course. We should not keep using or teaching the same instruments out of convention (and often the standard of practice is difficult to distinguish from habit, unless there is a fresh infusion of evidence). Teaching and practice could be improved by shifting resources from measures that lack evidence (including old standards) to those that do. A similarly radical but helpful change could be achieved by including more clinically oriented statistical methods in the core curriculum of clinical, counseling, developmental psychopathology, and school psychology programs by de-emphasizing hand computation this could be accomplished in many programs without increasing the number of required courses. Another method for promoting generalization of concepts into practice would be to craft homework exercises that involve doing statistics in assessment and therapy.

Historically, continuing education has been a weak method of imparting new information and skills in a way that influences practice. The situation might be improved by combining: (a) clear demonstrations of the clinical utility of new methods, (b) teaching the skills for locating new improvements (such as searching evidence-based mental health or Cochrane databases, or using MeSH terms to search PubMed), (c) teaching the Standards for Reporting of Diagnostic Accuracy (STARD; Bossuyt et al., 2003) and other guidelines for critically evaluating methods, and (d) giving practitioners opportunities to practice applying the new methods to existing cases, with corrective feedback and discussion. In the evidence-based medicine literature, there has been discussion of the leaky pipeline connecting research innovation to the improvement of care for a specific case. The pipeline has multiple leaks (at least eight in the discussion offered by Glasziou & Jeffrey, 2008), each of which is an opportunity for improved connection between research and practice.

Perhaps the most productive way to lead to improvement in the quality of assessment will be to teach an attitude and behaviors that continuously check for updates and improvements. Advocates of evidence-based medicine have captured this concept in a dramatic exhortation to "burn your textbooks." The point they hope to convey is that the ideas and data available when practitioners were completing training will become outdated, and the only solution is to regularly update knowledge and practices against the current evidence base. Computer software provides a convenient metaphor: Many programs now provide automated reminders to check for upgrades. Assessment upgrades will also become available, and hopefully practitioners and educators will get in the habit of applying them.

Acknowledgments

This work was supported in part by NIMH R01 MH066647. I would like to thank Megan Joseph, Melissa Noya, and David Miklowitz for their helpful comments.

References

Achenbach, T. M. (1991). *Manual for the Child Behavior Checklist/4-18 and 1991 profile*. Burlington: University of Vermont. Department of Psychiatry.

Achenbach, T. M. (1993). *Empirically based taxonomy: How to use syndromes and profile types derived from the CBCL/4-18, TRF, and YSR*. Burlington, VT: University of Vermont. Department of Psychiatry.

Achenbach, T. M. (1999). The child behavior checklist and related instruments. In M. E. Maruish, (Ed.), *The use of psychological testing for treatment planning and outcomes assessment* (2nd ed., pp. 429–466). Mahwah, NJ: Erlbaum.

Achenbach, T. M., & Edelbrock, C. (1983). *Manual for the Child Behavior Checklist and Revised Child Behavior Profile*. Burlington: University of Vermont, Department of Psychiatry.

Achenbach, T. M., McConaughy, S. H., & Howell, C. T. (1987). Child/adolescent behavioral and emotional problems: Implication of cross-informant correlations for situational specificity. *Psychological Bulletin, 101*, 213–232.

Achenbach, T. M., & Rescorla, L. A. (2001). *Manual for the ASEBA School-Age Forms & Profiles*. Burlington, VT: University of Vermont.

Aiken, L. S., & West, S. G. (1991). *Multiple regression: Testing and interpreting interactions*. Newbury Park, CA: Sage.

Aldenderfer, M. S., & Blashfield, R. K. (1984). *Cluster analysis*. Beverly Hills, CA: Sage.

Ambrosini, P. J., Bennett, D. S., Cleland, C. M., & Haslam, N. (2002). Taxonicity of adolescent melancholia: A categorical or dimensional construct? *Journal of Psychiatric Research, 36*, 247–256.

Angold, A., Costello, E. J., & Erkanli, A. (1999). Comorbidity. *Journal of Child Psychology and Psychiatry, 40*, 57–87.

Archer, R. P., & Newsom, C. R. (2000). Psychological test usage with adolescent clients: Survey update. *Assessment, 7*, 227–235.

Barkley, R. A. (2002). Major life activity and health outcomes associated with attention-deficit/hyperactivity disorder. *The Journal of Clinical Psychiatry, 63*, 10–15.

Baron, R. M., & Kenny, D. A. (1986). The moderator-mediator variable distinction in social psychological research: Conceptual, strategic, and statistical considerations. *Journal of Personality and Social Psychology, 51*, 1173–1182.

Beauchaine, T. P., & Beauchaine, R. J. (2002). A comparison of maximum covariance and k-means cluster analysis in classifying cases into known taxon groups. *Psychological Methods, 7*, 245–261.

Beck, A. T., & Steer, R. A. (1987). *Beck Depression Inventory manual*. San Antonio, TX: The Psychological Corporation.

Beck, A. T., Steer, R. A., & Garbin, M. G. (1988). Psychometric properties of the Beck Depression Inventory: Twenty-five years of evaluation. *Clinical Psychology Review, 8*, 77–100.

Bird, H. (1996). Epidemiology of childhood disorders in a cross-cultural context. *Journal of Child Psychology and Psychiatry, 37*, 35–49.

Bird, H., Yager, T., Staghezza, B., Gould, M., Canino, G., & Rubio-Stipec, M. (1990). Impairment in the epidemiological measurement of childhood psychopathology in the community. *Journal of the American Academy of Child & Adolescent Psychiatry, 29*, 796–803.

Blanchard, J. J., Gangestad, S. W., Brown, S. A., & Horan, W. P. (2000). Hedonic capacity and schizotypy revisited: A taxometric analysis of social anhedonia. *Journal of Abnormal Psychology, 109*, 87–95.

Bollen, K. A. (1989). *Structural equations with latent variables*. New York: Wiley.

Bossuyt, P. M., Reitsma, J. B., Bruns, D. E., Gatsonis, C. A., Glasziou, P. P., Irwig, L. M., et al. (2003). Towards complete and accurate reporting of studies of diagnostic accuracy: The STARD initiative. *British Medical Journal, 326*, 41–44.

Brooks, S. J., & Kutcher, S. (2001). Diagnosis and measurement of adolescent depression: A review of commonly utilized instruments. *Journal of Child and Adolescent Psychopharmacology, 11*, 341–376.

Brown, T. A. (2006). *Confirmatory factor analysis for applied research*. New York: Guilford.

Buros, O. K. (1965). Foreword. In O. K. Buros (Ed.), *The mental measurements yearbooks* (6th ed., pp. xxii) Lincoln, NE: University of Nebraska.

Camara, W., Nathan, J., & Puente, A. (1998). *Psychological test usage in professional psychology: Report of the APA practice and science directorates.*

Washington, DC: American Psychological Association.

Cantwell, D. P. (1996). Classification of child and adolescent psychopathology. *Journal of Child Psychology and Psychiatry, 37*, 3–12.

Carey, W. B. (1998). Temperament and behavior problems in the classroom. *School Psychology Review, 27*, 522–533.

Caron, C., & Rutter, M. (1991). Comorbidity in child psychopathology: Concepts, issues and research strategies. *Journal of Child Psychology and Psychiatry, 32*, 1063–1080.

Carson, R. C. (1997). Costly compromises: A critique of the Diagnostic and Statistical Manual of Mental Disorders. In S. Fisher & R. P. Greenberg (Eds.), *From placebo to panacea* (pp. 98–112). New York: Wiley.

Caspi, A., Sugden, K., Moffitt, T., Taylor, A., Craig, I., Harrington, H., et al. (2003). Influence of life stress on depression: Moderation by polymorphism in the 5-HTT Gene. *Science, 301*, 386–398.

Childs, R. A., & Eyde, L. D. (2002). Assessment training in clinical psychology doctoral programs: What should we teach? What do we teach? *Journal of Personality Assessment, 78*, 130–144.

Cicchetti, D., & Cohen, D. J. (1995). *Developmental psychopathology, Vol. 1: Theory and methods.* New York: Wiley.

Cohen, J. (1983). The cost of dichotomization. *Applied Psychological Measurement, 7*, 249–253.

Cohen, J. (1988). *Statistical power analysis for the behavioral sciences* (2nd ed.). Hillsdale, NJ: Lawrence Erlbaum.

Cohen, J. (1994). The earth is round (p < .05). *American Psychologist, 49*, 997–1003.

Cohen, J., & Cohen, P. (1983). *Applied multiple regression/correlation analysis for the behavioral sciences* (3rd ed.) Hillsdale, NJ: Lawrence Erlbaum.

Costello, E. J., Angold, A., Burns, B. J., Stangl, D. K., Tweed, D. L., Erkanli, A., et al. (1996). The Great Smoky Mountains Study of youth: Goals, design, methods, and the prevalence of *DSM-III-R* disorders. *Archives of General Psychiatry, 53*, 1129–1136.

Crits-Christoph, P., Baranackie, K., Kurcias, J. S., Beck, A. T., Carroll, K., Perry, K., et al. (1991). Meta-analysis of therapist effects in psychotherapy outcome studies. *Psychotherapy Research, 1*, 81–91.

Danielson, C. K. (2002). *The nature of major depression in youths: A taxometric analysis.* Cleveland, OH: Case Western Reserve University, Cleveland.

Denicoff, K. D., Smith-Jackson, E. E., Disney, E. R., Suddath, R. L., Leverich, G. S., & Post, R. M. (1997). Preliminary evidence of the reliability and validity of the prospective life-chart methodology (LCM-p). *Journal of Psychiatric Research, 31*, 593–603.

Depue, R. A., & Lenzenweger, M. F. (2001). A neurobehavioral dimensional model. In W. J. Livesley (Ed.), *Handbook of personality disorders: Theory, research, and treatment* (pp. 136–176). New York: Guilford.

Depue, R. A., Luciana, M., Arbisi, P., Collins, P., & Leon, A. (1994). Dopamine and the structure of personality: Relation of agonist-induced dopamine activity to positive emotionality. *Journal of Personality and Social Psychology, 67*, 485–498.

Derryberry, D., & Rothbart, M. K. (1997). Reactive and effortful processes in the organization of temperament. *Development and Psychopathology, 9*, 633–652.

Duke, M. P., Nowicki, S., & Martin, E. A. (1996). *Teaching your child the language of social success.* Atlanta, GA: Peachtree.

Duncan, T. E., Duncan, S. C., Strycker, L. A., Li, F., & Alpert, A. (1999). *An introduction to latent variable growth curve modeling: Concepts, issues, and applications.* Hillsdale, NJ: Lawrence Erlbaum.

Eisman, E. J., Dies, R. R., Finn, S. E., Eyde, L. D., Kay, G. G., Kubiszyn, T. W., et al. (1998). *Problems and limitations in the use of psychological assessment in contemporary health care delivery: Report of the Board of Professional Affairs Psychological Assessment Workgroup, Part II.* Washington, DC: American Psychological Association.

Embretson, S. E. (1996). The new rules of measurement. *Psychological Assessment, 8*, 341–349.

Evans, S. W., & Youngstrom, E. A. (2006). Evidence based assessment of attention-deficit hyperactivity disorder: Measuring outcomes. *Journal of the American Academy of Child and Adolescent Psychiatry, 45*, 1132–1137.

Fabrigar, L. R., Wegener, D. T., MacCallum, R. C., & Strahan, E. J. (1999). Evaluating the use of exploratory factor analysis in psychological research. *Psychological Methods, 4*, 272–299.

Faraone, S. V., Biederman, J., Mennin, D., Wozniak, J., & Spencer, T. (1997). Attention-deficit hyperactivity disorder with bipolar disorder: A familial subtype? *Journal of the American Academy of Child & Adolescent Psychiatry, 36*, 1378–1387.

Findling, R. L., McNamara, N. K., Gracious, B. L., Youngstrom, E. A., Stansbrey, R. J., Reed, M. D., et al. (2003). Combination lithium and divalproex in pediatric bipolarity. *Journal of the American*

Academy of Child & Adolescent Psychiatry, 42, 895–901.

Flanagan, D. J., McGrew, K. S., & Ortiz, S. O. (2000). *The Wechsler intelligence scales and Gf-Gc theory.* Needham Heights, MA: Allyn and Bacon.

Fletcher, J. M., Francis, D. J., Morris, R. D., & Lyon, G. R. (2005). Evidence-based assessment of learning disabilities in children and adolescents. *Journal of Clinical Child & Adolescent Psychology, 34,* 506–522.

Frank, E., Prien, R. F., Jarrett, R. B., Keller, M. B., Kupfer, D. J., Lavori, P. W., et al. (1991). Conceptualization and rationale for consensus definitions of terms in major depressive disorder:. Remission, recovery, relapse, and recurrence. *Archives of General Psychiatry, 48,* 851–855.

Frazier, T. W., & Youngstrom, E. A. (2006). Evidence based assessment of attention-deficit/hyperactivity disorder: Using multiple sources of information. *Journal of the American Academy of Child & Adolescent Psychiatry, 45,* 614–620.

Frazier, T. W., & Youngstrom, E. A. (2007). Historical increase in the number of factors measured by commercial tests of cognitive ability: Are we overfactoring? *Intelligence, 35,* 169–182.

Frazier, T. W., Youngstrom, E. A., & Naugle, R. I. (2007). The latent structure of attention-deficit/hyperactivity disorder in a clinic-referred sample. *Neuropsychology, 21,* 45–64.

Fristad, M. A. (2006). Psychoeducational treatment for school-aged children with bipolar disorder. *Development & Psychopathology, 18,* 1289–1306.

Garb, H. N. (1998). *Studying the clinician: Judgment research and psychological assessment.* Washington, DC: American Psychological Association.

Garfield, S. L. (1994). Research on client variables in psychotherapy. In S. L. Garfield & A. E. Bergin (Eds.), *Handbook of psychotherapy and behavior change* (4th ed., pp. 190–228). New York: Wiley.

Garfield, S. L. (1997). The therapist as a neglected variable in psychotherapy research. *Clinical Psychology: Science and Practice, 4,* 40–43.

Glasziou, P., & Aranson, Jeffrey (2008). *Evidence-based medical monitoring.* New York: Wiley-Blackwell.

Glorfeld, L. (1995). An improvement on Horn's parallel analysis methodology for selecting the correct number of factors to retain. *Educational and Psychological Measurement, 55,* 377–393.

Glutting, J. J., McDermott, P. A., Konold, T. R., Snelbaker, A. J., & Watkins, M. W. (1998). More ups and downs of subtest analysis: Criterion validity of the DAS with an unselected cohort. *School Psychology Review, 27,* 599–612.

Glutting, J. J., McDermott, P. A., Prifitera, A., & McGrath, E. A. (1994). Core profile types for the WISC-III and WIAT: Their development and application in identifying multivariate IQ-achievement discrepancies. *School Psychology Review, 23,* 619–639.

Glutting, J. J., McGrath, E. A., Kamphaus, R. W., & McDermott, P. A. (1992). Taxonomy and validity of subtest profiles on the Kaufman Assessment Battery for Children. *Journal of Special Education, 26,* 85–115.

Glutting, J. J., Youngstrom, E. A., Oakland, T., & Watkins, M. (1996). Situational specificity and generality of test behaviors for samples of normal and referred children. *School Psychology Review, 25,* 94–107.

Gottesman, I. I., & Gould, T. D. (2003). The endophenotype concept in psychiatry: Etymology and strategic intentions. *American Journal of Psychiatry, 160,* 636–645.

Gottfredson, L. S. (1997). Why g matters: The complexity of everyday life. *Intelligence, 24,* 79–132.

Gray, J. A., & McNaughton, N. (1996). The neuropsychology of anxiety: Reprise. In D. A. Hope (Ed.), *Perspectives in anxiety, panic and fear* (Vol. 43, pp. 61–134). Lincoln: University of Nebraska Press.

Greenberg, M. T., Kusche, C. A., Cook, E. T., & Quamma, J. P. (1995). Promoting emotional competence in school-aged children: The effects of the PATHS curriculum. *Development and Psychopathology, 7,* 117–136.

Grimm, L. G., & Yarnold, P. R. (1995a). Introduction to multivariate statistics. In L. G. Grimm & P. R. Yarnold (Eds.), *Reading and understanding multivariate statistics* (pp. 1–183). Washington, DC: American Psychological Association.

Grimm, L. G., & Yarnold, P. R. (1995b). *Reading and understanding multivariate statistics.* Washington, DC: American Psychological Association.

Grove, W. M., Zald, D. H., Lebow, B. S., Snitz, B. E., & Nelson, C. (2000). Clinical versus mechanical prediction: A meta-analysis. *Psychological Assessment, 12,* 19–30.

Guion, R. M. (1998). *Assessment, measurement, and prediction for personnel decisions.* Hillsdale, NJ: Erlbaum.

Guyatt, G. H., & Rennie, D. (Eds.). (2002). *Users' guides to the medical literature.* Chicago: AMA Press.

Hanley, J. A., & McNeil, B. J. (1983). A method of comparing the areas under receiver operating characteristic curves derived from the same cases. *Radiology, 148,* 839–843.

Harkness, A. R., & Lilienfeld, S. O. (1997). Individual differences science for treatment planning: Personality traits. *Psychological Assessment, 9,* 349–360.

Hasler, G., Drevets, W., Gould, T. D., Gottesman, I. I., & Manji, H. K. (2006). Toward constructing an endophenotype strategy for bipolar disorders. *Biological Psychiatry, 60,* 93–105.

Holmbeck, G. N. (1997). Toward terminological, conceptual, and statistical clarity in the study of mediators and moderators: Examples from the child-clinical and pediatric psychology literatures. *Journal of Consulting and Clinical Psychology, 65,* 599–610.

Horn, J. L. (1965). A rationale and test for the number of factors in factor analysis. *Psychometrika, 30,* 179–185.

Hudziak, J. J., Althoff, R. R., Derks, E. M., Faraone, S. V., & Boomsma, D. I. (2005). Prevalence and genetic architecture of Child Behavior Checklist-juvenile bipolar disorder. *Biological Psychiatry, 58,* 562–568.

Hudziak, J. J., Heath, A. C., Madden, P. F., Reich, W., Bucholz, K. K., Slutske, W., et al. (1998). Latent class and factor analysis of *DSM-IV* ADHD: A twin study of female adolescents. *Journal of the American Academy of Child & Adolescent Psychiatry, 37,* 848–857.

Hudziak, J. J., Wadsworth, M. E., Heath, A. C., & Achenbach, T. M. (1999). Latent class analysis of Child Behavior Checklist attention problems. *Journal of the American Academy of Child & Adolescent Psychiatry, 38,* 985–991.

Izard, C. E., Fine, S., Schultz, D., Mostow, A., Ackerman, B., & Youngstrom, E. A. (2001). Emotion knowledge as a predictor of social behavior and academic competence in children at risk. *Psychological Science, 12,* 18–23.

Jacobson, N. S., & Truax, P. (1991). Clinical significance: A statistical approach to defining meaningful change in psychotherapy research. *Journal of Consulting and Clinical Psychology, 59,* 12–19.

Jaeschke, R., Guyatt, G. H., & Sackett, D. L. (1994). Users' guides to the medical literature: III. How to use an article about a diagnostic test: B: What are the results and will they help me in caring for my patients? *Journal of the American Medical Association, 271,* 703–707.

Kagan, J. (1997a). Conceptualizing psychopathology: The importance of development profiles. *Development and Psychopathology, 9,* 321–334.

Kagan, J. (1997b). Temperament and the reactions to unfamiliarity. *Child Development, 68,* 139–143.

Kahana, S. Y., Youngstrom, E. A., & Glutting, J. J. (2002). Factor and subtest discrepancies on the Differential Abilities Scale: Examining prevalence and validity in predicting academic achievement. *Assessment, 9,* 82–93.

Kamphaus, R. W., Huberty, C. J., DiStefano, C., & Petoskey, M. D. (1997). A typology of teacher-rated child behavior for a national U.S. sample. *Journal of Abnormal Child Psychology, 25,* 453–463.

Kamphaus, R. W., Petoskey, M. D., Cody, A. H., Rowe, E. W., & Huberty, C. J. (1999). A typology of parent rated child behavior for a national U.S. sample. *Journal of Child Psychology and Psychiatry, 40,* 607–616.

Kaplan, D., & Elliott, P. R. (1997). A didactic example of multilevel structural equation modeling applicable to the study of organizations. *Structural Equation Modeling, 4,* 1–24.

Kaufman, A. (1994). *Intelligent testing with the WISC-III.* New York: Wiley.

Kazdin, A. E. (2005). Evidence-Based assessment for children and adolescents: Issues in measurement development and clinical application. *Journal of Clinical Child & Adolescent Psychology, 34,* 548–558.

Kazdin, A. E., & Kagan, J. (1994). Models of dysfunction in developmental psychopathology. *Clinical Psychology: Science and Practice, 1,* 35–52.

Keller, M. B., Lavori, P. W., Friedman, B., Nielsen, E., Endicott, J., McDonald-Scott, P., et al. (1987). The longitudinal interval follow-up evaluation:. A comprehensive method for assessing outcome in prospective longitudinal studies. *Archives of General Psychiatry, 44,* 540–548.

Kihlstrom, J. F. (2001). To honor Kraepelin: From symptoms to pathology in the diagnosis of mental illness. In L. E. Beutler & M. Malik (Eds.), *Rethinking the* DSM: *Psychological perspectives.* Washington, DC: American Psychological Association.

Konold, T. R., Glutting, J. J., & McDermott, P. A. (1997). The development and applied utility of a normative aptitude-achievement taxonomy for the Woodcock-Johnson Psycho-Educational Battery—Revised. *Journal of Special Education, 31,* 212–232.

Kraemer, H. C. (1992). *Evaluating medical tests: Objective and quantitative guidelines.* Newbury Park, CA: Sage.

Kraemer, H. C., Kazdin, A. E., Offord, D. R., Kessler, R. C., Jensen, P. S., & Kupfer, D. J. (1999). Measuring the potency of risk factors for clinical or policy significance. *Psychological Methods, 4,* 257–271.

Kraemer, H. C., Wilson, G. T., Fairburn, C. G., & Agras, W. S. (2002). Mediators and moderators of treatment effects in randomized clinical trials. *Archives of General Psychiatry, 59,* 877–883.

Lazarus, R. S. (1991). *Emotion and adaptation.* New York: Oxford University Press.

Lenzenweger, M. F., & Korfine, L. (1992). Confirming the latent structure and base rate of schizotypy: A taxometric analysis. *Journal of Abnormal Psychology, 101,* 567–571.

Lilienfeld, S. O. (2007). Psychological treatments that cause harm. *Perspectives on Psychological Science, 2,* 53–70.

Lipsey, M. W., & Wilson, D. B. (2001). *Practical meta-analysis* (vol. 49) Thousand Oaks, CA: Sage.

Lonigan, C. J., Vasey, M. W., Phillips, B. M., & Hazen, R. A. (2004). Temperament, anxiety, and the processing of threat-relevant stimuli. *Journal of Clinical Child & Adolescent Psychology, 33,* 8–20.

MacKinnon, D. P., Krull, J. L., & Lockwood, C. M. (2000). Equivalence of the mediation, confounding and suppression effect. *Prevention Science, 1,* 173–181.

Markon, K. E., & Krueger, R. F. (2005). Categorical and continuous models of liability to externalizing disorders: A direct comparison in NESARC. *Archives of General Psychiatry, 62,* 1352–1359.

McCutcheon, A. L. (1987). *Latent class analysis* (vol. 64). Thousand Oaks, CA: Sage.

McDermott, P. (1994). *National profiles in youth psychopathology: Manual of Adjustment Scales for Children and Adolescents.* Philadelphia: Edumetric and Clinical Science.

McDermott, P. (1998). MEG: Megacluster analytic strategy for multistage hierarchical grouping with relocations and replications. *Educational and Psychological Measurement, 58,* 677–686.

McDermott, P., Fantuzzo, J. W., & Glutting, J. J. (1990). Just say no to subtest analysis: A critique on Wechsler theory and practice. *Journal of Psychoeducational Assessment, 8,* 290–302.

McDermott, P., & Weiss, R. V. (1995). A normative typology of healthy, subclinical, and clinical behavior styles among American children and adolescents. *Psychological Assessment, 7,* 162–170.

McFall, R. M., & Treat, T. A. (1999). Quantifying the information value of clinical assessment with signal detection theory. *Annual Review of Psychology, 50,* 215–241.

Mechanic, D. (1989). *Mental Health and Social Policy.* Englewood Cliffs, NJ: Prentice-Hall.

Meehl, P. E. (1954). *Clinical versus statistical prediction: A theoretical analysis and a review of the evidence.* Minneapolis: University of Minnesota Press.

Meyer, G. J., & Handler, L. (1997). The ability of the Rorschach to predict subsequent outcome: A meta-analysis of the Rorschach Prognostic Rating Scale. *Journal of Personality Assessment, 69,* 1–38.

Mineka, S., Watson, D., & Clark, L. A. (1998). Comorbidity of anxiety and unipolar mood disorders. *Annual Review of Psychology, 49,* 377–412.

Moffitt, T. E., & Silva, P. A. (1987). WISC–R verbal and performance IQ discrepancy in an unselected cohort: Clinical significance and longitudinal stability. Special Issue: Eating disorders. *Journal of Consulting and Clinical Psychology, 55,* 768–774.

Mrazek, D. A. (2007). Current applications of clinical genetic testing for psychiatric practice. *Minnesota Medicine, 90,* 42–43.

MTA Cooperative Group. (1999). A 14-month randomized clinical trial of treatment strategies for Attention-Deficit/Hyperactivity Disorder. *Archives of General Psychiatry, 56,* 1073–1086.

Mufson, L. H., Dorta, K. P., Olfson, M., Weissman, M. M., & Hoagwood, K. (2004). Effectiveness research: Transporting interpersonal psychotherapy for depressed adolescents (IPT-A) from the lab to school-based health clinics. *Clinical child and family psychology review, 7,* 251–261.

Multimodal Treatment Study of ADHD (MTA) Cooperative Group. (1999). A 14-month randomized clinical trial of treatment strategies for Attention-Deficit/Hyperactivity Disorder. *Archives of General Psychiatry, 56,* 1073–1086.

Muthen, L., & Muthen, B. (2004). *M-Plus User's Guide* (3rd ed.) Los Angeles: Authors.

Neisser, U., Boodoo, G., Bouchard, T. J., Jr., Boykin, A. W., Brody, N., Ceci, S. J., et al. (1996). Intelligence: Knowns and unknowns. *American Psychologist, 51,* 77–101.

Nezu, A. M., Ronan, G. F., Meadows, E. A., & McClure, K. S. (2000). *Practitioner's guide to empirically based measures of depression.* New York: Kluwer Academic/Plenum Publishers.

O'Connor, B. P. (2000). SPSS and SAS programs for determining the number of components using parallel analysis and Velicer's MAP test. *Behavior Research Methods, Instruments & Computers, 32,* 396–402.

Oh, H. -J., Glutting, J. J., Watkins, M. W., Youngstrom, E. A., & McDermott, P. A. (2004). Correct interpretation of latent versus observed abilities: Implications from structural equation modeling applied to the WISC-III and WIAT linking sample. *Journal of Special Education, 38,* 159–173.

Panksepp, J. (2000). Emotions as natural kinds within the mammalian brain. In M. Lewis & J. M. Haviland-Jones (Eds.), *Handbook of emotions* (2nd ed. pp. 137–156). New York: Guilford.

Perloff, J. M., & Persons, J. B. (1988). Biases resulting from the use of indexes: An application to attributional style and depression. *Psychological Bulletin, 103,* 95–104.

Quay, H. C. (1993). The psychobiology of undersocialized aggressive conduct disorder: A theoretical perspective. Special Issue: Toward a developmental perspective on conduct disorder. *Development and Psychopathology, 5,* 165–180.

Quay, H. C. (1997). Inhibition and attention- deficit/hyperactivity disorder. *Journal of Abnormal Child Psychology, 25,* 7–13.

Raudenbush, S. W., & Bryk, A. S. (2002). *Hierarchical linear models: Applications and data analysis methods* (2nd ed.). Newbury Park, CA: Sage.

Richards, H. J., Casey, J. O., & Lucente, S. W. (2003). Psychopathy and treatment response in incarcerated female substance abusers. *Criminal Justice & Behavior, 30,* 251–276.

Robins, E., & Guze, S. B. (1970). Establishment of diagnostic validity in psychiatric illness: Its application to schizophrenia. *The American Journal of Psychiatry, 126,* 983–986.

Rubin, W. V., & Panzano, P. C. (2002). Identifying meaningful subgroups of adults with severe mental illness. *Psychiatric Services, 53,* 452–457.

Ruscio, A. M., & Ruscio, J. (2002). The latent structure of analogue depression: Should the Beck Depression Inventory be used to classify groups? *Psychological Assessment, 14,* 135–145.

Ruscio, J., & Marcus, D. K. (2007). Detecting small taxa using simulated comparison data: A reanalysis of Beach, Amir, and Bau's (2005) data. *Psychological Assessment, 19,* 241–246.

Sackett, D. L., Straus, S. E., Richardson, W. S., Rosenberg, W., & Haynes, R. B. (2000). *Evidence-based medicine: How to practice and teach EBM* (2nd ed.). New York: Churchill Livingstone.

Sattler, J. (2001). *Assessment of children: Cognitive applications* (4th ed.) San Diego: Author.

Sattler, J. M. (2002). *Assessment of children: Behavioral and clinical applications* (4th ed.). La Mesa, CA: Author.

Schmidt, N. B., Kotov, R., & Joiner, T. (2004). *Taxometrics: Toward a new diagnostic scheme for psychopathology.* Washington, DC: American Psychological Association.

Shiner, R. L. (1998). How shall we speak of children's personalities in middle childhood? A preliminary taxonomy. *Psychological Bulletin, 124,* 308–332.

Silverman, W. A. (1998). *Where's the evidence: Debates in modern medicine.* New York: Oxford University Press.

Silverman, W. K., & Ollendick, T. H. (2005). Evidence-based assessment of anxiety and its disorders in children and adolescents. *Journal of Clinical Child and Adolescent Psychology, 34,* 380–411.

Silverstein, A. B. (1993). Type I, Type II, and other types of errors in pattern analysis. *Psychological Assessment, 5,* 72–74.

Solomon, A., Haaga, D. A. F., & Arnow, B. A. (2001). Is clinical depression distinct from subthreshold depressive symptoms? A review of the continuity issue in depression research. *Journal of Nervous and Mental Disease, 189,* 498–506.

Stedman, J. M., Hatch, J. P., & Schoenfeld, L. S. (2001). The current status of psychological assessment training in graduate and professional schools. *Journal of Personality Assessment, 77,* 398–407.

Steer, R. A., Cavalieri, T. A., Leonard, D. M., & Beck, A. T. (1999). Use of the Beck Depression Inventory for primary care to screen for major depression disorders. *General Hospital Psychiatry, 21,* 106–111.

Straus, S. E., Richardson, W. S., Glasziou, P., & Haynes, R. B. (2005). *Evidence-based medicine: How to practice and teach EBM* (3rd ed.). New York: Churchill Livingstone.

Tabachnick, B. G., & Fidell, L. S. (2007). *Using multivariate statistics* (5th ed.) Boston: Allyn & Bacon.

Tengstroem, A., Grann, M., Langstroem, N., & Kullgren, G. (2000). Psychopathy (PCL-R) as a predictor of violent recidivism among criminal offenders with schizophrenia. *Law and Human Behavior, 24,* 45–58.

Teplin, L. A., Abram, K. M., McClelland, G. M., Dulcan, M. K., & Mericle, A. A. (2002). Psychiatric disorders in youth in juvenile detention. *Archives of General Psychiatry, 59,* 1133–1143.

The Psychological Corporation. (1992). *Wechsler Individual Achievement Test Manual.* San Antonio, TX: Author.

Thompson, B. (2000). Q-technique factor analysis: One variation on the two-mode factor analysis of variables. In L. G. Grimm & P. R. Yarnold (Eds.), *Reading and understanding more multivariate statistics* (pp. 207–226). Washington, DC: American Psychological Association.

Tillman, R., & Geller, B. (2005). A brief screening tool for a prepubertal and early adolescent bipolar disorder phenotype. *The American Journal of Psychiatry*, *162*, 1214–1216.

Velicer, W. F. (1976). Determining the number of components from the matrix of partial correlations. *Psychometrika*, *41*, 321–327.

Velicer, W. F., Eaton, C. A., & Fava, J. L. (2000). Construct explication through factor or component analysis: A review and evaluation of alternative procedures for determining the number of factors or components. In R. D. Goffin & E. Helmes (Eds.), *Problems and solutions in human assessment: A festschrift to Douglas Jackson at seventy* (pp. 41–71). Hillsdale, NJ: Erlbaum.

Wakefield, J. C. (1997). When is development disordered? Developmental psychopathology and the harmful dysfunction analysis of mental disorder. *Development and Psychopathology*, *9*, 269–290.

Waller, N. G., & Meehl, P. E. (1998). *Multivariate taxometric procedures: Distinguishing types from continua* (vol. 9) Thousand Oaks, CA: Sage.

Wampold, B. E. (2001). *The Great Psychotherapy Debate models, methods, and findings*. Mahwah, NJ: Lawrence Erlbaum.

Ware, J. E., Kosinski, M., & Keller, S. D. (1996). A 12-item short-form health survey: Construction of scales and preliminary tests of reliability and validity. *Medical Care*, *34*, 220–223.

Watkins, M. W., Glutting, J. J., & Youngstrom, E. A. (2005). Issues in subtest profile analysis. In D. P. Flanagan (Ed.), *Contemporary intellectual assessment: Theories, tests, and issues* (pp. 251–268). New York: Guilford.

Watkins, M. W., & Kush, J. C. (1994). Wechsler subtest analysis: The right way, the wrong way, or no way? *School Psychology Review*, *23*, 640–651.

Wechsler, D. (1974). *Manual for the Wechsler Intelligence Scale for Children—Revised Edition*. New York: The Psychological Corporation.

Wechsler, D. (1991). *Manual for the Wechsler Intelligence Scale for Children—Third Edition*. San Antonio, TX: The Psychological Corporation.

Wechsler, D. (2003). *Wechsler Intelligence Scale for Children—Fourth Edition: Technical and Interpretive Manual*. San Antonio, TX: The Psychological Corporation.

Whiting, P., Rutjes, A. W., Reitsma, J. B., Bossuyt, P. M., & Kleijnen, J. (2003). The development of QUADAS: A tool for the quality assessment of studies of diagnostic accuracy included in systematic reviews. *BMC Medical Research Methodology*, *3*, 25.

Wiggins, J. S. (1973). *Personality and prediction: Principles of personality assessment*. Reading, MA: Addison-Wesley.

Willett, J. B., & Singer, J. D. (1993). Investigating onset, cessation, relapse, and recovery: Why you should, and how you can, use discrete-time survival analysis to examine event occurrence. *Journal of Consulting and Clinical Psychology*, *61*, 952–965.

Wood, J. M., Nezworski, M. T., & Stejskal, W. J. (1996). The comprehensive system for the Rorschach: A critical examination. *Psychological Science*, *7*, 3–10.

Wellcome Trust Case Control Consortium (WTCCC). (2007). Genome-wide association study of 14,000 cases of seven common diseases and 3,000 shared controls. *Nature*, *447*, 661–678.

Youngstrom, E. A., & Duax, J. (2005). Evidence based assessment of pediatric bipolar disorder, part 1: Base rate and family history. *Journal of the American Academy of Child & Adolescent Psychiatry*, *44*, 712–717.

Youngstrom, E. A., Findling, R. L., Calabrese, J. R., Gracious, B. L., Demeter, C., DelPorto Bedoya, D., et al. (2004). Comparing the diagnostic accuracy of six potential screening instruments for bipolar disorder in youths aged 5 to 17 years. *Journal of the American Academy of Child & Adolescent Psychiatry*, *43*, 847–858.

Youngstrom, E. A., & Kogos Youngstrom, J. (2005). Evidence based assessment of pediatric bipolar disorder, part 2: Incorporating information from behavior checklists. *Journal of the American Academy of Child & Adolescent Psychiatry*, *44*, 823–828.

Youngstrom, E. A., Meyers, O., Youngstrom, J. K., Calabrese, J. R., & Findling, R. L. (2006a). Diagnostic and measurement issues in the assessment of pediatric bipolar disorder: Implications for understanding mood disorder across the life cycle. *Development and Psychopathology*, *18*, 989–1021.

Youngstrom, E. A., Meyers, O. I., Youngstrom, J. K., Calabrese, J. R., & Findling, R. L. (2006b). Comparing the effects of sampling designs on the diagnostic accuracy of eight promising screening instruments for pediatric bipolar disorder. *Biological Psychiatry*, *60*, 1013–1019.

Zwick, W. R., & Velicer, W. F. (1986). Comparison of five rules for determining the number of components to retain. *Psychological Bulletin*, *99*, 432–442.

Chapter 3

Generalized Anxiety Disorder

KAREN ROWA AND MARTIN M. ANTONY

Introduction

Generalized Anxiety Disorder (GAD) is characterized by excessive worry about a variety of topics. Until the publication of the revision of the third edition of the *Diagnostic and Statistical Manual of Mental Disorders* (*DSM-III-R;* American Psychiatric Association [APA], 1987), the diagnostic features of this disorder were not well established, and GAD was essentially a residual diagnostic category for individuals with persistent anxiety whose symptoms did not meet criteria for another anxiety disorder. In *DSM-III-R* and *DSM-IV* (APA, 1994) the key feature of GAD is chronic and excessive worry, and GAD is no longer considered a residual category. However, problems with unreliability in the diagnostic criteria, as well as considerable revisions from one version of *DSM* to the next, have taken their toll on the empirical status of knowledge about this disorder. Changing criteria have made it difficult for researchers to identify the essential biological and psychological underpinnings of this disorder. Until recently, treatment efforts were restricted by the inherent instability of the core features of this disorder. Recently, however, GAD has finally begun to receive the research emphasis it deserves, and studies have built upon a more stable foundation of theory and knowledge regarding the nature and phenomenology of this disorder.

Nature of Generalized Anxiety Disorder

DIAGNOSTIC CONSIDERATIONS

The central feature of GAD, according to the *Diagnostic and Statistical Manual of Mental Disorders Fourth Edition, Text Revision* (*DSM-IV-TR*; APA, 2000) is excessive worry occurring on more days than not, about a number of different topics. Worry must persist for at least 6 months, and can involve a wide variety of topics, such as finances, health, safety, and minor matters. Interestingly, the worries typically seen in GAD are indistinguishable in content from those reported by nonclinical samples (Abel & Borkovec, 1995), though they are distinguishable from cognitions seen in Panic Disorder (Breitholtz, Johansson, & Öst, 1999) and appear to be more future oriented than worry found in other anxiety disorders (Dugas et al., 1998). Further, the content of worry found in clinical versus community samples of individuals with GAD may differ slightly (Becker, Goodwin, Hölting, Hoyer, & Margraf, 2003). However, the features that seem to most clearly distinguish the worries found in GAD from normal worries include increased frequency and intensity and the individual's perceived inability to control the worry (Craske, Rapee, Jackel, & Barlow, 1989; Dupuy, Beaudoin, Rhéaume, Ladouceur, & Dugas, 2001). These features also distinguish the worries found in GAD from worries found in Social Phobia (Hoyer, Becker, & Roth, 2001). As a result of such findings, difficulty controlling the worry was added in *DSM-IV* as another criterion used to diagnose GAD.

In addition to the presence of uncontrollable and persistent worry, the diagnosis of GAD requires the presence of at least three out of six symptoms reflecting physiological or psychological arousal that accompany the worry. These include feeling keyed up, restless, or on edge, difficulty concentrating or having one's mind go blank due to worry, disrupted sleep due to worry, muscle tension, irritability, and fatigue.

Worry is a common feature of mood disorders; therefore, the *DSM-IV-TR* (APA, 2000) specifies that GAD cannot be diagnosed if the worry occurs exclusively in the context of a mood disorder. In other words, to establish a comorbid diagnosis of GAD with Unipolar or Bipolar Depression, the features of GAD must be evident at times other than when a person is symptomatic for a mood disorder. This can mean that the criteria for GAD predate the onset of a mood disorder, or that criteria for GAD continue to be met even during periods of remission from a mood disorder. For similar reasons, GAD is not diagnosed if it occurs exclusively during the course of Posttraumatic Stress Disorder, a psychotic disorder, or a pervasive developmental disorder.

As with other diagnoses in *DSM-IV-TR,* the worry and associated symptoms of GAD must lead to significant distress or impairment in a person's life. Further, the symptoms must not be better accounted for by another disorder (e.g., Social Phobia, an eating disorder), by a general medical condition, or by the use of a substance.

CASE EXAMPLE

Jennifer was a 20-year-old single woman entering her third year of college. At the urging of her parents, she presented at an anxiety disorders clinic for school-related stress. They had noticed a decline in Jennifer's ability to function over her first 2 years of school to the extent that she was debating her ability to return to her studies for a third year. A thorough assessment of Jennifer's difficulties with anxiety revealed significant difficulty with excessive worrying.

Jennifer was the third child in a family of five children, who lived in residence when attending college, but returned to her family home on weekends and holidays. Her parents were both professionals who described themselves as Type A personalities. They lived in an upper-middle-class neighborhood, and all the children except for Jennifer's eldest sister still resided at home. Jennifer was majoring in biology and had entered college on an academic scholarship. She described herself as hard working and perfectionistic, and had always achieved high grades in school. In fact, Jennifer had excelled in a number of activities in high school, including soccer and student government. In college, Jennifer had only peripherally maintained her involvement in extracurricular activities, and had mostly devoted herself to her studies. Although from an academic standpoint there was no objective threat for Jennifer to lose her scholarship, she found herself constantly worrying about her funding being taken away. This fear caused her to invest a significant amount of time in studying and working on school projects, to the exclusion of many extracurricular activities.

Although the focus of Jennifer's worry revolved around her school performance and the threat of losing her scholarship, she identified several other areas of worry. For example, she noted worrying excessively about the safety of her family and friends, especially her mother, who had a long commute to and from work. Jennifer reported that she often found herself unable to sleep if she was worrying about her mother being in a car accident, and stated that she needed to be sure that her mother had arrived home safely. To cope with this worry, Jennifer began asking her mother to call her on a daily basis, both when she arrived at work and again when she arrived home. Jennifer's mother had been compliant with this request, but noted that Jennifer often called her on her cell phone even before she had a chance to call Jennifer. Jennifer also reported worrying about her family's finances, even though her parents assured her there was no reason to worry. She began feeling very guilty about the money her parents provided for her living expenses. It took Jennifer excessively long periods of time to make decisions about any purchase that she perceived to be above and beyond daily necessities like food. For example, the purchase of new bedding almost paralyzed Jennifer, and she found herself worrying that she might find a better deal at another store if she could comparison shop further.

Finally, Jennifer had significant worries about her future. Jennifer had aspirations to complete a master's degree in biology, but worried about her ability to gain acceptance into a graduate program. She had consulted her academic advisor, who reassured Jennifer that she had the grade point average to be competitive for such programs, but Jennifer continued to worry. In fact, Jennifer's chain of worry led her down the following path: I won't be accepted to a graduate program, I won't be able to find a good job, I'll have to rely on my parents forever, I'll deplete their life savings, they'll lose their house, and none of us will have a place to live.

Jennifer's worrying had significant psychological and physical consequences. She reported difficulties sleeping, feeling as if she could not shut off her mind when she tried to sleep, despite feeling chronically tired. Even when Jennifer was able to fall asleep easily, she often woke up in the middle of the night and could not fall back asleep for several hours. Jennifer had also developed pain in her back and neck, likely due to the chronic tension she experienced when worrying. She described her mind as constantly active, and found it very difficult to shift her attention away from her worries once they began. As mentioned earlier, Jennifer had given up many valued activities and hobbies, and replaced them with devotion to her studies, checking flyers for the best deal on groceries, and checking on the safety of her loved ones (e.g., calling her mother).

HISTORICAL PERSPECTIVES ON GENERALIZED ANXIETY DISORDER

As mentioned earlier, the criteria required to make a diagnosis of GAD according to the *DSM-IV-TR* (APA, 2000) bears little resemblance to the criteria as first outlined in *DSM-III* (APA, 1980). To meet criteria for GAD according to the *DSM-III*, three of the following four symptoms needed to be met for at least one month: (1) symptoms reflecting startle, tension, and restlessness, (2) symptoms reflecting autonomic hyperactivity, (3) symptoms of anxious apprehension (e.g., worry, rumination), and (4) symptoms of hypervigilance. Thus, according to this diagnostic scheme, worry *could* be part of the diagnostic picture, but did not need to be present to meet criteria for a diagnosis of GAD. Further, according to *DSM-III,* GAD could only be diagnosed if all other anxiety disorders were ruled out, and none of the anxiety disorders could be diagnosed if another more pervasive problem had been diagnosed (e.g., a depressive or psychotic disorder). Thus, GAD was truly a residual category. The 1-month symptom duration also meant that a broader range of symptom presentations was able to meet criteria because of the inclusion of symptoms of short duration. Accordingly, the reliability of this diagnostic category was poor (Di Nardo, O'Brien, Barlow, Waddell, & Blanchard, 1983). Changes in the *DSM-III-R* attempted to rectify some of the difficulties with the original diagnostic criteria for GAD, though these changes only led to a small increase in the reliability of the diagnosis (Di Nardo, Moras, Barlow, Rapee, & Brown, 1993). For the first time, worry became the central feature of GAD in *DSM-III-R* (APA, 1987), with excessive worry about at least two life circumstances having to be present. Research confirms that excessive worry is elevated in people with GAD, as compared to individuals with other anxiety disorders and nonanxious individuals (Chelminski & Zimmerman, 2003). Further, symptoms had to be present for at least 6 months, raising the stringency for meeting criteria for GAD. Although establishing a minimum 6-month duration of symptoms appeared to be a reasonable strategy for increasing the meaningfulness of diagnoses, recent research questions whether this duration is necessary. Studies suggest that individuals who have GAD symptoms of less than 6 months did not significantly differ from those of greater than 6 months on a number of important variables, including impairment and comorbidity (Angst et al., 2006; Kessler et al., 2005).

DSM-III-R also addressed some of the hierarchical rule-outs that contributed to GAD's residual status, including allowing the diagnosis of GAD even in the presence of another disorder (except for a mood disorder), as long as the GAD symptoms were not better accounted for by the other disorder. Despite these changes, the associated symptoms of GAD remained somewhat problematic, with the list of possible associated symptoms being too broad (6 out of 18 associated symptoms were required for a GAD diagnosis in *DSM-III-R*). Subsequent research on the associated symptoms provided useful suggestions for further revision of this category. Marten and colleagues (1993) examined which associated symptoms could best distinguish individuals with GAD from control individuals. They found that symptoms of autonomic arousal (e.g., palpitations) were the least reliable symptoms of the current diagnostic scheme, and therefore these were removed in *DSM-IV.* Research on nonclinical worriers (i.e., individuals who report frequent and excessive worry that does not interfere with their functioning) suggests that muscle tension is specifically related to pathological worry, while difficulty concentrating is specifically related to depressive symptoms (Joormann & Stöber, 1999). Although these results have not resulted in changes to the diagnostic criteria for GAD, they suggest that further work may be necessary to pinpoint the essential associated symptoms that best characterize the specific syndrome of GAD.

EPIDEMIOLOGY AND DESCRIPTIVE PSYCHOPATHOLOGY

It has been difficult to establish prevalence estimates for GAD due the shifts in diagnostic criteria. The first prevalence estimates based on *DSM-III-R* criteria came from the

National Comorbidity Study. This study found that GAD was relatively rare in terms of current prevalence (1.6%), but was more common when lifetime prevalence was examined (approximately 5%; Wittchen, Zhao, Kessler, & Eaton, 1994). The recent replication of the National Comorbidity Study suggests a lifetime prevalence of GAD of 5.7% (Kessler, Berglund, et al., 2005). The 1-year prevalence rate of GAD in a representative German sample was 1.5%, with this rate increasing to 3.6% when subthreshold criteria were included (Carter, Wittchen, Pfister, & Kessler, 2001). Rates of GAD in primary care appear to be even higher. A review of prevalence rates in primary care suggests a median point prevalence of this disorder as 5.8%, suggesting that people with GAD may be more likely to seek medical attention than individuals with other disorders and are therefore more highly represented in a primary care setting than in the community (Roy-Byrne & Wagner, 2004).

In the recent replication of the National Comorbidity Study, the median age of onset of GAD was identified as 31 (Kessler et al., 2005). In a study of individuals who presented at an anxiety disorders clinic, mean age of onset was reported as 21 (Brown, Campbell, Lehman, Grisham, & Mancill, 2001). Studies suggest that earlier onset of this disorder is associated with higher levels of symptom severity, comorbidity, and vulnerability to other disorders (Campbell, Brown, & Grisham, 2003).

Studies of the long-term course of GAD suggest that it is a chronic and relapsing disorder with some fluctuation in course. A 16-month follow-up of clients diagnosed using *DSM-III-R* criteria found that half of the clients continued to be diagnosed with GAD at the time of follow-up, with no difference between remitted and nonremitted clients in terms of recent life stressors (Mancuso, Townsend, & Marcante, 1993). An even less encouraging outcome was found in a 5-year follow-up of clients with GAD, where only 18% of clients achieved full remission at the follow-up assessment compared to 45% of clients with Panic Disorder (Woodman, Noyes, Black, Schlosser, & Yagla, 1999). A recent 5-year prospective study found that the probability of full remission at some point during the 5 years was 38% and the probability of partial remission was 47%, with accompanying high levels of relapse (Yonkers, Dyck, Warshaw, & Keller, 2000). Predictors of a negative clinical course appear to be comorbid Axis I disorders (Bruce et al., 2005), personality disorders (especially cluster C personality features), decreased life satisfaction, and difficult family relationships (Yonkers et al., 2000). Results from a longitudinal study of individuals with GAD in primary care revealed a chronic course of illness in which many individuals experienced periods of symptom improvement or recovery over a 2-year follow-up, but the majority of these individuals went on to experience a recurrence of their symptoms (Rodriguez et al., 2006). In this study, predictors of chronicity included being female, having greater comorbidity (especially depression and anxiety disorders), and demonstrating more severe psychosocial impairment. In addition to the symptoms of GAD displaying a chronic course, the content of worry also appears to have some stability. Across a 12-month period, few originally identified worry domains in individuals with GAD had remitted, even though new worry topics were also identified (Constans, Barbee, Townsend, & Leffler, 2002).

GAD appears to be more common in women than men (Wittchen & Hoyer, 2001). One explanation for this gender difference is that women may use less effective strategies to manage worry. One study found that women were more likely than men to use thought suppression and to have a more negative problem orientation in response to worry (Robichaud, Dugas, & Conway, 2003).

Minimal research has examined differences in symptom presentation across different ethnic or cultural groups. A study by Scott, Eng, and Heimberg (2002) examined worry in a nonclinical population and found some differences across three ethnic groups. In this study, African American individuals reported less worry than Asian or Caucasian individuals on the topics of self-confidence, future goals, work competence, and relationship stability. Asian individuals reported more worry than the other groups on future goals. While Caucasians and Asians reported similar levels of worry across various domains of worry, African Americans reported the most frequent worry about financial issues. Although formal measures of socioeconomic status (SES) were not included in this study, ethnic groups did not differ in highest education level of education achieved by a parent, which was used by the authors as a proxy variable for SES. Thus, it does not appear that differences in worry about finances can be clearly explained by differences in SES levels. Another study compared somatic symptoms of anxiety in individuals with GAD from the United States and Nepal. This study found that individuals from Nepal endorsed higher scores on somatic symptoms of anxiety, whereas individuals from the United States scored higher on psychological symptoms of anxiety (i.e., being nervous) (Hoge et al., 2006). Thus, there is some preliminary evidence that different cultural groups may demonstrate differences in both the content of worries as well as in the focus of GAD symptoms.

Although once considered a minor disorder, the significant impairment associated with GAD is now well established. For example, individuals with GAD have similar functional impairment to individuals with Major Depression, and the impairment is worse for those with both conditions (Wittchen, 2002). One study found that 34% of individuals with pure GAD had at least 6 "impaired days" over the past month, in which the individual reported lost or limited days from work or activities (Wittchen et al., 2000).

COMORBIDITY

Even though GAD was once thought of as a residual or minor disorder that was most likely to occur as a secondary problem, research suggests that a primary diagnosis of GAD is common and numerous other psychiatric problems often co-occur with it. For example, data from the original National Comorbidity Study found that 80% of their respondents with a primary diagnosis of GAD also had a comorbid mood disorder (Judd et al., 1998). Another study using *DSM-III-R* criteria for GAD found significant rates of Comorbid Social Phobia (23%), simple (specific) phobias (21%), and Major Depressive Disorder (42%) (Brawman-Mintzer et al., 1993). Rates of comorbid personality disorders are also elevated in individuals with GAD, including avoidant (26%), paranoid (10%), and schizotypal (10%) personality disorders. The authors also found that anxiety symptoms per se did not contribute to personality disorder symptoms, suggesting that it is likely the presence of other variables in these patients (e.g., interpersonal sensitivity) that explains these high comorbidity rates (Mavissakalian, Hamann, Haidar, & de Groot, 1995). Comorbidity rates appear to diminish with successful treatment (Borkovec, Abel, & Newman, 1995).

More recently, the comorbidity of GAD has been studied using *DSM-IV* criteria. This research suggests that a current primary diagnosis of GAD is highly comorbid with other current Axis I disorders, including Panic Disorder With or Without Agoraphobia (41%), Social Phobia (42%), and Major Depressive Disorder (29%) (Brown, Campbell,

Lehman, Grisham, & Mancill, 2001). Comorbidity rates are even higher when lifetime diagnoses are studied. Some research suggests that high rates of comorbidity in GAD are associated with high levels of trait anxiety and negative affect, variables that are consistently elevated in GAD patients (Chambers, Power, & Durham, 2004).

The high rates of comorbidity found in GAD are associated with a more severe and chronic course of the disorder. Prospective studies find that rates of comorbidity increased over a 4-year follow-up period for individuals with GAD, and that this comorbidity had negative implications for the likelihood of remission from GAD symptoms (Bruce, Machan, Dyck, & Keller, 2001). The high rates of comorbidity in GAD are also associated with increased disability and use of the medical system (Stein, 2001).

Neurobiological and Psychological Underpinnings

NEUROBIOLOGY

Studies on the neurobiology of GAD are limited and therefore we do not have an integrated neurobiological theory of the development of this disorder. However, studies do implicate certain brain regions and neurotransmitters in understanding this disorder (see Sinha, Mohlman, and Gorman [2004] for a more thorough review). A number of neurotransmitter systems have been studied in GAD, in part because each of these systems has previously been implicated in understanding fear and anxiety. One such neurotransmitter is gamma-aminobutyric acid (GABA). Hypotheses involving GABA in GAD revolve around GABA's inhibitory role in the brain, aiding inhibition of subcortical circuits that are stimulated by threat (Thayer & Lane, 2000). It is thought that individuals with GAD and other anxiety disorders may have decreased GABA activity (Friedman, 2007), which leads to less inhibition of these threat-activated structures. Further, individuals with GAD may also have reduced benzodiazepine receptor sensitivity, which contributes to anxiety because the binding of a benzodiazepine receptor actually facilitates GABA binding, which then inhibits excitatory responses in the brain (Sinha, Mohlman, & Gorman, 2004). Research to support these ideas includes the findings that: (a) GABA receptors appear to be densely congregated in brain areas implicated in fear and anxiety, such as the frontal cortex, hippocampus, and amygdala (Petrovich & Swanson, 1997), (b) binding of a benzodiazepine to its receptor appears to increase the ability of GABA receptors to bind with available GABA (Goddard & Charney, 1997), and (c) benzodiazepines appear to be an effective treatment for GAD (reviewed later in this chapter).

Norepinephrine has also been implicated in GAD. Norepinephrine is the primary neurotransmitter in the sympathetic nervous system, the system responsible for the fight or flight response. Studies have demonstrated that norepinephrine levels are elevated in certain other anxiety disorders (e.g., Ballenger, 2001), raising the possibility that it may also be elevated in GAD. Further, venlafaxine, which affects the serotonin and norepinephrine systems, has been demonstrated to be an effective pharmacological treatment for GAD (Katz, Reynolds, Alexopoulos, & Hackett, 2002). However, other studies are equivocal thus far, and appear to include confounds that make definitive conclusions about the role of norepinephrine in GAD difficult (see Sinha, Mohlman, & Gorman, 2004).

Serotonin (5-HT) is also broadly implicated across the anxiety disorders, with studies suggesting that low levels of serotonin or serotonin receptor dysfunction are linked with increased anxiety (Goddard & Charney, 1997). However, studies of serotonin in GAD have yielded inconclusive results. Some studies have found that serotonin agonists lead to increased anxiety in GAD (Germine, Goddard, Woods, Charney, & Heninger, 1992) and that paroxetine (a selective serotonin reuptake inhibitor) shows reduced platelet binding in people with GAD compared to controls (Iny et al., 1994). However, other studies do not demonstrate differences in GAD patients versus controls on platelet binding of imipramine, which also affects the serotonergic system (Schneider, Munjack, Severson, & Palmer, 1987).

Cholecystokinin (CCK) has been linked to the panic attacks sometimes seen in GAD. One study found that a CCK agonist induced panic attacks in 71% of participants with GAD as compared to 14% of control participants (Brawman-Mintzer et al., 1997). Cholecystokinin is thought to be linked with both the serotonin and norepinephrine systems, and therefore may exert its effects in GAD through both of these systems, though one study suggested the effects of CCK appeared to be independent of the serotonin system (Goddard et al., 1999).

Cortisol levels, which suggest increased functioning of the limbic-hypothalamic-pituitary-adrenal axis, are also hallmark biochemical markers of stress and anxiety. Some evidence of overproduction of cortisol in GAD exists, though research is not consistent (Tiller, Biddle, Maguire, & Davies, 1988).

There have been few neuroimaging studies completed on GAD. Those that have been done suggest larger amygdala volumes in children with GAD (De Bellis et al., 2000), larger superior temporal gyrus volumes (De Bellis et al., 2002), lower metabolic rates in the basal ganglia (Wu et al., 1991), and hypermetabolism in the prefrontal cortex (Wu et al., 1991). A recent study suggested that a history of childhood trauma affected neurobiological markers in GAD (i.e., the N-acetylaspartate/creatine ratio in the prefrontal cortex, which is thought to be a marker of neuronal viability), suggesting an interplay between biological and psychological markers of this disorder (Mathew et al., 2004). Further, an imaging study of six patients with GAD (albeit with no control group) found that statements describing a personal worry yielded greater activation in prefrontal and thalamic-striatal regions for participants as compared to neutral statements (Hoehn-Saric, Schlund, & Wong, 2004).

In a study of adolescents with GAD, neuroimaging revealed greater activation in response to angry faces in the right ventrolateral prefrontal cortex, but this activation had a negative relationship with subjective anxiety levels, a finding that is inconsistent with other imaging studies, which have found a positive relationship between anxiety levels and prefrontal cortex activation (Monk et al., 2006). To explain this discrepancy, the authors postulated that activation in the prefrontal cortex may play a compensatory function, helping to regulate activation in subcortical structures. Interestingly, participants with GAD did not show greater activation in the amygdala than did controls, suggesting that the amygdala is not the subcortical structure of interest in understanding responses to angry faces. More research involving neuroimaging is required to resolve these types of discrepancies.

Chronic worry is also associated with reduced autonomic variability during stressful tasks (Borkovec & Inz, 1990) and elevated baseline muscle tension (Hoehn-Saric & Masek, 1981). For example, participants instructed to worry while exposed to a phobic image demonstrated less heart rate response to the image than did participants instructed to use relaxed or neutral thinking, though participants who received the worry instructions reported higher subjective fear (Borkovec & Hu, 1990). A more recent study suggested that worrying was associated with a slight increase in heart rate acceleration compared to relaxed thinking (Peasley-Miklus & Vrana, 2000), suggesting that worrying is associated with a gradual increase in physiological activation in the face of a stressor, rather than a suppression of physiological activation as suggested by the Borkovec and Hu (1990) study. Either way, GAD appears to be characterized by an autonomic rigidity. This more recent focus on the inhibitory function of the parasympathetic nervous system in addition to the excitatory function of the sympathetic nervous system has helped in understanding central nervous system functioning in GAD, as earlier studies tended to focus more exclusively on the excitation end of the equation (Friedman, 2007). However, as Friedman points out, physiological variability is actually the most effective way that organisms can maintain the stability of their systems. The more variability an organism can show in responding to (a sympathetic system function) and recovering from threat cues (a parasympathetic system function), the more able to adapt to the environment the organism is likely to be. Thus, autonomic rigidity is thought to lead to less adaptive behavioral and emotional responses to stressful events in comparison to an adaptive system where a more flexible autonomic system can help a person organize his or her physiological responses (Porges, 1995).

The most commonly used marker of autonomic rigidity is lower levels of heart rate variability in response to various stressors. Research suggests that individuals with GAD demonstrate lower heart rate variability during periods of worry and rest, decreased parasympathetic activity during periods of worry and rest (Thayer, Friedman, & Borkovec, 1996), and impaired habituation of heart rate activity to neutral words (Thayer, Friedman, Borkovec, Molina, & Johnsen, 2000). However, autonomic rigidity in worry has not been consistently demonstrated, with one recent study finding no evidence for autonomic rigidity as measured by heart rate variability in periods of relaxation, nonstressful cognitive tasks, worry, and negative imagery (Davis, Montgomery, & Wilson, 2002). Thus, more research is necessary to fully understand the rigidity of the physiological system underlying GAD.

In summary, neurobiological indexes suggest that individuals with GAD have a dysregulated central nervous system that may take longer to recover from a stressor than that of others. Further, the suppressed and rigid autonomic activity that is associated with worry may have implications for the maintenance of worry, providing individuals with short-term avoidance of physiological responses to stress, but impairing long-term adaptation to these stressors. These ideas will be discussed more thoroughly in the following sections (see, especially, the section on avoidance theories of worry). It is important to note, however, that there still exist many inconsistencies across studies on the neurobiology of GAD and further research is necessary to address these inconsistencies and aid in the development of a more coherent understanding of the neurobiology of GAD.

Cognitive and Behavioral Correlates

LIFE EVENTS

A small body of research has investigated the role that stressful life events may play in the development of chronic worry and GAD. An early study found that the presence of at least one stressful life event defined as unexpected, negative, and very important was associated with an increased risk of developing GAD symptoms (Blazer, Hughes, & George, 1987). This association was even more dramatic for men who had experienced more than four stressful life events; these men had a risk of GAD that was over eight times greater than men reporting zero to three life events. More specifically, Kendler, Hettema, Butera, Gardner, and Prescott (2003) found that themes of loss and danger in stressful life events specifically predicted onset of GAD. Further, Cougle, Reardon, and Coleman (2005) found elevated levels of generalized anxiety in women who had experienced abortions and Wenzel, Haugen, Jackson, and Robinson (2003) found elevated levels of generalized anxiety symptoms in new mothers. It appears that stressful life events may be a general risk factor for the development of a depressive or anxiety disorder, but life events involving loss and danger are more specific to anxiety and GAD in particular.

PROBLEM-SOLVING ABILITY

Researchers have also questioned the association between chronic, elevated worry and problem-solving ability in understanding GAD. Worrying has been conceptualized as an attempt to anticipate or solve real-life problems (Tallis, Davey, & Capuzzo, 1994) and research suggests that worry frequency is related to constructive, problem-focused coping (Davey, Hampton, Farrell, & Davidson, 1992). However, at some point, the worry process as constructive problem solving breaks down and becomes pathological. Davey et al. (1992) hypothesized that pathological worry may be associated with either poor problem-solving ability or poor confidence in problem solving, which thwarts the problem-solving cycle. They theorized that the presence of these deficits would prevent individuals from reaching acceptable solutions to perceived problems and thus lead to further worry.

Interestingly, research suggests that individuals with chronic worry do not have deficits in problem-solving ability (Davey, 1994; Dugas, Freeston, & Ladouceur, 1997), but rather have less confidence about their problem-solving abilities (Davey, 1994) and hold a negative problem orientation in response to problems (Belzer, D'Zurilla, & Maydeu-Olivares, 2002). Negative problem orientation refers to how a person thinks and feels about his or her ability to solve real-life issues. These findings are consistent in clinical samples of individuals with GAD (Dugas, Gagnon, Ladouceur, & Freeston, 1998; Ladouceur, Blais, Freeston, & Dugas, 1998). Further, the manipulation of problem-solving confidence has an impact on levels of anxiety and the tendency to catastrophize a personal worry, with lower confidence yielding higher anxiety and personal worry (Davey, Jubb, & Cameron, 1996). This study lends credence to the notion that meta-aspects of worry such as low problem-solving confidence may play a causal role on subsequent levels of worry.

Results for problem-solving ability versus orientation are similar to those found when examining the relationship between time management and worry. Worry has been found to have no relationship with time management behaviors (e.g., setting goals, organizational skills), but does have a negative relationship with time structure and purpose (e.g., possessing the notion that one's time use has a purpose, being present-focused, demonstrating persistence when completing tasks; Kelly, 2003). Thus, one maintenance factor of pathological worry as seen in GAD is likely influenced by the thoughts and feelings individuals have toward their problem-solving abilities and the purpose they attribute to their use of time.

Studies have also examined the strategies people with GAD use in response to their chronic worry. Similar to strategies used by individuals with other anxiety disorders, individuals with GAD reported a greater use of worry (e.g., think about more minor problems) and punishment (e.g., shout at oneself) strategies than did nonanxious controls, and less use of distraction (e.g., think about something else) and social control (e.g., talk to a friend) (Coles & Heimberg, 2005). Chronic worriers also appear to catastrophize positive aspects of their lives as well as hypothetical situations (e.g., worrying about being the Statue of Liberty) (Davey & Levy, 1998).

PROBABILITY OVERESTIMATION AND CATASTROPHIZING

Excessive worry, the defining feature of GAD, is essentially a cognitive phenomenon. Research confirms that individuals with GAD exhibit cognitive errors of probability overestimation (thinking a feared consequence is more likely to occur than it really is) and catastrophizing (assuming that an outcome will be much less manageable than it actually is) (Provencher, Freeston, Dugas, & Ladouceur, 2000) and these types of biases appear to be present in childhood worriers as well (Suarez & Bell-Dolan, 2001). Estimates of the cost of one's worry are related to worry severity, such that greater cost estimates are linked with greater worry severity (Berenbaum, Thompson, & Pomerantz, 2007).

INFORMATION-PROCESSING BIASES IN WORRY

Cognitive features of GAD and cognitive explanations for the phenomenon of chronic worry are plentiful. In this section we will review a number of cognitive features of this disorder.

Information-processing theories of the development and maintenance of GAD suggest that individuals with GAD pay greater attention to threatening stimuli, preferentially encode this information, interpret ambiguous stimuli as threatening, and have biases in memory for threatening events. Through such processes, individuals have greater access to frightening and threatening information, leading to increased states of anxiety. Indeed, one of the hallmark features of cognitive-behavioral interventions for GAD involves trying to modulate this bias in cognition.

Research using the emotional Stroop paradigm has provided evidence for a cognitive bias in GAD (see Mogg and Bradley, 2005, for a more detailed review of this topic). In the Stroop paradigm, participants are presented with threatening and neutral words presented in different colors. Participants are asked to quickly name the color of the word, while ignoring the meaning of the word. The inability to ignore the meaning of the word (thus suggesting preferential encoding of threat meanings) is deduced from slower color naming. Individuals with GAD appear to have difficulty with the Stroop task, taking longer to name the colors of threatening words (e.g., "disgrace") than nonthreatening words (e.g., "carpet"; Mathews & MacLeod, 1985). This result is consistent when words are presented in blocks (i.e., numerous words presented at once) (Mogg, Mathews, & Weinman, 1989), when stimuli involve general threat words (Martin, Williams, & Clark, 1991), when stimuli are relevant to the participant's idiosyncratic concerns (Mathews & Klug, 1993), and when stimuli are generally emotional words, including positive emotional words (Becker, Rinck, Magraf, & Roth, 2001). Further, the Stroop effect is also seen when word stimuli are blocked; that is, when words are followed by a masking stimulus designed to restrict the participant's conscious awareness of the word (Bradley, Mogg, Millar, & White, 1995). This attentional bias appears to be modifiable by treatment, such that color-naming interference in GAD participants is ameliorated by cognitive behavioral therapy (Mogg, Bradley, Millar, & White, 1995).

The visual dot probe task is another paradigm to study attentional biases in GAD. Individuals are asked to respond to a probe stimulus (e.g., a small dot) presented on a screen. Just prior to this probe stimulus, participants are presented with stimuli on the screen, one of which is the experimental stimulus (e.g., a threatening word or face). If participants respond quicker to a probe stimulus that appears in the same spot as the threatening stimulus, it is assumed that the participant was attending to that threat cue, and is therefore demonstrating an attentional bias for the threat cue. Research suggests that individuals with GAD demonstrate an attentional bias on this task, using threat words (MacLeod, Mathews, & Tata, 1986), negative words (Mogg, Bradley, & Williams, 1995), and emotional faces (Bradley, Mogg, White, Groom, & de Bono, 1999). Further, this bias is also demonstrated when stimuli are masked, suggesting that the processing of threat cues may not be at a conscious level (Mogg, Bradley, & Williams, 1995). Individuals with GAD were more likely to look toward threat faces rather than neutral faces in a visual probe task compared to nonanxious controls and individuals with depression (Mogg, Millar, & Bradley, 2000).

Individuals with GAD also appear to interpret ambiguous stimuli in a negative or threatening manner. For example, when presented with a number of homophones with both a threatening and nonthreatening meaning (e.g., "die" versus "dye") and asked to write out these words, individuals with GAD tend to write down a greater proportion of the threatening spellings of these words than do control participants (Mathews, Richards, & Eysenck, 1989; Mogg et al., 1994). Similarly, when GAD participants are presented with sentences that have a threatening or nonthreatening interpretation and are then asked to pick out recognized sentences whose meaning has been clarified by context, they have better recognition for the sentences that were given a threatening meaning by context (Eysenck, Mogg, May, Richards, & Mathews, 1991).

Biases in memory for threatening cues has also been studied in GAD. Researchers have hypothesized that individuals with GAD will demonstrate better memory for threatening than nonthreatening stimuli, and also enhanced memory for threatening stimuli than control participants. Results of a memory bias in GAD are not as consistent as those for other types of cognitive biases. Research has generally not found an explicit memory bias in GAD, such that individuals with GAD do not appear to preferentially recall more threatening stimuli (e.g., Becker, Roth, Andrich, & Margraf, 1999; Mathews, Mogg, May, & Eysenck, 1989; Mogg, Gardiner, Stavrou, & Golombok, 1992), though there are exceptions to these findings (e.g., Friedman, Thayer, & Borkovec, 2000). On the other hand, several studies have found an implicit memory bias in GAD, such that nonconscious memory for threatening stimuli has been demonstrated to affect performance on other tasks, even if these stimuli are not preferentially remembered. For example, MacLeod and McLaughlin (1995) presented threatening and nonthreatening words to individuals with GAD and nonanxious controls, and then asked participants to identify briefly presented words. Individuals with GAD demonstrated an implicit memory bias for threatening words, such that they were more readily able to identify these threatening words. Although the evidence for an implicit memory bias in GAD is more robust than that for an explicit memory bias, results are still equivocal (see MacLeod & Rutherford, 2004 for a review).

Clearly, individuals with GAD demonstrate a number of biases for threat-relevant information, suggesting that attentional biases are an important aspect of the development and maintenance of this disorder. What is still unclear is the relationship between these cognitive biases and the physiology of GAD. One would assume that preferentially encoding threat information would lead to sympathetic arousal, but, as reviewed earlier, individuals with GAD do not demonstrate such arousal. Further understanding of the relationship between attentional biases and physiology is necessary.

AVOIDANCE THEORIES OF WORRY

Researchers have proposed that worry is actually one of the ways that individuals respond to threat (see Borkovec, Alcaine, & Behar, 2004 for a comprehensive review of this theory). According to the cognitive avoidance theory of worry, worry is an attempt at cognitive avoidance, which is similar in function to the behavioral avoidance seen in many types of anxiety disorders. In other words, the verbal activity of worry is thought to distract individuals from the full experience of fear (e.g., feared imagery, sensations of arousal) associated with perceived danger. Evidence for the notion of worry as cognitive avoidance stems from a number of lines of research. Studies suggest that worry is a primarily verbal and linguistic activity, as compared to an image-based process (Behar, Zuellig, & Borkevec, 2005; Borkovec & Inz, 1990; Freeston, Dugas, & Ladouceur, 1996; Meyer, Miller, Metzger, & Borkovec, 1990). Further, imagery associated with worry is more concrete (i.e., less vivid, slower, and more difficult to access) (Stöber, 1998), making it less likely to evoke a fear reaction. Verbal recounting of feared material is thought to produce a less sympathetic nervous system response as compared to feared images. Thus, worry in the face of perceived threat would be negatively reinforced because it allows a person to experience a reduction in distress and arousal in the short term when confronted by a stressful trigger.

Self-reports by college students meeting criteria for GAD suggest that they use worry to distract themselves from more emotional topics, and this motivation for using worry distinguished the GAD group from control participants (Borkovec & Roemer, 1995). People with GAD report higher levels of experiential avoidance than do control individuals (Roemer, Salters, Raffa, & Orsillo, 2005), and worriers avoid anxiety-provoking images even when instructed to attend to them (Laguna, Ham, Hope, & Bell, 2004). Further, worrying before imagining giving a speech produces less heart rate response than relaxing beforehand, which does lead to increased heart rate (Borkovec & Hu, 1990; Borkovec, Lyonfields, Wiser, & Deihl, 1993). Similarly, participants instructed to worry after watching a horrific film experience less anxiety after the film is viewed (Wells & Papageorgiou, 1995).

Unfortunately, worrying appears to only provide short-term benefit, and is associated with increased arousal in the long term. For example, individuals in the Wells and Papageorgiou study found themselves experiencing increasingly intrusive thoughts about the film over the next several days. Borkovec et al. (2004) suggest that worrying may ultimately interfere with emotional processing of stressful stimuli. Thus, just as situational avoidance provides only short-term but not long-term benefit for reducing anxiety, worry does the same. Further, it has been proposed that suppressing distressing thoughts and feelings through worry may actually increase or intensify these thoughts and feelings in the long term (see Purdon, 1999; Wegner, 1994), though there is no evidence to suggest that suppression of worry leads to an increased frequency of worry (Mathews & Milroy, 1994;

Roemer & Borkovec, 1994). However, studies suggest that suppression is an impossible task (e.g., Behar, Vescio, & Borkovec, 2005) and therefore individuals with GAD might ascribe meaning to their inability to suppress worries that contributes to negative emotions and fears about being able to cope. One possible origin of the avoidance function of worry may be difficulties in people's ability to regulating emotions. This topic will be discussed in more detail in the "Emotional Correlates" section that follows on p. 93.

INTOLERANCE OF UNCERTAINTY

Dugas and colleagues (Dugas, Buhr, & Ladouceur, 2004) have proposed that a central difficulty in GAD involves an individual's tendency to react negatively to uncertain or ambiguous situations, sometimes preferring a negative outcome to an uncertain one. They suggest that intolerance of uncertainty is a cognitive filter through which a person with GAD views his or her world. Because many events and situations are characterized by uncertainty, the outcome of having this filter is an enhanced likelihood of worrying.

Studies suggest that intolerance of uncertainty is related to worry in nonclinical participants (Freeston, Rhéaume, Letarte, Dugas, & Ladouceur, 1994) and is elevated in individuals with GAD (Dugas et al., 1998). Moreover, elevated levels of intolerance of uncertainty appear to be specific to individuals with GAD as compared to those with other anxiety disorders (Dugas, Marchand, & Ladouceur, 2005). Experimental manipulations of intolerance of uncertainty have yielded changes in level of worry, such that increasing participants' level of intolerance of uncertainty leads to increased worry (Ladouceur, Gosselin, & Dugas, 2000). Further, time series analyses of the temporal sequence of change in CBT for GAD found that, for the majority of participants, changes in intolerance of uncertainty preceded changes in time spent worrying (Dugas, Langlois, Rhéaume, & Ladouceur, 1998). Thus, evidence is accumulating to suggest that intolerance of uncertainty may play a causal role in the development or exacerbation of pathological worry in GAD.

Researchers have also studied the relationship between intolerance of uncertainty and other variables demonstrated to be important in understanding GAD. For example, intolerance of uncertainty and negative problem orientation both contribute to the prediction of worry in a nonclinical sample (Dugas, Freeston, & Ladouceur, 1997). Intolerance of uncertainty has also been linked to an information-processing bias, such that participants high in intolerance of uncertainty recalled a greater proportion of words involving uncertainty (e.g., "inconclusive," "unclear") and were more concerned about ambiguous situations than participants low in intolerance of uncertainty (Dugas et al., 2005). Further, intolerance of uncertainty was related to a tendency to make more threatening interpretations of ambiguous situations (Dugas et al., 2005). The authors suggest that intolerance of uncertainty may lead to pathological worry by causing individuals to selectively process uncertain information and then interpret this information as threatening. Further, Dugas et al. (2004) theorize that intolerance of uncertainty might affect a person's perception of his or her problem-solving abilities, such that the individual feels less capable of effectively solving problems as they arise, leading to pathological worry instead of problem solution.

METACOGNITION AND GAD

Wells (1999) has proposed a metacognitive model of GAD that involves positive and negative beliefs about worry, as well as two types of worry content. *Metacognition* refers to the act of thinking about one's thought processes. Wells suggests that it is not typical worry, per se, that is the most significant problem in GAD, but rather the way one thinks about and reacts to this typical worry. *Type 1* worry refers to this so-called "typical" worry—worry about everyday events and triggers (e.g., worries about health, safety, or relationships). *Type 2* worry consists of worry about these cognitive processes; or in other words, worry about worry. In this model, Wells proposes that positive beliefs that a person holds about worry (e.g., "Worry will help me cope") cause a person to actively select worry as a coping strategy when faced with some sort of stressor. As a result, Type 1 worry is activated. In some circumstances, the process of worry is terminated by a felt sense that the person will be able to cope with the particular stressor. However, if this felt sense is not achieved, Type 2 beliefs about worry might be activated. These might include beliefs that worry is uncontrollable and/or beliefs that worrying might have negative mental or physical consequences for an individual. The activation of Type 2 worry is thought to produce excessive levels of anxiety, as well as to lead to unhelpful behavioral coping and thought control strategies, such that Type 2 worries cannot be disconfirmed and the worry cycle is maintained. For example, an increase in anxiety interferes with a person's ability to achieve a felt sense that he or she can cope, so he or she begins to avoid feared situations as means of coping. Unfortunately, avoidance of the situations that trigger worry does not allow a person to experience disconfirmatory information about the impact of worry on his or her functioning.

Studies confirm that individuals hold both positive and negative beliefs about worrying. For example, Davey, Tallis, and Capuzzo (1996) found that individuals' beliefs about worrying clustered into three factors representing negative consequences (i.e., worry disrupting performance, worry exaggerating the problem, and worry causing emotional distress), and two factors representing positive consequences (i.e., worry as motivation and worry as helping analytical thinking). The presence of both positive and negative beliefs about worry was associated with more psychopathology than simply the presence of negative beliefs about worry.

Cartwright-Hatton and Wells (1997) developed the Meta-Cognitions Questionnaire and found that three subscales uniquely predicted worry: positive beliefs about worry, negative beliefs about the controllability of thoughts, and cognitive confidence (i.e., lack of confidence in one's cognitive skills). In an independent study using this questionnaire, the presence of positive and negative beliefs about worry in GAD was confirmed (Davis & Valentiner, 2000). Positive beliefs about worry have been found to uniquely predict worry above and beyond the prediction of worry by general negative beliefs (Francis & Dugas, 2004). In a case study of CBT for an individual with GAD, modifying positive beliefs about worry led to positive treatment outcomes (Borkovec, Hazlett-Stevens, & Diaz, 1999). Although different research groups have found evidence for slight differences in the content of positive beliefs about worry, evidence is clear that positive beliefs are an important aspect of GAD.

Studies have also provided support for the presence of Type 2 worry and its unique association with pathological worry, even when Type 1 worries and trait anxiety are controlled (Wells & Carter, 1999). These results have also been replicated in a sample of older adults (Nuevo, Montorio, & Borkovec, 2004). Individuals with GAD scored higher on measures of meta-worry than did nonclincial control participants and nonworried anxious controls (Davis & Valentiner, 2000), as well as individuals with Social Phobia, Panic Disorder, and Depression (Wells & Carter, 2001). Individuals with GAD were not distinguishable from individuals with somatic anxiety (i.e., individuals who denied excessive worry but endorsed the somatic aspects of excessive worry) on a measure of meta-worry, though they had significantly higher scores on meta-worry than nonanxious controls (Wells, 2005). Clearly, the role of metacognitive factors in GAD (especially the presence of positive beliefs about the utility of worry) has provided a useful way of understanding why individuals with GAD routinely choose worry as a coping strategy (Coles & Heimberg, 2005). Further research on these factors is warranted.

Emotional Correlates

Some research suggests that individuals with GAD may have difficulties in regulating their emotional experience (Mennin, Heimberg, Turk, & Fresco, 2005). More specifically, individuals with GAD may experience more intense emotions, have more difficulty naming and understanding emotions, have more difficulty accepting their emotional experience (especially when this involves negative emotions), and demonstrate difficulty managing and regulating negative emotions when they do occur (Mennin et al., 2005). As a result of these difficulties, individuals often use strategies such as worry in the face of discomforting negative emotions. As worry becomes a more consistently used strategy, individuals have even more difficulty identifying and understanding their underlying emotional experience, motivating further emotional avoidance through worry. Initial research supports the notion that individuals with GAD symptoms, as well as individuals with a clinical diagnosis of GAD, experience more intense emotions than controls, have a more negative reaction to these emotions, and have fewer strategies to manage their emotions (Mennin et al., 2005). Individuals with GAD report being more fearful of depression and having more intense emotions than do those with Social Phobia and nonanxious controls (Turk, Heimberg, Luterek, Mennin, & Fresco, 2005). In addition, nonclinical samples of worriers experience more negative thought content during periods of relaxation as measured by objective raters, and report a lower sense of control over their mental activity than do nonworriers (Pruzinsky & Borkovec, 1990). Further, self-reported worry has been associated with general and specific emotion regulation deficits, including the ability to engage in goal-directed activity when distressed, control over impulses, acceptance of emotions, clarity of emotional state, and access to self-regulation strategies (Salters-Pedneault, Roemer, Tull, Rucker, & Mennin, 2006). These difficulties have been found to be consistent even when controlling for general negative affect. Finally, Mennin et al. (2005) found that students meeting criteria for GAD had a stronger physiological reaction to a mood induction than did controls, and demonstrated more difficulty managing this reaction (i.e., individuals endorsed that they had more difficulty accepting and influencing their emotional state than did controls). Thus, there is preliminary evidence that emotion regulation deficits may be an important variable for understanding the chronic worry seen in GAD.

Individuals with GAD may also find their worry process affected by preexisting negative emotional states. Davey and colleagues (Startup & Davey, 2001, 2003) have found evidence for a "mood-as-input" approach to understanding catastrophic worry like that found in GAD. They suggest that individuals who have pathological worry use rules in order to decide when to stop worrying. The "stop rules" they have identified are: (1) "feel like continuing," which is when an individual continues to try to solve a problem until he or she does not feel like continuing to work on it, and (2) "as many as can," which is when an individual persists with problem-solving attempts until he or she feels like as many possible responses have been generated as he or she possibly can (Davey, 2006). When the "as many as can" stop rule is paired with negative mood, the person is unlikely to feel that he or she has generated as many possible responses as possible after reasonable effort, leading to perseveration on a given task. Specifically applied to pathological worry, Davey (2006) suggests that worriers are likely candidates for perseveration. He notes that worriers are often in a negative mood state, the task of worrying has no obvious end point, and worriers often apply an "as many as can" rule to determine when to stop worrying. Thus, this model predicts that pathological worriers will frequently be subject to entering an iterative worry cycle that is not easily exited.

There is some empirical support for these assertions. According to their research, a negative mood induction actually increased the number of catastrophizing steps individuals made when asked to worry about a particular topic, and when worriers were asked to use an "as many as can" stop rule they generated more catastrophizing steps than nonworriers using this rule (Startup & Davey, 2001). Further, the interaction of negative mood and increased responsibility yielded greater catastrophizing for a sample of worriers, which suggests that levels of inflated responsibility may be one reason worriers use an "as many as can" stop rule (Startup & Davey, 2003).

Research has investigated the differences between worry and related symptoms such as rumination and obsessions. Researchers have long noted the similarities between these cognitive phenomena. Worry and rumination both involve repetitive, negative thinking. They have been found to be correlated in nonclinical (Fresco, Frankel, Mennin, Turk, & Heimberg, 2002) and clinical samples (Segerstrom, Tsao, Alden, & Craske, 2000). On a measure assessing numerous ways in which these cognitive processes might differ (i.e., frequency, duration, evaluation of the cognition, strategies used, and associated emotion), only seven significant differences emerged between ruminative and worrisome thoughts (Watkins, Moulds, & Mackintosh, 2005). Using a within-subjects methodology, this study found that worries were reported as having a longer duration, the content of worries was more strongly associated with future events than past events, worries were rated as more disturbing and less realistic, and worries were associated with greater feelings of insecurity. The authors suggest that worry, while similar in process to rumination, involves more future-oriented, threat-relevant content. More recent research suggests other significant differences between worry and rumination; specifically, worry was found to be related to both anxious and depressive symptoms, whereas rumination was more uniquely associated with depression. The perceived inability to cope mediated the relationship between worry and anxious and depressed mood (Hong, 2007).

On the other hand, research suggests little overlap between worry and obsessional thinking, though overlap still exists. Using the previously described questionnaire, Langlois, Freeston, and Ladouceur (2000) found that nonclinical participants rated their worrisome thoughts as being more realistic, less ego-dystonic, more persistent, and more verbally oriented than obsessions. Worry is more related to reactive obsessions (i.e., relatively realistic thoughts that are more triggered by environmental cues and are associated with perceived negative consequences) than autogenous obsessions (i.e., strongly ego-dystonic thoughts that are less related to environmental triggers) (Lee, Lee, Kim, Kwon, & Telch, 2005).

ENVIRONMENTAL FACTORS

Environmental factors appear to play a number of roles in understanding the development, phenomenology, and maintenance of GAD. For example, actual situations of enhanced risk appear to play a role in triggering a tendency to overestimate the likelihood of risk associated with a task. Participants in a statistics class were asked to complete risk questionnaires both on the first day of class as well as before their first exam (Constans, 2001). Measures of worry and anxiety were also given at both time periods. Results suggested that an increase in stress (i.e., the impending exam) was related to increased exam-related risk estimates for those with a propensity to worry. Risk assessment for issues unrelated to the exam stayed constant. Constans suggested that risk inflation related to a stressful life event may cause increases in anxiety.

FAMILY ENVIRONMENT

Factors related to family environment and parenting styles may also be relevant for understanding GAD. Although most studies on this topic have relied on self-report or retrospective reports of family environments, results converge to suggest that people with GAD may have experienced unpleasant, negative, and rejecting family environments. For example, a study of self-reported parenting styles and GAD symptoms found a relationship between perceived parental alienation and rejection with GAD symptoms in a sample of community adolescents (Hale, Engels, & Meeus, 2006). Further, college students who met self-reported criteria for GAD endorsed less secure attachment to their parents than did control participants (Eng & Heimberg, 2006). Similarly, individuals with GAD reported a higher rate of having a "dysfunctional family" than did those without GAD (Ben-Noun, 1998), and worry has been associated with an anxious or rejecting parenting style in children (Muris, Meesters, Merckelbach, & Hülsenbeck, 2000).

Other researchers have argued that interpersonal problems, in general, may play a causal role in the development of GAD. For example, Crits-Christoph, Gibbons, Narducci, Schamberger, and Gallop (2005) have suggested that there is a great deal of indirect evidence that individuals with GAD have interpersonal issues, including a high frequency of interpersonal themes in worry content, biases to social threat cues, and research suggesting that those with GAD show more parent-child boundary problems than do individuals without GAD (Cassidy & Shaver, 1999). Drawing from these ideas, they examined the change in interpersonal problems across the course of brief psychodynamic treatment for GAD and found that changes in interpersonal problems were significantly related to improvements in worry symptoms. Similarly, Borkovec, Newman, Pincus, and Lytle (2002) found that a subset of participants in a CBT trial for GAD demonstrated interpersonal difficulties at posttreatment, and that these difficulties were associated with fewer gains and improvements across follow-up. However, other research suggests that interpersonal problems in GAD may be more focused, with no evidence of disrupted peer relationships in a college sample meeting criteria for GAD (Eng & Heimberg, 2006). The role of interpersonal difficulties in GAD, therefore, is not clearly understood, including whether interpersonal difficulties are a cause or consequence of excessive worry and anxiety.

Assessment

As noted earlier, the inherent instability in the diagnostic criteria for GAD has made it difficult to reliably diagnose and assess this disorder. As diagnostic criteria have become more stable, reliable means of assessing GAD and chronic worry have also become more available. It has been suggested that a comprehensive assessment of GAD should include the following: worry, beliefs about worry, intolerance of uncertainty, anxiety, associated features (e.g., tension), comorbid symptoms, goals and areas of behavioral inactivation, and emotional avoidance (Roemer & Medaglia, 2001). In this section, we review several useful tools for the assessment of GAD, including those used to assess these constructs.

Two of the most extensively studied semistructured interviews for diagnosing anxiety-related problems, including GAD, are the *Anxiety Disorders Interview Schedule for* DSM-IV (ADIS-IV; Brown, Di Nardo, & Barlow, 1994; Di Nardo, Brown, & Barlow, 1994) and the *Structured Clinical Interview for* DSM-IV/*Axis I Disorders* (SCID-IV; First, Spitzer, Gibbon, & Williams, 1996). Both the SCID-IV and ADIS-IV provide systematic questions to establish a reliable current diagnosis of GAD and comorbid conditions (Brown, Di Nardo, Lehman, & Campbell, 2001; Segal, Hersen, & van Hasselt, 1994). Semistructured interviews also provide information about the content of a person's worry, areas of avoidance or behavioral inactivation, and the presence of comorbid conditions.

ANXIETY DISORDERS INTERVIEW SCHEDULE FOR *DSM-IV* (ADIS-IV)

The ADIS-IV (Di Nardo, Brown, & Barlow, 1994) is a clinician-administered semistructured interview that provides both diagnostic and dimensional information about a range of psychological problems, including anxiety disorders, mood disorders, somatoform disorders, and substance use disorders. Screening questions are provided for psychotic disorders, conversion symptoms, and the presence of a family history of psychiatric illness. Diagnoses are assigned based on *DSM-IV* criteria. Depending on the version of the ADIS-IV used (standard versus lifetime version), current and lifetime diagnoses can be assigned. Clinicians require extensive training in the administration of this interview, and the interview duration can be lengthy, particularly for the lifetime version (e.g., several hours). Despite these drawbacks for everyday practice, the ADIS-IV has the benefit of providing clear criteria to help determine the presence or absence of GAD (as well as common comorbid disorders).

The ADIS-IV has demonstrated good reliability. A recent study by Brown and colleagues examined the inter-rater reliability of diagnostic decisions made using the ADIS-IV (Brown, Di Nardo, Lehman, & Campbell, 2001). Interrater reliability was good both when GAD was diagnosed as the primary problem (kappa = .67) as well as when it was diagnosed as an additional clinical problem (kappa = .65). Sources of unreliability included one interviewer diagnosing GAD while the other diagnosed a disorder with overlapping clinical features (e.g., depression or Anxiety Disorder Not Otherwise Specified—subthreshold GAD), as well as shifts in patient report.

STRUCTURED CLINICAL INTERVIEW FOR *DSM-IV* (SCID-IV)

The SCID-IV (First, Spitzer, Gibbon, & Williams, 1996) is also a clinician-administered semistructured interview that provides diagnostic decisions about a wide range of psychiatric disorders. Two versions are available—a clinician version (SCID-CV) and a research version (SCID-I). The clinician version was designed for use in clinical settings and has a less extensive coverage of disorders. The research version has a broader focus and provides for assessment of mood disorders, anxiety disorders, somatoform disorders, substance disorders, eating disorders, adjustment disorders, and psychotic disorders. Current and lifetime diagnoses are obtained. Extensive training is also required to administer the SCID-IV, and administration can be lengthy, especially for the research version (i.e., 2 to 3 hours for a typical outpatient administration).

Studies using *DSM-III-R* criteria suggest that the SCID demonstrates adequate inter-rater reliability for GAD (kappa = .56) (Williams et al., 1992). A more recent study found interrater reliability of .63 and test-retest reliability of .44 for GAD using the SCID-IV (Zanarini et al., 2000). Thus, reliability is adequate, but not strong when using the SCID to diagnose GAD.

Self-Report Measures

Self-report measures of GAD have been developed for a number of purposes, including measuring the presence of diagnostic criteria, measuring the severity of worry, and assessing the range and content of worry topics. Further, there are a number of self-report measures designed to measure constructs thought to be important in the theoretical understanding of this disorder (e.g., measures of intolerance of uncertainty and meta-worry). In this section, we briefly review some of the most often-used self-report measures of worry and GAD.

Generalized Anxiety Disorder Questionnaire

The *Generalized Anxiety Disorder Questionnaire* (GADQ) (Roemer, Borkovec, Posa, & Borkovec, 1995) and its revised version (GADQ-IV) (Newman et al., 2002) is a self-report measure designed to assess the presence of *DSM-III-R* and *DSM-IV* criteria for GAD. It is a brief and simple measure to administer and score, making it a popular tool in research involving analogue samples. Most questions involve "yes/no" responses, two questions involve a severity scale, and one question is open-ended, asking for a list of frequent worries. Thus, the GADQ-IV provides both diagnostic and content-related information about a person's symptoms. The psychometric properties of this measure are quite strong, as it has demonstrated good test-retest reliability and good convergence with diagnoses made using the ADIS-IV and with scores on self-report measures of worry, while showing weaker relationships with theoretically distinct measures (Newman et al., 2002). The GADQ-IV has also demonstrated strong internal consistency and good convergence with diagnostic decisions as made using the ADIS-IV in a clinical sample (Luterek, Turk, Heimberg, Fresco, & Mennin, 2002). The GADQ-IV is an efficient and useful tool to assess the presence of the diagnostic criteria of GAD, especially when it is not practical to use a semistructured interview.

Self-Report Measures of Worry Severity and Worry Content

There are a few commonly used self-report measures of the general features of worry. For example, the *Penn State Worry Questionnaire* (PSWQ) (Meyer, Miller, Metzger, &

Borkovec, 1990) is a brief self-report measure that was designed to measure a person's tendency to worry excessively, without assessing the content of the worry. It is a widely used measure that has demonstrated strong psychometric properties (see Roemer, 2001 for a review). On the other hand, the *Worry Domains Questionnaire* (WDQ) (Tallis, Eysenck, & Mathews, 1992) provides an assessment of the content of worry. More specifically, it assesses the degree to which a person worries about relationships, lack of confidence, and his or her future, work, and finances. Its psychometric properties are also strong (Roemer, 2001). Another self-report measure of the content of worry is the *Anxious Thoughts Inventory* (AnTI) (Wells, 1994), which assesses social worry, health worry, and meta-worry. As reviewed earlier, social and health worry are seen as Type 1 worries while meta-worry is a Type 2 worry (i.e., having concerns about the consequences of one's worries on mental health, etc.). Consistent with this idea, scores on the meta-worry subscale have been shown to predict scores on the PSWQ, even after trait anxiety, social worry, and health worry are controlled (Wells & Carter, 1999).

Self-Report Measures of Theoretical Constructs Relevant to GAD

In addition to the meta-worry subscale of the Anxious Thoughts Inventory, several other self-report measures assess theoretical constructs believed to be important in understanding a person's GAD symptoms. For example, other meta-cognitions about worry can be assessed by the *Meta-Cognitions Questionnaire* (Cartwright-Hatton & Wells, 1997). This measure assesses positive beliefs about worry, the belief that worry is dangerous and harmful, lack of confidence in one's cognitive functioning, negative consequences or fears about worrying, and the degree to which an individual monitors his or her thinking. It has demonstrated good internal consistency and test-retest reliability (Cartwright-Hatton & Wells, 1997) and individuals with GAD score higher on this measure than do those with other anxiety disorders or related conditions (Wells & Carter, 2001). Positive beliefs about worry can be assessed using the *Why Worry Scale—I* and *II* (Freeston, Rhéaume, Letarte, Dugas, & Ladouceur, 1994), which measures the following positive beliefs about worry: worry helps problem-solving, worry helps motivate, worry protects against negative emotions, worry prevents negative outcomes, and worry is a positive personality trait. Both negative and positive beliefs about worry can be ascertained using the *Consequences of Worrying Scale* (Davey, Tallis, & Capuzzo, 1996).

As described earlier, intolerance of uncertainty has been proposed to be an important construct in understanding the development and maintenance of worry. The *Intolerance of Uncertainty Scale* (Freeston, Rhéaume, Letarte, Dugas, & Ladouceur, 1994) is a self-report measure designed to assess difficulties associated with uncertainty. The measure consists of statements describing how one might react to uncertainties (e.g., "I always want to know what the future has in store for me"), and respondents indicate how characteristic each statement is of them. This measure has demonstrated good psychometric properties (see Roemer, 2001).

Other Useful Self-Report Measures

As noted at the beginning of this section, in a thorough assessment of GAD, one may want to assess constructs such as general anxiety and emotional regulation. A number of measures have been used to assess the general features of anxiety, including the *State-Trait Anxiety Inventory* (Spielberger, Gorsuch, Lushene, Vagg, & Jacobs, 1983), the *Beck Anxiety Inventory* (Beck, Epstein, Brown, & Steer, 1988), and the *Hamilton Anxiety Rating Scale* (Hamilton, 1959). Emotion regulation has been assessed using the

Affective Control Scale (Williams, Chambless, & Ahrens, 1997) and the *Toronto Alexithymia Scale* (Bagby, Parker, & Taylor, 1994; Bagby, Taylor, & Parker, 1994).

ONGOING ASSESSMENT AND FOLLOW-UP

Assessment should not end after establishing a diagnosis and understanding the features of the disorder at hand. It is a continual process that needs to be reviewed and refined across the course of contact with a person, whether for a longitudinal research contact or for monitoring the progress and outcome of medication or psychological intervention. In therapy, it is essential to understand whether treatment strategies were helpful, in what way they were helpful, and on what dimensions strategies had their impact. In some instances, degree of improvement will have important implications for course and duration of treatment. In other cases, indicators of improvement will have implications for continued funding of treatment (e.g., by insurance companies or third-party payers).

All of the previously cited assessment tools can be used at any stage of contact, therapy, or follow-up. Indeed, it may be most beneficial to use a complement of diagnostic and descriptive tools in ongoing assessment to have a thorough understanding of the course of a person's symptoms and diagnosis. For example, follow-up studies of the outcome of interventions often assess diagnostic status (i.e., using the SCID-IV, ADIS-IV, or GADQ-IV), worry severity (i.e., using the PSWQ), as well as other constructs of interest to the particular study. In addition, ongoing and follow-up assessment often involves the assessment of more general constructs such as functional impairment due to anxiety symptoms, disability, interpersonal functioning, and quality of life.

Interventions

PSYCHOLOGICAL INTERVENTIONS

Research on the efficacy of psychological treatments for GAD is still in its infancy. With the advent of recent research and theoretical advances in the understanding of GAD and pathological worry, we can likely expect a surge of treatment outcome literature that tests interventions based on these theories. Some initial studies of these treatment advances are already available and will be reviewed in this section. Most advances in treatment are variations on a cognitive-behavioral protocol for treating GAD. Indeed, cognitive-behavioral therapy (CBT) for GAD is the best-studied psychological intervention for this disorder and has shown good outcomes in controlled trials. It is with traditional CBT interventions that this review begins.

COGNITIVE-BEHAVIORAL THERAPY

The majority of treatment outcome research has focused on the efficacy of cognitive-behavioral interventions for GAD. Although different CBT protocols contain somewhat different components, some of the most commonly used components include psychoeducation, relaxation training, monitoring of cues and triggers for worry, imaginal exposure, in vivo exposure (if necessary), and cognitive restructuring. For detailed reviews of these components see Lang (2004), Borkovec and Ruscio (2001), and Roemer, Orsillo, and Barlow (2002).

Psychoeducation involves providing information about GAD, worry, and anxiety. Further, individuals are provided with an overview of the rationale for CBT. Relaxation training can involve a number of strategies, including progressive muscle relaxation and breathing techniques. Monitoring forms are used to identify environmental triggers for worry and anxiety, to record the content of worries, and to become aware of behavioral and physiological consequences of worry. Imaginal and in vivo exposure techniques are used in a CBT protocol when relevant for a client's symptoms. For example, if someone is avoiding reading the newspaper for fear that it will trigger unwanted worries about world events, exposure to reading news stories would likely be an important component of treatment. Imaginal exposure is used to help individuals become more comfortable with the content of their most feared consequences, by repeated exposure to catastrophic images and fears. Cognitive restructuring is the process by which individuals are asked to challenge their fearful thoughts and to consider realistic alternatives.

In a number of investigations, CBT has proven superior to waitlist controls and non-specific alternative treatments (Borkevec & Ruscio, 2001; Mitte, 2005) and similar to pharmacological interventions (Gould, Otto, Pollack, & Yap, 1997; Mitte, 2005). In a meta-analysis of CBT for GAD, effect sizes for CBT interventions were large when compared to no treatment controls, and ranged from small to large when compared to alternative therapies or either behavior or cognitive therapy on its own (Borkevec & Ruscio, 2001). In a different meta-analysis focusing on the comparison of CBT with pharmacological interventions, effect sizes for CBT versus pharmacotherapy were similar, though the positive impact of pharmacotherapy was lost when individuals discontinued their medications, suggesting an advantage for CBT over the long term (Gould et al., 1997). Cognitive-behavioral therapy has also been found useful in helping individuals discontinue their benzodiazepine use (Gosselin, Ladouceur, Morin, Dugas, & Baillargeon, 2006). Cognitive-behavioral therapy appears to be effective not only for symptoms of worry, anxiety, and depression, but also for related symptoms such as insomnia (Bélanger, Morin, Langlois, & Ladouceur, 2004).

Studies have also studied the components of CBT protocols. For example, a study by Arntz (2003) compared applied relaxation to cognitive strategies. Both treatments were effective across a number of outcome measures, with an initial follow-up advantage for relaxation lost at the 6-month follow-up. Both treatments appeared to be effective at the 6-month follow-up with just over half of the sample demonstrating strong outcome on measures of anxiety. These results are similar to previous studies comparing these treatment components (e.g., Borkevec, Newman, Pincus, & Lytle, 2002; Öst & Breitholtz, 2000). In another study, problem-solving training (which is often used in CBT protocols for GAD) was compared to imaginal exposure, and again both treatment components yielded significant improvements on a variety of symptom measures (Provencher, Dugas, & Ladouceur, 2004).

Variables affecting the duration or mode of therapy have yet to have an impact on treatment outcome. For example, adding further sessions for individuals with a poor prognosis in treatment did not improve outcome (Durham et al., 2004). Further, although CBT appears to be an effective intervention for older individuals with GAD, it has not demonstrated superiority to supportive therapy (Stanley, Beck, & Glassco, 1996) and was only slightly superior to a discussion group (Wetherell, Gatz, & Craske, 2003) when offered in a group format.

RECENT ADVANCES IN CBT FOR GAD

As reviewed earlier in this chapter, there is considerable evidence that GAD is characterized by heightened levels of intolerance of uncertainty. Accordingly, treatment protocols have been developed that specifically target the difficulty individuals may have with uncertainty. Outcome studies are encouraging. In an initial study of this protocol, 26 individuals with GAD were assigned to active treatment or a delayed-treatment condition. Treatment was a modification of a CBT protocol that targeted difficulties with intolerance of uncertainty, positive and negative beliefs about worry, negative problem-solving orientation, and cognitive avoidance. This protocol led to significant and lasting improvements on GAD diagnostic status and associated symptoms (Ladouceur, Dugas, Freeston, Léger, Gagnon, & Thibodeau, 2000). Positive outcomes are also seen when this treatment is offered in a group format (Dugas et al., 2003).

Therapy based on Wells' metacognitive theory of GAD (Wells, 1995) has also demonstrated initial positive results. This treatment focuses on modifying individuals' negative beliefs about the uncontrollability of worry, negative beliefs about the danger of worry, and positive beliefs about the utility of using worry as a coping strategy (Wells, 2006). An open trial found strong effect sizes on measures of worry, anxiety, and depression, and recovery rates remained strong at the 12-month follow-up (Wells & King, 2006).

Another modification of a traditional CBT protocol for GAD has involved the incorporation of mindfulness and acceptance strategies into therapy. This change is based on evidence that individuals with GAD may be using worry to avoid negative emotional experiences. The inclusion of mindfulness and acceptance strategies encourages a client to accept his or her emotional experience and to move toward valued goals rather than engage in typical worry-related behaviors, and is based on acceptance-based therapies developed by Hayes, Strosahl, and Wilson (1999) and Linehan (1993). A case series (Orsillo, Roemer, & Barlow, 2002) and subsequent open trial (Roemer & Orsillo, 2007) suggest that the incorporation of these strategies shows promise for individuals with GAD, with clients in this study specifically acknowledging the mindfulness and acceptance elements of therapy as beneficial.

In summary, CBT has been shown to be an effective intervention for individuals with GAD, demonstrating superiority to waitlist controls and alternative therapies. It is still unclear which components of the CBT protocol are the most useful, and whether new variants can outperform standard CBT in randomized controlled trials. However, despite the benefits accrued by CBT, outcome data continue to be mediocre, with large percentages of clients continuing to experience significant symptoms at posttreatment and follow-up. It is clear that much more work is necessary to provide a high-quality psychological intervention for individuals with GAD.

BIOLOGICAL INTERVENTIONS

Conclusions about effective pharmacological interventions for GAD are limited by several factors. Most studies have examined benzodiazepines as a treatment for GAD, with only a handful of more recent studies investigating the utility of antidepressants and other medications for this condition. Further, most randomized controlled trials limit the comorbid psychological conditions that study participants can have, instead including only pure GAD cases. As noted earlier, GAD is highly comorbid with other disorders, making it difficult to find these pure cases and further limiting the general-izability of study results to the treatment of individuals with more complicated diagnos-tic profiles. The lack of consistent diagnostic criteria for GAD has also hampered our knowledge of effective pharmacological interventions, as many medication trials have used *DSM-III* or *DSM-III-R* criteria. The response of GAD to placebo appears to be particularly high (e.g., greater than 40%) (Schweizer & Rickels, 1997), making it more difficult to find active pharmacological agents that can demonstrate significantly better effects than this. Despite these limitations, there is an accumulating body of research on pharmacological agents for GAD.

Research generally supports the effectiveness of benzodiazepines when compared to placebo for GAD (see Anderson & Palm, 2006), although initial benefits were not main-tained across trials in some studies (e.g., Pourmotabbed, McLeod, Hoehn-Saric, Hipsley, & Greenblatt, 1996). Benzodiazepines appear to reduce symptoms of worry, tension, and concentration in addition to the somatic features of GAD. A recent meta-analysis of studies comparing pharmacotherapy (usually benzodiazepines) to CBT con-cluded that both interventions appear to be similarly effective, or that pharmacotherapy may have a slight advantage over CBT (Mitte, 2005). Different results emerged when different ways of examining outcome were used. Psychological and pharmacological approaches appeared to be similarly effective when studies that included a direct com-parison of these conditions were reviewed, and pharmacological interventions appeared more effective when effect sizes from different studies were compared across studies (i.e., when the effect size from a pharmacotherapy vs. placebo trial was compared to the effect size from an independent study examining CBT vs. a waitlist control). In this meta-analysis, Mitte also concluded that CBT appears to be better tolerated than pharmacotherapy.

In reviews of pharmacotherapy for GAD, selective serotonin reuptake inhibitors (SSRIs) are identified as a first-line therapy for GAD (see Goodman, 2004). More spe-cifically, approved medications include paroxetine, sertraline, and escitalopram, with all medications demonstrating efficacy as compared to pill placebo (Allgulander et al., 2004; Baldwin, Huusom, & Maehlum, 2006; Stocchi et al., 2003). Escitalopram may also be more efficacious than paroxetine (Baldwin et al., 2006), better tolerated than paroxetine (Bielski, Bose, & Chang, 2005), and is more effective than placebo in pre-venting relapse after successful pharmacotherapy of GAD symptoms (Allgulander, Ioana, & Huusom, 2006). Effective treatment with an SSRI has been shown to reduce the cognitive biases seen in GAD (e.g., interpreting ambiguous stimuli as threatening; Mogg, Baldwin, Brodrick, & Bradley, 2004). Further, an imaging study also suggested that effective pharmacotherapy with citalopram (another SSRI) reduced excessive brain activation in response to both neutral and worry statements in individuals with GAD (Hoehn-Saric et al., 2004).

Agents other than SSRIs have been studied in GAD. Although there is consistent evi-dence that buspirone is an effective medication, demonstrating a moderate effect size in a recent meta-analysis (Mitte, Noack, Steil, & Hautzinger, 2005), it appears to be less well tolerated in clinical practice (see Anderson & Palm, 2006; Goodman, 2004) and its efficacy and tolerability can be impaired when used in close proximity to a benzodiaze-pine (DeMartinis, Rynn, Rickels, & Mandos, 2000). Studies suggest that the serotonin-norepinephrine reuptake inhibitor, venlafaxine, is also effective for GAD, demonstrat-ing a moderate effect size across studies (Mitte et al., 2005) and showing similar effects as paroxetine (Kim et al., 2006). This medication has also demonstrated effectiveness over longer treatment trials (e.g., Gelenberg et al., 2000). However, some authors argue that it should remain a second-line treatment for GAD due to concerns about its safety in overdose and cardiac implications (see Anderson & Palm, 2006; Fricchione, 2004).

Two other antidepressants, imipramine and trazodone, have yielded some data suggesting effectiveness in GAD (e.g., Rickels, Downing, Schweizer, & Hassman, 1993), though results are not consistent across other studies. The antihistamine hydroxyzine was more effective than placebo for GAD (Llorca et al., 2002), though it took longer than the antidepressants to demonstrate therapeutic benefit. Recent evidence suggests that the herbal product Ginkgo biloba special extract EGb 761 is more effective than placebo on a number of outcome variables in patients who met *DSM-III-R* criteria for GAD (Woelk, Arnoldt, Kieser, & Hoerr, 2007), and it was found to be safe and well tolerated. Similarly, pregabalin has been shown to be more effective than placebo and similarly effective as venlafaxine in a recent trial (Montgomery, Tobias, Zornberg, Kasper, & Pande, 2006).

Summary and New Directions

Generalized Anxiety Disorder is a prevalent, chronic, debilitating disorder. Unfortunately, research on this condition has suffered due to the unreliable and changing diagnostic status of GAD. Compared to the other anxiety disorders, the criteria used to diagnose GAD have dramatically fluctuated with each edition of the *DSM*. Although this disorder has enjoyed more consistency in diagnostic criteria in recent years with the publication of the *DSM-IV* in 1994, there is still debate about the essential criteria and duration of symptoms required for diagnosis. For example, several studies suggest that the 6-month minimum duration of excessive worry and anxiety may not be necessary and may even miss out on a small but significant number of individuals who present with all other symptoms of GAD but for a shorter duration (e.g., Angst et al., 2006; Kessler et al., 2005). Thus, the first challenge in the field appears to be to address the diagnostic criteria of GAD to ensure that criteria are capturing the essence of this disorder but are not so restrictive as to exclude true cases of this disorder that have yet to reach the duration criterion. Any changes made to the diagnostic criteria should be made while considering the importance of maintaining the most consistency possible in the criteria so that we can continue to build upon the existing body of research that has used *DSM-III-R* and *DSM-IV* diagnostic criteria.

Increased reliability and validity in the diagnostic criteria of GAD needs to be translated into more reliable means of diagnosing this disorder. Although interrater reliability rates on the SCID-IV and ADIS-IV are adequate, rates fall below those for other psychological disorders. Studies suggest the source of diagnostic unreliability was often the difference between assigning GAD at a threshold level versus labeling it as a subthreshold constellation of symptoms (Brown et al., 2001). This suggests that, once again, the essential features and duration of this disorder may require further clarification.

More optimistically, the identification of excessive worry as the essential feature of GAD has led to a proliferation of theorizing and research on this disorder over the last 2 decades. Our understanding of the psychopathology of excessive worry and GAD is quite strong, with a number of complementary theories regarding the development and maintenance of GAD being extensively studied by numerous research groups. These research groups, each with their own ideas about the central issues in GAD, appear to have been able to incorporate others' ideas into their own understanding of this disorder. For example, more recent ideas about intolerance of uncertainty and meta-worry blend nicely with earlier theories of worry as a means of emotional avoidance (Borkovec et al., 2004). Furthermore, GAD is characterized by both positive and negative beliefs about the utility of worrying (Davey et al., 1996). As the field continues to evolve, it will be interesting to see if differing theoretical positions will continue to converge or if they will become increasingly divergent. It will also be interesting to see if neuroanatomical, physiological, and other biological studies will be consistent with the growing information on the psychopathology of GAD as well as add to our understanding of the essential components and processes of pathological worry.

Despite the complementary nature of existing theories of GAD and worry, there is less convergence in terms of understanding what the essential components of a cognitive-behavioral therapy program for GAD should involve. Different review articles and chapters recommend different CBT strategies for treating GAD. Ongoing research is focusing on multiple new components of psychotherapy for GAD, with minimal overlap with earlier components. Dismantling studies have yet to suggest exactly what therapists should be doing with their GAD clients. Furthermore, although CBT has been shown to be an effective therapy for GAD, effectiveness data are unconvincing. Thus, it is clear that much work is needed to better understand how we should treat GAD from a psychological perspective.

Similarly, much work remains to be done to understand effective biological treatments for GAD. Although recommendations exist for first- and second-line pharmacological treatments for GAD, progress in this area has been hampered by shifts in diagnostic criteria, by a focus on benzodiazepines as a first-line treatment, and by selecting individuals for medication trials who do not represent a typical individual with GAD. With the continued consistency of diagnostic criteria, it is hoped that some of these hurdles can be overcome to allow researchers to investigate new and potentially useful medications. Research has begun to examine the effectiveness of adjunctive treatments for GAD (e.g., Brawman-Mintzer, Knapp, & Nietert, 2005), but further research is warranted. Further understanding of biological, biochemical, and neuroanatomical aspects of GAD will also help in understanding what types of pharmacological agents might best help individuals with GAD.

It is clear that GAD has enormous personal and societal costs for the afflicted individual. Thus, effective treatment programs need to be balanced with research on the prevention of the onset or exacerbation of symptoms. We know that GAD shares a genetic diathesis with depression (Roy, Neale, Pedersen, Mathe, & Kendler, 1995), that anxiety disorders run in families (Merikangas, Avenevoli, Dierker, & Grillon, 1999), and that specific life events are associated with heightened symptoms of generalized anxiety (e.g., the postpartum period) (Wenzel et al., 2003). Prevention efforts need to make use of such information to target higher-risk populations before symptoms become debilitating.

References

Abel, J. L., & Borkovec, T. D. (1995). Generalizability of *DSM-III-R* generalized anxiety disorder to proposed *DSM-IV* criteria and cross-validation of proposed changes. *Journal of Anxiety Disorders*, *9*, 303–315.

Allgulander, C., Dahl, A. A., Austin, C., Morris, P. L., Sogaard, J. A., Fayyad, R., et al. (2004). Efficacy of sertraline in a 12-week trial for generalized anxiety disorder. *American Journal of Psychiatry*, *161*, 1642–1649.

Allgulander, C., Florea, I., & Huusom, A. K. T. (2006). Prevention of relapse in generalized anxiety disorder by escitalopram treatment. *International Journal of Neuropsychopharmacology*, *9*, 495–505.

American Psychiatric Association. (1980). *Diagnostic and statistical manual of mental disorders* (3rd ed.). Washington, DC: Author.

American Psychiatric Association. (1987). *Diagnostic and statistical manual of mental disorders* (3rd ed., revised). Washington, DC: Author.

American Psychiatric Association. (1994). *Diagnostic and statistical manual of mental disorders* (4th ed.). Washington, DC: Author.

American Psychiatric Association. (2000). *Diagnostic and statistical manual of mental disorders* (4th ed., text revision). Washington, DC: Author.

Anderson, I. M., & Palm, M. E. (2006). Pharmacological treatments for worry: Focus on generalized anxiety disorder. In G. C. L. Davey & A. Wells (Eds.), *Worry and its psychological disorders: Theory, assessment, and treatment* (pp. 305–334). Chichester, UK: Wiley.

Angst, J., Gamma, A., Bienvenu, O. J., Eaton, W. W., Ajdacic, V., Eich, D., et al. (2006). Varying temporal criteria for generalized anxiety disorder: Prevalence and clinical characteristics in a young age cohort. *Psychological Medicine*, *36*, 1283–1292.

Arntz, A. (2003). Cognitive therapy versus applied relaxation as a treatment of generalized anxiety disorder. *Behaviour Research and Therapy*, *41*, 633–646.

Bagby, R. M., Parker, J. D. A., & Taylor, G. J. (1994). The twenty-item Toronto Alexithymia Scale: II. Item selection and cross-validation of the factor structure. *Journal of Psychosomatic Research*, *38*, 23–32.

Bagby, R. M., Taylor, G. J., & Parker, J. D. A. (1994). The twenty-item Toronto Alexithymia Scale: II. Convergent, discriminant, and concurrent validity. *Journal of Psychosomatic Research*, *38*, 33–40.

Baldwin, D. S., Huusom, A. K. T., & Maehlum, E. (2006). Escitalopram and paroxetine in the treatment of generalized anxiety disorder: Randomized, placebo-controlled, double-blind study. *British Journal of Psychiatry*, *189*, 264–272.

Ballenger, J. C. (2001). Treatment of anxiety disorders to remission. *Journal of Clinical Psychiatry*, *62*, 5–9.

Beck, A. T., Epstein, N., Brown, G., & Steer, R. A. (1988). An inventory for measuring clinical anxiety: Psychometric properties. *Journal of Consulting and Clinical Psychology*, *56*, 893–897.

Becker, E. S., Goodwin, R., Hölting, C., Hoyer, J., & Margraf, J. (2003). Content of worry in the community: What do people with generalized anxiety disorder or other disorders worry about? *Journal of Nervous and Mental Disease*, *191*, 688–691.

Becker, E. S., Rinck, M., Margraf, J., & Roth, W. T. (2001). The emotional Stroop effect in anxiety disorders: General emotionality or disorder specificity? *Journal of Anxiety Disorders*, *15*, 147–159.

Becker, E. S., Roth, W. T., Andrich, M., & Margraf, J. (1999). Explicit memory in anxiety disorders. *Journal of Abnormal Psychology*, *108*, 153–163.

Behar, E., Vescio, K., & Borkovec, T. D. (2005). The effects of suppressing thoughts and images about worrisome stimuli. *Behavior Therapy*, *36*, 289–298.

Behar, E., Zuellig, A. R., & Borkovec, T. D. (2005). Thought and imaginal activity during worry and trauma recall. *Behavior Therapy*, *36*, 157–168.

Bélanger, L., Morin, C. M., Langlois, F., & Ladouceur, R. (2004). Insomnia and generalized anxiety disorder: Effects of cognitive behavior therapy for GAD on insomnia patients. *Journal of Anxiety Disorders*, *18*, 561–571.

Belzer, K. D., D'Zurilla, T. J., & Maydeu-Olivares, A. (2002). Social problem solving and trait anxiety as predictors of worry in a college student population. *Personality and Individual Differences*, *33*, 573–585.

Ben-Noun, L. (1998). Generalized anxiety disorder in dysfunctional families. *Journal of Behavior Therapy and Experimental Psychiatry*, *29*, 115–122.

Berenbaum, H., Thompson, R. J., & Pomerantz, E. M. (2007). The relation between worrying and concerns: The importance of perceived probability and cost. *Behaviour Research and Therapy*, *45*, 301–311.

Bielski, R. J., Bose, A., & Chang, C. (2005). A double-blind comparison of escitalopram and paroxetine in the long-term treatment of generalized anxiety disorder. *Annals of Clinical Psychiatry*, *17*, 65–69.

Blazer, D., Hughes, D., & George, L. K. (1987). Stressful life events and the onset of a generalized anxiety syndrome. *The American Journal of Psychiatry*, *144*, 1178–1183.

Borkovec, T. D., Abel, J. L., & Newman, H. (1995). Effects of psychotherapy on comorbid conditions in generalized anxiety disorder. *Journal of Consulting and Clinical Psychology*, *63*, 479–483.

Borkovec, T. D., Alcaine, O., & Behar, E. (2004). Avoidance theory of worry and generalized anxiety disorder. In R. G. Heimberg, C. L. Turk, & D. S. Mennin (Eds.), *Generalized anxiety disorder: Advances in research and practice*. New York: Guilford.

Borkovec, T. D., Hazlett-Stevens, H., & Diaz, M. L. (1999). The role of positive beliefs about worry in generalized anxiety disorder and its treatment. *Clinical Psychology and Psychotherapy*, *6*, 126–138.

Borkovec, T. D., & Hu, S. (1990). The effect of worry on cardiovascular response to phobic imagery. *Behaviour Research and Therapy*, *28*, 69–73.

Borkovec, T. D., & Inz, J. (1990). The nature of worry in generalized anxiety disorder: A predominance of thought activity. *Behaviour Research and Therapy*, *28*, 153–158.

Borkovec, T. D., Lyonfields, J. D., Wiser, S. L., & Deihl, L. (1993). The role of worrisome thinking in the suppression of cardiovascular response to phobic imagery. *Behaviour Research and Therapy*, *31*, 321–324.

Borkovec, T. D., Newman, M. G., Pincus, A. L., & Lytle, R. (2002). A component analysis of cognitive-behavioral therapy for generalized anxiety disorder and the role of interpersonal problems. *Journal of Consulting and Clinical Psychology*, *70*, 288–298.

Borkovec, T. D., & Roemer, L. (1995). Perceived functions of worry among generalized anxiety disorder subjects: Distraction from more emotional topics? *Journal of Behavior Therapy and Experimental Psychiatry*, *26*, 25–30.

Borkovec, T. D., & Ruscio, A. M. (2001). Psychotherapy for generalized anxiety disorder. *Journal of Clinical Psychiatry*, *62*, 37–42.

Bradley, B. P., Mogg, K., Millar, N., & White, J. (1995). Selective processing of negative information: Effects of clinical anxiety, concurrent depression, and awareness. *Journal of Abnormal Psychology*, *104*, 532–536.

Bradley, B. P., Mogg, K., White, J., Groom, C., & deBono, J. (1999). Attentional bias for emotional faces in generalised anxiety disorder. *British Journal of Clinical Psychology*, *38*, 267–278.

Brawman-Mintzer, O., Knapp, R. G., & Nietert, P. J. (2005). Adjunctive resperidone in generalized anxiety disorder: A double-blind, placebo-controlled study. *Journal of Clinical Psychiatry*, *66*, 1321–1325.

Brawman-Mintzer, O., Lydiard, B., Emmanuel, N., Payeur, R., Johnson, M., Roberts, J., et al. (1993). Psychiatric comorbidity in patients with generalized anxiety disorder. *American Journal of Psychiatry*, *150*, 1216–1218.

Brawman-Mintzer, O., Lydiard, R. B., Bradwejn, J., Villarreal, G., Knapp, R., Emmanuel, N., et al. (1997). Effects of the cholecystokinin agonist pentagastrin in patients with generalized anxiety disorder. *The American Journal of Psychiatry*, *154*, 700–702.

Breitholtz, E., Johansson, B., & Öst, L. G. (1999). Cognitions in generalized anxiety disorder and panic disorder patients. A prospective approach. *Behaviour Research and Therapy*, *37*, 533–544.

Brewerton, T. D., Lydiard, R. B., Johnson, M., Ballenger, J. C., Fossey, M. D., Zealberg, J. J., & Roberts, J. E. (1995). CSF serotonin: diagnostic and seasonal differences. *Biological Psychiatry*, *37*, 655.

Brown, T. A., Campbell, L. A., Lehman, C. L., Grisham, J. R., & Mancill, R. B. (2001). Current and lifetime comorbidity of the *DSM-IV* anxiety and mood disorders in a large clinical sample. *Journal of Abnormal Psychology*, *110*, 585–599.

Brown, T. A., DiNardo, P. A., & Barlow, D. H. (1994). *Anxiety Disorders Interview Schedule for* DSM-IV *(ADIS-IV)*. New York: Oxford.

Brown, T. A., DiNardo, P. A., Lehman, C. L., & Campbell, L. A. (2001). Reliability of *DSM-IV* anxiety and mood disorders: Implications for the classification of emotional disorders. *Journal of Abnormal Psychology*, *110*, 49–58.

Bruce, S. E., Machan, J. T., Dyck, I., & Keller, M. B. (2001). Infrequency of "pure" GAD: Impact of psychiatric comorbidity on clinical course. *Depression and Anxiety*, *14*, 219–225.

Bruce, S. E., Yonkers, K. A., Otto, M. W., Eisen, J. L., Weisberg, R. B., Pagano, M., et al. (2005). Influence of psychiatric comorbidity on recovery and recurrence in generalized anxiety disorder, social phobia, and panic disorder: A 12–year prospective study. *American Journal of Psychiatry, 162,* 1179–1187.

Campbell, L. A., Brown, T. A., & Grisham, J. R. (2003). The relevance of age of onset to the psychopathology of generalized anxiety disorder. *Behavior Therapy, 34,* 31–48.

Carter, R. M., Wittchen, H. -U., Pfister, H., & Kessler, R. C. (2001). One-year prevalence of subthreshold and threshold *DSM-IV* generalized anxiety disorder in a nationally representative sample. *Depression and Anxiety, 13,* 78–88.

Cartwright-Hatton, S., & Wells, A. (1997). Beliefs about worry and intrusions: The Meta-Cognitions Questionnaire and its correlates. *Journal of Anxiety Disorders, 11,* 279–296.

Cassidy, J. A., & Shaver, P. R. (Eds.). (1999). *Handbook of attachment: Theory, research, and clinical applications.* New York: Guilford.

Chambers, J. A., Power, K. G., & Durham, R. C. (2004). The relationship between trait vulnerability and anxiety and depressive diagnoses at long-term follow-up of generalized anxiety disorder. *Journal of Anxiety Disorders, 18,* 587–607.

Chelminski, I., & Zimmerman, M. (2003). Pathological worry in depressed and anxious patients. *Journal of Anxiety Disorders, 17,* 533–546.

Coles, M. E., & Heimberg, R. G. (2005). Thought control strategies in generalized anxiety disorder. *Cognitive Therapy and Research, 29,* 47–56.

Constans, J. I. (2001). Worry propensity and the perception of risk. *Behaviour Research and Therapy, 39,* 721–729.

Constans, J. I., Barbee, J. G., Townsend, M. H., & Leffler, H. (2002). Stability of worry content in GAD patients: A descriptive study. *Journal of Anxiety Disorders, 16,* 311–319.

Cougle, J. R., Reardon, D. C., & Coleman, P. K. (2005). Generalized anxiety following unintended pregnancies resolved through childbirth and abortion: A cohort study of the 1995 National Survey of Family Growth. *Journal of Anxiety Disorders, 19,* 137–142.

Craske, M. G., Rapee, R. M., Jackel, L., & Barlow, D. H. (1989). Qualitative dimensions of worry in *DSM-III-R* generalized anxiety disorder subjects and non-anxious controls. *Behaviour Research and Therapy, 27,* 397–402.

Crits-Christoph, P., Gibbons, M. B. C., Narducci, J., Schamberger, M., & Gallop, R. (2005). Interpersonal problems and the outcome of interpersonally oriented psychodynamic treatment of GAD. *Psychotherapy: Theory, Research, Practice, and Training, 42,* 211–224.

Davey, G. C. L. (1994). Worrying, social problem-solving abilities, and social problem-solving confidence. *Behaviour Research and Therapy, 32,* 327–330.

Davey, G. C. L. (2006). A mood-as-input account of perseverative worrying. In G. C. L. Davey & A.Wells (Eds.), *Worry and its psychological disorders: Theory, assessment, and treatment* (pp. 217–238). Chichester, UK: Wiley.

Davey, G. C. L., Hampton, J., Farrell, J., & Davidson, S. (1992). Some characteristics of worrying: Evidence for worrying and anxiety as separate constructs. *Personality and Individual Differences, 13,* 133–147.

Davey, G. C. L., Jubb, M., & Cameron, C. (1996). Catastrophic worrying as a function of changes in problem-solving confidence. *Cognitive Therapy and Research, 20,* 333–344.

Davey, G. C. L., & Levy, S. (1998). Catastrophic worrying: Personal inadequacy and a perseverative iterative style as features of the catastrophizing process. *Journal of Abnormal Psychology, 107,* 576–586.

Davey, G. C. L., Tallis, F., & Capuzzo, N. (1996). Beliefs about the consequences of worrying. *Cognitive Therapy and Research, 20,* 499–520.

Davis, M., Montgomery, I., & Wilson, G. (2002). Worry and heart rate variables: Autonomic rigidity under challenge. *Journal of Anxiety Disorders, 16,* 639–659.

Davis, R. N., & Valentiner, D. P. (2000). Does meta-cognitive theory enhance our understanding of pathological worry and anxiety? *Personality and Individual Differences, 29,* 513–526.

DeBellis, M. D., Casey, B. J., Dahl, R. E., Birmaher, B., Williamson, D. E., Thomas, K. M., et al. (2000). A pilot study of amygdala volumes in pediatric generalized anxiety disorder. *Biological Psychiatry, 48,* 51–57.

DeBellis, M. D., Keshavan, M. S., Shifflett, H., Iyengar, S., Dahl, R. E., Axelson, D. A., et al. (2002). Superior temporal gyrus volumes in pediatric generalized anxiety disorder. *Biological Psychiatry, 51,* 553–562.

DeMartinis, N., Rynn, M., Rickels, K., & Mandos, L. (2000). Prior benzodiazepine use and buspirone response in the treatment of generalized anxiety disorder. *Journal of Clinical Psychiatry, 61,* 91–94.

DiNardo, P., Brown, T. A., & Barlow, D. H. (1994). *Anxiety Disorders Interview Schedule for* DSM-IV. New York: Oxford University Press.

DiNardo, P., Moras, K., Barlow, D. H., Rapee, R. M., & Brown, T. A. (1993). Reliability of *DSM-III* anxiety disorder categories. *Archives of General Psychiatry, 50,* 251–256.

DiNardo, P. A., O'Brien, G. T., Barlow, D. H., Waddell, M. T., & Blanchard, E. B. (1983). Reliability of DSM-III anxiety disorder categories using a new structured interview. *Archives of General Psychiatry, 40*, 1070–1074.

Dugas, M. J., Buhr, K., & Ladouceur, R. (2004). The role of intolerance of uncertainty in etiology and maintenance. In R. G. Heimberg, C. L.Turk, & D. S. Mennin (Eds.), *Generalized anxiety disorder: Advances in research and practice* (pp. 143–163). New York: Guilford.

Dugas, M. J., Freeston, M. H., & Ladouceur, R. (1997). Intolerance of uncertainty and problem orientation in worry. *Cognitive Therapy and Research, 21*, 593–606.

Dugas, M. J., Gagnon, F., Ladouceur, R., & Freeston, M. H. (1998). Generalized anxiety disorder: A preliminary test of a conceptual model. *Behaviour Research and Therapy, 36*, 215–226.

Dugas, M. J., Gosselin, P., & Ladouceur, R. (2001). Intolerance of uncertainty and worry: Investigating specificity in a nonclinical sample. *Cognitive Therapy and Research, 25*, 551–558.

Dugas, M. J., et al. (2005). Intolerance of uncertainty and information processing: Evidence of biased recall and interpretation. *Cognitive Therapy and Research, 29*, 57–70.

Dugas, M. J., Langlois, F., Rhéaume, J., & Ladouceur, R. (1998, November). Intolerance of uncertainty and worry: Investigating causality. In J. Stöber (Chair), *Worry: New findings in applied and clinical research*. Symposium presented at the annual meeting of the Association for the Advancement of Behavior Therapy, Washington, DC.

Dugas, M. J., Ladouceur, R., Léger, E., Freeston, M. H., Langlois, F., Provencher, M. D., et al. (2003). Group cognitive-behavioral therapy for generalized anxiety disorder: Treatment outcome and long-term follow-up. *Journal of Consulting and Clinical Psychology, 71*, 821–825.

Dugas, M. J., Marchand, A., & Ladouceur, R. (2005). Further validation of a cognitive-behavioral model of generalized anxiety disorder: Diagnostic and symptom specificity. *Journal of Anxiety Disorders, 19*, 329–343.

Dupuy, J-B., Beaudoin, S., Rheaume, J., Ladouceur, R., & Dugas, M. J. (2001). Worry: Daily self-report in clinical and non-clinical populations. *Behaviour Research and Therapy, 39*, 1249–1255.

Durham, R. C., Fisher, P. L., Dow, M. G. T., Sharp, D., Power, K. G., Swan, J. S., et al. (2004). Cognitive behavior therapy for good and poor prognosis generalized anxiety disorder: A clinical effectiveness study. *Clinical Psychology and Psychotherapy, 11*, 145–157.

Eng, W., & Heimberg, R. G. (2006). Interpersonal correlates of generalized anxiety disorder: Self versus other perception. *Journal of Anxiety Disorders, 20*, 380–387.

Eysenck, M. W., Mogg, K., May, J., Richards, A., & Mathews, A. (1991). Bias in interpretation of ambiguous sentences related to threat in anxiety. *Journal of Abnormal Psychology, 100*, 144–150.

First, M. B., Spitzer, R. L., Gibbon, M., & Williams, J. B. W. (1996). *Structured Clinical Interview for Axis I DSM-IV Disorders—Patient Edition (SCID-I/P Version 2.0)*. New York: Biometrics Research Department, New York State Psychiatric Institute.

Francis, K., & Dugas, M. J. (2004). Assessing positive beliefs about worry: Validation of a structured interview. *Personality and Individual Differences, 37*, 405–415.

Freeston, M. H., Dugas, M. J., & Ladouceur, R. (1996). Thoughts, imagery, worry, and anxiety. *Cognitive Therapy and Research, 20*, 265–273.

Freeston, M. H., Rhéaume, J., Letarte, H., Dugas, M. J., & Ladouceur, R. (1994). Why do people worry? *Personality and Individual Differences, 17*, 791–802.

Fresco, D. M., Frankel, A. N., Mennin, D. S., Turk, C. L., & Heimberg, R. G. (2002). Distinct and overlapping features of rumination and worry: The relationship of cognitive production to negative affective states. *Cognitive Therapy and Research, 26*, 179–188.

Fricchione, G. (2004). Generalized anxiety disorder. *New England Journal of Medicine, 351*, 675–683.

Friedman, B. H. (2007). An autonomic flexibility-neurovisceral integration model of anxiety and cardiac vagal tone. *Biological Psychiatry, 74*, 185–199.

Friedman, B. H., Thayer, J. F., & Borkovec, T. D. (2000). Explicit memory bias for threat words in generalized anxiety disorder. *Behavior Therapy, 31*, 745–756.

Geleneberg, A. J., Lydiard, R. B., Rudolph, R. L., Aguiar, L., Haskins, J. T., & Salinas, E. (2000). Efficacy of venlafaxine extended-release capsules in nondepressed outpatients with generalized anxiety disorder: A 6–month randomized controlled trial. *Journal of the American Medical Association, 283*, 3082–3088.

Germine, M., Goddard, A. W., Woods, S. W., Charney, D. S., & Heninger, G. R. (1992). Anger and anxiety responses to m-chlorophenylpiperazine in generalized anxiety disorder. *Biological Psychiatry, 32*, 457–461.

Goddard, A. W., & Charney, D. S. (1997). Toward an integrated neurobiology of panic disorder. *Journal of Clinical Psychiatry, 58*, 4–12.

Goddard, A. W., Woods, S. W., Money, R., Pande, A. C., Charney, D. S., Goodman, W. K., et al. (1999). Effects of the CCK$_B$ antagonist CI-988 on responses to *m*CPP in generalized anxiety disorder. *Psychiatric Research, 85*, 225–240.

Goodman, W. K. (2004). Selecting pharmacotherapy for generalized anxiety disorder. *Journal of Clinical Psychiatry, 65* (Suppl. 13), 8–13.

Gosselin, P., Ladouceur, R., Morin, C. M., Dugas, M. J., & Baillargeon, L. (2006). Benzodiazepine discontinuation among adults with GAD: A randomized trial of cognitive-behavioral therapy. *Journal of Consulting and Clinical Psychology, 74*, 908–919.

Gould, R. A., Otto, M. W., Pollack, M. H., & Yap, L. (1997). Cognitive behavioral and pharmacological treatment of generalized anxiety disorder: A preliminary meta-analysis. *Behavior Therapy, 28*, 285–305.

Hale, W. W., Engels, R., & Meeus, W. (2006). Adolescent's perceptions of parenting behaviors and its relationship to adolescent generalized anxiety disorder symptoms. *Journal of Adolescence, 29*, 407–417.

Hamilton, M. (1959). The assessment of anxiety states by rating. *British Journal of Medical Psychology, 32*, 50–55.

Hayes, S. C., Strosahl, K. D., & Wilson, K. G. (1999). *Acceptance and commitment therapy: An experiential approach to behavior change.* New York: Guilford.

Hoehn-Saric, R., & Masek, B. J. (1981). Effects of naloxone on normals and chronically anxious patients. *Biological Psychiatry, 16*, 1041–1050.

Hoehn-Saric, R., McLeod, D. R., Funderburk, F., & Kowalski, P. (2004). Somatic symptoms and physiologic responses in generalized anxiety disorder and panic disorder: An ambulatory monitor study. *Archives of General Psychiatry, 61*, 913–921.

Hoehn-Saric, R., Schlund, M. W., & Wong, S. H. Y. (2004). Effects of citalopram on worry and brain activation in patients with generalized anxiety disorder. *Psychiatry Research: Neuroimaging, 131*, 11–21.

Hoge, E. A., Tamrakar, S. M., Christian, K. M., Mahara, N., Nepal, M. K., Pollack, M. H., et al. (2006). Cross-cultural differences in somatic presentation in patients with generalized anxiety disorder. *Journal of Nervous and Mental Disease, 194*, 962–966.

Hong, R. Y. (2007). Worry and rumination: Differential associations with anxious and depressive symptoms and coping behavior. *Behaviour Research and Therapy, 45*, 277–290.

Hoyer, J., Becker, E. S., & Roth, W. T. (2001). Characteristics of worry in GAD patients, social phobics, and controls. *Depression and Anxiety, 13*, 89–96.

Iny, L. J., Pecknold, J., Suranyi-Cadotte, B. E., Bernier, B., Luthe, L., Nair, N. P., et al. (1994). Studies of a neurochemical link between depression, anxiety, and stress from [3H]imipramine and [3H]paroxetine binding on human platelets. *Biological Psychiatry, 36*, 281–291.

Joormann, J., & Stober, J. (1999). Somatic symptoms of generalized anxiety disorder from the *DSM-IV*: Associations with pathological worry and depression symptoms in a nonclinical sample. *Journal of Anxiety Disorders, 13*, 491–503.

Judd, L. L., Kessler, R. C., Paulus, M. P., Zeller, P. V., Wittchen, H-U., & Kunovac, J. L. (1998). Comorbidity as a fundamental feature of generalized anxiety disorder: Results from the National Comorbidity Study (NCS). *Acta Psychiatrica Scandinavica, 98*, 6–11.

Katz, I. R., Reynolds, C. F., Alexopoulos, G. S., & Hackett, D. (2002). Venlafaxine ER as a treatment for generalized anxiety disorder in older adults: Pooled analysis of five randomized placebo-controlled clinical trials. *Journal of the American Geriatrics Society, 50*, 18–25.

Kelly, W. E. (2003). No time to worry: The relationship between worry, time structure, and time management. *Personality and Individual Differences, 35*, 1119–1126.

Kendler, K. S., Hettema, J. M., Butera, F., Gardner, C. O., & Prescott, C. A. (2003). Life event dimensions of loss, humiliation, entrapment, and danger in the prediction of onsets of major depression and generalized anxiety. *Archives of General Psychiatry, 60*, 789–796.

Kessler, R. C., Berglund, P., Demler, O., Jin, R., Merikangas, K. R., & Walters, E. E. (2005). Lifetime prevalence and age-of-onset distributions of *DSM-III-R* disorders in the National Comorbidity Survey replication. *Archives of General Psychiatry, 62*, 593–602.

Kessler, R. C., Brandenburg, N., Lane, M., Roy-Byrne, P., Stang, P. D., Stein, D. J., et al. (2005). Rethinking the duration requirement for generalized anxiety disorder: Evidence from the National Comorbidity Survey replication. *Psychological Medicine, 35*, 1073–1082.

Kim, T., Pae, C., Yoon, S., Bahk, W., Jun, T., Rhee, W., et al. (2006). Comparison of venlafaxine extended release versus paroxetine for treatment of patients with generalized anxiety disorder. *Psychiatry and Clinical Neurosciences*, *60*, 347–351.

Ladouceur, R., Dugas, M. J., Freeston, M. H., Léger, E., Gagnon, E., & Thibodeau, N. (2000). Efficacy of a new cognitive-behavioral treatment for generalized anxiety disorder: Evaluation in a controlled clinical trial. *Journal of Consulting and Clinical Psychology*, *68*, 957–964.

Ladouceur, R., Blais, F., Freeston, M. H., & Dugas, M. J. (1998). Problem solving and problem orientation in generalized anxiety disorder. *Journal of Anxiety Disorders*, *12*, 139–152.

Ladouceur, R., Gosselin, P., & Dugas, M. J. (2000). Experimental manipulation of intolerance of uncertainty: A study of a theoretical model of worry. *Behaviour Research and Therapy*, *38*, 933–941.

Laguna, L. B., Ham, L. S., Hope, D. A., & Bell, C. (2004). Chronic worry as avoidance of arousal. *Cognitive Therapy and Research*, *28*, 269–281.

Lang, A. J. (2004). Treating generalized anxiety disorder with cognitive-behavioral therapy. *Journal of Clinical Psychiatry*, *65*, 14–19.

Langlois, F., Freeston, M. H., & Ladouceur, R. (2000). Differences and similarities between obsessive intrusive thoughts and worry in a non-clinical population: Study 1. *Behaviour Research and Therapy*, *38*, 157–173.

Lee, H. J., Lee, S. H., Kim, H. S., Kwon, S. M., & Telch, M. J. (2005). A comparison of autogenous/reactive obsessions and worry in a nonclinical population: A test of the continuum hypothesis. *Behaviour Research and Therapy*, *43*, 999–1010.

Linehan, M. M. (1993). *Cognitive-behavioral treatment of borderline personality disorder*. New York: Guilford.

Llorca, P. M., Spadone, C., Sol, O., Danniau, A., Bougerol, T., Corruble, E., et al. (2002). Efficacy and safety of hydroxyzine in the treatment of generalized anxiety disorder: A 3–month double-blind study. *Journal of Clinical Psychiatry*, *63*, 1020–1027.

Luterek, J. A., Turk, C. L., Heimberg, R. G., Fresco, D. M., & Mennin, D. S. (2002, November). *Psychometric properties of the GADQ-IV among individuals with clinician-assessed generalized anxiety disorder: An update*. Poster presented at the annual meeting of Association for Advancement of Behavior Therapy, Reno, NV.

MacLeod, C., Mathews, A., & Tata, P. (1986). Attentional bias in emotional disorders. *Journal of Abnormal Psychology*, *95*, 15–20.

MacLeod, C., & McLaughlin, K. (1995). Implicit and explicit memory bias in anxiety: A conceptual replication. *Behaviour Research and Therapy*, *33*, 1–14.

MacLeod, C., & Rutherford, E. (2004). Information-processing approaches: Assessing the selective functioning of attention, interpretation, and retrieval. In R. G. Heimberg, C. L. Turk, & D. S. Mennin (Eds.), *Generalized anxiety disorder: Advances in research and practice* (pp. 109–142). New York: Guilford.

Mancuso, D. M., Townsend, M. H., & Mercante, D. E. (1993). Long-term follow-up of generalized anxiety disorder. *Comprehensive Psychiatry*, *34*, 441–446.

Marten, P. A., Brown, T. A., Barlow, D. H., Borkovec, T. D., Shear, M. K., & Lydiard, R. B. (1993). Evaluation of the ratings comprising the associated symptom criterion of *DSM-III-R* generalized anxiety disorder. *Journal of Nervous and Mental Disease*, *181*, 676–682.

Martin, M., Williams, R., & Clark, D. (1991). Does anxiety lead to selective processing of threat-related information? *Behaviour Research and Therapy*, *29*, 147–160.

Mathew, S. J., Mao, X., Coplan, J. D., Smith, E. L. P., Sackeim, H. A., Gorman, J. M., et al. (2004). Dorsolateral prefrontal cortical pathology in generalized anxiety disorder: A proton magnetic resonance spectroscopic imaging study. *American Journal of Psychiatry*, *161*, 1119–1121.

Mathews, A., & Klug, F. (1993). Emotionality and interference with color-naming in anxiety. *Behaviour Research and Therapy*, *31*, 57–62.

Mathews, A., & MacLeod, C. (1985). Selective processing of threat cues in anxiety states. *Behaviour Research and Therapy*, *23*, 563–569.

Mathews, A., & Milroy, R. (1994). Effects of priming and suppression of worry. *Behaviour Research and Therapy*, *32*, 843–850.

Mathews, A., Mogg, K., May, J., & Eysenck, M. (1989). Implicit and explicit memory bias in anxiety. *Journal of Abnormal Psychology*, *98*, 236–240.

Mathews, A., Richards, A., & Eysenck, M. (1989). Interpretation of homophones related to threat in anxiety states. *Journal of Abnormal Psychology*, *98*, 31–34.

Mavissakalian, M. R., Hamann, M. S., Haidar, S. A., & deGroot, C. M. (1995). Correlates of *DSM-III* personality disorder in generalized anxiety disorder. *Journal of Anxiety Disorders*, *9*, 103–115.

Mennin, D. S., Heimberg, R. G., Turk, C. L., & Fresco, D. M. (2005). Preliminary evidence for an emotion dysregulation model of generalized anxiety disorder. *Behaviour Research and Therapy*, *43*, 1281–1310.

Merikangas, K. R., Avenevoli, S., Dierker, L., & Grillon, C. (1999). Vulnerability factors among children at risk for anxiety disorders. *Society for Biological Psychiatry, 99*, 172–179.

Meyer, T. J., Miller, M. L., Metzger, R. L., & Borkovec, T. D. (1990). Development and validation of the Penn State Worry Questionnaire. *Behaviour Research and Therapy, 28*, 487–495.

Mitte, K. (2005). Meta-analysis of cognitive-behavioral treatments for generalized anxiety disorder: A comparison with pharmacotherapy. *Psychological Bulletin, 131*, 785–795.

Mitte, K., Noack, P., Steil, R., & Hautzinger, M. (2005). A meta-analytic review of the efficacy of drug treatment in generalized anxiety disorder. *Psychopharmacology, 176*, 141–150.

Mogg, K., Baldwin, D. S., Brodrick, P., & Bradley, B. P. (2004). Effect of short-term SSRI treatment on cognitive bias in generalized anxiety disorder. *Psychopharmacology, 176*, 466–470.

Mogg, K., & Bradley, B. P. (2005). Attentional bias in generalized anxiety disorder versus depressive disorder. *Cognitive Therapy and Research, 29*, 29–45.

Mogg, K., Bradley, B. P., Millar, N., Potts, H., Glenwright, J., & Kentish, J. (1994). Interpretation of homophones related to threat: Anxiety or response bias effects? *Cognitive Therapy and Research, 18*, 461–477.

Mogg, K., Bradley, B. P., Millar, N., & White, J. (1995). A follow-up study of cognitive bias in generalized anxiety disorder. *Behaviour Research and Therapy, 33*, 927–935.

Mogg, K., Bradley, B. P., & Williams, R. (1995). Attentional bias in anxiety and depression: The role of awareness. *British Journal of Clinical Psychology, 34*, 17–36.

Mogg, K., Gardiner, J. M., Stavrou, A., & Golombok, S. (1992). Recollective experience and recognition memory for threat in clinical anxiety states. *Bulletin of the Psychonomic Society, 30*, 109–112.

Mogg, K., Mathews, A., & Weinman, J. (1989). Selective processing of threat cues in clinical anxiety states: A replication. *Behaviour Research and Therapy, 27*, 317–323.

Mogg, K., Millar, N., & Bradley, B. P. (2000). Biases in eye movements to threatening facial expressions in generalized anxiety disorder and depressive disorder. *Journal of Abnormal Psychology, 109*, 695–704.

Monk, C. S., Nelson, E. E., McClure, E. B., Mogg, K., Bradley, B. P., Leibenluft, E., et al. (2006). Ventrolateral prefrontal cortex activation and attentional bias in response to angry faces in adolescents with generalized anxiety disorder. *American Journal of Psychiatry, 163*, 1091–1097.

Montgomery, S. A., Tobias, K., Zomberg, G. L., Kasper, S., & Pande, A. C. (2006). Efficacy and safety of pregabalin in the treatment of generalized anxiety disorder: A 6–week, multicenter, randomized, double-blind, placebo-controlled comparison of pregabalin and venlafaxine. *Journal of Clinical Psychiatry, 67*, 771–82.

Muris, P., Meesters, C., Merckelbach, H., & Hülsenbeck, P. (2000). Worry in children is related to perceived parental rearing and attachment. *Behaviour Research and Therapy, 38*, 487–497.

Newman, M. G., Zuellig, A. R., Kachin, K. E., & Constantino, M. J., Przeworski, A., Erickson, T., et al. (2002). Preliminary reliability and validity of the Generalized Anxiety Disorder Questionnaire–IV: A revised self-report diagnostic measure of generalized anxiety disorder. *Behavior Therapy, 33*, 215–233.

Nuevo, R., Montorio, I., & Borkovec, T. D. (2004). A test of the role of metaworry in the prediction of worry severity in an elderly sample. *Journal of Behavior Therapy and Experimental Psychiatry, 35*, 209–218.

Orsillo, S. M., Roemer, L., & Barlow, D. H. (2003). Integrating acceptance and mindfulness into existing cognitive-behavioral treatment for GAD: A case study. *Cognitive and Behavioural Practice, 10*, 222–230.

Öst, L. G., & Breitholtz, E. (2000). Applied relaxation vs. cognitive therapy in the treatment of generalized anxiety disorder. *Behaviour Research and Therapy, 38*, 777–790.

Peasley-Miklus, C., & Vrana, S. R. (2000). Effects of worrisome and relaxing thinking on fearful emotional processing. *Behaviour Research and Therapy, 38*, 129–144.

Petrovich, G. D., & Swanson, L. W. (1997). Projections from the lateral part of the central amygdalar nucleus to the postulated fear conditioning circuit. *Brain Research, 763*, 247–254.

Porges, S. W. (1995). Orienting in a defensive world: Mammalian modifications of our evolutionary heritage. A polyvagal theory. *Psychophysiology, 32*, 301–318.

Pourmotabbed, T., McLeod, D. R., Hoehn-Saric, R., Hipsley, P., & Greenblatt, D. J. (1996). Treatment, discontinuation and psychomotor effects of diazepam in women with generalized anxiety disorder. *Journal of Clinical Psychopharmacology, 16*, 202–207.

Provencher, M. D., Dugas, M. J., & Ladouceur, R. (2004). Efficacy of problem-solving training and cognitive exposure in the treatment of generalized anxiety disorder: A case replication series. *Cognitive and Behavioural Practice, 11,* 404–414.

Provencher, M. D., Freeston, M. H., Dugas, M. J., & Ladouceur, R. (2000). Catastrophizing assessment of worry and threat schemata among worriers. *Behavioral and Cognitive Psychotherapy, 28,* 211–224.

Pruzinsky, T., & Borkovec, T. D. (1990). Cognitive and personality characteristics of worriers. *Behaviour Research and Therapy, 28,* 507–512.

Purdon, C. (1999). Thought suppression and psychopathology. *Behaviour Research and Therapy, 37,* 1029–1054.

Rickels, K., Downing, R., Scheweizer, E., & Hassman, H. (1993). Antidepressants for the treatment of generalized anxiety disorder: A placebo-controlled comparison of imipramine, trazodone and diazepam. *Archives of General Psychiatry, 50,* 884–895.

Robichaud, M., Dugas, M. J., & Conway, M. (2003). Gender differences in worry and associated cognitive-behavioral variables. *Journal of Anxiety Disorders, 17,* 501–516.

Rodriguez, B. F., Weisberg, R. B., Pagano, M. E., Bruce, S. E., Spencer, M. A., Culpepper, L., et al. (2006). Characteristics and predictors of full and partial recovery from generalized anxiety disorder in primary care patients. *Journal of Nervous and Mental Disease, 194,* 91–97.

Roemer, L. (2001). Measures for generalized anxiety disorder. In M. M.Antony, S. M. Orsillo, & L. Roemer (Eds.), *Practitioner's guide to empirically based measures of anxiety* (pp. 197–210). New York: Springer.

Roemer, L., & Borkovec, T. D. (1994). Effects of suppressing thoughts about emotional material. *Journal of Abnormal Psychology, 103,* 467–474.

Roemer, L., Borkovec, M., Posa, S., & Borkovec, T. D. (1995). A self-report diagnostic measure of generalized anxiety disorder. *Journal of Behavior Therapy and Experimental Psychiatry, 26,* 345–350.

Roemer, L., & Medaglia, E. (2001). Generalized anxiety disorder: A brief overview and guide to assessment. In M. M. Antony, S. M. Orsillo, & L. Roemer (Eds.), *Practitioner's guide to empirically based measures of anxiety* (pp. 189–195). New York: Springer.

Roemer, L., & Orsillo, S. M. (2007). An open trial of an acceptance-based behavior therapy for generalized anxiety disorder. *Behavior Therapy, 38,* 72–85.

Roemer, L., Orsillo, S. M., & Barlow, D. H. (2002). Generalized anxiety disorder. In D. H. Barlow, *Anxiety and its disorders: The nature and treatment of anxiety and panic* (pp. 477–515). New York: Guilford.

Roemer, L., Salters, K., Raffa, S. D., & Orsillo, S. M. (2005). Fear and avoidance of internal experiences in GAD: Preliminary tests of a conceptual model. *Cognitive Therapy and Research, 29,* 71–88.

Roy, M., Neale, M. C., Pedersen, N. L., Mathe, A. A., & Kendler, K. S. (1995). A twin study of generalized anxiety disorder and major depression. *Psychological Medicine, 25,* 1037–1049.

Roy-Byrne, P., & Wagner, A. (2004). Primary care perspectives on generalized anxiety disorder. *Journal of Clinical Psychiatry, 65* (Suppl. 13), 20–26.

Salters-Pedneault, K., Roemer, L., Tull, M. T., Rucker, L., & Mennin, D. S. (2006). Evidence of broad deficits in emotion regulation associated with chronic worry and generalized anxiety disorder. *Cognitive Therapy and Research, 30,* 469–480.

Schneider, L. S., Munjack, D., Severson, J. A., & Palmer, R. (1987). Platelet [3H] imipramine binding in generalized anxiety disorder, panic disorder, and agoraphobia with panic attacks. *Biological Psychiatry, 22,* 59–66.

Schweizer, E., & Rickels, K. (1997). Placebo response in generalized anxiety: Its effect on the outcome of clinical trials. *Journal of Clinical Psychiatry, 58,* 30–38.

Scott, E. L., Eng, W., & Heimberg, R. G. (2002). Ethnic differences in worry in a nonclinical population. *Depression and Anxiety, 15,* 79–82.

Segal, D. L., Hersen, M., & vanHasselt, V. B. (1994). Reliability of the Structured Clinical Interview for *DSM-III-R*: An evaluative review. *Comprehensive Psychiatry, 35,* 316–327.

Segerstrom, S. C., Tsao, J. C. I., Alden, L. E., & Craske, M. G. (2000). Worry and rumination: Repetitive thought as a concomitant and predictor of negative mood. *Cognitive Therapy and Research, 24,* 671–688.

Sinha, S. S., Mohlman, J., & Gorman, J. M. (2004). Neurobiology. In R. G. Heimberg, C. L.Turk, & D. S. Mennin (Eds.), *Generalized anxiety disorder: Advances in research and practice* (pp. 187–216). New York: Guilford.

Spielberger, C. D., Gorsuch, R. L., Lushene, R., Vagg, P. R., & Jacobs, G. A. (1983). *Manual for the State-Trait Anxiety Inventory.* Palo Alto, CA: Consulting Psychologists.

Stanley, M. A., Beck, J. G., & Glassco, J. (1996). Treatment of generalized anxiety in older adults: A preliminary comparison of cognitive-behavioral and supportive approaches. *Behavior Therapy, 27*, 565–581.

Startup, H. M., & Davey, G. C. L. (2001). Mood as input and catastrophic worrying. *Journal of Abnormal Psychology, 110*, 83–96.

Startup, H. M., & Davey, G. C. L. (2003). Inflated responsibility and the use of stop rules for catastrophic worrying. *Behaviour Research and Therapy, 41*, 495–503.

Stein, D. J. (2001). Comorbidity in generalized anxiety disorder: Impact and implications. *Journal of Clinical Psychiatry, 62*, 29–34.

Stöber, J. (1998). Worry, problem elaboration and suppression of imagery: The role of concreteness. *Behaviour Research and Therapy, 36*, 751–756.

Stoicchi, F., Nordera, G., Jokinen, R. H., Lepola, U. M., Hewett, K., Bryson, H., et al. (2003). Efficacy and tolerability of paroxetine for the long-term treatment of generalized anxiety disorder. *Journal of Clinical Psychiatry, 64*, 250–258.

Suarez, L., & Bell-Dolan, D. (2001). The relationship of child worry to cognitive biases: Threat interpretation and likelihood of event occurrence. *Behavior Therapy, 32*, 425–442.

Tallis, F., Davey, G. C. L., & Capuzzo, N. (1994). The phenomenology of non-pathological worry: A preliminary investigation. In G. C. L. Davey & F. Tallis (Eds.), *Worrying: Perspectives on theory, assessment and treatment* (pp. 61–89). London: Wiley.

Tallis, F., Eysenck, M., & Mathews, A. (1992). A questionnaire for the measurement of nonpathological worry. *Personality and Individual Differences, 13*, 161–168.

Thayer, J. F., Friedman, T., & Borkovec, T. D. (1996). Autonomic characteristics of generalized anxiety disorder and worry. *Biological Psychiatry, 39*, 255–266.

Thayer, J. F., Friedman, T., Borkovec, T. D., Molina, S., & Johnsen, B. H. (2000). Phasic heart period reactions to cued threat and non-threat stimuli in generalized anxiety disorder. *Psychophysiology, 37*, 361–368.

Thayer, J. F., & Lane, R. D. (2000). A model of neurovisceral integration in emotion regulation and dysregulation. *Journal of Affective Disorders, 61*, 201–216.

Tiller, J. W., Biddle, N., Maguire, K. P., & Davies, B. M. (1988). The dexamethasone suppression test and plasma dexamethasone in generalized anxiety disorder. *Biological Psychiatry, 23*, 261–270.

Turk, C. L., Heimberg, R. G., Luterek, J. A., Mennin, D. S., & Fresco, D. M. (2005). Emotion dysregulation in generalized anxiety disorder: A comparison with social anxiety disorder. *Cognitive Therapy and Research, 29*, 89–106.

Watkins, E., Moulds, M., & Mackintosh, B. (2005). Comparisons between rumination and worry in a non-clinical population. *Behaviour Research and Therapy, 43*, 1577–1585.

Wegner, D. M. (1994). Ironic processes of mental control. *Psychological Review, 101*, 34–52.

Wells, A. (1994). A multi-dimensional measure of worry: Development and preliminary validation of the Anxious Thoughts Inventory. *Anxiety, Stress and Coping, 6*, 280–299.

Wells, A. (1995). Meta-cognition and worry: A cognitive model of generalised anxiety disorder. *Behavioural and Cognitive Psychotherapy, 23*, 301–320.

Wells, A. (1999). A metacognitive model and therapy for generalized anxiety disorder. *Clinical Psychology and Psychotherapy, 6*, 86–95.

Wells, A. (2005). The metacognitive model of GAD: Assessment of meta-worry and relationship with *DSM-IV* generalized anxiety disorder. *Cognitive Therapy and Research, 29*, 107–121.

Wells, A. (2006). The metacognitive model of worry and generalised anxiety disorder. In G. C. L. Davey & A. Wells (Eds.), *Worry and its psychological disorders: Theory, assessment, and treatment* (pp. 179–200). Chichester, UK: Wiley.

Wells, A., & Carter, K. (2001). Further tests of a cognitive model of generalized anxiety disorder: Metacognitions and worry in GAD, panic disorder, social phobia, depression, and nonpatients. *Behavior Therapy, 32*, 85–102.

Wells, A., & Carter, K. (1999). Preliminary tests of a cognitive model of generalized anxiety disorder. *Behaviour Research and Therapy, 37*, 585–594.

Wells, A., & King, P. (2006). Metacognitive therapy for generalized anxiety disorder: An open trial. *Journal of Behavior Therapy and Experimental Psychiatry, 37*, 206–212.

Wells, A., & Papageourgiou, C. (1995). Worry and the incubation of intrusive images following stress. *Behaviour Research and Therapy, 33*, 579–583.

Wenzel, A., Haugen, E. N., Jackson, L. C., & Robinson, K. (2003). Prevalence of generalized anxiety at eight weeks postpartum. *Archives of Women's Mental Health, 6*, 43–49.

Wetherell, J., Gatz, M., & Craske, M. G. (2003). Treatment of generalized anxiety disorder in older adults.

Journal of Consulting and Clinical Psychology, 71, 31–40.

Williams, J. B. W., Gibbon, M., First, M. B., Spitzer, R. L., Davies, M., Borus, J., et al. (1992). The Structured Clinical Interview for *DSM-III-R* (SCID): Multisite test-retest reliability. *Archives of General Psychiatry, 49,* 630–636.

Williams, K. E., Chambless, D. L., & Ahrens, A. (1997). Are emotions frightening? An extension of the fear construct. *Behaviour Research and Therapy, 35,* 239–248.

Wittchen, H-U. (2002). Generalized anxiety disorder: Prevalence, burden, and cost to society. *Depression and Anxiety, 16,* 162–171.

Wittchen, H. -U., Carter, R. M., Pfister, H., Montgomery, S. A., & Kessler, R. C. (2000). Disabilities and quality of life in pure and comorbid generalized anxiety disorder and major depression in a national survey. *International Journal of Clinical Psychopharmacology, 15,* 319–328.

Wittchen, H-U., & Hoyer, J. (2001). Generalized anxiety disorder: Nature and course. *The Journal of Clinical Psychiatry, 62,* 15–21.

Wittchen, H-U., Zhao, S., Kessler, R. C., & Eaton, W. W. (1994). *DSM-II-R* generalized anxiety disorder in the National Comorbidity Survey. *Archives of General Psychiatry, 51,* 355–364.

Woelk, H., Arnoldt, K. H., Kieser, M., & Hoerr, R. (2007). Ginkgo biloba special extract EGb 761 in generalized anxiety disorder and adjustment disorder with anxious mood: A randomized, double-blind, placebo-controlled trial. *Journal of Psychiatric Research, 41,* 472–480.

Woodman, C. L., Noyes, R., Jr., Black, D., Schlosser, S., & Yagla, S. (1999). A 5–year follow-up study of generalized anxiety disorder and panic disorder. *Journal of Nervous and Mental Disease, 187,* 3–9.

Wu, J. C., Buchsbaum, M. S., Hershey, T. G., Hazlett, E., Sicotte, N., & Johnson, J. C. (1991). PET in generalized anxiety disorder. *Biological Psychiatry, 29,* 1181–1199.

Yonkers, K. A., Dyck, I. R., Warshaw, M., & Keller, M. B. (2000). Factors predicting the clinical course of generalized anxiety disorder. *British Journal of Psychiatry, 176,* 544–549.

Zanarini, M. C., Skodol, A. E., Bender, D., Dolan, R., Sanislow, C., Schaefer, E., et al. (2000). The collaborative longitudinal personality disorder study: Reliability of Axis I and II diagnoses. *Journal of Personality Disorders, 14,* 291–299.

Chapter 4

Panic Disorder

Joanna Arch and Michelle G. Craske

The purpose of this chapter is to offer an up-to-date review on the nature, etiology, assessment, and treatment of panic disorder. The chapter aims to integrate a substantial body of previous research on panic disorder with the most recent advances in the field.

Description of Panic Disorder

Description of Symptoms and Criteria

A panic attack is an abrupt surge of intense fear or discomfort that is diagnostically characterized by a cluster of 13 physical and cognitive symptoms, including palpitations, shortness of breath, parasthesias, trembling, derealization, and fears of dying, going crazy, or losing control (American Psychiatric Association [APA], 1994). The panic attack is discrete, having a sudden, abrupt onset and relatively brief duration (with symptoms peaking within 10 minutes of onset), as opposed to gradually building anxious arousal. A *full-blown* panic attack is defined as four or more symptoms, whereas *limited symptom* attacks are defined as fewer than four symptoms.

Panic attacks are characterized by a unique action tendency: Specifically, urges to escape, and less often, urges to fight. In other words, panic attacks represent activation of the fight-flight system. Accordingly, panic attacks usually involve elevated autonomic nervous system arousal, needed to support such fight-flight reactivity. Furthermore, perceptions of imminent threat, such as death, loss of control, or social ridicule frequently accompany the fight-flight response. However, the urgency to escape, autonomic arousal, and perception of threat are not present in every self-reported occurrence of panic. For example, data gathered from ambulatory (portable) devices have found sympathetic nervous system activation (Wilkinson et al., 1998) although nonactivation has also been documented (for ~40% of self-reported panic attacks) (see Margraf, Taylor, Ehlers, Roth, & Agras, 1987; Taylor, Sheikh, Agras, Roth, Margraf, Ehlers, Maddock, & Gossard, 1986). Severe panic attacks are more autonomically based (Margraf et al., 1987). Self-reported panic in the absence of actual autonomic activation is assumed to reflect anticipatory anxiety versus true panic (Barlow, Brown, & Craske, 1994). Another discordant example occurs when perceptions of threat or danger are refuted, despite the report of intense fear and arousal. This has been termed *noncognitive* panic (Rachman, Lopatka, & Levitt, 1988).

Panic attacks may be experienced by individuals diagnosed with any of the anxiety disorders, and they are common in all of these disorders. Panic Disorder is distinguished by unexpected panic attacks, or attacks that occur without an obvious trigger, and at least 1 month of persistent apprehension about the recurrence of panic or its consequences, or a significant behavioral change. These behavioral changes may include safety behaviors, such as frequent attendance at medical facilities for fear of a medical problem, or agoraphobia. Agoraphobia refers to avoidance, or endurance with dread, of situations from which escape might be difficult or in which help might be unavailable in the event of a panic attack, or paniclike symptoms, such as loss of bowel control. Typical agoraphobic situations include shopping malls, waiting in line, movie theaters, traveling by car or bus, crowded restaurants and stores, and being alone.

A subset of individuals who have panic disorder also experience *nocturnal* panic attacks. Nocturnal panic refers to waking from sleep in a state of panic with symptoms that are very similar to panic attacks that occur during wakeful states (Uhde, 1994; Craske & Barlow, 1989). Nocturnal panic does *not* refer to waking from sleep and panicking after a lapse of waking time, or night-time arousals induced by nightmares or environmental stimuli (such as unexpected noises). Also, nocturnal panic is distinct from sleep terrors and sleep apnea (see Craske & Tsao, 2005, for a review).

Although epidemiological studies have not been conducted, surveys of select clinical groups suggest that nocturnal panic is relatively common among individuals with panic disorder, with 44% to 71% reporting nocturnal panic at least once, and 30% to 45% reporting repeated nocturnal panics (Craske & Barlow, 1989; Krystal, Woods, Hill, & Charney, 1991; Mellman & Uhde, 1989; Roy-Byrne, Mellman, & Uhde, 1988; Uhde, 1994). Individuals who suffer frequent nocturnal panics often become fearful of sleep and attempt to delay sleep onset. Avoidance of sleep may result in chronic sleep deprivation, in turn precipitating more nocturnal panics (Uhde, 1994).

CASE EXAMPLE

Sandy is a 30-year-old Caucasian mother of a 5 year old and a 3 year old, who lives with her husband of 6 years. For the past 2 years, she has been chronically anxious and panic stricken. Her panic attacks are described as intolerable and increasing in frequency. The first time that she panicked was 3 years ago, just after the birth of her second child. She recalls suddenly experiencing strong sensations of lightheadedness and weakness when she was at home with her newborn and 2-year-old children. She was convinced that she was about to pass out. She immediately laid down. The feelings passed within a few minutes, but Sandy remained very concerned that she would pass out. This concern was particularly worrisome since Sandy feared what would happen to her children if she lost consciousness. She felt anxious for a day or so but then forgot about the feelings until a few weeks later, when again, at home alone with her children, she was overcome with even stronger sensations of lightheadedness, weakness, and a cold sweat. She became very afraid, especially for her children, and called her husband, who left work to be with her. A visit to her primary care doctor the next day did not reveal any medical explanations for the symptoms. Nonetheless, Sandy began to pay close attention to her physical state and became very anxious about her husband's upcoming business trip. While her husband was away, she panicked daily, each time phoning her mother, who would come over to look after the children while Sandy laid down until the feelings subsided. From that time onward, Sandy was very anxious about being alone with her children.

Now Sandy has these feelings in many situations. She describes her panic attacks as intense feelings of lightheadedness, weakness, a sense of unreality and detachment, a racing heart, nausea, and fears of losing consciousness. It is the lightheadedness and unreality that scare her the most, for fear of passing out and leaving her children unattended. Consequently, Sandy is now sensitive to anything that produces lightheaded and unreal types of feelings, such as standing quickly from a seated position, heat, the semiconsciousness that occurs just before falling asleep, bright lights, alcohol, and drugs. Even though she has a prescription for Klonopin (a high-potency benzodiazepine), she rarely uses medication because of her fear of feeling "weird" and unable to take care of her children. She wants to be as alert as possible at all times, but she keeps the Klonopin with her in the event that she has no other escape route. She is very sensitive to her body in general—she becomes scared of anything that feels a little different than usual. Even coffee, which she used to enjoy, is distressing to her now because of its agitating and racy effects. She was never a big exerciser, but to think of exerting herself now is also scary. She reports that she is constantly waiting for the next panic to occur. She avoids being alone with her children and situations where she thinks she is more likely to pass out, such as driving, restaurants, and long distances from home. She avoids crowds and large groups as well, partly because of the feeling of too much stimulation and partly because she is afraid she might panic in front of others. Also, Sandy avoids unstructured time, in the event she might dwell on how she feels and, by so doing, panic. She tries to keep herself as busy as possible with her children but remains constantly anxious about the possibility of panicking and passing out. In general, she prefers to be with her husband or her mother.

In fact, her reliance on her husband and mother has strained those relationships. Her husband is frustrated with Sandy's behavior and the restrictions it has placed on his own life: he no longer goes on business trips, he spends every free moment with Sandy and the children, and sometimes he has to leave work to come home because Sandy's mother is not available to be with her. Similarly, while her mother offers to help as much as possible, she is also feeling that Sandy's reliance upon her is too much.

Sandy describes how different she is from the way she used to be: how weak and scared she is now. The only other incident that has any similarity to her current panic attacks occurred in her late teens when she smoked marijuana. Sandy recalls being very scared of the feeling of losing control and the sense that she would never return to reality. She has not taken drugs since then. Otherwise she has no history of serious medical conditions or any previous psychological treatment. Sandy was shy as a young child and throughout her teens. However, her social anxiety improved throughout her 20s to the point that, up until the onset of her panic attacks, she was mostly very comfortable around people. Since the onset of her panic attacks, she has become concerned that others will notice that she appears different or strange. However, her social anxiety is limited to panic attacks and does not reflect a broader social phobia.

In general, her appetite is good but her sleep is restless. At least once a week she wakes abruptly in the middle of the night with a panic attack, feeling short of breath and scared. Sandy is mostly worried about her panic attacks. She worries about what will happen to her children if she loses consciousness, but she also worries what will happen to them in the long term, if she continues to panic. She has some difficulty concentrating, but in general she functions well when she feels safe—that is, when her mother or husband are nearby. She sometimes becomes depressed about her panic and the limitations on her independence. She occasionally has times of feeling hopeless about the future, doubting if she will ever be able to get back to feeling like she did before these attacks began.

BRIEF HISTORY

Panic disorder was first regarded as a diagnostic entity with the publication of the *DSM III,* 25 years ago. Prior to that time, panic attacks were viewed as symptoms of a general neurosis, although accounts of a clinically similar syndrome appeared much earlier. These were labeled as *soldiers heart* (Wooley, 1982), *neurocirculatory asthenia* (Wheeler, White, Reed, & Cohen, 1950), and *effort syndrome* (Nixon, 1993). In the *DSM-III,* agoraphobia was considered a separate disorder, which might or might not be associated with panic attacks. Observations of clinical samples by Klein (1981) and others (Craske & Barlow, 1988; Turner, Williams, Beidel, & Mezzich, 1986) suggested that agoraphobia generally developed following panic attacks, and this led to a redefinition of agoraphobia as a secondary response to panic attacks in the *DSM-III-R* (Barlow, 2002). However, the debate continues (see the epidemiology section), and the latest *DSM* (*DSM-IV-TR* [American Psychiatric Association], 1994) retains agoraphobia without a history of Panic Disorder as a separate diagnosis.

In contrast to earlier *DSM* diagnostic criteria, greater recognition is given in *DSM-IV* to the notion that panic attacks may occur in the context of any anxiety disorder. Panic attacks are categorized as either situationally bound, situationally predisposed, or unexpected/uncued. Panic Disorder is diagnosed when there are repeated unexpected/uncued panic attacks and persistent apprehension about panic attacks and/or behavioral changes resultant from panic attacks.

EPIDEMIOLOGY

From the National Comorbidity Survey-Replication (NCS-R), prevalence estimates for Panic Disorder are 2.7% (12 month) and 4.7% (lifetime) (Kessler, Berglund, Demler, Jin, Merikangas, & Walters, 2005a; Kessler, Chiu, Demler, Merikangas, & Walters, 2005b). These rates are higher than those reported in the original NCS (Kessler et al., 1994) and the older Epidemiological Catchment Area (ECA) study (Myers et al., 1984). In addition, they are higher than recent estimates from the Ukraine (Bromet et al., 2005), Japan (Kawakami et al., 2005) and Germany (Goodwin, Fergusson, & Horwood, 2005). While data from the United States suggests increased prevalence over the past two decades (Goodwin 2003), the data from other countries raises the possibility that the range in prevalence rates reflects differences in diagnostic methodology as well as variations in diagnostic criteria.

In contrast to individuals with agoraphobia who seek treatment, who almost always report a history of panic that preceded development of their avoidance (Wittchen, Reed, & Kessler, 1998), epidemiological data indicate relatively high rates for agoraphobia without a history of panic disorder: 0.8% in the last 12 months (versus 2.8% for Panic

Disorder) (Kessler et al., 2005a) and 1.4% lifetime prevalence (versus 4.7% for Panic Disorder) (Kessler et al., 2005b). These rates are considerably lower than previous epidemiological estimates by Kessler and colleagues (1994) of 2.8% for agoraphobia without panic in the last 12 months and 5.3% over the lifetime. The more recent data still indicate that the rate of agoraphobia without a history of Panic Disorder occurs at nearly one third the rate of Panic Disorder. The earlier epidemiological data may have overestimated agoraphobia prevalence due to misdiagnosis of Generalized Anxiety, specific and social phobias, and reasonable cautiousness about certain situations (e.g., walking alone in unsafe neighborhoods) as agoraphobia (Horwath, Lish, Johnson, Hornig,& Weissman, 1993). The more general discrepancy between the clinical and epidemiology data may occur because individuals who panic are more likely to seek help (Boyd, 1986).

Rarely does the diagnosis of Panic Disorder, with or without agoraphobia, occur in isolation. Commonly co-occurring Axis I conditions include: specific phobias: Social Phobia, Dysthymia, Generalized Anxiety Disorder, Major Depressive Disorder, and substance abuse (e.g., 60% [Brown, Campbell, Lehman, Gishman, & Mancill, 2001]; 51% [Brown, Antony, & Barlow, 1995]; 51% [Kessler, Chiu, Demler, Merikangas, & Walker, 2005a]). Also, from 25% to 60% of persons with Panic Disorder meet criteria for a current comorbid personality disorder, mostly avoidant or dependent personality disorders (e.g., Chambless & Renneberg, September, 1988).

The modal age of onset for Panic Disorder is early adulthood, between age 21 and 23 (Kessler et al., 2006). In fact, a substantial proportion of adolescents report panic attacks (e.g., Hayward et al., 1992). Panic Disorder in children and adolescents tends to be chronic and comorbid with other anxiety, mood, and disruptive disorders (Biederman et al., 1997). Treatment is usually sought at a much later age, around 34 years (e.g., Noyes, Crowe, Harris, Hamra, McChesney, & Chaudhry, 1986). The overall ratio of females to males is approximately 2:1 (Kessler et al., 2006) although the ratio shifts dramatically in the direction of female predominance as the level of agoraphobia worsens (e.g., Thyer, Himle, Curtis, Cameron, & Nesse, 1985).

Most individuals with Panic Disorder With or Without Agoraphobia (approximately 72%) (Craske, Miller, Rotunda, & Barlow, 1990) report identifiable stressors around the time of their first panic attack. These include interpersonal stressors and stressors related to physical well-being, such as negative drug experiences, disease, or death in the family. However, the number of stressors does not differ from the number experienced prior to the onset of other types of anxiety disorders (Pollard, Pollard, & Corn, 1989; Rapee, Litwin, & Barlow, 1990; Roy-Byrne, Geraci, & Uhde, 1986). Approximately one half report having experienced panicky feelings at some time before their first full panic attack, suggesting that onset may be either insidious or acute (Craske et al., 1990).

Finally, Panic Disorder and agoraphobia tend to be chronic conditions, with severe financial and interpersonal costs. Individuals with Panic Disorder overutilize medical resources compared to the general public and to individuals with other psychiatric disorders (e.g., Roy-Byrne et al., 1999). Even with or following pharmacological treatment only a minority of patients remit without subsequent relapse ($\sim$30%), although a similar number experience notable improvement, albeit with a waxing and waning course (25–35%) (Roy-Byrne & Cowley, 1995; Katschnig & Amering, 1998). Nevertheless, the prognosis for Panic Disorder, especially in the absence of agoraphobia, is more positive than for Generalized Anxiety Disorder or Social Anxiety Disorder (Bruce et al., 2005).

Actual Dysfunction

NEUROBIOLOGY OF PANIC DISORDER

Genetics

The trait of neuroticism confers risk for emotional disorders, including Panic Disorder (e.g., Mineka, Watson, & Clark, 1998). Numerous multivariate genetic analyses of human twin samples consistently attribute approximately 50% of the variance in neuroticism to additive genetic factors (Lake, Eaves, Maes, Heath, & Martin, 2000). In addition, anxiety and depression appear to be variable expressions of the heritable tendency toward neuroticism (Kendler, Heath, Martin, & Eaves, 1987). Twin studies provide evidence that symptoms of fear (i.e., breathlessness, heart pounding) may be additionally explained by a unique source of genetic variance that is differentiated from symptoms of depression and anxiety (Kendler et al., 1987) and, at least in females, from neuroticism (Martin, Jardine, Andrews, & Heath, 1988).

Even though heritability studies of anxiety disorders rely on poorly validated lifetime diagnostic instruments (e.g., Diagnostic Interview Schedule), two broad but distinct genetic factors have been identified. The first is defined by high loadings for Generalized Anxiety Disorder and Major Depression, but only moderate loadings for Panic Disorder (Mineka, Watson, & Clark, 1998) and agoraphobia (Kendler, Neale, Kessler, Heath, & Eaves, 1993). The second is defined by high loadings for Panic Disorder (with and without agoraphobia) and phobias (Kendler et al., 1995). Support for these two broad diatheses exists in separate analyses of the Vietnam Era Twin Registry (Scherrer et al., 2000).

Analyses of specific genetic markers remain preliminary and inconsistent. For example, Panic Disorder has been linked to a locus on chromosome 13 (Hamilton et al., 2003; Schumacher et al., 2005) and chromosome 9 (Gagunashvili et al., 2003), but the exact genes remain unknown. Findings regarding markers for the cholecystokinin-BE receptor gene have been inconsistent (van Megen, Westenberg, Den Boer, & Kahn, 1996 versus Hamilton et al., 2001). Association and linkage studies implicate the adenosine receptor gene in panic disorder (Deckert et al., 1998; Hamilton et al., 2004). However, studies of genes involved in neurotransmitter systems associated with fear and anxiety have produced inconsistent results (see Roy-Byrne, Stein & Craske, in press).

BASIC NEUROCIRCUITRY

Amygdala

Current neural models focus on the role of the amgydala and related structures as central to the dysfunctional anxiety evaluation and response system in Panic Disorder (Gorman, Kent, Sullivan & Coplan, 2000). The amygdala serves as a mediator of input from the environment (via the thalamus and sensory cortex) and stored experience (via the frontal cortex and hippocampus), which then triggers the anxiety and panic response by activating brain regions involved in central panic symptoms, including the hypothalamus (HPA axis and autonomic system), locus ceruleus (heart rate and blood pressure), and parabrachial nucleus (changes in respiration; see Roy-Byrne, Stein & Craske, in press). Recent research on patients with Panic Disorder has found alterations in the amygdala and associated structures consistent with this model, including reduced volume in the amygdala (Massana et al., 2003) and left temporal lobe (Uchida et al.,

2003), decreased cerebral glucose metabolism in amygdala, hippocampus, thalamus, and brain stem (Sakai et al., 2005), and lowered levels of creatine and phosphocreatine metabolites in the right medial temporal lobe (Massana et al., 2002). Many of these findings occur in various combinations in other anxiety disorders such as Social Anxiety and Posttraumatic Stress Disorder (Kent & Rauch, 2003), indicating that they are not necessarily specific to Panic Disorder.

GABA/Benzodiazepine System

Another neurological system potentially implicated in the pathophysiology of Panic Disorder is the γ-aminobutyric acid (GABA) neuronal system. Studies demonstrate that patients with Panic Disorder exhibit low baseline GABA levels in the occipital cortex (Goddard et al., 2001) and, following acute benzodiazepine administration, show blunted benzodiazepine sensitivity (Roy-Byrne, Cowley, Greenblatt, Shader & Hommer, 1990) and GABA neuronal responses (Goddard et al., 2004). Potentially elucidating these findings, several (Bremner et al., 2000; Malizia et al., 1998) but not all (Brandt et al., 1998) studies have found lowered benzodiazepine receptor density in amygdala and perihippocampal areas in patients with Panic Disorder. However, GABA abnormalities have also been found in patients with other psychological disorders such as depression (Sanacora et al., 1999) and alcohol dependency (Behar et al., 1999), suggesting once again that these findings may not necessarily be specific to Panic Disorder.

HPA Axis and Autonomic Nervous System Functioning

Dysregulations of the autonomic nervous system and HPA axis have been hypothesized to be central to Panic Disorder. Previous research was mixed, although a carefully controlled examination of corticotropin and cortisol secretions over 24 hours revealed that individuals with Panic Disorder had significantly higher overnight cortisol levels, particularly the more severe individuals (Abelson & Curtis, 1996). In an attempt to reconcile seemingly contradictory findings, Abelson and colleagues (2006) recently reexamined four HPA studies from their laboratory, including the 24-hour study. They concluded that experimental contexts that are novel, uncontrollable, and/or threatening produce elevated HPA responses in Panic Disorder patients relative to healthy controls and account for disparate findings from previous studies. In other words, they found consistent evidence that individuals with Panic Disorder show elevated HPA reactivity to specific environmental cues, rather than elevated HPA responding in general (i.e., basally). The same effect has been observed with measures of the time course of startle eye blink responding (which is mediated by the amygdala) (Anders et al., 2004): baseline startle was enhanced in participants with Panic Disorder relative to controls, but the groups showed otherwise equivalent patterns of responding to approaching shock (Grillon, Ameli, Goddard, Woods, & Davis, 1994). Since baseline represents a state of anticipation about upcoming experimental procedures, the results are interpreted as elevated emotional reactivity to stressful conditions in general versus exaggerated responding to explicit threat cues (Grillon, 2002). Similarly, investigations of autonomic state, such as galvanic skin response, heart rate, respiration, and skin temperature generally indicate that persons with Panic Disorder show an elevated response to experimental contexts versus explicit threat stimuli (e.g., Roth et al., 1992).

Heart rate variability and specifically cardiac vagal tone, the high-frequency component of heart rate variability, have emerged as popular means of assessing parasympathetic responding. High cardiac vagal tone[1] facilitates the organism's capacity for quick, precise cardiac and behavioral adaptations to changes in internal states and environmental circumstances, whereas low vagal tone limits such flexible responding (Porges, 1992). In Panic Disorder, the evidence for abnormal heart rate variability and vagal tone is mixed. On one hand, compared to nonpanic controls, decreased spectral reserve and high-frequency (HF) power, increased low-frequency (LF) power, and an elevated LF/HF ratio have been found in Panic Disorder samples during both non-panic and panicogenic conditions (Friedman, Thayer & Borkovec, 1993; Friedman & Thayer, 1998). However, heart rate variability abnormalities have also been found among individuals with Generalized Anxiety Disorder (Thayer, Friedman, & Borkovec, 1996; Thayer et al., 2000), Posttraumatic Stress Disorder (e.g., Cohen et al., 1998, 2000) and Obsessive Compulsive Disorder (Hoehn-Saric, McLeod, & Hipsley, 1995, but see Slaap, Nielen, Boshuisen, van Roon, & den Boer, 2004 for the opposite finding). Thus, it remains unclear whether a distinct pattern of heart rate variability abnormalities characterizes Panic Disorder or whether similar abnormalities generalize across the anxiety disorders. More importantly, multiple well-controlled studies have failed to find heart rate variability differences in Panic Disorder patients versus healthy controls (Asmundson & Stein, 1994; Stein & Asmundson, 1994; McCraty, Atkinson, Tomasino & Stuppy, 2001; Slaap, et al., 2004) or produce contradictory results (Ito et al., 1999). Differences in time of testing, environmental and psychological conditions surrounding testing (e.g., Abelson et al., 2006), methods of recording and analysis, and subject demographic factors such as age, fitness, illness duration, and severity (e.g., Ito et al., 1999) may account for these inconsistencies.

Researchers also have focused on assessing sympathetic nervous system functioning in Panic Disorder. Evaluations of sympathetic nervous system functioning over extended periods of time in the natural environment have yielded mixed results. Some report no baseline differences between Panic Disorder and nonanxious controls in terms of respiratory and cardiovascular functioning (Clark et al., 1990; Shear et al., 1992), whereas others find differences (Anastasiades et al., 1990; Bystritsky, Craske, Maidenberg, Vapnik, & Shapiro, 1995). A recent study of patients who had remitted from Panic Disorder found evidence for a dysfunctional baroreflex regulation of sympathetic nerve activity before and after audiovisual stimulation (Shioiri et al., 2005). Another study (Lambert et al., 2002) failed to find differences in baroreflex response in Panic Disorder patients versus healthy controls at rest. However, Lambert and colleagues (2002) found evidence of higher reflex gain in arterial baroreflex control of the muscle sympathetic nerve activity in Panic Disorder patients, suggesting increased reactivity of vasoconstricting sympathetic nerves. Differences in the contextual threat value of the studies (anticipating and experiencing stressful stimuli versus resting) perhaps account for these seemingly contradictory findings (see Abelson et al., 2006).

Recently, Alvarenga and colleagues (2006) measured cardiac sympathetic nervous tone during resting baseline via rates of cardiac noradrenaline spillover and found no differences between individuals with and without panic disorder. Rather, they found reductions in measures of the noradrenaline transporter among Panic Disorder patients,

---

[1] Heart rate in humans is regulated by the sinoatrial node (SA), the natural pacemaker of the heart, located in the muscle fibers of the right atrial chamber. The SA is enervated by the sympathetic and parasympathetic branches of the autonomic nervous system, both of which modulate the regular rhythm set by the SA. The vagus, the 10th cranial nerve, serves as the principal source of parasympathetic communication between the SA and the central nervous system (Porges, 2003).

suggesting impaired neuronal uptake of noradrenaline in Panic Disorder. Interestingly, Middleton and Ashby (1995) found that Panic Disorder treatment in the form of CBT or imipramine increased plasma noradrenaline, suggesting that noradrenaline-associated dysregulations may be modifiable via treatment.

Despite one discrepant report (Schittecatte, Charles, Depauw, Mesters, & Wilmotte, 1988), the vast majority of studies (e.g., Abelson et al., 1992; Brambilla, Perna, Garberi, Nobile, & Bellodi, 1995) have shown that patients with panic disorder display blunted growth hormone responses to clonodine, an alpha2-adrenoreceptor partial agonist. However, Abelson and colleagues (2005) measured growth hormone secretion over a 24-hour period and found no differences between panic patients and non-patients, suggesting that growth hormone circadian patterns and basal secretory activity are normal in panic disorder. Hence, growth hormone abnormalities in panic disorder may be evidenced only in specific activation paradigms, most consistently with clonodine. These combined findings have been interpreted as consistent with subsensitivity in post-synaptic alpha2-adrenoreceptor in response to excessive central noradrenergic outflow.

Given the extent of the varied findings across multiple physiological indexes, opinion is mixed regarding whether instability of the autonomic nervous system is a necessary precondition for the development of Panic Disorder, either alone or coupled with cognitive distress (see Stein & Asmundson, 1994 versus Papp, Klein, and Gorman, 1993). As mentioned in the context of heart rate variability studies, the contradictory and inconsistent findings in the physiological literature on Panic Disorder may stem from differences in contextual, methodological, and sample demographic factors. Following the example of Abelson and associates (2006), future research would benefit from investigating hypotheses about specific factors that may account for disparate findings among studies.

BEHAVIORAL FEATURES OF PANIC DISORDER

The behavioral features of Panic Disorder involve actions taken or refrained from in order to increase perceived protection from panic attacks. These behaviors can be divided into categories of agoraphobic avoidance, interoceptive avoidance, safety behaviors, and experiential avoidance.

Agoraphobic Avoidance

Behaviors that involve enduring with dread or avoiding places and situations from which escape might be challenging or embarrassing or in which help may not be available in case of a panic attack are illustrations of agoraphobic avoidance (*DSM-IV*, APA, 1994). Typical agoraphobic avoidance behaviors include avoidance of buses or subways, large crowds, shopping malls, restaurants, sporting events, and being alone.

The relationship between agoraphobic avoidance and Panic Disorder remains a subject of debate (e.g., Craske, 2003). Among individuals with Panic Disorder, agoraphobic avoidance ranges widely (Craske & Barlow, 1988). Some individuals manifest few to no agoraphobic symptoms, whereas others spend years as virtual prisoners in their own homes. It is not uncommon for individuals with more severe agoraphobia to limit themselves to a safety zone of a few blocks or miles around their home and to not venture beyond its radius, unaccompanied or at all (Barlow, 2002).

What accounts for these wide discrepancies in the development of agoraphobia among individuals with Panic Disorder? Researchers have examined various predictors and correlates of agoraphobia. Although agoraphobia tends to increase as history of panic lengthens (Kikuchi et al., 2005), a significant proportion panic for many years without developing agoraphobic limitations. In addition, agoraphobia is not related to age of onset or frequency of panic attacks (Kikuchi et al., 2005; Cox, Endler, & Swinson, 1995; Craske & Barlow, 1988; Rapee & Murrell, 1988). Some investigators have found that panic attack symptomatology is more intense among more agoraphobic individuals (e.g., de Jong & Bouman, 1995; Goisman et al., 1994; Telch, Brouilard, Telch, Agras, & Taylor, 1989; Noyes, Clancy, Garvey, & Anderson, 1987) whereas others fail to find such differences (e.g., Kikuchi et al., 2005; Cox et al., 1995; Craske et al., 1990). Agoraphobic individuals with Panic Disorder do not differ from their non-agoraphobic counterparts in terms of fears of dying, going crazy, or losing control (Cox et al., 1995; Craske, Rapee, & Barlow, 1988). However, individuals with greater agoraphobia show more distress regarding the social consequences of panicking (Amering, Katschnig, Berger, Windhaber, Baischer, & Dantendorfer, 1997; de Jong & Bouman, 1995; Rapee & Murrell, 1988; Telch et al., 1989). A recent investigation by Kikuchi et al. (2005) found that individuals who developed agoraphobia within 6 months of the onset of Panic Disorder had a higher prevalence of Generalized Anxiety Disorder, but not major depression.[2] Whether the latter two findings serve an antecedent or secondary role in agoraphobia remains to be determined.

Occupational status also predicts agoraphobic avoidance, accounting for 18% of the variance: "the more one is forced to leave the house by means of employment, the less one is likely to suffer from agoraphobia" (de Jong & Bouman, 1995, p. 197). But perhaps the strongest predictor of agoraphobia is gender. As agoraphobia increases in severity, the proportion of females increases as well (e.g., Thyer et al., 1985). Socialized sex role expectations and behaviors may contribute to these effects, as socialization may reinforce activity, independence, and confrontation of feared stimuli and situations to a greater extent in boys than girls (Craske & Barlow, 1988; Craske 2003). Given the direct relevance of avoidance behaviors for the development of agoraphobia, the clinical implications are clear.

Interoceptive Avoidance

Strong sensitivity to and avoidance of the internal bodily symptoms associated with anxiety and panic is known as *interoceptive avoidance* (Rapee, Craske, & Barlow, 1995; Bouton, Mineka, & Barlow, 2001; White & Barlow, 2002). Behavioral manifestations include actions intended to minimize exposure to situations, substances, or activities that reproduce bodily sensations associated with symptoms of anxiety and/or panic attacks. Common examples include avoiding exercise, sex, caffeine, alcohol, wearing a necktie, watching arousing or scary movies, and situations that may produce anger. Assessing the specific interoceptive cues and situations Panic Disorder patients avoid is central to treatment.

Safety Behaviors

Safety behaviors are "behaviors which are intended to avoid *disaster*" (Salkovskis, Clark, Hackman, Wells, & Gelder, 1999, p. 573, italics in original). Within Panic Disorder, they are behaviors that help individuals feel more protected and secure in the

---

[2] Few individuals in the sample met *DSM-IV* criteria for social phobia (*n* = 1) or obsessive compulsive disorder (*n* = 4) (Kikuchi, 2005). Therefore, individuals with and without agoraphobia could not be compared on these anxiety disorders.

event of a panic attack (White & Barlow, 2002). Examples include checking to make sure that a bathroom or hospital is close by, taking one's pulse rate whenever cardiac concerns arise, and carrying cell phones, religious symbols, smelling salts, a special "safe" object, food or drink. Perhaps the most common safety behavior is carrying anti-anxiety medication, including empty pill bottles. Another widespread behavior is bringing along or checking on the location of a safe person, often a spouse, whose presence provides a sense of reassurance that facilitates venturing out to places that otherwise would be avoided. The "safe" person is generally considered as such because they know about the patient's panic attacks and can assist if the panic attack becomes overwhelming (White & Barlow, 2002).

Closely related to the concept of safety behaviors are safety signals, which refer to the safe objects, persons, and situations sought via safety behaviors. These include objects such as empty pill bottles, people such as the therapist or spouse, and situations such as the therapy room, which when present indicate that a given situation is safe from panic-related disaster. An extensive animal literature (see Hermans, Craske, Mineka, & Lovibond, 2006) demonstrates that the presence of safety signals functions as a conditioned inhibitor that interferes with extinction. Though somewhat limited methodologically, a few treatment studies indicate that exposure therapy targeting reductions of safety behaviors and signals is more successful than exposure therapy alone (Salkovskis et al., 1999; Telch, Sloan & Smits, 2000, as cited in Powers, Smits, & Telch, 2004). Also, the mere availability of safety signals rather than the actual use of them disrupted fear extinction in exposure treatment for claustrophobia (Powers, Smits and Telch). Hence, safety behaviors may reduce anxiety in the short term but likely serve to maintain Panic Disorder in the long term by preventing the disconfirmation of the patient's catastrophic predictions about panic (Salkovskis et al., 1999) and/or the extinction of the conditioned response (see Hermans et al., 2006).

Several investigators (Salkovskis et al., 1999; Thwaites & Freeston, 2005) have attempted to differentiate safety-seeking behaviors, which aim to prevent disaster, from adaptive coping strategies that aim to "reduce anxiety alone, with no further fears about the consequences of the anxiety" (Salkovskis et al., 1999, p. 573). However, as noted by Thwaites and Freeston (2005), this distinction is often blurry in practice. Perhaps the most general and clinically relevant definition of safety signals is any behavior intended to avert disasters associated with panic that inhibits corrective learning and eventual fear reduction of anxiety and panic-related stimuli.

Experiential Avoidance

Experiential avoidance occurs when an individual is "unwilling to remain in contact with particular private experiences [e.g., bodily sensations, emotions, thoughts, memories, behavioral predispositions] and takes steps to alter the form or frequency of these events and the contexts" in which they occur (Hayes et al., 1996, p. 1154). The types of avoidance discussed thus far, particularly interoceptive avoidance, also may be characterized as *experiential* avoidance. In addition, any form of distraction from anxiety- and panic-related symptoms falls under this category. Distraction behaviors include watching TV, playing video or computer games, and eating, among others. From the perspective of experiential avoidance, distraction represents an unwillingness to experience anxiety- and fear-related thoughts and emotions. Whether distraction interferes with exposure therapy for anxiety is a subject of debate (e.g., Devilly 2001a, 2001b versus Lipke, 2001; see also Rodriguez & Craske, 1993). However, several controlled, empirical studies (Rodriguez & Craske, 1995; Kamphuis & Telch, 2000; Telch et al., 2004) have found that distraction generally results in less effective fear reduction in the context of exposure therapy.

Experiential avoidance also includes avoidance and suppression of anxiety- and panic-related cognitions, such as "I'm having a heart attack." Evidence generally suggests that thought suppression has a negative impact. That is, thought suppression and to some extent emotional suppression have been shown to be relatively counterproductive, facilitating the return of the very thought or emotional arousal one hoped to avoid (Gross & Levenson, 1993, 1997; Wenzlaff & Wegner, 2000; Richards & Gross, 2000).

Researchers of experiential avoidance argue that psychopathology in general, including Panic Disorder, is caused and maintained by experiential avoidance. In other words, psychopathology stems from an unwillingness to experience whatever thoughts, feelings, memories, and so forth appear in the present (e.g., Hayes et al., 1996, 1999; Eifert & Forsyth, 2005). In claiming that altering thoughts is a form of avoidance, proponents of experiential avoidance argue against attempts to change or modify the content of anxiety- and panic-related thoughts, as is taught in traditional cognitive-behavioral therapy for Panic Disorder (see the following). They argue that psychopathology stems from unwillingness to accept and remain in contact with present experience. Hence, acceptance of inner experience (e.g., of anxiety- and panic-related thoughts, feelings, and sensations) is promoted over direct modification and change (Hayes et al, 2006; Eifert & Forsyth, 2005; Hayes et al, 1999).

COGNITIVE FEATURES OF PANIC DISORDER

Persons with Panic Disorder have strong beliefs and fears of physical or mental harm arising from bodily sensations that are associated with panic attacks (e.g., Chambless, Caputo, Bright, & Gallagher, 1984; McNally & Lorenz, 1987). They are more likely to interpret bodily sensations in a catastrophic fashion (Clark et al., 1988), and to allocate more attentional resources to words that represent physical threat, such as "disease" and "fatality" (e.g., Ehlers, Margraf, Davies, & Roth, 1988; Hope, Rapee, Heimberg, & Dombeck, 1990; Asmundson, Sandler, Wilson, & Walker, 1992) and catastrophe words, such as "death" and "insane" (e.g., Maidenberg, Chen, Craske, Bohn, & Bystritsky, 1996; McNally, Riemann, Louro, Lukach, & Kim, 1992). In one dot-probe study that used (what patients believed was) real heartbeat information rather than threat word stimuli, evidence for attentional bias toward the heartbeat stimuli was found in Panic Disorder patients but not healthy controls (Kroeze & van den Hout, 2000). Also, individuals with Panic Disorder are more likely to fear procedures that elicit bodily sensations similar to the ones experienced during panic attacks, including benign cardiovascular, respiratory, and audiovestibular exercises (Zarate, Rapee, Craske, & Barlow, 1988; Jacob, Furman, Clark, & Durrant, 1992) and carbon dioxide inhalations, compared to patients with other anxiety disorders (e.g., Rapee, 1986; Rapee, Brown, Antony, & Barlow, 1992; Perna, Bertani, Arancio, Ronchi, & Bellodi, 1995) or healthy controls (e.g., Gorman et al., 1994). Patients with Panic Disorder fear signals that ostensibly reflect heightened arousal and false physiological feedback (Ehlers, Margraf, Roth, Taylor, & Birnbaumer, 1988; Craske & Freed, 1995; Craske et al., 2002). The findings are not fully consistent, however, as patients with Panic Disorder did not differ from patients with Social Phobia in response to an epinephrine challenge (Veltman, Zijderveld, Tilders, & Dyck, 1996).

In addition, direct manipulation of appraisals can impact level of distress over physical symptoms. For example, persons with Panic Disorder and nonclinical panickers report significantly less fear and panic during laboratory-based panic provocation procedures, such as hyperventilation and carbon dioxide inhalation, when they perceive that the procedure is safe and/or controllable (e.g., Rapee, Mattick, & Murrell, 1986; Sanderson, Rapee, & Barlow, 1989), when accompanied by a safe person (Carter, Hollon, Carson, & Shelton, 1995), or after cognitive-behavioral treatment that reduces fears of bodily sensations (Craske, Lang, Aikins, & Mystkowski, 2005; Schmidt, Trakowski, & Staab, 1997). However, manipulations of predictability and controllability did not significantly affect frequency of panic responses among Panic Disorder patients in an epinephrine challenge study (Veltman, Zijderveld, van Dyck, & Bakker, 1998).

Individuals with Panic Disorder sometimes demonstrate memory abnormalities, although the results have been varied and contradictory. Studies of memory bias for physical threat and panic-related words include results supporting the existence of both implicit and explicit memory bias (Cloitre, Shear, Cancienne, & Zeitlin, 1994), explicit but not implicit memory bias (Lundh, Czyzykow, & Ost, 1997; Pauli, Dengler, & Wiedemann, 2005), implicit but not explicit memory bias (Neidhardt & Florin, 1999) and neither type of bias (Rapee, 1994; Baños, Medina & Pascual, 2001). Pauli and colleagues (2005) used event-related brain potentials to investigate implicit memory biases but found no differences between Panic Disorder patients and healthy controls. Differences in experimental methodology and context, instructional sets, sample size, sample demographic, and clinical characteristics may account for differences in these findings.

Recent studies have looked at dual versus single task memory in Panic Disorder patients and compared deficits in Panic Disorder to other anxiety disorders. Among inpatients with severe Panic Disorder (without co-occurring current or past disorders) Lautenbacher and associates (2002) found attentional deficits within a dual-task paradigm for divided attention, but not with a single-task paradigm for selective attention. These deficits also were seen among patients with severe depression (without co-occurring disorders) but not among healthy controls, suggesting that these two severe patient groups show similar deficits in tasks requiring high-attentional load. A small study of memory encoding for social threat and panic-related words found no memory differences between Panic Disorder and Social Phobia patients across various categories of threat encoding, including physical and social threat words (Heinrichs, Hofmann, & Barlow, 2004). The results, which await replication, suggest that threat may be encoded in more general rather than disorder-specific ways in these anxiety disorders. Alternatively, disorder-specific differences in memory encoding may require a larger sample size or more powerful manipulation of memory categories.

Studies utilizing event-related brain-potential EEG methodologies provide a more precise understanding of the time course of panic-related attentional and memory abnormalities. In contrast to healthy controls, panic patients failed to modulate prefrontal event-related brain potentials when responding to words with different affective connotations in a memory recognition task (Windmann, Sakhavat, & Kutas, 2002). The effect was found in the latency range of responding (300–500ms), which generally assumes greater influence of autonomic rather than controlled memory processes, but not at later processing stages (700ms+). Hence, the authors suggest that patients may "adopt conscious strategies to minimize the impact of these early processing abnormalities on overt behaviors" (p. 357). On a cautionary note, half of the patients had mild depression, making it unclear whether the results were due to panic- or depression-related functioning (or both). In a related set of findings, Pauli and colleagues (2005) found that panic patients—but not healthy controls—showed early enhanced brain potentials (at 100–200ms and 200 to 400ms) in response to panic-related words. The authors concluded that Panic Disorder may be characterized by an early, efficient, largely automatic processing bias toward panic-related stimuli.

Whereas event-related brain potential studies help identify the timing of cognitive processing abnormalities, fMRI brain imaging studies reveal their location. A small fMRI study of visual exposure to physical threat and neutral words (Maddock, Buonocore, Kile & Garrett, 2003), found that individuals with Panic Disorder showed greater activity in the left posterior cingulate and dorsolateral frontal cortices during threat words than healthy controls. The authors associated these brain regions with the link between affect and verbal memory processing, consistent with the notion of greater memory processing for threat-related words in Panic Disorder. However, memory for threat words was not tested directly. In an fMRI study of neuroanatomical correlates of the Stroop task across Panic Disorder, Obsessive-Compulsive Disorder (OCD), and hypochondriasis patient groups (van den Heuvel et al., 2005), panic patients showed activation patterns similar to hypochondriacal patients. Specifically, both patient groups displayed increased ventral and dorsal brain region activation, suggesting increased unconscious emotional processing as well as increased cognitive elaboration. The study generally did not find Panic Disorder-specific neuroanatomical correlates; rather, results differentiated a shared panic and hypochondriasis patient pattern from that of OCD patients. The grouping of results may reflect the exaggerated concern over body-related sensations shared by panic and hypochondriasis patients.

EMOTIONAL FEATURES OF PANIC DISORDER

The temperament variable most associated with anxiety disorders, including Panic Disorder, is neuroticism (Eysenck, 1967; Gray, 1982a, 1982b), or proneness to experience negative emotions in response to stressors. A closely linked construct is *negative affectivity*, or the tendency to experience an array of negative emotions across a variety of situations, even in the absence of objective stressors (Watson & Clark, 1984). Structural analyses confirm that negative affect is a higher-order factor that distinguishes each anxiety disorder and depression from controls with no mental disorder. The anxiety disorders load differentially on negative affectivity, with more pervasive anxiety disorders such as Generalized Anxiety Disorder loading more heavily, Panic Disorder loading at an intermediate level, and Social Anxiety Disorder loading the least (Brown et al., 1998).[3] Lower-order factors further discriminate among the anxiety disorders, with fear of fear being the factor that discriminates Panic Disorder from other anxiety disorders (Brown, Chorpita, & Barlow, 1998; Zinbarg & Barlow, 1996).

Longitudinal prospective evidence for the role of neuroticism in predicting the onset of Panic Disorder is relatively limited. However, neuroticism was found to predict the onset of panic *attacks* (Hayward, Killen, Kraemer, & Taylor, 2000; Schmidt, Lerew & Jackson, 1997, 1999), and emotional reactivity at age 3 was a significant variable in the

---

[3] Specific phobias were not assessed, but by being most circumscribed, SPs would be hypothesized to load the least on negative affectivity.

classification of Panic Disorder in 18- to 21-year-old males (Craske, Poulton, Tsao, & Plotkin, 2001). Ongoing studies, such as the Northwestern/UCLA Youth Emotion Project, are currently evaluating the relationships among neuroticism, various other risk factors, and Panic Disorder.

INTERACTION WITH ENVIRONMENTAL FACTORS

Environmental factors often interact with biologically and genetically related temper-amental factors to increase risk for anxiety disorders, including Panic Disorder. Several environmental factors are reviewed in the following. Early caregiving and parenting likely relate more to risk for psychopathology in general, whereas abuse and especially childhood experiences with illness may relate more specifically to Panic Disorder. Also, depending on their nature, life stressors may play a general or more direct role in the etiology and maintenance of Panic Disorder.

Early Caregiving and Infant Attachment

Emerging research supports the hypothesis that early experiences with infant care may play an important role in buffering or facilitating later proneness toward anxiety. Spe-cifically, early experiences with prediction and control may be associated with the de-velopment of adaptive emotional regulatory capacities in the face of negative stressors. In the context of emotional regulation in infants and children, prediction refers to a con-tingency (cause-effect) awareness of events in the environment as well as prediction of outcomes by virtue of one's own responding, and control refers to control over emotions and outcomes via one's own attention and behaviors (Craske, 2003). Evidence (e.g., Papousek & Papousek, 1997, 2002; Rochat & Striano, 1999) supports the assertion that parental monitoring and reactivity to infant signals enable infants to learn contingency-response relationships and hence, a sense of predictability. Initially, a sense of predict-ability may develop from the relationship between an infant's cues and the caretaker's response. Later, this may transfer to contingency knowledge of the relationship between an infant's own behaviors and responses (see Craske, 2003). According to attachment pioneer Bowlby (1969, 1980), caregiver responses that are characterized by unpredict-ability and unresponsiveness may lead to anxious attachment in which the child is chronically insecure and apprehensive.

However, this theorizing remains largely speculative since experimentally manipulat-ing predictability and control for extended periods of time in infant humans is not ethi-cally possible. Hence, the most compelling evidence of the effects of prolonged lack of predictability and control in infants comes from research with rhesus monkeys. Mineka, Gunnar, and Champoux (1986) demonstrated that infant rhesus monkeys who were granted control over toys and food habituated more quickly to novel stimuli, demon-strated more exploratory behavior in a novel playroom, and demonstrated enhanced coping responses during separation from peers compared to infants without control (but with equal exposure) over toys and food. In the same sample, administration of benzo-diazepine inhibitors resulted in increased distress and avoidance among the no control group, whereas the control group showed greater aggression. Mineka and Cook (1986) concluded that experiences with mastery and control buffer the effects of stressful expe-riences. Longitudinal studies of very young children are needed to more directly estab-lish the link between early caregiving, predictability, controllability, and subsequent stress reactivity.

Parenting

The literature on infant attachment (Bowlby 1969, 1980) and developmental models of anxiety (Craske, 1999, 2003) predicts that anxious, insecure attachment between caregiver and infant predict chronic emotional regulatory difficulties, including anxiety. General parental styles across situations may contribute to childhood trait anxiety, whereas situationally specific parental behaviors may contribute to the development of particular anxiety disorders in children (Craske, 1999). Although many previous studies examining these hypotheses are fraught with methodological difficulties, more recent studies on parent-child interactions with anxious children and/or anxious parents have been more informative. Though not specific to Panic Disorder, the research on parenting illuminates one risk factor for anxiety disorders in general.

One interesting line of studies examines children's current perceptions of their parents' behavior. Generally, children of anxious parents view their families as more conflictual, less independent, less cohesive, and more controlling than children with healthy, nonanxious parents (see Whaley, Pinto, & Sigman, 1999). In addition, children with anxiety disorders view their families as less independence promoting than nonanxious children. Another study has demonstrated that perceptions of low maternal caring and overprotectiveness were highest among children with anxiety disorders, slightly lower among high trait anxious children and lowest among low trait anxious children (Bennet & Stirling, 1998). These studies, however, are limited by reliance on self-report measures and cross-sectional designs, and they only assess influences of state anxiety on perceptions of family functioning (see Craske, 2003; Wood, McLeod, Sigman, Hwang, & Chu, 2003). Thus, little conclusive evidence exists for linking self-reported parenting style to offspring anxiety (Wood et al., 2003).

A more reliable body of research relies on behavioral coding of observed parent-child interactions. Fortunately, the findings generally converge with the self-report data. A descriptive review by Wood et al. (2003) concluded that observed parental control during parent-child interactions (defined as overprotectiveness, excessive regulation of activities, routines, and decision making) consistently was associated with child shyness and childhood anxiety disorders. Of note, the Wood et al. review did not include a study by Woodruff-Borden, Morrow, Bourland, & Cambron (2002), which found that parents with anxiety disorders were less engaged and more withdrawn though not more controlling than nonanxious parents. Wood et al. (2003) found mixed evidence for associations between parental acceptance (e.g., warmth, praise, active listening, responsiveness) and modeling of anxious behaviors (e.g., catastrophizing, emphasizing danger/threat, punishing coping behaviors) and childhood anxiety. Finally, Wood et al. (2003) concluded that the directionality and hence causality of the parent-child interactions remains to be determined. Furthermore, the specificity of parental behaviors to risk for anxiety disorders has not yet been demonstrated.

Hudson and Rapee (2001) have suggested that overinvolvement may represent a general parenting response to children who tend toward distress and psychopathology rather than to anxious children in particular. However, more evidence is needed to elucidate disparate findings. For example, Hudson and Rapee observed that mothers of anxious children were more negative, overinvolved, and intrusive than mothers of nonanxious control children. Similar to several other studies (e.g., Hibbs, Hamburger, Kruesi, & Lenane, 1993; but see Stubbe, Zahner, Goldstein, & Leckman, 1993, for the opposite finding), they failed to find a difference in maternal behaviors toward children with anxiety disorders versus children with oppositional disorders. Perhaps the most thorough attempt at disentangling the impact of child and maternal anxiety in a clinical sample is work by Whaley and Sigman (Whaley, Pinto & Sigman, 1999; Moore, Whaley, & Sigman, 2004). In comparison with nonanxious control mothers, anxious mothers were observed to criticize and catastrophize more, and to display less warmth and autonomy-granting toward their children. Maternal behaviors predicted children's anxiety levels, and children's anxiety levels predicted maternal autonomy-granting (Whaley et al., 1999). Finally, mothers of anxiety-disordered children, regardless of their own anxiety status, displayed less warmth and autonomy-granting (Moore et al., 2004). Though limited by cross-sectional design, these findings support an interactive model in which parenting behaviors predict offspring anxiety and offspring anxiety molds parenting behaviors.

Childhood Experiences with Illness and Abuse

Childhood experience with medical illness, personally or via observing others, may increase the risk for the subsequent development of anxiety disorders in general and Panic Disorder in particular. Experience with personal respiratory disturbance and parental illness in childhood predicted Panic Disorder onset at ages 18 or 21 in a large, longitudinal sample (Craske et al., 2001). This finding is consistent with reports of more respiratory disturbance in the history of Panic Disorder patients compared to other anxiety-disordered patients (Verburg, Griez, Meijer & Pols, 1995). Furthermore, a recent study found that first-degree relatives of Panic Disorder patients had a significantly higher prevalence of chronic obstructive respiratory disease and asthma, in particular, compared with first-degree relatives of patients with other anxiety disorders (van Beek, Schruers, & Friez, 2005).

Childhood experiences of sexual and physical abuse may also prime Panic Disorder. Retrospective reports of childhood abuse were associated with Panic Disorder onset at ages 16–21 in a recent longitudinal analysis of New Zealanders from birth to age 21 (Goodwin et al., 2005), a finding consistent with multiple cross-sectional studies in both clinical and community samples (e.g., Bandelow et al., 2002; Kendler et al., 2000; Kessler et al., 1997; Stein et al., 1996; Moisan & Engels, 1995). The link with childhood abuse was stronger for Panic Disorder than for other anxiety disorders such as Social Phobia (Safren et al., 2002; Stein et al., 1996) and Obsessive-Compulsive Disorder (Stein et al., 1996). In addition, some studies found an association between Panic Disorder and exposure to violence between other family members, usually interparental violence (e.g., Moisan & Engels, 1995; Bandelow et al., 2002), whereas the most recent study did not (Goodwin et al., 2005). Retrospective reporting of childhood abuse in all of these studies, however, limits their findings.

Stress

The relationship between external aversive events, also known as *stressful* events, and Panic Disorder has several facets. First, temperamental vulnerabilities, such as neuroticism, may contribute to more frequent and more potent stressful life events (Craske, 2003). Second, stressful life events may precipitate initial panic attacks and contribute to their repeated occurrence over time: As described earlier, a large percentage of individuals with Panic Disorder report the presence of identifiable stressors around the time of the first panic attack (Craske et. al., 1990; Faravelli & Pallanti, 1989; Pollard et al., 1989; Roy-Byrne, Geraci, & Uhde, 1986; although see Rapee, Litwin,

& Barlow, 1990 for contradictory findings). As alluded to earlier, significant child-hood adversity and stressful life events are both associated with increased risk for anxiety disorders as well as other psychopathology (Benjamin, Costello, & Warren, 1990; Brown, Harris, & Eales, 1993; Kessler et al., 1997). In addition, variations in anxiety symptom levels over time are influenced by life stress and other environmental factors (Mackinnon, Henderson, & Andrews, 1990). In addition, life stressors over multiple months and years predicted later anxious and depressive symptoms in adult (Cohen, McGowan, Fooskas, & Rose, 1984) though not adolescent samples (Cohen, Burt, & Bjork, 1987; Rueter, Scaramella, Wallace, & Conger, 1999).

A stress-diathesis perspective would hypothesize that stressful life events interact with preexisting vulnerabilities to produce panic attacks and Panic Disorder. For example, autonomic instability (e.g., the tendency to experience cardiac symptoms and shortness of breath) may develop into full-blown panic when instances occur in threatening contexts or following life stressors, when the sensations are more likely to be perceived as threatening (Craske, 1999). According to Bouton, Mineka, and Barlow (2001), evidence suggests that high anxiety elevates the likelihood of panic attacks. Hence, stressful life events may elevate levels of anxiety, particularly in vulnerable individuals, which in turn, increases the risk for panic. From a related perspective, a recent epidemiological study in a Russian sample examined the interaction of anxiety sensitivity, or the tendency to interpret anxiety symptoms as dangerous and threatening, and recent exposure to stressful life events (Zvolensky, Kotov, Antipova, & Schmidt, 2005). The study found that high levels of stressful life events interacted with a subscale of anxiety sensitivity (the physical concerns subscale) to predict panic attacks in the past week, and agoraphobic avoidance, beyond levels of negative affect. Their findings are consistent with a stress-diathesis model. However, the general notion of stress-diathesis does not offer specificity in the etiology of Panic Disorder relative to other anxiety disorders.

ETIOLOGICAL MODELS OF PANIC DISORDER

Barlow (1988; Barlow, Chorpita, & Turovsky, 1996) characterizes panic attacks as "false alarms," in which a fight-or-flight response is triggered in the absence of threatening stimuli. False alarms in the form of panic attacks occur relatively commonly in the general, nonclinical population (e.g., Wittchen & Essau, 1991; Norton, Cox, & Malan, 1992). This finding begs the question: What accounts for the difference between the majority of individuals, who display little to no distress over panic attacks, versus the minority, who develop Panic Disorder?

As described earlier, neuroticism is viewed as a higher-order factor characteristic of all anxiety disorders, with fear of fear being more singular to Panic Disorder. The construct of fear of fear overlaps with the construct of anxiety sensitivity, or the belief that anxiety and its associated symptoms may cause deleterious physical, social, and psychological consequences that extend beyond any immediate physical discomfort during an episode of anxiety or panic (Reiss, 1980). Anxiety sensitivity is elevated across most anxiety disorders, but it is particularly elevated in Panic Disorder (e.g., Taylor, Koch, & McNally, 1992; Zinbarg & Barlow, 1996), especially the physical concerns subscale (Zinbarg, Barlow, & Brown, 1997; Zinbarg & Barlow, 1996). Therefore, beliefs that physical symptoms of anxiety are harmful seem to be particularly relevant to Panic Disorder.

Anxiety sensitivity may be acquired insidiously from a lifetime of direct aversive experiences (such as personal history of significant illness or injury), vicarious observations (such as exposure to significant illnesses or death among family members, or family members who display fear of body sensations through hypochondriasis), and/or informational transmissions (such as parental warnings or overprotectiveness regarding physical well being; Craske & Rowe, 1997). In support, Watt, Stewart, and Cox (1998) reported that levels of anxiety sensitivity in young adulthood were positively correlated with retrospectively reported instrumental and vicarious conditioning experiences in childhood. Specifically, individuals with high anxiety sensitivity reported more learning experiences related to anxiety symptoms in the form of parental reinforcement (instrumental) and parental modeling (classical). Similarly, Watt and Stewart (2000) found that elevated anxiety sensitivity related to retrospectively reported parental responses to somatic symptoms in general but not specifically to anxiety-related symptoms. Unfortunately, data from all of these studies are retrospective and thus vulnerable to biased recall.

Anxiety sensitivity is posited to be a risk factor for Panic Disorder because it primes reactivity to bodily sensations. Consistent with this view is the finding that anxiety sensitivity predicts subjective distress and reported symptomatology in response to procedures that induce strong physical sensations such as carbon dioxide inhalation (Forsyth, Palav, & Duff, 1999), balloon inflation (Messenger & Shean, 1998), and hyperventilation (Sturges, Goetsch, Ridley, & Whittal, 1998), in nonclinical samples, even after controlling for the effects of trait anxiety (Rapee & Medoro, 1994). In addition, several longitudinal studies indicate that high scores on the Anxiety Sensitivity Index predict the onset of panic attacks over 1- to 4-year intervals in adolescents (Hayward, Killen, Kraemer, & Taylor, 2000), college students (Maller & Reiss, 1992), and community samples with specific phobias or no anxiety disorders (Ehlers, 1995). The predictive relationship remains after controlling for prior depression (Hayward, Killen, Kraemer & Taylor, 2000). In addition, Anxiety Sensitivity Index scores predicted spontaneous panic attacks and worry about panic during an acute military stressor (i.e., 5 weeks of basic training), even after controlling for history of panic attacks and trait anxiety (Schmidt, Lerew, & Jackson, 1997, 1999).

However, Bouton et al. (2001) argue that the relationship between anxiety sensitivity and panic attacks in these studies is relatively small, not exclusive to panic, and is weaker than the relationship between panic and general neuroticism. Furthermore, these studies have not evaluated the prediction of the development of full Panic Disorder as opposed to panic attacks.

Two other models offer accounts for the persistence of fear of bodily sensations. The first model, put forth primarily by Clark (1986, 1988, 1996) is cognitive in nature. Clark and others (e.g., Salkovskis, 1988) argue that catastrophic misappraisals of bodily sensations, including misinterpretation of panic- and anxiety-related bodily sensations as signs of imminent death, craziness, loss of control, and so forth, are central to the development and maintenance of Panic Disorder. As reviewed earlier, there is extensive evidence that persons with Panic Disorder judge certain bodily sensations to be detrimental. However, Bouton et al. (2001) take issue with Clark's cognitive misappraisal model for multiple reasons, including the fact that the model cannot account for panic attacks that lack conscious cognitive appraisal (e.g., nocturnal panic), without becoming untestable. They also note that although catastrophic cognitions often occur in panic patients, they do not necessarily play a causal role in

Panic Disorder. Finally, Bouton et al. (2001) critique the cognitive model for not specifying how and when such cognitions are acquired and for whom and under what circumstances they become catastrophic.

The second model was initially put forth by Eysenck more than four decades ago (Eysenck 1960); Eysenck & Rachman, 1965), expanded by Goldstein and Chambless (1978) and recently brought up-to-date by Bouton et al. (2001). This model emphasizes interoceptive conditioning, or the process by which low-level somatic sensations of arousal or anxiety (e.g., elevated heart rate or perspiration) become conditioned stimuli due to their association with intense fear, pain, or distress (Razran, 1961). In the context of Panic Disorder, the result is that early somatic components of the anxiety response come to elicit significant bursts of anxiety or panic. An extensive body of experimental literature attests to the robustness of interoceptive conditioning (e.g., Dworkin & Dworkin, 1999), particularly with regard to early interoceptive drug onset cues becoming conditioned stimuli for larger drug effects (e.g., Sokolowska, Siegel, & Kim, 2002). In addition, interoceptive conditioned responses are not dependent on conscious awareness of triggering cues (Razran, 1961) and are observed even under anesthesia in animals (e.g., Lennartz & Weinberger, 1992; Shibuki, Hamamura, & Yagi, 1984; Uno, 1970) and humans (e.g., Block, Ghoneim, Fowles, Kumar, & Pathak, 1987). Within this model, slight changes in relevant bodily functions that are not consciously recognized may elicit conditioned fear and panic due to previous pairings with the terror of panic (Barlow, 1988; Bouton, Mineka, & Barlow, 2001). Nevertheless, some researchers argue that the acquisition of interoceptive conditioned responding requires conscious awareness (Irie, Maeda, & Nagata, 2001; Lovibond & Shanks, 2002).

Expanding on this view, Bouton et al. (2001) argue that the similarity between conditioned and unconditioned stimuli creates very strong, easily conditioned responses, as occurs when initial bodily symptoms of panic (conditioned stimulus) signal the rest of the panic attack (unconditioned stimulus). Drawing on the extensive animal and human learning literature, they explain that interoceptive cues do not always produce conditioned panic due to factors such as the presence of safety signals and context effects (e.g., performance in one context does not always generalize to performance in another context). In addition, they cite evidence from Öhman and Mineka (2001) and others (e.g., LeDoux, 1996) to argue against the notion that conditioning necessarily involves propositional knowledge and cognitive awareness. Rather, Bouton et al. (2001) argue that catastrophic misappraisals may accompany panic attacks because they are part of the range of responses linked to panic or because they have been encouraged or reinforced. Such thoughts may become conditioned stimuli that trigger anxiety or they may simply be part of the conditioned response to anxiety- and panic-related cues.

Assessment of Panic Disorder

INTERVIEWS

An in-depth interview is the first step in establishing diagnostic and behavioral-cognitive profiles. The value of structured interviews lies in their contribution to differential diagnosis and interrater reliability. Several semi- and fully structured interviews exist. The Schizophrenia and Affective Disorders Schedule-Life Time Version (Anxiety Modified) produces reliable diagnoses for most of the anxiety disorders (Generalized Anxiety Disorder and simple phobia being the exceptions; Manuzza et al., 1989), as does the Structured Clinical Interview for *DSM-IV,* which covers all of the mental disorders (First, Spitzer, Gibbon, & Williams, 1994). However, the semistructured interview that most specifically focuses on assessment and differential diagnosis among the anxiety disorders is the Anxiety Disorders Interview Schedule-Fourth Edition (ADIS-IV; DiNardo, Brown, & Barlow, 1994). In addition to its primary focus on anxiety disorders, the ADIS-IV also evaluates mood disorders and somatoform disorders, as well as screens for psychotic and drug conditions. Differential diagnosis among the anxiety disorders is sometimes difficult because, as described earlier, panic is a ubiquitous phenomenon (Barlow, 1988), occurring across a wide variety of emotional disorders. It is not uncommon for persons with specific phobias, Generalized Anxiety Disorder, Obsessive-Compulsive Disorder, and Posttraumatic Stress Disorder to report panic attacks. Hence, the ADIS-IV facilitates a reliable method of gathering information to make differential diagnoses among the anxiety disorders and also offers the ability to distinguish between clinical and subclinical presentations of a disorder. Interrater agreement ranges from satisfactory to excellent for the various anxiety disorders using this instrument (Brown, DiNardo, Lehman, & Campbell, 2001).

CLINICAL RATING SCALES

There are no clinical rating scales specific to Panic Disorder and agoraphobia. However, a clinical rating of severity of distress and disablement (CSR; 0 = not at all, 8 = extreme) is often made based on the information gathered from the diagnostic interview. A CSR rating of 4 or higher indicates that the individual meets diagnostic criteria for a given disorder and evidences clinically significant distress and/or disablement stemming from the disorder. With proper training procedures, adequate reliabilities have been demonstrated for clinical severity ratings from the ADIS-IV interview (Brown, DiNardo, Lehman, & Campbell, 2001).

SELF-REPORT AND BEHAVIORAL MEASURES

Several standardized self-report inventories provide useful information for treatment planning, as well as being sensitive markers of therapeutic change. The Anxiety Sensitivity Index (Reiss, Peterson, Gursky, & McNally, 1986) has received wide acceptance as a trait measure of threatening beliefs about bodily sensations. It has good psychometric properties and tends to discriminate Panic Disorder from other types of anxiety disorders (e.g., Taylor, Koch, & McNally, 1992; Telch, Sherman, & Lucas, 1989). More specific information about which particular bodily sensations are feared the most, and what specific misappraisals occur most often, can be obtained from the Body Sensations and Agoraphobia Cognitions Questionnaires (Chambless, Caputo, Bright & Gallagher, 1984). Extensive psychometric and clinical research indicates that these questionnaires show strong psychometric properties (Chambless et al., & Arrindell, 1993), discriminate between individuals with panic and agoraphobia versus other anxiety disorders (Chambless & Gracely, 1989), and are sensitive to change following treatment (Chambless et al., 1984). Fears of interoceptive stimuli (e.g, caffeine, exercise) can be measured by the Albany Panic and Phobia Questionnaire, which has demonstrated good to excellent Cronbach alphas and adequate test-retest reliability (Rapee, Craske, & Barlow, 1995). The Mobility Inventory (Chambless, Caputo, Jasin, Gracely, & Williams, 1985) lists agoraphobic situations that are rated based on degree of avoidance, when alone, and when accompanied. This instrument is useful for establishing in vivo exposure hierarchies. Finally, Newman and colleagues (2006) recently developed the Panic Disorder Self-Report (PDSR), a self-report diagnostic measure based on *DSM-IV* Panic Disorder criteria. The PDSR demonstrates excellent sensitivity and specificity in diagnosing Panic Disorder, strong agreement with a structured diagnostic interview, and good retest reliability and convergent and discriminant validity (Newman et al., 2006).

Behavioral Tests

The behavioral test is a useful measure of degree of avoidance of specific situations. Behavioral approach tests can be standardized or individually tailored. The standardized behavioral test for agoraphobia usually involves walking or driving a particular route, such as a 1-mile loop around the clinic setting. Anxiety levels are rated at regular intervals and actual distance walked/driven is measured. The disadvantage is that the specific task may not be relevant to all clients, and hence, the value of individually tailored tasks that usually entail attempts at three to five individualized situations that the client has identified as being anywhere from somewhat to extremely difficult. These might include driving two exits on a freeway, waiting in a bank line, or shopping in a local supermarket for 15 minutes. Maximum levels of anxiety and degree of approach (i.e., refused task, attempted but escaped from task, or completed task) are assessed for each situation. Individually tailored behavioral tests are more informative for clinical practice, although they confound between-subject comparisons for research purposes. Standardized behavioral tests for individuals with Panic Disorder target interoceptive sensations and typically include exercises such as spinning, running in place, and hyperventilating. As with the behavioral tests for agoraphobia, anxiety levels are recorded continuously along with the duration for which the client continued each exercise.

Standardized and individually tailored behavioral tests are susceptible to demand biases for fear and avoidance prior to treatment and for improvement after treatment (Borkovec, Weerts, & Bernstein, 1977). On the other hand, behavioral tests are an important supplement to self-report of agoraphobic avoidance because clients tend to underestimate what they can actually achieve (Craske, Rapee, & Barlow, 1988). In addition, behavioral tests often reveal information of which the individual is not fully aware, and yet is important for treatment planning. For example, the safety-seeking behavior of remaining close to supports such as railings or walls may not be apparent until observing the client walk through a shopping mall.

ONGOING ASSESSMENT

Self-monitoring is a very important part of assessment and treatment for Panic Disorder and agoraphobia. Retrospective recall of past episodes of panic and anxiety, especially when made under anxious conditions, may inflate estimates of panic frequency and intensity (Margraf et al., 1987; Rapee, Craske, & Barlow, 1990). Moreover, such inflation may contribute to apprehension about future panic. Thus, to the degree that ongoing self-monitoring yields more accurate, less inflated estimates, it is a therapeutic tool (see

Craske & Tsao, 1999, for a comprehensive review of self-monitoring for panic and anxiety). Also, ongoing self-monitoring is believed to contribute to increased objective self-awareness that is essential to cognitive behavioral therapy approaches.

To assess the course and rate of change in treatment, as well as to investigate the mechanisms or mediators by which a given treatment exerts its effects (see Kraemer et al., 2002), it also is important to include psychometrically sound assessment of anxiety symptoms during treatment. Ongoing measures, also known as *process measures,* can be administered to patients at regular intervals during treatment to assess changes in panic symptomology. The Anxiety Sensitivity Index (Reiss et al., 1986) is one example of an appropriate symptom process measure for treatment of panic disorder. Finally, particularly at treatment follow-up, assessments may benefit from including broader quality of life (QOL) measures that capture the wider impact of Panic Disorder treatment. For example, the Quality of Life Inventory (Frisch, Cornell, Villanueva, & Retzlaff, 1992) assesses seventeen domains including the quality of clients' family relationships, friendships, and sense of meaning and life direction, whereas the frequently used, well-validated SF–36 (Ware, 1993; McHorney, Ware, & Raczek, 1993) assesses physical functioning, mental health, social functioning, vitality, and general health.

Neurobiological Assessment

A medical evaluation is generally recommended because several medical conditions should be ruled out before assigning the diagnosis of Panic Disorder and agoraphobia. These include thyroid conditions, caffeine or amphetamine intoxication, drug withdrawal, or pheochromocytoma (a rare, adrenal gland tumor). Furthermore, certain medical conditions can exacerbate Panic Disorder and agoraphobia, although panic and agoraphobia are likely to continue even when they are under medical control. Mitral valve prolapse, asthma, allergies, and hypoglycemia fall into this category. These medical conditions exacerbate Panic Disorder and agoraphobia to the extent that they elicit the types of physical sensations that are feared. For example, mitral valve prolapse sometimes produces the sensation of a heart flutter, asthma produces shortness of breath, and hypoglycemia produces dizziness and weakness.

Ongoing physiological measures are not very practical tools for clinicians, but can provide important information. In particular, the discrepancy described earlier between reports of symptoms and actual physiological arousal can serve as a therapeutic demonstration of the role of attention and appraisal in symptom production. Similarly, actual recordings provide data to disconfirm misappraisals such as "my heart feels like its going so fast that it will explode" or "I'm sure my blood pressure is so high that I could have a stroke at any minute." Finally, baseline levels of physiological functioning, which are sometimes dysregulated in anxious individuals, may be sensitive measures of treatment outcome (e.g., Craske et al., 2005).

Interventions

PSYCHOLOGICAL

The most widely studied and validated psychotherapeutic treatment for Panic Disorder is cognitive-behavioral therapy (CBT) in its various forms. The two major forms of CBT have been Barlow and Craske's Panic Control Treatment (PCT), and Clark's cognitive therapy for panic. Both treatments emphasize components of psychoeducation about panic to correct misconceptions regarding panic symptoms, cognitive restructuring to identify and correct distortions in thinking, and interoceptive exposure to feared bodily sensations (e.g., palpitations, dyspnea, dizziness) and in vivo exposure to feared situations (e.g., unfamiliar areas, driving) to obtain corrective information that disconfirms fearful misappraisals and eventually lessens fear responding. Breathing retraining as a means for helping patients cope with panic and anxiety is sometimes included. Although PCT and Clark's cognitive therapy for Panic Disorder have not been directly compared, the major difference lies in the reliance of PCT on both cognitive and conditioning models, with behavioral exposure functioning as a primary agent of therapeutic change. In Clark's model, cognitive models are more central and behavioral exposure serves as a vehicle for cognitive change.

Results for both of these forms of CBT typically yield panic-free rates in the range of 70% to 80% of those treated and high end-state rates (i.e., within normative ranges of functioning) in the range of 50% to 70% (e.g., Barlow, Craske, Cerny, & Klosko, 1989; Clark et al., 1994). Two meta-analyses reported very large effect sizes of 1.55 and 0.90 for CBT for panic disorder (Mitte, 2005; Westen & Morrison, 2001). Also, results generally are maintained over follow-up intervals for as long as 2 years (Craske, Brown, & Barlow, 1991). This contrasts with the higher relapse rates typically found with medication approaches to the treatment of panic disorder, particularly high-potency benzodiazepines (e.g., Gould, Otto & Pollack, 1995). One analysis of individual profiles over time suggested a less optimistic picture, in that one third of clients who were panic-free 24 months after CBT had experienced a panic attack in the preceding year, and 27% had sought additional treatment for panic over that same interval of time (Brown & Barlow, 1995). Nevertheless, this approach to analysis did not take into account the general trend toward continuing improvement over time. Thus, rates of eventual therapeutic success may be underestimated when success is defined by continuous panic-free status since the end of active treatment.

The effectiveness of CBT extends to patients who experience nocturnal panic attacks (Craske et al., 2005). Also, CBT has proven very helpful in lowering relapse rates upon discontinuation of high-potency benzodiazapines (e.g., Otto, Pollack, Sachs, Reiter, Meltzer-Brody, & Rosenbaum, 1993; Spiegel, Bruce, Gregg, & Nuzzarello, 1994). Moreover, treatment is effective even when there is comorbidity; indeed, some studies indicate that comorbidity does not reduce the effectiveness of CBT for Panic Disorder (e.g., Brown, Antony, & Barlow, 1995; McLean et al., 1998). Furthermore, CBT results in improvements in comorbid conditions (Brown, Antony & Barlow, 1995; Tsao, Lewin, & Craske, 1998; Tsao, Mystkowski, Zucker, & Craske, 2002, 2005). In other words, co-occurring symptoms of depression and other anxiety disorders tend to improve after CBT for panic disorder. However, one study assessing patients 2 years after treatment suggests that the benefits for comorbid conditions may lessen over time (Brown et al., 1995). Nonetheless, the general finding of improvement in comorbidity suggests the value of remaining focused on Panic Disorder treatment even when comorbidity is present, since the comorbidity will be benefited as well (for at least up to 1 year). In fact, there is preliminary evidence to suggest that attempting to simultaneously address panic disorder along with comorbidity (using CBT, tailored to each disorder) may be less effective on average than remaining focused on Panic Disorder (Craske et al., in press), although this finding is in need of replication.

Generally, CBT for agoraphobia involves more situational exposure than CBT for Panic Disorder alone. Randomized controlled studies of CBT for agoraphobia generally yield slightly less effective results than CBT for Panic Disorder with no or minimal agoraphobia (e.g., Williams & Falbo, 1996). Nonetheless, the trends suggest continuing improvement over time, after CBT is over. Furthermore, Fava, Zielezny, Savron, and Grandi (1995) found that only 18.5% of their panic-free clients relapsed over a period of 5 to 7 years after exposure-based treatment for agoraphobia. Some research suggests that the trend for improvement after acute treatment is facilitated by involvement of significant others in every aspect of treatment (e.g., Cerny, Barlow, Craske, & Himadi, 1987). Recently, an intensive 8-day treatment, using a sensation-focused PCT approach was developed for individuals with moderate to severe agoraphobia, and initial results are promising (Morissette, Spiegel, & Neinrichs, 2005).

Attempts have been made to dismantle the different components of CBT for panic and agoraphobia. The results are somewhat confusing, and depend on the samples used (e.g., mild versus severe levels of agoraphobia) and the exact comparisons made. It appears that the cognitive therapy component may be effective (e.g., Williams & Falbo, 1996) even when conducted in full isolation from exposure and behavioral procedures (e.g., Salkovskis, Clark, & Hackman, 1991), and is more effective than applied relaxation with exposure (e.g., Arntz & van den Hout, 1996; Clark et al., 1994). On the other hand, some studies find that cognitive therapy does not improve outcome when added to in vivo exposure treatment for agoraphobia (e.g., van den Hout, Arntz, & Hoekstra, 1994; Rijken, Kraaimaat, Ruiter, & Garssen, 1992). A recent meta-analysis (Chambless & Peterman, 2004) found no differences between CBT and behavioral therapies in the treatment of Panic Disorder. It appears that exposure alone, without the aid of tools such as cognitive restructuring or relaxation training, is effective for Panic Disorder and agoraphobia (e.g. Rijken, Kraaimaat, de Ruiter, & Garssen, 1992; van den Hout, Arntz, & Hoekstra, 1994). Another study found that breathing skills training and repeated interoceptive exposure to hyperventilation did not improve outcome beyond in vivo exposure alone for agoraphobia (de Beurs, van Balkom, Lange, Koele, & van Dyke, 1995), and we found that breathing skills training was slightly less effective than interoceptive exposure when each was added to cognitive restructuring (Craske, Rowe, Lewin, Noriega-Dimitri, 1997). Clearly, more dismantling research is needed.

Group formats appear to be as effective as individual treatment formats for CBT for panic and agoraphobia (Neron, Lacroix, & Chaput, 1995; Lidren et al., 1994). One possible exception is that individual, one-to-one formats may be better in the long term with respect to symptoms of generalized anxiety and depression (Neron et al., 1995). However, more direct comparison between group and individual formats is warranted before firm conclusions can be made.

Most of the Panic Disorder treatment studies described in the previous sections averaged around 11 to 12 treatment sessions. Four to six sessions of PCT (Craske, Maidenberg, & Bystritsky, 1995; Roy-Byrne et al., 2005) seemed effective also, although the results were not as strong as those typically seen with 11 or 12 treatment sessions. On the other hand, another study demonstrated equally effective results when delivering CBT for Panic Disorder across the standard 12 sessions versus approximately 6 sessions (Clark, Salkovskis, Hackmann, Wells, Ludgate, & Gelder, 1999), and a pilot study has indicated good effectiveness with intensive CBT over two days (Deacon & Abramowitz, 2006).

Self-directed treatments, with minimal direct therapist contact, are very beneficial to highly motivated and educated clients (e.g., Ghosh & Marks, 1987; Gould & Clum, 1995; Gould, Clum, & Shapiro, 1993). Computerized versions of CBT for Panic Disorder now exist. Computer-assisted and Internet versions of CBT are effective for Panic Disorder (e.g., Richards, Klein, & Carlbring, 2003). In one study, a 4-session computer-assisted CBT for Panic Disorder was less effective than a 12-session PCT at posttreatment, although they were equally effective at follow-up (Newman, Kenardy, Herman, & Taylor, 1997). However, findings from computerized programs for emotional disorders in general indicate that such treatments are more acceptable and successful when they are combined with therapist involvement (e.g., Carlbring, Ekselius, & Andersson, 2003).

BIOLOGICAL

Based on 19 placebo-controlled randomized clinical trials (Roy-Byrne & Cowley, 2002), SSRIs are the medication treatment of choice for Panic Disorder. Meta-analyses and reviews have reported medium to large effect sizes compared to placebo (e.g., Mitte, 2005; Bakker, van Balkom, & Spinhoven, 2002). The majority of trials have been short term, although several have examined and confirmed longer-term efficacy up to 1 year.

Benzodiazepines are effective agents for Panic Disorder as well. They work rapidly, within days to 1 week, and are even better tolerated than the very tolerable SSRI class of agents. However, they are limited by their risk of physiologic dependence and withdrawal, and the risk of abuse (Roy-Byrne & Cowley, 2002)

Numerous studies show clearly that discontinuation of medication results in relapse in a significant proportion of patients, with placebo-controlled discontinuation studies showing rates between 25% and 50% within 6 months, depending on study design (Roy-Byrne & Cowley, 2002). In addition, SSRIs, SNRIs, and benzodiazepines are associated with a time-limited withdrawal syndrome (considerably worse for the benzodiazepines), which itself may serve as an interoceptive stimulus that promotes or contributes to Panic Disorder relapse.

In terms of comparison between pharmacological and psychological approaches, a recent meta-analysis of 21 randomized trials involving over 1,700 patients with Panic Disorder With or Without Agoraphobia clearly showed that combined treatment with antidepressants and psychotherapy (behavior, CBT and "other") was superior to antidepressant alone and to psychotherapy alone in the acute phase (Furukawa, Watanabe, & Churchill, 2006). After treatment discontinuation, combined treatment was superior to medication only but was not different from psychotherapy alone, and specifically CBT alone. Furthermore, following medication discontinuation, the combination of medication and CBT fared worse than CBT alone, suggesting the possibility that state- or context-dependent learning in the presence of medication may have attenuated the new learning that occurs during CBT.

Findings from the combination of fast-acting anxiolytics, especially the high-potency benzodiazepines, with behavioral treatments for Panic Disorder With Agoraphobia are contradictory (e.g., Marks et al., 1993; Wardle, Hayward, Higgitt, Stabl, Blizard, & Gray, 1994). Nevertheless, several studies reliably show detrimental effects from chronic, naturalistic use of benzodiazepines on short-term and long-term outcome from cognitive-behavioral treatments for panic or agoraphobia (e.g., Fava et al., 2001; Otto, Pollack, & Sabatino, 1996; van Balkom, de Beurs, Koele, Lange,

& van Dyck, 1996; Westra, Stewart, & Conrad., 2002, for as-needed benzodiazepine use). Specifically, there is evidence for more attrition, poorer memory for CBT-related psychoeducation materials, poorer outcome, and greater relapse when cognitive-behavioral therapy is conducted in the context of the chronic, naturalistic use of benzodiazepines.

PREVENTION

Prevention for high-risk samples might not only halt the development of Panic Disorder but also ultimately prevent the development of other psychological disorders, since people who report panic attacks are at risk for other psychological problems including other anxiety disorders, depression, and substance abuse (e.g., Warren & Zgourides, 1988). Moreover, comorbid diagnoses such as depressive disorders (e.g., Roy-Byrne, Stang, Wittchen, Ustun, et al., 2000), and substance abuse (e.g., Marshall, 1997) are believed to sometimes develop as a direct function of having Panic Disorder.

In addition, prevention using a brief cognitive-behavioral intervention is likely to be highly cost efficient. Cognitive-behavioral therapy is among the least expensive treatments for Panic Disorder (Gould, Otto, & Pollack, 1995). Prevention may cut indirect costs as well, given that people with Panic Disorder are heavy users of the medical system (e.g., Roy-Byrne et al., 1999). However, research on prevention is very limited.

Swinson, Soulios, Cox, and Kuch (1992) briefly intervened with 33 patients who attended an emergency room with panic attacks. Within 24 hours of the panic attack, 17 were assigned to an exposure condition and the remaining 16 were assigned to a reassurance condition. The latter were informed that what they had experienced was a panic attack, and that a panic attack is not dangerous. Participants in the exposure group were told the same reassuring information, and were advised that the most effective way to reduce fear is to confront the situation in which the panic attack occurred. One week later, the mean frequency of panic attacks decreased from 2.53 to .76 in the exposure group, but increased in the reassurance group from 2.50 to 3.38. This pattern was consistent over time, 3 months and 6 months later, and generalized to measures of anxiety (Swinson et al., 1992). Unfortunately, neither diagnostic evaluations nor independent assessments were conducted.

We (Gardenswartz & Craske, 2002) conducted a selective/indicated prevention study that targeted Panic Disorder. College students were considered at risk for developing Panic Disorder if they reported at least one panic attack in the past year and had at least moderate anxiety sensitivity (as assessed by the Anxiety Sensitivity Index). Half of the participants ($n = 61$) attended a 5-hour, group cognitive-behavioral workshop, modified from empirically supported cognitive-behavioral treatment for Panic Disorder (Barlow & Cerny, 1998). The other half was wait-listed. Six months later, 13.6% of the individuals in the control group developed Panic Disorder, as opposed to only 1.8% of individuals in the workshop group.

Summary and Future Directions

As the many studies discussed in this chapter attest, Panic Disorder enjoys the position as the most-researched anxiety disorder. The outgrowth of this intensive research includes an emerging understanding of the interplay between environmental and individual factors in shaping risk for Panic Disorder, converging evidence on the neuro-circuitry of fear and panic, an integration of the latest advances in learning theory into models of etiology and maintenance, and the development of effective cognitive behavioral and pharmacological treatments. Nevertheless, despite a proliferation of studies and technological advances in methodology there remain areas in which the research is contradictory, including panic-related memory functioning and multiple areas of panic-related psychophysiology.

Looking toward the future, multiple new and continuing areas of investigation may attract increasing attention from researchers and clinicians alike. One rapidly expanding research area involves the role of genetics, and particularly the interaction of genetic and environmental factors, in increasing the risk for Panic Disorder. Future studies may range from investigating the interaction of specific genes with known environmental risk factors, to linking our emerging understanding of parent and child interactions in the etiology and maintenance of anxiety disorders (e.g. Whaley, Pinto & Sigman, 1999; Moore, Whaley, & Sigman, 2004) with specific genetic risk factors (i.e., familial/environmental x individual x genetics interactions). New studies on genetics and environment interactions for anxiety disorders are emerging on a monthly basis, and although few currently focus specifically on Panic Disorder, more focused studies likely will emerge as the field expands. Additional potentially emerging areas include associations between in-utero, birth-related and early childhood trauma and genetics in increasing risk for Panic Disorder, as well as other forms of psychopathology.

On the treatment front, the role of experiential avoidance as a risk and maintenance factor for Panic Disorder has led to the development of a new line of acceptance-oriented behavioral treatments for anxiety disorders. One of the most prominent of the new therapies is Acceptance and Commitment Therapy (ACT) (Hayes, Strosahl & Wilson, 1999). Eifert and Forsyth (2005) recently developed an ACT-based treatment manual for anxiety disorders, including Panic Disorder, and a randomized control trial is currently underway to test its efficacy. Whether ACT represents an improvement over traditional CBT therapies remains to be seen. Regardless, comparing ACT and traditional CBT presents an opportunity to examine the treatment process and outcome effects of mastery and control- versus acceptance-based strategies for Panic Disorder.

Acceptance and Commitment Therapy draws heavily on eastern-based mindfulness traditions.[4] Mindfulness meditation, in which mindfulness states are intentionally cultivated, forms the basis of an 8-week Mindfulness Based Stress Reduction (MBSR) program originally developed by Kabat-Zinn (1990) for patients with chronic pain. Since its initial application, MBSR has been applied to the treatment of Panic Disorder and Generalized Anxiety Disorder (Kabat-Zinn et al., 1992; Miller, Fletcher, & Kabat-Zinn, 1995), as well as an increasingly wide variety of psychological and medical conditions (e.g., Ramel, Goldin, Carmona & McQuaid, 2004; Robert-McComb, Tacon, Randolph & Caldera, 2004; Speca, Carolson, Goodey, & Angen, 2000). However, MBSR lacks randomized controlled trials for anxiety disorders, including Panic Disorder. Future research may see a proliferation of studies on ACT, MBSR, and other mindfulness and acceptance-oriented therapies for Panic Disorder (and other anxiety disorders), including much-needed randomized controlled trials. In addition, behavioral, physiological,

---

[4] Although scientifically defining the construct of mindfulness has been challenging (Bishop, 2002), it is thought to involve the cultivation of concentration, attention, and nonjudgmental acceptance toward whatever one is experiencing in the present moment (Bishop et al., 2004).

and brain experimental studies investigating mechanisms by which mindfulness and acceptance effect attention, mood, and emotional regulation (e.g. Davidson et al., 2003; Eifert & Heffner, 2003; Broderick, 2005; Takahashi et al., 2005; Arch & Craske, in press) are emerging. Finally, interest in experiential avoidance and mindfulness will likely spawn new self-report and behavioral measures to assess and validate these constructs; several such measures have emerged already (e.g., Brown & Ryan, 2003; Hayes et al., 2004; Baer, Smith, Hopkins, Krietemeyer, & Toney, 2006).

With the emergence of new therapy treatments and the existence of proven, effective ones (e.g., CBT), it is important to consider that treatments are only as effective as the patients and clinicians who know about and use them. Despite the existence for over a decade of effective cognitive-behavioral treatments, a significant portion of individuals with Panic Disorder never receive CBT or any other form of treatment. In fact, many individuals with Panic Disorder are never treated by mental health professionals, but nearly 85% initially seek medical help for their symptoms (Katerndahl & Realini, 1995). Notably, Panic Disorder is not well recognized in medical settings (e.g., 80% nonrecognition in general medical patients referred for psychiatric evaluation (Roy-Byrne & Katon, 2000); 98% not diagnosed in emergency departments (Fleet et al., 1996), and is not well treated (e.g. Yelin et al., 1996). Hence, panic researchers have begun adapting treatment models to the medical locations in which most (help-seeking) panic patients are seen: primary care and emergency room settings (Craske, Roy-Byrne, Stein, Donald-Sherbourne, Bystritsky, Katon, & Sullivan, 2002). Adaptations that depart from traditional clinical trials include treatment in the medical setting rather than a mental health clinic and use of mental health trainees with minimal treatment experience or nonmental health professionals, such as primary care nurses, for conducting therapy and managing care. A recent multisite Panic Disorder treatment study conducted in a primary care setting demonstrated that an enhanced CBT and medication-based intervention was more effective across a number of outcome measures than usual care (Roy-Byrne, Craske, Stein, Sullivan et al., 2005), a finding that replicates an earlier medication-only study (Roy-Byrne, Katon, Cowley & Russo, 2002). Given the significant unmet needs of medical patients for recognition and treatment of Panic Disorder and the success of these early trials, future work in this direction is expected to continue.

Finally, given the enormous financial, quality of life, familial, and societal costs of Panic Disorder (e.g., Greenberg et al., 1999; Ettigi, Meyerhoff, Chirban, Jacob & Wilsons, 1997; Katerndahl & Realini, 1997), efforts toward early detection and prevention of panic disorder will continue to demand the attention of researchers, mental health professionals, and policymakers. Significant strides have been made in the identification of general risk and buffering factors in the development of anxiety disorders (see Zucker & Craske, 2001). Individuals at risk may be defined broadly (e.g., females, high neurotics, high stress) or more narrowly (e.g., children of parents with anxiety disorders, individuals with disorder-specific genetic profiles or high-anxiety sensitivity). Similarly, prevention and early detection efforts can be directly broadly through mass media or school-based programs, or more specifically, toward individuals at risk for anxiety disorders (selective prevention) or individuals with subclinical anxiety symptoms (indicated prevention). Greater attention is currently needed to identify the most effective timing for prevention efforts, buffers that prevent high-risk or symptomatic individuals from developing full-blown anxiety disorders, and whether prevention efforts are better directed at broad vulnerability to anxiety or vulnerability to specific anxiety disorders (Zucker & Craske).

References

Abelson, J. L., & Curtis, G. C. (1996). Hypothalamic-pituitary-adrenal axis activity in panic disorder: 24-hour secretion of corticotropin and cortisol. *Archives of General Psychiatry, 53,* 323–331.

Abelson, J. L., Curtis, G. C., & Uhde, T. W. (2005). Twenty-four hour growth hormone secretion in patients with panic disorder. *Psychoneuroendocrinology, 30,* 72–79.

Abelson, J. L., Glitz, D., Cameron, O. G., Lee, M. A., Bronzo, M., & Curtis, G. C. (1992). Endocrine, cardiovascular, and behavioral responses to clonodine in patients with panic disorder. *Biological Psychiatry, 32,* 18–25.

Abelson, J. L., Khan, S., Liberzon, I., & Young, E. A. (2006). HPA axis activity in patients with panic disorder: Review and synthesis of four studies. *Depression and Anxiety, 24,* 66–76.

Aikins, D., & Craske, M. G. (in press). Autonomic expressions of anxiety: Heart rate and heart period variability in the anxiety disorders. In D. M. Barch (Ed.), *Cognitive and affective neuroscience of psychopathology.* New York: Oxford University Press.

Alvarenga, M. E., Richards, J. C., Lambert, G., & Esler, M. D. (2006). Psychophysiological mechanisms in panic disorder: A correlative analysis of noradrenaline spillover, neuronal noradrenaline reuptake, power spectral analysis of heart rate variability, and psychological variables. *Psychosomatic Medicine, 68,* 8–16.

American Psychiatric Association. (1994). *Diagnostic and statistical manual of mental disorders* (4th. ed.). Washington, DC: Author.

Amering, M., Katschnig, H., Berger, P., Windhaber, J., Baischer, W., & Dantendorfer, K. (1997). Embarrassment about the first panic attack predicts agoraphobia in panic disorder patients. *Behaviour Research and Therapy, 35,* 517–521.

Anastasiades, P., Clark, D. M., Salkovskis, P. M., Middleton, H., Hackman, A., Gelder, M. G., et al. (1990). Psychophysiological responses in panic and stress. *Journal of Psychophysiology, 4,* 331–338.

Anders, S., Martin, L., Erb, M., Grodd, W., & Birbaumer, N. (2004). Brain activity underlying emotional valence and arousal: A response-related fMRI study. *Human Brain Mapping, 23,* 200–209.

Arch, J. J., & Craske, M. G. (in press). Mechanisms of mindfulness: Emotion regulation following a focused breathing induction. *Behavior Research and Therapy.*

Arrindell, W. A. (1993). The fear of fear concept: Stability, retest artifact and predictive power. *Behaviour Research and Therapy, 31,* 139–148.

Arntz, A., & van den Hout, M. (1996). Psychological treatments of panic disorder without agoraphobia: Cognitive therapy versus applied relaxation. *Behaviour Research and Therapy, 34,* 113–121.

Asmundson, G. J., Sandler, L. S., Wilson, K. G., & Walker, J. R. (1992). Selective attention toward physical threat in patients with panic disorder. *Journal of Anxiety Disorders, 6,* 295–303.

Asmundson, G. J. G., & Stein, M. B. (1994). Vagal attenuation in panic disorder: An assessment of parasympathetic nervous system function and subjective reactivity to respiratory manipulations. *Psychosomatic Medicine, 56,* 187–193.

Baer, R. A., Smith, G. T., Hopkins, J., Krietemeyer, J., & Toney, L. (2006). Using self-report assessment methods to explore facets of mindfulness. *Assessment, 13,* 27–45.

Bakker, A., vanBalkom, A. J. L. M., & Spinhoven, P. (2002). SSRIs vs. TCAs in the treatment of panic disorder: A meta-analysis. *Acta Psychiatrica Scandinavica, 106,* 163–167.

Bandelow, B., Spath, C., Tichaner, G. A., Brooks, A., Hajak, G., & Ruther, E. (2002). Early traumatic life events, parental attitudes, family history, and birth risk factors in patients with panic disorder. *Comprehensive Psychiatry, 43,* 269–278.

Baños, R. M., Medina, P. M., & Pascual, J. (2001). Explicit and implicit memory biases in depression and panic disorder. *Behaviour Research and Therapy, 29,* 61–74.

Barlow, D. H. (1988). *Anxiety and its disorders: The nature and treatment of anxiety and panic.* New York: Guilford.

Barlow, D. H. (2002). *Anxiety and its disorders: The nature and treatment of anxiety and panic* (2nd ed.). New York: Guilford.

Barlow, D. H., Brown, T. A., & Craske, M. G. (1994). Definitions of panic attacks and panic disorder in the

DSM-IV: Implications for research. *Journal of Abnormal Psychology, 103,* 553–564.

Barlow, D. H., & Cerny, J. A. (1988). *Psychological treatment of panic.* New York: Guilford.

Barlow, D. H., Chorpita, B. P., & Turovsky, J. (1996). Fear, panic, anxiety, and disorders of emotion. In D. A. Hope (Ed.), *Perspectives on anxiety, panic, and fear* (The 43rd Annual Nebraska Symposium on Motivation) (pp. 251–328). Lincoln: University of Nebraska Press.

Barlow, D. H., Craske, M. G., Cerny, J. A., & Klosko, J. S. (1989). Behavioral treatment of panic disorder. *Behavior Therapy, 20,* 261–282.

Beck, J. G., Stanley, M. A., Baldwin, L. E., Deagle, E. A., & Averill, P. M. (1994). Comparison of cognitive therapy and relaxation training for panic disorder. *Journal of Consulting and Clinical Psychology, 62,* 818–826.

Behar K. L., Rothman D. L., Petersen K. F., Hooten M., Delaney R., Petroff, O. A. C., et al. (1999). Preliminary evidence of low cortical GABA levels in localized 1H-MR spectra of alcohol-dependent and hepatic encephalopathy patients. *American Journal of Psychiatry, 156,* 952–954.

Benjamin, R. S., Costello, E. J., & Warren, M. (1990). Anxiety disorders in a pediatric sample. *Journal of Anxiety Disorders, 4,* 293–316.

Bennet, A., & Stirling, J. (1998). Vulnerability factors in the anxiety disorders. *British Journal of Medical Psychology, 71,* 311–321.

Biederman, J., Faraone, S. V., Marrs, A., & Moore, P. (1997). Panic disorder and agoraphobia in consecutively referred children and adolescents. *Journal of the American Academy of Child & Adolescent Psychiatry, 36,* 214–223.

Bishop, S. R. (2002). What do we really know about mindfulness-based stress reduction?*Psychosomatic Medicine, 64,* 71–83.

Bishop, S. R., Lau, M., Shapiro, S., Carlson, L., Anderson, N. D., Carmody, J., et al. (2004). Mindfulness: A proposed operational definition. *Clinical Psychology: Science and Practice, 11,* 230–241.

Block, R. I., Ghoneim, M. M., Fowles, D. C., Kumar, V., & Pathak, D. (1987). Effects of a subanesthetic concentration of nitrous oxide on establishment, elicitation, and semantic and phonemic generalization of classically conditioned skin conductance responses. *Pharmacology, Biochemistry & Behavior, 28,* 7–14.

Borkovec, T. D., Weerts, T. C., & Bernstein, D. A. (1977). Assessment of anxiety. In Ciminero, A. R.

Calhoun, K. S. & Adams, H. E. (Eds.), *Handbook of Behavioral Assessment.* New York: Wiley.

Bouton, M. E., Mineka, S., & Barlow, D. H. (2001). A modern learning theory perspective on the etiology of panic disorder. *Psychological Review, 108,* 4–32.

Bowlby, J. (1969). Disruption of affectional bonds and its effects on behavior. *Canada's Mental Health Supplement, 59,* 12.

Bowlby, J. (1980). By ethology out of psycho-analysis: An experiment in interbreeding. *Animal Behaviour, 28,* 649–656.

Boyd, J. H. (1986). Use of mental health services for the treatment of panic disorder. *American Journal of Psychiatry, 143,* 1569–1574.

Brambilla, F., Perna, G., Garberi, A., Nobile, P., & Bellodi, L. (1995). Alpha2-adrenergic receptor sensitivity in panic disorder. I. GH response to GHRH and clonodine stimulation in panic disorder. *Psychoneuroendocrinology, 20,* 1–9.

Brandt, C. A., Meller, J., Keweloh, L., Hoschel, K., Staedt, J., Munz, D., et al. (1998). Increased benzodiazepine receptor density in the prefrontal cortex in patients with panic disorder. *Journal of Neural Transmission, 105,* 1325–1333.

Bremner, J. D., Innis, R. B., White, T., Masahiro, F., Silbersweig, D., Goddard, A. W., et al. (2000). SPECT [I-123] iomazenil measurement of the benzodiazepine receptor in panic disorder. *Biological Psychiatry, 47,* 96–106.

Broderick, P. C. (2005). Mindfulness and coping with dysphoric mood: Contrasts with rumination and distraction. *Cognitive Therapy and Research, 29,* 501–510.

Bromet, E. J., Gluzman, S. F., Paniotto, V. I., Webb, C. P. M., Tintle, N. L., Zakhozha, V., et al. (2005). Epidemiology of psychiatric and alcohol disorders in Ukraine: Findings from the Ukraine World Mental Health Survey. *Social Psychiatry and Psychiatric Epidemiology, 40,* 681–690.

Brown, G. W. (1993). The role of life events in the aetiology of depressive and anxiety disorders. In A. C. Stanford, P. Salmon, & J. A. Gray (Eds.), *Stress: From synapse to syndrome* (pp. 23–50). London: Academic Press.

Brown, G. W., Harris, T. O., & Eales, M. J. (1993). Aetiology of anxiety and depressive disorders in an inner-city population: II. Comorbidity and adversity. *Psychological Medicine, 23,* 155–165.

Brown, K. W., & Ryan, R. M. (2003). The benefits of being present: Mindfulness and its role in psychological well-being. *Journal of Personality and Social Psychology, 84,* 822–848.

Brown, T. A., Antony, M. M., & Barlow, D. H. (1995). Diagnostic comorbidity in panic disorder: Effect on treatment outcome and course of comorbid diagnoses following treatment. *Journal of Consulting and Clinical Psychology*, *63*, 408–418.

Brown, T. A., & Barlow, D. H. (1995). Long-term outcome in cognitive behavioral treatment of panic disorder: Clinical predictors and alternative strategies for assessment. *Journal of Consulting and Clinical Psychology*, *63*, 754–765.

Brown, T. A., Campbell, L. A., Lehman, C. L., Grishman, J. R., & Mancill, R. B. (2001). Current and lifetime comorbidity of the *DSM-IV* anxiety and mood disorders in a large clinical sample. *Journal of Abnormal Psychology*, *110*, 585–599.

Brown, T. A., Chorpita, B. F., & Barlow, D. H. (1998). Structural relationships among dimensions of the *DSM-IV* anxiety and mood disorders and dimensions of negative affect, positive affect, and autonomic arousal. *Journal of Abnormal Psychology*, *107*, 179–192.

Brown, T. A., DiNardo, P. A., Lehman, C. L., & Campbell, L. A. (2001). Reliability of *DSM-IV* anxiety and mood disorders: Implications for the classification of emotional disorders. *Journal of Abnormal Psychology*, *110*, 49–58.

Bruce, S. E., Yonkers, K. A., Otto, M. W., Eisen, J. L., Weisberg, R. B., Pagano, M., et al. (2005). Influence of psychiatric comorbidity on recovery and recurrence in generalized anxiety disorder, social phobia, and panic disorder: A 12-year prospective study. *American Journal of Psychiatry*, *162*, 1179–1187.

Bystritsky, A., Craske, M., Maidenberg, E., Vapnik, T., & Shapiro, D. (1995). Ambulatory monitoring of panic patients during regular activity: A preliminary report. *Biological Psychiatry*, *38*, 684–689.

Carlbring, P., Ekselius, L., & Andersson, G. (2003). Treatment of panic disorder via the Internet: A randomized trial of CBT vs. applied relaxation. *Journal of Behavior Therapy and Experimental Psychiatry*, *34*, 129–140.

Carter, M. M., Hollon, S. D., Carson, R., & Shelton, R. C. (1995). Effects of a safe person on induced distress following a biological challenge in panic disorder with agoraphobia. *Journal of Abnormal Psychology*, *104*, 156–163.

Cerny, J. A., Barlow, D. H., Craske, M. G., & Himadi, W. G. (1987). Couples treatment of agoraphobia: A two-year follow-up. *Behavior Therapy*, *18*, 401–415.

Chambless, D. L., Caputo, G. C., Bright, P., & Gallagher, R. (1984). Assessment of fear of fear in agoraphobics: The Body Sensations Questionnaire and the Agoraphobic Cognitions Questionnaire. *Journal of Consulting and Clinical Psychology*, *52*, 1090–1097.

Chambless, D. L., Caputo, G. C., Jasin, S. E., Gracely, E. J., & Williams, C. (1985). The Mobility Inventory for Agoraphobia. *Behaviour Research and Therapy*, *23*, 35–44.

Chambless, D. L., & Gracely, E. J. (1989). Fear of fear and the anxiety disorders. *Cognitive Therapy and Research*, *13*, 19–20.

Chambless, D. L., & Renneberg, B. (September, 1988). *Personality disorders of agoraphobics*. Paper presented at the World Congress of Behavior Therapy, Edinburgh, Scotland.

Clark, D. B., Taylor, C. B., Hayward, C., King, R., Margraf, J., Ehlers, A., et al. (1990). Motor activity and tonic heart rate in panic disorder. *Psychiatry Research*, *32*, 45–53.

Clark, D. M. (1986). A cognitive approach to panic. *Behaviour Research and Therapy*, *24*, 461–470.

Clark, D. M. (1988). A cognitive model of panic attacks. In S. Rachman & J. D. Maser (Eds.), *Panic: Psychological perspectives* (pp. 71–89). Hillside, NJ: Erlbaum.

Clark, D. M. (1996). Panic disorder: From theory to therapy. In P. M. Salkovskis (Ed.), *Frontiers of cognitive therapy* (pp. 318–344). New York: Guilford.

Clark, D. M., Salkovskis, P. M., Gelder, M., Koehler, C., Martin, M., Anastasiades, et al. (1988). Tests of a cognitive theory of panic. In I. Hand & H.-U. Wittchen (Eds.), *Panic and phobias II: Treatments and variables affecting course and outcome* (pp. 71–90). Berlin: Springer-Verlag.

Clark, D. M., Salkovskis, P. M., Hackmann, A., Middleton, H., Anastasiades, P., & Gelder, M. (1994). A comparison of cognitive therapy, applied relaxation, and imipramine in the treatment of panic disorder: A randomized controlled trial. *British Journal of Psychiatry*, *164*, 759–769.

Clark, D. M., Salkovskis, P. M., Hackmann, A., Wells, A., Ludgate, J., & Gelder, M. (1999). Brief cognitive therapy for panic disorder: A randomized controlled trial. *Journal of Consulting and Clinical Psychology*, *67*, 583–589.

Cloitre, M., Shear, K. M., Cancienne, J., & Zeitlin, S. B. (1994). Implicit and explicit memory for catastrophic associations to bodily sensation words in panic disorder. *Cognitive Therapy and Research*, *18*, 225–240.

Cohen, H., Benjamin, J., Geva, A. B., Matar, M. A., Kaplan, Z., & Kotler, M. (2000). Autonomic dysregulation in panic disorder and in post-traumatic stress disorders: Application of power spectrum analysis of heart rate variability at rest and in response to recollection of trauma or panic attacks. *Psychiatry Research, 96,* 1–13.

Cohen, H., Matar, A. M., Kaplan, Z., Miodownik, H., Cassuto, Y., & Kotler, M. (1998). Analysis of heart rate variability in post-traumatic stress disorder patients: At rest and in response to a trauma-related reminder. *Biological Psychiatry, 44,* 1054–1059.

Cohen, L. H., Burt, C. E., & Bjorck, J. P. (1987). Life stress and adjustment: Effects of life events experienced by young adolescents and their parents. *Developmental Psychology, 23,* 583–592.

Cohen, L., McGowan, J., Fooskas, S., & Rose, S. (1984). Positive life events and social support and the relationship between life stress and psychological disorder. *American Journal of Community Psychology, 12,* 567–587.

Cox, B. J., Endler, N. S., & Swinson, R. P. (1995). An examination of levels of agoraphobic severity in panic disorder. *Behaviour Research and Therapy, 33,* 57–62.

Craske, M. G. (1999). *Anxiety disorders: Psychological approaches to theory and treatment.* Boulder, CO: Westview.

Craske, M. G. (2003). *Origins of phobias and anxiety disorders: Why more women than men?* Oxford, UK: Elsevier.

Craske, M. G., & Barlow, D. H. (1988). A review of the relationship between panic and avoidance. *Clinical Psychology Review, 8,* 667–685.

Craske, M. G., & Barlow, D. H. (1989). Nocturnal panic. *Journal of Nervous and Mental Disease, 177,* 160–167.

Craske, M. G., Brown, T. A., & Barlow, D. H. (1991). Behavioral treatment of panic disorder: A two-year follow-up. *Behavior Therapy, 22,* 289–304.

Craske, M. G., Farchione, T. J., Allen, L. B., Barrios, V., Stoyanova, & Rose, R. (in press). Cognitive behavioral therapy for panic disorder and comorbidity: Single or multiple treatment focus. *Journal of Consulting and Clinical Psychology.*

Craske, M. G., & Freed, S. (1995). Expectations about arousal and nocturnal panic. *Journal of Abnormal Psychology, 104,* 567–575.

Craske, M. G., Lang, A. J., Aikins, D., & Mystkowski, J. L. (2005). Cognitive behavioral therapy for nocturnal panic. *Behavior Therapy, 36,* 43–54.

Craske, M. G., Lang, A. J., Rowe, M., DeCola, J. P., Simmons, J., Mann, C., et al. (2002). Presleep attributions about arousal during sleep: Nocturnal panic. *Journal of Abnormal Psychology, 111,* 53–62.

Craske, M. G., Maidenberg, E., & Bystritsky, A. (1995). Brief cognitive-behavioral versus non-directive therapy for panic disorder. *Journal of Behavior Therapy and Experimental Psychiatry, 26,* 113–120.

Craske, M. G., Miller, P. P., Rotunda, R., & Barlow, D. H. (1990). A descriptive report of features of initial unexpected panic attacks in minimal and extensive avoiders. *Behaviour Research and Therapy, 28,* 395–400.

Craske, M. G., Poulton, R., Tsao, J. C. I., & Plotkin, D. (2001). Paths to panic disorder/agoraphobia: An exploratory analysis from age 3 to 21 in an unselected birth cohort. *Journal of the American Academy of Child and Adolescent Psychiatry, 40,* 556–563.

Craske, M. G., Rapee, R. M., & Barlow, D. H. (1988). The significance of panic-expectancy for individual patterns of avoidance. *Behavior Therapy, 19,* 577–592.

Craske, M. G., & Rowe, M. K. (1997). Nocturnal panic. *Clinical Psychology: Science & Practice, 4,* 153–174.

Craske, M. G., Rowe, M., Lewin, M., & Noriego-Dimitri, R. (1997). Interoceptive exposure versus breathing retraining within cognitive-behavioural therapy for panic disorder with agoraphobia. *British Journal of Clinical Psychology, 36,* 85–99.

Craske, M. G., Roy-Byrne, P., Stein, M. B., Donald-Sherbourne, C., Bystritsky, A., Katon, W., & Sullivan, G. (2002). Treating panic disorder in primary care: A collaborative care intervention. *General Hospital Psychiatry, 24*(3), 148–155.

Craske, M. G., & Tsao, J. C. I. (1999). Self-monitoring with panic and anxiety disorders. *Psychological Assessment, 11,* 466–479.

Craske, M. G., & Tsao, J. C. I. (2005). Assessment and treatment of nocturnal panic attacks. *Sleep Medicine Reviews, 9,* 173–184.

Davidson, R. J., Kabat-Zinn, J., Schumacher, J., Rosenkranz, M., Muller, D., Santorelli, S. F., et al. (2003). Alterations in brain and immune function produced by mindfulness meditation. *Psychosomatic Medicine, 65,* 564–570.

Deacon, B., & Abramowitz, J. (2006). A pilot study of two-day cognitive-behavioral therapy for panic disorder. *Behaviour Research and Therapy, 44,* 807–817.

deBeurs, E., vanBalkom, A. J., Lange, A., Koele, P., & van Dyke, R. (1995). Treatment of panic disorder with agoraphobia: Comparison of fluvoxamine, placebo, and psychological panic management combined with exposure and of exposure in vivo alone. *American Journal of Psychiatry, 152,* 683–691.

Deckert, J., Nothen, M. M., Franke, P., Delmo, C., Fritze, J., Knapp, M., et al. (1998). Systematic mutation screening and association study of the A1 and A2a adenosine receptor genes in panic disorder suggest a contribution of the A2a gene to the development of disease. *Molecular Psychiatry, 3,* 81–85.

de Jong, G. M., & Bouman, T. K. (1995). Panic disorder: A baseline period. Predictability of agoraphobic avoidance behavior. *Journal of Anxiety Disorders, 9,* 185–199.

Devilly, G. J. (2001a). Effect size and methodological rigor in EMDR: A reply to Lipke's (2001) comment. *Behavior Therapist, 24,* 195–196.

Devilly, G. J. (2001b). The influence of distraction during exposure and researcher allegiance during outcome trials. *Behavior Therapist, 24,* 18–21.

DiNardo, P. A., Brown, T. A., & Barlow, D. H. (1994). Anxiety Disorders Interview Schedule for *DSM-IV:* Clinician's manual. New York: Graywind.

Dworkin B. R., & Dworkin, S. (1999). Heterotopic and homotopic classical conditioning of the baroreflex. *Integrative Physiological & Behavioral Science, 34,* 158–176.

Ehlers, A. (1995). A 1-year prospective study of panic attacks: Clinical course and factors associated with maintenance. *Journal of Abnormal Psychology, 104,* 164–172.

Ehlers, A., Margraf, J., Davies, S., & Roth, W. T. (1988). Selective processing of threat cues in subjects with panic attacks. *Cognition & Emotion, 2,* 201–219.

Ehlers, A., Margraf, J., Roth, W. T., Taylor, C. B., & Birbaumer, N. (1988). Anxiety induced by false heart rate feedback in patients with panic disorder. *Behaviour Research and Therapy, 26,* 1–11.

Eifert, G. H., & Forsyth, J. P. (2005). *Acceptance and commitment therapy for anxiety disorders: A practitioner's treatment guide to using mindfulness, acceptance, and values-based behavior change strategies.* Oakland, CA: New Harbinger.

Eifert, G. H., & Heffner, M. (2003). The effects of acceptance versus control contexts on avoidance of panic-related symptoms. *Journal of Behavioral Therapy and Experimental Psychiatry, 34,* 293–312.

Ettigi, P., Meyerhoff, A. S., Chirban, J. T., Jacobs, R. J., & Wilson, R. R. (1997). The quality of life and employments in panic disorder. *Journal of Nervous and Mental Disease, 185,* 368–372.

Eysenck, H. J. (Ed.). (1960). *Behavior therapy and the neuroses.* Oxford, England: Pergamon.

Eysenck, H. J. (1967). *The biological basis of personality.* Springfield, IL: C.C. Thomas.

Eysenck, H. J., & Rachman, S. (1965). *The causes and cures of neurosis.* London: Routledge & Kegan Paul.

Faravelli, C., & Pallanti, S. (1989). Recent life events and panic disorder. *American Journal of Psychiatry, 146,* 622–626.

Fava, G. A., Rafanelli, C., Grandi, S., Conti, S., Ruini, C., Mangelli, L., et al. (2001). Long-term outcome of panic disorder with agoraphobia treated by exposure. *Psychological Medicine, 31,* 891–898.

Fava, G. A., Zielezny, M., Savron, G., & Grandi, S. (1995). Long-term effects of behavioural treatment for panic disorder with agoraphobia. *British Journal of Psychiatry, 166,* 87–92.

First, M. B., Spitzer, R. L., Gibbon, M., & Williams, J. B. W. (1994). *Structured clinical interview for axis I DSM-IV disorders.* New York: Biometric Research Department, New York State Psychiatric Institute.

Fleet, R. P., Dupuis, G., Marchand, A., Burelle, D., & Beitman B. D. (1997). Detecting panic disorder in emergency department chest pain patients: A validated model to improve recognition. *Annals of Behavioral Medicine, 19*(2), 124–131.

Forsyth, J. P., Eifert, G. H., & Barrios, V. (in press). Fear conditioning in an emotion regulation context: A fresh perspective on the origins of anxiety disorders. In M. G. Craske, D. Hermans, & D. Vansteenwegen (Eds.), *Fear and learning: From basic processes to clinical implications.* Washington, DC: American Psychological Association.

Forsyth, J. P., Palav, A., & Duff, K. (1999). The absence of relation between anxiety sensitivity and fear conditioning using 20% versus 13% CO_2-enriched air as unconditioned stimuli. *Behaviour Research and Therapy, 37,* 143–153.

Friedman, B. H., & Thayer, J. F. (1998). Autonomic balance revisited: Panic anxiety and heart rate variability. *Journal of Psychosomatic Research, 44,* 133–151.

Friedman, B. H., Thayer, J. F., & Borkovec, T. D. (1993). Heart rate variability in generalized anxiety disorder [abstract]. *Psychophysiology, 30*(suppl), S28.

Frisch, M. B., Cornell, J., Villanueva, M., & Retzlaff, P. J. (1992). Clinical validation of the Quality of Life Inventory: A measure of life satisfaction for use in treatment planning and outcome assessment, *Psychological Assessment, 4,* 92–101.

Furukawa, T. A., Watanabe, N., & Churchill, R. (2006). Psychotherapy plus antidepressant for panic disorder with or without agoraphobia: Systematic review. *British Journal of Psychiatry, 188*, 305–312.

Gardenswartz, C. A., & Crraske, M. G. (2001). Prevention of panic disorder. *Behavior Therapy 32*(4), 725–737.

Ghosh, A., & Marks, I. M. (1987). Self-treatment of agoraphobia by exposure. *Behavior Therapy, 18*, 3–16.

Goddard, A. W., Mason, G. F., Almai, A., Rothman, D. L., Behar, K. L., Petroff, O. A. C., et al. (2001). Reductions in occipital cortex GABA levels in panic disorder detected with 1h-magnetic resonance spectroscopy. *Archives of General Psychiatry, 58*, 556–561.

Goddard, A. W., Mason, G. F. Appel, M., Rothman, D. L., Gueorguieva, R., Behar, K. L., et al. (2004). Impaired GABA neuronal response to acute benzodiazepine administration in panic disorder. *American Journal of Psychiatry, 161*, 2186–2193.

Goisman, R. M., Goldenberg, I., Vasile, R. G., & Keller, M. B. (1995). Comorbidity of anxiety disorders in a multicenter anxiety study. *Comprehensive Psychiatry, 36*, 303–311.

Goisman, R. M., Warshaw, M. G., Peterson, L. G., Rogers, M. P., Cuneo, P., Hunt, M. F., et al. (1994). Panic, agoraphobia, and panic disorder with agoraphobia: Data from a multicenter anxiety disorders study. *Journal of Nervous and Mental Disease, 182*, 72–79.

Goldstein, A. J., & Chambless, D. L. (1978). A reanalysis of agoraphobia. *Behavior Therapy, 9*, 47–59.

Goodwin, R. D., & Eaton, W. W. (2003). Asthma and the risk of panic attacks among adults in the community. *Psychological Medicine, 33*, 879–885.

Goodwin, R. D., Fergusson, D. M., & Horwood, L. J. (2005). Childhood abuse and familial violence and the risk of panic attacks and panic disorder in young adulthood. *Psychological Medicine, 35*, 881–890.

Gorman, J. M., Kent, J. M., Sullivan, G. M., & Coplan, J. D. (2000). Neuroanatomical hypothesis of panic disorder, revised. *American Journal of Psychiatry, 157*, 493–505.

Gould, R. A., & Clum, G. A. (1995). Self-help plus minimal therapist contact in the treatment of panic disorder: A replication and extension. *Behavior Therapy, 26*, 533–546.

Gould, R. A., Clum, G. A., & Shapiro, D. (1993). The use of bibliotherapy in the treatment of panic: A preliminary investigation. *Behavior Therapy, 24*, 241–252.

Gould, R. A., Otto, M. W., & Pollack, M. H. (1995). A meta-analysis of treatment outcome for panic disorder. *Clinical Psychology Review, 15*, 819–844.

Gray, J. A. (1982a). *The neuropsychology of anxiety: An enquiry into the functions of the septo-hippocampal system*. New York: Oxford University Press.

Gray, J. A. (1982b). Precis of "The neuropsychology of anxiety: An enquiry into the functions of the septo-hippocampal system."*Behavioural and Brain Sciences, 5*, 469–534.

Greenberg, P. E., Sisitsky, T., Kessler, R. C., Finkelstein, S. N., Berndt, E. R., Davidson, J. R. T., et al. (1999). The economic burden of anxiety disorders in the 1990s. *Journal of Clinical Psychiatry, 60*, 427–435.

Grillon, C. (2002). Startle reactivity and anxiety disorders: Aversive conditioning, context, and neurobiology. *Biological Psychiatry, 52*, 958–975.

Grillon, C., Ameli, R., Goddard, A., Woods, S. W., & Davis, M. (1994). Baseline and fear-potentiated startle in panic disorder patients. *Biological Psychiatry, 35*, 431–439.

Gross, J. J., & Levenson, R. W. (1993). Emotional suppression: Physiology, self-report & expressive behavior. *Journal of Personality and Social Psychology, 64*, 970–986.

Gross, J. J., & Levenson, R. W. (1997). Hiding feelings: The acute effects of inhibiting negative and positive emotion. *Journal of Abnormal Psychology, 106*, 95–103.

Hamilton, S. P., Fyer, A. J., Durner, M., Heiman, G. A., Baisre de Leon, A., Hodge, S. E., et al. (2003). Further genetic evidence for a panic disorder syndrome mapping to chromosome 13q. *Proceedings of National Academy of Science, 100*, 2550–2555.

Hamilton, S. P., Slager, S. L., De Leon, A. B., Heiman, G. A., Klein, D. F., Hodge, S. E., et al. (2004). Evidence for genetic linkage between a polymorphism in the adenosine 2A receptor and panic disorder. *Neuropsychopharmacology, 29*, 558–565.

Hamilton, S. P., Slager, S. L., Helleby, L., Heiman, G. A., Klein, D. F., Hodge, S. E., et al. (2001). No association or linkage between polymorphisms in the genes encoding cholecystokinin and the cholecystokinin B receptor and panic disorder. *Molecular Psychiatry, 6*, 59–65.

Hayes, S. C., Luoma, J. B., Bond, F. W., Masuda, A., & Lillis, J. (2006). Acceptance and commitment therapy: Model, processes and outcomes. *Behaviour Research and Therapy, 44*, 1–25.

Hayes, S. C., Strosahl, K. D., & Wilson, K. G. (1999). *Acceptance and commitment therapy: An experiential approach to behavior change*. New York: Guilford.

Hayes, S. C., Wilson, K. G., Giffore, E. V., Follette, V. M., & Strosahl, K. (1996). Experiential avoidance and behavioral disorders: A functional dimensional approach to diagnosis and treatment. *Journal of Consulting and Clinical Psychology, 64,* 1152–1168.

Hayward, C., Killen, J. D., Hammer, L. D., Litt, I. F., Wilson, D. M., Simmonds, B., et al. (1992). Pubertal stage and panic attack history in sixth- and seventh-grade girls. *American Journal of Psychiatry, 149,* 1239–1243.

Hayward, C., Killen, J. D., Kraemer, H. C., & Taylor, C. B. (2000). Predictors of panic attacks in adolescents. *Journal of American Academy of Child Adolescent Psychiatry, 39,* 207–214.

Heinrichs, N., Hofmann, S. G., & Barlow, D. H. (2004). Non-specific encoding of threat in social phobia and panic disorder. *Cognitive Behaviour Therapy, 33,* 126–136.

Hermans, D., Craske, M. G., Mineka, S., & Lovibond, P. F. (2006). Extinction in humans. *Biological Psychiatry, 60,* 361–368.

Hibbs, E. D., Hamburger, S. D., Kruesi, M. J. P., & Lenane, M. (1993). Factors affecting expressed emotion in parents of ill and normal children. *American Journal of Orthopsychiatry, 63,* 103–112.

Hoehn-Saric, R., McLeod, D. R., & Hipsley, P. (1995). Is hyperarousal essential to obsessive-compulsive disorder? Diminished physiologic flexibility, but not hyperarousal, characterizes patients with obsessive-compulsive disorder. *Archives of General Psychiatry, 52,* 688–693.

Hope, D. A., Rapee, R. M., Heimberg, R. G., & Dombeck, M. J. (1990). Representations of the self in social phobia: Vulnerability to social threat. *Cognitive Therapy & Research, 14,* 177–189.

Horwath, E., Lish, J. D., Johnson, J., Hornig, C. D., & Weissman, M. M. (1993). Agoraphobia without panic: Clinical reappraisal of an epidemiologic finding. *American Journal of Psychiatry, 150,* 1496–1501.

Hudson, J., & Rapee, R. (2001). Parent–child interactions and anxiety disorders: An observational study. *Behaviour Research and Therapy, 39,* 1411–1427.

Irie, M., Maeda, M., & Nagata, S. (2001). Can conditioned histamine release occur under urethane anesthesia in guinea pigs? *Physiology & Behavior, 72,* 567–573.

Ito, T., Inoue, Y., Sugihara, T., Yamada, H. Katayama, S. & Kawahara, R. (1999). Autonomic function in the early stage of panic disorder: Power spectral analysis of heart rate variability. *Psychiatry and Clinical Neurosciences, 53,* 667–672.

Jacob, R. G., Furman, J. M., Clark, D. B., & Durrant, J. D. (1992). Vestibular symptoms, panic, and phobia: Overlap and possible relationships. *Annals of Clinical Psychiatry, 4,* 163–174.

Kabat-Zinn, J. (1990). *Full catastrophe living: Using the wisdom of your body and mind to face stress, pain, and illness.* New York: Delta.

Kabat-Zinn, J., Massion, A. O., Kristeller, J., Peterson, L. G., Fletcher, K. E., Pbert, L., et al. (1992). Effectiveness of a meditation-based stress reduction program in the treatment of anxiety disorders. *American Journal of Psychiatry, 149,* 936–943.

Kamphuis, J. H., & Telch, M. J. (2000). Effects of distraction and guided threat reappraisal on fear reduction during exposure-based treatments for specific fears. *Behaviour Research and Therapy, 38,* 1163–1181.

Katerndahl, D. A., & Realini, J. P. (1997). Quality of life and panic-related work disability in subjects with infrequent panic and panic disorder. *Journal of Clinical Psychiatry, 58,* 153–158.

Katschnig, H., & Amering, M. (1998). The long-term course of panic disorder and its predictors. *Journal of Clinical Psychopharmacology, 18*(Suppl 2), 6S–11S.

Kawakami, N., Takeshima, T., Ono, Y., Uda, H., Hata, Y., Nakane, Y., et al. (2002). Twelve-month prevalence, severity, and treatment of common mental disorders in communities in Japan: Preliminary finding from the World Mental Health Japan Survey 2002–2003. *Psychiatry and Clinical Neurosciences, 59,* 441–452.

Kendler, K. S., Bulik, C. M., Silberg, J., Hettema, J. M., Myers, J. & Prescott, C. A. (2000). Childhood sexual abuse and adult psychiatric and substance use disorders in women: An epidemiological and co-twin analysis. *Archives of General Psychiatry, 57,* 953–959.

Kendler, K. S., Heath, A. C., Martin, N. G., & Eaves, L. J. (1987). Symptoms of anxiety and symptoms of depression: Same genes, different environments? *Archives of General Psychiatry, 44,* 451–457.

Kendler, K. S., Neale, M. C., Kessler, R. C., Heath, A. C., & Eaves, L. J. (1993). Major depression and phobias: The genetic and environmental sources of comorbidity. *Psychological Medicine, 23,* 361–371.

Kendler, K. S., Walters, E. E., Neale, M. C., Kessler, R. C., Heath, A. C., & Eaves, L. J. (1995). The structure of the genetic and environmental risk factors for six major psychiatric disorders in women. *Archives of General Psychiatry, 52,* 374–383.

Kent, J. M., & Rauch, S. L. (2003). Neurocircuitry of anxiety disorders. *Current Psychiatry Report, 5*, 266–273.

Kessler, R. C., Chiu, W. T., Demler, O., Merikangas, K. R., & Walters, E. E. (2005a). Lifetime prevalence and age-of-onset distributions of *DSM-IV* disorders in the National Comorbidity Survey Replication. *Archives of General Psychiatry, 62*, 593–602.

Kessler, R. C., Chiu, W. T., Demler, O., Merikangas, K. R., & Walters, E. E. (2005b). Prevalence, severity, and comorbidity of 12-month *DSM-IV* disorders in the National Comorbidity Survey Replication. *Archives of General Psychiatry, 62*, 617–627.

Kessler, R. C., Davis, C. G., & Kendler, K. S. (1997). Childhood adversity and adult psychiatric disorder in the U.S. National Comorbidity Survey. *Psychological Medicine 27*, 1101–1119.

Kessler, R. C., McGonagle, K., Zhao, S., Nelson, C., Hughes, M., Eshelman, S., et al. (1994). Lifetime and 12-month prevalence of *DSM-III-R* psychiatric disorders in the United States: Results from the National Comorbidity Survey. *Archives of General Psychiatry, 51*, 8–19.

Keyl, P. M., & Eaton, W. W. (1990). Risk factors for the onset of panic disorder and other panic attacks in a prospective, population-based study. *American Journal of Epidemiology, 131*, 301–311.

Kikuchi, M., Komuro, R., Hiroshi, O., Kidani, T., Hanaoka, A., & Koshino, Y. (2005). Panic disorder with and without agoraphobia: Comorbidity within a half-year of the onset of panic disorder. *Psychiatry and Clinical Neurosciences, 58*, 639–643.

Klein, D. F. (1981). Anxiety reconceptualized. In D. F. Klein & J. G. Rabkin (Eds.), *Anxiety: New research and changing concepts*. New York: Raven.

Kraemer, H. C., Wilson, G. T., Fairburn, C. G., & Agras, W. S. (2002). Mediators and moderators of treatment effects in randomized clinical trials. *Archives of General Psychiatry, 59*, 877–884.

Kroeze, S., & van den Hout, M. A. (2000). Selective attention for cardiac information in panic patients. *Behaviour Research and Therapy, 38*, 63–72.

Krystal, J. H., Woods, S. W., Hill, C. L., & Charney, D. S. (1991). Characteristics of panic attack subtypes: Assessment of spontaneous panic, situational panic, sleep panic, and limited symptom attacks. *Comprehensive Psychiatry, 32*, 474–480.

Lake, R. I. E., Eaves, L. J., Maes, H. H. M., Heath, A. C., & Martin, N. G. (2000). Further evidence against the environmental transmission of individual differences in neuroticism from a collaborative study of 45,850 twins and relatives of two continents. *Behavior Genetics, 30*, 223–233.

Lambert, E. A., Thompson, J., Schlaich, M., Laude, D., Elghozi, J. L., Esler, M. D., et al. (2002). *Journal of Hypertension, 20*, 2445–2451.

Lang, P. J. (1971). The application of psychophysiological methods to the study of psychotherapy and behavior modification. In A. Bergin & S. Garfield (Eds.), *Handbook of psychotherapy and behavior change*. New York: Wiley.

Lautenbacher, S., Spernal, J., & Krieg, J-C. (2002). Divided and selective attention in panic disorder: A comparative study of patients with panic disorder, major depression and healthy controls. *European Archives of Psychiatry and Clinical Neuroscience, 252*, 210–213.

LeDoux, J. E. (1996). *The emotional brain: The mysterious underpinnings of emotional life*. New York: Simon & Schuster.

Lennartz, R. C., & Weinberger, N. M. (1992). Analysis of response systems in Pavlovian conditioning reveals rapidly versus slowly acquired conditioned responses: Support for two factors, implications for behavior and neurobiology. *Psychobiology, 20*, 93–119.

Lipke, H. (2001). Response to Devilly's (2001) claims on distraction and exposure. *The Behavior Therapist, 24*(9), 195.

Lovibond, P. F., & Shanks, D. R. (2002). The role of awareness in Pavlovian conditioning: Empirical evidence and theoretical implications. *Journal of Experimental Psychology: Animal Behavior Processes, 28*, 3–26.

Lundh, L. G., Czyzykow, S., & Ost, L. G. (1997). Explicit and implicit memory bias in panic disorder with agoraphobia. *Behaviour Research and Therapy, 35*, 1003–1014.

Mackinnon, A. J., Henderson, A. S., & Andrews, G. (1990). Genetic and environmental determinants of the lability of trait neuroticism and the symptoms of anxiety and depression. *Psychological Medicine, 20*, 581–591.

Maddock, R. J., Buonocore, M. H., Kile, S. J., & Garrett, A. S. (2003). Brain regions showing increased activation by threat-related words in panic disorder. *NeuroReport, 14*, 325–328.

Maidenberg, E., Chen, E., Craske, M., Bohn, P., & Bystristsky, A. (1996). Specificity of attentional bias in panic disorder and social phobia. *Journal of Anxiety disorders, 10*, 529–541.

Malizia, A. L., Cunningham, V. J., Bell, C. J., Liddle, P. F., Jones, T. & Nutt, D. J. (1998). Decreased brain

GABA(A)-benzodiazepine receptor binding in panic disorder: Preliminary results from a quantitative PET study. *Archives of General Psychiatry*, *55*, 715–720.

Maller, R. G., & Reiss, S. (1992). Anxiety sensitivity in 1984 and panic attacks in 1987. *Journal of Anxiety Disorders*, *6*, 241–247.

Mannuzza, S., Fyer, A. J., Martin, L. Y., Gallops, M. S., Endicott, J., Gorman, J. M., et al. (1989). Reliability of anxiety assessment: I Diagnostic agreement. *Archives of General Psychiatry*, *46*, 1093–1101.

Margraf, J., & Heidmeier, K. (in press). Lack of chronic hyperventilation in panic disorder patients. *Journal of Abnormal Psychology*.

Margraf, J., Taylor, C. B., Ehlers, A., Roth, W. T., & Agras, W. S. (1987). Panic attacks in the natural environment. Special issue: Mental disorders in their natural settings: The application of time allocation and experience-sampling techniques in psychiatry. *Journal of Nervous and Mental Disease*, *175*, 558–565.

Marks, I. M., Swinson, R. P., Basoglu, M., Kuch, K., Noshirvani, H., O'Sullivan, G., et al. (1993). "Alprazolam and exposure alone and combined in panic disorder with agoraphobia: A controlled study in London and Toronto": Reply. *British Journal of Psychiatry*, *162*, 790–794.

Martin, N. G., Jardine, R., Andrews, G., & Heath, A. C. (1988). Anxiety disorders and neuroticism: Are there genetic factors specific to panic? *Acta Psychiatrica Scandinavica*, *77*, 698–706.

Massana, G., Gasto, C., Junque, C., Mercader, J. M., Gomez, B., Massana, J., et al. (2002). Reduced levels of creatine in the right medial temporal lobe region of panic disorder patients detected with (1)H magnetic resonance spectoscopy. *Neuroimage*, *16*(pt. 1), 836–842.

Massana, G., Serra-Grabulosa, J. M., Salgado-Pineda, P., Gasto, C., Junque, C., Massana, J., et al. (2003). Amygdalar atrophy in panic disorder patients detected by volumetric magnetic resonance imaging. *Neuroimage*, *19*, 80–90.

McCraty, R., Atkinson, M., Tomasino, D. & Stuppy, W. P. (2001). Analysis of twenty-four hour heart rate variability in patients with panic disorder. *Biological Psychiatry*, *56*, 131–150.

McHorney, C. A., Ware, J. E., & Raczek, A. E. (1993). The MOS 36-Item Short-Form Health Survey (SF–36): II. Psychometric and clinical tests of validity in measuring physical and mental health constructs. *Medical Care. 31*, 247–263.

McNally, R. J. (1994). *Panic disorder: A critical analysis*. New York: Guilford.

McNally, R. J., & Lorenz, M. (1987). Anxiety sensitivity in agoraphobics. *Journal of Behavior Therapy and Experimental Psychiatry*, *18*, 3–11.

McNally, R. J., Riemann, B. C., & Kim, E. (1990). Selective processing of threat cues in panic disorder. *Behaviour Research and Therapy*, *28*, 407–412.

McNally, R. J., Riemann, B. C., Louro, C. E., Lukach, B. M., & Kim, E. (1992). Cognitive processing of emotional information in panic disorder. *Behaviour Research & Therapy*, *30*, 143–149.

Mellman, T. A., & Uhde, T. W. (1989). Sleep panic attacks: New clinical findings and theoretical implications. *American Journal of Psychiatry*, *146*, 1024–1027.

Messenger, C., & Shean, G. (1998). The effects of anxiety sensitivity and history of panic on reactions to stressors in a non-clinical sample. *Journal of Behavior Therapy*, *29*, 279–288.

Middleton, H. C., & Ashby, M. (1995). Clinical recovery from panic disorder is associated with evidence of changes in cardiovascular regulation. *Acta Psychiatrica Scandinavica*, *91*, 108–113.

Miller, J. J., Fletcher, K., & Kabat-Zinn, J. (1995). Three-year follow-up and clinical implications of a mindfulness meditation-based stress reduction intervention in the treatment of anxiety disorders. *General Hospital Psychiatry*, *17*, 192–200.

Mineka, S., & Cook, M. (1986). Immunization against the observational conditioning of snake fear in rhesus monkeys. *Journal of Abnormal Psychology*, *95*, 307–318.

Mineka, S., Gunnar, M., & Champoux, M. (1986). Control and early socioemotional development: Infant rhesus monkeys reared in controllable versus uncontrollable environments. *Child Development*, *57*, 1241–1256.

Mineka, S., & Henderson, R. W. (1985). Controllability and predictability in acquired motivation. *Annual Review of Psychology*, *36*, 495–529.

Mineka, S., Watson, D., & Clark, L. A. (1998). Comorbidity of anxiety and unipolar mood disorders. *Annual Review of Psychology*, *49*, 377–412.

Mitte, K. (2005). A meta-analysis of the efficacy of psycho- and pharmacotherapy in panic disorder with and without agoraphobia. *Journal of Affective Disorders*, *88*, 27–45.

Moore, P. S., Whaley, S. E., & Sigman, M. (2004). Interactions between mothers and children: Impacts of maternal and child anxiety. *Journal of Abnormal Psychology*, *113*, 471–476.

Moisan, D. & Engels, M. L. (1995). Childhood trauma and personality disorder in 43 women with panic disorder. *Psychological Reports, 76*, 1133–1134.

Morisette, S. B., Spiegel, D. A., & Heinrichs, N. (2005). Sensation-Focused intensive treatment for panic disorder with moderate to severe agoraphobia. *Cognitive and Behavioral Practice, 12*, 17–29.

Myers, J. K., Weissman, M. M., Tischler, G. L., Holzer, C. E., Leaf, P. J., Orvaschel, H., et al. (1984). Six-month prevalence of psychiatric disorders in three communities. *Archives of General Psychiatry, 41*, 959–967.

Neidhardt, E., & Florin, I. (1999). Memory bias for panic-related material in patients with panic disorder. *Psychopathology, 32*, 260–266.

Néron, S., Lacroix, D., & Chaput, Y. (1995). Group vs. individual cognitive behaviour therapy in panic disorder: An open clinical trial with a six month follow-up. *Canadian Journal of Behavioural Science, 27*, 379–392.

Newman, M. G., Holmes, M., Zuellig, A. R., Kachin, K. E., & Behar, E. (2006). The reliability and validity of the panic disorder self-report: A new diagnostic screening measure of panic disorder. *Psychological Assessment, 18*, 49–61.

Newman, M. G., Kenardy, J., Herman, S., & Taylor, C. B. (1997). Comparison of palmtop-computer-assisted brief cognitive-behavioral treatment to cognitive-behavioral treatment for panic disorder. *Journal of Consulting and Clinical Psychology, 65*, 178–183.

Nixon, P. G. (1993). The grey area of effort syndrome and hyperventilation: From Thomas Lewis to today. *Journal of the Royal College of Physicians of London, 27*, 377–383.

Norton, G. R., Cox, B. J., & Malan, J. (1992). Non-clinical panickers: A critical review. *Clinical Psychology Review, 12*, 121–139.

Noyes, R., Clancy, J., Garvey, M., & Anderson, D. J. (1987). Is agoraphobia a variant of panic disorder or separate illness? *Journal of Anxiety Disorders, 1*, 3–13.

Noyes, R., Crowe, R. R., Harris, E. L., Hamra, B. J., McChesney, C. M., & Chaudhry, D. R. (1986). Relationship between panic disorder and agoraphobia: A family study. *Archives of General Psychiatry, 43*, 227–232.

Öhman, A., & Mineka, S. (2001). Fears, phobias, and preparedness: Toward an evolved module of fear and fear learning. *Psychological Review, 108*, 483–522.

Otto, M. W., Pollack, M. H., Sachs, G. S., Reiter, S. R., Meltzer-Brody, S., & Rosenbaum, J. F. (1993). Discontinuation of benzodiazepine treatment: Efficacy of cognitive-behavioral therapy for patients with panic disorder. *American Journal of Psychiatry, 150*, 1485–1490.

Papousek, H., & Papousek, M. (1997). Fragile aspects of early social integration. In L. Murray & P. J. Cooper (Eds.), *Postpartum depression and child development* (pp. 35–53). New York: Guilford.

Papousek, H., & Papousek, M. (2002). Intuitive parenting. In M. H. Bornstein (Ed.), *Handbook of parenting* (2nd ed., vol. 2). *Biology and ecology of parenting* (pp. 183–203). Mahwah, NJ: Lawrence Erlbaum.

Papp, L. A., Klein, D. F., & Gorman, J. M. (1993). Carbon dioxide hypersensitivity, hyperventilation, and panic disorder. *American Journal of Psychiatry, 150*, 1149–1157.

Pauli, P., Amrhein, C., Muhlberger, A., Dengler, W. & Wiedemann, G. (2005). Electrocortical evidence for an early abnormal processing of panic-related words in panic disorder patients. *International Journal of Psychophysiology, 57*, 33–41.

Pauli, P., Dengler, W., & Wiedemann, G. (2005). Implicit and explicit memory processes in panic patients as reflected in behavioral and electrophysiological measures. *Journal of Behavior Therapy and Experimental Psychiatry, 36*, 111–127.

Perna, G., Bertani, A., Arancio, C., Ronchi, P., & Bellodi, L. (1995). Laboratory response of patients with panic and obsessive-compulsive disorders to 35% CO_2 challenges. *American Journal of Psychiatry, 152*, 85–89.

Petersen, W. (1994). Parental relations, mental health, and delinquency in adolescents. *Adolescence, 29*, 975–990.

Pollard, C. A., Pollard, H. J., & Corn, K. J. (1989). Panic onset and major events in the lives of agoraphobics: A test of contiguity. *Journal of Abnormal Psychology, 98*, 318–321.

Porges, S. W. (1991). Vagal tone: An autonomic mediator of affect. In J. Garber & K. A. Dodge, (Eds.), *The development of emotion regulation and dysregulation*. Cambridge, UK: Cambridge University Press.

Porges, S. W. (1992). Autonomic regulation and attention. In B. A. Campbell, H. Hayne, & R. Richardson (Eds.), *Attention and information processing in infants and adults*. Hillsdale, NJ: Lawrence Erlbaum.

Porges, S. W. (2003). The polyvagal theory: Phylogenetic contributions to social behavior. *Physiology & Behavior, 79*, 503–513.

Powers, M. B., Smits, J. A. J., & Telch, M. J. (2004). Disentangling the effects of safety behavior utilization and safety-behavior availability during exposure based treatments: A placebo- controlled trial. *Journal of Consulting and Clinical Psychology*, *72*, 448–454.

Rachman, S., & Hodgson, R. (1974). Synchrony and desynchrony in fear and avoidance. *Behaviour Research and Therapy*, *12*, 311–318.

Rachman, S., Lopatka, C., & Levitt, K. (1988). Experimental analyses of panic: II. Panic patients. *Behaviour Research and Therapy*, *26*, 33–40.

Ramel, W., Goldin, P. R., Carmona, P. E., & McQuaid, J. R. (2004). The effects of mindfulness meditation on cognitive processes and affect in patients with past depression. *Cognitive Therapy and Research*, *28*, 433–455.

Rapee, R. M. (1986). Differential response to hyperventilation in panic disorder and generalied anxiety disorder. *Journal of Abnomal Psychology*, *95*, 24–28.

Rapee, R. M. (1994). Failure to replicate a memory bias in panic disorder. *Journal of Anxiety Disorders*, *8*, 291–300.

Rapee, R. M., Brown, T. A., Antony, M. M., & Barlow, D. H. (1992). Response to hyperventilation and inhalation of 5.5% carbon dioxide-enriched air across the *DSM-III-R* anxiety disorders. *Journal of Abnormal Psychology*, *101*, 538–552.

Rapee, R. M., Craske, M. G., & Barlow, D. H. (1990). Subject-described features of panic attacks using self-monitoring. *Journal of Anxiety Disorders*, *4*, 171–181.

Rapee, R. M., Craske, M. G., & Barlow, D. H. (1995). Assessment instrument for panic disorder that includes fear of sensation-producing activities: The Albany Panic and Phobia Questionnaire. *Anxiety*, *1*, 114–122.

Rapee, R. M., Litwin, E. M., & Barlow, D. H. (1990). Impact of life events on subjects with panic disorder and on comparison subjects. *American Journal of Psychiatry*, *147*, 640–644.

Rapee, R., Mattick, R., & Murrell, E. (1986). Cognitive mediation in the affective component of spontaneous panic attacks. *Journal of Behavior Therapy & Experimental Psychiatry*, *17*, 245–253.

Rapee, R. M., & Medoro, L. (1994). Fear of physical sensations and trait anxiety as mediators of the response to hyperventilation in nonclinical subjects. *Journal of Abnormal Psychology*, *103*, 693–699.

Rapee, R. M., & Murrell, E. (1988). Predictors of agoraphobic avoidance. *Journal of Anxiety Disorders*, *2*, 203–217.

Razran, G. (1961). The observable unconscious and the inferable conscious in current Soviet psychophysiology: Interoceptive conditioning, semantic conditioning, and the orienting reflex. *Psychological Review*, *69*, 81–150.

Reiss, S. (1991). Expectancy model of fear, anxiety and panic. *Clinical Psychology Review*, *11*, 141–155.

Reiss, S., Peterson, R. A., Gursky, D. M., & McNally, R. J. (1986). Anxiety sensitivity, anxiety frequency and the predictions of fearfulness. *Behaviour Research and Therapy*, *24*, 1–8.

Richards, J. M., & Gross, J. J. (2000) Emotion regulation and memory: The cognitive costs of keeping one's cool. *Journal of Personality and Social Psychology*, *79*, 410–424.

Richards, J., Klein, B., & Carlbring, P. (2003). Internet-based treatment for panic disorder. *Cognitive Behaviour Therapy*, *32*, 125–135.

Rijken, H., Kraaimaat, F., de Ruiter, C., & Garssen, B. (1992). A follow-up study on short-term treatment of agoraphobia. *Behaviour Research and Therapy*, *30*, 63–66.

Robert McComb, J. J., Tacon, A. M., Randolph, P., & Caldera, Y. (2004). A pilot study to examine the effects of a mindfulness-based stress-reduction and relaxation program on levels of stress hormones, physical functioning, and submaximal exercise responses. *Journal of Alternative and Complementary Medicine*, *10*, 819–827.

Rochat, P., & Striano, T. (1999). Social-cognitive development in the first year. In P. Rochat (Ed.), *Early social cognition: Understanding others in the first months of life* (pp. 3–34). Mahwah, NJ: Lawrence Erlbaum.

Rodriguez, B. I., & Craske, M. G. (1993). The effects of distraction during exposure to phobic stimuli. *Behaviour Research and Therapy*, *31*, 549–558.

Rodriguez, B. I., & Craske, M. G. (1995). Does distraction interfere with fear reduction during exposure? A test among animal-fearful subjects. *Behavior Therapy. Special Issue: Experimental pain as a model for the study of clinical pain*, *26*, 337–349.

Roth, W. T., Margraf, J., Ehlers, A., Taylor, C. B., Maddock, R. J., Davies, S., et al. (1992). Stress test reactivity in panic disorder. *Archives of General Psychiatry*, *49*(4), 301–310.

Roy-Byrne, P. P., & Cowley, D. S. (1995). Course and outcome in panic disorder: A review of recent follow-up studies. *Anxiety*, *1*, 151–160.

Roy-Byrne, P. P., & Cowley, D. S. (2002). Pharamcologic treatments for panic disorder, generalized anxiety disorder, specific phobia and social anxiety disorders. In Nathan P. E. & Gorman J. M. (Eds.), *A guide to treatments that work* (2nd ed.). 337–365. New York: Oxford University Press.

Roy-Byrne, P. P., Cowley, D. S., Greenblatt, D. J., Shader, R. I. & Hommer, D. (1990). Reduced benzodiazepine sensitivity in panic disorder. *Archives of General Psychiatry, 47,* 534–538.

Roy-Bryne, P. P., Craske, M. G., Stein, M. B., Sullivan, G., Bystritsky, A., Katon, W., et al. (2005). A randomized effectiveness trial of cognitive-behavioral therapy and medication for primary care treatment of panic disorder. *Archives of General Psychiatry, 62,* 290–298.

Roy-Byrne, P. P., Geraci, M., & Uhde, T. W. (1986). Life events and the onset of panic disorder. *American Journal of Psychiatry, 143,* 1424–1427.

Roy-Byrne, P. P., Katon, W., Cowley, D. S., & Russo, J. (2002). A randomized effectiveness trial of collaborative care for patients with panic disorder in primary care. *Archives of General Psychiatry, 58,* 869–876.

Roy-Byrne, P. P., Mellman, T. A., Uhde, T. W. (1988). Biologic findings in panic disorder: Neuroendocrine and sleep-related abnormalities. *Journal of Anxiety Disorders. Special Issue: Perspectives on panic-related disorders, 2,* 17–29.

Roy-Byrne, P. P., Sherbourne, C. D., Craske, M. G., Stein, M. G., Katon, W., Sullivan, G., et al. (2003). Moving treatment research from clinical trials to the real world *Psychiatric Services, 54,* 327–332.

Roy-Byrne, P. P., Stang, P., Wittchen, H. U., Ustun, B., Walters, E. E., & Kessler, R. C. (2000). Lifetime panic-depression comorbidity in the National Comorbidity Survey. Association with symptoms, impairment, course and help-seeking. *The British Journal of Clinical Psychiatry, 58*(Suppl. 2), 46–50.

Roy-Byrne, P. P., Stein, M. B., Russo, J., Mercier, E., Thomas, R., McQuaid, J., et al. (1999). Panic disorder in the primary care setting: Comorbidity, disability, service utilization, and treatment. *Journal of Clinical Psychiatry, 60,* 492–499.

Rueter, M. A., Scaramella, L., Wallace, L. E., & Conger, R. D. (1999). First onset of depressive or anxiety disorders predicted by the longitudinal course of internalizing symptoms and parent–adolescent disagreements. *Archives of General Psychiatry, 56,* 726–732.

Safren, S. A., Gershuny, B. S., Marzol, P., Otto, M. W. & Pollack, M. H. (2002). History of childhood abuse in panic disorder, social phobia, and generalized anxiety disorder. *Journal of Nervous and Mental Disease 190,* 453–456.

Sakai, Y., Kumano, H., Nishikawa, M., Sakano, Y., Kaiya, Hisanobu., et al. (2005). "Cerebral glucose metabolism associated with a fear network in panic disorder": Erratum. *Neuroreport: For Rapid Communication of Neuroscience Research, 16,* 1251.

Salkovskis, P. M. (1988). Phenomenology, assessment, and the cognitive model of panic. In S. M. J. D. Rachman (Ed.), *Panic: Psychological perspectives* (pp. 111–136). Hillsdale, NJ: Erlbaum.

Salkovskis, P. M., Clark, D. M., & Hackmann, A. (1991). Treatment of panic attacks using cognitive therapy without exposure or breathing retraining. *Behaviour Research and Therapy, 29,* 161–166.

Salkovskis, P. M., Clark, D. M., Hackman, A., Wells, A., & Gelder, M. G. (1999). An experimental investigation of the role of safety behaviours in the maintenance of panic disorder with agoraphobia. *Behaviour Research and Therapy, 37,* 559–574.

Sanacora, G., Mason, G. F., Rothman, D. L., Behar, K. L., Hyder, F., Petroff, O. A., et al. (1999). Reduced cortical gamma-aminobutyric acid levels in depressed patients determined by proton magnetic resonance spectroscopy. *Archives of General Psychiatry, 56,* 1043–1047.

Sanderson, W. C., Rapee, R. M., & Barlow, D. H. (1989). The influence of an illusion of control on panic attacks induced via inhalation of 5.5% carbon dioxide-enriched air. *Archives of General Psychiatry, 46,* 157–162.

Scherrer, J. F., True, W. R., Xian, H., Lyons, M. J., Eisen, S. A., Goldberg, J., et al. (2000). Evidence for genetic influences common and specific to symptoms of generalized anxiety and panic. *Journal of Affective Disorders, 57,* 25–35.

Schittecatte, M., Charles, G., Depauw, Y., Mesters, P., & Wilmotte, J. (1988). Growth hormone response to clonidine in panic disorder patients. *Psychiatry Research, 23,* 147–151.

Schmidt, N. B., Lerew, D. R., & Jackson, R. J. (1997). The role of anxiety sensitivity in the pathogenesis of panic: Prospective evaluation of spontaneous panic attacks during acute stress. *Journal of Abnormal Psychology, 106,* 355–364.

Schmidt, N. B., Lerew, D. R., & Jackson, R. J. (1999). Prospective evaluation of anxiety sensitivity in the pathogenesis of panic: Replication and extension. *Journal of Abnormal Psychology, 108,* 532–537.

Schmidt, N. B., Trakowski, J. H., & Staab, J. P. (1997). Extinction of panicogenic effects of a 35% CO_2 challenge in patients with panic disorder. *Journal of Abnormal Psychology, 106,* 630–638.

Schumaker, J., Abou Jamra, R., Becker, T., Klopp, N., Franke, P., Jacob, C., et al. (2005). Investigation of the DAO/G30 locus in panic disorder. *Molecular Psychiatry 10*(5), 428–429.

Shear, M. K., Polan, J. J., Harshfield, G., Pickering, T., Mann, J. J., Frances, A., et al. (1992). Ambulatory monitoring of blood pressure and heart rate in panic patients. *Journal of Anxiety Disorders*, *6*, 213–221.

Shibuki, K., Kamamura, M., & Yagi, K. (1984). Conditioned heart rate response: Testing under anaesthesia in rats. *Neuroscience Research*, *1*, 373–378.

Shioiri, T., Kojima, M., Toshihiro, H., Kitamura, H., Tanaka, A., Yoshizawa, M., et al. (2005). Dysfunctional baroreflex regulation of sympathetic nerve activity in remitted patients with panic disorder: A new methodological approach. *European Archives of Psychiatry and Clinical Neuroscience*, *255*, 293–298.

Slaap, B. R., Nielen, M. M., Boshuisen, M. L., van Roon, A. M., & den Boer, J. A. (2004). Five-minute recordings of heart rate variability in obsessive-compulsive disorder, panic disorder and healthy volunteers. *Journal of Affective Disorders*, *78*, 141–148.

Swinson, R. P., Soulios, C., Cox, B. J., & Kuch, K. (1992). Brief treatment of emergency room patients with panic attacks. *American Journal of Psychiatry*, *149*, 944–946.

Sokolowska, M., Siegel, S., & Kim. J. A. (2002). Intra-administration associations: Conditional hyperalgesia elicited by morphine onset cues. *Journal of Experimental Psychology: Animal Behavior Processes*, *28*, 309–320.

Speca, M., Carolson, L. E., Goodey, E., & Angen, M. (2000). A randomized, wait-list controlled clinical trial: The effect of a mindfulness meditation-based stress reduction program on mood and symptoms of stress in cancer outpatients. *Psychosomatic Medicine*, *62*, 613–622.

Spiegel, D. A., Bruce, T. J., Gregg, S. F., & Nuzzarello, A. (1994). Does cognitive behavior therapy assist slow-taper alprazolam discontinuation in panic disorder? *American Journal of Psychiatry*, *151*, 876–881.

Stein, M. B., & Asmundson, G. J. G. (1994). Autonomic function in panic disorder: Cardiorespiratory and plasma catecholamine responsivity to multiple challenges of the autonomic nervous system. *Biological Psychiatry*, *36*, 548–558.

Stein, M. B., Walker, J. R., Anderson, G., Hazen, A. L., Ross, C. A., Eldridge, G., et al. (1996). Childhood physical and sexual abuse in patients with anxiety disorders and a community sample. *American Journal of Psychiatry*, *153*, 275–277.

Stubbe, D. E., Zahner, G. E. P., Goldstein, M. J., & Leckman, J. F. (1993). Diagnostic specificity of a brief measure of expressed emotion: A community study of children. *Journal of Child Psychology and Psychiatry*, *34*, 139–154.

Sturges, L. V., Goetsch, V. L., Ridley, J., & Whittal, M. (1998). Anxiety sensitivity and response to hyperventilation challenge: Physiologic arousal, interoceptive acuity, and subjective distress. *Journal of Anxiety Disorders*, *12*, 103–115.

Takahashi, T., Murata, T., Hamada, T., Omori, M., Kosaka, H., Kikuchi, M., et al. (2005). Changes in EEG and autonomic nervous activity during meditation and their association with personality traits. *International Journal of Psychophysiology*, *55*, 199–207.

Taylor, S., Koch, W. J., & McNally, R. J. (1992). How does anxiety sensitivity vary across the anxiety disorders? *Journal of Anxiety Disorders*, *6*, 249–259.

Taylor, C. B., Sheikh, J., Agras, W. S., Roth, W. T., Margraf, J., Ehlers, A., et al. (1986). Ambulatory heart rate changes in patients with panic attacks. *American Journal of Psychiatry*, *143*, 478–482.

Telch, M. J., Brouilard, M., Telch, C. F., Agras, W. S., & Taylor, C. B. (1989). Role of cognitive appraisal in panic-related avoidance. *Behaviour Research and Therapy*, *27*, 373–383.

Telch, M. J., Shermans, M. D., & Lucas, J. A. (1989). Anxiety sensitivity: Unitary personality trait or domain-specific appraisals? *Journal of Anxiety Disorders*, *3*, 25–32.

Telch, M. J., Valentiner, D. P., Ilai, D., Young, P. R., Powers, M. B., & Smits, J. A. J. (2004). Fear activation and distraction during the emotional processing of claustrophobic fear. *Journal of Behavior Therapy and Experimental Psychiatry*, *35*, 219–232.

Thayer, J. F., Friedman, B. H., & Borkovec, T. D. (1996). Autonomic characteristics of generalized anxiety disorder and worry. *Biological Psychiatry*, *39*, 255–266.

Thayer, J. F., Friedman, B. H., Borkovec, T. D., Johnsen, B. H., & Molina, S. (2000). Phasic heart period reactions to cued threat and nonthreat stimuli in generalized anxiety disorder. *Psychophysiology*, *37*, 361–368.

Thorgeirsson, T. E., Oskarsson, H., Desnica, N., Kostic, J. P., Stefansson, J. G., Kolbeinsson, H., et al. (2003). Anxiety with panic disorder linked to chromosome 9q in Iceland. *American Journal of Human Genetics*, *72*, 1221–1230.

Thyer, B. A., Himle, J., Curtis, G. C., Cameron, O. G., & Nesse, R. M. (1985). A comparison of panic disorder and agoraphobia with panic attacks. *Comprehensive Psychiatry*, *26*, 208–214.

Thwaites, R., & Freeston, M. H. (2005). Safety-seeking behaviours: Fact or function? How can we clinically differentiate between safety behaviours and adaptive coping strategies across anxiety disorders? *Behavioural and Cognitive Psychotherapy, 33*, 177–188.

Tsao, J. C. I., Lewin, M. R., & Craske, M. G. (1998). The effects of cognitive-behavior therapy for panic disorder on comorbid conditions. *Journal of Anxiety Disorders, 12*, 357–371.

Tsao, J. C. I., Mystkowski, J. L., Zucker, B. G., & Craske, M. G. (2002). Effects of cognitive-behavioral therapy for panic disorder on comorbid conditions: Replication and extension. *Behavior Therapy, 33*, 493–509.

Tsao, J. C. I., Mystkowski, J. L., Zucker, B. G., & Craske, M. G. (2005). Impact of cognitive-behavioral therapy for panic disorder on comorbidity: A controlled investigation. *Behaviour Research and Therapy, 43*, 959–970.

Turner, S. M., Williams, S. L., Beidel, D. C., & Mezzich, J. E. (1986). Panic disorder and agoraphobia with panic attacks: Covariation along the dimensions of panic and agoraphobic fear. *Journal of Abnormal Psychology, 95*, 384–388.

Uchida, R. R., Del-Ben, C. M., Santos, A. C., Araujo, D., Crippa, J. A., Guiamaraes, F. S., et al. (2003). Decreased left temporal lobe volume of panic patients measured by magnetic resonance imaging. *Brazilian Journal of Medical and Biological Research, 36*, 925–929.

Uhde, T. W. (1994). Anxiety and growth disturbance: Is there a connection? A review of biological studies in social phobia. *Journal of Clinical Psychiatry, 55*(Suppl), 17–27.

Uno, T. (1970). The effects of awareness and successive inhibition on interoceptive and exteroceptive conditioning of the galvanic skin response. *Psychophysiology, 7*, 27–43.

van Balkom, A. J. L. M., de Beurs, E., Koele, P., Lange, A., & van Dyck, R. (1996). Long-term benzodiazepine use is associated with smaller treatment gain in panic disorder with agoraphobia. *Journal of Nervous and Mental Disease, 184*(2), 133–135.

van Beek, N., Schruers, K. R. J., & Friez, E. J. L. (2005). Prevalence of respiratory disorders in first-degree relatives of panic disorder patients. *Journal of Affective Disorders, 87*, 337–340.

van den Heuvel, O. A., Veltman, D. J., Groenewegen, H. J., Witter, M. P., Merkelbach, J., Cath, D. C., et al. (2005). Disorder-specific neuroanatomical correlates of attentional bias in obsessive-compulsive disorder, panic disorder, and hypochondriasis. *Archives of General Psychiatry, 62*, 922–933.

van den Hout, M., Arntz, A., & Hoekstra, R. (1994). Exposure reduced agoraphobia but not panic, and cognitive therapy reduced panic but not agoraphobia. *Behaviour Research and Therapy, 32*, 447–451.

van Megen, H. J., Westenberg, H. G., Den Boer, J. A., & Kahn, R. S. (1996). The panic-inducing properties of the cholecystokinin tetrapeptide CCK4 in patients with panic disorder. *European Neuropsychopharmacology, 6*, 187–194.

Veltman, D. J., van Zijderveld, G., Tilders, F. J. H., & van Dyck, R. (1996). Epinephrine and fear of bodily sensations in panic disorder and social phobia. *Journal of Psychopharmacology, 10*, 259–265.

Veltman, D. J., van Zijderveld, G. A., van Dyck, R., & Bakker, A. (1998). Predictability, controllability, and fear of symptoms of anxiety in epinephrine-induced panic. *Biological Psychiatry, 44*, 1017–1026.

Verburg, K., Griez, E., Meijer, J., & Pols, H. (1995). Respiratory disorders as a possible predisposing factor for panic disorder. *Journal of Affective Disorders, 33*, 129–134.

Wardle, J., Hayward, P., Higgitt, A., Stabl, M., Blizard, R., & Gray, J. (1994). Effects of concurrent diazepam treatment on the outcome of exposure therapy in agoraphobia. *Behaviour Research and Therapy, 32*, 203–215.

Ware, J. E. (1993). *SF–36 health survey manual and interpretation guide*. Boston: The Health Institute, New England Medical Center.

Warren, R., & Zgourides, G. (1988). Panic attacks in high school students: Implications for prevention and intervention. *Phobia Practice and Research Journal, 1*, 97–113.

Watson, D., & Clark, L. A. (1984). Negative affectivity: The disposition to experience aversive emotional states. *Psychological Bulletin, 96*, 465–490.

Watt, M. C., & Stewart, S. H. (2000). Anxiety sensitivity mediates the relationships between childhood learning experiences and elevated hypochondriacal concerns in young adulthood. *Journal of Psychosomatic Research, 49*, 107–118.

Watt, M. C., Stewart, S. H., & Cox, B. J. (1998). A retrospective study of the learning history origins of anxiety sensitivity. *Behaviour Research and Therapy, 36*, 505–525.

Wenzlaff, R. M., & Wegner, D. M. (2000). Thought suppression. *Annual Review of Psychology, 51*, 59–91.

Westen, D., & Morrison, K. (2001). A multidimensional meta-analysis of treatments for depression, panic, and generalized anxiety disorder: An empirical examination of the status of empirically supported therapies. *Journal of Consulting and Clinical Psychology, 69*, 875–899.

Westra, H. A., Stewart, S. H., & Conrad, B. E. (2002). Naturalistic manner of benzodiazepine use and cognitive behavioral therapy outcome in panic disorder with agoraphobia. *Journal of Anxiety Disorders 16*, 233–246.

Whaley, S. E., Pinto, A., & Sigman, M. (1999). Characterizing interactions between anxious mothers and their children. *Journal of Consulting and Clinical Psychology, 67*, 826–836.

Wheeler, E. O., White, P. D., Reed, E. W., & Cohen, M. E. (1950). Neurocirculatory asthenia, anxiety neurosis, effort syndrome, neurasthenia: A 20 year follow-up study of 173 patients. *Journal of the American Medical Association, 142*, 878–889.

White, K. S. & Barlow, D. H. (2002). Panic disorder and agoraphobia. In D. H. Barlow (Ed.), *Anxiety and its disorders: The nature and treatment of anxiety and panic*. New York: Guilford.

Wilkinson, D. J., Thompson, J. M., Lambert, G. W., Jennings, G. L., Schwarz, R. G., Jefferys, D., et al. (1998). Sympathetic activity in patients with panic disorder at rest, under laboratory mental stress, and during panic attacks. *Archives of General Psychiatry, 55*, 511–520.

Williams, S. L., & Falbo, J. (1996). Cognitive and performance-based treatments for panic attacks in people with varying degrees of agoraphobic disability. *Behaviour Research and Therapy, 34*, 253–264.

Windmann, S., Sakhavat, Z., & Kutas, M. (2002). Electrophysiological evidence reveals affective evaluation deficits early in stimulus processing in patients with panic disorder. *Journal of Abnormal Psychology, 111*, 357–369.

Wittchen, H. U., & Essau, C. A. (1991). The epidemiology of panic attacks, panic disorder and agoraphobia. In J. R. Walker, G. R. Norton, & C. A. Ross (Eds.), *Panic disorder and agoraphogia* (pp. 103–149). Monterey, CA: Brooks/Cole.

Wittchen, H. -U., Reed, V., & Kessler, R. C. (1998). The relationship of agoraphobia and panic in a community sample of adolescents and young adults. *Archives of General Psychiatry, 55*, 1017–1024.

Wood, J., McLeod, B., Sigman, M., Hwang, W., & Chu, B. (2003). Parenting and childhood anxiety: Theory, empirical findings, and future directions. *Journal of Child Psychology and Psychiatry and Allied Disciplines, 44*, 134–151.

Woodruff-Borden, J., Morrow, C., Bourland, S., & Cambron, S. (2002). The behavior of anxious parents: Examining mechanisms of transmission of anxiety from parent to child. *Journal of Clinical Child and Adolescent Psychiatry, 31*, 364–374.

Wooley, C. F. (1982). Jacob Mendez DaCosta: Medical teacher, clinician, and clinical investigator. *American Journal of Cardiology, 50*, 1145–1148.

Yelin, E., Mathias, S. D., Buesching, D. P., Rowland, C., et al. (1996). The impact on employment of an intervention to increase recognition of previously untreated anxiety among primary care physicians. *Social Science & Medicine, 42*(7), 1069–1075.

Zarate, R., Rapee, R. M., Craske, M. G., & Barlow, D. H. (1988). Response-norms for symptom induction procedures. Poster presented at 22nd Annual AABT convention, New York.

Zinbarg, R. E., & Barlow, D. H. (1996). Structure of anxiety and the anxiety disorders: A hierarchical model. *Journal of Abnormal Psychology, 105*, 184–193.

Zinbarg, R. E., Barlow, D. H., & Brown, T. A. (1997). Hierarchical structural and general factor saturation of the anxiety sensitivity index: Evidence and implications. *Psychological Assessment, 9*, 277–284.

Zucker, B. G., & Craske, M. G. (2001). Prevention of anxiety disorders: A model for intervention. *Applied & Preventive Psychology, 10*, 155–175.

Zvolensky, M. J., Kotov, R., Antipova, A. V., & Schmidt, N. B. (2005). Diathesis stress model for panic-related distress: A test in a Russian epidemiological sample. *Behaviour Research and Therapy, 43*, 521–532.

Chapter 5

Obsessive-Compulsive Disorder

Jonathan S. Abramowitz

The Nature of Obsessive-Compulsive Disorder

Obsessive-Compulsive Disorder (OCD) is one of the most devastating psychological disorders. Its symptoms often interfere with work, school, social, and emotional relationships, and with activities of daily living (e.g., using the bathroom, leaving the house). Moreover, the psychopathology of OCD is among the most complex of the psychological disorders. Sufferers appear to struggle against seemingly ubiquitous unwanted thoughts and urges that, while senseless on the one hand, are perceived as signs of danger on the other. The wide array and intricate associations between behavioral and cognitive symptoms can perplex even the most experienced of clinicians. This chapter will describe the nature of OCD symptoms, the leading explanatory theories, and empirically supported approaches to assessment and treatment.

OVERVIEW OF THE DIAGNOSTIC CRITERIA

According to the *Diagnostic and Statistical Manual of Mental Disorders* (*DSM-IV-TR*;), American Psychiatric Association [APA, 2000], OCD is an anxiety disorder defined by the presence of *obsessions* or *compulsions* that produce significant distress and cause noticeable interference with various aspects of functioning such as academic, occupational, social, leisure, or family settings (the *DSM-IV* diagnostic criteria for OCD are presented in Table 5.1). Obsessions are defined as intrusive thoughts, ideas, images, impulses, or doubts that the person experiences as senseless and that evoke affective

TABLE 5.1 *DSM-IV* **Diagnostic Criteria for OCD**

A. Either obsessions or compulsions.

Obsessions are:

(1) Repetitive and persistent thoughts, images or impulses that are experienced, at some point, as intrusive and inappropriate and that cause marked anxiety or distress

(2) The thoughts, images, or impulses are not worries about real-life problems

(3) The person tries to ignore or suppress the thoughts, images, or impulses, or neutralize them with some other thought or action

(4) The thoughts, images, or impulses are recognized as a product of one's own mind and not imposed from without

Compulsions are:

(1) Repetitive behaviors or mental acts that one feels driven to perform in response to an obsession or according to certain rules

(2) The behaviors or mental acts are aimed at preventing or reducing distress or preventing feared consequences; however the behaviors or mental acts are clearly excessive or are not connected in a realistic way with what they are designed to neutralize or prevent.

B. At some point during the disorder the person has recognized that the obsessions or compulsions are excessive or unreasonable.

C. The obsessions or compulsions cause marked distress, are time-consuming (take more than 1 hour a day), or significantly interfere with usual daily functioning.

D. The content of the obsessions or compulsions is not better accounted for by another Axis I disorder, if present. For example, concern with appearance in the presence of Body Dysmorphic Disorder, or preoccupation with having a serious illness in the presence of hypochondriasis.

E. Symptoms are not due to the direct physiological effects of a substance or a general medical condition.

Specify if:

With poor insight: if for most of the time the person does not recognize that their obsessions and compulsions are excessive or unreasonable.

Adapted from the *DSM-IV* diagnostic criteria for OCD (American Psychiatric Association, 1994, pp. 422–423). Adapted with permission.

distress (i.e., anxiety, doubt). Classic examples include unwanted ideas of germs and contamination, unwanted doubts that one has been negligent, and unwanted impulses to act in a violent or sexually inappropriate way. *Compulsions* are urges to perform overt (e.g., checking, washing) or mental *rituals* (e.g., praying). Such rituals are usually performed in response to obsessions and with a sense of pressure to act. The person typically perceives the rituals (or their extensiveness) as senseless or excessive.

Although the *DSM* definition implies that obsessions and compulsions are independent phenomena (i.e., one *or* the other is necessary and sufficient for a diagnosis of OCD), evidence from large studies (e.g., Foa & Kozak, 1995) suggests that 96% of OCD patients report both obsessions and compulsions. Another limitation of the *DSM*'s definition is its emphasis on the *repetitiveness* and *persistent* nature of obsessions and compulsions. Whereas these characteristics are the most readily observable signs of the disorder, the defining characteristic of OCD is actually the relationship between obsessions (which evoke distress) and compulsive rituals (which are anxiety-reduction strategies). That is, OCD is best understood as a disorder in which obsessional thoughts have become fear cues, and compulsive rituals represent attempts to resist or control the obsessions, or to reduce the probability of some feared consequence associated with the obsessions.

Obsessions

It may be tempting to label any kind of repetitive thought or preoccupation as an "obsession." Indeed, this term is used indiscriminately in everyday language to refer to various types of repetitive thinking such as worries about decisions, fascination with a type of car, romantic infatuation, or the tendency to pay close attention to details. The clinical term "obsession" however, is reserved for a very specific type of thought that is experienced as distressing and that leads to certain types of excessive responses. In general, obsessions are experienced as unwanted, repugnant, threatening, obscene, blasphemous, nonsensical, or all of the above. Although the content of obsessions is highly individualized and probably shaped by one's personal experiences, data from numerous studies converge to suggest that the themes of obsessions can be organized into several general categories (e.g., McKay et al., 2004). Observations from our own clinic, as presented in Table 5.2, show examples of these categories. Obsessions may also take various *forms*, including thoughts, doubts, images, impulses, and fears (Akhtar, Wig, Varma, Pershad, & Verma, 1975). Most patients evince multiple obsessional themes and forms, as well as shifts in the content of these phenomena.

Three characteristics set clinical obsessions apart from other types of repetitive thinking (e.g., worries, daydreams). First, regardless of their theme, obsessions are experienced as unwanted or uncontrollable in that they intrude into consciousness (often triggered by something in the environment). Second, while personally relevant, the content of obsessions is incongruent with the individual's belief system and is not the type of thought one would expect of him or herself. Third, obsessions are resisted; that is, they are accompanied by the sense that they must be "dealt with," neutralized, or

TABLE 5.2   Examples of Obsessions Reported by Clinic Patients with OCD

Category	Case Example
Contamination	My boss has a cold and touched my stapler, now I will get sick
	What if I stepped in dog feces and then spread the germs to my house?
Responsibility for harm	I might have put poison in the children's supper
	If I don't warn people that the floor is slippery, it will be my fault if they get hurt
	What if I hit someone with my car without realizing it?
Symmetry/order	Odd numbers are "incorrect"
	The books must be evenly placed on the shelf
Unacceptable thoughts with immoral, sexual, or violent content	Image of Jesus having sex with Mary
	Image of my grandparents having sex
	Impulse to stab my wife in her sleep

TABLE 5.3 Examples of Compulsive Rituals Reported by Clinic Patients with OCD

Category	Case Example
Decontamination	Handwashing for 45 minutes in response to using the bathroom
	Wiping down all objects brought into the house for fear of germs from recently applied pesticides on an adjacent lawn
Checking	Driving back to recheck that no accidents were caused at the intersection
	Returning home after seeing a fire engine to make sure the house wasn't on fire
Repeating routine activities	Going through a doorway over and over to prevent bad luck
	Retracing one's steps to make sure that no mistakes were made
Ordering/arranging	Saying the word left whenever one hears the word right
	Rearranging the books on the bookshelf until they are "just right"
Mental rituals	Cancelling a bad thought by thinking of a good thought
	Excessive praying to prevent feared disastrous consequences

altogether avoided. The motivation to resist is activated by the fear that if action is not taken, disastrous consequences may occur.

Compulsions

Compulsive rituals are the most conspicuous features of OCD and, in many instances, account for the most functional impairment. The *DSM* specifies that compulsions are motivated and intentional, in contrast to mechanical or robotic repetitive behaviors as observed in disorders such as Tourette's disorder. Moreover, compulsions are performed to reduce distress, in contrast to repetitive behaviors in addictive or impulse-control disorders (e.g., sexual addiction, trichotillomania), which are carried out because they produce pleasure or gratification.

Table 5.3 displays the various categories of compulsions as assessed in our clinical sample. In most instances, it is clear that compulsive rituals are performed with the intention of reducing obsessional anxiety about particular feared consequences. Examples include compulsively checking appliances to reduce fears of electrical fires, or cleaning rituals intended to remove contaminants and thereby avoid sickness. In other cases, patients have difficulty articulating the presence of particular feared consequences, and instead perform rituals to reduce anxiety or to achieve a feeling of "completeness." As Table 5.3 indicates, compulsive rituals can be overt behaviors or covert mental acts aimed at preventing a negative outcome. Examples of common mental rituals include repetition of special phrases, prayers, or numbers in a specific manner, and ritualistically going over (mentally reviewing, analyzing) one's behavior or conversations to reassure oneself that one has not made egregious mistakes or said anything offensive.

Neutralization and Compulsive Reassurance-Seeking

Most people with OCD use various overt and covert strategies that do not meet *DSM* criteria for compulsions (i.e., they are not stereotyped or repeated according to rigid rules) to control, remove, or prevent their obsessions (Freeston & Ladouceur, 1997; Ladouceur et al., 2000). On one hand, these *neutralization* strategies resemble compulsive rituals in that they are attempts to reduce anxiety. However, whereas compulsions are intended to prevent negative outcomes, patients use neutralization to offset obsessional thoughts; and this may or may not be an attempt to prevent a feared outcome (Rachman & Shafran, 1998; Salkovskis, 1985). Individuals may use different strategies to neutralize different thoughts and different strategies to cope with the same thought (Freeston & Ladouceur, 1997).

Researchers have identified several general categories of neutralization responses including overanalyzing and rational self-talk (i.e., to convince oneself of the unimportance of the thought), seeking reassurance, replacing the thought with another thought, performing a brief mental or behavioral act, distraction, and thought suppression (Ladouceur et al., 2000). The choice of neutralizing strategy may be influenced by the intensity of the obsessional thought, the context in which it occurs, how the thought is appraised, and how well particular strategies have technically worked to reduce anxiety in the past (Freeston & Ladouceur, 1997). Neutralizing can take infinitely diverse forms, and some of these strategies may be remarkably subtle.

The following examples illustrate various kinds of neutralization strategies.

- One man gripped the steering wheel more tightly (brief behavioral act) when he experienced distressing thoughts of intentionally killing his family by driving his car into opposing traffic.
- A woman with unwanted obsessional thoughts of her child drowning in the bathtub tried to suppress and/or dismiss such images when they came to mind (thought suppression).
- A woman with obsessional thoughts of harming her unsuspecting husband confessed these thoughts to him whenever they came to her mind (social strategy). She explained to her therapist, *"If I tell my husband that I'm thinking about hurting him, he'll be ready to stop me if I start to act."*

Many individuals with OCD also engage in repeated attempts to gain "ultimate" certainty that the feared consequences featured in obsessions will not (or did not) occur. Requests for assurance may take various overt and covert forms although the most straightforward style is asking similar questions over and over.

Avoidance and Concealment

Avoidance is present to some degree in most individuals with OCD and is intended to prevent exposure to situations that would evoke obsessional thoughts and compulsive urges. For some patients the aim of avoidance is to prevent specific consequences such as contamination or illness, whereas in other instances avoidance is focused on preventing obsessional thoughts from occurring in the first place. For example, one woman avoided using public staircases because they evoked thoughts and fears of impulsively pushing unsuspecting people down the steps. Other patients engage in avoidance so that they do not have to carry out tedious compulsive rituals. For instance a young man with obsessional fears of contamination from his family's home computer (because it had been used to view pornography) engaged in elaborate and time-consuming compulsive cleaning and showering rituals. During the morning and afternoon he avoided the computer room so that he would not have to perform these rituals during the day. In the evening, however, he relaxed his avoidance and allowed himself to enter the room and become contaminated knowing that he could "work in" his ritualistic showering before bedtime.

Newth and Rachman (2001) have elaborated upon a form of avoidance in which patients deliberately conceal from others the content and frequency of their intrusive and repugnant obsessions. Usually it is unacceptable sexual, blasphemous and violent images, impulses to harm loved ones, and senseless thoughts about contamination that are hidden from others. This concealment may occur for a variety of reasons, the most obvious of which is the fear that others will respond negatively to hearing about the thoughts, or regard the person as dangerous or sick.

Subtypes and Dimensions of OCD

Although there are grounds for conceptualizing OCD as a homogeneous disorder, research has identified reliable and valid subtypes or dimensions of OCD symptoms (for a review see McKay et al., 2004). These include: (a) harming (aggressive obsessions and checking rituals), (b) contamination (contamination obsessions and decontamination rituals), (c) symmetry (obsessions about order or neatness and arranging rituals), (d) unacceptable immoral or violent thoughts with mental rituals and neutralization, and (e) hoarding symptoms.

POOR INSIGHT AND OVERVALUED IDEATION

The *DSM-IV* criteria for OCD include the specifier "with poor insight" to denote individuals who view their obsessional fears and compulsive behavior as reasonable. Although the majority of people with OCD recognize at some point that their obsessions and compulsions are senseless and excessive, there exists a continuum of insight into the irrationality of these symptoms with 4% of patients convinced that these symptoms are realistic (i.e., they have poor insight; Foa & Kozak, 1995). Poorer insight appears to be associated most strongly with the presence of religious obsessions, fears of mistakes, and aggressive obsessional impulses (Tolin, Abramowitz, Kozak, & Foa, 2001).

Case Study #1

Kent, a 33-year-old married male, was referred by his family physician after revealing that he had been taking 2-hour long showers each night. Kent said that he would get "stuck" in the shower because he worried that he had not washed all of the soap out of his hair and off of his body. On further assessment, Kent revealed obsessional fears that he might come to be responsible for making his 2-year-old daughter, Rachel, sick by accidentally contaminating her with various chemicals that he thought might be carcinogenic. For this reason, Kent avoided contact with substances such as detergents, pesticides, paints, and aerosol sprays. He also avoided touching the floor, shoes, grass, and most public surfaces (e.g., railings, door knobs). If avoidance was not possible, Kent would wash his hands in a certain ritualistic manner (involving counting) to decontaminate himself from the feared chemicals, and also from the soap residue. Because of his fear of spreading contamination, Kent also avoided touching his daughter, his wife, and certain rooms in the house (such as his daughter's) unless he had completed a ritualistic shower and had put on his "clean" clothes. Other "dirty" areas of the house were carefully avoided so he would not contaminate the "clean" areas or clothes.

Case Study #2

Linda was a 22-year-old graduate student who considered herself a strongly religious Catholic. She had developed OCD symptoms as a child, which mainly involved counting and repeating rituals, such as having to tap the door 15 times or having to turn the light switch on and off an even number of times to avoid the death of her parents. Presently, Linda described persistent obsessional doubts that while taking communion at church some months ago, microscopic pieces of the wafter might have somehow made their way into her underwear. Although she had checked her clothes carefully, and even saved (and wrapped in plastic) everything she was wearing that day, she had begun having intrusive obsessional thoughts that perhaps she had had genital contact with the body of Jesus. Linda was appalled at the content of her thoughts and images and dared not tell anyone for fear that she would be excommunicated from the church. She also believed the sacrilegious thoughts were a horrible sin and that she would be "damned to hell" for thinking this way. To combat them, she tried to suppress and engaged in prayer rituals that sometimes took up to 3 hours to complete "perfectly." The prayers involved liturgical chants as well as personal apologies to God. Linda had also begun avoiding church (even driving past churches) because this triggered the unwanted sexual thoughts that, she believed, were inappropriate to have especially in or near a church.

Epidemiology

PREVALENCE

Although OCD was once considered extremely rare, data now suggest it is among the more common adult psychological disorders. Estimates of the lifetime prevalence range from 0.7% (Weissman et al., 1994) to 2.9% (Kolada, Bland, & Newman, 1994; Kessler et al., 2005) and studies report a slight preponderance of females (Rasmussen & Eisen, 1992a). OCD typically begins by the age of 25, although childhood or adolescence onset is not rare (Rasmussen & Tsuang, 1986). The mean age of onset is earlier in males (about 21 years of age) than in females (22 to 24 years) (Rasmussen & Eisen, 1992b).

COURSE

OCD is a chronic condition with a very low rate of spontaneous remission. Left untreated, symptoms fluctuate, with worsening during periods of increased life stress. Fortunately, more patients now receive effective treatments than ever before, leading to increased rates of symptom remission (Steketee, Eisen, Dyck, Warshaw, & Rasmussen, 1999). Full recovery, however, is the exception rather than the rule.

Differentiating OCD from Problems with Similar Features

Seeming overlaps between the symptoms of OCD and those of several other psychological disorders (e.g., Obsessive-Compulsive Personality Disorder [OCPD], impulse control disorders) have prompted the proposal of an OCD spectrum that includes various conditions involving repetitive "obsessional" thinking and "compulsive" behaviors (Hollander, Friedberg, Wasserman, Yeh, & Iyengar, 2005). The boundaries of such a spectrum (and its existence), however, are the subject of rigorous debate (Abramowitz & Deacon, 2005) since it is often not clear how to differentiate between OCD and these other problems. The following section therefore discusses similarities and distinctions between OCD and a number of disorders often considered to overlap with OCD.

Obsessive Compulsive Personality Disorder

It is regrettable that OCD and OCPD have a similar name since these two conditions share little else. The main features of OCPD are an enduring pattern of perfectionism, rigidity, stubbornness, and orderliness that interferes with task completion; preoccupation with rules, organization, and schedules so that the point of activities is lost; over-conscientiousness and inflexibility regarding ethical or moral issues (not accounted for by normal cultural or religious values); and excessive devotion to work and productivity to the exclusion of friendships or leisure time (APA, 2000).

Although some of these characteristics are informally referred to as "compulsive" and might be present among individuals with OCD, closer examination reveals differences in what motivates these symptoms. In OCD, the compulsive behavior is resisted. That is, the person with OCD wishes he or she did not feel compelled to behave this way; yet the person feels pressure to act in order to reduce anxiety or the perceived probability of feared disastrous consequences. In contrast, clinical observations suggest that people with OCPD do not have obsessional fears of catastrophic consequences. Instead, such individuals perceive their "compulsive" behaviors as functional, agreeable, and consistent with a world-view which includes highly rigid beliefs about morality, the importance of not making mistakes, the need for predictability and control, and the need for perfection. Thus, whereas OCD symptoms are associated with subjective resistance, individuals with OCPD do not resist their inflexible style (they often see it as an advantage) and are often insurgent when it is suggested that they adapt a less rigid approach.

Impulse Control Disorders

Excessive and repetitive behaviors are present in both OCD and impulse control disorders such as pathological gambling, pathological shopping/buying, trichotillomania, kleptomania, compulsive internet use (e.g., viewing pornography) and "sexual compulsions." For this reason, impulse control disorders are considered by some to overlap with OCD. Research suggests, however, that the repetitive behaviors in impulse control disorders are performed to achieve a thrill or rush, whereas compulsive rituals in OCD are performed in response to obsessional fear and function as an escape from distress (Abramowitz & Houts, 2002). Although individuals with impulse control disorders may experience guilt, shame, and anxiety associated with their problematic behaviors, their anxiety is not triggered by obsessional cues as in OCD. Obsessions are not present in impulse control disorders.

Tics and Tourette's Syndrome (TS)

Both OCD and TS sometimes involve stereotyped or rapid movements. Tics—the repetitive behaviors in TS—however, are spontaneous acts evoked by a sensory urge (Miguel et al., 1995). Tics also serve to reduce sensory tension rather than as an escape from obsessive fear. In contrast, compulsions in OCD are deliberate acts evoked by affective distress and the urge to reduce fear.

DELUSIONAL DISORDERS (E.G., SCHIZOPHRENIA)

Both OCD and delusional disorders involve bizarre, senseless, and fixed thoughts and beliefs. These thoughts might evoke affective distress in both conditions. Unlike obsessions, however, delusions do not lead to compulsive rituals. Schizophrenia is also accompanied by other negative symptoms of thought disorders (e.g., loosening associations) that are not present in OCD.

HYPOCHONDRIASIS

Persistent thoughts about illnesses and repetitive checking for reassurance can be present in both OCD and hypochondriasis. In OCD, however, patients evince additional obsessive themes (e.g., aggression, contamination), whereas in hypochondriasis, patients are singly obsessed with their physical health.

Body Dysmorphic Disorder (BDD)

Both BDD and OCD can involve intrusive, distressing thoughts concerning one's appearance and repeated checking might be observed in both disorders. However, the focus of BDD symptoms is limited to one's appearance, whereas people with OCD also have other obsessions.

GENERALIZED ANXIETY DISORDER

The main features of generalized anxiety disorder (GAD) include chronic, exaggerated worry and tension that is uncontrollable, unfounded, or much more frequent and severe than normal anxiety. People with GAD are unable to relax and often suffer from insomnia and other physical symptoms including fatigue, trembling, muscle tension, headaches, irritability and hot flashes.

Worries in GAD can be intrusive, unwanted, repetitive, and highly distressing to the individual. Therefore, it is common for the worrying symptoms of GAD to be mistaken for obsessions as in OCD. The content of worries in GAD, however, focuses upon real life circumstances such as finances, social and family relationships, health, work, and school performance. In contrast, obsessional content in OCD is typically somewhat bizarre and does not concern actual life problems. Worries also tend to involve verbal content whereas obsessions often involve imagery and impulses along with thoughts and doubts. Worry is also often ruminative with general pessimistic ideas about oneself, the world, and the future. These ruminative ideas frequently shift in content from one topic to another. In contrast, obsessions are typically stable (fixed) and concern improbable disastrous consequences. Finally, whereas obsessions elicit neutralizing responses such as compulsive rituals, worries and ruminations are not associated with neutralizing.

OBSESSIONS VERSUS SOCIOPATHY

Clinical presentations of OCD involving aggressive or violent obsessions can superficially resemble sociopathy. People who engage in antisocial or sociopathic behavior, however, experience their violent thoughts as ego-syntonic (i.e., welcomed). They voluntarily fantasize about committing harmful acts, typically have histories of acting on such thoughts, and often devalue the victims (or potential victims) of such acts. In contrast, people with OCD who experience recurring violent or aggressive obsessional thoughts describe distress over such thoughts and make desperate attempts to resist and control them. Those with OCD often worry that they *might* harm others just by thinking such thoughts, or that presence of such thoughts indicates something personally abhorrent.

SUMMARY

Parallels between OCD and other disorders can be observed at two levels. On one level, phenomena such as hair pulling, tics, rigidity, and recurring worries all possess repetitive qualities as do obsessions and compulsive rituals. Yet, similarities at this superficial level are not helpful in differentiating OCD from other disorders because many normal and pathological behaviors can be repetitive. At a functional level, however, we see more enlightening similarities and differences between OCD and other disorders based on the presence or absence of a specific psychological mechanism. Whereas OCD involves the perception of threat followed by behavior aimed at reducing the threat, this mechanism is not present in most other differential diagnoses (e.g., impulse control disorders, OCPD). The take-home message here is that distinguishing OCD from other disorders requires a careful consideration of the cognitive, behavioral, and affective components of the observable symptoms.

Neurobiological Models of OCD

As of yet, there is no definitive answer to the question of what causes OCD. Most likely, the cause is multifactorial. A number of theoretical models have been put forward to explain OCD symptoms, although none account completely for the symptom picture as discussed above. Biological models include the serotonin hypothesis and structural or neuroanatomical approaches.

THE SEROTONIN HYPOTHESIS

The serotonin hypothesis is the leading neurochemical theory of OCD. It proposes that obsessions and compulsions arise from abnormalities in the serotonin neurotransmitter system, specifically a hypersensitivity of the post-synaptic serotonergic receptors (Zohar & Insel, 1987). Three lines of evidence are cited to support the serotonin hypothesis: medication outcome studies, biological marker studies, and biological challenge studies in which OCD symptoms are evoked using serotonin agonists and antagonists. The most consistent findings come from the pharmacotherapy literature which suggests that selective serotonin reuptake inhibitor medications (SSRIs; e.g., fluoxetine) are more effective than medications with other mechanisms of action (e.g., imipramine) in reducing OCD symptoms. In contrast, studies of biological markers— such as blood and cerebrospinal fluid levels of serotonin metabolites— have provided inconclusive results regarding a relationship between serotonin and OCD (Insel, Mueller, Alterman, Linnoila, & Murphy, 1985). Similarly, results from studies

using the pharmacological challenge paradigm are largely incompatible with the serotonin hypothesis (Hollander et al., 1992).

STRUCTURAL MODELS

Structural models of OCD hypothesize that obsessions and compulsions are caused by
neuroanatomical and functional abnormalities in particular areas of the brain, specifically the orbitofrontal-subcortical circuits (Saxena, Bota, & Brody, 2001). These circuits are thought to connect regions of the brain involved in processing information
with those involved in the initiation of behavioral responses that are implemented with
little conscious awareness. The classical conceptualization of this circuitry consists of a
direct and an indirect pathway. The direct pathway projects from the cerebral cortex to
the striatum to the internal segment of the globus pallidus/substantia nigra, pars reticu-
lata complex, then to the thalamus and back to the cortex. The indirect pathway is similar, but projects from the striatum to the external segment of the globus pallidus to the
subthalamic nucleus before returning to the common pathway. Overactivity of the direct
circuit is thought to give rise to OCD symptoms.

Structural models of OCD have largely been derived from the results of neuroimaging studies in which activity levels in specific brain areas are compared between people
with and without OCD. Investigations using positron emission tomography (PET) have
found increased glucose utilization in the orbitofrontal cortex (OFC), caudate, thalamus,
prefrontal cortex, and anterior cingulate among patients with OCD as compared to non-
patients (Baxter et al., 1987; Baxter et al., 1988). Studies using single photon emission
computed tomography (SPECT) have reported decreased blood flow to the OFC, caudate, various areas of the cortex, and thalamus in OCD patients as compared to non-
patients (for a review see Whiteside, Port, & Abramowitz, 2004). Finally, studies
comparing individuals with OCD to healthy controls using magnetic resonance spectroscopy (MRS) have reported decreased levels of various markers of neuronal viability in
the left and right striatum, and in the medial thalamus (Ebert et al., 1997; Fitzgerald,
Paulson, Stewart, & Rosenberg, 2000). Although findings vary across studies, a meta-
analysis of ten PET and SPECT studies found that relative to healthy individuals, those
with OCD evince more activity in the orbital gyrus and the head of the caudate nucleus
(Whiteside et al., 2004).

EVALUATION OF BIOLOGICAL MODELS

A critical examination reveals some important limitations of existing biological models
of OCD. First, there is little correspondence between the patterns of symptoms that
patients report and the biological mechanisms proposed to account for them. That is, no
explanation has been offered for how neurotransmitter or neuroanatomical abnormalities translate into OCD symptoms (e.g., why does hypersensitivity of postsynaptic
receptors cause obsessional thoughts or compulsive rituals?). Second, biological
models are void of content. They are unable to explain the fact that OCD symptoms
concern certain themes, but not others. Why do obsessions focus on contamination,
symmetry, harm, mistakes, religion, sex, and so on? Also, why do some people
experience contamination-related obsessions whereas others have intrusive sexual
obsessions?

A third problem with biological models is their logical (as opposed to empirical) basis. Since the serotonin hypothesis *originated from* the findings of preferential efficacy of clomipramine (an SSRI) over non-serotonergic antidepressants (e.g., imipramine; Zohar & Insel, 1987), the assertion that the effectiveness of SSRIs supports the serotonin hypothesis is circular. Further still, models of etiology cannot be derived solely from knowledge of successful treatment response. This is an example of the logical error known as *ex juvantibus* reasoning, or "reasoning backward from what helps," which is a variation of the fallacy known as *post hoc ergo propter hoc*, or "after this therefore because of this." The logical fallacy is clear if you consider the following example: "When I take aspirin, my headache goes away. Thus, the reason I get headaches is that my aspirin level is too low." Just as there may be many possible mechanisms by which aspirin makes headaches go away, there may be many possible mechanisms by which SSRIs decrease OCD symptoms.

The serotonin hypothesis *could* be supported by evidence from controlled experimental studies demonstrating differences in serotonergic functioning between individuals with and without OCD. Especially convincing would be a demonstration that the administration of serotonin agonists produces the onset (or exacerbation) of OCD symptoms. Yet, the numerous biological marker and pharmacological challenge studies that have been conducted to date provide inconsistent results (for a review, see Gross, Sasson, Chorpa, & Zohar, 1998). So, although it is likely that obsessive-compulsive symptoms *involve* the serotonin system at some level (one is hard-pressed to find many human processes that do not involve the serotonin system), the existing evidence does not suggest that OCD is *caused* by an abnormally functioning serotonin system.

A fifth and final problem with biological theories of OCD is that serotonin and brain scan studies do not provide convincing evidence that neuroanatomic abnormalities *cause* OCD symptoms. That is, studies reporting differences in serotonin function or blood flow to the OFC between OCD patients and non-patients do not necessarily provide evidence for a neuroanatomical *abnormality*; nor, do they implicate serotonin or the OFC per se as involved in the production of OCD symptoms. This is because such studies are correlational and therefore cannot address whether (a) true *abnormalities* exist, and (b) whether the observed relationships are causal.

Learning Models of OCD

The leading behavioral (conditioning) models of OCD are based on Dollard and Miller's (1950) and Mowrer's (1960) two-stage theory of fear acquisition and maintenance. In the first stage (classical conditioning), a previously neutral stimulus (the conditioned stimulus, or CS) is paired with an aversive stimulus (the unconditioned stimulus, or UCS; for example, a traumatic experience), so that the CS comes to elicit a conditioned fear response (CR). As a result of this associative learning process, specific situations (e.g., driving, using the bathroom), objects (e.g., door handles, knives), and thoughts, images, doubts, or impulses (e.g., thoughts of curse words, impulses to harm) that pose no objective threat may come to evoke obsessional fear.

The second stage of the model (operant conditioning) proposes that avoidance behaviors develop as a means of reducing obsessional anxiety. Such avoidance is negatively reinforced by the immediate (albeit temporary) reduction in distress that it engenders. Unlike in phobias, however, where fear cues are typically external (situational) and can be more or less easily avoided (e.g., elevators, snakes), obsessional fear in OCD is often evoked by ubiquitous cues such as intrusive thoughts and other stimuli that cannot be avoided (e.g., odd numbers, using the bathroom). Thus, compulsive rituals are employed to escape from obsessional fear when avoidance is impossible. Because rituals are technically effective as short-term escape strategies, they are negatively reinforced and likely to be performed repeatedly under similar conditions of obsessional distress. Repetition of avoidance and escape behaviors, however, terminate exposure and prevent the individual from fully confronting his or her feared stimuli. As a result, these responses obstruct the natural extinction of obsessional fears, thereby maintaining such fear.

CRITICAL EVALUATION OF THE BEHAVIORAL MODEL

The behavioral model of OCD has some strengths and limitations. Neither empirical research nor clinical observation strongly supports a classical conditioning explanation for the development of obsessional fear. First, most patients tend not to ascribe the onset of their OCD symptoms to specific conditioning experiences, but instead to more general life stress. Second, when traumatic events and social learning influences (as described above) are reported, they often precede the onset of OCD symptoms by many years. Third, symptom onset is often gradual, which is not what would be predicted by the classical conditioning theory. Finally, many patients report multiple types of obsessions as well as the development of new obsessions that do not correspond with new or multiple traumatic conditioning experiences. Thus, traumatic conditioning alone cannot account for the acquisition of obsessions. Verbal transmission of dangerous thoughts, however, is likely to be involved in the genesis of obsessional fears (e.g., "my father told me that doorknobs and toilet seats are full of peoples' germs"). In addition, direct verbal conditioning may also occur in which a neutral idea is paired with a scary one (e.g., "I saw a 'filthy' person use the toilet and wash her hands before me, so I should be very careful in all bathrooms"; Mineka & Zinbarg, 2006).

In contrast, there is substantial evidence that operant conditioning (negative reinforcement) plays a role in the *maintenance* of OCD symptoms. Experimental research, for example, has demonstrated that exposure to obsessional stimuli evokes subjective distress and urges to perform compulsive behaviors; and that the performance of compulsive rituals and other neutralization behaviors leads to anxiety reduction (de Silva, Menzies, & Shafran, 2003; Hodgson, & Rachman, 1972; Rachman, 1976; Rachman, Shafran, Mitchell, Trant, & Teachman, 1996; Roper & Rachman, 1976). Overall, then, negative reinforcement provides an empirically valid explanation for the persistence of compulsive rituals and avoidance behavior in OCD.

Cognitive Deficit Models of OCD

MEMORY DEFICITS

Some theorists have proposed that OCD symptoms arise from abnormally functioning cognitive processes, such as memory. Compulsive checking, for example, could develop as a consequence of *not being able to remember* whether or not one has locked the door, turned off the oven, or unplugged the iron. Despite its face validity, a number of investigations have found no evidence of an overall memory deficit among individuals with OCD (Abbruzzese, Bellodi, Ferri, & Scarone, 1993; Muller & Roberts, 2005; Tolin, Abramowitz, Brigidi, Amir, Street, & Foa, 2001; Woods, Vevea, Chambless, & Bayen, 2002). Other theorists have proposed that individuals with OCD have memory problems *only where their obsessional fears are concerned*. This would explain, for example, why a patient who fears burglaries might spend hours rechecking that doors to the outside (e.g., the garage door) are securely locked, yet have no urges to check closet or bathroom doors. The few studies that have examined this selective memory hypothesis, however, suggest just the opposite: patients appear to have a selectively *better* memory for OCD-related information relative to non-OCD-relevant stimuli (Radomsky & Rachman, 1999; Radomsky, Rachman, & Hammond, 2001). Such a memory bias in favor of remembering threat-related information is adaptive and can be conceptualized as part of the normal fight-or-flight response that functions to protect organisms from harm. Paying attention to and being able to remember characteristics of stimuli perceived to be harmful serves a protective function.

REALITY MONITORING DEFICITS

If OCD is not caused by memory deficits, perhaps the symptoms are related to problems with *reality monitoring*—the ability to discriminate between memories of actual versus imagined events (Johnson & Raye, 1981). Ritualistic checking, for example, could be prompted by difficulties discerning whether an action (e.g., locking the door) was really carried out or merely imagined. Studies examining the reality monitoring skills of individuals with OCD have found inconsistent results. Whereas two investigations found that those with OCD did not discriminate between real and imagined actions as well as did healthy controls (Ecker & Engelkamp, 1995; Rubinstein, Peynircioglu, Chambless, & Pigott, 1993), the majority suggest that OCD is not characterized by a deficit in reality monitoring (Brown, Kosslyn, Breiter, Baer, & Jenike, 1994; Constans, Foa, Franklin, & Matthews, 1995; Hermans, Martens, De Cort, Pieters, & Eelen, 2003; McNally & Kohlbeck, 1993). A meta-analytic study found no differences in reality monitoring between OCD patients and control groups across five studies (Woods et al., 2002).

INHIBITORY DEFICITS

The intrusive, repetitious, and seemingly uncontrollable quality of obsessional thoughts has led some researchers to hypothesize that individuals with OCD have deficits in cognitive inhibition—the ability to dismiss extraneous mental stimuli. For example, Wilhelm, McNally, Baer, and Florin (1996) used a directed forgetting task to test whether those with OCD have a dysfunction in their ability to forget disturbing material. In this study, people with OCD and healthy control participants were presented with a series of negative, positive, and neutral words; and given instructions to either remember or to forget each word after it was presented. Tests of recall and recognition showed that those with OCD had more difficulty forgetting negative material relative to positive and neutral material, whereas non-clinical control subjects did not. Tolin, Hamlin, and Foa (2002) replicated and extended this finding by demonstrating that relevance to OCD, rather than threat-relevance alone, predicted impaired forgetting.

Synthesis of Cognitive Deficit Research

Cognitive deficit theories of OCD have intuitive appeal, especially in explaining compulsive checking symptoms. Research, however, provides limited support for global memory problems in OCD, and instead suggests that those with this condition have less confidence in their own memory as compared to non-patients (Radomsky et al., 2001). Reduced memory confidence, however, is not a deficit; it is an erroneous belief or *cognitive bias* (e.g., "I recall having locked the door, but I can't trust that my memory is accurate"). In the case of compulsive checking, it is possible that reduced confidence in memory is evoked by doubts that one may be (or may come to be) responsible for negative outcomes. Hence, checking becomes a way of reducing doubts about one's memory and pathological estimates of the probability of harm.

Additional limitations of cognitive deficit models of OCD should be noted. First, the models do not account for the heterogeneity of OCD symptoms (e.g., why do some people have washing compulsions while others have checking rituals?). Second, the models do not account for the fact that mild neuropsychological deficits (e.g., memory problems) have been found in many disorders, including panic disorder, social phobia, posttraumatic stress disorder, and bulimia nervosa (Taylor, Thordarson, & Sochting, 2002). Thus, the question remains as to why such deficits give rise to OCD instead of one of these other disorders. If dysfunctional information processing plays any causal role in OCD, it is most likely to be a nonspecific vulnerability factor, as opposed to a specific cause.

Cognitive-Behavioral Models of OCD

Among the most promising contemporary models of OCD are those based on Beck's (Beck, 1976) cognitive theory of emotion, which proposes that emotional disturbance is brought about not by situations and stimuli themselves, but by how one interprets or appraises such situations or stimuli. The theory posits that specific kinds of interpretations give rise to particular emotional problems. Depression, for example, is said to be associated with interpretations focusing on loss, failure, and self-denigration (e.g., "When my wife left me, it confirmed that I'm a failure"). Social phobia is thought to be associated with beliefs about rejection or ridicule by others (Beck & Emery, 1985; e.g., "It's terrible to be rejected"). Panic disorder is said to be associated with beliefs about impending death, insanity, or loss of control (Beck, Epstein, Brown, & Steer, 1988; Clark, 1986; e.g., "My heart will stop if it beats too fast").

In like fashion, theorists have proposed that obsessions and compulsions arise from specific sorts of dysfunctional beliefs, with the strength of these beliefs influencing the person's degree of insight into his or her OCD symptoms. Cognitive-behavioral models of OCD (Salkovskis, 1996) begin with the well-established finding that unpleasant mental intrusions (i.e., thoughts, images, and impulses that intrude into consciousness) are a normal and universal experience. Numerous studies indicate that people with and without OCD report intrusive thoughts with similar content (Rachman & de Silva, 1978). The major differences between so-called "normal" and clinical obsessions are that clinical obsessions occur more often, are associated with more anxiety, and are resisted more than normal obsessions. Thus, any theory of OCD must explain why only some people experience clinical obsessions when everyone has intrusive thoughts.

Salkovskis (1996) proposed that mental intrusions—whether wanted or unwanted—reflect a person's current concerns and are more or less automatically triggered by internal or external reminders of those concerns. For example, intrusive thoughts of being contaminated may be triggered by seeing certain objects (e.g., toilets). Salkovskis (1996) hypothesized that intrusions develop into obsessions only when the intrusions are *appraised* as posing a threat for which the individual is personally responsible. To illustrate, consider an intrusive doubt about one's home burning down while he or she is away on vacation. Most people experiencing such an intrusion would regard it as a meaningless cognitive event with no harm-related implications (i.e., "mental noise"). Such a senseless intrusion, however, can develop into a clinical obsession if the person appraises it as having serious consequences for which he or she is personally responsible; for example: "I must take extra precautions to ensure that it doesn't happen." Such appraisals evoke distress and motivate the person to try to suppress or remove the unwanted intrusion (e.g., by replacing it with a "good" thought), and to attempt to prevent any harmful events associated with the intrusion (e.g., by checking over and over that the appliances are turned off).

According to the cognitive-behavioral approach, compulsive rituals and avoidance represent efforts to remove intrusions and to prevent feared harmful consequences. Salkovskis (1996) advanced two main reasons why compulsions and avoidance habits become persistent and excessive. First, they are negatively reinforced by their ability to immediately reduce distress (as in the learning model) and to temporarily remove the unwanted obsessional thought. Second, they prevent the person from learning that their responsibility appraisals are unrealistic. That is, performing the ritual robs the person of the opportunity to discover that the anticipated negative outcome would not have occurred in the first place. If the individual avoids obsessional triggers, there is no opportunity to learn that such stimuli do not pose significant danger.

Compulsive rituals and avoidance behavior also influence the frequency of intrusions by serving as reminders and thereby triggering their reoccurrence. For example, compulsive checking can remind the person that fires or burglaries are *possible*. Ritualistic hand washing can remind the person that he or she may have become contaminated. Attempts at avoiding or distracting oneself from unwanted intrusions may paradoxically increase the frequency of intrusions, possibly because the distractors become reminders (retrieval cues) of the intrusions (Abramowitz, Tolin, & Steet, 2001). Rituals can also strengthen one's perceived responsibility for preventing harm. That is, when the feared consequence (e.g., a house fire) fails to occur after performing the ritual (e.g., checking) the belief that the person must perform the ritual to prevent the dreaded outcome is reinforced. Therefore, people with OCD often erroneously attribute the nonoccurrence of feared consequences to the fact that they performed rituals or avoided the situation in the first place.

In summary, the cognitive-behavioral model of OCD posits that when a person appraises intrusions as posing a threat for which he or she is personally responsible, he or she becomes distressed over the intrusion and attempts to remove it and prevent feared negative consequences. This paradoxically increases the frequency of intrusions, leading the intrusions to escalate into clinical obsessions. Compulsive rituals maintain the intrusions and prevent the person from evaluating the accuracy of his or her appraisals.

Although Salkovskis (1996) emphasized the importance of *responsibility* appraisals and beliefs, other cognitive-behavioral theorists have identified additional types of dysfunctional beliefs and appraisals in OCD (e.g., Frost & Steketee, 2002). One of the

TABLE 5.4 Domains of Dysfunctional Beliefs in OCD

Belief	Description
Inflated responsibility/Overestimation of threat	Belief that one has the power to cause and/or the duty to prevent negative outcomes
	Belief that negative events are likely and would be unmanageable
Exaggeration of the importance of thoughts and need to control thoughts	Belief that the mere presence of a thought indicates that the thought is significant
	Belief that complete control over one's thoughts is both necessary and possible
Perfectionism/Intolerance for uncertainty	Belief that mistakes and imperfection are intolerable
	Belief that it is necessary and possible to be 100% certain that negative outcomes will not occur

major contemporary belief and appraisal models was developed by the Obsessive Compulsive Cognitions Working Group (OCCWG; 1997). Extending the work of Salkovskis and others, the OCCWG identified the following empirically derived domains of beliefs thought to underlie OCD symptoms (OCCWG, 2003, 2005; also see Table 5.4):

Inflated sense of responsibility and overestimation of threat. Responsibility refers to the belief that one has the pivotal power to cause or prevent unwanted outcomes. Individuals with OCD often view themselves as responsible for the content featured in their intrusive thoughts. They may be as concerned about failing to prevent bad outcomes (sins of omission) as they are with directly causing them (sins of commission; Wroe & Salkovskis, 2000). Excessive responsibility evokes feelings of anxiety and guilt.

People with OCD also tend to exaggerate the probability and costs of negative events featured in their obsessions (e.g., mistakes, sickness, or harm). Though most people take for granted that a situation is safe unless there are clear signs of danger, those suffering from OCD assume obsessional situations are dangerous unless they have a guarantee of safety. The belief that anxiety itself will persist indefinitely and lead to physical or psychological damage might also be present in OCD. Overestimates of threat likely arise from anxious individuals' inaccuracies in judgment. Rather than using objective evidence, such people frequently rely on publicized cases or the content of nonsensical obsessional thoughts to make such predictions. Excellent examples include obsessional fears of relatively rare conditions that often gain media attention such as West Nile virus, SARS, or Lyme disease.

The overimportance of, and need to control, thoughts. Individuals with OCD often reason (incorrectly) that the mere presence of unwanted intrusive thoughts indicates that such thoughts are significant and meaningful. Thought-action fusion (TAF) refers to two particular beliefs: (a) that intrusive thoughts are morally equivalent to the corresponding actions (moral TAF; e.g., "it is just as immoral to think about cursing in a place of worship as it is to actually say curse words"), and (b) that thinking about something makes the corresponding event more likely (likelihood TAF; e.g., "because I am thinking about cursing, I will probably do it") (Shafran, Thordarson, & Rachman, 1996). People with OCD also attach exaggerated significance to intrusive unwanted thoughts by regarding them as repugnant, horrific, dangerous, disgusting, sinful, alarming, insane, and criminal, (Freeston, Ladouceur, Gagnon, & Thibodeau, 1993; Rachman, 2003). They might believe that intrusive thoughts reveal important but hidden aspects of their personality or character (e.g., "these thoughts mean that deep down I am an evil, dangerous, and unstable person").

Related to perceiving intrusive thoughts as important, individuals with OCD may believe that it is both possible and necessary to maintain complete control over one's unwanted thoughts (Purdon & Clark, 1994). A related assumption is that it is important to track and "keep a look out" for intrusive or unwanted mental events. Such beliefs are usually associated with repugnant obsessions concerning aggression, violence, unwanted sexual themes, and blasphemous or taboo subjects (religious/morality obsessions), and may be accompanied by the fear that not controlling such thoughts will have disastrous moral, behavioral, or psychological consequences. The resistance to obsessions that is commonly observed in OCD occurs as a result of such beliefs.

Intolerance of uncertainty and the need for perfectionism. Individuals with OCD often hold the erroneous belief that it is both important and possible to be absolutely (100 percent) certain that negative outcomes will not occur. Even the remote possibility of highly unlikely events can become a source of great concern. As a result, harmless intrusive doubts evoke great distress and the urge to make sure that, for example, one did not commit a sin, leave the oven on, make an egregious mistake, cause something terrible to happen, or get close enough to blood to contract HIV. If senseless intrusive thoughts about violence and aggression, sex, contamination, or mistakes are appraised as highly significant, these stimuli activate intolerance for uncertainty leading individuals with OCD to doubt whether something terrible has (or will) happen (Tolin, Abramowitz, Brigidi, & Foa, 2003).

OCD is also associated with an inability to tolerate mistakes or imperfection (Frost & Steketee, 1997). The perfectionism may relate to external stimuli, such as a need to fill out a form without making a single mistake; or to internal stimuli, such as a need to repeat a routine action until it feels "just right" (Coles, Frost, Heimberg, & Rheaume, 2003). Such beliefs are often observed among individuals with symmetry and ordering OCD symptoms; for example, the belief that *"I must keep working at something until it is exactly right"* and *"even minor mistakes mean a job is not complete"* (OCCWG, 1997).

In addition to the Salkovskis/OCCWG models designed to account for OCD in general, OCCWG members have also developed a number of "mini-models" to account for particular types of OCD symptoms, such as compulsive washing (Jones & Menzies, 1997). The development of such models is consistent with the view that OCD may be etiologically heterogeneous, in addition to being symptomatically heterogeneous as discussed above. The mini-models account for symptom heterogeneity in various ways, such as by proposing that particular beliefs or patterns of beliefs are important for specific types of OCD symptoms, including highly specific beliefs in addition to the broad belief domains mentioned in Table 5.4. To illustrate, compulsive hoarding is said to arise from a constellation of etiologic factors, including dysfunctional beliefs about the value of possessions (e.g., beliefs that even worthless objects might be highly valuable or useful in the future), perfectionism, intolerance of uncertainty, and difficulty making decisions (Frost & Hartl, 1996).

EMPIRICAL EVIDENCE FOR THE COGNITIVE-BEHAVIORAL APPROACH

Data from three lines of evidence—self-report questionnaire research, laboratory experiments, and naturalistic longitudinal studies—provide support for the cognitive-behavioral approach to OCD. Numerous questionnaire studies consistently indicate that people with OCD are more likely than those without to overestimate the probability of harm and interpret intrusive thoughts as significant, threatening, or in terms of responsibility for harm (e.g., Abramowitz, Whiteside, Lynam, & Kalsy, 2003; Freeston et al., 1993; OCCWG, 2003; Salkovskis et al., 2000; Shafran et al., 1996). In one study, Abramowitz et al. (2003) found that relative to a non-patient control group, individuals with OCD had higher scores on a measure of TAF. Although cross-sectional studies like this one demonstrate relationships between OCD and cognitive variables, these correlational data do not address whether cognitive biases play a causal role in OCD; that is, it cannot be ruled out that dysfunctional beliefs result from the presence of OCD symptoms. Only experimentally controlled studies in which variables of interest are manipulated can address causal factors.

Several laboratory experiments have addressed the effects of interpretations of intrusive thoughts on OCD symptoms (Ladouceur et al., 1995; Lopatka & Rachman, 1995; Rassin, Merckelbach, Muris, & Spaan, 1999). In one particularly clever study, Rassin et al. (1999) connected 45 psychologically naïve participants to electrical equipment that, participants were told, would monitor their thoughts for 15 minutes. To induce dysfunctional appraisals, participants who had been randomly assigned to the *experimental* condition were told that thinking the word "apple" would automatically result in a mild electric shock to another person (a confederate of the experimenter) whom they had met earlier. Participants were also informed that by pressing a certain button immediately after having an "apple" thought, they could prevent the shock— this was intended to be akin to a compulsive ritual. On the other hand, subjects in the *control* group were told only that the electrical equipment would monitor their thoughts. Results indicated that during the 15-minute monitoring period, the experimental group reported more intrusive "apple" thoughts, more guilt, greater subjective discomfort, and more intense resistance to thoughts about apples compared to the control group. Moreover, there was a strong association between the number of reported "apple" thoughts and the number of button presses. Thus, experimentally induced dysfunctional beliefs about the significance of intrusive thoughts (i.e., the belief that one's thoughts can produce harmful and preventable consequences) evoked intrusive distressing thoughts and compulsive behavior profoundly similar to clinical OCD symptoms.

The causal effects demonstrated under highly controlled laboratory conditions might or might not extend to the development of OCD in naturalistic settings. Thus, longitudinal studies in which individuals are assessed for cognitive variables and then followed up after some critical event are apt to be particularly informative. Because pregnancy and the postpartum period represent periods of inceased vulnerability to OCD onset, this is a particularly opportune time to examine hypotheses about cognitive determinants of OCD: in particular, will the presence of OCD-related cognitive distortions be related to postpartum OCD symptoms? To examine this question, Abramowitz and colleagues (Abramowitz, Khandher, Nelson, Deacon, & Rygwall, 2006; Abramowitz, Nelson, Rygwall, & Khandher, 2007) administered measures of OCD-related dysfunctional beliefs to two samples of first-time expecting parents (mothers *and* fathers-to-be) during the third trimester of pregnancy. Between 2 and 3 months after childbirth, these new parents were again contacted and assessed for the presence and intensity of unwanted intrusive thoughts about their newborn. Not surprisingly, 75% of these new parents reported unwanted infant-related thoughts ("normal obsessions"; e.g., an image of dropping the child down the stairs or off the balcony). Moreover, after controlling for baseline levels of OCD symptoms and trait anxiety, the pre-childbirth strength of OCD-related dysfunctional beliefs was a significant predictor of OCD symptom intensity in the postpartum period. This lends support to the cognitive-behavioral model and suggests that the tendency to overestimate the chances of harm and significance of intrusive thoughts is a risk factor for the development of more severe OCD symptoms.

IMPLICATIONS OF THE COGNITIVE-BEHAVIORAL APPROACH

The cognitive-behavioral approach provides a logically and empirically consistent account of OCD symptoms that assumes the presence of intact learning (conditioning) processes and normally functioning (albeit biased and maladaptive) cognitive processes. It is parsimonious in that there is no appeal to "chemical imbalances" or disease states to explain OCD symptoms. Even the maladaptive beliefs and appraisals that are hypothesized to lead to obsessions are viewed as "errors" rather than "disease processes." Furthermore, the use of avoidance and compulsive behaviors to reduce perceived threat could be considered adaptive if harm was indeed likely. However, OCD patients' obsessive fears are exaggerated. Therefore, their avoidance and rituals are not only irrational, but highly problematic since they perpetuate a vicious cycle of intrusion → misappraisal → anxiety, and so on.

The model also suggests that a successful treatment for OCD symptoms must accomplish two things: (a) the correction of maladaptive beliefs and appraisals that lead to obsessional fear and (b) the termination of avoidance and compulsive rituals that prevent the self-correction of maladaptive beliefs and extinction of anxiety. In short, the task of cognitive-behavior therapy (CBT) is to foster an evaluation of obsessional stimuli as non-threatening and therefore not demanding of further action. Patients must come to understand their problem not in terms of the risk of feared consequences, but in terms of how they are thinking and behaving in response to stimuli that objectively pose a low risk of harm.

Environmental Factors in OCD

Although most individuals with OCD do not identify clear-cut environmental precipitants of symptom onset, researchers have found evidence that stressful or traumatic events and experiences may play a role for some patients (Gershuny, Baer, Jenike, Minichiello, & Wilhelm, 2002; Kolada et al., 1994). As mentioned earlier, accumulating data also suggest that OCD symptoms occur at higher than expected rates among childbearing women and their partners (Abramowitz, Schwartz, Moore, & Luenzmann, 2003). From a cognitive-behavioral perspective it seems likely that in this case the abrupt increase in stress and responsibility that comes with caring for a newborn infant increases the chances that when negative thoughts regarding this baby's well-being occur naturally, they will be misappraised as highly significant. This, in turn, would lead to obsessions and rituals or avoidance.

Although the exact etiology of OCD remains unknown, it is quite clear that the environment plays an important role in influencing the *presentation* of OCD symptoms. The content of one's obsessions and compulsions is not random. For example in India, where purity and cleanliness are emphasized as part of Hindu religious doctrines, research has observed a heightened frequency of contamination obsessions (Akhtar et al., 1975; Khanna & Channabasavanna, 1988). Similarly, studies of OCD in Egypt and Turkey reveal a preponderance of obsessions related to Muslim culture, including contamination and moral/ethical obsessions. Further evidence for the role of cultural influences can be found in how the content of obsessional concerns has undergone shifts over time that correspond with changes in societal concerns. For example, the heightened awareness of Anthrax poisoning following the 2001 terrorist attacks in the eastern United States gave rise to increased obsessions about this particular contaminant. Similarly, obsessional fears about contracting syphilis and gonorrhea, which were prevalent among those with washing compulsions in the 1970s, were replaced with fears of AIDS in the 1980s.

There is mixed evidence regarding the role that other environmental factors might play in OCD. Studies that have examined the possible contributions of parental child-rearing practices to the development of OCD have yielded largely conflicting results. Some researchers found high levels of parental overprotection in OCD patients (Hafner, 1988; Merkel, Pollard, Wiener, & Staebler, 1993; Turgeon, O'Connor, Marchand, & Freeston, 2002), whereas others have reported greater rejection as compared to non-patients (Hoekstra, Visser, & Emmelkamp, 1989); or no significant differences between individuals with and without OCD (Alonso et al., 2004; Vogel, Stiles, & Nordahl, 1997). Thus, there is little empirical support for the notion that certain parenting styles contribute to the development of OCD.

Other authors (Rachman, 1997) have proposed that strict religious orthodoxy could give rise to obsessions if certain standards for behaving and thinking are repeatedly admonished by authority figures. For example, if one were to repeatedly be admonished by his or her religious school teachers that it is a sin to *think* aggressive, blasphemous, or adulterous thoughts, this could lead to efforts to suppress or neutralize such thoughts when they invariably occur as normal mental intrusions. Such habitual suppression in the presence of dysfunctional beliefs about the importance of intrusive thoughts (and the need to control them) could give rise to obsessions. The influence of religious background on OCD symptoms has been examined in several studies with largely consistent results lending support for this hypothesis. Abramowitz, Huppert, Cohen, Tolin, and Cahill (2002) found that the fear of God and fear of committing sin were associated with increased obsessive-compulsive symptoms (particularly doubting and checking). In a subsequent study, highly religious Protestants reported more obsessionality, contamination concerns, beliefs about the importance of thoughts, beliefs about the need to control thoughts, and inflated responsibility, compared to atheists and less religious Protestants (Abramowitz, Deacon, Woods, & Tolin, 2004). A similar investigation of Catholics conducted in Italy revealed almost identical results (Sica, Novara, & Sanavio, 2002).

Salkovskis, Shafran, Rachman, and Freeston (1999) hypothesized additional paths by which environmental factors could give rise to dysfunctional beliefs and appraisals of intrusive thoughts. For example, a childhood in which one's parents convey the message that certain situations or objects are very dangerous, or that the child is incapable of dealing with the resulting harm, could lead to obsessions regarding the specific harbinger of perceived danger. This idea is consistent with previous research findings that patients with severe contamination obsessions came from families in which cleanliness and perfectionism were emphasized (Hoover & Insel, 1984). Shafran, Thordarson, and Rachman (1996) proposed that certain experiences, such as a chance pairing between a thought and a negative event could lead to a heightened threat value for intrusive mental processes. Research on the environmental predictors of OCD remains in its infancy but will most likely ultimately show that the causes of OCD are multifactorial.

Assessment

DIAGNOSTIC INTERVIEWS

Three structured diagnostic interviews may be used for establishing the presence of OCD on the basis of *DSM* criteria: the Structured Clinical Interview for *DSM IV-TR* (SCID) (First, Spitzer, Gibbon, & Williams, 2002), the Mini International Neuropsychiatric Interview (MINI) (Sheehan et al., 1998), and the Anxiety Disorders Interview Schedule for *DSM-IV* (ADIS-IV) (Di Nardo, Brown, & Barlow, 1994).

The SCID and MINI allow the interviewer to establish the diagnosis of a broad range of psychiatric disorders. Items on each interview include forced choice ("yes-no") questions, a positive response to which prompts more in-depth questions to clarify the problem. Each instrument includes an OCD module that assesses the presence of obsessions, compulsions, and insight into the senselessness of these symptoms. These interviews are widely employed in research settings and the OCD modules have acceptable reliability.

The ADIS was developed to establish differential diagnosis among the anxiety disorders according to DSM criteria. An advantage of the ADIS over the SCID and MINI is that the ADIS provides considerably more detail about OCD. In addition, items assess the severity of the problem using a dimensional rating scale. For these reasons, the ADIS is used in both clinical and research settings. As with the SCID and MINI, items on the ADIS include "yes-no" questions, a positive response to which prompts a clarification. The reliability of the ADIS is supported by several studies (kappas between .60 and .88).

CLINICIAN-RATED SEVERITY SCALES

Yale-Brown Obsessive Compulsive Scale

The most widely used clinician-rated measure of OCD is the Yale-Brown Obsessive Compulsive Scale (Y-BOCS) (Goodman, Price, Rasmussen, Mazure, Delgado, et al., 1989; Goodman, Price, Rasmussen, Mazure, Fleischmann, et al., 1989), which contains three parts. In the first part, the interviewer provides the patient with practical definitions of obsessions and compulsions to help in identifying these symptoms. The second part consists of a symptom checklist of over 50 common obsessions and compulsions. The interviewer asks the patient to indicate whether each symptom is currently present, absent, or present only in the past. After completing the checklist, the clinician and patient generate a list of the three most severe obsessions, compulsions, and OCD-related avoidance behaviors. The third section of the Y-BOCS is a 10-item severity scale that assesses the (a) time spent, (b) interference from, (c) distress associated with, (d) efforts to resist, and (e) ability to control obsessions (items 1–5) and compulsions (items 6–10). Each item is rated on a scale from 0 (no symptoms) to 4 (extremely severe) and scores on the 10 items are summed to produce a total score ranging from 0 to 40. In most instances, scores of 0 to 7 represent subclinical OCD symptoms, those from 8 to 15 represent mild symptoms, scores of 16 to 23 relate to moderate symptoms, scores from 24 to 31 suggest severe symptoms, and scores of 32 to 40 imply extreme symptoms.

The Y-BOCS is unique among measures of OCD in that it is sensitive to multiple aspects of symptom severity independent of the *number* or *types* of different obsessions and compulsions. A limitation, however, is that the symptom checklist largely assesses symptoms on a descriptive level without concern for functionality. For example, patients are asked only *whether* they wash their hands excessively, as opposed to *what triggers* the washing and the *consequences* of washing. It is important to know about the presence of obsessions and rituals, but a thorough understanding of OCD symptoms also requires assessment of the relationship between obsessional stimuli and compulsive rituals (this type of *functional* assessment is described later in this section). A final issue with using the Y-BOCS is that the symptom checklist contains some items which are not genuine obsessions or compulsions (e.g., hair-pulling). Research indicates that the Y-BOCS possesses adequate reliability, validity, and sensitivity to treatment (Taylor et al., 2002).

Brown Assessment of Beliefs Scale

The Brown Assessment of Beliefs Scale (BABS) (Eisen et al., 1998) is a seven-item clinician-administered scale designed to assess degree of insight into the senselessness of a variety of psychiatric symptoms and disorders, including OCD. The individual's main obsessional belief is determined, and specific probes and anchors are used to rate various components of this belief. In OCD, a typical belief might be "If I do not perform a prayer ritual, my mother will die." Items on the BABS assess the following parameters of insight: (a) conviction (how convinced the person is that his/her belief is accurate); (b) perception of others' views (how certain the person is that most people think the belief makes sense); (c) explanation of differing views (the person's explanation for the difference between his/her and others' views of the belief); (d) fixity (whether the person could be convinced that the belief is wrong); (e) attempt to disprove beliefs (how actively the person tries to disprove his/her belief); (f) insight (whether the person recognizes that the belief has a psychiatric/psychological cause); and (g) referential thinking (an optional item that assesses ideas/delusions of reference). Each item is rated from 0 to 4, with higher scores indicating poorer insight; the first six items are summed to create a total score (range, 0 to 24). The seventh item is not included in the total score because referential thinking is characteristic of some disorders but not others. Eisen, Phillips, Coles, and Rasmussen (2004) reported a mean total score of 8.38 (*SD* = 4.14) on the BABS among 64 individuals with OCD.

The BABS has strong internal consistency (α = .87), strong interrater and test-retest reliability, and good convergent and discriminant validity. It has been used to study treatment-related changes in insight in individuals with OCD.

SELF REPORT MEASURES

Numerous self-report inventories have been developed to measure the content and severity of OCD symptoms (for a comprehensive review see Taylor et al., 2002). The Maudsley Obsessional Compulsive Inventory (MOCI) (Hodgson & Rachman, 1977) was one of the first and most widely used instruments for measuring observable compulsive behavior such as washing and checking. It contains 30 true-false items with subscales for cleaning, checking, doubting/conscientiousness, and obsessional slowness. Over the past 25 years, the MOCI has demonstrated adequate internal consistency, with good criterion, convergent, and discriminant validity (Emmelkamp, Kraaijkamp, & van den Hout, 1999). Despite its longevity as a clinical research instrument, the MOCI has several limitations. First, the slowness subscale has been criticized as being neither internally consistent nor factorially distinct (Taylor et al., 2002). Second, the instrument primarily assesses washing and checking rituals and does not measure obsessions and covert rituals. Third, the MOCI is not well suited to measuring changes with treatment due to its dichotomous response format and because several items refer to past and permanent events rather than current concerns (e.g., "My parents were rather strict"). Finally, difficulty occurs with item wording (e.g., a number of items are worded as double negatives) which frequently leads to difficulty with completing and scoring the measure.

Additional self-report measures of OCD symptoms exist, yet also have limitations. The Padua Inventory (PI) (Sanavio, 1988) contains four subscales: checking, contamination fears, mental dyscontrol, and fear of behavioral dyscontrol. Several items, however, were found to measure worry rather than obsessions and therefore the scale was revised (Burns, Keortge, Formea, & Sternberger, 1996). The revision, the PI-R, which comprises five subscales: obsessional thoughts about harm to oneself or others, obsessional impulses to harm oneself or others, contamination obsessions and washing compulsions, checking compulsions, and dressing and grooming compulsions, has good psychometric properties and is one of the most comprehensive self-report measures of OCD. A remaining limitation of the PI-R is that several important types of symptoms are not covered, such as ordering.

The Obsessive Compulsive Inventory (OCI) (Foa, Kozak, Salkovskis, Coles, & Amir, 1998) assesses the frequency and distress associated with washing, checking, doubting, ordering, obsessing, hoarding, and mental neutralizing. Each of the 42 items, however, is rated on two dimensions: frequency and distress. This essentially increases the size of the scale to 84 items and patients frequently report that the double-rating is confusing.

With new research emerging on the nature of OCD symptoms, novel measures that more broadly assess OCD-related symptoms have been developed, evaluated, and introduced. Two of these instruments, both of which are well-suited for clinical and research purposes, are described below.

Obsessive Compulsive Inventory-Revised

Practical problems with the OCI (described above) led to the development of a revised version: the OCI-R, which consists of 18 items (Foa et al., 2002). Each item (e.g., I check things more often than necessary) is rated on a 5-point scale of distress associated with that particular symptom. The OCI-R has six subscales: washing, checking, ordering, obsessing, hoarding, and neutralizing, each containing three items which are summed to produce subscale scores (range = 0 to 12). A total score (range = 0 to 72) may be calculated by summing all 18 items. The OCI-R is psychometrically sound

(Abramowitz & Deacon, 2006; Foa et al., 2002) and is sensitive to the effects of treatment (Abramowitz, Tolin, & Deifenbach, 2005). A cutoff score of 21 can differentiate OCD patients from nonpatients.

Vancouver Obsessional Compulsive Inventory

The Vancouver Obsessional Compulsive Inventory (VOCI; Thordarson et al., 2004) is considered a revision of the MOCI. It contains 55 items and is designed to assess a wide range of obsessions, compulsions, avoidance behavior, and personality characteristics of known or theoretical importance in OCD. Each item is rated on a 5-point Likert scale to enhance its sensitivity to therapeutic change. Factors include contamination, checking, obsessions, hoarding, just right, and indecisiveness. A rigorous study describing scale development and psychometric evaluation (Thordarson et al., 2004) suggests that the VOCI is best suited for measuring symptoms in clinical populations. The measure also appears to have good convergent and discriminant validity, and internal consistency.

THEORY-DRIVEN FUNCTIONAL ASSESSMENT

Functional assessment is the compiling of detailed patient-specific information about the antecedents and consequences of target behaviors and emotions, usually for the purposes of developing a treatment plan. Behavioral or cognitive-behavioral theory dictates what information is collected and how it is organized to form a conceptualization of the problem that will drive therapeutic intervention (usually cognitive-behavioral treatment). A framework for the functional assessment of OCD is provided below.

Assessment of Obsessional Stimuli

This includes compiling a comprehensive list of the external and internal stimuli that evoke obsessional fear. External triggers include objects, situations, places, etc. that give rise to obsessional thinking and urges to ritualize: for example, public bathrooms, knives, churches, the number "13," leaving the house, and driving in certain places. Examples of questions to elicit this information include:

- What kinds of situations make you feel anxious?
- What kinds of things do you avoid?
- What triggers you to want to do rituals?

Internal obsessional stimuli include recurring ideas, images, doubts, and impulses that the individual finds unwanted, upsetting, immoral, repulsive, or otherwise unacceptable (i.e., obsessional thoughts). Examples include thoughts of germs, ideas of injuries occurring to loved ones, doubts about making unlikely mistakes, and impulses to harm elderly people. Examples of questions to elicit this information include:

- What intrusive thoughts do you have that trigger anxiety?
- What thoughts do you try to avoid, resist, or dismiss?

It is similarly important to obtain information about the cognitive basis of the individual's obsessional anxiety (i.e., the feared consequences). For example, what does the person fear if they are exposed to obsessional stimuli? Examples of questions to elicit feared consequences include:

- What is the worst thing you imagine happening if you are exposed to _____ (obsessional trigger)?
- What do you think might happen if you didn't do your _____ rituals?

The cognitive-behavioral model proposes that misinterpretations of unwanted thoughts, impulses, and images give rise to OCD symptoms. Therefore, assessment should include identification of mistaken beliefs about the presence and meaning of such stimuli. For example, "Thinking about stabbing my wife could lead me to actually stab her," "God will punish me for thinking immoral thoughts," "I'm a pervert if I have unwanted thoughts about sex," and "Anyone who thinks gay thoughts must be gay." Examples of questions to elicit this information include:

- What do you think it means that you have this thought?
- What will happen if you think this thought too much?
- Why do you try to avoid or dismiss these thoughts?

Some individuals with OCD fear that if obsessional anxiety is evoked, anxiety and related bodily sensations will persist indefinitely or spiral "out of control." For example, "If I don't arrange the books on the shelf perfectly, I will always feel anxious that things aren't just right." Questions to help elicit these types of cognitions include:

- Do you worry that you will become anxious and that the anxiety will never go away?
- What might happen to you if you remained anxious for long periods of time?

Two self-report questionnaires, the Obsessive Beliefs Questionnaire (OBQ) and the Interpretation of Intrusions Inventory (III), have been developed to systematically measure a range of pertinent OCD-related beliefs and misinterpretations (OCCWG, 2003, 2005). These psychometrically validated instruments are useful to include in the functional assessment to augment interview data.

Assessment of Avoidance and Compulsive Rituals

The cognitive-behavioral model proposes that avoidance and compulsive behavior maintains obsessional fear. It is, therefore, necessary to include such behaviors in a functional assessment. Most individuals with OCD avoid obsessional stimuli in order to reduce anxiety over feared disasters. Examples include avoidance of certain people (e.g., AIDS patients), places (e.g., public restrooms), situations (e.g., being the last one to leave the house), and certain words (e.g., "penis"). Examples of questions to elicit this information include:

- What situations do you avoid because of obsessional fear?
- Can you ever confront this situation?
- How does avoiding _____ make you feel more comfortable?

If avoidance is impossible, compulsive behaviors are performed to escape from distress or reduce the probability of feared consequences. In addition to gathering detailed information about all rituals (e.g., cleaning, checking, repeating actions, arranging objects, and asking for reassurance), subtle "mini rituals" such as wiping, using special soaps, and brief checks must be assessed. The cognitive motivation of all rituals should also be clarified as well (e.g., checking to prevent fires, using a certain soap to target certain kinds of chemicals). Examples of questions to elicit this information include:

- What do you do when you can't avoid (insert situation)?
- Tell me about the strategies or rituals you use to reduce obsessional fear of (insert obsessional fear).
- How does doing this ritual reduce your discomfort?
- What might happen if you didn't engage in this ritual?

Mental rituals are often overlooked in the functional assessment of OCD because they are not directly observable. Thus, it is important to ascertain any cognitive strategies the patient uses in response to obsessional stimuli. Examples include thinking "safe" thoughts, repeating prayers in a set manner, excessively mentally reviewing one's own actions to gain assurance, and habitual thought suppression and mental distraction. As with overt rituals, it is necessary to ascertain the cognitive links between mental rituals and the obsessional thoughts: for example, repeating the phrase "God is good" to avoid punishment for having sacrilegious thoughts, and suppression of violent thoughts to prevent acting violently. Examples of questions to elicit this information include:

- What kinds of mental strategies do you use to dismiss unwanted thoughts?
- What might happen if you didn't use the strategy?

Self Monitoring

Self-monitoring of rituals and avoidance behavior is an excellent tool for collecting real-time data on OCD symptoms. A log sheet can be given to the patient on which he or she records (a) date, (b) time, (c) obsessional thought or stimulus that triggers anxiety, (d) level of anxiety on a 0 to 10 scale, and (e) the ritual or avoidance behavior employed. Self-monitoring helps both the clinician and patient gain an accurate picture of OCD symptom severity and the functional relationship between obsessions and compulsions. It also helps the patient identify obsessions and rituals that he or she might not be aware of.

Case Conceptualization

The main value of a functional assessment is that it yields information from which to synthesize a case conceptualization. The case conceptualization is an individualized "blueprint" of OCD symptoms and is derived by listing (a) the situations and thoughts that trigger obsessional fear, (b) the associated cognitive variables (i.e., dysfunctional beliefs and appraisals), and (c) avoidance and compulsive rituals. Next, using the cognitive-behavioral model of OCD (as discussed above) as a framework, links between these phenomena are sketched as is shown in Figure 5.1. The individual in this case had obsessional fears of contamination and decontamination rituals.

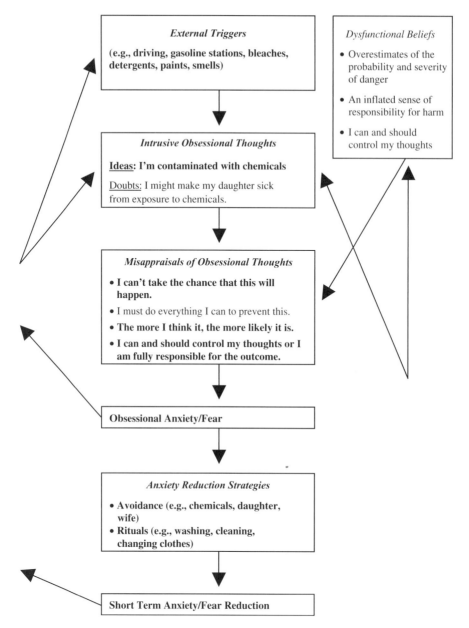

FIGURE 5.1   Case Conceptualization of an Individual with OCD.

Psychological Treatment

Cognitive-behavior therapy (CBT), a set of techniques derived from the cognitive-behavioral theoretical models described earlier, is considered the most effective approach to the psychological treatment of OCD. Two specific CBT methods have been examined in clinical studies: behavior therapy by exposure and response prevention (ERP) and cognitive therapy (CT). This section provides a concise description of these procedures and reviews research substantiating their effectiveness. Detailed guidelines for planning and implementing CBT techniques are provided in various treatment manuals (Abramowitz, 2006; Clark, 2004).

EXPOSURE AND RESPONSE PREVENTION

Exposure and response prevention entail confrontation with stimuli that provoke obsessional fear, but that objectively pose a low risk of harm. Exposure can occur in the form of repeated actual encounters with the feared situations (situational or *in vivo* exposure), and in the form of imaginal confrontation with the feared disastrous consequences of confronting these situations (imaginal exposure). For example, an individual with obsessional fears of hitting pedestrians while driving would be asked to practice driving through crowded streets for situational exposure. She would also practice imaginal exposure to thoughts of possibly having hit someone and being held responsible. A patient with fears of contaminating his daughter by accident might be asked to touch objects of increasing "dirtiness"—a doorknob, the floor, a toilet seat—for situational exposure. He would then confront thoughts of his daughter coming down with a serious illness as a result of his carelessness with these "contaminants."

As might be anticipated, initiating exposure tasks evokes the patient's anxiety. Patients are encouraged to engage in such tasks completely, and to allow this obsessional distress to increase. Over time, the anxiety (and associated physiological responding) naturally subsides—a process called *habituation*. With each repetition of the exposure task, habituation occurs more rapidly. The response prevention component of ERP entails refraining from compulsive rituals and other subtle avoidance behaviors that serve as an escape from obsessive fear. Response prevention helps to prolong exposure and facilitate the eventual extinction of obsessional anxiety. In the examples above, the first patient might practice refraining from any strategies she typically uses to reassure herself that no accidents have occurred, such as going in reverse to check out the scene, gazing in the rear-view mirror, asking a passenger for assurance, or checking with the police department about hit-and-run accidents in the vicinity. The second patient would be instructed to refrain from decontamination rituals such as washing or cleaning.

The Delivery of ERP

The way ERP is delivered can vary widely, although greater effectiveness is achieved when therapist-guided exposure sessions are held multiple times per week, as opposed to once-weekly (Abramowitz, 1996, 1997, 1998). One format that has been found to produce particularly potent effects includes a few hours of assessment and treatment planning followed by 15 (daily or twice-weekly) treatment sessions, lasting about 90 minutes each (Abramowitz, Foa, & Franklin, 2003). When pragmatic concerns render intensive regimens impractical, conducting the treatment sessions on a weekly basis works very well for individuals with less severe OCD (Warren & Thomas, 2001). Self-supervised exposure homework practice should be assigned for completion between sessions. It is important that home-based self-supervised exposure exercises (as with therapist-supervised exposure) last long enough for anxiety to dissipate; i.e., for habituation to occur.

A course of ERP ordinarily begins with the assessment of obsessions, compulsive rituals, avoidance strategies, and anticipated consequences of confronting feared situations. Information gathered during the assessment sessions is then used to plan the specific exposure exercises that will be pursued. Importantly, the term "response prevention" does not imply that the therapist physically restrains the patient from performing rituals. Instead, the therapist must convince patients to resist their own urges to carry out these behaviors. The therapist must also provide a cogent rationale for how exposure and response prevention will be helpful in reducing OCD. This rationale must motivate the patient to tolerate the distress that typically accompanies therapy. The treatment rationale also lets the patient know that this distress is temporary and that it subsides with repeated practice.

The exposure exercises in ERP typically begin with moderately distressing situations, stimuli, and images, and progress to the most distressing situations. Beginning with less anxiety-evoking exposure tasks increases the likelihood that the patient will learn to manage distress. This also increases confidence in the treatment. At the end of each treatment session, the therapist instructs the patient to continue exposure for several hours and in different environmental contexts, without the therapist. Exposure to the most anxiety-evoking situations—which must be faced—is completed during the middle third of the treatment program. This allows the patient ample opportunity to repeat such exposures in different contexts to allow generalization of treatment effects. During later sessions, the therapist emphases the importance of generalization and the individual continuing to apply the ERP procedures learned during treatment.

Mechanisms of Change

Foa and Kozak (1986) hypothesized that ERP produces its effects by correcting patients' overestimates of danger that underlie obsessional anxiety. These authors point to three requirements for successful outcome with ERP. First, physiological arousal and subjective fear must be evoked during exposure. Second, the fear responses must gradually diminish during the exposure session in the absence of compulsive rituals (within-session habituation). Third, the initial fear response at the beginning of each exposure session should decline across sessions (between-sessions habituation).

Several dismantling studies have examined the individual effects of exposure and response prevention techniques (Foa, Steketee, Grayson, Turner, & Lattimer, 1984; Foa, Steketee, & Milby, 1980). This research indicates that whereas exposure produces the greatest effects on obsessional anxiety, response prevention produces the greatest reduction of compulsive rituals. Nevertheless, there is an additive effect of combining the two techniques: using both exposure and response prevention is more effective than either of its individual components (Foa et al., 1984).

The Efficacy of ERP

A meta-analysis of 24 ERP studies revealed very large post-treatment (ES = 1.16 to 1.41) and follow-up (ES = 1.10 to 1.57) effect sizes (Abramowitz, 1996). Foa and Kozak (1996) found that across 13 ERP studies, 83% of patients were responders (defined as at least 30% symptom reduction) at post-treatment, and across 16 studies, 76% were responders at follow-up (mean follow-up was 29 months). In concert, these findings suggest that the majority of OCD patients who undergo treatment with ERP evidence substantial short- and long-term benefit. Data from individual studies reveal that patients who complete a trial of ERP consistently achieve 50% to 70% symptom reduction.

Randomized controlled studies have found that ERP is superior to waiting list, progressive muscle relaxation, anxiety management training, pill placebo, and pharmacotherapy by serotonergic medication (Foa et al., 2005; Nakatani et al., 2005). These studies indicate that the effects of CBT are due to the specific ERP techniques over and above the effects of nonspecific factors common to all interventions, such as the therapeutic relationship. Moreover, the effects of ERP are not limited to highly selected research samples or to treatment as delivered in specialty clinics. Effectiveness studies conducted with non-research patients (Franklin, Abramowitz, Foa, Kozak, & Levitt, 2000) show that over 80% of patients who complete CBT achieve clinically significant improvement.

COGNITIVE THERAPY

The basis of CT for OCD is the rational and evidence-based challenging and correction of faulty and dysfunctional thoughts and beliefs that underlie emotional distress (Beck & Emery, 1985). As is discussed above, individuals with OCD hold characteristic faulty beliefs that lead to obsessive fear. It is these beliefs that are targeted in CT, including overestimates of the probability and severity of danger and misinterpretations of intrusive thoughts as having implications for responsibility for harm.

Delivery of CT

Cognitive therapy typically begins with the therapist presenting a rationale for treatment that incorporates the notion that intrusive obsessional thoughts are normal experiences and not harmful or significant. The patient is then socialized to the cognitive-behavioral framework for understanding OCD as discussed earlier in this chapter. A central aim of CT is therefore to reduce obsessional fear and the need for compulsive rituals by helping the patient correct dysfunctional thinking and behavioral responses to obsessional stimuli (situations, thoughts, images) so that such situations no longer require avoidance and so that intrusive thoughts are no longer perceived as needing to be controlled or neutralized via rituals.

Various CT techniques are used to help patients identify and correct their erroneous appraisals, such as didactic presentation of educational material, Socratic dialogue, and cognitive restructuring aimed at helping patients recognize and remedy dysfunctional thinking patterns. "Behavioral experiments," in which the patient enters situations that exemplify their fears, are often used to facilitate the acquisition of corrective information about the realistic risks associated with obsessional fears. For a detailed manual describing the use of CT techniques for OCD see Wilhelm and Steketee (2006).

Van Oppen and Arntz (1994) outlined a 16-session CT intervention for OCD. This protocol included: (a) learning to conceptualize obsessive intrusions as normal stimuli; (b) identifying and challenging anxiety-provoking thoughts associated with obsessions with Socratic questioning; and (c) changing the dysfunctional assumptions to non-distressing beliefs, and (d) behavioral experiments to test out the new beliefs. This program was found to be effective in reducing OCD symptoms (Van Oppen et al., 1995).

CT versus ERP

A handful of studies have addressed the relative efficacy of CT and ERP by directly comparing variants of the two interventions. Although most of these studies have found that these treatments produced equivalent effects, methodological problems prevent definitive conclusions. In earlier studies, for example, both ERP and CT yielded minimal improvements in OCD symptoms. The efficacy of ERP was likely attenuated by the lack of therapist-supervised exposure; and CT programs were likely enhanced by the use of supervised behavioral experiments which mimic the effects of exposure. Vogel, Stiles, and Götestam (2004), however, found that the inclusion of CT was useful in reducing dropout from ERP. Thus, there are likely benefits to incorporating CT techniques along with ERP; perhaps CT techniques improve the acceptability of ERP.

Biological Treatments

SEROTONIN REUPTAKE INHIBITORS

Pharmacotherapy using selective serotonin reuptake inhibitor (SSRI) medication is the most widely used treatment for OCD. The specific agents in this class of drugs include fluoxetine, paroxetine, sertraline, citalopram, and fluvoxamine. Clomipramine, a tricyclic medication which also possesses serotonergic properties, is also used in the treatment of OCD. Problems with the serotonin hypothesis (as discussed earlier in this chapter) withstanding, it is this model that provides the rationale for the use of serotonergic medications to treat OCD. On average, serotonin medications produce a 20 to 40% reduction in obsessions and compulsions (Rauch & Jenike, 1998). The major strengths of a pharmacological approach to treating OCD include the convenience and the requirement of little effort on the patient's part. Limitations include the relatively modest improvement and likelihood of residual symptoms, high rate of non-response (40% – 60% of patients do not show any favorable response), and the prospect of unpleasant side effects (which can often be stabilized by adjusting the dose). Moreover, once SRIs are terminated, OCD symptoms typically return rapidly (Pato, Zohar-Kadouch, Zohar, & Murphy, 1988).

NEUROSURGICAL TREATMENT

Although they have received little in the way of controlled empirical evaluation, four neurosurgical procedures have been reported with OCD patients: (1) subcaudate tractotomy, (2) limbic leucotomy, (3) cingulotomy, and (4) capsulotomy. These operations involve severing interconnections between areas of the brain's frontal lobes and the limbic system. Recommended only in cases where severe and unmanageable OCD and depressive symptoms persist despite adequate trials of all other available treatments, the risks of neurosurgery include permanent alterations in cognitive functioning and personality. Although clinical improvement has been observed in some cases, it remains unknown why these procedures are only successful for a subset of OCD patients (Jenike, 2000). There is also an increased risk of suicide following failure with this approach.

Summary and New Directions

Few syndromes in psychopathology have generated as much curiosity and clinical exploration as has OCD. Since the 1970s, research on OCD has increased exponentially leading to a clearer understanding of the heterogeneity of the disorder, its boundaries with other syndromes, and the development of increasingly sophisticated theoretical models of etiology and maintenance. Perhaps most importantly, research has led to advances in treatment; and whereas the first line therapies (CBT and serotonergic medication) are not entirely effective for every sufferer, they have transformed OCD from an unmanageable lifetime affliction into a treatable problem that need not reduce quality of life.

Despite the aforementioned advances, a number of unresolved disagreements concerning OCD have emerged. Differences, for example, have surfaced over phenomenological issues, etiological models, and approaches to treatment. These disagreements occur predominantly along disciplinary lines between biologically oriented and cognitive-behaviorally oriented schools of thought. Biologically inclined theorists view OCD as a medical condition involving abnormal neurological processes, whereas psychosocial formulations emphasize the role of learning and dysfunctional cognitions. Yet, because of the relative insularity within each camp, theoretical conjecture and empirical findings from within different approaches are typically addressed toward distinct and narrow audiences. Clinicians, researchers, and students with broad interests are hindered from gaining a clear understanding of the diverse (and sometimes polarized) perspectives.

Presently, we stand at the dawn of a new century when we can look to the past and to the future with hope. In looking back, we can be glad that the days are gone when individuals with OCD had little hope of receiving the help that they needed, or worse, underwent years of ineffective treatment with false hopes of improvement. Today, we can see that there are treatments that are useful and oftentimes highly effective. We can also see that there is energetic disagreement among researchers in the OCD research communities, and it is the sort of disagreement that can lead to productive outcomes, fruitful debate, and more refined care of individuals with OCD. Although cognitive-behavioral treatments can be highly effective, one challenge for the future involves helping patients without good access to this therapy. Other challenges include helping individuals with motivational problems, and those with families and other social circles that reinforce OCD symptoms, to enter and succeed with treatment. In looking forward, we can also hope that investigators with differing backgrounds and research agendas will engage with one another as they pursue their own work so that at the close of the next century we will have an understanding of OCD that integrates the best methods of behavioral science with the best methods of neurochemistry and neurophysiology.

References

Abbruzzese, M., Bellodi, L., Ferri, S., & Scarone, S. (1993). Memory functioning in obsessive-compulsive disorder. *Behavioural Neurology, 6*, 119–122.

Abramowitz, J. S. (1996). Variants of exposure and response prevention in the treatment of obsessive-compulsive disorder: A meta-analysis. *Behavior Therapy, 27*, 583–600.

Abramowitz, J. S. (1997). Effectiveness of psychological and pharmacological treatments for obsessive-compulsive disorder: A quantitative review. *Journal of Consulting and Clinical Psychology, 65*, 44–52.

Abramowitz, J. S. (1998). Does cognitive-behavioral therapy cure obsessive-compulsove disorder? A Meta-analytic evaluation of clinical significance. *Behavior Therapy, 29*, 339–355.

Abramowitz, J. S. (2006). *Understanding and treating obsessive-compulsive disorder: A cognitive-behavioral approach.* Mahwah, NJ: Erlbaum.

Abramowitz, J. S., & Deacon, B. J. (2005). The OC spectrum: A closer look at the arguments and the data. In J. Abramowitz & A. C. Houts (Eds.), *Concepts and controversies in obsessive-compulsive disorder* (pp. 141–149). New York: Springer.

Abramowitz, J. S., & Deacon, B. J. (2006). Psychometric properties and construct validity of the Obsessive Compulsive Inventory-Revised: Replication and extension with a clinical sample. *Journal of Anxiety Disorders, 20*, 1016–1035.

Abramowitz, J. S., Deacon, B. J., Woods, C. M., & Tolin, D. F. (2004). Association between protestant religiosity and obsessive-compulsive symptoms and cognitions. *Depression and Anxiety, 20*, 70–76.

Abramowitz, J. S., Foa, E. B., & Franklin, M. E. (2003). Exposure and ritual prevention for obsessive-compulsive disorder: effects of intensive versus twice-weekly sessions. *Journal of Consulting and Clinical Psychology, 71*, 394–398.

Abramowitz, J. S., & Houts, A. C. (2002). What is OCD and what is not: Problems with the OCD spectrum concept. *Scientific Review of Mental Health Practice, 1*, 139–156.

Abramowitz, J. S., Huppert, J. D., Cohen, A. B., Tolin, D. F., & Cahill, S. P. (2002). Religious obsessions and compulsions in a non-clinical sample: The Penn Inventory of Scrupulosity (PIOS). *Behaviour Research and Therapy, 40*, 824–838.

Abramowitz, J. S., Khandher, M., Nelson, C., Deacon, B. J., & Rygwall, R. (2006). The role of cognitive factors in the pathogenesis of obsessive-compulsive symptoms: A prospective study. *Behaviour Research and Therapy, 44*, 1361–1374.

Abramowitz, J. S., Nelson, C., Rygwall, R., & Khandher, M. (2006). The cognitive mediation of obsessive-compulsive symptoms: A longitudinal study. *Journal of Anxiety Disorders, 21*, 91–104.

Abramowitz, J. S., Schwartz, S. A., Moore, K. M., & Luenzmann, K. R. (2003). Obsessive-compulsive symptoms in pregnancy and the puerperium: A review of the literature. *Journal of Anxiety Disorders, 17*, 461–478.

Abramowitz, J. S., Tolin, D. F., & Deifenbach, G. (2005). Measuring change in OCD: Sensitivity of the Obsessive-Compulsive Inventory-Revised. *Journal of Psychopathology and Behavioral Assessment, 27*, 317–324.

Abramowitz, J. S., Tolin, D., & Street, G. P. (2001). Paradoxical effects of thought suppression: a meta-analysis of controlled studies. *Clinical Psychology Review, 21*, 683–703.

Abramowitz, J. S., Whiteside, S., Lynam, D., & Kalsy, S. (2003). Is thought-action fusion specific to obsessive-compulsive disorder? A mediating role of negative affect. *Behaviour Research and Therapy, 41*, 1063–1079.

Akhtar, S., Wig, N. N., Varma, V. K., Pershad, D., & Verma, S. K. (1975). A phenomenological analysis of symptoms in obsessive-compulsive neurosis. *British Journal of Psychiatry, 127*, 342–348.

Alonso, P., Menchon, J. M., Mataix-Cols, D., Pifarre, J., Urretavizcaya, M., Crespo, M., et al. (2004). Perceived parental rearing style in obsessive-compulsive disorder: Relation to symptom dimensions. *Psychiatry Research, 127*, 267–278.

American Psychiatric Association (2000). *Diagnostic and statistical manual of mental disorders* (4th ed., text revision). Washington, DC: Author.

Baxter, L. R., Jr., Phelps, M. E., Mazziotta, J. C., Guze, B. H., Schwartz, J. M., & Selin, C. E. (1987). Local cerebral glucose metabolic rates in obsessive-compulsive disorder. A comparison with rates in unipolar depression and in normal controls. *Archives of General Psychiatry, 44*, 211–218.

Baxter, L. R., Jr., Schwartz, J. M., Mazziotta, J. C., Phelps, M. E., Pahl, J. J., Guze, B. H., et al. (1988). Cerebral glucose metabolic rates in nondepressed patients with obsessive-compulsive disorder. *American Journal of Psychiatry, 145*, 1560–1563.

Beck, A. T. (1976). *Cognitive therapy of the emotional disorders.* New York: International Universities Press.

Beck, A. T., & Emery, G. (1985). *Anxiety disorders and phobias: A cognitive perspective.* New York: Basic Books.

Beck, A. T., Epstein, N., Brown, G., & Steer, R. A. (1988). An inventory for measuring clinical anxiety: Psychometric properties. *Journal of Consulting and Clinical Psychology, 56*, 893–897.

Brown, H. D., Kosslyn, S., Breiter, H., Baer, L., & Jenike, M. (1994). Can patients with obsessive-compulsive disorder discriminate between percepts and mental images? A signal detection analysis. *Journal of Abnormal Psychology, 103*, 445–454.

Burns, G., Keortge, S. G., Formea, G. M., & Sternberger, L. G. (1996). Revision of the Padua Inventory of obsessive compulsive disorder symptoms: Distinctions between worry, obsessions, and compulsions. *Behaviour Research and Therapy, 34*, 163–173.

Clark, D. A. (2004). *Cognitive-Behavioral Therapy for OCD.* New York: Guilford.

Clark, D. M. (1986). A cognitive approach to panic. *Behaviour Research and Therapy, 24* (4), 461–470.

Coles, M. E., Frost, R. O., Heimberg, R. G., & Rheaume, J. (2003). "Not just right experiences": Perfectionism, obsessive-compulsive features and general psychopathology. *Behaviour Research and Therapy, 41*, 681–700.

Constans, J., Foa, E., Franklin, M. E., & Matthews, A. (1995). Memory for actual and imagined events in OC checkers. *Behaviour Research and Therapy, 33*, 665–671.

deSilva, P., Menzies, R. G., & Shafran, R. (2003). Spontaneous decay of compulsive urges: the case of covert compulsions. *Behaviour Research and Therapy, 41*, 129–137.

DiNardo, P., Brown, T., & Barlow, D. H. (1994). *Anxiety Disorders Interview Schedule for* DSM-IV: *Lifetime Version (ADIS-IV-LV).* San Antonio, TX: Psychological Corporation.

Dollard, J., & Miller, N. E. (1950). *Personality and psychotherapy: An analysis in terms of learning, thinking, and culture.* New York: McGraw-Hill.

Ebert, D., Speck, O., Konig, A., Berger, M., Hennig, J., & Hohagen, F. (1997). 1H-magnetic resonance spec-

troscopy in obsessive-compulsive disorder: Evidence for neuronal loss in the cingulate gyrus and the right striatum. *Psychiatry Research, 74*, 173–176.

Ecker, W., & Engelkamp, J. (1995). Memory for actions in obsessive-compulsive disorder. *Behavioural & Cognitive Psychotherapy, 23*, 349–371.

Eisen, J. L., Phillips, K. A., Baer, L., Beer, D. A., Atala, K. D., & Rasmussen, S. A. (1998). The Brown Assessment of Beliefs Scale: Reliability and validity. *American Journal of Psychiatry, 155*, 102–108.

Eisen, J. L., Phillips, K. A., Coles, M., & Rasmussen, S. (2004). Insight in obsessive compulsive disorder and body dysmorphic disorder. *Comprehensive Psychiatry, 45*, 10–15.

Emmelkamp, P., Kraaijkamp, H., & van denHout, M. (1999). Assessment of obsessive-compulsive disorder. *Behavior Modification, 23*, 269–279.

First, M. B., Spitzer, R. L., Gibbon, M., & Williams, J. (2002). *Structured Clinical Interview for the* DSM-IV *Axis 1 Disorders.* New York: Biometrics Research Department, New York State Psychiatric Institute.

Fitzgerald, K. D., Moorre, G. J., Paulson, L. A., Stewart, C. M., & Rosenberg, D. R. (2000). Proton spectroscopic imaging of the thalamus in treatment-naive pediatric obsessive-compulsive disorder. *Biological Psychiatry, 47*, 174–182.

Foa, E. B., Huppert, J. D., Leiberg, S., Langner, R., Kichic, R., Hajcak, G., et al. (2002). The Obsessive-Compulsive Inventory: Development and validation of a short version. *Psychological Assessment, 14*, 485–496.

Foa, E. B., & Kozak, M. (1986). Emotional processing of fear: Exposure to corrective information. *Psychological Bulletin, 99*, 20–35.

Foa, E. B., & Kozak, M. J. (1995). *DSM-IV* field trial: Obsessive-compulsive disorder. *American Journal of Psychiatry, 152*, 90–96.

Foa, E. B., & Kozak, M. J. (1996). Psychological treatment for obsessive-compulsive disorder. In M. R. Mavissakalian & R. F. Prien (Eds.), *Long-term treatments of anxiety disorders* (pp. 285–309). Washington, DC: American Psychiatric Press.

Foa, E. B., Kozak, M. J., Salkovskis, P. M., Coles, M. E., & Amir, N. (1998). The validation of a new obsessive-compulsive disorder scale: the obsessive-compulsive inventory. *Psychological Assessment, 10*, 206–214.

Foa, E. B., Liebowitz, M. R., Kozak, M. J., Davies, S., Campeas, R., Franklin, M. E., et al. (2005). Randomized, placebo-controlled trial of exposure and ritual prevention, clomipramine, and their combination in the treatment of obsessive-compulsive disorder. *American Journal of Psychiatry, 162*, 151–161.

Foa, E. B., Steketee, G., Grayson, J., Turner, R., & Lattimer, P. (1984). Deliberate exposure and blocking of obsessive-compulsive rituals: Immediate and long-term effects. *Behavior Therapy, 15*, 450–472.

Foa, E. B., Steketee, G., & Milby, J. (1980). Differential effects of exposure and response prevention in obsessive-compulsive washers. *Journal of Consulting and Clinical Psychology, 48*, 71–79.

Franklin, M., Abramowitz, J., Foa, E., Kozak, M., & Levitt, J. (2000). Effectiveness of exposure and ritual prevention for obsessive-compulsive disorder: randomized compared with nonrandomized samples. *Journal of Consulting and Clinical Psychology, 68*, 594–602.

Freeston, M. H., & Ladouceur, R. (1997). What do patients do with their obsessive thoughts? *Behaviour Research & Therapy, 35*, 335–348.

Freeston, M. H., Ladouceur, R., Gagnon, F., & Thibodeau, N. (1993). Beliefs about obsessional thoughts. *Journal of Psychopathology and Behavioral Assessment, 15*, 1–21.

Frost, R. O., & Hartl, T. L. (1996). A cognitive behavioral model of compulsive hoarding. *Behaviour Research and Therapy, 34*, 341–350.

Frost, R. O., & Steketee, G. (1997). Perfectionism in obsessive-compulsive disorder patients. *Behaviour Research and Therapy, 35*, 291–296.

Frost, R. O., & Steketee, S. (2002). *Cognitive approaches to obsessions and compulsions: Theory, assessment, and treatment.* Oxford, UK: Elsevier.

Gershuny, B. S., Baer, L., Jenike, M. A., Minichiello, W. E., & Wilhelm, S. (2002). Comorbid posttraumatic stress disorder: impact on treatment outcome for obsessive-compulsive disorder. *American Journal of Psychiatry, 159*, 852–854.

Goodman, W. K., Price, L. H., Rasmussen, S. A., Mazure, C., Delgado, P., Heninger, G. R., et al. (1989). The Yale-Brown Obsessive Compulsive Scale: validity. *Archives of General Psychiatry, 46*, 1012–1016.

Goodman, W. K., Price, L. H., Rasmussen, S. A., Mazure, C., Fleischmann, R. L., Hill, C. L., et al. (1989). The Yale-Brown Obsessive Compulsive Scale: development, use, and reliability. *Archives of General Psychiatry, 46*, 1006–1011.

Gross, R. C., Sasson, Y., Chorpa, M., & Zohar, J. (1998). Biological models of obsessive-compulsive disorder: The serotonin hypothesis. In R. P. Swinson,

M. Antony, S. Rachman, & M. Richter (Eds.), *Obsessive-compulsive disorder: Theory, research, and treatment* (pp. 141–153). New York: Guilford.

Hafner, R. J. (1988). Obsessive-compulsive disorder: A questionnaire study of a self-help group. *International Journal of Social Psychiatry, 34*, 310–315.

Hermans, D., Martens, K., DeCort, K., Pieters, G., & Eelen, P. (2003). Reality monitoring and metacognitive beliefs related to cognitive confidence in obsessive-compulsive disorder. *Behaviour Research and Therapy, 41*, 383–401.

Hodgson, R., & Rachman, S. (1972). The effects of contamination and washing in obsessional patients. *Behaviour Research and Therapy, 10*, 111–117.

Hodgson, R., & Rachman, S. (1977). Obsessional-compulsive complaints. *Behaviour Research and Therapy, 15*, 389–395.

Hoekstra, R. J., Visser, S., & Emmelkamp, P. M. G. (1989). A social learning formulation of the etiology of obsessive-compulsive disorders. In P. M. G. Emmelkamp (Ed.), *Fresh perspectives on anxiety disorders* (pp. 115–123). Amsterdam: Swets & Zeitlinger.

Hollander, E., DeCaria, C. M., Nitescu, A., Gully, R., Suckow, R. F., Cooper, T. B., et al. (1992). Serotonergic function in obsessive-compulsive disorder. Behavioral and neuroendocrine responses to oral m-chlorophenylpiperazine and fenfluramine in patients and healthy volunteers. *Archives of General Psychiatry, 49*, 21–28.

Hollander, E., Friedberg, J., Wasserman, S., Yeh, C. -C., & Iyengar, R. (2005). The case for the OCD spectrum. In J. Abramowitz & A. C. Houts (Eds.), *Concepts and controversies in obsessive-compulsive disorder* (pp. 95–118). New York: Springer.

Hoover, C., & Insel, T. R. (1984). Families of origin in obsessive-compulsive disorder. *Journal of Nervous and Mental Disease, 172*, 207–215.

Insel, T. R., Mueller, E. A., Alterman, I., Linnoila, M., & Murphy, D. L. (1985). Obsessive-compulsive disorder and serotonin: is there a connection? *Biological Psychiatry, 20*, 1174–1188.

Jenike, M. (2000). Neurosurgical treatment of obsessive-compulsive disorder. In W. Goodman, J. Maser, & M. V. Rudorfer (Eds.), *Obsessive-compulsive disorder* (pp. 457–482). Mahwah, NJ: Lawrence Erlbaum Associates.

Johnson, M. K., & Raye, C. L. (1981). Reality monitoring. *Psychological Review, 88*, 67–85.

Jones, M. K., & Menzies, R. G. (1997). The cognitive mediation of obsessive-compulsive handwashing. *Behaviour Research and Therapy, 35*, 843–850.

Kessler, R., Berglund, P., Demler, O., Jin, R., Merikangas, K., & Walters, E. (2005). Lifetime prevalence and age-of-onset distributions of *DSM-IV* disorders in the National Comorbidity Survey Replication. *Archives of General Psychiatry, 62,* 593–602.

Khanna, S., & Channabasavanna, S. M. (1988). Phenomenology of obsessions in obsessive-compulsive neurosis. *Psychopathology, 21,* 12–18.

Kolada, J. L., Bland, R. C., & Newman, S. C. (1994). Obsessive-compulsive disorder. *Acta Psychiatrica Scandinavica, 89,* 24–35.

Ladouceur, R., Freeston, M. H., Rheaume, J., Dugas, M. J., Gagnon, F., Thibodeau, N., et al. (2000). Strategies used with intrusive thoughts: a comparison of OCD patients with anxious and community controls. *Journal of Abnormal Psychology, 109,* 179–187.

Ladouceur, R., Rheaume, J., Freeston, M. H., Aublet, F., Jean, K., Lachance, S., et al. (1995). Experimental manipulations of responsibility: an analogue test for models of obsessive-compulsive disorder. *Behaviour Research and Therapy, 33,* 937–946.

Lopatka, C., & Rachman, S. (1995). Perceived responsibility and compulsive checking: An experimental analysis. *Behaviour Research and Therapy, 33,* 673–684.

McKay, D., Abramowitz, J. S., Calamari, J. E., Kyrios, M., Radomsky, A. S., Sookman, D., et al. (2004). A critical evaluation of obsessive-compulsive disorder subtypes: Symptoms versus mechanisms. *Clinical Psychology Review, 24,* 283–313.

McNally, R. J., & Kohlbeck, P. A. (1993). Reality monitoring in obsessive-compulsive disorder. *Behaviour Research and Therapy, 31,* 249–253.

Merkel, W., Pollard, C. A., Wiener, R. L., & Staebler, C. R. (1993). Perceived parental characteristics of patients with obsessive-compulsive disorder, depression, and panic disorder. *Child Psychiatry and Human Development, 24,* 49–57.

Miguel, E., Coffey, B., Baer, L., Savage, C. R., Rauch, S., & Jenike, M. (1995). Phenomenology of intentional repetitive behaviors in obsessive-compulsive disorder and Tourette's disorder. *Journal of Clinical Psychiatry, 56,* 246–255.

Mineka, S., & Zinbarg, R. (2006). A contemporary learning theory perspective on the etiology of anxiety disorders. *American Psychologist, 61,* 10–26.

Mowrer, O. (1960). *Learning theory and behavior.* New York: Wiley.

Muller, J., & Roberts, J. E. (2005). Memory and attention in obsessive-compulsive disorder: A review. *Journal of Anxiety Disorders, 19,* 1–28.

Nakatani, E., Nakagawa, A., Nakoa, T., Yoshizato, C., Nabeyama, M., Kudo, A., et al. (2005). A randomized controlled trial of Japanese patients with Obsessive-Compulsive Disorder: Effectiveness of behavior therapy and fluvoxamine. *Psychotherapy and Psychosomatics, 74,* 269–276.

Newth, S., & Rachman, S. (2001). The concealment of obsessions. *Behaviour Research and Therapy, 39,* 457–464.

Obsessive Compulsive Cognitions Working Group. (1997). Cognitive assessment of obsessive-compulsive disorder. *Behaviour Research and Therapy, 35,* 667–681.

Obsessive Compulsive Cognitions Working Group. (2001). Development and initial validation of the Obsessive Beliefs Questionnaire and the Interpretations of Intrusions Inventory. *Behaviour Research & Therapy, 39,* 987–1006.

Obsessive Compulsive Cognitions Working Group. (2003). Psychometric validation of the Obsessive Beliefs Questionnaire and the Interpretation of Intrusions Inventory: Part I. *Behaviour Research & Therapy, 41,* 863–878.

Obsessive Compulsive Cognitions Working Group. (2005). Psychometric validation of the Obsessive Belief Questionnaire and Interpretation of Intrusions Inventory: Part 2, factor analyses and testing of a brief version. *Behaviour Research and Therapy, 43,* 1527–1542.

Pato, M. T., Zohar-Kadouch, R., Zohar, J., & Murphy, D. L. (1988). Return of symptoms after discontinuation of clomipramine in patients with obsessive-compulsive disorder. *American Journal of Psychiatry, 145,* 1521–1525.

Purdon, C., & Clark, D. A. (1994). Obsessive intrusive thoughts in nonclinical subjects. Part II. Cognitive appraisal, emotional response and thought control strategies. *Behaviour Research and Therapy, 32,* 403–410.

Rachman, S. (1976). Obsessional-compulsive checking. *Behaviour Research and Therapy, 14,* 269–277.

Rachman, S. (1997). A cognitive theory of obsessions. *Behaviour Research and Therapy, 35,* 793–802.

Rachman, S. (2003). *The treatment of obsessions.* Oxford, UK: Oxford University Press.

Rachman, S., & deSilva, P. (1978). Abnormal and normal obsessions. *Behaviour Research and Therapy, 16,* 233–248.

Rachman, S., & Shafran, R. (1998). Cognitive and behavioral features of obsessive-compulsive disorder. In R. P. Swinson, M. M. Antony, S. Rachman, & M. A. Richter (Eds.), *Obsessive-Compulsive*

Disorder: Theory, research, and treatment (pp. 51–78). New York: Guilford.

Rachman, S., Shafran, R., Mitchell, D., Trant, J., & Teachman, B. (1996). How to remain neutral: An experimental analysis of neutralization. *Behaviour Research and Therapy, 34*, 889–898.

Radomsky, A. S., & Rachman, S. (1999). Memory bias in obsessive-compulsive disorder (OCD). *Behaviour Research and Therapy, 37*, 605–618.

Radomsky, A. S., Rachman, S., & Hammond, D. (2001). Memory bias, confidence and responsibility in compulsive checking. *Behaviour Research and Therapy, 39*, 813–822.

Rasmussen, S. A., & Eisen, J. L. (1992a). The epidemiology and clinical features of obsessive-compulsive disorder. *The Psychiatric Clinics of North America, 15*, 743–758.

Rasmussen, S. A., & Eisen, J. L. (1992b). The epidemiology and differential diagnosis of obsessive-compulsive disorder. *Journal of Clinical Psychiatry, 53*, 4–10.

Rasmussen, S. A., & Tsuang, M. T. (1986). Clinical characteristics and family history in *DSM-III* obsessive-compulsive disorder. *American Journal of Psychiatry, 143*, 317–322.

Rassin, E., Merckelbach, H., Muris, P., & Spaan, V. (1999). Thought-action fusion as a causal factor in the development of intrusions. *Behaviour Research and Therapy, 37*, 231–237.

Rauch, S., & Jenike, M. (1998). Pharmacological treatment of obsessive compulsive disorder. In P. E. Nathan & J. M. Gorman (Eds.), *A guide to treatments that work* (pp. 389–410). London: Oxford University Press.

Roper, G., & Rachman, S. (1976). Obsessional-compulsive checking: experimental replication and development. *Behaviour Research and Therapy, 14*, 25–32.

Rubinstein, C., Peynirciglu, Z., Chambless, D., & Pigott, T. (1993). Memory in sub-clinical obsessive-compulsive checkers. *Behaviour Research and Therapy, 31*, 759–765.

Salkovskis, P. (1996). Cognitive-behavioral approaches to the understanding of obsessional problems. In R. Rapee (Ed.), *Current controversies in the anxiety disorders* (pp. 103–133). New York: Guilford.

Salkovskis, P. M., Shafran, R., Rachman, S., & Freeston, M. H. (1999). Multiple pathways to inflated responsibility beliefs in obsessional problems: possible origins and implications for therapy and research. *Behaviour Research and Therapy, 37*, 1055–1072.

Salkovskis, P. M., Wroe, A. L., Gledhill, A., Morrison, N., Forrester, E., Richards, C., et al. (2000). Responsibility attitudes and interpretations are characteristic of obsessive compulsive disorder. *Behaviour Research and Therapy, 38*, 347–372.

Sanavio, E. (1988). Obsessions and compulsions: The Padua Inventory. *Behaviour Research and Therapy, 26*, 169–177.

Saxena, S., Bota, R. G., & Brody, A. L. (2001). Brain-behavior relationships in obsessive-compulsive disorder. *Seminars in Clinical Neuropsychiatry, 6*, 82–101.

Shafran, R., Thordarson, D. S., & Rachman, S. (1996). Thought-action fusion in obsessive compulsive disorder. *Journal of Anxiety Disorders, 10*, 379–391.

Sheehan, D., Lecrubier, Y., Harnett-Sheehan, K., Amoriam, P., Janavs, J., Weiller, E., et al. (1998). The Mini International Neuropsychiatric Interview (M.I.N.I.): The development and validation of a structured diagnostic interview for *DSM-IV* and ICD-10. *Journal of Clinical Psychiatry, 59* (Suppl. 20), 22–33.

Sica, C., Novara, C., & Sanavio, E. (2002). Religiousness and obsessive-compulsive cognitions and symptoms in an Italian population. *Behaviour Research and Therapy, 40*, 813–823.

Steketee, G., Eisen, J., Dyck, I., Warshaw, M., & Rasmussen, S. (1999). Predictors of course in obsessive-compulsive disorder. *Psychiatry Research, 89*, 229–238.

Taylor, S., Thordarson, D., & Sochting, I. (2002). Obsessive-compulsive disorder. In M. Antony & D. H. Barlow (Eds.), *Handbook of assessment and treatment planning for psychological disorders* (pp. 182–214). New York: Guilford.

Thordarson, D. S., Radomsky, A. S., Rachman, S., Shafran, R., Sawchuk, C. N., & Hakstian, A. (2004). The Vancouver Obsessional Compulsive Inventory (VOCI). *Behaviour Research and Therapy, 42*, 1289–1314.

Tolin, D. F., Abramowitz, J. S., Brigidi, B. D., & Foa, E. B. (2003). Intolerance of uncertainty in obsessive-compulsive disorder. *Journal of Anxiety Disorders, 17*, 233–242.

Tolin, D. F., Abramowitz, J. S., Kozak, M. J., & Foa, E. B. (2001). Fixity of belief, preceptual aberration, and magical ideation in obsessive-compulsive disorder. *Journal of Anxiety Disorders, 15*, 501–510.

Tolin, D. F., Abramowitz, J., Brigidi, B., Amir, N., Street, G., & Foa, E. (2001). Memory and memory confidence in obsessive-compulsive disorder. *Behaviour Research and Therapy, 39*, 913–927.

Tolin, D. F., Hamlin, C., & Foa, E. B. (2002). Directed forgetting in obsessive-compulsive disorder: Replication and extension. *Behaviour Research and Therapy, 40*, 792–803.

Turgeon, L., O'Connor, K., Marchand, A., & Freeston, M. (2002). Recollections of parent-child relationships in patients with obsessive-compulsive disorder and panic disorder with agoraphobia. *Acta Psychiatrica Scandinavica, 105*, 310–316.

VanOppen, P., & Arntz, A. (1994). Cognitive therapy for obsessive-compulsive disorder. *Behaviour Research and Therapy, 32*, 79–87.

VanOppen, P., DeHaan, E., VanBalkom, A. J. L. M., Spinhoven, P., Hoogduin, K., & VanDyck, R. (1995). Cognitive therapy and exposure *in vivo* in the treatment of obsessive compulsive disorder. *Behaviour Research and Therapy, 33*, 379–390.

Vogel, P. A., Stiles, T. C., & Gotestam, K. G. (2004). Adding cognitive therapy elements to exposure therapy for obsessive compulsive disorder: A controlled study. *Behavioural and Cognitive Psychotherapy, 32*, 275–290.

Vogel, P. A., Stiles, T. C., & Nordahl, H. (1997). Recollections of parent-child relationships in OCD outpatients compared to depressed outpatients and healthy controls. *Acta Psychiatrica Scandinavica, 96*, 469–474.

Warren, R., & Thomas, J. C. (2001). Cognitive-behavior therapy of obsessive-compulsive disorder in private practice: An effectiveness study. *Journal of Anxiety Disorders, 15*, 277–285.

Weissman, M. M., Bland, R. C., Canino, G. J., Greenwald, S., Hwu, H. -G., KyoonLee, C., et al. (1994). The Cross National epidemiology of obsessive compulsive disorder. *Journal of Clinical Psychiatry, 55*, 5–10.

Whiteside, S. P., Port, J. D., & Abramowitz, J. S. (2004). A metaanalysis of functional neuroimaging in obsessive-compulsive disorder. *Psychiatry Research: Neuroimaging, 132*, 69–79.

Wilhelm, S., McNally, R., Baer, L., & Florin, I. (1996). Directed forgetting in obsessive-compulsive disorder. *Behaviour Research and Therapy, 34*, 633–641.

Wilhelm, S., & Steketee, G. (2006). *Cognitive therapy for obsessive-compulsive disorder: A guide for professionals*. Oakland, CA: New Harbinger.

Woods, C. M., Vevea, J. L., Chambless, D. L., & Bayen, U. J. (2002). Are compulsive checkers impaired in memory? A meta-analytic review. *Clinical Psychology: Science and Practice, 9*, 353–366.

Wroe, A. L., & Salkovskis, P. M. (2000). Causing harm and allowing harm: A study of beliefs in obsessional problems. *Behaviour Research and Therapy, 38*, 1141–1162.

Zohar, J., & Insel, T. R. (1987). Obsessive-compulsive disorder: Psychobiological approaches to diagnosis, treatment, and pathophysiology. *Biological Psychiatry, 22*, 667–687.

Chapter 6

Social Anxiety Disorder

DEBORAH ROTH LEDLEY, BRIGETTE A. ERWIN, AND RICHARD G. HEIMBERG

Description of the Disorder

SYMPTOMS AND CRITERIA

Social Anxiety Disorder (SAD; also known as Social Phobia) is characterized by "a marked or persistent fear of social or performance situations" (American Psychiatric Association [APA], 1994, p. 411, Criterion A). People with Social Anxiety Disorder worry they will do or say something that will elicit negative evaluation from others, and they react with anxiety (Criterion B) to real or imagined anxiety-provoking situations. Adults with Social Anxiety Disorder may experience panic attacks in response to social or performance situations. Anxiety in children may manifest itself as crying, tantrums, or attempts to escape from feared situations.

To receive a diagnosis of Social Anxiety Disorder, individuals must realize that their fear of social or performance situations is unreasonable and excessive (Criterion C) and either avoid such situations or endure them with significant distress (Criterion D). Avoidance among individuals with Social Anxiety Disorder contributes substantially to broad impairment in social and occupational functioning (Criterion E).

Individuals with Social Anxiety Disorder who fear many social and performance situations are diagnosed with the generalized type of Social Anxiety Disorder, whereas persons with fears of a more limited nature (e.g., fearing only public speaking) have Nongeneralized Social Anxiety Disorder. Individuals with the generalized type of Social Anxiety Disorder fear a range of situations, including initiating and maintaining

198

conversations, performing in front of others, speaking to authority figures (e.g., bosses), or making requests of others (e.g., asking others to change their behavior, asking for a raise at work; Holt, Heimberg, Hope, & Liebowitz, 1992). Though the generalized type is associated with more severe social anxiety and greater impairment than the nongeneralized type (Heimberg, Holt, Schneier, Spitzer, & Liebowitz, 1993), a number of investigators have questioned whether the current approach to subtyping represents a meaningful distinction or rather the dichotimization of an inherently dimensional variable (e.g., Vriends, Becker, Meyer, Michael, & Margraf, 2007).

CASE EXAMPLE

Lucy was a 23-year-old woman who met the criteria for the generalized type of Social Anxiety Disorder. She had been shy and socially reticent for as long as she could remember. Midway through her senior year of college, Lucy had been offered an interview by a prestigious marketing firm. She told the recruiter that she would be unable to fly in for an interview, and they agreed to do the interview by phone. This was much easier for Lucy than a face-to-face interview, but even so, she went to her college career counseling service and sought extensive coaching for the interview. By the time her interview came around, she had memorized answers to numerous potential questions and she was offered the job.

Despite her extreme social anxiety, Lucy had functioned reasonably well until she left college to begin her job. Suddenly, social anxiety began to make both her work and social life very difficult. When she started working, Lucy was plagued by anxiety. She worried that her new colleagues would notice her blushing. As a redhead, her skin was very sensitive and she blushed easily. If a colleague asked her how her weekend had been, posed a job-related question to her, or asked her to do something, she immediately felt a surge of heat in her face and was convinced that she looked (in her words) "like a big, red tomato." In an attempt to prevent people from noticing her blushing, Lucy spent hours each morning before work selecting clothes that she felt would hide the redness (muted colors, turtlenecks) and applying thick make-up.

Lucy also worried a great deal about making mistakes—she worried about saying or doing the wrong thing, and that her new employers would conclude that she was not as smart or talented as they had believed. These fears caused Lucy to speak minimally during meetings, call in sick on days when she had to make presentations, and avoid most interactions with her superiors. Lucy's supervisors were perplexed by her behavior. When assigned a task, she did a wonderful job; yet, she hesitated to suggest new ideas or even casually chat about her weekend.

At this point in Lucy's life, she also started to suffer significant social impairment. She had attended her hometown college, living with her best friend of many years, occasionally going on dates with men with whom she had grown up, but making few new acquaintances. Living in a new city, Lucy now needed to meet new people for the first time, but her anxiety prevented her from doing so. She worried that she would not know what to say in casual conversations. She was concerned that people would find her boring or unintelligent. Of course, she also worried a great deal that others would notice her blushing and conclude from their observations that she must be nervous and incompetent. Lucy kept busy in her time away from work, mostly in solitary activities such as running or watching DVDs in her apartment. She craved companionship, but as she became more and more isolated, she began to feel regretful of her decision to move and felt increasingly depressed. When she came to our attention, she had been experiencing frequent thoughts that her life was no longer worth living, although she denied having an active suicidal plan.

BRIEF HISTORY

The term *Social Phobia* was coined by Janet in 1903 to describe patients who endorsed specific fears of being observed by others while speaking or writing. Based largely on the writings of Marks and Gelder (1966), Social Phobia was first included as a diagnostic category in the *Diagnostic and Statistical Manual of Mental Disorders* in 1980 with the publication of the *DSM-III* (APA, 1980). Consistent with Janet's initial conceptualization, Social Phobia was described in *DSM-III* as fear of a specific performance-related situation. Individuals who currently would be considered to have Generalized Social Anxiety Disorder would have been diagnosed under the *DSM-III* diagnostic rules as having Avoidant Personality Disorder. Once researchers began to recognize that social fears were often much more encompassing than fear of a single performance-related situation, the generalized subtype was added to the diagnostic criteria for Social Phobia in the *DSM-III-R* (APA, 1987). At the same time, a prominent group of researchers dubbed Social Phobia the "neglected anxiety disorder" (Liebowitz, Gorman, Fyer, & Klein, 1985, p. 729). This concern, along with improved diagnostic criteria for Social Phobia in both *DSM-III-R* and *DSM-IV* (APA, 1994), led to a burgeoning of research in this field.

EPIDEMIOLOGY

Social Anxiety Disorder is a highly prevalent disorder. In fact, findings from the National Comorbidity Survey Replication (NCS-R) indicate that Social Anxiety Disorder is one of the most prevalent psychiatric disorders in the United States, with a lifetime prevalence rate of 12.1% and a 1-year prevalence of 6.8% (Kessler et al., 2005; Kessler, Chiu, Demler, Merikangas, & Walters, 2005b). The mean age of onset for Social Anxiety Disorder ranges from 13 to 20 years old (Hazen & Stein, 1995), but many patients recall having struggled for all of their lives with shyness and fear of negative evaluation. In epidemiological studies, the disorder has been found to be more common in women than in men (Magee, Eaton, Wittchen, McGonagle, & Kessler, 1996), but in clinical samples, men slightly outnumber women (Chapman, Manuzza, & Fyer, 1995; Stein, 1997). This discrepancy is frequently explained by cultural norms for social behavior. The cost of not pursuing treatment may be higher for men, who are typically expected to be outgoing and assertive compared with women, for whom it is more acceptable to be shy and reticent (Weinstock, 1999).

Social Anxiety Disorder is associated with a high degree of Axis I comorbidity. In the original NCS, 81% of individuals with Social Anxiety Disorder met criteria for at least one other psychiatric disorder (Magee et al., 1996). In most cases, the onset of Social Anxiety Disorder was earlier than that of the comorbid disorder, the chronology of which suggests that Social Anxiety Disorder may be a risk factor for the development of other psychiatric disorders (Magee et al., 1996; Schneier, Johnson, Hornig, Liebowitz, & Weissman, 1992).

Social Anxiety Disorder most frequently co-occurs with other anxiety disorders. In the NCS, 56.9% of individuals with Social Anxiety Disorder met criteria for at least one other anxiety disorder (Magee et al., 1996). In the NCS-R, the occurrence of Social Anxiety Disorder was significantly related to the occurrence of Panic Disorder, Agoraphobia, Specific Phobia, Posttraumatic Stress Disorder, and Separation Anxiety Disorder (Kessler et al., 2005b).

Depression and alcohol use disorders are also common among individuals with Social Anxiety Disorder. Studies of both epidemiological (Kessler et al., 1994, 2005a, 2000b; Stein & Kean, 2000) and clinical samples (Brown & Barlow, 1992; Davidson et al., 1993; Gelernter et al., 1991; Lecrubier & Weiller, 1997) suggest that over one third of individuals currently diagnosed with Social Anxiety Disorder report having experienced Major Depressive Disorder at some time in their lives. The co-occurrence of Social Anxiety Disorder and depression is associated with greater impairment (Erwin, Heimberg, Juster, & Mindlin, 2002) and higher rates of attempted suicide (Lecrubier & Weiller, 1997) than Social Anxiety Disorder alone. Studies have also examined whether comorbid depression negatively affects the outcome of treatment for Social Anxiety Disorder. Some studies have suggested that patients with comorbid depression make as much improvement during treatment as patients without depression, but they end treatment with more severe social anxiety symptoms simply because they began treatment with more severe symptoms (e.g., Erwin et al., 2002). Other studies, however, suggest that higher levels of depressive symptoms are associated with poorer outcome and higher rates of treatment dropout (Chambless, Tran, & Glass, 1997; Ledley et al., 2005). In order to improve outcomes for this particularly impaired group, it might be necessary to lengthen treatments, pay greater attention to motivation and attrition, and perhaps add some depression-specific interventions to treatment protocols (i.e., behavioral activation; see Huppert, Roth, & Foa, 2003). Studies exploring the utility of these modifications would be useful contributions to the literature.

Within the realm of substance use disorders, most research attention has focused on alcohol use disorders, although cannabis use is also associated with Social Anxiety Disorder (Buckner, Mallott, Schmidt, & Taylor, 2006; Buckner, Schmidt, Bobadilla, & Taylor, 2006). Approximately 48% of individuals with a lifetime diagnosis of Social Anxiety Disorder also meet criteria for a lifetime diagnosis of Alcohol Use Disorder (Grant et al., 2005). The 12-month prevalence of Alcohol Use Disorder among individuals with Social Anxiety Disorder is 13.1% (Grant et al., 2005), compared to only 8.5% in the general population (Grant et al., 2004). As with depression, individuals with both Social Anxiety Disorder and Alcohol Use Disorder are more impaired than individuals with a sole diagnosis of Social Anxiety Disorder (Schneier, Martin, Leibowitz, Gorman, & Fyer, 1989). Whereas research on treatment outcome among patients with Comorbid Social Anxiety Disorder and depression is scant, research examining this same question in patients with Comorbid Social Anxiety Disorder and Alcohol Use Disorder is nonexistent. We examined the exclusion criteria in a sample of 33 recent papers on the treatment of Social Anxiety Disorder—eight of these studies made no mention of substance use disorders in their exclusion criteria and all others excluded patients with current alcohol or substance use disorders from participation. Therefore, we know little about how patients with Comorbid Social Anxiety Disorder and Alcohol Use Disorder fare during treatment. This is clearly a pressing research question.

The Axis II disorder that is most associated with Social Anxiety Disorder is Avoidant Personality Disorder (APD). Avoidant Personality Disorder is defined by "a pervasive pattern of social inhibition, feelings of inadequacy, and hypersensitivity to negative evaluation . . . in a variety of contexts" (*DSM-IV-TR*; APA, 2000, p. 721). Across studies, a median of 60% (Heimberg, 1996) of individuals with Generalized Social Anxiety Disorder meet diagnostic criteria for APD. This is not surprising given the considerable overlap in the criteria for these two disorders. Some researchers, including our group, have suggested that APD is simply a more severe form of Generalized Social Anxiety Disorder (Chambless, Fydrich, & Rodebaugh, in press; Heimberg, 1996). Even the *DSM-IV-TR* seems to concur, stating that "there appears to be a great deal of overlap between Avoidant Personality Disorder and Social Phobia, Generalized Type, so much so that they may be alternative conceptualizations of the same or similar conditions" (APA, 2000, p. 720).

Actual Dysfunction

Social Anxiety Disorder is caused by multiple biological and psychosocial factors and is associated with both biological and psychological dysfunction. In this section, the etiology and symptom presentation of Social Anxiety Disorder are reviewed.

GENETICS AND NEUROBIOLOGY

Genetics appear to be important in the development of Social Anxiety Disorder. Family studies have shown that there are higher rates of Social Anxiety Disorder in the relatives of individuals with the disorder than in the relatives of people without the disorder (see Tillfors, 2004, for a review). The generalized subtype of Social Anxiety Disorder demonstrates stronger familial aggregation than the nongeneralized subtype (Mannuzza et al., 1995; Stein et al., 1998). Twin studies offer the strongest support for the genetic contribution to the development of Social Anxiety Disorder. Studies by Kendler and his colleagues suggest that genetics account for about 50% of the variance in the familial transmission of Social Anxiety Disorder among female twins (Kendler, Karkowski, & Prescott, 1999) and a quarter of the variance in male twins (Kendler, Myers, Prescott, & Neale, 2001). Shared environmental effects (both within the family and the community) were found to have a significant effect on the incidence of Social Anxiety Disorder in men, but not in women (Kendler et al.). Kendler and his colleagues suggest that future research will be required to learn whether these gender differences are meaningful or due to chance alone (Kendler et al.). These interesting differences notwithstanding, the contribution of genetics to the development of Social Anxiety Disorder in both men and women is impressive (Kendler et al.; Kendler, Neale, Kessler, Heath, & Eaves, 1992).

   With respect to neurobiology, a few findings have been consistently demonstrated in the literature on Social Anxiety Disorder. The neurotransmitter serotonin has been implicated, but its role is unclear. In challenge studies, when individuals with Social Anxiety Disorder are given agents that release or mimic serotonin, they experience an increase in anxiety (e.g., Mathew, Coplan, & Gorman, 2001; Potts, Book, & Davidson, 1996). Nevertheless, the selective serotonin reuptake inhibitors (SSRIs), which make available greater levels of serotonin in the synaptic cleft, have been shown in numerous studies to reduce anxiety (Stein & Stahl, 2000). One plausible explanation for the inconsistency of this evidence is that increased levels of serotonin may have different short-term versus long-term effects. This conclusion is supported by clinical evidence that patients frequently experience an initial increase in anxiety, followed by improvement in their anxiety symptoms, when they begin taking SSRIs (Stein & Stahl).

Dopamine, a neurotransmitter, may also play a role in Social Anxiety Disorder. There a number of lines of evidence supporting this contention. First, the monoamine oxidase inhibitors (which work on both the dopaminergic and serotonin systems) are effective in the treatment of Social Anxiety Disorder (Blanco et al., 2003), whereas the tricyclic antidepressants (which work on the serotonin and norepinephrine systems) are not (Simpson et al., 1998). Second, low dopamine transporter density has been found in individuals with Social Anxiety Disorder (Tilhonen et al., 1997). Third, higher than expected rates of Social Anxiety Disorder are seen in individuals with Parkinson's disease. The drugs used to treat Parkinson's disease facilitate dopamine transmission (Stein, Heuser, Juncos, & Uhde, 1990). Finally, low dopamine receptor binding potential in the striatum region of the brain has also been found in individuals with Social Anxiety Disorder (Schneier et al., 2000). Interestingly, this same deficit has been found in animals with subordinate social status, which have been used as models for human Social Anxiety Disorder (see Schneier et al.).

Researchers have also examined whether specific brain regions play a role in Social Anxiety Disorder. In general, fear and anxiety are associated with the amygdala, the prefrontal cortex, and the hippocampus (see Tillfors, 2004). Imaging technology has been used to examine the brain function of patients with Social Anxiety Disorder under conditions of social threat (e.g., anticipation of making a speech, looking at faces). For example, Stein et al. (2002) demonstrated that patients with Generalized Social Phobia showed greater activity in the amygdala, uncus, and parahippocampal gyrus than healthy controls in response to angry and contemptuous faces (see Tillfors, 2004, for an excellent summary of studies). In a recent study, patients underwent positron emission tomography (PET) scans before and after either cognitive-behavioral therapy (CBT) or treatment with the SSRI, citalopram. Patients who received either CBT or citalopram improved significantly more than patients in a wait-list control group. These clinical improvements were accompanied by a decrease in right cerebral blood flow in the amygdaloid-hippocampal area (with no difference between treatments; Furmark et al., 2002). Furmark and colleagues explain that the amygdala and hippocampus are thought to act as an alarm system to aversive stimuli. They go on to suggest that "suppression of neural activity in the amygdalohippocampal and surrounding cortical regions might be an important mechanism by which both pharmacologic and psychological therapies exert their anxiolytic effect" (p. 430).

PSYCHOSOCIAL DYSFUNCTION

Individuals with Social Anxiety Disorder demonstrate numerous psychosocial dysfunctions. In the next section, we first discuss impairments in social functioning seen in this population. Then we discuss impairments that socially anxious individuals experience in their capacity to process information that is pertinent to their social world. Impairments in information processing are considered in relation to impairments in social functioning.

Impaired Social Functioning

How do patients with Social Anxiety Disorder function in the social world? As might be expected, numerous studies have demonstrated that socially anxious individuals have fewer social relationships than people without the disorder. This finding holds true across the lifespan. Children with Social Anxiety Disorder have fewer friends than children without the disorder (Beidel, Turner, & Morris, 1999; Spence, Donovan, & Brechman-Toussaint, 1999). Socially anxious college students date less, have fewer sexual experiences (Dodge, Heimberg, Nyman, & O'Brien, 1987; Leary & Dobbins, 1983), and have fewer friends (Jones & Carpenter, 1986) than their nonsocially anxious peers. Similarly, adults with Social Anxiety Disorder have fewer friends and are less likely to marry than individuals without the disorder (Schneier et al., 1994). Individuals with more severe social anxiety symptoms report greater dissatisfaction with the quality of their social lives (Eng, Coles, Heimberg, & Safran, 2005).

One reason for this dearth of relationships is avoidance. Because socially anxious individuals are so worried about being negatively evaluated and subsequently rejected by others, they often avoid the very behaviors that would get them into relationships in the first place—initiating and maintaining conversations, going to parties, and dating, for example. When socially anxious individuals do interact with others, they seem to engage in behaviors that may have a negative impact on the formation and maintenance of relationships. Alden and Taylor (2004) describe a "self-perpetuating interpersonal cycle" (p. 860) in which socially anxious people go into social interactions expecting negative evaluation, and therefore behave in ways that "'pull' on other people . . . to evoke responses that maintain . . . social assumptions" (p. 858).

There are numerous ways in which socially anxious individuals can exert this "pull" on others. First, they may exhibit behaviors or symptoms that can be interpreted as signs of anxiety or poor self-confidence, such as avoidance of eye contact, speaking softly, blushing, shaking, or sweating. Second, socially anxious individuals may distance themselves emotionally, engaging in less self-disclosure than nonsocially anxious people (e.g., see Alden & Bieling, 1998; Meleshko & Alden, 1993; Papsdorf & Alden, 1998). When they do engage in self-disclosure, socially anxious individuals tend to have difficulty describing emotional experiences (Turk, Heimberg, Luterek, Mennin, & Fresco, 2005). Patients with Social Anxiety Disorder often describe fearing that if people "really got to know them," they would ultimately reject them. This kind of core belief is likely related to attachment patterns that have their origins in early childhood. Specifically, individuals with Social Anxiety Disorder tend to exhibit insecure, fearful attachment patterns (Eng, Heimberg, Hart, Schneier, & Liebowitz, 2001; Wenzel, 2002). Not surprisingly, they have also been found to be more dependent in the relationships they do have than individuals without Social Anxiety Disorder (Davila & Beck, 2002). Some studies have also suggested that socially anxious individuals may behave angrily toward others. Erwin, Heimberg, Schneier, and Liebowitz (2003) have reported that patients with Social Anxiety Disorder have higher levels of state and trait anger than nonanxious controls, although they are also more likely to attempt to suppress the expression of angry feelings. Other research with normal populations (e.g., Butler et al., 2003) suggests that suppression of emotional expression is associated with reduced likeability. Taken together, these behaviors likely increase the probability that socially anxious individuals may indeed be judged negatively by others and that the formation and maintenance of interpersonal relationships will be negatively affected.

It is also important to emphasize that many individuals with Social Anxiety Disorder possess excellent social skills, and in a therapeutic relationship are very likeable and engaging. It is hard to imagine that these patients would be judged negatively by anybody! Numerous studies have shown, however, that individuals with social anxiety rate themselves more harshly than they are rated by others (e.g., Alden & Wallace, 1995; Rapee & Hayman, 1996; Rapee & Lim, 1992; Stopa & Clark, 1993). Individuals with Social Anxiety Disorder also become anxious when they receive positive feedback from others, believing that others will expect more of them in future interactions (Wallace & Alden, 1997). Holding such negative expectations for one's own social success might also lead to behaviors that attract negative reactions from others.

To summarize, individuals with Social Anxiety Disorder have fewer and more strained social relationships than people without the disorder. Many factors might contribute to this state of affairs, including biases in information processing. These biases can have an impact on both the initial development and maintenance of relationships. Three kinds of bias in information processing have been studied in individuals with social anxiety disorder: biases of attention, judgment and interpretation, and memory.

Impairments in Information Processing

Attentional Bias.   The literature examining attentional bias has primarily made use of the Stroop and dot-probe paradigms. In the so-called "emotional Stroop task," participants are shown socially threatening and neutral words printed in various colors and asked to respond by naming the color as quickly as possible, rather than reading the word. Slowed response suggests that the content of the word has diverted participants' attention, making it more difficult to quickly report the color. In the dot-probe paradigm, participants are typically shown two words (or other stimuli, such as faces), one neutral and one emotionally valenced. The stimuli are typically placed one above the other, and right after they are shown, a dot or other probe stimulus appears in the place of one of the words. If participants respond more quickly to a dot displayed in the same location as the emotionally valenced stimulus, they may still be attending to that stimulus instead of having looked away (or focused on the neutral stimulus).

Stroop studies have consistently shown that individuals with Social Anxiety Disorder selectively attend to social threat-related information as indicated by a longer latency to color-name social threat words than either neutral words or threatening words of a nonsocial nature (Hope, Rapee, Heimberg, & Dombeck, 1990; Lundh & Öst, 1996b; Maidenberg, Chen, Craske, Bohn, & Bystritsky, 1996; Mattia, Heimberg, & Hope, 1993). Recently, researchers have examined whether comorbidity has an effect on attentional bias. Surprisingly, patients with Social Anxiety Disorder and comorbid depression do not exhibit the attentional bias toward social threat words that has been repeatedly shown in patients with Social Anxiety Disorder alone (Musa, Lepine, Clark, Mansell, & Ehlers, 2003; see also Grant & Beck, 2006). Grant and Beck suggest that the reduced level of functioning seen in depression might, in effect, cancel out the attentional biases typically observed in socially anxious individuals who do not have comorbid depression.

Findings using the dot-probe paradigm are less consistent than those using the Stroop task. Asmundson and Stein (1994) found that individuals with Social Anxiety Disorder responded more quickly to the presentation of the dot when it was displayed in the same location as a social threat word than when it was displayed in the same location as a neutral word, providing evidence for an attentional bias. In contrast, Mansell, Ehlers, Clark, and Chen (2002) found no evidence of an attentional bias toward social threat words in a nonclinical sample of socially anxious individuals. This held true even after participants had been told that they would have to give a speech later in the study.

A clever variation on the dot-probe technique has been to replace social threat words with various facial expressions, on the assumption that these stimuli are more externally valid than words. Modified dot-probe studies in nonclinical samples have been inconsistent with one showing *delayed* responding to negative faces (Pishyar, Harris, & Menzies, 2004), one showing delayed responding to any emotional faces (positive or negative) but only after speech threat (Mansell, Clark, Ehlers, & Chen, 1999), and one failing to show delayed responding, even after a speech threat (Pineles & Mineka, 2005). An additional study by Chen, Ehlers, Clark, and Mansell (2002) found that patients with Social Anxiety Disorder responded more slowly to dots presented after any faces (positive, negative, or neutral) than dots presented after pictures of household items. Recently, Sposari and Rapee (2007) replicated the study by Mansell et al. (1999) in two separate clinical samples. In contrast to the findings of Mansell et al. and Chen et al. (2002), individuals with Social Anxiety Disorder showed greater vigilance (i.e., *faster* responding) to faces (regardless of expression) than did nonclinical controls after being presented with a speech threat.

It is difficult to put these divergent findings together. Some studies suggest vigilance toward social threat cues, including faces (Sposari & Rapee, 2007), words (Asmundson & Stein, 1994), and heart-rate feedback (Pineles & Mineka, 2005). Other studies suggest avoidance of faces (i.e., slowed responding; Chen et al., 2002; Mansell et al., 1999; Pishyar et al., 2004). The bottom line, however, is that vigilance is a precondition of avoidance. Avoidance manifests when individuals are vigilant to a cue, find it threatening, and then direct their attention away. Sposari and Rapee (2007) have suggested that "strategic attentional bias toward and away from faces may vary according to the degree of social threat or ambiguity incorporated in the instructional set given before the administration of . . . tasks" (p. 36). They go on to suggest that future studies should incorporate level of social threat into their experimental design. This might include obvious manipulations such as the use of speech threats. These authors also suggest, however, that more subtle variations in experimental design, such as varying the sex of the experimenter (e.g., female participants might be more nervous with a male experimenter) or how well the participant knows the experimenter might have an impact on findings.

If we conclude that individuals with Social Anxiety Disorder attend to social threat-relevant information in their environments, and often then divert their attention away from such information, it is important to consider how this pattern relates to difficulties with social relationships. It seems reasonable to conclude from the available literature that socially anxious individuals go into social interactions looking for cues that support the expectation that they will be negatively evaluated. In addition to the literature already presented, other studies support this notion. For example, individuals with Social Anxiety Disorder are quicker at finding an angry face in a crowd of neutral faces than they are at finding a happy face in a crowd of neutral faces. Although this tendency was also shown in nonclinical controls, it was particularly pronounced in individuals with Social Anxiety Disorder (Gilboa-Schechtman, Foa, & Amir, 1999). Veljaca and Rapee (1998) also found evidence that socially anxious individuals selectively attend to cues in the environment that might be indicative of criticism. In their study, participants who had scored either high or low on a measure of social anxiety were asked to give a speech to an audience of confederates who had been trained to engage in an equal number of positive (e.g., leaning forward) and negative (e.g., yawning) feedback behaviors, many of which included facial feedback of some sort. Whereas participants low in social anxiety detected more positive than negative feedback behaviors from audience members, participants high in social anxiety showed the opposite effect. Similar results were reported by Perowne and Mansell (2002).

Furthermore, the desire to divert attention away from faces (perhaps even those that display positive or neutral emotion) can negatively affect social interactions. If a person looks away during a conversation, he or she may miss out on important social cues that would make the conversation flow well. These might include positive cues like the other person's smiling or nodding that would indicate to the socially anxious person that he or she is doing well in the interaction. By looking away, socially anxious individuals might come across to others as bored, disinterested, or socially unskilled, potentially sabotaging a newly forming relationship. In established relationships, poor eye contact may make the nonanxious member of the dyad wonder if the anxious person is not being open or honest. Taken together, this seemingly simple protective stance can put strain on the quality of both new and established interpersonal relationships.

Judgment and Interpretation Bias

As we have repeatedly noted, socially anxious individuals go into social situations expecting negative evaluation from others. Research on judgment and interpretation bias provides further support for this notion. First, socially anxious individuals tend to be their own worst critics. Numerous studies have shown that socially anxious individuals (e.g., Rapee & Hayman, 1996), as well as those with social anxiety disorder (e.g., Alden & Wallace, 1995; Rapee & Lim, 1992; Stopa & Clark, 1993), judge themselves more negatively than they judge others and also judge themselves more negatively than they are judged by others. Furthermore, individuals with Social Anxiety Disorder are more likely than nonclinical controls to assume that other people interpret physical symptoms that they exhibit (like blushing, shaking, or sweating) as signs of an intense anxiety problem or some other psychiatric disorder, rather than some more benign explanation, such as being hot, cold, or tired (Roth, Antony, & Swinson, 2001). Given that socially anxious individuals judge themselves so harshly, it is not at all surprising that they enter social situations assuming that others will do the same (or worse).

Numerous studies have shown that individuals with Social Anxiety Disorder overestimate the probability that negative outcomes will occur for them in social situations (Foa, Franklin, Perry, & Herbert, 1996; Gilboa-Schechtman, Franklin, & Foa, 2000; Lucock & Salkovskis, 1988) and greatly overestimate the cost of these outcomes (Foa et al., 1996; Gilboa-Schechtman et al., 2000). Individuals with Social Anxiety Disorder tend to interpret both ambiguous social events (e.g., not obviously positively or negatively valenced; Amir, Foa, & Coles, 1998; see also Constans, Penn, Ihen, & Hope, 1999, for a similar study in a nonclinical sample) and mildly negative social events (Stopa & Clark, 2000) as extremely negative and catastrophic. Interpretation biases seem to resolve following a successful course of cognitive-behavioral therapy (Franklin, Huppert, Langner, Leiberg, & Foa, 2005).

Again, it is interesting to consider how bias relates to difficulties with social relationships. The literature on judgment and interpretation bias suggests that socially anxious individuals routinely put themselves into no-win situations. Almost any socially relevant information is perceived negatively and interpreted as costly, undoubtedly affecting the quality of social interactions. Taken together, these studies highlight why it is so compelling for socially anxious individuals to simply avoid social situations. To this point, laboratory studies of judgment and interpretation bias have generally involved asking participants what kind of judgments they would make if certain experiences happened to them (e.g., seeing a table of people laughing as you walk by). Basically, socially anxious individuals assume that they would make negative and costly judgments in these hypothetical situations. Researchers have not examined how individuals with Social Anxiety Disorder think about their own contributions to the development and maintenance of relationships. We do know that individuals with Social Anxiety Disorder have a difficult time with self-disclosure, and as noted earlier, our patients often express fears that people will reject them if they really got to know them. An interesting question is whether individuals with the disorder overestimate the probability that people will judge them negatively if they share relatively benign attributes about themselves (like being shy) and overestimate the cost of such self-disclosures (like being rejected). Certainly, this kind of bias might underlie difficulties with self-disclosure, thereby sabotaging the formation of new relationships and the maintenance of existing ones.

Memory Bias

Research on memory bias focuses on whether socially anxious individuals preferentially remember socially threatening information in contrast to neutral information or information that is threatening but lacking in personal salience (see Coles & Heimberg, 2002, for a review). In general, studies on memory bias have been inconsistent, with some providing support (e.g., Amir, Foa, & Coles, 2000) and some suggesting that memory biases do not exist in individuals with Social Anxiety Disorder (e.g., Lundh & Öst, 1997; Rapee, McCallum, Melville, Ravenscroft, & Rodney, 1994). Similar to research on attentional bias, memory researchers have tried to make their work more externally valid. For example, some studies have examined memory for personal feedback following social interactions. Again, findings are inconsistent, with one study (O'Banion & Arkowitz, 1977) showing that individuals high in social anxiety were better at recalling negative feedback about themselves than were individuals who were low in social anxiety and another failing to find evidence of such a bias (Wenzel & Holt, 2002).

Similar to the work on attentional biases, researchers have explored memory for faces in people with Social Anxiety Disorder. These studies suggest that patients with Social Anxiety Disorder are better than nonclinical controls at recalling which people had exhibited negative facial expressions following an encoding task (Foa, Gilboa-Schechtman, Amir, & Freshman, 2000, Experiment 1), as well as recognizing previously seen critical faces (Coles & Heimberg, 2005; Foa et al., 2000, Experiment 2; Lundh & Öst, 1996a). One study on memory bias among individuals with Social Anxiety Disorder reported conflicting results, finding that patients with social anxiety were actually slightly more likely to remember accepting faces than critical faces following a speech threat (Pérez-López & Woody, 2001).

The research on memory bias is somewhat difficult to interpret. Basically, earlier laboratory studies did not find much evidence for memory bias. However, more recently completed studies paint a more compelling picture, suggesting that socially anxious individuals exhibit preferential recall of critical faces.

Another consistent finding in the literature concerns memory for nonsocially threatening information in socially anxious individuals. Numerous studies (all conducted with nonclinical samples) have suggested that socially anxious individuals miss out on information during social interactions, such as information about their conversation partners' interests, appearance, and background (Hope, Heimberg, & Klein, 1990; Hope, Sigler, Penn, & Meier, 1998; see also Bond & Omar, 1990; Daly, Vangelisti, & Lawrence,

1989; Kimble & Zehr, 1982). In the earlier section on attentional bias, we alluded to this same concept. Specifically, we suggested that when people divert eye contact from faces (because they find them threatening), they might miss out on important social information. This group of studies provides further support for this notion—individuals with Social Anxiety Disorder fail to remember important information about social interactions, and it might be because of attentional focus. Diverting eye contact may prevent the encoding of information about the other person's appearance and focus attention on how one is coming across, rather than on the content of the conversation. Socially anxious individuals therefore might fail to encode all sorts of other details about the people they meet. Certainly, to the extent that these biases play out in real life, they increase the awkwardness of social interactions with people already met by people with Social Anxiety Disorder.

In a slightly different vein, researchers have examined memories of past social interactions and examined how they affect current functioning. As a whole, these studies suggest that individuals with Social Anxiety Disorder possess very negative and biased memories of themselves in social situations. Hackmann, Surawy, and Clark (1998) asked patients to recall a recent social situation in which they felt anxious and describe the image that they had of themselves during it. Compared to nonclinical controls, individuals with Social Anxiety Disorder were more likely to report having a clear, negative self-image that felt like a very accurate depiction of how they were coming across at the time of the event. Hackmann, Clark, and McManus (2000) asked patients if they associated this negative self-image with a particular event. Indeed, most could recall a specific past event in which they felt embarrassed and humiliated, with the image clearly connected to the most negative aspects of this recalled event. This finding fits nicely with a study by our group, studying autobiographical memories in Social Anxiety Disorder (Erwin, Heimberg, Marx, & Franklin, 2006). In our study, a majority of patients with Social Anxiety Disorder recall having experienced a socially stressful life event, like feeling humiliated after a poor public performance or being rejected by a potential romantic interest. These memories were accompanied by such significant symptoms of avoidance and hyperarousal that patients would have met criteria for Posttraumatic Stress Disorder (PTSD) had these events qualified as PTSD Criterion A events. It is likely that the patients in this study had negative self-images related to these socially stressful life events, just like the patients in the studies from Clark's group.

A number of studies have also examined memory perspective in individuals with Social Anxiety Disorder. Specifically, these studies have explored the perspective from which people recall social events. There are two perspectives from which to recall such events—either the observer perspective, in which people see themselves through the eyes of others (as if they are viewing themselves on videotape) or the field perspective, in which people recall situations as viewed through their own eyes. Socially anxious individuals are more likely to take an observer perspective when remembering themselves in social situations, in effect spectatoring on themselves. In contrast, individuals without the disorder tend to take the field perspective. In other words, when socially anxious individuals look back on social situations, they tend to remember them from the perspective of how they *think* they were viewed by others (e.g., Coles, Turk, Heimberg, & Fresco, 2001; Coles, Turk, & Heimberg, 2002; Hackmann et al., 1998; Wells, Clark, & Ahmad, 1998; Wells & Papageorgiou, 1999) rather than based on what actually occurred in the social situation. The problem with this information is that it is terribly biased, always in the negative direction. The bias comes about because socially anxious individuals believe that they know what other people are thinking about them. Unfortunately, as we often discuss in therapy, we are not mind-readers and can never know how people truly perceive us (unless they tell us, which they rarely do!). This biased information causes socially anxious individuals to come away from situations remembering themselves in a very negative light, undoubtedly affecting their willingness to enter similar situations in the future.

Recently, Hirsch, Clark, and Mathews (2006) have proposed that different kinds of cognitive biases interact with one another and are best understood in this way rather than in isolation. For example, memories of a poor self-image seem to have an important impact on how socially anxious individuals interpret social situations (and vice versa). Hirsch, Clark, Mathews, and Williams (2003) asked patients to have a conversation with a stranger, either holding their typical negative self-image in mind or a self-image that was more positive and benign. When they held the negative self-image in mind, they felt more anxious, rated their own performance more poorly, and were also rated more poorly by objective observers than when they held the positive self-image in mind. These findings were replicated in another study using a nonclinical sample (Hirsch, Meynen, & Clark, 2004). These studies suggest that negative self-imagery can color interpretations of current social situations as well as actual performance. The paper by Hirsch et al. (2006) will likely initiate a new trend in information-processing research, in which connections will be established between attentional bias, interpretation/judgment bias, and memory bias.

Interaction with Environmental Factors.   The research on cognitive biases is very helpful in explaining the experiences of individuals with Social Anxiety Disorder. They go into social situations with very negative expectancies—namely, that their interactions will turn out badly and be very costly. This leads to distress in or avoidance of social situations and also affects what they notice and recall in the situations that they do confront. Basically, socially anxious individuals notice and remember information that serves to confirm their expectations (e.g., critical faces) and fail to notice and remember information that would serve to disconfirm their expectations (e.g., a reassuring smile or nod). An additional consequence of the allocation of their attention to negative expectancies is that patients with Social Anxiety Disorder do not encode information that would help them function better in the social world (e.g., information about the person to whom they are talking).

The next reasonable question to pose is what environmental factors underlie the development of Social Anxiety Disorder. In the next section of this chapter, ways in which early experiences within the family and with peers relate to later problems in psychosocial functioning and cognitive bias will be discussed.

Factors Related to the Family Environment

Multiple factors related to the family environment may be related to the development of the social and information processing deficits seen in individuals with Social Anxiety Disorder. Two important factors begin to exert their effect at birth (or even before): infant temperament and the early attachment relationship that is formed between parents and their children. The temperament that has been most studied in relation to anxiety is the highly reactive or "behaviorally inhibited" temperament (see Kagan, 1994). This body of research began with a group of almost 400 4-month-old infants who were exposed in a controlled laboratory setting to a variety of visual, olfactory, and auditory stimuli (Kagan, 1994). Based on their reactions, the infants were classified as behaviorally inhibited or uninhibited. They were then brought back to the lab at 14 months and 21 months and exposed to both social and nonsocial events. Using stringent criteria, the number of events to which participants reacted with a fear response was coded. Behaviorally inhibited infants showed a fear response to a greater number of events than did uninhibited infants (75% of whom actually responded to none or only one of the events with fear).

The participants were next studied at age 4.5. At this age, the children were observed by examiners who were blind to their classification as they interacted with an examiner and with same-sex, same-age peers. Children who had been classified as inhibited made fewer comments to the examiners and smiled less at them than did the children who had been classified as uninhibited. Furthermore, almost half of the children who had been classified as behaviorally inhibited were rated as inhibited when interacting with peers. In contrast, only 10% of children who had been classified as uninhibited were rated as inhibited during this interaction.

At age 7.5, the children were interviewed again. At this time, the main issue of interest was whether the children had developed anxiety symptoms. As was expected, the children who had been classified as inhibited during infancy were more likely to exhibit anxiety symptoms at age 7.5 than were children who had been classified as uninhibited during infancy. Interestingly, the best predictor of the presence of anxiety symptoms at age 7.5 was exhibiting an inhibited style when interacting with peers at age 4.5. Schwartz, Snidman, and Kagan (1999) used structured clinical interviews to assess 13-year-olds who had been classified as behaviorally inhibited or uninhibited at age 2. In this study, there was a significant association between classification as behaviorally inhibited at age 2 and the presence of Generalized Social Anxiety Disorder at age 13. Interestingly, there was *not* an association between earlier behavioral inhibition and later performance anxiety, specific phobias, or separation anxiety. This pattern of results has been mirrored in retrospective studies of adolescents, college-age students, and adults (see Hayward, Killen, Kraemer, & Taylor, 1998; Gladstone, Parker, Mitchell, Wilhelm, & Malhi, 2005; Mick & Telch, 1998; Muris, Merckelbach, Wessel, & van de Ven, 1999). For example, Mick and Telch (1998) reported that socially anxious adolescents were more likely than adolescents with generalized anxiety to recall having been inhibited during childhood. Gladstone and Parker (2006) recently examined whether recalled behavioral inhibition during childhood was related to later depression. Their study found that indeed there was a relationship between childhood behavioral inhibition and depression, but that this relationship was mediated by the presence of Social Anxiety Disorder. Taken together, these results suggest that a reactive or inhibited temperament might be uniquely related to the later development of social anxiety. Social anxiety may then influence the onset of other problems, such as depression.

Since the children in Kagan's sample exhibited reactive tendencies from such a young age, it was reasonable to question whether genetics or other family factors may have played a role. In fact, studies have shown that parents of behaviorally inhibited children have increased rates of current Social Anxiety Disorder and also had increased rates of anxiety disorders when they themselves were children (Rosenbaum, Biederman, Bolduc, & Hirshfeld, 1992; Rosenbaum, Biederman, Hirshfeld, Bolduc, & Chaloff, 1991).

In addition to the possible role of genetics, it is likely that social learning also plays a role in the relationship between inhibited temperament during infancy and later problems with social anxiety. Behaviorally inhibited infants react to all novel stimuli, including new people, with fear. This kind of reaction undoubtedly has an impact on others. If a baby always cries when a family friend tries to hold her or him, it is quite likely that this friend will just stop trying. Similarly, parents might be inclined to protect their babies from having fear reactions, leaving the inhibited baby with less opportunity for exposure and subsequent habituation to people. Later in life, these individuals may continue to avoid social situations or may go into them with the expectation that they will be frightening and negative.

Another early factor that might play a role in the development of social anxiety is the attachment relationship that is formed between parents and their children. Attachment theorists posit that people develop schemas for understanding their social world via this earliest interpersonal relationship. The quality of this relationship is thought to affect personality development and the quality of subsequent relationships later in life (e.g., Bowlby, 1982; see also Greenberg, 1999).

Attachment theorists have long distinguished between secure and insecure attachment relationships (see Dozier, Stovall, & Albus, 1999). Securely attached children have parents who are attentive and responsive, whereas insecurely attached children have parents who are rejecting and undependable. Studies have shown that shyness and social anxiety during childhood are related to insecure attachment patterns during infancy (see Bohlin, Hagekull, & Rydell, 2000; LaFreniere & Sroufe, 1985). When asked to recall their early childhood, shy adults report having had parents who were rejecting and lacking in warmth (Schlette et al., 1998). Researchers have also examined adult attachment patterns, since the way that we relate to one another as adults likely has its roots in the early parent-child relationship. Relationships have been found between Social Anxiety Disorder in adulthood and insecure adult attachment patterns (e.g., Eng et al., 2001; Mickelson, Kessler, & Shaver, 1997).

Again, it is interesting to consider the role of social learning. For children who grow up having a secure attachment relationship with their parents, a template is set that defines people as accepting and dependable. In contrast, for children who grow up with an insecure attachment relationship, the template defines people as critical and unreliable. All interactions are evaluated against this template, thus setting the stage for the development of difficulties with social anxiety.

Parenting is another crucial familial factor that must be considered in the development of Social Anxiety Disorder. Though other factors may be important, there is no doubt that children primarily learn about how to relate to others from their parents. Studies looking at parenting and the family environment among people with social anxiety identify some interesting qualities. Perhaps most importantly, individuals with social anxiety recall growing up in homes with parents (predominantly mothers) who are themselves socially anxious (Tillfors, Furmark, Ekselius, & Fredrikson, 2001). Studies of shy children and children with Social Anxiety Disorder have shown that their parents have much higher rates of Social Anxiety Disorder than parents of nonshy children (Bögels, van Oosten, Muris, & Smulders, 2001; Cooper & Eke, 1999). Socially anxious individuals also report that their parents overemphasized the importance of making a good impression on others (Bruch, Heimberg, Berger, & Collins, 1989; Caster, Interbitzen, & Hope, 1999) and made their children feel ashamed of being shy (Caster et al., 1999).

Growing up with extremely shy parents can have a number of consequences. First, while growing up, children do not see their parents participating in strong, positive interpersonal relationships of their own (e.g., Bögels et al., 2001; Bruch et al., 1989; Caster et al., 1999). Similarly, they see their parents reacting anxiously in a variety of social situations. One study observed mothers and their 10-week-old babies during an interaction with a stranger (Murray, Cooper, Creswell, Schofield, & Sack, 2007). During this interaction, mothers with Social Anxiety Disorder exhibited more anxiety and were also less encouraging of their baby's interactions with the stranger than were mothers with Generalized Anxiety Disorder or nonanxious mothers. This study suggests that offspring of socially anxious mothers might begin to learn about (and even imitate) social anxiety from a very young age. A little later on in life, shy parents are less likely to facilitate peer interactions for their children (e.g., Bögels et al., 2001; Bruch et al., 1989; Caster et al., 1999). During the early years, parents are involved not only in planning play-dates with other parents, but they also socialize during these play-dates. In the study by Bögels et al. (2001), the finding that greater levels of social anxiety in children is associated with greater levels of social anxiety in parents was actually supported by the levels of social anxiety experienced by mothers. This is not surprising, given that it is mothers who tend to be more involved in the day-to-day social lives of their children. By the time children of socially anxious parents reach adolescence and can be more socially independent, it is quite likely that lack of experience and the usual anxieties of adolescence could make social interactions difficult to tolerate. Finally, if parents overemphasize the importance of making a good impression on others, they might instill in their children the belief that they should make the "perfect impression," an expectation that cannot be met. This is likely to result in distress and avoidance as well as biased attention toward cues in the environment that confirm failure.

Other events within the family environment have also been related to the development of Social Anxiety Disorder. One such event is marital conflict, including early parental separation or divorce (Chartier, Walker, & Stein, 2001; Davidson, Hughes, George, & Blazer, 1993). When parents divorce, children often move to new neighborhoods or start splitting time between both parents' homes. This can adversely affect the social lives of children, particularly for those who are already shy and reticent. Similarly, when parents divorce, their own social lives often become of greater concern to them as they begin to date and make new friends beyond the friendships that they shared with their former spouses. This new focus can negatively affect anxious children, who need all of the extra help that they can get with managing their own social lives.

Studies have also shown that lack of a close relationship with an adult during childhood (Chartier et al., 2001), long-lasting separation from either parent during childhood (Wittchen, Stein, & Kessler, 1999), and observing conflict between parents during childhood (Magee, 1999) are all are related to the development of Social Anxiety Disorder. These difficulties can come about because of divorce (as previously discussed), as well as other factors, such as parental psychopathology (Lieb et al., 2000). That these difficulties are related to the development of Social Anxiety Disorder fits well with research on the importance of attachment. Early relationships serve as a template for later relationships—if children do not form strong, safe attachments to adults in their lives early on, they might have life-long difficulties forming meaningful relationships or feeling confident of the stability of relationships that they are able to establish.

Factors Related to the Peer Environment

Early peer relations can also play a role in the development of the cognitive biases that are characteristic of individuals with Social Anxiety Disorder. Studies of young children who are socially anxious suggest that they are more likely than nonanxious children to experience negative peer relations, most notably peer neglect (La Greca, Dandes, Wick, Shaw, & Stone, 1988; Strauss, Lahey, Frick, Frame, & Hynd, 1988). These studies also suggest that negative peer relations in turn lead to the exacerbation and maintenance of social anxiety (see also Rubin & Mills, 1988; Vernberg, Abwender, Ewell, & Beery, 1992). Retrospective studies suggest a relationship between adult social anxiety and childhood peer victimization, including teasing (McCabe, Antony, Summerfeldt, Liss, & Swinson, 2003; Roth, Coles, & Heimberg, 2002). Recalled teasing in the social domain (e.g., being teased about looking shy, appearing nervous) was more strongly related to psychological distress during adulthood than recalled teasing in other domains, such as appearance or academics (e.g., being the teacher's pet; Storch et al., 2004). Interestingly, recalled childhood teasing has also been related to interpersonal functioning during early adulthood. Specifically, recalling frequent teasing during childhood was associated with less comfort with intimacy and closeness, less of an ability to trust and depend on others, as well as a greater degree of worry about being unloved or abandoned in relationships (Ledley et al., 2006).

Obviously, it is impossible to draw causal relationships from the findings just described, but it is interesting to consider why childhood teasing might contribute to interpersonal deficits in adulthood. In Ledley et al. (2006), we speculated that being victimized by peers during childhood may lead to the development of a negative inferential style, such as a tendency to be hopeless regarding one's ability to change negative events. This line of thought was consistent with Rose and Abramson's (1992) proposal that childhood maltreatment, particularly emotional maltreatment, may lead to a negative inferential style and thereby confer vulnerability to hopelessness depression. Rose and Abramson proposed that when children are subject to repeated emotional maltreatment, they are increasingly likely to attribute the maltreatment to stable and global negative characteristics of the self, leading to increasing hopelessness. This pathway of events, from peer victimization (undoubtedly a form a childhood maltreatment) to the development of a negative inferential style to hopelessness and depression might explain the interpersonal deficits that we identified in adults who recalled frequent teasing during childhood.

It is also interesting to consider how the research on peer relations correlates with the difficulties with avoidance, perceived social failure, and social behavior that attracts negative evaluation from others. First, it is quite evident that the difficulties seen in adults with social anxiety often emerge from shyness in childhood. Children likely become classified as "neglected" because their anxiety leads to avoidance. Shy children are unlikely to initiate contact with peers and might choose to avoid contact that is initiated by other, more outgoing children. Being teased about being shy (and about other topics) further chips away at a child's already poor social self-esteem. Shy children end up not having the opportunity to learn how to socialize from their more skilled peers. Furthermore, they never have the opportunity to gather evidence to disconfirm their beliefs about their inability to succeed in the social world. This might then affect how they navigate the social world as adults. They might be inclined to continue to avoid. They might continue to perceive that they lack social skills because it has been part of their self-perception for so long. And, they might in fact engage in behaviors that attract poor judgments from others, such as being overly dependent in relationships.

ASSESSMENT OF SOCIAL ANXIETY DISORDER

Clinical Interviews

In research settings, semistructured diagnostic interviews are used to establish diagnoses and, in some cases, to rate the severity of these diagnoses. Semistructured interviews present the assessor with a set of questions to guide decisions about the presence or absence of *DSM* diagnoses, but also allow for sufficient flexibility to gain a clear under-standing of the patient's primary concerns. In anxiety disorder research settings, the Structured Clinical Interview for *DSM-IV-TR* Axis I Disorders—Patient Edition (SCID I/P; First, Spitzer, Gibbon, & Williams, 2002) and the Anxiety Disorder Interview Schedule for *DSM-IV* (ADIS-IV) (Brown, DiNardo, & Barlow, 1994) are commonly used. A lifetime version of the ADIS, which assesses for both current and lifetime diag-noses, is also available (ADIS-IV-L) (DiNardo, Brown, & Barlow, 1994), as is a version to be used with children and adolescents (ADIS-IV, Child/Parent Version) (Silverman & Albano, 2005). A strength of the SCID is that it can be completed in a relatively efficient manner. It includes screening questions for each diagnosis that allow clinicians to skip out of sections that do not seem relevant to the given patient. It also allows clinicians to skip out of particular sections though they have begun questioning on a disorder, once they have ascertained that criteria for the given disorder are not met. A disadvantage of the SCID is that it does not cue clinicians to gather additional data on a patient's difficulties beyond *DSM* criteria. Thus, the information gathered during the SCID is not sufficiently detailed for use in treatment planning.

In contrast, the ADIS includes numerous questions that go beyond *DSM* criteria, in-cluding triggers for anxiety (e.g., feared social situations) and reactions to these triggers (e.g., the experience of situationally cued panic attacks). These additional questions mean that the ADIS can be lengthy to administer, but they provide extremely helpful information for treatment planning. Another strength of the ADIS is that it allows the clinician to assign a Clinician's Severity Rating (CSR) for each diagnosis. The CSR has clear utility in research settings, but is also helpful in clinical settings in terms of treat-ment planning (e.g., having a sense of symptom severity and how long treatment might last) and evaluating improvement over the course of treatment. The psychometric prop-erties of the ADIS have been examined within a clinical sample of individuals with anxiety disorders. In 362 patients with mixed diagnoses, Brown, DiNardo, Lehman, and Campbell (2001) reported a kappa of .77 for a primary diagnosis of Social Anxiety Dis-order using the ADIS-IV-L. For more detailed information concerning the reliability of structured interviews employed for the diagnosis of Social Anxiety Disorder, see Hart, Jack, Turk, and Heimberg (1999).

Clinical Rating Scales

The most commonly used clinician-administered measure of social anxiety is the Liebowitz Social Anxiety Scale (LSAS) (Liebowitz, 1987). The LSAS includes 24 items, 11 pertaining to social interaction situations (e.g., hosting a party) and 13 pertaining to performance situations (e.g., making a presentation to a small group). Each item is rated according to the degree to which clients have feared each situation and the degree to which they have avoided each situation over the past week. The LSAS includes numer-ous subscales, but its total score is also commonly used in research. A self-report version of the LSAS correlates highly with the original interviewer-rated version (Fresco et al., 2001). The LSAS has strong convergent validity, adequate discriminant validity, and is sensitive to treatment change (Fresco et al., 2001; Heimberg et al., 1999). It is also a highly reliable measure; Cronbach's alphas of .95 and .96 for the LSAS total score have been reported (Fresco et al., 2001; Heimberg et al., 1999). A version of the LSAS has been developed for use with children and adolescents and also has strong psychomet-ric properties (LSAS-CA) (Masia-Warner et al., 2003).

It is important to note that the LSAS is an excellent clinical tool. Because it gathers information on the various social and performance situations that patients fear and avoid, it can be used for treatment planning (e.g., creating a hierarchy of feared situations) and to assess improvement over the course of treatment (e.g., Heimberg et al., 1998; Liebowitz et. al., 1999). A score of 30 has been demonstrated to discriminate between patients with Social Anxiety Disorder and normal controls with good specificity and sensitivity (Mennin et al., 2002).

Another clinician-administered measure of Social Anxiety Disorder is the Brief Social Phobia Scale (BSPS; Davidson et al., 1991). The BSPS is an 18-item scale that assesses the symptoms of Social Anxiety Disorder that the patient has experienced in the past week. Patients are first presented with seven broadly defined social/performance situations (e.g., speaking in public, talking to strangers) and are asked to rate on a five-point scale how much they have feared each situation in the past week and the degree to which they have avoided each situation in the past week. If patients have not encountered a particular situation in the past week (due to avoidance or because it simply did not come up), they are asked to provide hypothetical ratings (e.g., "If you had been invited to a party this week, to what degree would you have feared it?"). In the second part of the interview, patients are asked to rate the severity of four physiological symptoms (e.g., sweating, blushing) that they sometimes experience when they are in social/performance situations or even when they are just thinking about such situations.

The BSPS yields three subscales—fear, avoidance, and physiological arousal. The scale has been shown to have strong internal consistency ($\alpha = .81$ for the total scale) and good retest reliability ($r = .91$ for the total scale over 1 week) (Davidson et al., 1997), but there is some concern about its convergent validity, particularly with respect to the physiological subscale. The BSPS has been shown to be sensitive to medication-related changes in social anxiety symptoms (Stein, Fyer, Davidson, Pollack, & Wiita, 1999).

Self-Report Measures

Numerous self-report measures are available to assess for social anxiety symptoms. For more extensive reviews of these measures, see Hart et al. (1999). For a review of measures to be used with children and adolescents, see Morris (2004). Common self-report measures for Social Anxiety Disorder in adults include the Social Interaction Anxiety Scale (SIAS) (Mattick & Clarke, 1998), the Social Phobia Scale (SPS) (Mattick & Clarke), the Brief Fear of Negative Evaluation Scale (BFNE) (Leary, 1983), and the Social Phobia and Anxiety Inventory (SPAI) (Turner, Beidel, Dancu, & Stanley, 1989). Each of these measures assess slightly different aspects of Social Anxiety Disorder. All can be used to establish severity of social anxiety at pretreatment, to assess treatment-related change in symptoms, and for treatment planning.

The SIAS measures anxiety that is experienced in dyads and groups (sample items: "I feel I will say something embarrassing when talking," "I have difficulty making eye contact with others"). The SPS measures anxiety in situations in which the person may be critically observed by others (sample items: "I get nervous that people are staring at me as I walk down the street" and "I worry I might do something to attract the attention of other people"). Both the SIAS and the SPS have been shown to be reliable instruments for the assessment of Social Anxiety Disorder and to possess a high degree of convergent validity with other indexes of social anxiety and avoidance (E. J. Brown et al., 1997; Heimberg, Mueller, Holt, Hope, & Liebowitz, 1992; Mattick & Clarke, 1998).

As its name implies, the BFNE assesses the core concern experienced by individuals with social anxiety—fear of negative evaluation (sample item: "I am frequently afraid of other people noticing my shortcomings"). The BFNE consists of 12 items. Recent research suggests that the scale is most valid when only the 8 items of the scale that are straightforwardly worded are used (omitting the 4 items that are reverse-worded; see Rodebaugh et al., 2004; Weeks et al., 2005). The BFNE has been shown to have strong psychometric properties (Weeks et al., 2005).

The SPAI inquires about the somatic, cognitive, and behavioral responses to social and performance situations. It also inquires about situations commonly feared by individuals with Panic Disorder and Agoraphobia. It consists of 45 items, but because some require multiple responses, respondents actually answer a total of 109 items. These items yield three subscales: a Social Phobia subscale, an Agoraphobia subscale, and a derived Difference (or total) score. The SPAI has been shown to be a valid scale, has demonstrated adequate reliability and good test-retest reliability, and is sensitive to treatment-related change (see Hart et al., 1999).

Ongoing Assessment and Follow-up

As noted previously, the measures that are commonly used with socially anxious patients are all useful in assessing treatment-related change. Our group has also developed a specific measure to assess session-by-session change over the course of treatment for Social Anxiety Disorder. The Social Anxiety Session Change Index (SASCI; Hayes, Miller, Hope, Heimberg, & Juster, in press) is a four-item scale that is completed prior to each treatment session to assess the progress the patient believes he or she has made since beginning treatment. Hayes et al. found the scale to be a valid measure with good internal consistency. Furthermore, the SASCI is sensitive to symptom improvement. Its strong psychometric properties, along with its brevity and ease of scoring, make the SASCI an excellent choice for assessing session-by-session change over the course of treatment for Social Anxiety Disorder.

Depending on the concerns of each specific patient, additional measures can be administered on a weekly basis to gather important information and aid in treatment planning. As an example, patients with co-occurring depression can complete the Beck Depression Inventory-II (Beck, Steer, & Brown, 1996) on a regular basis. Those with co-occurring alcohol use problems can complete the Alcohol Use Disorders Identification Test (Saunders, Aasland, Babor, de la Fuente, & Grant, 1993). Both of these measures are brief enough to be completed prior to each treatment session. Idiographically designed self-monitoring forms in which patients record aspects of their anxiety and behavior in feared social situations are also extremely useful in the treatment of Social Anxiety Disorder.

Neurobiological Assessment

As was mentioned earlier, imaging studies have been used to examine treatment-related changes in brain structure and function (e.g., Furmark et al., 2002). However, neurobiological assessments are not routinely used with patients who have Social Anxiety Disorder.

INTERVENTIONS

Psychological Interventions

The psychological intervention that has gained the most empirical support for the treatment of social anxiety disorder is CBT. Cognitive-behavioral therapy for Social Anxiety

Disorder most commonly includes three primary components: in-session exposures, cognitive restructuring, and homework assignments (see Heimberg & Becker, 2002). In-session exposures are designed to help patients face social and performance situations in which they experience distress and/or situations that they avoid completely. Cognitive restructuring helps patients to become more aware of their thoughts, examine these thoughts to see if they are dysfunctional, and for those that are, engage in a process of reframing. Cognitive restructuring helps patients to challenge the biases that we have discussed in detail earlier in this chapter, which allows them to view the world in a more accurate way so that they do not expect failure in every social situation. Homework—which is used for both exposures and cognitive restructuring—is assigned so that patients can apply what they have learned in therapy to their real lives. Homework compliance is associated with improved outcome in CBT for Social Anxiety Disorder (Leung & Heimberg, 1996).

The most studied CBT program for Social Anxiety Disorder is cognitive-behavioral group therapy (CBGT) (Heimberg & Becker, 2002). Cognitive-behavioral group therapy is typically administered to groups of five to six patients in 12 weekly, 2.5-hour-long sessions. During the first two sessions, patients are educated about social anxiety and are taught cognitive restructuring skills. During the third session, in-session exposures are initiated. These exposures are tailored to target each patient's unique concerns and are preceded and followed by therapist-directed cognitive restructuring exercises. At the end of each session, each patient is assigned homework that typically consists of exposures to real-life situations, with patient-directed pre- and post-exposure cognitive restructuring. As treatment proceeds, patients confront increasingly anxiety-provoking situations and are also helped to explore the core beliefs that underlie their difficulties with social anxiety. Multiple studies by our group (Heimberg et al., 1990, 1998; Hope, Heimberg, & Bruch, 1995; Liebowitz et. al., 1999) and others (Chambless et al., 1997; Edelman & Chambless, 1995; Gelernter et al., 1991; Lucas & Telch, 1993; Woody, Chambless, & Glass, 1997) support the efficacy of CBGT. Cognitive-behavioral group therapy has also been shown to have good long-term efficacy (Heimberg, Salzman, Holt, & Blendell, 1993) and is associated with significant improvements in quality of life (Eng, Coles, Heimberg, & Safren, 2001; Safren, Heimberg, Brown, & Holle, 1997). Other group treatments based on CBGT, such as comprehensive cognitive behavior therapy (CCBT) (Foa, Franklin, & Kozak, 2001; Franklin, Jaycox, & Foa, 1999) have also been shown to be efficacious (Davidson et al., 2004).

Although group treatment certainly holds appeal for the treatment of Social Anxiety Disorder, it can be logistically difficult to implement, particularly in clinical settings in which it can take a long time to gather a sufficient number of appropriate patients to form a group. Furthermore, meta-analytic studies suggest there is no difference in efficacy between group and individual treatment for Social Anxiety Disorder (Gould, Buckminster, Pollack, Otto, & Yap, 1997), and one study even suggests that individual treatment may be more efficacious (Stangier, Heidenreich, Peitz, Lauterbach, & Clark, 2003). Cognitive-behavioral group therapy has been adapted to an individual format (Hope, Heimberg, Juster, & Turk, 2000) and has been shown to be more effective than a wait-list control (Zaider, Heimberg, Roth, Hope, & Turk, 2003). Comprehensive cognitive-behavioral therapy has also recently been adapted to an individual format (Huppert et al., 2003). Clark and his colleagues have also developed an individual cognitive therapy program for Social Anxiety Disorder (Clark, 2001) that has shown very promising results. The treatment, based on Clark and Well's (1995) cognitive model of Social Anxiety Disorder, teaches patients to reduce safety behaviors and shift their attention externally (rather than on the self) to gather more accurate information about how they are evaluated by others. In the first randomized controlled trial, their cognitive therapy was found to be more effective than either fluoxetine plus instructions for self-exposure or placebo plus instructions for self exposure (Clark et al., 2003). In a second randomized controlled trial, cognitive therapy was found to be more effective than a wait-list control or a treatment that combined exposure (based on a habituation model) and applied relaxation (Clark et al., 2006).

Biological Interventions

Medications are also frequently used to treat Social Anxiety Disorder. The first-line pharmacological treatments for Social Anxiety Disorder are the SSRIs, including drugs like paroxetine and sertraline. These medications tend to yield relatively good outcomes, with mild side effects and low risk of overdose. Several controlled studies and meta-analyses support their efficacy (see Blanco et al., 2003; Davidson, 2003). Interesingly, two recent studies have suggested that the SSRI, fluoxetine, might not be particularly effective in the treatment of Social Anxiety Disorder (Clark et al., 2003; Kobak, Greist, Jefferson, & Katzelnick, 2002). Although fluoxetine was more effective than placebo in one large study (Davidson et al., 2004), these two studies are notable since they are the only published negative trials of SSRIs in the treatment of Social Anxiety Disorder.

Recent research has examined the efficacy of venlafaxine, a serotonin and norepinephrine reuptake inhibitor, in the treatment of Social Anxiety Disorder. It has been found to be more effective than pill-placebo in reducing social anxiety symptoms (e.g., Liebowitz, Mangano, Bradwejn, & Asnis, 2005; Liebowitz, Gelenberg, & Munjack, 2005) and has comparable efficacy to paroxetine (Liebowitz, Gelenberg, & Munjack).

Benzodiazepines have also been studied as treatments for Social Anxiety Disorder. Though studies with the benzodiazepine, clonazepam, have yielded very positive results (e.g., Davidson et al., 1993), studies of other benzodiazepines (e.g., alprazolam) have been less promising (Gelernter et al., 1991). Benzodiazepines are frequently prescribed but must be administered with adequate supervision because of their abuse potential and their sometimes difficult withdrawal effects (e.g., the phenomenon of rebound anxiety on withdrawal from alprazolam).

Finally, monamine oxidase inhibitors (MAOIs), such as phenelzine, have been found to be very effective for the treatment of social anxiety disorder (Blanco et al., 2003). However, patients who take them must adhere to strict dietary restrictions, avoiding any foods, beverages, and medications containing tyramine. Failure to adhere to this dietary regimen can lead to a sudden surge in blood pressure, with potentially serious effects. Given this risk, MAOIs are used only *after* other medications (e.g., SSRIs, benzodiazepines, venlafaxine) have proven ineffective for a given patient.

Prevention.   At the present time, research has not been conducted on the specific prevention of Social Anxiety Disorder. The field of anxiety prevention, more broadly defined, is still in its infancy, but shows great promise. Prevention programs, targeted at school-age children, teach skills that are part of thoroughly researched protocols used to treat children with anxiety disorders. Barrett and Turner (2001) targeted almost 500 sixth-grade students in their anxiety prevention program. Schools were randomly assigned to deliver either a teacher-led or a therapist-led anxiety prevention program based on Kendall's (1994) Coping Cat program. A third group of schools did not offer the intervention, allowing for a comparison group. The intervention included 10 weekly sessions, incorporated into classtime. Children were taught a number of skills, including cognitive restructuring and relaxation, and they also learned about exposure. Parents attended four evening sessions, learning how parenting skills can affect the development of problems with anxiety and how they could help their children confront feared situations. Children in both teacher-led and therapist-led intervention groups improved significantly more than children in the assessment-only control group. Furthermore, children who had been identified as being at greatest risk for the development of anxiety disorders were more likely to move into the normal range on measures of anxiety symptomatology if they had been assigned to one of the intervention groups. A similar study was completed by Lowry-Webster, Barrett, and Dadds (2001); they also found greater improvement among children who completed a teacher-led anxiety prevention program as compared to children who did not complete the program.

In contrast to the two studies cited previously, which were universal in that they included all children in a particular grade in a selected school, other studies have selected only at-risk children to participate. For example, in the first published anxiety prevention trial, children (ages 7–14) were selected for participation if they met criteria for an anxiety disorder but at a very mild level or if they did not meet criteria for an anxiety disorder but showed features of one (Dadds, Spence, Holland, Barrett, & Laurens, 1997). The purpose of the study was to see if intervention programs could ward off the onset of an anxiety disorder or prevent a mild one from worsening. Children were assigned to an intervention group, which consisted of a psychologist-led program based on the Coping Cat program, or to a control group. The intervention also included parent education. At 6 months post-intervention, children in the intervention group had lower rates of anxiety disorders (as assessed by a structured interview) than children in the control group. Of children who had only features of an anxiety disorder at baseline, fewer in the intervention group than in the control group progressed to having an anxiety disorder at the 6-month follow-up. Although these differences were no longer present by 12-month follow-up, they were again evident at a 2-year follow-up assessment (Dadds, Holland, Barrett, Laurens, & Spence, 1999).

In another study, Schmidt and Vasey (2000, 2002) delivered an intervention to college-aged women with high anxiety sensitivity, commonly seen as a risk factor for the development of anxiety disorders. Participants were assigned to an intervention group or a control group. The intervention included psychoeducation about anxiety and interoceptive exposure. Interoceptive exposure involves repeatedly confronting feared bodily sensations, like racing heart or dizziness, until the sensations no longer cause significant anxiety (e.g., fear of dying, fear of fainting). Following the program, participants in the intervention group showed a significant decrease in anxiety sensitivity as compared to participants in the control group. Furthermore, at a 1-year follow-up structured interview, participants in the intervention group had lower rates of anxiety disorders than participants in the control group.

As noted earlier, studies have not yet been directed at the specific prevention of Social Anxiety Disorder. Such studies would be a benefit to the field. As an example, it would be very interesting to enroll a group of behaviorally inhibited children in a prevention program based either on the Coping Cat program or on a treatment more specifically targeted to children with Social Anxiety Disorder, such Social Effectiveness Training for Children (Beidel, Turner, & Morris, 2000).

Summary and Future Directions

In the more than 20 years since Social Anxiety Disorder was termed the "neglected anxiety disorder" (Liebowitz et al., 1985, p. 729), great progress has been made in understanding the nature of the impairments observed in the disorder, advancing hypotheses on factors that might have contributed to these impairments, and developing and testing treatments for this prevalent and highly impairing disorder. There is however, still much to be done. One essential goal is for researchers to come to a clearer understanding of the nature of the social relationships of individuals with Social Anxiety Disorder. This might involve collaboration between social psychologists (experts on interpersonal relationships) and clinical psychologists (experts on Social Anxiety Disorder). Beginning with children, it will be important to elucidate not only why socially anxious individuals have fewer social relationships than their less anxious counterparts, but also what occurs within relationships that leads to dissatisfaction and other difficulties. As we gain a clearer understanding of the nature of these impairments, new components of treatment can be developed (Walker, 2003). These components need to extend beyond simple social skills training, which has generally not been shown to add much to Social Anxiety Disorder treatment protocols (although see Herbert et al., 2005). Rather, treatment might involve discussion of where to seek out new friends and potential romantic relationships, how to judge whether a person might become an appropriate friend, reasonable expectations about the development of a relationship from acquaintance to friend/romantic partner, and so on. Perhaps even more importantly, treatment could involve discussion of how the biases inherent in Social Anxiety Disorder can negatively affect relationships. For example, the research on interpretation bias tells us that individuals with Social Anxiety Disorder interpret neutral and mildly negative social cues as being terribly negative and costly. This might lead them to seek a lot of reassurance in relationships or to be highly defensive. It is important to frame these behaviors as "safety behaviors" (Wells et al., 1995), and then to instruct patients to discontinue their use. As we have noted earlier, individuals with Social Anxiety Disorder also seem to exaggerate the probability and cost of revealing personal information about themselves to others, particularly if they see the information as negative. Again, treatment should involve sharing increasing "negative" self-disclosures to test out the belief that people will reject them if they really get to know them. Research studies should explore whether these kinds of interventions lead to improved outcomes, as well as whether there are certain predictors that help clinicians decide which patients could benefit from them and which patients do not need them. It is important to note that these interventions are entirely consistent with existing treatment protocols (e.g., Hope et al., 2000), and therapists who are experienced with Social Anxiety Disorder routinely use them. For less experienced therapists, it would be very helpful to clearly articulate the social deficits seen in Social Anxiety Disorder, as well as the interventions best suited to targeting them.

Another essential goal is to develop a clearer understanding of the nature of the information processing deficits seen in Social Anxiety Disorder. As we have noted throughout the chapter, there are inconsistencies in the literature. Part of the reason for these inconsistencies is the use of divergent methodologies across a relatively small group of studies. Research groups should seek greater consistency in the methodologies that are used and should attempt to replicate the findings of others (as Sposari & Rapee,

2007, recently did with the study by Mansell et al., 1999). By working together, it is likely that clearer conclusions can be drawn about the nature of the impairments that are most central to understanding and treating Social Anxiety Disorder.

Another important direction is for researchers to stop seeing individual information-processing deficits in isolation. As recently pointed out by Hirsch et al. (2006), "one bias or its results influences another bias or the effects of that second bias, and vice versa" (p. 223). Understanding how biases interact to maintain Social Anxiety Disorder will be a strong contribution to the field. Most notably, therapeutic interventions can be (and have been) developed that target multiple biases. As an example, video feedback is being used to correct patients' biased self-images (Clark & Wells, 1995; Harvey, Clark, Ehlers, & Rapee, 2000). Patients are videotaped during a social or performance situation. They are then asked to make very clear and detailed predictions of what they expect they will see when viewing the tape. When the tape is played back, the patient is asked to view the tape as an unbiased observer, almost as if he or she is watching someone across the room at a cocktail party. Studies have shown that the video feedback technique corrects negative self-images and does so most effectively for individuals whose self-image is most extremely unrealistic (Rodebaugh, 2004; Rodebaugh & Rapee, 2005). Treatments that incorporate video feedback have yielded strong outcomes (e.g., Clark et al., 2003). The next step is to examine how the use of video feedback influences various cognitive biases. For example, it would be interesting to see whether patients respond less negatively to interpretation bias tasks after completing video feedback, or whether their attentional biases becomes less skewed toward negative social information in the environment. Some researchers have also developed cognitive training paradigms (e.g., Murphy, Hirsch, Mathews, Smith, & Clark, 2005) in which computerized tasks have been developed to induce a more benign interpretation bias. It has been suggested that these tasks might be useful adjuncts to traditional cognitive behavioral therapy (Hirsch et al., 2006).

Thus far, we have suggested various modifications to treatment as we have discussed further developing research on the interpersonal deficits and information-processing deficits seen among individuals with Social Anxiety Disorder. Other next steps in treatment research are also worth discussing. Current psychosocial and pharmacological treatments yield excellent results, but efforts should be made at further optimizing outcomes (see Ledley & Heimberg, 2005). These might include development of new pharmacological agents, new ways of using existing agents (e.g., combining medications to enhance outcomes), promulgation of new guidelines for action when a first-line agent does not work (e.g., increasing dose or switching to a new agent), and matching agents with particular patient symptom profiles. It is also important to explore how to best combine pharmacological and psychosocial treatments. One existing study (Davidson et al., 2004) found no advantage of combining medication and CBT over either treatment alone, but the two treatments were administered concurrently. It is possible that combined treatments would work better if treatments were sequenced—for example, adding CBT to medication once the medication has had a chance to take effect. This approach is currently being explored by our research group.

With psychosocial treatments, many interesting issues remain to be explored in addition to the increased focus on interpersonal issues mentioned previously. It is also important for investigators to learn more about patients with comorbid conditions, particularly depression and alcohol use disorders. These disorders often co-occur with Social Anxiety Disorder, but patients exhibiting these patterns of comorbidity are often excluded from treatment studies. Thus, we know little about how they fare in standard treatment for Social Anxiety Disorder. We know even less about the kinds of modifications to treatment that might improve outcomes for these particularly impaired groups.

Finally, it is essential that work is done on disseminating treatments for Social Anxiety Disorder. Epidemiological studies (e.g., Kessler, Stein, & Berglund, 1998) have suggested that individuals with Generalized Social Anxiety Disorder are twice as likely to report not seeking treatment as individuals with specific social fears (e.g., a fear of public speaking). Among individuals with three or more social fears, only 22.6% had ever sought treatment from a medical doctor, only 15.6% had ever sought treatment from another professional, and only 11.6% had taken medication more than once. Similar results were reported by Erwin, Turk, Heimberg, Fresco, and Hantula (2004), who surveyed individuals who sought information about social anxiety on the Internet. Among this particularly severe sample, only one third had received therapy and/or medication for Social Anxiety Disorder (Erwin et al., 2004). Even more extreme, Keller (2003) reported that only 5% of individuals with Social Anxiety Disorder seek help. When they do seek help, Social Anxiety Disorder is often unrecognized and undertreated. Unfortunately, when Social Anxiety Disorder is treated, it is often not treated according to current state-of-the-art research. Despite extensive research on the use of SSRIs in the treatment of Social Anxiety Disorder, benzodiazepines are still the most commonly prescribed agents (see Keller, 2003). Similarly, supportive therapy and psychodynamic therapy are used more commonly than cognitive-behavioral approaches, despite the complete lack of research support for use of the former and the extensive research support for use of the latter (Keller, 2003). Keller suggests that this trend might be explained partly by the lack of individuals trained to deliver cognitive-behavioral therapy. It is also possible, however, that the problem begins with referring doctors who suggest outdated treatments that they learned about years ago in medical school.

Future research efforts should focus on the best ways to make empirically supported treatments available to individuals with Social Anxiety Disorder. These efforts must include educating the public about Social Anxiety Disorder and available treatments for it, taking into account that a common barrier to treatment is that socially anxious individuals fear what others might think or say about them (Olfson et al., 2000). Referring doctors, particularly general practitioners and general psychiatrists, should receive similar education. Furthermore, it is important to disseminate empirically supported treatments for Social Anxiety Disorder to clinicians in the community. Such efforts should include the publication of treatment protocols that are relatively easy to implement (e.g., Hope, Heimberg, & Turk, 2006; Hope et al., 2000) and explorations into the best ways to train clinicians to use such protocols effectively.

References

Alden, L. E., & Bieling, P. (1998). Interpersonal consequences of the pursuit of safety. *Behaviour Research and Therapy, 36,* 53–64.

Alden, L. E., & Taylor, C. T. (2004). Interpersonal processes in social phobia. *Clinical Psychology Review, 24,* 857–882.

Alden, L. E., & Wallace, S. T. (1995). Social phobia and social appraisal in successful and unsuccessful social interactions. *Behaviour Research and Therapy, 33,* 497–505.

American Psychiatric Association (1980). *Diagnostic and statistical manual of mental disorders* (3rd edition). Washington, DC: Author.

American Psychiatric Association (1987). *Diagnostic and statistical manual of mental disorders* (3rd ed., revised). Washington, DC: Author.

American Psychiatric Association. (1994). *Diagnostic and statistical manual of mental disorders* (4th ed.). Washington, DC: Author.

American Psychiatric Association. (2000). *Diagnostic and statistical manual of mental disorders* (4th ed., text revision). Washington, DC: Author.

Amir, N., Foa, E. B., & Coles, M. E. (1998). Negative interpretation bias in social phobia. *Behaviour Research and Therapy, 36,* 959–970.

Amir, N., Foa, E. B., & Coles, M. E. (2000). Implicit memory bias for threat-relevant information in generalized social phobia. *Journal of Abnormal Psychology, 109,* 713–720.

Asmundson, G. J. G., & Stein, M. B. (1994). Selective processing of social threat in patients with generalized social phobia: Evaluation using a dot-probe paradigm. *Journal of Anxiety Disorders, 8,* 107–117.

Barrett, P., & Turner, C. (2001). Prevention of anxiety symptoms in primary school children: Preliminary results from a universal school-based trial. *British Journal of Clinical Psychology, 40,* 399–410.

Beck, A. T., Steer, R. A., & Brown, G. K. (1996). *Beck Depression Inventory Manual* (2nd ed.). San Antonio, TX: The Psychological Corporation.

Beidel, D. C., Turner, S. M., & Morris, T. L. (1999). Psychopathology of childhood social phobia. *Journal of the American Academy of Child and Adolescent Psychiatry, 38,* 643–650.

Beidel, D. C., Turner, S. M., & Morris, T. L. (2000). Behavioral treatment of childhood social phobia.

Journal of Consulting and Clinical Psychology, 68, 1072–1080.

Blanco, C., Schneier, F. R., Schmidt, A., Blanco-Jerez, C. -R., Marshall, R. D., Sanchez-Lacày, A., et al. (2003). Pharmacological treatment of social anxiety disorder: A meta-analysis. *Depression and Anxiety, 18,* 29–40.

Bögels, S. M., van Oosten, A., Muris, P., & Smulders, D. (2001). Familial correlates of social anxiety in children and adolescents. *Behaviour Research and Therapy, 39,* 273–287.

Bohlin, G., Hagekull, B., & Rydell, A. -M. (2000). Attachment and social functioning: A longitudinal study from infancy to middle childhood. *Social Development, 9,* 24–39.

Bond, C. F., Jr., & Omar, A. S. (1990). Social anxiety, state dependence, and the next-in-line effect. *Journal of Experimental Social Psychology, 26,* 185–198.

Bowlby Brown, E. J., Turovsky, J., Heimberg, R. G., Juster, H. R., Brown, T. A., et al. (1997). Validation of the Social Interaction Anxiety Scale and the Social Phobia Scale across the anxiety disorders. *Psychological Assessment, 9,* 21–27.

Brown, T. A., & Barlow, D. H. (1992). Comorbidity among anxiety disorders: Implications for treatment and *DSM-IV*. *Journal of Consulting and Clinical Psychology, 60,* 835–844.

Brown, T. A., DiNardo, P. A., & Barlow, D. H. (1994). *Anxiety Disorders Interview Schedule for* DSM-IV *(ADIS-IV)*. New York: Oxford University Press.

Brown, T. A., DiNardo, P. A., Lehman, C. L., & Campbell, L. A. (2001). Reliability of *DSM-IV* anxiety and mood disorders: Implications for the classification of emotional disorders. *Journal of Abnormal Psychology, 110,* 49–58.

Bruch, M. A., Heimberg, R. G., Berger, P., & Collins, T. M. (1989). Social phobia and perceptions of early parental and personal characteristics. *Anxiety Research, 2,* 57–65.

Buckner, J. D., Mallott, M. A., Schmidt, N. B., & Taylor, J. (2006). Peer influence and gender differences in problematic cannabis use among individuals with social anxiety. *Journal of Anxiety Disorders, 20,* 1087–1092.

Buckner, J. D., Schmidt, N. B., Bobadilla, L., & Taylor, J. (2006). Social anxiety and problematic cannabis use: Evaluating the moderating role of stress reactivity and perceived coping. *Behaviour Research and Therapy, 44,* 1007–1015.

Butler, E. A., Egloff, B., Wlhelm, F. H., Smith, N. C., Erickson, E. A., & Gross, J. J. (2003). The social consequences of expressive suppression. *Emotion, 3,* 48–67.

Caster, J. B., Inderbitzen, H. M., & Hope, D. (1999). Relationship between youth and parent perceptions of family environment and social anxiety. *Journal of Anxiety Disorders, 13,* 237–251.

Chambless, D. L., Tran, G. Q., & Glass, C. R. (1997). Predictors of response to cognitive-behavioral group therapy for social phobia. *Journal of Anxiety Disorders, 11,* 221–240.

Chambless, D. L., Fydrich, T., & Rodebaugh, T. L. (in press). Generalized social phobia and avoidant personality disorder: Meaningful distinction or useless duplication? *Depression and Anxiety.*

Chapman, T. F., Mannuzza, S., & Fyer, A. J. (1995). Epidemiology and family studies in social phobia. In R. G. Heimberg, M. R. Liebowitz, D. A. Hope, & F. R. Schneier (Eds.), *Social phobia: Diagnosis, assessment, and treatment* (pp. 21–40). New York: Guilford.

Chartier, M. J., Walker, J. R., & Stein, M. B. (2001). Social phobia and potential childhood risk factors in a community sample. *Psychological Medicine, 31,* 307–315.

Chen, Y. P., Ehlers, A., Clark, D. M., & Mansell, W. (2002). Patients with generalized social phobia direct their attention away from faces. *Behaviour Research and Therapy, 40,* 677–687.

Clark, D. M. (2001). A cognitive perspective on social phobia. In W. R. Crozier & L. E. Alden (Eds.), *International handbook of social anxiety: Concepts, research and interventions relating to the self and shyness* (pp. 405–430). Chichester, UK: Wiley.

Clark, D. M., Ehlers, A., Hackmann, A., McManus, F., Fennell, M., Grey, N., et al. (2006). Cognitive therapy versus exposure and applied relaxation in social phobia: A randomized controlled trial. *Journal of Consulting and Clinical Psychology, 74,* 568–578.

Clark, D. M., Ehlers, A., McManus, F., Hackmann, A., Fennell, M., Campbell, H., et al. (2003). Cognitive therapy vs. fluoxetine in generalized social phobia: A randomized placebo controlled trial. *Journal of Consulting and Clinical Psychology, 71,* 1058–1067.

Clark, D. M., & Wells, A. (1995). A cognitive model of social phobia. In R. G. Heimberg, M. R. Liebowitz,

D. A. Hope, & F. R. Schneier (Eds.), *Social phobia: Diagnosis, assessment, and treatment* (pp. 69–93). New York: Guilford.

Coles, M. E., & Heimberg, R. G. (2002). Memory biases in the anxiety disorders: Current status. *Clinical Psychology Review, 22,* 587–627.

Coles, M. E., & Heimberg, R. G. (2005). Recognition bias for critical faces in social phobia: A replication and extension. *Behaviour Research and Therapy, 43,* 109–120.

Coles, M. E., Turk, C. L., & Heimberg, R. G. (2002). The role of memory perspective in social phobia: Immediate and delayed memories for role-played situations. *Behavioural and Cognitive Psychotherapy, 30,* 415–425.

Coles, M. E., Turk, C. L., Heimberg, R. G., & Fresco, D. M. (2001). Effects of varying levels of anxiety within social situations: Relationship to memory perspective and attributions in social phobia. *Behaviour Research and Therapy, 39,* 651–665.

Constans, J. I., Penn, D. L., Ihen, G. H., & Hope, D. A. (1999). Interpretive biases for ambiguous stimuli in social anxiety. *Behaviour Research and Therapy, 37,* 643–651.

Cooper, P. J., & Eke, M. (1999). Childhood shyness and maternal social phobia: A community study. *British Journal of Psychiatry, 174,* 439–443.

Dadds, M. R., Holland, D., Barrett, P. M., Laurens, K., & Spence, S. (1999). Early intervention and prevention of anxiety disorders in children: Results at 2–year follow-up. *Journal of Consulting and Clinical Psychology, 67,* 145–150.

Dadds, M. R., Spence, S. H., Holland, D. E., Barrett, P. M., & Laurens, K. R. (1997). Prevention and early intervention for anxiety disorders: A controlled trial. *Journal of Consulting and Clinical Psychology, 65,* 627–635.

Daly, J. A., Vangelisti, A. L., & Lawrence, S. G. (1989). Self-focused attention and public speaking anxiety. *Personality and Individual Differences, 10,* 903–913.

Davidson, J. R. T. (2003). Pharmacotherapy of social phobia. *Acta Psychiatrica Scandinavica, 108* (suppl. 417), 65–71.

Davidson, J. R., Foa, E. B., Huppert, J. D., Keefe, F. J., Franklin, M. E., Compton, J. S., et al. (2004). Fluoxetine, comprehensive cognitive behavioral therapy, and placebo in generalized social phobia. *Archives of General Psychiatry, 61,* 1005–1013.

Davidson, J. R., Hughes, D. L., George, L. K., & Blazer, D. G. (1993). The epidemiology of social phobia: Findings from the Duke Epidemiological Catchment Area Study. *Psychological Medicine, 23,* 709–718.

Davidson, J. R. T., Miner, C. M., DeVeaugh-Geiss, J., Tupler, L. A., Colket, J. T., & Potts, N. L. S. (1997). The Brief Social Phobia Scale: A psychometric evaluation. *Psychological Medicine*, *27*, 161–166.

Davidson, J. R. T., Potts, N. L. S., Richichi, E. A., Ford, S. M., Krishnan, R. R., Smith, R. D., & Wilson, W. (1991). The Brief Social Phobia Scale. *Journal of Clinical Psychiatry*, *52*, 48–51.

Davidson, J. R. T., Potts, N., Richichi, E., Krishnan, R., Ford, S. M., Smith, R., et al. (1993). Treatment of social phobia with clonazepam and placebo. *Journal of Clinical Psychopharmacology*, *13*, 423–428.

Davila, J., & Beck, J. G. (2002). Is social anxiety associated with impairment in close relationships? A preliminary investigation. *Behavior Therapy*, *33*, 427–446.

DiNardo, P. A., Brown, T. A., & Barlow, D. H. (1994). *Anxiety Disorders Interview Schedule for* DSM-IV: *Lifetime Version (ADIS-IV-L)*. New York: Oxford University Press.

Dodge, C. S., Heimberg, R. G., Nyman, D. J., & O'Brien, G. T. (1987). Daily heterosocial interactions of high and low socially anxious college students: A diary study. *Behavior Therapy*, *18*, 90–96.

Dozier, M., Stovall, K. C., & Albus, K. E. (1999). Attachment and psychopathology in adulthood. In J. Cassidy & P. R. Shaver (Eds.), *Handbook of attachment: Theory, research, and clinical applications* (pp. 497–519). New York: Guilford.

Edelmann, R. E., & Chambless, D. L. (1995). Adherence during session and homework in cognitive-behavioral group treatment of social phobia. *Behaviour Research and Therapy*, *33*, 537–577.

Eng, W., Coles, M. E., Heimberg, R. G., & Safren, S. A. (2001). Quality of life following cognitive behavioral treatment for social anxiety disorder: Preliminary findings. *Depression and Anxiety*, *13*, 192–193.

Eng, W., Coles, M. E., Heimberg, R. G., & Safren, S. A. (2005). Domains of life satisfaction in social anxiety disorder: Relation to symptoms and response to cognitive-behavioral therapy. *Journal of Anxiety Disorders*, *19*, 143–156.

Eng, W., Heimberg, R. G., Hart, T. A., Schneier, F. R. & Liebowitz, M. R. (2001). Attachment in individuals with social anxiety disorder: The relationship among adult attachment styles, social anxiety and depression. *Emotion*, *1*, 365–380.

Erwin, B. A., Heimberg, R. G., Juster, H. R., & Mindlin, M. (2002). Comorbid anxiety and mood disorders among persons with social anxiety disorder. *Behaviour Research and Therapy*, *40*, 19–35.

Erwin, B. A., Heimberg, R. G., Marx, B. P., & Franklin, M. E. (2006). Traumatic and socially stressful life events among persons with social anxiety disorder. *Journal of Anxiety Disorders*, *20*, 896–914.

Erwin, B. A., Heimberg, R. G., Schneier, F. R., & Liebowitz, M. R. (2003). Anger experience and anger expression in social anxiety disorder: Pretreatment profile and predictors of attrition and response to cognitive-behavioral treatment. *Behavior Therapy*, *34*, 331–350.

Erwin, B. A., Turk, C. L., Heimberg, R. G., Fresco, D. M., & Hantula, D. A. (2004). The Internet: Home to a severe population of individuals with social anxiety disorder? *Journal of Anxiety Disorders*, *18*, 629–646.

First, M. B., Spitzer, R. L., Gibbon, M., & Williams, J. (2002). *Structured Clinical Interview for* DSM-IV-TR *Axis I disorders–Patient Edition (SCID-I/P)*. New York: Biometrics Research Department.

Foa, E. B., Franklin, M. E., & Kozak, M. J. (2001). Social phobia: An information processing perspective. In S. Hofman, & P. M. DiBartolo (Eds.), *From social anxiety to social phobia: Multiple perspectives* (pp. 268–280). Needham, MA: Allyn & Bacon.

Foa, E. B., Franklin, M. E., Perry, K. J., & Herbert, J. D. (1996). Cognitive biases in generalized social phobia. *Journal of Abnormal Psychology*, *105*, 433–439.

Foa, E. B., Gilboa-Schechtman, E., Amir, N., & Freshman, M. (2000). Memory bias in generalized social phobia: Remembering negative emotional expressions. *Journal of Anxiety Disorders*, *14*, 501–519.

Franklin, M. E., Huppert, J., Langner, R., Leiberg, S., & Foa, E. B. (2005). Interpretation bias: A comparison of treated social phobics, untreated social phobiics, and controls. *Cognitive Therapy and Research*, *29*, 289–300.

Franklin, M. E., Jaycox, L. H., & Foa, E. B. (1999). Social phobia: Social skills training. In M. Hersen & A. Bellack (Eds.), *Handbook of comparative treatments for adult disorders* (2nd ed; pp. 317–339). New York: Wiley.

Fresco, D. M., Coles, M. E., Heimberg, R. G., Liebowitz, M. R., Hami, S., Stein, M. B., et al. (2001). The Liebowitz Social Anxiety Scale: A comparison of the psychometric properties of self-report and clinician-administered formats. *Psychological Medicine*, *31*, 1025–1035.

Furmark, T., Tillfors, M., Marteinsdottir, I., Fischer, H., Pissiota, A., Langstroem, B., et al. (2002). Common changes in cerebral blood flow in patients with social phobia treated with citalopram or cognitive-behavioral therapy. *Archives of General Psychiatry*, *59*, 425–433.

Gelernter, C. S., Uhde, T. W., Cimbolic, P., Arnkoff, D. B., Vittone, B. J., & Tancer, M. E. (1991). Cognitive-behavioral approaches and pharmacological treatments of social phobia: A controlled study. *Archives of General Psychiatry, 48*, 938–945.

Gilboa-Schechtman, E., Foa, E. B., & Amir, N. (1999). Attentional biases for facial expressions in social phobia: The face-in-the-crowd paradigm. *Cognition and Emotion, 13*, 305–318.

Gilboa-Schechtman, E., Franklin, M. E., & Foa, E. B. (2000). Anticipated reactions to social events: Differences among individuals with generalized social phobia, obsessive compulsive disorder, and nonanxious controls. *Cognitive Therapy and Research, 24*, 731–746.

Gladstone, G. L. & Parker, G. B. (2006). Is behavioral inhibition a risk factor for depression? *Journal of Affective Disorders, 95*, 85–94.

Gladstone, G. L., Parker, G. B., Mitchell, P. B., Wilhelm, K. A., & Malhi, G. S. (2005). Relationship between self-reported childhood behavioral inhibition and lifetime anxiety disorders in a clinical sample. *Depression and Anxiety, 22*, 103–113.

Gould, R. A., Buckminster, S., Pollack, M. H., Otto, M. W., & Yap, L. (1997). Cognitive-behavioral and pharmacological treatment for social phobia: A meta-analysis. *Clinical Psychology: Science and Practice, 4*, 291–306.

Grant, B. F., Hasin, D. S., Blanco, C., Stinson, F. S., Chou, S. P., Goldstein, R. B., et al. (2005). The epidemiology of social anxiety disorder in the United States: Results from the National Epidemiologic Survey on Alcohol and Related Conditions. *Journal of Clinical Psychiatry, 66*, 1351–1361.

Grant, B. F., Stinson, F. S., Dawson, D. A., Chou, S. P., Ruan, J., & Pickering, R. P. (2004). Co-occurrence of 12–month alcohol and drug use disorders and personality disorders in the United States: Results from the National Epidemiologic Survey on Alcohol and Related Conditions. *Archives of General Psychiatry, 61*, 362–368.

Grant, D. M., & Beck, J. G. (2006). Attentional biases in social anxiety and dysphoria: Does comorbidity make a difference? *Journal of Anxiety Disorders, 20*, 520–529.

Greenberg, M. T. (1999). Attachment and psychopathology in childhood. In J. Cassidy & P. R. Shaver (Eds.), *Handbook of attachment: Theory, research, and clinical applications* (pp. 469–496). New York: Guilford.

Hackman, A., Clark, D. M., & McManus, F. (2000). Recurrent images and early memories in social phobia. *Behaviour Research and Therapy, 38*, 601–610.

Hackmann, A., Surawy, C., & Clark, D. M. (1998). Seeing yourself through others' eyes: A study of spontaneously occurring images in social phobia. *Behavioural and Cognitive Psychotherapy, 26*, 3–12.

Hart, T. A., Jack, M. S., Turk, C. L., & Heimberg, R. G. (1999). Issues for the measurement of social anxiety disorder. In H. G. M.Westenberg & J. A. Den Boer (Eds.), *Social anxiety disorder* (pp. 133–155). Amsterdam: Syn-Thesis.

Harvey, A. G., Clark, D. M., Ehlers, A., & Rapee, R. M. (2000). Social anxiety and self-impression: Cognitive preparation enhances the beneficial effects of video feedback following a stressful social task. *Behaviour Research and Therapy, 38*, 1183–1192.

Hayes, S. A., Miller, N. A., Hope, D. A., Heimberg, R. G., & Juster, H. R. (in press). Assessing client progress session-by-session: The Social Anxiety Session Change Index. *Cognitive and Behavioral Practice.*

Hayward, C., Killen, J. D., Kraemer, H. C., & Taylor, C. B. (1998). Linking self-reported childhood behavioral inhibition to adolescent social phobia. *Journal of the American Academy of Child and Adolescent Psychiatry, 37*, 1308–1316.

Hazen, A. L., & Stein, M. B. (1995). Clinical phenomenology and comorbidity. In M. B. Stein (Ed.), *Social phobia: Clinical and research perspectives* (pp. 3–41). Washington, DC: American Psychiatric Press.

Heimberg, R. G. (1996). Social phobia, avoidant personality disorder, and the multiaxial conceptualization of interpersonal anxiety. In P. Salkovskis (Ed.), *Trends in cognitive and behavioural therapies* (pp. 43–62). Sussex, UK: Wiley.

Heimberg, R. G., & Becker, R. E. (2002). *Cognitive-behavioral group therapy for social phobia: Basic mechanisms and clinical strategies.* New York: Guilford.

Heimberg, R. G., Dodge, C. S., Hope, D. A., Kennedy, C. R., Zollo, L., & Becker, R. E. (1990). Cognitive behavioral group treatment of social phobia: Comparison to a credible placebo control. *Cognitive Therapy and Research, 14*, 1–23.

Heimberg, R. G., Holt, C. S., Schneier, F. R., Spitzer, R. L., & Liebowitz, M. R. (1993). The issue of subtypes in the diagnosis of social phobia. *Journal of Anxiety Disorders, 7*, 249–269.

Heimberg, R. G., Horner, K. J., Juster, H. R., Safren, S. A., Brown, E. J., Schneier, F. R., et al. (1999).

Psychometric properties of the Liebowitz Social Anxiety Scale. *Psychological Medicine*, *29*, 199–212.

Heimberg, R. G., Liebowitz, M. R., Hope, D. A., Schneier, F. R., Holt, C. S., Welkowitz, L. A., et al. (1998). Cognitive-behavioral group treatment versus phenelzine in social phobia: 12 week outcome. *Archives of General Psychiatry*, *55*, 1133–1141.

Heimberg, R. G., Mueller, G. P., Holt, C. S., Hope, D. A., & Liebowitz, M. R. (1992). Assessment of anxiety in social interaction and being observed by others: The Social Interaction Anxiety Scale and the Social Phobia Scale. *Behavior Therapy*, *23*, 53–73.

Heimberg, R. G., Salzman, D., Holt, C. S., & Blendell, K. (1993). Cognitive behavioral group treatment of social phobia: Effectiveness at 5–year follow-up. *Cognitive Therapy and Research*, *17*, 325–339.

Herbert, J. D., Gaudiano, B. A., Rheingold, A. A., Myers, V. H., Dalrymple, K., & Nolan, E. M. (2005). Social skills training augments the effectiveness of cognitive behavioral group therapy for social anxiety disorder. *Behavior Therapy*, *36*, 125–138.

Hirsch, C., Clark, D. M., & Mathews, A. (2006). Imagery and interpretations in social phobia: Support for the combined cognitive biases hypothesis. *Behavior Therapy*, *37*, 223–236.

Hirsch, C. R., Clark, D. M., Mathews, A., & Williams, R. (2003). Self-images play a causal role in social phobia. *Behaviour Research and Therapy*, *41*, 909–921.

Hirsch, C. R., Meynen, T., & Clark, D. M. (2004). Negative self-imagery in social anxiety contaminates social interactions. *Memory*, *12*, 496–506.

Holt, C. S., Heimberg, R. G., Hope, D. A., & Liebowitz, M. R. (1992). Situational domains of social phobia. *Journal of Anxiety Disorders*, *6*, 63–77.

Hope, D. A., Heimberg, R. G., & Bruch, M. A. (1995). Dismantling cognitive- behavioral group therapy for social phobia. *Behaviour Research and Therapy*, *33*, 637–650.

Hope, D. A., Heimberg, R. G., Juster, H., & Turk, C. L. (2000). *Managing social anxiety: A cognitive-behavioral therapy approach (Client workbook)*. New York: Oxford University Press.

Hope, D. A., Heimberg, R. G., & Klein, J. F. (1990). Social anxiety and the recall of interpersonal information. *Journal of Cognitive Psychotherapy*, *4*, 185–195.

Hope, D. A., Heimberg, R. G., & Turk, C. L. (2006). *Therapist guide for Managing social anxiety: A cognitive-behavioral therapy approach*. New York: Oxford University Press.

Hope, D. A., Rapee, R. M., Heimberg, R. G., & Dombeck, M. J. (1990). Representations of the self in social phobia: Vulnerability to social threat. *Cognitive Therapy and Research*, *14*, 177–189.

Hope, D. A., Sigler, K. D., Penn, D. L., & Meier, V. (1998). Social anxiety, recall of interpersonal information, and social impact on others. *Journal of Cognitive Psychotherapy*, *12*, 303–322.

Huppert, J. D., Roth, D. A., & Foa, E. B. (2003). Cognitive behavioral treatment of social phobia: New advances. *Current Psychiatry Reports*, *5*, 289–296.

Janet, P. (1903). *Les obsessions et la psychasthénie*. Paris: F. Alcan.

Jones, W. H., & Carpenter, B. N. (1986). Shyness, social behavior, and relationships. In W. H. Jones, J. M.Cheek & S. R.Briggs (Eds.), *Shyness: Perspectives on research and treatment* (pp. 227–238). New York: Plenum.

Kagan, J. (1994). *Galen's prophecy*. New York: Basic Books.

Kendall, P. C. (1994). Treatment of anxiety disorders in children: A randomized clinical trial. *Journal of Consulting and Clinical Psychology*, *62*, 100–110.

Kendler, K. S., Karkowski, L. M., & Prescott, C. A. (1999). Fears and phobias: Reliability and heritability. *Psychological Medicine*, *29*, 539–553.

Kendler, K. S., Myers, J., Prescott, C. A., & Neale, M. C. (2001). The genetic epidemiology of irrational fears and phobias in men. *Archives of General Psychiatry*, *58*, 257–265.

Kendler, K. S., Neale, M. C., Kessler, R. C., Heath, A. C., & Eaves, L. J. (1992). The genetic epidemiology of phobias in women: The interrelationship of agoraphobia, social phobia, situational phobia, and simple phobia. *Archives of General Psychiatry*, *49*, 273–281.

Keller, M. B. (2003). The lifelong course of social anxiety disorder: A clinical perspective. *Acta Psychiatrica Scandinavica*, *108 (Suppl. 417)* 85–94.

Kessler, R. C., Berglund, P. D., Demler, O., Olga, J. R., Merikangas, K. R., & Walters, E. E. (2005). Lifetime prevalence and age-of-onset distributions of *DSM-IV* disorders in the National Comorbidity Survey Replication. *Archives of General Psychiatry*, *62*, 593–602.

Kessler, R. C., Chiu, W. T., Demler, O., Merikangas, K., & Walters, E. E. (2005). Prevalence, severity, and comorbidity of 12–month *DSM-IV* disorders in the National Comorbidity Survey Replication. *Archives of General Psychiatry*, *62*, 617–627.

Kessler, R. C., McGonagle, K. A., Zhao, S., Nelson, C. B., Hughes, M., Eshleman, S., et al. (1994). Lifetime and 12–month prevalence of *DSM-III-R* psychiatric disorders in the United States: Results from the National Comorbidity Survey. *Archives of General Psychiatry, 51*, 8–19.

Kessler, R. C., Stein, M. B., & Berglund, P. (1998). Social phobia subtypes in the National Comorbidity Survey. *American Journal of Psychiatry, 155*, 613–619.

Kimble, C. E., & Zehr, H. D. (1982). Self-consciousness, information load, self-presentation, and memory in a social situation. *Journal of Social Psychology, 118*, 39–46.

Kobak, K. A., Greist, J. H., Jefferson, J. W., & Katzelnick, D. J. (2002). Fluoxetine in social phobia: A double-blind, placebo-controlled pilot study. *Journal of Clinical Psychopharmacology, 22*, 257–262.

LaFreniere, P. J., & Sroufe, L. A. (1985). Profiles of peer competence in the preschool: Interrelations between measures, influence of social ecology, and relation to attachment history. *Developmental Psychology, 21*, 56–69.

LaGreca, A. M., Dandes, S. K., Wick, P., Shaw, K., & Stone, W. L. (1988). Development of the social anxiety scale for children: Reliability and concurrent validity. *Journal of Clinical Child Psychology, 17*, 84–91.

Leary, M. R. (1983). A brief version of the Fear of Negative Evaluation Scale. *Personality and Social Psychology Bulletin, 9*, 371–375.

Leary, M. R., & Dobbins, S. E. (1983). Social anxiety, sexual behavior, and contraceptive use. *Journal of Personality and Social Psychology, 45*, 1347–1354.

Lecrubier, Y., & Weiller, E. (1997). Comorbidities in social phobia. *International Clinical Psychopharmacology, 12*(suppl 6), S17–S21.

Ledley, D. R., & Heimberg, R. G. (2005). Social anxiety disorder. In M. M. Antony, D. R. Ledley, & R. G. Heimberg (Eds.), *Improving outcomes and preventing relapse in cognitive behavioral therapy* (pp. 38–76). New York: Guilford.

Ledley, D. R., Huppert, J. D., Foa, E. B., Davidson, J. R. T., Keefe, F. J., & Potts, N. L. S. (2005). The impact of depressive symptoms on the treatment of generalized social anxiety disorder. *Depression and Anxiety, 22*, 161–167.

Ledley, D. R., Storch, E. A., Coles, M. E., Heimberg, R. G., Moser, J., & Bravata, E. A. (2006). The relationship between childhood teasing and later interpersonal functioning. *Journal of Psychopathology and Behavioral Assessment, 28*, 33–40.

Leung, A. W., & Heimberg, R. G. (1996). Homework compliance, perceptions of control, and outcome of cognitive-behavioral treatment of social phobia. *Behaviour Research and Therapy, 34*, 423–432.

Lieb, R., Wittchen, H. U., Hofler, M., Fuetsch, M., Stein, M. B., & Merikangas, K. R. (2000). Parental psychopathology, parenting styles, and the risk of social phobia in offspring. *Archives of General Psychiatry, 57*, 859–866.

Liebowitz, M. (1987). Social phobia. *Modern Problems of Pharmacopsychiatry, 22*, 141–173.

Liebowitz, M. R., Gelenberg, A. J., & Munjack, D. (2005). Venlafaxine extended release vs. placebo and paroxetine in social anxiety disorder. *Archives of General Psychiatry, 62*, 190–198.

Liebowitz, M. R., Gorman, J. M., Fyer, A. J., & Klein, D. F. (1985). Social phobia: Review of a neglected anxiety disorder. *Archives of General Psychiatry, 42*, 729–736.

Liebowitz, M. R., Heimberg, R. G., Schneier, F. R., Hope, D. A., Davies, S., Holt, C. S., et al. (1999). Cognitive-behavioral group therapy versus phenelzine in social phobia: Long term outcome. *Depression and Anxiety, 10*, 89–98.

Liebowitz, M. R., Mangano, R. M., Bradwejn, J., & Asnis, G. (2005). A randomized controlled trial of venlafaxine extended release in generalized social anxiety disorder. *Journal of Clinical Psychiatry, 66*, 238–247.

Lowry-Webster, H. M., Barrett, P. M., & Dadds, M. R. (2001) A universal prevention trial of anxiety and depressive symptomatology in childhood: Preliminary data from an Australian study. *Behaviour Change, 18*, 36–50.

Lucas, R. A., & Telch, M. J. (1993, November). *Group versus individual treatment of social phobia.* Paper presented at the annual meeting of the Association for Advancement of Behavior Therapy, Atlanta, GA.

Lucock, M. P., & Salkovskis, P. M. (1988). Cognitive factors in social anxiety and its treatment. *Behaviour Research and Therapy, 26*, 297–302.

Lundh, L. G., & Öst, L. -G. (1996a). Recognition bias for critical faces in social phobics. *Behaviour Research and Therapy, 34*, 787–794.

Lundh, L. G., & Öst, L. -G. (1996b). Stroop interference, self-focus, and perfectionism in social phobics. *Personality and Individual Differences, 20*, 725–731.

Lundh, L. G., & Öst, L. -G. (1997). Explicit and implicit memory bias in social phobia: The role of subdiagnostic type. *Behaviour Research and Therapy, 35*, 305–317.

Magee, W. J. (1999). Effects of negative life experiences on phobia onset. *Social Psychiatry and Psychiatric Epidemiology, 34,* 343–351.

Magee, W. J., Eaton, W. W., Wittchen, H. -U., McGonagle, K. A., & Kessler, R. C. (1996). Agoraphobia, simple phobia, and social phobia in the National Comorbidity Survey. *Archives of General Psychiatry, 53,* 159–168.

Maidenberg, E., Chen, E., Craske, M., Bohn, P., & Bystritsky, A. (1996). Specificity of attentional bias in panic disorder and social phobia. *Journal of Anxiety Disorders, 10,* 529–541.

Mannuzza, S., Schneier, F. R., Chapman, T. F., Liebowitz, M. R., Klein, D. F., & Fyer, A. J. (1995). Generalized social phobia: Reliability and validity. *Archives of General Psychiatry, 52,* 230–237.

Mansell, W., Clark, D. M., Ehlers, A., & Chen, Y. -P. (1999). Social anxiety and attention away from emotional faces. *Cognition and Emotion, 13,* 673–690.

Mansell, W., Ehlers, A., Clark, D. M., & Chen, Y. (2002). Attention to positive and negative social-evaluative words: Investigating the effects of social anxiety, trait anxiety, and social threat. *Anxiety, Stress, and Coping, 15,* 19–29.

Marks, I. M., & Gelder, M. G. (1966). Different ages of onset in varieties of social phobia. *American Journal of Psychiatry, 123,* 218–221.

Masia-Warner, C., Storch, E. A., Pincus, D. B., Klein, R. G., Heimberg, R. G., & Liebowitz, M. R. (2003). The Liebowitz Social Anxiety Scale for Children and Adolescents: An initial psychometric investigations. *Journal of the American Academy of Child and Adolescent Psychiatry, 42,* 1076–1084.

Mathew, S. J., Coplan, J. D., & Gorman, J. M. (2001). Neurobiological mechanisms of social anxiety disorder. *American Journal of Psychiatry, 158,* 1558–1567.

Mattia, J. I., Heimberg, R. G., & Hope, D. A. (1993). The revised Stroop color-naming task in social phobics. *Behaviour Research and Therapy, 31,* 305–313.

Mattick, R. P., & Clarke, J. C. (1998). Development and validation of measures of social phobia scrutiny fear and social interaction anxiety. *Behaviour Research and Therapy, 36,* 455–470.

McCabe, R. E., Antony, M. M., Summerfeldt, L. J., Liss, A., & Swinson, R. P. (2003). Preliminary examination of the relationship between anxiety disorders in adults and self-reported history of teasing or bullying experiences. *Cognitive Behaviour Therapy, 32,* 187–193.

Meleshko, K. A., & Alden, L. E. (1993). Anxiety and self-disclosure: Toward a motivational model. *Journal of Personality and Social Psychology, 64,* 1000–1009.

Mennin, D. S., Fresco, D. M., Heimberg, R. G., Schneier, F. R., Davies, S. O., & Liebowitz, M. R. (2002). Screening for social anxiety disorder in the clinical setting: Using the Liebowitz Social Anxiety Scale. *Journal of Anxiety Disorders, 16,* 661–673.

Mick, M. A., & Telch, M. J. (1998). Social anxiety and history of behavioral inhibition in young adults. *Journal of Anxiety Disorders, 12,* 1–20.

Mickelson, K. D., Kessler, R. C., & Shaver, P. R. (1997). Adult attachment in a nationally representative sample. *Journal of Personality and Social Psychology, 73,* 1092–1106.

Morris, T. L. (2004). Diagnosis of social anxiety disorder in children. In B. Bandelow & D.Stein (Eds.), *Social anxiety disorder—More than shyness* (pp. 75–91). New York: Marcel Dekker.

Muris, P., Merckelbach, H., Wessel, I., & van deVen, M. (1999). Psychopathological correlates of self-reported behavioural inhibition in normal children. *Behaviour Research and Therapy, 37,* 575–584.

Murphy, R., Hirsch, C. R., Mathews, A., Smith, K., & Clark, D. M. (2005, July). *Training a benign interpretation bias in a high socially anxious population.* Paper presented at annual meeting of the British Association for Behavioural and Cognitive Psychotherapy, Canterbury, England.

Murray, L., Cooper, P., Cresswell, C., Schofield, E., & Sack, C. (2007). The effects of maternal social phobia on mother-infant interactions and infant social responsiveness. *Journal of Child Psychology and Psychiatry, 48,* 45–52.

Musa, C., Lépine, J. -P., Clark, D. M., Mansell, W., & Ehlers, A. (2003). Selective attention in social phobia and the moderating effect of a concurrent depressive disorder. *Behaviour Research and Therapy, 41,* 1043–1054.

O'Banion, K., & Arkowitz, H. (1977). Social anxiety and selective memory for affective information about the self. *Social Behavior and Personality, 5,* 321–328.

Olfson, M., Guardino, M., Struening, E., Schneier, F. R., Hellman, F., & Klein, D. F. (2000). Barriers to treatment of social anxiety. *American Journal of Psychiatry, 157,* 521–527.

Papsdorf, M. P., & Alden, L. E. (1998). Mediators of social rejection in socially anxious individuals. *Journal of Research in Personality, 32,* 351–369.

Pérez-López, J. R., & Woody, S. R. (2001). Memory for facial expressions in social phobia. *Behaviour Research and Therapy*, *39*, 967–975.

Perowne, S., & Mansell, W. (2002). Social anxiety, self-focused attention, and the discrimination of negative, neutral and positive audience members by their non-verbal behaviours. *Behavioural and Cognitive Psychotherapy*, *30*, 11–23.

Pineles, S. L., & Mineka, S. (2005). Attentional bias to internal and external sources of potential threat in social anxiety. *Journal of Abnormal Psychology*, *114*, 314–318.

Pishyar, R., Harris, L. M., & Menzies, R. G. (2004). Attentional bias for words and faces in social anxiety. *Anxiety, Stress, and Coping*, *17*, 23–36.

Potts, N. L. S., Book, S., & Davidson, J. R. T. (1996). The neurobiology of social phobia. *International Clinical Psychopharmacology*, *11*(suppl. 3) 43–48.

Rapee, R. M., & Hayman, K. (1996). The effects of video feedback on the self-evaluation of performance in socially anxious subjects. *Behaviour Research and Therapy*, *34*, 315–322.

Rapee, R. M., & Lim, L. (1992). Discrepancy between self- and observer ratings of performance in social phobics. *Journal of Abnormal Psychology*, *101*, 728–731.

Rapee, R. M., McCallum, S. L., Melville, L. F., Ravenscroft, H., & Rodney, J. M. (1994). Memory bias in social phobia. *Behaviour Research and Therapy*, *32*, 89–99.

Rodebaugh, T. L. (2004). I might look OK, but I'm still doubtful, anxious, and avoidant: The mixed effects of enhanced video feedback on social anxiety symptoms. *Behaviour Research and Therapy*, *42*, 1435–1451.

Rodebaugh, T. L., & Rapee, R. M. (2005). Those who think they look worst respond best: Self-observer discrepancy predicts response to video feedback following a speech task. *Cognitive Therapy and Research*, *29*, 705–715.

Rodebaugh, T. L., Woods, C. M., Thissen, D. M., Heimberg, R. G., Chambless, D. L., & Rapee, R. M. (2004). More information from fewer questions: The factor structure and item properties of the original and Brief Fear of Negative Evaluation Scale. *Psychological Assessment*, *16*, 169–181.

Rose, D. T., & Abramson, L. Y. (1992). Developmental predictors of depressive cognitive style: Research and theory. In D. Chicetti, & S. Toth (Eds.), *Rochester symposium of developmental psychopathology* (Vol. IV, pp. 323–349). Rochester, NY: University of Rochester Press.

Rosenbaum, J. F., Biederman, J., Bolduc, E. A., & Hirshfeld, D. R. (1992). Comorbidity of parental anxiety disorders as risk for childhood-onset anxiety in inhibited children. *American Journal of Psychiatry*, *149*, 475–481.

Rosenbaum, J. F., Biederman, J., Hirshfeld, D. R., Bolduc, E. A., & Chaloff, J. (1991). Behavioral inhibition in childhood: A possible precursor to panic disorder or social phobia. *Journal of Clinical Psychiatry*, *52*(Suppl.), 5–9.

Roth, D. A., Antony, M. M., & Swinson, R. P. (2001). Interpretations for anxiety symptoms in social phobia. *Behaviour Research and Therapy*, *39*, 129–138.

Roth, D. A., Coles, M., & Heimberg, R. G. (2002). The relationship between memories for childhood teasing and anxiety and depression in adulthood. *Journal of Anxiety Disorders*, *16*, 151–166.

Rubin, K. H., & Mills, R. S. L. (1988). The many faces of social isolation in childhood. *Journal of Consulting and Clinical Psychology*, *56*, 916–924.

Safren, S. A., Heimberg, R. G., Brown, E. J., & Holle, C. (1997). Quality of life in social phobia. *Depression and Anxiety*, *4*, 126–133.

Saunders, J. B., Aasland, O. G., Babor, T. F., de la Fuente, J. R., & Grant, M. (1993). Development of the Alcohol Use Disorders Identification Test (AUDIT): WHO collaborative project on early detection of persons with harmful alcohol consumption—II. *Addiction*, *88*, 791–804.

Schlette, P., Brändström, S., Eisemann, M., Sigvardsson, S., Nylander P.-O., Adolfsson, R., et al. (1998). Perceived parental rearing behaviours and temperament and character in healthy adults. *Personality and Individual Differences*, *24*, 661–668.

Schmidt, N. B., & Vasey, M. (2000). Primary prevention of psychopathology in a high risk youth population. *New Research in Mental Health*, *14*, 267–270.

Schmidt, N. B., & Vasey, M. (2002). Primary prevention of psychopathology in a high risk youth population. *New Research in Mental Health*, *15*, 203–209.

Schneier, F. R., Heckelman, L. R., Garfinkel, R., Campeas, R., Fallon, B. A., Gitow, A., et al. (1994). Functional impairment in social phobia. *Journal of Clinical Psychiatry*, *55*, 322–331.

Schneier, F. R., Johnson, J., Hornig, C. D., Liebowitz, M. R., & Weissman, M. M. (1992). Social phobia: Comorbidity and morbidity in an epidemiologic sample. *Archives of General Psychiatry*, *49*, 282–288.

Schneier, F. R., Liebowitz, M. R., Abi-Dargham, A., Zea-Ponce, Y., Lin, S-H, & Luruelle, M. (2000). Low dopamine D2 receptor binding potential in social phobia. *American Journal of Psychiatry*, *157*, 457–459.

Schneier, F. R., Martin, L. Y., Leibowitz, M. R., Gorman, J. M., & Fyer, A. J. (1989). Alcohol abuse in social phobia. *Journal of Anxiety Disorders*, *3*, 15–23.

Schwartz, C. E., Snidman, N., & Kagan, J. (1999). Adolescent social anxiety as an outcome of inhibited temperament in childhood. *Journal of the American Academy of Child and Adolescent Psychiatry*, *38*, 1008–1015.

Silverman, W. K., & Albano, A-M. (2005). *Anxiety Disorders Interview Schedule (ADIS-IV), Child/Parent Version*. New York: Oxford University Press.

Simpson, H. B., Schneier, F. R., Campeas, R., Marshall, R. D., Fallon, B. A., Davies, S., et al. (1998). Imipramine in the treatment of social phobia. *Journal of Clinical Psychopharmacology*, *18*, 132–135.

Spence, S. H., Donovan, C., & Brechman-Toussaint, M. (2000). The treatment of childhood social phobia: The effectiveness of a social skills training-based cognitive-behavioural intervention with and without parental involvement. *Journal of Child Psychology and Psychiatry and Allied Disciplines*, *41*, 713–726.

Sposari, J. A., & Rapee, R. M. (2007). Attentional bias toward facial stimuli under conditions of social threat in socially phobic and nonclinical participants. *Cognitive Therapy and Research*, *31*, 23–37.

Stangier, U., Heidenreich, T., Peitz, M., Lauterbach, W., & Clark, D. M. (2003). Cognitive therapy for social phobia: Individual versus group treatment. *Behaviour Research and Therapy*, *41*, 991–1007.

Stein, D. J., & Stahl, S. (2000). Serotonin and anxiety: Current models. *International Clinical Psychopharmacology*, *15*(Suppl. 2), S1–S6.

Stein, M. B. (1997). Phenomenology and epidemiology of social phobia. *International Clinical Psychopharmacology*, *12*(Suppl. 6), S23–S26.

Stein, M. B., Chartier, M. J., Hazen, A. L., Kozak, M. V., Tancer, M. E., Lander, S., et al. (1998). A direct interview family study of generalized social phobia, *American Journal of Psychiatry*, *155*, 90–97.

Stein, M. B., Fyer, A. J., Davidson, J. R. T., Pollack, M. H., & Wiita, B. (1999). Fluvoxamine treatment of social phobia (social anxiety disorder): A double-blind placebo-controlled study. *American Journal of Psychiatry*, *156*, 756–760.

Stein, M. B., Goldin, P. R., Sareen, J., Eyler Zorrilla, L. T., & Brown, G. G. (2002). Increased amygdala activation to angry and contemptuous faces in gen-eralized social phobia. *Archives of General Psychiatry, 59*, 1027–1034.

Stein, M. B., Heuser, I. J., Juncos, J. L., & Uhde, T. W. (1990). Anxiety disorders in patients with Parkinson's disease. *American Journal of Psychiatry*, *147*, 217–220.

Stein, M. B., & Kean, Y. (2000). Disability and quality of life in social phobia: Epidemiologic findings. *American Journal of Psychiatry*, *157*, 1606–1613.

Stopa, L., & Clark, D. M. (1993). Cognitive processes in social phobia. *Behaviour Research and Therapy*, *31*, 255–267.

Stopa, L., & Clark, D. M. (2000). Social phobia and interpretation of social events. *Behaviour Research and Therapy*, *38*, 273–283.

Storch, E. A., Roth, D., Coles, M. E., Heimberg, R. G., Bravata, E. A., & Moser, J. (2004). The measurement and impact of childhood teasing in a sample of young adults. *Journal of Anxiety Disorders*, *18*, 681–694.

Strauss, C. C., Lahey, B. B., Frick, P., Frame, C. L., & Hynd, G. W. (1988). Peer social status of children with social anxiety disorders. *Journal of Consulting and Clinical Psychology*, *56*, 137–141.

Tilhonen, J., Kuikka, J., Bergstrom, K., Lepola, U., Koponen, H., & Leinonen, E. (1997). Dopamine reuptake site densities in patients with social phobia. *American Journal of Psychiatry*, *154*, 239–242.

Tillfors, M. (2004). Why do some individuals develop social phobia? A review with emphasis on the neuro-biological influences. *Nordic Journal of Psychiatry*, *58*, 267–276.

Tillfors, M., Furmark, T., Ekselius, L., & Fredrikson, M. (2001). Social phobia and avoidant personality disorder as related to parental history of social anxiety: A general population study. *Behaviour Research and Therapy*, *39*, 289–298.

Turk, C. L., Heimberg, R. G., Luterek, J. A., Mennin, D. S., & Fresco, D. M. (2005). Emotion dysregulation in generalized anxiety disorder: A comparison with social anxiety disorder. *Cognitive Therapy and Research*, *29*, 89–106.

Turner, S. M., Beidel, D. C., Dancu, C. V., & Stanley, M. A. (1989). An empirically derived inventory to measure social fears and anxiety: The Social Phobia and Anxiety Inventory. *Psychological Assessment*, *1*, 35–40.

Veljaca, K., & Rapee, R. M. (1998). Detection of negative and positive audience behaviours by socially anxious subjects. *Behaviour Research and Therapy*, *36*, 311–321.

Vernberg, E. M., Abwender, D. A., Ewell, K. K., & Beery, S. H. (1992). Social anxiety and peer relationships in early adolescence: A prospective analysis. *Journal of Clinical Child Psychology, 21,* 189–196.

Vriends, N., Becker, E. S., Meyer, A., Michael, T., & Margraf, J. (2007). Subtypes of social phobia: Are they of any use? *Journal of Anxiety Disorders, 21,* 59–75.

Walker, J. (2003, March). *Bringing the interpersonal into cognitive-behavior therapy for social anxiety disorder.* Paper presented at the annual meeting of the Anxiety Disorders Association of America, Toronto, Ontario, Canada.

Wallace, S. T., & Alden, L. E. (1997). Social phobia and positive social events: The price of success. *Journal of Abnormal Psychology, 106,* 416–424.

Weeks, J. W., Heimberg, R. G., Fresco, D. M., Hart, T. A., Turk, C. L., Schnieier, F. R., et al. (2005). Empirical validation and psychometric evaluation of the Brief Fear of Negative Evaluation Scale in patients with social anxiety disorder. *Psychological Assessment, 17,* 179–190.

Weinstock, L. S. (1999). Gender differences in the presentation and management of social anxiety disorder. *Journal of Clinical Psychiatry, 60*(Suppl. 9), 9–13.

Wells, A., Clark, D. M., & Ahmad, S. (1998). How do I look with my mind's eye? Perspective taking in social phobic imagery. *Behaviour Research and Therapy, 36,* 631–634.

Wells, A., Clark, D. M., Salkovskis, P., Ludgate, J., Hackmann, A., & Gelder, M. (1995). Social phobia: The role of in-situation safety behaviors in maintaining anxiety and negative beliefs. *Behavior Therapy, 26,* 153–161.

Wells, A., & Papageorgiou, C. (1999). The observer perspective: Biased imagery in social phobia, agoraphobia, and blood/injury phobia. *Behaviour Research and Therapy, 37,* 653–658.

Wenzel, A. (2002). Characteristics of close relationships in individuals with social phobia: A preliminary comparison with nonanxious individuals. In J. H. Harvey & A. Wenzel (Eds.), *Maintaining and enhancing close relationships: A clinician's guide* (pp. 199–213). Mahwah, NJ: Lawrence Erlbaum.

Wenzel, A., & Holt, C. S. (2002). Memory bias against threat in social phobia. *British Journal of Clinical Psychology, 41,* 73–79.

Wittchen, H. -U., Stein, M. B., & Kessler, R. C. (1999). Social fears and social phobia in a community sample of adolescents and young adults: Prevalence, risk factors and co-morbidity. *Psychological Medicine, 29,* 309–323.

Woody, S. R., Chambless, D. L., & Glass, C. R. (1997). Self-focused attention in the treatment of social phobia. *Behaviour Research and Therapy, 35,* 117–129.

Zaider, T., Heimberg, R. G., Roth, D. A., Hope, D. A., & Turk, C. L. (2003, November). *Individual CBT for social anxiety disorder: Preliminary findings.* Paper presented at the annual meeting of the Association for Advancement of Behavior Therapy, Boston, MA.

Chapter 7

Posttraumatic Stress Disorder

PATRICIA A. RESICK, CANDICE M. MONSON, AND SHIREEN L. RIZVI

Description of Disorder

The study of Posttraumatic Stress Disorder (PTSD) began in 1980 with the introduction of the disorder into the psychological nomenclature following the Vietnam War, and in response to the women's movement, which began to highlight the psychological aftermath of rape, domestic violence, and child sexual abuse. Over the past three decades, study of the disorder has evolved through a large body of research that has established that the disorder exists and that it has associated biological, cognitive, and behavioral characteristics, and is highly treatable. For students of psychopathology, it should be pointed out that PTSD contrasts to most other disorders in that PTSD is a disorder of nonrecovery, whereas most other disorders have a developmental course. Posttraumatic Stress Disorder is one of the few disorders in which researchers and clinicians can pinpoint the genesis of the disorder and can study risk and resilience factors as people grapple with some of life's worst events. Prospective studies can be mounted from the time of a traumatic event, and in some cases before exposure, to study how people react and recover. The strongest emotions, biological reactions, thoughts, and behavioral escape-and-avoidance behaviors occur during and soon after the traumatic event. Those who are eventually diagnosed with PTSD do not typically develop greater symptoms over time—rather, they stall out in their recovery—while those who do not go on to have PTSD continue to recover over the months after the event has occurred (Gutner, Rizvi, Monson, & Resick, 2006; Rothbaum, Foa, Riggs, & Walsh, 1992). This chapter will provide an overview of this recovery process with regard to symptoms comprising the disorder, its epidemiology, the biological, cognitive, emotional, and behavioral components of the disorder, and comorbidity factors, assessment, and treatment.

DESCRIPTION OF SYMPTOMS AND CRITERIA

Posttraumatic Stress Disorder (PTSD) and Acute Stress Disorder are the only disorders in our current classification system that require an identifiable external event as a precursor to its existence. According to the *Diagnostic and Statistical Manual of Mental Disorders*, 4th edition (*DSM-IV*; American Psychiatric Association, 1994) and the *DSM-IV Text Revision* (*DSM-IV-TR*; American Psychiatric Association, 2000), in order for a diagnosis of PTSD to be considered, an individual must have experienced, witnessed, or otherwise been confronted with news of a traumatic event. An event is considered traumatic if it involved actual or threatened death, serious injury, or threat to physical integrity. Furthermore, at the time of the event, the individual must have responded with intense fear, helplessness, or horror. Thus, Criterion A for PTSD requires that an individual must have experienced strong negative affect in response to a traumatic event that involved death or serious injury to self or others.

The 17 symptoms of PTSD fall into three broad domains or clusters: reexperiencing symptoms (Criterion B), avoidance and numbing symptoms (Criterion C), and physiological hyperarousal (Criterion D). The five reexperiencing symptoms include persistent and distressing recollections of the trauma through intrusive memories, nightmares, or flashbacks. These recollections are often experienced as intrusive (i.e., out of the individual's control), spontaneous (i.e., without warning, or seemingly "out of the blue"), and repetitive. Upon exposure to the cues that evoke the trauma, the individual may experience intense psychological responses (e.g., extreme distress, terror) and/or physiological responses (e.g., rapid heart rate, perspiration, rapid or shallow breathing). In order to meet criteria for a diagnosis of PTSD, an individual must exhibit at least one Criterion B symptom.

The seven avoidance and numbing symptoms that comprise Criterion C, of which the individual must exhibit three for a diagnosis, include efforts to avoid thinking or talking about the event, efforts to avoid places or situations that are reminiscent of the event, inability to recall a part of what happened, diminished interest in activities or people since the trauma, feeling cut off or detached from others, feeling as though the future will be cut short, and experiencing a restricted range of affect, including both positive and negative emotions (i.e., blunting). These symptoms reflect strategies that individuals use in order to reduce coming into contact with events, places, thoughts, or emotions that remind them of the traumatic event.

Finally, Criterion D includes five symptoms of physiological arousal, of which an individual must experience at least two in order to meet criteria for a diagnosis of PTSD. These symptoms include sleep difficulties, concentration impairment, anger or irritability, hypervigilance, and exaggerated startle response. Although somewhat difficult to assess, especially in cases where the trauma occurred in the distant past or in the presence of a comorbid mood disorder, these symptoms can only have been present in the aftermath of the traumatic event.

This collection of symptoms from the three clusters must be present concurrently for at least 1 month in order to receive a diagnosis of PTSD, and they must be perceived as distressing or causing functional impairment. (Acute Stress Disorder is often the diagnosis given for symptoms that persist for less than a month following a particularly significant stressor or trauma.) Further specifiers of "Acute" and "Chronic" are based on the total duration of symptoms. Acute PTSD refers to symptom duration of less than 3 months, whereas Chronic PTSD refers to symptom duration of greater than 3 months. Furthermore, a diagnosis of PTSD with Delayed Onset can be made in cases in which the onset of the symptoms did not occur until at least 6 months after the traumatic event. Cases of true delayed onset are extremely rare and are more likely to occur as reactivation or exacerbation of prior symptoms (Andrews, Brewin, Philpott, & Stewart, 2007). That is, it is highly unlikely that an individual will be completely symptom-free following a trauma only to be diagnosed with PTSD at a later time.

Although not part of the *DSM-IV* diagnostic criteria, there are a number of associated features of PTSD that are worthy of mention and should be included in standardized assessments because of their high frequency of occurrence. Such features include feelings of guilt and shame surrounding the event, dissociative experiences (e.g., periods of derealization, depersonalization), and somatic complaints as a result of physical injury suffered during the trauma, somatic presentations, or exacerbations of preexisting pain problems (Shipherd et al., 2007). Guilt and shame could be related to a myriad of factors concerning the trauma, including humiliation that the event occurred (often related to hesitation to disclose, as in the case of sexual assault), guilt about surviving a situation when others did not (survivor guilt), feeling as though one could have done more to prevent the trauma from occurring in the first place, or shame about how one behaved or physiological responses *during* the event.

CASE EXAMPLE

Anne was a 30-year-old woman who presented for treatment wanting help to manage "anger and anxiety." She lived alone and, with the exception of two female friends, had no significant social relationships. She further reported that she had not had any romantic relationships during her adult life. She had been unemployed for the past 3 months, having been fired from her last job due to "anger problems." She was currently supporting herself with savings, which were quickly running out; however, she expressed ambivalence about finding another job because she stated she "didn't like being around most people."

During a standard intake interview, Anne, with much trepidation, acknowledged that she had been raped more than 10 years earlier. She stated that she had not told anyone about this previously. The rape occurred when she was out on a first date with a man that she knew casually from one of her college classes. After dinner, he suggested a walk on the beach, during which he became sexually suggestive and began to fondle her. Anne reported that she initially resisted his advances but he became more aggressive and eventually physically restrained her, pinning her down with his body and covering her mouth with his hand. Anne remarked that she "shut down" and felt numb all over during the rape. Immediately afterward, the man told her that she just got what she wanted and that if she told anyone about what occurred, he would deny it. He further said that since he was a popular person on campus, everyone would believe him and think that she was "easy." Anne remembered returning to her dormitory room, where she immediately showered and then told everyone that she wasn't feeling well so that she could stay alone in her room for several days.

Anne reported that since then she had thought about the rape every day, often with perseveration about how she might have prevented it or how she might get revenge against the rapist. She stated that she frequently had nightmares and would wake up in a sweat. In addition, she frequently exhibited a generalized response of anger toward men and reported feeling suspicious of all men, with only a few exceptions. She stated that she felt like "men were only after one thing" and were "manipulators and liars." Because of this, Anne reported that she avoided all social situations because she didn't want to interact with men on a social level. When she couldn't avoid it (e.g., family weddings), she would feel extreme anxiety and would often respond to fairly innocuous comments (e.g., "you look nice tonight") with an outburst of anger and nastiness. She reported that she had gained the reputation of being the black sheep of the family as a result. She further stated that the rape occurred on a beach while on a resort vacation with her family and that she had not been to a beach since because she feared it would bring up memories too intense to manage.

Anne reported that prior to the rape she had had good peer relationships, and stated that she had many life goals, including a career in journalism. She stated that after the rape she lost interest in her goals and in being with others, and barely graduated from college. She reported that she spent most of her time alone. Anne described feeling angry a good portion of the day and said that she felt like she had a "short fuse"; many things irritated her that wouldn't irritate others. Throughout her adult life she held a string of temporary jobs, mostly as a receptionist, and would often get fired due to complaints from customers that she was rude. She stated that she often only slept 3 to 4 hours a night and would wake up feeling frightened from her nightmares. When this occurred, she said she would go around her apartment to check the locks on the windows and doors because she felt unsafe and was worried that an intruder would break in. She stated that she often had intrusive images of the rapist's face and when this happened, she would have paniclike symptoms and be "filled with rage and self-loathing."

BRIEF HISTORY

Posttraumatic Stress Disorder was added to the *DSM* in its third edition, published in 1980. Prior to this publication, the condition we now know as PTSD went by many names, such as "Traumatic Neurosis," "Gross Stress Reaction," "War Neurosis," and "Combat Fatigue" (Monson, Friedman, & La Bash, 2007). Following the return of thousands of veterans from Vietnam, many of whom exhibited difficulties adjusting to civilian life following their experience, along with the women's movement, which heightened consciousness of the effects of sexual and physical victimization (e.g., Rape Trauma Syndrome, Battered Women's Syndrome), the modern diagnosis became known as PTSD. Despite the fact that most research and attention has been given to PTSD in the United States and Europe, there is growing appreciation of the cultural implications of the development and maintenance of PTSD, because the overwhelming majority of wars, violence, and natural disasters occur in the developing world (Keane, Brief, Pratt, & Miller, 2007).

EPIDEMIOLOGY

Results from several epidemiological studies indicate that experiencing a traumatic event in one's life is the rule rather than the exception. For example, in an examination of the prevalence and effects of trauma in individuals from the National Comorbidity

Survey, Kessler, Sonnega, Bromet, Hughes, and Nelson (1995) found that approximately 60.7% of men and 51.2% of women had experienced at least one trauma in their lifetime. In comparison with women, men were more likely to report experiencing a physical attack, being threatened with a weapon, being in an accident, or witnessing a trauma. Women were more likely to report rape, molestation, neglect, or physical abuse. In a random probability sample of 4,008 American women, Resnick, Kilpatrick, Dansky, Saunders, and Best (1993) found that 69% of women endorsed experiencing at least one trauma in their lifetime. Frequencies of type of stressor experienced included: completed rape (32%), other sexual assault (31%), physical assault (39%), homicide of family member or friend (22%), any crime victimization (26%), and other trauma (e.g., natural and manmade disasters, accidents [9%]). Furthermore, Norris (1992) has highlighted the significance of motor vehicle accidents (MVAs) in terms of both prevalence and rates of PTSD. Twenty-three percent of the population is estimated to experience at least one MVA in their lifetime and the incidence of PTSD from MVA is estimated at 12%.

It's important to note that most individuals exhibit PTSD symptoms immediately following trauma exposure. For example, after 2 weeks following a sexual assault, 80% to 94% of victims would meet criteria for PTSD if not for the duration requirement (Gutner et al., 2006; Rothbaum & Foa, 1993). However, 3 months after the rape, the rates of PTSD drop to approximately 50% (Gutner et al., 2006; Rothbaum & Foa, 1993). These statistics suggest that perhaps the important question to ask is not: "Who develops PTSD?" but rather "Who *fails to recover* following a traumatic event?" Different events considered to be more heterogenous in terms of severity and less personal—such as accidents or natural disasters—are associated with lower rates of PTSD (Kessler et al., 1995) than rape (see Epidemiology in the following).

In terms of prevalence, epidemiological studies suggest that less than 7% of the population will have had PTSD at some point in their lifetime. For example, in the recent National Comorbidity Survey Replication study (Kessler et al., 2005), lifetime prevalence rates of PTSD were reported at 6.8% and a 12-month prevalence of 3.6% for the general U.S. population. Rates of PTSD, however, are significantly higher in at-risk populations such as war veterans. The largest and most frequently cited study of combat veterans is the National Vietnam Veterans Readjustment Study (NVVRS; Kulka et al., 1990). This study was mandated by the U.S. Congress in 1983 for the purpose of assessing PTSD and other psychological sequelae following service in the Vietnam War.

The NVVRS included interviews and assessments with 1,632 Vietnam theater veterans, 730 Vietnam-era veterans who were not in combat, and 668 nonveteran controls for a total of over 3,000 interviews. Results indicate that 31% of male veterans and 27% of female veterans had a diagnosis of PTSD at some point after the war. Additionally, at the time of assessment, 15% of male and 9% of female veterans met criteria for PTSD more than a decade after the end of the war. Although not everyone who was exposed to the horrors of the Vietnam War developed PTSD, a significant minority of individuals did, suggesting that some Criterion A events, such as combat exposure, may be more directly linked to subsequent development of PTSD.

The NVVRS is not without its critics. Some have suggested that the NVVRS overestimated the rates of PTSD. In response to this criticism, the data were recently reevaluated using very strict criteria. Specifically, Criterion A combat events were only included if they could be verified as having occurred through historical records (Dohrenwend et al., 2006). Although rates of PTSD were lower than in the original study (18.7% of veterans met criteria for lifetime war-related PTSD and 9.1% still met criteria when assessed 11 to 12 years later), these results can be interpreted as very conservative estimates because there are a number of potential events that occurred that may not exist in historical accounts or were outside the narrow definition of combat (e.g., sexual assault, accidents, trauma to support personnel such as medical personnel or those involved in body handling). Dohrenwend and colleagues found a strong relationship between amount of combat exposure and rates of PTSD and very little evidence for falsification of events.

In contrast to the retrospective nature of the research on the effects of the Vietnam War, the recent wars in Iraq and Afghanistan have allowed for an ongoing assessment of PTSD and PTSD symptomatology in soldiers *during* the war. Studies by Hoge and colleagues (Hoge, Auchterlonie, & Milliken, 2006; Hoge, Castro, et al., 2004) indicate that the presence of mental health problems is significant following deployment, with estimates of up to 20% of individuals exceeding the cut-off score for likely PTSD by self report.

Additionally, the impact of recent large-scale manmade and natural disasters, such as the September 11, 2001, terrorist attacks, the Asian tsunami of December 2004, and Hurricane Katrina of August 2005, has been assessed in terms of large-scale population surveys. Although these studies typically do not use gold standard assessments to diagnose PTSD, they provide snapshot indexes of PTSD symptomatology in trauma-exposed communities.

A web-based survey of two thousand residents of New York City 1 to 2 months after the terrorist attacks found a prevalence rate of 11.2% "probable PTSD" (Schlenger et al., 2002). A phone survey of adult residents of Manhattan, also conducted 1 to 2 months after the event, found 7.5% of individuals to endorse symptoms suggestive of a PTSD diagnosis (Galea et al., 2002). This rate increased to 20% for individuals who lived in close proximity to the World Trade Center site.

A study of people affected by the Asian tsunami used a multistaged, cluster, population-based mental health survey (specifically, the Short-Form Health Survey [SF-36]) to assess outcomes. Participants were displaced and nondisplaced persons in the Phang Nga province of Thailand, where more than 5,000 individuals were confirmed dead. The researchers found that 12% of displaced persons and 7% of nondisplaced persons evidenced PTSD symptoms 8 weeks after the tsunami (van Griensven et al., 2006). A follow-up survey 9 months after the tsunami demonstrated that the percentage of individuals reporting PTSD symptomatology decreased to 7% of displaced persons and 3% of nondisplaced persons.

So far, research into the mental health effects of Hurricane Katrina has been limited. A web-based survey of more than one thousand residents of New Orleans conducted 6 months after the hurricane found nearly 20% endorsed symptoms consistent with a PTSD diagnosis, based on a self-report measure (Desalvo et al., 2007). Further, a Centers for Disease Control (CDC) study of firefighters and police officers in New Orleans at the time of the hurricane indicates that 22% of firefighters and 19% of police officers exhibit some PTSD symptoms 7 to 13 weeks later ("Health hazard evaluation," 2006).

Gender Differences. There appears to be a gender difference in rates of PTSD, with women nearly three times as likely to have a lifetime diagnosis (9.7% to 3.6%; Kessler et al., 2005). In Hoge et al.'s studies of men and women deployed to Iraq and Afghanistan, 23.6% of women reported mental health concerns compared with 18.6% of the men (Hoge et al., 2006). A recent meta-analysis of sex differences in risk for PTSD demonstrated that, consistent with the summarized data discussed previously, although females are more likely than males to meet criteria for PTSD, they are less likely to have experienced potentially traumatic events (Tolin & Foa, 2006). Moreover, even when type of trauma is controlled, women still appear to exhibit greater rates of PTSD, suggesting that risk of exposure to particular types of trauma only partially explains the differential PTSD rates in men and women A number of explanations for this difference have been offered, including biological, psychological, and sociocultural (Kimerling, Ouimette, & Wolfe, 2002).

In sum, epidemiological research on trauma and PTSD has consistently found that exposure to trauma is a common experience. Prevalence rates of PTSD in the general U.S. population are about 7% for a lifetime diagnosis, but increase substantially (up to 20 to 30%) when examining specific trauma-exposed groups. War veterans, rape victims, and victims of natural and manmade disasters have been the most frequently studied populations. Increasing attention by the research community to the effects of global events, as well as more sophisticated rapid assessment techniques, have allowed for a better understanding of the development and maintenance of PTSD symptomatology in trauma survivors.

Actual Dysfunction

PSYCHOBIOLOGY

A number of neurobiological systems have been implicated in the pathophysiology of PTSD, including alterations in the noradrenergic, hypothalamic-pituitary-adrenal (HPA) axis, GABA/glutamate, serotonin, and dopamine systems.

Noradrenergic System

Norepinephrine. A number of studies, using various methodologies, have provided compelling evidence for increased noradrenergic activity in traumatized humans with PTSD (e.g., Friedman & Southwick, 1995; Southwick et al., 1999; Yehuda et al., 1998). Heightened norepinephrine reactivity to pharmacological and behavioral challenge appears to be a more important marker of PTSD than high tonic or baseline levels of norepinephrine sampled at a single point in time (Blanchard, Kolb, Prins, Gates, & McCoy, 1991; McFall, Murburg, Ko, & Veith, 1990; Southwick et al., 1993). Moreover, the presence of comorbid depression appears to be an important moderator of the association between heightened noradrenergic output and PTSD. For example, Yehuda and colleagues (1998) found that combat veterans with PTSD but without comorbid depression had higher mean norepinephrine levels at nearly every time point compared with combat veterans with PTSD and comorbid depression, subjects with depression alone, and healthy controls.

Neuropeptide Y (NPY). Neuropeptide Y is an amino acid transmitter that inhibits the release of both norepinephrine and corticotrophin releasing factor (CRF; see the following). It is found in the peripheral sympathetic nervous system and in multiple stress-related brain regions, including the locus coeruleus, amygdala, hippocampus, periaquaductal gray, and prefrontal cortex (Heilig & Widerlöv, 1990). Neuropeptide Y is simultaneously released with norepinephrine during stress provocation and acts as an endogenous antiadrenergic, thereby having anxiolytic- and cognitive-enhancing effects.

Evidence of these effects is found in studies of Special Forces men undergoing military survival training involving high levels of uncontrollable stress. Morgan, Wang, and Southwick (2000) and Morgan et al. (2001) found a significant positive association between NPY release and superior performance in mock training situations, as well as a significant negative relationship between NPY and symptoms of dissociation. Compared with healthy controls, PTSD patients have also been found to exhibit low baseline levels of NPY and blunted NPY responses to yohimbine stimulation (Rasmusson et al., 2000).

Hypothalamic-Pituitary-Adrenal (HPA) Axis

Corticotropin Releasing Factor (CRF). Corticotropin releasing factor promotes the release of norepinephrine from the locus coeruleus as well as the release of corticotropin (ACTH) from the pituitary gland, which then promotes release of cortisol and other glucocorticoids from the adrenal cortex. Vietnam veterans with PTSD have been shown to have elevated resting levels of cerebrospinal fluid CRF (Baker et al., 1999; Bremner et al., 1997), and enhanced hypothalamic release of CRF (Yehuda, 2002).

Cortisol. Although excessive HPA dysregulation is consistently associated with trauma exposure and PTSD, there have been inconsistent results surrounding the nature of HPA dysfunction. Low urinary cortisol output has been found in male combat veterans and male and postmenopausal female Holocaust survivors. Conversely, high cortisol output has been found most consistently in premenopausal women and children with PTSD (e.g., Heim, Newport, & Heit, 2000; Lipschitz, Rasmusson, & Yehuda, 2003; Rasmusson, Vasek, & Lipschitz, 2004; Rasmusson, Vythilingam, & Morgan III, 2003; Young & Breslau, 2004). The inconsistency in these findings is likely related to other clinical and methodological factors associated with cortisol output and its measurement, including sex hormones, diagnostic comorbidity (especially depression), age of trauma exposure, substance use, medications, exercise, and ethnicity or genetic factors (Rasmusson et al., 2004).

Dehydroepiandrosterone (DHEA). Dehydroepiandrosterone is another adrenal steroid that is released in concert with cortisol in the face of stress. In the brain, DHEA may confer protective neurocognitive effects through its antiglucocorticoid properties. There has been one clinical study of DHEA in a sample of premenopausal women with PTSD (Rasmusson et al., 2003). In that study, they found an inverse relationship between DHEA reactivity and the severity of PTSD symptoms. A nonclinical study of the previously mentioned Special Forces soldiers undergoing intensive survival training also provides evidence of the possible protection that DHEA may confer in warding off the symptoms of PTSD. Morgan et al. (2004) found a negative relationship between the ratio of DHEAS (the sulfated version of DHEA) to cortisol and dissociation. They also found a positive correlation between the DHEAS/cortisol ratio and better behavioral performance in this sample.

Allotetrahydrodeoxycorticosterone/allopregnanolone. There have been a few studies on allotetrahydrodeoxycorticosterone and allopregnanolone in PTSD, which are neuroactive steroids that positively modulate the effects of GABA (see the following) and produce anxiolytic, sedative, and analgesic effects. In a study of premenopausal women with PTSD who were in the follicular phase of the menstrual cycle, CSF allopregnanolone levels in the PTSD subjects were less than 40% of those in the nontraumatized healthy subjects (Rasmusson, Pinna, & Paliwal, 2006). The allopregnanolone-to-DHEA ratio in these subjects was also negatively associated with reexperiencing and depressive symptoms in the PTSD participants (Rasmusson et al., 2006).

Glutamate and Gamma-Amino Butyric Acid (GABA)

Glutamate. Glutamate is the brain's primary excitatory neurotransmitter. In response to dangerous situations, glutamate is rapidly released and mediates nearly all fast excitatory point-to-point synaptic transmission in the brain. Although no studies on glutamate have been conducted with PTSD patients to date, a series of studies by Krystal et al., 1994, Krystal et al., 1998, and Krystal et al., 1999 provide support for the hypothesized role of glutamate in PTSD. These studies revealed that administration of the NMDA glutamate antagonist ketamine, which increases glutamate release, produced significant dose-dependent increases in dissociative symptoms often seen in patients with PTSD.

Gamma-Amino Butyric Acid (GABA). In contrast to glutamate, GABA is the brain's primary inhibitory neurotransmitter, which functions to counter excitatory glutamatergic synaptic transmission. At least two studies have found PTSD to be associated with decreased GABA levels. Bremner et al. (2000) found that benzodiazepine receptor density and/or affinity was reduced in the medial prefrontal cortex among patients with PTSD compared with controls, in a sample of accident victims. Vaiva and colleagues (2004) reported significantly lower plasma GABA levels in subjects who developed PTSD compared with subjects who did not.

Serotonin (5H-T)

Direct evidence of serotonin dysregulation in PTSD comes from clinical studies comparing patients with and without PTSD, at rest and upon neuroendocrine challenge. A resting state has been associated with decreased platelet serotonin uptake (Arora, Fichtner, O'Connor, & Crayton, 1993; Bremner, Southwick, & Charney, 1999), blunted prolactin response to d-fenfluramine (Davis, Clark, Kramer, Moeller, & Petty, 1999) and exaggerated panic/anxiety and heart rate reactions to a serotonergic probe (meta-chlorophenylpiperazine; Southwick et al., 1997), in individuals with PTSD compared with non-PTSD controls. Fitchner, Arora, O'Connor, and Crayton (1994) also found that PTSD patients who responded best to the medication paroxetine were those with the highest pretreatment platelet affinity for the drug.

Dopamine

Excessive dopamine release may play a role in the hyperarousal, hypervigilance, and brief psychotic states sometimes observed in individuals with PTSD. Surprisingly little research has focused on dopamine in comparison with the neurotransmitters previously reviewed. Elevated urinary and plasma dopamine concentrations have been found among PTSD subjects (Hamner & Diamond, 1993; Lemieux & Coe, 1995; Yehuda et al., 1994).

PSYCHOLOGY-COGNITION AND MEMORY

Posttraumatic Stress Disorder pathology is dominated by disruptions in cognition or memory, which is reflected in the *DSM-IV* criteria. The symptoms that comprise the B criterion include the hallmark symptoms of recurrent and intrusive recollections of the event, dreams about the event, or flashbacks. Within the C criterion, there are items about amnesia for the event, avoidance of trauma-related thoughts and images, and appraisals of having a foreshortened future. The D arousal criterion includes difficulty concentrating, which could reflect problems of attention, as well as arousal. Theorists and researchers have noted that traumatized people have problems both remembering and problems forgetting traumatic events, and that cognitive processes feature prominently in individuals' attempts to cope with intrusive memories and emotions.

Cognitions can be considered as cognitive processes or cognitive content. Cognitive processes include cognitive attempts to cope with intrusive recollections of the event (e.g., thought suppression, overaccommodation) or attentional bias to direct attention to potential danger cues. Cognitive content includes specific beliefs that become maladaptive ("Because one person assaulted me, that means no one can be trusted") or the outcome of cognitive or memory processes such as amnesia for the event, or fragmented memory. Most recent theories of PTSD have incorporated cognition along with considerations of arousal, emotions, and avoidance (Cahill & Foa, 2007). Some theorists have focused specifically on memory processes in PTSD (Brewin, 2007; Brewin, Dalgleish, & Joseph, 1996; Dalgleish, 2004).

Theories and Cognitive Processes

The study of memory in PTSD began with the observations of flashbacks, intrusive memories, amnesia, and fragmented memory among those with PTSD. In order to account for some of these phenomena, as well as incorporate extant theories, Brewin, Dalgleish, and Joseph (1996) proposed a dual representation theory of PTSD, in which memories of a traumatic experience are thought to be stored in two ways: autobiographical memories of the experience, referred to as *verbally accessible memories* (VAM) that include information the individual attended to before, during, and after the traumatic event with sufficient conscious processing to be transferred to long-term memory, and *situationally accessible memories* (SAM), which contain extensive, nonconscious information about the traumatic event that cannot be deliberately accessed or easily altered. They can, however, be triggered in the forms of flashbacks, nightmares, or intrusive images. Brewin et al. also propose two types of emotional reactions: primary emotions, conditioned during the traumatic event (e.g., fear, helplessness, horror) and secondary emotions that result from post-hoc consideration of the traumatic event (e.g., anger, shame, sadness). Brewin et al. propose that successful emotional processing of a traumatic event requires the activation of both VAM and SAM. Resolution of schema conflicts occurs through a conscious search for meaning during activation of SAM and VAM, resulting in an integrated view of the trauma.

Ehlers and Clark (2000) have focused on the apparent paradox of memory in PTSD, such that someone with PTSD may have trouble intentionally accessing his or her memory of the event but have involuntary intrusions of parts of it. Ehlers and Clark noted that anxiety disorders, within a cognitive framework, are focused on future danger, while PTSD appears to be focused about an event in the past. They resolve this discrepancy by suggesting that people with PTSD are processing their traumatic events in idiosyncratic ways that produce an appraisal of serious current threat. Ehlers and Clark propose that because the memory that is encoded at the time of the trauma is poorly elaborated and integrated with other memories with regard to details, context of time, sequence, and so forth, this might explain why people with PTSD may have poor autobiographical memory and yet may be triggered to have memory fragments that have a here-and-now quality (no time context) or may not have appropriate posttrauma appraisals (e.g., "I did not die"). Like the emotional processing models, Ehlers and Clark also propose that strong associative learning is paired with fear responses and can generalize.

In response to the perceptions of threat, people with PTSD adopt various maladaptive coping strategies, depending upon their appraisals. For example, people who believe they will go crazy if they think about the traumatic event will attempt to avoid thoughts about the trauma and will try to keep their minds occupied with other things as much as they can. Someone who believes that he or she must figure out why the traumatic event happened to keep it from happening again will ruminate about how it could have been prevented. Those who think that the traumatic event was punishment for prior actions may become immobilized and unable to make decisions. These maladaptive strategies, most often avoidance behaviors, may (1) increase symptoms, (2) prevent change in negative appraisals, or (3) prevent change in the trauma memory.

Another multirepresentational cognitive model, called Schematic Propositional Associative and Analogical Representational Systems (SPAARS) (Dalgleish, 2004) was originally proposed to explain everyday emotional experience and was later specifically applied to PTSD. The model proposes four types or levels of mental representation systems: the schematic, propositional, analogue, and associative representational systems. The schematic level represents abstract generic information, or schemas. Propositional-level information is verbally accessible meanings, similar to VAMs, whereas information at the analogue level is stored as "images" across all types of sensory systems, similar to SAMs. The associative system is similar to the fear structures hypothesized in emotional processing theory as representing the connections between other types of representations. In the SPAARS model, emotions are proposed to be generated through two routes. One, similar to Ehlers and Clark's (2000) cognitive model, is through appraisals at the schematic level, in which events are evaluated against important goals. For example, a person will appraise an event to be threatening if the event blocks an important goal, and will then experience fear. Because traumatic events are appraised as threats to the goal of survival, they elicit fear. The second route to emotion is through associative learning, which is automatic and similar to the fear activation described by Foa, Steketee, and Rothbaum (1989).

Within the SPAARS model, a traumatic event triggers intense appraisal-driven fear, helplessness, or horror, as well as a range of other emotions. Information about the traumatic event will be simultaneously encoded in the schematic, propositional, and analogue levels. Because the memory of the traumatic event represents an ongoing threat to goals, the person is left with low-level fear activation, cognitive bias to attend to threat appraisals, and intrusive sensory images and appraisals. The trauma memory exists across different levels of mental representation, but is unincorporated into the person's larger mental representations; the memory can be elicited as flashbacks or nightmares. Such strong memory and emotional intrusions result in efforts to cope through avoidance.

Social-cognitive theorists have observed that traumatic events dramatically alter basic beliefs about the self, world, and others. These theorists tend to focus on the content of altered cognitions and the processes by which trauma victims integrate traumatic events into their overall conceptual systems, either by assimilating the information into existing schemas or by altering existing schemas to accommodate the new information (Hollon & Garber, 1988). Janoff-Bulman (1992) focused primarily on three major assumptions that may be shattered in the face of a traumatic event: personal invulnerability, the world as a meaningful and predictable place, and the self as positive or worthy. McCann, Sakheim, & Abrahamson (1988) proposed six major areas of functioning, either self or other focused, that can be disrupted by traumatic victimization: agency, safety, trust, power, esteem, and intimacy. This theory suggests that difficulties with adaptation following traumatic events results if previously positive schemas (basic assumptions or conceptual systems) are disrupted by the experience or if previous negative schemas are seemingly confirmed by the experience.

In a similar vein, Resick (1992) has proposed that when traumatic events conflict with prior beliefs, the people affected have three possibilities: altering their interpretations of the event in an attempt to maintain previously held beliefs (assimilation), altering their beliefs just enough to accommodate the new information (accommodation), or changing their beliefs drastically (overaccommodation). Examples of these three processes would be for someone who was attacked by a friend to think "It's all my fault; I must have caused him to do this" (assimilation), "There must be something wrong with him that he would betray me this way" (accommodation), or "This means that I can't trust anyone (over-accommodation). Those people who have histories of traumatic events are particularly prone to overaccommodation and use experiences with disparate events as mounting proof of an extreme belief (McCann & Pearlman, 1990).

As part of a larger emotional processing theory (see the following), Foa and her colleagues (Cahill & Foa, 2007; Foa & Rothbaum, 1998) have proposed that cognitions of people with PTSD fall into two classes: one, that the world is dangerous, and two, they are completely incompetent. They propose that danger cognitions emanate from the large number of stimulus representations that can activate the mental fear structure that is thought to underlie PTSD. Incompetence beliefs are generated from erroneous mental representations of how the person behaved during the trauma and of subsequent symptoms.

Research on Cognitive Processes

There is evidence supporting the fragmentation of trauma memories, cognitive avoidance by way of thought suppression, as well as an attentional bias toward threat cues. Regarding fragmentation and content of memory for traumatic events, research has shown that recovery from a trauma event involves organizing and streamlining the traumatic memory (e.g., Foa & Kozak, 1986; Foa & Riggs, 1993; Rachman, 1980). Consistent with this notion, research has shown that trauma narratives that are disorganized are associated with increased PTSD symptom severity (Foa, Molnar, & Cashman, 1995; Halligan, Michael, Clark, & Ehlers, 2003; Harvey & Bryant, 1999; Jones, Harvey, & Brewin, 2007; Zoellner, Alvarez-Conrad, & Foa, 2002). Importantly, Jones and colleagues (2007) found that the disorganization of trauma narratives did not distinguish participants who suffered a traumatic brain injury during the traumatic event from those who did not. Therefore, the disorganization findings for trauma narratives do not appear to be merely the result of cognitive deficits associated with traumatic brain injury (e.g., physical assault, combat injury, motor vehicle accident).

Cognitive theories of PTSD have also emphasized the importance of memory vividness and accessibility (Brewin, 1996), and research has found that sections of trauma narratives that are reflective of a flashback contain more sensory words compared with other sections of the narrative (e.g., Brewin, 1996; Hellawell & Brewin, 2004). Foa and

Kozak's (1986) emotion-processing theory also suggests that effectively accessing a trauma memory should result in greater usage of words representing negative emotion and trauma-associated sensory content. Consistent with this theory, trauma narratives of PTSD individuals contain more sensory details and negative emotion content compared with trauma survivors who do not develop PTSD (Hellawell & Brewin, 2004; Jones et al., 2007; Zoellner et al., 2002). Underscoring the importance of the nature of the trauma memory in PTSD, Foa, Massie, and Yarczower (1995) found that pre- to post-treatment decreases in disorganization of the trauma narrative were correlated with successful treatment with prolonged exposure.

Evidence for the role of thought suppression is found by asking people to think about or not think about something (e.g., the white bear test), and then report on their thoughts (Wegner, Schneider, Carter, & White, 1987). The first studies examined normal populations following exposure to a stressful movie; researchers found that after being asked to suppress thoughts about the movie, a rebound effect occurred such that the participants had an increase in their negative thoughts about the movie. This thought-suppression paradigm has been used to examine the role of cognitive avoidance in the maintenance of PTSD symptoms (Davies & Clark, 1998; Harvey & Bryant, 1998; McNally & Riccardi, 1996). This rebound effect, an increase in thoughts after initial suppression, was assumed to parallel what naturally occurs when trauma survivors try to avoid intrusive trauma-related thoughts. In studies of recent trauma survivors with and without Acute Stress Disorder (ASD) (Harvey & Bryant, 1998) and in longer-term samples of women with or without PTSD (Shipherd & Beck, 1999), the rebound effect has been demonstrated in those with the stress-related disorders compared with those without the disorders. These findings were recently replicated when comparing motor vehicle accident survivors with and without PTSD (Shipherd & Beck, 2005). Together these studies support the theories that emphasize the role of cognitive avoidance as a maintaining factor in PTSD.

Research has also examined attentional bias toward threat cues through the use of a modified Stroop paradigm (Stroop, 1935). In the original Stroop paradigm, participants were instructed to name the color of a printed word while ignoring the meaning elements of that word. The modified Stroop paradigm has been used to study selective processing in people with or without PTSD by asking participants to name the color of words that do or don't relate to their trauma. Studies have demonstrated that people with PTSD are slower at naming the color of trauma-related words than positive words, general threat words, and neutral words. This Stroop effect has been demonstrated in a variety of trauma populations, including war veterans (Litz et al., 1996; McNally, English, & Lipke, 1993; McNally, Kaspi, Riemann, & Zeitlin, 1990), sexual assault survivors (Foa, Feske, Murdock, Kozak, & McCarthy, 1991), survivors of a ferry disaster (Thrasher, Dalgleish, & Yule, 1994), childhood sexual abuse survivors (Bremner et al., 2004; Field, Classen, Butler, Koopman, Zarcone et al., 2001), motor vehicle accident survivors (Beck, Freeman, Shipherd, Hamblen, & Lackner, 2001; Bryant & Harvey, 1995), and child and adolescent trauma survivors (Freeman & Beck, 2000; Moradi, Taghavi, Neshat Doost, Yule, & Dalgleish, 1999).

Although the Stroop effect could represent a conscious pause upon recognition of the trauma-related word, there is also evidence that the bias exists even when presented too quickly for conscious recognition of the words (Harvey, Bryant, & Rapee, 1996). In the Harvey et al. study, the PTSD group (victims of a motor vehicle accident) was slower to color name in both conscious and preconscious conditions than groups that had an accident but no PTSD and a no accident/no PTSD group. The PTSD group was also slower to name neutral words in each condition than the other two groups. Interference with processing at the preconscious level may provide evidence for a fear network, but greater interference with neutral words as well, seems to indicate a more generalized processing difficulty related to PTSD. Recently, Brewin, Kleiner, and Vasterling (in press) conducted a meta-analysis of 27 studies, including 660 people with PTSD and 812 controls, of memory for emotionally neutral information. They found a small- to moderate-sized decrement in memory performance, particularly verbal memory, among those with PTSD compared with controls.

There is also evidence regarding the relationship between cognitive content disturbance and PTSD. Strong correlations have been found between maladaptive beliefs regarding safety, trust, esteem, or intimacy beliefs and PTSD symptoms among survivors of child sexual abuse (Wenninger & Ehlers, 1998). Using the same scale (the Personal Beliefs and Reactions Scale; Resick, Schnicke, & Markway, 1991 November), Owens and Chard (2001) found similar findings among 53 adult survivors of child sexual abuse. Posttraumatic Stress Disorder severity was correlated with cognitive distortions on all seven subscales. Kubany (1994) specifically examined guilt cognitions among combat veterans and battered women and found that guilt cognitions correlated highly with several different PTSD measures.

Dunmore, Clark, & Ehlers (1999) examined 92 assault victims, with or without PTSD, in a cross-sectional study and found that the PTSD group reported more mental defeat, mental planning, mental confusion, and detachment during the traumatic event. They also reported more negative appraisals of their initial posttrauma symptoms, more negative perception of others' responses, lower positive perception of others' responses, and greater perception of perceived permanent damage. Furthermore, they reported a greater impact on their posttrauma beliefs. When those who had recovered from their PTSD and those who had persistent PTSD were compared, the important cognitive variables associated with persistence of PTSD were mental defeat, mental confusion, negative appraisals of emotions and symptoms, negative responses from others, and the belief they had permanently changed and altered beliefs posttrauma. In a related longitudinal study, Dunmore, Clark, and Ehlers (2001) examined assault victims within 4 months and then again at 6 and 9 months postcrime. They also found that cognitive variables were predictive of PTSD at 6 or 9 months postcrime either directly or indirectly, mediated by initial PTSD.

There have also been several treatment studies that have examined change in cognitions as a result of therapy, all of which found improvements in maladaptive cognitions along with improvements in PTSD (Foa & Rauch, 2004; Owens, Pike, & Chard, 2001; Resick, Nishith, Weaver, Astin, & Feuer, 2002). However, in examining predictors of treatment outcome with prolonged exposure, Ehlers and her colleagues (2001) divided a treatment sample into those who had good treatment versus inferior outcomes and then examined concepts that emerged during the exposures that had been mentioned earlier, such as mental defeat versus mental planning during the event, or perception of permanent damage. The investigators found that participants with good treatment outcome reported more mental planning, no mental defeat, and less perception of permanent change. Therefore, it appears that some cognitions that occurred during the traumatic event may predict better or poorer subsequent treatment outcome.

PSYCHOLOGY-BEHAVIORAL

The most prominently mentioned behaviors in the current *DSM* description of PTSD are avoidance behaviors. These criteria represent efforts to avoid thoughts, feelings, conversations, activities, places, or people that arouse recollections of the traumatic event. These avoidance symptoms were identified early in the study of trauma, (e.g., Keane, Fairbank, Caddell, Zimering, & Bender, 1985; Kilpatrick, Best, Veronen, Amick, Villeponteaux et al., 1985). The first theories of reactions to trauma, and subsequently PTSD, were based on two-factor theory (Mowrer, 1947), which proposed that anxiety is first acquired through classical conditioning in which an unconditioned stimulus (the traumatic event) becomes associated with other stimuli, which then elicit conditioned emotional responses. However, instead of extinguishing in the absence of further traumatic events, the person escapes or avoids the conditioned stimuli in an attempt to stop the negative emotional response. The avoidance behavior is negatively reinforced by the short-term reduction in anxiety but ultimately causes the initial anxious reaction to be maintained through the second factor of operant conditioning.

Avoidance behaviors have been implicated in maintenance of PTSD symptoms in more modern theories as well. Theories regarding the development of fear networks in PTSD have been offered by Foa and her colleagues (Cahill & Foa, 2007; Foa & Kozak, 1985, 1986; Rothbaum & Foa, 1996), following upon the work of Lang (1979). In these theories, it is suggested that following traumatic events a pathological fear structure develops that is composed of feared stimuli, responses, and meaning elements. The fear structure is activated by stimuli in the environment that match elements of the fear structure. When activated, cognitive, behavioral, and arousal anxiety reactions result. If the situation were in fact dangerous, it would be an effective program for escape or avoidance. However, a pathological fear network triggers false alarms because of the generalization of stimuli to nondangerous cues (Jones & Barlow, 1990). Fear elicits escape and avoidance behavior and subsequent emotional numbing. Resick and Schnicke (1992) have also suggested that avoidance is an important element in the maintenance of PTSD and have suggested that many of the symptoms and disorders that develop along with PTSD may develop as attempts to avoid the intrusive images and strong emotions. However, they have emphasized that fear is not the only emotion being avoided; many traumatic events elicit anger, sadness, guilt, and horror, which are overwhelming. These emotions, too, may trigger escape, avoidance, and numbing.

Emotional processing theorists such as Cahill and Foa (2007) propose that for natural recovery from trauma to occur or for therapy to work, the affected person must be able to activate his or her trauma memory, block the negative reinforcement that occurs with escape and avoidance behavior, and disconfirm erroneous beliefs through extinction of anxiety. As the anxiety diminishes, the person learns that he or she can tolerate fear and anxiety and begins to change his or her incompetence beliefs. Through exposure, the person also learns to discriminate true danger cues from false alarms and past experiences from the present.

Evidence for a fear network and activation/extinction of fear comes from two sources. Physiological reactivity to trauma cues is associated with PTSD (Keane et al., 1998; Shalev, Orr, Peri, & Schreiber, 1992; Tarrier et al., 2002), and this reactivity changes as a function of successful treatment (Blanchard et al., 2003; Boudewyns & Hyer, 1990). In a study of physiological reactivity comparing treatment responders with nonresponders, Griffin, Resick, & Galovski (2006) recently found that patients who responded to treatment exhibited overall decreases in physiological responding from pretreatment to posttreatment, whereas those who did not benefit from treatment showed no such change. Findings from two other studies that have examined whether pretreatment physiological reactivity could predict treatment outcome have been negative (Blanchard et al., 2003, 2002). However, both studies had small samples and neither measured the critical comorbidity factors that may have confounded their findings. Rather than assessing physiological activation, Foa et al. (1995) examined facial expressions during the first prolonged exposure (PE) session and found that greater facial displays of fear, assumed to reflect emotional engagement, were predictive of positive treatment outcomes.

There is also mixed evidence that habituation of pathological fear occurs in exposure treatments for PTSD. Jaycox, Foa, and Morral (1998) conducted cluster analyses of profiles of subjective units of distress (SUD) ratings over the course of therapy for 36 female sexual assault victims who were receiving PE. Three patterns emerged: 14 women reported a high initial SUD score and then a steady decrease over the remaining five sessions (high engagers/habituators), 14 women had even higher initial scores but didn't habituate, and 9 women had lower initial SUD and did not decrease. The first group had significantly better treatment outcome than the other two groups, providing support for the need for both emotional engagement and habituation across sessions.

Two studies of predictors of exposure treatment outcome were conducted by van Minnen and her colleagues (van Minnen, Arntz, & Keijsers, 2002; van Minnen & Hagenaars, 2002). The first study examined a range of predictors within two mixed clinical samples that had somewhat different compositions, possibly explaining why some variables correlated to treatment outcome in one study or the other, but not both. The only stable predictor of poorer posttreatment scores across both samples was greater severity of PTSD at pretreatment. The second sample also assessed use of benzodiazepines during treatment, which was related to poorer outcome. These investigators suggested that the use of benzodiazepines might interfere with fear activation during exposures, an element considered to be crucial in exposure treatment. In the second study, van Minnen and Hagenaars (2002) examined the question of fear activation during exposure treatment. They compared 21 treatment completers who improved with 13 who did not improve on indicators of within-session habituation and between-session habituation at sessions one and two. They found that clients who did not improve had greater anxiety at the start of session one, which was assumed to be anticipatory in nature and might have interfered with the clients' accessing their trauma memory. The improvers did not differ on within-session habituation, but they reported more habituation with at-home exposures, even though there were no differences in the number of times the two groups listened to their trauma accounts. The improvers reported greater decreases in distress between session one and session two, consistent with Jaycox et al. (1998).

PSYCHOLOGY-EMOTION

The emotion in PTSD that has received the lion's share of theoretical and research attention is fear. Posttraumatic Stress Disorder is classified as an anxiety disorder, thus theories regarding fear and anxiety have been applied to PTSD. There is ample evidence, as indicated by the psychophysiological arousal research reviewed in the previous section, that fear and anxiety play a large role in PTSD. However, clinicians and researchers have long noted that people with PTSD also have serious problems with anger (Andrews, Brewin, Rose, & Kirk, 2000; Chemtob, Hamada, Roitblat, & Muraoka, 1994; Chemtob, Novaco, Hamada, & Gross, 1997; McFall, Fontana, Raskind, & Rosenheck, 1999; Riggs, Dancu, Gershuny, Greenberg, & Foa, 1992), shame (Andrews et al., 2000; Leskela, Dieperink, & Thuras, 2002; Wong & Cook, 1992), and guilt (Beckham, Feldman, & Kirby, 1998; Henning & Frueh, 1997; Kubany, 1994; Kubany et al., 1996; Resick et al., 2002).

For example, Andrews et al. (2000) conducted a prospective study with crime victims. Within 1 month of a crime, 157 people (118 men and 28 women) completed interviews. Eighty-eight percent of them completed follow-up interviews 6 months later. This study examined shame and self- or other-directed anger in predicting PTSD at the two time points. After controlling for gender, education, and injury, results indicated that shame and anger at others significantly predicted PTSD at 1 month postcrime. In examining PTSD symptoms at 6 months postcrime, 1-month PTSD scores were entered first, followed by the other control variables. As expected, the severity of PTSD at 1 month was strongly predictive of PTSD at 6 months. However, beyond that, shame at 1 month was also a significant predictor of PTSD at 6 months.

Brewin, Andrews, and Rose (2000) found that in addition to fear, emotions of helplessness or horror experienced within 1 month of the crime were predictive of PTSD status 6 months later. Also, shame and anger predicted later PTSD status, even after controlling for intense emotions of fear, helplessness, and horror. Pitman, Orr, Forgue, & Altman (1990) also found that combat veterans with PTSD reported experiencing a range of emotions other than fear while listening to individualized traumatic scripts. In fact, veterans with PTSD were no more likely to report experiencing fear than other emotions. Similarly, in a study examining responses at the time of the trauma, Rizvi and colleagues (Rizvi, Kaysen, Gutner, Griffin, & Resick, in press), have demonstrated that rape victims reported a wide range of emotional responses during the rape and that emotions other than fear (e.g., sadness, humiliation, and anger) were more predictive of later PTSD symptomatology than was fear.

COMORBIDITY AND PERSONALITY

Posttraumatic Stress Disorder is associated with very high rates of comorbidity. Brown, Di Nardo, Lehman, & Campbell (2001) examined comorbidity patterns of 1,126 community outpatients and found that PTSD had the highest and most diverse rate of comorbid disorders (over 90%), with the most frequent comorbid disorder being Major Depressive Disorder (77%) followed by Generalized Anxiety Disorder (38%), and Alcohol Abuse/Dependence (31%). Studies of military veterans have found rates of comorbidity from 50% to 80% (Kulka et al., 1990; Orsillo et al., 1996). The most common comorbidity across studies is Major Depressive Disorder, which is typically present in 50% or more of PTSD cases (Kessler et al., 1995; North et al., 1999; Orsillo et al., 1996). Substance abuse and dependence are common but vary widely depending upon the population being studied (Green, Lindy, Grace, & Leonard, 1992; Kessler et al., 1995; Kulka et al., 1990; Orsillo et al., 1996). The question arises as to why comorbid conditions are so common in PTSD. Recent research on the dimensional nature of psychopathology may provide an explanation along with an understanding of the function of the comorbid symptoms in managing PTSD intrusion and arousal.

Although it has been recognized and studied for over 30 years in the child disorders literature (cf., Achenbach & Edelbrock, 1978; Achenbach & Edelbrock, 1984), only recently have psychopathology researchers examined the latent dimensions of internalizing and externalizing that underlie adult disorders. A series of factor analytic studies have determined that comorbid disorders fall along these dimensions (Cox, Clara, & Enns, 2002; Kendler, Prescott, Myers, & Neale, 2003; Krueger, Caspi, Moffitt, & Silva, 1998; Krueger, McGue, & Iacono, 2001) such that substance abuse disorders and antisocial personality load on the externalizing dimension while mood and anxiety disorders load on the internalizing dimension. Widiger and Simonsen (2005) have proposed a hierarchical structure to the Axis II disorders as well, with internalization and externalization at the highest level of this structure. Immediately beneath these higher-order dimensions are three to five broad domains of personality functioning, followed by personality trait constructs, and at the lowest level the more behaviorally specific diagnostic criteria.

Recent studies have examined whether the internalizing/externalizing model is relevant to patterns of posttraumatic psychopathology (Miller, Fogler, Wolf, Kaloupek, & Keane, in press; Miller, Greif, & Smith, 2003; Miller, Kaloupek, Dillon, & Keane, 2004; Miller & Resick, 2007), particularly with regard to explanations for the high levels of comorbidity among those with PTSD or the consideration of complex PTSD. Cox et al. (2002) examined where PTSD loaded on a factor analysis of Axis I disorders and found that it loaded best (although somewhat weakly, at .39) on the internalizing, anxious misery factor rather than the internalizing anxiety disorders factor. Subsequently, Miller and colleagues have shown evidence of internalizing and externalizing subtypes of PTSD in both male and female samples totaling over 1,000 subjects through a series of cluster analytic studies of personality inventories. Across these three studies, Miller et al. found that there are people who score low on both internalizing and externalizing who could be conceptualized as a subtype of *simple* PTSD.

A second subtype, *externalizing*, is characterized by the tendency to outwardly express distress through antagonistic interactions with others, blaming others, and coping through acting out. Individuals in this subgroup endorsed elevated levels of anger and aggression, substance-related disorders, and cluster B personality disorder features. They described themselves as impulsive, with little regard for the consequences of their actions, easily upset, and chronically stressed. On measures of Axis II symptoms, they described themselves as tending toward manipulative, exhibitionistic, and unconventional behavior. Externalizers described themselves as being emotionally labile, overactive, fearless, and feeling chronically betrayed and mistreated by others. In both studies of veterans, in which data on premilitary characteristics were available, those with externalizing tendencies reported higher rates of premilitary delinquency, suggesting the influence of externalizing personality traits that were present prior to the trauma.

The third subtype, the *internalizing* subtype, is characterized by the tendency to direct posttraumatic distress inwardly through shame, self-defeating and self-deprecating beliefs, anxiety, avoidance, depression, and withdrawal. Across the three studies, people in this subtype reported the highest levels of PTSD and reported high rates of comorbid Major Depression and Panic Disorder, Schizoid and Avoidant Personality Disorder features, and personality profiles defined by high negative emotionality combined with low positive emotionality. This subtype also described themselves as unenthusiastic, uninspired, easily fatigued, and lacking interests. They endorsed having few friends, being aloof and distant from others, preferring to spend time alone, a restricted range of emotions in interpersonal settings, feelings of social inhibition, inadequacy, and hyper-sensitivity to negative evaluation.

These findings suggest that the internalizing/externalizing substraits of psychopathology, originally developed to account for covariation among broad classes of mental disorders (cf. Krueger et al., 1998; Krueger et al., 2001), are relevant to the understanding of the heterogeneity of PTSD comorbidity. Earlier cluster analytic studies of U.S. and Australian veterans with PTSD found similar patterns that can now be interpreted as reflecting individual differences in internalizing and externalizing processes (Forbes et al., 2003; Hyer, Davis, Albrecht, Boudewyns, & Woods, 1994; Piekarski, Sherwood, & Funari, 1993).

INTERACTION WITH EXTERNAL, ENVIRONMENTAL FACTORS

By definition, external environmental factors play a key role in PTSD. Criterion A requires a traumatic stressor that evokes fear, helplessness, or horror. Interestingly, not all stressors have equal effects, which provided support for the idea that PTSD is not just a conditioned response to a fear-inducing situation. In the National Comorbidity Study, Kessler et al. (1995) found that the more personally directed events such as rape, molestation, assault, and combat were more likely to result in PTSD than more impersonal events, such as disasters or accidents, even though the latter were far more common. In fact, rape was the single event most likely to result in PTSD among both men and women. There is also a dose-response relationship such that the more traumatic events one experiences, the more likely he or she will develop PTSD (e.g., Fairbank, Keane, & Malloy, 1983; Foy, Carroll, & Donahoe, 1987; March, 1993; Rodriguez, Vande-Kemp, & Foy, 1998).

Importance of Social Support and Additional Life Stress

Among risk factors for the development or maintenance of PTSD, social support has emerged as one of the most important variables. A number of studies have found that lack of social support is a risk factor for PTSD among people exposed to trauma (e.g., Egendorf, Kadushin, Laufer, Rothbart, & Sloan, 1981; Keane, Scott, Chavoya, Lamparski, & Fairbank, 1985; King, King, Foy, Keane, & Fairbank, 1999; Solomon & Mikulincer, 1990; Solomon, Mikulincer, & Avitzur, 1988; Solomon, Mikulincer, & Flum, 1989). Brewin, Andrews and Valentine (2000) conducted a meta-analysis of 77 studies to evaluate risk factors for PTSD. They examined 14 predictors of PTSD that were typically examined in these studies, including various demographics, psychiatric and trauma history, trauma severity, lack of social support, and additional life stress. Brewin et al. included 11 studies that measured lack of social support and 8 studies that assessed additional life stressors. They found that factors occurring during or after the trauma (trauma severity, lack of social support, additional life stress) had stronger effects on PTSD than pretrauma factors. Ozer, Best, Lipsey, & Weiss (2003) also found a moderate, albeit slightly weaker, association between social support and PTSD.

Research regarding the impact of additional life stressors suggests that this is also a risk factor for PTSD (Brewin et al., 2000; King et al., 1998). Additional life stressors demonstrated the second-highest effect size in the Brewin et al. (2000) meta-analysis. The role that additional life stressors have on recovery has been a particular focus of the work of Hobfall (1989, 1991) regarding the conservation of resources.

Intimate Relationships and PTSD

An external or interpersonal factor associated with vulnerability to PTSD is intimate relationship dysfunction. Epidemiological studies indicate that those with PTSD are as likely as those without PTSD to be married, but they are substantially more likely to divorce, and divorce multiple times (Kessler, Walters, Forthofer, 1998). Posttraumatic Stress Disorder has also been found to be associated with relationship discord, domestic violence, sexual dysfunction, and mental health problems in the partners of those with PTSD (e.g., Glenn et al., 2002; Jordan et al., 1992; Bramsen, Van der Ploeg, & Twisk, 2002). Avoidance and numbing symptoms of PTSD have been specifically implicated in relationship satisfaction (Riggs, Byrne, Weathers, & Litz, 1998), and the hyperarousal symptoms have been associated with violence perpetration (Byrne & Riggs, 1996). Most of the research in this area has been cross-sectional in nature, which does not allow for conclusions about the directionality of this association. However, there is likely a reciprocal relationship between intimate relationship functioning and PTSD, wherein each may serve to facilitate or exacerbate the other (Monson, Price, & Ranslow, 2005, October).

Conservation of Resources

Another way in which trauma interacts with the environment to interfere with recovery from PTSD, is through the loss of resources. For example, if people have severe PTSD such that they do not sleep and cannot concentrate at work, they may lose their jobs. Without a job, they may lose social and family support. Hobfall (1989, 1991) has proposed a theory of stress called Conservation of Resources (COR) which he has subsequently applied to, and tested with, traumatic stress. The underlying tenet of COR is that people "*will strive to obtain, retain, and protect what they value*" (Hobfoll, 1991, p. 187). Stress occurs when resources are threatened or lost, or when resources don't increase adequately following their initial investment. By resources, Hobfall is referring to four types: conditions (e.g., stable marriage or work), objects (e.g., housing, car), personal characteristics (e.g., self-efficacy, skills), and energies, such as credit or insurance. Because the expenditure of resources to offset losses may deplete the person's resources, loss spirals may result.

According to COR theory, traumatic stress results in sudden and rapid loss of resources and the resources that are most valued (e.g., trust in self and others, perception of control, sense of well-being). Furthermore, traumatic events make excessive demands for which people have little experience and therefore fewer strategies for coping. Because the demands of traumatic stressors are excessive, there is typically no amount of resources that would prevent an initial reaction. However, those who possess abundant personal, social, and financial resources will recover more quickly. Those who are already facing additional life stressors or whose resources are depleted by the trauma will face loss spirals and a downward trajectory of functioning.

Assessment of Disorder

Given the high prevalence of traumatic events in the general population as well as the shame and guilt that often accompanies certain types of trauma, assessment of PTSD requires a careful and sensitive assessment. The first task of a comprehensive assessment is to determine whether a life event meets the seriousness and subjective response requirements of a traumatic stressor (Criterion A). Following this, the presence and severity of the 17 associated symptoms which comprise Criteria B to D must be determined. Interviews are considered the most reliable and valid method for assessing PTSD; however, a number of self-report questionnaires have been developed that may provide a valid, yet quicker and less costly alternative to an interview (Monson et al., 2007). These measures are summarized in the following section.

ASSESSMENT OF TRAUMATIC EVENTS

In order to determine whether the diagnosis of PTSD is plausible, the first step in assessment is to identify traumatic events that the individual experienced in his or her lifetime. This history can be extraordinarily difficult to obtain, depending on the experiences and the level of shame, self-blame, or embarrassment the person may be suffering. For example, although individuals may have little trouble disclosing that they experienced a natural disaster like a hurricane or tornado, rape or child sexual abuse victims may have greater difficulty spontaneously disclosing what happened to them. This inhibition of disclosure is also consistent with general patterns of avoidance of trauma-related reminders or cues (i.e., Criterion C symptoms of avoiding talking about or thinking about what occurred).

Kilpatrick (1983) has suggested several other reasons victims might not be forthcoming with this information, including fear of a negative reaction to disclosure, especially if previous disclosure has resulted in disbelief or blame. The terminology used in the assessment can have an impact on disclosure as well. For example, many trauma victims may not recognize or label their experiences as "trauma," "rape," or "assault," especially if the perpetrator was known to them, or if the experience was one suffered by many, such as combat or a natural disaster. Therefore, it is important for the assessor to use sensitive language and, early in the assessment, be more willing to include false positives for traumatic events than risk losing important information. Later questioning can reduce the error of being overly inclusive. Finally, it should be clear that a strong alliance between the clinician and interviewee is necessary in order to increase the likelihood and level of self-disclosure. It is recommended that the clinician be straightforward about the purpose of the questioning, specify any limits of confidentiality, and explain how the obtained information may be used (e.g., diagnosis, treatment planning, or research purposes).

The use of behavioral, descriptive, and nonjudgmental prompts is recommended when asking about past trauma experiences. For example, instead of asking "Have you ever been raped?", a preferable alternative would be to ask "Has anyone ever made you have unwanted sexual contact by physical force or threat of force?" Similarly, instead of asking "Were you abused as a child?", an interviewer could ask "Did anyone ever hit you or use physical punishment when you were a child?" An interviewee may say "no" to the first question, but readily admit that she or he was hit with a belt routinely as a child. In general, it is recommended that the clinician always begin with broad questions about experiences and then move to more specific behaviorally anchored questions.

An alternative to this relatively lengthy approach to assessing past traumas is to use a self-report measure, such as a checklist, to acquire initial information that can then be explored further through interview. There are a number of such checklists that can be used as a springboard for further inquiry. For example, the Life Events Checklist (Gray, Litz, Hsu, Lombardo, 2004) was developed as part of the CAPS interview (discussed in the following). Other scales include the Traumatic Stress Schedule (Norris, 1990), the Trauma History Questionnaire (THQ) (Green, 1996), the Traumatic Life Events Questionnaire (TLEQ) (Kubany et al., 2000), and the Traumatic Events Scale (Vrana & Lauterbach, 1994). The Posttraumatic Stress Diagnostic Scale (PDS) (Foa, 1995) has two sections prior to assessing symptoms. The first section assesses 13 potentially traumatic events, while the second section has questions to determine if an event meets the definition of Criterion A. With regard to combat in particular, the Combat Exposure Scale (Keane, Fairbank, Caddell, & Zimering, 1989), has been used widely to assess the degree of combat exposure. Although these are useful tools that can be administered to shorten the overall diagnostic interview, clinicians are discouraged from relying on them exclusively without follow-up questions due to the possibility of misreporting or lack of understanding on the part of the individual answering the questions. That is, just because an individual endorses an event on a checklist, it doesn't necessarily indicate that this event would meet criteria for a traumatic event. With the exception of the Combat Exposure Scale, most of these measures assess a number of different types of potentially traumatic events, including accidents, natural and manmade disasters, sexual assault, child abuse, and physical assault.

DIAGNOSTIC INTERVIEWS

A number of interviews exist that allow for a clinician to make a diagnosis of PTSD as well as assess its overall severity. The measure often considered to be the gold standard diagnostic assessment for PTSD is the Clinician-Administered PTSD Scale (CAPS) (Blake et al., 1995). The CAPS has questions to assess both the severity and frequency of each of the PTSD symptoms and contains very specific behavioral anchors to increase reliability. Additionally, beyond the 17 core symptoms assessed, the CAPS includes questions on associated features of PTSD, including survivor guilt, depersonalization and derealization, and social and occupational impairment. The CAPS has a large body of research demonstrating its reliability and validity across a wide variety of populations (see Weathers, Keane, & Davidson, 2001 for a review). Because of these strengths, the CAPS is probably the most widely used diagnostic interview for PTSD (Weathers et al., 2001); (Weathers, Ruscio, & Keane, 1999). A disadvantage to the CAPS is its length of administration, which can last over an hour, which makes it an unlikely candidate for studies using rapid assessment or telephone methodologies, or for studies that are assessing a wide range of psychiatric disorders and not just PTSD.

The Structured Clinical Interview for *DSM-IV* (SCID) (First, Spitzer, Williams, & Gibbon, 1995) is a widely used interview for Axis I disorders generally and includes a section on PTSD. The SCID was developed for use by experienced clinicians and assesses the presence or absence of all the symptoms of PTSD, thus yielding a decision about diagnosis. However, the SCID, in its present form, does not assess for frequency or severity of individual symptoms, and only a count of number of symptoms (in addition to a diagnosis) is possible to obtain. Further, the SCID was not necessarily designed for traumatized populations, and the one question determining whether a Criterion A event occurred includes a myriad of life-threatening events that may be perceived as overwhelming to the interviewee. In response to this, Resnick, Kilpatrick, & Lipovsky

(1991) recommend certain modifications for use of the SCID with rape victims, which include five more sensitive screening questions for history of rape and other major traumatic events. Other modifications can be made for use with different traumatized populations.

The Diagnostic Interview Schedule (DIS; Robins, Helzer, Croughan, & Ratcliff, 1981) is another structured interview that has the advantage of requiring less training and experience than the CAPS and SCID. As with the SCID, one can make a diagnosis of PTSD with the DIS but not assess its level of severity. Finally, the PTSD Symptom Scale-Interview (PSS-I; Foa, Riggs, Dancu, & Rothbaum, 1993) contains 17 items that match the 17 PTSD criteria and results in both diagnosis and continuous scores of frequency of each symptom. It also has a companion self-report measure (PSS-SR) that can be used on a more frequent basis (e.g., to assess weekly symptom change in treatment outcome studies). It is important to note that the PSS-I assesses symptoms over the most recent 2-week period; thus, if one wants to make a *DSM-IV* diagnosis of PTSD, the timeframe must first be modified to 1 month.

SELF-REPORT MEASURES

A large number of self-report scales for PTSD have been developed, many with excellent psychometric properties. One potential problem with using a self-report measure for PTSD is that the measure often has to rely on the participant's judgment about what constitutes a traumatic event. In addition, some were developed with specific trauma populations in mind and thus may only be appropriate for a certain subset of individuals or may require knowledge about the traumatic event prior to administering. As with any self-report measure, it is important to recognize potential limitations in diagnosis or assessment of symptom severity. However, these limitations can be overcome in part by using self-report measures in conjunction with a structured interview. In this capacity, the self-report measures can be used as a quick screening tool or to demonstrate changes in symptomatology over time.

Among the measures originally developed to assess PTSD in veteran populations are the Mississippi Scale for Combat-Related PTSD (Keane, Caddell, & Taylor, 1988) and the PTSD Checklist (PCL) (Weathers, Litz, Huska, & Keane, 1994). The Mississippi Scale is one of the oldest self-report measures; it contains 35 items designed to assess both the diagnostic criteria as well as associated features of PTSD. The PCL is widely used in VA and military settings. It contains all the *DSM-IV* criteria of PTSD and can be scored dimensionally to assess global severity. The PCL also has established cutoffs so that it can be scored categorically as well (Blanchard, Jones-Alexander, Buckley, & Forneris, 1996; Forbes, Creamer, & Biddle, 2001), and has recently been shown to be valid in assessing changes in symptoms over time and as a result of treatment (Monson et al., 2007). Civilian versions of both the Mississippi Scale and the PCL have since been developed to assess symptomatology in response to other types of traumas.

The PTSD Symptom Scale–Self-Report (PSS-SR) (Foa et al., 1993) was originally developed for rape victims and matches the items in the interview version (see the previous discussion). Other measures include the Purdue PTSD Scale-Revised (Lauterbach & Vrana, 1996), the Impact of Event Scale (IES) (Horowitz, Wilner, & Alvarez, 1979), the Distressing Event Questionnaire (DEQ) (Kubany, Leisen, Kaplan, & Kelly, 2000), and the Posttraumatic Stress Diagnostic Scale (Foa, 1995). The IES is useful for measuring trauma impact, and has been revised from its original version which included only intrusion and avoidance symptoms, to include arousal symptoms as well, and thus maps onto the *DSM-IV* criteria (IES-R) (Weiss & Marmar, 1997). The PDS is a 49-item scale that was designed to assess all five criteria of PTSD. It has strong psychometric properties (PDS) (Foa, Cashman, Jaycox, & Perry, 1997; Griffin, Uhlmansiek, Resick, & Mechanic, 2004).

There are two additional measures of PTSD that have been empirically derived from other existing scales. Posttraumatic Stress Disorder subscales have been derived from the Symptom Checklist-90-R (SCL-90-R) (Derogatis, 1983) from different sets of items for female crime victims (Saunders, Arata, & Kilpatrick, 1990) and combat veterans (Weathers et al., 1999). The Keane-PTSD Scale (PK) of the MMPI and MMPI-2 has been used successfully to discriminate Vietnam combat veterans with and without PTSD (Keane, Malloy, & Fairbank, 1984; Weathers & Keane, 1999).

In response to the recent need to screen mass numbers of people for PTSD after combat or disasters, or in primary care medical settings when time is limited, a brief PTSD screen, the PTSD-PC (Prins et al., 2004), has been developed. The PTSD-PC is now being routinely used in the United States following military service and for those individuals receiving treatment in VA medical centers (Hoge et al., 2006). The scale has four yes-no items that represent the four major symptom clusters found in most PTSD factor analysis studies that separate effortful avoidance from numbing. These four items were found to be highly associated with PTSD as measured by the CAPS. The authors recommend a cutoff score of 3 for an optimally efficient score and a cutoff of 2 is recommended for maximum sensitivity (Prins et al., 2004).

Finally, of all these measures, it should be noted that only one trauma-related scale, the Trauma Symptom Inventory (TSI) (Briere, 1995) includes scales to assess response bias. For forensic purposes, in which response bias may be of particular concern, the assessor may wish to include the TSI or administer the MMPI-2, which contains the PK scale as well as validity subscales. In addition to clinical scales, the TSI also includes subscales assessing tendencies to over-endorse unusual or bizarre symptoms, to respond in an inconsistent or random manner, and to deny symptoms others commonly endorse. The clinical scales include PTSD-related scales, such as intrusive experiences, defensive avoidance, and anxious arousal, as well as subscales that measure frequently observed problems with depression, anger, dissociation, tension-reduction behaviors, and disruptions in self-perception and sexual functioning. Unfortunately, the TSI does not assess exposure to specific traumatic events, thus requiring the clinician to establish the presence of a Criterion A event prior to administration.

PHYSIOLOGICAL ASSESSMENT

There have now been a number of studies documenting psychophysiological differences between individuals with PTSD and individuals without PTSD who have also been exposed to trauma (see Orr, Metzger, Miller, & Kaloupek, 2004 for a review). Given the fact that physiological reactivity to trauma cues is one of the criteria of the disorder, a comprehensive assessment of PTSD should include psychophysiological testing, especially when the validity of the diagnosis for a particular individual is questioned.

Studies of Vietnam veterans have found that those individuals with PTSD are consistently more reactive to combat imagery (presented through pictures and accompanying sounds) than Vietnam veterans without PTSD (Keane, Kolb et al., 1998; Pitman et al., 1990; Pitman, Orr, Forgue, de Jong, & Claiborn, 1987). These differences emerge even when the non-PTSD sample has other anxiety disorders or psychological problems, suggesting that the key difference is that of PTSD, not other psychopathology. Similar differences between PTSD and non-PTSD individuals have been found in motor vehicle accident survivors (Blanchard, Hickling, Buckley, & Taylor, 1996) and childhood sexual abuse victims (Orr et al., 1998).

The largest study of physiological reactivity was conducted in a multisite study of over 1,300 Vietnam veterans (Keane, Kaloupek, & Kolb, 1998). Using four psychophysiological measures, the researchers were able to correctly classify two-thirds of those who had PTSD (using diagnoses based on the CAPS as the criterion). Although this indicates that psychophysiological reactivity on specified measures can predict a diagnosis of PTSD for the majority of individuals, it's important to caution that psychophysiological responding to trauma cues should not be used as the sole measure of PTSD. There are a number of factors that can affect physiological reactivity, and these must be taken into account when assessing the validity of psychophysiological findings. For example, the presence of psychotropic drugs, especially benzodiazepines and beta-adrenergic blockers, can affect an individual's response. Furthermore, it has been demonstrated that antisocial characteristics can suppress levels of psychophysiological responding (Miller, Kaloupek, & Keane, 1999, October).

In addition to those people who do not physiologically respond, for various reasons, there appear to be some who have an alternative physiological response to trauma cues, which must also be taken into account. In a study of psychophysiological reactivity in recent rape victims, Griffin, Resick, and Mechanic (1997) examined reactivity as a function of the degree to which the individual experienced peritraumatic dissociation. Peritraumatic dissociation (PD) refers to the extent to which someone dissociated *during* the traumatic event. Griffin et al. (1997) found that women with a high degree of PD differed from women with low to medium levels of PD in terms of their psychophysiological responses while talking about their rape. Although both groups of women reported similar levels of subjective distress, skin conductance and heart rate of those with lower PD scores increased as expected while they were talking about the rape, whereas those with high PD scores showed a decrease in the physiological measures. Griffin and colleagues speculated that there may be a dissociative subtype of PTSD who physiologically responds quite differently than the more phobic type of PTSD.

Interventions

PSYCHOPHARMACOLOGICAL TREATMENT

There are currently two medications, both considered antidepressants, that have received indication from the U.S. Food and Drug Administration (FDA) for the treatment of PTSD: sertraline and paroxetine. Both of these medications are selective serotonin reuptake inhibitors (SSRIs), the class of medications considered to be the frontline pharmacological treatment for PTSD in four different clinical practice guidelines (American Psychiatry Association, 2004; Davidson et al., 2005; Friedman, Davidson, Mellman, & Southwick, 2000; VA/DoD, 2004). In addition to improving PTSD symptoms, there is some evidence that paroxetine improves cognitive deficits associated with PTSD as assessed with neuropsychological testing and magnetic resonance imaging (MRI; Vermetten, Vythilingam, Southwick, Charney, & Bremner, 2003). Other medications have yielded various results in the treatment of PTSD.

Other Antidepressants

Antidepressant medications have been the most studied class of drugs in the treatment of PTSD. Some tricyclic antidepressants have been found to decrease symptoms of PTSD. Both imipramine (Kosten, Frank, Dan, McDougle, & Giller, 1991) and amitryptyline (Davidson et al., 1990) have shown efficacy in reducing PTSD symptoms, although desipramine has not (Reist, Kauffman, Haier, Sangdahl, DeMet et al., 1989). Studies testing monoamine oxidase inhibitors (MAOIs) in the treatment of PTSD have produced mixed results. A randomized controlled trial (RCT) of phenelzine with Vietnam combat veterans successfully reduced reexperiencing and hyperarousal symptoms of PTSD (Kosten et al., 1991). However, uncontrolled trials of this drug have yielded no effects (Milanes, Mack, Dennison, & Slater, 1984), and one study reported symptom worsening (Shestatzky, Greenberg, & Lerer, 1988). Investigating a different MAOI, moclobemide, Neal, Shapland, and Fox (1997) reported improvements across the PTSD symptom clusters. Mirtazepine and venlafaxine, which work on both the serotonin and norepinephrine systems, have been shown to reduce PTSD symptoms in RCTs (Davidson et al., 2006; Davidson et al., 2003). Only case studies and open trials support the use of bupropion, which has noradrenergic and dopaminergic effects, in treating PTSD (Canive, Clark, Calais, Qualls, & Tuason, 1998).

Antiadrenergics (Drugs Acting on the Epinephrine and Norepinephrine Systems)

Research with prazosin reveals improvements in trauma-related nightmares and other PTSD symptoms (Raskind, Peskind, Kanter, Petrie, Radont et al., 2003). A large multi-site study within the U.S. Veterans' Administration is underway to further investigate this medication in the treatment of PTSD. In addition, there is some evidence that propranolol is not only an efficacious treatment for PTSD (e.g., Famularo, Kinscherff, & Fenton, 1988), but also an effective prophylactic agent to prevent acutely traumatized individuals from later PTSD (e.g., Pitman et al., 2002; Vaiva, Ducrocq, Jezequel, Averland, Lestavel et al., 2003).

Mood Stabilizers

Only one small RCT of a medication within this class, lamotrigine, has been conducted, and this trial found improvements in PTSD (Hertzberg, 1999). Case studies and small, open-label trials suggest that other mood stabilizers, including carbamazepine, valproate, topirimate, gabapentin, tiagabine, and vigabatrin may hold promise in the treatment of PTSD symptoms (e.g., Berigan, 2002; Berlant & van Kammen, 2002; Brannon, Labbate, & Huber, 2000; Clark, Canive, Calais, Qualls, & Tuason, 1999; Lipper et al., 1986; Macleod, 1996). However, these medications have not yet been submitted to the rigors of RCTs.

GABA-ergic Agonists (Anti-Anxiety Medication)

An RCT of the benzodiazepine alprazolam showed no reduction in PTSD symptoms (Braun, Greenberg, Dasberg, & Lerer, 1990). Moreover, trials testing other benzodiazepines (i.e., clonazepam, temazepam) with acutely traumatized emergency room patients have failed to find that these drugs are efficacious in reducing the likelihood of later PTSD symptoms (Gelpin, 1996; Mellman, Bustamante, David, & Fins, 2002).

Augmentation with Partial NMDA Agonist

D-cycloserine is a partial NMDA glutamatergic receptor agonist that has positive effects on memory deficits in elderly volunteers (Jones, Wesnes, & Kirby, 1991) and Alzheimer's disease patients (Schwartz, Hashtroudi, Herting, Schwartz, & Deutsch, 1996). An RCT of D-cycloserine as an augmentation to other medications for PTSD revealed significantly greater reductions in PTSD and anxiety, but not depressive symptoms, compared with placebo augmentation (Heresco-Levy et al., 2002).

Augmentation with Atypical Antipsychotics

Two RCTs report improvements in PTSD as a result of using risperidone as an adjunctive therapy to other medications for PTSD (Bartzokis, Lu, Turner, Mintz, & Saunders, 2005; Hamner, Faldowski et al., 2003). Similarly, an open trial of quetiapine as an adjunctive agent to other pharmacological treatments has revealed positive effects on PTSD symptoms (Hamner, Deitsch, Brodrick, Ulmer, & Lorberbaum, 2003). The results regarding olanzapine, another atypical antipsychotic, as an adjunctive agent have been mixed. One RCT indicates its efficacy among chronic PTSD patients who had failed to respond to other agents (Stein, Kline, & Matloff, 2002), but another RCT failed to find an adjunctive effect (Butterfield et al., 2001).

PSYCHOSOCIAL TREATMENT

There have now been over 40 RCTs of psychotherapy for PTSD. Early trials compared active treatment to wait-list control, while later trials have compared different psychotherapies to one another or to therapies controlling for the nonspecific elements of any good psychotherapy. More recent efforts have been aimed at comparing the additive value of different types of interventions and at determining the essential elements of a given therapy using dismantling designs. Cognitive-behavioral therapy has the most evidence supporting its efficacy. There are several other types of therapies with growing evidence of efficacy based on RCTs.

Cognitive-Behavioral Therapy

A number of RCTs have established the efficacy of behavioral exposure to trauma-related material in the treatment of PTSD compared to a waiting-list control condition. The exposure interventions come in the form of exposure to the trauma memory, as in imaginal exposure, or through exposure to trauma-related stimuli in the environment, in vivo exposure. One of the most thoroughly researched exposure therapies is prolonged exposure (PE) (Foa et al., 1991; Foa, Hearst, Dancu, Hembree, & Jaycox, 1994), which includes both imaginal and *in vivo* exposure techniques. Prolonged exposure has been shown to be efficacious in the treatment of sexual assault-related PTSD in several trials (Foa et al., 1999; Foa & Rothbaum, 1998), and there is some evidence of its efficacy in other trauma populations (Cigrang, Peterson, & Schobitz, 2005; Marshall & Suh, 2003). Similarly, several trials have established the efficacy of different forms of cognitive therapy that have not included behavioral exposure interventions in the treatment of PTSD (Bryant, Moulds, & Guthrie, 2003; Gillespie, Duffy, Hackmann, & Clark, 2002; Kubany et al., 2004; Marks, Lovell, Noshirvani, Livanou, & Thrasher, 1998; Tarrier et al., 1999). Cognitive Processing Therapy (CPT) (Resick & Schnicke, 1993), a predominantly cognitive therapy for PTSD that includes some behavioral elements, has established efficacy in the treatment of PTSD in a variety of traumatized populations (Chard, 2005; Monson et al., 2006; Resick & Schnicke, 1992; Schulz, Resick, Huber, & Griffin, 2006). There are a few nontrauma-focused cognitive-behavioral therapies that have been found to be more efficacious than waiting list. For example, Stress Inoculation Therapy (SIT) without any trauma-specific interventions has been shown to be efficacious in the treatment of PTSD (Foa et al., 1999).

A few trials have compared CBT to nonspecific therapy, to control for therapist effects. For example, Schnurr et al. (2007) conducted a large, multisite trial comparing PE with present-centered therapy (PCT), which included support and problem solving, in a sample of women veterans with PTSD. They found that PE was more efficacious than PCT in treating PTSD and other comorbid conditions. In head-to-head trials comparing different forms of CBT, very few differences between the therapies in their ability to treat PTSD have generally emerged. For example, in Resick et al.'s (2002) trial, there were no statistical differences between CPT and PE in PTSD symptoms at any assessment point.

There have been a few potentially important differences between these treatments found at follow-up assessments and in the treatment of comorbid conditions. In Foa's early trial comparing PE and SIT, there were no differences between the two treatments at post-treatment assessment; however, starting at 3-month follow-up, there was an advantage of PE over SIT in treating PTSD symptoms (Foa, Rothbaum, Riggs, & Murdock, 1991). At 5-year follow-up of their trial comparing imaginal exposure and cognitive therapy, Tarrier and Sommerfield (2004) found an advantage of cognitive therapy over imaginal exposure in maintaining diminished PTSD symptoms. With regard to conditions often co-occurring with PTSD, Resick et al. (2002) found statistical advantages of CPT over PE in some aspects of trauma-related guilt.

The latest generation of studies examining specific cognitive and behavioral interventions and their combination in the treatment of PTSD generally suggests that interventions with a singular element are as efficacious as combined elements. Findings supporting this conclusion come from Foa et al.'s study (1999) comparing PE to SIT and their combination (PE/SIT), and Foa et al.'s (2005) study comparing PE to PE plus cognitive therapy. Similarly, in Resick et al.'s (2005) dismantling study comparing full CPT with the written trauma account-only element of CPT (Writing Exposure or WE) and the cognitive therapy-only element of CPT (CPT-C), there were no differences at posttreatment or 6-month follow-up assessment. However, Resick et al. also found that the CPT-C version improved faster during treatment, differed significantly from CPT until the exposure component was completed, and differed from the WE condition until the end of treatment.

An exception to the trend for equivalent efficacy in singular and combined therapies comes from Bryant et al.'s (2001) study revealing advantages to combined imaginal exposure and cognitive restructuring over imaginal exposure alone. An additional caveat to the conclusion that therapies with a singular element are equally efficacious to combined therapies is that studies heretofore have equated the amount of time spent in treatment sessions for methodological reasons. Therefore, it is difficult to determine if additional elements delivered with extra time might yield more efficacious treatment.

Eye Movement Densitization and Reprocessing (EMDR)

Several studies have shown that EMDR is more effective than waiting list in the treatment of PTSD (e.g., Rothbaum, 1997; Wilson, Becker, & Tinker, 1995), and a recent trial comparing EMDR with PE found no differences between the two groups in their efficacy in treating PTSD (Rothbaum, Astin, & Marsteller, 2005). Although EMDR may lead to improvements in PTSD symptoms, there is much debate surrounding the active ingredients of EMDR that are considered responsible for improvements. Randomized controlled trials in which patients have received the treatment with and without the manipulation of eye movements, or with eye movements versus other irrelevant movements have yielded no evidence supporting the specific efficacy of eye movements (e.g., Devilly & Spence, 1999; Pitman et al., 1996). These results have led many to conclude that the active ingredients of EMDR are really cognitive-behavioral in nature (Monson et al., 2007).

Other Therapies with Controlled Evidence

Several other therapies have been shown to be efficacious relative to waiting list and other control conditions. Brief eclectic psychotherapy (BEP) combines cognitive-behavioral and psychodynamic approaches and includes five basic elements: (1) psychoeducation about PTSD, (2) imaginal exposure, (3) writing tasks and memorabilia aimed at uncovering difficult feelings, (4) meaning and integration, and (5) farewell ritual. It has been shown to be efficacious compared with waiting lists, in samples of police officers (Gersons, Carlier, & Lamberts, 2000) and outpatients with a range of traumas (Lindauer, Vlieger, & Jalink, 2005). Narrative Exposure Therapy (NET; Schauer, Neuner, & Elbert, 2005) involves patients providing a detailed chronological report of his or her own biography, with a special focus on traumatic experiences. This report is recorded in written form and read during sessions with the goal of developing a coherent narrative of the traumatic event and the habituation of emotional responses to reminders of the traumatic event. There have been two controlled trials of NET showing it to be efficacious compared with psychoeducation and supportive counseling in survivors of political detention (Bichescu, Neuner, Schauer, & Elbert, in press) and refugees (Neuner, Schauer, Klaschik, Karunakara, & Elbert, 2004). In a sample of childhood abuse survivors, Cloitre, Koenen, Cohen, and Han (2002) also found that behavioral interventions to improve affect regulation and interpersonal skills followed by a modified form of PE was more efficacious than a waiting-list control.

Treatment Summary

There are several efficacious pharmacological and psychosocial treatments that are capable of ameliorating the symptoms of PTSD for many individuals. We are aware of only one head-to-head trial comparing medications and psychotherapy in the treatment of PTSD, and that trial compared EMDR to fluoxetine (van der Kolk et al., 2007). EMDR yielded greater symptom reductions that were better sustained over time compared with fluoxetine. These results, favoring psychotherapy over medications for PTSD, are consistent with prior meta-analyses directly comparing medications and psychotherapies generally (Van Etten & Taylor, 1998), as well as effect size comparisons of meta-analyses of drugs (Mooney, Oakley, Ferriter, & Travers, 2004; Stein, Seedat, & van der Linden, 2000) and meta-analyses of psychotherapy (Bisson et al., 2007; Bradley, Greene, Russ, Dutra, & Westen, 2005) for PTSD. It is also important to note that discontinuation of medication is associated with relapse of PTSD symptoms (e.g., Martenyi, Brown, Zhang, Koke, & Prakash, 2002), whereas long-term follow-up of patients in PTSD psychotherapy trials indicates maintenance of gains across different types of therapy (e.g., Resick et al., 2002; Schnurr et al., 2007; Tarrier & Sommerfield, 2004).

Future studies that examine the combination and sequencing of current evidence-based medication and psychosocial treatments (e.g., Rothbaum et al., 2006), as well as the use of medications like D-cycloserine, which might potentiate the effects of psychotherapy for PTSD, are needed to increase the percentage of individuals who respond to treatment.

Moreover, there is still room for psychosocial and pharmacological treatment innovations for the approximately 50% of individuals in intention-to-treat samples who do not have a remission in their PTSD diagnosis as a result of treatment. Several psychotherapies for PTSD in development have at least uncontrolled trial data supporting their efficacy, including such therapies as Imagery Rescripting (Smucker, Dancu, & Foa, 1995), Interapy (Lange, Rietdijk, & Hudcovicova, 2003), Virtual Reality Exposure (Rothbaum, Hodges, & Ready, 2001), Acceptance and Commitment Therapy (Walser & Hayes, 2006), Behavioral Activation Therapy (Jakupcak et al., 2006), and Cognitive-Behavioral Conjoint Therapy for PTSD (Monson, Schnurr, Stevens, & Guthrie, 2004). Likewise, there are new drugs in development that are theoretically likely to improve PTSD symptoms, such as the corticotrophin releasing factor antagonist antalarmin, which has been shown to reduce stress-induced fearful behavior in preclinical studies (Friedman & Davidson, 2007). There are also existing drugs like hydrocortisone, a glucocorticoid, or mifepristone (RU-486), which blocks glucocorticoid receptors, that might be considered with new indications, if diminished or excessive cortisol levels (respectively), prove to be consistently associated with the disorder (Friedman & Davidson). Treatments that address PTSD and comorbid disorders, such as Seeking Safety (Najavits, 2003), designed for comorbid PTSD and substance abuse, and a cognitive-behavioral treatment developed by Mueser, Rosenberg, Jankowski, Hamblen, & Descamps (2004) that simultaneously addresses PTSD and severe mental illness appear promising.

Summary and Future Directions

Over the past 3 decades of study on the effects and treatment of traumatic stress, we have made great gains in understanding posttraumatic responses and recovery. We now understand that most people experience traumatic events in their lives that are of sufficient magnitude to trigger serious posttraumatic responses. Nevertheless, with time, the majority of people go on to recover from these events. However, there does appear to be a limit as to how much trauma people can absorb, as demonstrated by a strong dose-response relationship. The more traumas that people experience, the more difficulty they will have returning to healthy and balanced functioning without some type of assistance. A person's biological make-up and alterations that occur as a result of trauma will interact with memory, cognition, emotions, and behavior to promote or interfere with recovery. The external environment also has an important effect on recovery or maintenance of PTSD symptoms. Positive and sufficient social support, lack of negative reactions (which has a disproportionate influence compared with good support), and sufficient resources are important in recovery. Additional life stressors such as family adjustment problems and problems with work or housing can all complicate and delay, or prevent, recovery. One only has to look at situations like Hurricane Katrina, with the prolonged duration of the event and the area's slow recovery, or the war in Iraq, with its multiple deployments of military personnel into highly volatile and unpredictable violence, to understand how continued environmental instability prevents the return to homeostasis.

Fortunately, we have treatments that work with the majority of people with PTSD (40% to 80% fully remit, depending upon the population and sampling method). Although there is no specific PTSD medication thus far that is as effective as cognitive-behavioral therapy, many medications can provide some relief for some symptoms. Both cognitive therapy and exposure treatments are effective and, unlike some other disorders, there is little evidence of relapse over time. However, because PTSD is maintained over time by avoidance and numbing, people often refuse to seek treatment. even when they know it is available, and they may drop out at rather high rates (20% to 40%). Also, because PTSD is most often accompanied by other disorders, treatment may be complicated by substance abuse, chronic pain, severe depression, and personality disorders. The recent wars in Iraq and Afghanistan are highlighting the problem of head injury and PTSD, although this may have been an unidentified complication in other cases of PTSD in which head injuries are common, such as domestic violence, child abuse, and motor vehicle accidents.

Challenges for the future will be to incorporate what we have learned about PTSD into future diagnostic schemes as we move toward the *DSM-V* and *ICD-XX*. Although most current theories of PTSD are concerned with memory and cognition, there is very little mention of either in the diagnostic criteria. Because PTSD has been categorized with the anxiety disorders, most of the research and treatment focus has been on fear and anxiety to the exclusion of other important emotions, such as anger, sadness, shame, or horror. There is sufficient research on these topics to indicate that they may interfere with recovery and predict poorer outcome with treatment than fear and anxiety. Diagnostic criteria and treatment research need to attend to these other emotions as well. Furthermore, if the diagnostic criteria move to a more dimensional than categorical organization, there will be a question as to how PTSD should be considered. People with PTSD appear to have either a simple case of PTSD, in which they have the core symptoms of intrusive images/nightmares, arousal and emotions, and avoidance, or a more complex picture, which can include a broad range of externalizing or internalizing attempts to cope with their unacceptable memories. Posttraumatic Stress Disorder appears to fall on both the internalizing and externalizing dimensions for large numbers of people.

Research on treatment is beginning to push into areas of comorbidity, and is questioning the current wisdom of treating comorbid conditions separately and sequentially. Research on systems of delivery such as telehealth or Internet-based therapies are currently underway. Research on dissemination of evidence-based treatments is also underway, with a growing understanding that books and workshops are not sufficient to train clinicians; built-in follow-up supports and actual system change may be needed. Finally, there is a great deal of research currently being conducted on the underlying biology of PTSD, including neurotransmitters, hormones, and brain structures, which will fuel our understanding of the interaction of biology, individual differences, and environment in PTSD over the next decade.

References

Achenbach, T. M., & Edelbrock, C. S. (1978). The classification of child psychopathology: A review and analysis of empirical efforts. *Psychological Bulletin*, *85*, 1275–1301.

Achenbach, T. M., & Edelbrock, C. S. (1984). Psychopathology of childhood. *Annual Review of Psychology*, *35*, 227–256.

American Psychiatric Association. (1994). *Diagnostic and statistical manual of mental disorders* (4th ed.). Washington, DC: Author.

American Psychiatric Association. (2000). *Diagnostic and statistical manual of mental disorders* (4th ed., text revision [*DSM-IV-TR*]). Washington, DC: Author.

American Psychiatry Association. (2004). Practice guideline for the treatment of patients with acute stress disorder and posttraumatic stress disorder. *American Journal of Psychiatry*, *161*, November supplement.

Andrews, B., Brewin, C. R., Philpott, R., & Stewart, L. (2007). Delayed onset posttraumatic stress disorder: A systematic review of the evidence. *American Journal of Psychiatry*, *164*, 1319–1326.

Andrews, B., Brewin, C. R., Rose, S., & Kirk, M. (2000). Predicting PTSD symptoms in victims of violent crime: The role of shame, anger, and childhood abuse. *Journal of Abnormal Psychology*, *109*, 69–73.

Arora, R. C., Fichtner, C. G., O'Connor, F., & Crayton, J. W. (1993). Paroxetine binding in the blood platelets of post-traumatic stress disorder patients. *Life Sciences*, *53*, 919–928.

Baker, D. G., West, S. A., Nicholson, W. E., Ekhator, N. N., Kasckow, J. W., Hill, K. K., et al. (1999). Serial CSF corticotropin-releasing hormone levels and adrenocortical activity in combat veterans with posttraumatic stress disorder. *American Journal of Psychiatry*, *156*, 585–588.

Bartzokis, G., Lu, P. H., Turner, J., Mintz, J., & Saunders, C. S. (2005). Adjunctive resperidone in the treatment of chronic combat-related posttraumatic stress disorder. *Biological Psychiatry*, *57*, 474–479.

Beck, J. G., Freeman, J. B., Shipherd, J. C., Hamblen, J. L., & Lackner, J. M. (2001). Specificity of Stroop interference in patients with pain and PTSD. *Journal of Abnormal Psychology*, *110*, 536–543.

Beckham, J. C., Feldman, M. E., & Kirby, A. C. (1998). Atrocities exposure in Vietnam combat veterans with chronic posttraumatic stress disorder: Relationship to combat exposure, symptom severity, guilt, and interpersonal violence. *Journal of Traumatic Stress*, *11*, 777–785.

Berigan, T. (2002). Treatment of posttraumatic stress disorder with tiagabine. *Canadian Journal of Psychiatry*, *8*, 788.

Berlant, J. L., & vanKammen, D. P. (2002). Open-label topiramate as primary or adjunctive therapy in chronic civilian post-traumatic stress disorder: A preliminary report. *Journal of Clinical Psychiatry*, *63*, 15–20.

Bichescu, D., Neuner, F., Schauer, M., & Elbert, T. (in press). Narrative exposure therapy for political imprisonment-related chronic posttraumatic stress disorder and depression. *Behaviour Research and Therapy*.

Bisson, J., Ehlers, A., Matthews, R., Pilling, S., Richards, D., & Turner, S. (2007). Psychological treatments for chronic post-traumatic stress disorder: Systematic review and meta-analysis. *British Journal of Psychiatry*, *190*, 97–104.

Blake, D. D., Weathers, F. W., Nagy, L. M., Kaloupek, D. G., Gusman, F. D., Charney, D. S., et al. (1995). The development of a clinician-administered PTSD scale. *Journal of Traumatic Stress*, *8*, 75–90.

Blanchard, E. B., Hickling, E. J., Buckley, T. C., & Taylor, A. E. (1996). Psychophysiology of posttraumatic stress disorder related to motor vehicle accidents: Replication and extension. *Journal of Consulting and Clinical Psychology*, *64*, 742–751.

Blanchard, E. B., Hickling, E. J., Malta, L. S., Jaccard, J., Devineni, T., Veazey, C. H., et al. (2003). Prediction of response to psychological treatment among motor vehicle accident survivors with PTSD. *Behavior Therapy*, *34*, 351–363.

Blanchard, E. B., Jones-Alexander, J., Buckley, T. C., & Forneris, C. A. (1996). Psychometric properties of the PTSD Checklist (PCL). *Behaviour Research and Therapy*, *34*, 669–673.

Blanchard, E. B., Kolb, L. C., Prins, A., Gates, S., & McCoy, G. C. (1991). Changes in plasma norepinephrine to combat-related stimuli among Vietnam veterans with posttraumatic stress disorder. *Journal of Nervous and Mental Disease*, *179*, 371–373.

Boudewyns, P. A., & Hyer, L. (1990). Physiological response to combat memories and preliminary treatment outcome in Vietnam veteran PTSD patients treated with direct therapeutic exposure. *Behavior Therapy, 21*, 63–87.

Bradley, R., Greene, J., Russ, E., Dutra, L., & Westen, D. (2005). A multidimensional meta-analysis of psychotherapy for PTSD. *American Journal of Psychiatry, 162*, 214–227.

Bramsen, I., Van der Ploeg, H. M., & Twisk, J. W. R. (2002). Secondary traumatization in Dutch couples of World War II survivors. *Journal of Consulting and Clinical Psychology, 70*, 241–245.

Brannon, N., Labbate, L., & Huber, M. (2000). Gabapentin treatment for posttraumatic stress disorder. *Canadian Journal of Psychiatry, 45*, 84.

Braun, P., Greenberg, D., Dasberg, H., & Lerer, B. (1990). Core symptoms of posttraumatic stress disorder unimproved by alprazolam treatment. *Journal of Clinical Psychology, 51*, 236–238.

Bremner, J. D., Innis, R. B., Southwick, S. M., Staib, L., Zoghbi, S., & Charney, D. S. (2000). Decreased benzodiazepine receptor binding in prefrontal cortex in combat-related posttraumatic stress disorder. *American Journal of Psychiatry, 157*, 1120–1126.

Bremner, J. D., Licinio, J., Darnell, A., Krystal, J. H., Owens, M. J., & Southwick, S. M., et al. (1997). Elevated CSF corticotropin-releasing factor concentrations in posttraumatic stress disorder. *American Journal of Psychiatry, 154*, 624–629.

Bremner, J. D., Southwick, S., & Charney, D. (1999). The neurobiology of posttraumatic stress disorder: An integration of animal and human research. In P. A. Saigh & J. D. Bremner (Eds.), *Posttraumatic stress disorder: A comprehensive text* (pp. 103–143). Boston: Allyn and Bacon.

Bremner, J. D., Vermetten, E., Vythilingan, M., Afzal, N., Schmahl, C., Elzinga, B., et al. (2004). Neural correlates of the classic color and emotional Sstroop in women with abuse-related posttraumatic stress disorder. *Biological Psychiatry, 55*, 612–620.

Brewin, C. R. (1996). Theoretical foundations of cognitive-behavioral therapy for anxiety and depression. *Annual Review of Psychology, 47*, 33–57.

Brewin, C. R. (2007). Remembering and forgetting. In M. J. Friedman, T. M. Keane & P. A. Resick (Eds.), *Handbook of PTSD: Science and practice* (pp. 116–134). New York: Guilford.

Brewin, C. R., Andrews, B., & Rose, S. (2000). Fear, helplessness, and horror in posttraumatic stress disorder: Investigating *DSM-IV* criterion A2 in victims of violent crime. *Journal of Traumatic Stress, 13*, 499–509.

Brewin, C. R., Andrews, B., & Valentine, J. D. (2000). Meta-analysis of risk factors for posttraumatic stress disorder in trauma-exposed adults. *Journal of Consulting and Clinical Psychology, 68*, 748–766.

Brewin, C. R., Dalgleish, T., & Joseph, S. (1996). A dual representation theory of posttraumatic stress disorder. *Psychological Review, 103*, 670–686.

Brewin, C. R., Kleiner, J. S., & Vasterling, J. J. (in press). Memory for emotionally neutral information in posttraumatic stress disorder: A meta-analytic investigation. *Journal of Abnormal Psychology.*

Briere, J. (1995). *The Trauma Symptom Inventory (TSI): Professional manual.* Odessa, FL: Psychological Assessment Resources.

Brown, T. A., DiNardo, P. A., Lehman, C. L., & Campbell, L. A. (2001). Reliability of *DSM-IV* anxiety and mood disorders: Implications for the classification of emotional disorders. *Journal of Abnormal Psychology, 119*, 49–58.

Bryant, R. A., & Harvey, A. G. (1995). Processing threatening information in posttraumatic stress disorder. *Journal of Abnormal Psychology, 104*, 537–541.

Bryant, R. A., Moulds, M. L., & Guthrie, R. M. (2003). Imaginal exposure alone and imaginal exposure with cognitive restructuring in treatment of posttraumatic stress disorder. *Journal of Consulting and Clinical Psychology, 71*, 706–712.

Burnett, A., & Peel, M. R. (2001). Asylum seekers and refugees in Britain: The health of survivors of torture and organised violence. *British Medical Journal, 322*, 606–609.

Butterfield, M. I., Becker, M. E., Connor, K. M., Sutherland, S., Churchill, L. E., & Davidson, J. R. T. (2001). Olanzapine in the treatment of post-traumatic stress disorder: A pilot study. *International Clinical Psychopharmacology, 16*, 197–203.

Byrne, C. A., & Riggs, D. S. (1996). The cycle of trauma: Relationship aggression in male Vietnam veterans with symptoms of posttraumatic stress disorder. *Violence and Victims, 11*, 213–225.

Cahill, S. P., & Foa, E. B. (2007). Psychological theories of PTSD. In M. J. Friedman, T. M. Keane, & P. A. Resick (Eds.), *Handbook of PTSD: Science and practice* (pp. 55–77). New York: Guilford.

Canive, J. M., Clark, R. D., Calais, L. A., Qualls, C., & Tuason, V. B. (1998). Bupropion treatment in veterans with posttraumatic stress disorder: An open study. *Journal of Clinical Psychopharmacology, 18*, 379–383.

Chard, K. M. (2005). Cognitive processing therapy for sexual abuse: A treatment outcome study. *Journal of Consulting and Clinical Psychology*, *73*, 965–971.

Chemtob, C. M., Hamada, R. S., Roitblat, H. L., & Muraoka, M. Y. (1994). Anger, impulsivity, and anger control in combat-related posttraumatic stress disorder. *Journal of Consulting and Clinical Psychology*, *62*, 827–832.

Chemtob, C. M., Novaco, R. W., Hamada, R. S., & Gross, D. M. (1997). Cognitive-behavioral treatment for severe anger in posttraumatic stress disorder. *Journal of Consulting and Clinical Psychology*, *65*, 184–189.

Cigrang, J. A., Peterson, A. L., & Schobitz, R. P. (2005). Three American troops in Iraq: Evaluation of a brief exposure therapy treatment for the secondary prevention of combat-related PTSD. *Pragmatic Case Studies in Psychotherapy*, *1*, 1–25.

Clark, R. D., Canive, J. M., Calais, L. A., Qualls, C. R., & Tuason, V. B. (1999). Divalproex in posttraumatic stress disorder: An open-label clinical trial. *Journal of Traumatic Stress*, *12*, 395–401.

Cloitre, M., Koenen, K. C., Cohen, L. R., & Han, H. (2002). Skills training in affective and interpersonal regulation followed by exposure: A phase-based treatment for PTSD related to childhood abuse. *Journal of Consulting and Clinical Psychology*, *70*, 1067–1074.

Cox, B. J., Clara, I. P., & Enns, M. W. (2002). Posttraumatic stress disorder and the structure of common mental disorders. *Depression and Anxiety*, *15*, 168–171.

Dalgleish, T. (2004). Cognitive approaches to posttraumatic stress disorder: The evolution of multirepresentational theorizing. *Psychological Bulletin*, *130*, 228–260.

Davidson, J., Rothbaum, B. O., Tucker, P., Asnis, G., Benattia, I., & Musgnung, J. J. (2006). Venlafaxine extended release in posttraumatic stress disorder: A sertraline- and placebo-controlled study. *Journal of Clinical Psychopharmacology*, *26*, 259–267.

Davidson, J. R. T., Bernick, M., Connor, K. M., Friedman, M. J., Jobson, K., Kim, Y., et al. (2005). A psychopharmacology algorithm for treating posttraumatic stress disorder. *Psychiatric Annals*, *35*, 887–898.

Davidson, J. R. T., Kudler, H., Smith, R., Mahorney, S. L., Lipper, S., Hammett, E. B., et al. (1990). Treatment of post-traumatic stress disorder with amitriptyline and placebo. *Archives of General Psychiatry*, *47*, 259–266.

Davidson, J. R. T., Weisler, R. H., Butterfield, M. I., Casat, C. D., Connor, K. M., Barnett, S., et al. (2003). Mirtazapine vs. placebo in posttraumatic

stress disorder: A pilot trial. *Biological Psychiatry*, *53*, 188–191.

Davies, M. I., & Clark, D. M. (1998). Thought suppression produces a rebound effect with analogue posttraumatic intrusions. *Behaviour Research and Therapy*, *36*, 571–582.

Davis, L., Clark, D., Kramer, G., Moeller, F., & Petty, F. (1999). D-fenfluramine challenge in posttraumatic stress disorder. *Biological Psychiatry*, *45*, 928–930.

Derogatis, L. R. (1983). *SCL-90-R: Administration, scoring and procedures manual-II*. Towson, MD: Clinical Psychometric Research.

Desalvo, K. B., Hyre, A. D., Ompad, D. C., Menke, A., Tynes, L. L., & Muntner, P. (2007). Symptoms of posttraumatic stress disorder in a New Orleans workforce following Hurricane Katrina. *Journal of Urban Health*, *84*, 142–152.

Devilly, G. J., & Spence, S. H. (1999). The relative efficacy and treatment distress of EMDR and a cognitive-behavior trauma treatment protocol in the amelioration of posttraumatic stress disorder. *Journal of Anxiety Disorders*, *13*, 131–157.

Dohrenwend, B. P., Turner, J. B., Turse, N. A., Adams, B. G., Koenen, K. C., & Marshall, R. (2006). The psychological risks of Vietnam for U.S. veterans: A revisit with new data and methods. *Science*, *313*, 979–982.

Dunmore, E., Clark, D. M., & Ehlers, A. (1999). Cognitive factors involved in the onset and maintenance of posttraumatic stress disorder (PTSD) after physical or sexual assault. *Behaviour Research and Therapy*, *37*, 809–829.

Dunmore, E., Clark, D. M., & Ehlers, A. (2001). A prospective investigation of the role of cognitive factors in persistent posttraumatic stress disorder (PTSD) after physical or sexual assault. *Behaviour Research and Therapy*, *39*, 1063–1084.

Egendorf, A., Kadushin, C., Laufer, R. S., Rothbart, G., & Sloan, L. (1981). *Legacies of Vietnam: Comparative adjustment of veterans and their peers*. New York: Center for Policy Research.

Ehlers, A., & Clark, D. M. (2000). A cognitive model of posttraumatic stress disorder. *Behaviour Research and Therapy*, *38*, 319–345.

Fairbank, J. A., Keane, T. M., & Malloy, P. F. (1983). Some preliminary data on the psychological characteristics of Vietnam veterans with posttraumatic stress disorder. *Journal of Consulting and Clinical Psychology*, *51*, 912–919.

Famularo, R., Kinscherff, R., & Fenton, T. (1988). Propranolol treatment for childhood posttraumatic stress disorder, acute type. *American Journal of Diseases of Children, 142*, 1244–1247.

Fichtner, C., Arora, R., O'Connor, F., & Crayton, J. (1994). Platelet paroxetine binding and fluoxetine pharmacotherapy in posttraumatic stress disorder: Preliminary observations on a possible predictor of clinical treatment response. *Life Sciences, 54*, 39–44.

Field, N. P., Classen, C., Butler, L. D., Koopman, C., Zarcone, J., & Spiegel, D. (2001). Revictimization and information processing in women survivors of childhood sexual abuse. *Journal of Anxiety Disorders, 15*, 459–469.

First, M. B., Spitzer, R. L., Williams, J. B. W., & Gibbon, M. (1995). *Structured Clinical Interview for* DSM-IV-*Patient Edition (SCID-P)*. Washington, DC: American Psychiatric Press.

Foa, E. B. (1995). *Posttraumatic Stress Diagnostic Scale (manual)*. Minneapolis, MN: National Computer Systems.

Foa, E. B., Cashman, L., Jaycox, L., & Perry, K. (1997). The validation of a self-report measure of posttraumatic stress disorder: The Posttraumatic Diagnostic Scale. *Psychological Assessment, 9*, 445–451.

Foa, E. B., Dancu, C. V., Hembree, E. A., Jaycox, L. H., Meadows, E. A., & Street, G. P. (1999). A comparison of exposure therapy, stress inoculation training, and their combination for reducing posttraumatic stress disorder in female assault victims. *Journal of Consulting and Clinical Psychology, 67*, 194–200.

Foa, E. B., Feske, U., Murdock, T. B., Kozak, M. J., & McCarthy, P. R. (1991). Processing of threat-related information in rape victims. *Journal of Abnormal Psychology, 100*, 156–162.

Foa, E. B., Hearst, D. E., Dancu, C. V., Hembree, E., & Jaycox, L. H. (1994). *Prolonged exposure (PE) manual*. Unpublished manuscript. Medical College of Pennsylvania, Eastern Pennsylvania Psychiatric Institute.

Foa, E. B., Hembree, E. A., Cahill, S. P., Rauch, S. A., Riggs, D. S., Feeny, N. C., et al. (2005). Randomized trial of prolonged exposure for posttraumatic stress disorder with and without cognitive restructuring: Outcome at academic and community clinics. *Journal of Consulting and Clinical Psychology, 73*, 953–964.

Foa, E. B., & Kozak, M. J. (1985). Treatment of anxiety disorders: Implications for psychopathology. In A. H. Tuma & J. D. Maser (Eds.), *Anxiety and the anxiety disorders*. Hillsdale, NJ: Lawrence Erlbaum.

Foa, E. B., & Kozak, M. J. (1986). Emotional processing of fear: Exposure to corrective information. *Psychological Bulletin, 99*, 20–35.

Foa, E. B., Molnar, C., & Cashman, L. (1995). Change in rape narratives during exposure therapy for posttraumatic stress disorder. *Journal of Traumatic Stress, 8*, 675–690.

Foa, E. B., & Rauch, S. A. (2004). Cognitive changes during prolonged exposure versus prolonged exposure plus cognitive restructuring in female assault survivors with posttraumatic stress disorder. *Journal of Consulting and Clinical Psychology, 72*, 879–884.

Foa, E. B., & Riggs, D. S. (1993). Posttraumatic stress disorder in rape victims. In J. Oldham, M. B. Riba, & A. Tasman (Eds.), *American Psychiatric Press Review of Psychiatry* (pp. 273–303). Washington, DC: American Psychiatric Press.

Foa, E. B., Riggs, D. S., Dancu, C. V., & Rothbaum, B. O. (1993). Reliability and validity of a brief instrument for assessing post-traumatic stress disorder. *Journal of Traumatic Stress, 6*, 459–473.

Foa, E. B., Riggs, D. S., Massie, E. D., & Yarczower, M. (1995). The impact of fear activation and anger on the efficacy of exposure treatment for posttraumatic stress disorder. *Behavior Therapy, 26*, 487–499.

Foa, E. B., & Rothbaum, B. O. (1998). *Treating the trauma of rape: Cognitive-behavioral therapy for PTSD*. New York: Guilford.

Foa, E. B., Rothbaum, B. O., Riggs, D. S., & Murdock, T. B. (1991). Treatment of posttraumatic stress disorder in rape victims: A comparison between cognitive-behavioral procedures and counseling. *Journal of Consulting and Clinical Psychology, 59*, 715–723.

Foa, E. B., Steketee, G., & Rothbaum, B. O. (1989). Behavioral/cognitive conceptualizations of posttraumatic stress disorder. *Behavior Therapy, 20*, 155–176.

Forbes, D., Creamer, M., Allen, N., Elliott, P., McHugh, T., Debenham, P., et al. (2003). MMPI-2 based subgroups of veterans with combat-related PTSD: Differential patterns of symptom change after treatment. *Journal of Nervous and Mental Disease, 191*, 531–537.

Forbes, D., Creamer, M., & Biddle, D. (2001). The validity of the PTSD checklist as a measure of symptomatic change in combat-related PTSD. *Behaviour Research and Therapy, 39*, 977–986.

Foy, D. W., Carroll, E. M., & Donahoe, C. P. (1987). Etiological factors in the development of PTSD in clinical samples of Vietnam combat veterans. *Journal of Clinical Psychology, 43*, 17–27.

Freeman, J. B., & Beck, J. G. (2000). Cognitive interference for trauma cues in sexually abused adolescent girls with posttraumatic stress disorder. *Journal of Clinical Child Psychology, 29,* 245–256.

Friedman, M. J., & Davidson, J. R. T. (2007). Pharmacotherapy for PTSD. In M. Friedman, T. M. Keane, & P. A. Resick (Eds.), *PTSD: Science and practice—A comprehensive handbook* (pp. 37–52). New York: Guilford.

Friedman, M. J., Davidson, J. R. T., Mellman, T. A., & Southwick, S. M. (2000). Guidelines for pharmacotherapy and position paper on practice guidelines. In E. B. Foa, T. M. Keane, & M. J. Friedman (Eds.), *Effective treatments for post-traumatic stress disorder: Practice guidelines from the International Society for Traumatic Stress Studies* (pp. 84–105). New York: Guilford.

Friedman, M. J., & Southwick, S. M. (1995). Towards pharmacotherapy for post-traumatic stress disorder. In M. J. Friedman, D. S. Charney, & A. Y. Deutch (Eds.), *Neurobiological and clinical consequences of stress* (pp. 465–482). Philadelphia: Lippincott-Raven.

Galea, S., Ahern, J., Resnick, H., Kilpatrick, D., Bucuvalas, M., Gold, J., et al. (2002). Psychological sequelae of the September 11 terrorist attacks in New York City. *New England Journal of Medicine, 346,* 982–987.

Gelpin, E., Bonne, O., Peri, T., Brandes, D., & Shalev, A. Y. (1996). Treatment of recent trauma survivors with benzodiazepines: A prospective study. *Journal of Clinical Psychiatry, 57,* 390–394.

Gersons, B. P. R., Carlier, I. V. E., & Lamberts, R. D. (2000). Randomized clinical trial of brief eclectic psychotherapy for police officers with posttraumatic stress disorder. *Journal of Traumatic Stress, 13,* 333–347.

Gillespie, K., Duffy, M., Hackmann, A., & Clark, D. M. (2002). Community based cognitive therapy in the treatment of posttraumatic stress disorder following the Omagh bomb. *Behaviour Research and Therapy, 40,* 345–357.

Glenn, D. M., Beckham, J. C., Feldman, M. E., Kirby, A. C., Hertzberg, M. A., & Moore, S. D. (2002). Violence and hostility among families of Vietnam veterans with combat-related posttraumatic stress disorder. *Violence and Victims, 17,* 473–489.

Gray, M. J., Litz, B. T., Hsu, J. L., & Lombardo, T. W. (2004). Psychometric properties of the life events checklist. *Assessment, 11,* 330–341.

Green, B. L. (1996). Trauma History Questionnaire. In B. H. Stamm, (Ed.), *Measurement of stress, trauma, and adaptation* (pp. 366–369). Lutherville, MD: Sidran.

Green, B. L., Lindy, J. D., Grace, M. C., & Leonard, A. C. (1992). Chronic posttraumatic stress disorder and diagnostic comorbidity in a disaster sample. *Journal of Nervous and Mental Disease, 180,* 760–766.

Griffin, M. G., Resick, P. A., & Galovski, T. E. (2006, November). Psychobiological assessment following cognitive behavioral treatment for PTSD in rape and physical assault survivors. Paper presented in Psychobiology and Treatment of PTSD symposium, International Society for Traumatic Stress Studies, Hollywood, CA.

Griffin, M. G., Resick, P. A., & Mechanic, M. B. (1997). Objective assessment of peritraumatic dissociation: Psychophysiological indicators. *American Journal of Psychiatry, 154,* 1081–1088.

Griffin, M. G., Uhlmansiek, M. H., Resick, P. A., & Mechanic, M. B. (2004). Comparison of the posttraumatic stress disorder scale versus the clinician-administered posttraumatic stress disorders scale in domestic violence survivors. *Journal of Traumatic Stress, 17,* 497–504.

Gutner, C., Rizvi, S. L., Monson, C. M., & Resick, P. A. (2006). Changes in coping strategies, relationship to the perpetrator, and posttraumatic stress disorder in female crime victims. *Journal of Traumatic Stress, 19,* 813–823.

Halligan, S. L., Michael, T., Clark, D. M., & Ehlers, A. (2003). Posttraumatic stress disorder following assault: The role of cognitive processing, trauma memory, and appraisals. *Journal of Consulting and Clinical Psychology, 71,* 419–431.

Hamner, M., & Diamond, B. (1993). Elevated plasma dopamine in posttraumatic stress disorder: A preliminary report. *Biological Psychiatry, 33,* 304–306.

Hamner, M. B., Deitsch, S. E., Brodrick, P. S., Ulmer, H. G., & Lorberbaum, J. P. (2003). Quetiapine treatment in patients with posttraumatic stress disorder: An open trial of adjunctive therapy. *Journal of Clinical Psychopharmacology, 23,* 15–20.

Hamner, M. B., Faldowski, R. A., Ulmer, H. G., Frueh, B. C., Huber, M. G., & Arana, G. W. (2003). Adjunctive risperidone treatment in post-traumatic stress disorder: A preliminary controlled trial of effects on comorbid psychotic symptoms. *International Clinical Psychopharmacology, 18,* 1–8.

Harvey, A. G., & Bryant, R. A. (1998). The effect of attempted thought suppression in acute stress disorder. *Behaviour Research and Therapy, 36,* 583–590.

Harvey, A. G., & Bryant, R. A. (1999). A qualitative investigation of the organization of traumatic memories. *British Journal of Clinical Psychology, 38,* 401–405.

Harvey, A. G., Bryant, R. A., & Rapee, R. M. (1996). Preconcious processing of threat in posttraumtic stress disorder. *Cognitive Therapy and Research, 20,* 613–623.

Health hazard evaluation of police officers and firefighters after Hurricane Katrina—New Orleans, October 17–28 and November 30–December 5. (2006). *Morbidity and Mortality Weekly Report, 55,* 456–458.

Heilig, M., & Widerlöv, E. (1990). Neuropeptide Y: An overview of central distribution, functional aspects, and possible involvement in neuropsychiatric illnesses. *Acta Psychiatrica Scandinavica, 82,* 95–114.

Heim, C., Newport, D. J., & Heit, S. (2000). Pituitary-adrenal and autonomic responses to stress in women after sexual and physical abuse in childhood. *Journal of the American Medical Association, 284,* 592–597.

Hellawell, S. J., & Brewin, C. R. (2004). A comparison of flashbacks and ordinary autobiographical memories of trauma: Content and language. *Behaviour Research and Therapy, 42,* 1–12.

Henning, K. R., & Frueh, B. C. (1997). Combat guilt and its relationship to PTSD symptoms. *Journal of Clinical Psychology, 53,* 801–808.

Heresco-Levy, U., Kremer, I., Javitt, D. C., Goichman, R., Reshef, A., Blanaru, M., et al. (2002). Pilot-controlled trial of D-cycloserine for the treatment of post-traumatic stress disorder. *International Journal of Neuropsychopharmacology, 5,* 301–307.

Hertzberg, M. A., Butterfield, M. I., Feldman, M. E., Beckham, J. C., Sutherland, S. M., Connor, K. M., et al. (1999). A preliminary study of lamotrigine for the treatment of posttraumatic stress disorder. *Biological Psychiatry, 45,* 1226–1229.

Hobfoll, S. E. (1989). Conservation of resources: A new attempt at conceptualizing stress. *American Psychologist, 44,* 513–524.

Hobfoll, S. E. (1991). Traumatic stress: A theory based on rapid loss of resources. *Anxiety Research, 4,* 187–197.

Hoge, C. W., Auchterlonie, J. L., & Milliken, C. S. (2006). Mental health problems, use of mental health services, and attrition from military service after returning from deployment to Iraq or Afghanistan. *Journal of the American Medical Association, 295,* 1023–1032.

Hoge, C. W., Castro, C. A., Messer, S. C., McGurk, D., Cotting, D. I., & Koffman, R. L. (2004). Combat duty in Iraq and Afghanistan, mental health prob-lems, and barriers to care. *New England Journal of Medicine, 351,* 13–22.

Hollon, S. D., & Garber, J. (1988). Cognitive therapy. In L. Y. Abramson (Ed.), *Social cognition and clinical psychology: A synthesis* (pp. 204–253). New York: Guilford.

Horowitz, M. J., Wilner, N., & Alvarez, W. (1979). Impact of Event Scale: A measure of subjective stress. *Psychosomatic Medicine, 41,* 209–218.

Hyer, L., Davis, H., Albrecht, W., Boudewyns, P., & Woods, G. (1994). Cluster analysis of MCMI and MCMI-II on chronic PTSD victims. *Journal of Clinical Psychology, 50,* 502–515.

Jakupcak, M., Roberts, L., Martell, C., Mulick, P., Michael, S., Reed, R., et al. (2006). A pilot study of behavioral activation for veterans with posttraumatic stress disorder. *Journal of Traumatic Stress, 19,* 387–391.

Janoff-Bulman, R. (1992). *Shattered assumptions: Towards a new psychology of trauma.* New York: The Free Press.

Jaycox, L. H., Foa, E. B., & Morral, A. R. (1998). Influence of emotional engagement and habituation on exposure therapy for PTSD. *Journal of Consulting and Clinical Psychology, 66,* 185–192.

Jones, C., Harvey, A. G., & Brewin, C. R. (2007). The organisation and content of trauma memories in survivors of road traffic accidents. *Behaviour Research and Therapy, 45,* 151–162.

Jones, J. C., & Barlow, D. H. (1990). The etiology of posttraumatic stress disorder. *Clinical Psychology Review, 10,* 299–328.

Jones, R. W., Wesnes, K. A., & Kirby, J. (1991). Effects of NMDA modulation in scopolamine dementia. *Annals of the New York Academy of Sciences, 640,* 241–244.

Jordan, B. K., Marmar, C. R., Fairbank, J. A., Schlenger, W. E., Kulka, R. A., & Hough, R. L. (1992). Problems in families of male Vietnam veterans with posttraumatic stress disorder. *Journal of Consulting and Clinical Psychology,* 916–926.

Keane, T. M., Brief, D., Pratt, L., & Miller, M. W. (2007). Assessment and diagnosis of PTSD and its comorbidities. In M. Friedman, T. M. Keane, & P. Resick (Eds.), *PTSD: Science and practice—A comprehensive handbook* (pp. 279–305). New York: Guilford.

Keane, T. M., Caddell, J. M., & Taylor, K. L. (1988). Mississippi Scale for Combat-Related Posttraumatic Stress Disorder: Three studies in reliability and validity. *Journal of Consulting and Clinical Psychology, 56,* 85–90.

Keane, T. M., Fairbank, J. A., Caddell, J. M., & Zimering, R. T. (1989). Implosive (flooding) therapy reduces symptoms of PTSD in Vietnam combat veterans. *Behavior Therapy, 20*, 245–260.

Keane, T. M., Fairbank, J. A., Caddell, J. M., Zimering, R. T., & Bender, M. E. (1985). A behavioral approach to assessing and treating posttraumatic stress disorder in Vietnam veterans. In C. R.Figley (Ed.), *Trauma and its wake* (pp. 257–294). New York: Brunner/Mazel.

Keane, T. M., Kaloupek, D. G., & Kolb, L. C. (1998). VA Cooperative Study #334: I. Summary of findings on the psychological assessment of PTSD. *PTSD Research Quarterly, 9*, 1–4.

Keane, T. M., Kolb, L. C., Kaloupek, D. G., Orr, S. P., Blanchard, E. B., Thomas, R. G., et al. (1998). Utility of psychophysiology measurement in the diagnosis of posttraumatic stress disorder: Results from a department of Veterans Affairs cooperative study. *Journal of Consulting and Clinical Psychology, 66*, 914–923.

Keane, T. M., Malloy, P. F., & Fairbank, J. A. (1984). Empirical development of an MMPI subscale for the assessment of combat-related posttraumatic stress disorder. *Journal of Consulting and Clinical Psychology, 52*, 888–891.

Keane, T. M., Scott, W. O., Chavoya, G. A., Lamparski, D. M., & Fairbank, J. A. (1985). Social support in Vietnam veterans with posttraumatic stress disorder: A comparative analysis. *Journal of Consulting and Clinical Psychology, 53*, 95–102.

Kendler, K. S., Prescott, C. A., Myers, J., & Neale, M. C. (2003). The structure of genetic and environmental risk factors for common psychiatric and substance use disorders in men and women. *Archives of General Psychiatry, 60*, 929–937.

Kessler, R. C., Berglund, P., Demler, O., Jin, R., Merikangas, K. R., & Walters, E. E. (2005). Lifetime prevalence and age-of-onset distributions of *DSM-IV* disorders in the National Comorbidity Survey Replication. *Archives of General Psychiatry, 62*, 593–602.

Kessler, R. C., Sonnega, A., Bromet, E., Hughes, M., & Nelson, C. B. (1995). Posttraumatic stress disorder in the National Comorbidity Survey. *Archives of General Psychiatry, 52*, 1048–1060.

Kessler, R. C., Walters, E. E., & Forthofer, M. A. (1998). The social consequences of psychiatric disorders, III: Probability of marital stability. *American Journal of Psychiatry, 155*, 1092–1096.

Kilpatrick, D. G. (1983). Rape victims: Detection, assessment and treatment. *Clinical Psychologist, 36*, 92–95.

Kilpatrick, D. G., Best, C. L., Veronen, L. J., Amick, A. E., Villeponteaux, L. A., & Ruff, G. A. (1985). Mental health correlates of criminal victimization: A random community survey. *Journal of Consulting and Clinical Psychology, 53*, 866–873.

Kimerling, R., Ouimette, P. C., & Wolfe, J. (Eds.). (2002). *Gender and PTSD*. New York: Guilford.

King, D. W., King, L. A., Foy, D. W., Keane, T. M., & Fairbank, J. A. (1999). Posttraumatic stress disorder in a national sample of female and male Vietnam veterans: Risk factors, war-zone stressors, and resilience-recovery variables. *Journal of Abnormal Psychology, 108*, 164–170.

King, L. A., King, D. W., Fairbank, J. A., Keane, T. M., & Adams, G. A. (1998). Resilience-recovery factors in post-traumatic stress disorder among female and male Vietnam veterans: Hardiness, postwar social support, and additional stressful life events. *Journal of Personality and Social Psychology, 74*, 420–434.

Kosten, T. R., Frank, J. B., Dan, E., McDougle, C. J., & Giller, E. L. (1991). Pharmacotherapy for posttraumatic stress disorder using phenelzine or imipramine. *Journal of Nervous and Mental Disease, 179*, 366–370.

Krueger, R. F., Caspi, A., Moffitt, T. E., & Silva, P. A. (1998). The structure and stability of common mental disorders (*DSM-III-R*): A longitudinal-epidemiological study. *Journal of Abnormal Psychology, 107*, 216–227.

Krueger, R. F., McGue, M., & Iacono, W. G. (2001). The higher-order structure of common *DSM* mental disorders: Internalization, externalization, and their connections to personality. *Personality and Individual Differences, 30*, 1245–1259.

Krystal, J. H., D'Souza, D. C., Karper, L. P., Bennett, A., Abi-Dargham, A., Abi-Saab, D., et al. (1999). Interactive effects of subanesthetic ketamine and haloperidol in healthy humans. *Psychopharmacology (Berl), 145*, 193–204.

Krystal, J. H., Karper, L. P., Bennett, A., D'Souza, D. C., Abi-Dargham, A., Morrissey, K., et al. (1998). Interactive effects of subanesthetic ketamine and subhypnotic lorazepam in humans. *Psychopharmacology (Berl), 135*, 213–229.

Krystal, J. H., Karper, L. P., Seibyl, J. P., Freeman, G. K., Delaney, R., & Bremner, J. D., et al. (1994). Subanesthetic effects of the noncompetitive NMDA antagonist, ketamine, in humans. Psychotomimetic, perceptual, cognitive, and neuroendocrine responses. *Archives of General Psychiatry, 51*, 199–214.

Kubany, E. S. (1994). A cognitive model of guilt typology in combat-related PTSD. *Journal of Traumatic Stress*, 7, 3–19.

Kubany, E. S., Haynes, S. N., Abueg, F. R., Manke, F. P., Brennan, J. M., & Stahura, C. (1996). Development and validation of the Trauma-Related Guilt Inventory (TRGI). *Psychological Assessment*, 8, 428–444.

Kubany, E. S., Haynes, S. N., Leisen, M. B., Owens, J. A., Kaplan, A. S., Watson, S. B., et al. (2000). Development and preliminary validation of a brief broad-spectrum measure of trauma exposure: The Traumatic Life Events Questionnaire. *Psychological Assessment*, 12, 210–224.

Kubany, E. S., Hill, E. E., Owens, J. A., Iannce-Spencer, C., McCaig, M. A., Tremayne, K. J., et al. (2004). Cognitive trauma therapy for battered women with PTSD (CTT-BW). *Journal of Consulting and Clinical Psychology*, 72, 3–18.

Kubany, E. S., Leisen, M. B., Kaplan, A. S., & Kelly, M. P. (2000). Validation of a brief measure of posttraumatic stress disorder: The Distressing Event Questionnaire (DEQ). *Psychological Assessment*, 12, 197–209.

Kulka, R. A., Schlenger, W. E., Fairbank, J. A., Hough, R. L., Jordan, B. K., Marmar, C. R., et al. (1990). *Trauma and the Vietnam war generation: Report of findings from the National Vietnam Veterans Readjustment Study*. New York: Brunner/Mazel.

Lang, P. J. (1979). A bio-informational theory of emotional imagery. *Psychophysiology*, 16, 495–512.

Lange, A., Rietdijk, D., & Hudcovicova, M. (2003). Interapy: A controlled randomized trial of the standardized treatment of posttraumatic stress through the Internet. *Journal of Consulting and Clinical Psychology*, 71, 901–909.

Lauterbach, D., & Vrana, S. R. (1996). Three studies on the reliability and validity of a self-report measure of posttraumatic stress disorder. *Assessment*, 3, 17–25.

Lemieux, A. M., & Coe, C. L. (1995). Abuse-related posttraumatic stress disorder: Evidence for chronic neuroendocrine activation in women. *Psychosomatic Medicine*, 57, 105–115.

Leskela, J., Dieperink, M., & Thuras, P. (2002). Shame and posttraumatic stress disorder. *Journal of Traumatic Stress*, 15, 223–226.

Lindauer, R. J. L., Vlieger, E. -J., & Jalink, M. (2005). Effects of psychotherapy on hippocampal volume in out-patients with post-traumatic stress disorder: An MRI investigation. *Psychological Medicine*, 35, 1421–1431.

Lipper, S., Davidson, J. R. T., Grady, T. A., Edinger, J. D., Elliott, B., Hammet, M. D., et al. (1986).

Preliminary study of carbamazepine in posttraumatic stress disorder. *Psychosomatics*, 27, 849–854.

Lipschitz, D. S., Rasmusson, A. M., & Yehuda, R. (2003). Salivary cortisol responses to dexamethasone in adolescents with posttraumatic stress disorder. *Journal of the American Academy of Child and Adolescent Psychiatry*, 42, 1301–1317.

Litz, B. T., Weathers, F. W., Monaco, V., Herman, D. S., Wulfsohn, M., Marx, B., et al. (1996). Attention, arousal, and memory in posttraumatic stress disorder. *Journal of Traumatic Stress*, 9, 497–518.

Macleod, A. D. (1996). Vigabatrin and posttraumatic stress disorder. *Journal of Clinical Psychopharmacology*, 2, 190–191.

March, J. S. (1993). What constitutes a stressor? In J. R. T. Davidson & E. B. Foa (Eds.), *The "Criterion A" issue. Posttraumatic stress disorder:* DSM-IV *and beyond* (pp. 37–54). Washington, DC: American Psychiatric.

Marks, I., Lovell, K., Noshirvani, H., Livanou, M., & Thrasher, S. (1998). Treatment of posttraumatic stress disorder by exposure and/or cognitive restructuring: A controlled study. *Archives of General Psychiatry*, 55, 317–325.

Marshall, R. D., & Suh, E. J. (2003). Contextualizing trauma: Using evidence-based treatments in a multicultural community after 9/11. *Psychiatric Quarterly*, 74, 401–420.

Martenyi, F., Brown, E. B., Zhang, H., Koke, S. C., & Prakash, A. (2002). Fluoxetine v. placebo in prevention of relapse in post-traumatic stress disorder. *British Journal of Psychiatry*, 315–320.

McCann, I. L., & Pearlman, L. A. (1990). *Psychological trauma and the adult survivor: Theory, therapy, and transformation*. New York: Brunner/Mazel.

McCann, I. L., Sakheim, D. K., & Abrahamson, D. J. (1988). Trauma and victimization: A model of psychological adaptation. *The Counseling Psychologist*, 16, 531–594.

McFall, M., Fontana, A., Raskind, M., & Rosenheck, R. (1999). Analysis of violent behavior in Vietnam combat veteran psychiatric inpatients with posttraumatic stress disorder. *Journal of Traumatic Stress*, 12, 501–517.

McFall, M. E., Murburg, M. M., Ko, G. N., & Veith, R. C. (1990). Autonomic responses to stress in Vietnam combat veterans with posttraumatic stress disorder. *Biological Psychiatry*, 27, 1165–1175.

McNally, R. J., English, G. E., & Lipke, H. J. (1993). Assessment of intrusive cognition in PTSD: Use of the modified Stroop paradigm. *Journal of Traumatic Stress*, 6, 33–41.

McNally, R. J., Kaspi, S. P., Riemann, B. C., & Zeitlin, S. B. (1990). Selective processing of threat cues in posttraumatic stress disorder. *Journal of Abnormal Psychology*, *99*, 398–402.

McNally, R. J., & Riccardi, J. N. (1996). Suppression of negative and neutral thoughts. *Behavioural and Cognitive Psychotherapy*, *24*, 17–25.

Mellman, T. A., Bustamante, V., David, D., & Fins, A. I. (2002). Hypnotic medication in the aftermath of trauma (personal comm.). *Journal of Clinical Psychiatry*, *63*, 1183–1184.

Milanes, F. J., Mack, C. N., Dennison, J., & Slater, V. L. (1984). Phenelzine treatment of post-Vietnam stress syndrome. *VA Practitioner*, 40–49.

Miller, M. W., Fogler, J., Wolf, E. J., Kaloupek, D. G., & Keane, T. M. (in press). The internalizing and externalizing structure of psychiatric comorbidity in combat veterans. *Journal of Traumatic Stress*.

Miller, M. W., Greif, J. L., & Smith, A. A. (2003). Multidimensional Personality Questionnaire profiles of veterans with traumatic combat exposure: Externalizing and internalizing subtypes. *Psychological Assessment*, *15*, 205–215.

Miller, M. W., Kaloupek, D. G., Dillon, A. L., & Keane, T. M. (2004). Externalizing and internalizing subtypes of combat-related PTSD: A replication and extension using the PSY-5 scales. *Journal of Abnormal Psychology*, *113*, 636–645.

Miller, M. W., Kaloupek, D. G., & Keane, T. M. (1999, October). Antisociality and physiological hyporesponsivity during exposure to trauma-related stimuli in patients with PTSD. Poster presented at the 39th Annual Meeting of the Society for Psychophysiological Research, Granada, Spain.

Miller, M. W., & Resick, P. A. (2007). Internalizing and externalizing subtypes in female sexual assault survivors: Implications for the understanding of complex PTSD. *Behavior Therapy*, *38*, 58–71.

Monson, C. M., Friedman, M., & LaBash, H. A. J. (2007). A psychological history of PTSD. In M. J. Friedman, T. M. Keane, & P. A. Resick (Eds.), *PTSD: Science and practice—A comprehensive handbook* (pp. 37–52). New York: Guilford.

Monson, C. M., Price, J. L., & Ranslow, E. (2005, October). Treating combat PTSD through cognitive processing therapy. *Federal Practitioner*, 75–83.

Monson, C. M., Schnurr, P. P., Resick, P. A., Friedman, M. J., Young-Xu, Y., & Stevens, S. P. (2006). Cognitive processing therapy for veterans with military-related posttraumatic stress disorder. *Journal of Consulting and Clinical Psychology*, *74*, 898–907.

Monson, C. M., Schnurr, P. P., Stevens, S. P., & Guthrie, K. A. (2004). Cognitive-behavioral couple's treatment for posttraumatic stress disorder: Initial findings. *Journal of Traumatic Stress*, *17*, 341–344.

Mooney, P., Oakley, J., Ferriter, M., & Travers, R. (2004). Sertraline as a treatment for PTSD: A systematic review and meta-analysis. *Irish Journal of Psychological Medicine*, *21*, 100–103.

Moradi, A. R., Taghavi, M. R., Neshat Doost, H. T., Yule, W., & Dalgleish, T. (1999). Performance of children and adolescents with PTSD on the Stroop colour-naming task. *Psychological Medicine*, *29*, 415–419.

Morgan, C. A., III, Hazlett, G., Wang, S., Richardson, E. G., Jr., Schnurr, P., & Southwick, S. M. (2001). Symptoms of dissociation in humans experiencing acute, uncontrollable stress: A prospective investigation. *American Journal of Psychiatry*, *158*, 1239–47.

Morgan, C. A., III, Southwick, S., Hazlett, G., Rasmusson, A., Hoyt, G., Zimolo, Z., et al. (2004). Relationships among plasma dehydroepiandrosterone sulfate and cortisol levels, symptoms of dissociation, and objective performance in humans exposed to acute stress. *Archives of General Psychiatry*, *61*, 819–825.

Morgan, C. A., III, Wang, S., & Southwick, S. M., (2000). Plasma neuropeptide-Y concentrations in humans exposed to military survival training. *Biological Psychiatry*, *47*, 902–909.

Mowrer, O. H. (1947). On the dual nature of learning— A re-interpretation of "conditioning" and "problem-solving." *Harvard Educational Review*, *14*, 102–148.

Mueser, K. T., Rosenberg, S. D., Jankowski, M. K., Hamblen, J. L., & Descamps, M. (2004). Cognitive behavioral treatment program for posttraumatic stress disorder in persons with severe mental illness. *American Journal of Psychiatric Rehabilitation*, *7*, 107–146.

Najavits, L. M. (2003). *Seeking safety: A treatment manual for PTSD and substance abuse*. New York: Guilford.

Neal, L. A., Shapland, W., & Fox, C. (1997). An open trial of moclobemide in the treatment of posttraumatic stress disorder. *International Journal of Clinical Psychopharmacology*, *12*, 231–232.

Neuner, F., Schauer, M., Klaschik, C., Karunakara, U., & Elbert, T. (2004). A comparison of narrative exposure therapy, supportive counseling, and psychoeducation for treating posttraumatic stress disorder in an African refugee settlement. *Journal of Consulting and Clinical Psychology*, *72*, 579–587.

Norris, F. H. (1990). Screening for traumatic stress: A scale for use in the general population. *Journal of Applied Social Psychology, 20,* 1704–1718.

Norris, F. H. (1992). Epidemiology of trauma: Frequency and impact of different potentially traumatic events on different demographic groups. *Journal of Consulting and Clinical Psychology, 60,* 409–418.

North, C. S., Nixon, S. J., Shariat, S., Mallonee, S., McMillen, J. C., Spitznagel, E. L., et al. (1999). Psychiatric disorders among survivors of the Oklahoma City bombing. *Journal of the American Medical Association, 282,* 755–762.

Orr, S. P., Lasko, N. B., Metzger, L. J., Berry, N. J., Ahern, C. E., & Pitman, R. K. (1998). Psychophysiologic assessment of women with posttraumatic stress disorder resulting from childhood sexual abuse. *Journal of Consulting and Clinical Psychology, 66,* 906–913.

Orr, S. P., Metzger, L. J., Miller, M. W., & Kaloupek, D. G. (2004). Psychophysiological assessment of posttraumatic stress disorder. In J. P. Wilson & T. M. Keane (Eds.), *Assessing psychological trauma and PTSD* (2nd ed., pp. 289–343). New York: Guilford.

Orsillo, S. M., Weathers, F. W., Litz, B. T., Steinberg, H. R., Huska, J. A., & Keane, T. M. (1996). Current and lifetime psychiatric disorders among veterans with war zone-related posttraumatic stress disorder. *Journal of Nervous and Mental Disease, 184,* 307–313.

Owens, G. P., & Chard, K. M. (2001). Cognitive distortions among women reporting childhood sexual abuse. *Journal of Interpersonal Violence, 16,* 178–191.

Owens, G. P., Pike, J. L., & Chard, K. M. (2001). Treatment effects of cognitive processing therapy on cognitive distortions of female child sexual abuse survivors. *Behavior Therapy, 32,* 413–424.

Ozer, E. J., Best, S. R., Lipsey, T. L., & Weiss, D. S. (2003). Predictors of posttraumatic stress disorder and symptoms in adults: A meta-analysis. *Psychological Bulletin, 129,* 52–73.

Piekarski, A. M., Sherwood, R., & Funari, D. J. (1993). Personality subgroups in an inpatient Vietnam veteran treatment program. *Psychological Reports, 72,* 667–674.

Pitman, R. K., Orr, S. P., Altman, B., Longpre, R. E., Poiré, R. E., Macklin, M. L., et al. (1996). Emotional processing during eye movement desensitisation and reprocessing therapy of Vietnam veterans with chronic posttraumatic stress disorder. *Comprehensive Psychiatry, 37,* 419–429.

Pitman, R. K., Orr, S. P., Forgue, D. F., & Altman, B. (1990). Psychophysiologic responses to combat imagery of Vietnam veterans with posttraumatic stress disorder versus other anxiety disorders. *Journal of Abnormal Psychology, 99,* 49–54.

Pitman, R. K., Orr, S. P., Forgue, D. F., deJong, J., & Claiborn, J. M. (1987). Psychophysiologic assessment of posttraumatic stress disorder imagery in Vietnam combat veterans. *Archives of General Psychiatry, 44,* 970–975.

Pitman, R. K., Sanders, K. M., Zusman, R. M., Healy, A. R., Cheema, F., Lasko, N. B., et al. (2002). Pilot study of secondary prevention of posttraumatic stress disorder with propranolol. *Biological Psychiatry, 51,* 189–192.

Prins, A., Ouimette, P., Kimerling, R., Cameron, R. P., Hugelshofer, D. S., Shaw-Hegwer, J., et al. (2004). The primary care PTSD screen (PC-PTSD): Development and operating characteristics. *Primary Care Psychiatry, 9,* 9–14.

Rachman, S. (1980). Emotional processing. *Behaviour Research and Therapy, 18,* 51–60.

Raskind, M. A., Peskind, E. R., Kanter, E. D., Petrie, E. C., Radont, A., Thompson, C., et al. (2003). Prazosin reduces nightmares and other PTSD symptoms in combat veterans: A placebo-controlled study. *American Journal of Psychiatry, 160,* 371–373.

Rasmusson, A. M., Hauger, R. L., Morgan, C. A., III, Bremner, J. D., Southwick, S. M., & Charney, D. S. (2000). Low baseline and yohimbine stimulated plasma neuropeptide Y (NPY) levels in combat-related PTSD. *Biological Psychiatry, 47,* 526–539.

Rasmusson, A. M., Pinna, G., & Paliwal, P. (2006). Decreased cerebrospinal fluid allopregnanolone levels in women with posttraumatic stress disorder. *Biological Psychiatry, 60,* 704–713.

Rasmusson, A. M., Vasek, J., & Lipschitz, D. S. (2004). An increased capacity for adrenal DHEA release is associated with decreased avoidance and negative mood symptoms in women with PTSD. *Neuropsychopharmacology, 29,* 1546–1557.

Rasmusson, A. M., Vythilingam, M., & Morgan, C. A. III, (2003). The neuroendocrinology of posttraumatic stress disorder: New directions. *CNS Spectrums, 8,* 651–667.

Reist, C., Kauffman, C. D., Haier, R. J., Sangdahl, C., DeMet, E. M., Chicz-DeMet, A., et al. (1989). A controlled trial of desipramine in 18 men with post-traumatic stress disorder. *American Journal of Psychiatry, 146,* 513–516.

Resick, P. A. (1992). Cognitive treatment of a crime-related post-traumatic stress disorder. In R. D.

Peters, R. J. McMahon, & V. L. Quinsey (Eds.), *Aggression and violence throughout the life span.* (pp. 171–191). Newbury Park, CA: Sage.

Resick, P. A. (2001). *Stress and trauma* (1st ed.). Hove, UK: Psychology Press Ltd.

Resick, P. A., Galovski, T., Phipps, K., Uhlmansiek, M., Ansel, J., & Griffin, M. (2005). A dismantling study of the components of cognitive processing therapy. In Innovative use of cognitive processing therapy for treating PTSD symposium. Presented at the 39th annual meeting of the Association for Behavioral and Cognitive Therapies, Washington, DC.

Resick, P. A., Nishith, P., Weaver, T. L., Astin, M. C., & Feuer, C. A. (2002). A comparison of cognitive processing therapy, prolonged exposure and a waiting condition for the treatment of posttraumatic stress disorder in female rape victims. *Journal of Consulting and Clinical Psychology, 70,* 867–879.

Resick, P. A., & Schnicke, M. K. (1992). Cognitive processing therapy for sexual assault victims. *Journal of Consulting and Clinical Psychology, 60,* 748–756.

Resick, P. A., & Schnicke, M. K. (1993). *Cognitive processing therapy for rape victims: A treatment manual.* Newbury Park, CA: Sage.

Resick, P. A., Schnicke, M. K., & Markway, B. G. (1991 November). The relation between cognitive content and PTSD. Paper presented at the 25th Annual Convention of the Association for the Advancement of Behavioral Therapy, New York.

Resnick, H. S., Kilpatrick, D. G., Dansky, B. S., Saunders, B. E., & Best, C. L. (1993). Prevalence of civilian trauma and posttraumatic stress disorder in a representative national sample of women. *Journal of Consulting and Clinical Psychology, 61,* 984–991.

Resnick, H. S., Kilpatrick, D. G., & Lipovsky, J. A. (1991). Assessment of rape-related posttraumatic stress disorder: Stressor and symptom dimensions. Special Section: Issues and methods in assessment of posttraumatic stress disorder. *Psychological Assessment, 3,* 561–572.

Riggs, D. S., Byrne, C. A., Weathers, F. W., & Litz, B. T. (1998). The quality of the intimate relationships of male Vietnam veterans: Problems associated with posttraumatic stress disorder. *Journal of Traumatic Stress, 11,* 87–101.

Riggs, D. S., Dancu, C. V., Gershuny, B. S., Greenberg, D., & Foa, E. B. (1992). Anger and post-traumatic stress disorder in female crime victims. *Journal of Traumatic Stress, 5,* 613–625.

Rizvi, S. L., Kaysen, D., Gutner, C. A., Griffin, M. G., & Resick, P. A. (in press). Beyond fear: The role of peritraumatic responses in posttraumatic stress and depressive symptoms among female crime victims. *Journal of Interpersonal Violence.*

Robins, L. N., Helzer, J. E., Croughan, J., & Ratcliff, K. S. (1981). National Institute of Mental Health Diagnostic Interview Schedule: Its history, characteristics, and validity. *Archives of General Psychiatry, 38,* 381–389.

Rodriguez, N., Vande-Kemp, H., & Foy, D. W. (1998). Posttraumatic stress disorder in survivors of childhood sexual and physical abuse: A critical review of the empirical research. *Journal of Child Sexual Abuse, 7,* 17–45.

Rothbaum, B. O. (1997). A controlled study of eye movement desensitisation and reprocessing in the treatment of posttraumatic stress disordered sexual assault victims. *Bulletin of the Menninger Clinic, 61,* 317–334.

Rothbaum, B. O., Astin, M. C., & Marsteller, F. (2005). Prolonged exposure versus eye movement desensitization and reprocessing (EMDR) for PTSD rape victims. *Journal of Traumatic Stress, 18,* 607–616.

Rothbaum, B. O., Cahill, S., Foa, E., Davidson, J., Compton, J., Connor, K., et al. (2006). Augmentation of sertraline with prolonged exposure in the treatment of posttraumatic stress disorder. *Journal of Traumatic Stress, 19,* 625–638.

Rothbaum, B. O., & Foa, E. B. (1993). Subtypes of posttraumatic stress disorder and duration of symptoms. In J. R. T. Davidson & E. B. Foa (Eds.), *Posttraumatic stress disorder:* DSM-IV *and beyond* (pp. 23–35). Washington, DC: American Psychiatric Press.

Rothbaum, B. O., & Foa, E. B. (1996). Cognitive-behavioral therapy for posttraumatic stress disorder. In B. A. van der Kolk & A. C. McFarlane (Eds.), *Traumatic stress: The effects of overwhelming experience on mind, body, and society* (pp. 491–509). New York: Guilford.

Rothbaum, B. O., Foa, E. B., Riggs, D. S., & Walsh, W. (1992). Posttraumatic stress disorder in rape victims: A prospective examination of posttraumatic stress disorder and rape victims. *Journal of Traumatic Stress, 5,* 455–475.

Rothbaum, B. O., Hodges, L. F., & Ready, D. (2001). Virtual reality exposure therapy for Vietnam veterans with posttraumatic stress disorder. *Journal of Clinical Psychiatry, 62,* 617–622.

Saunders, B. E., Arata, C. M., & Kilpatrick, D. G. (1990). Development of a crime-related posttraumatic stress disorder scale for women within the symptom checklist-90–revised. *Journal of Traumatic Stress, 3,* 439–448.

Schauer, M., Neuner, F., & Elbert, T. (2005). *Narrative exposure therapy: A short-term intervention for traumatic stress disorders after war, terror, or torture*. Ashland, OH: Hogrefe & Huber.

Schlenger, W. E., Caddell, J. M., Ebert, L., Jordan, B. K., Rourke, K. M., Wilson, D., et al. (2002). Psychological reactions to terrorist attacks: Findings from the National Study of Americans' Reactions to September 11. *Journal of the American Medical Association*, 288, 581–588.

Schnurr, P. P., Friedman, M. J., Engel, C. C., Foa, E. B., Shea, T., Chow, B. K., et al. (2007). Cognitive-behavioral therapy for posttraumatic stress disorder in women: A randomized controlled trial. *Journal of the American Medical Association*, 297, 820–830.

Schulz, P. M., Resick, P. A., Huber, L. C., & Griffin, M. G. (2006). The effectiveness of cognitive processing therapy for PTSD with refugees in a community setting. *Cognitive and Behavioral Practice*, 13, 322–331.

Schwartz, B. L., Hashtroudi, S., Herting, R. L., Schwartz, P., & Deutsch, S. I. (1996). D-cycloserine enhances implicit memory in Alzheimer patients. *Neurology*, 46, 420–444.

Shalev, A. Y., Orr, S. P., Peri, T., & Schreiber, S. (1992). Physiologic responses to loud tones in Israeli patients with posttraumatic stress disorder. *Archives of General Psychiatry*, 49, 870–875.

Shestatzky, M., Greenberg, D., & Lerer, B. (1988). A controlled trial of phenelzine in posttraumatic stress disorder. *Psychiatry Research*, 24, 149–155.

Shipherd, J. C., & Beck, J. G. (1999). The effects of suppressing trauma-related thoughts on women with rape-related posttraumatic stress disorder. *Behaviour Research and Therapy*, 37, 99–112.

Shipherd, J. C., & Beck, J. G. (2005). The role of thought suppression in posttraumatic stress disorder. *Behavior Therapy*, 36, 277–287.

Shipherd, J. C., Keyes, M., Jovanovic, T., Ready, D., Baltzell, D., Worley, V., et al. (2007). PTSD treatment seeking veterans: What about comorbid chronic pain? *Journal of Rehabilitation Research and Development*, 44, 153–166.

Smucker, M. R., Dancu, C., & Foa, E. B. (1995). Imagery rescripting: A new treatment for survivors of childhood sexual abuse suffering from posttraumatic stress. *Journal of Cognitive Psychotherapy: An International Quarterly*, 9.

Solomon, Z., & Mikulincer, M. (1990). Life events and combat-related posttraumatic stress disorder: The intervening role of locus of control and social support. *Military Psychology*, 2, 241–256.

Solomon, Z., Mikulincer, M., & Avitzur, E. (1988). Coping, locus of control, social support, and combat-related posttraumatic stress disorder: A prospective study. *Journal of Personality and Social Psychology*, 55, 279–285.

Solomon, Z., Mikulincer, M., & Flum, H. (1989). The implications of life events and social integration in the course of combat-related post-traumatic stress disorder. *Social Psychiatry and Psychiatric Epidemiology*, 24, 41–48.

Southwick, S. M., Bremner, J. D., Rasmusson, A., Morgan, C. A., III, Arnsten, A., & Charney, D. S. (1999). Role of norepinephrine in the pathophysiology and treatment of posttraumatic stress disorder. *Biological Psychiatry*, 46, 1192–1204.

Southwick, S. M., Krystal, J. H., Bremner, J. D., Morgan, C. A., Nicolaou, A. L., Nagy, L. M., et al. (1997). Noradrenergic and serotonergic function in posttraumatic stress disorder. *Archives of General Psychiatry*, 54, 749–758.

Southwick, S. M., Krystal, J. H., Morgan, C. A., Johnson, D., Nagy, L. M., Nicolaou, A., et al. (1993). Abnormal noradrenergic function in posttraumatic stress disorder. *Archives of General Psychiatry*, 50, 266–274.

Stein, D. J., Seedat, S., & van derLinden, G. J. H. (2000). Selective serotonin reuptake inhibitors in the treatment of post-traumatic stress disorder: A meta-analysis of randomized controlled trials. *International Clinical Psychopharmacology*, 15, S31–S39.

Stein, M. B., Kline, N. A., & Matloff, J. L. (2002). Adjunctive olanzapine for SSRI-resistant combat-related PTSD: A double-blind, placebo-controlled study. *American Journal of psychiatry*, 159, 1777–1779.

Stroop, J. R. (1935). Studies of inference in serial verbal reactions. *Journal of Experimental Psychology*, 18, 643–662.

Tarrier, N., Pilgrim, H., Sommerfield, C., Faragher, B., Reynolds, M., Graham, E., et al. (1999). A randomized trial of cognitive therapy and imaginal exposure in the treatment of chronic post-traumatic stress disorder. *Journal of Consulting and Clinical Psychology*, 67, 13–18.

Tarrier, N., & Sommerfield, C. (2004). Treatment of chronic PTSD by cognitive therapy and exposure: 5 year follow-up. *Behavior Therapy*, 35, 231–246.

Tarrier, N., Sommerfield, C., Connell, J., Deakin, B., Pilgrim, H., & Reynolds, M. (2002). The psychophysiological responses to PTSD patients: Habituation, responses to stressful and neutral vignettes and association with treatment outcome. *Behavioral and Cognitive Psychotherapy*, *30*, 129–142.

Thrasher, S., Dalgleish, T., & Yule, W. (1994). Information processing in post-traumatic stress disorder. *Behaviour Research and Therapy*, *32*, 247–254.

Tolin, D. F., & Foa, E. B. (2006). Sex differences in trauma and posttraumatic stress disorder: A quantitative review of 25 years of research. *Psychological Bulletin*, *132*, 959–092.

VA/DoD clinical practice guideline for management of post-traumatic stress-Veterans Health Administration. (2004). Retrieved from http://www.oqp.med.va.gov/cpg/PTS/PTS_base.htm.

Vaiva, G., Ducrocq, F., Jezequel, K., Averland, B., Lestavel, P., Brunet, A., et al. (2003). Immediate treatment with propranolol decreases posttraumatic stress disorder two months after trauma. *Biological Psychiatry*, *54*, 947–949.

Vaiva, G., Thomas, P., Ducrocq, F., Fontaine, M., Boss, V., & Devos, P., et al. (2004). Low posttrauma GABA plasma levels as a predictive factor in the development of acute posttraumatic stress disorder. *Biological Psychiatry*, *55*, 250–254.

van derKolk, B., Spinazzola, J., Blaustein, M., Hopper, J., Hopper, E., Korn, D., et al. (2007). A randomized clinical trial of eye movement desensitization and reprocessing (EMDR), fluoxetine, and pill placebo in the treatment of posttraumatic stress disorder: Treatment effects and long-term maintenance. *Journal of Clinical Psychiatry*, *68*, 37–46.

VanEtten, M. L., & Taylor, S. (1998). Comparative efficacy of treatment for posttraumatic stress disorder: A meta-analysis. *Clinical Psychology and Psychotherapy*, *5*, 126–144.

vanGriensven, F., Chakkraband, M. L., Thienkrua, W., Pengjuntr, W., Lopes Cardozo, B., Tantipiwatanaskul, P., et al. (2006). Mental health problems among adults in tsunami-affected areas in southern Thailand. *Journal of the American Medical Association*, *296*, 537–548.

vanMinnen, A., Arntz, A., & Keijsers, G. P. (2002). Prolonged exposure in patients with chronic PTSD: Predictors of treatment outcome and dropout. *Behaviour Research and Therapy*, *40*, 439–457.

vanMinnen, A., & Hagenaars, M. (2002). Fear activation and habituation patterns as early process predictors of response to prolonged exposure treatment in PTSD. *Journal of Traumatic Stress*, *15*, 359–367.

Vermetten, E., Vythilingam, M., Southwick, S. M., Charney, D. S., & Bremner, J. D. (2003). Long-term treatment with paroxetine increases verbal declarative memory and hippocampal volume in posttraumatic stress disorder. *Biological Psychiatry*, *54*, 693–702.

Vrana, S., & Lauterbach, D. (1994). Prevalence of traumatic events and post-traumatic psychological symptoms in a nonclinical sample of college students. *Journal of Traumatic Stress*, *7*, 289–302.

Walser, R. D., & Hayes, S. C. (2006). Acceptance and commitment therapy in the treatment of posttraumatic stress disorder: Theoretical and applied issues. In V. M. R. Follette & I. Josef (Eds.), *Cognitive-behavioral therapies for trauma* (2nd ed., pp. 146–172). New York: Guilford.

Weathers, F. W., Litz, B., Huska, J. A., & Keane, T. (1994). *PTSD symptom checklist*. Washington, DC: National Center for PTSD, Behavioral Science Division.

Weathers, F. W., & Keane, T. M. (1999). Psychological assessment of traumatized adults. In P. A. Saigh & J. D. Bremner (Eds.), *Posttraumatic stress disorder: A comprehensive text* (pp. 219–247). Boston: Allyn & Bacon.

Weathers, F. W., Keane, T. M., & Davidson, J. R. (2001). Clinician-administered PTSD scale: A review of the first ten years of research. *Depression and Anxiety*, *13*, 132–156.

Weathers, F. W., Ruscio, A. M., & Keane, T. M. (1999). Psychometric properties of nine scoring rules for the Clinician-Administered Posttraumatic Stress Disorder Scale. *Psychological Assessment*, *11*, 124–133.

Wegner, D. M., Schneider, D. J., Carter, S. R., & White, T. L. (1987). Paradoxical effects of thought suppression. *Journal of Personality and Social Psychology*, *53*, 5–13.

Weiss, D. S., & Marmar, C. R. (1997). The Impact of Events Scale—Revised. In J. P. Wilson & T. M. Keane (Eds.), *Assessing psychological trauma and PTSD* (pp. 399–411). New York: Guilford.

Wenninger, K., & Ehlers, A. (1998). Dysfunctional cognitions and adult psychological functioning in child sexual abuse survivors. *Journal of Traumatic Stress*, *11*, 281–300.

Widiger, T. A., & Simonsen, E. (2005). Alternative dimensional models of personality disorder: Finding a common ground. *Journal of Personality Disorders*, *19*, 110–130.

Wilson, S. A., Becker, L. A., & Tinker, R. H. (1995). Eye movement desensitisation and reprocessing (EMDR) treatment for psychologically traumatized individuals. *Journal of Consulting and Clinical Psychology*, *63*, 928–937.

Wong, M. R., & Cook, D. (1992). Shame and its contribution to PTSD. *Journal of Traumatic Stress*, *5*, 557–562.

Yehuda, R. (2002). Current status of cortisol findings in post-traumatic stress disorder. *Psychiatric Clinics of North America*, *2*, 341–348.

Yehuda, R., Giller, E. L., Southwick, S. M., Kahana, B., Boisneau, D., Ma, X., et al. (1994). Relationship between catecholamine excretion and PTSD symptoms in Vietnam combat veterans and holocaust survivors. In M. M. Murburg (Ed.), *Catecholamine function in post-traumatic stress disorder: Emerging concepts* (pp. 203–220). Washington, DC: American Psychiatric Press.

Yehuda, R., Siever, L. J., Teicher, M. H., Levengood, R. A., Gerber, D. K., Schmeidler, J., et al. (1998). Plasma norepinephrine and 3–methoxy-4–hydroxyphenylglycol concentrations and severity of depression in combat posttraumatic stress disorder and major depressive disorder. *Biological Psychiatry*, *44*, 56–63.

Young, E. A., & Breslau, N. (2004). Cortisol and catecholamines in posttraumatic stress disorder: An epidemiologic community study. *Archives of General Psychiatry*, *61*, 394–401.

Zoellner, L. A., Alvarez-Conrad, J., & Foa, E. B. (2002). Peritraumatic dissociative experiences, trauma narratives, and trauma pathology. *Journal of Traumatic Stress*, *15*, 49–57.

Chapter 8

Major Depressive Disorder

W. Edward Craighead, Lorie A. Ritschel, Eirikur O. Arnarson, and Charles F. Gillespie

Introduction

Descriptions of individuals suffering from Major Depressive Disorder (MDD) have been remarkably similar for centuries, though the designation of specific criteria for diagnosis of this disorder has been relatively recent. One of the very earliest examples is the biblical description of Job's depression. In U.S. history, a number of well-known individuals from all walks of life have suffered from MDD. These include: Abraham Lincoln, who suffered at least two episodes of MDD, the late U.S. Senator Thomas Eagleton from Missouri; William James, one of the founders of psychology and the primary force in establishing it as a discipline at Harvard University in the 1890s; entertainers such as Brooke Shields and Billy Joel; astronaut Buzz Aldrin, who was the second human to walk on the moon; television personalities such as newscaster Mike Wallace, and night show host Dick Cavett; former editor of the L.A. Times and head of CNN Tom Johnson; and, athletes such as Terry Bradshaw, who led the Pittsburgh Steelers to four Super Bowl championships during the 1970s, and Dorothy Hamill, who was a 1976 Olympic Gold Medal figure skater. Although each had a somewhat different experience and course of the disorder, the symptoms and defining characteristics were remarkably similar.

It is fairly common to hear someone remark, "I am so depressed," because almost everyone has experienced a sad mood, one of the indicators of clinical MDD. Most often, however, this comment describes transient feelings of sadness, dysphoria, or disappointment that dissipate within a fairly brief period of time. Major Depressive Disorder, while episodic, is clearly distinguishable from such transient dysphoric states that most people are experiencing when they somewhat casually refer to themselves as "depressed." The feelings of sadness and anhedonia indicative of clinical MDD are of much greater intensity, depth, and duration and are more encompassing than the typical negative mood states accompanying the more casual complaint of being "normally" depressed. Furthermore, clinical depression, by definition, is terribly disruptive to the individual's life and

279

environment, including characteristic patterns of behavioral, cognitive, and biological dysfunction far beyond the level of disruption caused by blue, sad, or depressed transient mood states, even when this dysphoria might continue for several days.

Clinical depression gives rise to extraordinary personal and family suffering. It also produces significant societal burdens, such as an increased use of social and medical services (Johnson, Weissman, & Klerman, 1992). There are also enormous financial costs for its treatment and for lost productivity due to absenteeism from work (Greenberg, Stiglin, Finkelstein, & Berndt, 1993). In fact, when considered among all diseases, MDD is the world's fourth leading cause of disability-adjusted life years (Murray & Lopez, 1997). Furthermore, MDD is very strongly related to suicide attempts and completions (Johnson et al., 2002; Kessler & Walters, 1998), particularly when depressed individuals reach a state of hopelessness regarding the disorder or about not finding a way to overcome it.

Diagnostic Criteria

Major Depressive Disorder, then called *melancholia*, was first described in a systematic fashion by the Greek physician, Hippocrates (ca. 460–370 BCE). He based his naturalistic classification system on the writings of Greek philosophers such as Thales, who had lived about a century earlier. At that point in history, Greek philosophers posited that the basic elements of the world were composed of earth, fire, water, and air. Hippocrates maintained that each of these elements was represented by a respective humour in the body. In a healthy person these humours were maintained in balance, but disease occurred when the humours were out of balance. Melancholia, specifically, resulted from the presence of too much black bile, one of the four humours. Diseases were based on this scientific view of humans, and thus their origins were distinct from religious interpretations. This naturalistic model was sustained by another great Greek physician, Galen (128 to ca. 200 AD), who actually interpreted it in such as fashion as to make it palatable to the Christian religion, so it found some favor through the Middle Ages.

In relatively modern times, the German psychiatrist, Emil Kraepelin (1856–1926) first used the word *depression* to describe a clinical condition.[1] In the sixth edition of his *Textbook of Psychiatry*, published in 1899, Kraepelin described both "dementia praecox" (which he had described previously in its fourth edition in 1893) and "manic-depressive insanity" (see Decker, 2004). These disorders roughly correspond, respectively, to current diagnoses of Schizophrenia (dementia praecox) and Bipolar Disorder (manic-depressive). Kraeplin's diagnostic categories were based on clinical observations in several German hospitals where he served as chief psychiatrist. Depression continued to be viewed as one pole of Manic-Depressive Disorder for much of the twentieth century. The major exceptions to this were Adolf Meyer's more psychosocially based description of a "Depressive Reaction" to negative life experiences, and the psychodynamic descriptions of depression by Abraham (1911) and Freud (1917). Even within these alternative conceptual frameworks, the descriptions of the phenomenology of depression remained essentially the same as those that had been described for depressive states by Kraepelin when he had written about Manic-Depressive Disorder. Over the

---

[1] Though infrequently noted, in addition to his medical education, Kraepelin trained in experimental psychology with Wundt, who continued to mentor him during the rough beginnings he experienced as a psychiatrist, and much of Kraepelin's experimental work was based on the methods utilized in Wundt's laboratory.

course of the last half of the twentieth century, empirical data and theoretical developments led to the separation of MDD from Manic-Depressive Disorder (Bipolar Disorder). Consequently, criteria for MDD were developed and presented formally as a psychiatric diagnosis in the American Psychiatric Association *Diagnostic and Statistical Manual*—first as a Depressive Reaction (*DSM-II*) and then as Major Depressive Disorder (*DSM-III*).

Within the *DSM-IV* (APA, 1994), the primary clinical forms of depression are: Major Depressive Disorder, Dysthymia (discussed in the Chronic Depression chapter in this book), and Bipolar Depression. This chapter focuses on Major Depressive Disorder. In order to receive a diagnosis of *Major Depressive Disorder*, a person must experience marked distress or a decrease in level of functioning for at least 2 weeks. In addition, the 2 weeks before a diagnosis of Major Depressive Disorder (MDD) must be characterized by the almost daily occurrence of a dysphoric mood (sad, empty, or tearful) or a loss of interest or pleasure in almost all activities (APA, 1994). The individual must also experience at least four (only three if *both* dysphoric mood and loss of interest or pleasure are present) of the following seven symptoms (with the second through sixth occurring nearly every day).

1. Significant weight loss (while not trying to lose weight), significant weight gain, or a change in appetite.
2. Insomnia or hypersomnia.
3. Psychomotor agitation or retardation.
4. Fatigue or loss of energy.
5. Feelings of worthlessness or excessive or inappropriate guilt.
6. Decreased concentration or indecisiveness.
7. Recurrent thoughts of death or suicidal ideation, plan, or attempt.

Thus, one can meet criteria for Major Depressive Disorder (MDD) without exhibiting all the listed symptoms; different people may have different combinations of the symptoms of the disorder.

When diagnosing MDD, it is important to consider other disorders that might cause an individual to experience depression. In particular, *DSM-IV* specifies that when the depressive symptoms are substance-induced (either by prescribed medications or by recreational drugs) or another general medical illness, then MDD is not the appropriate primary diagnosis. For example, a person with hypothyroidism may meet all the criteria for MDD, but MDD should not be the primary diagnosis; this underscores the importance of assessing for all the related medical illnesses, substances that cause depression, and other possible primary Axis-I disorders when conducting a diagnostic evaluation.

There are a number of *specifiers*, or diagnostic elements, that need to be incorporated into a clinical assessment of MDD. Perhaps the most important one is the chronicity of the disorder. Thus, this book devotes an entire chapter to Chronic Depression, which also includes another mood disorder, Dysthymia. A second important specifier is the level of depression severity, because the most severe forms of MDD (e.g., MDD with psychotic features) are likely to necessitate a pharmacological intervention and are more clearly indicative of an underlying pathophysiology (Schatzberg et al., 1983). Another specifier that frequently has treatment implications is atypical depression, which characterizes approximately 15% of depressed patients. Atypical depression is marked by mood reactivity (mood brightens in response to positive events or potential positive events) hypersomnia, extended fatigue, heightened sensitivity to criticism, and significant increase in appetite and weight gain (APA, 1994).

Two other specifiers, melancholia and seasonal pattern, while remaining in *DSM-IV* terminology, do not appear to be of great clinical significance. Knowing that a person may be more vulnerable to depression onset in the fall (or even another season) might help in earlier identification of an episode, but the data for differing treatments based on either of these specifiers are meager.

Postpartum depression is another important specifier, because various treatment decisions must take the baby into account. Furthermore, the information is significant in planning future pregnancies, particularly when the disorder is prolonged or the treatment has included antidepressant medications. It is also essential to differentiate postpartum MDD from postpartum psychosis.

Prevalence of MDD

Major Depressive Disorder is one of the most commonly diagnosed psychiatric disorders among adults, with U.S. lifetime prevalence rates of approximately 17%, with rates of 20% to 25% for women and 9% to 12% for men; point prevalence rates are approximately 6% and 3% for women and men, respectively (Kessler, Chiu, Demler, & Walters, 2005). These point-prevalence rates and gender differences are relatively constant across the *adult* life span.

Although it is a debated issue (see Costello, Erkanli, & Angold, 2006), the prevalence of MDD appears to have increased among recent birth cohorts (Fergusson, Horwood, Ridder, & Beautrais, 2005; Hankin et al., 1998; Lewinsohn, Hops, Roberts, Seeley, & Andrews, 1993), which suggests that the lifetime prevalence ultimately will be higher for current younger cohorts. The age at which the first episode of MDD occurs has also been decreasing (Burke, Burke, Regier, & Rae, 1990; Lewinsohn, Clarke, Seeley, & Rohde, 1994;), so that the peak years for first onset are presently between 15 and 29 years of age (Burke et al., 1990; Fergusson et al., 2005; Weissman et al., 1996). At least one-half of these individuals will experience multiple episodes of MDD, and a substantial minority will go on to experience Chronic Depression (see Klein chapter in this book; also see Mueller et al., 1999). Thus, MDD is a major health problem for which it is important to develop better understanding and interventions.

CASE EXAMPLE

Mary is a 57–year-old single woman from a small town in the southeastern United States. She has been hospitalized for MDD with psychotic features. For most of her adult life, she has been successfully employed as a hospital nurse, working in a variety of hospital settings. About 2 years ago her father became terminally ill and was unable to care for himself. She volunteered to quit her job and take care of her father because she had the needed nursing skills and because she was the only one of her siblings without a spouse and children. Though her siblings felt she provided excellent care for their father, Mary spent most of her time alone with her dying father and grew to believe that her father's deterioration in health was due, in part, to her lack of adequate care. Toward the end of his life, Mary developed all the symptoms of MDD. As her depression deepened her cognitive distortions about his care deteriorated until she developed a delusion that she had in some way actually contributed directly to his death. When she was hospitalized because of her depression, she strongly believed this delusion to be true, and she believed that it would be only a few days until the "authorities" figured this out and would arrest her. Rather than go to jail, she had decided to kill herself; thus, she was hospitalized. Her delusions continued in the hospital, and each time the security guards made their rounds outside the hospital window, she would hide in the closet of her hospital room.

During the last few months of her father's life, Mary had been treated with moderate success with antidepressant medications. However, upon her father's death, the MDD became much worse and overrode the ameliorative effects of the medicines. Upon hospitalization, her medical regimen was changed to include antipsychotic medications; an unsuccessful attempt also was made to conduct Cognitive Behavior Therapy (CBT) for her delusions and depression. After several days of unsuccessful treatment with this plan, a decision was made to treat her with Electroconvulsive Shock Therapy (EST), to which she had a very successful response. After the hospitalization, she chose to live in an apartment at a sibling's house and chose not to return to work; she did, however, become involved in community volunteer and church activities.

PSYCHOLOGY OF MAJOR DEPRESSION

Depression is frequently thought of as a disturbance in emotion (Engel & DeRubeis, 1993). As discussed earlier, however, not everyone who meets criteria for depression reports feeling sad. In fact, a quick review of the nine primary diagnostic criteria for a major depressive episode reveals that only one criterion is specifically related to mood disturbance; whereas, five of nine possible symptoms are related to changes in behavior or physiology, while one of the remaining symptoms focuses on emotional states and three of cognitive changes (*DSM-IV*, 1994). The *DSM-IV* symptoms of MDD can be categorized as follows:

Emotional Symptoms of Depression:
• Depressed mood most of the day, nearly every day

Behavioral/Physiological Symptoms of Depression:
• Markedly diminished interest or pleasure in all, or almost all, activities most of the day, nearly every day (anhedonia)
• Significant weight loss when not dieting, or weight gain, or decrease or increase in appetite nearly every day
• Insomnia or hypersomnia nearly every day
• Psychomotor agitation or retardation nearly every day
• Fatigue or loss of energy nearly every day

Cognitive Symptoms of Depression:
• Feelings of worthlessness or excessive or inappropriate guilt nearly every day
• Diminished ability to think or concentrate, or indecisiveness, nearly every day
• Recurrent thoughts of death, recurrent suicidal ideation without a specific plan, or a suicide attempt or a specific plan for committing suicide

Hence, it is possible to receive a diagnosis of MDD simply by endorsing predominantly behavioral/biological *or* predominantly cognitive symptoms. Because both behaviors and cognitions play such an important role in the etiology and maintenance of depression, it is critical to understand both categories of dysfunctions for research and clinical purposes. To further that understanding we now turn to an overview of the major behavioral, cognitive, and biological theories and research regarding MDD.

Behavioral Models of Depression

The 1960s–1970s were marked by the development and expansion of behavioral models of the etiology and maintenance of depression (e.g., Ferster, 1965, 1966, 1973; Lewinsohn, 1974). Skinner (1953) had previously proposed the idea that depression is related to a reduction in behaviors that elicit positive reinforcement from the environment. Ferster elaborated Skinner's ideas and postulated that three proximal causes were likely to contribute to a depressive shift in affect. First, infrequent positive reinforcement is likely to lead to a decline in behavior in general. Second, behaviors are further inhibited by the presence of anxiety. Third, unexpected changes in environmental stimuli (including human relationships) decrease the frequency of behaviors. In other words, Ferster proposed that people tend to withdraw in the absence of positive reinforcement, anxiety, or unexpected environmental changes. Ferster (1973) also posited that a decrease in positive environmental reinforcement is likely to result in a narrowing of an individual's behavioral repertoire in an effort to prevent further loss of positive reinforcement. Hence, depression is caused by behavioral inhibition and maintained through a process of escape (negative reinforcement) or avoidance.

Lewinsohn and colleagues (Lewinsohn, 1974; Lewinsohn & Gotlib, 1995; Lewinsohn, Youngren, & Grosscup, 1979) further refined Ferster's work with a focus on positive reinforcement schedules. Lewinsohn agreed with his behavioral predecessors that depression develops when individuals experience a low rate of positive reinforcement for their behavior. He extended previous conceptualizations with a theory that the rate of positive reinforcement is contingent upon three elements: (1) the number of reinforcing activities in which an individual engages; (2) the amount of positive reinforcement that the environment is able to provide; and (3) the skillfulness of the individual in eliciting reinforcement from the environment (i.e., social skills deficiencies are fundamentally related to low rates of environmental reinforcement). Lewinsohn further hypothesized that, in addition to low rates of positive reinforcement, depression also could be caused by high amounts of aversive experiences or events.

Some scholars theorize that depression results from the interaction of cognitive and behavioral difficulties associated with depression. For example, Pyszczynski and Greenberg (1987) concur with early behaviorists that depression is related to decreases in environmental reinforcement. They posit, however, that cognitive and emotional changes initiate and perpetuate behavioral changes in depression. Specifically, they hypothesize that onset and maintenance of depression are predicated upon a loss of a source of self-esteem that is followed by an increase in self-focused attention (see Mor & Winquist, 2002). They posit that this process increases the salience of the lost source of esteem as well as the negative affect induced by the loss. The resulting self-criticism interferes with social performance, which the individual perceives as validation of the self-criticism. As a result, self-criticism and negative affect increase, thereby perpetuating the cycle.

Taken together, these behavioral theories call attention to the importance of both positive and negative reinforcement in the etiology and maintenance of depression. The question, then, is how these models translate into observable human behaviors. In the next section, we turn our attention to the clinical presentation of behavioral symptoms of depression and to the empirical evidence in support of behavioral theories of depression.

BEHAVIORAL DEFICITS IN MDD

Three symptom classes commonly found in MDD are anhedonia, amotivation, and avoidance. Together, they weave a vicious web that perpetuates depressive episodes. As individuals lose interest in activities that previously brought them pleasure (anhedonia), they subsequently lose the desire to continue to attempt those activities (amotivation). As energy and motivation decrease, individuals often prefer *not* to engage in activities or spend time with other people because these activities (a) require energy they do not have, and (b) are no longer rewarding. Hence, they find greater satisfaction in doing nothing (avoidance). As a result, motivation and avoidance are targeted as primary behavioral deficits in the behavioral treatment of MDD.

AMOTIVATION AND ANHEDONIA

One of the most commonly reported symptoms of depression is a loss of motivation or ability to carry out the necessary tasks of one's life. Unlike the cognitive symptoms of depression, which affect patients' perceptions of themselves, their future, and their environments, most depressed individuals know what they need to do; they simply lack the motivation or energy to engage in tasks of living. For example, it is not unusual for patients to report that they have difficulty getting out of bed in the morning and going to work or school. They also may be neglecting activities at home, such as washing the dishes or cleaning the house. In more extreme cases, they may not even be attending to personal tasks, such as exercise, dressing, or showering.

Beck, Rush, Shaw, and Emery (1979) proposed that two factors interfere with motivation in depressed individuals. First, many people who are depressed hold the belief that they cannot complete a task (this is generally a cognitive distortion and is addressed as such in cognitive therapy). Second, depressed individuals believe that they will not derive satisfaction from having completed a task, and hence their motivation declines. This belief is addressed as a behavioral deficit, and patients are encouraged to counter amotivation by engaging in graded task assignments. This type of intervention helps patients break tasks down into small elements so that they are less overwhelming. Completing small tasks often has the effect of helping patients build self-efficacy (Bandura, 1977) or even mastery as well as increasing the likelihood that they will receive positive reinforcement from their environment. Hence, patients are encouraged to engage in behaviors despite their lack of motivation, under the assumption that motivation will follow activity.

Neuropsychological research suggests that behavioral symptoms in depression are related to deficits in the behavioral activation system (BAS). Gray (1987) proposed that behavior is largely monitored by two systems: the behavioral activation system (BAS), which is responsive to reward cues; and, the behavioral inhibition system (BIS), which is responsive to punishment cues (i.e., the BAS is posited to be behavior generating, while the BIS is behavior inhibiting). Applying Gray's model, Davidson (1992) posited that an underactive BAS is related to reductions in positive emotion and motivation. These reductions, in turn, are risk factors for depression. Davidson (1992, 1998) has proposed a model suggesting that behavioral activation is modulated by activity in the left prefrontal cortex, while behavioral inhibition (or withdrawal) is modulated by activity in the right prefrontal cortex. Several studies support this hypothesis (see McFarland, Shankman, Tenke, Bruder, & Klein, 2006, for a review). In one study, self-reported deficits in behavioral activation predicted the number of depressive symptoms, weekly level of depression, and time to recovery at 6-month follow-up (McFarland et al., 2006).

Other recent research avenues support the notion that activity (rather than passivity) is helpful in ameliorating symptoms of depression. Burns and Nolen-Hoeksema (1991) showed that depressed individuals who engaged in active coping strategies were significantly less depressed than their more passive peers at the end of 12 weeks of therapy and again at 12–week follow-up. These results remained intact even after controlling for initial levels of depression.

AVOIDANCE AND PASSIVITY

Emotions and emotional states frequently can be identified by the biological drives or urges that accompany them. For example, if an individual desires to punch another person, we can infer that he or she is feeling angry. Or, if we observe an individual running away from a particular situation (e.g., a burning building), it would be reasonable to assume that he is feeling fear. At one level, this is because our own experiences tell us that the behavioral pattern associated with anger is to lash out and the behavior associated with fear is to run away (see Linehan, 1993a, 1993b). Similarly, sadness has a behavioral correlate: to isolate oneself. Clinically, it is common for a depressed patient to report that she no longer calls or sees her friends, or that she has difficulty getting out of bed in the morning. In more extreme cases, patients may report that they are no longer going to work or even leaving the house.

Avoidance has long been recognized as a common consequence of depression (Ferster, 1973). For depressed individuals, however, avoidance functions to minimize distress and hence is its own reward (i.e., it is a negative reinforcer). For example, if a patient calls in sick to work because she would rather lie in bed all day, she feels better in the moment because she does not have to go to work and interact with others. In this way, calling in sick (avoidance) has been reinforced as a solution to the experience of dread about work.

The consequences of avoidant behaviors, however, are twofold. First, avoidance is a passive, short-term strategy that often results in ever-mounting long-term difficulties. For example, repeatedly calling in sick is likely to cause problems with coworkers and bosses, and the patient may soon face disciplinary action or termination for repeated absences. This, of course, creates a new set of problems to be solved.

The second consequence of avoidance is that it reduces the opportunity for depressed individuals to encounter positive reinforcement in their environment (see Dimidjian, Martell, Addis, & Herman-Dunn, 2007; Lewinsohn, 1974; Lewinsohn & Graf, 1973); that is, it is hard to be told that you are doing a good job at work if you are not going to work! It is also difficult to derive pleasure from friendly interactions when friends are avoided. This combination of negative reinforcement and lack of positive reinforcement fuels the cycle of avoidant behavior, and depressed individuals become more and more withdrawn. As time goes on, an individual's behavioral repertoire narrows further until passivity is the dominant behavioral response (Dimidjian et al., 2007).

Avoidance has long been a major target in the treatment of anxiety, and it recently has received more attention in the treatment of MDD. More recent behavior therapies (sometimes called *third wave therapies*[2]) such as Dialectical Behavior Therapy (DBT; Linehan, 1993a) and Acceptance and Commitment Therapy (ACT; Hayes, Strosahl, & Wilson, 1999) focus more heavily on blocking or reversing avoidant behaviors in depression (i.e., the skill of "opposite action" in DBT). In addition, Behavioral Activation (BA) is a recently manualized therapy that views avoidance behaviors as a primary target when treating MDD (Dimidjian et al., 2007). In fact, Dimidjian et al. (2006) proposed that avoidance-blocking strategies might have accounted for the superior performance of BA over cognitive-behavioral therapy (CBT) in a recent clinical trial of treatments for MDD.

Some data suggest that therapies targeting only MDD behavioral deficits may be comparable to those that focus on a combination of behavioral and cognitive symptoms (Jacobson et al., 1996). Component analyses have shown that the behavioral elements alone of classic CBT are capable of producing change equal to the full package of CBT (Jacobson et al., 1996). Furthermore, behavioral interventions for depression have been shown to be equal to CBT in relapse prevention over a 2-year period (Gortner, Gollan, Dobson, & Jacobson, 1998). Dimidjian et al. (2006) reported that BA was equal to antidepressant medication and superior to cognitive therapy for patients with more severe depression. Taken together, these findings suggest that: (a) behavioral symptoms of depression can and should be evaluated and targeted in the course of treatment; (b) alleviating behavioral deficits in depressed individuals has an impact on overall mood; and (c) further research is needed to determine what works for whom.

Cognitive Models of MDD

Although depressed individuals experience different combinations of symptoms, most people who are suffering from depression report some type of cognitive disturbance. From self-blame to suicidal ideation, abnormal cognitions are present in most cases of depression.

In the late 1960s and early 1970s, there was a veritable explosion of research regarding cognitive theories of depression, led in large part by Aaron Beck and Martin Seligman and their colleagues. Beck's cognitive theory (1967, 1987) emphasized the direct relationship between thoughts and emotions and posited that cognitive symptoms were central rather than peripheral symptoms of the disorder (Engel & DeRubeis, 1993). Beck hypothesized that the thoughts of depressed individuals were often distorted in a negative way, and these types of cognitions were fundamentally linked to feelings of depression (Beck, 1976). Seligman (1975) hypothesized that depression developed from a sense of helplessness, which arose from situations that were uncontrollable and unpleasant. These two theories spawned a plethora of research into the cognitive aspects

---

[2] Behaviorally based therapies are sometimes discussed as having occurred in three waves (Eifert & Forsyth, 2005). Using this terminology, the first wave comprises traditional behavior therapies, and the second wave comprises Cognitive Therapy and Cognitive-Behavioral Therapy. The third-wave therapies build upon their predecessors with the inclusion of strategies such as acceptance, mindfulness, spirituality, dialectics, and values. Hence, DBT and ACT are referred to as *third-wave therapies*.

of depression and the cognitive deficits experienced by individuals who suffer from depression. We will review the relevant cognitive models that continue to guide current research regarding the major cognitive deficits present in MDD (for more extensive reviews, see Alloy, Abramson, Walshaw, & Neeren, 2006; Dobson, 2001; Ingram, Miranda, & Segal, 2006; Pyszcynski & Greenberg, 1987).

BECK'S COGNITIVE MODEL

Beck's cognitive theory of depression (1968, 1976; Beck, Rush, Shaw, & Emery, 1979) grew out of his experiences working with depressed patients, who often made personally evaluative statements that were negatively biased. His model comprises three components: negative self-statements, cognitive errors, and underlying schemas or core beliefs. In this model, the combination of information-processing deficits (cognitive errors) and enduring negative cognitive patterns (schemas) contribute to the development and maintenance of depression. That is, Beck postulates that the processes and ways that people think about a situation are critical elements in the development of depression. This model is presented in Figure 8.1 Furthermore, CBT focuses on teaching the patient to change these statements, processes, and beliefs so they become more adaptive and the more positive views are internalized.

Automatic Thoughts

Beck et al. (1979) have stated that depressed individuals tend to have negative automatic thoughts or self-statements. These thoughts may be about themselves, the world, and the future (frequently referred to as the *cognitive triad*). Although depressed individuals generally are aware of these thoughts, they often are unaware that their thoughts contain distortions that serve to maintain or exacerbate negative mood. Consider a situation in which you are walking down the hallway at work and you pass by a colleague who does not acknowledge you. Assuming that you are not depressed, you might say something to yourself like, "Tom must be awfully busy today," or, "I wonder what Tom was reading—he looked like he was really into it." According to Beck's

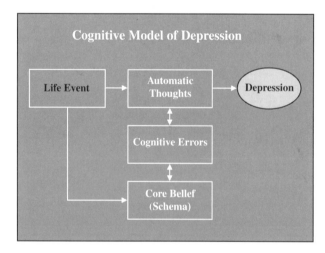

FIGURE 8.1   A Graphic View of Beck's Cognitive Model of Depression.

model, a depressed individual would be more likely to say, "Tom probably didn't acknowledge me because he doesn't like me. Nobody does—I'm not a very likable person. I guess I'll never fit in or have friends." Hence, the depressed individual tells herself that she is inherently unlikeable (negative view of himself), that she does not fit in (negative view of the world), and that this condition will last indefinitely (negative view of the future). In this example, the depressed individual is aware of her thoughts but does not seem to question them as invalid. Rather, she believes them to be true. For someone vulnerable to depression, the emotional response is similar to what it would be if her distorted thoughts actually were true.

Cognitive Distortions

A central tenet of Beck's cognitive theory of depression is that the thinking of a depressed individual is not only negatively biased and automatic, but it is also fraught with cognitive errors.[3] According to Beck, these errors are activated by continuous negative self-statements or they derive from the individual's self-schema or core beliefs. Some examples of cognitive errors are as follows (Beck, 1995):

All-or-nothing thinking: viewing things in black and white terms, rather than as occurring on a continuum.
Example: "If I'm not perfect, then I'm a terrible person."

Arbitrary inference: drawing negative conclusions in the absence of corroborating evidence.
Example: "My husband always comes home late from work; he must be having an affair."

Overgeneralization: drawing conclusions that far exceed the bounds of the current situation.
Example: "I don't get along with Mary, so I'll never get along with anyone."

Selective abstraction: concentrating on one detail about a situation and ignoring others, thereby not seeing the whole picture.
Example: "My teacher took two points off my essay. I'm a terrible writer."

Magnification/minimization: tending to unreasonably magnify the negative aspects of a person or situation and minimizing the positive aspects.
Example: "Just because I got a good performance evaluation does not mean I am a good worker."

Personalization: believing that external events happen because of inherent inadequacy, weakness, or other flaw; disregarding contradictory evidence.
Example: "That person just cut me off in traffic because they think I'm a terrible driver."

Emotional reasoning: thinking something must be true because of the strength of the feeling behind the thought.
Example: "I know my boyfriend says I'm a great person with lots of great qualities, but I just feel like such a terrible, worthless person."

---

[3] It is important to note that depressed individuals have also been shown to have a more realistic appraisal of reality than nondepressed individuals (Ackerman & DeRubeis, 1991). Empirical support for depressive realism is equivocal, though (see Dunning & Story, 1991).

As is evident in these examples, these kinds of perceptual processing errors function to screen out positive information and to bias negative or neutral information in a negative way.

Core Beliefs

Sacco and Beck (1995) noted that the cognitive theory of depression is predicated on a diathesis-stress model. That is, depressogenic schemas begin to develop early in life (diathesis) and are latent until they are activated by negative life events (stress). Hence, they ultimately predispose individuals to depression because they increase the likelihood of cognitive errors and negative self-statements or automatic thoughts. In addition to the cognitive triad, Beck postulated that depressed individuals also show a stable, negative cognitive pattern when interpreting information in their environments. These patterns are based on fundamental beliefs or assumptions they hold about themselves. Beck refers to these fundamental beliefs as *schemas*. These depressogenic schemas become activated in the presence of a negative life event and serve as a filter for incoming information.

Humans use various schemas to organize incoming data and to enhance processing speed in everyday life. For example, if you are sitting in a booth and someone hands you a menu and gives you silverware, your "restaurant schema" will be activated and you will have a certain set of expectations about what will happen next (e.g., a person will soon come to the table and ask you what you want to drink). Hence, schemas can effectively streamline cognitive processing by consolidating mental effort. In depression, however, people often hold fundamental beliefs about themselves that are far less innocuous. For example, a depressed individual might believe he is unlovable, that he must be perfect, or that he is worthless. Hence, all incoming information is organized according to these precepts, which results in cognitive distortions or errors when basic beliefs do not match reality.

According to the cognitive model, there are a variety of pathways by which information may be processed incorrectly. These cognitive distortions (see preceding examples) help the depressed individual maintain her negative cognitive style even in the face of contradictory evidence. According to Beck et al. (1979), depressive symptoms such as tearfulness, unjustified guilt, and feelings of worthlessness flow from this type of negative cognitive pattern. It is important to note, again, that depressive schemas are typically latent and become active in the face of one or more situational stressors; that is, an individual may not always believe he is inadequate, but this schema may become activated when he is fired.

LEARNED HELPLESSNESS MODEL AND EXPLANATORY STYLE

Seligman's learned helplessness theory (1975; Peterson, Maier, & Seligman, 1993) proposed that individuals become depressed because they view their situations as futile, and they view themselves as unable to bring about changes in these situations. He posited that people begin to experience feelings of helplessness in situations where outcomes are perceived to be independent of behavior. In essence, people give up trying when they have determined that an aversive situation is not likely to change, no matter what they do. Furthermore, Seligman hypothesized that helplessness was related to the motivational, emotional, behavioral, and cognitive deficits often seen in depression (Engel & DeRubeis, 1993).

As Seligman and his colleagues refined his research on helplessness, they began to explore the concept of attributional styles. Specifically, they posited that the crux of helplessness did not develop because people *perceived* there was no relationship between their actions and situational outcomes; rather, it was the way people *explained* this lack of a contingency to themselves that was crucial (Seligman, Abramson, Semmel, & von Baeyer, 1979; Abramson, Metalsky, & Alloy, 1989).

According to the *revised model of learned helplessness* (Abramson, Seligman, & Teasdale, 1978; Abramson, Metalsky, & Alloy, 1989) three essential belief dimensions are considered with regard to the preponderance of depressive symptoms: personalization, pervasiveness, and permanence. Personalization refers to the extent to which an individual believes that he or she caused an event to happen. People may make attributions about causality that run the gamut from "not at all my fault" to "completely my fault." Abramson and colleagues refer to these attributions as *external* or *internal* styles. For example, the student from a previous example may attribute her test failure to her teacher by saying "that teacher is so unfair" (external style). Alternatively, she may blame herself for her failure by saying "I am so stupid" (internal style). The second dimension in the learned helplessness model, pervasiveness, refers to the specificity or universality of a belief. For example, an individual who gets into a fender bender may say to herself, "I am a terrible driver" (specific style); on the other hand, she may say "I am always terrible at everything" (global style). Finally, permanence refers to the extent to which an individual believes that a problem is either temporary or permanent. Someone who recently went through the breakup of a relationship may say "This is hard, but I learned a lot that will help me in my next relationship" (unstable or temporary style). Alternatively, she may say "I am destined to be alone for the rest of my life" (stable or permanent style).

Abramson and colleagues (1989) found that the most depressed individuals have explanatory styles for negative events that are internal, global, and stable. In the relationship example, this individual might say to herself, "This breakup is all my fault. If only I weren't so annoying and clingy, I wouldn't have to be alone forever." As a corollary, depressed individuals attribute positive events to causes that are external, unstable, and specific (Seligman et al., 1979). For example, our student might say "Oh sure, I passed this test, but that's only because the teacher made this one so easy. It is only one test, and it will be different next time."

HOPELESSNESS THEORY OF DEPRESSION

Abramson, Metalsky, & Alloy (1989) published an updated and further refined, if not alternative, version of the earlier revised model of learned helplessness called the *hopelessness theory* of depression. They hypothesize that "hopelessness depression" is a subtype of depression, wherein hopelessness is "an expectation that highly desired outcomes will not occur or that highly aversive outcomes will occur coupled with an expectation that no response in one's repertoire will change the likelihood of occurrence" (Abramson et al., p. 359). They view hopelessness as a proximal, sufficient cause of depression; in other words, if hopelessness is present, symptoms of depression likely will be present as well.

The authors of hopelessness theory posit that depression is more likely to occur under the following circumstances: negative events that are considered important by the individual are attributed to global and stable causes; negative events are predicted by the individual to lead to additional negative consequences; and situations in which an individual makes a causal attribution about the relationship between the negative event and his or her inherent deficiencies (Abramson et al., 2002; Alloy et al., 2006). In other words, hopelessness develops from a combination of negative events and a negative cognitive style. Hopelessness theory also takes into account the perceived importance of the negative event to the individual and notes that unimportant events are not likely to contribute to the etiology of depression, regardless of one's attribution.

In summary, these theories emphasize the importance of the contributions of thoughts, attributions, and schema to the etiology and maintenance of depression. What, however, do the data say about the contributions of distorted thinking to mood disturbance?

COGNITIVE DEFICITS IN MDD

The common thread in the cognitive theories of depression is that they posit that depression is associated with disturbances in cognitive processes. Specifically, cognitive models have proposed that the thinking of depressed individuals tends to be negatively biased (Sacco & Beck, 1995). When compared to nondepressed controls, empirical support for this hypothesis of negative bias in depressed individuals has been shown for memory processes (Kennedy & Craighead, 1988; Mathews & MacLeod, 2005) and attentional processes (Gotlib et al., 2004). Data also indicate higher negative content in thoughts about the self, the world, the future, and life in general (see Engel & DeRubeis, 1993; Sacco & Beck, 1995).

Information Processing, Learning, and Memory

Cognitive distortions and negative attentional and memory biases are thought to play a major role in the development of negative cognitions (Sacco & Beck, 1995). All of the aforementioned cognitive theories of depression posit that a major vulnerability to depression occurs when depressed individuals orient toward negatively biased self-referential information. This is the primary premise behind Beck's theory of schemas 1967, 1987 and has long been observed in depressed individuals (see Ingram, Miranda, & Segal, 1998). Alloy and Abramson (1999) found that individuals with negative cognitive styles who were considered to be at higher risk (HR) for depression were more strongly oriented toward negative self-referential adjectives (e.g., "failure," "useless") than individuals with lower risk (LR) for depression. In addition, HR individuals were less strongly oriented toward positive self-referential adjectives (e.g., "worthy," "competent") compared to LR individuals. Importantly, these findings held for people who were currently depressed as well as those who were not currently depressed but who were considered high risk because of their cognitive style (Alloy et al., 2006). In other studies, depressed individuals also had more difficulty recalling positive self-referential adjectives and less difficulty recalling negative adjectives compared to nondepressed controls (Gotlib et al., 2004; Matt, Vazquez, & Campbell, 1992). In fact, Johnson, Joorman, and Gotlib (2007) found that improved recall of positive self-referential information predicted symptomatic improvement in depressed individuals in a naturalistic 9–month follow-up.

Multiple studies have shown that memory processes, both verbal and visual, are affected in the course of depression (Austin, Mitchell, & Goodwin, 2001). In addition, depressed individuals frequently show deficits in learning and episodic memory

(Goodwin, 1997). In some studies, depressed individuals show more negative bias in recognition memory and event recall (Haaga, Dyck, & Ernst, 1991) as well as autobiographical memory (Lyubomirsky, Caldwell, & Nolen-Hoeksema, 1998); in other words, these individuals are more likely to remember bad experiences rather than good experiences. Additionally, Nelson and Craighead (1977) demonstrated that depressed individuals recall more negative feedback and less positive feedback when compared to nondepressed individuals. Other studies, however, have shown that anxiety may be an important component in the recall of feedback. For example, Kennedy and Craighead (1988) found that both depressed individuals who are also anxious and anxious but nondepressed individuals are more accurate in their recall of negative feedback than nondepressed, nonanxious people. The distortion of recall of positive feedback, however, seemed to be a function of depression, with depressed individuals consistently recalling having received less positive feedback than they, in fact, had received, whereas anxious nondepressed individuals and nonanxious nondepressed individuals accurately recalled positive feedback.

Clinically, these data are relevant for the treatment of depression. First, given that depressed individuals interpret and recall information and events with a negative bias, they also are likely to report this information to therapists as though it is factual. For example, the work of Alloy and Abramson (1999) and others demonstrates the following: If a student gets a paper back from a teacher that contains both positive and negative feedback, she is more likely to orient toward the negative feedback and disregard the positive. Furthermore, she may report only the negative feedback to her therapist, *because the negative feedback is more salient in memory than the positive feedback for the depressed individual*. Clearly, this presents a dilemma for the clinician; although the patient is not purposefully withholding information, it is possible that she still is not presenting a complete picture due to the memory deficits associated with her depression.

In addition, clinicians should understand that attentional biases are compounded by negative memory biases. Depressed individuals are not only more likely to orient toward negative stimuli in their environments, they are also more likely to recall negative information than positive information. For example, the work of Lyubomirsky et al. (1998) demonstrates that a depressed individual may report to her therapist that she did not get on base in her softball game last night, but that she may not report that she struck out eight batters and won the game.

Taken together, these data highlight three important clinical points: (a) information presented in therapy may be distorted due to impaired attentional and memory processes; (b) the therapist will likely need to inquire directly about positive experiences that may have occurred; and (c) shifts in the proportion of positive to negative events that are reported in therapy should be carefully tracked, as they may be indicative of clinical progress.

Rumination

According to Response Styles Theory (RST; Nolen-Hoeksema, 1987), *rumination* involves self-focused attention accompanied by a repetitive focus on negative emotional causes, symptoms, and consequences (Lyubomirsky & Nolen-Hoeksema, 1993; Morrow & Nolen-Hoeksema, 1990; Nolen-Hoeksema, 1991, 2000; Nolen-Hoeksema, Larson, & Grayson, 1999; Treynor, Gonzalez, & Nolen-Hoeksema, 2003). Depressed individuals who ruminate will often report that they have difficulty disengaging from thoughts about their symptoms (e.g., "I cry all the time and can't seem to stop") or about possible causes of their depression (e.g., "If only my marriage hadn't ended"). Individuals with ruminative response styles also report focusing on potential consequences of their depression (e.g., "If I continue to stay home in bed, I'm probably going to lose my job"). They report feeling "stuck" with their depressive thoughts and unable to focus their attention on anything else.

Although ruminative thoughts are similar in form and function to the automatic thoughts described by Beck et al. (1979), they differ in style. Both automatic and ruminative thoughts are often depressogenic; however, rumination is a repetitive pattern of thinking that is characterized by a failure to disengage attention from the thought content. This repetitious style differentiates rumination from automatic thoughts, which may have a profound effect on mood but are often time-limited occurrences (Nolen-Hoeksema, 1991). In addition, the grist for the cognitive-behavioral mill lies in the distortions in depressive thinking; that is, automatic thoughts are posited to contain cognitive errors. Ruminative thoughts, however, are often accurate reflections of reality (Nolen-Hoeksema, Morrow, & Fredrickson, 1993). For example, there is some truth to the thought, "If I continue to stay home from work because I am so depressed, I will probably get fired." Although both types of thought processes are related to changes in mood, they are distinct from one another. Note also that the ruminative individual spends a considerable amount of time thinking about her symptoms and their consequences, leaving little opportunity for the individual to be distracted from her negative mood.

Rumination is a passive rather than active problem-solving strategy (Nolen-Hoeksema, 2000). The individual's thought content is centered on the symptoms and consequences of depression but not on how to alleviate those symptoms. Several studies have shown that people who endorse a ruminative thinking style are less likely than nonruminators to engage in active problem solving (Carver, Scheier, & Weintraub, 1989; Nolen-Hoeksema & Morrow, 1991; Nolen-Hoeksema, Parker, & Larson, 1994). Moreover, in laboratory studies they have a harder time generating solutions to problems (Morrow, 1990). To complicate matters to a greater degree, rumination exhausts cognitive resources, further interfering with problem-solving and decision-making processes (Nolen-Hoeksema, 1991; Riso et al., 2003).

The processes and outcomes of ruminative thought patterns are similar to the previously discussed information-processing problems. Individuals who ruminate show distortions of memories (Bower, 1981; Clark & Teasdale, 1982) and present-day interpretations of events (Forgas, Bower, & Krantz, 1984; Forgas & Bower, 1987; Schwarz & Clore, 1988). In addition, they show increasingly distorted thinking about their futures (Lyubomirsky, Caldwell, & Nolen-Hoeksema, 1998; Lyubomirsky & Nolen-Hoeksema, 1995). These progressive distortions of the cognitive triad lead to an increased sense of hopelessness and decreased problem-solving abilities (Nolen-Hoeksema, 2002).

Since the initial description of RST, a number of studies have shown that rumination is a useful predictor of both the onset of depressive episodes and the intensity of depressive symptoms (Just & Alloy, 1997; Nolan, Roberts, & Gotlib, 1998; Roberts, Gilboa, & Gotlib, 1998; Spasojevic & Alloy, 2001). Empirical evidence has shown that ruminative styles tend to maintain or even worsen symptoms of depression (Morrow & Nolen-Hoeksema, 1990; Needles & Abramson, 1990; Nolen-Hoeksema, Morrow, & Frederickson, 1993). In addition, people who have strong ruminative patterns experience longer periods of depression and depressive symptoms (Nolen-Hoeksema et al., 1993).

After studying students' reactions to the 1989 Loma Prieta earthquake in the San Francisco Bay area, Nolen-Hoeksema and Morrow (1991) concluded that rumination is more aptly classified as a response style rather than as a symptom of depression. Indeed, even ruminating about daily struggles is related to increased distress and sadness (Wood, Saltzberg, Neale, Stone, & Rachmiel, 1990). Recent findings also have shown that rumination mediates the relationship between risk factors for depression (e.g., negative cognitive style, prior history of depression) and the onset of a major depressive episode (Spasojevic & Alloy, 2001).

Attentional Deficits

Gotlib and colleagues (2004) have shown that mood is related to attentional biases regarding emotional expression on human faces. Depressed individuals have a stronger bias than nondepressed individuals toward sad rather than angry, neutral, or happy faces. In addition, Gotlib and colleagues (2004) found that symptom severity in MDD was related to a tendency to look away from happy faces. Some evidence suggests that such attentional biases hold even when depression has remitted (Gilboa & Gotlib, 1997; Joormann & Gotlib, 2007; Timbremont & Braet, 2004).

Similarly, data show that depressed individuals are more strongly oriented toward unhappy faces in their environment. Hence, a depressed patient may report that "it just seems like everyone around me is sad—I probably make everyone else miserable." Gotlib and colleagues' work (2004) demonstrated that it may be that the depressed person in this example failed to notice all of the happy, neutral, or angry people around him and oriented instead to the other sad people in his environment. Again, this individual is not purposefully misrepresenting his experience in the world (i.e., "poor me"); rather, he is experiencing a common cognitive pattern characteristic of MDD.

Depressed individuals also tend to show difficulty shifting their attention from one task to another (Murphy et al., 1999). MacCoon, Abramson, Mezulis, Hanking, & Alloy (2006) recently proposed the Attention Mediated Hopelessness (AMH) theory, which is an expansion of the hopelessness theory of depression. Attention Mediated Hopelessness theory proposes that when there is a discrepancy between a desired and actual outcome, one's attention shifts to that discrepancy, which one then attempts to resolve or reduce. These investigators (MacCoon et al., 2006) have proposed that individuals at higher risk for depression are likely to have greater difficulty solving the problem of the discrepancy between the goal state and the actual state. Hence, they "become trapped in a recursive self-regulatory cycle" (Smith, Alloy, & Abramson, 2006, p. 444). In other words, they are more likely to ruminate. In a test of the AMH theory, Smith et al., Alloy, and Abramson (2006) reported three important findings: (a) vulnerability to depression, rumination, and hopelessness were related to suicidal ideation; (b) hopelessness mediated the relationship between rumination and the duration of suicidal ideation; and (c) rumination mediated the relationship between cognitive risk and suicidal ideation.

Negative Cognitive Style

Most people encounter negative events over the course of their lives, but not everyone goes on to develop clinically significant depression as a result of these events. Hopelessness theory posits that people who encounter negative life events and who go on to develop depression are more likely to have a negative cognitive style than their nondepressed counterparts (Abramson et al., 1989).[4] Recent research lends strong support to this theory (Abramson et al., 1999; Alloy et al., 1999; Clark, Beck, & Alford, 1999; Ingram et al., 1998).

Alloy and Abramson (1999) have spearheaded recent research efforts regarding negative cognitive styles and depression in the Temple-Wisconsin Cognitive Vulnerabilities to Depression (CVD) project. Similar to Beck's theory, they have proposed that individuals with negative cognitive styles, compared to individuals without a negative cognitive style, are at greater risk for developing depression in the face of negative life events. The Temple-Wisconsin CVD project screened college freshmen with no history of Axis I pathology for the presence of negative cognitive styles. Those who showed evidence of a negative cognitive style were considered to be at high risk (HR) for depression, while those without a negative cognitive style were considered to be at low risk (LR) for depression. The results of the CVD project showed that people with negative cognitive styles were significantly more likely to have a lifetime history of depressive episodes as well as greater recurrences of depressive episodes (Alloy & Abramson, 1999; Alloy et al., 2000; Alloy et al., 2006; Alloy et al., 1999). Another compelling finding showed that negative cognitive style predicted both first onset as well as recurrences of major depressive episodes (Alloy, Abramson, Walshaw, & Nereen, 2006; Alloy, Abramson, Whitehouse, Hogan, et al., 2006). These findings lend critical support to the hypothesis that negative cognitive style increases vulnerability to depression.

Other studies have shown that negative cognitive styles are related to a greater number of depressive episodes, more intense episodes, and more chronic depressive episodes than individuals without a negative cognitive style (Haeffel et al., 2003; Iacoviello, Alloy, Abramson, Whitehouse, & Hogan, 2006). In addition, negative style also has been shown to predict increases in number of symptoms during an episode (Iacoviello et al., 2006). It should be noted, however, that virtually all of their studies have not included Axis II symptomatology and when comorbid Axis II symtomatology is considered simultaneously with negative cognitive styles, most of the predictive power is attributable to the comorbid Axis II symptoms rather than to the cognitive styles (Ilardi & Craighead, 1999).

Individuals with cognitive vulnerabilities to depression (i.e., negative cognitive styles) are thought to be at particularly high risk for ruminating due to problems in self-regulatory processes (Abramson et al., 2002; Alloy, Abramson, Murray, Whitehouse, & Hogan, 1997). Abramson and colleagues (2002) proposed a model to explain the relationship between cognitive vulnerability and rumination. They note that self-focused attention, as discussed earlier, has been shown to increase the intensity of an individual's current mood state (Ingram, 1990; Mor & Winquist, 2002); this is true for both positive and negative mood states (Scheier & Carver, 1977). According to self-regulatory theories, one's attention shifts in response to a negative or unexpected event that occurs, allowing the individual to evaluate what (if anything) needs to be done to take care of the problem that has arisen (Gray, 1994). Of course, this attentional shift is adaptive in many ways, as it allows one to modify her behaviors such that the individual's external environments and internal goal states are in line. Recall, however, that the occurrence of a negative or unexpected event is posited by cognitive theorists to be the first event in a causal chain that culminates in depression for vulnerable individuals. Abramson and colleagues (2002) posited that this is due to a failure to disengage

---

[4] Please see Gibb (2002) for a review of the etiology of negative cognitive styles.

one's attention from the negative event and the attributions being made about that event. In essence, these individuals continue to evaluate the discrepancy between their current and desired states, resulting in a repetitious self-regulatory process, or rumination (Pyszcynski & Greenberg, 1987).

Biology of Major Depression

Major Depressive Disorder is characterized by complex genetics and diverse symptomatology suggestive of the disruption of a variety of neural systems within the central nervous system (CNS) that participate in the regulation of mood, sleep, motivation, energy balance, and cognition (Nestler et al., 2002). In addition to disrupted functioning of the CNS, other organ systems of the body, including the endocrine and immune systems, are also dysregulated in patients with MDD, and this contributes to depressive pathophysiology within the CNS as well. In this portion of the chapter, we provide a brief and selected overview of relevant genetic and biological research.

GENETICS

Major Depressive Disorder is in part a heritable disorder. Heritability estimates for MDD based on estimates from twin studies range from 40% to 50% (Bierut et al., 1999; Kendler, Gardner, Neale, & Prescott, 2001; Kendler, Neale, Kellser, Heath, & Eaves, 1993; McGuffin, Katz, and Rutherford, 1991; McGuffin, Katz, Watkins, & Rutherford, 1996; Sullivan, Neale, & Kendler, 2000; Torgersen, 1986) and suggest that genetic influences on resilience to depression may be as important as the genetic influence on vulnerability to depression (Rijsdijk et al., 2003). Adoption studies also support the notion of a substantial genetic component of risk for major depression (Cadoret, 1978; Mendlewicz & Rainer 1977; Wender et al., 1986). Quantitatively, the relative risk ratio for major depression probands is 2–3 (Gershon et al., 1982; Maier et al., 1992; Weissman et al., 1984) and risk for MDD is increased by exposure to detrimental environmental factors such as childhood abuse and neglect or other forms of early life stress that promote vulnerability to depression (Kendler, Gardner, & Prescott, 2002; Kendler, Kuhn, & Prescott, 2004).

The mode of inheritance for MDD is unclear (Marazita et al., 1997; Moldin, Reich, & Rice, 1991; Price, Kidd, & Weissman, 1987). Genetic research on depression historically has focused on the use of single-gene models that likely do not apply to MDD or other psychiatric disorders. Like many common medical illnesses, MDD is a clinical syndrome that likely evolves from the differential contribution of multiple, variably penetrant genes with differing modes of inheritance. Their expression is likely influenced by environmental exposures and possibly architectural changes within the genome such as chromosomal rearrangement or copy number variation. As a consequence, MDD, as well as other forms of depression such as minor depression, dysthymia, and bipolar depression may be termed *complex* genetic disorders (Baron, 2001; Jaffee & Price, 2007; Lee & Lupski, 2006; Risch, 2000). The term, *complex*, stands in distinction to classic genetic diseases such as Huntington's disease or phenylketonuria (which are often referred to as Mendelian disorders in honor of the Augustinian monk, Gregor Mendel), in which mutations of a single gene are completely or largely responsible for the presence of the disease. In the context of complex genetic disease, additive and multiplicative models of genetic risk may be useful in dissecting the genetic contribution to depression (Orstavik, Kendler, Czajkowski, Tambs, & Reichborn-Kjennerud, 2007; Rijsdijk et al., 2003).

An enormous body of research examining candidate genes for MDD exists. Much of this research has attempted to identify candidate genes whose allelic variants are thought to predict differences in risk for MDD or depressive symptomatology either alone, as genetic main effects, or in concert with the environment. In some cases, these variants are single nucleotide polymorphisms (SNPs) that may have an identified function such as alteration of gene regulation or the structure of the protein for which the gene codes. Some of the better-known genes that have been investigated include the serotonin transporter gene (Caspi et al., 2003; Chorbov et al., 2007; Kaufman et al., 2006; Kendler, Kuhn, Vittum, Prescott, & Riley, 2005), the brain-derived neurotrophic factor gene (Kaufman et al., 2006), the glucocorticoid receptor chaperone protein gene, *FKBP5* (Binder et al., 2004) and the Type 1 corticotrophin-releasing hormone receptor gene (Bradley et al., 2007; Licinio et al., 2004).

The candidate gene literature is complex, and the frequently discordant results between well-designed studies of candidate genes make interpretation of the literature challenging (Caspi et al., 2003; Chorbov et al., 2007). Although a comprehensive review of this literature is beyond the scope of this chapter, many useful reviews are available (see Craddock & Forty 2006; Kato, 2007; Levinson, 2006).

Neurochemistry of Depression

Serotonin and Depression

Serotonin (5–hydroxytryptamine, 5–HT) is an indoleamine neurotransmitter synthesized from the amino acid, tryptophan, within the neurons of the rostral and caudal raphe nuclei of the brainstem. Neural fibers originating from the raphe are widespread and project through a variety of forebrain structures, including the hypothalamus, amygdala, basal ganglia, thalamus, hippocampus, cingulate cortex, and prefrontal cortex (Azmitia & Gannon, 1986). Fourteen 5–HT receptors have now been identified (Baez, Krusar, Helton, Wainscott, & Nelson, 1995). Following release from synaptic terminals, 5–HT is removed from extracellular fluid by the serotonin transporter (SERT), located on the presynaptic terminal, and is either repackaged into synaptic vesicles or degraded by monoamine oxidase (MAO).

Several lines of evidence suggest a role for deficient 5–HT signaling in depression and suicide (Owens & Nemeroff, 1994; Risch & Nemeroff, 1992). A reduction in platelet 5–HT$_2$ receptor binding, suggesting peripheral normalization of 5–HT levels, is associated with clinical improvement among patients treated with antidepressants (Biegon et al., 1990; Biegon et al., 1987). A novel experimental paradigm to investigate the effect of acute alterations of serotonergic neurotransmission on depressive symptomatology involves experimental depletion of tryptophan, the amino acid precursor from which serotonin is synthesized. Such acute depletion of tryptophan in patients with remitted depression, who had previously been responsive to selective serotonin reuptake inhibitors (SSRIs), has been found to rapidly precipitate recurrence of depression (Booij et al., 2002; Smith, Fairburn, & Cowen, 1997). Finally, a large body of clinical data supports the efficacy of serotonin reuptake inhibitors (e.g., fluoxetine, paroxetine, citalopram, and sertraline) in the treatment of depression (Nemeroff, 2007).

Norepinephrine and Depression

Norepinephrine (NE) is a catecholamine neurotransmitter synthesized from the amino acid, tyrosine, by neurons of the locus coeruleus (LC) and to a lesser extent by neurons of the lateral tegmental fields of the midbrain. Projections originating from the LC innervate a variety of forebrain structures including the cerebral cortex, thalamus, cerebellar cortex, hippocampus, hypothalamus, and the amygdala (Moore & Bloom, 1979). NE acts through activation of alpha (α-) and beta (β-) adrenergic receptors. Following release, NE is taken up on the presynaptic element by the norepinephrine transporter (NET) and is either repackaged into synaptic vesicles or degraded by MAO. Within the peripheral nervous system, NE is released from the postganglionic terminals of the sympathetic division of the autonomic nervous system as well as from the adrenal medulla and peripheral adrenal chromaffin cells.

Although the NE research may not be as extensive or diverse as the evidence for the contribution of serotonin to depression, findings related to NE concentrations within the CNS, experimental depletion, and antidepressant efficacy also implicate NE in the pathophysiology and treatment of depression (Ressler & Nemeroff, 2001). Elevated CSF concentrations of the major NE metabolite (3–methoxy-4–hydroxyphenylglycol; MHPG) have been consistently observed for many years among depressed patients, as well as those with mania and schizoaffective disorder (Schildkraut, 1965). In addition to studies of CNS pools of NE metabolites, NE and its metabolites have also been found to be increased in the plasma and urine of depressed patients (Roy, Pickar, DeJong, Karoum, & Linnoila, 1988; Veith et al., 1994). Selective serotonin reuptake inhibitor treatment of depression results in decreased concentrations of CSF MHPG (Sheline, Bardgett, & Csernansky, 1997), while treatment of depressed patients with tricyclic antidepressants (TCAs) results in decreased plasma (Charney, Heninger, Sterngberg, & Roth, 1981) and urinary (Golden et al., 1988; Linnoila et al., 1986) metabolites of NE.

As is the case with serotonin, experimental depletion of NE in depressed patients who have had a therapeutic response to treatment with an antidepressant such as desipramine (which works predominantly to increase NE within the CNS) can precipitate relapse of depression (Charney, 1998). This suggests that a state of relative NE deficiency may play a role in the production of depressive symptomatology. Taking this approach a step further, the experimental depletion of catecholamine neurotransmitters (which depletes NE as well as dopamine) in euthymic, unmedicated patients with a history of depression has also been shown to precipitate relapse of depressive symptoms (Berman et al., 1999). Consistent with a role of dysregulated NE signaling in depression, suicide completers exhibit increased activity of the rate-limiting enzyme in NE synthesis, tyrosine hydroxylase (TH), within the locus coeruleus in postmortem tissue studies (Ordway 1997). The finding of compensatory upregulation of TH is indicative of the increased NE synthetic capacity required to support the high NE turnover that has been observed in severely depressed patients. Finally, a large body of clinical data supports the efficacy of NE reuptake inhibitors (including reboxetine and desipramine) in the treatment of depression (Nemeroff, 2007).

Brain-Derived Neurotrophic Factor (BDNF) and Depression

Brain-derived neurotrophic factor is a neuropeptide neurotransmitter that plays a substantial role in the regulation of neuronal survival, differentiation, and function within the developing and adult central nervous system. It also performs important regulatory roles in short- and long-term synaptic plasticity, the process whereby connections between neurons are altered (Bramham, 2007; Poo, 2001). These effects appear to be driven in part by activity of the tyrosine kinase B receptor (TrkB, encoded by the *NTRK2* locus) through which BDNF acts. Functionally, BDNF appears to be important in episodic as well as emotion-related memory. Preclinical research using animal models of fear conditioning indicate a central role for BDNF and the TrkB receptor in the development of fear-related memory (Berton et al., 2006; Chhatwal, Stanek-Rattiner, Davis, & Ressler, 2006; Rattiner & Ressler, 2004; Rattiner, Davis, French, & Ressler, 2004). Clinical research with humans has identified a functional polymorphism (Val66-Met) within the BDNF gene that impacts hippocampal function and episodic memory (Egan et al., 2003; Duncan, Hutchison, & Craighead, 2007) as well as function of the hypothalamic-pituitary-adrenal axis in depressed patients (Schule et al., 2006).

The complex relationship that exists between stress and mood disorders may be mediated in part by the activity of BDNF and other neurotrophic factors (Duman & Monteggia, 2006; Schmidt & Duman, 2007); this may provide a window for the development of novel antidepressants (Berton & Nestler, 2006; though also see Groves, 2007). Using rodent models, stress has been found to decrease BDNF expression within the hippocampus using restraint (Smith, Makino, Kim, & Kvetnansky, 1995; Smith, Makino, Kvetnansky, & Post, 1995), maternal deprivation (Roceri, Hendriks, Racagni, Ellenbroek, & Riva, 2002), and social defeat (Tsankova et al., 2006) paradigms, among others. Notably, reductions in other neurotrophic factors, including nerve growth factor (Ueyama et al., 1997), vascular endothelial growth factor (VEGF) and VEGF receptors (Heine, Zareno, Maslam, Joels, & Lucassen, 2005) are also reduced by stress. Increased hippocampal BDNF-like immunoreactivity, an index of BDNF protein levels, has been observed in depressed patients treated with antidepressants (Chen, Dowlatshahi, MacQueen, Wang, & Young, 2001). Serum BDNF is also lower in depressed patients (Shimizu et al., 2003), and it appears to be normalized by antidepressant treatment (Aydemir, Deveci, & Taneil, 2005; Gervasoni et al., 2005; Gonul et al., 2005).

Neuroendocrinology

Hypothalamic-Pituitary-Adrenal (HPA) Axis

Excess secretion of cortisol (Carpenter & Bunney, 1971; Gibbons & McHugh, 1962) and its metabolites (Sachar, Hellman, Fukushima, & Gallagher, 1970) was first observed in depressed patients over 40 years ago. The prominent presence of depression and anxiety in patients with endocrinopathies affecting the hypothalamic-pituitary-adrenal (HPA) axis (e.g., Cushing's Disease; Dorn et al., 1997). in conjunction with the observation of increased secretion of cortisol in healthy patients exposed to stress contributed to the development of the stress-diathesis model of depression. This model hypothesizes that individual predisposition to excess reactivity of the neural and endocrine stress response systems plays a central role in susceptibility to depression. The presence of acute or prolonged stress in vulnerable individuals is believed to play a significant role in both the onset and relapse of certain forms of depression and may also contribute to the burden of medical illness in patients with depression (Brown, Varghese, & McEwen, 2004). This model highlights the interaction of life events, cognitive styles, and neurobiology in the etiology of MDD.

Functional Organization of the HPA Axis

The discovery of corticotrophin-releasing factor (CRF; Vale, Speiss, Rivier, & Rivier, 1981) greatly accelerated research into the biology of stress and helped clarify the organization of the HPA axis, a collection of neural and endocrine structures that function collectively to facilitate the adaptive response to stress. Parvocellular neurons of the paraventricular nucleus (PVN) within the hypothalamus project to the median eminence, where they secrete CRF into the primary plexus of blood vessels that comprise the hypothalamo-hypophyseal portal system (Swanson, Sawchenko, River, & Vale, 1983). The secreted CRF is then transported to the anterior pituitary gland, where it activates CRF receptors on pituitary corticotrophs, resulting in increased secretion of adrenocorticotrophic hormone (ACTH). The ACTH released from the anterior pituitary into the systemic circulation subsequently stimulates the production and release of cortisol from the adrenal cortex. With elevated activity of the HPA axis, circulating levels of cortisol increase and feedback inhibition reduces stress-induced activation of the HPA axis and limits excess secretion of glucocorticoids, effectively dampening the stress response (Jacobson & Sapolsky, 1991).

In addition to its major role in the regulation of the HPA axis, CRF is widely distributed in areas of the brain outside of the hypothalamus, including the amygdala, septum, bed nucleus of the stria terminalis, and the cerebral cortex (Swanson et al., 1983). CRF also functions, along with the hypothalamic CRF system, as a neurotransmitter in coordinating the behavioral, autonomic, endocrine, and immune responses to stress (Arborelius, Owens, Plotsky, & Nemeroff, 1999).

Injection of CRF into the CNS of laboratory animals initiates changes in the activity of the autonomic nervous system that results in the elevation of peripheral catecholamines, reduced gastrointestinal activity, increased heart rate, and elevated blood pressure. Further, behavioral changes similar to those observed in humans with depression, such as disturbed sleep, diminished food intake, reduced grooming, decreased reproductive behavior, and enhanced fear-conditioning also occur following central administration of CRF in rodents and primates (Dunn & Berridge, 1990; Owens & Nemeroff, 1991). Similarly, experimental induction of these physiological changes using behavioral stress paradigms is reduced by pretreatment with CRF receptor antagonists (Gutman, Owens, Skelton, Thrivikraman, & Nemeroff, 2003).

Depression and Pathophysiology of the HPA Axis

The dexamethasone suppression test (DST), which was originally designed to aid in the diagnosis of Cushing's Disease, was one of the first endocrine challenge tests to be studied in psychiatric patients. The DST is useful as a clinical index of HPA axis activity. It consists of the administration of a low dose (1 mg) of the synthetic glucocorticoid, dexamethasone, at 11:00 p.m. followed by measurement of plasma cortisol concentrations at 2 or 3 time points the following day. Dexamethasone acts at the level of the anterior pituitary corticotrophs to reduce the secretion of ACTH, resulting in a decrease in the synthesis and release of cortisol from the adrenal cortex. Failure to suppress plasma cortisol concentrations after dexamethasone administration suggests impaired feedback regulation and hyperactivity of the HPA axis.

A large percentage of drug-free patients with major depression fail to suppress secretion of cortisol following administration of dexamethasone, a finding known as dexamethasone nonsuppression (Carroll, Martin, & Davies, 1968). This suggests that DST nonsuppression (DST-NS) is a biological marker for depression (Carroll, 1982). Dexamethasone nonsuppression status and hypercortisolemia are both common in depression, although they certainly are not universal. Meta-analyses have revealed that DST-NS status is most commonly found in patients with psychotic depression or mixed bipolar states, as previously reported by several investigators (Evans & Nemeroff, 1983; Schatzberg, Rothschild, Bond, & Cole, 1984). Dexamethasone nonsuppression status also generally predicts a more severe course of illness (Arana, Baldessarin, & Orsteen, 1985). Additional meta-analytic data have provided further support for the relationship between hypercortisolemia and psychotic depression as assessed with the DST (Nelson & Davis, 1997). Finally, a meta-analysis conducted by Ribeiro, Tandon, Grunhaus, and Greden (1993) concluded the following: (a) baseline DST status was not predictive of response to treatment; (b) DST-NS status was associated with poor response to placebo; and (c) post-treatment DST-NS was identified as a significant risk factor for relapse and poor outcome as initially reported by Greden et al. (1980) with subsequent confirmation by Nemeroff and Evans (1984).

Substantial rates of DST-NS have been reported in patients with a variety of other Axis-I and Axis II diagnoses (Baxter, Edell, Gerner, Fairbanks, & Gwirtsman, 1984; Gerner & Gwirtsman, 1981; Hubain, Simonnet, & Mendlewicz, 1986), calling into question its specificity as a diagnostic test. However, the greatest contribution of the DST was to serve as an impetus for subsequent studies exploring the underlying pathophysiology of the HPA axis in depression.

Considerable data support the hypothesis that the dysregulation of the HPA axis observed in depression is a state phenomenon, rather than a trait phenomenon. In this context, state dependence implies the presence of pathophysiological phenomena that are related to a particular phase of depression rather than being constitutively present, that is, trait based. Among depressed patients who secrete abnormally high amounts of cortisol into the bloodstream (hypercortisolemia), plasma cortisol levels (Sachar et al., 1970), dexamethasone suppression test-nonsuppression status (Arana et al., 1985), blunting of the ACTH response to CRF infusion (Amsterdam et al., 1988), hypersecretion of CRF (Nemeroff, Bissette, Akil, & Fink, 1991), and adrenal hypertrophy (Rubin, Phillips, Sadow, & McCracken, 1995) all normalize following resolution of clinical symptoms.

There appear to be a variety of ways in which the presence of depression, as a function of patient population, is reflected in altered functioning of the HPA axis. For example, patients with psychotic depression demonstrate hyperactivity of the HPA axis along with the highest rates of nonsuppression on the dexamethasone suppression test (Schatzberg et al., 1983), while depressed patients without psychosis may have either decreased or normal activity of the HPA axis (Posener et al., 2000). Alternatively, patients who have a history of childhood adversity show elevated secretion of ACTH and cortisol in response to a laboratory stress test (Heim, Newport, Bonsall, Miller, & Nemeroff, 2000) as well as abnormal responses to neuroendocrine challenge tests (Heim, Mletzko, Purselle, Musselman, & Nemeroff, 2007) whereas those without such history do not (for review see Gillespie & Nemeroff, 2007). A multisite treatment study found that patients with chronic depression with a history of trauma during childhood responded preferentially to treatment with cognitive-behavioral therapy compared to the antidepressant, nefazodone, suggesting that particular subtypes of depression may require different approaches to treatment (Nemeroff et al., 2003).

Psychoneuroimmunology

Inflammation is another key component of the adaptive response to stress (Chrousos, 1995). Stress stimulates the inflammatory response so that the body may appropriately respond to injury and contamination by infectious agents. The principal way this occurs is by the stress-induced secretion by white blood cells of small peptides known as proinflammatory cytokines that stimulate the development of inflammation (Elenkov, Iezzoni, Daly, Harris, & Charousos, 2005; Glaser & Kiecolt-Glaser, 2005; McEwen, 1998). In addition to proinflammatory cytokines, other important chemical components of the inflammatory response include acute phase proteins that promote resistance to infection and tissue repair (e.g., fibrinogen and c-reactive protein) and nuclear factor kappa-B, a candidate mediator for some of the CNS effects related to the inflammatory response (Bierhaus et al., 2003). Finally, cortisol (secreted following activation of the HPA axis) acts on intracellular signaling pathways that help to terminate the inflammatory response after cessation of acute stress (Chrousos, 1995). The relationship between the HPA axis and systemic inflammation may be especially pertinent in view of the findings that patients with a history of early-life stress have an impaired capacity to regulate the HPA axis in the presence of psychosocial stress (Heim et al., 2000); this suggests that control of the inflammatory response (as a consequence of HPA axis dysregulation) may be impaired as well.

Increasingly, research evidence indicates that systemic inflammation may play a key role in the etiology of a number of common medical diseases and depression (Evans et al., 2005; Raison, Capuron, & Miller, 2006). This may be due, in part, to the body's inability to down-regulate short-term physiological adaptations to stress, (e.g., inflammation and HPA activation) back to baseline levels following exposure to stressful circumstances in susceptible individuals. Administration of proinflammatory cytokines to laboratory animals results in a syndromal pattern of behavioral and neurovegetative symptoms known as *sickness behavior* that is similar to the pattern of signs of depression in human patients and includes psychomotor slowing, fatigue, elevated pain sensitivity, disrupted sleep, and anxiety (Kent, Bluthe, Kelley, & Dantzer, 1992). Clinical research in humans has identified an array of proinflammatory cytokines including interleukin (IL)-6, IL-1, and tumor necrosis factor-alpha (TNF-α) and inflammatory markers such as CRP (Alesci et al., 2005; Danner, Kasl, Abramson, & Vaccarino, 2003; Ford & Erlinger, 2004; Kahl et al., 2005; Miller, Stetler, Carney, Freedland, & Banks, 2002; Musselman, Miller et al., 2001; Panagiotakos et al., 2004; Penninx et al., 2003) that are elevated in patients with depression. Humans treated with interferon-α, which promotes the release of IL-6, IL-1b, and TNF-α, commonly develop symptoms of depression, and a significant subset of these individuals fulfill diagnostic criteria for an episode of major depression that may be effectively treated with SSRIs (Musselman, Lawson et al., 2001; Raison et al., 2005).

Inflammation may be particularly relevant to three populations of depressed patients: those with treatment-resistant depression (Maes, 1999; Sluzewska, Sobieska, & Ryabakowski, 1997), chronic medical illness comorbid with depression (Evans et al., 2005), and depression associated with early-life stress (Pace et al., 2006). In some patients, exposure to trauma or stressful childhood experiences may be a variable connecting risk for depression, chronic medical illness, and inflammation. For example, patients with histories of childhood trauma have an elevated risk for depression that is often chronic in course (Hayden & Klein, 2001; Kendler et al., 2004; Lara, Klein, & Kasch, 2000) and also elevated risk for a variety of common, chronic, and progressive medical diseases, including coronary artery disease (Goodwin & Stein, 2004).

Brain Imaging

HIPPOCAMPUS

Owing to its major role in the regulation of both stress and learning, the hippocampus has been a major focus of neuroanatomical studies in patients with depression. Functionally, the hippocampus plays a central role in adaptation to stress, as it is involved in the regulation of HPA-axis activity as well as the registration of explicit memory and learning context. Further, the hippocampus is a remarkably plastic structure, being a major site of neurogenesis in the adult brain on the one hand and possessing a well-demonstrated vulnerability to stress on the other. For example, neurons in one particular region of the hippocampus, CA3, exhibit morphological changes involving the loss of dendritic spines, reduced dendritic branching, and impaired neurogenesis in response to stress exposure (Duman & Monteggia, 2006; Fuchs & Gould, 2000; Nestler et al., 2002).

Hippocampal vulnerability to stress may be, in part, a consequence of the high concentration of type I and type II corticosteroid receptors present within the hippocampus. These receptors enable the hippocampus to exert an inhibitory role on activity of the HPA axis (Jacobson & Sapolsky, 1991). Prolonged exposure to large amounts of corticosteroids results in hippocampal damage in rodents (Magarinos & McEwen, 1995a; Magarinos & McEwen, 1995b) and nonhuman primates (Magarinos, McEwen, Flugge, & Fuchs, 1996; Sapolsky, Uno, Rebert, & Finch, 1990; Uno et al., 1994; Uno, Tarara, Else, Suleman, & Sapolsky, 1989). In humans, bilateral hippocampal atrophy has been observed in patients with Cushing's Disease, among whom the extent of hippocampal atrophy correlates with the magnitude of corticosteroid hypersecretion (Starkman, Gebarski, Berent, & Schteingart, 1992).

Hippocampal atrophy has been documented in a wide variety of neuropsychiatric disorders (Geuze, Vermetten, & Bremner, 2005). With respect to mood disorders, reduced hippocampal volume has been found in some studies (Bremner, Narayan, Andersen, Miller, & Charney, 2000; Frodl et al., 2002; Sheline, 1996), but not all studies of patients with unipolar depression (Campbell & Macqueen, 2004; Rusch, Abercrombie, Oakes, Schaefer, & Davidson, 2001; Vakili et al., 2000). In patients with a history of depression who also have hippocampal atrophy, the extent of atrophy is positively correlated with total lifetime duration of depression (Sheline, Sanghavi, Minturn, & Gado, 1999; Sheline, Wang, Gado, Csernansky, & Vannier, 1996). The finding of reduced hippocampal volume in patients with remitted unipolar depression has also suggested the possibility that small hippocampal size may be a risk factor for depression (Neumeister et al., 2005).

Exposure to traumatic stress, either early in life or during adulthood is associated with loss of hippocampal volume and has been documented in individuals with combat-induced (Bremner et al., 1995; Vythilingam et al., 2005), childhood-related (Bremner et al., 2003) and chronic (Kitayama, Vaccarino, Kutner, Weiss, & Bremner, 2005) Posttraumatic Stress Disorder as well as Dissociative Identity Disorder (Vermetten,

Schmahl, Linder, Loewenstein, & Bremner, 2006). Vythilingham and colleagues (2002) reported that depressed women with a history of childhood sexual abuse, but not depressed women without such a history, had a reduction in hippocampal volume compared with control subjects. This suggests that previous reports of reduced hippocampal size in patients with depression may, in fact, be related specifically to a history of childhood trauma rather than depression in general.

SUBGENUAL CINGULATE

Another area of the brain that has received considerable attention in studies of patients with mood disorders is the subgenual cingulate (Brodmann's area—Cg25). Brain imaging studies have suggested the importance of limbic-cortical pathways in the pathogenesis of major depression (Brody, Barsom, Bota, & Sexena, 2001; Drevets, 1999; Mayberg, 1994). Additional research (Mayberg et al., 1999; Seminowicz et al., 2004) has demonstrated the importance of Cg25 in the modulation of acute sadness and response to antidepressant treatment response, indicating that Cg25 likely plays a role in the regulation of negative affect states. Cg25 possesses descending projections to a variety of brain regions (brainstem, hypothalamus, and insula) implicated in regulating neurovegetative and motivational states associated with depression (Barbas, Saha, Rempel-Clower, & Ghasghaei, 2003; Freedman, Insel, & Smith, 2000; Jurgens & Muller-Preuss, 1977; Ongur, An, & Price, 1998). Further, a number of pathways link Cg25 to the orbitofrontal, medial prefrontal, and anterior and posterior cingulate cortices that provide a means through which autonomic and homeostatic processes influence learning, reward, and motivation (Barbas et al., 2003; Carmichael & Price, 1996; Haber, 2003; Vogt & Pandya, 1987). Decreased activity of Cg25 has been associated with positive clinical responses to a variety of antidepressant treatments (Dougherty et al., 2003; Goldapple et al., 2004; Mayberg et al., 2000; Mottaghy et al., 2002; Nobler et al., 2001). More recently, the technique of deep brain stimulation (DBS), originally developed for the treatment of Parkinson's Disease (Benabid, 2003), has been shown to produce significant clinical benefits for patients with treatment-resistant depression (Mayberg et al., 2005); in the treatment of MDD, the stimulating electrode is placed in Cg25.

Summary

We have provided a brief overview of the pathobiology of depression with respect to the integrated involvement of the central nervous system and the endocrine and immune systems. Research into the genetics of depression is an evolving endeavor, and data derived from genetic methods have validated previous research into the biology of depression with respect both to the general heritability of biological risk for depression and for genetic variation as it affects specific neurotransmitter and neuroendocrine systems. An extensive body of research into the neurochemistry and neuroendocrinology of depression has implicated the monoamine neurotransmitters, serotonin and norepinephrine, the neurotrophic peptide, BDNF, and elements of the HPA axis (particularly cortisol, CRF, and FKBP5) as playing particularly key roles in the initiation and maintenance of depression. Similarly, a host of findings from the field of psychoneuroimmunology have demonstrated a role for the immune system and inflammatory response in the biology of depression. Structural and functional brain imaging research has identified abnormalities at most levels of the brain in depressed individuals. We chose to focus on the hippocampus and subgenual cingulate in this chapter. The hippocampus is both a major regulator of the stress response and may be affected by the stress response as well in individuals exposed to early life stress. CG25 resides at the crossroads of many information conduits of the brain, and it has been identified as a brain area responsive to mood state and antidepressant treatment response as well as a possible target for treatment-refractory depression. Finally, a recurring theme in the biology of depression is the preeminent role of stress as a developmental force that shapes biological vulnerability to depression and stress as a factor in the relapse of depression.

An Integrative Model

It is important to understand the psychological and biological research within the context of an overall interactive and developmental conceptual model. A schematic representation of the model we follow is presented in Figure 8.2. The empirical data reviewed within this chapter fit nicely within such a theoretical framework. It also serves heuristically to guide research and clinical intervention. For example, we draw this model on a notepad when conducting individual therapy or on a "smart" board in group therapy.

Earlier we referred to a diathesis/stress model. Within our model, the diathesis may be biological (e.g., genetic, neural connections) or psychological (e.g., cognitive, emotional, behavioral). As we have maintained for many years (Craighead, 1980), the key concept is that the diathesis is neither *unidimensional* nor singular in its etiological role. Rather, it may include more than one variable in any of the domains categorized as "Person" variables.

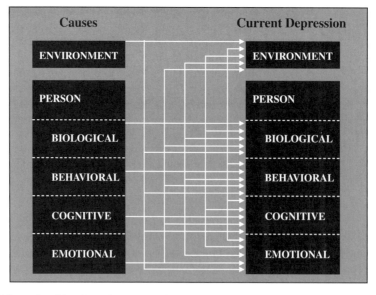

FIGURE 8.2   A Graphic View of an Integrative Model of Depression.

This schematic representation is to be viewed as a shapshot or static description of a dynamic and interacting set of variables within each domain and across all domains. Within this model, the various depressive symptoms, as categorized earlier in this chapter, occur within an environmental context. As a child grows and develops, she interacts with the environment, which also comprises numerous dimensions of causative influence in all domains of the person. By the processes described as *reciprocal determinism* (Bandura, 1969), the external environment influences the person, but it is a two-way street—and the person has a reciprocal impact on the environment. This process of interactive development affects both those variables within and outside the individual. Furthermore, within the individual (the "Person" variables) there are interactive processes across the various domains. For example, emotional regulation is an important variable in the development of depression and other disorders. Emotional arousal may be regulated from the "bottom up" because it may be triggered by a limbic system reaction to some environmental stimulus; on the other hand, recent research has shown that emotions may also be regulated by cortical activity by so-called "top down" processes (see Ochsner & Gross, 2007). The process of unraveling these processes and increasing our understanding of their interrelationships will be essential to enhance the prevention and treatment of MDD.

It is posited that each environmental and person sphere or domain is multidimensional in its *impact* in both causing and ameliorating MDD. Thus, a neurobiological intervention changes not only somatic symptoms of depression; it exerts influence on cognitive activity, emotional states, and behavioral actions (bottom up). At the same time, and with equal importance, cognitive changes, for example, impact neurobiology as well as emotions and behavioral patterns (top down), and so on for each of the domains. Thus, this model also implies that a clinician may intervene in any of the domains and expect to have an impact on all other domains. The impact of the intervention may be most direct within the same domain, but clearly there is cross talk between all the domains and resultant changes in all the categories of symptoms of depression. Hence, antidepressant medications affect not only neurobiology but also cognitions, emotions, and behaviors. In the same manner, cognitive-behavior therapy modifies cognitions, behaviors, *and* neurobiological pathways associated with MDD (see Goldapple et al., 2004). In contrast to unidimensional causative models of MDD, this approach underscores both the interactive and developmental aspects of all domains of human functioning. Consequently, it is essential to study MDD from a multidisciplinary approach in order to elucidate these pathways of etiological and treatment significance. It further underscores the importance of identifying which types of interventions may be most effective for which patterns of empirically determined subtypes of MDD.

Assessment of Depression

CLINICAL INTERVIEWS

The *Structured Clinical Interview for DSM-IV Axis I Disorders, Clinician Version* (SCID-CV; First, Spitzer, Gibbon, & Williams, 1997) is a semistructured interview that helps clinicians and researchers systematically inquire about possible Axis I symptomatology based on *DSM-IV* criteria. The interviewer asks a series of questions and elicits examples that allow for diagnostic determinations to be made. The SCID-I takes approximately 45 to 90 minutes to administer, depending on the extent of the pathology evinced (First & Gibbon, 2004). It inquires about both current and lifetime diagnoses, and it allows for the interviewer to "skip out" of a section if it is clear that a diagnosis will not be met.

The SCID comprises six modules: (1) Mood Episodes, Dysthymia, Mood Disorder due to a General Medical Condition, and Substance-Induced Mood Disorder; (2) Psychotic and Associated symptoms; (3) Psychotic Disorders; (4) Mood Disorders; (5) Substance Use Disorders; and (6) Anxiety and Other Disorders. The first two modules assess for the presence of mood and psychotic symptoms, whereas the remaining four modules assess more specifically for the presence or absence of the symptoms necessary to meet criteria for *DSM-IV* diagnoses. During the interview, the client's responses to questions about particular behaviors and symptoms are rated as follows: "present" if the behavior or symptom is endorsed by the interviewee; "absent" if the behavior or symptom is not endorsed or is subthreshold; or "unsure" if the client does not give enough information to make an accurate assessment, including follow-up questioning. The Mood Disorders subsection of the SCID-I aids the clinician in determining whether the interviewee meets criteria for Major Depressive Disorder and helps rule out bipolar and depressive disorders due to medical conditions or substance-use disorders.

Research on the reliability of the SCID-I has been equivocal. Reliability for categorical constructs (such as diagnostic status for MDD) is reported in terms of the Kappa statistic, which assesses the agreement between independent raters while correcting for chance agreement. Kappa scores range from 0 (no agreement between two raters) to 1.00 (perfect agreement), with higher scores indicating a greater degree of agreement. Viera & Garrett (2005) report that levels of agreement may be slight (kappa ranges 0.21–.40), fair (.41–.60), moderate (.61–.80), or substantial (.81–.99). Kappa ratings for MDD across several studies have ranged from moderate (.61) to substantial (.93), with typical scores being about .80 (First & Gibbon, 2004).

Validity ratings for the SCID have been more difficult to establish, based on the fact that no gold standard for diagnosing mental illness exists. In fact, the SCID is often regarded as the gold standard in assessing psychopathology (Shear et al., 2000; Steiner, Tebes, Sledge, & Walker, 1995). Using Spitzer's best-estimate diagnosis technique, the SCID was superior to standard clinical intake interviews in two studies (Basco et al., 2000; Kranzler et al., 1995).

The *Longitudinal Interval Follow-Up Evaluation* (LIFE) (Keller et al., 1987) is a semistructured interview created to assess the longitudinal course of *DSM-IV* Axis I symptoms and disorders including MDD. Specific dates of onset, remission, relapse, and recurrence are recorded, which makes the LIFE the most appropriate measure for conducting longitudinal or treatment outcome studies of MDD. The LIFE is designed to be administered every 6 months; if, however, a patient or research participant misses an interview, information for the missing period can be collected at the next scheduled interview. High interrater reliability has been demonstrated for the interview (Keller et al., 1987). The interview takes between 30–60 minutes to administer.

SELF-REPORT MEASURES

The most widely used self-report measure is the *Beck Depression Inventory-II* (BDI-II) (Beck, Steer, & Brown, 1996), which can be administered to patients aged 13–80. The

BDI-II is a 21–item instrument that measures the intensity of both cognitive and somatic-affective symptoms of depression. Symptoms are presented categorically, and each item has four possible response choices. For example, the item inquiring about a patient's mood reads as follows:

0   Mood
1   I do not feel sad.
2   I feel blue or sad.
3   I am blue or sad all the time and I can't snap out of it.
4   I am so sad or unhappy that I can't stand it.

Point values from each item are combined into a total score; scores range from 0 to 64, with higher scores indicating higher levels of depression. The BDI-II demonstrates high internal consistency across a wide variety of populations (average coefficient $\alpha = .91$). It also has high convergent validity, demonstrating strong correlations with the Hamilton Rating Scale for Depression ($r = .71$), the Beck Hopelessness Scale ($r = .68$), and with previous versions of the BDI ($r = .93$) (Dozois & Covin, 2004).

CLINICAL RATING SCALES OF MDD SEVERITY

The *Hamilton Rating Scale for Depression* (HAM-D; Hamilton, 1960) is a 17–item, clinician-administered interview designed to measure intensity of depression (i.e., it is not intended to be a diagnostic instrument). There are various longer versions of the HAM-D, but the 17–item is the most frequently used version. Nine of the HAM-D items are rated on a 5–point scale, and eight items are rated on a 3–point scale. Ratings from each item are summed to derive a total score, with possible scores ranging from 0 to 52 points. The HAM-D demonstrates good internal consistency (average coefficient $\alpha = .78$) as well as interrater reliability (range = .70 to .96; Kovak, 2004).[5] The HAM-D correlates highly with the BDI-II as well as the Montgomery-Asberg Depression Rating Scale (MADRS; Kovak, 2004). The HAM-D is especially useful for detecting change in participants' level of depression over time, which makes it particularly attractive for research purposes. In fact, it is the most commonly used measure of depression change by pharmaceutical companies testing new antidepressant medications (Kovak, 2004).

The *Quick Inventory of Depression Symptomatology* (QIDS) (Rush et al., 2003) is available as both a clinician-administered scale (QIDS-C) and as a self-report measure (QIDS-SR). The QIDS is a 16–item measure designed to assess symptom severity across the nine *DSM-IV-TR* (2000) symptom domains. Each item is rated on a scale from 0 to 3, with total scores ranging from 0 to 27. The QIDS has demonstrated high internal consistency ($\alpha = .87$), and scores on the QIDS-SR have been shown to be highly correlated with scores on the HAM-D (.86) (Rush et al., 2003). In addition, Rush and colleagues (2003, 2006) report that the QIDS-SR is comparable to the HAM-D with regard to sensitivity to symptomatic change; in fact, they have suggested that the QIDS-SR is sufficiently sensitive to change that it could effectively replace clinician-administered ratings in clinical trials.

---

[5] It is important to note that these ratings are affected by the interviewer's level of training, and the numbers reported here include studies that used raters who were not highly trained.

Psychological Treatment of MDD

Although several types of psychosocial interventions have been employed in the treatment of depression, most clinical research has examined the effectiveness of behavioral and cognitive treatments. Both types of interventions have been shown to be effective for patients with MDD. Although a thorough review of these and other interventions for depression (e.g., Interpersonal Psychotherapy) is beyond the scope of this chapter, we will review briefly the evidence for behavior therapy (BT) and cognitive-behavioral therapy (CBT).[6]

BEHAVIORAL TREATMENTS

Historically, behavioral interventions for depression have focused on decreasing unpleasant events and increasing pleasant activities, largely by teaching patients to increase behaviors likely to generate positive reinforcement from the environment (Craighead, Hart, Craighead, & Ilardi, 2002). Multiple interventions based on this principle have demonstrated empirical success, beginning with Lewinsohn, Sullivan, and Grosscup's (1980) 12–session program (Lewinsohn & Gotlib, 1995). Over time, additional skills have been added to Lewinsohn's original formulation, including social skills training (Becker, Heimberg, & Bellack, 1987; Bellack, Hersen, & Himmelhoch, 1983; Hersen, Bellack, Himmelhoch, & Thase, 1984; McLean & Hakstian, 1990), self-monitoring and self-reinforcement (Antonuccio, Ward, & Tearnan, 1991), and problem-solving (Nezu, Nezu, & Perri, 1989; Nezu & Perri, 1989).

In more recent years, behavioral treatments have been overshadowed by increased research regarding cognitive-behavioral interventions. In one study, however, Jacobson et al. (1996) found that the behavioral components alone of CBT were equal to the full package of CBT. Dimidjian et al. (2006) recently presented a manualized version of this intervention, called Behavioral Activation (BA), which builds on the principles of the older behavior therapies by emphasizing the link between avoidance and depression. Behavioral Activation aims to augment an individual's behavioral repertoire to increase opportunities for positive reinforcement from the environment. In a recent study, BA was equal to antidepressant medication and superior to cognitive-behavior therapy in the treatment of severely depressed patients (Dimidjian et al., 2006). Although more research is needed, the preliminary findings are encouraging.

COGNITIVE-BEHAVIOR THERAPY

Cognitive-behavior therapy (CBT) for depression is based on Beck's work and theory (Beck et al., 1979). Cognitive-behavior therapy is a short-term (16 to 20 sessions over 12 to 16 weeks) structured treatment that aims to teach patients to recognize and correct cognitive errors and help them change underlying core beliefs about themselves. In the final sessions of CBT, the focus of therapy shifts to consolidating gains to help prevent future depressive episodes.

[6] For thorough reviews regarding the effectiveness of psychological interventions for depression, please see Craighead et al., 2002; Hollon et al., 2002; and Roth & Fonagy, 2005.

Cognitive-behavior therapy has been empirically subjected to more than 80 controlled clinical trials (American Psychiatric Association, 2000), and numerous studies have documented its effectiveness in treating depression (see Hollon, Thase, & Markowitz, 2002; Roth & Fonagy, 2005). However, results comparing CBT to antidepressant medications have been equivocal. Several studies have found that CBT and medications are equally efficacious in the treatment of depression (for a review, see Craighead et al., 2002; Hollon, Haman, & Brown, 2002). The most notable exception to this finding is the National Institute of Mental Health Treatment of Depression Collaborative Research Project (TDCRP), which found medications to be superior to CBT in the treatment of depressed outpatients (Elkin et al., 1989). Concerns about the TDCRP have been noted, and additional studies have since been conducted comparing medications to CBT; these studies have failed to find differences between the two interventions (DeRubeis et al., 2005; see Vittengl, Clark, Dunn, & Jarrett, 2007).

In sum, both behavioral and cognitive-behavioral interventions have been shown to be effective at attenuating the symptoms of MDD. Many empirical questions remain, however. How should treatments be selected based on severity of the depressive episode? Which treatments produce the most enduring effects? What are the mechanisms of action of the psychosocial interventions? When are combination therapies (i.e., psychotherapy plus medication) indicated? These and other questions are under investigation, and results from these studies will inform a new generation of research and treatment.

Somatic Treatments

The observation that the induction of seizure activity was useful in the treatment of psychiatric illness (Fink, 2001) was first noted among asylum patients treated with convulsion-inducing chemical agents such as camphor and then later with metrazole and insulin. The subsequent development of electrical methods of seizure induction and technical refinements to its application (Loo, Schweitzer, & Pratt, 2006) led to modern electroconvulsive therapy (ECT), the prototypic brain stimulation treatment. Reviews of the efficacy of ECT in the treatment of depression date from as early as 1963 (Riddell, 1963) to the present (Pagnin, de Queiroz, Pini, & Cassano, 2004; Van der Wurff, Stek, Hoogendijk, & Beekman, 2003).

Since the initial observations of the antidepressant effects of convulsion-inducing compounds on depressed patients, clinical options for the biological treatment of depression have grown extensively. The serendipitous discovery of the first antidepressants, the monoamine oxidase inhibitors (MAOIs), during the course of drug treatment for tuberculosis, led over time to the development of additional empirically validated antidepressant medications (Slattery, Hudson, & Nutt, 2004). In parallel, other somatic treatments for depression have been developed. These include: light therapy (Terman & Terman, 2005; Wirz-Justice, 2006) and newer brain stimulation paradigms such as transcranial magnetic stimulation (Loo & Mitchell, 2005; Ridding & Rothwell 2007; Schlaepfer et al., 2003), magnetic seizure therapy (Lisanby et al., 2003), and deep brain stimulation (Mayberg et al., 2005).

At present, medication is the most common somatic treatment employed for depression. Several classes of antidepressant medications exist for the treatment of Unipolar Depression and, in some circumstances, Bipolar Depression (Nemeroff, 2007). With respect to class, these medications include the monoamine oxidase inhibitors (MAOIs—e.g., phenelzine, tranylcypromine, selegiline), tricyclic antidepressants (TCAs—e.g., imipramine, desipramine, clomipramine, amitriptyline), selective serotonin reuptake inhibitors (SSRIs—e.g., fluoxetine, sertraline, paroxetine, citalopram, escitalopram, fluvoxamine), serotonin and norepinephrine reuptake inhibitors (SNRIs—e.g., venlafaxine & duloxetine), and the "atypical" antidepressants (e.g., trazodone, bupropion, nefazodone, mirtazipine). In addition, a wide variety of additional medications may be used in conjunction with andidepressants as augmentation strategies to optimize antidepressant response (Fava & Rush, 2006). Examples of augmenting medications include lithium carbonate, valproic acid, lamotrigine, atypical antipsychotic medications (e.g., ziprasidone, risperidone, olanzipine, aripiprazole, quetiapine), thyroid agents (e.g., triiodothyronine), psychostimulants (e.g., dextroamphetamine and methylphenidate), and anxiolytic medications (e.g., buspirone).

The common thread linking the various classes of currently available antidepressants is activity directed toward alteration of monoamine neurotransmitter activity, primarily serotonin and norepinephrine (Slattery et al., 2004). However, the development of novel antidepressants is an area of active investigation (Holtzheimer & Nemeroff, 2006). Most antidepressants work by altering synaptic concentrations of monoamines. Mechanistically, this may occur through the inhibition of enzymes such as monoamine oxidase, which catabolizes neurotransmitters within the synapse following their release. Alternatively, antidepressants (e.g., TCAs, SSRIs, and SNRIs) may inhibit cellular transport proteins, such as the serotonin and norepinephrine transporters that physically remove serotonin or norepinephrine from the synapse (a process known as *reuptake*). Like conventional antidepressants, some atypical antidepressants also have dose-dependent effects on reuptake inhibition but additionally appear to have complex effects on individual subtypes of serotonin and norepinephrine receptors.

The key advances that have been made with respect to antidepressant pharmacology have been substantial improvement in the safety and tolerability of antidepressants (Schatzberg, 2007). For example, the use of MAOIs requires particular dietary restrictions that, if disregarded, may result in a potentially life-threatening elevation of blood pressure known as a hypertensive crisis; TCAs, as a drug class, and lithium carbonate are both potentially lethal in overdose; and particular TCAs as well as lithium carbonate have sometimes burdensome dose-dependent side-effect profiles as well. Despite these issues, MAOIs, TCAs, and lithium (in the case of Bipolar Depression) may produce remission of depressive symptoms in instances when many other medications do not; thus, they remain core elements of the antidepressant armamentarium. As with any medication, close monitoring of patient mental status and side effects is central to effective treatment.

A major current focus of clinical trials research in depression is the derivation of treatment algorithms to guide effective implementation of antidepressant therapy, such as with the Sequenced Treatment Alternatives to Relieve Depression (STAR*D) trial (Rush et al., 2006; Thase et al., 2007; Trivedi, Fava, et al., 2006; Trivedi, Rush et al., 2006) and the integration of psychological and pharmacological treatments for depression (Keller et al., 2000; Thase et al., 2007). In addition, the discovery of biological predictors of treatment response (Binder et al., 2004; Ising et al., 2007) and treatment-emergent symptoms such as suicidal ideation (Laje et al., 2007) and adverse effect burden (Hu et al., 2007) are additional major areas of investigation.

Prevention

As noted, the probability of an episode of MDD is about 20%, but for those individuals who have one episode, the probability of a second episode is 50%; hence, MDD is a recurrent disorder. The probability of a recurrence of MDD is greater among those who have their first episode earlier in life (Lewisohn, Rohde, Seeley, Klein, & Gotlib, 2003). Therefore, it is important to develop programs to prevent the first episode. There is a rapid increase in the rates of initial episodes beginning at age 15; therefore, the optimal time for preventive interventions is before that age. Universal prevention programs designed for application to all adolescents have largely failed to work (Horowitz & Garber, 2006).

More encouraging results have been obtained for those programs targeted to at-risk adolescents. The term *at risk* has typically been defined as having some depressive symptoms or a negative cognitive style. Family-based (Beardslee, Gladsone, Wright, & Cooper, 2003), HMO-based (Clarke, Hawkins, Murphy, Sheeber, Lewinsohn, & Seeley, 1995), and school-based CBT programs for at-risk adolescents have provided promising results, significantly reducing an initial episode of MDD for up to a year (Arnarson & Craighead, 2007). Obviously, longer-term follow-ups are needed; it will be extremely important to determine if these programs actually prevent MDD or merely delay the initial episode. Of course, a significant delay in MDD onset would be valuable because the adolescent would be more mature, would have completed more education, and would have reached a different level of neural, cognitive, and social development. How these prevention programs affect brain development is perhaps the most intriguing question raised by these apparently successful preventive interventions.

Summary and Future Directions

Major Depressive Disorder is a prevalent and debilitating disorder resulting in suffering at the individual, family, and societal levels. It can be reliably diagnosed, even though it is a heterogeneous disorder with multiple etiological pathways. In this chapter, we have described the psychological, genetic, and neurobiological markers of MDD. We have described how the extant effective treatments have been derived and implemented.

Clearly, great advances have been made in the evolution of clinical science research regarding MDD. It seems that the most significant future questions need to address how the multiple pathways of the etiology of the disorder interact in the development of MDD. Though we have made great progress in developing effective treatments, results still indicate that only about 30%–35% of MDD patients completely remit from their episode when treated; we need to work toward better understanding of the disorder(s) so a greater percentage of the patients suffering from MDD will be successfully treated. We have reached a stage of clinical scientific development at which we can begin to ask which patients respond best to which treatment; this should provide badly needed evidence to guide clinical intervention. Finally, it is extremely important to develop programs designed to prevent the initial episode of MDD.

References

Abraham, K. (1911). Notes on the psychoanalytic investigation and treatment of manic-depressive insanity and allied conditions. In D. Bryan & A. Strachey (Eds.), *Selected papers on psychoanalysis* (pp. 137–156). New York: Basic Books.

Abramson, L. Y., Alloy, L. B., Hankin, B. L., Haeffel, G. J., MacCoon, D. G., & Gibb, B. E. (2002). Cognitive vulnerability-stress models of depression in a self-regulatory and psychobiological context. In I. H. Gotlib & C. L. Hammen (Eds.), *Handbook of depression* (pp. 268–294). New York: Guilford.

Abramson, L. Y., Alloy, L. B., Hogan, M. E., Whitehouse, W. G., Donovan, P., Rose, D. T., et al. (1999). Cognitive vulnerability to depression: Theory and evidence. *Journal of Cognitive Psychotherapy: An International Quarterly, 13*, 5–20.

Abramson, L. Y., Metalsky, G. I., & Alloy, L. B. (1989). Hopelessness depression: A theory-based subtype of depression. *Psychological Review, 96*, 358–372.

Abramson, L. Y., Seligman, M. E. P., & Teasdale, J. (1978). Learned helplessness in humans: Critique and reformulation. *Journal of Abnormal Psychology, 87*, 49–74.

Ackerman, R., & DeRubeis, R. (1991). Is depressive realism real? *Clinical Psychology Review, 11*, 565–584.

Alesci, S., Martinez, P. E., Kelkar, S., Ilias, I., Ronsaville, D. S., Listwak, S. J., et al. (2005). Major depression is associated with significant diurnal elevations in plasma interleukin-6 levels, a shift of its circadian rhythm, and loss of physiological complexity in its secretion: Clinical implications. *Journal of Clinical Endocrinology and Metabolism, 90*, 2522–2530.

Alloy, L. B., & Abramson, L. Y. (1999). The Temple–Wisconsin Cognitive Vulnerability to Depression (CVD) Project: Conceptual background, design, and methods. *Journal of Cognitive Psychotherapy: An International Quarterly, 13*, 227–262.

Alloy, L. B., Abramson, L. Y., Hogan, M. E., Whitehouse, W. G., Rose, D. T., Robinson, M. S., et al. (2000). The Temple–Wisconsin Cognitive Vulnerability to Depression (CVD) Project: Lifetime history of Axis I psychopathology in individuals at high and low cognitive risk for depression. *Journal of Abnormal Psychology, 109*, 403–418.

Alloy, L. B., Abramson, L. Y., Murray, L. A., Whitehouse, W. G., & Hogan, M. E. (1997). Self–referent information processing in individuals at high and low cognitive risk for depression. *Cognition and Emotion, 11*, 539–568.

Alloy, L. B., Abramson, L. Y., Walshaw, P. D., & Neeren, A. M. (2006). Cognitive vulnerability to unipolar and bipolar mood disorders. *Journal of Social and Clinical Psychology, 25*, 726–754.

Alloy, L. B., Abramson, L. Y., Whitehouse, W. G., Hogan, M. E., Panzarella, C., & Rose, D. T. (2006). Prospective incidence of first onsets and recurrences of depression in individuals at high and low cognitive risk for depression. *Journal of Abnormal Psychology, 115*, 145–156.

Alloy, L. B., Abramson, L. Y., Whitehouse, W. G., Hogan, M. E., Tashman, N. A., Steinberg, D. L., et al. (1999). Depressogenic cognitive styles: Predictive validity, information processing and personality characteristics, and developmental origins. *Behaviour Research and Therapy, 37*, 503–531.

American Psychiatric Association. (1994). *Diagnostic and statistical manual of mental disorders* (4th ed.) Washington, DC: Author.

American Psychiatric Association. (2000). Practice guidelines for the treatment of patients with major depressive disorder (revision). *American Journal of Psychiatry, 157*(suppl. 4), 1–45.

Amsterdam, J. D., Maislin, G., Winokur, A., Berwish, N., Kling, M., & Gold, P. (1988). The oCRH stimulation test before and after clinical recovery from depression. *Journal of Affective Disorder, 14*, 213–222.

Antonuccio, D. O., Ward, C. H., & Tearnan, B. H. (1991). The behavioral treatment of unipolar depression in adult outpatients. In M. Hersen, R. M. Eisler, & P. M. Miller (Eds.), *Progress in behavior modification* (vol. 24, pp. 152–191). Newbury Park, CA: Sage.

Arana, G. W., Baldessarini, R. J., & Orsteen, M. (1985). The dexamethasone suppression test for diagnosis and prognosis in psychiatry. Commentary and review. *Archives of General Psychiatry, 42*, 1193–1204.

Arborelius, L. Owens, M. J., Plotsky, P. M., & Nemeroff, C. B. (1999). The role of corticotropin-releasing factor in depression and anxiety disorders. *Journal of Endocrinology*, *160*, 1–12.

Arnarson, E. O., & Craighead, W. E. (August, 2007). Prevention of depression among Icelandic adolescents. Paper presented at the Annual Meeting of the American Psychological Association. San Francisco, CA.

Austin, M-P., Mitchell, P., & Goodwin, G. M. (2001). Cognitive deficits in depression: Possible implications for functional neuropathology. *British Journal of Psychiatry*, *178*, 200–206.

Aydemir, O., Deveci, A., & Taneli, F. (2005). The effect of chronic antidepressant treatment on serum brain-derived neurotrophic factor levels in depressed patients: A preliminary study. *Progress in Neuro-Psychopharmacology & Biological Psychiatry*, *29*, 261–265.

Azmitia, E. C., & Gannon, P. J. (1986). The primate serotonergic system: A reviewof human and animal studies and a report on Macaca fascicularis. *Advances in Neurology*, *43*, 407–468.

Baez, M., Kursar, J. D., Helton, L. A., Wainscott, D. B., & Nelson, D. L. (1995). Molecular biology of serotonin receptors. *Obesity Research 3*, (Suppl. 4), 441S–447S.

Bandura, A. (1969). *Principles of behavior modification*. New York: Holt, Rinehart, & Winston.

Bandura, A. (1977). Self-efficacy: Toward a unifying theory of behavioral change. *Psychological Review*, *84*, 191–215.

Barbas, H., Saha, S., Rempel-Clower, N., & Ghasghaei, T. (2003). Serial pathways from primate prefrontal cortex to autonomic areas may influence emotional expression. *BMC Neuroscience*, *4*, 25.

Baron, M. (2001). The search for complex disease genes: Fault by linkage or fault by association? *Molecular Psychiatry*, *6*, 143–149.

Basco, M. R., Bostic, J. Q., Davies, D., Rush, A. J., Witte, B., Hendrickse, W. A., et al. (2000). Methods to improve diagnostic accuracy in a community mental health setting. *American Journal of Psychiatry*, *157*, 1599–1605.

Baxter, L., Edell, W., Gerner, R., Fairbanks, L., & Gwirtsman, H. (1984). Dexamethasone suppression test and Axis I diagnoses of inpatients with *DSM-III* borderline personality disorder. *Journal of Clinical Psychiatry*, *45*, 150–153.

Beardslee, W. R., Gladstone, T. R. G., Wright, E. J., & Cooper, A. B. (2003). A family-based approach to the prevention of depressive symptoms in children at risk: Evidence of parental and child change. *Pediatrics*, *112*, 119–131.

Beck, A. T. (1967). *Depression: Clinical, experimental, and theoretical aspects*. New York: Harper & Row.

Beck, A. T. (1968). *Depression: Causes and treatment*. Philadelphia: University of Pennsylvania Press.

Beck, A. T. (1976). *Cognitive therapy and the emotional disorders*. New York: International Universities Press.

Beck, A. T. (1987). Cognitive models of depression. *Journal of Cognitive Psychotherapy: An International Quarterly*, *1*, 5–37.

Beck, A. T., Rush, A. J., Shaw, B. F., & Emery, G. (1979). *Cognitive therapy of depression*. New York: Guilford.

Beck, A. T., Steer, R. A., & Brown, G. K. (1996). *Beck Depression Inventory Manual* (2nd ed.). San Antonio, TX: Psychological Corporation.

Beck, J. S. (1995). *Cognitive therapy: Basics and beyond*. New York: Guilford.

Becker, R. E., Heimberg, R. G., & Bellack, A. S. (1987). *Social skills training treatment for depression*. Elmsford, NY: Pergamon.

Bellack, A. S., Hersen, M., & Himmelhoch, J. (1983). A comparison of social skills training, pharmacotherapy, and psychotherapy for depression. *Behaviour Research and Therapy*, *21*, 101–107.

Benabid, A. L. (2003). Deep brain stmulation for Parkinson's disease. *Current Opinion in Neurobiology*, *13*, 696–706.

Berman, R. M., Narasimhan, M., Miller, H. L., Anand, A., Cappiello, A., Oren, D. A., et al. (1999). Transient depressive relapse induced by catecholamine depletion: Potential phenotypic vulnerability marker?*Archives of General Psychiatry*, *56*, 395–403.

Berton, O., McClung, C. A., Dileone, R. J., Krishnan, V., Renthal, W., Russo, S. J., et al. (2006). Essential role of BDNF in the mesolimbic dopamine pathway in social defeat stress. *Science*, *311*, 864–868.

Berton, O., & Nestler, E. J. (2006). New approaches to antidepressant drug discovery: Beyond monoamines. *Nature Reviews Neuroscience*, *7*, 137–151.

Biegon, A., Essar, N., Israeli, M., Elizur, A., Bruch, S., & Bar-Nathan, A. A. (1990). Serotonin 5–HT2 receptor binding on blood platelets as a state dependent marker in major affective disorder. *Psychopharmacology*, *102*, 73–75.

Biegon, A., Weizman, A., Karp, L., Ram, A., Tiano, S., & Wolff, M. (1987). Serotonin 5–HT2 receptor binding on blood platelets—A peripheral marker for depression? *Life Science*, *41*, 2485–2492.

Bierhaus, A., Wolf, J., Andrassy, M., Rohleder, N., Humpert, P. M., Petrov, D., et al. (2003). A mechanism converting psychosocial stress into mononuclear cell activation. *Proceedings of the National Academy of Sciences, 100,* 1920–1925.

Bierut, L. J., Heath, A. C., Bucholz, K. K., Dinwiddie, S. H., Madden, P. A., Statham, D. J., et al. (1999). Major depressive disorder in a community-based twin sample: Are there different genetic and environmental contributions for men and women? *Archives of General Psychiatry, 56,* 557–563.

Binder, E. B., Salyakina, D., Lichtner, P., Wochnik, G. M., Ising, M., Putz, B., et al. (2004). Polymorphisms in FKBP5 are associated with increased recurrence of depressive episodes and rapid response to antidepressant treatment. *Nature Genetics, 36,* 1319–1325.

Booij, L., Van derDoes, W. I., Benkelfat, C., Bremner, J. D., Cowen, P. J., Fava, M., et al. (2002). Predictors of mood response to acute tryptophan depletion: A reanalysis. *Neuropsychopharmacology, 27,* 852–861.

Bower, G. H. (1981). Mood and memory. *American Psychologist, 36,* 129–148.

Bradley, R. G., Binder, E. B., Epstein, M. P., Tang, Y., Nair, H. P., Wei, L., et al. (2007). Influence of child abuse and trauma on adult depression is moderated by the corticotropin releasing hormone receptor gene. *Society of Biological Psychiatry Abstracts.*

Bramham, C. R. (2007) Control of synaptic consolidation in the dentate gryrus: Mechanisms, functions, and therapeutic implications. *Progress in Brain Research, 163,* 453–471.

Bremner, J. D., Narayan, M., Andersen, E., Miller, H., & Charney, D. (2000). Hippocampal volume reduction in major depression. *American Journal of Psychiatry, 154,* 624–629.

Bremner, J. D., Randall, P., Scott, T. M., Bronen, R. A., Seibyl, J. P., Southwick, S. M., et al. (1995). MRI-based measurement of hippocampal volume in patients with combat-related posttraumatic stress disorder. *American Journal of Psychiatry, 152,* 973–981.

Bremner, J. D., Randall, P., Vermetten, E., Staib, L., Bronen, R. A., Mazure, C., et al. (1997). Magnetic resonance imaging-based measurement of hippocampal volume in posttraumatic stress disorder related to childhood physical and sexual abuse: A preliminary report. *Biological Psychiatry, 41,* 23–32.

Bremner, J. D.Vythilingam, M., Vermetten, E., Southwick, S. M., McGlashan, T., Mazeer, A., et al. (2003). MRI and PET study of deficits in hippocampal structure and function in women with childhood sexual abuse and posttraumatic stress disorder. *American Journal of Psychiatry, 160,* 924–932.

Brody, A. L., Barsom, M. W., Bota, R. G., & Saxena, S. (2001). Prefrontal-subcortical and limbic circuit mediation of major depressive disorder. *Seminars in Clinical Neuropsychiatry, 6,* 102–112.

Brown, E. S., Varghese, F. P., & McEwen, B. S. (2004). Association of depression with medical illness: Does cortisol play a role? *Biological Psychiatry, 55,* 1–9.

Burke, K. C., Burke, J. D., Regier, P. A., & Rae, P. S. (1990). Age at onset of selected mental disorders in five community populations. *Archives of General Psychiatry, 47,* 511–518.

Burns, D., & Nolen-Hoeksema, S. K. (1991). Coping styles, homework assignments, and the effectiveness of cognitive-behavioral therapy. *Journal of Consulting and Clinical Psychology, 59,* 305–311.

Cadoret, R. J. (1978). Evidence for genetic inheritance of primary affective disorder in adoptees. *The American Journal of Psychiatry, 135,* 463–466.

Campbell, S., & Macqueen, G. (2004). The role of the hippocampus in the pathophysiology of major depression. *Journal of Psychiatry Neuroscience, 29,* 417–426.

Cannon, T. D., & Keller, M. C. (2006). Endophenotypes in the genetic analyses of mental disorders. *Annual Review of Clinical Psychology, 2,* 267–290.

Carmichael, S. T., & Price, J. L. (1996). Connectional networks within the orbital and medial prefrontal cortex of macaque monkeys. *Journal of Comparative Neurology, 371,* 179–207.

Carpenter, W. T., Jr., & Bunney, W. E., Jr. (1971). Adrenal cortical activity in depressive illness. *American Journal of Psychiatry, 128,* 31–40.

Carroll, B. J. (1982). Use of the dexamethasone suppression test in depression. *The Journal of Clinical Psychiatry, 43,* 44–50.

Carroll, B. J., Martin, F. I., & Davies, B. (1968). Pituitary-adrenal function in depression. *Lancet, 1,* 1373–1374.

Carver, C. S., Scheier, M. F., & Weintraub, J. K. (1989). Assessing coping strategies: A theoretically based approach. *Journal of Personality and Social Psychology, 56,* 267–283.

Caspi, A., Sugden, K., Moffitt, T. W., Taylor, A., Craig, I. W., Harrington, H., et al. (2003). Influence of life stress on depression: Moderation by a polymorphism in the 5-HTT gene. *Science, 301,* 386–389.

Charney, D. S. (1998). Monoamine dysfunction and the pathophysiology and treatment of depression. *The Journal of Clinical Psychiatry, 59*(Suppl. 14) 11–14.

Charney, D. S., Heninger, G. R., Sternberg, D. E., & Roth, R. H. (1981). Plasma MHGP in depression:

Effects of acute and chronic desipramine treatment. *Psychiatry Research, 5,* 217–229.

Chen, B., Dowlatshahi, D., MacQueen, G. M., Wang, J. F., & Young, L. T. (2001). Increased hippocampal BDNF immunoreactivity in subjects treated with antidepressant medication. *Biological Psychiatry, 50,* 260–265.

Chhatwal, J. P., Stanek-Rattiner, L., Davis, M., & Ressler, K. J. (2006). Amygdala BDNF signaling is required for consolidation but not encoding extinction. *Nature Neuroscience, 9,* 870–872.

Chorbov, V. M., Lobos, E. A., Todorov, A. A., Heath, A. C., Botteron, K. N., & Todd, R. D. (2007). Relationship of 5-HTTLPR genotypes and depression risk in the presence of trauma in a female twin sample. *American Journal of Medical Genetics Part B Neuropsychiatric Genetics, 144b,* 830–833.

Chrousos, G. P. (1995). The hypothalamic-pituitary-adrenal axis and immune-mediated inflammation. *The New England Journal of Medicine, 332,* 1351–1362.

Clark, D. A., Beck, A. T., & Alford, B. A. (1999). *Scientific foundations of cognitive theory and therapy of depression.* New York: Wiley.

Clark, D. M., & Teasdale, J. D. (1982). Diurnal variation in clinical depression and accessibility of memories of positive and negative experiences. *Journal of Abnormal Psychology, 91,* 87–95.

Clarke, G. N., Hawkins, W., Murphy, M., Sheeber, L. B., Lewinsohn, P. M., & Seeley, J. R. (1995). Targeted prevention of unipolar depressive disorder in an at-risk sample of high school adolescents: A randomized trial of a group cognitive intervention. *Journal of the American Academy of Child and Adolescent Psychiatry, 34,* 312–321.

Costello, E. J., Erkanli, A., & Angold, A. (2006). Is there an epidemic of child or adolescent depression? *Journal of Child Psychology and Psychiatry, 47,* 1263–1271.

Craddock, N. & Forty, L. (2006). Genetics of affective (mood) disorders. *European Journal of Human Genetics, 14,* 660–668.

Craighead, W. E. (1980). Away from a unitary model of depression. *Behavior Therapy, 11,* 123–129.

Craighead, W. E., Hart, A. B., Craighead, L. W., & Ilardi, S. S. (2002). Psychosocial treatment for major depressive disorder. In P. E. Nathan & J. M. Gorman (Eds.), *A guide to treatments that work* (2nd ed, pp. 245–262). New York: Oxford University Press.

Danner, M., Kasl, S. V., Abramson, J. L., & Vaccarino, V. (2003). Association between depression and elevated C-reactive protein. *Psychosomatic Medicine, 65,* 347–356.

Davidson, R. J. (1992). Anterior cerebral symmetry and the nature of emotion. *Brain and Cognition, 20,* 125–151.

Davidson, R. J. (1998). Affective style and affective disorders: Perspectives from affective neuroscience. *Cognition and Emotion, 12,* 307–330.

Decker, H. S. (2004). The psychiatric works of Emil Kraepelin: A many-faceted story of modern medicine. *Journal of the History of Neuroscience, 13,* 248–276.

DeRubeis, R. J., Hollon, S. D., Amsterdam, J. D., Shelton, R. C., Young, P. R., Salomon, R. M. et al. (2005). Cognitive therapy vs. medications in the treatment of moderate to severe depression. *Archives of General Psychiatry, 62,* 409–416.

Dimidjian, S., Hollon, S. D., Dobson, K. S., Schmaling, K. B., Kohlenberg, R. J., Addis, M. E., et al. (2006). Randomized trial of behavioral activation, cognitive therapy, and antidepressant medication in the acute treatment of adults with major depression. *Journal of Consulting and Clinical Psychology, 74*(4), 658–670.

Dimidjian, S., Martell, C. R., Addis, M. E., & Herman-Dunn, R. (2007). Behavioral activation for depression. In D. H. Barlow (Ed.), *Clinical handbook of psychological disorders: A step-by-step treatment manual* (4th ed., pp. 328–364). New York: Guilford.

Dobson, K. S. (2001). *Handbook of cognitive-behavioral therapies* (2nd ed.). New York: Guilford.

Dorn, L. D., Burgess, E. S., Dubbert, B., Simpson, S. E., Friedman, T., Kling, M., et al. (1995). Psychopathology in patients with endogenous Cushing's syndrome after correction of hypercortisolism. *Journal of Clinical Endocrinology Metabolism, 82,* 912–919.

Dorn, L. D., Burgess, E. S., Friedman, T. C., Dubbert, B., Gold, P. W., & Chrousos, G. P. (1997). The longitudinal course of psychopathology in Cushing's syndrome after correction of hypercortisolism. *Journal of Clinical Endocrinology & Metabolism, 82,* 912–919.

Dougherty, D. D., Weiss, A. P., Cosgrove, G. R., Alpert, N. M., Cassem E. H., Nierenberg, A. A., et al. (2003). Cerebral metabolic correlates as potential predictors of response to anterior cingulotomy for treatment of major depression. *Journal of Neurosurgery, 99,* 1010–1017.

Dozois, D. J. A., & Covin, R. (2004). The Beck Depression Inventory (BDI-II), Beck Hopelessness Scale (BHS), and Beck Scale for Suicide Ideation (BSS). In M. J. Hilsenroth & D. L. Segal (Eds.), *Comprehensive handbook of psychological assessment* (pp. 50–69) Hoboken, NJ: Wiley.

Drevets, W. C. (1999). Prefrontal cortical-amygdalar metabolism in major depression. *Annals of the New York Academy of Sciences, 887,* 617–637.

Duman, R. S., & Monteggia, L. M. (2006). A neurotrophic model for stress-related mood disorders. *Biological Psychiatry, 59,* 1116–1127.

Duncan, L. E., Hutchison, K. E., & Craighead, W. E. (2007, November). Variation in Brain-Derived Neurotrophic Factor (BDNF) gene: Association with cognitive-affective factor of depression. Paper presented at the Annual Meeting of the Association of Cognitive and Behavioral Therapies, Philadelphia, PA.

Dunn, A. J., & Berridge, C. W. (1990). Physiological and behavioral responses to corticotropin-releasing factor administration: Is CRF a mediator of anxiety or stress responses? *Brain Research Brain Research Reviews, 15,* 71–100.

Dunning, D., & Story, A. L. (1991). Depression, realism, and the overconfidence effect: Are the sadder wiser when predicting future actions and events? *Journal of Personality and Social Psychology, 61,* 521–532.

Egan, M. F., Kokima, M., Callicott, J. H., Goldberg, T. E., Kolachana, B. S., Bertolino, A. et al. (2003). The BDNF val66met polymorphism affects activity-dependent secretion of BDNF and human memory and hippocampal function. *Cell, 112,* 257–269.

Eifert, G. H., & Forsyth, J. P. (2005). *Acceptance and Commitment Therapy for anxiety disorders: A practitioner's treatment guide to using mindfulness, acceptance, and values-based behavior change strategies.* Oakland, CA: New Harbinger.

Elenkov, I. J., Iezzoni, D. G., Daly, A., Harris, A. G., & Chrousos, G. P. (2005). Cytokine dysregulation, inflammation, and well-being. *Neuroimmunomodulation, 12,* 255–269.

Elkin, I., Shea, M. T., Watkins, J. T., Imber, S. D., Sotsky, S. M., Collins, J. F., et al. (1989). National Institute of Mental Health Treatment of Depression Collaborative Research Program: General effectiveness of treatments. *Archives of General Psychiatry, 46,* 971–982.

Engel, R. A., & DeRubeis, R. J. (1993). The role of cognition in depression. In K. S. Dobson & P. C. Kendall (Eds.), *Psychopathology and cognition* (pp. 83–119). San Diego, CA: Academic Press.

Evans, D. L., Charney, D. S., Lewis, L., Golden, R. N., Gorman, J. M., Krishnan, K. R., et al. (2005). Mood disorders in the medically ill: Scientific review and recommendations. *Biological Psychiatry, 58,* 175–189.

Evans, D. L., & Nemeroff, C. B. (1983). The dexamethasone suppression test in mixed bipolar disorder. *American Journal of Psychiatry, 140,* 615–617.

Fava, M., & Rush, A. J. (2006). Current status of augmentation and combination treatments for major depressive disorder: A literature review and a proposal for a novel approach to improve practice. *Psychotherapy and Psychosomatics, 75,* 139–153.

Fergusson, D. M., Horwood, J., Ridder, E. M., & Beautrais, A. L. (2005). Subthreshold depression in adolescence and mental health outcomes in adulthood. *Archives of General Psychiatry, 62,* 66–72.

Ferster, C. B. (1965). Classification of behavioral pathology. In L. Krasner & L. P. Ullmann (Eds.), *Research in behavior modification* (pp. 6–26). New York: Holt, Rinehart, & Winston.

Ferster, C. B. (1966). Animal behavior and mental illness. *Psychological Record, 16,* 345–356.

Ferster, C. B. (1973). A functional analysis of depression. *American Psychologist, 28,* 857–870.

Fink, M. (2001). Convulsive therapy: A review of the first 55 years. *Journal of Affective Disorders, 63,* 1–15.

First, M. B., & Gibbon, M. (2004). The structured clinical interview for *DSM-IV* Axis-I disorders (SCID-I) and the structured clinical interview for *DSM-IV* Axis-II disorders (SCID-II). In M. J. Hilsenroth & D. L.Segal (Eds.), *Comprehensive handbook of psychological assessment* (pp. 134–143) Hoboken, NJ: Wiley.

First, M. B., Spitzer, R. L., Gibbon, M., & Williams, J. B. W. (1997). *User's guide for the structured clinical interview for DSM-IV Axis I disorders, clinician version.* Washington, DC: American Psychiatric Association.

Ford, D. E., & Erlinger, T. P. (2004). Depression and C-reactive protein in U.S. adults: Data from the Third National Health and Nutrition Examination Survey. *Archives of Internal Medicine, 164,* 1010–1014.

Forgas, J. P., & Bower, G. H. (1987). Mood effects on person-perception judgments. *Journal of Personality and Social Psychology, 53,* 53–60.

Forgas, J. P., Bower, G. H., & Krantz, S. E. (1984). The influence of mood on perception of social interactions. *Journal of Experimental Social Psychology, 20,* 497–513.

Freedman, L. J., Insel, T. R., & Smith, Y. (2000). Subcortical projections of area 25 (subgenual cortex) of the macaque monkey. *The Journal of Comparative Neurology, 421,* 172–188.

Freud, S. (1917 [1950]). Mourning and melancholia. In *Collected papers,* Vol. 4. London: Hogarth Press.

Frodl, T., Neisenzahl, E. M., Zetzsche, T., Born, C., Groll, C., Jager, M. et al. (2002). Hippocampal changes in patients with a first episode of major depression. *American Journal of Psychiatry, 159,* 1112–1118.

Fuchs, E., & Gould, E. (2000). Mini-review: In vivo neurogenesis in the adult brain: Regulation and functional implications. *European Journal of Neuroscience, 12,* 2211–2214.

Gerner, R. H., & Gwirtsman, H. E. (1981). Abnormalities of dexamethasone suppression test and urinary MHPG in anorexia nervosa. *American Journal of Psychiatry, 138,* 650–653.

Gershon, E. S., Hamovit, J., Guroff, J. J., Dibble, E., Leckman, J. F., Sceery, W., et al. (1982). A family study of schizoaffective, bipolar I, bipolar, II, unipolar, and normal control probands. *Archives of General Psychiatry, 39,* 1157–1167.

Gervasoni, N., Aubry, J. M., Bondolfi, G., Osek, C., Schwald, M., Bertschy, G., et al. (2005). Partial normalization of serum brain-derived neurotrophic factor in remitted patients after a major depressive episode. *Neuropsychobiology, 51,* 234–238.

Geuze, E., Vermetten, E., & Bremner, J. D. (2005). MR-based in vivo hippocampal volumetrics: 2 findings in neuropsychiatric disorders. *Molecular Psychiatry,10,* 160–184.

Gibb, B. E. (2002). Childhood maltreatment and negative cognitive styles: A quantitative and qualitative review. *Clinical Psychology Review, 22,* 223–246.

Gibbons, J. L., & McHugh, P. R. (1962). Plasma cortisol in depressive illness. *Journal of Psychiatric Research, 1,* 162–171.

Gilboa, E., & Gotlib, I. H. (1997). Cognitive biases and affect persistence in previously dysphoric and never-dysphoric individuals. *Cognition & Emotion, 11,* 517–538.

Gillespie, C. F., & Nemeroff, C. B. (2007). Corticotropin-releasing facor and the psychobiology of early life stress. *Current Directions in Psychological Science, 16,* 85–89.

Glaser, R., & Kiecolt-Glaser, J. K. (2005). Stress induced immune dysfunction: Implications for health. *National Review of Immunology, 5,* 243–251.

Goldapple, K., Segal, Z., Garson, C., Lau, M., Bieling, P., Kennedy, S., et al. (2004). Modulation of cortical-limbic pathways in major depression: Treatment-specific effects of cognitive behavior therapy. *Archive of General Psychiatry, 61,* 34–41.

Golden, R. N., Markey, S. P., Risby, E. D., Rudorfer, M. V., Cowdry, R. W., & Potter, W. Z. (1988). Antidepressants reduce whole-body norepinephrine turnover while enhancing 6–hydroxymelatonin output. *Archives of General Psychiatry, 45,* 150–154.

Gonul, A. S., Akdeniz, F., Taneli, F., Donat, O., Eker, C., & Vahip, S. (2005). Effect of treatment on serum brain-derived neurotrophic factor levels in depressed patients. *European Archives of Psychiatry and Clinical Neuroscience, 255,* 381–386.

Goodwin, G. M. (1997). Neuropsychological and neuroimaging evidence for the involvement of the frontal lobes in depression. *Journal of Psychopharmacology, 11,* 115–122.

Goodwin, R. D., & Stein, M. B. (2004). Association between childhood trauma and physical disorders among adults in the United States. *Psychological Medicine, 34,* 509–520.

Gortner, E. T., Gollan, J. K., Dobson, K. S., & Jacobson, N. S. (1998). Cognitive behavioral treatment for depression: Relapse prevention. *Journal of Consulting and Clinical Psychology, 66,* 377–384.

Gotlib, I. H., Kasch, K. L., Traill, S., Joormann, J., Arnow, B. A., & Johnson, S. L. (2004). Coherence and specificity of information-processing biases in depression and social phobia. *Journal of Abnormal Psychology, 113*(3), 386–398.

Gray, J. A. (1987). *The psychology of fear and stress* (2nd ed.). New York: Cambridge University Press.

Gray, J. A. (1994). Three fundamental emotions systems. In P. Ekman & R. J. Davidson (Eds.), *The nature of emotion: Fundamental questions* (pp. 243–247). New York: Oxford University Press.

Greden, J. F., Albala, A. A., Haskett, R. F., James, N. M., Goodman, L., Steiner, M., et al. (1980). Normalization of dexamethasone suppression test: A laboratory index of recovery from endogenous depression. *Biological Psychiatry, 15,* 449–458.

Greenberg, P. E., Stiglin, L. E., Finkelstein, S. N., & Berndt, E. R. (1993). The economic burden of depression in 1990. *Journal of Clinical Psychiatry, 54,* 405–418.

Groves, J. O. August, 2007. Is it time to reassess the BDNF hypothesis of depression?*Molecular Psychiatry.* doi/10.1038/sj.mp.4002075.

Gutman, D. A., Owens, M. J., Skelton, K. H., Thrivikraman, K. V., & Nemeroff, C. B. (2003). The corticotropin-releasing factor1 receptor antagonist R121919 attenuates the behavioral and endocrine responses to stress. *Journal of Pharmacological and Experimental Therapy, 304,* 874–880.

Haaga, D. A. F., Dyck, M. J., & Ernst, D. (1991). Empirical status of cognitive theory of depression. *Psychological Bulletin, 110,* 215–236.

Haber, S. N. (2003). The primate basal ganglia: Parallel and integrative networks. *Journal of Chemical Neuroanatomy, 26*, 317–330.

Haeffel, G. J., Abramson, L. Y., Voelz, Z. R., Metalsky, G. I., Halberstadt, L., Dykman, B. M., et al. (2003). Cognitive vulnerability to depression and lifetime history of Axis I psychopathology: A comparison of negative cognitive styles (CSQ) and dysfunctional attitudes (DAS). *Journal of Cognitive Psychotherapy: An International Quarterly, 17*, 3–22.

Hamilton, M. (1960). A rating scale for depression. *Journal of Neurology, Neurosurgery, and Psychiatry, 23*, 56–62.

Hankin, B. L., Abramson, L. Y., Moffitt, T. E., Silva, P. A., McGee, R., & Angell, K. E. (1998). Development of depression from preadolescence to young adulthood: Emerging gender differences in a 10-year longitudinal study. *Journal of Abnormal Psychology, 107*, 128–140.

Hayden, E. P., & Klein, D. N. (2001). Outcome of dysthymic disorder at 5–year follow-up: The effect of familial psychopathology, early adversity, personality, comorbidity, and chronic stress. *American Journal of Psychiatry, 158*, 1864–1870.

Hayes, S. C., Strosahl, K. D., & Wilson, K. G. (1999). *Acceptance and commitment therapy: An experiential approach to behavior change.* New York: Guilford.

Heim, C., Mletzko, T., Purselle, D., Musselman, D. L., & Nemeroff, C. B. (2007). The dexamethasone/corticotropin-releasing factor test in men with major depression: Role of childhood trauma. *Biological Psychiatry.*

Heim, C., Newport, J., Heit, S., Graham, Y. P., Wilcox, M., Bonsall, R., Miller, A. H., & Nemeroff, C. B. (2000). Pituitary-adrenal and autonomic responses to stress in women after sexual and physical abuse in childhood. *Journal of the American Medical Association, 284*, 592–597.

Heine, V. M., Zareno, J., Maslam, S., Joels, M., & Lucassen, P. J. (2005). Chronic stress in adult dentate gyrus reduces cell proliferation near the casculature and VEGF and Flk-1 protein expression. *The European Journal of Neuroscience, 21*, 1304–1314.

Hersen, M., Bellack, A. S., Himmelhoch, J., & Thase, M. E. (1984). Effects of social skills training, amitriptyline, and psychotherapy in unipolar depressed women. *Behavior Therapy, 15*, 21–40.

Hollon, H. D., Haman, K. L., & Brown, L. L. (2002). Cognitive-behvioral treatment of depression. In I. H. Gotlib & C. L. Hammen (Eds.), *Handbook of depression* (pp. 383–403) New York: Guilford.

Hollon, S. D., Thase, M. E., & Markowitz, J. C. (2002). Treatment and prevention of depression. *Psychological Science in the Public Interest, 3*, 39–77.

Holtzheimer, P. E., & Nemeroff, C. B. (2006). Advances in the treatment of depression. *NeuroRx, 3*, 42–56.

Horowitz, J. L., & Garber, J. (2006). The prevention of depressive symptoms in children and adolescents: A meta-analytic review. *Journal of Consulting and Clinical Psychology, 74*, 401–415.

Hu, X. Z., Rush, A. J., Charney, D., Wilson, A. F., Sorant, A. J., Papanicolaous, G. J., et al. (2007). Association between a functional serotonin transporter promoter polymorphism and citalopram treatment in adult outpatients with major depression. *Archives of General Psychiatry, 64*, 783–792.

Hubain, P. P., Simonnet, M. P., & Mendlewicz, J. (1986). The dexamethasone suppression test in affective illnesses and schizophrenia: Relationship with psychotic symptoms. *Neuropsychobiology, 16*, 57–60.

Iacoviello, B. M., Alloy, L. B., Abramson, L. Y., Whitehouse, W. G., & Hogan, M. E. (2006). The course of depression in individuals at high and low cognitive risk for depression: A prospective study. *Journal of Affective Disorders, 93*, 61–69.

Ilardi, S. S., & Craighead, W. E. (1999). The relationship between personality pathology and dysfunctional cognitions In previously depressed adults. *Journal of Abnormal Psychology, 108*, 51–57.

Ingram, R. E. (1984). Toward an information-processing analysis of depression. *Cognitive Therapy and Research, 8*, 443–478.

Ingram, R. E. (1990). Self-focused attention in clinical disorders: Review and a conceptual model. *Psychological Bulletin, 107*, 156–176.

Ingram, R. E., Miranda, J., & Segal, Z. V. (1998). *Cognitive vulnerability to depression.* New York: Guilford.

Ingram, R. E., Miranda, J., & Segal, Z. V. (2006) Cognitive vulnerability to depression. In L. B. Alloy and J. H. Riskind (Eds.), *Cognitive vulnerability to emotional disorders* (pp. 63–91). Mahwah, NJ: Lawrence Erlbaum.

Ising, M., Horstmann, S., Kloiber, S., Lucae, S., Binder, E. B., Kern, N., et al. (2007). Combined dexamethasone/corticotropin releasing hormone test predicts treatment response in major depression—A potential biomarker? *Biological Psychiatry, 62*, 47–54.

Jacobson, L., & Sapolsky, R. (1991). The role of the hippocampus in feedback regulation of the hypothalamic-pituitary-adrenocortical axis. *Endocrine Reviews, 12*, 118–134.

Jacobson, N. S., Dobson, K. S., Truax, P. A., Addis, M. E., Koerner, K., Gollan, J. K., et al. (1996). A component analysis of cognitive-behavioral treatment for depression. *Journal of Consulting and Clinical Psychology, 64,* 295–304.

Jaffee, S. R., & Price, T. S. (2007). Gene-environment correlations: A review of the evidence and implications for prevention of mental illness. *Molecular Psychiatry, 12,* 432–442.

Johnson, S. L., Joormann, J., & Gotlib, I. H. (2007). Does processing of emotional stimuli predict symptomatic improvement and diagnostic recovery from major depression? *Emotion, 7,* 201–206.

Johnson, J., Weissman, M. M., & Klerman, G. L. (1992). Service utilization and social morbidity associated with depressive symptoms in the community. *Journal of the American Medical Association, 267,* 1478–1483.

Joormann, H., & Gotlib, I. H. (2007). Selective attention to emotional faces following recovery from depression. *Journal of Abnormal Psychology, 116,* 80–85.

Just, N., & Alloy, L. B. (1997). The response styles theory of depression: Tests and an extension of the theory. *Journal of Abnormal Psychology, 106*(2), 221–229.

Jurgens, U., & Muller-Preuss, P. (1977). Convergent projections of different limbic vocalization areas in the squirrel monkey. *Experimental Brain Research, 29,* 75–83.

Kahl, K. G., Rudolf, S., Stoeckelhuber, B. M., Dibbelt, L., Gehl, H. B., Markhof, K., et al. (2005). Bone mineral density, markers of bone turnover, and cytokines in young women with borderline personality disorder with and without comorbid major depressive disorder. *The American Journal of Psychiatry, 162,* 168–174.

Kato, T. (2007). Molecular genetics of bipolar disorder and depression. *Psychiatry and Clinical Neurosciences, 61,* 3–19.

Kaufman, J., Yang, B. Z., Douglas-Palumberi, H., Grasso, D., Lipschitz, D., Houshyar, S., et al. (2006). Brain-derived neurotrophic factor-5-HTTLPR gene interactions and environmental modifiers of depression in children. *Biological Psychiatry, 59,* 673–680.

Keller, M. B., McCullough, J. P., Klein, D. N., Arnow, B., Dunner, D. L., Gelenberg, A. J., et al. (2000). A comparison of nefazdone, the cognitive behavioral-analysis system of psychotherapy, and their combination for the treatment of chronic depression. *New England Journal of Medicine, 342,* 1462–1470.

Kendler, K. S., Gardner, C. O., Neale, M. C., & Prescott, C. A. (2001). Genetic risk factors for major depression in men and women: Similar or different heritabilites and same or partly distinct genes? *Psychological Medicine, 31,* 605–616.

Kendler, K. S., Gardner, C. O., & Prescott, C. A. (2002). Toward a comprehensive developmental model for major depression in women. *The American Journal of Psychiatry, 159,* 1133–1145.

Kendler, K. S., Kuhn, J. W., & Prescott, C. A. (2004). Childhood sexual abuse, stressful life events, and risk for major depression in women. *Psychological Medicine, 34,* 1475–1482.

Kendler, K. S., Kuhn, J. W., Vittum, J., Prescott, C. A., & Riley, B. (2005). The interaction of stressful life events and a serotonin transporter polymorphism in the prediction of episodes of major depression: A replication. *Archives of General Psychiatry, 62,* 529–535.

Kendler, K. S., Neale, M. C., Kessler, R. C., Heath, A. C. & Eaves, L. J. (1993). The lifetime history of major depression in women: Reliability of diagnosis and heritability. *Archives of General Psychiatry, 50,* 863–870.

Kennedy, R., & Craighead, W. E. (1988). Differential effects of depression and anxiety on recall of feedback in a learning task. *Behavior Therapy, 19,* 437–454.

Kent, S., Bluthe, R. M., Kelley, K. W., & Dantzer, R. (1992). Sickness behavior as a new target for drug development. *Trends of Pharmacological Science, 13,* 24–28.

Kessler, R. C., Chiu, W. T., Demier, O., & Walters, E. E. (2005). Prevalence, Severity, and Comorbidity of 12-month *DSM-IV* disorders in the National Cormorbidity Survey replication. *Archives of General Psychiatry, 62,* 617–627.

Kessler, R. C., & Walters, E. E. (1998). Epidemiology of *DSM-III-R* major depression and minor depression among adolescents and young adults in the national comorbidity survey. *Depression and Anxiety, 7,* 3–14.

Kitayama, N., Vaccarino, V., Kutner, M., Weiss, P., & Bremner, J. D. (2005). Magnetic resonance imaging (MRI) measurement of hippocampal volume in posttraumatic stress disorder: A meta-analysis. *Journal of Affective Disorders, 88,* 79–86.

Kovak, K. A. (2004). The Hamilton Depression Rating Scale (HAMD). In M. J. Hilsenroth & D. L. Segal (Eds.), *Comprehensive handbook of psychological assessment* (pp. 87–98) Hoboken, NJ: Wiley.

Kranzler, H. R., Kadden, R., Burleson, J., Babor, T. F., Apter, A., & Rounsaville, B. J. (1995). Validity of psychiatric diagnoses in patients with substance use disorders—Is the interview more important than the interviewer? *Comprehensive Psychiatry, 36,* 278–288.

Laje, G., Paddock, S., Manji, H., Rush, A. J., Wilson, A. F., Charney, D., et al. (2007). Genetic markers of suicidal ideation emerging during citalopram treatment of major depression. *American Journal of Psychiatry, 109,* 6444–6450.

Lara, M. E., Klein, D. N., & Kasch, K. L. (2000). Psychosocial predictors of the short-term course and outcome of major depression: A longitudinal study of a nonclinical sample with recent-onset episodes. *Journal of Abnormal Psychology, 109,* 644–650.

Lee, J. A., & Lupski, J. R. (2006). Genomic rearrangements and gene copy-number alterations as a cause of nervous system disorders. *Neuron, 52,* 103–121.

Levinson, D. F. (2006). The genetics of depression: A review. *Biological Psychiatry, 60,* 84–92.

Lewinsohn, P. M., & Graf, M. (1973). Pleasant activities and depression. *Journal of Consulting and Clinical Psychology, 41,* 261–268.

Lewinsohn, P. M. (1974). A behavioral approach to depression. In R. J. Friedman & M. Katz (Eds.), *The psychology of depression: Contemporary theory and research* (pp. 157–178). Oxford, England: Wiley.

Lewinsohn, P. M., Clarke, G. N., Seeley, J. R., & Rohde, P. (1994). Major depression in community adolescents: Age at onset, episode duration, and time to recurrence. *Journal of the American Academy of Child and Adolescent Psychiatry, 33,* 809–818.

Lewinsohn, P. M., Hops, H., Roberts, R. E., Seeley, J. R., & Andrews, J. A. (1993). Adolescent psychopathology: I. Prevalence and incidence of depression and other *DSM-III-R* disorders in high school students. *Journal of Abnormal Psychology, 102,* 133–144.

Lewinsohn, P. M., Sullivan, J. M., & Grosscup, S. J. (1980). Changing reinforcing events: An approach to treatment of depression. *Psychotherapy: Theory, Research, and Practice, 47,* 322–334.

Lewinsohn, P. M., & Gotlib, I. H. (1995). Behavioral therapy and treatment of depression. In E. E. Beckham & W. R. Leber (Eds.), *Handbook of depression* (2nd ed., pp. 352–375). New York: Guilford.

Lewinsohn, P. M., Rohde, P., Seeley, J. R., Klein, D. N., & Gotlib, I. (2003). Psychosocial functioning of young adults who have experienced and recovered from major depressive disorder during adolescence. *Journal of Abnormal Psychology, 112,* 353–363.

Lewinsohn, P. M., Youngren, M. A., & Grosscup, S. J. (1979). Reinforcement and depression. In R. A. Dupue (Ed.), *The psychobiology of depressive disorders: Implications for the effects of stress.* New York: Academic Press.

Licinio, J., O'Kirwan, F., Irizarry, K., Merriman, B., Thakur, S., Jepson, R., et al. (2004). Association of a corticotropin-releasing hormone receptor 1 haplotype and antidepressant treatment response in Mexican-Americans. *Molecular Psychiatry, 9,* 1075–1082.

Linehan, M. M. (1993a). *Cognitive-behavioral treatment of borderline personality disorder.* New York: Guilford.

Linehan, M. M. (1993b). *Skills training manual for treating borderline personality disorder.* New York: Guilford.

Linnoila, M., Guthrie, S., Lane, E. A., Karoum, F., Rudorfer, M., & Potter, W. Z. (1986). Clinical norepinephrine metabolism: How to interpret the numbers. *Psychiatry Research, 17,* 229–239.

Lisanby, S. H., Morales, O., Payne, N., Kwon, E., Fitzsimmons, L., Luber, B., et al. (2003). New developments in electroconvulsive therapy and magnetic seizure therapy. *CNS Spectrums, 8,* 529–536.

Loo, C. K., & Mitchell, P. B. (2005). A review of the efficacy of transcranial magnetic stimulation (TMS) treatment for depression and current and future strategies to optimize efficacy. *Journal of Affective Disorders, 88,* 255–267.

Loo, C. K., Schweitzer, I., & Pratt, C. (2006). Recent advances in optimizing electroconvulsive therapy. *Australian and New Zealand Journal of Psychiatry, 40,* 632–638.

Lyubomirsky, S., Caldwell, N. D., & Nolen-Hoeksema, S. (1998). Effects of ruminative and distracting responses to depressed mood on the retrieval of autobiographical memories. *Journal of Personality and Social Psychology, 75,* 166–177.

Lyubomirsky, S., & Nolen-Hoeksema, S. (1993). Self-perpetuating properties of dysphoric rumination. *Journal of Personality and Social Psychology, 65*(2), 339–349.

Lyubomirsky, S., & Nolen-Hoeksema, S. (1995). Effects of self-focused rumination on negative thinking and interpersonal problem-solving. *Journal of Personality and Social Psychology, 69,* 176–190.

MacCoon, D. G., Abramson, L. Y., Mezulis, A. H., Hanking, B., & Alloy, L. B. (2006). *The Attention-Mediated Hopelessness (AMH) Theory: The role of attention in connecting cognitive vulnerability to rumination in depression.* Manuscript under review.

Maes, M. (1999). Major depression and activation of the inflammatory response system. *Advances in Experimental Medicine and Biology*, *461*, 25–46.

Magarinos, A. M., & McEwen, B. S. (1995a). Stress-induced atrophy of apical dendrites of hippocampal CA3c neurons: Comparison of stressors. *Neuroscience*, *69*, 83–88.

Magarinos, A. M., & McEwen, B. S. (1995b). Stress-induced atrophy of apical dendrites of hippocampal CA3c neurons: Involvement of glucocorticoid secretion and excitatory amino acid receptors. *Neuroscience*, *69*, 89–98.

Magarinos, A. M., McEwen, B. S., Flugge, G., & Fuchs, E. (1996). Chronic psychosocial stress casues apical dendritic atrophy of hippocampal CA3 pyramidal neurons in subordinate tree shrews. *Journal of Neuroscience*, *16*, 3534–3540.

Magarinos, A. M., Verdugo, J. M., & McEwen, B. S. (1997). Chronic stress alters synaptic terminal structure in hippocampus. *Proceedings of the National Academy of Sciences*, *97*, 14002–14008.

Maier, W., Lichtermann, D., Minges, J., Heun, R., Hallmayer, J., & Benkert, O. (1992). Schizoaffective disorder and affective disorders with mood-incongruent psychotic features: Keep separate or combine? Evidence from a family study. *American Journal of Psychiatry*, *149*, 1666–1673.

Marazita, M. L., Neiswanger, K., Cooper, M., Zubenko, G. S., Giles, D. E., Frank, E., et al. (1997). Genetic segregation analysis of early-onset recurrent unipolar depression. *American Journal of Human Genetics*, *61*, 1370–1378.

Mathews, A., & MacLeod, C. M. (2005). Cognitive vulnerability to emotional disorders. *Annual Review of Clinical Psychology*, *1*, 167–195.

Matt, G. E., Vasquez, C., & Campbell, W. K. (1992). Mood-congruent recall of affectively toned stimuli: A meta-analytic review. *Clinical Psychology Review*, *12*, 227–255.

Mayberg, H. S. (1994). Frontal lobe dysfunction in secondary depression. *The Journal of Neuropsychiatry and Clinical Neurosciences*, *6*, 428–442.

Mayberg, H. S., Brannan, S. K., Tekell, J. L., Silva, J. A., Mahurin, R. K., McGinnis, S., et al. (2000). Regional metabolic effects of fluoxetine in major depression: Serial changes and relationship to clinical response. *Biological Psychiatry*, *48*, 830–843.

Mayberg., H. S., Liotti, M., Brannan, S. K., McGinnis, S., Mahurin, R. K., Jerabek, P. A., et al. (1999). Reciprocal limbic-cortical function and negative mood: Convergin PET findings in depression and normal sadness. *The American Journal of Psychiatry*, *156*, 675–682.

Mayberg, H. S., Lozano, A. M., Voon, V., McNeely, H. E., Seminowicz, D., Hamani, C., et al. (2005). Deep brain stimulation for treatment resistant-depression. *Neuron*, *45*, 651–660.

McEwen, B. S. (1998). Protective and damaging effects of stress mediators. *The New England Journal of Medicine*, *338*, 171–179.

McFarland, B. R., Shankman, S. A., Tenke, C. E., Bruder, G. E., & Klein, D. N. (2006). Behavioral activation system deficits predict the six-month course of depression. *Journal of Affective Disorders*, *91*, 229–234.

McGuffin, P., Katz, R., & Rutherford, J. (1991). Nature, nurture, and depression: A twin study. *Psychological Medicine*, *21*, 329–335.

McGuffin, P., Katz, R., Watkins, S., & Rutherford, J. (1996). A hospital-based twin register of the heritability of *DSM-IV* unipolar depression. *Archives of General Psychiatry*, *53*, 129–136.

McLean, P. D., & Hakstian, A. R. (1990). Relative endurance of unipolar depression treatment effects: Longitudinal follow-up. *Journal of Consulting and Clinical Psychology*, *58*, 482–488.

Mendlewicz, J., & Rainer, J. D. (1977). Adoption study supporting genetic transmission in manic-depressive illness. *Nature*, *268*, 327–329.

Miller, G. E., Stetler, C. A., Carney, R. M., Freedland, K. E., & Banks, W. A. (2002). Clinical depression and inflammatory risk markers for coronary heart disease. *American Journal of Cardiology*, *90*, 1279–1283.

Moldin, S. O., Reich, T., & Rice, J. P. (1991). Current perspectives on the genetics of unipolar depression. *Behavioral Genetics*, *21*, 211–242.

Moore, R. Y., & Bloom, F. E. (1979). Central catecholamine neuron systems: Anatomy and physiology of the norepinephrine and epinephrine systems. *Annual Review of Neurosience*, *2*, 113–168.

Mor, N., & Winquist, J. (2002). Self-focused attention and negative affect: A meta-analysis. *Psychologcal Bullletin*, *128*, 638–662.

Morrow, J. (1990). *The effects of rumination, distraction, and negative mood on memories, evaluations, and problem solving*. Unpublished manuscript, Stanford University, Stanford, CA.

Morrow, J., & Nolen-Hoeksema, S. (1990). Effects of responses to depression on the remediation of depressive affect. *Journal of Personality and Social Psychology*, *58*, 519–527.

Mottaghy, F. M., Keller, C. E., Gangitano, M., Ly, J., Thall, M., Parker, J. A., et al. (2002). Correlation of cerebral blood flow and treatment effects of repetitive transcranial magnetic stimulation in depressed patients. *Psychiatry Research*, *115*, 1–14.

Mueller, T. I., Leon, A. C., Keller, M. B., Solomon, D. A., Endicott, J., Coryell, W., Warshaw, M., & Maser, J. D. (1999). Recurrence after recovery from major depressive disorder during 15 years of observational follow-up. *American Journal of Psychiatry*, *156*, 1000–1006.

Murphy, F. C., Sahakian, B. J., Rubinsztein, J. S., Michael, A., Rogers, R. D., Robbins, T. W., et al. (1999). Emotional bias and inhibitory control processes in mania and depression. *Psychological Medicine*, *29*, 1307–1321.

Murray, J. L., & Lopez, A. D. (1997). Global mortality, disability, and the contribution of risk factors: Global Burden of Disease Study. *Lancet*, *349*, 1436–1442.

Musselman, D. L., Lawson, D. H., Gumncik, J. F., Manatunga, A. K., Penna, S., Goodkin, R. S., et al. (2001). Paroxetine for the prevention of depression induced by high-dose interferon alfa. *New England Journal of Medicine*, *344*, 961–96.

Musselman, D. L., Miller, A. H., Porter, M. R., Manatunga, A., Gao, F., Penna, S., et al. (2001). Higher than normal plasma interleukin-6 concentrations in cancer patients with depression: Preliminary findings. *American Journal of Psychiatry*, *158*, 1252–1257.

Needles, D. J., & Abramson, L. Y. (1990). Positive life events, attributional style, and hopefulness: Testing a model of recovery from depression. *Journal of Abnormal Psychology*, *99*, 156–165.

Nelson, R. E., & Craighead, W. E. (1977). Selective recall of positive and negative feedback, self-control behaviors, and depression. *Journal of Abnormal Psychology*, *86*(4), 379–388.

Nelson, J. C., & Davis, J. M. (1997). DST studies in psychotic depression: A meta-analysis. *American Journal of Psychiatry*, *154*, 1497–1503.

Nemeroff, C. B. (2007). The burden of severe depression: A review of diagnostic challenges and treatment alternatives. *Journal of Psychiatric Research*, *41*, 189–206.

Nemeroff, C. B., Bissette, G., Akil, H., & Fink, M. (1991). Neuropeptide concentrations in the cerebrospinal fluid of depressed patients treated with electroconvulsive therapy. Corticotrophin-releasing factor, beta-endorphin, and somatostatin. *British Journal of Psychiatry*, *158*, 59–63.

Nemeroff, C. B., & Evans, D. L. (1984). Correlation between the dexamethasone suppression test in depressed patients and clinical response. *American Journal of Psychiatry*, *141*, 247–249.

Nemeroff, C. B., Heim, C. M., Thase, M. E., Klein, D. N., Rush, A. J., Schatzberg, A. F., et al. (2003). Differential responses to psychotherapy versus pharmacotherapy in patients with chronic forms of major depression and childhood trauma. *Proceedings of the National Academy of Sciences*, *100*, 14293–14296.

Nestler, E. J., Barrot, M., DiLeone, R. J., Eisch, A. J., Gold, S. J., & Montteggia, L. M. (2002). Neurobiology of depression. *Neuron*, *34*, 13–25.

Neumeister, A., Wood, S., Bonne, O., Nugent, A. C., Luckenbaugh, D. A., Young, T., et al. (2005). Reduced hippocampal volume in unmedicated, remitted patients with major depression versus control subjects. *Biological Psychiatry*, *57*, 935–937.

Nezu, A. M., Nezu, C. M., & Perri, M. G. (1989). *Problem-solving therapy for depression: Theory, research, and clinical guidelines*. New York: Wiley.

Nezu, A. M., & Perri, M. G. (1989). Social problem-solving therapy for unipolar depression: An initial dismantling investigation. *Journal of Consulting and Clinical Psychology*, *57*, 408–413.

Nobler, M. S., Oquendo, M. A., Kegeles, L. S., Malone, K. M., Campbell, C. C., Sackeim, H. A., et al. (2001). Decreased regional brain metabolism after ECT. *American Journal of Psychiatry*, *158*, 305–308.

Nolan, S. A., Roberts, J. E., & Gotlib, I. H. (1998). Neuroticism and ruminative response style as predictors of change in depressive symptomatology. *Cognitive Therapy and Research*, *22*(5), 445–455.

Nolen-Hoeksema, S. (1987). Sex differences in unipolar depression: Evidence and theory. *Psychological Bulletin*, *101*, 259–282.

Nolen-Hoeksema, S. (1991). Responses to depression and their effects on the duration of the depressive episode. *Journal of Abnormal Psychology*, *100*, 569–582.

Nolen-Hoeksema, S. (2000). The role of rumination in depressive disorders and mixed anxiety/depressive symptoms. *Journal of Abnormal Psychology*, *109*(3), 504–511.

Nolen-Hoeksema, S. (2002). Gender differences in depression. In I. H. Gotlib & C. L. Hammen (Eds.), *Handbook of depression* (pp. 492–510) New York: Guilford.

Nolen-Hoeksema, S., Larson, J., & Grayson, C. (1999). Explaining the gender difference in depressive symptoms. *Journal of Personality and Social Psychology*, *77*(5), 1061–1072.

Nolen-Hoeksema, S., & Morrow, J. (1991). A prospective study of depression and posttraumatic stress symptoms after a natural disaster: The 1989 Loma Prieta earthquake. *Journal of Personality and Social Psychology, 61*(1), 115–121.

Nolen-Hoeksema, S., Morrow, J., & Fredrickson, B. L. (1993). Response styles and the duration of episodes of depressed mood. *Journal of Abnormal Psychology, 102*(1), 20–28.

Nolen-Hoeksema, S., Parker, L., & Larson, J. (1994). Ruminative coping with depressed mood following loss. *Journal of Personality and Social Psychology, 67*, 92–104.

Ochsner, K. N., & Gross, J. J. (2007). The neural archtecture of emotion regulation. In J. J. Gross (Ed.), *Handbook of emotion regulation*. New York: Guilford.

Ongur, D., An, X., & Price, J. L. (1998). Prefrontal cortical projections to thehypothalamus in macaque monkeys. *Journal of Comparative Neurology, 401*, 480–505.

Ordway, G. A. (1997). Pathophysiology of the locus coeruleus in suicide. *Annals of the New York Academy of Sciences, 836*, 233–252.

Orstavik, R. E., Kendler, K. S., Czajkowski, N., Tambs, K., & Reichborn-Kjennerud (2007). Genetic environmental contributions to depressive personality disorder in a population-based sample of Norwegian twins. *Journal of Affective Disorders, 99*, 181–189.

Owens, M. J., & Nemeroff, C. B. (1991). Physiology and pharmacology of corticotropin-releasing factor. *Pharmacological Review, 43*, 425–473.

Owens, M. J., & Nemeroff, C. B. (1994). Role of serotonin in the pathophysiology of depression: focus on the serotonin transporter. *Clinical Chemistry, 40*, 288–295.

Pace, T. W., Mletzko, T. C., Alagbe, O., Musselman, D. L., Nemeroff, C. B., Miller, A. H., et al. (2006). Increased stress-induced inflammatory responses in male patients with major depression and increased early life stress. *American Journal of Psychiatry, 163*, 1630–1633.

Pagnin, D., de Queiroz, V., Pini, S., & Cassano, G. B. (2004). Efficacy of ECT in depression: A meta-analytic review. *Journal of ECT, 20*, 13–20.

Panagiotakos, D. B., Pitsavos, C., Chrysohoou, C., Tsetsekou, E., Papageorgiou, C., Christodoulou, G., et al. (2004). Inflammation, coagulation, and depressive symptomatology in cardiovascular disease-free people: The ATTIC study. *European Heart Journal, 25*, 492–499.

Penninx, B. W., Kritchevsky, S. B., Yaffe, K., Newman, A. B., Simonsick, E. M., Rubin, S., et al. (2003). Inflammatory markers and depressed mood in older persons: Results from the Health, Aging, and Body Composition Study. *Biological Psychiatry, 54*, 566–572.

Peterson, C., Maier, S. F., & Seligman, M. E. P. (1993). *Learned helplessness: A theory for the age of personal control*. New York: Oxford University Press.

Poo, M. M. (2001). Neurotrophins as synaptic modulators. *National Review of Neuroscience, 2*, 24–32.

Posener, J. A., DeBattista, C., Williams, G. H., Chmura-Kraemer, H., Kalehzan, B. M., & Schatzberg, A. F. (2000). 24-Hour monitoring of cortisol and corticotropin secretion in psychotic and nonpsychotic major depression. *Archives of General Psychiatry, 44*, 434–440.

Price, R. A., Kidd, K. K., & Weissman, M. M. (1987). Early onset (under age 30 years) and panic disorder as markers for etiologic homogeneity in major depression. *Archives of General Psychiatry, 44*, 434–440.

Pyszcynski, T., & Greenberg, J. (1987). Self-regulatory perseveration and the depressive self-focusing style: A self-awareness theory of reactive depression. *Psychological Bulletin, 102*, 122–138.

Raison, C. L., Borisoy, A. S., Broadwell, S. D., Capuron, L., Woolwine, B. J., Jacobson, I. M., et al. (2005). Depression during pegylated interferon-alpha ribavirin therapy: Prevalence and prediction. *Journal of Clinical Psychiatry, 66*, 41–48.

Raison, C. L., Capuron, L., & Miller, A. H. (2006). Cytokines sing the blues: Inflammation and the pathogenesis of depression. *Trends in Immunology, 27*, 24–31.

Rattiner, L., & Ressler, K. J. (2004). BDNF and amygdala dependent learning. *Neuroscientist*

Rattiner, L. M., Davis, M., French, C. T., & Ressler, K. J. (2004). Brain-derived neurotrophic factor and tyrosine kianse receptor B involvement in amygdala-dependent fear conditioning. *Journal of Neuroscience, 24*, 4796–4806.

Ressler, K. J., & Nemeroff, C. B. (2001). Role of norepinephrine in the pathophysiology of neuropsychiatric disorders. *CNS Spectrums, 6*, 663–666, 670.

Ribeiro, S. C., Tandon, R. Grunhaus, L., & Greden, J. F. (1993). The DST as a predictor of outcome in depression: A meta-analysis. *The American Journal of Psychiatry, 150*, 1618–1629.

Riddell, S. A. (1963). The therapeutic efficacy of ECT: A review of the literature. *Archives of General Psychiatry, 8*, 546–556.

Ridding, M. C., & Rothwell, J. C. (2007). Is there a future for therapeutic use of transcranial magnetic stimulation? *Nature Reviews Neuroscience, 8,* 559–567.

Rijsdijk, F. V., Snieder, H., Ormel, J., Sham, P., Goldberg, D. P., & Spector, T. D. (2003). Genetic and environmental influences on psychological distress in the population: General Health Questionnaire analyses in UK twins. *Psychological Medicine, 33,* 793–801.

Risch, N. J. (2000). Searching for genetic determinants in the new millennium. *Nature, 405,* 847–856.

Risch, S. C., & Nemeroff, C. B. (1992). Neurochemical alterations of serotonergic neuronal systems in depression. *Journal of Clinical Psychiatry, 53,* Suppl 3–7.

Riso, L. P., du Toit, P. L., Blandino, J. A., Penna, S., Dacey, S., Duin, J. S., et al. (2003). Cognitive aspects of chronic depression. *Journal of Abnormal Psychology, 112*(1), 72–80.

Roberts, J. E., Gilboa, E., & Gotlib, I. H. (1998). Ruminative response style and vulnerability to episodes of dysphoria: Gender, neuroticism, and episode duration. *Cognitive Therapy and Research, 22*(4), 401–423.

Roceri, M., Hendriks, W., Racagni, G., Ellenbroek, B. A., & Riva, M. A. (2002). Early maternal deprivation reduces the expression of BDNF and NMDA receptor stimulus in rat hippocampus. *Molecular Psychiatry, 7,* 606–616.

Roth, A., & Fonagy, P. (2005). *What works for whom?* (2nd ed.). New York: Guilford.

Roy, A., Pickar, D., DeJong, J., Karoum, F., & Linnoila, M. (1988). Norepinephrine and its metaboites in cerebrospinal fluid, plasma, and urine. Relationship to hypothalamic-pituitary-adrenal axis function in depression. *Archives of General Psychiatry, 45,* 849–857.

Rubin, R. T., Phillips, J. J., Sadow, T. F., & McCracken, J. T. (1995). Adrenal gland volume in major depression: Increase during depressive episode and decrease with successful treatment. *Archives of General Psychiatry, 52,* 213–218.

Rusch, B. D., Abercrombie, H. C., Oakes, T. R., Schaefer, S. M., & Davidson, R. J. (2001). Hippocampal morphometry in depressed patients and control subjects: Relations to anxiety symptoms. *Biological Psychiatry, 50,* 960–964.

Rush, A. J., Berstein, I. H., Trivedi, M. H., Carmody, T. J., Wisniewski, S., Mundt, J. C., et al., (2006). An evaluation of the quick inventory of depressive symptomatology and the Hamilton rating scale for depression: A sequenced treatment alternatives to relieve depression trial report. *Biological Psychiatry, 59,* 493–501.

Rush, A. J., Trivedi, M. H., Ibrahim, H. M., Carmody, T. J., Arnow, B., Klein D. N., et al., (2003). The 16–Item Quick Inventory of Depressive Symptomatology (QIDS), clinician rating (QIDS-C), and self-report (QIDS-SR): A psychometric evaluation in patients with chronic major depression, *Biological Psychiatry, 54,* 573–583.

Sacco, W. P., & Beck, A. T. (1995). Cognitive theory and therapy. In E. E. Beckham & W. R. Leber (Eds.), *Handbook of depression* (pp. 329–351). New York: Guilford.

Sachar, E. J., Hellman, L., Fukushima, D. K., & Gallagher, T. F. (1970). Cortisol production in depressive illness. A clinical and biochemical clarification. *Archives of General Psychiatry, 23,* 289–298.

Sapolsky, R. M., Uno, H., Rebert, C. S., & Finch, C. E. (1990). Hippocampal damage associated with prolonged glucocorticoid exposure in primates. *Journal of Neuroscience, 10,* 2897–2902.

Schatzberg, A. F. (2007). Safety and tolerability of antidepressants: Weighing the impact on treatment decisions. *Journal of Clinical Psychiatry, 68* (Suppl 8), 26–34.

Schatzberg, A. F., Rothschild, A. J., Bond, T. C., & Cole, J. O. (1984). The DST in psychotic depression: Diagnostic and pathophysiologic implications. *Psychopharmacology Bulletin, 20,* 362–364.

Schatzberg, A. F., Rothschild, A. J., Stahl, J. B., Bond, T. C., Rosenbaum, A. H., Lofgren, S. B., et al. (1983). The dexamethasone suppression test: Identification of subtypes of depression. *American Journal of Psychiatry, 140,* 88–91.

Scheier, M. F., & Carver, C. S. (1977). Self-focused attention and the experience of emotion: Attraction, repulsion, elation, and depression. *Journal of Personality and Social Psychology, 35,* 625–636.

Schildkraut, J. J. (1965). The catecholamine hypothesis of affective disorders: A review of supporting evidence. *American Journal of Psychiatry, 122,* 509–522.

Schmidt, H. D., & Duman, R. S. (2007). The role of neurotrophic factors in adult hippocampal neurogenesis, antidepressant treatments and animal models of depressive-like behavior. *Behavioural Pharmacology, 18,* 391–418.

Schule, C., Zill, P., Baghai, T. C., Eser, D., Zwanzger, P., Wenig, N., et al. (2006). Brain-derived neurotrophic factor Val66Met polymorphism and dexamethasone/CRH test results in depressed patients. *Psychoneuroendocrinology*, *31*, 1019–1025.

Schwarz, N., & Clore, G. L. (1988). How do I feel about it? The informative function of affective states. In K. Fiedler & J. Forgas (Eds.), *Affect, cognition, and social behavior* (pp. 44–62). Toronto: Hogrefe.

Seligman, M. E. P. (1975). *Helplessness: On depression, development, and death*. San Francisco: Jossey-Bass.

Seligman, M. E. P., Abramson, L. Y., Semmel, A., & von Baeyer, C. (1979). Depressive attributional style. *Journal of Abnormal Psychology*, *88*, 242–247.

Seminowicz, D. A., Mayberg, H. S., McIntosh, A. R., Goldapple, K., Kennedy, S., Segal, Z., et al. (2004). Limbic-frontal circuitry in major depression: A path modeling meta analysis. *NeuroImage*, *22*, 409–418.

Shear, M. K., Greeno, C., Kang, J., Ludewig, D., Frank, E., Swartz, H. A., et al. (2000). Diagnosis of non-psychotic patients in community clinics. *American Journal of Psychiatry*, *157*, 581–587.

Sheline, Y. I. (1996). Hippocampal atrophy in major depression: A result of depression-included neurotoxicity? *Molecular Psychiatry*, *1*, 298–299.

Sheline, Y. I., Bardgett, M. E., & Csernansky, J. G. (1997). Correlated reductions in cerebrospinal fluid 5-HIAA and MHGP concentrations after treatment with selective serotonin reuptake inhibitors. *Journal of Clinical Psychopharmacology*, *17*, 11–14.

Sheline, Y. I., Sanghavi, M., Mintum, M. A., & Gado, M. H. (1999). Depression duration but not age predicts hippocampal volume loss in medically healthy women with recurrent major depression. *Journal of Neuroscience*, *19*, 5034–5043.

Sheline, Y. I., Wang, P. W., Gado, M. H., Csernansky, J. G., & Vannier, M. W. (1996). Hippocampal atrophy in recurrent major depression. *Proceedings of the National Academy of Sciences*, *93*, 3908–3913.

Shimizu, E., Hashimoto, K., Okamura, N., Koike, K., Komatsu, N., Kumakiri, C., et al. (2003). Alterations of serum levels of brain-derived neurotrophic factor (BDNF) in depressed patients with or without antidepressants. *Biological Psychiatry*, *54*, 70–75.

Skinner, B. F. (1953). *Science and human behavior*. New York: Macmillan.

Slattery, D. A., Hudson, A. L., & Nutt, D. J. (2004). Invited review: The evolution of antidepressant mechanisms. *Fundamental & Clinical Pharmacology*, *18*, 1–21.

Sluzewska, A., Sobieska, M., & Rybakowski, J. K. (1997). Changes in acute-phase proteins during lithium potentiation of antidepressants in refractory depression. *Neuropsychobiology*, *35*, 123–127.

Smith, J. M., Alloy, L. B., & Abramson, L. Y. (2006). Cognitive vulnerability to depression, rumination, hopelessness, and suicidal ideation: Multiple pathways to self-injurious thinking. *Suicide and Life-Threatening Behavior*, *36* (4), 443–454.

Smith, M. A., Makino, S., Kim, S. Y., & Kvetnansky, R. (1995). Stress increases brain-derived neurotrophic facto messanger ribonucleic acid in the hypothalamus and pituitary. *Endocrinology*, *136*, 3743–3750.

Smith, M. A., Makino, S., Kvetnansky, R., & Post, R. M. (1995). Stress and glucocorticoids affect the expression of brain-derived neurotrophic factor and neurotrophin-3 mRNAs in the hippocampus. *Journal of Neuroscience*, *15*, 1768–1777.

Smith, K. A., Fairburn, C. G., & Cowen, P. J. (1997). Relapse of depression after rapid depletion of tryptophan. *Lancet*, *349*, 915–919.

Spasojevic, J., & Alloy, L. B. (2001). Rumination as a common mechanism relating depressive risk factors to depression. *Emotion*, *1*, 25–37.

Starkman, M. N., Gebarski, S. S., Berent, S., & Schteingart, D. E. (1992). Hippocampal formation volume, memory dysfunction, and cortisol levels in patients with Cushing's syndrome. *Biological Psychiatry*, *32*, 756–765.

Steiner, J. L., Tebes, J. K., Sledge, & Walker, M. L. (1995). A comparison of the Structured Clinical Interview for the *DSM-III-R* and clinical diagnoses. *Journal of Nervous and Mental Disease*, *183*, 365–369.

Sullivan, P. F., Neale, M. C., & Kendler, K. S. (2000). Genetic epidemiology of major depression: Review and meta-analysis. *American Journal of Psychiatry*, *157*, 1552–1562.

Swanson, L. W., Sawchenko, P. E., Rivier, J., & Vale, W. W. (1983). Organization of ovine corticotropin-releasing factor immunoreactive cells and fibers in the rat brain: An immunohistochemical study. *Neuroendocrinology*, *36*, 165–186.

Terman, M., & Terman, J. S. (2005). Light therapy for seasonal and nonseasonal depression: Efficacy, protocol, safety, and side effects. *CNS Spectrums*, *10*, 647–663.

Thase, M. E., Friedman, E. S., Biggs, M. M., Wisniewski, S. R., Trivedi, M. H., Luther, J. F., et al. (2007). Cognitive therapy versus medication in augmentation and switch strategies as second-step treatments: a STAR*D report. *American Journal of Psychiatry*, *164*, 739–752.

Timbremont, B., & Braet, C. (2004). Cognitive vulnerability in remitted depressed children and adolescents. *Behavior Research and Therapy*, *42*, 423–437.

Torgersen, S. (1986). Genetic factors in moderately severe and mild affective disorders. *Archives of General Psychiatry*, *43*, 222–226.

Treynor, W., Gonzalez, R., & Nolen-Hoeksema, S. (2003). Rumination reconsidered: Apsychometric analysis. *Cognitive Therapy and Research*, *27*(3), 247–259.

Trivedi, M. H., Fava, M., Wisniewski, S. R., Thase, M. E., Quitkin, F., Warden, D., et al. (2006). Medication augmentation after the failure of SSRIs for depression. *New England Journal of Medicine*, *354*, 1243–1252.

Trivedi, M. H., Rush, A. J., Wisniewski, S. R., Nierenberg, A. A., Warden, D., Ritz, L., et al. (2006). Evaluation of outcomes with citalopram for depression using measurement-based care in STAR*D: Implications for clinical practice. *American Journal of Psychiatry*, *163*, 28–40.

Tsankova, N. M., Berton, O., Renthal, W., Kumar, A., Neve, R. L., & Nestler, E. J. (2006). Sustained hippocampal chromatin regulation in a mouse model of depression and ntidepressant action. *Nature Neuroscience*, *9*, 519–525.

Ueyama, T., Kawai, Y., Nemoto, K., Sekimoto, M., Tone, S., & Senba, E. (1997). Neurotoxicity of glucocorticoids in the primate brain. *Hormones and Behavior*, *28*, 336–348.

Uno, H., Eisele, S., Sakai, A., Shelton, S., Baker, E., DeJesus, O., et al. (1994). Neurotoxicity of glucocorticoids in the primate brain. *Hormones and Behavior*, *28*, 336–348.

Uno, H., Tarara, R., Else, J. G., Suleman, M. A., & Sapolsky, R. M. (1989). Hippocampal damage associated with prolonged and fatal stress in primates. *Journal of Neuroscience*, *9*, 1705–17111.

Vakili, K., Pillay, S. S., Lafer, B., Fava, M., Renshaw, P. F., Bonello-Cintron, C. M., et al. (2000). Hippocampal volume in primary unipolar major depression: A magnetic resonance imaging study. *Biological Psychiatry*, *47*, 1087–1090.

Vale, W., Spiess, J., Rivier, C., & Rivier, J. (1981). Characterization of 41–residue ovine hypothalamic peptide that stimulates secretion of corticotropin and beta-endorphin. *Science (New York, NY) 213*, 1394–1397.

Van der Wurff, F. B., Stek, M. L., Hoogendijk, W. L., & Beekman, A. T. (2003). Electroconvulsive therapy for the depressed elderly. *Cochrane Database Syst Rev*, C0003593.

Veith, R. C., Lewis, N., Linares, O. A., Barnes, R. F., Raskind, M. A., Villacres, E.C., et al. (1994). Sympathetic nervous system activity in major depression: Basal and desipramine-induced alterations in plasma norepinephrine kinetics. *Archives of General Psychiatry*, *51*, 411–422.

Vermetten, E., Schmahl, C., Linder, S., Loewenstein, R. J., & Bremner, J. D. (2006). Hippocampal and amygdalar volumes in dossociative identity disorder. *American Journal of Psychiatry*, *163*, 630–636.

Viera, A. J. & Garrett, J. M. (2005). Understanding interobserver agreement: The kappa statistic. *Family Medicine*, *37*, 360–363.

Vittengl, J. R., Clark, L. A., Dunn, T. W., & Jarrett, R. B. (2007). Reducing relapse and recurrence in unipolar depression: A comparative meta-analysis of cognitive therapy's effects. *Journal of Consulting and Clinical Psychology*, *75*, 475–488.

Vogt, B. A., & Pandya, D. N. (1987). Cingulate cortex of the rhesus monkey: II. Cortical afferents. *The Journal of Comparative Neurology*, *262*, 271–289.

Vythilingam, M., Heim, C., Newport, J., Miller, A. H., Anderson, E., Bronen, R., et al. (2002). Childhood trauma associated with smaller hippocampal volume in women with major depression. *American Journal of Psychiatry*, *159*, 2072–2080.

Vythilingam, M., Luckenbaugh, D. A., Lam, T., Morgan, C. A., 3rd., Lipschitz, D., Charney, D. S., et al. (2005). Smaller head of the hippocampus in Gulf War-related posttraumatic stress disorder. *Psychiatry Research*, *139*, 89–99.

Weissman, M. M., Gerson, E. S., Kidd, K. K., Prusoff, B. A., Leckman, J. F., Dibble, E., et al. (1984). Psychiatric disorders in the relatives of probands with affective disorders. *Archives of General Psychiatry*, *41*, 13–21.

Wender, P., Kety, S. S., Rosenthal, D., Schulsinger, F., Ortmann, J., & Lunde, I. (1986). Psychiatric disorders in the biological and adoptive families of adopted individuals with affective disorders. *Archives of General Psychiatry*, *43*, 923–929.

Wirz-Justice, A. (2006). Biological rhythm disturbances in mood disorders. *International Clinical Psychopharmacology, 21* (Suppl 1), S11–15.

Weissman, M. M., Bland, R. C., Canino, G. J., Faravelli, C., Greenwald, S., Hwu, H., et al. (1996). Cross-national epidemiology of major depression and bipolar disorder. *JAMA*, *276*, 293–299.

Wood, J. V., Saltzberg, J. A., Neale, J. M., Stone, A. A., & Rachmiel, T. B. (1990). Self focused attention, coping responses, and distressed mood in everyday life. *Journal of Personality and Social Psychology*, *58*, 1027–1036.

Chapter 9

Dysthymia and Chronic Depression

Daniel N. Klein

Depressive disorders have traditionally been conceptualized as episodic, remitting conditions. Only within the past 10 to 20 years has it been widely recognized that a significant proportion of depressive disorders have a chronic course (Akiskal, 1983; Kocsis & Frances, 1987). Indeed, 36% to 47% of patients with mood disorders in outpatient mental health settings are chronically depressed (Rounsaville, Sholomskas, & Prusoff, 1980; Benazzi, 1997). Nonetheless, chronicity is frequently overlooked as an important aspect of depression in the research literature, and chronic depression is often undertreated, even in patients seeking psychological or medical treatment (Shelton, Davidson, Yonkers, & Koran, 1997). In this chapter, we review current thinking and research on dysthymia and chronic major depression, and present evidence that chronicity is a key aspect of the clinical and etiological heterogeneity of depression that should be considered in both clinical practice and research.

Description of Disorder

Current Diagnostic Criteria

Chronic depressions can take a number of forms, which vary in their pattern of severity over time. The two major categories of chronic depression in the fourth edition of the *Diagnostic and Statistical Manual of Mental Disorders* (*DSM-IV*) (American Psychiatric Association, 1994) are Dysthymic Disorder and Major Depressive Disorder, chronic type.

Dysthymic Disorder

Dysthymic disorder is defined by a chronic course (depressed most of the day, more days than not, for at least 2 years), persistent symptoms (no symptom-free periods of longer than 2 months), and an insidious onset (no major depressive episode within the first 2 years of the disturbance). It can present with the full gamut of depressive symptoms, although cognitive (e.g., low self-esteem, hopelessness), affective (dysphoric mood), and social-motivational (e.g., social withdrawal) symptoms are more common than vegetative symptoms (e.g., sleep or appetite disturbance; Keller et al., 1995; Serretti et al., 1999). The *DSM-IV* currently requires at least two of the following six sets of symptoms: decreased energy or fatigue, insomnia or hypersomnia, increased or decreased appetite, low self-esteem, poor concentration or difficulty making decisions, and helplessness. However, patients who meet the chronicity and persistence criteria for dysthymic disorder typically have many more than the required two depressive symptoms (Klein et al., 1996). As described in the following, although dysthymic disorder may appear to be relatively mild at any given point, the cumulative burden of persistent depressive symptoms and impaired functioning is substantial and can be greater than many episodic major depressions (Holm-Denoma, Berlim, Fleck, & Joiner, 2006; Klein, Schwartz, Rose, & Leader, 2000).

There have been proposals to change the symptom criteria for Dysthymic Disorder to better reflect the more common cognitive, affective, and social-motivational symptoms (Gwirtsman, Blehar, McCullough, Kocsis, & Prien, 1997), and an alternative set of symptom criteria was included in the *DSM-IV* Appendix. However, as almost all the variance in assigning the diagnosis is due to the chronicity and persistence criteria, revising the symptom criteria would increase descriptive validity but have little impact on who qualifies for the diagnosis (Klein et al., 1996). Hence, Dunner's (2005) suggestion to use the same set of symptom criteria for dythymic disorder as is currently used for Major Depressive Disorder merits consideration in the interests of greater parsimony.

Most persons with Dysthymic Disorder experience exacerbations that meet criteria for a major depressive episode (Klein et al., 2000). Indeed, the development of a superimposed major depressive episode is often what leads individuals with Dysthymic Disorder to seek treatment. Though it is not a formal category in the current nosology, the superimposition of a major depressive episode on an antecedent dysthymic disorder has been referred to as "double depression" (Keller & Shapiro, 1982). In *DSM-IV*, such patients receive both Major Depressive Disorder and Dysthymic Disorder diagnoses. Unfortunately, this implies that these are two distinct, comorbid conditions. Instead, it is more likely that the dysthymia and major depressive episodes in patients with double depression represent different phases of a single condition that waxes and wanes, often in response to stressful life events (Keller & Lavori, 1984; Moerk & Klein, 2000).

Major Depressive Episode, Chronic Type

Major Depressive Episode, Chronic Type refers to a depressive episode that meets the full criteria for major depression continuously for a minimum of 2 years. Approximately 20% of patients with a major depressive episode meet these critiera (Gilmer et al., 2005; Mueller et al., 1996).

The *DSM-IV* includes several additional episode and course specifiers relevant to chronic depression. In coding the severity of the current major depressive episode, *DSM-IV* includes an option for patients who are in partial remission. This refers to patients who have recovered to the point they no longer meet full criteria for a major depressive episode but continue to experience significant symptoms. The distinction between full and partial remission is important because the persistence of subthreshold symptoms is associated with significant functional impairment and an increased risk of recurrence (Judd et al., 2000). In many cases, these subthreshold depressive symptoms can persist for many years. Such cases can be considered another form of chronic depression. If these patients experience a recurrence, they qualify for the *DSM-IV* longitudinal course specifier, "recurrent major depression without full interepisode recovery." If the total continuous duration of illness is greater than 2 years, this can also be viewed as a form of chronic depression.

CASE EXAMPLE OF DYSTHYMIC DISORDER WITH SUPERIMPOSED RECURRENT MAJOR DEPRESSIVE EPISODES

RG is a 48-year-old caucasian female, a high school English teacher, and a divorcé. She sought psychotherapy for depression from a clinical psychologist at a medical school after reading about his work on the Internet. She is slightly overweight, neatly dressed, speaks softly, and is hesitant to make eye contact. RG reports feeling depressed, anxious, and lonely. She has diminished interest in the things that she usually enjoys (e.g., reading and gardening), and she has little energy, reporting that she feels as if she has to drag herself through the day. She has had difficulty concentrating on everyday activities, trouble falling and staying asleep, and feels as if she has little value and purpose. In addition, she feels worried and pessimistic about the future, blames herself for not being able to shake off the depressed mood and be more productive, and ruminates about not having made more of her life. While RG has never had an active social life, she is avoiding social contact to a greater extent than usual. She frequently thinks about death, but denies current or past suicidal ideation or behavior.

RG reports that she has felt depressed for most of her life, but some periods have been worse than others. The current period of more severe depression began several months ago during summer vacation. Without the structure of the school year, she began to feel purposeless and lacking direction, and she became increasingly withdrawn. RG reports that she has had approximately half a dozen episodes like this in the past, with the first one occurring during her first year of high school.

RG was an only child who was raised in an intact family. She reports that her mother, a librarian (who died several years ago from natural causes), was distant and critical. RG feels like she was a disappointment to her mother in a way that she could not understand, but also suspects that her mother may have been depressed throughout much of RG's childhood. RG felt closer to her father, a midlevel manager for a large corporation, who died when she was a young adult. She reported, however, that he traveled a great deal for work and was not able to spend much time with her.

RG was a good student, but describes herself as being shy and never having more than one or two friends. She met her husband at college. He was an energetic, dominant individual, and she reports being flattered by his interest. After being married for 10 years, RG's husband left her for another woman. They did not have children because RG did not believe that she could be a good mother. During the past 17 years since the divorce, RG has briefly dated several men, but has not had any significant romantic relationships. She has several friends whom she sees regularly, but she rarely discusses personal matters with them. She has worked as a teacher for almost 25 years, but derives little satisfaction from it. She feels that most of her students are uninterested in literature, and that she has little impact on them. RG indicates that, if she could do it over again, she would have chosen another career.

RG has been in psychotherapy several times, once for approximately 2 years. She has also taken several antidepressant medications, although only one medication trial lasted longer than 6 weeks. The various courses of treatment have been somewhat helpful, but have never completely relieved RG's symptoms or prevented recurrences.

HISTORY OF CONSTRUCT

The antecedents of the contemporary constructs of Dysthymic Disorder and Chronic Major Depression include the older clinical constructs of neurotic depression, the depressive temperament and personality, and earlier descriptions of chronic depression (see Klein, Riso, & Anderson, 1993). The concept of neurotic depression grew out of attempts by Kraepelin and other classical European descriptive psychopathologists to distinguish between biological and psychogenic forms of mood disorders. Referred to as "depressive neurosis" in *DSM-II* (American Psychiatric Association, 1968), it was the most frequently diagnosed form of mood disorder in the 1960s and 1970s (Akiskal, Bitar, Puzantian, Rosenthal, & Walker, 1978). However, neurotic depression was a confusing term because it was used in a number of different ways, including: mild depression; chronic depression; depression with a nonbiological etiology; the absence of psychotic features; the absence of endogenous (or melancholic) features; the presence of mood reactivity to external events (i.e., nonautonomous); depressive episodes that appeared to be precipitated by stressful life events; the presence of co-occuring "neurotic" personality traits (e.g., anxious, dependent, or histrionic features); and an etiology that was rooted in intrapsychic conflicts (Klerman et al., 1979). The concordance between these definitions was low (Klerman et al.), interrater reliability was poor, and patients with neurotic depression were extremely heterogenous with respect to long-term outcome (Akiskal et al., 1978). Hence, the diagnosis of *depressive neurosis* was replaced by *dysthymic disorder* in *DSM-III* (American Psychiatric Association, 1980).

The concepts of depressive personality, depressive temperament, and characterological depression also date back to classical European descriptive psychopathologists (see Phillips, Gunderson, Hirschfeld, & Smith, 1990). For example, Kraepelin (1921) used the term "depressive temperament" to refer to a pattern of traits (e.g., gloomy, lacking self-confidence, self-reproachful, ruminative, introverted, and lacking in vitality and initiative) that often characterized the premorbid personalities of depressed inpatients and was common in their biological relatives. This was subsequently elaborated by Schneider (1958), who rejected the idea of a genetic link between depressive personality and the major mood disorders. Schildkraut and D.F. Klein's (1975) concept of *chronic characterological depression* was closely related to the depressive personality—however, they argued that this category was heterogeneous and included several more specific subgroups, including some that were responsive to antidepressant medication. Finally, the concepts of depressive personality and depressive character have been widely used by psychoanalytic investigators (e.g., Bemporad, 1976), some of whom also linked it with masochistic, or self-defeating, traits (Kernberg, 1988).

The original version of the Research Diagnostic Criteria (RDC), the precursor to the explicit diagnostic criteria pioneered by the *DSM-III*, included a depressive personality category. However, this was later replaced by the categories of Intermittent Depressive

Disorder and Chronic Minor Depressive Disorder (Spitzer, Endicott, & Robins, 1978). Like the subsequent *DSM-III* formulation of Dysthymic Disorder, intermittent and chronic minor depression were defined as symptomatically mild, chronic depressive conditions. Intermittent and chronic minor depression differed in that the former was characterized by a fluctuating course, while the latter had a more stable chronic course, a distinction that was abandoned in *DSM-III*.

The text of *DSM-III-R* (American Psychiatric Association, 1987) indicates that depressive personality is an alternative label for dysthymia. However, in light of evidence for the conceptual and empirical distinctiveness of Dysthymic Disorder and depressive personality (see the following), the *DSM-IV* introduced a separate category for depressive personality in the Appendix for conditions requiring further study.

Finally, in the 1960s and 1970s, there was increasing recognition that a substantial number of depressed patients experienced a chronic, rather than remitting, course. In a landmark paper, Weissman and Klerman (1977) reported that 12% of a cohort of 150 depressed women remained chronically symptomatic throughout a 20-month follow-up. Chronic depression was not formally included in the nosology until *DSM-III-R*, when Major Depression, chronic type was introduced for patients who failed to recover from a major depressive episode within 2 years. This category was tightened in *DSM-IV*, which required that patients had to continue to meet full criteria for major depression for the entire 2 years. As noted, patients with persisting depressive symptoms that fell beneath full diagnostic threshold are coded as being in partial remission.

EPIDEMIOLOGY, COMORBIDITY, SOCIAL FUNCTIONING

Epidemiology

There are a number of studies of the prevalence of dysthymic disorder using large, representative community samples. For example, in the Epidemiological Catchment Area (ECA) Study, Weissman, Leaf, Bruce, & Florio (1988) reported that the lifetime prevalence of *DSM-III* Dysthymic Disorder was 3.1%. In the National Comorbidity Study (NCS), Kessler et al. (1994) reported 12-month and lifetime prevalences of 2.5% and 6.4%, respectively for *DSM-III-R* Dysthymia. Similarly, in the National Health and Nutrition Examination Survey III, the lifetime prevalence of *DSM-III-R* Dysthymia was 6.1% (Riolo, Nguyen, Greden, & King, 2005). Finally, the rates were somewhat lower in the recent NCS replication, where the 12-month and lifetime prevalences of *DSM-IV* dysthymic disorder were 1.5% and 2.5%, respectively (Kessler, Berglund, Demler, Jin, & Walters, 2005).

Rates of Dysthymic Disorder are somewhat higher in medical settings. For example, Browne et al. (1999) reported that the 12-month prevalence of Dysthymic Disorder in a large primary care sample was 5.1%. The prevalence of Dysthymic Disorder is even higher in psychiatric settings, with studies reporting rates of 22%–36% in outpatient mental health clinics (Klein, Dickstein, Taylor, & Harding, 1989; Markowitz, Moran, Kocsis, & Frances, 1992).

The median age of onset of dysthymia in the NCS-R was 31 years (Kessler et al., 2005). The prevalence of Dysthymic Disorder is approximately two times higher in women than men (Weisman et al., 1988; Kessler et al., 1994). Several studies have reported that the prevalence of dysthymia is negatively associated with income (Weissman et al., 1988; Riolo et al., 2005). However, data on the associations between

Dysthymic Disorder and education and ethnicity are inconsistent (Riolo et al., 2005; Weissman et al., 1988).

Few data are available on the prevalence of chronic major depression, which is combined with nonchronic major depression in most epidemiological studies. However, in an unpublished manuscript using the NCS sample, Swartz, Kessler, McGonagle, and Blazer (1993) reported that the lifetime prevalence of *DSM-III-R* chronic major depression was 6.2%, compared to 10.8% for nonchronic major depression. Although women were more likely to have chronic major depression than men, the sex ratio was no different from nonchronic major depression.

Impairment

Depressive disorders are often accompanied by significant functional impairment. Indeed, the level of impairment associated with depression is equal to or greater than most common general medical conditions, including hypertension, arthritis, diabetes, congestive heart failure, and recent myocardial infarction (Hays, Wells, Sherbourne, Rogers, & Spritzer, 1995). Severity and chronicity appear to contribute additively to functional impairment in depression (Leader & Klein, 1996). Thus, Dysthymic Disorder is associated with as much or more impairment as nonchronic major depression, and double depression is associated with greater impairment than both (Evans, Cloitre, Kocsis, & Gniwesch, 1995; Goodman, Schwab-Stone, Lahey, Schaffer, & Jensen, 2000; Hays et al., 1995). The impairment is evident in many areas, including occupational, interpersonal, marital, and family functioning (Adler et al., 2004; Evans et al., 1995; Leader & Klein, 1996).

Comorbidity

As noted earlier, almost all patients with Dysthymic Disorder experience superimposed major depressive episodes at some point in the course of the dysthymia (Keller et al., 1995). Chronic depressions are also frequently accompanied by nonaffective disorders, particularly anxiety, substance use, and personality disorders. For example, in the ECA study, 46% of individuals with dysthymia had a history of anxiety disorders, and 30% had a history of substance use disorders (Weissman et al., 1988). Rates of Axis II disorders are also very high (Garyfallos et al., 1999; Markowitz et al., 1992; Spalletta et al., 1996). For example, Pepper et al. (1995) reported that 60% of patients with Dysthymic Disorder met criteria for a personality disorder based on a semistructured diagnostic interview. Similarly, 60% had a personality disorder based on an independent interview with a knowledgeable informant. The most frequent co-occurring Axis II conditions are Avoidant, Borderline, and Dependent Personality Disorder (Garyfallos et al., 1999; Markowitz et al., 1992; Pepper et al., 1995; Spalletta et al., 1996).

Classification

There have been a variety of questions and controversies regarding where chronic depressions, particularly Dysthymic Disorder, should be placed in the classification system. In the 1980s and early 1990s, the debate focused on whether Dysthymic Disorder should be placed on Axis I with the mood disorders or on Axis II with the personality disorders. This stimulated research exploring its relationship to both types of psychopathology. More recent work has focused on the distinctions between the various forms of chronic depression and between Dysthymic Disorder and Depressive Personality Disorder.

DYSTHYMIC DISORDER: RELATIONSHIP TO MOOD AND PERSONALITY DISORDERS

The introduction of Dysthymic Disorder as a category within the mood disorders section of *DSM-III* precipitated a controversy over whether it was best conceptualized as a form of mood disorder or personality disorder (Kocsis & Frances, 1987; Klein et al., 1993). Critics argued that because of its chronic course, often early onset, and lower rates of vegetative symptoms, Dysthymic Disorder appeared to be more like a personality disorder than a classical mood disorder with an episodic/remitting course, adult onset, and melancholic features. Moreover, as previously noted, persons with Dysthymic Disorder frequently exhibit significant personality pathology and meet criteria for personality disorders. However, there are three lines of evidence indicating that Dysthymic Disorder also has a close relationship to Major Depressive Disorder.

First, in retrospective studies, approximately 75% of persons with Dysthymic Disorder report having experienced a major depressive episode at some point in their lives (e.g., Keller et al., 1995), and longitudinal studies indicate that the rate may be as high as 95% (Klein, Shankman, & Rose, 2006). Conversely, approximately 25% of patients presenting with a major depressive episode have an antecedent dysthymic disorder (Keller & Shapiro, 1982).

Second, there is a strong familial relationship between Dysthymic Disorder and Major Depressive Disorder. Family studies indicate that the first-degree relatives of individuals with Dysthymic Disorder have an elevated rate of Major Depressive Disorder (Klein et al., 1995; Klein, Shankman et al., 2004), and there is an elevated rate of Dysthymic Disorder in the offspring of parents with Major Depressive Disorder (Klein, Clark, Dansky, & Margolis, 1988; Lieb, Höffler, Pfister, & Wittchen, 2002). Third, antidepressant medications are effective in treating Dysthymic Disorder (Thase et al., 1996).

In light of this evidence, the classification of Dysthymic Disorder in the mood disorders section is now commonly accepted. However, there is also evidence for relationships between Dysthymic Disorder and at least some of the main-text *DSM-IV* personality disorders. In addition to the high comorbidity between Dysthymic Disorder and many personality disorders (Garyfallos et al., 1999; Markowitz et al., 1992; Pepper et al., 1995), there appear to be shared etiological influences. For example, Riso et al. (1996) found an elevated rate of Borderline Personality Disorder in the first-degree relatives of patients with Dysthymic Disorder. In addition, in a 5-year prospective follow-up study, Klein and Schwartz (2002) used structural equation modeling to compare several models of the relationship between Dysthymic Disorder and Borderline Personality Disorder. They found that a model specifying a single latent factor that influenced the course and relationship between the two disorders over time provided a better fit to the data than models in which borderline traits had a direct influence on depressive symptoms and/or depressive symptoms had a direct influence on borderline traits.

DISTINCTION BETWEEN CHRONIC AND NONCHRONIC DEPRESSIONS

In light of the close relationship between Dysthymic Disorder and Major Depressive Disorder, an important question is whether the two conditions should be distinguished at all. In other words, perhaps Dysthymic Disorder and Major Depressive Disorder should be combined into a single depressive disorder category.

Despite their similarities, there are a number of differences between Dysthymic Disorder (both with and without superimposed major depressive episodes) and Major Depressive Disorder (at least in its nonchronic form) that support their separation. First, persons with Dysthymic Disorder have greater Axis I (Holm-Denoma et al., 2006) and Axis II (Garyfallos et al., 1999; Pepper et al., 1995; Spalletta et al., 1996) comorbidity than nonchronic Major Depressive Disorder. In addition, Dysthymic Disorder is associated with more extreme normal-range personality traits (Hirschfeld, 1990; Klein, Taylor et al., 1988), higher levels of at least some depressive cognitive biases (Klein, Taylor et al.; Riso et al., 2003), and greater suicidality (Holm-Denoma et al., 2006; Klein, Taylor et al., 1988b; Klein et al., 2000).

Second, individuals with Dysthymic Disorder report having experienced greater early adversity and maladaptive parenting than persons with nonchronic major depression (Lizardi et al., 1995). Third, Dysthymic Disorder aggregates specifically in families. Thus, the relatives of probands with Dysthymic Disorder have significantly higher rates of Dysthymic Disorder than the relatives of patients with nonchronic major depression (Klein et al., 1995; Klein, Shankman et al., 2004).

Finally, consistent with their definitions, Dysthymic Disorder predicts a more chronic course and poorer outcomes than nonchronic Major Depressive Disorder. For example, in a 10-year follow-up study, patients with Dysthymic Disorder had a significantly higher level of depressive symptomatology, spent a significantly greater portion of the follow-up meeting criteria for a depressive disorder, and a significantly smaller proportion of the follow-up recovered from all depressive disorders, and had a greater number of suicide attempts and hospitalizations than patients with nonchronic Major Depressive Disorder (Klein, Schwartz, Rose, & Leader, 2000; Klein et al., 2006).

In summary, though Dysthymic Disorder is closely related to Major Depressive Disorder, the two conditions appear to differ in important ways. Interestingly, dysthymia, which is conceptualized as the milder of the two conditions, appears to be more severe than nonchronic major depression on virtually all variables that distinguish the two conditions.

A related question concerns the validity of the distinction between chronic and nonchronic major depression. The literature addressing this issue is somewhat less than consistent. Nonetheless, persons with chronic Major Depressive Disorder have been reported to be older (Gilmer et al., 2005; Rush et al., 1995), have an earlier onset of major depression (Garvey, Tollefson, & Tuason, 1986: Klein, Shankman et al., 2004), a higher rate of attempted suicide (Garvey et al., 1986; Gilmer et al., 2005; Szádóczky, Fazekas, Rihmer, & Arato, 1994), greater comorbidity with anxiety disorders (Gilmer et al., 2005; Klein, Shankman et al., 2004); greater medical illness burden (Gilmer et al., 2005), higher levels of neuroticism (Hirschfeld et al., 1986), poorer work and social adjustment (Gilmer et al., 2005), and a stronger family history of mood disorder (Klein, Shankman et al., 2004; Scott et al., 1988; Vocisano, Klein, Keefe, Dienst, & Kincaid, 1996) than individuals with nonchronic Major Depressive Disorder.

Thus, there is evidence suggesting that both Dysthymic Disorder and chronic Major Depressive Disorder differ from nonchronic Major Depressive Disorder in fairly similar ways. This suggests that it may be useful to recognize a broader distinction between chronic and nonchronic depressions. Indeed, there are several lines of evidence that support such a broader distinction. First, in a study comparing heterogeneous forms of chronic depression to nonchronic depression, Mondimore et al. (2006) reported that chronic depression was associated with an earlier age of onset of depression, higher rates of attempted suicide, Panic Disorder, substance use disorders, and a higher rate of chronic depression in first-degree relatives.

Second, the distinction between chronic and nonchronic depression is relatively stable over time. Over the course of a 10-year follow-up, Klein et al. (2006) found that patients with Dysthymic Disorder and double depression were 14 times more likely to exhibit a chronic course than patients with nonchronic major depression. Conversely, patients with nonchronic major depression were 12 times more likely to exhibit a nonchronic depressive course than patients with Dysthymic Disorder and double depression.

Finally, although direct comparisons are rare (see Thase et al., 1994, for an exception), chronic depressions appear to require somewhat different approaches to treatment than nonchronic depressions. Thus, rates of treatment response tend to be lower in chronic than nonchronic depressions (Kocsis, 2003). In addition, it appears that chronic depressions require a longer duration of pharmacotherapy (Koran et al., 2001) and may be more likely to benefit from combined pharmacotherapy and psychotherapy (Keller et al., 2000) than nonchronic major depression.

RELATIONSHIP BETWEEN FORMS OF CHRONIC DEPRESSION

The multiple *DSM* chronic depression categories, subtypes, and specifiers enhance the descriptive validity of the nomenclature by reflecting the variation in the longitudinal course of depression. However, it is unclear how meaningful these often-subtle distinctions are in terms of etiology, prognosis, and treatment.

Only a handful of studies have compared different forms of chronic depression. A series of papers from two different research groups found virtually no differences between patients with Dysthymic Disorder and those with double depression on comorbidity, personality, coping style, childhood adversity, familial psychopathology, and 10-year course and outcome (Lizardi et al., 1995; Klein et al., 1995, 2006; McCullough et al., 1990; Pepper et al., 1995).

Two studies have compared patients with Dythymic Disorder and those with chronic Major Depressive Disorder (Cassano & Savino, 1993; Yang & Dunner, 2001). Both studies found few differences, although Cassano and Savino (1993) reported that patients with Dysthymic Disorder were more likely to report a family history of Bipolar Disorder.

Finally, two large studies found virtually no differences between patients with double depression, patients with chronic Major Depressive Disorder, and patients with chronic major depressive episodes superimposed on Dysthymic Disorder (a more chronic form of double depression that had not been previously described in the literature) on comorbidity, psychosocial functioning, depressive cognitions, coping style, early adversity, family history, and treatment response (McCullough et al., 2000, 2003). Moreover, the latter of these studies also included a fourth group of patients with major depression in partial remission or recurrent major depression with incomplete recovery between episodes and a total continuous duration of at least 2 years. This group also failed to differ from patients with double depression, chronic major depression, and chronic major depression superimposed on dysthymia on the broad range of variables assessed in the study (McCullough et al., 2003).

The lack of distinctiveness between the various forms of chronic depression is also supported by within-subject longitudinal data. As noted previously, almost all patients with Dysthymic Disorder experience exacerbations that meet criteria for major depressive episodes, suggesting that Dysthymic Disorder and double depression are different phases of the same condition (Keller & Lavori, 1984; Klein et al., 2000). In addition, in a 10-year follow-up study, Klein et al. (2006) found that although patients with Dysthymic Disorder and double depression often experienced recurrences of chronic depression, the form of chronic depression varied. Of the patients who experienced a recurrence of chronic depression, 28% met criteria for Dysthymic Disorder, 24% met criteria for a chronic major depressive episode, and 48% had a period of chronic depression that did not meet criteria for either category (e.g., major depression with partial remission and a continuous duration of over 2 years).

Thus, there is little evidence that the distinctions between the various forms of chronic depression are stable, etiologically meaningful, or clinically useful. On the other hand, as previously discussed, there appear to be important differences between chronic and nonchronic forms of depression. This suggests that in the interest of parsimony, the different forms of chronic depression recognized in the *DSM-IV* can be combined into a single chronic depression category and contrasted with nonchronic depression (Dunner, 2005; Klein, Shankman et al., 2004; McCullough et al., 2003).

If the various patterns of chronic depression were to be combined into a single, more parsimonious, category, how could that category be defined? Several groups of investigators have demonstrated that a relatively global judgment of chronicity may be sufficient (Mondimore et al., 2006; Stewart, McGrath, & Quitkin, 2002). For example, Mondimore et al. (2006) used a three-point scale to assess course: remitting (good remissions, substantially longer than episodes); frequent/brief (<3 weeks) episodes without prolonged remissions; and double or chronic depression (frequent mood symptoms most or all of the time). Applying this definition to a large sample of depressed patients and their depressed relatives, Mondimore et al. found strong evidence for the familial aggregation of chronic depression. Moreover, in a follow-up paper, these investigators compared their global rating of chronicity to the *DSM* categories of Dysthymic Disorder and chronic Major Depression, and found that the global rating resulted in stronger evidence for familial aggregation than the *DSM* categories (Mondimore et al., in press).

Relationship to Depressive Personality Disorder

As noted earlier, one of the precursors of the construct of Dysthymic Disorder was Depressive Personality. Indeed, the *DSM-III* suggested that they were equivalent constructs. However, there appear to be important differences between these two diagnoses, at least as they are currently formulated. As previously discussed, the *DSM-IV* criteria for Dysthymic Disorder require a persistent depressed mood and include several vegetative symptoms in the list of associated symptoms. In contrast, Depressive Personality is defined in terms of personality traits, often of a cognitive nature, and does not require a persistent depressed mood. As a result, the concordance between the two diagnoses is actually surprisingly modest. Fewer than one-half of individuals with Dysthymic Disorder meet criteria for Depressive Personality, and fewer than one-half of individuals with Depressive Personality Disorder meet criteria for Dysthymic Disorder (see Klein & Bessaha, in press). In addition, there is evidence for the incremental validity of a diagnosis of Depressive Personality over and above that of Dysthymic Disorder in predicting the course of depression, as patients with both diagnoses exhibit a slower rate of improvement over time than patients with Dysthymic Disorder alone (Laptook, Klein, & Dougherty, 2006). In light of the uncertain relationship between these constructs, Depressive Personality Disorder was included in the *DSM-IV* Appendix as a category requiring further study.

Nonetheless, Dysthymic Disorder and Depressive Personality Disorder are related, and family and follow-up study data suggest that it is reasonable to view depressive personality as part of a spectrum of chronic depressive conditions. Thus, the relatives of patients with chronic depressions have higher levels of depressive personality traits than relatives of patients with nonchronic depressions and the relatives of healthy controls (Klein, 1999; Klein, Clark et al., 1988). In addition, persons with Depressive Personality are at increased risk for developing Dysthymic Disorder (but not Major Depressive Disorder) over time (Kwon et al., 2000).

SUBTYPES

Chronic depression is probably heterogeneous, even if this heterogeneity is not adequately captured by the distinctions between the various *DSM-IV* chronic depression subtypes and course specifiers. Based on Akiskal's (1983) work, the *DSM-III* and subsequent editions have divided Dysthymic Disorder into early (< age 21) and late (≥ age 21) onset subtypes. Although it is unclear whether age 21 is the optimal cutoff point (or indeed whether age of onset is better conceptualized dimensionally), there is considerable support for this distinction. Thus, early-onset Dysthymic Disorder is associated with a higher familial loading for mood disorders, greater childhood adversity, increased comorbidity with Axis I and II disorders, and greater neuroendocrine dysregulation compared to late-onset Dysthymic Disorder (Devanand et al., 2004; Garyfallos et al., 1999; Klein, Taylor et al., 1988a; Klein, Schatzberg, McCullough, Keller, et al., 1999; Szádoöczky et al., 1994). In contrast, late-onset Dysthymic Disorder may be closely associated with stressful life events (Barzega, Maina, Venturello, & Bogetta, 2001; Devanand et al., 2004), particularly chronic stressors related to general medical disorders (Devanand et al.; Hays et al., 1997) or the illness or loss of loved ones (Dura, Stukenberg, & Kielcolt-Glaser, 1990). These data suggest that early- and late-onset Dysthymic Disorder may reflect at least two different etiological pathways. Interestingly, the early-late onset distinction may also be relevant for chronic Major Depressive Disorder. Klein, Schatzberg, McCullough, Dowling et al. (1999) reported that patients with early-onset chronic Major Depressive Disorder had a longer duration of the index episode, were more likely to have a history of recurrent episodes, and had greater Axis I and II comorbidity and a trend for a higher familial loading for mood disorders than patients with late-onset chronic major depression.

Akiskal (1983) also suggested that early-onset dysthymia could be further divided into subaffective and character spectrum subtypes. Akiskal et al. (1980) divided a group of patients with early-onset dysthymia according to their response to antidepressant medication. The medication-responsive group exhibited more melancholic and depressive personality features, fewer personality disorders, a lower rate of early object loss, a higher rate of mood disorders and a lower rate of alcoholism in relatives, and shortened rapid eye movement latencies, a sleep electrophysiological marker that characterizes many patients with Major Depressive Disorder. Based on these data, Akiskal (1983) proposed criteria for the subaffective type that included depressive personality traits and mild forms of melancholic symptoms, and defined the character spectrum group by the absence of these features. However, the few studies that have applied Akiskal's (1983) criteria for subaffective dysthymia have provided only limited support for this distinction (e.g., Anderson et al., 1996; Rihmer & Szádóczky, 1993).

More recently, however, there has been some suggestive support for Akiskal's (1983) general conceptualization, although not for his specific criteria. Dougherty, Klein, and Davila (2004) examined the role of chronic stress in the maintenance of early-onset Dysthymic Disorder. They found that patients with a greater familial loading for chronic depression were unaffected by chronic stress, whereas chronic stressors were closely associated with subsequent changes in depressive symptoms among patients with a history of early adversity. Moreover, in a large clinical trial for chronic depression, Nemeroff et al. (2003) reported that patients who had a history of early adversity had a significantly greater chance of remission in response to cognitive-behavioral psychotherapy than to pharmacotherapy, whereas patients without early adversity exhibited a trend for higher remission rates with pharmacotherapy than psychotherapy. Taken together, these data suggest that there may be several distinct developmental pathways in Dysthymic Disorder, one of which is characterized by a strong familial liability and the other by early adversity and increased sensitivity of behavioral and neurobiological stress response systems.

Pathogenesis and Maintenance

FAMILIAL AGGREGATION/GENETICS

Family studies are the first line of evidence in testing the role of genetic factors in a disorder. Unfortunately, twin and adoption studies of chronic depression have not been conducted, so it is impossible to go further and untangle genetic from environmental effects. Moreover, no genetic linkage or association studies of chronic depression have been published.

We are aware of four family studies of chronic depression (Goodman et al., 1994/1995; Klein et al., 1995; Klein, Shankman et al., 2004; Mondimore et al., 2006). These studies indicate that the first-degree relatives of probands with Dysthymic Disorder and chronic Major Depressive Disorder exhibit higher rates of both chronic and nonchronic depressive disorders than the relatives of healthy controls (Klein et al., 1995; Klein, Shankman et al., 2004). In addition, there is some specificity of familial transmission, as the first-degree relatives of probands with chronic depressions have higher rates of chronic depression than the relatives of probands with nonchronic Major Depressive Disorder (Goodman et al., 1994/1995; Klein et al., 1995; Klein, Shankman et al., 2004; Mondimore et al., 2006). However, some studies have reported that the relatives of probands with chronic depression also have a higher rate of nonchronic major depression than the relatives of probands with nonchronic depression (Klein, Shankman et al., 2004). There is no evidence of differences in familial aggregation between dysthymia/double depression and chronic major depression (Klein, Shankman et al.). Finally, the familial transmission of chronic depression appears to be greatest in probands with an early onset (Mondimore et al., 2006).

These studies suggest several alternative models of the relationship between chronic and nonchronic depressions: (a) chronic depression is qualitatively similar to, but more severe than, nonchronic major depression with respect to familial liability; (b) chronic depression is associated with a qualitatively distinct familial liability; and (c) chronic depression is associated with both a general familial liability for mood disorder as well as a more specific familial liability to chronic depression. Unfortunately, the data are insufficient to choose between these models at the present time.

NEUROBIOLOGY

Given the voluminous and rapidly growing literature on the neurobiology of mood disorders, research on the biological correlates of chronic depression is surprisingly sparse (see Riso, Miyatake, & Thase, 2002 for a review). Moreover, the research that has been done tends to be relatively unsystematic and has yielded inconclusive results. In this section we briefly review the current literature on chronic depression in the areas of neuroendocrinology, neurotransmission, sleep electrophysiology, and neuroimaging.

Neuroendocrinology

There has been extensive documentation of neuroendocrine dysregulation in the major mood disorders, particularly involving the hypothalamic-pituitary-adrenal (HPA) axis (Thase & Howland, 2002). However, the evidence for HPA-axis abnormalities in chronic depression is weaker. For example, a common index of HPA-axis dysregulation is failure to suppress the production of cortisol after ingestion of the synthetic corticosteriod dexamethasone (referred to as the dexamethasone suppression test, or DST, Carroll et al., 1981). Patients with dysthymia, double depression, and/or chronic major depression tend to have rates of DST nonsuppression that are lower than those in depressed comparison groups (Gastó et al., 1994; Ravindran, Bialik, & Lapierre, 1994; Szádóczky et al., 1994), and similar to healthy controls (Roy, Sutton, & Pickar, 1985; Watson et al., 2002). Studies examining other hormones, such as thyrotropin-releasing hormone and growth hormone, have also failed to reveal consistent abnormalities in chronic depression (Riso et al., 2002). However, several recent studies have reported differences using more sensitive measures of HPA-axis dysfunction. Watson et al. (2002) found that persons with chronic major depression exhibited a marginally increased rate of cortisol nonsuppression on the more sensitive dexamethasone/corticotrophin-releasing hormone test. Subsequently, Watson et al. (2006) argued that if chronic depression is associated with chronically elevated glucocorticoid levels, then arginine vasopressin (AVP) may play a greater role in regulating the HPA axis. In support of this hypothesis, they reported that patients with chronic depression exhibited significantly higher levels of post-DST AVP than normal controls. Hence, further work is needed to elucidate the role of the HPA axis in chronic depression, and delineate differences between chronic and nonchronic depressions in HPA system regulation.

Neurotransmission

Numerous lines of research have implicated the monoamine neurotransmitters serotonin, norepinephrine, and possibly dopamine in the pathophysiology of the mood disorders (Thase & Howland, 2002). However, research on neurotransmitter function in chronic mood disorders has been extremely limited. In general, peripheral measures of norepinephrine have not distinguished patients with dysthymia and double depression from patients with nonchronic major depression and healthy controls (Ravindram, Griffiths, Merali, & Anisman, 1996; Roy, Pickar, Douillet, Karoum, & Linnoila, 1986). Similarly, there has not been consistent evidence of serotonergic dysfunction in chronic depression (Riso et al., 2002).

Sleep Electrophysiology

A number of abnormalities in sleep electrophysiology have been documented in the major mood disorders, including reduced rapid eye movement (REM) latency, increased REM density, and reduced slow wave sleep (Thase & Howland, 2002). A handful of studies and published abstracts have compared patients with chronic depression to those with nonchronic depression and/or healthy controls on polysomnographic measures (Riso et al., 2002). The results, unfortunately, have been inconsistent. Some studies have reported that patients with dysthymia and double depression exhibit REM latencies that are similar to or even shorter than those in depressed controls (e.g., Akiskal et al., 1984; Arriaga, Cavaglia, Matos-Pires, Lara, & Paiva, 1995), while others have found few differences from healthy controls (e.g., Arriaga, Rosado, & Paiva, 1990).

NEUROIMAGING

Structural and functional neuroimaging studies have identified possible abnormalities in a number of brain regions in patients with major mood disorders, including the dorsolateral and orbital prefrontal cortex, anterior cingulate cortex, amygdala, and hippocampus (Davidson, Pizzagalli, Nitschke, & Putnam, 2002). However, there have been very few neuroimaging studies of chronic depression. Shah and colleagues (Shah, Ebmeier, Glabus, & Goodwin, 1998; Shah, Glabus, Goodwin, & Ebmeier, 2002) reported that patients with chronic Major Depression exhibited right frontal-striatal atrophy and reduced grey matter density in the left temporal cortex, including the hippocampus, compared to patients who had recovered from a major depressive episode and healthy controls. Lyoo et al. (2002) reported structural differences in the frontal region, as women with early-onset dysthymia or depressive personality exhibited significantly smaller genu of the corpus callosum compared to healthy controls. Hence, there is suggestive evidence that patients with chronic depression exhibit structural abnormalities in some of the same regions as patients with mood disorders more generally. We are unaware, however, of any functional brain imaging studies with chronically depressed patients.

EARLY ADVERSITY

Childhood early adversity, including emotional abuse and neglect, physical abuse and neglect, sexual abuse, and maladaptive parenting, appears to play an important role in chronic depression. A number of prospective longitudinal studies (e.g., Lara, Klein, & Kasch, 2000; Zlotnick, Warshaw, Meredith, Shea, & Keller, 1997) have reported that various forms of early adversity predict a poorer course and outcome of depression. Moreover, Brown and colleagues found that early adversity predicted the subsequent development of chronic (duration > 1 year) depression in both clinical

(Brown, Harris, Hepworth, & Robinson, 1994) and community (Brown & Moran, 1994) samples. Finally, several studies have found that patients with Dysthymic Disorder and double depression report greater childhood adversity than patients with nonchronic Major Depression and healthy controls (Alnaes & Torgerson, 1989; Lizardi et al., 1995).

There are a number of issues to consider in evaluating the role of early adversity in chronic depression. First, the literature is based on retrospective assessments of childhood events conducted many years later. This raises concerns about recall biases, as depressed mood tends to increase the accessibility of negative memories and persons with depression may magnify past adversities in an effort to understand and explain their condition. However, several lines of evidence suggest that retrospective assessments of childhood adversity are at least moderately valid. A number of studies have found that depressed patients' reports of childhood adversity are stable despite clinically significant changes in mood state (e.g., Lizardi & Klein, 2005). In addition, retrospective reports of early adversity have relatively high test-retest reliability over periods of 10 to 20 years (Lizardi & Klein; Wilhelm, Niven, Parker, & Hadzi-Pavlovic, 2005). Finally, there is at least moderate agreement between family members regarding retrospective reports of childhood adversity (Bifulco, Brown, & Lillie, 1997).

Second, childhood adversity is probably not specific to chronic depression, because it is also a risk factor for many other Axis I and II disorders. Indeed, this may help to explain why there is such high comorbidity between chronic depression and other forms of psychopathology. Importantly, however, comorbidity cannot account for the association between adversity and chronic depression, as the association remains after controlling for other disorders (Lizardi et al., 1995).

Third, it is unclear whether chronic depression is more closely associated with some forms of early adversity than others. Unfortunately, this is difficult to determine, as most forms of early adversity tend to be highly correlated with one another (Klein, 2006). Harkness and Wildes (2002) recently examined the specificity of the associations between early adversity, dysthymia, anxiety disorders, and major depression in a sample of women with Major Depressive Disorder. They found that physical abuse was specifically associated with double depression; parental indifference and apathy were associated with the combination of double depression and anxiety disorders; and sexual and psychological abuse were associated with the combination of nonchronic Major Depression and anxiety disorders.

Fourth, early adversity may be associated with chronic depression without necessarily having a causal influence. The link could be due to a third variable, such as particular genes that predispose both to maladaptive parenting (perhaps via parental depression) and to chronic depression in offspring. Importantly, childhood adversity is significantly related to chronic depression even after controlling for the parental psychopathology (Lizardi & Klein, 2000). Nonetheless, further work is needed to establish a causal relationship between early adversity and chronic depression.

A final issue concerns how distal events occurring many years earlier can have persisting effects on the course of adult depression. Some possible pathways include childhood adversity influencing the development of maladaptive interpersonal styles (Brown et al., 1994) and depressogenic cognitive schemas (Gibb, 2002), and persisting abnormalities in neurobiological stress response systems (Heim et al., 2000), all of which may increase risk for chronic depression.

NEURODEVELOPMENTAL FACTORS

There has been very little research on the role of neurodevelopmental factors in the pathogenesis of chronic depression. However, a few studies have suggested that patients with chronic depression have higher rates of birth-related problems, significant medical conditions or disabilities in infancy, and poorer premorbid social functioning than patients with nonchronic Major Depression (Klein, Taylor, Dickstein, & Harding, 1988b; Vocisano et al., 1996).

PERSONALITY/TEMPERAMENT

Some theorists have viewed the depressive personality (discussed previously) as a temperamental substrate for mood disorders (Akiskal, 1983; Kraepelin, 1921). However, it is more likely that it represents a socially and cognitively mediated elaboration of more fundamental temperamental processes. Most models of child temperament and adult personality include the higher-order dimensions of positive emotionality (PE) and negative emotionality (NE). Positive emotionality, which is similar to extroversion, encompasses features like exuberance, engagement with the environment, and sociability. Negative emotionality, which is analogous to neuroticism, reflects sensitivity to negative stimuli resulting in a range of negative moods, such as sadness, fear, anxiety, and anger. Watson and Clark (1995) have hypothesized that low PE and high NE form the core of the depressive temperament and predispose to depressive disorders.

Positive and negative emotionality may play a particularly important role in chronic depression. A number of studies have reported that, in samples of individuals with Major Depressive Disorder, higher NE predicts a poorer course and outcome (Klein, Durbin, Shankman, & Santiago, 2002). In addition, patients with dysthymia and double depression report higher levels of NE and lower levels of PE than patients with nonchronic major depression and healthy controls, although the differences have not always reached statistical significance (Angst, 1998; Hirschfeld, 1990; Klein Taylor et al., 1988b; McCullough et al., 1994). A problem in interpreting these data is that the depressed state influences assessments of personality. Hence, it noteworthy that Hirschfeld (1990) found that individuals who had recovered from dysthymia exhibited significantly greater NE and significantly less PE than individuals who had recovered from major depression, as well as individuals with no history of psychopathology.

While finding differences after recovery is important in ruling out the confound of clinical state, they cannot exclude the possibility that the experience of depression alters personality ("scar" effects). Two lines of evidence suggest that low PE and high NE may also be evident prior to the development of chronic depression. First, in laboratory observations, preschool-aged children of depressed mothers exhibit significantly lower levels of PE and higher levels of some forms of NE, compared to children of nondepressed mothers (Durbin et al., 2005). Moreover, child PE was negatively associated with the chronicity of maternal depression.

Second, several longitudinal studies of large birth cohorts of children have reported evidence suggesting that low PE and high NE may predict the subsequent development of chronic depression. Based on examiner's ratings of the laboratory behavior of a large sample of 3-year-olds in New Zealand, Caspi, Moffitt, Newman, and Silva (1996) identified a cluster of "inhibited" children who were characterized by a combination of low PE and high NE behaviors, including sluggishness, low approach, social reticence, and fearfulness. Children in this cluster had elevated rates of interview-assessed depressive disorders and suicide attempts (but not anxiety disorders, alcoholism, or antisocial behavior) at age 21. As these children had also exhibited significantly higher levels of parent-rated internalizing behavior problems at ages 13 and 15 (Caspi, 2000), it is likely that many had depressions that persisted since adolescence. Finally, in a large British birth cohort, Van Os, Jones, Lewis, Wadsworth, and Murray (1997) found that physicians' ratings of behavioral apathy, an indicator of low PE, during childhood predicted chronic depression in middle age.

COGNITIVE FACTORS

Given the central role of cognitive theories in depression (Christensen, Carney, & Segal, 2006), there has been surprisingly little research on the role of cognitive variables in chronic depression. A number of studies have indicated that cognitive variables such as dysfunctional attitudes, depressive attributions, a ruminative response style, and overly general autobiographical memory are associated with a poorer course of depression (e.g., Iacoviello, Alloy, Abramson, Whitehouse, & Hogan, 2006; Peeters, Wessel, Merckelbach, & Boon-Vermeeren, 2002). However, few studies have directly examined cognitive variables in chronic depression. McCullough et al. (1994) found that a nonclinical sample with dysthymia and double depression exhibited more stable and global attributions for negative events and less stable attributions for positive events than healthy controls. Similarly, Riso et al. (2003) reported that patients with chronic depression exhibited more stable and global attributions for negative events, a higher level of dysfunctional attitudes, a more ruminative response style, and higher scores on a measure of maladaptive schemas and core beliefs than healthy controls. Comparisons between patients with chronic and nonchronic depressions have yielded inconsistent results for dysfunctional attitudes (Klein, Taylor et al., 1988b; Miller, Norman, & Dow, 1986; Riso et al., 2003), and the two groups have not differed on attributional and ruminative response styles (Klein, Taylor et al., 1988b; Riso et al., 2003). However, patients with dysthymic disorder and double depression report higher levels of self-criticism (Klein, Taylor et al., 1988b) and maladaptive schemas (Riso et al., 2003) than patients with nonchronic major depression.

Few prospective studies have been conducted in order to determine whether cognitive variables precede the development of chronicity, they are a consequence of persistent depression, cognitive variables and depression have reciprocal effects on one another, or both depressive cognitions and symptoms are caused by a third variable. In one of the few studies that have addressed this issue, Arnow, Spangler, Klein, & Burns (2004) modeled the associations between rumination, distraction, and depressive symptomatology over the course of 12 weeks in a large sample of patients with double depression and chronic major depression. A model positing that depression and rumination are both caused by the same factors provided a better fit to the data than models positing that rumination causes subsequent depression or that depression causes subsequent rumination.

Studies of cognitive factors in chronic depression have all relied on self-report measures of cognitions. As a result, little is known about the role of more automatic and implicit processes in chronic depression, such as the attentional and memory biases that have been associated with depression in general (Christensen et al., 2006).

INTERPERSONAL FACTORS

Coyne (1976) proposed that interpersonal difficulties play an important role in maintaining and prolonging depressive episodes. According to Coyne, the depressed individual has a negative impact on others, particularly family members and friends, by excessively seeking assurances of love and support. These demands eventually become aversive and begin to erode relationships. The depressed individual perceives that the support he or she is receiving is diminishing and thus escalates his or her demands on others, resulting in a vicious cycle. Joiner (2000) has extended this model by describing a variety of self-propagating processes that might serve to maintain depression, including stress generation, negative feedback-seeking, excessive reassurance-seeking, conflict avoidance, and blame maintenance.

Numerous studies have found that low social support, conflicted family and marital relationships, and interpersonal difficulties are associated with a poorer course and outcome of depression (Lara & Klein, 1999). Several cross-sectional studies have reported that chronic depression is associated with poorer interpersonal relationships. McCullough et al. (1994) found that individuals with dysthymia and double depression reported having more submissive and hostile interpersonal styles, less social support, and greater family dysfunction than healthy controls. Klein, Taylor et al. (1988b) and Hays et al. (1997) found that patients with chronic depression reported having less social support than patients with nonchronic depression. In addition, Brown and colleagues found that interpersonal difficulties predicted subsequent chronic depression in two prospective studies in clinical (Brown, Harris, & Hepworth, 1994) and community (Brown & Moran, 1994) samples.

Individuals with Dysthymic Disorder continue to experience greater interpersonal difficulties after recovery than individuals who have recovered from Major Depressive Disorder and never mentally ill controls (Klein, Lewinsohn, & Seeley, 1997). This is important, because it suggests that these deficits are not simply due to the depressed state. However, longitudinal studies are required to untangle the direction of the association between chronic depression and dysfunctional interpersonal relationships. As Coyne and Joiner have suggested, it is unlikely that the influences are simple and unidirectional. Rather, depression and maladaptive interpersonal processes probably have reciprocal effects, with each perpetuating the other.

CHRONIC STRESS

Although depressive episodes are frequently preceded by stressful life events (Monroe & Hadjiyannakis, 2002), chronic and nonchronic depressions do not appear to differ in this respect (Klein, Taylor et al., 1988b; Moerk & Klein, 2000; Ravindran et al., 1995). However, chronic depression is associated with a higher level of chronic stress and daily hassles than nonchronic depression (Klein, Taylor et al., 1988; Ravindran et al., 1995).

The direction of this relationship is difficult to determine: chronic stress may cause or maintain depression, but chronic depression can also create long-term difficulties. Determining the direction of these effects is particularly challenging because it is often difficult to date the onsets of both chronic depression and chronic stressors in order to establish the temporal sequence. However, there is some evidence that chronic stress may play a causal role in the onset or maintenance of chronic depression.

In a multiwave longitudinal study of dysthymia and double depression, Dougherty et al. (2004) found that after controlling for prior level of depression, chronic stress predicted the subsequent level of depression at each follow-up assessment. In contrast, depressive symptoms did not predict subsequent chronic stress. It also appears that chronic depression can develop in the face of an incapacitating medical illness or the chronic illness of a loved one. Dura et al. (1990) found that there was a significantly higher rate of dysthymia in spouses caring for partners with dementia than in noncaregiving controls. Importantly, the groups did not differ on personal or family history of depression prior to caregiving.

While chronic stress appears to maintain depression, Brown, Adler, and Bifulco (1988) reported that a reduction in ongoing difficulties was associated with recovery from chronic (duration ≥ 1 year) depression. In addition, Brown et al. (1988) found that life events that reduced or neutralized an ongoing difficulty and "fresh-start" events (events that signal hope and offer an opportunity to start over), also predicted recovery from chronic depression.

Course and Prognosis

There are only a few longitudinal studies of the naturalistic course of chronic depression. *Naturalistic* refers to the fact that the investigators did not attempt to influence treatment. Thus, patients in these studies varied widely with respect to the type and duration of treatment received, and many did not receive any treatment for substantial portions of the study period.

Most follow-up studies of Dysthymic Disorder and double depression have been no longer than 2 years in duration, which is relatively brief for a chronic illness (e.g., Agosti, 1999; Keller et al., 1983; McCullough et al., 1988). However, Klein et al. (2006) recently reported a 10-year study of Dysthymic Disorder and double depression that included four follow-up assessments at 30-month intervals. Using survival analysis, the estimated 10-year recovery rate for dysthymia was 74%, with a median time to recovery of 52 months. Of patients who recovered, the estimated risk of relapse into another episode of chronic depression was 71%. Six percent of patients developed manic or hypomanic episodes, and 84% experienced superimposed major depressive episodes during the course of the follow-up.

These investigators used mixed-effects growth curve models to examine baseline predictors of the course trajectories and estimated level of depressive symptoms at 10-year outcome (Klein, Shankman, & Rose, in press). Concurrent anxiety disorder, a greater familial loading of chronic depression in first-degree relatives, a history of a poorer maternal relationship in childhood, and a history of childhood sexual abuse predicted higher levels of depressive symptoms 10 years later; the presence of comorbid personality predicted a slower rate of improvement over time. As previously noted, an earlier report from this sample reported that chronic stress also played a role in the maintenance of Dysthymic Disorder, albeit only for patients with a history of early adversity and those with a lower familial loading for chronic depression (Dougherty et al., 2004).

There are even fewer prospective data on the course of chronic Major Depressive Disorder. However, Mueller et al. (1996) described the 10-year course and outcome of a small group of patients with major depressive episodes who had not remitted during the first 5 years of prospective follow-up. Only 38% of these patients recovered in years 6 through 10 of follow-up. Failure to recover was associated with never having been married and a longer duration of depression prior to entry into the study.

Chronic Depression in Youth and the Elderly

Chronic depression can be evident throughout the life span, including childhood, adolescence, and old age. Most of the literature on chronic depression in youth and the elderly is limited to Dysthymic Disorder and double depression, hence that will be the focus in this section.

CHRONIC DEPRESSION IN CHILDREN AND ADOLESCENTS

The *DSM-IV* criteria for Dysthymic Disorder are modified when applied to children and adolescents. The minimum duration is 1 year instead of 2, and irritable mood can substitute for depressed mood. The point prevalence of Dysthymic Disorder appears to be just over 0.1% in children (Costello et al., 1996), and approximately 0.5% in adolescents, with a lifetime prevalence of 3% by late adolescence (Lewinsohn et al., 1993). As in adults with Dysthymic Disorder, cognitive and affective symptoms are more common than vegetative/somatic symptoms (Kovacs, Akiskal, Gatsonis, & Parrone, 1994; Masi et al., 2003). Most children and adolescents with Dysthymic Disorder eventually experience superimposed major depressive episodes. For example, in a long-term follow-up study of children with dysthymia, Kovacs et al. (1994) estimated that the risk for developing a first lifetime major depressive episode was 81%. Comorbid nonmood disorders, particularly anxiety disorders, Attention Deficit Hyperactivity Disorder, and oppositional and conduct disorders, are also common, and are evident in over 50% of cases (Kovacs & Devlin, 1998).

In children and adolescents, the onset of Dysthymic Disorder is generally earlier than that of Major Depressive Disorder (Goodman et al., 2000; Kovacs et al., 1994; Lewinsohn, Rohde, Seeley, & Hops, 1991). Youth with dysthymia and Major Depressive Disorder tend to exhibit similar depressive symptoms (Ferro, Carlson, Greyson, & Klein, 1994; Flament, Cohen, Choquet, Jeammet, & Ledoux, 2002). Levels of impairment are also similar, and children and adolescents with double depression exhibit greater impairment than those with Dysthymic Disorder or major depression alone (Goodman et al., 2000). Studies comparing rates of comorbidity between Dysthymic Disorder and Major Depressive Disorder have yielded inconsistent findings (Ferro et al., 1994; Flament et al., 2002; Goodman et al., 2000; Kovacs et al., 1984). Similar to the findings from retrospective studies of adults, children and adolescents with Dysthymic Disorder experience greater familial dysfunction and parental maltreatment than youths with Major Depressive Disorder (Flament et al., 2002; Goodman et al., 2000).

The naturalistic course of Dysthymic Disorder in children and adolescents is generally similar to adults. In a 9-year longitudinal study of 8–13-year-old outpatients with Dysthymic Disorder, almost all of the children eventually recovered, although the median duration of the episode was about 4 years (Kovacs et al., 1994). However, the risk for developing Bipolar Disorder appears to be greater in children than adults. Kovacs et al. (1994) reported that there was a 21% risk for developing manic or hypomanic episodes in their sample of children with Dysthymic Disorder.

CHRONIC DEPRESSION IN THE ELDERLY

The prevalence of Dysthymic Disorder in community samples of individuals over the age of 65 has been estimated to be between 2% and 6% (Beekman et al., 2004). Differences between elderly and nonelderly individuals with Dysthymic Disorder mirror those between early- and late-onset dysthymia, which is not surprising, given that the majority of the elderly with dysthymia have an adult onset (Devanand et al., 1994; Kirby, Bruce, Coakley, & Lawlor, 1999). Thus, older individuals with Dysthymic Disorder exhibit lower rates of Axis I and II comorbidity and higher rates of recent life events and more concomitant general medical conditions than younger persons with dysthymia (Beekman et al., 2004; Bellino, Patria, Ziero, Rocca, & Bogetto, 2001; Devanand et al., 1994; Kirby et al., 1999). When elderly individuals with Dysthymic Disorder and Major Depressive Disorder are compared, most depressive symptoms are similar, but the age of onset of depression is earlier among those with dysthymia (Beekman et al., 2004).

In follow-up studies ranging from 15 months to 6 years, 12%–38% of elderly individuals with dysthymia recover (Beekman et al., 2004; Kivelä, Pahkala, & Laippala, 1991). Predictors of a poorer course of dysthymia in the aged include greater severity of depressive symptoms, social isolation/low social support, and poor self-reported health (Kivelä et al., 1991).

Assessment

The assessment and diagnosis of chronic depressive disorders can be challenging and requires considerable clinical skill. Clinicians often overlook the presence of chronic depression and focus on a superimposed acute major depressive episode or comorbid nonaffective Axis I or II conditions (Markowitz et al., 1992). Many chronically depressed patients, especially those with an early-onset, consider dysphoria to be "normal" or a part of their "usual self," and therefore fail to report it to clinicians or consider that it may be an appropriate target for treatment (Akiskal, 1983). Residual depressive symptoms are often overlooked as patients and clinicians focus on the improvement from an acute major depressive episode. Finally, it can be difficult to distinguish between the various forms of chronic depression in the *DSM-IV*. These differential diagnoses require a very careful and detailed history of the onset and changes in the severity of depressive symptoms over the course of the disorder.

In order to assess and diagnose chronic depressive disorders, clinicians must take a careful history of the patient's past course of depression. If the patient has a history of nonchronic major depressive episodes, it is critical to explore the presence of milder depression before and after the major episodes. It is often helpful to construct a life-chart or timeline with the patient that graphs his or her level of depression over time (McCullough et al., 1996). It is also critical to explain to the patient that depression can exist at varying levels of severity, and that it is important to describe both the milder and more severe periods. Unfortunately, these procedures have not been incorporated into the standard versions of widely used diagnostic instruments.

Most fully structured (or respondent-based) interviews (e.g., the Diagnostic Interview Schedule and the Composite International Diagnostic Interview) and semistructured (or interviewer-based) interviews (e.g., the Structured Clinical Interview for *DSM-IV* [SCID]) include a section assessing Dysthymic Disorder. However, these interviews generally only assess current Dysthymic Disorder, and they fail to collect information on a past history of dysthymia. Thus, epidemiological data on the prevalence of lifetime psychopathology probably underestimate the rate of Dythymic Disorder, particularly in comparison to other disorders that are assessed on a lifetime basis.

Fully structured diagnostic interviews collect only limited information about onset, course, and interepisode symptomatology. Hence, it is often difficult to distinguish between chronic and nonchronic depressions, and virtually impossible to make the subtle distinctions between the various forms of chronic depression. Semistructured diagnostic interviews allow greater flexibility to obtain data on course. However, it is almost always necessary to go beyond the standard interview probes in order to obtain sufficient information to distinguish between chronic and recurrent nonchronic depressions and between the various forms of chronic depression.

It is also important to be aware that diagnostic interviews vary in their conventions about how and when to assess chronic depression, and that these conventions may not reflect the *DSM* criteria. For example, the *DSM-III-R* version of the SCID (Spitzer, Williams, Gibbon, & First, 1990) instructed interviewers to skip out of dysthymia if there had been a major depressive syndrome present for more than 50% of the past 2 years. This instruction was dropped from the *DSM-IV* version; however the *DSM-IV* SCID *User's Guide* (First, Gibbon, Spitzer, & Williams, 1996) instructs individual investigators to establish their own study-specific conventions regarding when the Dysthymic Disorder section should be skipped (e.g., if there has been a major depressive episode in the past year; if there have been recurrent major depressive episodes in the past year). These conventions simplify and shorten the administration of the interview. However, they are not empirically justified, undoubtedly result in missing many cases of double depression, and create problems in comparing findings across studies.

Most widely used depression rating scales and self-report inventories are limited to assessing the severity of depressive symptoms during a particular time period, and do not collect the information on course necessary to make diagnoses of the various forms of chronic depression. However, these measures may be useful in assessing symptom severity and monitoring treatment response. Nonetheless, many widely used depression rating scales have limitations when applied to chronic depressive conditions (Gwirtsman et al., 1997). For example, the widely used 17- and 21-item versions of the Hamilton Rating Scale for Depression (HAM-D) do not assess many of the most common symptoms of Dysthymic Disorder (e.g., cognitive symptoms; Keller et al., 1995). Hence, it is advisable to use modified versions of the HAM-D (e.g., Miller et al., 1985) or other rating scales (e.g., the clinician-rated Inventory of Depressive Symptomatology; Rush et al., 2003) that include cognitive symptoms (helplessness, hopelessness, and worthlessness) and reversed vegetative features. In addition, the HAM-D rates patients' symptoms on the basis of a difference from their normal or usual behavior. However, for patients with early-onset chronic depressions, their normal or usual state may be depressed. Hence, symptoms may be overlooked if questions are phrased in terms of change or worsening from the usual state. In order to address these problems, Mason et al. (1995) developed the Cornell Dysthymia Rating Scale, which has greater content validity, a broader range of symptom severity, and greater sensitivity to change than the HAM-D (Hellerstein, Batchelder, Lee, & Borisovskaya, 2002).

The General Behavior Inventory (GBI) (Depue, Krauss, Spoont, & Arbisi, 1989) is the only self-report measure that was explicitly developed to screen for chronic mood disorders. It assesses symptoms on a trait basis, rather than during a recent, discrete time period. The GBI has good psychometric properties and exhibits relatively good concordance with semistructured interview-based diagnoses in community and clinical samples and in adolescents and adults (Depue et al., 1989; Danielson, Youngstrom, Findling, & Calabrese, 2003; Klein et al., 1989). Other self-report inventories, such the Beck Depression Inventory-II (Beck, Steer, & Brown, 1996) and the self-report version of the IDS (Rush et al., 2003) are useful in assessing symptom severity and monitoring change. Finally, the Longitudinal Interview Follow-up Examination (LIFE; Keller et al., 1987) is a semistructured interview that can be useful in assessing the longitudinal course of acute and chronic depressive disorders in follow-up and treatment studies.

ACUTE-PHASE PHARMACOTHERAPY

Randomized, placebo-controlled clinical trials have indicated that most antidepressant medications are efficacious in the acute-phase treatment of chronic depression. While most studies have focused on patients with double depression and chronic major depression, antidepressants are also efficacious in patients with "pure" dysthymia (Thase et al., 1996).

Antidepressants in the tricyclic, selective serotonin reuptake inhibitor, and atypical antidepressant classes appear to have similar efficacy for chronic depression, and all have been demonstrated to be superior to placebo (DeLima, Hotoph, & Wessely, 1999; Kocsis, 2003). Despite these encouraging results, however, 40%–50% of patients do not respond to a trial of antidepressant medication, and only about 25%–30% achieve full remission. One problem is that patients with chronic depression appear to take longer to respond to medication. Therefore, it may be advisable to extend medication trials for longer than is customary in nonchronic major depression (Koran et al., 2001). In addition, it is common to have to switch or augment medications or add psychotherapy for patients who cannot tolerate, fail to respond, or respond only partially to a drug (see the following).

ACUTE-PHASE PSYCHOTHERAPY

There has been only limited research on the efficacy of psychotherapy for chronic depression, and many commonly used approaches, such as cognitive therapy and psychodynamic psychotherapy, have not been tested. The approach with the strongest empirical support is McCullough's (2000) Cognitive Behavioral Analysis System of Psychotherapy (CBASP). Cognitive behavioral analysis system of psychotherapy is one of the few approaches specifically designed to treat chronic depression. It is highly structured and uses behavioral and cognitive techniques to help patients to develop better interpersonal problem solving skills. In a large multisite clinical trial, 48% of patients with double depression, chronic major depression, or recurrent major depression with incomplete recovery between episodes responded after 12 weeks (16 sessions) of CBASP. This was identical to the 48% response rate for antidepressant medication (Keller et al., 2000). Patients in the pharmacotherapy condition responded more quickly, but CBASP caught up by the sixth week of treatment.

Interpersonal Psychotherapy (IPT; Klerman et al., 1984) has also been tested in several clinical trials. Interpersonal psychotherapy is a short-term therapy that focuses on current interpersonal problems such as grief, interpersonal conflicts, change in an important social role, and social isolation/skills deficits. Interpersonal psychotherapy has demonstrated efficacy for Acute Major Depression, and it was modified for use with Dysthymic Disorder by Markowitz (1998). The evidence for efficacy in symptom reduction in dysthymia has not been encouraging, although IPT may help reduce medical and social service costs and increase compliance with medication. In a 16-week study of patients with Dysthymic Disorder, Markowitz, Kocsis, Bleiberg, Chritos, and Sacks (2005) reported that antidepressant medication and medication plus IPT were superior to IPT alone and Brief Supportive Therapy alone. Browne et al. (2002) compared IPT, medication, and the combination of IPT plus medication in a large sample of patients with Dysthymic Disorder and double depression. Medication, both alone and in combination with IPT, was superior to IPT alone. However, it is important to note that the number and frequency of sessions of IPT in this study were unusually low. While the standard dose of IPT is 16 sessions over 16 weeks, Browne et al.'s patients averaged 10 sessions over the course of 6 months. At 2-year follow-up, patients in the IPT-alone group still had poorer outcomes. However the IPT-alone and combination groups had lower health and social services costs than the medication-alone group, resulting in combination treatment being the most cost-effective approach. In addition, IPT appeared to increase medication compliance, as patients in the combination group were less likely to discontinue medication than patients in the medication-alone condition.

Two studies have examined Problem-Solving Therapy for Primary Care (PST-PC) (Mynors-Wallis, Gath, Lloyd-Thomas, & Tomlinson, 1995) in patients with dysthymia in primary care settings. The intensity of psychotherapy was low, consisting of six sessions over the course of 12 weeks. One study focused on adults under the age of 60 (Barrett et al., 2001) and the other focused on adults 60 years and older (Williams et al., 2000). In the first study, pharmacotherapy was more effective than PST-PC, which was more effective than placebo. In the second study, with older adults, PST-PC did not differ significantly from either pharmacotherapy or placebo.

The limited data suggest that some forms of psychotherapy may be more effective for chronic depression than others, although head-to-head comparisons have not been conducted. In addition, a study that compared cognitive therapy in patients with chronic and nonchronic depressions suggested that chronic depression requires more frequent sessions (Thase et al., 1994). Hence, it is probably not surprising that studies that administered more intensive psychotherapy have yielded stronger evidence of efficacy than studies with less intensive psychotherapy.

Common factors that cut across specific forms of therapy, such as the therapeutic alliance, also play a significant role in fostering change in psychotherapy with chronically depressed patients (Klein et al., 2003). In a recent comparison of the effects of common and specific factors, Santiago et al. (2005) reported that they had additive effects in predicting outcome, with common factors accounting for somewhat more variance than specific factors.

On balance, it appears that antidepressant medication may be somewhat more efficacious than psychotherapy in treating chronic depression. However, some forms of psychotherapy, or psychotherapy administered with sufficient intensity, may be as effective as pharmacotherapy. Given the broad range of treatment options available, an important question is whether there are predictors of differential treatment response to help guide treatment selection. Unfortunately, few predictors of differential response to different medications or to pharmacotherapy versus psychotherapy have been identified. However, as noted earlier, Nemeroff et al. (2003) found that CBASP produced a significantly higher rate of remission than pharmacotherapy in the subgroup of chronically depressed patients with a history of childhood adversity. In contrast, patients without a history of childhood adversity exhibited a nonsignificantly higher remission rate in pharmacotherapy. These findings are potentially important, but require replication.

COMBINATION THERAPY

There is some evidence that the combination of at least some forms of psychotherapy with antidepressant medication may be superior to either approach alone for the treatment of chronic depression (Arnow & Constantino, 2003). For example, Keller et al. (2000) reported that 73% of patients with chronic depression responded to the combination of CBASP and nefazodone, compared to response rates of 48% to both CBASP alone and nefazodone alone. In addition, although studies of IPT plus medication have not revealed an advantage with respect to symptom reduction, combination treatment was associated with greater cost-effectiveness at 2-year follow-up (Browne et al., 2002). As combination treatment is more costly than monotherapy, though, there is a need to explore the efficacy of sequenced approaches in which patients initially receive a single treatment and additional treatments are added if the patient does not have a full response to the initial treatment.

TREATMENT OF NONRESPONDERS

As noted earlier, approximately half of patients fail to respond to an initial trial of treatment. However, recent studies of chronic depression indicate that failure to respond to one medication does not reduce the chance of responding to another medication in a different class (Thase et al., 2002). In addition, psychotherapy can be effective for many chronically depressed patients who fail to respond to pharmacotherapy, and pharmacotherapy is effective for many patients with chronic depression who fail to respond to psychotherapy (Schatzberg et al., 2005).

Unfortunately, there is a small group of chronically depressed patients who fail to respond to numerous trials of medication and psychotherapy. There are few data on how to best treat these highly treatment-resistant patients. The best established option is electroconvulsive therapy (ECT). Although response rates are lower for patients with a longer duration of illness, ECT is a reasonable choice for patients with established treatment resistance (Nobler & Sackeim, 2006). Several other neurostimulation techniques such as transcranial magnetic stimulation (TMS), vagal nerve stimulation (VNS), and deep brain stimulation (DBS) are currently under investigation. Initial findings for TMS and VNS have been equivocal, and few data on DBS are available (George et al., 2006; Nobler & Sackeim, 2006).

CONTINUATION AND MAINTENANCE TREATMENT

Due to the high risk of relapse and recurrence (Klein et al., 2006), continuation and maintenance pharmacotherapy is an important consideration for patients with chronic depression. The continuation phase consists of the first 4 to 6 months of treatment after recovery; the maintenance phase consists of treatment after that point. Several double-blind placebo-discontinuation studies have demonstrated that continuation (Koran et al., 2001) and maintenance (Keller et al., 1998; Kocsis et al., 1996) treatment of patients who have recovered from chronic depression are associated with a significantly lower risk of recurrence than placebo. There are fewer studies of the efficacy of psychotherapy in preventing relapse and recurrence in chronic depression. However, Klein, Santiago et al. (2004) reported that CBASP appears to be effective as a maintenance phase treatment. Chronically depressed patients who responded to 12 weeks of acute phase treatment and 16 weeks of continuation treatment were randomly assigned to continue to receive either one session of CBASP per month or assessment-only for 12 months. Patients who received maintenance CBASP had a significantly lower risk of recurrence than patients who were assigned to the assessment-only condition.

PREVENTION

The topic of prevention raises important questions about how chronic depression should be conceptualized. If chronic depressions are prolonged versions of nonchronic depressions, then preventive efforts should focus on the effective treatment of acute depression. On the other hand, if chronic depression is a distinct form of depression, then the appropriate target is the prevention of the onset of the initial episode. There may be some validity to both perspectives. Untreated, poorly treated, and difficult-to-treat depressions can become chronic, hence more aggressive public education and treatment may have important preventive effects. On the other hand, as discussed earlier, chronic and nonchronic depressions are distinguished by a number of factors that are evident prior to onset (e.g., family history of chronic depression, early adversity, particular temperamental features). From this perspective, it is important to identify young children with these risk factors and target them for preventive interventions.

Summary and Future Directions

Only within the past several decades has it been widely recognized that depressive disorders often exhibit a chronic course. Indeed, chronic depressions account for one third to one half of cases of mood disorders in clinical settings. The *DSM-IV* includes a number of forms of chronic depression, including Dysthymic Disorder and chronic major depression. The existing literature suggests that these various forms of chronic depression are more alike than different, and may represent variants or different phases of the same underlying disorder. For example, almost all patients with Dysthymic Disorder eventually experience superimposed major depressive episodes; patients with Dysthymic Disorder frequently have recurrences that are manifested as other forms of chronic depression; and few differences have been identified when different groups of chronic depressives are compared on clinical features, comorbidity, psychosocial functioning, family history, and treatment response.

In contrast, chronic depression differs from nonchronic depression in a number of important respects. Chronic depression aggregates specifically within families. Persons with chronic depression are more likely to have a history of early adversity, exhibit higher rates of Axis I and Axis II comorbidity, and report higher levels of NE and lower levels of PE than individuals with nonchronic major depression. In addition, chronic depression is associated with higher levels of suicidality, at least some forms of depressotypic cognitions, interpersonal dysfunction, and chronic stress. Finally, the distinction between chronic and nonchronic depression is stable over time. Taken together, these data suggest that the chronic-nonchronic distinction is an important source of heterogeneity in nonbipolar depression that should be considered in both clinical practice and research.

Despite the lack of meaningful differences between the various forms of chronic depression in the *DSM-IV*, chronic depression is probably not a unitary condition. One important source of variation is age at onset. Early-onset chronic depression is associated with greater familial aggregation of mood disorders, greater childhood adversity, and more comorbidity. In contrast, major life events and poor physical health appears to play a greater role in late-onset chronic depression. In addition, there may be distinct family-genetic and early adversity-stress reactivity pathways within early-onset chronic depression.

Although the episodes can last for many years, most patients with chronic depression eventually recover. However, the risk of recurrence is high. Predictors of a poorer long-term course and outcome include a family history of chronic depression, childhood adversity, comorbid anxiety and personality disorders, and chronic stress.

Chronic depression is often challenging to treat due to the entrenched psychopathology, presence of comorbid disorders, longstanding interpersonal deficits, and chronic helplessness and hopelessness. In many instances, chronic depression has become partially ego-syntonic, and it has been integrated into the individual's self-image and daily routine (Markowitz, 1998). Nonetheless, approximately 50% of persons with chronic depression respond to an initial trial of antidepressant medication, and approximately 25% achieve full remission. In addition, nonresponders have close to a 50% chance of responding to a second pharmacological agent.

There are fewer and less consistent data on the efficacy of psychotherapy for chronic depression. However, there is evidence that some structured and intensive short-term psychotherapies, such as CBASP, are as effective as pharmacotherapy in treating chronic depression. Moreover, the combination of medication plus psychotherapy may be more effective than either monotherapy alone. Finally, there is evidence that maintenance pharmacotherapy and psychotherapy can prevent recurrences.

The existing research has implications for revising the diagnostic nomenclature in *DSM-V*. Findings indicate there are clinically and etiologically relevant differences between chronic and nonchronic depression, but few meaningful differences between the various forms of chronic depression in *DSM-IV*. This suggests that it may be possible to simplify the classification of depressive disorders by combining the various forms of chronic depression and introducing a distinction between chronic and episodic depression. As severity is clinically important for treatment planning and monitoring, these groups could be subdivided by severity, producing a four-fold classification consisting of moderate-severe chronic (double depression and chronic major depression), mild chronic (dysthymia), moderate-severe acute (episodic major depression), and mild acute (minor depression) depressive conditions.

There are a number of areas in which further research is needed. One of the challenges in conducting and interpreting research on chronic depression is that most assessment instruments are geared to nonchronic depression, and they are not well-suited to assess chronic forms of depression. For example, diagnostic interviews emphasize the assessment of depressive symptoms and generally fail to assess course with sufficient detail. In addition, the most frequently used rating scales do not include some of the most common symptoms in Dysthymic Disorder, and they rate symptoms in terms of change from normal, which is problematic when the patient's usual state is depressed. Investigators need to be more aware of these problems when designing and interpreting studies. Further work on instrument development is warranted.

In addition, research on the etiopathogenesis of Dysthymic Disorder and chronic major depression has been limited. Genetically informative studies have not been conducted to determine the relative impact of genetic and environmental factors, nor have genetic linkage and association studies been reported. Another potentially important area for future research is gene by environment interactions. However, rather than focusing on major life events and the onset of depressive episodes, as recent studies of gene-by-environment interactions in depression in general (e.g., Caspi et al., 2003), it may be more fruitful to search for genetic polymorphisms that increase susceptibility to the effects of chronic stress.

Research on the neurobiology of chronic depression has been unsystematic and inconclusive. Two key areas for future research are neuroendocrine reactivity to stress and regional brain activation in response to emotional and stressful stimuli. Studies of the neurobiology of chronic depression have generally examined variables that have been shown to be associated with nonchronic depression. However, it is important to consider the possibility that the nature and manifestations of neurobiological dysregulation in chronic depression may differ from nonchronic depression, both because chronic and nonchronic depressions may have somewhat different pathophysiologies, and because there may be neurobiological adaptations to persisting depression that alter the nature of the dysfunction (e.g., Watson et al., 2006).

It is well-established that chronic depression is associated with particularly high rates of Axis I and II comorbidity. However, the causal processes that produce these comorbidities require elucidation (e.g., shared risk factors). In addition, although comorbidity appears to contribute to the maintenance of chronic depression, the mediating processes remain obscure. For example, it is conceivable that anxiety and personality disorders prolong depressive episodes by increasing avoidance behavior or interpersonal conflict.

More generally, there is a need for research delineating the pathways involved in the development of Dysthymic Disorder and chronic Major Depressive Disorder. As Dysthymic Disorder often has an onset in childhood or adolescence, this will require a developmental perspective. Moreover, chronic depression is probably etiologically heterogeneous, indicating that multiple pathways are likely to be involved. The current literature suggests that some of the key variables involved in these pathways include family history of mood disorders (particularly chronic depression), early adversity, temperamental low PE and high NE, and the development of neurobiological stress response systems. As these are fairly distal variables, it is also important to trace these pathways and examine the more proximal processes and mechanisms (e.g., cognitive and interpersonal deficits, stress reactivity) that mediate these effects. In addition, it is important to identify protective factors and environmental variables that facilitate recovery (e.g., "fresh-start" events).

Finally, a number of aspects of the treatment of chronic depression require further study. First, there are only limited data on the efficacy of psychotherapy for Dysthymic Disorder and chronic Major Depressive Disorder, either alone or in conjunction with pharmacotherapy. Research is needed to determine the specificity and range of efficacious psychotherapeutic treatments and to identify the active ingredients and processes in order to develop optimal treatment packages. In addition, there are remarkably few data available to help determine the optimal parameters of psychosocial interventions, such as the frequency of sessions and the duration of treatment. Finally, despite the existence of efficacious treatments, only a minority of patients achieve full remission with a single medication or course of time-limited psychotherapy. Hence, there is a need for research to develop and validate algorithms for the optimal sequencing and combination of psychosocial and pharmacological treatments.

References

Adler, D. A., Irish, J., McLaughlin, T. J., Perissinotto, C., Chang, H., Hood, M., et al. (2004). The work impact of dysthymia in a primary care population. *General Hospital Psychiatry*, *26*, 269–276.

Agosti, V. (1999). One year clinical and psychosocial outcomes of early-onset chronic depression. *Journal of Affective Disorders*, *54*, 171–175.

Akiskal, H. S. (1983). Dysthymic disorder: Psychopathology of proposed chronic depressive subtypes. *American Journal of Psychiatry*, *140*, 11–20.

Akiskal, H. S., Bitar, A. H., Puzantian, V. R., Rosenthal, T. L., & Walker, P. W. (1978). The nosological status of neurotic depression: A prospective three-four year follow-up examination in light of the primary-secondary and unipolar-bipolar dichotomies. *Archives of General Psychiatry*, *35*, 757–766.

Akiskal, H. S., Lemmi, H., Dickson, H., King, D., Yerevanian, B., & van Valkenburg, C. (1984). Chronic depressions: Part 2. Sleep EEG differentiation of primary dysthymic disorders from anxious depressions. *Journal of Affective Disorders*, *6*, 287–295.

Akiskal, H. S., Rosenthal, T. L., Haykal, R. F., Lemmi, H., Rosenthal, R. H., & Scott-Strauss, A. (1980). Characterological depressions: Clinical and sleep EEG findings separating "subaffective dysthymias" from "character spectrum disorders." *Archives of General Psychiatry*, *37*, 777–783.

Alnaes, R., & Torgersen, S. (1989). Characteristics of patients with major depression in combination with dysthymic or cyclothymic disorders: Childhood and precipitating events. *Acta Psychiatrica Scandinavica*, *79*, 11–18.

American Psychiatric Association. (1968). *Diagnostic and Statistical Manual of Mental Disorders* (2nd ed.). Washington, DC: Author.

American Psychiatric Association. (1980). *Diagnostic and Statistical Manual of Mental Disorders* (3rd ed.). Washington, DC: Author.

American Psychiatric Association. (1987). *Diagnostic and Statistical Manual of Mental Disorders* (3rd ed., rev.). Washington, DC: Author.

American Psychiatric Association. (1994). *Diagnostic and Statistical Manual of Mental Disorders* (4th ed.). Washington, DC: Author.

Anderson, R. L., Klein, D. N., Riso, L. P., Ouimette, P. C., Lizardi, H., & Schwartz, J. E. (1996). The subaffective-character spectrum subtyping distinction in primary early-onset dysthymia: A clinical and family study. *Journal of Affective Disorders*, *38*, 13–22.

Angst, J. (1998). Dysthymia and personality. *European Psychiatry*, *13*, 188–197.

Arnow, B. A., & Constantino, M. J. (2003). Effectiveness of psychotherapy and combination treatment for chronic depression. *Journal of Clinical Psychology*, *59*, 893–905.

Arnow, B. A., Spangler, D., Klein, D. N., & Burns, D. D. (2004). Rumination and distraction among chronic depressives in treatment: A structural equation analysis. *Cognitive Therapy and Research*, *28*, 67–83.

Arriaga, F., Cavaglia, F., Matos-Pires, A., Lara, E., & Paiva, T. (1995). EEG sleep characteristics in dysthymia and major depressive disorder. *Neuropsychobiology*, *32*, 128–131.

Arriago, F., Rosado, P., & Paiva, T. (1990). The sleep of dysthymic patients: A comparison with normal controls. *Biological Psychiatry*, *27*, 649–656.

Barrett, J. E., Williams, J. W., Oxman, T. E., Frank, E., Katon, W., Sullivan, M., et al. (2001). Treatment of dsythymia and minor depression in primary care: A randomized trial in patients aged 18 to 59 years. *Journal of Family Practice*, *50*, 405–412.

Barzega, G., Maina, G., Venturello, S., & Bogetto, F. (2001). Dysthymic Disorder: Clinical characteristics in relation to age at onset. *Journal of Affective Disorders*, *66*, 39–46.

Beck, A. T., Steer, R. A., & Brown, G. K. (1996). *Manual for the Beck Depression Inventory-II*. San Antonio, TX: Psychological Corporation.

Beekman, A. T. F., Deeg, D. J. H., Smit, J. H., Comijs, H. C., Braam, A. W., de Beurs, E., et al. (2004). Dysthymia in later life: A study in the community. *Journal of Affective Disorders*, *81*, 191–199.

Bellino, S., Patria, L., Ziero, S., Rocca, G., & Bogetto, F. (2001). Clinical features of dysthymia and age: A clinical investigation. *Psychiatry Research*, *103*, 219–228.

Bemporad, J. (1976). Psychotherapy of the depressive character. *Journal of the American Academy of Psychoanalysis and Dynamic Psychiatry*, *4*, 347–372.

Benazzi, F. (1997). Chronic depression: A case series of 203 outpatients treated at a private practice. *Journal of Psychiatry and Neuroscience*, *23*, 51–55.

Bifulco, A., Brown, G. W., Lillie, A., & Jarvis, J. (1997). Memories of childhood neglect and abuse: Corroboration in a series of sisters. *Journal of Child Psychology and Psychiatry, 38*, 365–374.

Brown, G. W., Adler, Z., & Bifulco, A. (1988). Life events, difficulties and recovery from chronic depression. *British Journal of Psychiatry, 152*, 487–498.

Brown, G. W., Harris, T. O., Hepworth, C., & Robinson, R. (1994). Clinical and psychosocial origins of chronic depressive episodes II: A patient inquiry. *British Journal of Psychiatry, 165*, 457–465.

Brown, G. W., & Moran, P. (1994). Clinical and psychosocial origins of chronic depressive episodes: I. A community survey. *British Journal of Psychiatry, 165*, 447–456.

Browne, G., Steiner, M., Roberts, J., Gafni, A., Byrne, C., Bell, B., et al. (1999). Prevalence of dysthymic disorder in primary care. *Journal of Affective Disorders, 54*, 303–308.

Browne, G., Steiner, M., Roberts, J., Gafni, A., Byrne, C., Dunn, E., et al. (2002). Sertraline and/or interpersonal psychotherapy for patients with dysthymic disorder in primary care: 6–month comparison with longitudinal 2–year follow-up of effectiveness and costs. *Journal of Affective Disorders, 68*, 317–330.

Carroll, B. J., Feinberg, M., Greden, J. F., Tarika, J., Albala, A. A., Haskett, R. F., et al. (1981). A specific laboratory test for the diagnosis of melancholia: Standardization, validity, and clinical utility. *Archives of General Psychiatry, 38*, 15–22.

Caspi, A. (2000). The child is father of the man: Personality continuities from childhood to adulthood. *Journal of Personality and Social Psychology, 78*, 158–172.

Caspi, A., Moffitt, T. E., Newman, D. L., & Silva, P. A. (1996). Behavioral observations at age 3 years predict adult psychiatric disorders. *Archives of General Psychiatry, 53*, 1033–1039.

Caspi, A., Sugden, K., Moffitt, T. E., Taylor, A., Craig, I., et al. (2003). Influence of life stress on depression: Moderation by a polymorphism on the 5–HTT gene. *Science, 301*, 386–389.

Cassano, G. B., & Savini, M. (1993). Chronic major depressive episode and dysthymia: Comparison of demographic and clinical characteristics. *European Psychiatry, 8*, 277–279.

Christenson, B. K., Carney, C. E., & Segal, Z. V. (2006). Cognitive processing models of depression. In D. J. Stein, D. J. Kupfer, and A. F. Schatzberg (Eds.), *The American Psychiatric Publishing Textbook of Mood Disorders* (pp. 131–144). Washington, DC: American Psychiatric Publishing.

Costello, E. J., Angold, A., Burns, B. J., Stangl, D. K., Tweed, D. L., Erkanli, A. et al. (1996). The Great Smokey Mountain Study of Youth: Goals, designs, methods, and the prevalence of DSM-III-R disorders. *Archives of General Psychiatry, 53*, 1137–1143.

Coyne, J. C. (1976). Depression and the response of others. *Journal of Abnormal Psychology, 43*, 43–48.

Danielson, C. K., Youngstrom, E. A., Findling, R. L., & Calabrese, J. R. (2003). Discriminative validity of the General Behavior Inventory using youth report. *Journal of Abnormal Child Psychology, 31*, 29–39.

Davidson, R. J., Pizzagalli, D., Nitschke, J. B., & Putnam, K. (2002). Depression: Perspectives from affective neuroscience. *Annual Review of Psychology, 53*, 545–574.

DeLima, M. S., Hotoph, M., & Wessely, S. (1999). The efficacy of drug treatments for dysthymia: A systematic review and meta-analysis. *Psychological Medicine, 29*, 1273–1289.

Depue, R. A., Krauss, S., Spoont, M. R., & Arbisi, P. (1989). General Behavior Inventory identification of unipolar and bipolar affective conditions in a nonclinical university population. *Journal of Abnormal Psychology, 98*, 117–126.

Devanand, D. P., Adorno, E., Cheng, J., Burt, T., Pelton, G. H., Roose, S. P., & Sackeim, H. A. (2004). Late onset dysthymic disorder and major depression differ from early onset dysthymic disorder and major depression in elderly outpatients. *Journal of Affective Disorders, 78*, 259–267.

Devanand, D. P., Nobler, M. S., Singer, T., Keirsky, J. E., Turret, N., Roose, S. P., et al. (1994). Is dysthymia a different disorder in the elderly? *American Journal of Psychiatry, 151*, 1592–1599.

Dougherty, L. R., Klein, D. N., & Davila, J. (2004). A growth curve analysis of the effects of chronic stress on the course of dysthymic disorder: Moderation by adverse parent-child relationships and family history. *Journal of Consulting and Clinical Psychology, 72*, 1012–1021.

Dunner, D. (2005). Dysthymia and double depression. *International Review of Psychiatry, 17*, 3–8.

Dura, J. R., Stukenberg, K. W., & Kiecolt-Glaser, J. K. (1990). Chronic stress and depressive disorders in older adults. *Journal of Abnormal Psychology, 99*, 284–290.

Durbin, C. E., Klein, D. N., Hayden, E. P., Buckley, M. E., & Moerk, K. C. (2005). Temperamental emotionality in preschoolers and parental mood disorders. *Journal of Abnormal Psychology, 114*, 28–37.

Evans, S., Cloitre, M., Kocsis, J. H., Keitner, G. I., Holzer, C. P., & Gniwesch, L. (1995). Social-vocational adjustment in unipolar mood disorders: Results of the *DSM-IV* field trial. *Journal of Affective Disorders, 38*, 73–80.

Ferro, T., Carlson, G. A., Grayson, P., & Klein, D. N. (1994). Depressive disorders: Distinctions in children. *Journal of the American Academy of Child and Adolescent Psychiatry, 33*, 664–670.

First, M. B., Gibbon, M., Spitzer, R. L., & Williams, J. B. W. (1996). *User's Guide for the Structured Clinical Interview for DSM-IV*. New York: New York State Psychiatric Institute, Biometrics Research.

Flament, M. E., Cohen, D., Choquet, M., Jeammet, P., & Ledoux, S. (2002). Phenomenology, psychosocial correlates, and treatment seeking in major depression and dysthymia of adolescence. *Journal of the American Academy of Child and Adolescent Psychiatry, 40*, 1070–1078.

Garyfallos, G., Adamopoulou, A., Karastergiou, A., Voikli, M., Sotiropoulou, A., Donias, S. et al. (1999). Personality disorders in dysthymia and major depression. *Acta Psychiatrica Scandinavica, 99*, 332–340.

Garvey, M. J., Tollefson, G. D., & Tuason, V. B. (1986). Is chronic primary major depression a distinct depression subtype? *Comprehensive Psychiatry, 27*, 446–448.

Gastó, C., Vallejo, J., Menchón, J. M., Catalán, R., Otero, a., Martínez de Osaba, M. J., et al. (1994). Platelet serotonin-binding and dexamethasone suppression test in melancholia and dysthymia. *European Psychiatry, 9*, 281–287.

George, M. S., Nahas, Z., Bohning, D. E., Kozel, F. A., Anderson, B., Mu, C., et al. (2006). Vagus nerve stimulation and deep brain stimulation. In D. J. Stein, D. J. Kupfer, and A. F. Schatzberg (Eds.), *The American Psychiatric Publishing Textbook of Mood Disorders* (pp. 337–349). Washington, DC: American Psychiatric Publishing.

Gibb, B. E. (2002). Childhood maltreatment and negative cognitive styles: A quantitative and qualitative review. *Clinical Psychology Review, 22*, 223–246.

Gilmer, W. S., Trivedi, M. H., Rush, A. J., Wisniewski, S. R., Luther, J., Howland, R. H., et al. (2005). Factors associated with chronic depressive episodes: A preliminary report from the STAR-D project. *Acta Psychiatrica Scandinavica, 112*, 425–433.

Goodman, D. W., Goldstein, R. B., Adams, P. B., Horwath, E., Sobin, C., Wickramaratne, P., et al. (1994/1995). Relationship between dysthymia and major depression: An analysis of family study data. *Depression, 2*, 252–258.

Goodman, S. H., Schwab-Stone, M., Lahey, B. B., Shaffer, D., & Jensen, P. S. (2000). Major depression and dysthymia in children and adolescents: Discriminant validity and differential consequences in a community sample. *Journal of the American Academy of Child and Adolescent Psychiatry, 39*, 761–770.

Gwirtsman, H. E., Blehar, M. C., McCullough, J. P., Kocsis, J. H., & Prien, R. F. (1997). Standardized assessment of dysthymia: Report of a National Institute of Mental Health conference. *Psychopharmacology Bulletin, 33*, 3–11.

Harkness, K. L., & Wildes, J. E. (2002). Child adversity and anxiety versus dysthymia comorbidity in major depression. *Psychological Medicine, 32*, 1239–1249.

Hays, J. C., Krishnan, K. R. R., George, L. K., Pieper, C. F., Flint, E. P., & Blazer, D. G. (1997). *Psychosocial and physical correlates of chronic depression. Psychiatry Research, 72*, 149–159.

Hays, R. D., Wells, K. B., Sherbourne, C. D., Rogers, W., & Spritzer, K. (1995). Functioning and well-being outcomes of patients with depression compared with chronic general medical illnesses. *Archives of General Psychiatry, 52*, 11–19.

Heim, C., Newport, D. J., Heit, S., Graham, Y. P., Wilcox, M., Bonsall, R., et al. (2000). Pituitary-adrenal and autonomic responses to stress in women after sexual and physical abuse in childhood. *Journal of the American Medical Association, 284*, 592–597.

Hellerstein, D. J., Batchelder, S. T., Lee, A., & Borisovskaya, M. (2002). Rating dysthymia: An assessment of the construct and content validity of the Cornell Dysthymia Rating scale. *Journal of Affective Disorders, 71*, 85–96.

Hirschfeld, R. M. A., Klerman, G. L., Andreasen, N. C., Clayton, P. J., & Keller, M. B. (1986). Psychosocial predictors of chronicity in depressed patients. *British Journal of Psychiatry, 148*, 648–654.

Hirschfeld, R. M. A. (1990). Personality and dysthymia. In S. W. Burton and H. S. Akiskal (Eds.), *Dysthymic disorder* (pp. 69–77). Gaskell: London.

Holm-Denoma, J. M., Berlim, M. T., Fleck, M. P. A., & Joiner, T. E. (2006). Double depression in adult psychiatric outpatients in Brazil: Distinct from major depression? *Psychiatry Research, 144*, 191–196.

Iacoviello, B. M., Alloy, L. B., Abramson, L. Y., Whitehouse, W. G., & Hogan, M. E. (2006). The course of depression in persons at high and low cognitive risk for depression: A prospective study. *Journal of Affective Disorders, 93*, 61–69.

Joiner, T. E. (2000). Depression's vicious scree: Self-propagating and erosive processes in depression chronicity. *Clinical Psychology: Science and Practice, 7*, 203–218.

Judd, L. L., Paulus, M. J., Schettler, P. J., Akiskal, H. S., Endicott, J., Leon, A. C., et al. (2000). Does incomplete recovery from first lifetime major depressive episode herald a chronic source of illness? *American Journal of Psychiatry, 157*, 1501–1504.

Keller, M. B., Klein, D. N., Hirschfeld, R. M. A., Kocsis, J. H., McCullough, J. P., Miller, I., et al. (1995). Results of the *DSM-IV* Mood Disorders Field Trial. *American Journal of Psychiatry, 152*, 843–849.

Keller, M. B., Kocsis, J. H., Thase, M. E., Gelenberg, A. J., Rush, A. J., Koran, L., et al. (1998). Maintenance phase efficacy of sertraline for chronic depression: A randomized controlled trial. *Journal of the American Medical Association, 280*, 1665–1672.

Keller, M. B., & Lavori, P. W. (1984). Double depression, major depression, and dysthymia: Distinct entities or different phases of a single disorder? *Psychopharmacology Bulletin, 20*, 399–402.

Keller, M. B., Lavori, P. W., Endicott. J., Coryell, W., & Klerman, G. L. (1983). "Double Depression": Two-year follow-up. *American Journal of Psychiatry, 140*, 689–694.

Keller, M. B., Lavori, P. W., Friedman, B., Nielson, E., Endicott, J., McDonald-Scott, P., et al. (1987). The longitudinal interval follow-up evaluation: A comprehensive method for assessing outcome in prospective longitudinal studies. *Archives of General Psychiatry, 44*, 540–548.

Keller, M. B., McCullough, J. P, Klein, D. N., Arnow, B., Dunner, D. L., Gelenberg, A. J., et al. (2000). A comparison of nefazodone, the cognitive behavioral-analysis system of psychotherapy, and their combination for the treatment of chronic depression. *New England Journal of Medicine, 342*, 1462–1470.

Keller, M. B., & Shapiro, R. W. (1982). "Double depression": Superimposition of acute depressive episodes on chronic depressive disorders. *American Journal of Psychiatry, 139*, 438–442.

Kernberg, O. F. (1988). Clinical dimensions of masochism. *Journal of the American Psychoanalytic Association, 36*, 1005–1029.

Kessler, R. C., Berglund, P., Demler, O., Jin, R., & Walters, E. E. (2005). Lifetime prevalence and age of onset distributions of *DSM-IV* disorders in the National Comorbidity Study Replication. *Archives of General Psychiatry, 62*, 593–602.

Kessler, R. C., McGonagle, K. A., Zhao, S., Nelson, C. B., Hughes, M., Eshleman, S., et al. (1994). Lifetime and 12–month prevalence of *DSM-III-R* psychiatric disorders in the United States: Results from the National Comorbidity Survey. *Archives of General Psychiatry, 51*, 8–19.

Kirby, M., Bruce, I., Coakley, D., & Lawlor, B. A. (1999). Dysthymia among the community-dwelling elderly. *International Journal of Geriatric Psychiatry, 14*, 440–445.

Kivelä, S.-L., Pahkala, K., & Lappala, P. (1991). A one-year prognosis of dysthymic disorder and major depression in old age. *International Journal of Geriatric Psychiatry, 6*, 81–87.

Klein, D.N. (1999). Depressive personality in the relatives of outpatients with dysthymic disorder and episodic major depressive disorder and normal controls. *Journal of Affective Disorders, 55*, 19–27.

Klein, D. N. (2006). Depression and childhood adversity and abuse. *Depression: Mind and Body, 2*, 89–93.

Klein, D. N., Bessaha, M., (in press). Depressive and self-defeating (masochistic) personality disorders. In T. Millon, P. Blaney, & R. Davis (Eds.), *Oxford Textbook of Psychopathology* (2nd ed.). New York: Oxford University Press.

Klein, D. N., Clark, D. C., Dansky, L., & Margolis, E. T. (1988). Dysthymia in the offspring of parents with primary unipolar affective disorder. *Journal of Abnormal Psychology, 97*, 265–274.

Klein, D. N., Dickstein, S., Taylor, E. B., & Harding, K. (1989). Identifying chronic affective disorders in outpatients: Validation of the General Behavior Inventory. *Journal of Consulting and Clinical Psychology, 57*, 106–111.

Klein, D. N., Durbin, C. E., Shankman, S. A., & Santiago, N. J. (2002). Depression and personality. In I. H. Gotlib & C. L. Hammen,(Eds.), *Handbook of depression* (pp. 115–140). New York: Guilford.

Klein, D. N., Kocsis, J. H., McCullough, J. P., Holzer, C. P., III, Hirschfeld, R. M. A., & Keller, M. B. (1996). Symptomatology in dysthymia. *Psychiatric Clinics of North America, 19*, 41–55.

Klein, D. N., Lewinsohn, P. M., & Seeley, J. R. (1997). Psychosocial characteristics of adolescents with a past history of dysthymic disorder: Comparison with adolescents with past histories of major depressive and non-affective disorders, and never mentally ill controls. *Journal of Affective Disorders, 42*, 127–135.

Klein, D. N., Riso, L. P., & Anderson, R. L. (1993). DSM-III-R dysthymia: Antecedents and underlying assumptions. In L. Chapman, J. Chapman, and D. Fowles (Eds.), *Progress in experimental personality and psychopathology research,* vol. *16* (pp. 222–253). New York: Springer.

Klein, D. N., Riso, L. P., Donaldson, S. K., Schwartz, J. E., Anderson, R. L., Ouimette, P. C., et al. (1995). Family study of early-onset dysthymia: Mood and personality disorders in relatives of outpatients with dysthymia and episodic major depression and normal controls. *Archives of General Psychiatry, 52,* 487–496.

Klein, D. N., Santiago, N. J., Vivian, D., Arnow, B. A., Blalock, J. A., Dunner, D. L., et al. (2004). Cognitive-behavioral analysis system of psychotherapy as a maintenance treatment for chronic depression. *Journal of Consulting and Clinical Psychology, 72,* 681–688.

Klein, D. N., Schatzberg, A. F., McCullough, J. P., Dowling, F., Goodman, D., Howland, R. H., et al. (1999). Age of onset in chronic major depression: Relation to demographic and clinical variables, family history, and treatment response. *Journal of Affective Disorders, 55,* 149–157.

Klein, D. N., Schatzberg, A. F., McCullough, J. P., Keller, M. B., Dowling, F., Goodman, D., et al. (1999). Early- versus late-onset dysthymic disorder: Comparison in outpatients with superimposed major depressive episodes. *Journal of Affective Disorders, 52,* 187–196.

Klein, D. N., & Schwartz, J. E. (2002). The relation between depressive symptoms and Borderline Personality Disorder features over time in Dysthymic Disorder. *Journal of Personality Disorders, 16,* 523–535.

Klein, D. N., Schwartz, J. E., Rose, S., & Leader, J. B. (2000). Five-year course and outcome of dysthymic disorder: A prospective, naturalistic follow-up study. *American Journal of Psychiatry, 157,* 931–939.

Klein, D. N., Schwartz, J. E., Santiago, N. J., Vivian, D., Vocisano, C., Castonguay, L. G., et al. (2003). Therapeutic alliance in depression treatment: Controlling for prior change and patient characteristics. *Journal of Consulting and Clinical Psychology, 71,* 997–1006.

Klein, D. N., Shankman, S. A., Lewinsohn, P. M., Rohde, P., & Seeley, J. R. (2004). Family study of chronic depression in a community sample of young adults. *American Journal of Psychiatry, 161,* 646–653.

Klein, D. N., Shankman, S. A., & Rose, S. (2006). Ten-year prospective follow-up study of the naturalistic course of dysthymic disorder and double depression. *American Journal of Psychiatry, 163,* 872–880.

Klein, D. N., Shankman, S. A., Rose, S. (in press). Dysthymic disorder and double depression: Baseline predictors of 10–year course and outcome. *Journal of Psychiatric Research.*

Klein, D. N., Taylor, E. B., Dickstein, S., & Harding, K. (1988a). The early-late onset distinction in DSM-III-R dysthymia. *Journal of Affective Disorders, 14,* 25–33.

Klein, D. N., Taylor, E. B., Dickstein, S., & Harding, K. (1988b). Primary early-onset dysthymia: Comparison with primary non-bipolar, non-chronic major depression on demographic, clinical, familial, personality, and socioenvironmental characteristics and short-term outcome. *Journal of Abnormal Psychology, 97,* 387–398.

Klerman, G. L., Endicott, J., Spitzer, R. L., Hirschfeld, R. M. A. et al. (1979). Neurotic depression: A systematic analysis of multiple criteria and meanings. *American Journal of Psychiatry, 136,* 57–61.

Klerman, G. L., Weissman, M. M., Rounsaville, B. J., & Chevron, E. S. (1984). *Interpersonal psychotherapy of depression.* New York: Basic Books.

Kocsis, J. H. (2003). Pharmacotherapy and chronic depression. *Journal of Clinical Psychology, 59,* 885–892.

Kocsis, J. H., & Frances, A. J. (1987). A critical discussion of DSM-III dysthymic disorder. *American Journal of Psychiatry, 144,* 1534–1542.

Kocsis, J. H., Friedman, R. A., Markowitz, J. C., Leon, A. C., Miller, N. L., Gniwesch, L., et al. (1996). Maintenance therapy for chronic depression: A controlled clinical trial of desipramine. *Archives of General Psychiatry, 53,* 769–774.

Koran, L. M., Gelenberg, A. J., Kornstein, S. G., Howland, R. H., Friedman, R. A., DeBattista, C., et al. (2001). Sertraline versus imipramine to prevent relapse in chronic depression. *Journal of Affective Disorders, 65,* 27–36.

Kovacs, M., Akiskal, H. S., Gatsonis, C., & Parrone, P. L. (1994). Childhood-onset dysthymic disorder: Clinical features and prospective naturalistic outcome. *Archives of General Psychiatry, 51,* 365–374.

Kovacs, M., & Devlin, B. (1998). Internalizing disorders in childhood. *Journal of Child Psychology and Psychiatry, 39,* 47–63.

Kraepelin, E. (1921). *Manic depressive insanity and paranoia.* Edinburgh: E and S Livingstone.

Kwon, J. S., Kim, Y.-M., Chang, C.-G., Park, B.-J., Kim, L., et al. (2000). Three-year follow-up of women with the sole diagnosis of depressive personality disorder: subsequent development of dysthymia and major depression. *American Journal of Psychiatry, 157,* 1966–1972.

Laptook, R. S., Klein, D. N., & Dougherty, L. R. (2006). Ten-year stability of depressive personality disorder in depressed outpatients. *American Journal of Psychiatry, 163,* 865–871.

Lara, M. E., & Klein, D. N. (1999). Psychological processes underlying the maintenance and persistence of depression: Implications for understanding chronic depression. *Clinical Psychology Review, 19*, 553–570.

Lara, M. E., Klein, D. N., & Kasch, K. L. (2000). Psychosocial predictors of the short-term course and outcome of major depression: A longitudinal study of a non-clinical sample with recent-onset episodes. *Journal of Abnormal Psychology, 109*, 644–650.

Leader, J. B., & Klein, D. N. (1996). Social adjustment in dysthymia, double depression, and episodic major depression. *Journal of Affective Disorders, 37*, 91–101.

Lewinsohn, P. M., Hops, H., Roberts, R. E., Seeley, J. R., & Andrews, J. A. (1993). Adolescent psychopathology: I. Prevalence and incidence of depression and other *DSM-III-R* disorders in high school students. *Journal of Abnormal Psychology, 102*, 133–144.

Lewinsohn, P. M., Rohde, P., Seeley, J. R., & Hops, H. (1991). Comorbidity of unipolar depression: I. Major depression with dysthymia. *Journal of Abnormal Psychology, 100*, 205–213.

Lieb, R., Isensee, B., Höffler, M., Pfister, H., & Wittchen, H.-U. (2002). Parental major depression and the risk of depression and other mental disorders in offspring: A prospective- longitudinal community study. *Archives of General Psychiatry, 59*, 365–374.

Lizardi, H., & Klein, D. N. (2000). Parental psychopathology and reports of the childhood home environment in adult early-onset dysthymic disorder. *Journal of Nervous and Mental Disease, 188*, 63–70.

Lizardi, H., & Klein, D. N. (2005). Long term stability of parental representations in depressed outpatients utilizing the Parental Bonding Instrument. *Journal of Nervous and Mental Disease, 193*, 183–188.

Lizardi, H., Klein, D. N., Ouimette, P. C., Riso, L. P., Anderson, R. L., & Donaldson, S. K. (1995). Reports of the childhood home environment in early-onset dysthymia and major depression. *Journal of Abnormal Psychology, 104*, 132–139.

Lyoo, I. K., Kwon, J. S., Lee, S. J., Han, M. H., Chang, C.-G., Seo, C. S., et al. (2002). Decrease in genu of the corpus callosum in medication-naïve, early-onset dysthymia and depressive personality disorder. *Biological Psychiatry, 52*, 1134–1143.

Markowitz, J. C. (1998). *Interpersonal psychotherapy for dysthymic disorder*. Washington, DC: American Psychiatric Press.

Markowitz, J. C., Kocsis, J. H., Bleiberg, K. L., Christos, P. J., & Sacks, M. (2005). A comparative trial of psychotherapy and pharmacotherapy for "pure" dysthymic patients. *Journal of Affective Disorders, 89*, 167–175.

Markowitz, J. C., Moran, M. E., Kocsis, J. H., & Frances, A. J. (1992). Prevalence and comorbidity of dysthymic disorder among psychiatric outpatients. *Journal of Affective Disorders, 24*, 63–71.

Masi, G., Millepiedi, S., Mucci, M., Pascale, R. R., Perugi, G., & Akiskal, H. S. (2003). Phenomenology and comorbidity of dysthymic disorder in 100 consecutively referred children and adolescents: Beyond *DSM-IV*. *Canadian Journal of Psychiatry, 48*, 99–105.

Mason, B. J., Kocsis, J. H., Leon, A. C., Thompson, S., Frances, A. J., Morgan, R. O., et al. (1995). Assessment of symptoms and change in dysthymic disorder. In J. H. Kocsis and D. N. Klein (Eds.), *Diagnosis and treatment of chronic depression* (pp. 73–88). New York: Guilford.

McCullough, J. P. (2000). *Treatment for chronic depression: Cognitive behavioral analysis system of psychotherapy*. New York: Guilford.

McCullough, J. P., Braith, J. A., Chapman, R. C., Kasnetz, M. D., Carr, K. F., Cones, J. H., et al. (1990). Comparison of dysthymic major and nonmajor depressives. *Journal of Nervous and Mental Disease, 178*, 596–597.

McCullough, J. M., McCune, K. J., Kaye, A. L., Braith, J. A., Friend, R., Roberts, W. C., et al. (1994). One-year prospective replication study of an untreated sample of community dysthymia subjects. *Journal of Nervous and Mental Disease, 182*, 396–401.

McCullough, J. P., Kornstein, S. G., McCullough, J. P., Belyea-Caldwell, S., Kaye, A. L., Roberts, W. C., et al. (1996). Differential diagnosis of chronic depressive disorders. *Psychiatric Clinics of North America, 19*, 55–71.

McCullough, J. P., Klein, D. N., Borian, F. E., Howland, R. H., Riso, L. P., Keller, M. B., et al. (2003). Group comparisons of DSM-IV subtypes of chronic depression: Validity of the distinctions, Part 2. *Journal of Abnormal Psychology, 112*, 614–622.

McCullough, J. P., Klein, D. N., Keller, M. B., Holzer, C. E., Davis, S. M., Kornstein, S. G., et al. (2000). Comparison of *DSM-III-R* chronic major depression and major depression superimposed on dysthymia (double depression): A study of the validity and value of differential diagnosis. *Journal of Abnormal Psychology, 109*, 419–427.

Miller, I. W., Bishop, S., Norman, W. H., & Maddever, H. (1985). The modified Hamilton Rating Scale for Depression: Reliability and validity. *Psychiatry Research, 14*, 131–142.

Miller, I. W., Norman, W. H., & Dow, M. G. (1986). Psychosocial characteristics of "double depression."

American Journal of Psychiatry, *143*, 1032–1044.

Moerk, K. C., & Klein, D. N. (2000). The development of major depressive episodes during the course of dysthymic and episodic major depressive disorders: A retrospective examination of life events. *Journal of Affective Disorders*, *58*, 117–123.

Mondimore, F. M., Zandi, P. P., MacKinnon, D. F., McInnis, M. G., Miller, E. B., Crowe, R., et al. (2006). Familial aggregation of illness chronicity in recurrent, early-onset depression pedigrees. *American Journal of Psychiatry*, *163*, 1554–1560.

Mondimore, F. M., Zandi, P. P., MacKinnon, D. F., McInnis, M. G., Miller, E. B., Schweizer, B., et al. (in press). Comparison of the familiality of chronic depression in recurrent early-onset depression pedigrees using different definitions of chronicity. *Journal of Affective Disorders*.

Monroe, S. M., & Hadjiyannakis, K. (2002). The social environment and depression: Focusing on severe life stress. In I. H. Gotlib & C. L. Hammen (Eds.), *Handbook of depression* (pp. 314–340). New York: Guilford.

Mueller, T. I., Keller, M. B., Leon, A. C., Solomon, D. A., Shea, M. T., Coryell, W., et al. (1996). Recovery after 5 years of unremitting major depressive disorder. *Archives of General Psychiatry*, *53*, 794–799.

Mynors-Wallis, L. M., Gath, D. H., Lloyd-Thomas, A. R., & Tomlinson, D. (1995). Randomized controlled trial comparing problem solving treatment with amitryptaline and placebo for major depression in primary care. *British Medical Journal*, *310*, 441–445.

Nemeroff, C. G., Heim, C. M., Thase, M. E., Klein, D.N., Rush, A. J., Schatzberg, A. F., et al. (2003). Differential responses to psychotherapy versus pharmacotherapy in the treatment for patients with chronic forms of major depression and childhood trauma. *Proceedings of the National Academy of Sciences*, *100*, 14293–14296.

Nobler, M. S., & Sackeim, H. A. (2006). Electroconvulsive therapy and transcranial magnetic stimulation. In D. J. Stein, D. J. Kupfer, and A. F. Schatzberg (Eds.), *The American Psychiatric Publishing Textbook of Mood Disorders* (pp. 317–335). Washington, DC: American Psychiatric Publishing, Inc.

Peeters, F., Wessel, I., Merckelbach, H., & Boon-Vermeeren, M. (2002). Autobiographical memory specificity and the course of major depressive disorder. *Comprehensive Psychiatry*, *43*, 344–350.

Pepper, C. M., Klein, D. N., Anderson, R. L., Riso, L. P., Ouimette, P. C., & Lizardi, H. (1995). Axis II

comorbidity in dysthymia and major depression. *American Journal of Psychiatry*, *152*, 239–247.

Phillips, K. A., Gunderson, J. G., Hirschfeld, R. M., & Smith, L. E. (1990). A review of the depressive personality. *American Journal of Psychiatry*, *147*, 830–837.

Ravindran, A. V., Bialik, R. J., & Lapierre, Y. D. (1994). Primary early onset dysthymia, biochemical correlates of the therapeutic response to fluoxetine: I. Platelet monoamine oxidase activity and the dexamethasone suppression test. *Journal of Affective Disorders*, *31*, 111–117.

Ravindran, A. V., Griffiths, J., Waddell, C., & Anisman, H. (1995). Stressful life events and coping styles in relation to dysthymia and major depressive disorder: Variations associated with alleviation of symptoms following pharmacotherapy. *Progress in Neuropsychopharmacology and Biological Psychiatry*, *19*, 637–653.

Rihmer, Z., & Szádóczky, E. (1993). Dexamethasone suppression test and TRH-TSH test in subaffective dysthymia and character-spectrum disorder. *Journal of Affective Disorders*, *28*, 287–291.

Riolo, S. A., Nguyen, T. A., Greden, J. F., & King, C. A. (2005). Prevalence of depression by race/ethnicity: Findings from the National Health and Nutrition Examination Survey III. *American Journal of Public Health*, *95*, 998–1000.

Riso, L. P., du Toit, P. L., Blandino, J. A., Penna, S., Darcy, S., Duin, J. S., et al. (2003). Cognitive aspects of chronic depression. *Journal of Abnormal Psychology*, *112*, 72–80.

Riso, L. P., Klein, D. N., Ferro, T., Kasch, K. L., Pepper, C. M., Schwartz, J. E., et al. (1996). Understanding the comorbidity between early-onset dysthymia and cluster B personality disorders: A family study. *American Journal of Psychiatry*, *153*, 900–906.

Riso, L. P., Miyatake, R., & Thase, M. E. (2002). The search for determinants of chronic depression: A review of six factors. *Journal of Affective Disorders*, *70*, 103–116.

Rounsaville, B. J., Sholomskas, D., & Prusoff, B. (1980). Chronic mood disorders in depressed outpatients: Diagnosis and response to pharmacotherapy. *Journal of Affective Disorders*, *2*, 73–88.

Roy, A., Sutton, M., & Pickar, D. (1985). Neuroendocrine and personality variables in dysthymic disorder. *American Journal of Psychiatry*, *142*, 94–97.

Roy, A., Pickar, D., Douillet, P., Karoum, F., & Linnoila, M. (1986). Urinary monoamines and monoamine metabolites in subtypes of unipolar depressive disorder and normal controls. *Psychological Medicine, 16*, 541–546.

Rush, A. J., Laux, L., Giles, D. E., Jarrett, R. B., Weissenburger, J., Feldman-Koffler, F., et al. (1995). Clinical characteristics of outpatients with chronic major depression. *Journal of Affective Disorders, 34*, 25–32.

Rush, A. J., Trivedi, M. H., Ibrahim, H. M., Carmody, T. J., Arnow, B., Klein, D. N., et al. (2003). The 16-item Quick Inventory of Depressive Symptomatology (QIDS) Clinician Rating (QIDS-C) and Self-Report (QIDS-SR): A psychometric evaluation in patients with chronic major depression. *Biological Psychiatry, 54*, 573–583.

Santiago, N. J., Klein, D. N., Vivian, D., Arnow, B. A., Blalock, J. A., Kocsis, J. H., et al. (2005). The therapeutic alliance and CBASP-specific skill acquisition in the treatment of chronic depression. *Cognitive Therapy and Research, 29*, 803–817.

Schatzberg, A. F., Rush, A. J., Arnow, B. A., Banks, P., Blalock, J. A., Borian, et al. (2005). Chronic depression: Medication (Nefazodone) or psychotherapy (CBASP) is effective when the other is not. *Archives of General Psychiatry, 62*, 513–520.

Schildkraut, J. J., & Klein, D. F. (1975). The classification and treatment of depressive disorders. In R. I. Shader (Ed.), *Manual of psychiatric therapeutics* (pp. 39–61). Boston: Little Brown.

Schneider, K. (1958). *Psychopathic personalities*. London: Cassell.

Scott, J. (1988). Chronic depression. *British Journal of Psychiatry, 153*, 287–297.

Serretti, A., Jori, M. C., Casadei, G., Ravizza, L., Smeraldi, E., et al. (1999). Delineating psychopathologic clusters within dysthymia: A study of 512 outpatients without major depression. *Journal of Affective Disorders, 56*, 17–25.

Shah, P. J., Ebmeier, K. P., Glabus, M. F., & Goodwin, G. M. (1998). Cortical grey matter reductions associated with treatment-resistant chronic unipolar depression. *British Journal of Psychiatry, 172*, 537–542.

Shah, P. J., Glabus, M. F., Goodwin, G. M., & Ebmeier, K. P. (2002). Chronic, treatment-resistant depression and right fronto-striatal atrophy. *British Journal of Psychiatry, 180*, 434–440.

Shelton, R. C., Davidson, J., Yonkers, K. A., & Koran, L. (1997). The undertreatment of dysthymia. *Journal of Clinical Psychiatry, 58*, 59–65.

Spalleta, G., Troisi, A., Saracco, M., Ciani, N., & Augusto, P. (1996). Symptom profile, Axis II comorbidity, and suicidal behavior in young males with *DSM-III-R* depressive illness. *Journal of Affective Disorders, 39*, 141–148.

Spitzer, R. L., Endicott, J., & Robins, E. (1978). *Research Diagnostic Criteria (RDC) for a selected group of functional disorders* (3rd ed.) New York: New York State Psychiatric Institute, Biometrics Research.

Stewart, J. W., McGrath, P. J., & Quitkin, F. M. (2002). Do age of onset and course of illness predict different treatment outcome among DSM-IV depressive disorders with atypical features? *Neuropsychopharmacology, 26*, 237–245.

Swartz, M. S., Kessler, R. C., McGonagle, K., & Blazer, D. G. (1993). *Lifetime chronic major depression in the community: Results from the National Comorbidity Survey*. Durham, NC: Department of Psychiatry, Duke Unviersity Medical Center.

Szádóczky, E., Fazekas, I., Rihmer, Z., & Arato, M. (1994). The role of psychosocial and biological variables in separating chronic and non-chronic major depression and early-late onset dysthymia. *Journal of Affective Disorders, 32*, 1–11.

Thase, M. E., Fava, M., Halbreich, U., Kocsis, J. H., Koran, L., Davidson, J., et al. (1996). A placebo-controlled, randomized clinical trial comparing sertraline and imipramine for the treatment of dysthymia. *Archives of General Psychiatry, 53*, 777–784.

Thase, M. E., Jindal, R., & Howland, R. H. (2002). Biological aspects of depression. In I. H. Gotlib & C. L. Hammen. *Handbook of depression* (pp. 192–218). New York: Guilford

Thase, M. E., Reynolds, C. F., Frank, E., Simons, A. D., Garamoni, G. D., McGeary, J., et al. (1994). Response to cognitive-behavioral therapy in chronic depression. *Journal of Psychotherapy Practice and Research, 3*, 204–214.

Thase, M. E., Rush, A. J., Howland, R. H., Kornstein, S. B., Kocsis, J. H., Gelenberg, A. J., et al. (2002). Double-blind switch study of imipramine or sertraline treatment of antidepressant-resistant chronic depression. *Archives of General Psychiatry, 59*, 233–239.

van Os, J., Jones, P., Lewis, G., Wadsworth, M., & Murray, R. (1997). Developmental precursors of affective illness in a general population birth cohort. *Archives of General Psychiatry, 54*, 625–631.

Vocisano, C., Klein, D. N., Keefe, R. S. E., Dienst, E. R., & Kincaid, M. M. (1996). Demographics, family history, premorbid functioning, developmental characteristics, and course of patients with deteriorated affective disorder. *American Journal of Psychiatry, 153*, 248–255.

Watson, D., & Clark. L. A. (1995). Depression and the melancholic temperament. *European Journal of Personality*, *9*, 351–366.

Watson, S., Gallagher, P., Del-Estal, D., Hearn, A., Ferrier, I. N., & Young, A. H. (2002). Hypothalamic-pituitary-adrenal axis function in patients with chronic depression. *Psychological Medicine*, *32*, 1021–1028.

Watson, S., Gallagher, P., Ferrier, I. N., & Young, A. H. (2006). Post-dexamethasone arginine vasopressin levels in patients with severe mood disorders. *Journal of Psychiatric Research*, *40*, 353–359.

Weissman, M. M., & Klerman, G. L. (1977). The chronic depressive in the community: Unrecognized and poorly treated. *Comprehensive Psychiatry*, *18*, 523–532.

Weissman, M. M., Leaf, P. J., Bruce, M. L., & Florio, L. (1988). The epidemiology of dysthymia in five communities: Rates, risks, comorbidity, and treatment. *American Journal of Psychiatry*, *145*, 815–819.

Wilhelm, K., Niven, H., Parker, G., & Hadzi-Pavlovic, D. (2005). The stability of the Parental Bonding Instrument over a 20–year period. *Psychological Medicine*, *35*, 387–393.

Williams, J. W., Barrett, J., Oxman, T., Frank, E., Katon, W., Sullivan, M., et al. (2001). Treatment of dysthymia and minor depression in primary care: A randomized controlled trial in older adults. *Journal of the American Medical Association*, *284*, 1519–1526.

Yang, T., & Dunner, D. L. (2001). Differential subtyping of depression. *Depression and Anxiety*, *13*, 11–17.

Zlotnick, C., Warshaw, M., Meredith, S., Shea, M. T., & Keller, M. B. (1997). Trauma and chronic depression among patients with anxiety disorders. *Journal of Consulting and Clinical Psychology*, *65*, 333–336.

Chapter 10

Bipolar Disorder

DAVID J. MIKLOWITZ AND SHERI L. JOHNSON

The endless questioning finally ended. My psychiatrist looked at me, there was no uncertainty in his voice. "Manic-depressive illness." I admired his bluntness. I wished him locusts on his lands and a pox upon his house. Silent, unbelievable rage. I smiled pleasantly. He smiled back. The war had just begun.

—Jamison (1995)

Bipolar Disorder is a highly debilitating psychiatric illness that may affect as many as 1 in every 25 persons (Kessler, Berglund, Demler, Jin, & Walters, 2005). People with the disorder have highly disruptive episodes, frequent recurrences, and severe psychosocial impairments—even when not symptomatic. The illness typically has its onset in adolescence and even late childhood in some patients—much earlier than was once thought.

Bipolar Disorder represents a conundrum on many fronts—how to reliably diagnose it and distinguish it from "near-neighbor" disorders; to what extent recurrences can be reliably predicted; the relative contributions of genetic, biological, and psychosocial factors at various phases of development; and the role of medications and psychotherapy in its acute and maintenance treatment. Nonetheless, the outlook for people with Bipolar Disorder is more optimistic than ever before because of notable advances in research on its diagnosis, etiology, prognosis, and treatment.

This chapter discusses the current state of knowledge on Bipolar Disorder. Relative to similar chapters that might appear in medical texts, this chapter emphasizes the role of psychosocial variables as predictors of recurrence and psychosocial interventions as adjunctive to pharmacotherapy. Special emphasis is placed on knowledge gained from laboratory-based studies of psychosocial stressors and randomized clinical trials, which have proliferated in the past decade. We conclude with recommendations for the next generation of research on this disorder.

Description of the Disorder

Symptoms and *DSM-IV* Criteria

Bipolar Disorder is characterized by severe changes in mood, thinking, and behavior—from extreme highs to debilitating lows. In its most classic presentation, mania and depression alternate in distinctive episodes that can last anywhere from a few days to a year or more. During manic episodes, patients experience an elated, expansive, or irritable mood with at least three of the following (four if the mood is only irritable): inflated self-esteem (grandiosity), decreased need for sleep, racing thoughts or flight of ideas, rapid or pressured speech, reckless and impulsive behavior (e.g., indiscreet sexual liaisons, spending sprees, reckless driving), enhanced energy, increased goal-directed activity, and distractibility. According to the fourth edition of the *Diagnostic and Statistical Manual of Mental Disorders* (American Psychiatric Association, 2000), manic episodes are defined by symptoms occurring for at least 1 week, evidence of functional impairment (deterioration in family, work, or social functioning), or—if lasting less than 1 week—the need for hospitalization or emergency treatment.

Hypomanic episodes are defined by symptoms of shorter duration (i.e., 4 or more days) and noticeable changes in behavior that do not meet the *DSM-IV* definition of functional impairment. Mania and hypomania are more distinguished by severity and impairment.

Depressive phases are defined by the criteria used for Major Depressive Disorder—2 or more weeks of intense sadness and loss of interests—with five or more of the following symptoms: insomnia or hypersomnia, psychomotor agitation or retardation, changes in weight or appetite, loss of energy, difficulty concentrating or making decisions, feelings of worthlessness or guilt, and suicidal ideation or behavior.

When manic and depressive episodes occur simultaneously (i.e., severely irritable mood along with racing thoughts, decreased need for sleep, suicidal thoughts, feelings of worthlessness, and insomnia), patients are diagnosed with a bipolar, *mixed* episode. The *DSM-IV* criteria for mixed episodes are considered too strict in many cases: patients must simultaneously fulfill the criteria for syndromal mania and depression for at least one week. At least 40% of patients with Bipolar Disorder have mixed episodes (Calabrese, Fatemi, Kujawa, & Woyshville, 1996), although the rate is probably much higher when subsyndromal mixed presentations are taken into account (e.g., depression with simultaneous hypomania: states that are clearly impairing but fall short of the number of symptoms required for mania or depression; Akiskal, Benazzi, Perugi, & Rihmer, 2005). Mixed states appear to be more pharmacologically treatment-resistant than manic episodes (e.g., Kupfer, Frank, et al., 2000; Strober et al., 1995).

Bipolar Subtypes

Persons with Bipolar Disorder who have had at least one manic or mixed episode are diagnosed with Bipolar I Disorder, and those who have had no manic or mixed episode, recurrent major depression and one hypomanic episode are diagnosed with Bipolar II Disorder. Patients need not have had a depressive episode to have Bipolar I Disorder. Unipolar mania is commonly reported within community studies of mania. Indeed, in the first National Comorbidity Survey (NCS) 20% of persons with a history of mania did not report episodes of depression (Kessler, Rubinow, Holmes, Abelson, & Zhao,

1997). Similarly, in the National Institute of Mental Health (NIMH) Collaborative Study of the Psychobiology of Depression, a large scale study of 903 probands, 27% of Bipolar I participants reported no history of major depressive episodes (Coryell et al., 1995). Nonetheless, most patient samples are characterized by high rates of depression—perhaps because depression is related to more aggressive help-seeking (Calabrese, Hirschfeld, Frye, & Reed, 2004). Interestingly, a 20-year follow-up of patients with unipolar mania found that the majority (20 of 27 participants, or 74%) had at least one episode of depression at follow-up (Solomon et al., 2003). On the other hand, in the NCS, the proportion of unipolar mania cases did not relate to age (Kessler et al., 1997). Thus, there is controversy concerning how common unipolar mania is and whether unipolar mania is stable over the life course.

Although it is not clear whether the treatment of Bipolar II Disorder is different from Bipolar I Disorder, the two subtypes are distinct in other ways. In a study involving a 10-year follow-up, only about 1 in 10 Bipolar II patients eventually developed a full manic or mixed episode and could then be diagnosed with Bipolar I (Coryell et al., 1995). Perhaps because Bipolar II Disorder is defined by recurrent depressive episodes (whereas Bipolar I Disorder requires no depression-related criterion), patients with Bipolar II Disorder spend the majority of their weeks ill in depressive rather than hypomanic states (with a ratio of 37 to 1), whereas the ratio of depressed versus manic weeks in Bipolar I Disorder is about 3:1 (Judd et al., 2002). Patients with Bipolar II Disorder are also more likely to be rapid cyclers (to have four or more illness episodes in a single year) than patients with Bipolar I Disorder (Schneck et al., 2004). This difference may reflect that the diagnostic criteria for Bipolar II Disorder require the occurrence of at least two distinct episodes (severe depression and hypomania) and (more typically) recurrences of depression—whereas Bipolar I Disorder can be diagnosed from a single manic or mixed episode.

DSM-IV devotes two categories to conditions that are considered part of a broader bipolar spectrum (Akiskal et al., 2000). *Cyclothymia* is characterized by two or more years of switching between hypomanic and depressive symptoms that do not meet the full *DSM-IV* criteria for a hypomanic or a major depressive episode. *DSM-IV* includes the diagnosis of Bipolar Not Otherwise Specified (NOS) for patients with manic symptoms that do not meet the criteria for other Bipolar Disorders. Bipolar NOS has not been adequately operationalized, although a recent study of children and adolescents offered the following definition: a distinct period of abnormally elevated, expansive, or irritable mood plus two (three if irritable mood only) *DSM-IV* symptoms of mania that caused a change in functioning, lasted for at least one day, and was present for a total of at least four days in a patient's lifetime (Birmaher et al., 2006). This study found that 25% of childhood and adolescent patients who began with a bipolar NOS diagnosis converted to Bipolar I or II within a 15-month follow-up. They also had considerable psychosocial impairment, suggesting that Bipolar NOS is a category worthy of continued study and clarification (NIMH, 2001).

PHENOMENOLOGY OF THE MANIC SYNDROME

Recent studies have attempted to distinguish the key characteristics of patients with euphoric mania and irritable (or aggressive) mania. A principal component analysis using data from 576 Bipolar I, manic patients identified seven stable underlying factors: pure manic symptoms, depressive mood, depressive inhibition, irritable aggression, insomnia, emotional lability and agitation, and psychosis (Sato, Bottlender, Kleindienst, & Moller, 2002). Manic episodes could be differentiated by their accompanying levels of aggressive, psychotic, or depressive symptoms—despite parallels in the manifestations of core manic symptoms.

A meta-analysis of seven studies examining the characteristics of mania among youths (aged 5–18; Kowatch, Youngstrom, Danielyan, & Findling, 2005) revealed that the most common symptoms were increased energy, distractibility, and pressure of speech. Approximately 80% showed irritability and grandiosity, whereas 70% had the cardinal manic symptoms of elated mood, decreased need for sleep, or racing thoughts. Less frequent symptoms included hypersexuality and psychotic symptoms. Thus, most manic children show symptoms that also characterize adult mania. Clearly, however, mania is not always experienced as a pleasurable state in either children or adults—it can be experienced as an angry, depressed, unfocused, tired but wired, and suicidal state.

CASE EXAMPLE

Robert, age 45, managed a landscape architecture firm. According to his girlfriend Jessie, his most recent manic episode began when—over a 1-week period—he became increasingly "expressive," impulsive, loud, and "took on a physical dominance stance." For example, he screamed inappropriately at the coach while watching his daughter's basketball game and "barked" orders at the waitress in a restaurant. He agreed that he was being "hyper" but also felt that he saw things more clearly than ever before. Things deteriorated when Robert, angry that his son Brian (age 21) had not returned his phone calls, confronted Brian at the record store where he worked. A shouting match laden with obscenities ensued, and Brian's boss nearly fired him.

In the next couple of days Robert became frantic. He became highly irritable and fixated on ideas about a musical career (he had only recently begun taking guitar lessons). He slept less and less. Toward the end of the week he impulsively moved out of his home with Jessie and into his office. He called her in a state of panic one night, saying that either he was dying or that he might kill himself—he was unsure of which. Jessie called the police, who found him at his office staring at the ceiling. He was admitted to the hospital and stayed for 2 weeks (Miklowitz & Goldstein, 1997).

EPIDEMIOLOGY

The large-scale National Comorbidity Survey replication study (NCS-R; N = 9,282) estimated that 2.1% of the general population meets lifetime *DSM-IV* criteria for Bipolar I (1.0%) or II (1.1%) Disorder (Merikangas et al., 2007). Another 2.4% meets criteria for Subthreshold Bipolar Disorder (i.e., recurrent threshold or subthreshold hypomanic episodes, with or without intercurrent major depressive episodes). Although it has not been studied as systematically, Cyclothymia appears to affect as much as 4.2% of the population (Regeer et al., 2004). By contrast, Major Depressive Disorder is at least four times more prevalent than Bipolar Disorder or Cyclothymia (17% lifetime prevalence in the population; Kessler et al., 2005).

It is less certain how common Bipolar Disorder is in youth. In a large community sample, Lewinsohn, Klein, and Seeley (1995) reported that approximately 1% of high school students met diagnostic criteria for bipolar spectrum disorders, most typically Bipolar II or Cyclothymic Disorder. This is probably an underestimate, however, since diagnoses were based on adolescent report only and teens are known to underreport bipolar symptoms relative to parents (Youngstrom, Findling, & Calabrese, 2004). Other estimates of Bipolar Disorder in children or adolescents are as high as 2% (Kessler, Avenevoli, & Ries-Merikangas, 2001) and 6% in treatment-seeking samples (Youngstrom, Findling, Youngstrom, & Calabrese, 2005). Interestingly, in the Lewinsohn study 6% of the adolescents reported having experienced at least one period of abnormally and persistently elated or irritable mood—even though they did not meet the *DSM-IV* criteria for Bipolar Disorder.

The onset of mood disorders appears to be getting younger in successive birth cohorts (e.g., Ryan et al., 1992). In the NCS-R, Kessler et al. (2005) reported that the lifetime risk of Bipolar I or II Disorder in 18- to 29-year-olds was 22 times higher than in persons over 60. It is likely, however, that younger persons are more likely to report mood disorder (notably manic) symptoms than older persons.

AGE AT ONSET

There is considerable variability in age at onset from study to study, depending upon whether onset is defined as the first fully syndromal manic episode, the first depressive episode, or the first onset of any symptoms. In the NCS-R, the mean age at onset of Bipolar I Disorder (defined as the first manic/hypomanic or depressive episode) was 18.2 years; for Bipolar II it was 20.3 years, with the inter-quartile range (25–75 percentile) between 12.6 and 24.9 years (Merikangas et al., 2007). Another large-scale study found that between 50% and 67% of Bipolar I and II patients had onset before age 18, and between 15% and 28% before age 13 (Perlis et al., 2004). Earlier age at onset (for example, prior to age 17) is associated with rapid cycling and other negative illness outcomes in adulthood (Coryell et al., 2003; Schneck et al., 2004; Suppes et al., 2001).

SUICIDALITY

Patients with Bipolar Disorder are at 15 times greater risk for completed suicide than the general population (Harris & Barraclough, 1997; Jamison & Baldessarini, 1999) and four times greater risk than patients with Major Depressive Disorder (Brown, Beck, Steer, & Grisham, 2000). In a 40–44-year follow-up of 406 mood disorder inpatients (unipolar, Bipolar I, and Bipolar II), Angst, Angst, Gerber-Werder, and Gamma (2005) found that 11% had died by suicide. Risk factors for completed suicide include younger age, recent illness onset, male gender, prior suicide attempts, a family history of suicide, comorbid alcohol or substance abuse, rapid cycling course, social isolation, anxious mood, and impulsive aggression (Fawcett, Golden, & Rosenfeld, 2000; Angst et al., 2005; Jamison, 2000; Marangell et al., 2006; Bridge, Goldstein, & Brent, 2006). On a more hopeful note, Angst et al. (2005) found that patients who were treated with lithium, antipsychotics, or antidepressants—particularly in combination regimens—had a lower suicide rate than those who did not. Not surprisingly, patients with a more severely depressive course of illness were more likely to commit suicide than were those with a more severely manic course.

COMORBID DISORDERS

Virtually all Bipolar patients have a lifetime history of other psychiatric disorders. Among Bipolar adults, the most frequent lifetime comorbid disorders are anxiety disorders (75%), impulse control disorders (63%), and substance use disorders (42%; Merikangas et al., 2007). The comorbidity of Bipolar Disorder and Attention Deficit Hyperactivity Disorder (ADHD) in youth is between 60% and 90%, even when over-lapping symptoms are removed from consideration (Geller et al., 2002; Kim & Miklo-witz, 2002). Differentiation of the two disorders usually requires a careful diagnostic screening, information from multiple informants (i.e., parents, teachers), and longitudi-nal observation of the course of illness. Children and adult Bipolar Disorder patients with comorbid disorders have poorer long-term prognoses than patients without comor-bid features (Feske et al., 2000; Frank et al., 2002; Masi et al., 2004; Otto et al., 2006; Tohen, Waternaux, & Tsuang, 1990).

IMPAIRMENT IN FUNCTIONING

Many patients experience ongoing functional impairments even between episodes (Fagiolini et al., 2005; Coryell et al., 1993; Suppes et al., 2001; Goldberg, Harrow, & Grossman, 1995). In a 12-month follow-up of hospitalized manic or mixed patients, 48% recovered symptomatically by 12 months but only 24% showed full recovery of function (Keck et al., 1998). The functional consequences of manic episodes—impaired family, work, and interpersonal relationships—can be observed for 5 years after an acute manic episode (Coryell et al., 1993). Only about one in three patients with Bipolar Disorder taking lithium had good functioning over a 4.5-year follow-up (Goldberg et al., 1995).

In a Stanley Foundation Network study of 253 adult patients with Bipolar Disorder, only about one in three worked full-time outside of the home. More than half were un-able to work or worked only in sheltered settings (Suppes et al., 2001). These results are similar to those of an earlier study by Dion, Tohen, Anthony, & Waternaux (1988) who found that one-third of patients were unable to work at all, and only one in five work at their expected level in the 6 months after a hospitalized episode of illness. The disorder is also associated with high rates of family or marital distress, dysfunction, separation, divorce, and problems in the adjustment of patients' offspring (Coryell et al., 1993; Hodgins, Faucher, Zarac, & Ellenbogen, 2002; Simoneau, Miklowitz, & Saleem, 1998).

As one would expect, a broad range of variables predict functional impairment. Symptom status is one such predictor, although it accounts for only modest variance (Gitlin et al., 1995). Hammen, Gitlin, and Altshuler (2000) found that higher personality disorder symptoms predicted occupational dysfunction even after symptom-status vari-ables were covaried. The presence of a supportive relationship was the best predictor of successful employment.

MANIA AND CREATIVITY

Mania has been described as a highly productive, creative state of exuberance (Jamison, 2005). It appears that creativity output is unlikely to occur during manic episodes, although it may occur during hypomania. Many historical figures in the arts, literature, and politics are believed to have had Bipolar Disorder—Vincent Van Gogh, Ernest Hemingway, and Winston Churchill are examples (Jamison, 1993). There may be com-monalties of temperament among patients with Bipolar Disorder and highly creative persons, including novelty seeking and openness to new experiences (Nowakowska, Strong, Santosa, Wang, & Ketter, 2005). The unaffected first-degree relatives of patients with Bipolar Disorder demonstrate higher creativity than do the affected relatives (Johnson, 2005b; Richards, Kinney, Lunde, Benet, & Merzel, 1988). Furthermore, children diagnosed with Bipolar Disorder and children who are the offspring of bipolar parents score higher on a measure related to creativity than healthy control children do (Simeonova, Chang, Strong, & Ketter, 2005).

Etiology, Risk Factors, and Protective Factors: The Biopsychosocial Perspective

Modern perspectives on Bipolar Disorder view the illness as a continuous interaction between genetic vulnerability, neurobiological dysregulation, and environmental events. The mechanisms by which genetic, biological, cognitive, emotional, and contextual factors interact across different phases of development, however, have only recently received serious study. Notably, in proposing the *kindling effect,* Post (1992) hypothesized that environmental stress has its greatest impact at the beginning phases of the illness, and that early episodes are more likely to be precipitated by psychosocial stressors than later episodes. Eventually, one episode kindles another and the cycling of the illness takes on an autonomous course.

Not all studies support this view (Coryell, Endicott, & Keller, 1990). In an alternate perspective—the *sensitization model*—patients with Bipolar Disorder become highly reactive to stress as the illness progresses, such that minor stressors are more likely to precipitate the rapid onset of recurrences later in the illness than early in the illness (Hammen & Gitlin, 1997). Evidence for the main effects of and interactions between genetic, neurobiological, and stress variables in the onset and course of Bipolar Disorder is presented below.

GENETIC STUDIES

Bipolar Disorder is among the most heritable of disorders. Heritability estimates from twin studies are as high as .85 to .93 (Kieseppa, Partonen, Haukka, Kaprio, & Lonnquist, 2004; McGuffin et al., 2003). At least a dozen studies have examined the risk of Bipolar Disorder among first-degree relatives of those with Bipolar Disorder, with estimates ranging from 5 to 12% (Alda, 1997), and between 20–25% when all forms of mood disorder in first-degree relatives are considered (Smoller & Finn, 2003). A meta-analysis of 17 studies suggested that children of bipolar parents are at a four-fold increased risk of affective disorders compared to children of parents without a psychiatric diagnosis (LaPalme, Hodgins, & LaRoche, 1997). Finally, the few available adoption studies confirm the highly heritable nature of Bipolar Disorder (Wender et al., 1986).

Some meta-analyses find consistent evidence for the 13q32 and 22q11 sites (Badner & Gershon, 2002) and for the serotonin transporter promoter region (Anguelova, Benkelfat, & Turecki, 2003; Lasky-Su, Faraone, Glatt, & Tsuang, 2005). The results of meta-analyses, however, differ depending on study sampling methods. Whereas previous analyses had compiled only published data (which accentuates positive findings), Segurado and colleagues (2003) gathered original data from 18 different teams with samples of more than 20 affected probands, so as to be able to analyze even the negative, unpublished findings for genetic regions. Their meta-analysis, weighted for sample size, provided the strongest support for links of Bipolar Disorder to 14q 9p-q, 10q, 18p-q, and 8-q. However, their analyses suggested that no genetic region has replicated in more than 10 of the 18 studies. Readers are referred to more comprehensive reviews of this literature (Badner & Gershon, 2002; Hasler, Drevets, Gould, Gottesman, & Manji, 2006; Kato, 2007; Lotrich & Pollock, 2004).

SHARED GENETIC VULNERABILITIES OF BIPOLAR DISORDER WITH DEPRESSION AND SCHIZOPHRENIA

When examining the first-degree relatives of Bipolar Disorder probands, there is an increased risk for major depressive disorders (Smoller & Finn, 2003) as well as Schizophrenia. Increasingly, a key question is understanding the extent of overlap in the phenotypes and genotypes for these disorders. One twin study found that the heritability for unipolar depression and mania was modestly correlated, but 71% of the genetic liability to mania was distinct from that of depression (McGuffin et al., 2003). A polymorphism in the serotonin transporter promotor region has been documented across at least some studies of Bipolar Disorder (Levinson, 2006) and has been documented as a risk factor for Unipolar Depression in the context of life events within several large scale studies (Caspi et al., 2003; Kendler, Kuhn, Vittum, Prescott, & Riley, 2005; Taylor et al., 2005).

In parallel, researchers have begun to examine overlap in the genetic risk of Schizophrenia and Bipolar Disorder. In regard to Schizophrenia, the monozygotic twins of persons with Schizophrenic Disorder are at increased risk for mania (8.2%) as well as Schizophrenia (40.8%). Likewise, the monozygotic twins of manic patients are at an increased risk for Schizophrenia (13.6%) and mania (36.4%) (Cardno, Rijsdijk, Sham, Murray, & McGuffin, 2002).

Of the genetic regions hypothesized to be involved in Bipolar Disorder, several appear to overlap with those proposed to increase risk for Schizophrenia, including 13q32 and 22q11 (Badner & Gershon, 2002). The findings, however, are inconsistent: two recent meta-analyses failed to suggest overlap in the genetic regions involved in Schizophrenia and Bipolar Disorder (Lewis, Levinson, & Wise, 2003; Segurado et al., 2003). Hence, while there is considerable hope that eventually genetic research will identify regions that increase vulnerability to both Bipolar Disorder and Schizophrenia, or to Bipolar Disorder and Depression, early findings have not been replicated.

NEUROTRANSMITTER DYSREGULATION

Over the past decade, models of neurotransmitter disturbance in Bipolar Disorder have shifted from a focus on absolute levels of neurotransmitters to an emphasis on the overall functioning of systems. Increasingly sophisticated technologies facilitate examining facets of the system that contribute to overall functioning, such as the binding of neurotransmitters to receptors or individual differences in sensitivity to pharmacological challenges. Dopamine and serotonin dysfunctions likely interact with deficits in other neurotransmitter systems, such as GABA and Substance P, to produce symptoms of mood disorders (e.g., Stockmeier, 2003). For the sake of brevity, we focus our review on the evidence regarding dysregulation in dopamine and serotonin systems. We do not focus on norepinephrine here—although norepinephrine levels have been found to be increased during mania and diminished during depression, it is less clear whether changes in norepinephrine levels are a product or cause of mood symptoms (Thase, Jindal, & Howland, 2002).

Dopamine

Current theory suggests that dopamine function is enhanced during mania and diminished during depression. Among people without Bipolar Disorder, dopaminergic agonists have been found to trigger manic symptoms such as increased mood, energy, and talkativeness (Willner, 1995). Manic symptoms in response to amphetamine are more pronounced among people with Bipolar Disorder than among people without Bipolar Disorder, probably because amphetamine increases the bioavailability of dopamine as well as other catecholamines (Anand et al., 2000).

Beyond pharmacological studies, a fair amount of research has been conducted on sleep deprivation, which has been found to interfere with normalizing the sensitivity of dopamine receptors (Ebert, Feistel, Barocks, Kaschka, & Pirner, 1994). Consistent with a role of dopamine in manic symptoms, about 10% of people with a history of mania demonstrate manic symptoms the morning after a night of sleep deprivation (Barbini et al., 1998).

Theories of bipolar disorders have long placed emphasis on the dopaminergic pathways involved in reward sensitivity (Depue, Collins, & Luciana, 1996; Hestenes, 1992) including the nucleus accumbens and the ventral tegmentum (Naranjo, Tremblay, & Busto, 2001). Behavioral sensitization paradigms—in which repeated, intermittent doses of psychomotor stimulants produce a progressively greater and longer-lasting behavioral response—provide one window into studying these pathways (Sax & Strakowski, 2001). Increased sensitivity to stimulants appears to be a result of enhanced sustained release of dopamine (Robinson & Becker, 1986), particularly within reward pathways (Kalivas, Duffy, DuMars, & Skinner, 1988).

First episode patients with Bipolar Disorder and Schizophrenia demonstrate less behavioral sensitivity than do those not diagnosed with these disorders, perhaps indicating that dopaminergic receptors have already developed increased sensitivity (Strakowski, Sax, Setters, & Keck, 1996; Strakowski, Sax, Setters, Stanton, & Keck, 1997). This is consistent with the hypothesis (discussed below) that Bipolar Disorder is characterized by greater sensitivity to reward, as mediated by changes in the regulation of dopaminergic reward pathways.

Serotonin

Substantial evidence now suggests that Bipolar Disorder is related to diminished function of the serotonin system. As serotonin constrains other neurotransmitter systems, deficits in the function of the serotonin system are believed to allow for greater variability in the function of dopamine. Neuroimaging studies indicate mood disorders are generally associated with decreased sensitivity of the serotonin receptors (Stockmeier, 2003). Research on Unipolar Disorder has examined how people respond to fluctuations in serotonin, induced by either the depleting or augmenting of tryptophan—the precursor to serotonin (Staley, Malison, & Innis, 1998). Persons with a positive family history of Bipolar Disorder display more cognitive deficits after serotonin-depletion and serotonin-augmentation procedures than persons without a positive family history (Sobcazk, Honig, Schmitt, & Riedel, 2003; Sobczak et al., 2002). The nature of this dysregulation in serotonergic systems remains undefined.

BRAIN REGIONS INVOLVED IN BIPOLAR DISORDER

The brain regions involved in emotional reactivity and regulation are being mapped in healthy individuals (Phillips, Drevets, Rauch, & Lane, 2003). For example, the amygdala is involved in identifying the significance of emotionally relevant stimuli of both negative and positive valence (Aggleton, 2000). Signals from the amygdala activate relevant structures involved in emotion processing and planning—such as the hippocampus, which is hypothesized to facilitate encoding and retrieval of emotion-relevant memories, and the prefrontal cortex (PFC), which appears to be involved in the regulation of emotion (Ochsner & Gross, 2005).

Not surprisingly, these same regions have been implicated in the pathophysiology of Bipolar Disorder. In functional studies, Bipolar I Disorder is associated with elevated activity in the amygdala in PET studies (Kruger, Seminowicz, Goldapple, Kennedy, & Mayberg, 2003), as well as in functional MRI studies of activity during cognitive or emotional tasks (Chang et al., 2004; Lawrence et al., 2004). In structural studies, above-average volumes of the amygdala have been reported (Phillips, Drevets, Rauch, & Lane, 2003). One would expect that the elevated activity and size of the amygdala would contribute to an emotional sensitivity. Beyond this, several functional studies suggest diminished activity of the hippocampus and prefrontal cortex among persons with Bipolar Disorder (Chang et al., 2004; Kruger et al., 2003), as well as diminished volume in the prefrontal cortex, basal ganglia, hippocampus, and anterior cingulate (Phillips, Drevets, Rauch, & Lane, 2003). Diminished activity of the PFC and related cortical regions might interfere with the ability to inhibit emotions and to conduct effective planning and goal pursuit in the context of emotion. Taken together, these structural and functional deficits are consistent with the models of limbic-cortical dysfunction proposed for Unipolar Depression (Davidson, Pizzagalli, & Nitschke, 2002; Mayberg, Keightley, Mahurin, & Brannan, 2004).

Neural activity in brain regions related to emotion processing changes during manic episodes. For example, persons with Bipolar Disorder show less neural reactivity to negative stimuli during mania than during healthy periods (Lennox, Jacob, Calder, Lupson, & Bullmore, 2004). Other studies have found that both at rest and during motor tasks, activity in the basal ganglia—a reward pathway structure (Knutson, Adams, Fong, & Hommer, 2001)—is positively correlated with concurrent manic symptoms (Blumberg et al., 1999; Caligiuri et al., 2003). Hence, manic symptoms may be associated with diminished neural responsivity to cues of threat and increased activity in reward processing regions.

Psychosocial Predictors of the Course of Bipolar Disorder

By the end of the 1980s, it was relatively well established that genetic models of Bipolar Disorder did not explain the enormous heterogeneity in the course of the illness over time (Prien & Potter, 1990). Given this, researchers began to consider the role of psychosocial factors in predicting the course of disorder. Several early findings established that psychosocial variables were robust predictors of the course of disorder. For example, Ellicott, Hammen, Gitlin, Brown, & Jamison (1990) found that bipolar patients with high levels of life-events were at 4.5 greater risk for relapse within 2 years than were patients with medium or low levels of life events, even when the focus of the analyses was on life events that were not caused by the person. Intriguingly, life events have also been found to predict the onset of mood disorders among the adolescent children of parents with Bipolar Disorder (Hillegers et al., 2004; Wals et al., 2005).

Miklowitz, Goldstein, Nuechterlein, Snyder, and Mintz (1988) found that manic inpatients who returned home to families rated high on expressed emotion (EE) attitudes (criticism, hostility, or emotional overinvolvement) or who showed high levels of caregiver-to-patient affective negativity (criticism, hostility, or guilt-induction) during face-to-face interactions were at 94% risk for relapse within 9 months. This figure compares to a 17% risk of relapse among those who returned to families that were low on both EE and affective negativity.

Although these earlier studies established the predictive value of psychosocial variables, they did not differentiate manic versus depressive symptoms in studying outcomes. Recent research has systematically examined how psychosocial variables influence the course of depression versus mania within Bipolar Disorder.

PSYCHOSOCIAL PREDICTORS OF DEPRESSION WITHIN BIPOLAR DISORDER

The symptomatology and neurobiology of Unipolar and Bipolar Depression have many strong parallels (Cuellar, Johnson, & Winters, 2005). Given this, it is not surprising that many of the psychosocial predictors of Unipolar Depression also predict the course of Bipolar Depression. Predictors of both the Unipolar and Bipolar depressive recurrences or severe symptoms include low social support (Johnson, Winett, Meyer, Greenhouse, & Miller, 1999), family EE (Kim & Miklowitz, 2004; Yan, Hammen, Cohen, Daley, & Henry, 2004), and neuroticism (Heerlein, Richter, Gonzalez, & Santander, 1998; Lozano & Johnson, 2001).

In considering the role of life events in Bipolar Disorder, it becomes important for investigators to use interview-based methods that exclude life events caused by symptoms (Johnson, 2005a). Three cross-sectional studies that used this methodology found that negative life events are equally common before episodes of Bipolar Depression and Unipolar Depression (Malkoff-Schwartz et al., 2000; Pardoen et al., 1996; Perris, 1984).

Prospective interview-based studies suggest that stressful life events lengthen the time to recovery from a depressive episode (Johnson & Miller, 1997), and predict increases in Bipolar Depression over several months (Johnson, 2005a). Kim, Miklowitz, Biuckians, and Mullen (2007) followed 38 adolescents with Bipolar Depression who were enrolled in a randomized trial of a family treatment program. Adolescents who experienced more chronic stress in family and romantic relationships during the follow-up period also experienced more sustained depressive symptoms over time.

Several studies have examined moderators of life events effects. Two studies of undergraduates with a history of hypomanic or depressive symptoms found that negative life events predicted increases in depressive symptoms only among students with negative cognitive styles (Alloy, Reilly-Harrington, Fresco, Whitehouse, & Zechmeister, 1999; Reilly-Harrington, Alloy, Fresco, & Whitehouse, 1999). Despite theories of kindling (Post & Weiss, 1998), studies have not consistently found that life events are more potent in provoking initial episodes than later episodes in either adult (Hammen & Gitlin, 1997; Hlastala et al., 2000) or adolescent samples (Hillegers et al., 2004).

One cross-sectional study of an adult sample (Dienes, Hammen, Henry, Cohen, & Daley, 2006) found that, contrary to the kindling model, the number of prior episodes of illness did not interact with life events stress in predicting recurrences among bipolar adults. Consistent with a stress sensitization model, patients who reported severe early adversity (such as parental neglect or sexual/physical abuse) reported less stress prior to recurrences and an earlier age at onset of Bipolar Disorder than patients who reported no early adversity. Thus, early adversity may create a vulnerability that decreases the threshold at which stress provokes symptoms of Bipolar Disorder.

Although negative cognitive styles are often documented in Bipolar Disorder, the negativity of cognitive styles appears to be related to the severity of depression (Cuellar, Johnson, & Winters, 2005). That is, cognitions appear to be more negative during depressive periods compared with well periods (Knowles, Tai, Christensen, & Bentall, 2005; Seligman et al., 1988; Thomas & Bentall, 2002) and they can be explained by the presence of depressive history rather than manic history (Alloy et al., 1999). Furthermore, negative cognitive styles and low self-esteem predict increases in depression over time (Johnson & Fingerhut, 2004; Johnson, Meyer, Winett, & Small, 2000). In sum, variables that influence the course of Unipolar Depression also influence Bipolar Disorder depression—including poor social support, EE, neuroticism, negative cognitive styles, and negative life events.

PSYCHOSOCIAL PREDICTORS OF MANIA

Compared with Bipolar Disorder depression, less is known about the psychosocial variables influencing mania. Three models focus on the predictors of mania: the manic-defense model (emphasizing negative threats and defensiveness), goal dysregulation (emphasizing reward sensitivity), and life events involving sleep or schedule disruption.

The Manic-Defense Model

Psychodynamic models have long conceptualized mania as a defense against loss experiences and painful awareness of negative feelings about the self (Abraham, 1911). As reviewed by Johnson (2005a), most prospective studies using life event interviews do not indicate that negative life events directly predict increases in mania (Alloy et al., 1999; Johnson et al., 2000; McPherson, Herbison, & Romans, 1993; Reilly-Harrington et al., 1999). For example, Kim, Miklowitz, Biukians, and Mullen (2007) found that adolescents with ongoing manic symptoms do not report more chronic peer-related stress.

There is evidence, however, that persons with Bipolar Disorder are defensive in the way they describe themselves. Although their responses are in the normative range on self-esteem measures, they demonstrate more negative responses on measures of blame for hypothetical negative life events or on measures of attention to negative words (Lyon, Startup, & Bentall, 1999; Winters & Neale, 1985). One hypothesis is that persons with Bipolar Disorder engage in coping efforts that are excessively activating in the face of stress, promoting the genesis of manic symptoms. Consistent with this idea, researchers have found that people with Bipolar Disorder endorse more sensation seeking (Knowles et al., 2005). Other research shows that people at high risk for mania used more defensive responses to threatening lab tasks (such as writing about one's own mortality) than did those at low risk (Johnson, Joiner, & Ballister, 2005). In sum, literature on the manic defense theory provides evidence for certain maladaptive coping styles, but less is known about whether these prospectively predict manic symptoms.

Goal Dysregulation

As described above, it has long been hypothesized that Bipolar Disorder relates to dysregulation in reward pathways. As a consequence, one might expect that people with Bipolar Disorder might be more reactive to rewards and successes in their environment (Johnson, 2005b). People with a history of mania and students vulnerable to mania describe themselves as more reward sensitive—more likely to react with strong emotions to reward or achievement (Meyer, Johnson, & Carver, 1999; Meyer, Johnson, & Winters, 2001). People with Bipolar Disorder place a stably high emphasis on achieving goals (Lam, Wright, & Smith, 2004). Indeed, several studies suggest that people with Bipolar Disorder and those at risk for the disorder endorse highly ambitious life goals (Johnson, Eisner, & Carver, 2007; Johnson & Carver, 2006). Studies that have examined these characteristics find that reward sensitivity and ambitious goal setting are trait-like features that do not appear to be explained by current symptoms of mania (Johnson & Carver, 2006; Lam et al., 2004).

Johnson, Sandrow et al. (2000) hypothesized that excess reward sensitivity may heighten reactivity to success, such that manic symptoms would be more likely after life events involving goal attainment. Results of a longitudinal study of Bipolar I Disorder patients supported this hypothesis: goal-attainment life events predicted increases in manic symptoms but not depressive symptoms. Such effects were apparent even after controlling for baseline manic symptoms and excluding life events that could have been caused by the symptoms.

Laboratory studies provide a means to study processes that could contribute to manic symptoms after an initial success. With increases in manic symptoms and even mild increases in positive affect, people with Bipolar Disorder remember more positive than negative memories (Eich, Macaulay, & Lam, 1997), pay less attention to negative stimuli (Murphy et al., 1999), are less willing to take advice (Mansell & Lam, 2006), and become impaired in the ability to detect negative facial expressions (Lembke & Ketter, 2002). Impulsivity, or the tendency to pursue rewards without awareness of potential negative consequences, also becomes elevated as people become manic (Swann, Dougherty, Pazzaglia, Pham, & Moeller, 2004).

These shifts in cognitive processing may contribute to changes in confidence. In studies of responses to standardized (false) success feedback, people vulnerable to Bipolar Disorder demonstrate more robust increases in confidence than nonvulnerable people (Johnson, 2005b; Stern & Berrenberg, 1979). Mood-state dependent increases in confidence may also contribute to increased goal engagement (Johnson et al., 2005). Longitudinal evidence suggests that increases in goal engagement (setting new goals and spending time pursuing goals) predict increases in manic symptoms over several months (Lozano & Johnson, 2001). In sum, goal attainments and successes appear to inspire bursts of confidence, which then fuel increased goal engagement for persons with Bipolar Disorder. This excess goal engagement may accelerate the development of manic symptoms (Johnson, 2005b).

Schedule Disruption

Drawing on extensive clinical observations Wehr and colleagues (Wehr, Sack, & Rosenthal, 1987; Wehr, Goodwin, Wirz-Justice, Breitmaier, & Craig, 1982) hypothesized that sleep disruption might trigger episodes of Bipolar Disorder. As mentioned above, sleep deprivation has been found to interfere with normalizing the sensitivity of dopamine receptors (Ebert et al., 1994). Empirical research since that time has shown that sleep deprivation is a potent predictor of manic symptoms (Barbini et al., 1998). In an 18-month naturalistic study of more modest sleep changes, diminished time sleeping predicted next day increases in manic symptoms (Leibenluft, Albert, Rosenthal, & Wehr, 1996).

Wehr also hypothesized that sleep deprivation might mediate the effects of life events on episodes of Bipolar Disorder, noting that the life events triggering episodes might often interfere with the ability to sleep (e.g., transmeridian flights, childbirth). This theory was expanded by Ehlers and colleagues (Ehlers, Frank, & Kupfer, 1988; Ehlers, Kupfer, Frank, & Monk, 1993). In the elaborated model, environmental and interpersonal influences serve the role of timekeepers ("social zeitgebers") whereas other social influences ("social zeitstorers") disrupt the ability of the Bipolar Disorder person to maintain daily rhythms (e.g., a job with shifting work hours). Ehlers and colleagues also suggested that social rhythm disruptions (e.g., to daily routines, social plans, and sleep-wake cycles) might predict symptoms above and beyond the role of disruptions specific to sleep.

The social rhythm metric (SRM) has been most widely used to test the constancy of the daily schedule (Monk, Flaherty, Frank, Hoskinson, & Kupfer, 1990) and has been well validated against measures of schedule and sleep disruption (Monk, Reynolds, Buysse, DeGrazia, & Kupfer, 2003). Social rhythm regularity scores on the SRM are lower among persons with rapid cycling Bipolar Disorder compared to healthy controls (Ashman et al., 1999). A study using actigraphy found that parents with Bipolar Disorder, as well as their children with early onset mood disorders, evidenced dysregulation in their daily activity patterns (Jones, Tai, Evershed, Knowles, & Bentall, 2006). Stabilization of SRM scores after an acute episode were associated with longer well intervals prior to recurrences in a randomized treatment trial (Frank et al., 2005).

Malkoff-Schwartz et al. (1998) conducted interviews with Bipolar Disorder patients to assess the life events before their most recent illness episode. Patients reported more life events that disrupted social rhythms in the eight weeks before mania recurrences than in the eight weeks before depressive recurrences. These results remained parallel in a publication with an enlarged sample (Malkoff-Schwartz et al., 2000). Such findings provide one more potential mechanism for understanding how life events affect the onset of mania.

In sum, it has long been hypothesized that sleep disruption could be a trigger for manic episodes, and both naturalistic and experimental data support this idea. Although people with Bipolar Disorder and their offspring show more varied patterns of day-to-day social activities, this variability does not predict symptoms. Nonetheless, people with Bipolar Disorder do report that their manic episodes—but not depressive episodes—were often preceded by changes in social rhythms.

Thus, the variables most consistently associated with the onset of mania include life events involving maladaptive coping and defensiveness in response to threats, reward sensitivity and goal engagement, and life events involving sleep/wake cycle disruption. Later in this chapter, we will describe an intervention geared towards addressing sleep/wake cycle disruptions (interpersonal and social rhythm therapy).

Diagnostic Assessment

STRUCTURED INTERVIEWS

Traditionally, Bipolar Disorder has been established via structured or semistructured clinical interview. Some clinicians are reluctant to diagnose the disorder unless they actually see the patient in a manic state—others rely on the history offered by the patient or family members.

The most prominent diagnostic interview in the United States is the Structured Diagnostic Interview for *DSM-IV* (SCID) (First, Spitzer, Gibbon, & Williams, 1995). The Schedule for Affective Disorders and Schizophrenia (SADS) is also a commonly used interview. Both the SCID and the SADS have achieved excellent inter-rater reliability and validity for the diagnosis of Bipolar I Disorder (Rogers, Jackson, & Cashel, 2001; Williams et al., 1992). The SCID is time-consuming, however, and some researchers are now using the Mini International Neuropsychiatric Interview (Sheehan et al., 1998), which simply requires patients to respond with yes or no to various questions about current and previous symptom states. The chance for false negative responses, however, increases with a yes/no format.

For patients under the age of 18, the Kiddie Schedule for Affective Disorders and Schizophrenia, Present and Lifetime Version (KSADS-PL) (Chambers et al., 1985; Kaufman et al., 1997) or the Washington University KSADS (Geller et al., 2002) is preferred. In childhood samples, parent report is generally more reliable than child report, but most studies obtained K-SADS data from both parent and child (Youngstrom et al., 2004).

Even with structured interviews, the diagnosis of Bipolar II Disorder can be quite difficult. When interviewers rate the same tapes, reliability estimates for Bipolar II Disorder are inadequate for the SADS in some (Keller et al., 1981) but not all studies (Simpson et al., 2002; Spitzer, Endicott, & Robins, 1978). As might be expected given low inter-rater reliability, test-retest reliability over a six-month period was quite poor for Bipolar II Disorder ($r = .06$) and even poorer for Cyclothymia (Andreasen et al., 1981). In a five-year test-retest study, SADS diagnoses of Bipolar II Disorder achieved kappa scores of only .09 (Rice et al., 1986), and in a 10-year study only 40% of persons initially diagnosed with Bipolar II Disorder on the SADS experienced further episodes of hypomania or mania (Coryell et al., 1995). Dunner and Tay (1993) found that the SCID under-identified hypomanic episodes when comparing with diagnoses based on unstandardized interviews conducted by clinicians.

To gain a thorough assessment of the disorder and its subsyndromal forms, structured diagnostic assessments like the SCID should be supplemented by self-report questionnaires, family history interviews, and life charting (timeline records of the frequency, severity, and timing of prior episodes (e.g., Leverich & Post, 1998). However, patients' insight tends to diminish as symptoms become more severe; as a result, any of these measures can yield questionable information when patients are highly symptomatic. Given this, it is important to gather input from family members.

QUESTIONNAIRE MEASURES OF RISK FOR BIPOLAR DISORDER

As described above, structured clinical interviews do not fare well in identifying the milder forms of Bipolar Disorder. Subsyndromal or spectrum forms of Bipolar Disorder—notably Cyclothymia or hyperthymia—may precede the onset of fully syndromal Bipolar

Disorder (Akiskal et al., 2005). Several investigators have attempted to capture these spectrum conditions with self-report questionnaires. The Temperament Evaluation of Memphis, Pisa, Paris, and San Diego, autoquestionnaire version (TEMPS-A) yields five factors with high internal consistency: cyclothymic (0.91), depressive (0.81), irritable (0.77), hyperthymic (0.76), and anxious (0.67; Akiskal et al., 2005). Moreover, in a prospective study using a questionnaire measure adapted from the TEMPS-A cyclothymic scale for children, baseline cyclothymic-hypersensitive TEMPS-A scores predicted the onset of Bipolar Disorder in a 2-year follow-up of clinically depressed youth (Kochman et al., 2005).

Other clinical investigators have focused on identifying mild symptoms of mania as a means of identifying persons at high risk of onset. The 79-item General Behavior Inventory (GBI) (Depue, Kleinman, Davis, Hutchinson, & Krauss, 1985) measures hyperthymia, dysthymia, or biphasic/cyclothymic temperaments. High GBI scores during adolescence are associated with psychosocial impairment in adulthood (Klein & Depue, 1984). Among teens with depression, higher scores on the depression subscale of the GBI were associated with Bipolar Disorder at 5-year follow-up (Reichart et al., 2005). The Hypomanic Personality Scale, a self-report instrument for measuring hypomanic temperaments among college students, predicted the onset of bipolar spectrum disorders over 13 years (Kwapil et al., 2000).

ASSESSMENT OF LONGITUDINAL OUTCOME

Studies focused on recovery or recurrence often use the Longitudinal Interval Follow-up Evaluation (LIFE; Keller, Lavori, & Friedman, 1987), originally developed for the Psychobiology of Depression collaborative study. The LIFE is a semi-structured interview given to the patient at 3–6 month intervals. The 0–6 ratings of psychiatric status are given for each week of follow-up and cover the severity of mania, hypomania, major depression, delusions, hallucinations, and comorbid disorders (e.g., anxiety, ADHD). From these ratings, the timing, duration, and frequency of recoveries and recurrences can be tabulated—along with functional outcomes such as school performance, household duties, interpersonal relationships, family relationships, satisfaction, and global functioning. An adolescent version of the LIFE was used in the Course and Outcome of Bipolar Youth Study (Birmaher et al., 2006), with inter-rater reliabilities (intraclass correlations) of ≥ .80 for mood disorder ratings. Moreover, ratings on the A-LIFE enabled investigators to identify conversion rates from Bipolar NOS to Bipolar II or Bipolar I (25% over an average of 2 years of prospective follow-up).

Treatment: Pharmacotherapy

Considerable strides have been made in the drug treatment of Bipolar Disorder within the past two decades. Drug treatment serves at least three purposes: (a) to stabilize an acute manic, depressed, or mixed/cycling episode; (b) to prevent relapse (maintenance pharmacotherapy); and (c) to reduce the severity of symptoms and to improve functioning in between episodes. For comprehensive reviews of the literature on drug treatment of bipolar depression and mania in adults and children, the reader is referred to Thase (2006), Goldberg (2004), DelBello and Kowatch (2006), and Kowatch, Fristad, et al. (2005).

In the past decade, the most significant change in pharmacological treatment for Bipolar Disorder has been the increasing use of anticonvulsant and antipsychotic medications. Although lithium continues to be the mainstay of treatment, psychiatrists increasingly are substituting divalproex sodium, lamotrigine, or atypical antipsychotics such as olanzapine, risperidone, quetiapine, ziprasidone, or aripiprazole to control acute manic or mixed episodes, to alleviate depressive symptoms, and to prevent recurrences. The increased popularity is generally attributed to more tolerable side effect profiles among anticonvulsants and atypical antipsychotics. In fact, these agents have different side effect profiles than lithium, as elaborated in the following sections.

TREATMENT OF MANIA

Approximately 60–70% of patients with Bipolar Disorder improve on lithium during a manic episode, although not all responders fully remit (Goldberg, 2004). Lithium, however, is difficult to tolerate: patients experience sedations, weight gain, tremors of the hands, stomach irritation, thirst, and kidney clearance problems. Divalproex sodium is as effective as lithium in controlling manic episodes but generally has more benign side effects (Bowden et al., 1994; Kowatch et al., 2000). A recent 18-month maintenance study comparing lithium to divalproex among children with Bipolar Disorder revealed equal efficacy in preventing recurrences (Findling et al., 2005). Divalproex, however, causes stomach pain, nausea, weight gain, elevated liver enzymes, and lowering of blood platelet counts.

Olanzapine, an atypical antipsychotic medication, appears to have strong antimanic properties and may be particularly useful for mixed episodes or rapid cycling (Frazier et al., 2001; Gonzalez-Pinto et al., 2002; Tohen et al., 2000). Its prophylaxis against recurrences of mania or mixed episodes is as good as or better than lithium or divalproex (Tohen et al., 2003; Tohen, Kryzhanovskaya et al., 2005; Tohen, Greil et al., 2005). A combination treatment, olanzapine with fluoxetine (Prozac)—usually called OFC or Symbiax—has a strong record of stabilizing both mania and depression (Tohen et al., 2003).

Although olanzapine emerged as the most clinically effective atypical antipsychotic in the large scale CATIE Schizophrenia trial, it also had a more difficult side effect profile than other atypical or typical antipsychotics—including weight gain and increases in glucose or lipid metabolism (Lieberman et al., 2005). Concerns about weight gain and more generally, the *metabolic syndrome* (abdominal obesity, elevated blood pressure, abnormal blood lipids, glucose intolerance) on olanzapine has made physicians favor other antipsychotics for mania, especially if they are going to be used in maintenance treatment. Quetiapine and risperidone appear to be associated with intermediate risk of weight gain and metabolic dysfunction, whereas aripiprazole and ziprasidone are of lowest risk (Newcomer, 2007). Quetiapine is increasingly used to control manic symptoms in adolescents, either alone or in combination with divalproex (Delbello, Schwiers, Rosenberg, & Strakowski, 2002; DelBello et al., 2006).

TREATMENT OF DEPRESSION

Although many clinicians use antidepressants in combination with mood stabilizers to control bipolar, depressive episodes, it is not clear that they are effective (Ghaemi, Lenox, & Baldessarini, 2001). A multi-site naturalistic study found that bipolar, depressed patients who were stabilized on mood stabilizers in combination with selective serotonin reuptake inhibitors (SSRIs) were less likely to relapse into depression and no more likely to develop mania or rapid cycling (treatment-emergent affective switch) if they continued antidepressants for 6 months after remission, when compared to patients who discontinued antidepressants (Altshuler et al., 2003). In contrast, the multi-site randomized Systematic Treatment Enhancement Program for Bipolar Disorder trial (STEP-BD) (Sachs et al., 2007) found that patients receiving mood stabilizers plus buproprion or paroxetine did not stabilize any faster than patients receiving mood stabilizers plus placebo, nor were they any more likely to have treatment-emergent affective switches.

One study found that combining lithium and divalproex is as effective in treating bipolar depression as combining mood stabilizers with an SSRI, raising the question of whether antidepressants are worth the risk of more frequent mood cycles (Young et al., 2000). Given these conflicting results, treatment guidelines for Bipolar depression recommend adding antidepressants to mood stabilizers or atypical antipsychotics only if other agents have failed (e.g., Yatham et al., 2005; Kowatch et al., 2005).

Other options for Bipolar depression, mania, and rapid cycling include lamotrigine (Bowden et al., 2003) and quetiapine (DelBello & Kowatch, 2006). Lamotrigine appears to be more effective than lithium as an antidepressant but not as an anti-manic agent (Goodwin et al., 2004). Concerns about a serious skin rash that, in a small number of patients can progress into Stevens-Johnson syndrome—a potentially fatal dermatological condition—has made clinicians cautious about the use of lamotrigine. Quetiapine can cause dizziness and sleepiness and, along with olanzapine, weight gain.

MEDICATION NONADHERENCE

Perhaps the biggest limitation to mood stabilizers is the high rates of nonadherence among patients who are expected to take them continuously. Between 40% and 60% of patients are fully or partially nonadherent with mood stabilizer regimens in the year after a manic episode (Strakowski et al., 1998) (Keck, McElroy, Strakowski, Bourne, & West, 1997; Colom et al., 2000). Rates of noncompliance in community mental health clinics are especially high—one study estimated that patients took lithium for an average of only 2–3 months (Johnson & McFarland, 1996). Rapid discontinuation of lithium places patients at considerably higher risk for recurrence and suicide (Suppes, Baldessarini, Faedda, Tondo, & Tohen, 1993; Tondo & Baldessarini, 2000).

Originally, nonadherence was believed to be due to a desire to recreate high periods or resenting having one's moods controlled by medications (Jamison, Gerner, & Goodwin, 1979). Although these beliefs undoubtedly contribute to nonadherence in some patients, more recent studies have emphasized the additional role of side effects, comorbid personality disorders, substance or alcohol abuse disorders, and more severe, recurrent forms of the illness in nonadherence (Colom et al., 2000). Difficulties with accepting the disorder and high rates of denial of the illness also contribute to medication inconsistency or discontinuation (Greenhouse, Meyer, & Johnson, 2000).

Treatment: Psychotherapy

Given the high rates of recurrence among bipolar patients, even when maintained on optimal pharmacotherapy, investigators are increasingly looking to combining pharmacotherapy with psychotherapy. Early trials of cognitive-behavioral therapy (Cochran,

1984) and family therapy (Clarkin et al., 1990) had shown positive benefits in enhancing medication compliance, reducing recurrences, and improving functioning among Bipolar patients. More recently, treatments have become manual-based and disorder-specific.

Four forms of psychotherapy have emerged as effective in the long-term maintenance of Bipolar Disorder. These treatments are each psychoeducational in focus, although their length and format vary considerably. Recent studies on these modalities are reviewed here. For a more comprehensive review see Miklowitz (2006).

Group Psychoeducation

A study conducted at the University of Barcelona, Spain (Colom et al., 2003) assessed the efficacy of psychoeducation and support groups among 120 adult patients with Bipolar I Disorder who had been in remission for at least six months. All patients received mood-stabilizing medications. One group received 21 weekly sessions of structured group psychoeducation and another received 21 unstructured, nondidactic group sessions. At the end of two years, fewer of the group psychoeducation patients (67%) than the control patients (92%) had relapsed, and fewer had been hospitalized. Patients in group psychoeducational treatment were also more likely to maintain lithium levels within the therapeutic range (Colom et al., 2005).

Bauer and colleagues (2006) tested a collaborative care management program for bipolar patients ($N = 306$) at 11 participating Veterans' Administration sites. The intervention centered on a group psychoeducational treatment to improve patients' self-management skills, but also included enhanced access to care through a nurse coordinator and medication practice guidelines for the treating psychiatrist. Patients were followed over 3 years. Those patients in the collaborative care management program spent fewer weeks in manic episodes than patients who received continued care as usual. They also showed greater improvements in social functioning, quality of life, and treatment satisfaction. The CCM treatment did not have an effect on mean levels of manic and depressive symptoms over the 3-year period. Dismantling studies will be necessary to determine the unique contribution of the group psychoeducation to the effectiveness of the full CCM program.

A similar study was conducted in a group health network (Simon, Ludman, Bauer, Unutzer, & Operskalski, 2006). The study randomly assigned 441 patients who were part of a prepaid group health plan to a 2-year multicomponent care-management intervention or treatment-as-usual. Patients were in various clinical states (some asymptomatic, some fully syndromal) and were receiving health care within the same managed care network. Care-management consisted of pharmacotherapy, telephone-based monitoring, interdisciplinary care planning, relapse prevention planning, and group psychoeducational treatment. Over 2 years, patients in the program had significantly lower mania scores and spent less time in manic or hypomanic episodes than those in the treatment-as-usual comparison group, but there were no effects on depressive symptoms. The results were strongest for patients who were symptomatic at baseline.

One study has examined the relative efficacy of two group psychoeducational treatments for bipolar adults who had comorbid substance dependence (Weiss et al., 2007). Bipolar patients with substance dependence ($N = 62$) were assigned randomly to 20 weeks of either integrated group therapy or traditional group drug counseling. The integrated group used a cognitive behavioral relapse prevention framework focused on the relationships between the two disorders (i.e., the overlap between the cognitions and behaviors of both conditions during recovery and relapse). The group counseling did not address mood issues, and instead focused on encouraging abstinence and teaching ways to cope with substance craving. The integrated, dual-focus groups were better in maintaining abstinence over 8 months: patients in these groups had half as many days of substance use as those receiving only drug counseling. The results were only significant for days of alcohol use, not drug use. The groups did not differ in the number of episodes of Bipolar Disorder. Surprisingly, patients in the integrated groups had higher subsyndromal depression and mania scores during treatment and follow-up than patients in drug counseling. The significance of this higher level of subsyndromal symptoms is unclear; it is possible that the dual diagnosis focus of the groups increased the likelihood that patients recognized and reported such symptoms. Alternatively, successful treatment of alcohol use disorders may unmask or even increase mood disorder symptoms. Integrated group treatment deserves further study in randomized trials involving substance dependent patients.

RELAPSE PREVENTION STRATEGIES

Perry, Tarrier, Morriss, McCarthy, & Limb (1999) examined a 7–12 session individual psychoeducational treatment and medication combination therapy, in comparison with routine care and medication. Psychoeducation sessions instructed patients how to identify early warning signs of recurrence and obtain emergency medical intervention. The investigators observed a 30% reduction in manic relapses, a longer time before manic relapse, and enhanced social functioning in the relapse prevention condition. The intervention was not associated with time to depressive relapse. Thus, a brief relapse prevention intervention may be a cost-effective way of reducing manic symptoms.

FAMILY PSYCHOEDUCATIONAL APPROACHES

Miklowitz & Goldstein (1990, 1997) designed a family-focused treatment (FFT) for recently episodic Bipolar Disorder patients. This approach is based on the idea that improving knowledge about Bipolar Disorder, reducing high EE attitudes, and enhancing communication will reduce relapse rates. It also involved the first use of a relapse prevention drill—a well-known technique in the substance dependence literature (e.g., Marlatt, 1985)—for Bipolar Disorder. The treatment involves three stages: psychoeducation for the patient and family members about Bipolar Disorder (including sessions devoted to identifying and learning to intervene early with prodromal symptoms of relapse), communication-enhancement training, and problem-solving skills training.

In a randomized trial, FFT was combined with standard pharmacotherapy and compared with a brief psychoeducational control (two sessions of family psychoeducation plus crisis intervention sessions as needed over 9 months). Patients had Bipolar I Disorder ($N = 101$) and were recruited during or shortly after a manic, mixed, or depressive episode. Over a two-year follow-up, patients in FFT were three times more likely to complete the study without relapsing (52% versus 17%) and had longer periods of stability without relapse (73.5 weeks versus 53.2 weeks). They also had greater improvements over time in depression, lower mania symptoms, and better adherence to medications than patients in the comparison group (Miklowitz, George, Richards, Simoneau, & Suddath, 2003). An analysis of mediating variables revealed that patients in

FFT demonstrated more improved communication with their relatives than patients in the control treatment, and further, that improved communication was associated with the alleviation of mood symptoms over 1 year (Simoneau, Miklowitz, Richards, Saleem, & George, 1999).

Rea and colleagues (2003) compared FFT plus pharmacotherapy to an equally intensive (21 session) individually focused patient management treatment plus pharmacotherapy for Bipolar I patients hospitalized for a manic episode ($N = 53$). In the first study year, no treatment differences were observed in relapse or rehospitalization rates. Over a 1- to 2-year post-treatment follow-up, however, patients in FFT had much lower rates of rehospitalization (12%) and symptomatic relapse (28%) than patients in the individual therapy (60% were rehospitalized and 60% had symptomatic relapse).

Two open trials (Miklowitz, Biuckians, & Richards, 2006; Pavuluri et al., 2004) demonstrated the benefits for FFT—either alone or in combination with CBT—in stabilizing symptoms among adolescent or school-aged bipolar patients. In sum, family interventions have been shown to be effective adjuncts to drug treatment for Bipolar Disorder.

COGNITIVE-BEHAVIORAL THERAPY

Two major trials of CBT have been conducted, both in the United Kingdom. Lam and colleagues (Lam, Hayward, Watkins, Wright, & Sham, 2005; Lam et al., 2003) compared 6 months of CBT (12–18 sessions, plus two booster sessions after 6 months) with pharmacotherapy, to treatment-as-usual with pharmacotherapy for 103 bipolar patients who had been in remission for at least six months. At one year, relapse rates were 44% in the CBT condition and 75% in the usual care condition. Patients in CBT also spent fewer days in illness episodes. Twelve to 30 months after treatment, CBT no longer prevented relapse relative to usual care but did continue to show a positive influence on mood and days spent in episodes. The effects of CBT were stronger on depression than mania.

A United Kingdom multicenter trial conducted across five sites ($N = 253$; Scott et al., 2006) compared 22 sessions of CBT plus medication to treatment-as-usual and medication. The patients had been in various clinical states before entry into the trial. A total of 60% of the patients had a recurrence during the 18-month follow-up, but no effects were found for CBT versus treatment-as-usual on time to recurrence. A posthoc analysis revealed that patients with less than 12 prior episodes had fewer recurrences if treated with CBT than treatment-as-usual. However, the opposite pattern was apparent among patients with 13 or more episodes—who were more likely to have recurrences in CBT than treatment-as-usual.

These results suggest that CBT may be most suited to patients in the early stages of their disorder or those with a less recurrent course. Because the study sites varied in experience in treating people with Bipolar Disorder, analyses of cross-site effects will probably be necessary to clarify these results.

INTERPERSONAL AND SOCIAL-RHYTHM THERAPY

As discussed above, one model suggests that Bipolar Disorder symptoms are triggered by disruptions in daily routines and sleep/wake cycles. Frank (2005) developed interpersonal and social-rhythm therapy (IPSRT) as a means to alter this pathway to recurrence. IPSRT begins during or shortly following an acute illness episode and includes techniques to stabilize social rhythms and resolve interpersonal problems that preceded that episode. Patients learn to track their daily routines and sleep/wake cycles and identify events (e.g., job changes, transatlantic travel) that may provoke changes in these routines.

In the Pittsburgh Maintenance Therapies study (Frank et al., 2005), acutely ill patients (N = 175) were randomly assigned to one of two weekly psychosocial treatments in combination with medication management: IPSRT or active clinical management. Clinical management was focused on symptom control and medication adherence. Once patients were stabilized, they were randomly reassigned to IPSRT or active clinical management for a two-year maintenance phase. IPSRT in the acute phase was associated with more time prior to recurrences in the maintenance phase than was the active clinical management. Moreover, IPSRT was most effective in delaying recurrences in the maintenance phase when patients succeeded in stabilizing their daily routines and sleep/wake cycles during the acute phase. IPSRT during the maintenance phase, however, was not superior to active clinical management in delaying recurrences.

In a nonrandomized open trial with an historical comparison group (N = 100), Miklowitz, George, Richards, Simoneau, and Suddath, (2003) examined the effects of individual IPSRT sessions in combination with FFT sessions for Bipolar I and II patients who had had an episode of illness within the prior 3 months. All patients received standard medication management. Over the study year, patients in the combined integrated family and individual therapy had longer periods of wellness prior to relapse and less severe depressive symptoms than patients in the comparison condition. The combination treatment did not affect manic symptoms.

Little is known about the mechanisms involved in treatment response with IPSRT, although it would appear from the Maintenance Therapies Trial that sleep/wake stabilization is one such mechanism. Interestingly, two case studies show that sleep regulation alone can improve bipolar mood symptoms (Wehr et al., 1998).

The STEP-BD Study

One study has compared the effectiveness of psychotherapies found to be effective in single-site trials. The STEP-BD study (Miklowitz, Otto, Frank, Reilly-Harrington, Wisniewski, et al., 2007) examined the effectiveness of IPSRT, FFT, and CBT (30 sessions over 9 months) compared to a 3-session psychoeducational control intervention (collaborative care; CC). Bipolar Disorder I and II patients (N = 293) were treated at 15 STEP-BD sites and began in a major depressive episode. All patients received pharmacotherapy with at least one mood stabilizer—and, often, adjunctive atypical antipsychotics, antidepressants, or anxiolytics.

Over 1 year, patients in the intensive therapy conditions were more likely to recover from depression (64%) and recovered more rapidly (mean 169 days) than patients in CC (52%, 279 days). One-year rates of recovery—which did not statistically differ across the intensive therapy groups—were 77% for FFT, 65% for IPSRT, 60% for CBT. Patients in the intensive therapies were also more likely to remain well in any given month of the 12-month study than patients in CC (Miklowitz, Otto, Frank, Reilly-Harrington, Wisniewski, et al., 2007). Moreover, patients in intensive therapy had better overall functioning, relationship functioning, and life satisfaction over time than patients in CC and they did not differ in vocational functioning (Miklowitz, Otto, Frank, Reilly-Harrington, Kogan, et al., 2007).

The STEP-BD program suggests that intensive psychotherapy is a vital part of the effort to stabilize episodes of depression and enhance functioning in Bipolar Disorder. Possibly, the emphasis on pharmacological maneuvering to combat mood dysregulation has obscured the potential role of psychotherapy in addressing life stressors associated with depression. Given that Bipolar patients often spend up to one-third of their lives in states of depression (Judd et al., 2002), and that mood stabilizing medications are generally more effective in controlling mania than depression (Keck, McElroy, Richtand, & Tohen, 2002), the integration of pharmacological and psychosocial treatments seems increasingly important.

Summary and Future Directions

Patients with Bipolar Disorder experience a highly recurrent course of illness with substantial psychosocial impairment. Although considerable advances have been made in understanding the diagnostic boundaries, etiology, prognostic factors, and pharmacological and psychosocial treatment of the illness, much remains to be learned.

Genetic and Neurobiological Markers of Risk

A family history of Bipolar Disorder clearly puts people at risk for the illness but genetic markers with disease specificity have not been identified. Certain genetic loci appear promising as candidates for identifying persons at risk. Ongoing efforts are directed at identifying genes that overlap between Bipolar Disorder and Schizophrenia.

Changes in the regulation of dopaminergic reward pathways and a decreased sensitivity of serotonin receptors have been implicated in bipolar mood symptoms. Serotonin deficits may contribute to a general dysregulation of emotion systems that increases vulnerability to a wide range of disorders (Carver, Johnson, & Joormann, 2007). Further research will be necessary to determine the exact nature and diagnostic specificity of these neurotransmitter system dysfunctions, and the degree to which such dysfunctions are evident during euthymic as well as symptomatic states.

What Are the Unique Predictors of Depression versus Mania?

Similar to recurrent Major Depressive Disorder, Bipolar Disorder is characterized by pathology in the brain systems involved in emotion regulation. The psychosocial variables that trigger negative emotional states—such as negative life events and high EE in caregivers—exert a major influence on the depressive course of the disorder. But what are the unique predictors of mania? Patients whose Bipolar Disorder is in remission have high sensitivity to reward and ambitious goal setting; during mania, they may develop cognitions that contain overly optimistic biases (Johnson, 2005b). Relatedly, excess goal engagement appears to predict increases in mania.

Sleep deprivation has also been found to predict manic symptoms. Life events that disrupt social rhythms are more common before manic recurrences than before depressive recurrences. The unique pathways that lead to mania versus depression, then, have begun to be clarified—but there have been relatively few prospective studies, and of those, most have focused on a single model rather than integrating a set of risk variables.

WHAT ARE THE OPTIMAL TREATMENT REGIMENS FOR BIPOLAR PATIENTS?

Pharmacotherapy trials have become more sophisticated, and increasing evidence points to the utility of anticonvulsants and atypical antipsychotics in stabilizing depression and mania. Few of these trials have considered long-term maintenance. We do not know, for example, whether bipolar patients are best maintained on combination therapy or monotherapy, or whether Bipolar II patients whose illness is primarily depressive could benefit equally from psychotherapy alone instead of mood stabilizing medications. The idea of treating certain forms of Bipolar Disorder without medication runs against the grain of current psychiatric practice, but in fact the data are not there to justify long-term medication maintenance in every case.

Randomized controlled trials indicate that adding psychotherapy onto medication helps stabilize the disorder and prevent recurrences. It is not clear whether the effect sizes for adjunctive psychotherapy are the same for manic or depressive symptoms, or whether the polarity of the episode at entry into treatment is an important determinant of treatment outcomes. The next generation of psychosocial research should examine treatment moderators to determine under what conditions psychotherapies are more and less successful.

More and more practical trials are appearing in the literature, in which treatment regimens are not set in stone and clinicians have the flexibility to change strategies when patients do not respond adequately. A recent example is the STAR-D trial (Rush, 2007). Studies have only begun to explore the effectiveness of algorithms for the drug treatment of Bipolar Disorder. Likewise, investigators could propose treatment staging strategies that combine psychopharmacology with psychotherapy—such as treating Bipolar depressed patients to remission with mood stabilizers or atypical antipsychotics and then determining whether adding a psychosocial intervention enables quicker discontinuation of the adjunctive agent.

PREVENTION OF ONSET

The potential application of psychosocial interventions to the prevention of onset of Bipolar Disorder has considerable promise. Bipolar Disorder can be conceptualized within a developmental psychopathology framework: how do bipolar symptoms emerge over time as a function of risk and protective processes within the genetic, biological, social, familial, and cultural domains, and how might one intervene in these developmental pathways to maximize protection and minimize risk (Miklowitz & Cicchetti, 2006)? These interventions may be both psychosocial and pharmacological. Prevention of the onset of first manic episodes may mean fewer or less severe mood symptoms over time, less risk of suicide, and enhanced psychosocial functioning.

Chang, Howe, Gallelli, & Miklowitz (2006) have offered the following hypothesis regarding how early intervention might stave off the onset of full Bipolar Disorder. Areas of the prefrontal cortex, along with other structures in the limbic system, suffer neurodegeneration after repeated episodes of bipolar illness. The stress of repeated episodes may interfere with prefrontal mood regulation, which may lead to increased cycling and increasing resistance to pharmacological interventions (kindling).

Preventative interventions (i.e., those administered before the first full manic episode) that interfere with this kindling process, and successfully restore healthy prefrontal neural circuitry and neuronal integrity would, theoretically, reduce the patient's chances of having recurrences (Chang et al., 2006).

PREVENTION OF SUICIDE

Finally, psychosocial interventions have not directly addressed the prevention of suicide in Bipolar Disorder—despite the fact that it is an expectionally high-risk illness. Given that some psychosocial interventions have greater effects on depression than mania, and can enhance life satisfaction, it follows that they may also reduce suicidal risk. However, these questions have not been addressed in samples that are adequately powered by sample sizes or adequate lengths of follow-up. Nonetheless, this is a key area for investigation in the next generation of psychosocial research on Bipolar Disorder.

References

Abraham, K. (1911). Notes on the psychoanalytic investigations and treatment of manic-depressive insanity and allied conditions. In E. Jones (Ed.), *Selected papers of Karl Abraham* (pp. 418–480). London: Hogarth.

Aggleton, J. P. (2000). *The amygdala: A functional analysis* (2nd Ed.). Oxford: Oxford University Press.

Akiskal, H. S., Benazzi, F., Perugi, G., & Rihmer, Z. (2005). Agitated "unipolar" depression re-conceptualized as a depressive mixed state: Implications for the antidepressant-suicide controversy. *Journal of Affective Disorders, 85*, 245–258.

Akiskal, H. S., Bourgeois, M. L., Angst, J., Post, R., Moller, H., & Hirschfeld, R. (2000). Re-evaluating the prevalence of and diagnostic composition within the broad clinical spectrum of Bipolar Disorders. *Journal of Affective Disorders, 59(Suppl. 1)* S5–S30.

Akiskal, H. S., Mendlowicz, M. V., Jean-Louis, G., Rapaport, M. H., Kelsoe, J. R., Gillin, J. C., et al. (2005). TEMPS-A: Validation of a short version of a self-rated instrument designed to measure variations in temperament. *Journal of Affective Disorders, 85* (1–2), 45–52.

Alda, M. (1997). Bipolar disorder: From families to genes. *Canadian Journal of Psychiatry, 42*, 378–387.

Alloy, L.B., Reilly-Harrington, N., Fresco, D. M., Whitehouse, W. G., & Zechmeister, J. S. (1999). Cognitive styles and life events in subsyndromal unipolar and Bipolar Disorders: Stability and prospective prediction of depressive and hypomanic mood swings. *Journal of Cognitive Psychotherapy, 13*, 21–40.

Altshuler, L., Suppes, T., Black, D., Nolen, W. A., Keck, P. E., Jr., Frye, M. A., et al. (2003). Impact of antidepressant discontinuation after acute bipolar depression remission on rates of depressive relapse at 1-year follow-up. *American Journal of Psychiatry, 160*, 1252–1262.

American Psychiatric Association. (2000). *Diagnostic and statistical manual of mental disorders (Text Revision)*. Washington, DC: Author.

Anand, A., Verhoeff, P., Seneca, N., Zoghbi, S. S., Seibyl, J. P., Charney, D. S., et al. (2000). Brain SPECT imaging of amphetamine-induced dopamine release in euthymic Bipolar Disorder patients. *American Journal of Psychiatry, 157*, 1109–1114.

Andreasen, N. C., Grove, W. M., Shapiro, R. W., Keller, M. B., Hirschfeld, R. M., & McDonald-Scott, P. (1981). Reliability of lifetime diagnosis. A multicenter collaborative perspective. Archives of General Psychiatry, *38*, 400–405.

Angst, J., Angst, F., Gerber-Werder, R., & Gamma, A. (2005). Suicide in 406 mood-disordered patients with and without long-term medication: A 40 to 44 years' follow-up. *Archives of Suicide Research, 9* (3), 279–300.

Anguelova, M., Benkelfat, C., & Turecki, G. (2003). A systematic review of association studies investigating genes coding for serotonin receptors and the serotonin transporter: I. Affective disorders. *Molecular Psychiatry, 8*, 574–591.

Ashman, S. B., Monk, T. H., Kupfer, D. J., Clark, C. H., Myers, F. S., Frank, E., et al. (1999). Relationship between social rhythms and mood in patients with rapid cycling Bipolar Disorder. *Psychiatry Research, 86* (1), 1–8.

Badner, J. A., & Gershon, E. S. (2002). Meta-analysis of whole-genome linkage scans of Bipolar Disorder and Schizophrenia. *Molecular Psychiatry, 7*, 405–411.

Barbini, B., Colombo, C., Benedetti, F., Campori, E., Bellodi, L., & Smeraldi, E. (1998). The unipolar-bipolar dichotomy and the response to sleep deprivation. *Psychiatry Research, 79*, 43–50.

Bauer, M. S., McBride, L., Williford, W. O., Glick, H., Kinosian, B., Altshuler, L., et al. (2006). Collaborative care for Bipolar Disorder: Part II. Impact on clinical outcome, function, and costs. *Psychiatric Services, 57*, 937–945.

Birmaher, B., Axelson, D., Strober, M., Gill, M. K., Valeri, S., Chiappetta, L., et al. (2006). Clinical course of children and adolescents with bipolar spectrum disorders. *Archives of General Psychiatry, 63* (2), 175–183.

Blumberg, H. P., Stern, E., Ricketts, S., Martinez, D., de Asis, J., White, T., et al. (1999). Rostral and orbital prefrontal cortex dysfunction in the manic state of Bipolar Disorder. *American Journal of Psychiatry, 156*, 1986–1988.

Bowden, C. L., Brugger, A. M., Swann, A. C., Calabrese, J. R., Janicak, P. G., Petty, F., et al. (1994). Efficacy of divalproex vs lithium and placebo in the treatment of mania. The Depakote Mania Study Group. *Journal of the American Medical Association*, *271*, 918–924.

Bowden, C. L., Calabrese, J. R., Sachs, G., Yatham, L. N., Asghar, S. A., Hompland, M., et al. (2003). A placebo-controlled 18-month trial of lamotrigine and lithium maintenance treatment in recently manic or hypomanic patients with Bipolar I Disorder. *Archives of General Psychiatry*, *60*, 392–400.

Bridge, J. A., Goldstein, T. R., & Brent, D. A. (2006). Adolescent suicide and suicidal behavior. *Journal of Child Psychology and Psychiatry*, *47* (3–4), 372–394.

Calabrese, J. R., Fatemi, S. H., Kujawa, M., & Woyshville, M. J. (1996). Predictors of response to mood stabilizers. *Journal of Clinical Psychopharmacology*, *16(Suppl. 1)* 24–31.

Calabrese, J. R., Hirschfeld, R. M. A., Frye, M. A., & Reed, M. L. (2004). Impact of depressive symptoms compared with manic symptoms in Bipolar Disorder: Results of a U.S. community-based sample. *Journal of Clinical Psychiatry*, *65*, 1499–1504.

Caligiuri, M. P., Brown, G. G., Meloy, M. J., Eberson, S. C., Kindermann, S. S., Frank, L. R., et al. (2003). An fMRI study of affective state and medication on cortical and subcortial regions during motor performance in Bipolar Disorder. *Psychiatry Research: Neuroimaging*, *123*, 171–182.

Cardno, A. G., Rijsdijk, F. V., Sham, P. C., Murray, R. M., & McGuffin, P. (2002). A twin study of genetic relationships between psychotic symptoms. *American Journal of Psychiatry*, *159*, 539–545.

Carver, C., Johnson, S. L., & Joormann, J. (2007). Serotonin function, two modes of self-regulation, and the nature of depression. Manuscript submitted for publication.

Caspi, A., Sugden, K., Moffitt, T., Taylor, A., Craig, I. W., Harrington, H., et al. (2003). Influence of life stress on depression: Moderation by a polymorphism in the 5-HTT gene. *Science*, *301*, 386–390.

Chambers, W. J., Puig-Antich, J., Hirsch, M., Paez, P., Ambrosini, P. J., Tabrizi, M. A., et al. (1985). The assessment of affective disorders in children and adolescents by semi-structured interview: test-retest reliability. *Archives of General Psychiatry*, *42*, 696–702.

Chang, K., Adleman, N. E., Dienes, K., Simeonova, D. J., Menon, V., & Reiss, A. (2004). Anomalous prefrontal-subcortical activation in familial pediatric Bipolar Disorder: A functional magnetic resonance imaging investigation. *Archives of General Psychiatry*, *61* (8), 781–792.

Chang, K., Howe, M., Gallelli, K., & Miklowitz, D. (2006). Prevention of pediatric Bipolar Disorder: Integration of neurobiological and psychosocial processes. *Annals of the New York Academy of Sciences*, *1094*, 235–247.

Clarkin, J. F., Glick, I. D., Haas, G. L., Spencer, J. H., Lewis, A. B., Peyser, J., et al. (1990). A randomized clinical trial of inpatient family intervention: V. Results for affective disorders. *Journal of Affective Disorders*, *18*, 17–28.

Cochran, S. D. (1984). Preventing medical noncompliance in the outpatient treatment of bipolar affective disorders. *Journal of Consulting and Clinical Psychology*, *52*, 873–878.

Colom, F., Vieta, E., Martinez-Aran, A., Reinares, M., Benabarre, A., & Gasto, C. (2000). Clinical factors associated with treatment noncompliance in euthymic bipolar patients. *Journal of Clinical Psychiatry*, *61*, 549–555.

Colom, F., Vieta, E., Martinez-Aran, A., Reinares, M., Goikolea, J. M., Benabarre, A., et al. (2003). A randomized trial on the efficacy of group psychoeducation in the prophylaxis of recurrences in bipolar patients whose disease is in remission. *Archives of General Psychiatry*, *60*, 402–407.

Colom, F., Vieta, E., Sanchez-Moreno, J., Martinez-Aran, A., Reinares, M., Goikolea, J. M., et al. (2005). Stabilizing the stabilizer: Group psychoeducation enhances the stability of serum lithium levels. *Bipolar Disorders*, *7(Suppl. 5)* 32–36.

Coryell, W., Endicott, J., & Keller, M. (1990). Outcome of patients with chronic affective disorder: A five-year follow-up. *American Journal of Psychiatry*, *147*, 1627–1633.

Coryell, W., Endicott, J., Maser, J. D., Keller, M. B., Leon, A. C., & Akiskal, H. S. (1995). Long-term stability of polarity distinctions in the affective disorders. *American Journal of Psychiatry*, *152*, 385–390.

Coryell, W., Scheftner, W., Keller, M., Endicott, J., Maser, J., & Klerman, G. L. (1993). The enduring psychosocial consequences of mania and depression. *American Journal of Psychiatry*, *150*, 720–727.

Coryell, W., Solomon, D., Turvey, C., Keller, M., Leon, A. C., Endicott, J., et al. (2003). The long-term course of rapid-cycling Bipolar Disorder. *Archives of General Psychiatry*, *60*, 914–920.

Cuellar, A., Johnson, S. L., & Winters, R. (2005). Distinctions between bipolar and unipolar depression. *Clinical Psychology Review*, *25*, 307–339.

Davidson, R. J., Pizzagalli, D., & Nitschke, J. B. (2002). The representation and regulation of emotion in depression: perspectives from affective neuroscience. In C. L. Hammen & I. H. Gotlib (Eds.), *Handbook of depression* (pp. 219–244). New York: Guilford.

DelBello, M. P., & Kowatch, R. (2006). Pharmacological interventions for bipolar youth: developmental considerations. *Development and Psychopathology, 18* (4), 1231–1246.

DelBello, M. P., Kowatch, R. A., Adler, C. M., Stanford, K. E., Welge, J. A., Barzman, D. H., et al. (2006). A double-blind randomized pilot study comparing quetiapine and divalproex for adolescent mania. *Journal of the American Academy of Child & Adolescent Psychiatry, 45* (3), 305–313.

Delbello, M. P., Schwiers, M. L., Rosenberg, H. L., & Strakowski, S. M. (2002). A double-blind, randomized, placebo-controlled study of quetiapine as adjunctive treatment for adolescent mania. *Journal of the American Academy of Child & Adolescent Psychiatry, 41*, 1216–1223.

Depue, R. A., Collins, P. F., & Luciana, M. (1996). A model of neurobiology–environment interaction in developmental psychopathology. In M. F. Lenzenweger & J. J. Haugaard (Eds.), *Frontiers of developmental psychopathology* (pp. 44–77). New York: Oxford University Press.

Depue, R. A., Kleinman, R. M., Davis, P., Hutchinson, M., & Krauss, S. P. (1985). The behavioral high-risk paradigm and bipolar affective disorder: VII. Serum free cortisol in nonpatient cyclothymic subjects selected by the General Behavior Inventory. *American Journal of Psychiatry, 142*, 175–181.

Dienes, K. A., Hammen, C., Henry, R. M., Cohen, A. N., & Daley, S. E. (2006). The stress sensitization hypothesis: Understanding the course of Bipolar Disorder. *Journal of Affective Disorders, 95* (1–3), 43–49.

Dion, G., Tohen, M., Anthony, W., & Waternaux, C. (1988). Symptoms and functioning of patients with Bipolar Disorder six months after hospitalization. *Hospital and Community Psychiatry, 39*, 652–656.

Dunner, D. L., & Tay, L. K. (1993). Diagnostic reliability of the history of hypomania in Bipolar II patients and patients with major depression. *Comprehensive Psychiatry, 34* (5), 303–307.

Ebert, D., Feistel, H., Barocks, A., Kaschka, W. P., & Pirner, A. (1994). SPECT assessment of cerebral dopamine D2 receptor blockade in depression before and after sleep deprivation. *Biological Psychiatry, 35*, 880–885.

Ehlers, C. L., Frank, E., & Kupfer, D. J. (1988). Social zeitgebers and biological rhythms: a unified approach to understanding the etiology of depression. *Archives of General Psychiatry, 45*, 948–952.

Ehlers, C. L., Kupfer, D. J., Frank, E., & Monk, T. H. (1993). Biological rhythms and depression: the role of zeitgebers and zeitstorers. *Depression, 1*, 285–293.

Eich, E., Macaulay, D., & Lam, R. W. (1997). Mania, depression, and mood dependent memory. *Cognition and Emotion, 11*, 607–618.

Ellicott, A., Hammen, C., Gitlin, M., Brown, G., & Jamison, K. (1990). Life events and the course of Bipolar Disorder. *American Journal of Psychiatry, 147*, 1194–1198.

Fagiolini, A., Kupfer, D. J., Masalehdan, A., Scott, J. A., Houck, P. R., & Frank, E. (2005). Functional impairment in the remission phase of Bipolar Disorder. *Bipolar Disorders, 7*, 281–285.

Fawcett, J., Golden, B., & Rosenfeld, N. (2000). *New hope for people with Bipolar Disorder.* Roseville, CA: Prima Health.

Feske, U., Frank, E., Mallinger, A. G., Houck, P. R., Fagiolini, A., Shear, M. K., et al. (2000). Anxiety as a correlate of response to the acute treatment of Bipolar I Disorder. *American Journal of Psychiatry, 157*, 956–962.

Findling, R. L., McNamara, N. K., Youngstrom, E. A., Stansbrey, R. J., Gracious, B. L., Reed, M. D., et al. (2005). Double-blind 18-month trial of lithium versus divalproex maintenance treatment in pediatric Bipolar Disorder. *Journal of the American Academy of Child & Adolescent Psychiatry, 44*(5), 409–417.

First, M. B., Spitzer, R. L., Gibbon, M., & Williams, J. B. W. (1995). *Structured clinical interview for DSM-IV axis I disorders.* New York: Biometrics Research.

Frank, E. (2005). *Treating Bipolar Disorder: A clinician's guide to interpersonal and social rhythm therapy.* New York: Guilford.

Frank, E., Cyranowski, J. M., Rucci, P., Shear, M. K., Fagiolini, A., Thase, M. E., et al. (2002). Clinical significance of lifetime panic spectrum symptoms in the treatment of patients with Bipolar I Disorder. *Archives of General Psychiatry, 59*, 905–911.

Frank, E., Kupfer, D. J., Thase, M. E., Mallinger, A. G., Swartz, H. A., Fagiolini, A. M., et al. (2005). Two-year outcomes for interpersonal and social rhythm therapy in individuals with Bipolar I Disorder. *Archives of General Psychiatry, 62* (9), 996–1004.

Frazier, J. A., Biederman, J., Tohen, M., Feldman, P. D., Jacobs, T. G., Toma, V., et al. (2001). A prospective open-label treatment trial of olanzapine monotherapy in children and adolescents with

Bipolar Disorder. *Journal of Child and Adolescent Psychopharmacology, 11*, 239–250.

Geller, B., Zimerman, B., Williams, M., Bolhofner, K., Craney, J. L., Frazier, J., et al. (2002). *DSM-IV* mania symptoms in a prepubertal and early adolescent Bipolar Disorder phenotype compared to attention deficit hyperactive and normal controls. *Journal of the American Academy of Child and Adolescent Psychopharmacology, 12*, 11–25.

Ghaemi, S. N., Lenox, M. S., & Baldessarini, R. J. (2001). Effectiveness and safety of long-term antidepressant treatment in Bipolar Disorder. *Journal of Clinical Psychiatry, 62*, 565–569.

Goldberg, J. F. (2004). The changing landscape of psychopharmacology. In S. L. Johnson, & R. L. Leahy (Eds.), *Psychological Treatment of Bipolar Disorder* (pp. 109–138). New York.

Goldberg, J. F., Harrow, M., & Grossman, L. S. (1995). Course and outcome in bipolar affective disorder: A longitudinal follow-up study. *American Journal of Psychiatry, 152*, 379–385.

Gonzalez-Pinto, A., Tohen, M., Lalaguna, B., Perez-Heredia, J. L., Fernandez-Corres, B., Gutierrez, M., et al. (2002). Treatment of Bipolar I rapid cycling patients during dysphoric mania with olanzapine. *Journal of Clinical Psychopharmacology, 22*, 450–454.

Goodwin, G. M., Bowden, C. L., Calabrese, J. R., Grunze, H., Kasper, S., & White, R. et al. (2004). A pooled analysis of 2 placebo-controlled 18-month trials of lamotrigine and lithium maintenance in Bipolar I Disorder. *Journal of Clinical Psychiatry, 65*, 432–441.

Greenhouse, W. J., Meyer, B., & Johnson, S. L. (2000). Coping and medication adherence in Bipolar Disorder. *Journal of Affective Disorders, 59* (3), 237–241.

Hammen, C., Gitlin, M., & Altshuler, L. (2000). Predictors of work adjustment in Bipolar I patients: A naturalistic longitudinal follow-up. *Journal of Consulting and Clinical Psychology, 68*, 220–225.

Hammen, C., & Gitlin, M. J. (1997). Stress reactivity in bipolar patients and its relation to prior history of the disorder. *American Journal of Psychiatry, 154*, 856–857.

Harris, E. C., & Barraclough, B. (1997). Suicide as an outcome for mental disorders: A meta-analysis. *British Journal of Psychiatry, 170*, 205–208.

Hasler, G., Drevets, W. C., Gould, T. D., Gottesman, I. I., & Manji, H. K. (2006). Toward constructing an endophenotype strategy for Bipolar Disorders. *Biological Psychiatry, 60*, 93–105.

Heerlein, A., Richter, P., Gonzalez, M., & Santander, J. (1998). Personality patterns and outcome in depressive and Bipolar Disorders. *Psychopathology, 31*, 15–22.

Hestenes, D. (1992). A neural network theory of manic-depressive illness. In D. S. Levine & S. J. Leven (Eds.), *Motivation, emotion, and goal direction in neural networks* (pp. 209–257). Hillsdale, NJ: Lawrence Erlbaum.

Hillegers, M. H., Burger, H., Wals, M., Reichart, C. G., Verhulst, F. C., Nolen, W. A., et al. (2004). Impact of stressful life events, familial loading and their interaction on the onset of mood disorders. *British Journal of Psychiatry, 185*, 97–101.

Hlastala, S.A., Frank, E., Kowalski, J., Sherrill, J. T., Tu, X. M., Anderson, B., et al. (2000). Stressful life events, Bipolar Disorder, and the "kindling model". *Journal of Abnormal Psychology, 109*, 777–786.

Hodgins, S., Faucher, B., Zarac, A., & Ellenbogen, M. (2002). Children of parents with Bipolar Disorder: A population at high risk for major affective disorders. *Child and Adolescent Psychiatric Clinics of North America, 11*, 533–553.

Jamison, K. R. (2005). Exuberance: The passion for life. London: Vintage.

Jamison, K. R. (2000). Suicide and Bipolar Disorder. *Journal of Clinical Psychiatry, 61 (Suppl. 9)* 47–56.

Jamison, K. R. (1993). *Touched with fire: manic-depressive illness and the artistic temperament.* New York: Maxwell Macmillan International.

Jamison, K. R. (1995). *An Unquiet Mind.* New York: Alfred A. Knopf.

Jamison, K. R., & Baldessarini, R. J. (1999). Effects of medical interventions on suicial behavior. *Journal of Clinical Psychiatry, 60 (Suppl. 2)*, 4–6.

Jamison, K. R., Gerner, R. H., & Goodwin, F. K. (1979). Patient and physician attitudes toward lithium: Relationship to compliance. *Archives of General Psychiatry, 36*, 866–869.

Johnson, R. E., & McFarland, B. H. (1996). Lithium use and discontinuation in a health maintenance organization. *American Journal of Psychiatry, 153*, 993–1000.

Johnson, S. L. (2005a). Life events in Bipolar Disorder: Towards more specific models. *Clinical Psychology Review, 25* (8), 1008–1027.

Johnson, S. L. (2005b). Mania and dysregulation in goal pursuit. *Clinical Psychology Review, 25*, 241–262.

Johnson, S. L., & Carver, C. (2006). Extreme goal setting and vulnerability to mania among undiagnosed young adults. *Cognitive Therapy and Research, 30*, 377–395.

Johnson, S. L., Eisner, L., & Carver, C. (2007). Unrealistic goal setting among persons diagnosed with Bipolar Disorders. Manuscript submitted for publication.

Johnson, S. L., & Fingerhut, R. (2004). Negative cognitions predict the course of bipolar depression, not mania. *Journal of Cognitive Psychotherapy: An International Quarterly, 18,* 149–162.

Johnson, S. L., Joiner, T. E. J., & Ballister, C. (2005). Hypomanic vulnerability, terror management, and materialism. *Personality and Individual Differences, 38,* 287–296.

Johnson, S. L., Meyer, B., Winett, C., & Small, J. (2000). Social support and self-esteem predict changes in bipolar depression but not mania. *Journal of Affective Disorders, 58,* 79–86.

Johnson, S. L., & Miller, I. (1997). Negative life events and time to recovery from episodes of Bipolar Disorder. *Journal of Abnormal Psychology, 106,* 449–457.

Johnson, S. L., Sandrow, D., Meyer, B., Winters, R., Miller, I., Solomon, D., et al. (2000). Increases in manic symptoms following life events involving goal-attainment. *Journal of Abnormal Psychology, 109,* 721–727.

Johnson, S. L., Winett, C. A., Meyer, B., Greenhouse, W. J., & Miller, I. (1999). Social support and the course of Bipolar Disorder. *Journal of Abnormal Psychology, 108,* 558–566.

Jones, S. H., Tai, S., Evershed, K., Knowles, R., & Bentall, R. (2006). Early detection of Bipolar Disorder: A pilot familial high-risk study of parents with Bipolar Disorder and their adolescent children. *Bipolar Disorders, 8,* 362–372.

Judd, L. L., Akiskal, H. S., Schettler, P. J., Endicott, J., Maser, J., Solomon, D. A., et al. (2002). The long-term natural history of the weekly symptomatic status of Bipolar I Disorder. *Archives of General Psychiatry, 59,* 530–537.

Kalivas, P. W., Duffy, P., DuMars, L. A., & Skinner, C. (1988). Behavioral and neurochemical effects of acute and daily cocaine administration in rats. *Journal of Pharmacology and Experimental Therapeutics, 245* (2), 485–492.

Kato, T. (2007). Molecular genetics of Bipolar Disorder and depression. *Psychiatry and Clinical Neurosciences, 61,* 3–19.

Kaufman, J., Birmaher, B., Brent, D., Rao, U., Flynn, C., Moreci, P., et al. (1997). Schedule for affective disorders and Schizophrenia for school-age children-present and lifetime version (K-SADS-PL): Initial reliability and validity data. *Journal of the American Academy of Child and Adolescent Psychiatry, 36,* 98–988.

Keck, P. E., Jr., McElroy, S. L., Richtand, N., & Tohen, M. (2002). What makes a drug a primary mood stabilizer? *Molecular Psychiatry, 7(Suppl. 1)* S8–S14.

Keck, P. E., Jr., McElroy, S. L., Strakowski, S. M., Bourne, M. L., & West, S. A. (1997). Compliance with maintenance treatment in Bipolar Disorder. *Psychopharmacology Bulletin, 33,* 87–91.

Keck, P. E., Jr., McElroy, S. L., Strakowski, S. M., West, S. A., Sax, K. W., Hawkins, J. M., et al. (1998). Twelve-month outcome of patients with Bipolar Disorder following hospitalization for a manic or mixed episode. *American Journal of Psychiatry, 155,* 646–652.

Keller, M. B., Lavori, P. W., & Friedman, B. (1987). The longitudinal interval follow-up evaluation: A comprehensive method for assessing outcome in prospective longitudinal studies. *Archives of General Psychiatry, 44,* 540–548.

Keller, M. B., Lavori, P. W., McDonald-Scott, P., Scheftner, W. A., Andreasen, N. C., Shapiro, R. W., et al. (1981). Reliability of lifetime diagnoses and symptoms in patients with current psychiatric disorder. *Journal of Psychiatry Research, 16,* 229–240.

Kendler, K. S., Kuhn, J. W., Vittum, J., Prescott, C. A., & Riley, B. (2005). The interaction of stressful life events and a serotonin transporter polymorphism in the prediction of episodes of major depression: a replication. *Archives of General Psychiatry, 62* (5), 529–535.

Kessler, R. C., Avenevoli, S., & Ries-Merikangas, K. (2001). Mood disorders in children and adolescents: An epidemiologic perspective. *Biological Psychiatry, 49,* 1002–1014.

Kessler, R. C., Berglund, P., Demler, O., Jin, R., & Walters, E. E. (2005). Lifetime prevalence and age-of-onset distributions of *DSM-IV* disorders in the National Comorbidity Survey replication. *Archives of General Psychiatry, 62,* 593–602.

Kessler, R. C., Rubinow, D. R., Holmes, C., Abelson, J. M., & Zhao, S. (1997). The epidemiology of *DSM-III-R* Bipolar I Disorder in a general population survey. *Psychological Medicine, 27,* 1079–1089.

Kieseppa, T., Partonen, T., Haukka, J., Kaprio, J., & Lonnquist, J. (2004). High concordance of Bipolar I Disorder in a nationwide sample of twins. *American Journal of Psychiatry, 161,* 1814–1821.

Kim, E. Y., & Miklowitz, D. J. (2002). Childhood mania, attention deficit hyperactivity disorder, and conduct disorder: A critical review of diagnostic dilemmas. *Bipolar Disorders, 4*, 215–225.

Kim, E. Y., & Miklowitz, D. J. (2004). Expressed emotion as a predictor of outcome among bipolar patients undergoing family therapy. *Journal of Affective Disorders, 82*, 343–352.

Kim, E. Y., Miklowitz, D. J., Biuckians, A., & Mullen, K. (2007). Life stress and the course of early-onset Bipolar Disorder. *Journal of Affective Disorders, 99* (1), 37–44.

Klein, D. N., & Depue, R. A. (1984). Continued impairment in persons at risk for Bipolar Disorder: Results of a 19-month follow-up. *Journal of Abnormal Psychology, 93*, 345–347.

Knowles, R., Tai, S., Christensen, I., & Bentall, R. (2005). Coping with depression and vulnerability to mania: A factor analytic study of the Nolen-Hoeksema (1991) Response Styles Questionnaire. *British Journal of Clinical Psychology, 44*, 99–112.

Knutson, B., Adams, C. M., Fong, G. W., & Hommer, D. (2001). Anticipation of increasing monetary reward selectively recruits nucleus accumbens. *Journal of Neuroscience, 21* (16), RC 159.

Kochman, F. J., Hantouche, E. G., Ferrari, P., Lancrenon, S., Bayart, D., & Akiskal, H. S. (2005). Cyclothymic temperament as a prospective predictor of bipolarity and suicidality in children and adolescents with major depressive disorder. *Journal of Affective Disorders, 85* (1–2), 181–189.

Kowatch, R. A., Fristad, M., Birmaher, B., Wagner, K. D., Findling, R. L., Hellander, M., et al. (2005). Treatment guidelines for children and adolescents with Bipolar Disorder. *Journal of the American Academy of Child & Adolescent Psychiatry, 44* (3), 213–235.

Kowatch, R. A., Suppes, T., Carmody, T. J., Bucci, J. P., Hume, J. H., Kromelis, M., et al. (2000). Effect size of lithium, divalproex sodium, and carbamazepine in children and adolescents with Bipolar Disorder. *Journal of the American Academy of Child and Adolescent Psychiatry, 39*, 713–720.

Kowatch, R. A., Youngstrom, E. A., Danielyan, A., & Findling, R. L. (2005). Review and meta-analysis of the phenomenology and clinical characteristics of mania in children and adolescents. *Bipolar Disorders, 7* (6), 483–496.

Kruger, S., Seminowicz, S., Goldapple, K., Kennedy, S. H., & Mayberg, H. S. (2003). State and trait influences on mood regulation in Bipolar Disorder: Blood flow differences with an acute mood challenge. *Biological Psychiatry, 54*, 1274–1283.

Kupfer, D. J., Frank, E., Grochocinski, V. J., Luther, J. F., Houck, P. R., Swartz, H. A., et al. (2000). Stabilization in the treatment of mania, depression, and mixed states. *Acta Neuropsychiatrica, 12*, 110–114.

Kwapil, T. R., Miller, M. B., Zinser, M. C., Chapman, L. J., Chapman, J., & Eckblad, M. (2000). A longitudinal study of high scorers on the hypomanic personality scale. *Journal of Abnormal Psychology, 109*, 222–226.

Lam, D., Wright, K., & Smith, N. (2004). Dysfunctional assumptions in Bipolar Disorder. *Journal of Affective Disorders, 79*, 193–199.

Lam, D. H., Hayward, P., Watkins, E. R., Wright, K., & Sham, P. (2005). Relapse prevention in patients with Bipolar Disorder: Cognitive therapy outcome after 2 years. *American Journal of Psychiatry, 162*, 324–329.

Lam, D. H., Watkins, E. R., Hayward, P., Bright, J., Wright, K., Kerr, N., et al. (2003). A randomized controlled study of cognitive therapy of relapse prevention for bipolar affective disorder: Outcome of the first year. *Archives of General Psychiatry, 60*, 145–152.

LaPalme, M., Hodgins, S., & LaRoche, C. (1997). Children of parents with Bipolar Disorder: A mata-analysis of risk for mental disorders. *Canadian Journal of Psychiatry, 42*, 623–631.

Lasky-Su, J. A., Faraone, S. V., Glatt, S. J., & Tsuang, M. T. (2005). Meta-analysis of the association between two polymorphisms in the serotonin transporter gene and affective disorders. *American Journal of Medical Genetics, 133*, 110–115.

Lawrence, N. S., Williams, A. M., Surguladze, S., Giampietro, V., Brammer, M. J., Andrew, C., et al. (2004). Subcortical and ventral prefrontal responses to facial expressions distinguish patients with BPD and major depression. *Biological Psychiatry, 55*, 578–587.

Leibenluft, E., Albert, P. S., Rosenthal, N. E., & Wehr, T. A. (1996). Relationship between sleep and mood in patients with rapid-cycling Bipolar Disorder. *Psychiatry Research, 63*, 161–168.

Lembke, A., & Ketter, T. (2002). Impaired recognition of facial emotion in mania. *American Journal of Psychiatry, 159*, 302–304.

Lennox, R., Jacob, R., Calder, A. J., Lupson, V., & Bullmore, E. T. (2004). Behavioral and neurocognitive responses to sad facial affect are attenuated in patients with mania. *Psychological Medicine, 34*, 795–802.

Leverich, G. S., & Post, R. M. (1998). Life charting of affective disorders. *CNS Spectrums, 3*, 21–37.

Levinson, D. F. (2006). The genetics of depression: A review. *Biological Psychiatry, 60*, 84–92.

Lewinsohn, P. M., Klein, D. N., & Seeley, J. R. (1995). Bipolar disorders in a community sample of older adolescents: prevalence, phenomenology, comorbidity, and course. *Journal of the American Academy of Child and Adolescent Psychiatry, 34*, 454–463.

Lewis, C. M., Levinson, D. F., & Wise, L. H. (2003). Genome scan meta-analysis of Schizophrenia and Bipolar Disorder, part II: Schizophrenia. *American Journal of Human Genetics, 73* (1), 34–48.

Lieberman, J. A., Stroup, T. S., McEvoy, J. P., Swartz, M. S., Rosenheck, R. A., Perkins, D. O., et al. (2005). Effectiveness of antipsychotic drugs in patients with chronic Schizophrenia. *New England Journal of Medicine, 353* (12), 1209–1223.

Lotrich, F. E., & Pollock, B. G. (2004). Meta-analysis of serotonin transporter polymorphisms and affective disorders. *Psychiatric Genetics, 14*, 121–129.

Lozano, B. L., & Johnson, S. L. (2001). Can personality traits predict increases in manic and depressive symptoms? *Journal of Affective Disorders, 63*, 103–111.

Lyon, H. M., Startup, M., & Bentall, R. P. (1999). Social cognition and the manic defense: Attributions, selective attention, and self-schema in bipolar affective disorder. *Journal of Abnormal Psychology, 108*, 273–282.

Malkoff-Schwartz, S., Frank, E., Anderson, B., Sherrill, J. T., Siegel, L., Patterson, D., et al. (1998). Stressful life events and social rhythm disruption in the onset of manic and depressive bipolar episodes: A preliminary investigation. *Archives of General Psychiatry, 55*, 702–707.

Malkoff-Schwartz, S., Frank, E., Anderson, B. P., Hlastala, S. A., Luther, J. F., Sherrill, J. T., et al. (2000). Social rhythm disruption and stressful life events in the onset of bipolar and unipolar episodes. *Psychological Medicine, 30*, 1005–1016.

Mansell, W., & Lam, D. (2006). "I won't do what you tell me!": Elevated mood and the assessment of advice-taking in euthymic Bipolar I Disorder. *Behaviour Research and Therapy, 44* (12), 1787–1801.

Marangell, L. B., Bauer, M., Dennehy, E. B., Wisniewski, S. R., Allen, M., Miklowitz, D. J., et al. (2006). Prospective predictors of suicide and suicide attempts in 2000 patients with Bipolar Disorders followed for 2 years. *Bipolar Disorders, 8*(5, Pt. 2), 566–575.

Marlatt, G. A. (1985). *Relapse prevention*. New York: Guilford.

Masi, G., Perugi, G., Toni, C., Millepiedi, S., Mucci, M., Bertini, N., et al. (2004). Obsessive-compulsive bipolar comorbidity: Focus on children and adolescents. *Journal of Affective Disorders, 78*, 175–183.

Mayberg, H. S., Keightley, M., Mahurin, R. K., & Brannan, S. K. (2004). Neuropsychiatric aspects of mood and affective disorders. In R. E. Hales & S. C. Yudofsky (Eds.), *Essentials of neuropsychiatry and clinical neurosciences* (pp. 489–517). Washington, DC: American Psychiatric Publishing.

McGuffin, P., Rijsdijk, F., Andrew, M., Sham, P., Katz, R., & Cardno, A. (2003). The heritability of bipolar affective disorder and the genetic relationship to unipolar depression. *Archives of General Psychiatry, 60*, 497–502.

McPherson, H., Herbison, P., & Romans, S. (1993). Life events and relapse in established bipolar affective disorder. *British Journal of Psychiatry, 163*, 381–385.

Merikangas, K. R., Akiskal, H. S., Angst, J., Greenberg, P. E., Hirschfeld, R. M. A., Petukhova, M., et al. (2007). Lifetime and 12-month prevalence of bipolar spectrum disorder in the National Comorbidity Survey replication. *Archives of General Psychiatry, 64* (5), 543–552.

Meyer, B., Johnson, S. L., & Carver, C. S. (1999). Exploring behavioral activation and inhibition sensitivities among college students at-risk for bipolar-spectrum symptomatology. *Journal of Psychopathology and Behavioral Assessment, 21*, 275–292.

Meyer, B., Johnson, S. L., & Winters, R. (2001). Responsiveness to threat and incentive in Bipolar Disorder: Relations of the BIS/BAS scales with symptoms. *Journal of Psychopathology and Behavioral Assessment, 23*, 133–143.

Miklowitz, D. J. (2006). A review of evidence-based psychosocial interventions for Bipolar Disorder. *Journal of Clinical Psychiatry, 67(Suppl. 11)* 28–33.

Miklowitz, D. J., Biuckians, A., & Richards, J. A. (2006). Early-onset Bipolar Disorder: A family treatment perspective. *Development and Psychopathology, 18* (4), 1247–1265.

Miklowitz, D. J., & Cicchetti, D. (2006). Toward a lifespan developmental psychopathology perspective on Bipolar Disorder. *Development and Psychopathology, 18* (4), 935–938.

Miklowitz, D. J., George, E. L., Richards, J. A., Simoneau, T. L., & Suddath, R. L. (2003). A randomized study of family-focused psychoeducation and pharmacotherapy in the outpatient management of

Bipolar Disorder. *Archives of General Psychiatry*, *60*, 904–912.

Miklowitz, D. J., & Goldstein, M. J. (1990). Behavioral family treatment for patients with bipolar affective disorder. *Behavior Modification*, *14*, 457–489.

Miklowitz, D. J., & Goldstein, M. J. (1997). *Bipolar disorder: A family-focused treatment approach*. New York: Guilford.

Miklowitz, D. J., Goldstein, M. J., Nuechterlein, K. H., Snyder, K. S., & Mintz, J. (1988). Family factors and the course of bipolar affective disorder. *Archives of General Psychiatry*, *45*, 225–231.

Miklowitz, D. J., Otto, M. W., Frank, E., Reilly-Harrington, N. A., Kogan, J. N., Sachs, G. S., et al. (2007). Intensive psychosocial intervention enhances functioning in patients with bipolar depression: Results from a 9-month randomized controlled trial *American Journal of Psychiatry*, *164* (9), 1–8.

Miklowitz, D. J., Otto, M. W., Frank, E., Reilly-Harrington, N. A., Wisniewski, S. R., Kogan, J. N., et al. (2007). Psychosocial treatments for bipolar depression: A 1-year randomized trial from the Systematic Treatment Enhancement Program. *Archives of General Psychiatry*, *64*, 419–427.

Miklowitz, D. J., Richards, J. A., George, E. L., Suddath, R. L., Frank, E., Powell, K., et al. (2003). Integrated family and individual therapy for Bipolar Disorder: Results of a treatment development study. *Journal of Clinical Psychiatry*, *64*, 182–191.

Monk, T. H., Flaherty, J. F., Frank, E., Hoskinson, K., & Kupfer, D. J. (1990). The social rhythm metric: An instrument to quantify daily rhythms of life. *Journal of Nervous and Mental Disease*, *178*, 120–126.

Monk, T. H., Reynolds, C. F., Buysse, D. J., DeGrazia, J. M., & Kupfer, D. J. (2003). The relationship between lifestyle regularity and subjective sleep quality. *Chronobiology International*, *20* (1), 97–107.

Murphy, F. C., Sahakian, B. J., Rubinsztein, J. S., Michael, A., Rogers, R. D., Robbins, T. W., et al. (1999). Emotional bias and inhibitory control processes in mania and depression. *Psychological Medicine*, *29*, 1307–1321.

Naranjo, C. A., Tremblay, L. K., & Busto, U. E. (2001). The role of the brain reward system in depression. *Progress in Neuropsychopharmacological and Biological Psychiatry*, *25*, 781–823.

Newcomer, J. W. (2007). Metabolic considerations in the use of antipsychotic medications: A review of recent evidence. *Journal of Clinical Psychiatry*, *68(Suppl. 1) 20–27*.

National Institute of Mental Health. (2001). Research roundtable on prepubertal Bipolar Disorder. *Journal of the American Academy of Child and Adolescent Psychiatry*, *40*, 871–878.

Nowakowska, C., Strong, C. M., Santosa, C. M., Wang, P. W., & Ketter, T. A. (2005). Temperamental commonalities and differences in euthymic mood disorder patients, creative controls, and healthy controls. *Journal of Affective Disorders*, *85*, 207–215.

Ochsner, K. N., & Gross, J. J. (2005). The cognitive control of emotion. *Trends in Cognitive Sciences*, *9*, 242–249.

Otto, M. W., Simon, N. M., Wisniewski, S. R., Miklowitz, D. J., Kogan, J., Reilly-Harrington, N. A., et al. (2006). Prospective 12-month course of Bipolar Disorder in outpatients with and without comorbid anxiety disorders. *British Journal of Psychiatry*, *189*, 20–25.

Pardoen, D., Bauewens, F., Dramaix, M., Tracy, A., Genevrois, C., Staner, L., et al. (1996). Life events and primary affective disorders: A one-year prospective study. *British Journal of Psychiatry*, *169*, 160–166.

Pavuluri, M. N., Graczyk, P. A., Henry, D. B., Carbray, J. A., Heidenreich, J., & Miklowitz, D. J. (2004). Child and family-focused cognitive behavioral therapy for pediatric Bipolar Disorder: Development and preliminary results. *Journal of the American Academy of Child & Adolescent Psychiatry*, *43*, 528–537.

Perlis, R. H., Miyahara, S., Marangell, L. B., Wisniewski, S. R., Ostacher, M., DelBello, M. P., et al. (2004). Long-term implications of early onset in Bipolar Disorder: data from the first 1000 participants in the Systematic Treatment Enhancement Program for Bipolar Disorder (STEP-BD). *Biological Psychiatry*, *55*, 875–881.

Perris, H. (1984). Life events and depression: Part 2. Results in diagnostic subgroups and in relation to the recurrence of depression. *Journal of Affective Disorders*, *7*, 25–36.

Perry, A., Tarrier, N., Morriss, R., McCarthy, E., & Limb, K. (1999). Randomised controlled trial of efficacy of teaching patients with Bipolar Disorder to identify early symptoms of relapse and obtain treatment. *British Medical Journal*, *16*, 149–153.

Phillips, M. L., Drevets, W. C., Rauch, S. L., & Lane, R. (2003). Neurobiology of emotion perception II: Implications for major psychiatric disorders. *Biological Psychiatry*, *54*, 515–528.

Post, R. M. (1992). Transduction of psychosocial stress into the neurobiology of recurrent affective disorder. *American Journal of Psychiatry*, *149*, 999–1010.

Post, R. M., & Weiss, S. R. B. (1998). Sensitization and kindling phenomena in mood, anxiety, and obsessive-compulsive disorders: The role of serotonergic mechanisms in illness progression. *Biological Psychiatry, 44,* 193–206.

Prien, R. F., & Potter, W. Z. (1990). NIMH Workshop report on treatment of Bipolar Disorder. *Psychopharmacology Bulletin, 26,* 409–427.

Rea, M. M., Tompson, M., Miklowitz, D. J., Goldstein, M. J., Hwang, S., & Mintz, J. (2003). Family focused treatment vs. individual treatment for Bipolar Disorder: Results of a randomized clinical trial. *Journal of Consulting and Clinical Psychology, 71,* 482–492.

Regeer, E. J., ten Have, M., Rosso, M. L., Hakkaart-van Roijen, L., Vollebergh, W., & Nolen, W. A. (2004). Prevalence of Bipolar Disorder in the general population: A reappraisal study of the Netherlands Mental Health Survey and Incidence Study. *Acta Psychiatrica Scandinavaca, 110,* 374–382.

Reichart, C. G., van derEnde, J., Wals, M., Hillegers, M. H., Nolen, W. A., Ormel, J., et al. (2005). The use of the GBI as predictor of Bipolar Disorder in a population of adolescent offspring of parents with a Bipolar Disorder. *Journal of Affective Disorders, 89* (1–3), 147–155.

Reilly-Harrington, N. A., Alloy, L. B., Fresco, D. M., & Whitehouse, W. G. (1999). Cognitive styles and life events interact to predict bipolar and unipolar symptomatology. *Journal of Abnormal Psychology, 108,* 567–578.

Rice, J. P., McDonald-Scott, P., Endicott, J., Coryell, W., Grove, W. M., Keller, M. B., et al. (1986). The stability of diagnosis with an application to Bipolar II Disorder. *Journal of Psychiatry Research, 19,* 285–296.

Richards, R., Kinney, D. K., Lunde, I., Benet, M., & Merzel, A. P. (1988). Creativity in manic-depressives, cyclothymes, their normal relatives, and control subjects. *Journal of Abnormal Psychology, 97,* 281–288.

Robinson, T. E., & Becker, J. B. (1986). Enduring changes in brain and behavior produced by chronic amphetamine administration: A review and evaluation of animal models of amphetamine psychosis. *Brain Research Review, 11,* 157–198.

Rogers, R., Jackson, R. L., & Cashel, M. (2001). The schedule for affective disorders and Schizophrenia (SADS). In R. Rogers, (Ed.), *Handbook of diagnostic and structural interviewing* (pp. 84–102). New York: Guilford.

Rush, A. J. (2007). STAR*D: What have we learned? *American Journal of Psychiatry, 164* (2), 201–204.

Ryan, N. D., Williamson, D. E., Iyengar, S., Orvaschel, H., Reich, T., Dahl, R. E., et al. (1992). A secular increase in child and adolescent onset affective disorder. *Journal of the American Academy of Child and Adolescent Psychiatry, 31,* 600–605.

Sachs, G. S., Nierenberg, A. A., Calabrese, J. R., Marangell, L. B., Wisniewski, S. R., Gyulai, L., et al. (2007). Effectiveness of adjunctive antidepressant treatment for bipolar depression. *New England Journal of Medicine, 356* (17), 1711–1722.

Sato, T., Bottlender, R., Kleindienst, N., & Moller, H. J. (2002). Syndromes and phenomenological subtypes underlying acute mania: A factor analytic study of 576 manic patients. *American Journal of Psychiatry, 159* (6), 968–974.

Sax, K. W., & Strakowski, S. M. (2001). Behavioral sensitization in humans. *Journal of Addictive Diseases, 20,* 55–65.

Schneck, C. D., Miklowitz, D. J., Calabrese, J. R., Allen, M. H., Thomas, M. R., Wisniewski, S. R., et al. (2004). Phenomenology of rapid cycling Bipolar Disorder: data from the first 500 participants in the Systematic Treatment Enhancement Program for Bipolar Disorder. *American Journal of Psychiatry, 161,* 1902–1908.

Scott, J., Paykel, E., Morriss, R., Bentall, R., Kinderman, P., Johnson, T., et al. (2006). Cognitive behaviour therapy for severe and recurrent Bipolar Disorders: A randomised controlled trial. *British Journal of Psychiatry, 188,* 313–320.

Segurado, R., Detera-Wadleigh, S. D., Levinson, D. F., et al. (2003). Genome scan meta-analysis of Schizophrenia and Bipolar Disorder, part III: Bipolar disorder. *American Journal of Human Genetics, 73* (1), 49–62.

Seligman, M. E. P., Castellon, C., Cacciola, J., Schulman, P., Luborsky, L., Ollove, M., et al. (1988). Explanatory style change during cognitive therapy for unipolar depression. *Journal of Abnormal Psychology, 97,* 13–18.

Sheehan, D. V., Lecrubier, Y., Sheehan, K. H., Amorim, P., Janavs, J., Weiller, E., et al. (1998). The Mini-International Neuropsychiatric Interview (M.I.N.I.): The development and validation of a structured diagnostic psychiatric interview for *DSM-IV* and ICD-10. *Journal of Clinical Psychiatry, 59* (Suppl. 20) 22–33.

Simeonova, D. I., Chang, K. D., Strong, C., & Ketter, T. A. (2005). Creativity in familial Bipolar Disorder. *Journal of Psychiatric Research, 39* (6), 623–631.

Simon, G. E., Ludman, E. J., Bauer, M. S., Unutzer, J., & Operskalski, B. (2006). Long-term effectiveness and cost of a systematic care program for Bipolar Disorder. *Archives of General Psychiatry, 63* (5), 500–508.

Simoneau, T. L., Miklowitz, D. J., Richards, J. A., Saleem, R., & George, E. L. (1999). Bipolar disorder and family communication: Effects of a psychoeducational treatment program. *Journal of Abnormal Psychology, 108*, 588–597.

Simoneau, T. L., Miklowitz, D. J., & Saleem, R. (1998). Expressed emotion and interactional patterns in the families of bipolar patients. *Journal of Abnormal Psychology, 107*, 497–507.

Simpson, S. G., McMahon, F. J., McInnis, M. G., MacKinnon, D. F., Edwin, D., Folstein, S. E., et al. (2002). Diagnostic reliability of Bipolar II Disorder. *Archives of General Psychiatry, 59*, 746–750.

Smoller, J. W., & Finn, C. T. (2003). Family, twin, and adoption studies of Bipolar Disorder. *American Journal of Medical Genetics, Part C: Seminars in Medical Genetics, 123* (1), 48–58.

Sobcazk, S., Honig, A., Schmitt, J. A. J., & Riedel, W. J. (2003). Pronounced cognitive deficits following an intravenous L-Tryptophan challenge in first-degree relatives of bipolar patients compared to healthy controls. *Neuropsychopharmacology, 28*, 711–719.

Sobczak, S., Riedel, W.J., Booij, L., Aan het Rot, M., Deutz, N. E. P., & Honig, A. (2002). Cognition following acute tryptophan depletion: Differences between first-degree relatives of Bipolar Disorder patients and matched healthy control volunteers. *Psychological Medicine, 32*, 503–515.

Solomon, D. A., Leon, A. C., Endicott, J., Coryell, W. H., Mueller, T. I., Posternak, M. A., et al. (2003). Unipolar mania over the course of a 20-year follow-up study. *American Journal of Psychiatry, 160*, 2049–2051.

Spitzer, R. L., Endicott, J., & Robins, E. (1978). Research diagnostic criteria: Rationale and reliability. *Archives of General Psychiatry, 35*, 773–782.

Staley, J. K., Malison, R. T., & Innis, R. B. (1998). Imaging of the serotonergic system: Interactions of neuroanatomical and functional abnormalities of depression. *Biological Psychiatry, 44*, 534–549.

Stern, G. S., & Berrenberg, J. L. (1979). Skill-set, success outcome, and mania as determinants of the illusion of control. *Journal of Research in Personality, 13*, 206–220.

Stockmeier, C. A. (2003). Involvement of serotonin in depression: Evidence from postmortem and imaging studies of serotonin receptors and the serotonin transporter. *Journal of Psychiatric Research, 37*, 357–373.

Strakowski, S. M., Keck, P. E., McElroy, S. L., West, S. A., Sax, K. W., Hawkins, J. M., et al. (1998). Twelve-month outcome after a first hospitalization for affective psychosis. *Archives of General Psychiatry, 55*, 49–55.

Strakowski, S. M., Sax, K.W., Setters, M. J., & Keck, P. E. J. (1996). Enhanced response to repeated d-amphetamine challenge: Evidence for behavioral sensitization in humans. *Biological Psychiatry, 40*, 827–880.

Strakowski, S. M., Sax, K. W., Setters, M. J., Stanton, S. P., & Keck, Jr., P. E. (1997). Lack of enhanced behavioral response to repeated d-amphetamine challenge in first-episode psychosis: Implications for a sensitization model of psychosis in humans. *Biological Psychiatry, 42*, 749–755.

Strober, M., Schmidt-Lackner, S., Freeman, R., Bower, S., Lampert, C., & DeAntonio, M. (1995). Recovery and relapse in adolescents with bipolar affective illness: A five-year naturalistic, prospective follow-up. *Journal of the American Academy of Child and Adolescent Psychiatry, 34*, 714–731.

Suppes, T., Baldessarini, R. J., Faedda, G. L., Tondo, L., & Tohen, M. (1993). Discontinuation of maintenance treatment in Bipolar Disorder: risks and implications. *Harvard Review of Psychiatry, 1*, 131–144.

Suppes, T., Leverich, G. S., Keck, P.E., Nolen, W. A., Denicoff, K. D., Altshuler, L. L., et al. (2001). The Stanley Foundation Bipolar Treatment Outcome Network. II. Demographics and illness characteristics of the first 261 patients. *Journal of Affective Disorders, 67*, 45–59.

Swann, A. C., Dougherty, D. M., Pazzaglia, P. J., Pham, M., & Moeller, F. G. (2004). Impulsivity: A link between Bipolar Disorder and substance abuse. *Bipolar Disorders, 6*, 204–212.

Taylor, W. D., Steffens, D. C., Payne, M. E., MacFall, J. R., Marchuk, D. A., Svenson, I. K., et al. (2005). Influence of serotonin transporter promoter region polymorphisms on hippocampal volumes in late-life depression. *Archives of General Psychiatry, 62*(5), 537–544.

Thase, M. E. (2006). Pharmacotherapy of bipolar depression: An update. *Current Psychiatry Reports, 8* (6), 478–488.

Thase, M. E., Jindal, R., & Howland, R. H. (2002). Biological aspects of depression. In C. L. Hammen & I. H.Gotlib,(Eds.), *Handbook of Depression* (pp. 192–218). New York: Guilford.

Thomas, J., & Bentall, R. (2002). Hypomanic traits and response styles to depression. *British Journal of Clinical Psychology, 41*, 309–314.

Tohen, M., Greil, W., Calabrese, J. R., Sachs, G. S., Yatham, L. N., Oerlinghausen, B. M., et al. (2005). Olanzapine versus lithium in the maintenance treatment of Bipolar Disorder: A 12-month, randomized, double-blind, controlled clinical trial. *American Journal of Psychiatry, 162,* 1281–1290.

Tohen, M., Jacobs, T. G., Grundy, S. L., McElroy, S. L., Banov, M. C., Janicak, P. G., et al. (2000). Efficacy of olanzapine in acute bipolar mania: A double-blind, placebo-controlled study. The Olanzapine HGGW Study Group. *Archives of General Psychiatry, 57,* 841–849.

Tohen, M., Kryzhanovskaya, L., Carlson, G., DelBello, M. P., Wozniak, J., R., K., et al. (2005). Olanzapine in the treatment of acute mania in adolescents with Bipolar I Disorder: A 3-week randomized double-blind placebo-controlled study. *Neuopsychopharmacology, 30(Suppl. 1)* 176.

Tohen, M., Vieta, E., Calabrese, J., Ketter, T. A., Sachs, G., Bowden, C., et al. (2003). Efficacy of olanzapine and olanzapine-fluoxetine combination in the treatment of Bipolar I depression. *Archives of General Psychiatry, 60,* 1079–1088.

Tohen, M., Waternaux, C. M., & Tsuang, M. T. (1990). Outcome in mania: A 4-year prospective follow-up of 75 patients utilizing survival analysis. *Archives of General Psychiatry, 47,* 1106–1111.

Tondo, L., & Baldessarini, R. J. (2000). Reducing suicide risk during lithium maintenance treatment. *Journal of Clinical Psychiatry, 61(Suppl. 9)* 97–104.

Wals, M., Hillegers, M. H. J., Reichart, C. G., Verhulst, F. C., Nolen, W. A., & Ormel, J. (2005). Stressful life events and onset of mood disorders in children of bipolar parents during 14-month follow-up. *Journal of Affective Disorders, 87,* 253–263.

Wehr, R., Turner, E., Shimada, J., Lowe, C., Barker, C., & Leibenluft, E. (1998). Treatment of a rapidly cycling bipolar patient by using extended bed rest and darkness to stabilize the timing and duration of sleep. *Biological Psychiatry, 43,* 822–828.

Wehr, T., Goodwin, F., Wirz-Justice, A., Breitmaier, J., & Craig, C. (1982). 48-hour sleep-wake cycles in manic-depressive illness: Naturalistic observations and sleep deprivation experiments. *Archives of General Psychiatry, 39,* 559–565.

Wehr, T. A., Sack, D. A., & Rosenthal, N. E. (1987). Sleep reduction as a final common pathway in the genesis of mania. *American Journal of Psychiatry, 144,* 210–214.

Weiss, R. D., Griffin, M. L., Kolodziej, M. E., Greenfield, S. F., Najavits, L. M., Daley, D. C., et al. (2007). A randomized trial of integrated group therapy versus group drug counseling for patients with Bipolar Disorder and substance dependence. *American Journal of Psychiatry, 164* (1), 100–107.

Wender, P. H., Kety, S. S., Rosenthal, D., Schulsinger, F., Ortmann, J., & Lunde, I. (1986). Psychiatric disorders in the biological and adoptive families of adopted individuals with affective disorders. *Archives of General Psychiatry, 43,* 923–929.

Williams, J. B. W., Gibbon, M., First, M. B., Spitzer, R. L., Davies, M., Borus, J., et al. (1992). The structured clinical interview for the *DSM-III-R* (SCID). II. Multisite Test-Retest Reliability. *Archives of General Psychiatry, 49,* 630–636.

Willner, P. (1995). Sensitization of dopamine D-sub-2- or D-sub-3-type receptors as a final common pathway in antidepressant drug action. *Clinical Neuropharmacology, 18(Suppl. 1)* S49–S56.

Winters, K. C., & Neale, J. M. (1985). Mania and low self-esteem. *Journal of Abnormal Psychology, 94,* 282–290.

Yan, L. J., Hammen, C., Cohen, A. N., Daley, S. E., & Henry, R. M. (2004). Expressed emotion versus relationship quality variables in the prediction of recurrence in bipolar patients. *Journal of Affective Disorders, 83,* 199–206.

Yatham, L. N., Kennedy, S. H., O'Donovan, C., Parikh, S., MacQueen, G., McIntyre, R., et al. (2005). Canadian Network for Mood and Anxiety Treatments (CANMAT) guidelines for the management of patients with Bipolar Disorder: Consensus and controversies. *Bipolar Disorders, 7(Suppl. 3)* 5–69.

Young, L. T., Joffe, R. T., Robb, J. C., MacQueen, G. M., Marriott, M., & Patelis-Siotis, I. (2000). Double-blind comparison of addition of a second mood stabilizer versus an antidepressant to an initial mood stabilizer for treatment of patients with bipolar depression. *American Journal of Psychiatry, 157,* 124–126.

Youngstrom, E. A., Findling, R. L., & Calabrese, J. R. (2004). Effects of adolescent manic symptoms on agreement between youth, parent, and teacher ratings of behavior problems. *Journal of Affective Disorders, 82(Suppl. 1)* S5–S16.

Youngstrom, E. A., Findling, R. L., Calabrese, J. R., Gracious, B. L., Demeter, C., DelPorto-Bedoya, D., et al. (2004). Comparing the diagnostic accuracy of six potential screening instruments for Bipolar Disorder in youths age 5 to 17 years. *Journal of the American Academy of Child and Adolescent Psychiatry, 43,* 847–858.

Youngstrom, E. A., Findling, R. L., Youngstrom, J. K., & Calabrese, J. R. (2005). Towards an evidence-based assessment of pediatric Bipolar Disorder. *Journal of Clinical Child and Adolescent Psychology, 34* (3), 433–448.

Chapter 11

Schizophrenia and the Psychotic Spectrum

ELAINE WALKER, VIJAY MITTAL, KEVIN TESSNER, AND HANAN TROTMAN

I can't find the words to describe it. Schizophrenia is like a disconnect. My thoughts and my feelings are not connected. I'm not connected with other people. I don't understand them and they don't understand me. It is like life is just passing me by, and it is out of my control. My mind is out of my control and it is frightening.

The quote above is from a man in his 40s who was diagnosed with Schizophrenia in his 20s. Unlike most patients, he was able to make it through college, despite the gradual onset of clinical symptoms in his late teens. But the illness impaired his ability to form close relationships, to develop his talents, and to achieve economic independence. The story is similar for most people who suffer from Schizophrenia.

Schizophrenia is a mental illness that falls in the general category of *psychotic disorders*. The term *psychosis* is used to refer to disorders that involve an impairment in the individuals' perception of reality. Thus, psychotic symptoms include abnormalities in sensory perception (e.g., auditory, visual, and tactile hallucinations) and ideations (e.g., delusions, thought disorders). Although psychotic symptoms often accompany mood disorders, Schizophrenia is the most common psychotic disorder.

Because the symptoms of Schizophrenia are manifested in the core human functions of thought and sensation, it is among the most debilitating of mental illnesses. Further, for the majority of patients there are repeated episodes of the illness throughout their life even when the patient receives treatment (Carpenter & Buchanan, 1994; Menezes, Arenovich, & Zipursky, 2006). The story of Dr. John Nash—professor and mathematician at Princeton, as told in the movie *A Beautiful Mind*—illustrates this point quite well. Although John Nash achieved a level of cognitive functioning far beyond the average person, he experienced negative symptoms and intermittent episodes of psychosis throughout his adult life.

The fact that Schizophrenia is usually first diagnosed when the individual is in the prime of life—between 20 and 25 years of age—further adds to the burden of the illness (DeLisi, 1992). The critical developmental processes of gaining independence from parents, developing enduring romantic relationships, pursuing educational goals, and beginning work or career endeavors, are interrupted by the emergence of psychotic symptoms. As a result most patients are unable to complete college or achieve economic independence, and few marry or have children. Not only does the patient suffer, but family members must also confront the challenge of seeing their loved one loose hope about their future.

Unlike some disorders listed in the *Diagnostic and Statistical Manual of Mental Disorders* (*DSM*), Schizophrenia is observed at approximately the same rate across diverse cultures. Estimates of the lifetime prevalence of Schizophrenia are around 1% (1 out of 100) in both industrialized and nonindustrialized societies (Arajarvi et al., 2005; Keith, Regier, & Rae, 1991; Kulhara & Chakrabarti, 2001; Torrey, 1987). It is, therefore, assumed that vulnerability to Schizophrenia is present in some individuals in every ethnic and racial group.

Although scientific research has not yet succeeded in yielding a clear-cut picture of the origins of the disorder, it has gotten us much closer to a realistic picture. Virtually all experts in the field now agree on the following: (a) the collection of symptoms we label *Schizophrenia* is not a single disease with one cause, but rather a syndrome with multiple causes; (b) Schizophrenia is a behavioral manifestation of brain dysfunction; (c) its etiology involves the interplay between genetic and environmental factors, including psychosocial stressors; (d) multiple developmental pathways lead to disease onset; and (e) brain maturational processes play a role in the etiological process. The primary goal in this chapter is to provide an historical perspective on Schizophrenia, as well as a selective overview of the current state of our knowledge. The term *selective* is used because the research literature on Schizophrenia is voluminous and a comprehensive review of even a single area of investigation is beyond the scope of this chapter. Further, for convenience we use the singular term *Schizophrenia* although many of the research findings described in this chapter suggest that Schizophrenia is a syndrome or a group of disorders—rather than a single disease entity with a single cause.

A Contemporary Diathesis-Stress Model

To set the stage for our discussion, the model in Figure 11.1 summarizes key assumptions about the etiology of Schizophrenia and other psychotic disorders. The model is a contemporary version of the *diathesis-stress model* that postulates constitutional vulnerability (i.e., the diathesis) emanates from both inherited and acquired constitutional factors (Walker & Diforio, 1997). The inherited factors are genetically determined characteristics of the brain that influence its structure and function. Acquired vulnerabilities arise mainly from prenatal events and delivery complications that compromise fetal brain development. Whether the constitutional vulnerability is a consequence of genetic factors or environmental factors or a combination of both, the model assumes that vulnerability is, in most cases, congenital. But the assumption that vulnerability is present at birth does not imply that it will be clinically expressed at any particular point in the life span. Rather, the model posits that two sets of factors determine the postnatal

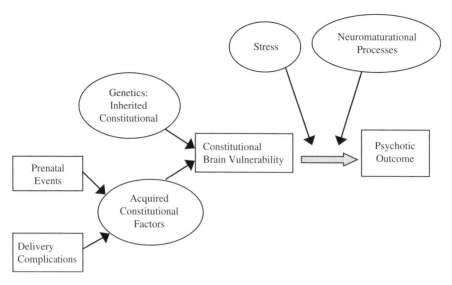

FIGURE 11.1   A Diathesis-Stress Model of the Etiology of Schizophrenia and Other Psychotic Disorders.

course of the vulnerable individual. First, external stressors influence the expression of the vulnerability. In addition, the model assumes that neuromaturation is a key element. In particular, adolescence/early adulthood appears to be a critical period for the expression of the vulnerability for Schizophrenia. Thus, some aspects of brain maturational processes during the post-pubertal period are likely to play important roles in triggering the clinical expression of latent liabilities (Walker, 2004; Corcoran et al., 2003).

Within the framework of this general model, we now turn to a discussion of the history and phenomenology of Schizophrenia and then proceed to a description of some of the findings that have shed light on the illness. In particular, we will highlight recent findings that have challenged researchers to change some of their long-held assumptions about etiology. Although some discussions of research on Schizophrenia are pessimistic with respect to our progress in identifying the origins of this devastating mental disorder, we believe there is reason for optimism.

The Nature of Schizophrenia: Historical Aspects of Our Understanding

Descriptions of people manifesting psychotic symptoms have been recorded since antiquity. But it was not until the mid- to late-nineteenth century that physicians began to systematically explore the etiology and classification of various types of psychosis. At that time, the most common cause of psychotic symptoms was syphilis although researchers were not aware that there was any link between psychosis and syphilis. Syphilis is due to infection with the spirochete, *treponema pallidum*. Infection of the brain by syphilis occurs in 15 to 20% of all late or tertiary syphilis infections, and emerges about 10 to 20 years after the primary infection with progressive, life-threatening complications. The form referred to as general paresis involves psychotic symptoms that parallel those of Schizophrenia and mental hospitals were filled with general paresis patients into the early 1900s. Then, in the early twentieth century advances in diagnostic methods conclusively linked general paresis to syphilis, and with the discovery of effective antibiotic treatments for syphilis general paresis became rare.

The discovery that many individuals in mental hospitals were suffering from general paresis was important because it served to illustrate how an infectious agent can produce a psychological syndrome. It also sensitized researchers to the possibility that a psychological syndrome assumed to represent a single disorder might, in fact, have multiple causes. Most researchers in the field now agree that this is the case for Schizophrenia (Jablensky, 2006). To date, no single etiological factor or clinical symptom has been found to characterize all patients with the illness. For example, no specific genetic risk factor has been identified, although several genes are known to be associated with Schizophrenia. Similarly, Schizophrenia patients vary in symptom profiles, developmental histories, family backgrounds, cognitive functions, and even brain morphology and neurochemistry. We now recognize that Schizophrenia is a syndrome with multiple etiologies.

Emil Kraepelin (1856–1926) was the first to differentiate Schizophrenia, which he referred to as "dementia praecox" (or early onset dementia), from manic-depressive psychosis (Kraepelin, 1913). He did not believe that any one symptom was diagnostic of dementia praecox, but instead based diagnosis on a collection of symptoms and the nature of their change over time. If a psychotic patient deteriorated over an extended period of time (months or years) the condition was assumed to be dementia praecox. Kraepelin also proposed that "hebephrenia," "paranoia," and "catatonia"—which were previously assumed to be distinct disorders—should be classified as variants of dementia praecox. He based this on similarities in age-of-onset and poor prognosis.

At the beginning of the 20th century Eugen Bleuler (1857–1939)—a Swiss psychiatrist—introduced the term *Schizophrenia* (Bleuler, 1911/1950; Howells, 1991, p. xii, p. 95). The word is derived from two Greek words: *schizo*, which means to tear or to split, and *phren*, which meant "the intellect" or "the mind". Thus, the word Schizophrenia literally means the splitting of the mind. Bleuler classified the symptoms of Schizophrenia into *fundamental* and *accessory* symptoms. The fundamental symptoms of Schizophrenia are disturbances of association (loose, illogical thought processes), disturbances of affect (indifference, apathy, or inappropriateness), ambivalence (conflicting thoughts, emotions, or impulses that are present simultaneously or in rapid succession), autism (detachment from social life with an inner preoccupation), abulia (lack of drive or motivation), and dementia. According to Bleuler, these symptoms are present in all patients, at all stages of the illness, and are diagnostic of Schizophrenia. The accessory symptoms of Schizophrenia include delusions, hallucinations, movement disturbances, somatic symptoms, and manic and melancholic states. In contrast to fundamental symptoms, Bleuler believed that accessory symptoms often occurred in other illnesses and were not present in all Schizophrenia patients or diagnostic of Schizophrenia.

Subsequent revisions to the diagnostic criteria for Schizophrenia were proposed by Kurt Schneider in the mid-1900s. Like Bleuler, Schneider thought that certain key symptoms were diagnostic of Schizophrenia (Schneider, 1959). He referred to these symptoms as *first rank symptoms* (see Table 11.1), and made the diagnosis of Schizophrenia if one or more of the first rank symptoms was present. Subsequent diagnostic criteria for Schizophrenia have been heavily influenced by Schneider's approach.

TABLE 11.1   The Schneiderian "First Rank Symptoms"

Thought echoing or audible thoughts (the patient hears his thoughts out loud).

Thought broadcasting (patient believes that others can hear his thoughts out loud).

Thought intrusion (patient feel that some of his thought are from outside; that is, not originating in his own mind).

Thought withdrawal (patient believes that the cause of having lost track of a thought is that someone taking his thoughts away).

Somatic hallucinations (unusual, unexplained sensations in one's body).

Passivity feelings (patient believes that his thoughts, feelings or actions are controlled by another or others).

Delusional perception (a sudden, fixed, false belief about an particular everyday occurrence or perception).

The Bleulerian and Schneiderian diagnostic systems allowed for a wider range of psychotic patients to be diagnosed with Schizophrenia. In contrast, the Kraepelinian tradition—with its longitudinal emphasis—identified patients with poorer long-term prognosis. Thus, the patients diagnosed with this system tended to have a poorer prognosis than those diagnosed with Bleuler's or Schneider's systems. During the middle of the twentieth century different diagnostic criteria became popular in different parts of the world and these discrepancies had a detrimental effect on research progress. Research findings using different diagnostic criteria could not be generalized across countries.

Concerns about diagnostic inconsistency inspired the next generation of researchers to focus on the development of a uniform diagnostic system with the intent of improving diagnostic reliability and validity. Notable among these attempts were the Feighner—or St Louis—diagnostic criteria (Feighner, Robins, & Guze, 1972), and the Research Diagnostic Criteria developed by Spitzer, Endicott, and Robins (1978). These two approaches to the diagnosis of Schizophrenia strongly influenced modern day diagnostic systems, most notably, the *Diagnostic and Statistical Manual of Mental Disorders (DSM)*.

The *DSM* is now the most widely used system for diagnosing Schizophrenia and other mental disorders. The most recent version of the *DSM* is the *DSM-IV-TR* (APA, 2000). Using the *DSM-IV-TR* criteria (Table 11.2), Schizophrenia can be diagnosed when signs and symptoms of the disorder have been present for six months or more (including prodromal and residual phases). The characteristic symptom criteria for Schizophrenia include: (a) hallucinations, (b) delusions, (c) disorganized speech (e g., frequent derailment or incoherence), (d) grossly disorganized or catatonic behavior, and (e) negative symptoms (i.e., affective flattening, alogia, or avolition).

At least two or more of these psychotic symptoms must be present for at least one month (or less if successfully treated). Only one of the above is necessary if the delusions are bizarre, or the hallucinated voices consist of a running commentary or of two voices conversing (both of these are derived from Schneider's first rank symptoms in Table 11.1). In addition to the clinical symptoms there must be social or occupational dysfunction (or both). Further, significant mood disorder, such as depression or manic symptoms, must not be present. This would exclude individuals who meet criteria for Major Depressive Disorder with psychotic symptoms and Bipolar Disorder with psychotic symptoms. Finally, general medical conditions or substance abuse that might lead to psychotic symptoms must be ruled out.

TABLE 11.2 *DSM-IV* Subtypes of Schizophrenia

Subtype	Prognosis
Paranoid	*Good*
- Preoccupation with one or more persecutory delusions or auditory hallucinations	
- No prominent disorganized speech, disorganized or catatonic behavior or flat or inappropriate affect	
Disorganized	*Poor*
- Prominent disorganized speech and behavior, and flat or inappropriate emotional expressions	
Catatonic	*Poor*
- Motoric immobility or excessive motor activity, and/or peculiar or stereotyped movements	
- Echoing of words spoken by others, imitations of others movements	
Undifferentiated	
- Display of schizophrenic symptomatology in a pattern that does not fit the above categories	

The four subtypes of Schizophrenia described in the *DSM-IV* are *paranoid, disorganized, catatonic*, and *undifferentiated*. The paranoid type is characterized by a preoccupation with delusions or hallucinations involving threat, but there is no disorganized speech, disorganized or catatonic behavior or flat or inappropriate affect. This subtype has the best prognosis. In the disorganized type, disorganized speech, disorganized behavior, and flat or inappropriate affect are all prominent but the criteria for the catatonic subtype are not met. In terms of the course of illness, this subtype is considered to have a very poor prognosis. The *catatonic* type involves a clinical syndrome that is dominated by at least two of the following: motoric immobility, excessive, purposeless motor activity (catatonic excitement), extreme negativism (purposeless resistance to movement or all instructions or both), mutism (absence of speech), peculiar voluntary movements (voluntary assumption of bizarre or unusual postures), stereotyped movements (repetitive, nonfunctional, yet voluntary), prominent mannerisms (repetitive gestures or expressions), prominent facial grimacing, echolalia (repetition of another person's words or phrases), or echopraxia (repetition of another person's actions).

There are two other *DSM* diagnostic categories in the Schizophrenia spectrum. One category, the *residual* type, is for individuals who have met criteria for Schizophrenia in the past but no longer do. This diagnosis is applied when there is a prominence of negative symptoms or two or more attenuated characteristic symptoms, but no prominent delusions, hallucinations, catatonic symptoms, or disorganized behavior or speech. The other category, *Schizophreniform Disorder*, is for individuals whose symptoms do not meet the six-month criterion. This diagnosis is frequently met prior to the diagnosis of Schizophrenia when the patient presents for treatment early in the course of the disorder. A small (5 to 10%) portion of individuals who fall into this category, however, will recover completely and not suffer further episodes of psychosis (Menezes et al., 2006).

It is important to emphasize that, despite advances in diagnosis, the diagnostic boundaries of Schizophrenia subtypes are still quite unclear (Jablensky, 2006; Wolff, 1991). Moreover, the boundaries between Schizophrenia and mood disorders are sometimes obscure (Kempf, Hussain, & Potash, 2005). Many individuals who meet criteria for Schizophrenia show marked signs of depression or manic tendencies prior to and following the onset of psychotic symptoms. As a result, the *DSM-IV* includes a diagnostic category called Schizoaffective Disorder. This disorder can be conceived of as a hybrid between the mood disorders (Bipolar Disorder or Major Depression with psychotic features) and Schizophrenia. The two sub-types of schizoaffective disorder are the depressive subtype (i.e, if the mood disturbance includes only depressive episodes) and the bipolar subtype (i.e., where the symptoms of the disorder have included either a manic or a mixed episode). Interestingly, the prognosis for patients with Schizoaffective Disorder is, on average, somewhere between that of Schizophrenia and the mood disorders. There are also diagnostic categories in the *DSM* for mood disorders (unipolar and bipolar) with psychotic features.

In the 1980s, investigators began to make a distinction between positive and negative symptoms of Schizophrenia, with the assumption that these two classes of symptoms involved different neural mechanisms (Harvey & Walker, 1987). The positive symptoms are those that involve an excess of ideas, sensory experiences, or behavior. Hallucinations, delusions, and bizarre behaviors fall in this category. Most of the first rank symptoms described by Schneider would also be classified as positive symptoms. In contrast, negative symptoms involve a decrease in behavior, such as blunted or flat affect, anhedonia, and lack of motivation. Although research has not yielded support for the notion that the positive and negative symptom dimensions reflect different neural abnormalities, the distinction is commonly used by researchers and clinicians. Further, it has been shown that more severe negative symptoms are associated with a poorer prognosis for recovery (Malla & Payne, 2005).

The Origins of Schizophrenia

PSYCHOLOGICAL INFLUENCES

Not more than three centuries ago, individuals who suffered from psychotic symptoms were assumed to be suffering from demonic possession (Mirsky & Duncan, 2005). These religious views were gradually replaced by more benevolent attitudes that stemmed from a more compassionate view of psychotic symptoms as a manifestation of an illness of the mind. By the twentieth century the mental health movement was firmly established in western nations, and individuals with psychotic symptoms were assumed to have a mental disorder (Mirsky & Duncan, 2005). The recognition of psychotic disorders—particularly Schizophrenia—as mental illnesses set the stage for a new debate. This debate mirrored the ongoing conceptual dilemma about the distinction between mind and brain (Schwartz & Begley, 2002)—some argued that psychosis was the product of disordered mental processes that arose in response to adverse psychosocial factors, while others took the position that impaired brain function was the critical and final pathway in psychotic disorders. During the twentieth century, theorizing about the origins of Schizophrenia has shifted from a primary focus on psychosocial factors in the first half, to a greater emphasis on biological factors in the later part of the twentieth century.

Most psychosocial theories were grounded in the basic assumption that adverse social experiences produced psychotic symptoms. For example, Sigmund Freud—the father of psychoanalysis—wrote extensively on Schizophrenia in the early 1900s and proposed that traumatic interpersonal experiences led to intrapsychic conflicts that exceeded the individuals capacity to cope using normal psychological defense mechanisms (Howells, 1991). Freud believed that psychosocial trauma could disturb personality formation and bring about a mental state of ego fragmentation (Grotstein, 1989). Psychotic symptoms were assumed to be symbolic representations of repressed, unconscious conflicts accompanied by strong emotions that could not be adequately expressed or discharged. Other analytic theorists viewed Schizophrenia as a psychological state that arose from a disturbance in the early formation of object relations, specifically attachment to others (Novey, 1958). Arlow and Brenner (1969) reformulated analytic theory and focused on the ways in which mental object representations are cathected (i.e., associated with positive or negative emotion) by Schizophrenia patients. Schizophrenia was thus viewed as a cathectic withdrawal, such that attachments to others were severely compromised, as was the ability to resolve intrapsychic conflict between drives and defenses.

In 1948, Frieda Fromm-Reichmann proposed a psychological theory of Schizophrenia that postulated that the disorder arose in response to rearing by a schizophrenogenic mother (Fromm-Reichmann, 1948). Although this hypothesis has fallen in disfavor because of lack of support from empirical research, many believed it caused considerable suffering for families. Specifically, they believed that the theory added to the stigma and burden on family members seeking treatment for their loved one.

Another example of a highly influential psychological perspective is the *double-bind theory* of Schizophrenia (Bateson, Jackson, Haley, & Weakland, 1956). Double-bind theorists proposed that symptoms of Schizophrenia were a result of maladaptive patterns of interaction in the family. Gregory Bateson and his colleagues posited that psychotic symptoms emerge when a developing child is unable to adequately respond to repeated conflicting injunctions from family members. For example, a child receives a contradictory message if he is repeatedly exposed to interactions with a father who tells his son that he loves him but refuses to engage with him (e g., showing disgust at the child's approach). Over time, the child who is the recipient of such conflicting messages about the nature of his relationship with a family member will begin to react with social withdrawal, and the psychological distress will be reflected in psychotic symptoms, such as incoherent speech, thought disorder, and flattened affect. Although the double-bind theory has not garnered empirical support, it did set the stage for the development of other theories about the role of family interactions in Schizophrenia (Howells, 1991). Although few of these have had a sustained influence, some have contributed to our understanding of the etiology of Schizophrenia and the importance of the family in providing support for the recovering patient.

In particular, some theorists focused on the affective component of family communication and the role it might play in precipitating or exacerbating psychosis. These theories assume that maladaptive communication patterns in the interactions among family members of Schizophrenia patients can have deleterious effects (Singer & Wynne,

1963; Leff & Vaughn, 1985; Vaughn & Leff, 1976). Singer and Wynne (1963) were pivotal in launching this area of investigation through their studies that revealed communication abnormalities in the families of Schizophrenia patients. Eventually the phrase *expressed emotion* was introduced to refer to family members' communications with the patient that are critical, negative, or emotionally over-involved. Studies of expressed emotion indicated that negative expressed emotion may contribute to relapse in Schizophrenia (Leff & Vaughn, 1985; Vaughn & Leff, 1976). A meta-analysis of expressed emotion studies showed that Schizophrenia patients returning to families with highly critical communication styles have a 50% chance of relapse, compared to 15% for patients returning to families that are less critical (Butzlaff & Hooley, 1998). These findings suggested an important role for psychosocial factors in the recurrence of psychotic episodes in schizophrenic patients.

Other investigators, however, raised questions about the nature of the causal relationship. Do family members' negative communications contribute to risk for relapse, *or* are family members reacting to the patients impending relapse? In other words, does the patient's worsening behavior and symptoms elicit frustration and criticism from the family? Recent research indicates that this is indeed the case. At least in part, the relation between the family's expressed emotion and the patient's illness course reflects the reactions of family members to the patient's symptoms (King, Ricard, Rochon, Steiger, & Nelis, 2003). But there is also longitudinal evidence that negative expressed emotion can contribute to symptom exacerbation and relapse independent of the patient's symptom levels at baseline. Research has shown that family communication style (Goldstein, 1987) and quality of support (O'Brien et al., 2006) are significant predictors of the course of Schizophrenia spectrum symptoms. A recent study followed diagnosed patients over seven years and found that negative expressed emotion in family members was associated with higher rates of rehospitalization (Marom, Munitz, Jones, Weizman, & Hermesh, 2005). These findings indicate that the psychosocial environment does matter.

Contemporary conceptualizations of the role of psychosocial factors in the etiology and course of Schizophrenia view them as stressors that can act to trigger or worsen the illness in vulnerable individuals (Walker & Diforio, 1997). Empirical research has provided evidence that episodes of Schizophrenia follow periods of increased life stress (Horan et al., 2005; Ventura, Neuchterlein, Hardesty, & Gitlin, 1992). Thus, just as stress exposure can trigger or exacerbate physical illnesses, it is assumed that stress can increase risk for Schizophrenia and other psychotic disorders. Although the evidence does not indicate that individuals who are vulnerable to Schizophrenia experience significantly more stress than other persons, it does suggest that vulnerable individuals are more sensitive to stress when it occurs. This assumption is the essence of the model in Figure 11.1 where the interaction between vulnerability and stress is viewed as critical.

Biological Factors

Although early writers on Schizophrenia—such as Kraepelin and Bleuler—did not offer specific theories about the origins of Schizophrenia, they did suggest that there might be a biological basis for at least some cases of the illness. Likewise, contemporary ideas about the origins of Schizophrenia focus on biological (i.e., constitutional) vulnerabilities that are assumed to be present at birth. Researchers have identified two sources of constitutional vulnerability: genetic factors and prenatal or obstetric factors. Both appear to have implications for brain development.

The Genetics of Schizophrenia

One of the most well established findings in Schizophrenia research is that vulnerability to the illness can be inherited (Gottesman, 1991). Behavior genetic studies utilizing twin, adoption, and family history methods have all yielded evidence that the risk for Schizophrenia is elevated in individuals who have a biological relative with the disorder—the closer the level of genetic relatedness, the greater the likelihood the relative will also suffer from Schizophrenia.

In a review of family, twin, and adoption studies conducted from 1916 to 1989, Irving Gottesman (1991) outlined the compelling evidence for the role of genetic factors in Schizophrenia. For example, family studies have shown that as the genetic relatedness of the relative to the patient becomes closer—such as from 2nd-degree relatives (grand-parents, half siblings, aunts, and uncles) to 1st-degree (parents and siblings)—the relative's lifetime risk for Schizophrenia is increased. Similarly, monozygotic (MZ) twins, who essentially share 100% of their genes, have the highest concordance rate for Schizophrenia. Among monozygotic cotwins of patients with Schizophrenia, 25% to 50% will develop the illness. Dizygotic (DZ) twins and other siblings share, on average, only about half of their genes. About 10% to 15% of the DZ cotwins of patients are also diagnosed with the illness.

Adoption studies have also yielded evidence that the tendency for Schizophrenia to run in families is due to genetic factors, rather than being solely attributable to the environmental stressor of growing up in close proximity to a mentally ill family member. In a seminal adoption study, Heston (1966) examined the rates of Schizophrenia in adoptees with and without a biological parent who was diagnosed with the illness. He found higher rates of Schizophrenia and other mental illnesses, in the biological offspring of parents with Schizophrenia, when compared to adoptees with no mental illness in biological parents. Similarly, in a Danish sample, Kety (1988) examined the rates of mental illness in the relatives of adoptees with and without Schizophrenia. He found that the biological relatives of adoptees who suffered from Schizophrenia had a significantly higher rate of Schizophrenia than the adoptive relatives who reared them. Also, the rate of Schizophrenia in the biological relatives of adoptees with Schizophrenia was higher than in the biological relatives of healthy adoptees. Taken together, these behavioral genetic studies provide ample evidence for a significant genetic component in the etiology of Schizophrenia. In addition, behavioral genetic studies have shed light on environmental factors.

Findings from an adoption study conducted in Finland indicate that genetic influences act in concert with environmental factors. Like others, Tienari, Wynne, Moring, and Lahti (1994) found that the rate of psychosis and other severe disorders was significantly higher in the adopted offspring of biological mothers with Schizophrenia than in the matched control adoptees. However, the difference between the groups was only detected in children from adoptive families that were rated as dysfunctional. Thus, the genetic vulnerability was mainly expressed in association with a disruptive adoptive environment and less pronounced in adoptees reared in a healthy, possibly protective, family environment. Along these same lines, it has been shown that high-risk children—offspring of parents with Schizophrenia—are more likely to develop schizophrenic symptoms if they were raised in institutional rather than familial environments (Walker, Cudeck, Mednick, & Schulsinger, 1981). These findings, which highlight a biological vulnerability to environmental events, are consistent with the prevailing diathesis-stress models of etiology (Walker & Diforio, 1997).

The Nature of the Genetic Predisposition

Although some initially hoped to find a single gene that accounted for Schizophrenia, the findings from behavioral and molecular genetic studies of Schizophrenia lead to the conclusion that the disorder involves multiple genes—rather than a single gene (Gottesman, 1991). This conclusion is based on several observations, most notably the fact that the pattern of familial transmission does not conform to what would be expected from a single genetic locus or even a small number of genes. Consistent with this assumption, attempts to identify a genetic locus that accounts for a significant proportion of cases of Schizophrenia have not met with success. Instead, researchers using molecular genetic and other techniques have identified a number of candidate genes each of which may account for a very small proportion of cases.

Candidate gene analyses and linkage and association studies have provided some evidence for the involvement of several chromosomal regions (i e., regions on chromosomes 6, 8, 13, and 22) and several specific genes, including genes that code for hormones, nerve growth factors, and serotonin and dopamine (DA) receptors, (Mowry & Nancarrow, 2001; Riley & Kendler, 2006). Although a review of this vast literature is beyond the scope of this chapter, one of the most noteworthy genetic discoveries is a line of research concerning genetic abnormalities that affect dopamine activity. The Catecho-O-methyltransferase (COM-T) gene codes for the enzyme that breaks down DA. While a majority of people inherit two copies, approximately one in 4000 children are born with one copy of the COM-T gene: this is referred to as 22q11 deletion syndrome or *velocardiofacial syndrome*. The 22q11 deletion occurs in about 0.025% of the general population, involves a microdeletion on chromosome 22q112, and is often accompanied by physical syndrome that includes structural anomalies of the face, head, and heart. Roughly 30% of 22q11 deletion patients manifest Schizophrenia (Murphy, Jones, & Owen, 1999), and people with Schizophrenia show an 80 fold increased prevalence of 22q11 deletion compared to the general population (Chow, Watson, Young, & Bassett, 2006; Karayiorgou, Morris, & Morrow, 1995). Furthermore, the rate of 22q11 deletion may be higher in patients with an earlier onset of Schizophrenia (Bassett et al., 1998; Karayiorgou et al., 1995). Other studies of Schizophrenia patients have also suggested that certain alleles of the COM-T gene are linked with risk for Schizophrenia (Riley & Kendler, 2006).

The Specificity of the Genetic Predisposition

Beyond the findings described here, there are some larger ongoing controversies surrounding the genetics of Schizophrenia. One of these controversies concerns the specificity of the genetic liability for Schizophrenia. Early behavioral genetic studies were guided by the assumption that there were separable genetic liabilities for Schizophrenia and the major affective disorders—namely, Bipolar Disorder and Psychotic Depression. But more recent evidence indicates that this may not be the case. Using quantitative genetic techniques with large twin samples, researchers have shown that there is significant overlap in the genes that contribute to Schizophrenia, Schizoaffective Disorder, and mood disorders (Cardno, Rijsdijk, Sham, Murray, & McGuffin, 2002; Riley & Kendler, 2006). Other research methodologies have yielded similar results, leading many in the field to conclude that the genetic vulnerability does not conform to the

diagnostic boundaries listed in the *DSM* and other taxonomic
Rather, it appears that there may be a genetic vulnerability to p
that the expression of this vulnerability can take the form of Schiz
tive psychosis, depending on other genetic and acquired risk facto
2005). This new perspective continues to refine our conceptualizations of

The Magnitude of the Genetic Predisposition

The second major controversy in the field concerns the magnitude and extent o
genetic vulnerability for Schizophrenia. In other words, what is the relative importan
of inherited vulnerability versus external factors. As described below, we now know
that the environment begins to have an impact before birth. Thus, in order to index environmental events that contribute to nongenetic constitutional vulnerability, we must
include the prenatal period. At this point, however, researchers are not in a position to
estimate with precision the relative magnitude of the inherited and environmental contributors to the etiology of Schizophrenia. Moreover, we do not yet know whether
genetic vulnerability is present in all cases of Schizophrenia. It is possible that some
cases of the illness are solely attributable to environmental risk factors.

Further, we do not know whether the genetic predisposition to Schizophrenia is always expressed. There is substantive evidence to indicate that it is not. We know that
the concordance rate for Schizophrenia in MZ twins is nowhere near 100%, suggesting
that some genetically vulnerable individuals do not develop the illness. It is possible,
however, that the genetic liability for Schizophrenia sometimes results from a mutation
that occurs in only the affected member of discordant MZ pairs. But findings from studies of discordant MZ twins indicate that the rate of Schizophrenia is elevated in the
offspring of both the affected and nonaffected co-twins (Gottesman & Bertelsen, 1989;
Kringlen & Cramer, 1989). In other words, the offspring of the normal MZ twin have a
rate of Schizophrenia similar to the offspring of the ill co-twin, even though they were
not raised by a schizophrenic parent. This provides support for the notion that some
individuals possess a genetic vulnerability for Schizophrenia that they pass on to their
offspring, despite the fact that they are never diagnosed with the illness.

Thus, unexpressed genetic vulnerabilities for Schizophrenia may be common in the
general population. The presence of individuals who have an unexpressed genetic vulnerability to Schizophrenia makes the work of genetic researchers much more difficult.
At the same time, the evidence of unexpressed genotypes for Schizophrenia leads us
to inquire about factors that trigger the expression of illness in vulnerable individuals,
and the hope that this knowledge may, some day, lead to effective preventative
interventions.

PRENATAL AND OBSTETRICAL FACTORS

As noted, the fact that at least 50% of MZ co-twins of Schizophrenia patients do not
manifest Schizophrenia clearly illustrates the importance of environmental factors in
the etiology of Schizophrenia. Identifying these factors is a focus of many investigations, and the prenatal period has received greater attention in recent years. There is
extensive evidence that obstetrical complications (OCs) have an adverse impact on the
developing fetal brain, and may contribute to vulnerability for Schizophrenia. Birth cohort studies have shown that Schizophrenia patients are more likely to have a history of
OCs (Buka, Tsuang, & Lipsitt, 1993; McNeil, 1988; Dalman Allebeck, Cullberg,

akagai et al., 2006). Included among these are prenatal
preeclampsia, and labor and delivery complications. A
Cannon (1997) concluded that among the different types
with fetal hypoxia (oxygen deprivation) were the most
zophrenia. In general, the odds of developing adult onset
ase linearly with an increasing number of hypoxia-related
den, & Hadley, 1997; Cannon, 1998; Zornberg, Buka, &

it has been linked with increased risk for Schizophrenia is
earchers have found that the risk rate for Schizophrenia is
rn shortly after a flu epidemic (Barr, Mednick, & Munk-
nes, O'Callaghan, & Takei, 1992; Limosin, Rouillon, Pay-
en, Cohen., Brown et al., 2004), or after being prenatally exposed to
rubella (Brown, Cohen, narkavy-Friedman, & Babulas, 2001). The critical period of
exposure appears to be between the fourth and sixth months of pregnancy. The findings
from research on prenatal viral infection might help explain the season-of-birth effect
in Schizophrenia. Several studies have found that a disproportionate number of
schizophrenic patients are born during the winter months (Bradbury & Miller, 1985;
Torrey, Miller, Rawlings, & Yolken, 1997; Narita et al., 2000). This timing may reflect
seasonal exposure to viral infections, which are most common in late fall and early winter. Thus the fetus would have been exposed to the infection during the 2nd trimester, a
critical period for fetal brain development. Disruptions during this stage may give rise
to brain abnormalities that confer vulnerability.

Indirect support for the relationship between second trimester fetal insult and
Schizophrenia also comes from the observation that many patients show subtle physical
aberrations in body features referred to as minor physical anomalies (MPAs; Smith,
1982; Ismail, Cantor-Graai, & McNeil, 2000). External craniofacial and limb features
and the central nervous system (CNS) originate in the same germinal (ectoderm) layer
during the same period of fetal development. The presence of MPAs is assumed to be an
outward manifestation of abnormal CNS development. In addition to evidence of second trimester insult, there are also data suggesting that exposure to nutritional deficiency during the first trimester is linked with an increased risk for Schizophrenia
(Susser & Brown, 1999).

Studies of rodents and nonhuman primates have shown that prenatal maternal stress
can interfere with fetal brain development, and is associated with elevated glucocorticoid release and hippocampal abnormalities in the offspring (Smythe, McCormick,
Rochford, & Meaney, 1994; Weinstock, 1996; Coe et al., 2003). Along the same lines,
in humans there is evidence that stressful events during pregnancy are associated with
greater risk for Schizophrenia and other psychiatric disorders in adult offspring. Researchers have found higher rates of Schizophrenia in the offspring of women whose
spouses died during their pregnancies (Huttunen, 1989) and in women who were exposed to a military invasion during their pregnancies (van Os & Selten, 1998). It is
likely that prenatal stress triggers the release of maternal stress hormones, which can
disturb fetal neurodevelopment and subsequent functioning of the hypothalamic-
pituitary-adrenal axis, and in turn influence behavior and cognition (Welberg &
Seckl, 2001).

One of the chief questions confronting researchers is whether OCs act independently
to increase risk for Schizophrenia, or have their effect by interacting with a genetic

(e.g., Potash et al., 2001).
ychosis in general, and
ophrenia or an affec-
(Kempf et al.,
outcome.

f the
e

vulnerability. One possibility is that the genetic vulnerability for Schizophrenia involves an increased sensitivity to prenatal factors that interfere with fetal neurodevelopment (Cannon, 1997, 1998; Preti, 2005, Walshe et al., 2005). As an example, genes associated with the immune process are potential candidates; individuals with certain genotypes may be more sensitive to the adverse effects of prenatal exposure to maternal viral infection. Indeed, researchers have recently posited that functional polymorphisms on interleukin genes are candidates for genetic research (Brown, 2006). This serves as an illustrative example of the gene X environment interactions that may be involved.

It is also plausible that obstetrical events act independently of genetic vulnerabilities, although such effects would likely entail interactions among factors (Susser & Brown, 1999). For example, in order to produce the neurodevelopmental abnormalities that confer risk for Schizophrenia, it may be necessary for a specific OC to occur during a critical period of cellular migration and/or in conjunction with other factors such as maternal fever or immune response.

Cognitive Deficits in Schizophrenia: Signs of Brain Dysfunction

One of the earliest and most well established observations about Schizophrenia was that it is often associated with impairments in cognitive performance. Schizophrenia patients manifest performance deficits on a broad range of mental tasks, from simple sensory processing and attention to abstract thinking (Green, Kern, Braff, & Mintz, 2000; Bozikas, Kosmidis, Kiosseoglou, & Karavatos, 2006). In fact, many investigators have argued that one or more cognitive deficits may be the core feature of the illness (Elvevag & Goldberg, 2000).

Some of the most basic deficits in Schizophrenia are detected in the very earliest stages of visual and auditory information processing. Using a laboratory procedure called backward masking, researchers have shown that—compared to both healthy individuals and psychiatric controls—Schizophrenia patients are slower in the initial processing of visual stimuli (Green, Nuechterlein, Breitmeyer, & Mintz, 1999; Green, Nuechterlein, Breitmeyer, & Mintz, 2006). In the auditory modality, researchers have found abnormalities in a process called sensory gating. Sensory gating refers to the habituation of responses to repeated exposure to the same sensory stimulus. The inhibition of responsiveness to repetitive stimulation provides humans with the ability to block out irrelevant or redundant stimuli. P50 is an electroencephalogram (EEG) event-related potential waveform used to assess sensory gating. There is a large body of evidence suggesting that a significant proportion of patients with Schizophrenia have sensory gating impairments (Potter, Summerfelt, Gold, & Buchanan, 2006). In other words, Schizophrenia patients fail to habituate and instead continue to show P50 responses to auditory stimuli even after continued presentation.

Among the higher-level cognitive functions, Schizophrenia patients show deficits in verbal and spatial memory, abstract reasoning, and executive functions such as planning and organization (Kuperberg & Heckers, 2000; Caspi et al., 2003). Deficits in executive functions—which are subserved by the frontal lobes—have been of particular interest to researchers because they may contribute to the impaired insight manifested by so many patients (Shad, Tamminga, Cullum, Haas & Keshavan, 2006). Impaired insight is a clinically important phenomenon because it is associated with a failure among patients to acknowledge their illness and comply with treatment.

Given the deficits in both basic and higher level cognitive processes, it is not surprising that research has consistently shown that Schizophrenia is associated with lower scores on tests of intelligence (Aylward, Walker, & Bettes, 1984). Although, on average, Schizophrenia patients do not score in the 'retarded' range, they do score below their healthy siblings and these differences are apparent in childhood, long before the onset of the illness. Also, for some patients there appears to be a decline in intellectual functioning with advanced age greater than the decline associated with normal aging (Kurtz, 2005).

In addition to the deficits in basic sensory processing and cognitive functions, Schizophrenia patients also show deficits in thinking about social phenomena. Studies of social-cognitive abilities in Schizophrenia patients have consistently shown that patients are impaired in their ability to comprehend and solve social problems (Penn, Waldheter, Perkins, Mueser, & Lieberman, 2005; Niendam et al., 2006). Further, they are less accurate than normal comparison subjects in their ability to label facial expressions of emotion (Penn et al., 2000; Walker et al., 1981; Martin, Baudouin, Tiberghien, & Franck, 2005; Bigelow et al., 2006). As described previously, one of the diagnostic criteria for Schizophrenia is blunted or inappropriate affect. It is, therefore, not surprising that patients show abnormalities in the expression of emotion in both their faces and verbal communications—specifically, less positive and more negative emotion (Brozgold et al., 1998; Tremeau et al., 2005). It has been suggested that these deficits may be linked with the problems patients manifest in recognizing emotions in others. Alternatively, it has been proposed that Schizophrenia patients' deficits in social cognition may be due to limitations in more basic cognitive processes, such as memory and reasoning. However, basic cognitive impairments do not account completely for the more pervasive and persistent social-cognitive dysfunction observed in Schizophrenia (Penn et al., 2000).

Biological Indicators of Vulnerability: The Nature of the Brain Impairment

Research on genetics and obstetrical factors have provided clues about the likely origin of brain dysfunction in Schizophrenia, and the vast literature on cognitive functions illustrates its association with performance deficits. We now turn to the question of which brain regions or processes are impaired. Since the turn of the century, writers in the field of psychopathology had suspected that Schizophrenia involved some abnormality in the brain (Bleuler, 1965). This assumption was based, in part, on the severity of the symptoms and the deteriorating clinical course. However, it was not until the advent of neuroimaging techniques that solid, empirical data were available to support this assumption. As described below, research on Schizophrenia has revealed abnormalities in brain structure, neurotransmitters and functional activity.

ABNORMALITIES IN BRAIN STRUCTURE

Early reports on brain structure in Schizophrenia patients were based on computerized axial tomography (CAT) scans, and showed that affected individuals had enlarged brain ventricles, especially increased volume of the lateral ventricles (Dennert & Andreasen, 1983). As new techniques for brain scanning were developed, these findings were replicated and additional abnormalities were detected (Henn & Braus, 1999). Magnetic resonance imaging (MRI) revealed decreased frontal, temporal, and whole brain volume (Lawrie & Abukmeil, 1998) among people with Schizophrenia. More fine-grained analyses demonstrated reductions in the size of structures such as the thalamus and hippocampus. In fact, of all the regions studied the hippocampus is one that has most consistently been identified as distinguishing people with Schizophrenia from healthy controls (Schmajuk, 2001).

A landmark study of monozygotic (MZ) twins discordant for Schizophrenia was the first to demonstrate that these brain abnormalities were not solely attributable to genetic factors (Suddath, Christison, Torrey, Casanova & Weinberger, 1990). When compared to their healthy identical cotwins, twins with Schizophrenia were found to have smaller temporal lobe volumes—with the hippocampal region showing the most dramatic difference between the affected and nonaffected co-twins. Subsequent studies have confirmed smaller brain volumes among affected twins than among their healthy identical co-twins (Baare et al., 2001). These studies lend support to the hypothesis that the brain abnormalities observed in Schizophrenia are at least partially due to factors that interfere with prenatal brain development.

Despite the plethora of research findings indicating the presence of abnormalities in the brains of patients with Schizophrenia, no specific abnormality has yet been shown to be pathognomonic. In other words, there is no evidence that a specific morphological abnormality is unique to Schizophrenia or characterizes all Schizophrenia patients. It is likely, therefore, that the structural brain abnormalities observed in Schizophrenia are gross manifestations of the occurrence of a deviation in neurodevelopment that has implications for neurocircuitry function.

NEUROTRANSMITTERS

The idea that Schizophrenia involves an abnormality in neurotransmission has a long history. Initial neurotransmitter theories focused on epinephrine and norepinephrine. Subsequent approaches have hypothesized that serotonin, glutamate, and/or GABA abnormalities are involved in Schizophrenia. But—compared to other neurotransmitters—dopamine has played a more enduring role in theorizing about the biochemical basis of Schizophrenia. In this section we review the major neurotransmitter theories of Schizophrenia, with an emphasis on dopamine.

In the early 1950s, investigators began to suspect that dopamine might be playing a central role in Schizophrenia. Dopamine is widely distributed in the brain and is one of the neurotransmitters that enables communication in the circuits that link subcortical with cortical brain regions (Jentsch, Roth, & Taylor, 2000). Since the 1950s, support for this idea has waxed and waned. In the past decade, however, there has been a resurgence of interest in dopamine—largely because research findings have offered a new perspective.

The initial support for the role of dopamine in Schizophrenia was based on two indirect pieces of evidence: (a) drugs that reduce dopamine activity also serve to diminish psychotic symptoms, and (b) drugs that heighten dopamine activity exacerbate or trigger psychotic episodes (Carlsson, 1988). It was eventually discovered that antipsychotic drugs had their effect by blocking dopamine receptors, especially the D2 subtype that is prevalent in subcortical regions of the brain. The newer antipsychotic drugs—or atypical antipsychotics—act on more neurotransmitter systems (including both dopamine and serotonin) and have the advantage of causing fewer motor side effects. Nonetheless, they also act on the dopamine system by blocking various subtypes of dopamine receptors.

The relationship between dopamine and psychotic symptoms can be demonstrated by studies examining compounds such as levodopa. Levodopa increases dopamine transmission and is used to treat Parkinson's. The motor abnormalities associated with Parkinson's disease (i.e., hypokinesias; rigidity, tremors) are due to the low levels of dopamine that characterize the disease. However, researchers have observed that patients with Parkinson's disease who are being treated with dopamine agonists (i.e., levodopa which elevates striatal dopamine) show drug-induced dyskinesias (i.e., increased involuntary writhing movements; Hoff, Plas, Wagemans, & van Hilten, 2001), and in some cases psychotic symptomatology (Papapetropoulos & Mash, 2005). In a similar vein, researchers have observed that stimulants—such as cocaine and amphetamine—increase dopamine activity and can cause both hyperkinesias and psychotic symptoms (Weiner, Rabinstein, Levin, Weiner, & Shulman, 2001). The relation between dopamine and movement can also be seen in research examining genetics and drug response in Schizophrenia. For example, Schizophrenia patients with certain genotypes (specific alleles of the CYP2D6 gene) related to poor metabolization of antipsychotic drugs show a heightened rate of dyskinesias (Ellingrod, Schultz, & Arndt, 2002).

Early studies of dopamine in Schizophrenia sought to determine whether there was evidence of excess neurotransmitter in Schizophrenia patients. But concentrations of dopamine and its metabolites were generally not found to be elevated in body fluids from Schizophrenia patients. When investigators examined dopamine receptors, however, there was some evidence of increased densities. Both postmortem and functional MRI studies of patients' brains yielded evidence that the number of dopamine D2 receptors tends to be greater in patients than normal controls (for a review, Kestler, Walker, & Vega, 2001). Controversy has surrounded this literature because antipsychotic drugs can change dopamine receptor density. Nonetheless, even studies of never-medicated patients with Schizophrenia have shown elevations in dopamine receptors.

Other abnormalities in dopamine transmission have also been found. It appears, for example, that dopamine synthesis and release may be more pronounced in the brains of people with Schizophrenia than among non-Schizoprenics (Lindstrom et al., 1999). When Schizophrenia patients and normal controls are given amphetamine, a drug that enhances dopamine release, the patients exhibit a greater augmentation of dopamine release (Abi-Dargham et al., 1998; Soeares & Innis, 1999).

Glutamate—an excitatory neurotransmitter—may also play a role in the neurochemistry of Schizophrenia. Glutamatergic neurons are part of the pathways that connect the hippocampus, prefrontal cortex, and thalamus—all regions that have been implicated in Schizophrenia. There is evidence of diminished activity at glutamatergic receptors in these brain regions among Schizophrenia patients (Carlsson, Hansson, Waters, & Carlsson, 1999; Goff & Coyle, 2001; Tsai & Coyle, 2002). One of the chief receptors for glutamate in the brain is the N-methyl-D-aspartic acid (NMDA) subtype receptor. It has been suggested that these receptors may be abnormal in Schizophrenia. Blockade of NMDA receptors produces some of the symptomatic manifestations of Schizophrenia in normal subjects, including negative symptoms and cognitive impairments. For example, administration of NMDA receptor antagonists—such as phencyclidine (PCP) and ketamine—induces a broad range of schizophrenic-like symptomatology in humans and these findings have contributed to a hypoglutamatergic hypothesis of Schizophrenia. Conversely, drugs that indirectly enhance NMDA receptor function can reduce negative symptoms and improve cognitive functioning in Schizophrenia patients. It is important to note that the idea of dysfunction of glutamatergic transmission is not inconsistent with the dopamine hypothesis of Schizophrenia because there are reciprocal connections between forebrain dopamine projections and systems that use glutamate. Thus dysregulation of one system would be expected to alter neurotransmission in the other.

In addition, there is evidence that GABA—an inhibitory neurotransmitter—may have excessive inhibitory effects in psychotic disorders (Squires & Saederup, 1991). Related to this, the uptake and the release of GABA has been shown to be abnormal in some studies of postmortem brain tissue from Schizophrenia patients (Lewis, Pierri, Volk, Melchitzky, & Woo, 1999) and there are abnormalities in the interconnections among GABA neurons (Benes & Berretta, 2001). More specifically, there is evidence of a loss of cortical GABA interneurons. Current theories about the role of GABA in Schizophrenia assume that it is important because cortical processes require an optimal balance between GABA inhibition and glutamatergic excitation.

The true picture of the neurochemical abnormalities in Schizophrenia may be more complex than we would like to assume. All neurotransmitter systems interact in intricate ways at multiple levels in the brain's circuitry (Carlsson et al., 2001; Walker, 1994). Consequently, an alteration in the synthesis, re-uptake or receptor density, and/or affinity for any one of the neurotransmitter systems would be expected to have implications for one or more of the other neurotransmitter systems. Further, because neural circuits involve multiple segments that rely on different transmitters, it is easy to imagine how an abnormality in even one specific subgroup of receptors could result in the dysfunction of all the brain regions linked by a particular brain circuit.

Premorbid Development, Course and Prognosis

Assuming genetic and obstetrical factors set the stage for the brain impairment that is the basis of vulnerability for Schizophrenia, the diathesis must be present at birth. Yet, Schizophrenia is typically diagnosed in late adolescence or early adulthood—with the average age of diagnosis in males about four years earlier than for females (Riecher-Rossler & Hafner, 2000). This raises intriguing questions about the developmental course prior to the clinical onset. Is the vulnerability dormant prior to late adolescence or is it manifested in other ways?

PREMORBID DEVELOPMENT

There is compelling evidence that there are signs of vulnerability to Schizophrenia long before the illness is diagnosed. Most of these signs are subtle and do not reach the severity of clinical disorder. Nonetheless, when compared to children with healthy adult outcomes, children who later develop Schizophrenia manifest deficits in multiple domains. In some of these domains, the deficits are apparent as early as infancy.

In the area of cognitive functioning, children who later develop Schizophrenia tend to perform below their healthy siblings and classmates. This is reflected in lower scores on measures of intelligence and achievement, and poorer grades in school (Aylward et al., 1984; Jones, Rodgers, Murray, & Marmot, 1994). Preschizophrenic children also show abnormalities in social behavior. They are less responsive in social situations, exhibit less positive emotion (Walker & Lewine, 1990; Walker, Grimes, Davis, & Smith, 1993), show abnormalities in gestural behavior (Mittal et al., 2006), and have poorer social adjustment than children with healthy adult outcomes (Done, Crow, Johnstone, & Sacker, 1994). In studies of the childhood home movies of Schizophrenia patients, it was found that the preschizophrenic children showed more negative facial expression of emotion than their siblings as early as the first year of life—indicating that the vulnerability for Schizophrenia is subtly manifested in the earliest interpersonal interactions (Walker et al., 1993).

Vulnerability to Schizophrenia is also apparent in motor functions. When compared to their siblings with healthy adult outcomes, preschizophrenic children show more delays and abnormalities in motor development—including deficits in the acquisition of early motor milestones such as bimanual manipulation and walking (Walker, Savoi, & Davis, 1994). Deficits in motor function extend throughout the premorbid period (Walker, Lewis, Loewy, & Palyo, 1999) and persist after the onset of the clinical illness (McNeil & Cantor-Graae, 2000). Further—as mentioned previously—abnormal gesture behavior has been found in both the premorbid period (Mittal et al., 2006) and in unmedicated individuals with Schizophrenia (Troisi, Spalletta, & Pasini, 1998). These data imply that the movement abnormalities recognized in Schizophrenia may be associated with abnormalities in communication and motor planning centers.

It is important to note that neuromotor abnormalities are not pathognomonic for Schizophrenia, in that they are observed in children at risk for a variety of disorders—including learning disabilities, and conduct and mood disorders. But they are one of several important clues pointing to the involvement of brain dysfunction in Schizophrenia. Also, it is important to distinguish between *tardive dyskinesia*—a movement disorder that can be induced by antipsychotic medications—and the involuntary movements which have been demonstrated to be present in nonmedicated infants (Fish, 1987) and adolescents (Walker et al., 1999) at risk for Schizophrenia, and diagnosed Schizophrenia patients who are not on medication (Khot & Wyatt, 1991).

Despite the subtle signs of abnormality that have been identified in children at risk, most adult patients with Schizophrenia do not manifest diagnosable mental disorders in childhood. Thus, while their parents typically recall some irregularities in their development, most preschizophrenic children were not viewed as clinically disturbed. But the picture often changes in adolescence. Many adolescents who go on to develop Schizophrenia show a pattern of escalating adjustment problems—including feelings of depression, social withdrawal, irritability, and noncompliance (Walker & Baum, 1998). Further, this developmental pattern is not unique to Schizophrenia—adolescence is also the critical period for the expression of the first signs of mood disorders, substance abuse, and some other behavioral disorders. As a result, researchers view adolescence as a critical period for the emergence of various kinds of behavioral dysfunction (Walker, 2002; Corcoran et al., 2003).

Schizotypal Personality Disorder

Among the behavioral risk indicators sometimes observed in preschizophrenic adolescents are subclinical' signs of psychotic symptoms. These signs are also the defining features of a *DSM* Axis II disorder, namely, Schizotypal Personality Disorder (SPD). The diagnostic criteria for SPD includes social anxiety and withdrawal, affective abnormalities, eccentric behavior, unusual ideas (e.g., persistent belief in ESP, aliens, extrasensory phenomena), and unusual sensory experiences (e.g., repeated experiences with confusing noises with peoples' voices, or seeing objects move). Although the individual's unusual ideas and perceptions are not severe or persistent enough to meet criteria for delusions or hallucinations, they are recurring and atypical of the person's cultural context.

An extensive body of research demonstrates genetic and developmental links between Schizophrenia and SPD. The genetic link between SPD and Schizophrenia has been documented in twin and family history studies (Kendler, McGuire, Gruenberg, & Walsh, 1995; Kendler, Neale, & Walsh, 1995; Raine & Mednick, 1995). The developmental transition from schizotypal signs to Schizophrenia in young adulthood has been followed in several recent longitudinal studies—with researchers reporting that a substantial proportion of schizotypal individuals eventually show an Axis I Schizophrenia spectrum disorder (Miller et al., 2002; Yung et al., 1998). The remainder of individuals with SPD either show other adjustment problems or a complete remission of symptoms in young adulthood. Given the elevated rate of progression to Schizophrenia, researchers are now attempting to determine whether schizotypal youth who will eventually manifest Schizophrenia can be identified prior to the onset of the illness. This step is considered to be pivotal in efforts to develop secondary prevention programs.

Recent investigations have revealed that adolescents with SPD manifest some of the same functional abnormalities observed in patients with Schizophrenia. For example, SPD youth show motor abnormalities (Neumann & Walker, 2003; Mittal et al., 2006; Walker et al., 1999), cognitive deficits (Diforio, Kestler, & Walker, 2000; Harvey, Reichenberg, Romero, Granholm, & Siever, 2006), and an increase in cortisol—a stress hormone that is elevated in several psychiatric disorders, including Schizophrenia (Mitropoulou et al., 2004; Walker and Diforio, 1997; Weinstein, Diforio, Schiffman, Walker, & Bonsall, 1999). These findings may eventually aid in the identification of SPD adolescents who are at greatest risk for developing Schizophrenia. Moreover, the finding that stress hormones are elevated in SPD and Schizophrenia suggests that risk for Schizophrenia may be associated with heightened sensitivity to psychosocial stress.

THE ILLNESS COURSE AND PROGNOSIS

The onset of the first-episode of Schizophrenia may be sudden or gradual. But as mentioned above, it is usually preceded by escalating adjustment problems and subclinical symptoms, a period referred to as the *prodromal phase* (Lencz, Smith, Auther, Correll, & Cornblatt, 2003; Lieberman et al., 2001). The prodromal phase often involves the manifestation of schizotypal symptoms as well as mood disturbances, such as depression. There has been an increased research focus on identifying individuals who are in the prodromal period because there is some evidence that the longer the duration of untreated psychosis the worse the prognosis (Harris et al., 2004; Perkins et al., 2004; Davidson & McGlashan, 1997). These findings have contributed to the idea that it is important to provide treatment as early as possible after the onset of the first psychotic episode. However, controversy still surrounds this notion, and some researchers suggest that the relation between longer duration of untreated psychosis and worse prognosis may be a product of poorer premorbid functioning and an insidious onset (Larsen et al., 2001).

Several demographic and clinical factors are associated with prognosis. Being male, having a gradual onset, an early age of onset, poor premorbid functioning, and a family history of Schizophrenia are all associated with poorer prognosis (Gottesman, 1991). In addition, some environmental factors have been found to contribute to a worse outcome. For example, Schizophrenia patients who live in homes where family members express more negative emotions are more likely to relapse (Rosenfarb, Bellack, & Aziz, 2006; Butzlaff & Hooley, 1998). Similarly, exposure to stress has been found to exacerbate Schizophrenia symptoms. As noted, researchers have found an increase in the number of stressful events in the months immediately preceding a Schizophrenia relapse (Horan et al., 2005; Ventura et al., 1992).

Despite advances in treatment, the prognosis for many Schizophrenia patients is very poor. Only 20 to 30% are able to live independently and/or maintain a job (Grebb & Cancro, 1989). The majority experience a more debilitating course, with 20 to 30% manifesting continued moderate symptoms and over half experiencing significant impairment the rest of their lives. Harrow and colleagues (2005) evaluated a group of patients with Schizophrenia over a fifteen-year period and found that only about 40% of the patients showed one or more periods of recovery. Further, patients with Schizophrenia showed poorer courses than those with other psychotic and nonpsychotic disorders (Harrow, Grossman, Jobe, & Herbener, 2005). Further, patients with Schizophrenia often suffer from other comorbid (i.e., co-occurring) conditions. For example, the rate of substance abuse among Schizophrenia patients is very high—with as many as 47% of patients in the community and 90% in prison settings meeting lifetime *DSM-IV* criteria for substance abuse or dependence (Regier et al., 1990).

More recently, there is evidence to suggest that the use of certain recreational drugs can also be a bioenvironmental risk factor. To the surprise of many scientists—as well as the general public—it has been shown that adolescent use of marijuana can contribute to risk for psychosis (Verdoux, Tournier, & Cougnard, 2005). Evidence to support this relation has come from retrospective and prospective studies. Although the mechanisms involved are not yet known, there is reason to suspect that the principal active ingredient of cannabis—Δ-9-tetrahydrocannabinol (Δ-9-THC)—increases risk for psychosis by augmenting dopamine neurotransmission and stress hormone release (D'Souza et al., 2005; Viveros, Llorente, Moreno, & Marco, 2005).

Finally, patients with Schizophrenia have a higher rate of early morbidity than the general population and suicide is a leading cause of death. It has been estimated that 25–50% of Schizophrenia patients attempt suicide and 4 to 13% successfully commit suicide (Meltzer, 2001). Risk factors associated with suicide in this population include more severe depressive symptoms, being male, having an earlier onset, and suffering recent traumatic events (Schwartz & Cohen, 2001).

THE ASSESSMENT AND TREATMENT OF SCHIZOPHRENIA

There are currently no biological or psychological cures for Schizophrenia; however, significant progress has been made in treatments that greatly improve the prognosis. As a result of this research progress, the quality of life for individuals with Schizophrenia is dramatically better now than it was just 20 years ago. This is largely due to the availability of more effective medications.

The treatment of Schizophrenia can be divided into three phases: acute, stabilization, and maintenance (Kaplan & Sadock, 1999). In the acute phase, the goal of treatment is to reduce the severity of symptoms and this usually involves the administration of medication. In the stabilization phase, the goal is to consolidate treatment gains and help the patient attain a stable living situation. Finally, during the maintenance phase, when the symptoms are in remission (partial or complete), the goal is to reduce residual symptoms, prevent relapse, and improve functioning.

Antipsychotic Medication

The mainstay of the biological treatment of Schizophrenia is antipsychotic medication. First introduced in the 1950s, these medications had an enormous impact on the lives of people afflicted with Schizophrenia. Their psychotic symptoms improved and many were able to leave psychiatric hospitals (deinstitutionalization). Chlorpromazine (Thorazine) was among the first in a line of medications now referred to as the typical antipsychotics or neuroleptics. All of the typical antipsychotics act by decreasing dopamine activity via receptor blockade. In addition to reducing psychotic symptoms, however, they can also induce movement disorders—most notably tardive dyskinesia.

Concerns about the motor side effects of typical antipsychotic drugs served as an impetus for the development of new compounds. In the late 1980s, a new generation of antipsychotic medications was introduced. The new class of medication is commonly referred to as the atypical or second generation antipsychotics. Medications in this class share a lower risk of movement disorders. The atypical antipsychotics include Risperdal (risperidone), Zyprexa (olanzapine), Seroquel (quetiapine), Geodon (ziprazadone), Abilify (aripiprazole), and Clozaril (clozapine). These medications differ from one another in the neurotransmitter receptors that they occupy. Although all block dopamine neurotransmission to some extent, they vary in the extent to which they affect serotonin, glutamate, and other neurotransmitters. Since their introduction, the atypical antipsychotics have become first-line in the treatment of Schizophrenia. The efficacy of the atypical antipsychotics for the treatment of positive symptoms is at least equivalent to that of the typical antipsychotics, and some studies suggest that they are more effective for negative symptoms and the cognitive impairments associated with the disorder (Forster, Buckley, & Phelps, 1999; Kaplan & Sadock, 2000). Nonetheless, there are still side effects, including the risk of developing a metabolic syndrome, substantial weight gain, new onset or worsening of diabetes mellitus, and lipid abnormalities (Newcomer, 2005).

Antipsychotic medications are usually administered orally. For patients who are not compliant with oral medication, injectible, long-lasting (depot) antipsychotic medication may be administered every two to four weeks. Benefits of injectable antipsychotics include the ease of use for the patient and the fact that the clinician can monitor compliance.

It is fortunate that the rate of tardive dyskinesia has declined since the introduction of atypical antipsychotics. Nonetheless, a recent collaborative national study comparing the effectiveness of typical and atypical antipsychotics did not reveal significant differences among the medications with regard to their ability to enhance patient's social functioning (Swartz et al., 2007). Thus, the advantages of the new generation of antipsychotics may be limited.

Another issue to be addressed in the evaluation and treatment of Schizophrenia is the patient's safety. Given the high rate of suicide among patients with Schizophrenia, the risk of self-harm and violence is important to assess (McGirr et al., 2006; Siris, 2001). Also, a medical examination is typically conducted in order to rule out other illnesses that can cause or exacerbate psychotic symptoms. This examination includes a review of the medical history, a physical examination, and laboratory tests.

Antipsychotic Medication for the Prodromal Phase of Schizophrenia

Several reports indicate that antipsychotics may be effective in reducing the progression of prodromal syndromes into Axis I psychotic disorders. As noted, prodromal signs include subclinical psychotic symptoms, social adjustment problems, and mood changes, and many prodromal patients meet criteria for SPD. An early study suggested that a low-dose typical antipsychotic could prevent the onset of Schizophrenia (Falloon, 1992). Subsequent studies indicate that atypical antipsychotics have the same potential. In one study, prodromal young adults were identified based on the administration of a standardized diagnostic interview that is designed to measure prodromal signs (McGorry et al., 2002). They were then randomly assigned to either low-dose risperidone with cognitive therapy or to usual care alone. After six months, the rate of conversion to psychosis was 9.7% for those receiving risperidone and cognitive treatment, and 35.7% for usual care. For risperidone compliant patients, protection against progression extended for 6 months after cessation of drug treatment. In another study, investigators conducted a double-blind, randomized, placebo-controlled trial with 60 patients who met prodromal criteria (Wood et al., 2004). Olanzapine, an atypical antipsychotic, or placebo was administered for eight weeks. Although both groups showed a decline in prodromal symptoms, analyses revealed that the olanzapine–placebo difference was significant by week eight—with those on Olanzapine shower fewer and less severe symptoms. There were some adverse side effects, however, with Olanzapine patients gaining significantly more weight.

Despite these preliminary reports, most agree that we must proceed with caution in administering antipsychotic medications to prodromal subjects. First, as described previously, we know that not all who meet standard criteria for the prodrome will actually develop a psychotic disorder. Thus, some would receive medication and be subjected to side effects unnecessarily. Further, the prodrome typically emerges in adolescence/early adulthood and we know relatively little about the long-term effects of antipsychotics on development. It is, therefore, important for researchers to conduct naturalistic prospective studies aimed at elucidating the developmental course of symptoms in youth who are receiving antipsychotics (Simeon, Milin, & Walker, 2002). As our knowledge of the effects of psychotropic medication on adolescent growth and development increases we will be in a better position to weigh any adverse effects against potential benefits, both short-term and long-term (Jensen et al., 1999).

Psychosocial Treatments for Schizophrenia

Although antipsychotic medication is the crucial first step in the treatment of Schizophrenia, there is substantial evidence that psychosocial interventions can also be beneficial for both the patient and the family. It is unfortunate that such treatments are not always available because of limited mental health resources. Nonetheless, it is generally agreed that the optimal treatment approach is one that combines medication and psychosocial interventions.

Research supports the use of family therapy—which includes psycho-educational and behavioral components—in treatment programs for Schizophrenia (Bustillo, Lauriello, Horan, & Keith, 2001). Family therapy has been shown to reduce the risk of relapse, reduce family burden, and improve family members' knowledge of and coping with Schizophrenia.

Comprehensive programs for supporting the patient's transition back into the community have also been effective in enhancing recovery and reducing relapse. One such program, called Assertive Community Treatment (ACT), was originally developed in the 1970's by researchers in Madison, Wisconsin (Udechuku et al., 2005; Bustillo et al., 2001; Kaplan & Sadock, 2000). ACT is a comprehensive treatment approach for the seriously mentally ill living in the community. Patients are assigned to a multidisciplinary team (nurse, case manager, general physician, and psychiatrist) that has a fixed caseload and a high staff/patient ratio. The team delivers all services to the patient when and where he or she needs them and is available to the patient at all times. Services include home delivery of medication, monitoring of physical and mental health status, in vivo social skills training, and frequent contact with family members. Studies suggest that ACT can reduce time spent in hospital, improve housing stability, and increase patient and family satisfaction (Udechuku et al., 2005).

Social skills training seeks to improve the overall functioning of patients by teaching the skills necessary to improve performance of daily living activities, employment related skills, and interpersonal relationships (Bustillo et al., 2001). Research indicates that social skills training can improve social competence in the laboratory and in the clinic (Bustillo et al., 2001). However, it remains unclear to what extent this improvement in social competence translates into better functioning in the community.

Because the rate of competitive employment for the severely mentally ill is low (Lehman, 1995), vocational rehabilitation has been a major focus of many treatment programs. Vocational rehabilitation programs have a positive influence on work-related activities, although they have not yet been shown to have a substantial impact on patients' abilities to obtain employment in the community (Lehman, 1995). Some evidence suggests that supported employment programs produce better results than traditional vocational rehabilitation programs—as measured by patients' ability to obtain competitive, independent employment. Nonetheless, job retention remains a significant problem (Bustillo et al., 2001; Lehman et al., 2002).

Finally, cognitive behavior therapy for Schizophrenia draws on the tenants of cognitive therapy that were originally developed by Beck and Ellis (Beck, 1976; Ellis, 1986). The theory posits that dysfunctional cognitions can contribute to specific psychotic symptoms. Cognitive-behavioral therapy (CBT) for psychosis challenges the notion of a discontinuity between psychotic and normal thinking. Rather, it assumes that the normal cognitive mechanisms are being employed by the patient during periods of nonpsychotic thinking, and that these processes can be used to help the psychotic individuals deal directly with their symptoms (Kingdon & Turkington, 2005). Individual CBT emphasizes a collaborative relationship between patient and therapist. Psychotic beliefs are never directly confronted, although specific psychotic symptoms such as hallucinations, delusions, and related problems are targeted for intervention (Dickerson, 2000). The few published randomized controlled trials available for review suggest that CBT is at least somewhat effective in reducing hallucinations and delusions in medication-resistant patients and as a complement to pharmacotherapy in acute psychosis (Wykes et al., 2005; Bustillo et al., 2001). A recent meta-analysis examining 14 studies including 1,484 patients concluded that CBT produced significant improvements in patient functioning, especially for acute patients, compared to those individuals suffering from chronic Schizophrenia (Zimmerman, Favrod, Trieu, & Pomini, 2005). However, the investigators acknowledge that many moderating factors still need to be evaluated—including the therapeutic alliance, as well as the extent of cognitive deficits during the pretreatment period (Zimmerman et al., 2005).

Summary and Future Directions

The accumulated findings from decades of research have documented the tremendous personal and social costs of Schizophrenia and other psychotic disorders. They are debilitating and often chronic mental disorders. Although we have not yet identified their causes, we have made substantial progress in understanding their nature. First, and most important, we now know that early assumptions that Schizophrenia was a single disorder and that it involved only one or a few etiologic factors were inaccurate. Instead, contemporary researchers generally agree that Schizophrenia is a syndrome that has multiple causes and that some of these involve complex interactions among genetic and environmental factors. In this sense, Schizophrenia appears to be similar to many serious physical illnesses, like cancer and cardiovascular disease.

The volume of research literature on Schizophrenia and other psychotic disorders is so vast that it is beyond the scope of any chapter. Nonetheless, we reviewed some key scientific findings that bear on how we conceptualize the nature and origins of these disorders. The findings have provided the framework for recently developed models of etiology, such as that illustrated in Figure 11.1. The emergent picture is an elaborated version of the diathesis-stress model that has dominated the field for several decades.

What does the future hold? Several trends are plausible. First, it is likely that research efforts will gradually identify more of the genetic and bioenvironmental factors that contribute to Schizophrenia. In the process, we will probably discover subgroups of patients who are characterized by the same etiologic process. In other words, just as general paresis was found to account for a subgroup of individuals with psychotic syndromes, we will isolate other subgroups that have distinct etiologic processes. Some of these subgroups will undoubtedly share specific genetic risk factors.

Second, parallel with this, we can expect more progress in our understanding of the brain dysfunction that gives rise to psychotic symptoms. Advances in neuroimaging have made it possible to explore the brain from the gross level of anatomy to the molecular level of receptor function. Again, we are likely to find that the neural circuit(s) that subserve psychotic symptoms can be disrupted at multiple stages via different neurotransmitter systems. This information will play a major role in the development of new drug treatments.

Third, we can expect that advances will be made in our understanding of the way environmental factors—from prenatal complications to postnatal stress exposure and stimulant and cannabis use—can trigger the expression of latent vulnerabilities. Advances in this area will set the stage for efforts at prevention, including public health strategies aimed at the general population and preventive interventions for at-risk individuals.

Finally, we can expect that scientific progress in our understanding of adolescent brain development will move the field forward (Walker, 2002). The fact that the overwhelming majority of individuals who are diagnosed with a major mental disorder, including both psychotic and mood disorders, experience a clinical decline that begins within years after the onset of puberty highlights the importance of brain developmental processes in the etiology of psychotic disorders.

Whether or not these predicted trends in research progress unfold, we can be reasonably confident that future investigations will confirm our assumption that Schizophrenia and other psychotic disorders often involve interactions between genetic and environmental factors. Thus, simplistic nature *versus* nurture assumptions will give way to more complex and accurate accounts of etiology.

References

Abi-Dargham, A., Gil, R., Krystal, J., Baldwin, R. M., Seibyl, J. P., Bowers, M., et al. (1998). Increased striatal dopamine transmission in Schizophrenia: Confirmation in a second cohort. *American Journal of Psychiatry*, *155* (6), 761–767.

American Psychiatric Association. (2000). *Diagnostic and statistical manual of mental disorders* (4th Ed.) Washington, DC: Author.

Arajarvi, R., Suvisaari, J., Suokas, J., Schreck, M., Haukka, J., Hintikka, J., et al. (2005). Prevalence and diagnosis of Schizophrenia based on register, case record and interview data in an isolated Finnish birth cohort born 1940–1969. *Social Psychiatry and Psychiatric Epidemiology*, *40* (10), 808–816.

Arlow, J. A., & Brenner, C. (1969). The psychopathology of the psychoses: A proposed revision. *International Journal of Psychoanalysis*, *50* (1), 5–14.

Aylward, E., Walker, E., & Bettes, B. (1984). Intelligence in Schizophrenia: Meta-analysis of the research. *Schizophrenia Bulletin*, *10*, 430–459.

Baare, W. F., van Oel, C. J., Pol, H. E., Schnack, H. G., Durston, S., Sitskoorn, M. M., et al. (2001). Volumes of brain structures in twins discordant for Schizophrenia. *Archives of General Psychiatry*, *58* (1), 33–40.

Barr, C. E., Mednick, S. A., & Munk-Jorgensen, P. (1990). Exposure to influenza epidemics during gestation and adult Schizophrenia: A 40-year study. *Archives of General Psychiatry*, *47*, 869–874.

Bassett, A. S., Hodgkinson, K., Chow, E. W., Correia, S., Scutt, L. E., & Weksberg, R. (1998). 22q11 deletion syndrome in adults with Schizophrenia. *American Journal of Medical Genetics*, *81* (4), 328–337.

Bateson, G., Jackson, D. D., Haley, J., & Weakland, J. (1956). Toward a theory of Schizophrenia. *Behavioral Science*, *1*, 251–264.

Benes, F. M., & Berretta, S. (2001). GABAergic interneurons: Implications for understanding Schizophrenia and bipolar disorder. *Neuropsychopharmacology*, *25* (1), 1–27.

Bigelow, N. O., Paradiso, S., Adolphs, R., Moser, D. J., Arndt, S., Heberlein, A., et al. (2006). Perception of socially relevant stimuli in Schizophrenia. *Schizophrenia Research*, *83* (2–3), 257–267.

Bleuler, E. (1950). Group of Schizophrenias (J. Zinkin, Trans.). New York: International Universities Press. (Original work published in 1911)

Bleuler, M. (1965). Conception of Schizophrenia within the last fifty years and today. *International Journal of Psychiatry*, *1* (4), 501–523.

Bozikas, V. P., Kosmidis, M. H., Kiosseoglou, G., & Karavatos, A. (2006). Neuropsychological profile of cognitively impaired patients with Schizophrenia. *Comprehensive Psychiatry*, *47*(2), 136–143.

Bradbury, T. N., & Miller, G. A. (1985). Season of birth in Schizophrenia: A review of evidence, methodology, and etiology. *Psychological Bulletin*, *98*, 569–594.

Brown, A. S. (2006). Prenatal infection as a risk factor for Schizophrenia. *Schizophrenia Bulletin*, *32* (2), 200–202.

Brown, A. S., Begg, M. D., Gravenstein, S., Schaefer, C. A., Wyatt, R. J., Bresnahan, M., et al. (2004). Serologic evidence of prenatal influenza in the etiology of Schizophrenia. *Archives of General Psychiatry*, *61* (8), 774–780.

Brown, A. S., Cohen, P., Harkavy-Friedman, J., & Babulas, V. (2001). Prenatal rubella, premorbid abnormalities, and adult Schizophrenia. *Biological Psychiatry*, *49*, 473–486.

Brozgold, A. Z., Borod, J. C., Martin, C. C., Pick, L. H., Alpert, M., & Welkowitz, J. (1998). Social functioning and facial emotional expression in neurological and psychiatric disorders. *Applied Neuropsychology*, *5* (1), 15–23.

Buka, S. L., Tsuang, M. T., & Lipsitt, L. P. (1993). Pregnancy/delivery complications and psychiatric diagnosis: A prospective study. *Archives of General Psychiatry*, *50*, 151–156.

Bustillo, J. R., Lauriello, J., Horan, W. P., & Keith, S. J. (2001). The psychosocial treatment of Schizophrenia: An update. *The American Journal of Psychiatry*, *158* (2), 163–175.

Butzlaff, R. L., & Hooley, J. M. (1998). Expressed emotion and psychiatric relapse. *Archives of General Psychiatry*, *55* (6), 547–552.

Cannon, T. D. (1998). Genetic and perinatal influences in the etiology of Schizophrenia: A neurodevelopmental model. In M. F. Lenzenweger & R. H. Dworkin (Eds.), *Origins and Development of Schizophrenia* (pp. 67–92). Washington, DC: American Psychological Association.

Cannon, T. D. (1997). On the nature and mechanisms of obstetric influences in Schizophrenia: A review and synthesis of epidemiologic studies. *International Review of Psychiatry, 9,* 387–397.

Cannon, T. D., Hollister, J. M., Bearden, C. E., & Hadley, T. (1997). A prospective cohort study of genetic and perinatal influences in Schizophrenia. *Schizophrenia Research, 24,* 248.

Cardno, A. G., Rijsdijk, F. V., Sham, P. C., Murray, R. M., & McGuffin, P. (2002). A twin study of genetic relationships between psychotic symptoms. *American Journal of Psychiatry, 159* (4), 539–545.

Carlsson, A. (1988). The current status of the dopamine hypothesis of Schizophrenia. *Neuropsychopharmacology, 1* (3), 179–186.

Carlsson, A., Hansson, L. O., Waters, N., & Carlsson, M. L. (1999). A glutamatergic deficiency model of Schizophrenia. *British Journal of Psychiatry, 37,* 2–6.

Carlsson, A., Hansson, L. O., Waters, N., & Carlsson, M. L. (1997). Neurotransmitter aberrations in Schizophrenia: New perspectives and therapeutic implications. *Life Sciences, 61* (2), 75–94.

Carlsson, A., Waters, N., Holm-Waters, S., Tedroff, J., Nilsson, M., & Carlsson, M. L. (2001). Interactions between monoamines, glutamate, and GABA in Schizophrenia: New evidence. *Annual Review of Pharmacology & Toxicology, 41,* 237–260.

Carpenter, W. T., & Buchanan, R. W. (1994). Schizophrenia. *New England Journal of Medicine 330* (10), 681–690.

Caspi, A., Reichenberg, A., Weiser, M., Rabinowitz, J., Kaplan, Z. E., Knobler, H., et al. (2003). Cognitive performance in Schizophrenia patients assessed before and following the first psychotic episode. *Schizophrenia Research, 65* (2–3), 87–94.

Chow, E. W., Watson, M., Young, D. A., & Bassett, A. S. (2006). Neurocognitive profile in 22q11 deletion syndrome and Schizophrenia. *Schizophrenia Research. 87* (1–3), 270–278.

Coe, C. L., Kramer, M., Czeh, B., Gould, E., Reeves, A. J., Kirschbaum, C., et al. (2003). Prenatal stress diminishes neurogenesis in the dentate gyrus of juvenile rhesus monkeys. *Biological Psychiatry, 54* (10), 1025–1034.

Corcoran, C., Walker, E. F., Huot, R., Mittal, V. A., Tessner, K., Kestler, K., et al. (2003). The stress cascade and Schizophrenia: Etiology and onset. *Schizophrenia Bulletin, 29* (4), 671–692.

Dalman, C., Allebeck, P., Cullberg, J., Grunewald, C., & Koester, M. (1999). Obstetric complications and the risk of Schizophrenia: A longitudinal study of a national birth cohort. *Archives of General Psychiatry, 56* (3), 234–240.

Davidson, L., & McGlashan, T. H. (1997). The varied outcomes of Schizophrenia. *Canadian Journal of Psychiatry, 42,* 34–43.

De Lisi, L. E. (1992). The significance of age of onset for Schizophrenia. *Schizophrenia Bulletin, 18,* 209–215.

Dennert, J. W., & Andreasen N. C. (1983). CT scanning and Schizophrenia: A review. *Psychiatric Developments, 1* (1), 105–122.

Dickerson, F. B. (2000). Cognitive behavioral psychotherapy for Schizophrenia: A review of recent empirical studies. *Schizophrenia Research, 43,* 71–90.

Diforio, D., Kestler, L., & Walker, E. (2000). Executive functions in adolescents with schizotypal personality disorder. *Schizophrenia Research, 42,* 125–134.

Done, D. J., Crow, T. J., Johnstone, E. C., & Sacker, A. (1994). Childhood antecedents of Schizophrenia and affective illness: Social adjustment at ages 7 and 11. *British Medical Journal, 309* (6956), 699–703.

D'Souza, D. C., Abi-Saab, W. M., Madonick, S., Forselius-Bielen, K., Doersch, A., Braley, G., et al. (2005). Delta-9-tetrahydrocannabinol effects in Schizophrenia: implications for cognition, psychosis, and addiction. *Biological Psychiatry, 57* (6), 594–608.

Ellingrod, V. L., Schultz, S. K., & Arndt, S. (2002). Abnormal movements and tardive dyskinesia in smokers and nonsmokers with Schizophrenia genotyped for cytochrome P450 2 D6. *Pharmacotherapy, 22* (11), 1416–1419.

Ellis, A. (1986). Rational-emotive therapy and cognitive-behavioral therapy: Similarities and differences. In A. Ellis & R. Grieger (Eds.), *Handbook of rational-emotive therapy* (Vol. 2, pp. 31–45). New York: Springer.

Elvevag, B., & Goldberg, T. E. (2000). Cognitive impairment in Schizophrenia is the core of the disorder. *Critical Reviews in Neurobiology, 14* (1), 1–21.

Falloon, I. R. H. (1992). Early intervention for first episodes of Schizophrenia: A preliminary exploration. *Psychiatry, 55,* 4–15.

Feighner, J. P., Robins, E., & Guze, S. B. (1972). Diagnostic Criteria for use in psychiatric research. *Archives of General Psychiatry, 26,* 57–63.

Fish, B., Marcus, J., Hans, S. L., Auerbach, J. G., & Purdue, S. (1992). Infants at risk for Schizophrenia: Sequelae of a genetic neurointegrative defect. *Archives of General Psychiatry, 49,* 221–235.

Forster, P. L., Buckley, R., & Phelps, M. A. (1999). Phenomenology and treatment of psychotic disorders in the psychiatric emergency service. *Psychiatric Clinics of North America, 22* (4), 735–754.

Fromm-Reichmann, F. (1948). Notes on the treatment of Schizophrenia by psychoanalytic psychotherapy. *Psychiatry, 11*, 263.

Goff, D. C., & Coyle, J. T. (2001). The emerging role of glutamate in the pathophysiology and treatment of Schizophrenia. *American Journal of Psychiatry, 158* (9), 1367–1377.

Goff, D. C., Heckers, S., & Freudenreich, O. (2001). Advances in the pathophysiology and treatment of psychiatric disorders: Implications for internal medicine. *Medical Clinics of North America, 85* (3), 663–689.

Goldstein, M. J. (1987). The UCLA High-Risk Project. *Schizophrenia Bulletin, 13* (3), 505–514.

Gottesman, I. (1991a). *Psychiatric genesis: The origins of madness*. New York: Freeman.

Gottesman, I. (1991b). *Schizophrenia genesis: The origins of madness*. New York: Freeman.

Gottesman, I. I., & Bertelsen, A. (1989). Confirming unexpressed genotypes for Schizophrenia: Risks in the offspring of Fischer's Danish identical and fraternal discordant twins. *Archives of General Psychiatry, 46* (10), 867–872.

Grebb, J. A., & Cancro, R. (1989). Schizophrenia: Clinical features. In J. I. Kaplian & B. J. Sadock (Eds.), *Synopsis of psychiatry: Behavioral sciences, clinical psychiatry* (5th Ed. pp. 757–777). Baltimore: Williams & Wilkins.

Green, M. F., Kern, R. S., Braff, D. L., & Mintz, J. (2000). Neurocognitive deficits and functional outcome in Schizophrenia: Are we measuring the "right stuff"? *Schizophrenia Bulletin, 26* (1), 119–136.

Green, M. F., Nuechterlein, K. H., Breitmeyer, B., & Mintz, J. (1999). Backward masking in unmedicated schizophrenic patients in psychotic remission: Possible reflection of aberrant cortical oscillation. *American Journal of Psychiatry, 156* (9), 1367–1373.

Green, M. F., Nuechterlein, K. H., Breitmeyer, B., & Mintz, J. (2006). Forward and backward visual masking in unaffected siblings of schizophrenic patients. *Biological Psychiatry, 59* (5), 446–451.

Grotstein, J. S. (1989). A revised psychoanalytic conception of Schizophrenia. *Psychoanalytic Psychology, 6*, 253–275.

Harris, M. G., Henry, L. P., Harrigan, S. M., Purcell, R., Schwartz, O. S., Farrelly, S. E., et al. (2005). The relationship between duration of untreated psychosis and outcome: An eight-year prospective study. *Schizophrenia Research, 79* (1), 85–93.

Harrow, M., Grossman, L. S., Jobe, T. H., & Herbener, E. S. (2005). Do patients with Schizophrenia ever show periods of recovery? *A 15-year multi-follow-up study. Schizophrenia Bulletin, 31* (3), 723–734.

Harvey, P. D., Reichenberg, A., Romero, M., Granholm, E., & Siever, L. J. (2006). Dual-task processing in Schizotypal personality disorder: Evidence of impaired processing capacity. *Neuropsychology, 20* (4), 453–460.

Harvey, P. D., & Walker, E. F. (Eds.). (1987). *Positive and negative symptoms of psychosis: Description, research, and future directions*. Hillsdale, UK: Lawrence Erlbaum.

Henn, F. A., & Braus, D. F. (1999). Structural neuroimaging in Schizophrenia. An integrative view of neuromorphology. *European Archives of Psychiatry & Clinical Neuroscience, 249 (Suppl. 4)* 48–56.

Heston, L. L. (1966). Psychiatric disorders in foster home reared children of schizophrenic mothers. *British Journal of Psychiatry, 112*, 819–825.

Hoff, J., van den Plas, A. A., Wagemans, E. A., & van Hilten, J. J. (2001). Accelerometric assessment of levodopa-induced dyskinesias in Parkinson's disease. *Movement Disorders, 16* (1), 58–61.

Howells, J. G. (1991). *The concept of Schizophrenia: Historical perspectives*. Washington, DC: American Psychiatric Press.

Huttunen, M. (1989). Maternal stress during pregnancy and the behavior of the offspring. In S. Doxiadis & S. Stewart (Eds.), *Early influences shaping the individual. NATO Advanced Science Institute Series: Life Sciences* (Vol. 160) New York: Plenium.

Ismail, B., Cantor-Graae, E., & McNeil, T. F. (2000). Minor physical anomalies in Schizophrenia: Cognitive, neurological and other clinical correlates. *Journal of Psychiatric Research, 34*, 45–56.

Jablensky, A. (2006). Subtyping Schizophrenia: Implications for genetic research. *Molecular Psychiatry, 11* (9), 815–836.

Jentsch, J. D., Roth, R. H., & Taylor, J. R. (2000). Role for dopamine in the behavioral functions of the prefrontal corticostriatal system: Implications for mental disorders and psychotropic drug action. *Progress in Brain Research, 126*, 433–453.

Jones, P., Rodgers, B., Murray, R., & Marmot, M. (1994). Child developmental risk factors for adult Schizophrenia in the British 1946 birth cohort. *Lancet, 344*, 1398–1402.

Karayiorgou, M., Morris, M. A., & Morrow, B. (1995). Schizophrenia susceptibility associated with interstitial deletions of chromosome 22q11. *Proceedings of the National Academy of Science 92*, 7612–7616.

Keith, S. J., Regier, D. A., & Rae, D. S. (1991). Schizophrenic disorders. In L. N., Robins & D. A., Regier (Eds.), *Psychiatric disorders in America: The epidemiologic catchment area study* (pp. 33–52). New York: Free Press.

Kempf, L., Hussain, N., & Potash, J. B. (2005). Mood disorder with psychotic features, schizoaffective disorder, and Schizophrenia with mood features: Trouble at the borders. *International Review of Psychiatry, 17* (1), 9–19.

Kendler, K. S., McGuire, M., Gruenberg, A. M., & Walsh, D. (1995). Schizotypal symptoms and signs in the Roscommon Family Study: Their factor structure and familial relationship with psychotic and affective disorders. *Archives of General Psychiatry, 52*, 296–303.

Kendler, K. S., Neale, M. C., & Walsh, D. (1995). Evaluating the spectrum concept of Schizophrenia in the Roscommon Family Study. *American Journal of Psychiatry, 152*, 749–754.

Kestler, L. P., Walker, E., & Vega, E. M. (2001). Dopamine receptors in the brains of Schizophrenia patients: A meta-analysis of the findings. *Behavioural Pharmacology, 12* (5), 355–371.

Kety, S. S. (1988). Schizophrenic illness in the families of schizophrenic adoptees: Findings from the Danish national sample. *Schizophrenia Bullletin, 14*, 217–222.

Khot, V., & Wyatt, R. J. (1991). Not all that moves is tardive dyskinesia. *American Journal of Psychiatry, 148*, 661–666.

King, S., Ricard, N., Rochon, V., Steiger, H., & Nelis, S. (2003). Determinants of expressed emotion in mothers of Schizophrenia patients. *Psychiatry Research, 117* (3), 211–222.

Kingdon, D. G., & Turkington, D. (2005). *Cognitive therapy of Schizophrenia*. J. B., Persons (Series Ed.). New York: Guilford.

Kraepelin, E. (1913). Psychiatrie (8th Ed.). In R. M. Barclay (Trans.), *Dementia Praecox and Paraphrenia* (Vol. *3*, Pt. 2) Edinburgh, UK: Livingstone.

Kringlen, E., & Cramer, G. (1989). Offspring of monozygotic twins discordant for Schizophrenia. *Archives of General Psychiatry, 46* (10), 873–877.

Kulhara, P., & Chakrabarti, S. (2001). Culture and Schizophrenia and other psychotic disorders. *Psychiatric Clinics of North America, 24* (3), 449–464.

Kuperberg, G., & Heckers, S. (2000). Schizophrenia and cognitive function. *Current Opinion in Neurobiology, 10* (2), 205–210.

Kurtz, M. M. (2005). Neurocognitive impairment across the lifespan in Schizophrenia: An update. *Schizophrenia Research, 74* (1), 15–26.

Lane, H.-Y., Liu, Y.-C., Huang, C.-L., Chang, Y.-C., Wu, P.-L., Lu, C.-T., et al. (2006). Risperidone-related weight gain: Genetic and nongenetic predictors. *Journal of Clinical Psychopharmacology, 26* (2), 128–134.

Larsen, T. K., Friis, S., Haahr, U., Joa, I., Johannessen, J. O., Melle, I., et al. (2001). Early detection and intervention in first-episode Schizophrenia: A critical review. *Acta Psychiatrica Scandinavic, 103* (5), 323–334.

Lawrie, S. M., & Abukmeil, S. S. (1998). Brain abnormality in Schizophrenia: A systematic and quantitative review of volumetric magnetic resonance imaging studies. *British Journal of Psychiatry, 172*, 110–120.

Leff, J., & Vaughn, C. (1985). *Expressed emotion in families: Its significance for mental illness*. New York: Guilford.

Lehman, A. F. (1995). Vocational rehabilitation in Schizophrenia. *Schizophrenia Bulletin, 21* (4), 64–66.

Lehman, A. F., Goldberg, R., Dixon, L., McNary, S., Postrado, L., Hackman, A., et al. (2002). Improving employment outcomes for persons with severe mental illnesses. *Archives of General Psychiatry, 59* (2), 165–172.

Lencz, T., Smith, C. W., Auther, A. M., Correll, C. U., & Cornblatt, B. A. (2003). The assessment of "Prodromal Schizophrenia": Unresolved issues and future directions. *Schizophrenia Bulletin, 29* (4), 717–728.

Lewis, D. A., Pierri, J. N., Volk, D. W., Melchitzky, D. S., & Woo, T. U. (1999). Altered GABA neurotransmission and prefrontal cortical dysfunction in Schizophrenia. *Biological Psychiatry, 46* (5), 616–626.

Lieberman, J. A., Perkins, D., Belger, A., Chakos, M., Jarskog, F., Boteva, K., et al. (2001). The early stages of Schizophrenia: Speculations on pathogenesis, pathophysiology, and therapeutic approaches. *Biological Psychiatry, 50* (11), 884–897.

Lima, A. R., Soares-Weiser, K., Bacaltchuk, J., & Barnes, T. R. (2002). Benzodiazepines for neuroleptic-induced acute akithisia. *Cochrane Database System Review, 1*, CD001950.

Limosin, F., Rouillon, F., Payan, C., Cohen, J., & Strub, N. (2003). Prenatal exposure to influenza as a risk factor for adult Schizophrenia. *Acta Psychiatrica Scandinavica, 107* (5), 331–335.

Lindstrom, L. H., Gefvert, O., Hagberg, G., Lundberg, T., Bergstrom, M., Hartvig, P., et al. (1999). Increased dopamine synthesis rate in medial prefrontal cortex and striatum in Schizophrenia indicated by L-(beta-11C) DOPA and PET. *Biological Psychiatry, 46* (5), 681–688.

Malla, A., & Payne, J. (2005). First-episode psychosis: Psychopathology, quality of life, and functional outcome. *Schizophrenia Bulletin, 31* (3), 650–671.

Marom, S., Munitz, H., Jones, P. B., Weizman, A., & Hermesh, H. (2005). Expressed emotion: *Relevance to rehospitalization in Schizophrenia over 7 years. Schizophrenia Bulletin, 31* (3), 751–758.

Martin, F., Baudouin, J.-Y., Tiberghien, G., & Franck, N. (2005). Processing emotional expression and facial identity in Schizophrenia. *Psychiatry Research, 134* (1), 43–53.

McGirr, A., Tousignant, M., Routhier, D., Pouliot, L., Chawky, N., Margolese, H., et al. (2006). Risk factors for completed suicide in Schizophrenia and other chronic psychotic disorders: A case-control study. *Schizophrenia Research, 84* (1), 132–143.

McGorry, P. D., Yung, A. F., Phillips, L. J., Yuen, H. P., Francey, S., & Cosgrave E. M. (2002). Randomized controlled trial of interventions designed to reduce the risk of progression to first-episode psychosis in a clinical sample with subthreshold symptoms. *Archives of General Psychiatry, 59*, 921–928.

McNeil, T. F. (1988). Obstetric factors and prerinatal injuries. In M. T. Tsuang & J. C. Simpson. (Eds.), *Handbook of Schizophrenia: Nosology, epidemiology and genetics* (Vol. *3*, pp. 319–343). Amsterdam: Elsevier Science.

McNeil, T. F., Cantor-Graae, E., & Weinberger, D. R. (2000). Relationship of obstetric complications and differences in size of brain structures in monozygotic twin pairs discordant for Schizophrenia. *American Journal of Psychiatry, 157* (2), 203–212.

Meltzer, H. J. (2001). Treatment of suicidality in Schizophrenia. In H. Hendin & J. J. Mann (Eds.), *The clinical science of suicide prevention. Annals of the New York Academy of Sciences* (Vol. *932*, pp. 44–60). New York: New York Academy of Sciences.

Menezes, N. M. Arenovich, T., & Zipursky, R. B. (2006). A systematic review of longitudinal outcome studies of first-episode psychosis. *Psychological Medicine, 36* (10), 1349–1362.

Miller, T. J., McGlashan, T. H., Rosen, J. L., Somjee, L., Markovich, P. J., Stein, K., et al. (2002). Prospective diagnosis of the initial prodrome for Schizophrenia based on the Structured Interview for Prodromal Syndromes: Preliminary evidence of interrater reliability and predictive validity. *American Journal of Psychiatry, 159* (5), 863–865.

Mirsky, A. F., & Duncan, C. (2005). Pathophysiology of mental illness: A view from the fourth ventricle. *International Journal of Psychophysiology, 58*, 162–178.

Mitropoulou, V., Goodman, M., Sevy, S., Elman, I., New, A. S., Iskander, E. G., et al. (2004). Effects of acute metabolic stress on the dopaminergic and pituitary-adrenal axis activity in patients with schizotypal personality disorder. *Schizophrenia Research, 70* (1), 27–31.

Mittal, V. A., Tessner, K., Sabuwalla, Z., McMillan, A., Trottman, H. & Walker, E. F. (2006). Gesture behavior in unmedicated schizotypal adolescents. *Journal of Abnormal Psychology, 115* (2), 351–358.

Mowry, B. J., & Nancarrow, D. J. (2001). Molecular genetics of Schizophrenia. *Clinical & Experimental Pharmacology & Physiology, 28*, 66–69.

Murphy, K. C., Jones, L. A., & Owen, M. J. (1999). High rates of Schizophrenia in adults with velo-cardio-facial syndrome. *Archives of General Psychiatry, 56*, 940–945.

Murray, R. M., Jones, P. B., O'Callaghan, E., & Takei, N. (1992). Genes, viruses and neurodevelopmental Schizophrenia. *Journal of Psychiatric Research, 26*, 225–235.

Narita, K., Sasaki, T., Akaho, R., Okazaki, Y., Kusumi, I., Kato, T., et al. (2000). Human leukocyte antigen and season of birth in Japanese patients with Schizophrenia. *American Journal of Psychiatry, 157* (7), 1173–1175.

Neumann, C. S., & Walker, E. F. (2003). Neuromotor functioning in adolescents with schizotypal personality disorder: Associations with symptoms and neurocognition. *Schizophrenia Bulletin, 29* (2), 285–298.

Neumann, C., Walker, E. Lewine, R., & Baum, K. (1996). Childhood behavior and adult neuropsychological dysfunction in Schizophrenia. *Neuropsychiatry, Neuropsychology and Behavioral Neurolog, 9*, 221–229.

Newcomer, John W. (2005). Second-generation (atypical) antipsychotics and metabolic effects: A comprehensive literature review. *CNS Drugs, 19* (*Suppl. 1*) 1–93.

Niendam, T. A., Bearden, C. E., Johnson, J. K., McKinley, M., Loewy, R., O'Brien, M., et al. (2006). Neurocognitive performance and functional disability in the psychosis prodrome. *Schizophrenia Research, 84* (1), 100–111.

Norton, N., Williams, H. J., & Owen, M. J. (2006). An update on the genetics of Schizophrenia. *Current Opinion in Psychiatry, 19* (2), 158–164.

Nurnberger, J., (2006). Meeting report for molecular psychiatry, 2005. *Psychiatric Genetics*, *16* (3), 89–90.

O'Brien, M. P., Gordon, J. L., Bearden, C. E., Lopez, S. R., Kopelowicz, A., & Cannon, T. D. (2006). Positive family environment predicts improvement in symptoms and social functioning among adolescents at imminent risk for onset of psychosis. *Schizophrenia Research*, *81* (2–3), 269–275.

Papapetropoulos, S., & Mash, D. C. (2005). Psychotic symptoms in Parkinson's disease: From description to etiology. *Journal of Neurology*, *252* (7), 753–764.

Penn, D. L., Combs, D. R., Ritchie, M., Francis, J., Cassisi, J., Morris, S., et al. (2000). Emotion recognition in Schizophrenia: Further investigation of generalized versus specific deficit models. *Journal of Abnormal Psychology*, *109* (3), 512–516.

Penn, D. L., & Mueser, K. T. (1996). Research update on the psychosocial treatment of Schizophrenia. *American Journal of Psychiatry*, *153* (5), 607–617.

Penn, D. L., Waldheter, E. J., Perkins, D. O., Mueser, K. T., & Lieberman, J. A. (2005) Psychosocial treatment for first-episode psychosis: A research update. *American Journal of Psychiatry*, *162* (12), 2220–2232.

Perkins, D. O., Lieberman, J. A., Gu, H., Tohen, M., McEvoy, J., Green, A. I., et al. (2004). Predictors of antipsychotic treatment response in patients with first-episode Schizophrenia, schizoaffective and schizophreniform disorders. *British Journal of Psychiatry*, *185* (1), 18–24.

Potash, J. B., Willour, V. L., Chiu, Y. F., Simpson, S. G., MacKinnon, D. F., Pearlson, G. D., et al. (2001). The familial aggregation of psychotic symptoms in bipolar disorder pedigrees. *American Journal of Psychiatry*, *158* (8), 1258–1264.

Potter, D., Summerfelt, A., Gold, J., & Buchana, R. W. (2006) Review of clinical correlates of P50 sensory gating abnormalities in patients with Schizophrenia. *Schizophrenia Bulletin*, *32* (4), 692–700.

Preti, A. (2005). Obstetric complications, genetics and Schizophrenia. *European Psychiatry*, *20* (4), 354.

Raine, A., & Mednick, S. (Eds.). (1995). *Schizotypal personality disorder*. London: Cambridge University.

Regier, D. A., Farmer, M. E., Rae, D. S., Locke, B. Z., Keith, S. J., Judd, L. L., et al. (1990). Comorbility of mental disorders with alcohol and other drug abuse. Results from the Epidemiologic Catchment Area (ECA) Study. *Journal of the American Medial Association*, *264*, 2511–2518.

Riecher-Rossler, A., & Hafner, H. Gender aspects in Schizophrenia: Bridging the border between social and biological psychiatry. *Acta Psychiatrica Scandinavica, 102*(407), 58–62.

Riley, B., & Kendler, K. S. (2006) Molecular genetic studies of Schizophrenia. *European Journal of Human Genetics*, *14* (6), 669–680.

Roffman, J. L., Weiss, A. P., Goff, D. C., Rauch, S. L., & Weinberger, D. R. (2006). Neuro-imaging-genetic paradigms: A new approach to investigate the pathophysiology and treatment of cognitive deficits in Schizophrenia. *Harvard Review of Psychiatry*, *14* (2), 78–91.

Rosenfarb, I. S., Bellack, A. S., & Aziz, N. (2006). Family interactions and the course of Schizophrenia in African American and White patients. *Journal of Abnormal Psychology*, *115* (1), 112–120.

Sadock, B. J., & Sadock, V. A. (Eds.). (2000). *Kaplan & Sadock's comprehensive textbook of psychiatry* (7th Ed. *Vol. 1*) New York: Lippincott, Williams & Wilkins.

Schmajuk, N. A. (2001). Hippocampal dysfunction in Schizophrenia. *Hippocampus*, *11* (5), 599–613.

Schmidt-Kastner, R., van Os, J., Steinbusch, H. W., & Schmitz, C. (2006). Gene regulation by hypoxia and the neurodevelopmental origin of Schizophrenia. *Schizophrenia Research*, *84* (2–3), 253–271.

Schneider, K. (1959). *Clinical Psychopathology*. New York: Grune & Stratton.

Schwartz, J. M., & Begley, S. (2002) *The mind and the brain: Neuroplasticity and the power of mental force*. New York: Harper Collins.

Schwartz, R. C., & Cohen, B. N. (2001). Risk factors for suicidality among clients with Schizophrenia. *Journal of Counseling & Development*, *79* (3), 314–319.

Schwarz, M. J., Kronig, H., Riedel, M., Dehning, S., Douhet, A., Spellmann, I., et al. (2006). IL-2 and IL-4 polymorphisms as candidate genes in Schizophrenia. *European Archives of Psychiatry and Clinical Neuroscience*, *256* (2), 72–76.

Shad, M. U., Tamminga, C. A., Cullum, M., Haas, G. L., & Keshavan, M. S. (2006) Insight and frontal cortical function in Schizophrenia: A review. *Schizophrenia Research*, *86* (1-3), 54–70.

Simeon, J., Milin, R., & Walker, S. (2002). A retrospective chart review of risperidone use in treatment-resistant children and adolescents with psychiatric disorders. *Progress in Neuropsychopharmacology and Biological Psychiatry*, *26* (2), 267–275.

Singer, M., & Wynne, L. (1963). Differentiating characteristics of parents of childhood schizophrenics, childhood neurotics, and young adult schizophrenics. *American Journal of Psychiatry*, *120*, 234–243.

Siris, S. G. (2001). Suicide and Schizophrenia. *Journal of Psychopharmacology*, *1* (2), 127–135.

Smith, D. (1982). *Recognizable Patters of Human Malformation*. London: Saunders.

Smythe, J. W., McCormick, C. M., Rochford, J., & Meaney, M. J. (1994). The interaction between prenatal stress and neonatal handling on nociceptive response latencies in male and female rats. *Physiology and Behavior*, *55*, 971–974.

Soares, J. C., & Innis, R. B. (1999). Neurochemical brain imaging investigations of Schizophrenia. *Biological Psychiatry*, *46* (5), 600–615.

Spitzer, R. L., Endicott, J., & Robins, E. (1978). *Research diagnostic criteria (RDC) for a selected group of functional disorders*. New York: Biometrics Research.

Squires, R. F., & Saederup, E. (1991). A review of evidence for GABergic redominance/glutamatergic deficit as a common etiological factor in both Schizophrenia and affective psychoses: More support for a continuum hypothesis of "functional" psychosis. *Neurochemical Research*, *16* (10), 1099–1111.

Suddath, R. L., Christison, G. W., Torrey, E. F., Casanova, M. F., & Weinberger, D. R. (1990). Anatomical abnormalities in the brains of monozygotic twins discordant for Schizophrenia. *New England Journal of Medicine*, *322* (12), 789–794.

Sullivan, P. F., Owen, M. J., O'Donovan, M. C., & Freedman, R. (2006). Genetics. In J. A. Lieberman, T. S. Stroup, & D. O. Perkins (Eds.), *Textbook of Schizophrenia*. Washington, DC: American Psychiatric Publishing.

Susser, E. S., & Brown, A. S. (Eds.). (1999). *Prenatal exposures in Schizophrenia. Progress in psychiatry*. Washington, DC: American Psychiatric Press.

Swartz, M. S., Perkins, D. O., Stroup, T. S., Davis, S. M., Capuano, G., Rosenheck, R. A., et al. (2007). CATIE Investigators. Effects of antipsychotic medications on psychosocial functioning in patients with chronic Schizophrenia: Findings from the NIMH CATIE study. *American Journal of Psychiatry164* (3), 428–436.

Takagai, S., Kawai, M., Tsuchiya, K. J., Mori, N., Toulopoulou, T., & Takei, N. (2006). Increased rate of birth complications and small head size at birth in winter-born male patients with Schizophrenia. *Schizophrenia Research*, *83* (2–3), 303–305.

Talkowski, M. E., Seltman, H, Bassett, A. S., Brzustowicz, L. M., Chen, X., Chowdari, K. V., et al. (2006). Evaluation of a susceptibility gene for Schizophrenia: genotype based meta-analysis of RGS4 polymorphisms from thirteen independent samples. *Biological Psychiatry*, *60* (2), 152–162.

Tienari, P., Wynne, L. C., Moring, J., & Lahti, I. (1994). The Finnish adoptive family study of Schizophrenia: Implications for family research. *British Journal of Psychiatry*, *164* (Suppl. 23) 20–26.

Torrey, E. F. (1987). Prevalence studies in Schizophrenia. *British Journal of Psychiatry*, *150*, 598–608.

Torrey, E. F., Bowler, A. E., & Taylor, E. H. (1994). *Schizophrenia and manic-depressive disorder: The biological roots of mental illness as revealed by the landmark study of identical twins*. New York: Basic Books.

Torrey, E. F., Miller, J., Rawlings, R., & Yolken, R. H. (1997). Seasonality of births in Schizophrenia and bipolar disorder: A review of the literature. *Schizophrenia Research*, *28*, 1–38.

Tremeau, F., Malaspina, D., Duval, F., Correa, H., Hager-Budny, M., Coin-Bariou, L., et al. (2005). Facial expressiveness in patients with Schizophrenia compared to depressed patients and nonpatient comparison subjects. *American Journal of Psychiatry*, *162* (1), 92–101.

Troisi, A., Spalletta, G., & Pasini, A. (1998). Nonverbal behavior deficits in Schizophrenia: An ethological study of drug-free patients. *Acta Psychiatrica Scandinavica*, *97*, 109–115.

Tsai, G., & Coyle, J. T. (2002). Glutamatergic mechanisms in Schizophrenia. *Annual Review of Pharmacology & Toxicology*, *42*, 165–179.

Udechuku, A., Olver, J., Hallam, K., Blyth, F., Leslie, M., Nasso, M., et al. (2005). Assertive community treatment of the mentally ill: Service model and effectiveness. *Australasian Psychiatry*, *13* (2), 129–134.

van Os, J., & Selten, J. (1998). Prenatal exposure to maternal stress and subsequent Schizophrenia: The May 1940 invasion of The Netherlands. *British Journal of Psychiatry*, *172*, 324–326.

Vaughn, C., & Leff, J. (1976). The measurement of expressed emotion in families of psychiatric patients. *British Journal of Social and Clinical Psychology*, *15* (2), 157–165.

Verdoux, H., Tournier, M., & Cougnard, A. (2005). Impact of substance use on the onset and course of early psychosis. *Schizophrenia Research*, *79* (1), 69–75.

Viveros, M. P., Llorente, R., Moreno, E., & Marco, E. M. (2005). Behavioural and neuroendocrine effects of cannabinoids in critical developmental periods. *Behavioural Pharmacology*, *16* (5–6), 353–362.

Ventura, J., Nuechterlein, K. H., Hardesty, J. P., & Gitlin, M. (1992). Life events and schizophrenic relapse after withdrawal of medication. *British Journal of Psychiatry*, *161*, 615–620.

Walder, D., Walker, E., & Lewine, R. J. (2000). The relations among cortisol release, cognitive function and symptom severity in psychotic patients. *Biological Psychiatry, 48*, 1121–1132.

Walker, E. (2002). Adolescent neurodevelopment and psychopathology. *Current Directions in Psychological Science, 11*, 24–28.

Walker, E. (1994). Developmentally moderated expressions of the neuropathology underlying Schizophrenia. *Schizophrenia Bulletin, 20*, 453–480.

Walker, E., & Baum, K. (1998). Developmental changes in the behavioral expression of the vulnerability for Schizophrenia. In M. Lenzenweger & R. Dworkin (Eds.), *Origins and development of Schizophrenia: Advances in experimental psychopathology* (pp. 469–491). Washington, DC: American Psychological Association.

Walker, E., & Diforio, D. (1997). Schizophrenia: A neural diathesis-stress model. *Psychological Review, 104*, 1–19.

Walker, E., Grimes, K., Davis, D., & Smith, A. (1993). Childhood precursors of Schizophrenia: Facial expressions of emotion. *American Journal of Psychiatry, 150*, 1654–1660.

Walker, E., & Lewine, R. J. (1990). Prediction of adult-onset Schizophrenia from childhood home movies of the patients. *American Journal of Psychiatry, 147*, 1052–1056.

Walker, E., Lewine, R. J., & Neumann, C. (1996). Childhood behavioral characteristics and adult brain morphology in Schizophrenia patients. *Schizophrenia Research, 22*, 93–101.

Walker, E., Lewis, N., Loewy, R., & Palyo, S. (1999). Motor dysfunction and risk for Schizophrenia. *Development and Psychopathology, 11*, 509–523.

Walker, E., Lewis, N., Loewy, R., & Paylo, S. (1999). Motor functions and psychopathology. *Development and Psychopathology, 11(Special Ed.)*, 509–523.

Walker, E., Savoie, T., & Davis, D. (1994). Neuromotor precursors of Schizophrenia. *Schizophrenia Bulletin, 20*, 441–452.

Walker, E., Walder, D., & Reynolds, F. (2001). Developmental changes in cortisol secretion in normal and at-risk youth. *Development and Psychopathology, 13*, 719–730.

Walshe, M., McDonald, C., Taylor, M., Zhao, J., Sham, P., Grech, A., et al. (2005). Obstetric complications in patients with Schizophrenia and their unaffected siblings. *European Psychiatry, 20* (1), 28–34.

Weiner, W. J., Rabinstein, A., Levin, B., Weiner, C., & Shulman, L. (2001). Cocaine-induced persistent dyskinesias. *Neurology, 56* (7), 964–965.

Weinstein, D., Diforio, D., Schiffman, J., Walker, E., & Bonsall, B. (1999). Minor physical anomalies, dermatoglyphic asymmetries and cortisol levels in adolescents with schizotypal personality disorder. *American Journal of Psychiatry, 156*, 617–623.

Weinstock, M. (1996). Does prenatal stress impair coping and regulation of hypothalamic-pituitary-adrenal axis? *Neuroscience and Biobehavioral Reviews, 21*, 1–10.

Welberg, L. A., & Seckl, J. R. (2001). Prenatal stress, glucocorticoids and the programming of the brain. *Journal of Neuroendocrinology, 2*, 113–128.

Wolff, S. (1991). 'Schizoid' personality in childhood and adult life I: The vagaries of diagnostic labeling. *British Journal of Psychiatry, 159*, 615–620.

Wonodi, I., Hong, L., Avila, M. T., Buchanan, R. W., Carpenter, W. T., Jr., Thaker, G. K., et al. (2005). Association between polymorphism of the SNAP29 gene promoter region and Schizophrenia. *Schizophrenia Research, 78* (2–3), 339–341.

Wood, G. E., Young, L. T., Reagan, L. P., Chen, B., & McEwen, B. S., (2004). Stress-induced structural remodeling in hippocampus: Prevention by lithium treatment. *Proceedings of the National Acadamy of Scences U.S.A., 101* (11), 3973–3978.

Wykes, T., Hayward, P., Thomas, N., Green, N., Surguladze, S., Fannon, D., et al. (2005). What are the effects of group cognitive behaviour therapy for voices? A randomised control trial. *Schizophrenia Research, 77* (2–3), 201–210.

Yung, A. R., Phillips, L. J., McGorry, P. D., Hallgren, M. A., McFarlane, C. A., Jackson, H. J., et al. (1998). Prediction of psychosis: A step towards indicated prevention of Schizophrenia. *British Journal of Psychiatry, 172* (Suppl. 33) 14–20.

Zhao, X., Li, H., Shi, Y., Tang, R., Chen, W., Liu, J., et al. (2006). Significant association between the genetic variations in the 5' end of the N-Methyl-D-Aspartate receptor subunit gene GRIN1 and Schizophrenia. *Biological Psychiatry, 59* (8), 747–753.

Zimmermann, G., Favrod, J., Trieu, V., & Pomini, V. (2005). The effect of cognitive behavioral treatment on the positive symptoms of Schizophrenia spectrum disorders: A meta-analysis. *Schizophrenia Research, 77* (1), 1–9.

Zornberg, G. L., Buka, S. L., & Tsuang, M. T. (2000). Hypoxic-ischemia-related fetal/neonatal complications and risk of Schizophrenia and other nonaffective psychoses: A 19-year longitudinal study. *American Journal of Psychiatry, 157* (2), 196–202.

Chapter 12

Eating Disorders: Bulimia Nervosa and Binge Eating

LINDA W. CRAIGHEAD AND LUCY T. SMITH

Disordered eating can take a variety of forms, with the core problem behaviors identified as restrictive eating, binge eating, and compensatory behaviors. The current classification system *DSM-IV-TR* (American Psychiatric Association [APA], 2000) includes two specific diagnoses for eating disorders: Anorexia Nervosa (AN), and Bulimia Nervosa (BN), as well as a nonspecific diagnosis Eating Disorder Not Otherwise Specified (EDNOS) that applies to the wide variety of distressing and impairing patterns that do not meet criteria for a specific disorder. Anorexia Nervosa is discussed separately (in Chapter 13) because its diagnosis and treatment has been dominated by a focus on weight (rather than behavior), and the most important criterion for therapy outcome has been weight restoration. AN has traditionally been viewed as having a fairly distinct etiology compared to BN. However, individuals achieve and maintain low weight through a variety of methods, so the behaviors and attitudes associated with AN overlap considerably with the patterns of binge eating that will be discussed in this chapter.

The primary emphasis here will be the two patterns of binge eating that have been studied most extensively—BN and the EDNOS pattern labeled Binge Eating Disorder (BED). BED is currently a provisional diagnosis but some version is likely to be approved in the forthcoming revision of the *DSM*, so we refer to BED as a disorder in this chapter. Unlike the binge-purge subtype of AN, neither of these patterns has a weight criterion and neither diagnosis is assigned unless the binge eating behavior occurs

435

outside the course of an episode of AN (i.e., low weight). These two maladaptive eating patterns are characterized by: (a) objective binge eating (distressing feelings of loss of control over the process of eating) and/or (b) "compensatory" behaviors (deliberate efforts to minimize intake or minimize its impact on weight). We also address the current diagnostic controversies that are highlighted by the fact that eating behaviors and weight have a complex and uncertain relationship. It is not clear how best to fit behaviors and weight criteria into the diagnostic system, since weight status clearly impacts treatment decisions.

Symptoms and Diagnostic Criteria

BULIMIA NERVOSA (BN)

BN is characterized by recurrent binge eating episodes and recurrent compensatory behavior designed to minimize the impact of those episodes (preventing weight gain). The individual must also highly value body shape and weight, and those must disproportionately factor into the individual's self-evaluation and self-worth (overconcern with weight and shape). Specific criteria—as described in the *Diagnostic and Statistical Manual of Mental Disorders* (*DSM-IV*; APA, 2000)—require that the binge episodes be objectively large (objective binge episodes, called OBEs), which is defined as eating more than most people would eat in a similar situation and in a discrete period of time (e.g., two hours). A binge is defined by the subjective experience of loss of control at some point during an eating episode. Defining loss of control has been fairly problematic since most individuals can (and do) stop eating if there is an unexpected external disruption such as another person entering the situation. The general guideline for defining objectively large is a portion at least three times the typical portion size for that food. The OBEs and compensatory behaviors often occur together, forming a distinct binge-purge episode—but that is not always the case and is not a requirement for diagnosis. Nonetheless, both OBEs and compensatory behavior must occur, on average, at least twice a week for three months. Subjective binge episodes (called SBEs)—which may or may not trigger compensatory behaviors—are also frequently reported but those do not count toward meeting the frequency criterion for binge episodes.

Subtypes

The two subtypes of BN are based on the primary type of compensatory behavior employed: *purging* (self-induced vomiting or misuse of laxatives, diuretics, or enemas) or *nonpurging* (fasting or excessive physical activity). Some individuals rely primarily on one method—such as self-induced vomiting—but many utilize several methods and their use patterns vary over time. In clinical settings, the purging subtype of BN is reported more frequently than the nonpurging subtype: 80 to 90% of treatment seeking individuals with BN report engaging in vomiting behaviors, while one-third of individuals with BN report using laxatives after binge eating (APA, 2000). However, data suggest that the nonpurging subtype may be more common (or at least as common as the purging subtype) in the general population (Favaro, Ferrara, & Santonastaso, 2003). If such individuals have not become overweight due to their binge eating, they may not view their problem as a potentially treatable disorder and they are generally less motivated to seek treatment. Individuals with the nonpurging subtype of BN report less severe psychopathology than those who purge—especially in terms of mood disturbance, body dissatisfaction, and physical abnormalities (APA, 2000)—although they are typically quite distressed about their weight and tend to be heavier than individuals with the purging subtype. Individuals who meet most but not all of the criteria (e.g., frequency) are considered to have subclinical BN, although officially they would receive a diagnosis of EDNOS.

Clearly identifiable binge/purge episodes tend to occur when the individual is alone. The behaviors are often quite secretive and are typically associated with high levels of shame and embarrassment. Oftentimes binges are comprised of high fat, high calorie foods such as pastries or ice cream, but a binge may be large amounts of healthy foods. Individuals often restrict their food intake between binge/purge episodes, and they often binge on the same foods they are trying to restrict. Meals are frequently skipped. The most typical pattern is little to no breakfast or lunch, with intake postponed as long as possible in the day. Frequency of eating is minimized as the individual is trying to limit total intake and feels at risk for binge or overeating whenever they do eat. Both type and amount of food may be severely limited by a set of rules—for example, only healthy foods, no fat, no processed foods, no meat. Binges are often unplanned (normal eating turns into overeating and then binge eating), at least early in the course of the disorder. As the pattern crystallizes, it becomes more common that individuals fight the urge to binge and purge. They are then very vulnerable when they are alone and have the opportunity to binge and purge. When the urge to binge builds, the person typically plans to binge at a time when they will not be detected. Some individuals then experience a period of relief from the urges and can refrain for several days. Evenings are especially high-risk times for many individuals with BN (Deaver, Miltenberger, Smyth, Meidinger, & Crosby, 2003).

Common triggers for binges/purges include emotions (both positive and negative), interpersonal stressors, presence of tempting food, feeling like a dieting rule has been broken, body image dissatisfaction, and skipping meals or getting too hungry. Eating disordered behaviors often serve to distract individuals from unpleasant emotions, to comfort or soothe the individual, to numb unpleasant emotions, or to provide a sense of control. However, after binging/purging individuals typically report feeling intense guilt and shame. In more chronic cases, the binge-purge pattern is so well established it feels more like a habit rather than a response to current distress. Nonetheless, the individual becomes very distressed when they attempt to refrain from either the binge eating or the purging. Due to the high levels of distress that accompany binge/purge symptoms in addition to fears about weight, individuals with bulimia are more likely to seek treatment voluntarily than are women with AN (Fairburn & Harrison, 2003; Klein & Walsh, 2004; Polivy & Herman, 2002). However, individuals typically struggle to stop on their own for a long period of time, often as long as 5 to 10 years before they seek treatment.

Individuals with BN are typically within the normal weight range (APA, 2000; Fairburn & Harrison, 2003), though many are at the higher levels of that range—levels that they consider "overweight." Regardless of their actual weight, these individuals are either wanting to be considerably thinner or they are convinced that they will gain weight if they stop their compensatory behaviors. Thus, while they are highly motivated to stop binge eating, they are ambivalent about stopping the compensatory behaviors. While the initiation of purging behaviors may initially be associated with some weight loss, most individuals find that this effect is not maintained, and many report some weight gain over time because the frequency of binge eating tends to escalate once individuals know they have a way to compensate. As one client stated,

This disorder turns out to be a cruel trick. You think you have found a solution for occasional overeating. You believe you are only going to resort to purging occasionally, but you end up eating more, feeling more out of control, and purging more and more often. The solution stops working but you are afraid to stop purging. (Craighead, personal communcation, 2006)

Medical Complications of Bulimia

Medical complications arise most often from the purging behaviors—for example, self-induced vomiting and laxative abuse (Mitchell & Crow, 2006)—especially at high levels of use. In a moderately severe case the frequency of purging is limited to a few times a week, but in the most severe cases an individual may purge several times a day or purge after any food is eaten. Extended episodes that include multiple periods of eating and then purging are not uncommon. Persons with BN may develop fluid or electrolyte abnormalities (leading to potentially fatal arrhythmias), esophageal complications, GI symptoms, renal system problems, menstrual irregularities, thyroid dysfunction, and Russell's sign (scarring or calluses on the top of the hands from repeatedly inducing vomiting) (APA, 2000; Klein & Walsh, 1996; Mitchell & Crow, 2006). However, many individuals show few medical indicators for extended periods of time. Dental concerns (dental enamel erosion, gum disease) and enlarged parotid glands (chipmunk-like cheeks) are often the only obvious signs of chronic vomiting. Dentists are now being trained to assess for purging when atypical dental problems are evident. Laboratory tests (salivary amalase) can be used as an indicator of inflammation of the parotid glands and positive results may mean the person is purging, but this test is not a specific indicator so it is not currently widely used. BN is very difficult to detect early in the course of the disorder if a person is motivated to hide their problem. Social difficulties related to atypical eating patterns, social isolation, unexplained absences, secretive behavior, missing food (or money), and excessive bathroom use are more often the observable signs that a person's problems have reached clinically significant levels.

Decreased stomach motility can contribute to a patient's complaints that they feel very full after eating normal or small amounts of food (making it more difficult to resist urges to purge). Preliminary evidence suggests that individuals with BN have blunted postprandial cholecystokinin (CCK) release, which may contribute to their difficulty feeling satisfied with normal amounts of food. Keel, Wolfe, Liddel, De Young, and Jimerson (1997) reported findings suggesting that this blunted release may be fairly specific to those who eat large amounts when they binge. Women who purged after normal to small amounts of food were not significantly lower than controls on CCK release.

Over time some individuals find certain methods of eating (or types of foods) that make it easier to self-induce vomiting. Using those strategies escalates the frequency of both bingeing and purging. Some individuals find they can now induce vomiting simply by flexing their stomach muscles. Other find that inducing vomiting becomes more and more difficult. A few individuals resort to using ipecac to induce vomiting, a method which is medically very dangerous as it can lead to irreversible damage to heart muscle tissue. Individuals with diabetes are at particular risk for medical problems as they can misuse their medication as a form of compensatory behavior. Many women with BN seek treatment from a medical doctor for physical concerns before they consider seeking psychological treatment for the disorder (Crow & Peterson, 2003; Mitchell & Crow, 2006). It is not clear if people fail to seek treatment due to stigma, reluctance to tell parents, lack of financial resources, or failure to perceive BN as a treatable problem.

BINGE EATING DISORDER (BED)

BED is diagnosed when an individual reports OBEs (same as defined for BN), but no regular, inappropriate (unhealthy) compensatory behaviors that warrant a diagnosis of BN. Another difference is that overconcern about weight and shape is not a required criterion for BED, although marked distress regarding binge eating is required. Overconcern is generally reported as part of the clinical picture but this is less clearly a distinguishing aspect of the disorder as the majority of those with BED are overweight (or obese) or have appropriate concerns associated with their medical problems. Also, many do not endorse the excessively thin weight goals that are common in BN. Individuals with BED often report low levels of restrictive eating between binge episodes so they have less clearly delineated episodes of binge eating than those with BN (where the end of an episode is more clearly marked by the compensatory behavior). With BED, binges can be difficult to distinguish from normal overeating when a "grazing" pattern is present in which an individual snacks over a more extended period of time—such as all afternoon or evening—yet the overall amount consumed is objectively large and the person feels loss of control. The caloric value reported by Bartholome, Raymong, Lee, Peterson, and Warren (2006) for an objective binge episode averaged 1900 calories (about 8 cups in volume), and for a subjective binge episode about 700 calories (about 4 cups). Binge eating is most typically a long-term, chronic concern but the frequency is very reactive to situational factors and stressors. Thus, the frequency of binge eating within a given person often varies considerably over time. For these reasons, the frequency criteria for BED are slightly different from BN; binge eating must occur on average at least two *days* a week (rather than two episodes) for six (instead of three) months. The eating patterns of individuals with BED who are not objectively overweight more closely resemble the nonpurging subtype of BN—in that their eating is generally fairly restrictive but their compensatory behaviors (e.g., dieting and exercise) are not clearly inappropriate. These individuals may be characterized as chronic, excessively concerned/distressed dieters.

Medical Problems Associated with BED

Immediate medical problems associated with the binge eating specifically are relatively uncommon except for reports of gastrointestinal (GI) distress. More commonly, the medical concerns relate to the comorbid obesity. The incidence of diagnosable BED increases with an increase of weight over normal. Thus, individuals with BED are at risk for the development of obesity and its complications even if they are not currently overweight. The co-occurrence of BED with obesity raises significant treatment issues. For obese binge eaters, it is their weight that is most distressing and they are primarily motivated to seek treatment for weight loss. Many overweight individuals do not endorse loss of control so they are not diagnosable with BED, even though they may have significant health issues exacerbated by their weight status and they may eat large amounts and fail to lose weight. There are some characteristics that differentiate the nonbinge eating obese from obese binge eaters, but this distinction seems to be less useful the more overweight the individual. Some obese individuals do not endorse loss of control while eating but acknowledge that overall they have lost control over their eating or indicate they have given up trying to control their eating. These individuals have been described as "burnt out" dieters, and they are similar to those meeting criteria for BED (who endorse loss of control during eating).

As long as the amount of food eaten is clearly large (whether this is feeling very full or grazing to excess) and the person is obese, the degree to which loss of control is reported appears to be less important—at least in terms of the treatment that is needed. In an attempt to distinguish BED from more normative types of overeating, current *DSM* criteria require that the binge eating in BED not only be characterized as out of control but it must also be associated with three (or more) of the following: (a) eating more rapidly than normal, (b) eating until uncomfortably full, (c) eating large amounts when not physically hungry, (d) eating alone due to embarrassment about amounts eaten, and (e) feeling disgusted, depressed, or very guilty after overeating. An individual's experience of an OBE varies widely. Although many binges in BN are triggered by restriction—that is, waiting until quite hungry to eat—this is less common in BED. In BED, binges are more often experienced as psychologically motivated—the person may recognize that they are not hungry and that they are eating for emotional reasons. Binges may have an obvious trigger—such as a breakup or work stress—but they are often triggered by less intense feelings such as feeling generally deprived, feeling bored or lonely, or feeling unsatisfied with life. Many people downplay the significance of (or even deny) these less intense feelings and report little insight about why they binge.

In some cases binges are clearly a non-normative experience in which an individual dissociates, may eat unusual types or combinations of food, may steal or otherwise take food inappropriately, and may report no enjoyment associated with the eating. One example, identified early on by Stunkard (1959), is night eating where individuals wake from sleep but report an almost trancelike state and extreme difficulty preventing or limiting eating when food is available—yet they rarely leave the house to seek more food. They often have difficulty recalling the episode in the morning. More research is needed to understand these episodes and to determine if they require different intervention than the more normative variations of binge eating.

Eating Disorder Not Otherwise Specified (EDNOS)

In addition to BED, the EDNOS category includes any pattern of disordered eating that is distressing and impairing but does not meet full criteria for AN or BN. Some of the examples given in *DSM-IV* describe what are typically labeled subclinical cases of AN or BN. However, these presentations do not differ significantly on many indices of distress and impairment so the utility of designating certain levels as subclinical has been challenged. In particular, current work (Binford & Le Grange, 2005) describing BN-like patterns among adolescents points out the importance of establishing criteria that are more appropriate for clinical presentations at that age. Intervention early in the course of eating disorders is generally more successful so it is helpful to note developmental stage when making diagnoses. The onset of subclinical BN in a 15-year-old needs to be treated urgently and will likely benefit from a different approach than a pattern of chronic, subclinical BN in a 25-year-old which reflects partial recovery from an earlier period of full BN symptoms.

Diagnostic Controversies

Wonderlich, Joiner, Keel, Williamson, and Crosby (2007) reviewed the evidence supporting the current (*DSM*) classification scheme and concluded that while there is substantial evidence supporting the utility of broad distinctions between AN and BN, there is little evidence to support the specific criteria that are currently in use. Furthermore, the overall scheme is limited because the EDNOS category is so broad. These authors describe current sophisticated statistical approaches that are paving the way for the development of a more empirically based classification scheme. Latent class analysis, a multivariate method that identifies subtypes of related cases, has been used to help identify different patterns as well as to determine the optimal number of categories that should be considered distinct. Their summary suggests there are at least six patterns that will be useful to study. The data support the utility of making a distinction between the two subtypes of AN and support consideration of BED as a distinct pattern, but the data provide no support for the current distinction between the subtypes of BN. Two other distinct patterns emerged: purging disorder (purging after normal to small amounts of food) and subjective binge-eating disorder (loss of control or distress associated with eating normal to small amounts of food).

Taxometric analysis is the other tool that was used to determine if a pattern represented a single underlying condition or if it represented more distinct entities. The studies cited in their review suggest that the behavior of binge eating (large amounts) appeared to be qualitatively distinct from normal (nonbinge) eating, regardless of actual weight status. Evidence also suggested that binge-purge behavior represented a qualitatively different class of behaviors than binge eating by itself. These results suggest it may be more appropriate to group the AN binge-purge subtype with the BN purging subtype, and group BN nonpurging subtype with BED. On the other hand, the evidence suggested that restriction (eating very little) was not qualitatively different from normal eating and simply represented the extreme end of a continuum that included normal eating. These new approaches to classification are significantly altering current conceptualizations about eating disorders, so we expect significant changes in the next revision of the *DSM*. Two alternative models for classification have already been proposed.

Three Dimensional Model. Williamson, Gleaves, and Stewart (2005) described a three-dimensional model in which binge eating is considered a categorical dimension (high versus low) while fear of fatness/compensatory behaviors and extreme drive for thinness are viewed as continuous variables. Wonderlich and his colleagues discuss two implications of this model that are particularly interesting. First, if binge eating is best viewed as a taxon—that is a separate dimension—it may be that a specific genetic vulnerability, perhaps a phenotype related to low impulse control, could be identified. Such a vulnerability could be unique to eating, but it might also show up as problematic in areas other than eating behavior. If impulsivity is implicated, psychological and pharmacological interventions might be targeted more specifically to address that mechanism. Second, if restricting behavior is best viewed as on a continuum with normal eating, problems with restriction may be better conceptualized as similar to personality disorders (since those are also thought to be extreme ends of a normal continuum of psychological traits). If that view is correct, one would expect longer term treatment might be required, and one would predict that restrictive behavior would be less likely to respond to pharmacological intervention. Within this viewpoint, the binge-purge subtype of AN might represent an individual with both difficulties—which could explain why this pattern seems different from BN and why it is generally less responsive to current treatments than BN. While much remains to be done, it seems likely that identifying and studying this wider range of very specific, behaviorally anchored patterns of disordered eating will promote a better understanding of the etiology and psychopathology of disordered eating. Weight status may well have treatment implications, but may have limited utility as a criterion for classification.

Transdiagnostic Model. Taking a different approach, Fairburn and colleagues (Fairburn & Bohn, 2005; Fairburn, Cooper, & Shafran, 2003) have proposed reducing current diagnostic categories to a single diagnosis, a solution that seems useful in terms of simplifying clinical diagnosis and treatment recommendations. This transdiagnostic approach is based on the argument that a similar core psychopathology—the over-evaluation of eating, shape, and weight (or their control)—characterizes the entire range of disordered eating patterns. This explains the significant overlap in symptoms, the fact that many patients migrate across diagnostic categories over time and the fact that a chronic course of residual symptoms is a common outcome. Consistent with this view, Eddy et al. (2002) suggests that the pure restricting type of AN might be better viewed as a phase that typically would occur early in the course of the disorder. Effective treatment might be able to prevent its progression, but if this theory is correct patients who did not respond to intervention would be likely to progress to some type of bingeing or compensating as they fail to be able to maintain their excessive restriction over long periods of time. Consistent with this view, the average age of onset of AN is clearly younger than for BN. On the other hand, there is a subset of patients with AN who are able to maintain chronic restriction and low weight without progressing to binge eating who do not appear to fit that model. Further research is needed to determine what allows certain individuals to maintain chronic restriction long term while most cannot. If poor treatment responders could be identified early on in the course of the disorder, more targeted or more intense interventions might be developed to prevent the restriction pattern from becoming so well entrenched, and/or prevent progression to bingeing/purging.

Within the transdiagnostic view, overconcern is viewed as the core pathology that drives the restriction/dieting which leads to, and perpetuates disordered eating patterns. This pattern is quite evident in BN as overconcern drives the dieting that often triggers binge eating, as well as the compensatory behaviors when the threat of weight gain cannot be tolerated. Overconcern also provides the best explanation for the patterns labeled purging disorder and subjective binge eating disorder. When normal to small amounts of food are experienced as loss of control or as requiring purging, overconcern with weight and shape would appear to be the driving force. This conceptualization is less obviously applicable to BED—as many individuals report the onset of binge eating before the onset of either weight concerns or dieting (Mussell et al., 1995). However, it is not clear that early "overeating/binge eating" would escalate to the point of diagnosable BED if it did not occur within the context of overconcern about weight and shape. Thus, overconcern may be the important factor differentiating those who simply overeat and/or become overweight from those who develop BED. The transdiagnostic approach provides a useful way to conceptualize the varied presentations of disordered eating, provides a unifying framework for treatment, and identifies overconcern as the most important target both for prevention efforts and for relapse prevention once unhealthy eating behaviors are eliminated.

History

Cultural norms have long supported a variety of forms of overeating (even to the point of discomfort) as part of celebrations of the harvest or other social events. The degree to which overeating has always been considered normative complicates the identification of binge eating. Today, the term binge is used quite loosely by the general public, and a person may or may not mean the large amount or the feeling of loss of control that characterizes *DSM*-defined objective binge episodes.

Stunkard (1993) described the early history and development of the term binge eating and the fairly early recognition of purging behaviors that sometimes accompanied this phenomenon. He noted that Liddell & Scott (1972) refer to several early Greek authors, and later Galen, who used the term *boulimos*—meaning a great deal of (or ravenous) hunger, which was viewed as different from normal hunger. This term came to refer both to hunger and to the overeating that extreme hunger triggers. As early as James (1743), a variety of case accounts of atypical preoccupation with food and overeating were described. James described a variant "caninus appetite" that involved overeating followed by vomiting.

As first used, the term bulimia referred primarily to excessive and unusual overeating and this aspect was seen as more central than the vomiting that sometimes occurred afterwards. Stunkard, Grace, and Wolff (1955) may be best credited with drawing researchers' attention to the phenomenon of binge eating. They described a night-eating syndrome, which they conceptualized as primarily a deficit within the satiety regulation system. These patients did not report high levels of hunger during the day but ate a lot at night (often waking up to eat). They had extreme difficulty stopping eating as long as food was available but did not seem highly motivated to seek out food. In contrast, Stunkard (1959) described a binge eating syndrome which was conceptualized primarily as a problem within the hunger regulation system. In the latter case, patients would report high levels of hunger, would seek out food, and would typically not stop eating until physically uncomfortable. Vomiting was sometimes induced but often that was more to relieve abdominal pain than specifically to prevent weight gain. Patients reported guilt, remorse, and self-contempt related more to their failure to control their own behavior. This work broadened thinking about overeating; overeating might be due to decreased sensations of satiety (failure to stop eating) instead of (or in addition to) being due primarily to increased hunger (drive to eat).

Boskind-Lodahl and White (1973) modified this more biological view of binge eating when they published a feminist formulation of "bulimarexia," describing a binge-purge syndrome among normal weight women. It was conceptualized as a culture-bound syndrome resulting from modern Western culture's obsession with female thinness—which was also thought to be part of a larger picture of restricted options for women. A few years later, Russell (1979) described similar cases, which he labeled as "bulimia nervosa" and viewed as a variant of AN that was particularly difficult to treat.

As a result of this attention to difficulties related to binge eating, bulimia was added to the 3rd edition of the *Diagnostic and Statistical Manual of Mental Disorders (DSM-III)* as a disorder distinct from AN. It was not until *DSM-III-R* (APA, 1987) that the term bulimia nervosa was introduced. At that point the criteria required some type of inappropriate compensatory behavior, thereby relegating large numbers of individuals with binge eating to the EDNOS category. To address this difficulty, BN was retained as a specific diagnosis in *DSM-IV* but Binge Eating Disorder (BED) was added as a provisional diagnosis. The incidence of bulimia significantly increased in the years following its identification, reaching a peak in 1996 (Currin, Schmidt, Treasure, & Jick, 2005; Keel & Klump, 2003). Interestingly, in one sample of college students the rate of BN decreased from 1982 to 2002. In this sample the prevalence of binge eating decreased over time, but the prevalence of purging remained consistent (Keel, Heatherton, Dorer, Joiner, & Zalta, 2006).

As discussed earlier, empirical support has been found for at least six patterns of disordered eating. Stunkard (1993) suggests that binge eating (i.e., BED) is the pattern that has the clearest historical roots, being observed even in early cultures. This observation is consistent with the current notion that vulnerability to binge eating might reflect a distinct taxon, probably with some genetic basis. Binge eating without compensation is still the most common presentation of disordered eating and furthermore there is less evidence of sex differences than in other presentations. Empirical studies have failed to support the differentiation of nonpurging BN from BED, also suggesting that regular eating of large amounts is likely a distinct syndrome. The degree to which a person adopts compensatory behaviors may be a separate issue, possibly more culturally determined.

The second oldest pattern (which has always had a very low base rate), Stunkard called "uninterrupted dieting," which refers to the restricting type of AN. It is notable that the binge-purge subtype of AN appears to have emerged somewhat later in history and that recent analyses suggest it might be better grouped with BN. Patterns of regular compensation as a method of weight control—especially the currently most typical ones (vomiting and laxatives)—were not reported that often before 1960. Thus, binge-purge patterns may well constitute more culturally bound syndromes, reflecting the degree of subjectively experienced pressure to be thin. It will be instructive to see what is discovered about the two new patterns that have emerged in recent research. Will subjective binge eating disorder turn out to be a less severe (or early) form of restricting AN? What keeps some women from escalating their pursuit to more unhealthy weights? Will purging disorder turn out to be a particularly serious form of restriction since such an individual is motivated to compensate yet does not seem to be vulnerable to binge eating?

EPIDEMIOLOGY

Prevalence

Prevalence estimates for BN range from 1 to 3% of the population (APA, 2000; Hoek, 2006). The prevalence of partial syndrome BN (5.4%) is substantially higher than full criteria manifestations (Whitehouse, Cooper, Vize, Hill, & Vogel, 1992). Women in late adolescence or early adulthood (ages 18–24) appear to be at the highest risk for onset of BN (Currin et al., 2005; Fairburn & Harrison, 2003; Hoek & van Hoeken, 2003). Prevalence rates for BED are higher (15 to 30%) than for BN.

The vast majority (90%) of those affected by bulimia nervosa are women (APA, 2000), and the majority of patients presenting for treatment with BED are women as well. However, in community samples the rates of BED are similar for males and females, which provides some support for the hypothesis that binge eating (large amounts) may be associated with certain biological vulnerabilities while patterns involving compensatory behaviors may be more culture bound.

Although eating disorders were initially thought to be more prevalent among white females from higher income families, a recent review found that binge eating and purging were equally common among white (Caucasian) females compared to minority females. However, dieting behaviors were reported to be more common in the white sample (Crago & Shisslak, 2003). This report reflects a growing body of literature suggesting that disordered eating and diagnosable eating disorders has increased in recent years among non-white races and ethnicities and among young women in all social classes and within all religions (Walcott, Pratt, & Patel, 2003). Evidence does suggest that living in (or moving to) a Western culture puts one at increased risk for the development of BN (Fairburn & Harrison, 2003; Keel & Klump, 2003).

Course

Typical age of onset for BN is late adolescence or early adulthood (APA, 2000). Studies suggest that a minority of individuals with BN—only about 6%—receive mental health treatment (Fairburn, Welch, Norman, O'Connor, & Doll, 1996; Hoek, 2006), and when treatment is sought the average length of history at presentation is about 5 years (Mitchell, Hatsukami, Eckert, & Pyle, 1985). It is not uncommon for individuals with BN to have had an earlier episode of AN: in community samples, 10 to 14% of those with BN had an earlier episode of AN (Favaro et al., 2003; Kendler, MacLean, Neale, & Kessler, 1991), whereas in clinical samples, the percentage of those with past AN increases to 25 to 37% (Braun, Sunday, & Halmi, 1994; Sullivan, Bulik, & Kendler, 1998). Herzog et al. (1999) found that over a 7 year period, 16% of women with restricting AN developed BN but only 7% of women with BN developed AN—providing some support for the argument that restricting AN may be an early phase that evolves to include binge eating or compensating.

While the age of onset of objective binge eating varies widely and is often quite young ("I can't even remember when I didn't binge"), the age at which an individual would meet full criteria for BED and/or would present for treatment is somewhat later than other EDs, commonly over 25. Once established, BN and BED both tend to run a chronic course—even though this may comprise a number of discrete episodes, often initiated by life transitions or stressors (APA, 2000; Fairburn, Cooper, Doll, Norman, & O'Connor, 2000; Fairburn, Stice, Cooper, Doll, Norman, & O'Connor, 2003; Quadflieg & Fichter, 2003). The chronic course of BN and high relapse rates are consistent across both clinical and community samples. In a five-year prospective study, Fairburn et al. (2000), 15% of the sample originally diagnosed with BN still met criteria at the last assessment, 32% had residual symptoms (EDNOS), and 7% met criteria for BED. Of those originally diagnosed with BED, 9% still met criteria, 12% had residual symptoms (EDNOS), and 3% met criteria for BN.

Even among those who fully recover from BN, relapse rates are high: approximately one-third relapse during follow-up periods (Herzog et al., 1999; Keel & Mitchell, 1997). There is also great flux in clinical status over time. Herzog et al. (1999) found that each year during the 5-year follow-up period, one-third remitted and an additional one-third relapsed.

Comorbidity

BN and BED both overlap with several other forms of psychopathology, including mood, anxiety, substance use, and personality disorders (O'Brien & Vincent, 2003). Mood disorders, especially major depression and dysthymia, are common with estimates ranging from 36% to 50% (O'Brien & Vincent, 2003; Williamson, Zucker, Martin, & Smeets, 2001). A recent review suggests that lifetime prevalence of anxiety disorders among those with bulimia ranges from 41% to 75% (Godart, Flament, Perdereau, & Jeammet, 2002). Posttraumatic stress disorder was the only anxiety disorder that occurred significantly (three times) more often in BN than AN (Kaye et al., 2005). There is also a strong relationship—in the range of 30% overlap—between substance abuse and binge or purge behaviors, regardless of whether the behaviors occur within the context of AN or BN (O'Brien & Vincent, 2003) or in the context of BED (Eldredge & Agras, 1996).

In terms of Axis II disorders, borderline personality disorder is diagnosed most frequently with BN, with a prevalence rate ranging from 20–28%. However, there is overlap in the criteria as eating disturbance is considered evidence of impulsivity in diagnosing the latter. Avoidant, Dependent, Histrionic, and Paranoid Personality Disorders are also fairly common—with prevalence rates ranging from 9 to 20% each (Cassin & von Ranson, 2005; Sansone, Levitt, & Sansone, 2005). Sansone et al. (2005) reported that one-third of the cases of BED had comorbid Axis II disorders; however, Obsessive-Compulsive Personality Disorder was the most common type.

Biological Aspects of Bulimia Nervosa and Binge Eating Disorder

In their recent review of risk factors for eating disorders, Striegel-Moore and Bulik (2007) summarized current work on genetic factors. First, they noted that virtually all studies had been done with European populations so conclusions were correspondingly limited. Nonetheless, there is substantial evidence suggesting high heritability estimates (in the range of 50% to 80%) in twin studies in which BN has been defined in a variety of ways. Heritability effects were strong for the specific symptoms of self-induced vomiting and binge eating, but shared and unique environmental effects better accounted for the cognitive symptom of overconcern with weight and shape. Work by Keski-Rahkonen et al. (2005) showed sex differences in heritability patterns for the symptoms of drive for thinness and body-dissatisfaction. Only one study specifically investigated a syndrome approximating BED (i.e., binge eating without purging) but this study reported a fairly similar heritability estimate (41%) as found for BN. Thus a definite level of familial transmission for both these disorders has been established, but little is known about the specific genes or the mechanisms through which they could influence relevant eating behaviors. Keel, Klump, Miller, McGue, and Iacono (2005) demonstrated shared transmission between EDs and anxiety disorders, but again the basis for this similarity is not known.

In short, little is conclusive at this point in time, but simple answers—that is, main effects for genes—seem unlikely. Genetic variation may largely account for certain core symptoms (possibly binge eating or the ability to maintain low weight without binge eating). When the environment shifts (as in the emergence of the ultra thin ideal or the increased availability of high fat foods) these genetic vulnerabilities are differentially elicited, which can make the shift appear to be culturally mediated. Thus, gene by environment interaction models are most likely to be useful explanations. Current thinking also proposes that it will be more useful to investigate specific endo- and subphenotypes that have narrow effects on certain core behaviors (e.g., impulsivity) rather than attempting to identify genetic influences for specific diagnoses.

Several specific physiological mechanisms that are believed to be involved in the regulation of eating are currently being explored. It is not clear if differences in the processes of digesting food encourage overeating because it is more difficult for certain individuals to sense satiety or if regular eating of large amounts alters digestive processes. Geliebter and Hashim (2001) found that gastric capacity was specifically related to binge eating. Women with BN and binge-eating obese women had similar, increased capacity compared to either normal weight or nonbinge eating obese women. Larger stomach capacity is hypothesized to contribute to lower satiety both directly and by delaying release of CCK in the duodenum. Evidence suggests that women with BN have blunted postprandial release of CCK (Pirke, Kellner, Friess, Drieg, & Fichter, 1994), and that women with BED have similar disturbances in satiety (Sysko, Devlin, Walsh, Zimmerli, & Kesseleff, 2007). As suggested by the significant overlap between mood disorders and eating disorders, neurotransmitters are also likely to be involved. Recent work utilizing brain imaging (Kaye et al., 2005) identified disturbances in individuals with BN and AN in specific brain areas that persisted after recovery. Dysregulation in serotonin pathways in the brain is hypothesized to influence the hedonic aspects of feeding behavior as well as its well documented effects on mood and impulse control.

Psychosocial Aspects of BN and BED

PERSONALITY TRAITS

Several personality traits have been associated with eating disorders. Some of these seem to be predisposing factors whereas others are thought to be more secondary to the eating disturbance. Methodologically speaking, research in this area varies in terms of the samples that are selected, with some studies collapsing across ED diagnostic groups, some examining one or more distinct ED groups, and others creating groups based on behavioral patterns (e.g., purging vs. nonpurging behaviors). Each type of study provides unique information and, taken together, results across multiple samples leads to a more comprehensive picture of the relation of personality traits to eating pathology. The following sections describe several personality traits with consistent and robust empirical support: impulsivity, compulsivity/obsessionality, perfectionism, sensation seeking, harm avoidance, and self-directedness.

Impulsivity

High impulsivity is commonly reported by individuals with BN, and levels of impulsivity are higher in this group as compared to individual with AN or psychiatric controls (Cassin & von Ranson, 2005; Engel et al., 2005). Evidence suggests that impulsive behavior is related to purging—be it in the context of AN or BN—and is associated with higher levels of psychological and eating disordered symptomatology (Favaro et al., 2005). Importantly, evidence suggests that degree of impulsivity abates with recovery, suggesting that the high levels of impulsivity during an episode of BN might be due, in part, to the uncontrolled eating behaviors and associated emotional instability (Cassin & von Ranson, 2005).

Compulsivity and Obsessionality

Obsessive/compulsive features tend to be common in women with eating disorders, both in university and clinical samples (Cassin & von Ranson, 2005). These traits tend to persevere even after recovery from the eating disorder (Cassin & von Ranson, 2005; Lilenfeld, Wonderlich, Riso, Crosby, & Mitchell, 2006), suggesting that they are not simply a concomitant of the eating pathology. A recent study (Engel et al., 2005) examined the prevalence and effects of both impulsivity and compulsivity in women with BN. Women with high levels of both impulsivity and compulsivity exhibited the highest levels of impairment and psychopathology (in terms of comorbid personality disorders, substance use, eating pathology, and depression), while those women with low levels of both impulsivity and compulsivity demonstrated the lowest levels of functional impairment and comorbid psychopathology. Women who scored high on measures of impulsivity and low on measures of compulsivity had the highest levels of drug and alcohol related problems, while the reverse pattern (low impulsivity and high compulsivity) was associated with higher levels of eating disordered and depressive symptoms.

Perfectionism

Important facets of perfectionism include high expectations of one's own performance, self-criticism, belief that others critically evaluate one, fear of failure, and excessive concern over mistakes (Cassin & von Ranson, 2005; Fairburn et al., 2003; Franco-Paredes, Mancilla-Diaz, Vazquez-Arevalo, Lopez-Aguilar, & Alvarez-Rayon, 2005). Perfectionism has been noted as a risk factor for bulimic pathology and a maintenance factor for more general eating pathology (Stice, 2002). Based on a multidimensional assessment of perfectionism, individuals with BN have elevated levels of perfectionism in both the acute and recovery phases of the disorder (Cassin & von Ranson, 2005; Franco-Paredes et al., 2005). Recent studies suggest that perfectionism combines with low self-efficacy and perceived overweight to predict subsequent onset of eating disordered symptoms (Bardone-Cone, Abramson, Vohs, Heatherton, & Joiner, 2006; Lilenfeld et al., 2006). Interestingly, associations with perfectionism were strongest for fasting and purging and the relationship between perfectionism and binge eating was mediated by fasting (Forbush, Heatherton, & Keel, 2007). As a testament to its important role in eating pathology, perfectionism is one of four key maintaining factors described in the transdiagnostic cognitive-behavioral model of eating disorders (Fairburn, Cooper, et al., 2003).

Other Traits

Three additional personality characteristics have shown some promise and warrant further investigation: sensation or novelty seeking, harm avoidance, and self-directedness. Individuals with binge-purge variants of eating disorders report higher levels of sensation seeking or novelty seeking when compared to either individuals with restricting eating disorder (Cassin & von Ranson, 2005; Favaro et al., 2005; Vervaet, van Heeringen, & Audenaert, 2004) or controls (Cassin & von Ranson, 2005). Individuals with BN also report high levels of harm avoidance (Berg, Crosby, Wonderlich, & Hawley, 2000; Cassin & von Ranson, 2005), and when compared to the restrictive subtype, individuals who binge and purge tend to score low in self-directedness (Cassin & von Ranson, 2005; Vervaet et al., 2004).

EMOTION DISREGULATION

Women with eating disorders typically report intense mood states and increased mood lability. Several studies have examined the association between negative affect and eating disorder symptoms, as well as the interaction between negative affect and other known risk factors for eating pathology. There is strong support for a relationship between negative affect and bulimic symptoms, such that increased levels of neuroticism or negative affect prospectively predict onset of eating pathology (Leon, Fulkerson, Perry, Keel, & Klump, 1999; Lilenfeld et al., 2006; Stice, Akutagawa, Gaggar, & Agras, 2000). In addition to increasing the risk of eating disorders, negative affect maintains binge eating in individuals who struggle with disordered eating (Stice et al., 2000) and the elevated levels of negative affect seem to persist even after recovery from the eating disorder (Lilenfeld et al., 2006). Negative affect is also related to other eating disorder risk factors, suggesting that negative affect might impact eating pathology through multiple pathways. Research suggests that negative affect mediates the relationship between body dissatisfaction and bulimic symptoms (Sim & Zeman, 2005; Stice, Nemeroff, & Shaw, 1996) and that it moderates the relationship between dieting and binge eating (Stice et al., 2000). In addition, increases in negative affect lead to increased body dissatisfaction (Stice, 2002).

Binge eating and purging behaviors (as well as other ED behaviors) have been conceptualized as strategies to regulate emotions. Women with eating disorders have a hard time identifying their feelings, are unsure about how to cope with emotions, and have difficulty tolerating adverse mood states (Fairburn, Cooper, & Shafran, 2003; Sim & Zeman, 2005). To manage these difficulties in emotion regulation they turn to bingeing and/or purging as a way to distract from or modulate negative feelings. Conversely, negative affect has also been found to exacerbate ED symptoms (Polivy & Herman, 2002), often leading to a downward spiral of increased negative affect and increased eating pathology. From a behavioral perspective, the binge-purge episodes become highly reinforcing. In the moment, binge eating decreases negative affect, which serves to negatively reinforce the behavior (Deaver et al., 2003). However, this momentary relief is soon followed by feelings of guilt, shame, and anxiety about having binged (Corstorphine, Waller, Ohanian, & Baker, 2006). The original negative emotions are then replaced by negative feelings centered on eating behavior and body shape and weight concerns, presumably an area with more perceived control. In the context of BN, compensatory behaviors arise to reduce the negative feelings about having binged. In this manner, compensatory behaviors are negatively reinforced since they help to mitigate unpleasant emotions and decrease sensations of fullness, which often feel distressing (Corstorphine et al., 2006; Williamson, White, York-Crowe, & Stewart, 2004). The purging behavior is also positively reinforced since it increases levels of happiness and relief (Corstorphine et al., 2006). The entire binge-purge episode is reinforced because it serves to control emotions that otherwise feel overwhelming.

COGNITIVE DYSFUNCTION

Cognitive manifestations of BN can be organized into four main areas: (a) appearance overvaluation, (b) internalization of the thin ideal, (c) cognitive biases, and (d) rigid and obsessive thinking patterns. As mentioned previously, appearance overvaluation is one of the diagnostic criteria for BN, occurring when an individual's self-worth is disproportionately affected by physical attributes such as body shape and weight (Williamson et al., 2004; Fairburn, Cooper, et al., 2003; Polivy & Herman, 2002). Focus becomes narrowed on eating and control over eating as a means to achieve the desired physical outcome. Appearance overvaluation prospectively predicts later onset of eating disordered symptoms (Lilenfeld et al., 2006; Stice, Presnell, & Spangler, 2002), and overvaluation of eating, weight, and shape has been implicated as the central maintaining feature in eating pathology (Fairburn, Cooper, et al., 2003).

Current Western culture endorses an ultra-thin ideal for women's body shape and size. Thin-ideal internalization is the degree to which an individual adopts and subscribes to this cultural standard. Internalization of the thin ideal is hypothesized to increase body dissatisfaction, since women who highly value a thin ideal are more likely to be dissatisfied with their weight and shape and are more likely to engage in behaviors to help them achieve the thin ideal. Research confirms that a high level of thin ideal internalization is a risk factor for body dissatisfaction, dieting, and negative affect (Stice, 2002). Internalization of the thin ideal also prospectively predicts later onset of binge eating and bulimic pathology, as well as maintaining bulimic pathology (Stice, 2002).

Women with eating disorders exhibit cognitive biases when processing information related to food and to weight and shape, and evidence suggests that these biases affect both attention and memory processes. Women with eating disorders tend to pay increased attention to stimuli that are eating, shape, or weight related. In addition, such individuals are better able to encode and recall eating, weight, and shape related information in comparison to other categories of information. Another manifestation of cognitive bias is overestimation of body shape and size, which leads to increased body dissatisfaction and increased desire to lose weight (Polivy & Herman, 2002; Williamson et al., 2004). These biased ways of thinking are thought to increase negative affect; conversely, increases in negative affect are thought to increase the biases in information processing (Williamson, White, York-Crowe, & Stewart, 2005). Importantly, some evidence suggests that the biased thinking might be more a result of—rather than a cause of—the eating disorder (Polivy & Herman, 2007).

Women with BN demonstrate a thinking pattern that tends to be characterized by obsessive thought patterns and rigid, dichotomous thinking. The obsessive thought patterns manifest as high levels of preoccupation with eating, weight, and shape (Cooper, 2005; Polivy & Herman, 2002). Rigid and dichotomous thinking leads to categorization of food as good or bad, as well as leading to very inflexible expectations for eating behaviors (and often for life in general). Dichotomous thinking is hypothesized to give rise to the Abstinence Violation Effect. Individuals have rigid dietary rules and when they break one of these rules even to a small extent, they feel like they have blown it completely so there is no reason to try further. Thus, small slips become full binges.

Cooper, Todd, and Wells (2004) described four categories of automatic thoughts that result in and maintain bulimic pathology: (a) thoughts of no control (e.g., I will never be able to stop eating if I have that piece of candy), (b) permissive thoughts (e.g., buying a whole bag of bagels really is not that big a deal; it won't hurt), (c) positive thoughts (e.g., eating the pizza will make me feel much better), and (d) negative thoughts (e.g., I am going to gain a ton of weight). The positive thoughts are hypothesized to promote binge eating, while the negative thoughts encourage compensatory behaviors.

OTHER PSYCHOSOCIAL VARIABLES SPECIFIC TO EATING DISORDERS

Body Dissatisfaction

Body dissatisfaction is a consistent and robust risk factor for eating pathology, as well as a maintenance factor (Lilenfeld et al., 2006; Stice, 2002; Young, Clopton, & Bleckley, 2004). In addition to its direct impact on eating pathology, body dissatisfaction leads to dieting and negative affect, which in turn further impact eating disorder symptoms (Stice, 2002; Stice & Shaw, 2002). It is also hypothesized that other causal factors impact eating pathology through body dissatisfaction (Polivy & Herman, 2002). For example, increased sociocultural pressure to be thin and elevated thin ideal internalization lead to increases in body dissatisfaction (Stice, 2002) which directly increases eating pathology.

Dieting

Elevated dieting and dietary restraint prospectively predict binge eating onset, level of bulimic pathology, and negative affect (Jacobi, Hayward, de Zwann, Kraemer, & Agras, 2004; Stice, 2002; Stice et al., 2002). In addition, self-reported dieting is a maintenance factor for bulimic pathology (Stice, 2002), where binge eating arises in response to rigid, stringent efforts at dietary control (Fairburn, Cooper, et al., 2003). In fact, many individuals with BN cycle between restrictive eating and binge-purge behaviors. Evidence suggests that dieting may result, in part, from body dissatisfaction (Polivy & Herman, 2002; Stice, 2002), where it serves as an attempt to fix the weight and body problem. More recent studies demonstrate that successful caloric deprivation (dieting) does not lead to increased eating disorder symptoms (Stice, 2002), suggesting that unsuccessful dieting or struggles with dieting may be more problematic than actual dieting, per se. However, excessively restrictive dieting increases the likelihood of struggle and can trigger binge eating, so extreme dieting is problematic in its own right. However, the level of restriction that is experienced as problematic (difficult) appears to vary widely among individuals making it hard to identify a particular point at which dieting becomes more harmful than helpful.

Interoceptive Awareness

Interoceptive awareness refers to the ability to identify internal sensations, with regard to both physiological and emotional states. Women with eating disorders report poor interoceptive awareness (Jacobi, Hayward, de Zwann, Kraemer, & Agras, 2004), and this inability to identify internal sensations prospectively predicts onset of eating disorder symptoms (Killen et al., 1996; Leon, Fulkerson, Perry, & Early-Zald, 1995). Some research suggests that even after recovery these women continue to struggle in identifying their internal states (Lilenfeld et al., 2006). However, specific intervention to train appetite awareness has been shown to improve awareness of internal hunger and satiety cues.

Body Mass

Individuals with higher premorbid body mass were found to be at increased risk for perceived pressure to be thin, body dissatisfaction, and dieting (Stice, 2002). However, higher initial body mass did not predict either negative affect or eating pathology (Stice, 2002). Hence, it seems that body mass influences other risk factors to eating pathology, rather than directly being a risk factor itself.

Childhood Sexual Abuse/Stress

Physical and sexual abuse have been hypothesized to be significant risk factors for disordered eating. However, recent evidence suggests that childhood abuse is a risk factor for general psychopathology, as opposed to a risk factor specific to eating disorders (Hund & Espelage, 2005; Katerndahl, Burge, & Kellogg, 2005; Moyer, DiPietro, Merkowitz, & Stunkard, 1997; Schmidt, 2003). In a similar vein, Striegel-Moor et al. (2007) reported that elevated levels of perceived stress prior to the age of 14 constituted one pathway to binge eating (BN and BED), but this pathway only accounted for 13% of the cases, and no specific stressors were detected. Thus, the etiology of BN as well as BED likely involves multiple pathways, some of which include childhood abuse and other early stressors.

Environmental Factors

SOCIOCULTURAL PRESSURE TO BE THIN

With the obvious deluge of images of overly thin women in the mass media, one misperception is that eating disorders are largely due to misguided efforts (excessive dieting) to attain our culture's thin ideal. As just noted, it has been difficult to establish the degree to which dieting is a direct risk factor. Similarly, efforts to document a clear causal relationship between the level of media exposure and eating disorders have not shown consistent, strong effects. A more pervasive or indirect transmission of the thin ideal may be occurring because research does more clearly indicate that individuals who immigrate to a Western culture and those living in relatively more urban than rural areas are at increased risk for eating disorders (Becker, Keel, Anderson-Fry, & Thomas, 2004). Two points are worth noting here. First, individuals clearly differ in the extent to which they personally adopt the thin ideal. The degree of internalization of the thin ideal and the degree to which a person personally feels pressured by others to be thin appear to be more important than simply degree of media exposure (Stice, Presnell, & Spangler, 2002). Furthermore, while media exposure appears to increase risk of body dissatisfaction and subsequent dieting as well as binge eating, media exposure appears to play less of a role in maintaining already established eating disorder symptoms (Stice, 2002).

FAMILY

The family may serve as one of the important ways that the thin-ideal is transmitted and internalized. The attitudes and behaviors of family members and peers (e.g., feeding patterns, critical comments, weight-related teasing, modeling of restrictive eating or other disordered eating behaviors)—seem to be stronger influences than the less personal media exposure. It is also useful to note that parental obesity is a risk factor for eating disorders (Jacobi et al., 2004). While this could be a result of shared genetic vulnerability to obesity (or impulsivity), it may also reflect more subtle environmental influences. Individuals with overweight family members are more likely to have been exposed to negative societal attitudes towards obesity (stigma), and thus may impose excessive pressure on themselves. Similarly, parents who are overweight may exert excessive and unhelpful pressure on children to be thin as they hope to prevent them from developing weight problems. Beyond transmitting the pressure of the thin ideal, family environment may also play a role by failing to teach adaptive eating behavior or coping skills to build self-esteem (which would reduce risk for EDs). Families of individuals with BN have been described as as more chaotic, conflicted, and critical, and as low in positive expressiveness, cohesion, and caring. A negative family environment would increase anxiety and depression which would make individuals more vulnerable to emotional eating and therefore possible development of obesity or EDs.

Assessment

Currently, the most widely used assessment for disordered eating behaviors (across all diagnoses) is the semistructured interviewer-administered Eating Disorder Examination (EDE) (Fairburn & Cooper, 1993). It primarily assesses attitudes and behaviors over the past four weeks and takes about an hour to administer. Such an assessment is important to use in the research context where highly reliable diagnoses are required, but it can be useful in a clinical context because the interview format allows for greater clarification of complex eating disorder concepts that use terms (e.g., binge eating and overconcern about weight) about which there is less agreement. Furthermore, the interview insures that many important constructs are assessed which might not be elicited in an unstructured format due to the secrecy and shame associated with many of the behaviors. However, the training required to achieve reliability and the burden for staff and patients is sufficiently high that briefer methods are more typically used in clinical work.

A 36 item self-report version (EDE-Q) (Fairburn & Beglin, 1994) provides the basis for a possible diagnosis as well as the same four subscales (continuous scores for restraint, eating concern, shape concern, and weight concern) as the EDE. However, a recent factor analysis suggested that a three-factor solution is more appropriate for the EDE-Q (Peterson et al., 2007). Correlations between the interview and self-report versions and between change on the two measures were reasonable (Sysko et al., 2007) even though within individuals discrepancies were common, particularly in terms of frequency of types of binge episodes. It is not clear if clients are more willing to disclose information in a self-report or if an interviewer is more likely to elicit accurate information. Regardless, more objective (interviewer) ratings and more subjective/self reports of constructs such as overconcern and distress each convey useful information.

A number of other self-reports are widely used. The more global, continuous measures provide indices of degree of improvement that can be useful to provide a broader picture than simple frequency counts of specific behaviors. Many of these measures contain multiple subscales that attempt to capture the wide rage of important constructs associated with disordered eating. The Eating Disorder Inventory (EDI-3) (Garner, 2005) and the Bulimia Test Revised (Thelen, Farmer, Wonderlich and Smith, 1991) are most commonly used in assessing outcome. In addition, very specific self-reports are available to assess narrower constructs that may be of interest—such as specific cognitions, body dissatisfaction, restraint, dietary intent, or food avoidance (see review by Anderson & Paulosky, 2004). Body checking is a specific construct that has only recently been identified as an important aspect of disordered eating that needs to be assessed. The Body Checking Questionnaire (Reas, Whisenhunt & Netemeyer, 2002) is a 23 item self-report of the frequency and nature of those behaviors.

Assessment of eating disorders in children and adolescents is not as well developed, but several inventories and interviews are available. The Children's Eating Attitudes Test (Ch-EAT) (Garner and Garfinkle, 1979) has been used and the use of a shorter, 26-item version was reported by Wallin, Kronovall and Majewski (2000). Shapiro et al.'s (2007) report on the Children's Binge Eating Disorder Scale, a brief structured interview, suggests that this type of assessment would be more appropriate if one's purpose was just to assess the degree to which overeating had become problematic for a child.

Treatment outcomes in BN and BED trials are reported in a number of ways. Sometimes successful outcome is defined as percent reduction of the core behaviors or as no longer meeting criteria for the disorder, which allows for some residual level of symptoms. Often, outcome is reported in terms of abstinence from the core symptoms, generally defined as no binges or purges in the past four weeks as assessed by the EDE. This time frame is needed to determine abstinence because eating behaviors tend to fluctuate over time and a week or two is not necessarily representative. If used to evaluate treatment outcome, the four-week time frame should be the four weeks after the end of treatment rather than the last four weeks of treatment. Abstinence may be a bit too strict a criteria, as many individuals improve dramatically but do not become abstinent. However, there is support for abstinence being an important outcome. Individuals who still have residual symptoms at the end of treatment generally fare more poorly during follow-up than those who become abstinent by the end of treatment.

Abstinence from purging is relatively easy to assess, but abstinence from binge eating can be more problematic and thus may not be as useful as an outcome measure. Elimination of clear OBEs is usually obvious, but the line between OBEs and SBEs typically becomes even more blurred after treatment as the size of OBEs is often greatly diminished. This issue is sometimes addressed in BN studies by simply reporting binges (i.e., combining OBEs and SBEs) but this can also be misleading as SBEs don't count as diagnostic criteria. Eliminating SBEs that lead to purging is clearly important in BN. However, abstinence from SBEs in the absence of purging may be too strict a criterion to be useful. Clients may not clearly endorse loss of control, especially after treatment. Some clients describe having "bingey" feelings—episodes that do not quite feel normal but do not involve really large amounts and not clear loss of control. Clinically, it is useful to have clients continue to monitor and report such feelings even though the obvious OBEs (and purges) may have been eliminated. Residual "urges to binge and/or urges to purge," are useful to monitor as they can indicate the need to continue with treatment until the urges become infrequent.

In addition to self-reports, daily self-monitoring records (of food, binges and purges) are frequently an important aspect of assessment as well as treatment. Self-monitoring avoids the difficulty of retrospective recall, and has greater validity in terms of specific behaviors. However, monitoring does not provide as useful an index of the more global attitudes of the person. Thus, both monitoring and self-reports continue to be important. Monitoring of appetite rather than food intake (Craighead, 2006) is a relatively recent development that can provide useful indices of clinically relevant variables. For example, episodes can be identified as hunger violations (waited until very hungry to start eating), satiety violations (continued to eat past moderate sensations of stomach fullness), or both. This kind of specific assessment of behavioral patterns may be particularly useful in treatment planning and evaluating response to treatment.

Treatment

INTERVENTIONS FOR BULIMIA NERVOSA

Psychosocial and pharmacological treatments are available that substantially reduce the core problem behaviors associated with BN and BED. However, only about half of the individuals treated for BN achieve (and maintain) full remission of their primary symptoms (binge eating and unhealthy compensatory behavior). Though much improved, many patients show a chronic course of residual symptoms—that is, restrictive eating patterns, preoccupation with eating and food, and impaired social functioning due to those issues. Negative body image tends to persist as most individuals fail to achieve a weight that is psychologically satisfactory to them or they remain dissatisfied with aspects of their shape. While a higher percentage of individuals with BED (70–80 %) achieve remission from their primary symptom (objectively large binge episodes), very few are able to lose substantial weight. Since most of these individuals are objectively overweight and have health as well as body image concerns, most are not totally satisfied with the outcome of treatment. Thus, more effective ways to address issues related to residual restrictive eating, weight goals, and negative body image remains a high priority.

A substantial number of reasonably powered clinical trials for BN have been reported (see review by Wilson, Grilo, & Vitousek, 2007). These have clearly established cognitive-behavior therapy (CBT) as the first line treatment, either alone or in combination with medications. Interpersonal psychotherapy (IPT) is a second established option. Initial outcome is not as positive, but individuals receiving IPT continue to show improvement over the course of follow-up so that by one year follow-up those individuals are not significantly different from those who received CBT.

Several antidepressants have demonstrated overall effectiveness equivalent to CBT, but an even smaller proportion of individuals (20%) achieve abstinence by the end of treatment and relapse following medication withdrawal is a significant problem (see Mitchell, Agras, & Wonderlich, 2007). Medication is generally equally effective whether or not the individual has diagnosable comorbid depression, therefore the mechanism through which it works remains unclear. Evidence suggests that medication enhances restraint while CBT clearly works through reducing restraint—which may account for some of the difficulties with relapse following medication withdrawal. Thus, medication alone is not currently recommended for BN, but medication combined with CBT is recommended when comorbid depression is present, and medication may be useful to add if an individual does not respond adequately to CBT alone.

Clinical trials have been almost exclusively done with young adult women, but what is known about treatment for males or older women suggests that the CBT treatment effect is quite robust and does not require significant modifications for other adult populations. Recent work by Lock (2005) and others (Schapman, Lock, & Couturier, 2006) demonstrates that CBT can be successfully adapted for adolescents. Similarly, Le Grange, Crosby, Rathouz, & Levanthal (2007) have reported positive results for their adaptation of family-based therapy for AN to address BN in adolescents.

In clinical trials, CBT has been provided as individual (or group) outpatient therapy, most typically 12 to 24 sessions. In clinical practice the format and time frame vary. Three elements form the core of CBT. First, clients engage in daily self-monitoring based on what they are eating and when, to encourage careful examination of their eating patterns. Second, clients are strongly encouraged to adopt a structured plan of three meals and two snacks a day to replace the chaotic and unhelpful restraint strategies they have developed in their struggle to restrict intake. Third, clients learn to utilize behavioral analysis and problem-solving to develop effective alternatives for bingeing and purging and to do cognitive challenging to address dysfunctional thought patterns and their underlying overconcern with weight and shape. For patients who respond to CBT, rapid change in symptoms over the first six to eight weeks is reported. Then, therapy may address more individualized concerns and plans to prevent relapse are put into place.

To address the problem of partial response, Fairburn and colleagues (Fairburn, Cooper, et al., 2003) developed (and are currently evaluating) an extended CBT model in which four specific mechanisms that may be impeding treatment are directly addressed: severe clinical perfectionism, unconditional and pervasive low self-esteem, and significant difficulties with either mood regulation or interpersonal relationships. This version of CBT stems from the transdiagnostic model and is being applied to all variants of eating disorders—including BED.

Several other modifications of CBT have been developed and are currently being evaluated. Preliminary data suggest these are viable alternatives, providing therapists with options that may be more acceptable or effective with some clients. Safer, Telch, and Agras (2001) reported on the use of dialectical behavior therapy (DBT)—which directly targets the emotion disregulation hypothesized to trigger many binge-purge episodes. Dicker and Craighead (2004) and Hill (2007) reported on the use of appetite awareness training (Craighead, 2006), an approach providing specific training to focus on internal cues—particularly stomach fullness. In this approach, food monitoring is replaced with self-monitoring of hunger and fullness to shift client attention away from their typical overfocus on food type. Individuals with a range of disordered eating patterns have rated appetite monitoring as significantly more helpful and acceptable than monitoring food.

To address issues of accessibility and affordability, several CBT-based versions of self-help have been developed and evaluated (Mitchell, Agras, & Wonderlich, 2007). Generally, results from these studies indicate that self-help is somewhat (but not significantly) less effective than traditional therapy—abstinence is lower and drop-out higher. However, self-help is clearly more cost effective. Guided self-help fares somewhat better than pure self-help, and guidance provided by a mental health professional is generally more effective than guidance provided by other professionals. Thus, guided self-help appears to be a positive and cost effective first step within a stepped care model of treatment, but it does not appear to be adequate to achieve remission for the majority of individuals with BN.

Perhaps the most important outcome from the many studies of CBT for BN is the observation that change early in treatment is the best predictor of ultimate outcome. Current treatments are quite effective for about half of the clients, so the field must now turn its attention to predicting the poor and partial responders. Currently, the only reliable predictor of poor response is initial severity. Dicker and Craighead (2004) reported that baseline purging once a day or more best differentiated their partial and poor responders from those who attained abstinence by the end of treatment. Other studies show that extending weekly outpatient treatment beyond 24 weeks is of limited benefit in getting partial responders to remission. Similarly, individuals who fail to respond to their initially assigned therapy are not generally helped significantly by switching to different approaches. Thus, more intensive and comprehensive treatments are being developed. Such interventions require more highly trained therapists and are typically longer term, but they may be cost effective for the initially more severe and they may help those who do not respond adequately to first line treatment. For example, Wonderlich, Mitchell, Peterson, and Crow (2001) have developed a promising integrative cognitive therapy for BN that draws heavily on self-discrepancy theory, attachment theory, and personality theories.

At the current time, there are few indications to warrant expensive inpatient hospitalizations for BN. Various types of partial programs and intensive outpatient programs (e.g., several evenings a week) are now available in many clinical settings but little is known about their effectiveness compared to more typical outpatient treatment because such programs have not been carefully evaluated. Current clinical wisdom suggests that individuals who present with high frequencies of purging (daily) and anyone who fails to respond well within 8 to 10 weeks to a first line treatment is likely to be best served by referral to more intensive treatment rather than continued on a weekly outpatient regime. Research on these intensive programs is needed to answer questions about effectiveness and cost effectiveness.

INTERVENTIONS FOR BINGE EATING DISORDER

Most of the treatments that have been used to treat BN have also been applied to BED (Brownley, Berkman, Sedway, Lohr, & Bulik, 2007). Interestingly, CBT does not have the short-term advantage over interpersonal psychotherapy as it does for BN. Various types of cognitive behavioral therapy such as appetite awareness training, and dialectical behavior therapy all produce similar, quite large reductions in frequency of binge eating when applied to BED, but none have led to significant weight loss (on average). It is not clear why this is the case. If the calories previously consumed as binges are just distributed more appropriately throughout the day in meals and snacks, eating may not feel out of control, but the overall intake may not be reduced adequately to trigger weight loss. Across treatments, remission rates—defined as abstinence from binge eating (generally no OBEs in the past month)—range from about 70 to 85%. It is not clear if this general effectiveness across interventions is more of a placebo response, or structured CBT has less of an advantage because its primary mechanism is reduction of restraint. Since individuals with BED already have lower levels of restraint than those with BN perhaps the more critical aspect of treating BED is reducing emotional triggers for binge eating. All of the interventions may accomplish this in different ways.

Since a variety of interventions appear to be viable for treating BED, client preference and therapist training/availability may dictate the preferred treatment approach. Many clients with BED respond positively to the structure of CBT but a substantial subgroup, particularly the burned out dieters, appear to respond more positively to alternatives that do not require food monitoring. Craighead, Elder, Niemeier, and Pung (2002) found that about a third of their participants with BED assigned to appetite monitoring indicated they would not be willing to monitor food. Similarly, it may turn out that certain clients respond better to the explicit focus on emotions and interpersonal issues that form the core of interventions such as DBT and IPT. An internet-based self-help program developed by Shapiro et al. (2007) has shown promise as a highly accessible self-help option. Such a program has great potential to provide cost effective interactive support.

For BED with comorbid obesity, behavioral weight loss (BWL) is another viable option, but the most recent direct comparison to CBT found the modest initial weight loss shown in BWL did not continue. By one year the effects of the two treatments were not different on either binges or weight (Munsch et al., 2007). However, as found in earlier studies, individuals who had achieved abstinence from binge eating lost more weight than those who continued some binge eating. The concern in using BWL was that it might increase bingeing as it is designed to increase restriction (in the sense of increasing awareness of, and accountability for, limiting overall caloric intake). However, both BWL and CBT promote the same structure (a regular three meal and two snack pattern). Thus, it appears that restriction/dieting in this way (eating smaller amounts but eating often) is not problematic and in fact may be helpful. Notably, BWL has typically been provided in a group format, both for reasons of cost effectiveness and to provide social support for lifestyle change. Fairburn and colleagues (Cooper, Fairburn, & Hawker, 2004) hypothesize that behavioral treatment provided in individual sessions is likely to be more effective for weight loss, regardless of the presence or absence of binge eating. If their current study evaluating individual therapy for weight loss supports the greater effectiveness of that approach, individual BWL may turn out to be the first line treatment for BED with comorbid obesity.

It is useful to note that, if not treated, BED is characterized by a chronic but fluctuating course (often linked to life stressors). Thus, although all interventions seem to be equally effective in the short run, it will be particularly important for future research to examine extended follow-up to determine if some interventions fare better over the long run. However, obesity is now being conceptualized as a chronic medical problem that is likely to need extended or intermittent intervention over a long period of time. Therefore, BED with obesity is likely to need the same. Flexible, long term access to treatment may be needed to help individuals maintain treatment gains (both binge abstinence and weight loss), especially through periods of crisis or high stress.

As with BN, several classes of antidepressant medications have shown similar effectiveness as psychotherapy in the treatment of BED. Again, there is little evidence regarding mechanisms of action, but anti-depressants appear to increase restraint in BN so that is likely to be the mechanism. Recent work investigating the effects of topirimate (a mood stabilizer) suggests a promising new approach. This medication is hypothesized to reduce binge eating by moderating general tendencies toward impulsivity. Initial studies on BED with comorbid obesity reported topirimate was associated with modest weight loss in addition to significant reduction of binge eating (about 58% abstinence) but rates of medication discontinuation were 30% (McElroy et al., 2007). This percent abstinence from binge eating is not quite as high as reported for most psychosocial interventions. Given the genetic vulnerabilities hypothesized to effect binge eating as well as weight, it is highly likely that treatments combining biological and psychosocial interventions will ultimately be most effective for BED.

PREVENTION OF EATING DISORDERS

There has been an explosion of eating disorder prevention research over the past decade, with the publication of over 50 distinct investigations (Neumark-Sztainer et al., 2006). Two recent meta-analyses (Fingeret, Warren, Cepeda-Benito, & Gleaves, 2006; Stice & Shaw, 2004) have synthesized relevant literature and key findings from these reviews will be delineated. Approximately two-thirds of the programs targeted a college-aged population, while the remaining targeted high school students. Most of the participants were female. The majority of studies targeting college students were selected programs in that they targeted high-risk individuals. Overall, prevention programs had a positive impact on knowledge, established risk factors for eating pathology, and eating pathology itself. The effect size for knowledge was large, while the effects sizes for general eating pathology and dieting were in the small range. Both reviews concluded that targeted and selected prevention programs had a larger impact than universal prevention programs. Stice and Shaw (2004) reasoned that high-risk individuals (who would be targeted by selected prevention programs) and older individuals might have more subjective distress and might thereby have been more motivated to engage in the preventive interventions.

Although both meta-analyses converged in certain findings, each study also contributed unique perspectives. Stice and Shaw (2004) found that, in addition to risk status, the following characteristics strengthened the impact of preventive programs: interactive (versus didactic), multisession, females only, participants over age 15, no psychoeducational content, and trials that used validated measures (Stice & Shaw, 2004). The authors hypothesized that programs with multiple sessions were more impactful than single session programs because participants in the multisession programs had more time to consolidate new knowledge and skills, and were able to try out new skills between sessions and problem solve at later sessions. The authors also raised the idea that repeated sessions may be helpful due to increased social support. Fingeret et al. (2006) reported there was no evidence to suggest that preventive interventions produce iatrogenic effects. Secondly, with regard to type of intervention, those researchers found that purely psychoeducational approaches were just as effective as skills-based approaches so that issue of the most effective content requires further investigation.

Summary and Future Directions

Extensive research is summarized describing the differences in symptoms, course, prevalence, etiology, and response to treatment for the two patterns of disordered eating that involve episodes of objectively large binge eating, Bulimia Nervosa, and Binge Eating Disorder. Recent empirical approaches to classification confirm that objective binge eating and compensatory behaviors each constitute a distinct class of behavior while restrictive eating is better conceptualized as the end of the continuum of normal eating. This approach to classifying eating disorders by focusing on specific behavioral patterns and considering weight as a separate, primarily medical concern is likely to be useful as we seek to better understand the genetic vulnerabilities, and the interactions between those vulnerabilities and the environment that result in the development of multiple pathways to disordered eating. Since weight is influenced by numerous other factors besides eating behavior—such as exercise behavior and possible biological determinants of weight that are not yet fully understood, it is not particularly surprising that attempting to include weight as a diagnostic criteria introduces unhelpful variance if one's goal is to understand behavioral patterns. Weight status (either under or over) must of course be taken into consideration with treatment recommendations, but identifying specific behavioral patterns may be more helpful in understanding different etiologies—and perhaps genetic vulnerabilities associated with various behavioral patterns.

Since current empirical approaches suggest that binge-purge behaviors constitute a distinct typology regardless of weight status, the current BN and AN binge-purge sub-types may be better treated as one category while the BN nonpurging type may best be grouped with BED (neither includes specific purging behaviors). Current evidence also suggests that the nonbingeing obese are more similar to normal weight individuals than to the binge-eating obese on a number of psychological and biological variables—suggesting it would not be most useful to limit the diagnosis of BED to those who are overweight, but instead to consider obesity as a separate, comorbid condition that may need to be addressed. However, the frequency of binge eating increases with degree of overweight so making a distinction between binge eating and significant "over"(but not binge) eating is less likely to be useful the more overweight the individual is.

Making a distinction between objective and subjective binge eating remains one of the most difficult and controversial aspects of assigning current eating disorder diagnoses. However, empirical approaches to classification tend to uphold the utility of identifying regular eating of clearly large amounts as a problematic and pathological type of eating. In contrast, the utility of identifying "clearly small" amounts seems less clear and likely less useful. In addition to AN, which is based primarily on weight not eating behavior, two behavioral eating patterns have been described as potentially useful subtypes of EDNOS that specifically exclude eating large amounts (OBEs) but do not require "clearly small" amounts. The first, labeled subjective binge eating disorder, is similar to BED but the binges do not involve clearly large amounts, and the second is purging disorder, which involves purging after normal to small amounts of food. Current thinking suggests that a genetic vulnerability—perhaps higher impulsivity—might make it more likely that a person would eat large amounts. If so, then BED and BN would share this vulnerability but subjective binge-eating, purging disorder and restricting type AN would not. Cultural pressures to be thin may be more highly implicated in those patterns as distress is triggered even though the amounts eaten are relatively normal. AN binge-purge type could fall in either category as size of binges varies considerably.

Two alternative classification schemes have been proposed. The three dimensional model (Williamson, Gleaves and Stewart, 2005) suggests at least six behavioral patterns that may be useful to study. A better understanding of specific behavior patterns may encourage the development of novel biological and psychological interventions to target those patterns, particularly during periods of acute symptoms. The alternative approach to classification is the transdiagnostic model of Fairburn and colleagues (Fairburn and Bohn, 2005) that proposes collapsing current categories into a single ED diagnosis. Overconcern with weight, shape, or controlling eating is viewed as the core pathology that must be addressed for successful treatment, regardless of the specific problem behaviors. Both of these approaches are likely to make useful contributions to our overall understanding of the development of disordered eating. Since the current culture promotes excessive eating yet endorses the thin ideal, a certain level of concern with weight and shape is expected. Normative discontent and normative dieting may be unavoidable and not necessarily predictive of the emergence of significant eating pathology. What is needed is to find ways to identify critical points when normal concern becomes overconcern, and when normal dieting escalates to the point that binge eating is triggered. In the current environment, even weak genetic vulnerabilities related to regulation of eating behavior (e.g.,vulnerabilities that intensify or reduce the experience of hunger, and those that intensify or reduce impulsive or compulsive behaviors) are likely to be expressed. Initial success, or lack of success, in managing weight may send individuals down various different pathways, only some of which end in eating disorders. As far as treatment is concerned, the emphasis at initial presentation is likely to be on specific maladaptive eating patterns. Somewhat more specific interventions and medications could hopefully be developed to target specific behaviors more effectively. However, for prevention and for long-term maintenance of recovery from eating disorders, the transdiagnostic model clearly suggests that the underlying overconcern with weight and shape motivates disordered eating behaviors. This overconcern needs to be targeted at some point regardless of specific problematic behavioral patterns.

Extensive research examining personality traits that are associated with eating disorders was also reviewed. Sample selection in most of these studies is not consistent with the *DSM* diagnostic groupings, which means that many of the findings are not specific to BN or BED. However, there is substantial evidence—at least for BN—that individuals diagnosed with this disorder experience increased impulsivity, compulsivity and obsessionality, perfectionism, sensation seeking, and harm avoidance, and that they have comparatively low levels of self-directedness. Thus, regardless of the decisions that will be made regarding the official diagnostic classification system, further work is clearly needed to understand how the interaction of personality and biology leads to different presentations of disordered eating. In addition, ability to lose weight varies widely and needs to be better understood. Are there important biological differences— for example in the experience of hunger and satiety that impact an individual's ability to restrict or to maintain a thin weight? Do some people experience more intense hunger or are some just better able to tune out or tolerate hunger? Does impulsivity or lack of satiety account for the inability to stop eating after normal amounts? Does overconcern drive inappropriate compensatory behaviors? What prevents some individuals from resorting to those methods? Are there differences in prohibitions against compensatory behaviors or is the difference due to lower levels of overconcern? Future research to answer these questions will improve our understanding of the complex presentations of disordered eating and improve the treatment options currently available.

References

American Psychiatric Association. (2000). *Diagnostic and statistical manual of mental disorders* (4th ed., text rev.). Washington, DC: Author.

American Psychiatric Association. (1987). *Diagnostic and statistical manual of mental disorders* (3rd ed. Rev.). Washington, DC: Author.

Anderson, D. A., & Paulosky, C. A. (2004). Psychological assessment of eating disorders and related features. In J. K. Thompson (Ed.), *Handbook of eating disorders and obesity* (pp. 112–129). Washington, DC: American Psychiatric Press.

Bardone-Cone, A. M., Abramson, L. Y., Vohs, K. D., Heatherton, T. F., & Joiner, T. E. (2006). Predicting bulimic symptoms: An interactive model of self-efficacy, perfectionism, and perceived weight status. *Behaviour Research and Therapy, 44*, 27–42.

Bartholome, L. T., Raymond, N. C., Lee, S. S., Peterson, C. B., & Warren, C. S. (2006). Detailed analysis of binges in obese women with binge eating disorder: Comparisons using multiple methods of data collection. *International Journal of Eating Disorders, 36*, 685–693.

Becker, A. E., Keel, P., Anderson-Fye, E. P., & Thomas, J. J. (2004). Genes and/or jeans?: Genetic and socio-cultural contributions to risk for eating disorders. *Journal of Addictive Diseases, 23*, 81–103.

Berg, M. L., Crosby, R. D., Wonderlich, S. A., & Hawley, D. (2000). Relationship of temperament and perceptions of nonshared environment in bulimia nervosa. *International Journal of Eating Disorders, 28*, 148–154.

Binford, R. B., & Le Grange, D. (2005). Adolescents with bulimia nervosa and eating disorder not otherwise specified-purging only. *International Journal of Eating Disorders, 38*(2), 157–161.

Braun, D. L., Sunday, S. R., & Halmi, K. A. (1994). Psychiatric comorbidity in patients with eating disorders. *Psychological Medicine, 24*, 859–867.

Brownley, K. A., Berkman, N. D., Sedway, J. A., Lohr, K. N., & Bulik, C. M. (2007). Binge eating disorder treatment: A systematic review of randomized clinical trials. *International Journal of Eating Disorders, 40*, 337–3480.

Boskind-Lodahl, M., & White, W. C. (1973). The definition and treatment of bulimarexia in college women—a pilot study. *Journal of the American Health Association. 27*, 84–97.

Cassin, S. E., & von Ranson, K. M. (2005). Personality and eating disorders: A decade in review. *Clinical Psychology Review, 25*, 895–916.

Cooper, M. J. (2005). Cognitive theory in anorexia nervosa and bulimia nervosa: Progress, development and future directions. *Clinical Psychology Review, 25*, 511–531.

Cooper, Z., Fairburn, C. G., & Hawker, D. M. (2004). Cognitive-behavioral Treatment of Obesity: A clinician's guide. New York: Guilford.

Corstorphine, E., Waller, G., Ohanian, V., & Baker, M. (2006). Changes in internal states across the binge-vomit cycle in bulimia nervosa. *The Journal of Nervous and Mental Disease, 194*, 446–449.

Crow, S. J., & Peterson, C. B. (2003). The economic and social burden of eating disorders: A review. In M. Maj, K. Halmi, J. J. Lopez-Ibor, & N. Sartorius (Eds.), *Eating disorders*. Chichester, UK: Wiley.

Crago, M., & Shisslak, C. M. (2003). Ethnic differences in dieting, binge eating, and purging behaviors among American females: A review. *Eating Disorders, 11*, 289–304.

Craighead, L. W. (2006). The appetite awareness workbook: How to listen to your body and overcome binge eating, overeating, and obsession with food. Oakland, CA: New Harbinger.

Craighead, L. W., Elder, K. E., Niemier, H. M., & Pung, M. (November 2002). Food versus appetite monitoring in CBWL for binge eating disorder. Paper presented at the meetings of the Association for Behavior Therapy. Reno, Nevada.

Currin, L., Schmidt, U., Treasure, J., & Jick, H. (2005). Time trends in eating disorder incidence. *British Journal of Psychiatry, 186*, 132–135.

Deaver, C. M., Miltenberger, R. G., Smyth, J., Meidinger, A., & Crosby, R. (2003). An evaluation of affect and binge eating. *Behavior Modification, 27*, 578–599.

Dicker, S., & Craighead, L. W. (2004). Appetite-focused cognitive behavioral therapy in the treatment of binge eating with purging. *Cognitive Behavioral Practice, 11*(2), 213–221.

Eddy, K. T., Keel, P. K., Dorer, D. J., Delinshky, S. S., Franko, D. L., & Herzog, D. B. (2002). A longitudinal comparison of anorexia nervosa subtypes. *International Journal of Eating Disorders*, *32*, 191–201.

Eldredge, K. L., & Agras, W. S. (1996). Weight and shape overconcern and emotional eating in binge eating disorder. *International Journal of Eating Disorders*, *19*, 73–82.

Engel, S. G., Corneliussen, S. J., Wonderlich, S. A., Crosby, R. A., LeGrange, D., Crow, S., et al. (2005). Impulsivity and compulsivity in bulimia nervosa. *International Journal of Eating Disorders*, *38*, 244–251.

Fairburn, D. G., & Beglin, S. J. (1994). Assessment of eating disorders: Interview or self-report questionnaire? *International Journal of Eating Disorders*, *16*, 363–370.

Fairburn, C. G., & Bohn, K. (2005). Eating disorder NOS (EDNOS): An example of the troublesome "not otherwise specified" (NOS) category in *DSM-IV*. *Behaviour Research and Therapy*, *43*, 691–701.

Fairburn, C. G., & Cooper, Z. (1993). The Eating Disorder Examination (12th ed.). In C. G. Fairburn & G. T. Wilson (Eds.), *Binge eating: Nature, assessment and treatment* (pp. 317–360). New York: Guilford.

Fairburn, C. G., Cooper, Z., Doll, H. A., Norman, P., & O'Connor, M. (2000). The natural course of bulimia nervosa and binge eating disorder in young women. *Archives of General Psychiatry*, *57*, 659–665.

Fairburn, C. G., Cooper, Z., & Shafran, R. (2003). Cognitive behaviour therapy for eating disorders: A "transdiagnostic" theory and treatment. *Behaviour Research and Therapy*, *41*, 509–528.

Fairburn, C. G., & Harrison, P. J. (2003). Eating disorders. *Lancet*, *361*, 407–416.

Fairburn, C. G., Stice, E., Cooper, Z., Doll, H. A., Norman, P., & O'Connor, M. (2003). Understanding persistence in bulimia nervosa: A 5-year naturalistic study. *Journal of Consulting and Clinical Psychology*, *71*, 103–109.

Fairburn, C. G., Welch, S. L., Norman, P. A., O'Connor, M. E., & Doll, H. A. (1996). Bias and bulimia nervosa: How typical are clinic cases? *American Journal of Psychiatry*, *153*, 386–391.

Favaro, A., Ferrara, S., & Santonastaso, P. (2003). The spectrum of eating disorders in young women: A prevalence study in a general population sample. *Psychosomatic Medicine*, *65*, 701–708.

Favaro, A., Zanetti, T., Tenconi, E., DeGortes, D., Ronzan, A., Veronese, A., et al. (2005). The relationship between temperament and impulsive behaviors in eating disordered subjects. *Eating Disorders*, *13*, 61–70.

Fingeret, M. C., Warren, C. S., Cepeda-Benito, A., & Gleaves, D. H. (2006). Eating disorder prevention research: A meta-analysis. *Eating Disorders*, *14*, 191–213.

Forbrush, K., Hatherton, T. F., & Keel, P. K. (2007). Relationship between perfectionism and specific disordered eating behaviors. *International Journal of Eating Disorders*, *40* (1), 37–41.

Franco-Paredes, K., Mancilla-Diaz, J. M., Vazquez-Arevalo, R., Lopez-Aguilar, X., & Alvarez-Rayon, G. (2005). Perfectionism and eating disorders: A review of the literature. *European Eating Disorders Review*, *13*, 61–70.

Garner, D. M. (2005). Eating Disorder Inventory-3. Lutz, FL: Psychological Assessment Resources.

Garner, D. M., & Garfinkle, P. (1979). The Eating Attitude Test: An index of the symptoms of anorexia nervosa. *Psychological Medicine*, *9*, 273–279.

Geliebter, A., & Hashim, S. A. (2001). Gastric capacity in normal, obese, and bulimic women. *Physiology & Behavior*, *74*, 743–746.

Godart, N. T., Flament, M. F., Perdereau, F., & Jeammet, P. (2002). Comorbidity between eating disorders and anxiety disorders: a review. *International Journal of Eating Disorders*, *32*, 253–270.

Herzog, D. B., Dorer, D. J., Keel, P. K., Selwyn, S. E., Ekeblad, E. R., Flores, A. T., et al. (1999). Recovery and relapse in anorexia and bulimia nervosa: A 7.5 year follow-up study. *Journal of the American Academy of Child and Adolescent Psychiatry*, *38*, 829–837.

Hill, D. (2007). Appetite-focused dialectical behavior therapy for the treatment of binge eating with purging: A randomized controlled trial. University of Colorado, Unpublished Dissertation.

Hoek, H. W. (2006). Incidence, prevalence and mortality of anorexia nervosa and other eating disorders. *Current Opinion in Psychiatry*, *19*, 389–394.

Hoek, H. W., & van Hoeken, D. (2003). Review of the prevalence and incidence of eating disorders. *International Journal of Eating Disorders*, *34*, 383–396.

Hund, A. R., & Espelage, D. L. (2005). Childhood sexual abuse, disordered eating, alexithymia, and general distress: A mediation model. *Journal of Consulting Psychology*, *52*, 559–573.

Jacobi, C., Hayward, C., de Zwann, M., Kraemer, H. C., & Agras, W. S. (2004). Coming to terms with risk factors for eating disorders: Application of risk terminology and suggestions for a general taxonomy. *Psychological Bulletin*, *130*, 19–65.

James, R. (1743). *A medical dictionary*. London: Osborne.

Katerndahl, D., Burge, S., & Kellogg, N. (2005). Predictors of development of adult psychopathology in female victims of childhood sexual abuse. *The Journal of Nervous and Mental Disease, 193*, 258–264.

Kaye, W. H., Frank, G. K., Bailer, U. F., Henry, S. E., Meltzer, C. C., Price, J. C., et al. (2005). Serotonin alternations in anorexia and bulimia nervosa: New insights from imaging studies. *Physiology & Behavior, 85*, 73–81.

Keel, P. K., Heatherton, T. F., Dorer, D. J., Joiner, T. E., & Zalta, A. K. (2006). Point prevalence of bulimia nervosa in 1982, 1992, and 2002. *Psychological Medicine, 36*, 119–127.

Keel, P. K., & Klump, K. L. (2003). Are eating disorders culture-bound syndromes? Implications for conceptualizing their etiology. *Psychological Bulletin, 129*, 747–769.

Keel, P. K., Klump, K. L., Miller, K. B., McGue, M., & Iacono, W. G. (2005). Shared transmission of eating disorders and anxiety disorders. *International Journal of Eating Disorders, 38*(2), 199–205.

Keel, P. K., & Mitchell, J. E. (1997). Outcome in bulimia nervosa. *American Journal of Psychiatry, 154*, 313–321.

Keel, P. K., Wolfe, B. E., Lidlde, R. A., De Young, K. P., & Jimerson, D. C. (2007). Clinical features and physiological response to a test meal in purging disorder and bulimia nervosa. *Archives of General Psychiatry, 64*(9), 1058–1066.

Kendler, K. S., MacLean, C., Neale, M., & Kessler, R. C. (1991). The genetic epidemiology of bulimia nervosa. *American Journal of Psychiatry, 148*, 1627–1637.

Keski-Rahkonen, A., Bulik, C. M., Neale, B. M., Rose, R. J., Rissanen, A., & Kaprio, J. (2005). Body dissatisfaction and drive for thinness in young adult twins. *International Journal of Eating Disorders, 37*, 188–199.

Killen, J. D., Barr Taylor, C., Hayward, C., Farish Haydel, K., Wilson, D. M., Hammer, L., et al. (1996). Weight concerns influence the development of eating disorders: A 4-year prospective study. *Journal of Consulting and Clinical Psychology, 64*, 936–940.

Klein, D. A., & Walsh, B. T. (2004). Eating disorders: Clinical features and pathophysiology. *Physiology and Behavior, 81*, 359–374.

Le Grange, D., Crosby, R., Rathouz, P., & Levanthal, B. (2007). A randomized controlled comparison of family-based treatment and supportive psychotherapy for adolescent bulimia nervosa. *Archives of General Psychiatry, 64*, 1049–1056.

Leon, G. R., Fulkerson, J. A., Perry, C. L., & Early-Zald, M. B. (1995). Prospective analysis of personality and behavioral vulnerabilities and gender influences in the later development of disordered eating. *Journal of Abnormal Psychology, 104*, 140–149.

Leon, G. R., Fulkerson, J. A., Perry, C. L., Keel, P. K., & Klump, K. L. (1999). Three to four year prospective evaluation of personality and behavioral risk factors for later disordered eating in adolescent girls and boys. *Journal of Youth and Adolescence, 28*, 181–196.

Liddell, H. G., & Scott, R. (1972). Greek and English Lexicon. Oxford: Clarendon Press.

Lilenfeld, L. R. R., Wonderlich, S., Riso, L. P., Crosby, R., & Mitchell, J. (2006). Eating disorders and personality: A methodological and empirical review. *Clinical Psychology Review, 26*, 299–320.

Lock, J. (2005). Adjusting cognitive behavior therapy for adolescents with bulimia nervosa: Results of case series. *American Journal of Psychotherapy, 59*(3), 267–281.

McElroy, S. L., Hudson, J. I., Capece, K. B., Beyers, K., Fisher, A. C. & Rosenthal, N. R. (2007). Topiramate for the treatment of binge eating disorder associated with obesity: A placebo-controlled study. *Biological Psychiatry, 61*, 1039–1048.

Mitchell, J. E., Agras, S., & Wonderlich, S. (2007). Treatment of bulimia nervosa: Where are we and where are we going? *International Journal of Eating Disorders, 40*(2), 95–101.

Mitchell, J. E. & Crow, S. (2006). Medical complications of anorexia nervosa and bulimia nervosa. *Current Opinion in Psychiatry, 19*, 438–443.

Mitchell, J. E., Hatsukami, D., Eckert, E. D., & Pyle, R. L. (1985). Characteristics of 275 patients with bulimia. *American Journal of Psychiatry, 142*, 482–485.

Moyer, D. M., DiPietro, L., Merkowitz, R. I., & Stunkard, A. J. (1997). Child sexual abuse and precursors of binge eating in an adolescent female population. *International Journal of Eating Disorders, 21*, 21–30.

Munsch, S., Biedert, E., Meyer, A., Michael, T., Schllup, B., Tuch, A., et al. (2007). A randomized comparison of cognitive behavioral therapy and behavioral weight loss treatment for overweight individuals with Binge Eating Disorder. *International Journal of Eating Disorders, 40*(2), 102–113.

Mussell, M. P., Mitchell, J. E., Weller, C. L., Raymond, N. C., Crow, S. J., & Crosby, R. D. (1994). Onset of binge eating, dieting, obesity, and mood disorders among subjects seeking treatment for binge eating. *International Journal of Eating Disorders, 17*(4), 395–401.

Neumark-Sztainer, D., Levine, M. P., Paxton, S. J., Smolak, L., Piran, N., & Wertheim, E. H. (2006). Prevention of body dissatisfaction and disordered eating: What next? *Eating Disorders, 14,* 265–285.

O'Brien, K. M., & Vincent, N. K. (2003). Psychiatric comorbidity in anorexia and bulimia nervosa: Nature, prevalence, and causal relationships. *Clinical Psychology Review, 23,* 57–74.

Peterson, C. B., Crosby, R. D., Wonderlich, S. A., Joiner, T., Crow, S. J., Mitchell, J. E., et al. (2007) Psychometric properties of the Eating Disorder Examination-Questionnaire: Factor structure and internal consistency. *International Journal of Eating Disorders, 4,* 386–389.

Pirke, K. M., Kellner, M. M., Friess, E., Krieg, J. C., & Fichter, M. M. Satiety and cholecystokinin. *International Journal of Eating Disorders, 15,* 63–69.

Polivy, J., & Herman, C. P. (2002). Causes of eating disorders. *Annual Review of Psychology, 53,* 187–213.

Quadflieg, N., & Fichter, M. M. (2003). The course and outcome of bulimia nervosa. *European Child and Adolescent Psychiatry, 12 (Suppl. 1),* 99–109.

Rheas, D. L., Whisenhunt, B., & Netemeyer, R. (2002). Development of the Body Checking Questionnaire: A self-report measure of body checking behaviors. *International Journal of Eating Disorders, 31*(3), 324–333.

Russell, G. (1979). Bulimia nervosa: An ominous variant of anorexia nervosa. *Psychological Medicine, 9,* 429–448.

Safer, D. L., Telch, C. F., & Agras, W. S. (2001). Dialectical behavior therapy for bulimia nervosa. *American Journal of Psychiatry, 158,* 632–634.

Sansone, R. A., Levitt, J. L., & Sansone, L. A. (2005). The prevalence of personality disorders among those with eating disorders. *Eating Disorders, 13,* 7–21.

Schapman, A. M., Lock, J., & Couturier, J. (2006). Cognitive-behavioral therapy for adolescents with binge eating syndromes: A case series. *International Journal of Eating Disorders, 39*(3), 1–4.

Schmidt, U. (2003). Aetiology of eating disorders in the 21st century: New answers to old questions. *European Child and Adolescent Psychiatry, 12 (Suppl. 1),* 30–37.

Shapiro, J. R., Reba-Harrelson, L., Dymek-Valentine, M., Woolson, S. L., Hamer, R. M., & Bulik, C. M. (2007). Feasibility and acceptability of CD-ROM based cognitive-behavioural treatment for binge eating disorder. *European Eating Disorders Review, 15,* 175–184.

Shapiro, J. R., Woolson, S. L., Hamer, R. M., Kalarchian, M. A., Marcus, M. D., & Bulik, C. M. (2007).

Evaluating binge eating disorder in children: Development of the Children's Binge Eating Disorder Scale (C-BEDS). *International Journal of Eating Disorders, 40,* 82–89.

Sim, L., & Zeman, J. (2005). Emotion regulation factors as mediators between body dissatisfaction and bulimic symptoms in early adolescent girls. *Journal of Early Adolescence, 25,* 478–496.

Striegel-Moore, R. H., & Bulik, C. M. (2007). Risk factors for eating disorders. *American Psychologist, 62*(3), 181–198.

Striegel-Moore, R. H., Dohm, F. A., Kraemer, H. C., Schreiber, G. B., Taylor, C. B., & Daniels, S. R. (2007). Risk factors for binge-eating disorders: An exploratory study. *International Journal of Eating Disorders, 40*(6), 481–487.

Stice, E. (2002). Risk and maintenance factors for eating pathology: A meta-analytic review. *Psychological Bulletin, 128,* 825–848.

Stice, E., Akutagawa, D., Gaggar, A., & Agras, W. S. (2000). Negative affect moderates the relation between dieting and binge eating. *International Journal of Eating Disorders, 27,* 218–229.

Stice, E., Nemeroff, C., & Shaw, H. E. (1996). Test of the dual pathway model of bulimia nervosa: Evidence for dietary restraint and affect regulation mechanisms. *Journal of Social and Clinical Psychology, 15,* 340–363.

Stice, E., Presnell, K., & Spangler, D. (2002). Risk factors for binge eating onset in adolescent girls: A 2-year prospective investigation. *Health Psychology, 21,* 131–138.

Stice, E. & Shaw, H. (2004). Eating disorder prevention programs: A meta-analytic review. *Psychological Bulletin, 130,* 206–227.

Stice, E., & Shaw, H. E. (2002). Role of body dissatisfaction in the onset and maintenance of eating pathology: A synthesis of research findings. *Journal of Psychosomatic Research, 53,* 985–993.

Stunkard, A. J. (1959). Eating patterns and obesity. *Psychiatric Quarterly, 33,* 284–295.

Stunkard, A. J. (1993). A history of binge eating. In C. G.Fairburn & G. T. Wilson (Eds.), *Binge eating: Nature, assessment and treatment.* New York: Guildford.

Stunkard, A. J., Grace, W. J., & Wolff, H. G. (1955). The night-eating syndrome: A pattern of food intake among certain obese patients. *American Journal of Medicine, 19,* 78–86.

Sullivan, P. F., Bulik, C. M., & Kendler, K. S. (1998). The Epidemiology and classification of bulimia nervosa. *Psychological Medicine, 28,* 599–610.

Sysko, R., Devlin, M. J., Walsh, B. T., Zimmerli, E., & Kissileff, H. R. (2007). Satiety and test meal intake among women with binge eating disorder. *International Journal of Eating Disorders, 40*(6), –561.

Thelen, M. H., Farmer, J., Wonderlich, S., & Smith, M. (1991). A revision of the bulimia test: the BULIT-R. *Psychological Assessment, 3,* 119–124.

Vervaet, M., van Heeringen, C., & Audenaert, K. (2004). Personality-related characteristics in restricting versus binging and purging eating disordered patients. *Comprehensive Psychiatry, 45,* 37–43.

Walcott, D. D., Pratt, H. D., & Patel, D. R. (2003). Adolescents and eating disorders: Gender, racial, ethnic, sociocultural and socioeconomic issues. *Journal of Adolescent Research. Special Issue: Eating disorders in adolescents, 18,* 223–243.

Wallin, U., Kronovall, P., and Majewski, M. (2000). Body awareness therapy in teenage Anorexia Nervosa: Outcome after 2 years. *European Eating Disorders Review, 8,* 19–30.

Whitehouse, A. M., Cooper, P. J., Vize, C. V., Hill, C., & Vogel, L. (1992). Prevalence of eating disorders in three Cambridge general practices: Hidden and conspicuous morbidity. *British Journal of General Practice, 42,* 57–60.

Williamson, D. A., Gleaves, D. H., & Stewart, T. M. (2005). Categorical versus dimensional models of eating disorders: An examination of the evidence. *International Journal of Eating Disorders, 37,* 1–10.

Williamson, D. A., White, M. A., York-Crowe, E., & Stewart, T. M. (2004). Cognitive-behavioral theories of eating disorders. *Behavior Modification, 28,* 711–738.

Williamson, D. A., Zucker, N. L., Martin, C. K., & Smeets, M. A. M. (2001). Etiology and management of eating disorders. In P. B. Sutker & H. E. Adams (Eds.), *Comprehensive Handbook of Psychopathology* (3rd Ed., pp. 61–670). New York: Kluwer Academic/Plenum.

Wilson, G. T., Grilo, C. M., & Vitousek, K. M. (2007). Psychological treatment of eating disorders. *American Psychologist, 62*(3), 199–216.

Wonderlich, S. A., Joiner, T. E., Jr., Keel, P. K., Williamson, D. A., & Crosby, R. D. (2007). Eating disorder diagnoses: Empirical approaches to classification. *American Psychologist, 62* (3), 181–198.

Wonderlich, S. A., Mitchell, J. E., Peterson, C. B., & Crow, S. (2001). Integrative cognitive therapy for bulimic disorder. In R. Striegel-Moore & L. Smolak (Eds.), *Eating disorders: Innovative directions in research and practice* (pp. 173–196). Washington, DC: American Psychological Association.

Young, E. A., Clopton, J. R., & Bleckley, M. K. (2004). Perfectionism, low self-esteem, and family factors as predictors of bulimic behavior. *Eating Behaviors, 5,* 273–283.

Chapter 13

Eating Disorders: Anorexia Nervosa

JAMES LOCK AND NINA KIRZ

Description

SYMPTOMS AND DIAGNOSTIC CRITERIA

Eating disorders are characterized by pathological eating behaviors combined with abnormal thoughts and beliefs about food and weight, including overvaluation of thinness, distorted body image, or obsessively ruminating about food or weight (Fairburn & Harrison, 2003). The *DSM-IV* has three eating disorder diagnoses: Anorexia Nervosa (AN), Bulimia Nervosa (BN), and Eating Disorder Not Otherwise Specified (EDNOS) (American Psychiatric Association, 1994). Of these, AN is the oldest type of eating disorder described in the medical literature and arguably the most serious of them (Gull, 1874; Lasègue, 1883). The *DSM-IV* describes four main criteria for diagnosing AN: refusal to maintain body weight in a normal range, an irrational fear of fat or of gaining weight in the context of low weight, body image distortion or denial of the medical seriousness of extreme low weight, and in postmenarcheal females, three consecutive months of amenorrhea. There is a purely restrictive subtype and a binge/purge subtype of AN described in *DSM-IV* (APA, 1994).

The core features of AN include behavioral, psychological, and physiological factors. There is a clear and unwavering behavioral refusal to obtain or maintain weight acceptable for height and health. The behaviors that illustrate this refusal include a highly restrictive and selective eating pattern, excessive exercise, and in some cases purging behaviors (e.g., vomiting and laxative use). Often these behaviors appear initially innocuous, even consistent with age appropriate developmental concerns about appearance; however, over time, these behaviors take on an urgent and insistent nature while other important social and emotional pursuits are deferred or avoided all together. Hours may be spent calculating calories and planning meals. Exercise deviates from normal activity levels and it becomes a compulsive activity where attempts to interrupt the behavior are met with extreme resistance. Purging behaviors develop in 15 to 20% of cases as an attempt to limit the potential for weight gain even in the context of extremely limited intake. Over time the experiences of starvation, exercise, and even purging behaviors become self-reinforcing and are experienced as a source of support and comfort for the person with AN.

The psychological basis for these behaviors is usually considered to be an intense fear of fat or of gaining weight. The triggers for the development of this specific type of anxiety and fear about fat and weight gain are extremely variable but commonly include the onset of puberty, development of an extreme health or nutrition focus, being teased about weight or appearance, initiating social or academic transitions (e.g. starting middle school or high school), emergence of a medical illness that initiates weight loss, attempting to improve athletic performance, and experiences of physical and sexual abuse. Whatever the specific trigger may be, the development of this extreme anxiety and fear is the psychological underpinning that putatively supports the behaviors that lead to extreme weight loss. The fear of weight gain and fat is relieved—albeit temporarily—by the various weight loss inducing behaviors. This is accomplished directly because the behaviors lead to weight loss and that reduces the anxiety and fear; and indirectly, by providing a focus for the obsessive worry that accompanies these fears.

Another psychological aspect of AN is the disturbance in the appreciation of current body weight and shape, leading to overestimating body size relative to true body size. This *body-image distortion* likely results from a consistent and persistent over focus on the body as a whole or on specific parts of the body (e.g. thighs, buttocks, cheeks) in an attempt to assess the success of efforts to lose weight or fat. Initially, this focus may be a source of limited reassurance, much in the way that constant checking of weight on as scale may be, because changes can be seen and measured. However, over time the hyper focus on the body leads to greater and greater distortions and misperceptions. This can also lead to a severe distortion in evaluating the medical consequences of being severely underweight. This denial of the seriousness of malnutrition is a major source of treatment avoidance and represents a significant psychological hazard for both psychological and medical treatment.

The result of the interaction between the psychological factors of fear, distortion, and denial and the behaviors precipitating extreme weight loss is *physiological malnutrition*. A commonly used figure for determining malnutrition in adults is a BMI of 17.5 or below, or an Ideal Body Weight (IBW) of 85% or below. However, in children and adolescents these figures can be misleading and growth and pubertal status greatly affect these types of norms. Malnutrition affects most organ systems, as the body responds to manage a starvation state and conserves energy by cutting back on all but the most essential functions. Blood flow to the periphery is decreased, leading to cold extremities. Skin becomes dry and hair falls out, while the body becomes coated with lanugo, a fine downy hair meant to conserve warmth. Menstruation stops or becomes irregular, and fertility is impaired. Along with these hormonal changes, calcium is lost from the bones leading to osteopenia, or in severe cases to osteoporosis. In children who are still growing, growth can be slowed or stopped. Heart and brain function are preserved for as long as possible but eventually the cardiac muscle weakens, leading to low heart rate, low blood pressure, and possible death. Brain scans have shown shrinkage of the brain during the illness (Katzman, Christensen, Young, & Zipursky, 2001).

Of all these complications, the only one known to definitely persist after weight restoration is osteoporosis—the severity of which depends on the duration of the illness.

The *DSM-IV* attempts to describe discrete eating disorder syndromes, but given the paucity of knowledge about eating disorders it has been less successful with AN than with many other disorders (Fairburn & Bohn, 2005). There is a significantly higher incidence of Eating Disorder Not Otherwise Specified (EDNOS) than of AN or BN—while many patients with ED NOS are just as compromised as patients with AN or BN, but do not meet full criteria (Fairburn & Bohn, 2005). Several of the current criteria for AN are problematic and exclude patients who have the same types of thoughts and behaviors as patients who meet criteria for AN.

Some authors have contested the current suggested weight criterion of 85% or below of ideal body weight (Herzog & Delinsky, 2001). It is extremely difficult to be accurate when calculating IBW to take into account body frame, pubertal status, and ethnicity, and thus difficult to determine when a patient is below 85% of his or her individual ideal body weight. Determination of ideal body weight is even more complicated in younger patients who may be growth retarded due to malnutrition: Should their current ideal body weight be calculated based on current height, or the height they would have been if they had continued their previous growth curve? This criterion excludes patients who start off overweight and lose to a normal weight, who may have just as severe thoughts, behaviors, and medical consequences. Finally, the cut point of 85% or BMI of 17.5 is arbitrary and has varied considerably in various iterations of the *DSM* over time. Even in the current version, these weight cut-points are given as examples, not absolutes, though many clinicians and researchers appear to treat them as such.

Lee (1995) objected to the requirement for weight phobia on cultural grounds. Patients diagnosed with AN in non-Western countries are less likely to report fear of fatness as a motivation for their weight loss, as are younger adolescents and preadolescents (Nicholls & Bryant-Waugh, 2003). Clinically, patients without weight phobia—but who otherwise meet criteria for AN—do not seem to be significantly different from patients who do present with weight phobia, although Strober, Freeman, and Morrell (1997, 1999)—in a 10–15 year follow up study—found patients without weight phobia to be less likely to have a chronic course or engage in binge eating, and more likely to be fully weight recovered Amenorrhea is also a problematic criterion. Amenorrhea may occur before weight loss, or may not occur in patients with severe weight loss. Studies suggest no difference in patients with and without amenorrhea in terms of severity of illness, body image disturbance, depression, or personality disorders (Cachelin & Maher, 1998; Garfinkel et al., 1996). This criterion does not apply to males or to premenarcheal girls, and can be confusing in young adolescent girls who normally have irregular periods or with girls on oral steroids for birth control.

As noted above, the *DSM-IV* gives two subtypes of AN—restricting and binge/purge. The evidence supporting these subtypes as clinically discrete entities is controversial. There is some evidence that patients with the binge-purge subtype have a more complicated course (Herzog & Delinsky, 2001; Herzog et al., 1999; Pryor, Wiedermann, & McGilley, 1996) and other studies have found more depression, substance abuse, and personality disorders in binge-purge patients (Dacosta & Halmi, 1992; Herzog et al., 1996). Other studies have found no difference in recovery rates or psychopathology (Eddy et al., 2002). Many patients appear to cross back and forth between the two subtypes as well as between AN, BN, and EDNOS over the course of the their lives. Thus there remains considerable controversy about the validity of the *DSM* diagnostic scheme insofar as it relates to eating disorders and to AN specifically, especially for younger patients with these disorders (Nicholls, Chater, & Lask, 2000). Development of reliable ways to differentiate early stage AN from nonproblematic, genetically-based "thinness," and normative dieting and body discontent remains a challenge, but are needed as intervention early in the disorder is more successful and prevents medical complications.

CASE EXAMPLE

Lisa is a 17 year old female who reports "according to other people I'm not eating safely." About six months ago she decided to "lose a few pounds" for her junior prom. She is 5'5", and initially wanted to decrease her weight from 130lbs to 120lbs. She initiated her dieting by eating what she described as "healthier": she cut out junk food, desserts, and fast food, and limited her portion sizes. She also started an exercise routine of running three miles and doing 100 sit-ups and 100 pushups every day. Her weight dropped to 120lbs by prom, but she still felt overweight. She cut more and more foods from her diet until she was eating mostly fruits and vegetables and was skipping lunch at school. She kept careful track of calories and tried not to eat more than 500kcal/day. Her parents noticed that she was losing too much weight and tried to keep her from exercising, but Lisa felt too guilty about "all those calories just sitting there" and was afraid of gaining weight. She started secretly doing jumping jacks and running in place in her room at night. As her weight decreased further she became more and more irritable, especially when her parents tried to encourage her to eat. Her menses ceased, she felt cold all the time, and her hair started falling out. She stopped spending time with friends because she was worried they would comment on her not eating, and because she just did not have the energy to go out. Her parents became concerned enough to bring her to the pediatrician, who found that her weight was down to 100 lbs and her heart rate was 42 beats per minute. She was admitted to the hospital, which Lisa thought was completely unnecessary. She was furious at being made to gain weight in the hospital as she felt her thighs were still "huge."

HISTORY OF ANOREXIA NERVOSA

Although there are reports of disturbed eating patterns and food refusal throughout history, the association with disturbed body image and fear of weight gain did not arise until the late nineteenth century (Saraf, 1998). In 1873 the French physician Charles Lasègue and the British physician Sir William Gull independently described an illness, which Lasègue dubbed "anorexia hystérique" and Gull called "anorexia hysterica," primarily affecting girls and young women and consisting of severe weight loss, amenorrhea, constipation, and restlessness, without evidence of any organic pathology (Gull, 1874; Lasègue, 1883). Gull later called this illness Anorexia Nervosa in a lecture the next year, but it did not receive much attention. In 1914 a German pathologist named Morris Simmonds found lesions in the pituitaries of some emaciated patients (Simmonds, 1914). AN was theorized to have an endocrine etiology and was called "Simmond's disease" or "pituitary cachexia." This notion was refuted after World War II. Psychoanalytic thinking was popular at this time and AN was thought of as a fear of oral impregnation (Thoma, 1967). AN did not receive widespread attention until the work of the psychiatrist Hilde Bruch, who published her pioneering work in the 1970s (Bruch, 1973, 1978). Her formulation emphasized the issues of core low self-esteem, limited self-concept, and distorted body image that she saw in AN patients. Arthur Crisp's formulation of AN as an effort to avoid the difficulties, physical, emotional, and familial problems related to the onset of adolescence, offers a related psychological formulation to that of Bruch (Crisp, 1997). Theories about family psychopathology related to intrusiveness and over control as contributors to the psychological vulnerability in adolescents with AN were advanced by Minuchin, Rosman, and Baker (1978), and Selvini Palazzoli (1974). At the same time, cognitive behavioral therapies were being developed to address other mental health problems, particularly depression and anxiety (Beck, Rush, Shaw, & Emery, 1979). The application of purely behavioral treatments for AN has been limited and largely confined to inpatient treatment programs (Jenkins, 1987); however, the success of cognitive-behavioral therapy (CBT) for bulimia nervosa, a related eating disorder, has lead to preliminary examination of this approach for AN as well (Fairburn, 1981; Fairburn, Cooper, & Safran, 2002; Pike, Walsh, Vitousek, Wilson, & Bauer, 2004). To date, although each of these proposed psychological theories has its adherents, little substantive research supports any of them.

EPIDEMIOLOGY

Estimates of the incidence and prevalence of AN vary depending on the population studied (community versus clinical samples), but most estimates for point prevalence range from 0.1 to 0.9% of the population, while rates of subthreshold AN (meeting all but one of the *DSM-IV* criteria) are higher (Hoek & Hoeken, 2003; Hoek et al., 2005). Approximately 5 to 10% of patients with AN are male, although the true incidence in males may be higher as males are less likely to come to clinical attention. The peak age of onset in females may be bimodal at 14 and 18 years of age, but onset of the disorder is seen as young as seven years old and throughout adulthood (Halmi, Brodland, & Loney, 1973). Contrary to previous beliefs, the disorder is prevalent across ethnicities and socioeconomic status. Nevertheless, the prevalence is higher in industrialized Westernized countries, and increases in other countries as they become more industrialized and exposed to Western media. There is controversy over whether the incidence of AN is increasing. Many studies show an increased incidence over the past 50 years, but this may be due to an increase in detection or to a relative increase in the most vulnerable population (i.e., young women). A study by Lucas, Beard, and O'Fallon (1991) that looked at the population of Rochester, Minnesota, over the course of fifty years found that while the incidence in women over 24 years old remained constant, the incidence in the 15 to 24 group went from 16.6/100,000 in 1935–1939, to 7 in 1950–1954, but then rose to 26.3 in 1980–1984 (Lucas, Crowson, O'Fallon, & Melton, 1999). More recent data suggest that this increased incidence in younger age groups continues to the present (van Son et al., 2006).

Dysfunction

NEUROBIOLOGY

The study of the neurobiology of eating disorders is still relatively unexplored. The current avenues of exploration are the investigation of neurotransmitters and appetite related peptides, and the use of neuroimaging techniques to examine the possibility of structural and functional brain contributions to AN.

Serotonin has been the most popular neurotransmitter targeted for investigation so far, as 5-HT systems are involved in mood and obsessiveness, appetite regulation, and impulse control. Patients with AN have been found to have low levels of 5-HT metabolites in the cerebrospinal fluid and abnormal hormonal response to 5-HT specific challenges. However, specific abnormalities in the serotonin system have not been identified. More recently, interest in the dopaminergic neurotransmitter system has developed because of the role of this neurotransmitter in reward systems and obsessive compulsive thinking and behavior. Some suggest that hypersensitivity of the dopameningic system may account for the extreme reactions of patients with AN to novel stimuli (Kaye, Strober, & Jimerson, in press).

Recent studies suggest a neural disturbance in eating disorders (Trummer, Eustacchio, Unger, Tillich, & Flaschka, 2002; Uher et al., 2004; Ward, Tiller, Treasure, & Russell, 2000). Indirect evidence in support of a neural basis of eating disorders can be inferred from neuropsychological, electrophysiological, neuropharmacological, structural neuroimaging, and functional neuroimaging investigations (Uher, Treasure, & Campbell, 2002). Although there is a fairly substantial brain imaging literature in AN—including positron emission tomography (PET) and single-photon emission computed tomography (SPECT) studies that show regional differences in metabolism and neurotransmitter (usually receptor) alternations, and fMRI studies demonstrating differences in activation response to stimuli (usually food)—these studies are only on adults and are generally small scale and variable in terms of patient subtypes, state of illness, and regional neuroanatomy examined (Frank et al., 2002; Kaye, Strober, & Jimerson, in press; 1998; Kaye, Grendall, & Strober, 1998; Kaye, Gwirtsman, George, & Ebert, 1991; Uher et al., 2004).

Neuroimaging generally reveals decreased brain mass and enlarged sulci in patients in the acute malnourished phase of the disorder. This is thought to be an effect either directly of malnutrition or of the effect of increased cortisol on brain tissue, and seems to resolve with weight restoration. There is some question whether the grey matter mass returns completely to normal, as some studies have found continued decreased grey matter after recovery (Katzman, Kapstein, & Kirsh, 1997; Salzer, Bickman, & Lambert, 1999). SPECT studies have shown unilateral hypoperfusion in specific areas of most patients with AN—most commonly in the temporal lobe—that seems to persist after recovery. Rastam, Bjure, and Vestergren (2001) found decreased blood flow to the temporal lobe in 14 of 21 patients seven years after recovery, with no correlation between the blood flow and BMI or IQ. Chowdhury, Gordon, and Lask (2003) found unilateral hypoperfusion correlated with eating disorder psychopathology and not with BMI. Lask et al. (2006) found decreased temporal blood flow to correlate with eating disorder psychopathology and impaired executive functioning, and no correlation between blood flow and BMI, mood, or length of illness. On the three year follow up these investigators found persistent hypoperfusion in 86% associated with persistent eating disorder psychopathology and persistent cognitive impairment (visuospatial processing and memory, and cognitive inhibition) (Lask, 2006). These authors hypothesize that this unilateral hypoperfusion represents a preexisting deficit—likely either genetic or due to perinatal insult—that predisposes patients to develop AN.

Further, there are increasing data supportive of a variety of neurocognitive alterations in AN and BN subjects (Godley, Tchanturia, MacLeod, & Schmidt, 2001; Tchanturia et al., 2004; Tchanturia, Morris, Brecelj, Nikolau, & Treasure, in press; Tchanturia,

Morris, Surguladze, & Treasure, 2002; Tchanturia, Serpell, Troop, & Treasure, 2001). These include problems with attention, executive functioning, divided attention, working memory, response inhibition, and mental inflexibility. These variables, among others, are likely not only to play a role on the etiology and maintenance of AN symptoms, but also to have an impact on treatment response. Attention problems would make it difficult to participate in most psychological treatments, problems in working memory would likely inhibit insight-oriented therapies and cognitive therapies, and mental inflexibility might increase resistance to new ideas and behaviors proposed across a variety of treatments.

Studies also suggest a biological basis in genetics for AN, though the mechanism for this is unclear. Family aggregate studies suggest that AN is familial (Lilenfeld et al., 1998; Strober, Freeman, Lampert, Diamond, & Kaye, 2000) and more recent studies suggest that genetic contributions appear to account for more than 50% of the heritable risk for developing AN (Bulik, 2004; Bulik et al., 2006). The specific genetic mechanism for increasing heritability risk is still unknown but may relate to inherited vulnerabilities related to temperament and anxiety (Wagner et al., 2006).

BEHAVIORAL

There are a number of psychosocial factors related to the emergence, maintenance, or recovery from AN that complicate the course. AN often starts with dieting or exercising to lose just a little weight; very few patients start saying "I want to become anorexic." Anorexia Nervosa may start after an identifiable trigger such as being called fat by a classmate or sibling, or a loss such as death of a grandparent or parental divorce. The patient may want to lose weight for a specific occasion, such as a spring break trip or a Quinceanera. The patient may want to improve athletic performance. Over time the weight loss becomes an end in and of itself and spirals out of the patient's control. Many patients firmly believe the behavior is within their control until they try to stop, at which point they sometimes realize that their symptoms actually control them.

The stereotype of the person with AN is someone who does not eat at all, but this is usually not the case. Most people with AN restrict their intake in some form: by eating smaller portions, skipping meals, or avoiding foods they believe will make them gain weight or are unhealthy. Converting to vegetarianism in the context of dieting can be an early sign of AN. Only certain foods will be *safe* to consume and this group typically becomes smaller over time until often a patient eats the exact same thing every day. Some patients drink excessive amounts of water to control hunger, while others will consume very little water because it appears to increase their weight or makes them feel bloated. They may weigh themselves frequently and may feel the day is ruined if their weight has not decreased. Exercise is another common method of weight loss. Exercise may initially be fairly normal in quantity and quality, but often becomes obsessive. Some patients feel so compelled to exercise they will not miss a day despite illness, injury, or other engagements. The patient may feel he or she must exercise in order to be allowed to eat, or may exercise after meals to burn off the calories consumed. In some cases this is called *exercise anorexia* and the individual exercises at such a high level (training for a marathon or participation in intensive sports) that their caloric intake may be in the normal range. However, such individuals refuse to eat "unhealthy" foods and to increase calories sufficiently to achieve or maintain a healthy weight.

Patients with the binge-purge type of AN usually restrict and/or over-exercise, but they also engage in other, more harmful weight loss behaviors. They may use laxatives, diuretics, or enemas that lead to dehydration rather than true weight loss; they may abuse medications, notably diabetics on insulin. However, even the feeling of decreased weight provides temporary reassurance about the fear of weight gain. They may also vomit after eating to avoid absorbing calories, although a large portion of the calories are actually absorbed before the patient is able to vomit them up. Some patients also binge eat, but for many these are subjective binge episodes where the patient feels he or she has over eaten and feels out of control after consuming only a small amount of foods, particularly those considered "forbidden."

Patients with AN are usually extremely preoccupied with food and food preparation, a symptom that is seen with any form of starvation (Franklin, Schiele, Brozek, & Keys, 1948). They may spend hours a day tallying up calories or planning what to eat at the next meal. Some will become very interested in cooking and will cook elaborate meals for others, but will not eat the meal themselves. Others become critical of family members' "fatty" and "unhealthy" diets. This preoccupation can make it difficult to concentrate on anything else. For example, some patients report they find it difficult to pay attention in school because they are too busy planning the next day's meals and analyzing the nutritional content.

Cognitive

There are a variety of cognitive problems associated with AN, the most common of which is body image distortion. When body image distortion is present, it can be near-delusional. Some patients may recognize their overall thinness but still believe a particular body part is grossly overweight, while others see themselves as fat all over. Being told by everyone around him or her that they are actually very underweight does little to shake this belief. Patients may have other fixed beliefs such as how food is processed in the body, which also do not yield despite education and reassurance from dieticians or other knowledgeable individuals. Patients with AN typically place a very high value on thinness, making it a large part of how they define their self-worth. Some state "I'd rather be dead than fat." Hours will be spent in front of the mirror looking for any change in weight, or trying on clothes to see if they still fit. Being overweight—or even of normal weight—is equated with being ugly, disgusting, or out of control.

Denial and deception are very common features of patients with AN. Early in the disorder most patients do not want to recover, and even later on with increased insight they likely will have mixed feelings about recovery (Couturier & Lock, 2006a). Many state, "I want to get better, but I don't want to gain weight." They can be very deceptive about how much they eat and exercise and whether they vomit. This is very distressing for parents, spouses, and clinicians trying to help them, as in most instances these individuals have been particularly honest and trustworthy people and remain so in other areas of their lives not related to eating and weight. Patients employ a variety of strategies to hide how little they are eating, claiming they have already eaten with friends or at school, hiding food while at the table, discreetly disposing of food, and spreading food over the plate to make it look like more has been eaten. They may vomit while in the shower, or have the faucet running in the bathroom to cover up the noise of vomiting. Early in the disorder many patients deny trying to lose weight. They may say they are just trying to be healthier or appear mystified by their weight loss. Early teens and preadolescents commonly give nausea, abdominal pain, or just feeling full as reasons for eating less, and the weight phobia is only admitted to over the course of treatment (Couturier & Lock, 2006a). These younger patients may not be completely feigning their confusion: they may not be completely conscious of what they are doing and why (Nicholls & Bryant-Waugh, 2003).

Perfectionism is another common characteristic of patients with AN (Halmi et al., 2000). Patients with AN tend to do very well in school, not because they are more intelligent, but because they work harder than others (Bryant-Waugh & Lask, 1995). As a result of their drive and perfectionism, they often see things in all-or-nothing terms. Perfection is an impossible goal and the pursuit of it leads to lower self-esteem and a lower sense of self-efficacy (Forsberg & Lock, 2006). In the context of AN, as the patient reaches each goal weight they feel they could still lose more so they set yet another, lower, goal weight. Other common personality traits are obsessionality, a sense of ineffectiveness, rigidness, and harm-avoidance (Klump et al., 2000). A fearful, constrained temperament may be an inherited risk factor for Anorexia Nervosa. A recent study by Wagner et al. (2006) found persistent high harm avoidance, high persistence, and low self-directedness in patients with a history of AN or BN that was still evident one year or greater after recovery, indicating that these characteristics are not just results of current malnutrition, and may be premorbid risk factors associated with temperament (Wagner et al., 2006).

EMOTIONAL

Anxiety and depression are common features in AN (Godart, Flament, Perdereau, & Jeammet, 2002; Herzog, Nussbaum, & Marmor, 1996; Klump et al., 2000; Rastram, 1992). Some symptoms of anxiety and depression are a direct effect of malnutrition because as people lose weight they have less energy, are more irritable, and become more obsessive. Social withdrawal and isolation are common as the patient has less energy to go out with friends. Patients may also want to avoid social situations with food, may worry about friends commenting on their weight and eating habits, or may find that socializing interferes too much with their rigid eating and exercise routines. Thus, symptoms of depression and obsessive-compulsive disorder (OCD) that start after the onset of an eating disorder sometimes resolve with improved nutrition. However, there is evidence of increased incidence of a history of anxiety disorders—especially OCD, generalized anxiety, and social phobia in patients who develop AN (Herzog, Nussbaum, et al., 1996). Depression is less likely to predate the AN, but patients with a history of AN have a higher incidence of depression than in the general population (Herzog, Nussbaum, et al., 1996). In follow-up studies, even after recovery from the acute symptoms of AN, a significant minority continue to have anxiety and depression disorders (Herzog, Nussbaum, et al., 1996; Lock, Couturier, & Agras, 2006; Steinhausen, 2002).

INTERACTION WITH EXTERNAL AND ENVIRONMENTAL FACTORS

The impact of severe malnutrition on overall physical health is considerable. The short and long-term medical complications of AN include changes in growth hormone, hypothalamic hypogonadism, bone marrow hypoplasia, structural abnormalities of the brain, cardiac dysfunction, and gastrointestinal difficulties (Fisher et al., 1995; Rome & Ammerman, 2003). The more important medical problems for adolescents are the potential for growth retardation, pubertal delay or interruption, and peak bone mass reduction (Fisher et al., 1995). Vomiting, laxatives, diuretics, and enemas can all lead to electrolyte imbalances in the blood as well as dehydration; vomiting can also cause bleeding in the stomach or esophagus, and over time causes erosions in the tooth enamel. The mortality rates associated with AN are higher than for any other psychiatric disorder (Herzog et al., 2000). Follow-up studies of varying lengths suggest that the aggregate mortality rate is approximately 5.6% per decade (Sullivan, 1995). These findings were confirmed in a more recent 11-year follow-up study with a crude mortality rate of 5.1% (Herzog et al., 2000). The standardized mortality ratios for death and suicide in this study were substantially higher than those expected in the general population. Overall, about half the deaths were due to suicide and the remainder due to the physical complications of AN.

Sociocultural factors likely play an important factor in triggering behaviors leading to AN. Social pressures to be thin, especially in females, are considerable (Anderson-Fye & Becker, 2004; Levine & Harrison, 2004). Various media presentations of ideal beauty continue to glamorize an overly thin ideal. Silverstein, Peterson, and Perdue 1986 found that rates for AN are highest immediately after periods when the beauty ideal for women is the thinnest. Cultures that value plumpness tend to have lower rates of AN, and non-Western countries tend to have increased rates of AN after being exposed to Western media. For example, a study of ethnic Fijian adolescent girls found an increased incidence of eating disorders following novel exposure to the Western aesthetic ideal via television after it was first introduced in the mid-1990s (Becker, Burnwell, Herzog, Hamberg, & Gilman, 2002). In general, males with AN have very much the same presentation as females, although they may come to clinical attention later in the disorder because of a lower clinical index of suspicion for these problems in males. Some males are more likely to be concerned with having a low percent body fat or being very muscular, rather than low weight per se (Carlat, Camargo, & Herzog, 1997; Pope, Gruber, Choi, Olivardia, & Phillips, 1997). Although there is still less cultural pressure on males to diet in order to accomplish the thin ideal, over the eighties and nineties the male ideal has become more and more lean and muscular (Leit, Pope, & Gray, 2001; Pope, Olivardia, Gruber, & Borowiecki, 1999). Male action figures have become extremely muscular and are now just as unrealistic for a male body type as the Barbie doll is for a female body type (Pope, Olivardia, Gruber, & Borowiecki, 1999). Despite the similarities between boys and girls with AN at presentation, some data suggests that males with AN have a generally better prognosis than their female counterparts (Strober et al., 2006).

The overvaluation of this thin ideal leads to destructive weight loss behaviors in many people, but only in a relatively few instances do these concerns lead to the extreme weight loss associated with AN. Thus, it is likely an interaction between the overvaluation of the ideal of thinness with personality characteristics such as perfectionism, obsessiveness, and suppression of emotions that increases the risk that sociocultural factors will lead to AN. Parents often describe their children who develop AN as having been perfect before the onset of the disorder (i.e., compliant, high-achieving, and never having had any problems). Difficulty expressing negative feelings is thought to be a factor in the disorder; controlling one's own body is felt to be more manageable than expressing negative emotions and coping with interpersonal conflicts. Low self-esteem is another aspect of these difficulties: negative feelings about oneself become focused on weight and appearance, giving the false hope that if only one's weight were low enough the patient would feel better about him or herself.

AN emerges in some children as a reaction to puberty, with its dramatic physical, cognitive, and social changes. Crisp (1997) formulates AN specifically as a flight from the developmental challenges of adolescence related to changes in body composition, separation from parents, taking up social and sexualized gender roles, and other issues related to autonomy. The behaviors of AN effectively stifle many of these efforts and the extreme weight loss returns the body to a preadolescent state, or in younger patients forestalls that physical development altogether.

As is the case with many psychiatric disorders, major psychosocial stressors can trigger AN. The stressor can be a loss, such as the death of a much-loved grandparent or parental divorce, or a major change such as a move or starting high school or college. A history of sexual or physical abuse can be a risk factor (Neumark-Sztainer, Story, Hannan, Beuhring, & Resnick, 2000). However, triggers that initiate AN can also be more minor events, such as being teased and called fat by a sibling or peer, or being told by a well-intentioned and obesity-conscious pediatrician to lose weight. Although much emphasis is often placed on uncovering these triggers in psychotherapy for AN, their specific relationship to AN and its resolution remains unclear.

Familial attitudes about food, dieting, and appearance may affect the development of AN (Woodside et al., 2002). Families who place a high emphasis on thinness and appearance, or who view dieting as normal, can instill these values into their children perhaps putting them at higher risk for AN. Early work by Minuchin, Rosman, and Baker 1978 hypothesized that "psychosomatic families" contribute to the maintenance of the behaviors related to AN. They described these families as having rigid organization and diffuse boundaries, as being emotionally enmeshed with one another, and as avoiding expressing conflict whenever possible. The authors proposed that this constellation of behaviors made supporting individuation during the adolescent period extremely challenging and provided the family milieu for developing AN. Others suggested that AN may develop and be maintained as a way to divert attention from other, deeper difficulties within the family, such as marital tension (Selvini Palazzoli & Viaro, 1988). Bruch also believed that family dysfunction played an important role in the etiology of AN (Bruch, 1973). She described an "anorexigenic" mother who is poorly attuned to her infant's needs and feeds the child on her own schedule, not according to the infant's hunger. The infant learns not to trust her own ability to distinguish her inner states and develops a sense of ineffectiveness.

While these ideas about family dysfunction may be credible theories and clearly dominated clinical work for many years, there is only limited support for them in published research at this point (Strober & Humphrey, 1987). It is difficult to determine whether family problems are a result of coping with a severe behavioral and psychological problem such as AN, or whether these problems antedated the onset of the disorder. Given the low base rates of AN, it is unlikely that large prospective studies of families will be undertaken to clarify this question, but recent treatments that have focused more on utilizing the strengths of families—rather than pointing out their presumed liabilities—have resulted in good response rates, at least among adolescents with AN (Dare & Eisler, 1997). These results lend credence to the notion that in many cases presumed to be caused by family psychopathology that factor may not be central to the development or maintenance of AN.

Assessment

There are a variety of structured interviews and assessments available for eating disorders and AN (Alison, 1995). The Eating Disorders Examination (EDE) is a semi-structured interview lasting about one hour and is the most commonly used measure in eating disorder treatment studies (Cooper, Cooper, & Fairburn, 1989; Cooper & Fairburn, 1987). The investigator is required to ask certain key questions about eating disorder behaviors and cognitions, but is also allowed to ask additional questions to clarify a response. It is considered the gold standard in assessment of psychopathology in eating disorders; however, it takes about an hour to administer and the interviewer must have gone through thorough training to achieve adequate reliability. The EDE gives categorical data for diagnosis based on the *DSM-IV*, and continuous data for four subscales (restraint, eating concern, shape concern, and weight concern). It has two behavioral indexes (overeating and methods of extreme weight control). The EDE focuses mostly on the previous four weeks, although some questions go back three or six months as this is required to determine clinical diagnoses. It has been shown to have good reliability and good discriminant and concurrent validity. A child version (ChEDE) is available and has been found to be both reliable and valid for children ages 8–14 (Bryant-Waugh, Cooper, Taylor, & Lask, 1996). In addition, the EDE-Q is a self-report from of the EDE that is also useful because it reduces subject and assessor burden and because it can be completed in less that 15 minutes. Reports suggest that it is a reliable measure for symptom change in adolescents with eating disorders (Passi, Bryson, & Lock, 2003; Binford, Le Grange, & Jellar, 2005). Although the Schedule for Affective Disorders and Schizophrenia for School-Aged Children (6-18 years; K-SADS) is a widely used interview for detecting psychiatric disorders in children and adolescents and includes diagnosis specific impairment ratings and generates *DSM-IV* diagnoses, it does not provide sufficiently detailed evaluation of eating disorder related thoughts and behaviors needed to assess treatment response, hence the EDE is the preferred treatment outcome measure (Kaufman et al., 1997). Multiple self-report measures to assess eating disorders are available. Two of the most popular are the Eating Attitudes Test (EAT) and the Eating Disorders Inventory (EDI). The EAT consists of 40 items that employ a 6-point Likert rating scale (Garner & Garfield, 1979). The EAT-26 takes 26 of the 40 items which tend to account for most of the variance in total score, and is very highly correlated with the EAT (Garner, Olmsted, Bohr, & Garfinkel, 1982). It is easy to administer and takes less than 10 minutes. The EAT has good internal consistency and test-retest reliability (Carter & Moss, 1984), and has good concurrent and discriminant validity with other eating disorders measures (Garner, 1997). The EAT consists of seven factors: food preoccupation, body image for thinness, vomiting and laxative abuse, dieting, slow eating, clandestine eating, and perceived social pressure to gain weight.

The EDI is a 64-item measure designed to assess symptoms of AN and BN (Garner, Olmsted, & Polivy, 1983). It consists of eight subscales: drive for thinness, bulimia, body dissatisfaction, ineffectiveness, perfectionism, interpersonal distrust, interoceptive awareness, and maturity fears. It was revised in 1991 to include 27 more items and three more subscales (i.e., asceticism, impulse regulation, and social insecurity; Garner, 1991). The EDI is used as a screening measure, and to measure symptom severity and treatment outcome. It has good test-retest reliability and good concurrent validity with the EAT (Garner et al., 1982). However, the EDI is unable to discriminate well between AN, BN, and EDNOS, so it is not a good diagnostic tool. At the same time, as noted above, the boundaries between these disorders are not systematically derived. Thus, the EDI provides a clear measure of severity of eating disordered problems that is a reliable measure of symptom change regardless of diagnosis.

The Morgan-Russell assessment battery is an interviewed based assessment consisting of 5 rating scales (nutritional status, menstrual function, mental state, sexual adjustment, and socioeconomic status) based on the six month period preceding the interview (Morgan & Russell, 1988). In addition, a general outcome category is made based on weight and menstruation status alone. For a good outcome, body weight has been maintained within 15% of average weight for height and menstrual cycles are regular; for an intermediate outcome, body weight is within 15% of the average weight for height, but this has not been sustained or there are continuing menstrual disturbances; for a poor outcome, weight has remained below 15% of average weight for height and menstruation is absent. Although the Morgan-Russell Scales are the most commonly used outcome measures for AN in treatment studies, they are limited by poor interrater reliability and difficulty in applying the categories in those with primary amenorrhea, those who are taking oral steroids, and males (Freeman, Walker, & Ben-Tovim, 1996; Couturier & Lock, 25,27). Also, menstrual cycles are quite difficult to evaluate, as they are often irregular in healthy adolescents.

Interventions

A range of psychological, behavioral, and environmental treatments are used for AN. However, there are few systematic studies of treatments for AN despite the seriousness of the condition. The low base rate and medical complications/risks contribute to the difficulty of conducting randomized trials. Outpatient treatments include psychodynamic, cognitive-behavioral, and family therapy. Behavioral and nutritional treatments characterize most hospital or residential treatment regimes.

OUTPATIENT

Variants of three psychological approaches for AN have been studied in controlled outpatienttrials: individual psychodynamic psychotherapy, cognitive-behavioral therapy (CBT), and family-based therapy (FBT). The results of these studies are summarized in Table 13.1 using the Morgan-Russell Outcome Scales as an outcome wherein a good or intermediate categorical outcome was defined as having achieved normal weight or menstruation or both (Morgan & Russell, 1988). In general, the studies suggest for adolescents with AN, some type of family therapy is superior to other treatments, though most of the studies are small in scale (Le Grange & Lock, 2005; Russell, Szmukler, Dare, & Eisler, 1987). For adults with AN, the treatment studies are characterized by high drop out rates and small numbers of subjects (Halmi et al., 2005). For AN, client reluctance to even engage in treatment creates multiple issues, especially for those over 18 years old. Thus, there is little evidence to support any specific treatment approach for this population, though both CBT for relapse prevention (Pike et al., 2004) and specialist individual treatment have shown some promise (Mcintosh et al., 2005).

TABLE 13.1 Outpatient Psychotherapy Trials for Anorexia Nervosa

Study	Type of therapy	N	Age	Treatment Duration (months)	# sessions	Drop-out rate	End of Tx outcome Morgan-Russell good + intermediate
Studies of adolescent patients							
Russell, Szmukler, Dare, Eisler (1987)*	Whole family vs. individual therapy	21	16.6	6–12	13	19%	Family therapy = 90%* Individual therapy = 18%
Le Grange, Eisler, Dare, & Russell (1992)	Whole family vs. separated family therapy	18	15.3	6	9	12%	68% overall; no differences between groups
Robin et al. (1999)**	Family therapy vs. individual therapy	37	13.9	12–18	47	11%	Family therapy = 81%* Individual therapy = 66%
Eisler et al. (2000)	Whole family vs. separated family therapy	40	15.5	12	16	10%	63% overall; No differences between groups
Lock, Agras, Bryson, & Kraemer (2005)	Family treatment, 6 vs. 12 months	86	15.1	6 or 12	10 or 20 sessions	12%	No differences in outcome between groups 96% overall
Studies of adult patients							
Russell, Szmukler, Dare, & Eisler (1987)*	Family therapy vs. individual therapy	36	24.1	12	13	29%	Family = 29% Individual = 60%
Hall & Crisp (1987)	Dietary advice vs. family/individual therapy combined	30	19.6	6–12	12	17%	Psychotherapy = 46% Dietary advice = 33%
Channon, de Silva, Hemsley, & Perkins (1989)	CAT, behavior therapy and no treatment	24	22.4	6–12	24	13%	No differences between groups
Crisp et al. (1991)	Assessment, inpatient vs. outpatient psychotherapy	90	22	10	11	24%	Assessment = 0%** Inpatient = 63% Outpatient = 63%
Treasure et al. (1995)	Cognitive-analytic therapy (CAT) vs. education	30	25	5	20	33%	63% overall; no difference between groups
Dare, Eisler, Russell, Treasure, & Dodge (2001)	Focal, family, CAT or treatment as usual (TAU)	84	26.3	7–12	16	46%	Focal = 33% Family = 36% CAT = 27% TAU = 5%**

480

| Pike, Walsh, Vitousek, Wilson, & Bauer (2004) | CBT vs. nutritional counseling (NC) (for relapse prevention) | 33 | 25 | 12 | 44 (CBT) 27 (NC) | 45% | CBT = 44% NC = 7% |
| McIntosh et al. (2005) | CBT vs. IPT vs. Specialist Supportive Individual Treatment (SSIT) | 56 | 17–40 Years (no mean available) | 5 or more | More than 20 | 38% | Specialist = 56%*, CBT = 32%, IPT = 10% |

*Denotes statistically significant advantage for this approach.
**Denotes statistically significant disadvantage for this approach.

FAMILY THERAPY

In the 1970s adolescent AN became a focus of interest by structural and strategic schools of family therapy (Liebman, Minuchin, & Baker, 1974; Minuchin, Rosman, & Baker, 1978; Rosman, Minuchin, Baker, & Liebman, 1977; Selvini Palazzoli, 121,122; Selvini Palazzoli & Viaro, 1988). These approaches view the family as a system whose processes affect usual adolescent development. They emphasize the family system as a potential solution for the dilemmas of AN in the adolescent patient, stressing family process, communication, and negotiation of adolescent developmental issues. More recently, a form of family-based treatment (FBT) for AN in adolescents was developed by Dare and Eisler and has been studied in a series of randomized clinical trials (Lock, Le Grange, Agras, & Dare, 2001). In FBT, parents are empowered to restore the child's weight at home. Brief hospitalization is used only for emergencies. The first phase is aimed at assisting parents at taking charge of refeeding their adolescent with AN. This represents a significant shift from the way parents have typically been responding to the child. The second phase focuses on assisting the adolescent with taking back control of eating once healthy patterns have been re-established under parental supervision. The third phase consists of an exploration of adolescent developmental issues, particularly as they may have been affected by AN. Principle features of the approach, which make it quite different from prior family work, are an agnostic view of the cause of AN—viewing the parents as the primary agent of change, and separation of the illness from the patient (externalization). Although the majority of time is spent meeting with the family as a whole, a portion of each session is spent individually with the adolescent to ascertain their perspective on progress and to identify issues relevant to the overall family treatment.

INDIVIDUAL THERAPIES

Individual Psycho-Dynamic Therapy for AN

Derived from the psycho-dynamic tradition, individually based psychotherapy is one of the main outpatient treatment approaches for adolescent AN. As formulated by Crisp (1997), individual therapy aims to address maturational issues associated with puberty and adolescence. In two trials, Crisp and colleagues report substantial improvements in their patient groups (these included both adolescents and adults) in terms of both medical and nutritional recovery and psychological improvement (Crisp et al., 1991; Hall & Crisp, 1987). More recently, Robin et al. (1999) developed Ego-Oriented Individual Therapy (EOIT), a manualized form of individual psychodynamic therapy. EOIT, devised specifically for adolescents, posits that individuals with AN manifest deficits in self-concept and confuse control with biological needs. AN is viewed as a disruption in normal individuation processes. In order to recover, patients must develop sufficient self-efficacy to successfully separate and individuate from the family of origin.

For adults with AN, McIntosh et al. (2005) developed and evaluated a specialist supportive individual therapy (SSIT) that focuses on utilizing the therapeutic relationship, and encouraging adequate nutritional intake and weight restoration though education, support, and promoting adherence to clinical management. SSIT shares many clinical features with EOIT, except for the emphasis on adolescent development issues in the latter. However, SSIT had been originally devised as a control for nonspecifics of treatment, so it was not based on a specific theory of etiology or intervention. In the only trial reported, SSIT turned out to be superior to both CBT and interpersonal pschother-apy (IPT), raising the question of what may be the mechanism of change (McIntosh et al., 2005). A careful reading of the manual suggests that SSIT maintains a consistent focus on making behavioral changes in eating patterns within a supportive, motivation-enhancing therapeutic stance that appears to minimize patient resistance, perhaps by reducing fears of losing control over the change process. In the trial, IPT was less effective than CBT, suggesting that this less directive, client-focused approach is not a viable alternative treatment for adult AN even thought IPT had been more promising in treatment of BN, and especially Binge Eating Disorder (BED). The common element of SSIT and CBT seems to be the explicit focus on setting behavioral goals. It has been suggested that CBTs direct challenging of distorted cognitions may elicit greater client resistance in AN than it does in BN since the symptoms of AN are more ego-syntonic. If this hypothesis is supported by subsequent research, it would provide guidance to clinicians regarding differential foci of treatment of disordered eating when low weight is the primary target.

COGNITIVE-BEHAVIORAL THERAPY FOR RELAPSE PREVENTION

Cognitive-Behavioral Therapy (CBT) for AN is based on the approach originally developed by Beck for treating depression and anxiety (Beck, Rush, Shaw, & Emery, 1979). CBT was first applied to BN and was quickly established as the first line of treatment (Fairburn, 36,37). Refinements of the approach—to take into account the challenges of AN—were made by Vitousek and Pike, including addressing the ego-syntonic nature of the disorder, the interaction of physical and psychological contributions to symptoms, distorted beliefs about food and weight, and pervasive deficits in self-esteem (Garner & Bemis, 1982; Pike, Walsh, Vitousek, Wilson, & Bauer, 2000). CBT focuses on cognitive and behavioral features associated with the maintenance of eating-related pathology. It aims to reduce concerns related to eating and weight, modify beliefs about weight and food, and over time to shift the focus from the focal symptoms of AN to more general aspects of the self that may predispose the individual to AN. Initial reports are promising, but further evaluation is needed. Furthermore, CBT for AN has been studied exclusively in adults with the disorder (Pike et al., 2004; Serfaty, 1999). However, many of these are young adults, suggesting it may be applicable to older adolescents. At the current time, it appears CBT may be more useful to offer after weight restoration rather than during acute treatment, when weight regain is the primary target (Pike et al., 2004).

INPATIENT, DAY-HOSPITAL, AND RESIDENTIAL TREATMENTS

In addition to outpatient treatment approaches, more intensive treatment in hospital, day hospital, or residential programs is frequently utilized for more severe and/or chronic AN. The approaches used are usually based on behavioral principles as weight restoration is the initial goal (Jenkins, 1987). Although these treatment approaches have not been systematically investigated, they are often used for medical urgencies that develop in the context of AN due to malnutrition and as respite care for families and providers when outpatient approaches are not perceived as making adequate progress. The single review summarizing the effectiveness of inpatient and outpatient care for AN concluded that outpatient treatment in a specialist eating disorder service was as effective as inpatient treatment among those who did not warrant emergency admission (Meads, Gold, & Burls, 2001). As outpatient care is significantly less expensive than inpatient care, reliance on such care is likely to increase and, hopefully, more rigorous evaluation of these programs will be undertaken in the future (Lock, 2003; Streigel-Moore, Leslie, Petrill, Garvin, & Rosenheck, 2000).

Inpatient psychiatric treatment programs vary greatly but most involve a combination of nutritional rehabilitation, education, medical intervention, psychotherapeutic treatment, psychosocial rehabilitation, and family therapies. Longer-term residential care programs provide intensive services (24 hour programming) and stays are generally between one and two months. Objective and systematic data on the outcomes of patients treated in residential centers is not available. Reports from these proprietary programs themselves suggest that treatment promotes recovery, prevents relapse, and reduces the development of a chronic course of AN. Because of the high cost and uncertain outcomes of these programs it is important that evaluation of residential treatment for AN be undertaken (Frisch, Franko, & Herzog, 2006). Day hospital programs for AN are also available for adults and older adolescent patients (Birchell, Palmer, Waite, Gadsby, & Gatward, 2002; Gerlinghoff, Backmund, & Franzen, 1998; Robinson, 2003; Zipfel, Lowe, Deter, & Herzog, 2000). These programs usually provide services 4 to 7 days per week and include supervised meals, therapeutic groups, and individual therapy (Olmsted, 2002). Intensive outpatient programs (IOPs) are somewhat less intensive programs, such as three hours twice a week, and often serve a transitional role between hospital and outpatient care.

PSYCHOPHARMACOLOGIC

A variety of medications have been tried in treating AN (Attia, Mayer, & Killory, 2001). To date, none of them appears to be systematically useful. The use of fluoxetine has been suggested as being useful in preventing relapse after weight restoration, but more recent studies suggest that this may not be as helpful as initially believed (Kaye et al., 2001; Walsh et al., 2006). Newer antipsychotic medications may also be of use, but systematic studies are not yet available (Malina et al., 2003).

TREATMENT RECOMMENDATIONS

What is the clinician to make of the current data about treatment? It is sobering to see the paucity of research currently available to guide treatment. Fewer than 600 patients have been studied in systematic treatment trials (Le Grange & Lock, 2005). Further, there is no theoretical agreement about the best approach. For adolescents, all systematic studies have included a family treatment component. In all cases, family therapy has been as good as or better than individual treatment for this age group. Clinicians might reasonably take from this that family involvement in treatment of adolescent AN is likely to be beneficial. However, only one type of family treatment, FBT, has been systematically studied to date. This approach would appear to be the current first line approach for adolescent AN and has received tentative recommendation from several groups in this regard (Agency for Healthcare Resource and Quality, 2006; National Institute for Health and Clinical Excellence, 2004). The data supporting individual approaches for adolescent AN is quite limited (Robin et al., 1999). What data is available suggests that individual therapy could be a valuable treatment as well for adolescents, but even these individually focused therapies involve parents to support adolescent development and autonomy.

It is interesting to postulate why FBT appears to be an effective treatment for AN given the psychopathology of the disorder. First, FBT takes seriously the notion that the degree of cognitive distortion is severe in AN, enough so that trusting the patient to make judgments about appropriate care in relation to food, weight, and exercise is dubious at best. The treatment approach is responsive to the extraordinarily ego-syntonic nature of AN. Instead of expecting the patient to be motivated for recovery, FBT encourages parents to recognize that this is highly unlikely given the patient's attachment to these disordered beliefs and, therefore, initially gives the parents the responsibility to make the necessary decisions. FBT also stresses the importance of behavioral disruption of weight loss and has an explicit behavioral focus. AN is maintained, to a large degree, by these behaviors and disrupting them is seen as a key intervention. In addition, by reducing the role of professionals as intermediaries between the adolescent and AN by helping parents to make these behavioral changes at home, a major opportunity for splitting, deception, and confusion is eliminated—any of which may increase the likelihood that the patient will be able to maintain their unhealthy behaviors. It should be noted that FBT targets relatively short duration AN and recognizes the likely negative effects of long-term behavioral maintenance on the developing sense of identity increasingly aligned with AN thinking. In contrast to FBT, individual approaches rely more directly on the therapeutic relationship to develop trust so that, ultimately, the patient may decide to follow the therapist's advice to eat and gain weight as well as challenge her distorted cognitions. Unfortunately, developing a trusting relationship takes time and may not be successful, especially because of the ego-syntonic nature of AN. Both of these eventualities may limit the usefulness of individual therapy for AN. Furthermore, quick decisive intervention may prevent unhealthy behaviors from becoming more firmly entrenched, ultimately shortening the course of the disorder and reducing medical complications.

For adults with AN, the available data provides little in the way of guidance. In addition to the problem of few studies and small numbers of participants in these studies, the retention rate in adult treatment studies is less than 50% on average (Halmi et al., 2005). This compares with retention rates of 80 to 85% in adolescent AN treatment studies. Nonetheless, the two largest studies provide conflicting conclusions about what type of treatment to use for adults with AN. Dare, Eisler, Russell, Treasure, and Dodge (2001) reported that specific therapies outperformed nonspecific supportive care, while McIntosh et al. 2005 found that nonspecific treatment outperformed specific treatments. In Dare's study, nonspecific care was provided by nonspecialists and was perhaps a truer control for nonspecific treatment effects. McIntosh and colleague's SSIT introduced the specialist's experience and clinical guidance, including specific encouragement of behavior change. This formulation of therapy brings into question the purely supportive, that is nonspecific, nature of the approach. In addition, individual CBT—another specific treatment—appears to be useful, at least for relapse after weight restoration for adults with AN (Pike et al., 2004). Thus, it might be reasonably concluded that for adults with AN specialist care and specific treatments are the best current strategies, though none of the specific approaches has truly demonstrated efficacy for low weight AN in this age group.

The failure to identify any psychopharmacologic interventions for AN may seem surprising, especially as antidepressants have been useful for adults with BN (Walsh et al.,

1997). As is the case with psychotherapy research for AN, few studies, low numbers of participants, and poor retention make definitive conclusions about the usefulness of medications for AN impossible. Even in the study by Walsh and colleagues, where the authors concluded that fluoxetine was not of benefit in relapse prevention after weight restoration for adults with AN, the dropout rate was over 50% calling into question the study's conclusions because of the lack of sufficient follow-up data (Walsh et al., 2006). Instead, it may be that medications are helpful for a subset of patients with AN, while for the majority medication use is unacceptable rather than ineffective. Treatment of any type is often rejected because of the ego-syntonic nature of AN, but medications in particular tend to be refused (Halmi et al., 2005). Current enthusiasm for the possible benefit of atypical antipsychotics for AN is dampened by reports of patient refusal to take these medications for fear of weight gain—a known side effect of these mediations. Although there is not systematic evidence yet available to support the use of any medications for AN, there is reason—based on case reports—to believe that both antidepressants and atypical antipsychotics can be useful in some cases. Use of medications for the primary symptoms of AN should be considered as a second or third line approach, but should not be discounted as not useful in all cases. The use of medications to assist with extreme anxiety, severe obsessive thinking and compulsive behavior, and depression remains an important adjunctive therapy in many instances.

Discouraging as the current state is about data from treatment studies for AN, there are some clear directions for future research. For adolescent AN the priority is to establish the relative importance of family therapy, particularly FBT in relation to age appropriate individual treatments and other family therapies. Studies are currently underway to examine just these issues. In addition, studies of medication use in adolescent AN, where compliance may be less of an issue, are needed. Again, a study to examine the role of antidepressant use as an adjunct to therapy is in process.

For adults with AN, the need to develop strategies to engage and keep patients in therapy (both psychological and psychopharmacological) is the next key advance needed (Halmi et al., 2005). Until this problem is resolved, it will be difficult to mount studies to provide efficacy data because of poor retention. At the same time, smaller studies to develop innovative approaches are needed as none of our current therapies are robust even among those who stay in treatment (Agras et al., 2004). It may be necessary, particularly with adults with AN and highly resistant adolescents with AN, to address key cognitive processes prior to addressing weight gain in order to make progress. A new therapy, cognitive-remediation therapy (CRT) aimed at cognitive abnormalities in AN including overall inflexibility of thinking and extensive attention to detail (difficulties with set-shifting, perseveration, and focusing on details compromising context) is a possible candidate (Tchanturia, Morris, Surguladze, & Treasure, 2002; Holliday, Tchanturia, Landau, Collier, & Treasure, 2005; Tchanturia, Whitney, & Treasure, in press; Whitney, Easter, & Tchanturia, in press; Davies & Tchanturia, 2005). Because many potentially effective psychological treatments (e.g., CBT) depend on fundamentally intact executive cognitive functions, cognitive impairments likely have a significant negative impact on both therapeutic engagement and the usefulness of such treatments. This, in turn, may explain in part why such treatments are rejected by patients, are not as effective as they might be, or both. Preliminary data suggests that CRT is both acceptable and feasible for adults with AN while also improving general cognitive skills needed to make use of more specific psychotherapies (Davies & Tchanturia, 2005). Future treatment studies that include CRT as a pretreatment for other more behaviorally or cognitive specific treatments for AN may be a rewarding direction for treatment research (Baldock & Tchanturia, in press).

Summary and Future Directions

Anorexia Nervosa is a serious psychiatric illness that typically begins during adolescence. The disorder also appears to be on the rise in this age group. The disorder is characterized by extreme fear of fat and/or weight gain that leads to behaviors such as extreme dieting, exercising, and purging. These behaviors in turn lead to extreme malnutrition and serious medical deterioration. Genetic, social, personality, and developmental factors likely contribute to the etiology of the disorder. There are few effective treatments for the disorder, especially in adults with more chronic illness. Mortality rates related to AN are extraordinarily high for a psychiatric disorder and long-term, comorbid psychiatric disorders are a common outcome.

There are important areas for future research in all aspects of AN. Little is known about the brain functioning of these individuals and studies using newer technologies—such as functional neuroimaging—could lead to innovations in our understanding of both the etiology and treatment of the disorder. Currently, there is a critical need for more studies of treatments and the development of new treatments for AN. Such treatments need to span the range from prevention of the development of AN—through developmentally tailored approaches for adolescents—to rehabilitation, medication and cognitive interventions for adults with chronic illness.

References

Agras, W. S., Brandt, H., Bulik, C. M., Dolan-Sewell, R., Fairburn, C. G., Halmi, C. A., et al. (2004). Report of the National Institutes of Health workshop on overcoming barriers to treatment research in anorexia nervosa. *International Journal of Eating Disorders, 35,* 509–521.

Agency for Healthcare Resource and Quality. (2006). Management of Eating Disorders. In *Evidence Report/Technology Assessment* (Vol. 135) Rockville, MD: Author.

Alison, D. (1995). *Handbook of assessment methods for eating behavior and weight-related problems.* Thousand Oaks, CA: Sage.

American Psychiatric Association. (1994). *Diagnostic and statistical manual of mental disorders* (4th Ed.) Washington, DC: Author.

Anderson-Fye, E. P., & Becker, A. E. (2004). Sociocultural Aspects of Eating Disorders. In J. Thompson (Ed.), *Handbook of eating disorders and obesity* (pp. 565–589). Hoboken, NJ: Wiley.

Attia, E., Mayer, L., & Killory, E. (2001). Medication response in the treatment of patients with anorexia nervosa. *Journal of Psychiatric Practice, 7,* 157–162.

Baldock, E., & Tchanturia, K.(in press). Translating laboratory research into practice: Foundations, functions, and future of cognitive remediation therapy for anorexia nervosa. Therapy.

Beck, A., Rush, A., Shaw, B., & Emery, R. (1979). *Cognitive therapy for depression.* New York: Guilford.

Becker, A. E., Burnwell, R. G., Herzog, D. B., Hamberg, P., & Gilman, S. E. (2002). Eating behaviors and attitudes following prolonged exposure to television among ethnic Fijian adolescent girls. *British Journal of Psychiatry, 180,* 509–514.

Binford, R., Le Grange, D., & Jellar, C. (2005). EDE and adolescent bulimia nervosa: Interview or self-report? *International Journal of Eating Disorders, 37,* 44–49.

Birchell, H., Palmer, R., Waite, J., Gadsby, K., & Gatward, N. (2002). Intensive day programme treatment for severe anorexia nervosa—the Leicester experience. *Psychiatric Bulletin, 26,* 334–336.

Bruch, H. (1973). *Eating disorders: Obesity, anorexia nervosa, and the person within.* New York: Basic Books.

Bruch, H. (1978). *The golden cage: The enigma of anorexia nervosa.* Cambridge, MA: Harvard University Press.

Bryant-Waugh, R., Cooper, P., Taylor, C., & Lask, B. (1996). The use of the eating disorders examination with children: A pilot study. *International Journal of Eating Disorders, 19,* 391–397.

Bryant-Waugh, R., & Lask, B. (1995). Eating disorders in children. *Journal of Child Psychology and Psychiatry, 36,* 191–202.

Bulik, C. M. (2004). Genetic and biological risk factors. In J. Thompson (Ed.), *Handbook of eating disorders and obesity* (pp. 3–16). Hoboken, NJ: Wiley.

Bulik, C. M., Sullivan, P. F., Tozzi, F., Furberg, H., Lichtenstein, M., & Pedersen, N. (2006). Prevalence, heritability, and prospective risk factors for anorexia nervosa. *Archives of General Psychiatry, 63,* 305–312.

Cachelin, F., & Maher, B. (1998). Is amenorrhea a critical criterion for anorexia nervosa? *Journal of Psychosomatic Research, 44,* 435–440.

Carlat, D. J., Camargo, C. A., Jr., & Herzog, D. B. (1997). Eating disorders in males: A report on 135 patients. *American Journal of Psychiatry, 154* (8), 1127–1132.

Carter, P., & Moss, R. (1984). Screening for anorexia and bulimia in a college population: Problems and limitations. *Addictive Behaviors, 9,* 417–419.

Channon, S., de Silva, P., Hemsley, D., & Perkins, R. (1989). A controlled trial of cognitive-behavioural and behavioural treatment of anorexia nervosa. *Behavioral Research Therapy, 27* (5), 529–535.

Chowdhury, U., Gordon, I., & Lask, B. (2003). Early onset anorexia nervosa: Is there evidence of limbic system imbalance. *International Journal of Eating Disorders, 33,* 388–396.

Cooper, Z., Cooper, P. J., & Fairburn, C. G. (1989). The validity of the eating disorder examination and its subscales. *British Journal of Psychiatry, 154,* 807–812.

Cooper, Z., & Fairburn, C. G. (1987). The Eating Disorder Examination: A semi-structured interview for the assessment of the specific psychopathology of eating disorders. *International Journal of Eating Disorders, 6,* 1–8.

Couturier, J., & Lock, J. (2006a). Denial and minimization in adolescent anorexia nervosa. *International Journal of Eating Disorders, 39*, 175–183.

Couturier, J., & Lock, J. (2006b). What constitutes remission in adolescent anorexia nervosa: a review of various conceptualizations and a quantitative analysis. *International Journal of Eating Disorders, 39*, 175–183.

Couturier, J., & Lock, J. (2006c). What is recovery in adolescent anorexia nervosa? *International Journal of Eating Disorders, 39*, 550–555.

Crisp, A. H. (1997). Anorexia Nervosa as flight from growth: Assessment and treatment based on the model. In D. M. Garner & P. Garfinkel (Eds.), *Handbook of treatment for eating disorders* (pp. 248–277). New York: Guilford.

Crisp, A. H., Norton, K., Gowers, S., Halek, C., Bowyer, C., Yeldham, D., et al. (1991). A controlled study of the effect of therapies aimed at adolescent and family psychopathology in anorexia nervosa. *British Journal of Psychiatry, 159*, 325–333.

Dacosta, M., & Halmi, C. A. (1992). Classification of anorexia nervosa: Question of subtypes. *International Journal of Eating Disorders, 11*, 305–311.

Dare, C., & Eisler, I. (1997). Family therapy for anorexia nervosa. In D. M. Garner & P. Garfinkel (Eds.), *Handbook of treatment for eating disorders* (pp. 307–324). New York: Guilford.

Dare, C., Eisler, I., Russell, G., Treasure, J. L., & Dodge, E. (2001). Psychological therapies for adults with anorexia nervosa: Randomized controlled trial of outpatient treatments. *British Journal of Psychiatry, 178*, 216–221.

Davies, M., & Tchanturia, K. (2005). Cognitive remediation therapy as an intervention for acute anorexia nervosa: A case report. *European Eating Disorders Review, 13*, 311–316.

Eddy, K., Keel, P., Dorer, D., Delinsky, S., Franko, D., & Herzog, D. B. (2002). Longitundinal comparison of anorexia nervosa subtypes. *International Journal of Eating Disorders, 31*, 191–202.

Eisler, I., Dare, C., Hodes, M., Russell, G., Dodge, E., & Le Grange, D. (2000). Family therapy for adolescent anorexia nervosa: The results of a controlled comparison of two family interventions. *Journal of Child Psychology and Psychiatry, 41* (6), 727–736.

Fairburn, C. G. (1981). A cognitive behavioural approach to the treatment of bulimia. *Psychological Medicine, 11* (4), 707–711.

Fairburn, C. G. (1988). The current status of the psychological treatments for bulimia nervosa. *Journal of Psychosomatic Research, 32* (6), 635–645.

Fairburn, C. G., & Bohn, K. (2005). Eating disorder NOS (EDNOS): An example of the troublesome eating disorder not otherwise specified (NOS) category in DSM-IV. *Behavioral Research and Therapy, 43*, 691–701.

Fairburn, C. G., Cooper, Z., & Safran, R. (2002). Cognitive behavioral therapy for eating disorders: A "transdiagnostic" theory and treatment. *Behavioral Research and Therapy, 41*, 509–528.

Fairburn, C. G., & Harrison, P. J. (2003). *Eating Disorders. The Lancet 361*, 407–416.

Fisher, M., Golden, N. H., Katzman, D. K., Kreipe, R. E., Rees, J., Schebendach, J., et al. (1995). Eating disorders in adolescents: A background paper. *Journal of Adolescent Health, 16*, 420–437.

Forsberg, S., & Lock, J. (2006). The relationship between perfectionism, eating disorders and athletes: A review. *Journal Minerva Pediatrica, 58* (6), 525–536.

Frank, G., Kaye W. H., Meltzer C. C., Price J. C., Greer P., McConaha C., et al. (2002). Reduced 5-HT2A receptor binding after recovery from anorexia nervosa. *Biological Psychiatry, 52*, 896–906.

Franklin, J., Schiele, B., Brozek, J., & Keys, A. (1948). Observations on human behavior in experimental semistarvation and rehabilitation. *Journal of Clinical Psychology, 4*, 28–45.

Freeman, R., Walker, M., & Ben-Tovim, D. (1996). Low levels of interrater reliability in a standard measure of outcome in eating disorders (the modified Morgan-Russell Assessment Schedule). *International Journal of Eating Disorders, 20*, 51–56.

Frisch, J., Franko, D., & Herzog, D. B. (2006). Residential treatment for eating disorders. *International Journal of Eating Disorders, 39*, 434–439.

Garfinkel, P., Lin, E., Goering, P., Spegg, C., Goldbloom, D. S., &Kennedy, S. H. (1996). Should amenorrhea be necessary for the diagnosis of anorexia nervosa? Evidence from a Canadian community sample. *British Journal of Psychiatry, 168*, 500–506.

Garner, D. M. (1991). *Eating Disorder Inventory-2 manual*. Odessa, FL: Psychological Assessment Resources.

Garner, D. M. (1997). Psychoeducational principles in treatment. In D. M. Garner & P. Garfinkel (Eds.), *Handbook of treatment for eating disorders* (2nd Ed. pp. 145–177). New York: Guilford.

Garner, D. M., & Bemis, K. (1982). A cognitive-behavioral approach to the treatment of anorexia nervosa. *Cognitive Therapy and Research, 6*, 123–150.

Garner, D. M., & Garfield, P. (1979). The Eating Attitudes Test: An index of the symptoms of anorexia nervosa. *Psychological Medicine, 9*, 273–279.

Garner, D. M., Olmsted, M., Bohr, Y., & Garfinkel, P. (1982). The Eating Attitudes Test: Psychometric features and clinical correlates. *Psychological Medicine, 12*, 871–878.

Garner, D. M., Olmsted, M., & Polivy, J. (1983). Development and validation of a multidimensional eating disorder inventory for anorexia nervosa and bulimia. *International Journal of Eating Disorders, 2*, 15–34.

Malina, A., Gaskill, J., McConaha, C., Frank, G., LaVia, M., Scholar, L., et al. (2003). Olanzapine treatment of anorexia nervosa: A retrospective study. *International Journal of Eating Disorders, 33*, 234–237.

Gerlinghoff, M., Backmund, H., & Franzen, U. (1998). Evaluation of a day treatment programme for eating disorders. *European Eating Disorders Review, 6*, 96–106.

Godart, N., Flament, M., Perdereau, F., & Jeammet, P. (2002). Comorbidity between eating disorders and anxiety disorders: A review. *International Journal of Eating Disorders, 32*, 253–270.

Godley, J., Tchanturia, K., MacLeod, A., & Schmidt, U. (2001). Future directed thinking in eating disorders. *British Journal of Clinical Psychology, 40*, 281–296.

Gull, W. (1874). Anorexia nervosa (apepsia hysterica, anorexia hysterica). *Transactions of the Clinical Society of London, 7*, 222–228.

Hall, A., & Crisp, A. H. (1987). Brief psychotherapy in the treatment of anorexia nervosa: Outcome at one year. *British Journal of Psychiatry, 151*, 185–191.

Halmi, C. A., Agras, W. S., Crow, S. J., Mitchell, J., Wilson, G. T., Bryson, S., et al. (2005). Predictors of treatment acceptance and completion in anorexia nervosa: implications for future study designs. *Archives of General Psychiatry, 62*, 776–781.

Halmi, C. A., Sunday, S., Strober, M., Kaplan, A. S., Woodside, B., Fichter, M., et al. (2000). Perfectionism in anorexia nervosa: Variation by clinical subtype, obsessionality, and pathological eating behavior. *American Journal of Psychiatry, 157*, 1799–1805.

Halmi, K., Brodland, G., & Loney, J. (1973). Progress in anorexia nervosa. *Annals of Internal Medicine, 78*, 907–909.

Herzog, D. B., & Delinsky, S. (2001). *Classification of eating disorders.* Washington, DC: American Psychological Association.

Herzog, D. B., Dorer, D. J., Keel, P. K., Selwyn, S. E., Ekeblad, E. R., Flores, A. T., et al. (1999). Recovery and relapse in anorexia and bulimia nervosa: A 7.5-year follow-up study. *Journal of the American Acad-*

emy of Child & Adolescent Psychiatry, 38 (7), 829–837.

Herzog, D. B., Field, A. E., Keller, M. B., West, J. C., Robbins, W. M., Staley, J., et al. (1996). Subtyping eating disorders: is it justified? *Journal of the American Academy of Child & Adolescent Psychiatry, 35* (7), 928–936.

Herzog, D. B., Greenwood, D. N., Dorer, D. J., Flores, A. T., Ekeblad, E. R., Richards, A., et al. (2000). Mortality in eating disorders: A descriptive study. *International Journal of Eating Disorders, 28*, 20–26.

Herzog, D. B., Nussbaum, K. M., & Marmor, A. K. (1996). Comorbidity and outcome in eating disorders. *Psychiatric Clinics of North America, 19* (4), 843–859.

Hoek, H., & Hoeken, D. V. (2003). Review of prevalence and incidence of eating disorders. *International Journal of Eating Disorders, 34*, 383–396.

Hoek, H., van Harten, P. N., Hermans, K. M., Katzman, M. A., Matroos, G. E., & Susser, E. S. (2005). The incidence of anorexia nervosa on Curacao. *American Journal of Psychiatry, 162*, 748–752.

Holliday, J., Tchanturia, K., Landau, S., Collier, D., & Treasure, J. L. (2005). Is impaired set shifting an endophenotype of anorexia nervosa? *American Journal of Psychiatry, 162*, 2269–2275.

Jenkins, M. (1987). An outcome study of anorexia nervosa on an adolescent unit. *Journal of Adolescence, 10*, 71–81.

Katzman, D., Christensen, G., Young, A., & Zipursky, R. (2001). Structural abnormalities and cognitive impairment in adolescents with anorexia nervosa. *Seminars in Clinical Neuropsychiatry, 6*, 146–152.

Katzman, D., Kapstein, S., & Kirsh, C. (1997). A longitudinal magnetic resonance imaging study of brain changes in adolescents with anorexia nervosa. *Comprehensive Psychiatry, 1997*, 321–326.

Kaufman, J., Birmhaher, B., Brent, D., Rao, U., Flynn, C., Moreci, P., et al. (1997). Schedule for affective disorders and schizophrenia for school-age children—present and lifetime version (KSADS-PL): Initial reliability and validity data. *Journal of the American Academy of Child & Adolescent Psychiatry, 36*, 980–988.

Kaye, W., Strober, M., & Jimerson, D. (in press). The neurobiology of eating disorders. In D. S. Charney & E. J. Nestler (Eds.), *The neurobiology of mental illness.* New York: Oxford Press.

Kaye, W. H., Greeno, C., Moss, H., Fernstrom, J., Fernstrom, M., Lilenfeld, L., et al. (1998).

Alterations in serotonin activity and psychiatric symptoms after recovery from bulimia nervosa. *Archives of General Psychiatry, 55,* 927–935.

Kaye, W. H., Grendall, K., & Strober, M. (1998). Serotonin neuronal function and selective serotonin reuptake inhibitor treatment in anorexia nervosa. *Biological Psychiatry, 44,* 825–838.

Kaye, W. H., Gwirtsman, H. E., George, D., & Ebert, M. H. (1991). Altered serotonin activity in anorexia nervosa after long-term weight restoration. Does elevated cerebrospinal fluid 5-hydroxyindoleacetic acid level correlate with rigid and obsessive behaviors? *Archives of General Psychiatry, 48,* 556–562.

Kaye, W. H., Nagata, T., Weltzin, T., Hsu, B., Sokol, M., McConaha, C., et al. (2001). Double-blind placebo controlled administration of fluoxetine in restricting and restricting-purging type anorexia nervosa. *Biological Psychiatry, 49,* 644–652.

Klump, K., Bulik, C. M., Pollice, C., Halmi, C. A., Fichter, M., Berrettini, W., et al. (2000). Temperament and character in women with anorexia nervosa. *Journal of Nervous and Mental Disease, 188,* 559–567.

Lasègue, E. (1883). De l'anorexie hysterique. *Archives Generales De Medecine, 21,* 384–403.

Lask, B. (2006). Functional neuroimaging in early-onset anorexia nervosa. *International Journal of Eating Disorders, 37,* S49–S51.

Le Grange, D., Eisler, I., Dare, C., & Russell, G. (1992). Evaluation of family treatments in adolescent anorexia nervosa: A pilot study. *International Journal of Eating Disorders, 12* (4), 347–357.

Le Grange, D., & Lock, J. (2005). The dearth of psychological treatment studies for anorexia nervosa. *International Journal of Eating Disorders, 37,* 79–81.

Lee, S. (1995). Self-starvation in context: Towards a culturally sensitive understanding of anorexia nervosa. *Social Science Medicine, 41,* 25–36.

Leit, R., Pope, H. G., & Gray, J. (2001). Cultural expectations of muscularity in men: The evolution of the playgirl centerfolds. *International Journal of Eating Disorders, 29,* 90–93.

Levine, M., & Harrison, K. (2004). Media's role in the perpetuation and prevention of negative body image and disordered eating. In J. Thompson (Ed.), *Handbook of eating disorders and obesity* (pp. 695–717). Hoboken, NJ: Wiley.

Liebman, R., Minuchin, S., & Baker, I. (1974). An integrated treatment program for anorexia nervosa. *American Journal of Psychiatry, 131,* 432–436.

Lilenfeld, L., Kaye, W. H., Greeno, C., Merikangas, K., Plotnicov, K., Pollice, C., et al. (1998). A controlled family study of anorexia nervosa and bulimia nervosa: Psychiatric disorders in first-degree relatives and effects of proband comorbidity. *Archives of General Psychiatry, 55,* 603–610.

Lock, J. (2003). A health services perspective on anorexia nervosa. *Eating Disorders, 11,* 197–208.

Lock, J., Agras, W. S., Bryson, S., & Kraemer, H. (2005). A comparison of short- and long-term family therapy for adolescent anorexia nervosa. *Journal of the American Academy of Child and Adolescent Psychiatry, 44,* 632–639.

Lock, J., Couturier, J., & Agras, W. S. (2006). Comparison of long term outcomes in adolescents with anorexia nervosa treated with family therapy. *American Journal of Child and Adolescent Psychiatry, 45,* 666–672.

Lock, J., Le Grange, D., Agras, W. S., & Dare, C. (2001). *Treatment manual for anorexia nervosa: A family-based approach.* New York: Guildford.

Lucas, A. R., Beard, C. M., & O'Fallon, W. M. (1991). 50-year trends in the incidence of anorexia nervosa in Rochester, Minn: A population-based study. *American Journal of Psychiatry, 148,* 917–929.

Lucas, A. R., Crowson, C., O'Fallon, W. M., & Melton, L. (1999). The ups and downs of anorexia nervosa. *International Journal of Eating Disorders, 26,* 397–405.

Malina, A., Gaskill, J., McConaha, C., Frank, G., LaVia, M., Scholar, L., et al. (2003). Olanzapine treatment of anorexia nervosa: A retrospective study. *International Journal of Eating Disorders, 33,* 234–237.

McIntosh, V. W., Jordan, J., Carter, F. A., Luty, S. E., McKenzie, J. M., Bulik, C. M., et al. (2005). Three psychotherapies for anorexia nervosa: a randomized, controlled trial. *American Journal of Psychiatry, 162,* 741–747.

Meads, C., Gold, L., & Burls, A. (2001). How effective is outpatient compared to inpatient care for treatment of anorexia nervosa? A systematic review. *European Eating Disorders Review, 9,* 229–241.

Minuchin, S., Rosman, B., & Baker, I. (1978). *Psychosomatic families: Anorexia nervosa in context.* Cambridge, MA: Harvard University Press.

Morgan, H., & Russell, G. (1988). Clinical assessment of anorexia nervosa: The Morgan-Russell outcome assessment schedule. *British Journal of Psychiatry, 152,* 367–371.

National Institute for Health and Clinical Excellence. (2004). *Core interventions in the treatment and management of anorexia nervosa, bulimia nervosa, and binge eating disorder*. London: British Psychological Society.

Neumark-Sztainer, D., Story, M., Hannan, P., Beuhring, T., & Resnick, M. (2000). Disordered eating among adolescents: Associations with sexual/physical abuse and other familial/psychosocial factors. *International Journal of Eating Disorders, 28*, 249–258.

Nicholls, D., & Bryant-Waugh, R. (2003). Children and adolescents. In J. L. Treasure, U. Schmidt, & E. van Furth (Eds.), *Handbook of eating disorders* (2nd Ed., pp. 415–434). Chichester, UK: Wiley.

Nicholls, D., Chater, R., & Lask, B. (2000). Children into *DSM* don't go: A comparison of classification systems for eating disorders in childhood and adolescence. *International Journal of Eating Disorders, 28*, 317–324.

Olmsted, M. (2002). Day hospital treatment of anorexia nervosa and bulimia nervosa. In C. G. Fairburn & K. Brownell (Eds.), *Eating disorders and obesity: A comprehensive review* (pp. 330–334). New York: Guilford.

Passi, V., Bryson, S., & Lock, J. (2003). Assessment of eating disorders in adolescents with anorexia nervosa: Self-report versus interview. *International Journal of Eating Disorders, 33*, 45–54.

Pike, K., Walsh, B. T., Vitousek, K., Wilson, G. T., & Bauer, J. (2000). *Cognitive-behavioral therapy in the relapse prevention of anorexia nervosa*. Kyoto, Japan: Third International Congress of Neuropsychology.

Pike, K., Walsh, B. T., Vitousek, K., Wilson, G. T., & Bauer, J. (2004). Cognitive-behavioral therapy in the posthospitalization treatment of anorexia nervosa. *American Journal of Psychiatry, 160*, 2046–2049.

Pope, H. G., Gruber, A., Choi, P., Olivardia, R., & Phillips, K. (1997). Muscle dysphoria: An under-recognized form of body dysmorphic disorder. *Psychosomatics, 38*, 548–557.

Pope, H. G., Olivardia, R., Gruber, A., & Borowiecki, J. (1999). Evolving ideals of male body image as seen through action toys. *International Journal of Eating Disorders, 26*, 65–72.

Pryor, T., Wiedermann, M., & McGilley, B. (1996). Clinical correlates of anorexia nervosa subtypes. *International Journal of Eating Disorders, 19*, 371–379.

Rastram, M. (1992). Anorexia nervosa in 51 Swedish adolescents: Premorbid problems and comorbidity. *Journal of the American Academy of Child & Adolescent Psychiatry, 31*, 819–828.

Rastram, M., Bjure, J., & Vestergren, E. (2001). Regional cerebral blood flow in weight-restored anorexia nervosa: A preliminary study. *Developmental Medicine and Child Neurology, 43*, 239–242.

Robin, A., Siegal, P., Moye, A., Gilroy, M., Dennis, A., & Sikand, A. (1999). A controlled comparison of family versus individual therapy for adolescents with anorexia nervosa. *Journal of the American Academy of Child & Adolescent Psychiatry, 38* (12), 1482–1489.

Robinson, P. (2003). Day treatments. In J. L. Treasure, U. Schmidt, & E. van Furth (Eds.), *Handbook of eating disorders* (pp. 333–347). Hoboken, NJ: Wiley.

Rome, E., & Ammerman, S. (2003). Medical complications of eating disorders: An update. *Journal of Adolecent Health, 33*, 418–426.

Rosman, B., Minuchin, S., Baker, L., & Liebman, R. (1977). A family approach to anorexia nervosa: study, treatment and outcome. In R. A. Vigersky (Ed.), *Anorexia nervosa* (pp. 341–348). New York: Raven.

Russell, G. F., Szmukler, G. I., Dare, C., & Eisler, I. (1987). An evaluation of family therapy in anorexia nervosa and bulimia nervosa. *Archives of General Psychiatry, 44* (12), 1047–1056.

Salzer, M., Bickman, L., & Lambert, E. (1999). Dose-effect relationship in children's psychotherapy services. *Journal of Consulting & Clinical Psychology, 67*, 228–238.

Saraf, M. (1998). Holy anorexia an anorexia nervosa: Society and concept of disease. *The Pharos, 61*, 2–4.

Selvini Palazzoli, M. (1974). *Self-starvation: From the intrapsychic to the transpersonal approach*. London: Chaucer.

Selvini Palazzoli, M. (1988). *The work of Mara Selvini Palazzoli*. New Jersey: Jason Aronson.

Selvini Palazzoli, M., & Viaro, M. (1988). The anorectic process in the family: A six-stage model as a guide for individual therapy. *Family Process, 27*, 129–148.

Serfaty, M. (1999). Cognitive therapy versus dietary counselling in the outpatient treatment of anorexia nervosa. *European Eating Disorders Review, 7*, 334–350.

Silverstein, B., Peterson, B., & Perdue, L. (1986). Some correlates of the thin standard of bodily attractiveness for women. *International Journal of Eating Disorders, 5*, 895–905.

Simmonds, M. (1914). Ueber embolische Prozesse in der Hypophyis. *Archives of Pathology and Anatomy, 217*.

Steinhausen, H. (2002). The outcome of anorexia nervosa in the 20th century. *American Journal of Psychiatry, 159*, 1284–1293.

Streigel-Moore, R., Leslie, D., Petrill, S. A., Garvin, V., & Rosenheck, R. A. (2000). One-year use and cost of inpatient and outpatient services among female and male patients with an eating disorder: Evidence from a national database of health insurance claims. *International Journal of Eating Disorders, 27*, 381–389.

Strober, M., Freeman, A., Lampert, C., Diamond, J., & Kaye, W. H. (2000). Controlled family study of anorexia nervosa and bulimia nervosa: evidence of shared liability and transmission of partion syndromes. *American Journal of Psychiatry, 157*, 393–401.

Strober, M., Freeman, A., & Morrell, W. (1997). The long-term course of severe anorexia nervosa in adolescents: Survival analysis or recovery, relapse, and outcome predictors over 10–15 years in a prospective study. *International Journal of Eating Disorders, 22*, 339–360.

Strober, M., Freeman, A., & Morrell, W. (1999). Atypical anorexia nervosa: Separation from typical cases in course and outcome in a long-term prospective study. *International Journal of Eating Disorders, 25*, 135–142.

Strober, M., Freeman, R., Lampert, C., Diamond, J., Teplinsky, C., & DeAntonio, M. (2006). Are there gender differences in core symptoms, temperament, and short-term prospective outcome in anorexia nervosa. *International Journal of Eating Disorders, 39*, 570–575.

Strober, M., & Humphrey, L. (1987). Family contributions to the etiology and course of anorexia nervosa and bulimia nervosa. *Journal of Consulting and Clinical Psychology, 55*, 654–659.

Sullivan, P. F. (1995). Mortality in anorexia nervosa. *American Journal of Psychiatry, 152*, 1073–1074.

Tchanturia, K., Brecelj, M., Sanchez, P., Morris, R., Rabe-Hesketh, S., & Treasure, J. L. (2004). An examination of cognitive flexibility in eating disorders. *Journal of International Neuropsycholgoical Society, 10*, 1–8.

Tchanturia, K., Morris, R., Brecelj, M., Nikolau, V., & Treasure, J. L. (in press). Set shifting in anorexia nervosa: An examination before and after weight gain in full recovery and the relationship to childhood and adult OCDP traits. *Journal of Psychiatric Research.*

Tchanturia, K., Morris, R., Surguladze, S., & Treasure, J. L. (2002). An examination of perceptual and cognitive set shifting tasks in acute anorexia nervosa and following recovery. *Journal of Eating and Weight Disorders, 7*, 312–316.

Tchanturia, K., Serpell, L., Troop, N. A., & Treasure, J. L. (2001). Perceptual illusions in eating disorders: Right and fluctuating styles. *Journal of Behavior Therapy and Experimental Psychiatry, 32*, 107–115.

Tchanturia, K., Whitney, J., & Treasure, J. L. (in press). Can cognitive exercises help treat anorexia nervosa? *Journal of Eating and Weight Disorders.*

Thoma, H. (1967). *Anorexia nervosa.* New York: International Universities Press.

Treasure, J. L., Todd, G., Brolly, M., Tiller, J., Nehmed, A., & Denman, F. (1995). A pilot study of a randomized trial of cognitive-behavioral analytical therapy vs educational behavioral therapy for adult anorexia nervosa. *Behavioral Research and Therapy, 33*, 363–367.

Trummer, M., Eustacchio, S., Unger, F., Tillich, M., & Flaschka, G. (2002). Right hemispheric frontal lesions as a cause for anorexia nervosa report of three cases. *Acta Neurochirurgica (Wien), 144*, 797–287.

Uher, R., Murphy, T., Brammer, M., Dalgleish, T., Philllips, M., Ng, V., et al. (2004). Medial prefrontal cortex activity associated with symptom provocation in eating disorders. *American Journal of Psychiatry, 161*, 1238–1246.

Uher, R., Treasure, J. L., & Campbell, I. (2002). Neuroanatomical bases of eating disorders. In H. D'Haenen, J. den Boer, & P. Willner (Eds.), *Biological psychiatry* (pp. 1173–1180). Chichester, UK: Wiley.

van Son, G., van hoeken, D., Aad, I., Bartelds, A., van Furth, E., & Hoek, H. (2006). Time trends in the incidence of eating disorders: A primary care study in the Netherlands. *International Journal of Eating Disorders, 39*, 565–569.

Wagner, A., Barbarich-Marstellar, N., Frank, G. K., Bailer, U., Wonderlich, S., Crosby, R., et al. (2006). Personality traits after recovery from eating disorders: Do subtypes differ. *International Journal of Eating Disorders, 39*, 276–284.

Walsh, B. T., Kaplan, A. S., Attia, E., Olmsted, M., Parides, M., Carter, J., et al. (2006). Fluoxetine after weight restoration in anorexia nervosa: A randomized clinical trial. *JAMA, 295*, 2605–2612.

Walsh, B. T., Wilson, G. T., Loeb, K. L., Devlin, M. J., Pike, K. M., Roose, S. P., et al. (1997). Medication and psychotherapy in the treatment of bulimia nervosa. *American Journal of Psychiatry, 154*(4), 523–531.

Ward, A., Tiller, J., Treasure, J. L., & Russell, C. (2000). Eating disorders: Psyche or soma? *International Journal of Eating Disorders*, *27*, 279–287.

Whitney, J., Easter, A., & Tchanturia, K. (in press). Service users' feedback on cognitive training in the treatment of anorexia nervosa: a qualitative study. *International Journal of Eating Disorders*.

Woodside, B., Bulik, C. M., Halmi, C. A., Fichter, M., Kaplan, A. S., Berrettini, W., et al. (2002). Personality, perfectionism, and attitudes toward eating in parents of individuals with eating disorders. *International Journal of Eating Disorders*, *31*, 290–299.

Zipfel, S., Lowe, B., Deter, H. C., & Herzog, W. (2000). Long-term prognosis in anorexia nervosa: Lessons from a 21-year follow-up study. *Lancet*, *355*, 721–722.

Chapter 14

Alcohol Use Disorders: History, Theory, and Diagnosis

Lara A. Ray, Kent E. Hutchison, and Monika Hauser

Introduction

Alcohol use is highly prevalent in the United States as in most Western countries. As many as 90% of Americans have had some experiences with alcohol during their lives, and a great number of those have developed one or more problems related to alcohol. Alcohol use disorders constitute a frequently occurring psychiatric problem. The lifetime prevalence of Alcohol Dependence (the more severe form) is approximately 15% in the general population, whereas the point prevalence is approximately 5%—suggesting that about 5% of the adult population in the United States meets criteria for Alcohol Dependence in a single year (American Psychological Association, 1994). Alcohol Abuse, a diagnosis given in cases where alcohol use causes significant interference in one or more domains of functioning, affects approximately 4 to 5% of the adult population in the United States (Grant et al., 2004). The National Comorbidity Survey revealed that over 90% of the nationally representative sample reported consuming alcohol and 14% had a history of Alcohol Dependence (Anthony, Warner, & Kessler, 1994). The prevalence of alcohol problems is high and increasing among U.S. college students, with studies suggesting that the prevalence of binge drinking (i.e., consuming five or more drinks on a single occasion) among college students may be as high as 44% (Wechsler, Davenport, Dowdall, Moeykens, & Castillo, 1994), and that approximately 25% of U.S. college students met criteria for an Alcohol Use Disorder within the past 12 months (13.1% met criteria for Alcohol Abuse and 11.4% for Dependence) (Clements, 1999).

More recent findings from a major epidemiological study, the National Epidemiological Survey on Alcohol and Related Conditions (NESARC) conducted between 2001–2002 by the National Institute on Alcohol Abuse and Alcoholism (Dawson et al., 2005), indicated that the prevalence of *DSM-IV* Alcohol Dependence in the general population of adults in the United States was 3.8%—with a higher incidence of the disorder among males (5.4%), as compared to females (2.3%). The prevalence of alcohol use disorders also varied by age, such that individuals between the ages of 18–29 had the highest rates of *DSM-IV* Alcohol Dependence with a prevalence estimate of 9.2% compared to 3.8% for individuals between the ages of 30–44 (Grant et al., 2004). A similar finding emerged for *DSM-IV* Alcohol Abuse, where individuals aged 18–29 had the highest rates of the disorder and a prevalence rate of 7%, followed by a 6% prevalence estimate among individuals aged 30–44 (Grant et al., 2004). Importantly, according to the current diagnostic system (*DSM-IV*) the diagnosis of Alcohol Abuse is preempted by that of Alcohol Dependence such that Alcohol Abuse is only diagnosed among nondependent individuals. Recent research revealed that among individuals with a lifetime diagnosis of Alcohol Dependence, 13.9% did not additionally meet lifetime criteria for Alcohol Abuse (10.1% for men, 22.1% for women). Those individuals would have skipped the less severe stage of the disorder (Alcohol Abuse), illustrating that serious problems may develop quickly rather than being simply a gradual progression from abuse (Hasin & Grant, 2004).

Results from NESARC compared to previous epidemiological studies of alcohol use disorders suggest that while the 12-month prevalence of Alcohol Dependence declined over the past decade—from 4.4 to 3.8%—prevalence rates significantly decreased among males but remained relatively unchanged among females (Grant et al., 2004). Conversely, the 12-month prevalence rate for Alcohol Abuse increased in the last decade from 3.0% in 1991–1992 to 4.7% in 2001–2002, with a significant increase among males, females, and all age groups except 18–29 year olds (Grant et al., 2004). The decrease in the prevalence of Alcohol Dependence is consistent with a slight decline in measures of alcohol consumption (National Center for Health Statistics, 2002), but the increase in the prevalence of Alcohol Abuse remains puzzling. It is not clear if there have been changes in drinking norms or if drinking patterns associated with Alcohol Abuse may be different from those underlying Alcohol Dependence (Grant et al., 2004). Taken together, results from the most recent epidemiological study of alcohol use disorders suggest that 8.5% of the adult population in the United States suffers from an alcohol use disorder in a given year, totaling 17.6 million individuals affected by Alcohol Abuse or Dependence (Grant et al., 2004). These figures clearly underscore the significance of alcohol use disorders as an important public health concern and are corroborated by studies estimating that the economic cost of Alcohol Abuse and Dependence were 184.6 billion dollars for 1998 (when figures are available; Harwood, 1998), representing an astounding but preventable financial burden.

OVERVIEW

The purpose of this chapter is to provide a comprehensive overview of alcohol use disorders, including history, theory, and diagnosis, followed by a brief discussion of the effective treatments for Alcoholism. First, we will review the history of alcohol use disorders in the United States and across Western societies. Second, we will discuss a theoretical conceptualization of Alcoholism based on a biopsychosocial model of psychiatric disorders and will present a review of psychosocial and biological factors thought to influence the etiology of Alcohol Abuse and Dependence. Third, we will review diagnostic considerations including research and clinical questions as the field prepares for *DMS-V*. Finally, we will briefly discuss empirically supported treatment approaches for alcohol use disorders, including psychosocial and pharmacological interventions.

History

ALCOHOL USE DISORDERS IN THE UNITED STATES

Even after the legalization of alcohol in the United States in the mid-1930s, societal and political views on alcohol consumption have varied considerably throughout the years. After the drug-friendly culture of the 1960s and early 1970s, the end of the 20th century saw increased public concern with heavy alcohol and drug use, and underage drinking (McCrady, 2001). The drinking age was increased to 21 again, after it had been lowered to 18 during the Vietnam War era, and the government started increasing their efforts to stop illegal alcohol and drug use. But not only was the government concerned about underage drinking, increased deaths from drunk driving received increased public attention. Groups such as Mothers against Drunk Driving helped promote stricter drunk driving laws. Moreover, news covering stories about binge drinking and deaths resulting from alcohol on college campuses have received increased attention for several years now, and the implementation of programs to stop underage drinking is a major priority and concern for most colleges in the United States (McCrady, 2001). It appears that society has taken two opposing approaches to deal with alcohol use: a conservative attitude that promotes more punishment for irresponsible alcohol use (especially any alcohol use for underage individuals), and a more liberal approach that focuses primarily on reducing the harm that may be caused by alcohol use.

As much as the perspectives on alcohol use have shifted throughout the years, the treatment modalities for alcohol use disorders have likewise changed. Until the mid-1930s individuals who did not have the financial means to pay for inpatient treatment at a private hospital were forced to use state hospitals, rescue missions, jails, the Salvation Army, or public ministries. Alcoholics Anonymous (AA), which was founded in 1935 by two alcohol dependent individuals—Bill Wilson, a stock speculator, and Dr. Bob Smith, a medical doctor—provided the first community-based approach to supporting the recovery of alcohol dependent individuals regardless of their financial status by offering free peer-delivered group treatment to all comers. For many years, AA has been one of the few outpatient treatment approaches individuals could turn to for help with alcohol problems. In addition, AA was also the first approach to combine religion, medicine, and the help of sponsors (individuals with a history of recovery from alcohol problems who were committed to helping others stay sober). AA has since become a well-known and highly utilized organization with over 100,000 groups in over 150 countries, with approximately 2 million members world wide (Alcoholics Anonymous, 2006). From the perspective of psychology, AA and other self-help groups that were developed following the AA model (e.g., Narcotics Anonymous, Cocaine Anonymous) have been criticized for their emphasis on the individuals' powerlessness over addiction, and for the spiritual focus of their Twelve-Step-Program. As a response to these criticisms, alternative self-help groups have evolved that are based on more rational and humanistic approaches. Abstinence-based programs such as the Self-Management and Recovery Training (SMART) and self-help groups emphasizing moderation in drinking (e.g., Moderation Management; MM) promote the use of cognitive-behavioral principles within a self-help environment to help individuals achieve desired outcomes. One of the best known of these alternative self-help programs is Rational Recovery (RR; Trimpey, 1992). Rational Recovery emphasizes self-empowerment and one's ability to replace harmful behaviors with healthier choices. The process of achieving sobriety using the Rational Recovery framework involves education and awareness, and the recognition of instances when the old brain (i.e., the addicted part of the brain) may try to tempt the new brain. Currently, research evaluating the effectiveness of RR is based primarily on self-reports about the patients' sobriety without research evidence from randomized controlled trials, which have recently become available for Twelve-Step Facilitation (Project MATCH Research Group, 1997). Nevertheless, results suggest that RR may be comparable to AA (Galanter, Egelko, & Edwards, 1993) and, thus, constitute a viable self-help alternative. There is, however, little research investigating other variables important in understanding the effectiveness of self-help treatment, such as defensiveness, resistance to recovery, and denial (Schmidt, Carns, & Chandler, 2001). Because of its low cost and accessibility, self-help is likely to remain a core element of treatment and more research is needed to evaluate the effectiveness of self-help programs using objective measures, as well as multiple outcome variables.

Throughout the past 20 years, treatment of alcohol use disorders evolved primarily from two approaches: rehabilitation and harm reduction. Examples of the rehabilitative approach are employee assistance programs (EAP) or education classes for individuals who have been convicted of drunk driving or other alcohol offenses (e.g., underage drinking). Rehabilitative programs are based on the belief that treatment is a better alternative to punishment, and that treatment will increase one's chances of returning to one's baseline of productive functioning in society (McCrady, 2001). Conversely, harm reduction models are based on the belief that human beings will continue to engage in behaviors that are potentially dangerous. In addition to emphasizing the reduction of alcohol intake, the goal of these models is to minimize harm by providing individuals with safer ways to engage in such risky behaviors (e.g., designated drivers). Individuals are encouraged to make changes in their use of alcohol that do not have to be as radical as complete and sustained abstinence. Controlled drinking, for example, is one approach thought to promote a decrease in risky alcohol use behaviors and, as a result, a decrease in the negative consequences of drinking. Although the harm reduction model remains widely debated, there is a great deal of research supporting its effectiveness and efficacy in the treatment *and* prevention of alcohol problems (Witkiewitz & Marlatt, 2006).

The issue of abstinence versus moderation as alternative treatment goals remains a highly debated topic. The more traditional approach contends that abstinence is the only acceptable goal given the progressive nature of Alcohol Dependence. Abstinence remains the most standard clinical practice for Alcoholism treatment in the United States. Conversely, drinking moderation has been introduced as an alternative to abstinence in which patients are taught how to moderate their use of alcohol. This approach has been better accepted as an alternative for the treatment of Alcohol Abuse, but it is often criticized when suggested as an option for treating Alcohol Dependence. The empirical findings suggest that having clients select their treatment goals (i.e., abstinence versus controlled drinking) may increase compliance and improve outcomes (Ojehegan &

Berlund, 1989; Oxford & Keddie, 1986). Hc
of abstinence as a preferred treatment goal (Mc
selecting moderation as a goal may reinforce a
important to their functioning and therefore shc
Interestingly, recent research has found that the
predicted outcome in a moderation-oriented tr
higher on impaired control were less likely to
ment program at six-month follow-up (Heather
drinking was found to be more appropriate fc
levels of dependence and withdrawal, have a h
tion, have no medical or psychological probler
drinking, and do not have a family history pos

These findings are consistent with the clinical impression that moderation-oriented approaches may be appropriate for individuals with overall lower levels of Alcohol Dependence. As noted by McCrady (2001), clinicians should consider any initial drinking
goal (abstinence or moderation) as tentative, such that goals need to be reevaluated during the course of therapy. To that end, clients who are not succeeding in their efforts to
drink in moderation need to reconsider their drinking goal and reevaluate the extent of
their alcohol problems. Such clients may not be able to recover from alcohol addiction
without embracing abstinence as their goal.

The diagnosis of alcohol use disorders has changed significantly over the years,
which has been reflected in the various editions of the *DSM*. In the *first* edition of the
Diagnostic and Statistical Manual of Mental Disorders (*DSM-I*) (American Psychiatric
Association, 1952) Alcoholism was classified as a Personality Disorder, reflecting the
notion that Alcoholism stemmed from an addictive personality. More than 20 years
later, Edward and Gross (1976) published a very influential paper describing Alcohol
Dependence Syndrome (ADS), which led to a major shift in the way substance use disorders were conceptualized. Specifically, Edwards and Gross (1976) emphasized the
salience that a given substance of abuse was occupying in a person's life, thereby expanding the concept of dependence to various substances—many of which did not have
clinically relevant withdrawal syndromes or tolerance (e.g., cannabis). As a result, the
diagnosis of alcohol problems in the third edition of the *Diagnostic and Statistical Manual of Mental Disorders* (*DSM-III*) (APA, 1980) was based heavily on this notion that
multiple substances of abuse could lead to a dependence syndrome based on their impact on one's life and functioning. Importantly, up until *DSM-II* only diagnostic labels
and brief descriptions of the major illnesses had been provided. It was not until *DSM-III*
that specific diagnostic criteria were provided for substance use disorders, an approach
which found rapid acceptance in the United States and internationally (Hasin et al.,
2003). The use of specific diagnostic criteria in *DSM-III* was predated and heavily influenced by the Feighner Diagnostic Criteria (Feighner et al., 1972) for Alcohol Dependence, which was developed mainly for research purposes. An important change
implemented in *DSM-III* was the distinction between abuse and dependence. According
to *DSM-III*, Alcohol Abuse was characterized by a pattern of pathological alcohol use,
impairment in social or occupational functioning, and duration of disturbance of at
least one month. *DSM-III-R* (APA, 1987) and *DSM-IV* (APA, 1994) expanded the characterization of Alcohol Abuse by providing a more concrete operational definition
of the abuse criteria, which in turn increased the reliability of the Alcohol Abuse
diagnosis.

lcohol Dependence required that either the tolerance or withdrawal cri-
en met. However, in *DSM-III-R* these were no longer a necessary require-
e diagnosis of Alcohol Dependence. Furthermore, *DSM-III-R* established a
e criterion, quantifying the increase in the amount of drinking necessary to
ve a level of intoxication or desired effect—intake must be at least 50% higher
n baseline levels of use to demonstrate tolerance. However, *DSM-IV* dropped that
concept and suggested that tolerance needed to be established on a case-by-case basis.
The *DSM-IV* expanded on the *DSM-III-R* definition for tolerance by introducing the
concept that a casual user's behavior could be impaired with the same level of blood
alcohol at which an individual with Alcohol Dependence might function adequately. In
summary, the changes in the definition of Alcohol Abuse and Dependence across versions of the *DSM* over the years highlight the history of alcohol use disorders conceptualization and reflect societal views of alcohol use. Specifically, the field started with a
conceptualization of Alcohol Dependence that was largely based on personality traits
and the idea of an addictive personality, but has evolved into the current conceptualization of Alcohol Dependence that emphasizes the interplay between biological and psychological processes leading to significant impairments in functioning as a result of
excessive alcohol use.

ALCOHOL USE DISORDERS CROSS-CULTURALLY

Many studies have examined differences in alcohol use and misuse cross-culturally.
Although most of the literature is limited to simple descriptions of alcohol use patterns
in different cultures, these studies highlight the importance of examining cultural factors
influencing alcohol use and, ultimately, alcohol pathology. Cross-cultural comparisons
of drinking behaviors typically describe cultural factors that could account for the observed differences in drinking patterns across cultures. For example, a comparison of
drinking habits between Finish and Canadian samples found a higher prevalence of
binge drinking in Finish men (Cunningham & Makela, 2003). The authors discussed
these observed differences in the context of the cultural view of alcohol as an intoxicant
in Finland, a society in which there is a higher cultural acceptance of drunkenness
(Cunningham & Makela, 2003). A study comparing alcohol problems in Germany and
the United States found that at matched drinking levels more Americans reported
alcohol-related problems as compared to Germans. The authors hypothesized that those
differences in problem endorsement may reflect greater cultural ambivalence about the
use of alcohol in the United States (Bloomfield, Greenfield, Kraus, & Augustin, 2002).

Cross-cultural studies of alcohol use among adolescents have highlighted important
cultural factors influencing the initiation and maintenance of alcohol use, as well as the
development of alcohol-related problems. A recent study comparing alcohol use among
adolescents in the United States and Puerto Rico found higher rates of alcohol use
among United States youth (Warner et al., 2001). Interestingly, there were also significant differences in the symptoms endorsed, such that youth from Puerto Rico were more
likely to report "failure to fulfill obligations." The authors hypothesized that these findings may reflect differences in familial attachment between the two cultures (Warner,
Canino, & Colön, 2001). A larger study examining alcohol use among 15-year-olds in
22 European and North American countries found significant geographical differences
in adolescent drinking patterns, with higher drinking levels in the Nordic countries
(Schmid et al., 2003). It was hypothesized that geographical location served as a proxy

for drinking culture. The authors also noted that gender differences in alcohol use were higher in male-dominated drinking cultures, marked by more classic gender roles (Schmid et al., 2003). Interestingly, analyses of a multicultural sample of adolescents in the United States suggested that *DSM-IV* symptom endorsement patterns and the diagnosis of alcohol use disorders varied as a function of ethnicity and gender (Wagner, Lloyd, & Gil, 2002). Results from NESARC revealed stable high-risk subgroups for alcohol use disorders, which included: Whites, Native Americans, and males (Grant et al., 2004). Young adult Asian American males also showed a sharp increase in prevalence rates for alcohol use disorders, a group that has traditionally not received much attention as being at elevated risk. Based on the results of this large epidemiological study of alcohol use disorders, Grant and colleagues (2004) argued for new prevention programs designed with the observed gender and racial-ethnic differences in mind, as well as early prevention efforts for youth.

Cross-cultural differences in the relationship between alcohol use and gender are well documented in the literature (de Lima, Dunn, Novo, Tomasi, & Reisser, 2003; Schmid et al., 2003; Wilsnack, Vogeltanz, Wilsnack, & Harris, 2000). Wilsnack and colleagues (2000), reporting on data from the International Research Group on Gender and Alcohol, examined gender differences in 10 countries. The main findings were that women and men differed little in the likelihood of current drinking versus abstaining, but men reported significantly higher drinking frequencies, quantities, and rates of heavy drinking. The authors proposed that gender roles may magnify biological differences in pharmacological responses to alcohol and that gender differences in drinking may be impacted by culturally bound constructs such as gender roles (Wilsnack et al., 2000). In short, these findings underscore the complex nature of the relationship between cultural factors and alcohol use.

Although most cross-cultural studies have focused on comparing alcohol use among various cultures and nations, a few studies have examined moderators and mediators of the effects of culture on alcohol use and abuse. Studies have focused primarily on examining beliefs about the use and effects of alcohol in various cultures. In attempting to capture belief systems and "drinking cultures," a number of typologies for cultural views of drinking have been proposed. Those typologies include distinctions between "wet" and "dry" cultures, where the primary factor is whether or not alcohol use is integrated into daily life—for example, acceptance of having wine with meals. This typology refers primarily to European societies, especially those in Mediterranean cultures (Room, 1998). Another model proposed by Partanen (1991) consists of a two-dimensional typology with the following two axes: (1) engagement with alcohol, and (2) serious drinking. According to this typology, cultural views of alcohol should be analyzed in both domains. An additional typology for alcohol culture is Levine's distinction between temperance and non-temperance cultures (Levine, 1992). The distinction is based on both religion (temperance cultures are mostly Protestant) and societal position towards alcohol (e.g., temperance cultures are highly concerned about alcohol misuse and are often active in combating alcoholism). Studies have found that temperance cultures consume less alcohol and have more AA groups (Peele, 1993, 1997).

Finally, a few studies have attempted to understand cultural factors associated with alcohol use by examining cognitive factors, such as alcohol expectancies, (Lindman, Sjoholm, & Land, 2000) and other cultural factors, such as the role of the family (Bjarnason et al., 2003; Johnson & Johnson, 1999). Regarding alcohol expectancies, results from a large cross-cultural comparison revealed that expectations of increased positive affect when drinking were influenced by culture, in addition to the direct pharmacological effects of alcohol (Lindman et al., 2000). Furthermore, cross-cultural studies of the family system and adolescent alcohol use revealed that the adverse effects of living in a nonintact family on drinking behaviors were greater in societies with higher alcohol availability and where adolescent heavy drinking was more common (Bjarnason et al., 2003). These results are consistent with the hypothesized role of the family in influencing the negative meaning of alcohol, which in turn is thought to delay the initiation of drinking and reduce alcohol use (Johnson & Johnson, 1999). In summary, most cross-cultural studies to date have focused on comparing drinking patterns and alcohol misuse cross-culturally, while a few studies have begun to examine factors that mediate or moderate the relationship between culture and alcohol use. These efforts represent an important step towards increasing our understanding of the role of cultural factors in the initiation, progression, and maintenance of alcohol use and abuse.

Theory

Theory refers to a conceptualization of a phenomenon of interest. It represents an attempt to capture and summarize the empirical findings into a cohesive set of rules that can in turn be used to generate hypotheses. Theories may vary widely in scope (e.g., broad versus narrow) and focus (e.g., focus on the social bases of behavior versus focus on biological processes). In contemporary psychology theories have become increasingly circumscribed. Nevertheless, theories are essential to fulfill the scientific purpose of "connecting empirical relations with statements of mechanisms and processes" (Kazdin, 2002, p. 127). In short, we want to make sense of the world by understanding the *why* and *how* of phenomena and theories represent our attempts to do so.

The overarching framework adopted throughout this chapter for examining specific theories about factors influencing the development and maintenance of alcohol use disorders is a *biopsychosocial model* of psychiatric disorders. Specifically, the biopsychosocial model applied to alcohol use disorders posits that the etiology of Alcoholism represents a complex interplay between *psychosocial* (e.g., cognitions, personality traits, and environmental variables such as peer groups and norms) and *biological* (e.g., genetics and neurobiology) factors. We will next present a discussion of important psychosocial and biological factors thought to influence the development and maintenance of alcohol use disorders, and will do so by working with the premise that these factors interplay in the development of the complex and heterogeneous phenomenon known as alcohol use disorders. As with all complex diseases, Alcoholism can be thought of as a clinical outcome resulting from a combination of many risk factors, both biological and psychosocial in nature. Importantly, the alcohol-dependent population represents a spectrum of individuals arriving at the diagnosis through diverse pathways and displaying different sets of symptoms.

PSYCHOSOCIAL FACTORS

In recent years, a number of psychological theories of alcohol use and abuse have been developed by focusing on specific factors relevant to alcohol use and Alcoholism. These theoretical frameworks represent attempts to conceptualize the phenomenon of alcohol use disorders and to explain why some individuals become dependent on alcohol and by which mechanisms (i.e., how). It has become increasingly clear that individuals may develop alcohol-related problems by different mechanisms resulting from a complex interaction among multiple, and often interrelated, causal factors. In this section we discuss some of the more widely researched psychosocial factors and their related theories. These conceptual models examine the complex pathways to alcohol use disorders from diverse vantage points, which in turn further highlight the phenotypic complexity of addictive behaviors.

Expectancy theory provides an explanation for a broad range of psychological phenomena, and it is often used to integrate psychological processes with their underlying biological mechanisms. Expectancy refers to processes within the nervous system that use neurobiological and cognitive residues of previous experience to guide future behavior. It is thought that the activation of an expectancy template can directly initiate a behavioral sequence previously associated with a recognized stimulus. Such a template can directly activate an affective experience. In a more indirect fashion, activation of expectancy can elicit a behavior that is associated with, or results from, the activation of an affective state. For example, persons may become more socially outgoing because they are affectively aroused.

The cognitive processes associated with expectancies are theorized to influence all behaviors and have been applied to understanding drinking and Alcohol Dependence (Brown, Goldman, Inn, & Anderson, 1980; Del Boca, Darkes, Goldman, & Smith, 2002). In this application, information that reflects the reinforcement value of alcohol acquired as a function of biological, psychological, or environmental risk variables is viewed as being stored as memory templates (Goldman & Darkes, 2004). The memory systems that retain this information are conceptualized as a kind of information-based buffer. Once acquired, these templates have the capacity to influence alcohol use and its associated behavioral patterns over widely varying periods of time. In short, alcohol expectancy refers to information that reflects the reinforcement value of alcohol, is stored as memory templates, and can influence alcohol use.

Although most research has focused on alcohol expectancies as moderators of drinking risk, some theorists argue that alcohol expectancies may serve as a mediator of alcohol use risk (Goldman, Del Boca, & Darkes, 1999). Expectancy theory is one of the most widely researched and empirically supported psychological theories of alcohol misuse. Results have largely and consistently supported an association between alcohol expectancies and drinking behaviors, such that higher positive expectancies regarding the effects of alcohol are strong predictors of heavier alcohol use. Importantly, expectancy theory has often been integrated into models that take into account additional risk factors for alcohol misuse such as personality constructs and genetic factors (Del Boca et al., 2002; Schuckit et al., 2006). Recent work using functional magnetic resonance imaging (fMRI) has suggested that decreased inhibitory neural processing may be associated with more positive and less negative alcohol outcome expectancies (Anderson, Schweinsburg, Paulus, Brown, & Tapert, 2005). In conclusion, expectancy theory represents an advanced cognitive model of alcohol use with strong empirical support from a wide array of research methodologies. Expectancies represent information processing systems that are proximally related to alcohol use patterns and capture the incentive value of drinking, which in turn is best conceptualized as a dynamic and unfolding process.

The central tenet of the *tension-reduction theory* of alcohol use is the assertion that individuals drink alcohol because of its ability to reduce tension. This theory was initially influenced by the drive reduction theory of the 1940s (Hull, 1943), which emphasized motivational aspects underlying drinking. Although there is significant intuitive appeal to the notion that individuals drink to reduce tension, an early review by Cappell and Herman (1972) suggested that empirical support for the theory was limited. A related theory was developed in the 1980s, which focused on the stress-response dampening (SRD) effects of alcohol (Levenson, Sher, Grossman, Newman, & Newlin, 1980; Sher & Levenson, 1982). The stress-response dampening model (SRD) focused on refining the operational definition and laboratory manipulation of stressors (e.g., electric shock, public speaking task) and examining individual differences in the stress-response dampening effects of alcohol, making it a more focused and testable theory (Greeley & Oei, 1999). As stated by Greeley & Oei (1999) in reviewing the empirical support for the tension reduction theory, "the general consensus has been that alcohol, at certain dosages, is capable of reducing some signs of tension in some humans, under certain contextual conditions" (p. 23).

More recent work on the tension-reduction model and related theories emphasizes understanding the pharmacological and neurobiological mechanisms by which alcohol may dampen a stress-response as well as the individual and contextual differences that may moderate those effects. Examples of such moderators include hostility (Zeichner, Giancola, & Allen, 1995), anxiety sensitivity (Stewart, Karp, Pihl, & Petterson, 1997), gender (Sinha, Robinson, & O'Malley, 1998), and the type of social situation (Armeli et al., 2003) or life stressor (Hart & Fazaa, 2004). In short, the tension-reduction theory and its most widely researched offshoot, the stress-response dampening model, identify alcohol's ability to reduce tension and stress-reactivity as central to the motivation to drink and the development of alcohol-related problems. Recent work on these theories has focused on understanding the pharmacological mechanisms by which alcohol may reduce tension and on describing potential moderators of a heightened stress-dampening response.

Personality theory has been applied to alcohol use disorders for many years. The notion that personality played a causal role in Alcoholism had so much intuitive appeal that many past studies sought to identify the alleged "alcoholic personality." As noted earlier, Alcoholism was classified as a personality disorder in the first edition of the *DSM*. Over the past five decades, researchers have shown that although personality traits may account for some of the variance in vulnerability to alcohol use disorders, personality characteristics are not necessarily a core component of the disorder and there is clearly not a specific personality dimension that can reliably predict Alcoholism (Sher, Trull, Bartholow, & Vieth, 1999).

Recent research has focused on the role of personality in the etiology of alcohol use disorders, and in establishing a causal link between personality traits and the development of alcohol pathology. In addition, personality characteristics have been used to identify possible subtypes of Alcohol Dependence. For example, Cloninger's (1987) model of type 1 and type 2 alcoholics suggests that the first group is marked by an early onset of Alcoholism and by antisocial personality traits while the later group is characterized by a late onset of problems and a tendency towards negative emotionality. A related typology was proposed by Babor (1996) who recommended parsing out the Alcohol Dependence phenotype into either type A or type B. The type A alcohol dependent cluster is characterized by later onset, fewer childhood risk factors, less severe dependence, fewer alcohol-related problems, and less psychopathological dysfunction, whereas the type B cluster is characterized by childhood risk factors, familial alcoholism, early onset of alcohol-related problems, greater severity of dependence, polydrug use, a more chronic treatment history, greater psychopathological dysfunction, and more life stress (Babor et al., 1992). Results from a randomized clinical trial based on the A and B typology found that type A alcoholics did better in group psychotherapy and more poorly with coping skills training, whereas type B alcoholics had better outcomes with the coping skills treatment and did worse with interactional group therapy; these results maintained at two year follow-up (Litt, Babor, DelBoca, Kadden, & Cooney, 1992). A recent review of the clinical subtyping of alcohol use disorders found mixed results in terms of construct, concurrent, and predictive validity of these classifications and concluded that further research is needed before these typologies could be useful in clinical practice (Babor & Caetano, 2006).

In addition to the clinical subtypes developed largely on the basis of personality characteristics, several studies to date have suggested a relationship—at times causal in nature—between certain personality traits and Alcoholism. The personality dimension of impulsivity/disinhibition, which includes traits such as impulsivity and sensation/experience seeking, appears to be the one most relevant to one's risk for developing Alcoholism (Finn, Earleywine, & Pihl, 1992). As proposed by Sher et al. (1999), personality traits may be most informative in terms of elucidating the etiology of Alcoholism. In order to reach this ultimate goal, personality researchers in the addictions field have begun to integrate personality constructs with parallel lines of research on behavioral genetics, stress and coping, pharmacological responses to alcohol, and developmental theories.

Social learning theory (SLT) emphasizes learning from social environments and cognitions as important determinants of behavior. SLT is a general theory of human behavior whose most notable proponent is Albert Bandura (1977, 1986). Social learning theory has heavily influenced the cognitive-behavioral approach to alcohol use disorders (Dimeff & Marlatt, 1995; Marlatt & Gordon, 1985). Applying SLT to the study of Alcoholism often entails focusing on three aspects of behavior: social-environmental, coping skills, and cognitive factors (Maisto, Carey, & Bradizza, 1999).

Social environmental variables include focusing on situational factors that may be associated (i.e., paired) with alcohol use; these are generally conceptualized as triggers. Coping skills, in turn, focuses on the patient's ability to cope with stressful events without reverting to the use of alcohol. This approach has been emphasized in cognitive-behavioral interventions for Alcoholism that focus on skills building—such as drinking refusal skills, coping with urges, and coping with negative thoughts and feelings. SLT also highlights two cognitive factors thought to be relevant for the development and maintenance of alcoholism: self-efficacy and outcome expectancies. Self-efficacy refers to one's belief in one's ability to enact a given behavior or obtain a certain outcome. Abstinence self-efficacy has been found to be a strong predictor of treatment outcome for alcohol use disorders (Ilgen, McKellar, Tiet, 2005). Alcohol expectancies—which refer to one's beliefs about the consequences of alcohol use—have received extensive empirical support for their role in alcohol use disorders (for details, see the previous section on expectancy theory).

One important application of SLT has been the conceptualization of the relapse process (Marlatt & Gordon, 1985). In brief, this model conceptualizes lapses as resulting from the patient's lack of skills for coping with high risk situations, which in turn leads to low levels of self-efficacy beliefs about his or her ability to cope with stressful situations, and expectancies that alcohol use would help them cope effectively with situations in the future. Relapse represents an important theoretical and clinical issue in alcohol use disorders. Recent research on relapse has attempted to develop multivariate models that can account for both distal and proximal factors likely to influence the relapse process in order to capture its complex nature. For example, distal factors found to predict relapse include less active coping efforts, lower self-efficacy, higher craving, and lower participation in self-help groups and treatment (McKay, Franklin, Patapis, & Lynch, 2006). Proximal factors, in turn, seek to identify personal characteristics and experiences that are likely to trigger a particular relapse episode. The understanding of proximal factors in relapse has been improved by recent advances in assessment methods, such as ecological momentary assessment (EMA), which allow for near real-time assessments of the circumstances surrounding a relapse episode. Studies of proximal relapse factors using EMA suggested that greater anxiety predicted higher alcohol use later in the day, especially among men (Swendsen et al., 2000). For an in-depth review of the relapse literature see Maisto and Connors (2006) and the special issue of *Clinical Psychology Review* (volume 26, issue 2). In short, SLT emphasizes social environments, coping skills, and cognitions as important determinants of behavior and SLT concepts have been widely applied to the current cognitive behavioral conceptualization and related treatment models for alcohol use disorders.

BIOLOGICAL FACTORS

As noted previously, Alcohol Dependence is a complex disorder resulting from the interplay between biological and psychosocial factors (for reviews on the neurobiology of addiction see Volkow & Li, 2005; Kalivas & Volkow, 2005). While several neurotransmitter systems are activated by alcohol administration, initial models in the literature focused on the role of mesolimbic dopamine and the stimulatory and reinforcing effects of alcohol (Samson & Harris, 1992; Littleton & Little, 1994). Both alcohol consumption and alcohol cue exposure prior to drinking increase dopamine activity in the nucleus accumbens (NAC), suggesting that prior learning and anticipation of reinforcement activates a dopamine response that is isomorphic to the effect of alcohol on mesolimbic dopamine activation (Weiss, Lorang, Bloom, & Koob, 1993). An important question that has only been partially answered is how alcohol might influence mesolimbic dopamine activity. Some researchers have suggested that the consumption of alcohol triggers the release of endogenous opiates, which in turn may mediate mesolimbic dopamine activity (Volpicelli, Pettinati, McLellan, & O'Brien, 2001; Gianoulakis, 1993; Gianoulakis, de Waele, & Thavundayil, 1996; Schuckit & Smith, 1996). The release of endogenous opiates is also thought to inhibit gamma-aminobutyric acid (GABA) interneurons that subsequently release dopaminergic neurons from inhibition (Kalivas & Stewart, 1991). This notion is consistent with a study demonstrating that the administration of ethanol increased dopamine activity in the NAC, and that naltrexone—a μ-opiate receptor antagonist—reduced dopaminergic activity in the NAC (Benjamin, Grant, & Pohorecky, 1993). In conjunction, these studies highlight the multiple neurotransmitter systems underlying the pharmacological and behavioral effects of alcohol.

One of the early theories regarding biological mechanisms that influence the development of Alcohol Dependence was the *psychostimulant theory of addiction*. According to the psychomotor stimulant theory of addictions, substances with high abuse potential—including alcohol—have the ability to produce psychomotor stimulation. This theory proposes that the stimulatory and rewarding effects of a vast range of addictive substances share an underlying biological mechanism (Wise & Bozarth, 1987). Consequently, individuals who experience greater alcohol-induced reward are thought to be more likely to develop alcohol problems. Specifically, Wise and Bozarth (1987) based their theory on three major assertions: (1) that all addictive substances produce psychomotor stimulation, (2) that the stimulant effects of these addictive substances share a common biological mechanism, and (3) that the stimulant effects of these substances produce their positive reinforcement. Importantly, the common neural pathway involved in the stimulant and reinforcing properties of several substances—including alcohol—is thought to be mediated by mesocorticolimbic dopamine activity in the reward circuitry in the brain.

Although early models of addiction focused on dopamine and the stimulatory and reinforcing effects of alcohol and drugs, subsequent biological models shifted the focus from reward to incentive salience and craving (Robinson & Berridge, 1993, 2001; Berridge & Robinson, 2003). These models suggest that activation along mesolimbic dopamine substrates is critical to the development of the motivational and appetitive properties of tobacco, alcohol, and other drugs. The model also suggests that the mechanisms that serve the motivational properties of alcohol and other drugs may be distinct from those that mediate reward. This assertion then led to a biological conceptualization of alcohol craving, which has recently been articulated as an incentive sensitization model of craving stipulating that mesolimbic dopamine activation influences the motivational and appetitive properties of alcohol and drug use by controlling the attribution of incentive salience to neural representations of alcohol related stimuli (Berridge & Robinson, 1998; Wise, 1988; Robinson & Berridge, 1993). Thus, the acquisition and sensitization of incentive salience (i.e., craving) for substances of abuse—including alcohol—is produced by repeated drug/alcohol ingestion and the associated release of dopamine. After these pathways have become sensitized the expression of incentive salience (i.e., craving) can be activated by the release of dopamine that is initiated in response to drug cues or priming doses of the drug itself (de Wit, 1996; Stewart, de Wit, & Eikelboom, 1984).

A recent biological model of Alcohol Dependence that is more broadly focused is known as the *allostatic model of dependence* (Koob, 2003; Koob & LeMoal, 2001; Koob & LeMoal, 2005). This model is an important development because it is one of the first models to integrate the neurobiology of the acute rewarding effects of alcohol and drugs with mechanisms related to negative reinforcement associated with alcohol withdrawal and the influence of stress. Conceptually, the development of Alcohol Dependence is characterized as an allostatic process that involves changes in reward and stress circuits that become dysregulated with repeated exposure to alcohol. More specifically, this process putatively involves alterations of corticotrophin-releasing factor (CRF) and neuropeptide Y (NPY) in the central nucleus of the amygdala and bed nucleus of the stria terminalis. In turn, these changes confer vulnerability to relapse among alcohol dependent patients. One of the primary advantages of this model is that it integrates a considerable amount of data on molecular, cellular, and neuronal changes that are associated with the pathophysiology of Alcohol Dependence.

Finally, no discussion of the biological factors underlying alcohol use disorders would be complete without considering the role of *behavior genetics*. Although behavioral genetics research does not offer a complete model for understanding alcoholism, the role of genetic factors in the etiology of the disorder is well established (Dick & Beirut, 2006). One of the most important contributions of genetic research is the demonstration that genetic factors account for a significant proportion of the variability in alcohol use disorders, with recent heritability estimates—based on twin and adoption studies—of approximately 50–60% (Heath et al., 1997). In addition, twin studies have shown that a number of alcohol-related traits, or phenotypes, are also heritable—such as alcohol sensitivity (Health & Martin, 1991; Viken, Rose, Morzoati, Christian, & Li, 2003), alcohol metabolism (Martin et al., 1985), and alcohol use (Koopmans & Boomsma, 1996). More recent behavioral genetics research has focused on identifying specific genes underlying individual differences in the vulnerability for the development of an Alcohol Use Disorder. In light of such efforts, the identification of more narrow behavioral phenotypes—or endophenotypes—for Alcoholism has received increased attention (Hines, Ray, Hutchison, & Tabakoff, 2005), as is the case for most psychiatric disorders (Burmeister, 1999; Gottesman & Gould, 2003). A good endophenotype must be narrowly defined, readily identifiable, and related to the disorder of interest (Hutchison, McGeary, Smolen, Bryan, & Swift, 2002). When used correctly, endophenotypes for psychiatric disorders are expected to increase the power to detect specific genes underlying the risk for a given disorder. Endophenotypes are thought to be more closely linked to specific neurobiological processes than full psychiatric syndromes, which are often quite heterogeneous phenotypes (Burmeister, 1999; Gottesman & Gould, 2003). Importantly, one should recognize that Alcoholism represents a disorder of complex genetics, such that no single gene is likely to fully explain its genetic liability. As stated by McGue (1999), future research on behavioral genetics of Alcoholism should focus on processes intervening between genetic effects and behavior as well as mechanisms by which environmental factors may interact with one's genetic predisposition and contribute to the behavioral outcome currently classified as Alcoholism.

Diagnosis

A pattern of maladaptive alcohol use may lead to two alcohol use disorders, namely Alcohol Abuse and Alcohol Dependence. The current version of the *Diagnostic and Statistical Manual of Mental Disorders, DSM-IV* (APA, 1994), requires that for the diagnosis of *Alcohol Dependence* three or more of the following symptoms occur at any time within the same 12-month period and these symptoms must cause significant impairment or distress: (a) tolerance, the need for greater amounts of the alcohol to achieve the same intoxication level or desired effect; (b) withdrawal, physiological and cognitive maladaptive symptoms that occur when the blood concentration of alcohol declines after prolonged and heavy use; (c) the substance is often taken in larger amounts and/or over longer periods of time as intended; (d) persistent desire or unsuccessful efforts to stop or cut down; (e) increased amount of time is spent consuming, obtaining, or recovering from the effects of alcohol; (f) important occupational, social or recreational activities are given up or reduced because of alcohol use; and (g) alcohol consumption continues despite the knowledge of having persistent or recurrent physiological and psychological difficulties (e.g., blackouts, depression, worsening of an ulcer). Consistent with the polythetic nature of the *DSM*, any combination of three of the symptoms described above is necessary and sufficient for a diagnosis of alcohol dependence. As a result, one individual may exhibit psychological difficulties after alcohol consumption, may drink in larger amounts than planned, and may neglect important occupational or social activities because of drinking, thus arriving at a diagnosis of alcohol dependence, while another patient may experience withdrawal, tolerance, and an inability to quit drinking, and receive the same diagnosis. This is an example of how our current nosology system allows clinicians to assign the same diagnosis to a variety of presentations of the same syndrome, which in turn reflects the phenotypic heterogeneity previously discussed as problematic from a behavioral genetics viewpoint.

Alcohol dependence can be diagnosed with or without physiological dependence, a specifier thought to be clinical relevant. Alcohol dependence *with* physiological dependence is diagnosed when an individual meets criteria for tolerance, withdrawal, or both. The presence of physiological dependence is believed to be associated with a higher risk for immediate medical problems and a higher rate of relapse (APA, 2000). If physiological dependence is associated with a history of withdrawal, it is often an indication of a more severe clinical course of the disorder including, but not limited to, an earlier onset, higher levels of alcohol consumption, and more alcohol-related problems (APA, 2000). Only about 5% of alcohol dependent individuals experience very severe withdrawal symptoms, such as delirium tremens (DTs) and grand mal seizures. Conversely, a substantial minority of individuals with alcohol dependence never experience clinically relevant withdrawal symptoms. The following alcohol withdrawal symptoms are specified in the *DSM-IV*: (a) autonomic hyperactivity (e.g., sweating or racing heart); (b) increased hand tremor; (c) insomnia; (d) nausea or vomiting; (e) transient visual, tactile, or auditory hallucinations or illusions; (f) psychomotor agitations; (g) anxiety; and (h) grand mal seizures. Additionally, these withdrawal symptoms must cause clinically significant distress or impairment in functioning and must not be due to a general medical condition or be better accounted for by another mental disorder. Importantly, withdrawal and intoxication symptoms presented in *DSM-IV* are unique to each substance of abuse and they are largely based on the pharmacological and behavioral effects of a substance when acutely present (i.e., intoxication) or acutely absent (i.e., withdrawal).

In addition to the previously mentioned specifiers, there are four course specifiers for the diagnosis of alcohol dependence. Because individuals are at particularly high risk for relapse in the first 12 months after dependence symptoms remit, the *DSM-IV* distinguishes between *early* remission, in the first 12 months, and *sustained* remission, for periods of 12 months and longer. *DSM-IV* also proposes two symptom remission specifiers that are used in conjunction with the duration specifiers: *full* remission is used when no criteria for alcohol dependence are met, whereas *partial* remission is used if one or more criteria for dependence are met.

Alcohol Abuse is only diagnosed if the absence of alcohol dependence has been established. In other words, an individual is not given both diagnoses; however, possible clinical and research utility of diagnosing Alcohol Abuse with co-existing Alcohol Dependence has been recently raised (Scuckit & Saunders, 2006). Currently, in order to receive a diagnosis of Alcohol Abuse an individual has to meet one (or more) criteria from the following list of problematic drinking behaviors: (a) recurrent alcohol use resulting in a failure to fulfill major role obligations at work, school, or home; (b) recurrent alcohol use in situations in which it is physically hazardous; (c) recurrent alcohol-related legal problems; and (d) continued alcohol use despite having persistent or recurrent social or interpersonal problems caused or exacerbated by the effects of alcohol. Although only one of the alcohol-related problems listed above is necessary for the abuse diagnosis, the symptom must have been recurrent within a 12-month period and must lead to clinically significant impairment or distress.

Recently, there has been great debate about the reliability and validity of the *DSM-IV* diagnostic criteria for Alcohol Abuse and Dependence. In light of the preparations for the fifth edition of *DSM*, researchers are considering various alternative approaches to the classification of alcohol use disorders (AUDs). Some researchers have proposed conceptualizing alcohol use disorders in terms of a "disease-progression model" in which Alcohol Abuse is considered a precursor, and a more mild form, of Alcohol Dependence (Alterman, Cacciola, Mulvaney, Rutherford, & Langenbucher, 2002; Martin, Langenbucher, Kaczynski, & Chung, 1996). The conceptualization of alcohol use disorders following this model is not without controversy, however, as others argue that abuse represents a separate disease category that has its own trajectory, and is not necessarily a preparatory stage to dependence (Hasin, Van Rossen, McCloud, & Endicott, 1997). Nevertheless, according to the *DSM-IV* a diagnosis of Alcohol Abuse is preempted by a diagnosis of Alcohol Dependence, which fits well with the disease-progression model. One problem for this model is that it has been reported that the ratios for *DSM-IV* Alcohol Abuse to Alcohol Dependence range from 12 to 1 (Langenbucher, Morgenstern, Labouvie, & Nathan, 1994) or even 99 to 1 (Grant, 1999). These ratios of severe to mild illness are unusual in other mental health areas as well as in medicine (Langenbucher et al., 1994), and suggest that Alcohol Abuse may represent a distinct diagnostic entity from Alcohol Dependence.

Another concern that has been raised is the reliability and validity of the *DSM-IV* abuse category. Studies have shown that its reliability is lower than expected (Chatterji et al., 1997), is less concordant across diagnostic systems (Grant, 1996; Hasin et al., 1997; Langebucher et al., 1994), and is less distinct from nonproblematic use (Pollock & Martin, 1999). Thus, researchers are currently considering alternative ways of diagnosing alcohol use disorders. One of such alternatives is the *Withdrawal-Gate-Model*, in which alcohol withdrawal would be a necessary—as well as sufficient—criterion for diagnosing Alcohol Dependence (Langenbucher et al., 2000). This change in the diagnostic criteria for Alcohol Dependence would likely result in larger proportions of individuals receiving a diagnosis of abuse rather than dependence. Another alternative diagnostic model consists of eliminating the abuse-dependence distinction and instead conceptualizing alcohol use disorders on a continuum of severity (Saha, Chou, & Grant, 2006; Martin, Chung, Kirisci, & Langenbucher, 2006). Recent research using item response theory (IRT) has shown that the present criteria for Alcohol Dependence may reflect the more severe end of the spectrum, and researchers and clinicians may need to identify other criteria that capture the mild to intermediate range of the continuum (Saha et al., 2006). Discussion and research on these important diagnostic issues are currently underway as the field prepares to revise *DSM-IV*.

Alcohol use disorders often co-occur with a number of other mental disorders. One of the most frequent Axis I comorbidities to alcohol use disorders is another substance use disorder (e.g., abuse or dependence on cannabis, cocaine, heroin, sedatives, hypnotics)—with recent research indicating that individuals with a drug use disorder are nine times more likely to report an AUD after adjusting for demographic characteristics and 5.6 times more likely to report an AUD after controlling for demographics and other psychiatric disorders (Compton, Thomas, Stinson, & Grant, 2007). Mood and anxiety disorders are also very common among alcohol dependent patients (Grant et al., 2004), and may precede, co-occur, or follow the use of alcohol. Regarding Axis II disorders, the most common comorbid condition to alcohol use disorders is Antisocial Personality Disorder, with recent estimates suggesting that approximately 9% of lifetime

Alcohol Use Disorder diagnoses meet criteria for antisocial personality disorder and up to 29% meet criteria for syndromal adult antisocial behavior without conduct disorder (Goldstein et al., 2007). The commorbidity with antisocial syndromes was associated with a more severe clinical presentation of the Alcohol Use Disorder (Goldstein et al., 2007). Additionally, AUDs are generally associated with an increased risk for accidents, suicide, and violence including murder, such that approximately 40% of people in the United States experience an alcohol-related accident at some point in their lives and 55% of all fatal driving accidents are related to alcohol (APA, 2000). Furthermore, alcohol use disorders are also associated with difficulties in cognitive functioning, in particular memory, abstract reasoning, and problem solving (Parsons, 1998), physical health (Rehm, Gmel, Sempos, & Trevisan, 2003), interpersonal relationships (Grant, 2000; Greenfield, 1998), and employment (Stewart, Ricci, Chee, Hahn, & Morganstein, 2003; Goetzel, Hawkins, & Ozminkowski, 2003).

Perhaps the most serious effect of alcohol on the brain is the condition known as Korsakoff's syndrome. The area of brain that is mainly affected by heavy chronic alcohol use is the one responsible for one's ability to remember recent events and to learn new information. Korsakoff's syndrome is caused by alcohol-mediated thiamine deficiency, and improvement of symptoms—even with thiamine treatment—can take several months and most patients with Korsakoff's syndrome remain memory-impaired for the rest of their lives. A study comparing Korsakoff and non-Korsakoff alcohol dependent patients on a series of neuropsychological measures revealed that abnormalities of frontal system functioning were most apparent in alcohol dependent patients with Korsakoff's syndrome, although more mild cognitive deficits were noted in the non-Korsakoff alcohol dependent controls (Oscar-Berman, Kirkely, Gansler, & Couture, 2004). A study of the memory impairments in Korsakoff's syndrome suggested that separate cortical and limbic brain systems are the principal neural substrates of the remote and anterograde memory deficits observed in Korsakoff's syndrome (Fama, Marsh, & Sullivan, 2004). The alcohol consumption threshold for the development of Korsakoff's syndrome is unclear as this syndrome represents an interplay between alcohol consumption and other factors, such as nutrition and likely biological and genetic predispositions. Importantly, even alcohol dependent patients who have not developed Korsakoff's syndrome may display a range of neuropsychological impairments, mostly mild to moderate in severity, especially after chronic and sustained heavy drinking (Fama et al., 2004).

Alcohol consumption in large amounts not only leads to social, occupational, and cognitive impairment or difficulties, it can also underlie the etiology of a number of other psychological disorders. Specifically, *DSM-IV* proposes a total of nine alcohol-induced disorders, namely Alcohol Intoxication Delirium, Alcohol Withdrawal Delirium, Alcohol-Induced Persisting Dementia, Alcohol-Induced Persisting Amnestic Disorder, Alcohol-Induced Psychotic Disorder, Alcohol-Induced Mood Disorder, Alcohol-Induced Sleep Disorder, and Alcohol-Induced Sexual Dysfunction. In the *DSM-IV* these alcohol-induced disorders are included in the sections of the manual with the disorders with which they share phenomenology. The underlying commonality for these disorders is that they are all thought to be etiologically linked to a maladaptive pattern of alcohol use. Importantly, diagnosing an Alcohol-Induced Disorder often requires careful assessment in order to distinguish whether the psychological presentation is alcohol induced or is simply comorbid with an alcohol use disorder. An accurate diagnosis is important as it may guide the choice of treatment. In conclusion, this review of diagnostic considerations for alcohol use disorders underscores the phenotypic complexity of these disorders, likely reflecting their multifaceted phenomenological underpinnings.

Treatment

It is estimated that approximately 700,000 individuals receive treatment for Alcoholism on any given day (Fuller & Hiller-Sturmhofel, 1999), with most patients receiving care on an outpatient basis. This reflects a trend in Alcoholism treatment, which has largely moved from primarily residential or inpatient programs to intensive outpatient treatment programs, often preceded by detoxification, when recommended. Recent analyses based on the National Epidemiological Survey on Alcohol and Related Conditions (NESARC) suggested that the vast majority (85%) of individuals who met lifetime criteria for an alcohol use disorders never receive formal treatment or participate in self-help groups (Cohen, Feinn, Arias, & Kranzler, 2007). The most common treatment modalities include detoxification, behavioral treatments (including AA and 12-Step facilitation), pharmacotherapy, and brief primary care interventions (Fuller & Hiller-Sturmhofel, 1999). Most treatment-seeking alcohol dependent patients receive some form of psychosocial intervention for Alcoholism. Pharmacotherapies for Alcoholism are less commonly used; however, the development of new and more efficacious medications for alcohol use disorders has received increased research attention over the last decade.

PSYCHOSOCIAL TREATMENTS

The majority of psychosocial treatments currently available for alcohol use disorders are highly eclectic in nature and have not been evaluated for efficacy. Empirically supported psychosocial treatments for Alcohol Abuse and Dependence include the following:

1. *Brief interventions* focus on providing feedback, negotiating behavioral change, and promoting some form of follow-up. These interventions are often delivered by health care professionals in opportunistic samples. Meta analyses have concluded that brief interventions are superior to no treatment controls but should not replace specialist-delivered extended treatment approaches (Moyer, Finney, Swearingen, & Vergun, 2002).

2. Motivational interviewing or *motivational enhancement therapy* (MET) focuses on enhancing individuals' motivation and commitment to change by adopting an empathetic and nonconfrontational therapeutic manner (Miller & Rollnick, 2002). Results of a recent meta-analysis have supported its efficacy (Vasilaki, Hosier, & Cox, 2006).

3. *Cognitive behavioral therapies* focus on teaching skills for coping with drinking urges including identifying triggers and preventing relapse (Monti, Kadden, Rohsenow, Cooney, & Abrams, 2002). CBT for alcohol use disorders has received empirical support over no-treatment or minimal treatment control conditions (Carroll, 1996).

4. *Behavioral marital therapy* (BCT) treats the substance abusing person along with their spouse to insure the spouse's support. A sobriety contract is negotiated,

communication skills are taught, and positive alternative activities are scheduled. BCT has been found to be superior to individual treatment in enhancing motivation to seek treatment, increasing abstinence, and improving relationship functioning (O'Farrell & Fals-Stewart, 2003). BCT has also been found to reduce domestic violence and emotional problems in the couple's children.

5. *Behavioral treatments* for alcohol use disorders generally take the form of the community reinforcement approach (CRA) and contingency management (CM) programs. Behavioral treatments operate on the assumption that alcohol use is reinforcing and that in order to decrease alcohol use its reinforcing value must decrease while alternative sources of reinforcement must increase. Controlled studies have found support for this approach in the treatment of Alcoholism (Smith, Meyers, & Delaney, 1998).

6. *Cue-exposure therapy* focuses on repeated exposure to alcohol cues to produce a decrease in alcohol craving and an increase in self-efficacy for coping with urges and high-risk situations. Cue exposure treatment has received empirical support in comparison to cognitive behavioral approaches (Loeber, Croissant, Heinz, Mann, & Flor, 2006; Rohsenow et al., 2001) and in conjunction with pharmacotherapies (Monti et al., 2001). However, other studies suggest that cue-exposure (CE) does not significantly add to CBT approaches (Kavanagh et al., 2006).

7. *Twelve-step therapies*, which are based on the philosophy of Alcoholics Anonymous (AA), represent the most widely used resource for individuals with alcohol problems. They promote the goal of long-term complete abstinence and generally discourage the use of any psychiatric medications (Rychtarik, Connors, Dermen, & Stasiewicz, 2000). This later aspect can be problematic and needs to be specifically addressed in the treatment of individuals with comorbid disorders that benefit from medications.

In short, many psychosocial treatment approaches have received some empirical support for treating alcohol use disorders, but no one treatment has emerged as highly successful in treating this complex problem.

A large multi-site Alcoholism study of outpatient treatments, called Project MATCH, attempted to identify specific patient characteristics that might predict which patients would respond better to a particular treatment. Project MATCH compared the efficacy of three widely used psychosocial treatments, namely cognitive behavioral therapy (CBT), motivational enhancement therapy (MET), and twelve-step facilitation (TSF) (Project MATCH Research Group, 1997, 1998). In addition, Project MATCH compared two types of enrollment into the study. One group of patients were enrolled in a traditional outpatient services, but the other group was enrolled into the study as an aftercare program, immediately following discharge from inpatient treatment for Alcoholism. Results from Project MATCH revealed only small differences between the three psychosocial treatment modalities at one-year follow-up, such that TSF patients were more likely to remain abstinent at one-year follow-up than CBT and MET patients (Project MATCH Research Group, 1997). One hypothesis is that patients assigned to TSF may have done slightly better because they would have been encouraged to continue attending AA meetings once the intervention ended. However, by three-year follow-up, drinking outcomes for all of the three treatment groups were similar, with about 30% of all patients reporting total abstinence in follow-up months 37–39 (Project MATCH Research Group,

1998). Type of enrollment showed a moderate effect as somewhat more (35%) of the patients in the aftercare condition were found to be continuously abstinent from alcohol one year following treatment compared to 20% of patients in the outpatient condition (Project MATCH Research Group, 1998). Perhaps those individuals just coming out of inpatient care were more highly motivated to take advantage of the outpatient treatment.

Results from Project MATCH lent only moderate support for the hypothesis that matching individuals to treatment on the basis of patient variables might improve outcomes. Only four of the possible 21 matches were found to improve treatment outcomes for Alcoholism, with initial client level of anger being the most consistent moderator of treatment response. Specifically, clients who initially scored higher in anger faired better in MET as compared to CBT and TSF, whereas clients who scored lower in anger did better after CBT and TSF treatment than in MET. Additionally, at three-year follow-up there was a significant effect from the client's pretreatment drinking social network, such that clients whose social networks were more supportive of drinking responded better to TSF treatment than to MET. In summary, results from Project MATCH as well as the recent literature on psychosocial treatment for Alcoholism make it clear that alternative, more effective psychosocial approaches to treating alcohol use disorders are still needed.

PHARMACOLOGICAL TREATMENT

Pharmacotherapy for Alcoholism is used less often than psychosocial interventions. Aside from detoxification treatment, when pharmacological agents are often used to manage withdrawal symptoms, few community programs combine pharmacotherapy and psychosocial interventions to treat Alcohol Dependence. The limited use of pharmacotherapy for Alcoholism is due, in part, to the relative lack of effective pharmacological options to treat alcohol use disorders. Specifically, the only pharmacotherapies currently approved by the Food and Drug Administration (FDA) for the treatment of Alcohol Dependence are disulfiran (Antabuse), naltrexone, acamprosate, and vivitrol—an injectable longer acting form of naltrexone (Petrakis, 2006; Pettinati & Rabinowitz, 2006).

Naltrexone is perhaps the most studied of these medications. Shortly after two initial trials suggested that naltrexone resulted in significantly fewer drinking days and lower rates of relapse (23% relapse rate for naltrexone versus 54% relapse rate for placebo) after three months of treatment (O'Malley et al., 1992; Volpicelli, Altermana, Hayahida, & O'Brien, 1992), naltrexone was advanced as one of the more promising pharmacological interventions for decreasing alcohol consumption and treating Alcohol Dependence (Litten, Allen, & Fertig, 1996; Schuckit & Smith, 1996). These finding also suggested that the effects of naltrexone were more prominent among individuals who consumed alcohol during the trial, with 95% relapse among placebo-treated individuals versus 50% relapse among naltrexone treated patients (Volpicelli et al., 1992). The initial results have been largely supported by more recent trials of naltrexone that generally demonstrate beneficial effects on heavy drinking rates, particularly among those who are compliant with the medication (Anton et al., 1999; Chick et al., 2000; Monterosso et al., 2001; Monti et al., 2001; Morris, Hopwood, Whelan, Gardner, & Drummond, 2001). However, the support for naltrexone is not uniform. A few trials, including a recent large multisite trial, have reported no significant outcome differences between naltrexone and placebo treated patients (e.g., Krystal, Cramer, Krol, Kirk, & Rosenheck, (2001); Kranzler, Modesto-Lowe, & Van Kirk, (2000)). Moreover, the effect sizes of previous findings are often modest even when they reach statistical significance. In sum, studies of naltrexone to date suggest only a modest effect on the reduction of alcohol use among treatment seeking alcoholics.

Ondansetron and topiramate are two recent pharmacotherapies currently under study that show promise for the treatment of Alcohol Dependence. Ondansetron is a 5-HT3 antagonist that has demonstrated effectiveness, relative to placebo, in the reduction of drinking among early onset alcoholics (Johnson, Ait-Daoud, & Prihoda, 2000). Although the mechanism of action is unclear, it has been speculated that ondansetron might address the serotonergic dysfunction thought to characterize early onset Alcohol Dependence (Johnson et al., 2000; Johnson & Ait Daoud, 2000). In addition, it has been suggested that ondansetron might reduce craving for alcohol, possibly through the influence of 5-HT3 projection to mesolimbic dopaminergic connections in the midbrain (Johnson et al., 2000; Johnson & Ait Daoud, 2000). Topiramate is an anticonvulsant medication that was only recently tested with alcohol dependent patients. This recent trial found that topiramate reduced drinking and alcohol craving over a 12 week treatment period (Johnson et al., 2003). The effects of topiramate were not limited to early onset alcoholics, as was the case with ondansetron. The mechanism of action of topiramate, however, remains unclear. In general, topiramate reduces neuronal excitability through inhibition at glutamate AMPA/kainate receptors and L-type calcium channels. This could conceivably decrease the distress of protracted withdrawal. Topiramate also facilitates brain GABA function and may even increase GABA levels. Both of these effects (i.e., glutamate blockade, GABA facilitation) can reduce or inhibit mesolombic DA activity. It has been suggested that topiramate may indirectly influence midbrain dopaminergic activity, thereby reducing craving (Johnson et al., 2003). Two additional medications that have shown promise include quetiapine (Monnelly, Ciraulo, Knapp, LoCastro, & Sepulveda, 2004) and olanzapine (Hutchison et al., 2003; Hutchison et al., 2006). Both of these medications may show promise, in part, because of their ability to reduce craving by targeting mesocorticolimbic dopamine function.

In summary, randomized clinical trials have provided sufficient evidence of the efficacy, albeit modest efficacy, of acamprosate, naltrexone, and vivitrol for the treatment of Alcoholism (Kranzler et al., 2000; Mann, 2004; Myrick, Brady, & Malcolm, 2001; Schaffer & Naranjo, 1998). In addition, there are a number of opportunities for research in the field of pharmacotherapies for alcohol-use disorders, including the need to identify psychosocial predictors of medication compliance and efficacy (Kranzler et al., 2000), expand our knowledge of dosing issues in relation to the pharmacotherapy of Alcoholism (Mason, 1996), improve the dissemination of research findings to clinicians in the field (Meza & Kranzler, 1996), examine the combined effects of psychosocial and pharmacotherapy treatments (McCaul & Petry, 2003), and study the role of genetic factors in predicting treatment response to pharmacotherapies, as a means of matching patients to treatments on the basis of genetic variables (Hutchison et al., 2006; Ray & Hutchison, in press). Consistent with the goal of advancing the treatment of alcohol use disorders by effectively combining pharmacotherapies and psychotherapies, NIAAA has recently completed a large multisite trial of naltrexone, acamprosate, or placebo in combination with a behavioral intervention (combine behavioral intervention; CBI) or medication management, using a multi-factorial research design (The COMBINE Study Research Group, 2003a, 2003b). Interestingly, CBI was designed to combine several elements of empirically supported treatments previously tested in Project MATCH, such as motivation enhancement therapy, cognitive-behavioral therapy, and facilitation of involvement in mutual-help groups (Miller, 2004). Recently published results from the COMBINE Study revealed that patients receiving naltrexone with medical management (MM), CBI, or both, had better drinking outcomes. Conversely, there was no evidence of efficacy for acamprosate, with or without CBI. Importantly, no combination produced better efficacy than naltrexone or CBI in addition to medical management (Anton et al., 2006). One of the main conclusions from the COMBINE Study, thus far, is that naltrexone in combination with MM can be delivered to alcohol dependent patients in health care settings—including primary care. Future studies, including analyses of moderators of treatment outcome in the COMBINE study, are needed to inform efforts at optimizing pharmacological, psychosocial, and combined treatments for alcoholism.

Summary and Future Directions

Alcohol use disorders are multifaceted in their etiology, maintenance, and relapse processes. Research reviewed in this chapter has underscored the complex nature of alcohol use disorders, which are currently best accounted for by a biopsychosocial model which proposes that alcohol pathology results from the interplay between biological and psychosocial variables. Importantly, the factors contributing to the etiology and development of alcohol problems may be different for different individuals, such that patients may arrive at an Alcohol Abuse or Dependence diagnosis through multiple pathways. Likewise, within a given patient the factors underlying the development of Alcoholism may be different from the factors maintaining the disorder or subserving a relapse. The historical, cultural, diagnostic, theoretical, and treatment considerations reviewed in this chapter clearly speak to the complexity of the alcohol addiction phenomenon. Importantly, the research reviewed here also highlights the progress of the field over the past several decades, as marked by an increased understanding of the psychological and biological factors underlying Alcoholism. This knowledge has been used to guide the development of more effective treatments and more informative diagnostic categories, yet current rates of recovery are modest even for the best treatments. Future progress in the field hinges upon our ability as clinicians and researchers to capture the complexity of alcohol use disorders in ways that are both cognizant of the empirical literature in our field and sensitive to each patient's presenting problems.

References

Alcoholics Anonymous (AA). (2007). AA at a glance. Retrieved February 6, 2007, from http://www.alcoholics-anonymous.org

Alterman, A. I., Cacciola, J. S., Mulvaney, F. D., Rutherford, M. J., & Langenbucher, J. (2002). Alcohol dependence and abuse in three groups at varying familial alcoholism risk. *Journal of Consulting and Clinical Psychology, 70,* 336–343.

American Psychological Association. (1952). *Diagnostic and statistical manual of mental disorders.* Washington, DC: Author.

American Psychological Association. (1980). *Diagnostic and statistical manual of mental disorders* (3rd Ed.) Washington, DC: Author.

American Psychological Association (1987). *Diagnostic and statistical manual of mental disorders* (3rd Ed., Rev.). Washington, DC: Author.

American Psychological Association (1994). *Diagnostic and statistical manual of mental disorders* (4th Ed.) Washington, DC: Author.

American Psychological Association (2000). *Diagnostic and statistical manual of mental disorders* (Text Rev.). Washington, DC: Author.

Anderson, K. G., Schweinsburg, A., Paulus, M. P., Brown, S. A., & Tapert, S. (2005). Examining personality and alcohol expectancies using functional magnetic resonance imaging (fMRI) with adolescents. *Journal of Studies on Alcohol, 66,* 323–331.

Anthony, J. C., Warner, L. A., & Kessler, R. C. (1994). Comparative epidemiology of dependence on tobacco, alcohol, controlled substances, and inhalants: Basic findings from the National Comorbidity Survey. *Experimental and Clinical Psychopharmacology, 2,* 244–268.

Anton, R. F., Moak, D. H., Waid, L. R., Latham, P. K., Malcom, R. J., & Dias, J. K. (1999). Naltrexone and cognitive behavioral therapy for the treatment of out-patient alcoholics: Results of a placebo-controlled trial. *American Journal of Psychiatry, 156,* 1758–1764.

Anton, R. F., O'Malley, S. S., Ciraulo, D. A., Cisler, R. A., Couper, D., Donavan, D. M., et al. (2006). Combined pharmacotherapies and behavioral interventions for alcohol dependence, the COMBINE study: A randomized controlled trial. *JAMA, 295,* 2003–2017.

Armeli, S., Tennen, H., Todd, M., Carney, M. A., Mohr, C., Affleck, G., et al. (2003). A daily process examination of the stress-response dampening effects of alcohol consumption. *Psychology of Addictive Behaviors, 17,* 266–276.

Babor, T. F. (1996). The classification of alcoholics: Typology theories from the 19th century to the present. *Alcohol Health and Research World, 20,* 6–17.

Babor, T. F., & Caetano, R. (2006). Subtypes of substance dependence and abuse: Implications for diagnostic classification and empirical research. *Addiction, 101* (Suppl.1), 104–110.

Babor, T. F., Hofmann, M., DelBoca, F. K., Hesselbrock, V., Meyer, R. E., Dolinsky, Z. S., et al. (1992). Types of alcoholics, I: Evidence for an empirically derived typology based on indicators of vulnerability and severity. *Archives of General Psychiatry, 49,* 599–608.

Bandura, A. (1986). *Social foundations of thought and action: A social cognitive theory.* Englewood Cliffs, NJ: Prentice-Hall.

Bandura, A. (1977). *Social learning theory.* Englewood Cliffs, NJ: Prentice-Hall.

Benjamin, D., Grant, E. R., & Pohorecky, L. A. (1993). Naltrexone reverses ethanol-induced dopamine release in the nucleus accumbens in awake, freely moving rats. *Brain Research, 621,* 137–140.

Berridge, K. C., & Robinson, T. E. (1998). What is the role of dopamine in reward: Hedonic impact, reward learning, or incentive salience? *Brain Research Reviews, 28,* 309–369.

Berrdige, K. C., & Robinson, T. E. (2003). Parsing reward. *Trends in Neuroscience, 26,* 507–513.

Bjarnason, T., Andersson, B., Choquet, M., Elekes, Z., Morgan, M., & Rapinett, G. (2003). Alcohol culture, family structure and adolescent alcohol use: Multi-level modeling of frequency of heavy drinking among 15–16 year old students in 11 European countries. *Journal of Studies on Alcohol, 64,* 200–208.

Bloomfield, K., Greenfield, T. K., Kraus, L., & Augustin, R. (2002). A comparison of drinking patterns and alcohol-use-related problems in the United States and Germany, 1995. *Substance Use and Misuse, 37,* 399–428.

Brown, S. A., Goldman, M. S., Inn, A., & Anderson, L. R. (1980). Expectations of reinforcement from alcohol: Their domain and relation to drinking problems. *Journal of Consulting and Clinical Psychology, 48*, 419–426.

Burmeister, M. (1999). Basic concepts in the study of diseases with complex genetics. *Biological Psychiatry, 45*, 522–532.

Cappell, H., & Herman, C. P. (1972). Alcohol and tension reduction: A review. *Journal of Studies on Alcohol, 33*, 33–64.

Carroll, K. M. (1996). Relapse prevention as a psychosocial treatment: A review of controlled clinical trials. *Experimental and Clinical Psychopharmacology, 4*, 46–54.

Chatterji, S., Saunders, J. B., Vrasti, R., Grant, B. F., Hasin, D., & Mager, D. (1997). Reliability of the alcohol and drug modules of the Alcohol Use Disorders and Associated Disabilities Interview Schedule-Alcohol/Drug-Revised (AUDADIS-ADR): An international comparison. *Drug and Alcohol Dependence, 47*, 171–185.

Chick, J., Anton, R., Checinski, K., Croop, R., Drummond, D. C., Farmer, R., et al. (2000). A multicentre, randomized, double-blind, placebo-controlled trial of naltrexone in the treatment of alcohol dependence or abuse. *Alcohol and Alcoholism, 35*, 587–593.

Clements, R. (1999). Prevalence of alcohol-use disorders and alcohol-related problems in a college student sample. *Journal of American College Health, 48*, 111–118.

Cloninger, C. R. (1987). Neurogenetic adaptive mechanisms in alcoholism. *Science, 236*, 410–16.

Cohen, E., Feinn, R., Arias, A., & Kranzler, H. (2007). Alcohol treatment utilization: Findings from the National Epidemiologic Survey on Alcohol and Related Conditions. *Drug and Alcohol Dependence, 86*, 214–221.

COMBINE Study Research Group (2003a). Testing combined pharmacotherapies and behavioral interventions in alcohol dependence: Rationale and methods. *Alcoholism: Clinical and Experimental Research, 27*, 1107–1122.

COMBINE Study Research Group (2003b). Testing combined pharmacotherapies and behavioral interventions in alcohol dependence (The COMBINE Study): A pilot feasibility study. *Alcoholism: Clinical and Experimental Research, 27*, 1123–1131.

Compton, W. M., Thomas, Y. F., Stinson, F. S., & Grant, B. F. (2007). Prevalence, correlates, disability, and comorbidity of *DSM-IV* drug abuse and dependence in the United States. *Archives of General Psychiatry, 64*, 566–576.

Cunningham, J. A., & Mäkelä, P. (2003). Comparing drinking patterns in Finland and Ontario (Canada). *Contemporary Drug Problems, 30*, 685–699.

Dawson, D. A., Grant, B. F., Stinson, F. S., Chou, P. S., Huang, B., & Ruan, W. J. (2005). Recovery from *DSM-IV* alcohol dependence: United States, 2001–2002. *Addiction, 100*, 281–292.

Del Boca, F. K., Darkes, J., Goldman, M. S., & Smith, G. T. (2002). Advancing the expectancy concept via the interplay between theory and research. *Alcoholism: Clinical and Experimental Research, 26*, 926–935.

de Lima, M. S., Dunn, J., Novo, I. P., Tomasi, E., & Reisser, A. A. P. (2003). Gender differences in the use of alcohol and psychotropics in a Brazilian population. *Substance Use and Misuse, 38*, 51–65.

de Wit, H. (1996). Priming effects with drugs and other reinforcers. *Experimental and Clinical Psychopharmacology, 4*, 5–10.

Dick, D. M., & Bierut, L. J. (2006). The genetics of alcohol dependence. *Current Psychiatry Reports, 8*, 151–157.

Dimeff, L. A., & Marlatt, G. A. (1995). Relapse prevention. In R. H. Hester & W. R. Miller (Eds.), *Handbook of alcoholism treatment approaches* (pp. 176–194). Needham Heights, MA: Allyn & Bacon.

Edwards, G., & Gross, M. (1976). Alcohol dependence: Provisional description of a clinical syndrome. *British Medical Journal, 1*, 1058–1061.

Fama, R., Marsh, L., & Sullivan, E. V. (2004). Dissociation of remote and anterograde memory impairment and neural correlates in alcoholic Korsakoff syndrome. *Journal of the International Neuropsychological Society, 10*, 427–441.

Feighner, J. P., Robins, E., Guze, S. B., Woodruff, R. A. J., Winokur, G., & Munoz, R. (1972). Diagnostic criteria for use in psychiatric research. *Archives of General Psychiatry, 26*, 57–63.

Finn, P. R., Earleywine, M., & Pihl, R. O. (1992). Sensation seeking, stress reactivity, and alcohol dampening discriminate the density of a family history of alcoholism. *Alcoholism: Clinical and Experimental Research, 16*, 585–590.

Fuller, R. K., & Hiller-Sturmhofel, S. (1999). Alcoholism treatment in the United States: An overview. *Alcohol Research & Health, 23*, 69–77.

Galanter, M., Egelko, S., & Edwards, H. (1993). Rational recovery: Alternative to AA for addiction. *American Journal of Drug and Alcohol Abuse, 19*, 499–510.

Gianoulakis, C. G. (1993). Endogenous opioids and excessive alcohol consumption. *Journal of Psychiatry and Neuroscience, 18*, 148–156.

Gianoulakis, C. G., de Waele, J. P., & Thavundayil, J. (1996). Implication of the endogenous opioid system in excessive ethanol consumption. *Alcohol, 13*, 19–23.

Goetzel, R. Z., Hawkins, K., & Ozminkowski, R. J. (2003). The health and productivity cost burden of the "top 10" physical and mental conditions affecting six large U.S. employers in 1999. *Journal of Occupational and Environmental Medicine, 45*, 5–14.

Goldman, M. S., & Darkes, J. (2004). Alcohol expectancy multiaxial assessment: A memory network-based approach. *Psychological Assessment, 16*, 4–15.

Goldman, M. S., Del Boca, F. K., & Darkes, J. (1999). Alcohol expectancy theory: The application of cognitive neuroscience. In K. E. Leonard & H. T. Blane (Eds.), *Psychological theories of drinking and alcoholism* (pp. 203–246). New York: Guildford.

Goldstein, R. B., Dawson, D. A., Saha, T. D., Ruan, W. J., Compton, W. M., & Grant, B. F. (2007). Antisocial behavioral syndromes and *DSM-IV* alcohol use disorders: Results from the National Epidemiologic Survey on Alcohol and Related Conditions. *Alcoholism: Clinical and Experimental Research, 31*, 814–828.

Gottesman, I. I., & Gould, T. D. (2003). The endophenotype concept in psychiatry: Etymology and strategic intentions. *American Journal of Psychiatry, 160*, 636–645.

Grant, B. F. (1996). *DSM-IV, DSM-III, DSM-III-R,* and ICD-10 alcohol and drug abuse/harmful use and dependence, United States: 1992: A nosological comparison. *Alcoholism: Clinical and Experimental Research, 20*, 309–316.

Grant, B. F. (2000). Estimates of U.S. children exposed to alcohol abuse and dependence in the family. *American Journal of Public Health, 90*, 112–115.

Grant, B. F., Dawson, D. A., Stinson, F. S., Chou, S. P., Dufour, M. C., & Pickering, R. P. (2004). The 12-month prevalence and trends in *DSM-IV* alcohol abuse and dependence: United States, 1991–1992 and 2001–2002. *Drug and Alcohol Dependence, 74*, 223–234.

Grant, K. A., (1999), Strategies for understanding the pharmalogical effects of ethanol with drug discrimination procedures. *Pharmacology, Biochemistry and Behavior, 64*, 261–267.

Greenfield, L. A. (1998). *Alcohol and crime: An analysis of national data on the prevalence of alcohol in crime.* Washington, DC: U.S. Department of Justice.

Greeley, J., & Oei, T. (1999). Alcohol and tension reduction. In K. E. Leonard & H. T. Blane (Eds.), *Psychological theories of drinking and alcoholism* (pp. 14–53). New York: Guildford.

Hart, K. E., & Fazaa, N. (2004). Life stress events and alcohol misuse: Distinguishing contributing stress events from consequential stress events. *Substance Use & Misuse, 39*, 1319–1339.

Harwood, H. (1998). *Updating estimates of the economic cost of alcohol abuse in the United States: Estimates, update methods and data.* Bethesda, MD: National Institute on Alcohol Abuse and Alcoholism.

Hasin, D. S., & Grant, B. F. (2004). The co-occurrence of *DSM-IV* alcohol abuse in *DSM-IV* alcohol dependence. *Archives of General Psychiatry, 61*, 891–896.

Hasin, D. S., Schuckit, M. A., Martin, C. S., Grant, B. F., Bucholz, K. K., & Helzer, J. E. (2003). The validity of the *DSM-IV* alcohol dependence: What do we know and what do we need to know? *Alcoholism: Clinical and Experimental Research, 27*, 244–252.

Hasin, D., Van Rossem, R., McCloud, S., & Endicott, J. (1997). Alcohol dependence and diagnoses: Validity in a community sample of heavy drinkers. *Alcoholism: Clinical and Experimental Research, 21*, 213–219.

Heath, A. C., Bucholz, K. K., Madden, P. A., Dinwiddie, S. H., Slutske, W. S., Bierut, L. J., et al. (1997). Genetic and environmental contributions to alcohol dependence risk in a national twin sample: Consistency of findings for women and men. *Psychological Medicine, 27*, 1381–1391.

Heath, A. C., & Martin, A. G. (1991). Intoxication after an acute dose of alcohol: An assessment of its association with alcohol consumption patterns by using twin data. *Alcoholism: Clinical and Experimental Research, 15*, 122–128.

Heather, N., & Dawe, S. (2005). Level of impaired control predicts outcome of moderation-oriented treatment for alcohol problems. *Addiction, 100*, 945–952.

Hines, L., Ray, L. A., Hutchison, K. E., & Tabakoff, B. (2005). Alcoholism: The dissection for endophenotypes. *Dialogues in Clinical Neuroscience, 7*, 153–163.

Hull, C. L. (1943). *Principles of behavior.* New York: Appleton-Century-Crofts.

Hutchison, K. E., Ray, L. A., Sandman, E., Rutter, M. C., Peters, A., & Swift, R. (2006). The effect of olanzapine on craving and alcohol consumption. *Neuropsychopharmacology, 31*, 1310–1317.

Hutchison, K. E., Wooden, A., Swift, R. M., Smolen, A., McGeary, J., & Adler, L. (2003). Olanzapine reduces craving for alcohol: A DRD4 VNTR polymorphism by pharmacotherapy interaction. *Neuropsychopharmacology, 28,* 1882–1888.

Hutchison, K. E., McGeary, J., Smolen, A., Bryan, A., & Swift, R. M. (2002). The DRD4 VNTR polymorphism moderates craving after alcohol consumption. *Health Psychology, 21,* 139–146.

Ilgen, M., McKellar, J., & Tiet, Q. (2005). Abstinence self-efficacy and abstinence 1 year after substance use disorder treatment. *Journal of Consulting and Clinical Psychology, 73,* 1175–1180.

Johnson, B. A., & Ait-Daoud, N. (2000). Neuropharmacological treatments for alcoholism: Scientific basis and clinical findings. *Psychopharmacology, 149,* 327–344.

Johnson, B. A., Ait-Daoud, N., & Prihoda, T. J. (2000). Combining ondansetron and naltrexone effectively treats biologically predisposed alcoholics: From hypotheses to preliminary clinical evidence. *Alcoholism: Clinical and Experimental Research, 24,* 737–742.

Johnson, B. A., O'Malley, S. S., Ciraulo, D. A., Roache, J. D., Chambers, R. A., Sarid-Segal, O., et al. (2003). Dose-ranging kinetics and behavioral pharmacology of naltrexone and acamprosate, both alone and combined, in alcohol dependent subjects. *Journal of Clinical Psychopharmacology, 23,* 281–293.

Johnson, P. B., & Johnson, H. L. (1999). Cultural and familial influences that maintain the negative meaning of alcohol. *Journal of Studies on Alcohol, 13,* 79–83.

Kalivas, P. W., & Stewart, J. (1991). Dopamine transmission in the initiation and expression of drug- and stress-induced sensitization of motor activity. *Brain Research Reviews, 16,* 223–244.

Kalivas, P. W., & Volkow, N. D. (2005). The neural basis of addiction: A pathology of motivation and choice. *American Journal of Psychiatry, 162,* 1403–1413.

Kavanagh, D. J., Sitharthan, G., Young, R. M., Sitharthan, T., Saunders, J. B., Shockley, N., et al. (2006). Addition of cue exposure to cognitive-behaviour therapy for alcohol misuse: A randomized trial with dysphoric drinkers. *Addiction, 101,* 1106–1116.

Kazdin, A. E. (2002). *Research design in clinical psychology* (4th Ed.). Boston: Allyn & Bacon.

Koob, G. F. (2003). Neuroadaptive mechanisms of addiction: Studies on the extended amygdale. *European Neuropsychopharmacology. Special Issue: Neuropsychopharmacology of Addiction, 13,* 442–452.

Koob, G. F., & LeMoal, M. (2001). Drug addiction, dysregulation of reward, and allostasis. *Neuropsychopharmacology, 24,* 97–129.

Koob, G. F., & LeMoal, M. (2005). Plasticity of reward neurocircuitry and the 'dark side' of drug addiction. *Nature Neuroscience, 8,* 1442–1444.

Koopmans, J. R., & Boomsma, D. L. (1996). Familial resemblances in alcohol use: Genetic or cultural transmission? *Journal of Studies on Alcohol, 57,* 19–28.

Kranzler, H. R., Modesto-Lowe, V., & Van Kirk, J. (2000). Naltrexone vs. nefazedone for treatment of alcohol dependence: A placebo-controlled trial. *Neuropsychopharmacology, 22,* 493–503.

Krystal, J. H., Cramer, J. A., Krol, W. F., Kirk, G. F., & Rosenheck, R. A. (2001). Naltrexone in the treatment of alcohol dependence. *New England Journal of Medicine, 345,* 1734–1739.

Langenbucher, J. W., Morgenstern, J., Labouvie, E., & Nathan, P. E. (1994). Diagnostic concordance of substance use disorders in *DSM-III, DSM-IV* and ICD-10. *Drug and Alcohol Dependence, 36,* 193–203.

Langenbucher, J. W., Martin, C. S., Labouvie, E., Sanjuan, P. M., Bavly, L., & Pollock, N. K. (2000). Toward the *DSM-V:* The Withdrawal-Gate Model versus the *DSM-IV* in the diagnosis of alcohol abuse and dependence. *Journal of Consulting and Clinical Psychology, 68,* 799–809.

Levenson, R. W., Sher, K. J., Grossman, L. M., Newman, J., & Newlin, D. B. (1980). Alcohol and stress-response dampening: Pharmacological effects, expectancy, and tension reduction. *Journal of Abnormal Psychology, 89,* 528–538.

Levine, H. G. (1992). Temperance cultures: Alcohol as a problem in Nordic and English-speaking cultures. In M. Lader, G. Edwards, & C. Drummond (Eds.), *The nature of alcohol and drug-related problems* (pp. 16–36). New York: Oxford University Press.

Lindman, R. E., Sjöholm, B. A., & Lang, A. R. (2000). Expectations of alcohol-induced positive affect: A cross-cultural comparison. *Journal of Studies on Alcohol, 61,* 681–687.

Litt, M. D., Babor, T. F., DelBoca, F. K., Kadden, R. M., & Cooney, N. L. (1992). Types of alcoholiscs, II: Application of an empirically derived typology to treatment matching. *Archives of General Psychiatry, 49,* 609–614.

Litten, R. Z., Allen, J., & Fertig, J. (1996). Pharmacotherapies for alcohol problems: A review of research with focus on developments since 1991. *Alcoholism: Clinical and Experimental Research, 20,* 859–876.

Littleton, J., & Little, H. (1994). Current concepts of ethanol dependence. *Addiction, 89,* 1397–1412.

Loeber, S., Croissant, B., Heinz, A., Mann, K., & Flor, H. (2006). Cue exposure in the treatment of alcohol dependence: Effects on drinking outcome, craving and self-efficacy. *British Journal of Clinical Psychology, 45,* 515–529.

Maisto, S. A., & Connors, G. J. (2006). Relapse in the addictive behaviors: Integration and future directions. *Clinical Psychology Review, 26,* 229–231.

Maisto, S. A., Carey, K. B., & Bradizza, C. M. (1999). Social learning theory. In K. E. Leonard & H. T. Blane (Eds.), *Psychological theories of drinking and alcoholism* (pp. 106–163). New York: Guildford.

Mann, K. (2004). Pharmacotherapy of alcohol dependence: A review of the clinical data. *CNS Drugs, 18,* 485–504.

Marlatt, G. A., & Gordon, J. R. (1985). *Relapse prevention.* New York: Guilford.

Martin, C. S., Chung, T., Kirisci, L., & Langenbucher, J. W. (2006). Item response theory analysis of diagnostic criteria for alcohol and cannabis use disorders in adolescents: Implications for the *DSM-V. Journal of Abnormal Psychology, 115,* 807–814.

Martin, C. S., Langenbucher, J. W., Kaczynski, N. A., & Chung, T. (1996). Staging in the onset of *DSM-IV* alcohol symptoms in adolescents: Survival/hazard analyses. *Journal of Studies on Alcohol, 57,* 549–558.

Martin, N. G., Oakeshott, J. G., Gibson, J. B., Starmer, G. A., Perl, J., & Wilks, A. V. (1985). A twin study of psychomotor and physiological responses to an acute dose of alcohol. *Behavior Genetics, 15,* 305–347.

Mason, B. J. (1996). Doing issues in the pharmacotherapy of alcoholism. *Alcoholism: Clinical and Experimental Research, 20,* 10–16.

McCaul, M. E., & Petry, N. M. (2003). The role of psychosocial treatment in pharmacotherapy for alcoholism. *American Journal of Addictions, 12,* S41–S52.

McCrady, B. S. (2001). Alcohol use disorders. In D. H. Barlow (Ed.), *Clinical handbook of psychological disorders* (pp. 376–433). New York: Guilford.

McCrady, B. S. (1992). A reply to Peele: Is this how you treat your friends? *Addictive Behaviors, 17,* 67–72.

McGue, M. (1999). Behavioral genetic models of alcoholism and drinking. In K. E. Leonard & H. T. Blane (Eds.), *Psychological theories of drinking and alcoholism* (pp. 372–421). New York: Guildford.

McKay, J. R., Franklin, T. R., Patapis, N., & Lynch, K. G. (2006). Conceptual, methodological, and statistical issues in the study of relapse. *Clinical Psychology Review, 26,* 109–127.

Meza, E., & Kranzler, H. R. (1996). Closing the gap between alcoholism research and practice: The case for pharmacotherapy. *Psychiatric Service, 47,* 917–920.

Miller, W. R. (Ed.). (2004). Combined behavioral intervention manual: A clinical research guide for therapists treating people with alcohol dependence. *COMBINE Monograph Series, 1*(NIH 04-5288) Bethesda, MD: National Institute on Alcohol Abuse and Alcoholism.

Miller, W. R., & Rollnick, S. (2002). Motivational interviewing: Preparing people for change. *Journal of Studies of Alcohol, 63,* 776–777.

Monterosso, J. R., Flannery, B. A., Pettinati, H. M., Oslin, D. W., Rukstalis, M., O'Brien, C. P., et al. (2001). Predicting treatment response to naltrexone: The influence of craving and family history. *American Journal of Addictions, 10,* 258–268.

Monti, P. M., Kadden, R. M., Rohsenow, D. J., Cooney, N. L., & Abrams, D. B. (2002). *Treating alcohol dependence: A coping skills training guide.* New York: Guilford.

Monti, P. M., Rohsenow, D. J., Swift, R. M., Gulliver, S. B., Colby, S. M., Mueller, T. I., et al. (2001). Naltrexone and cue exposure with coping and communication skills training for alcoholics: Treatment-process and 1-year outcomes. *Alcoholism: Clinical and Experimental Research, 25,* 1634–1647.

Monnelly, E. P., Ciraulo, D. A., Knapp, C., LoCastro, J., & Sepulveda, I. (2004). Quetiapine for treatment of alcohol dependence. *Journal of Clinical Psychopharmacology, 24,* 532–535.

Morris, P. L., Hopwood, M., Whelan, G., Gardner, J., & Drummond, E. (2001). Naltrexone for alcohol dependence: A randomized control trial. *Addiction, 96* (11), 1565–1573.

Moyer, A., Finney, J. W., Swearingen, C. E., & Vergun, P. (2002). Brief interventions for alcohol problems: A meta-analytic review of controlled investigations in treatment-seeking and non-treatment-seeking populations. *Addiction, 97,* 279–292.

Myrick, H., Brady, K. T., & Malcolm, R. (2001). New developments in the pharmacotherapy of alcohol dependence. *American Journal of Addictions, 10,* 3–15.

National Center for Health Statistics. (2002). *Health, United States, 2002. With chartbook and trends in the health of Americans.* Hyattsville, MD: Author.

O'Farrell, T. J., & Fals-Stewart, W. (2003). Alcohol abuse. *Journal of Marital and Family Therapy, 29,* 121–146.

Ojehegan, A., & Berglund, M. (1989). Changes in drinking goals in a two-year outpatient alcoholic treatment program. *Addictive Behaviors, 14*, 1–10.

O'Malley, S. S., Jaffe, A. J., Chang, G., Schottenfeld, R. S., Meyer, R. E., & Rounsaville, B. (1992). Naltrexone and coping skills therapy for alcohol dependence. *Archives of General Psychiatry, 49*, 881–887.

Orford, J., & Keddie, A. (1986). Abstinence or controlled drinking in clinical practice: A test of the dependence and persuasion hypotheses. *British Journal of Addiction, 81*, 495–504.

Oscar-Berman, M., Kirkely, S. M., Gansler, D. A., & Couture, A. (2004). Comparisons of Korsakoff and non-Korsakoff alcoholics on neuropsychological tests of prefrontal brain functioning. *Alcoholism: Clinical and Experimental Research, 28*, 667–675.

Parsons, O. A. (1998). Neurocognitive deficits in Alcoholics and social drinkers: A continuum? *Alcoholism: Clinical and Experimental Research, 22*, 954–961.

Partenen, J. (1991). *Sociability and intoxication: Alcohol and drinking in Kenya, Africa and the modern world* (Vol. 39). Helsinki, Finland: Finish Foundation for Alcohol Studies.

Peele, S. (1993). The conflict between public health goals and the Temperance mentality. *American Journal of Public Health, 83*, 805–810.

Peele, S. (1997). Utilizing culture and behavior in epidemiological models of alcohol consumption and consequences for Western nations. *Alcohol and Alcoholism, 32*, 51–64.

Petrakis, I. L. (2006). A rational approach to the pharmacotherapy of alcohol dependence. *Journal of Clinical Psychopharmacology, 26*, S3–12.

Pettinati, H. M., & Rabinowitz, A. R. (2006). Choosing the right medication for the treatment of alcoholism. *Current Psychiatry Reports, 8*, 383–388.

Pollock, N. K., & Martin, C. S. (1999). Diagnostic orphans: Adolescents with alcohol symptoms who do not qualify for *DSM-IV* abuse or dependence diagnoses. *American Journal of Psychiatry, 156*, 897–901.

Project MATCH Research Group. (1998). Matching alcoholism treatments to client heterogeneity: Project MATCH three-year drinking outcomes. *Alcoholism: Clinical and Experimental Research, 22*, 1300–1311.

Project MATCH Research Group. (1997). Matching alcoholism treatment to client heterogeneity: Project MATCH posttreatment drinking outcomes. *Journal of Studies on Alcohol, 58*, 7–29.

Ray, L. A., & Hutchison, K. E. (2007). Effects of naltrexone on alcohol sensitivity and genetic moderators of medication response: A double-blind placebo-controlled study. *Archives of General Psychiatry, 64* (9), 1069–1077.

Rehm, J., Gmel, G., Sempos, C. T., & Trevisan, M. (2003). Alcohol-related morbidity and mortality. *Alcohol Research and Health, 27*, 39–51.

Robinson, T. E., & Berridge, K. C. (1993). The neural basis of drug craving: An incentive sensitization theory of addiction. *Brain Research Reviews, 18*, 247–291.

Robinson, T. E., & Berridge, K. C. (2001). Incentive-sensitization and addiction. *Addiction, 96*, 103–114.

Rohsenow, D. J., Monti, P. M., Rubonis, A. V., Gulliver, S. B., Colby, S. M., Binkoff, J. A., et al. (2001). Cue exposure with coping skills training and communication skills training for alcohol dependence: 6- and 12-month outcomes. *Addiction, 96*, 1161–1174.

Room, R. (1998). Drinking patterns and alcohol-related social problems: Frameworks for analysis in developing societies. *Drug and Alcohol Review, 17*, 389–398.

Rosenberg, H. (1993). Prediction of controlled drinking by alcoholics and problems drinkers. *Psychological Bulletin, 113*, 129–139.

Rycgtarik, R. G., Connors, G. J., Dermen, K. H., & Stasiewicz, P. R. (2000). Alcoholics anonymous and the use of medications to prevent relapse: An anonymous survey of member attitudes. *Journal of Studies on Alcohol, 61*, 134–138.

Saha, T. D., Chou, S. P., & Grant, B. F. (2006). Toward an alcohol use disorder continuum using item response theory: Results from the National Epidemiologic Survey on Alcohol and Related Conditions. *Psychological Medicine, 36*, 931–941.

Samson, H. H., & Harris, R. A. (1992). Neurobiology of alcohol abuse. *TiPS, 13*, 206–211.

Schaffer, A., & Naranjo, C. A. (1998). Recommended drug treatment strategies for the alcoholic patient. *CNS Drugs, 56*, 571–585.

Schmid, H., Bogt, T. T., Godeau, E., Hublet, A., Dias, S. F., & Fotiou, A. (2003). Drunkenness among young people: A cross-national comparison. *Journal of Studies on Alcohol, 64*, 650–661.

Schmidt, E. A., Carns, A., & Chandler, C. (2001). Assessing the efficacy of rational recovery in the treatment of alcohol/drug dependence. *Alcoholism Treatment Quarterly, 19*, 97–106.

Schuckit, M. A., & Saunders, J. B. (2006). The empirical basis of substance use disorders diagnosis: Research recommendations for the diagnostic and statistical manual of mental disorders, fifth edition (*DSM-V*). *Addiction, 101* (Suppl. 1) 170–173.

Schuckit, M. A., Windle, M., Smith, T. L., Hesselbrock, V., Ohannessian, C., Averna, S., et al. (2006). Searching for the fullpicture: Structural equational modeling in alcohol research. *Alcoholism: Clinical and Experimental Research, 26*, 194–202.

Schuckit, M. A., & Smith, T. L. (1996). An 8-year follow-up of 450 sons of alcoholic and control subjects. *Archives of General Psychiatry, 53*, 202–210.

Sher, K. J., Trull, T. J., Bartholow, B. D., & Vieth, A. (1999). Personality and alcoholism: Issues, methods, and etiological processes. In K. E. Leonard & H. T. Blane (Eds.), *Psychological theories of drinking and alcoholism* (pp. 54–105). New York: Guildford.

Sher, K. J., & Levenson, R. W. (1982). Risk for alcoholism and individual differences in the stress-response dampening of alcohol. *Journal of Abnormal Psychology, 91*, 350–367.

Sinha, R., Robinson, J., & O'Malley, S. (1998). Stress response dampening: Effects of gender and family history of alcoholism and anxiety disorders. *Psychopharmacology, 137*, 311–320.

Smith, J. E., Meyers, R. J., & Delaney, H. D. (1998). Community reinforcement approach with homeless alcohol-dependent individuals. *Journal of Consulting and Clinical Psychology, 66*, 541–548.

Stewart, J., de Wit, H., & Eikelboom, R. (1984). Role of unconditioned and conditioned drug effects in the self-administration of opiates and stimulants. *Psychological Review, 91*, 251–268.

Stewart, S. H., Karp, J., Pihl, R. O., & Peterson, R. A. (1997). Anxiety sensitivity and self-reported reasons for drug use. *Journal of Substance Abuse, 9*, 223–240.

Stewart, W. F., Ricci, J. A., Chee, E., Hahn, S. R., & Morganstein, D. (2003). Cost of lost productive work time among U.S. workers with depression. *Journal of the American Medical Association, 289*, 3134–3144.

Swendsen, J. D., Tennen, H., Carney, M. A., Affleck, G., Willard, A., & Hromi, A. (2000). Mood and alcohol consumption: An experience sampling test of the self-medication hypothesis. *Journal of Abnormal Psychology, 109*, 198–204.

Trimpey, J. (1992). *The small book.* New York: Delacorte.

Vasilaki, E. I., Hosier, S. G., & Cox, W. M. (2006). The efficacy of motivational interviewing as a brief intervention for excessive drinking: A meta-analytic review. *Alcohol and Alcoholism, 41*, 328–335.

Viken, R. J., Rose, R. J., Morzoati, S. L., Christian, J. C., & Li, T. K. (2003). Subjective intoxication in response to alcohol challenge: Heritability and covariation with personality, breath alcohol level, and drinking history. *Alcoholism: Clinical and Experimental Research, 27*, 795–803.

Volkow, N., & Li, T. K. (2005). The neuroscience of addiction. *Nature Neuroscience, 8*, 1429–1430.

Volpicelli, J. R., Altermana, A. I., Hayahida, M., & O'Brien, C. P. (1992). Naltrexone in the treatment of alcohol dependence. *Archives of General Psychiatry, 49*, 876–880.

Volpicelli, J. R., Pettinati, H. M., McLellan, A., & O'Brien, C. P. (2001). *Combining medication and psychosocial treatments for addictions: The BRENDA approach.* New York: Guilford.

Wagner, E. F., Lloyd, D. A., & Gill, A. G. (2002). Racial/ethnic and gender differences in the incidence and onset age of *DSM-IV* alcohol use disorders symptoms among adolescents. *Journal of Studies on Alcohol, 63*, 609–619.

Warner, L. A., Canino, G., & Colön, H. M. (2001). Prevalence and correlates of substance use disorders among older adolescents in Puerto Rico and the United States: A cross-cultural comparison. *Drug and Alcohol Dependence, 63*, 229–243.

Wechsler, H., Davenport, A., Dowdall, G., Moeykens, B., & Castillo, S. (1994). Health and behavioral consequences of binge drinking in college: A national survey of students at 140 campuses. *The Journal of the American Medical Association, 272*, 1672–1677.

Weiss, F., Lorang, M. T., Bloom, F. E., & Koob, G. F. (1993). Oral alcohol self-administration stimulates dopamine release in the rat nucleus accumbens: Genetic and motivational determinants. *Journal of Pharmacology and Experimental Therapeutics, 267*, 250–258.

Wilsnack, R. W., Vogeltanz, N. D., Wilsnack, S. C., & Harris, T. R. (2000). Gender differences in alcohol consumption and adverse drinking consequences: Cross-cultural patterns. *Addiction, 95*, 251–265.

Wise, R. A. (1988). The neurobiology of craving: Implications for the understanding and treatment of addiction. *Journal of Abnormal Psychology, 97*, 118–132.

Wise, R. A., & Bozarth, M. A. (1987). A psychomotor stimulant theory of addiction. *Psychological Review, 94*, 469–492.

Witkiewitz, K., & Marlatt, G. A. (2006). Overview of harm reduction treatments for alcohol problems. *International Journal of Drug Policy, 17*, 285–294.

Zeichner, A., Giancola, P. R., & Allen, J. D. (1995). Effects of hostility on alcohol stress-response dampening. *Alcoholism: Clinical and Experimental Research, 19*, 977–983.

Chapter 15

Sleep Disorders

ALLISON G. HARVEY, POLINA EIDELMAN, AND LISA S. TALBOT

We spend approximately one third of our lives sleeping. Although the study of human sleep is a relatively young science and many fascinating mysteries remain to be solved, there have been great advances in knowledge on the function of sleep. For example, it is increasingly evident that sleep has a critical role in many domains of health (Zee & Turek, 2006) and psychological functioning (Walker & Stickgold, 2006). Another example of a domain in which great advances in knowledge have been made relates to the nature and treatment of sleep disorders. Moreover, sleep disturbance is a characteristic of psychiatric disorders and, as we will discuss below, may play a critical role in the maintenance of several psychiatric disorders (Harvey, 2001). In this chapter we focus on Insomnia, as it is the most common sleep disorder. Insomnia is a chronic difficulty that involves problems getting to sleep, maintaining sleep, or waking in the morning not feeling restored. It is a prevalent problem, reported by approximately 10% of the population (Ancoli-Israel & Roth, 1999). The consequences are severe and include functional impairment, work absenteeism, impaired concentration and memory, increased use of medical services (Roth & Ancoli-Israel, 1999), and increased risk of accident (Ohayon, Caulet, Philip, Guilleminault, & Priest, 1997). Not surprisingly, given the prevalence and associated impairments, the cost to society is enormous (Martin, Aikens, & Chervin, 2004). As will become evident later in this chapter, there are a wide range of other sleep disorders, all of which also have significant adverse consequences.

Sleep Basics

Human sleep can be divided into (a) non-rapid eye movement (NREM) sleep that can be subdivided into four stages (Stages 1, 2, 3, and 4) through which sleep progressively deepens and (b) rapid eye movement (or REM) sleep. In adults, each NREM-REM cycle spans 70 to 120 minutes Shneerson (2000). NREM sleep is thought to be important for conservation of energy and restoration. It is this phase of sleep that is associated with the most rapid cell division in some tissues as well as with increased protein synthesis (Shneerson, 2000). The functions of REM sleep is understood to include a role in learning (Karni, Tanne, Rubenstien, Askenasy, & Sagi, 1994) and in the unlearning of irrelevant information (Crick & Mitchison, 1983), as well as for memory consolidation (Walker & Stickgold, 2006), emotional processing, and mood/emotion regulation (Harvey, in press). It is well established that sleep deprivation has detrimental effects on many domains of health (Zee & Turek, 2006), including on the immune system, the neuroendocrine system, and on the cardiovascular system (Dinges, Rogers, & Baynard, 2005). Given these important functions, sleep disorders have major public health implications.

Description of the Disorder

DESCRIPTION OF SYMPTOMS AND CRITERIA

There are three main classification systems for sleep disorders: the second edition of the *International Classification of Sleep Disorders* (ICSD) (American Academy of Sleep Medicine, 2005), the Research Diagnostic Criteria (RDC) (Edinger et al., 2004), and the fourth edition of the *Diagnostic and Statistical Manual of Mental Disorders* (*DSM-IV-TR*; American Psychiatric Association, 2000). In keeping with the other chapters in this book, we will focus on the *DSM-IV-TR* criteria—however, readers are encouraged to consult the ICSD-2 manual and RDC criteria for further information about the other two nosologies commonly used in both clinical and research settings.

Within the *DSM-IV-TR* a diagnosis of Insomnia may be given when there is a subjective complaint of trouble falling asleep, staying asleep, or obtaining restorative sleep. Additionally, these difficulties must be associated with daytime impairment and must not be better accounted for by another medical or psychiatric condition. Because Insomnia can be associated with a wide range of medical illnesses and psychiatric disorders, the *DSM-IV-TR* distinguishes between primary and secondary Insomnia, with the latter referring to when the sleep difficulty is thought to be caused by a medical illness, psychiatric illness, medication, or substance. However, a recent National Institute of Health report (NIH, 2005) concluded that the term secondary should be replaced with comorbid on the basis that Insomnia which is comorbid with another disorder likely contributes to the maintenance of the disorder (Harvey, 2001; Smith, Huang, & Manber, 2005).

A recent advance has been to supplement the diagnostic criteria just described with quantitative criteria. The quantitative criteria for Insomnia requires that self-reported sleep onset latency (SOL) and/or wake after sleep onset (WASO) must be equal to or longer than 31 minutes for at least 3 nights per week over a period of at least 6 months (Lichstein, Durrence, Taylor, Bush, & Riedel, 2003).

CASE EXAMPLES

Insomnia without Comorbidity

Susan had never been a sound sleeper, but over the past five years Insomnia had caused her significant distress and difficulty coping during the day, so much so that she took early retirement from her job as a preschool teacher. Susan could never predict whether or not she would sleep poorly. When she did sleep poorly, she suffered from a combination of difficulty getting to sleep at the beginning of the night (on a bad night taking between 40 minutes and 2 hours to get to sleep) and experiencing six or more awakenings over the course of the night, each varying from 10 minutes in duration to two hours. Following a poor night of sleep, Susan would spend much of the next day sleeping or resting.

Insomnia that Is Comorbid with Another Psychiatric Disorder

Jerry had just dropped out of his third year as an undergraduate at university because of episodes of mania and depression. He was diagnosed with bipolar disorder, experienced Insomnia between episodes, and it worsened approximately two weeks prior to a relapse. Jerry was aware of the damage each episode caused in his life—and that sleep disturbance was an early warning signal of an impending episode—so he had come to fear poor sleep and he was worried about his sleep. He no longer had a social life in the evening in an attempt to ensure a good night of sleep, and would nap during the day to try to guarantee he was getting enough sleep. Some days he would not get out of bed at all. Jerry felt he should aim to get over 10 hours of sleep a day to avoid episodes of mania and depression, and if he did not get 10 hours he would become worried and preoccupied with his sleep.

Insomnia that Is Comorbid with a Medical Problem

Gemma's sleep difficulties led her to resign her job as a bank manager three months prior to coming for treatment. Gemma thought that her sleep difficulties were due to a urinary tract disorder (which she had been told was called irritable bladder). This problem caused her to get up between five and eight times each night to go to the bathroom. After getting back into bed she found it hard to get to sleep and would worry about the consequences of the disturbed sleep on her health and her ability to cope the next day. She had had two surgeries in an attempt to correct the bladder problem and they had not helped. Although Gemma felt that this medical problem was the major contributor to her Insomnia she came for treatment because she was so worried about her sleep. Interestingly, a treatment focused on Gemma's anxiety about sleep substantially reduced the number of bathroom visits during the night.

BRIEF HISTORY

Jacobson's presentation of progressive muscle relaxation treatment in 1934 was the first approach to treating Insomnia. The primary rationale for this treatment—and for many others that followed—was that heightened arousal disturbed sleep and predisposed individuals to a host of medical problems (Jacobson, 1934). Progressive muscle relaxation, as well as some of the treatments developed subsequently, was couched in the prevailing notion that Insomnia was always secondary to other medical or psychiatric illnesses, a view that was particularly prevalent through the 1960s.

During the rise of behaviorist thinking in the 1960s and 1970s, sleep disturbance came to be seen as a result of conditioning—where the bedroom environment and heightened arousal became associated with Insomnia, leading to a learned sleep disturbance (Bootzin, 1979). As a correlate to this theoretical shift, empirical work began to focus more specifically on primary, rather than secondary, Insomnia. In the 1980s, biofeedback—which requires patients to learn to monitor their electromyography or sensory-motor rhythm levels—became a popular treatment for Insomnia. In a review of nonpharmacologic treatments of sleep disturbance published in the 1990s, Chesson and colleagues (1999) listed biofeedback as an efficacious treatment option. However, the growing popularity of cognitive behavioral therapy (CBT) as well as the time-consuming nature of biofeedback has rendered it significantly less popular as a contemporary intervention. Currently, cognitive behavioral theoretical and treatment approaches are the most commonly accepted and practiced modalities (Perlis & Lichstein, 2003). These approaches will be discussed in greater detail in the following sections.

EPIDEMIOLOGY

It is estimated that about 6% of the general adult population meets diagnostic criteria for a formal diagnosis of Insomnia. Approximately one-third of the general population reports some significant symptoms of Insomnia. Additionally, as many as 12% of individuals in the general adult population suffer from the daytime sequelae of sleep disturbance (Hohagen et al., 1993; Ohayon, 2002). In 2006, a random telephone survey conducted with a sample of 2001 French-speaking Quebec adults revealed that 9.5% met diagnostic criteria for Insomnia, 13% had a lifetime history of seeking treatment for sleeping difficulties, and 29.9% reported some significant symptoms of Insomnia at the time of the survey (Morin, LeBlanc, Daley, Gregoire, & Merette, 2006).

For older adults Insomnia is often accompanied by medical illnesses, which may complicate issues of assessment and treatment—further compounding burden and cost (Morin et al., in press). In a large epidemiological study, Ford and Kamerow (1989) found that there is approximately a 50% comorbidity rate between Insomnia and other psychiatric or medical illnesses. More recent studies have yielded a rate as high as 75% (Lichstein, 2000). In cases of comorbid Insomnia, additional empirical and clinical attention may be especially important as there appears to be a cyclical influence of sleep disturbance and medical or psychiatric illness, with worsening sleep problems leading to a decline in general health as well as the maintenance of daytime distress and symptoms, and daytime distress and symptoms worsening the sleep problems (Dahl, 1992; Harvey, Mullin, & Hinshaw, 2006; Smith et al., 2005).

Actual Dysfunction

This section begins by discussing an influential overarching framework, the Spielman model. Then a sample of the behavioral, cognitive, hyperarousal, neurocognitive, and hybrid models of Insomnia are described.

THREE-FACTOR MODEL

The three-factor model is a diathesis-stress model and is often referred to as either the three-factor model or the three-P model. According to Spielman, Caruso, & Glovinsky (1987), acute or short-term Insomnia occurs as a result of predisposing factors (e.g., genetic traits) and precipitating factors (e.g., life stressors). This acute form can then develop into a chronic or longer-term disorder as a result of perpetuating factors (e.g., poor coping strategies). Predisposing factors (such as a tendency to worry) constitute vulnerability for Insomnia, and this vulnerability remains across the life of the disorder. Precipitating factors trigger acute Insomnia but their influence tends to wane over time. In contrast, perpetuating factors take hold and serve to maintain Insomnia.

BEHAVIORAL MODEL: STIMULUS CONTROL MODEL

The most important behavioral model is the stimulus control model (Bootzin, 1972). It is based on the conditioning principle that Insomnia occurs when the bed or bedroom ceases to be paired specifically with sleep, but has become paired with many possible responses (e.g., being awake and anxious about not sleeping). As will become evident later in this chapter, this theory has led to the development of an intervention with strong efficacy (Morin et al., 2006).

COGNITIVE MODEL

One cognitive model of Insomnia aims to specify the cognitive processes that serve to perpetuate the disorder (Harvey, 2002). According to this conceptualization, Insomnia is maintained by a cascade of cognitive processes that operate at night and during the day. The equal emphasis on the night time and day time processes is an important feature of this model. The key cognitive processes that comprise the cascade are (a) worry and rumination, (b) selective attention and monitoring, (c) misperception of sleep and daytime deficits, (d) dysfunctional beliefs about sleep (Morin, 1993), and (e) counterproductive safety behaviors that serve to maintain beliefs. Many of the specific predictions generated by this model have been empirically tested, leading to refinement of the model (Harvey, 2005) and a new cognitive therapy treatment approach that has preliminary support in an open trial (Harvey, Sharpley, Ree, Stinson, & Clark, 2007).

HYPERAROUSAL MODELS

The hypothesis that physiological hyperarousal serves to perpetuate Insomnia has attracted interest for several decades, since the classic work of Monroe (1967) in which significantly increased physiological activation (increased rectal temperature, heart rate, basal skin resistance, and aphasic vasoconstrictions) was found 30 minutes before and during sleep in persons with Insomnia—as compared to good sleepers. More recently, in a series of elegant studies Bonnet and Arand (1992) experimentally induced a chronic physiological activation via caffeine intake in good sleepers. The caffeine resulted in decreased sleep efficiency and increased daytime fatigue. In addition, Bonnet and Arand (1995) measured whole body VO_2—which was conceptualized as an index of hyperarousal—at intervals across the day and during sleep. VO_2 was consistently elevated at all measurement points in the Insomnia, relative to the good sleepers. The authors concluded that the 24-hour increase in metabolic rate observed may be an important maintainer of Insomnia.

NEUROCOGNITIVE MODEL

The neurocognitive model (Perlis, Giles, Mendelson, Bootzin, & Wyatt, 1997; Perlis, Merica, Smith, & Giles, 2001) extends the behavioral model by explicitly allowing for the possibility that conditioned arousal may act as a perpetuating factor. The concept of arousal is expressed in terms of somatic, cognitive, and cortical arousal.

Somatic arousal corresponds to measures of metabolic rate, *cognitive arousa* typically refers to mental constructs like worry rumination, and *cortical arousal* refers to the level of cortical activation (but may also include all of CNS arousal). Cortical arousal, it is hypothesized, occurs as a result of classical conditioning and allows for abnormal levels of sensory and information processing, and long-term memory formation. These phenomena, in turn, are directly linked to sleep continuity disturbance or sleep state misperception or both. Specifically, enhanced sensory processing (detection of a stimuli and potentially the emission of a startle and/or orienting responses) around sleep onset and during NREM sleep is thought to make the individual particularly vulnerable to perturbation by environmental stimuli (e.g., a noise outside on the street), which in turn interferes with sleep initiation and/or maintenance. Enhanced information processing (detection of, and discrimination between, stimuli and the formation of a short term memory of the stimulating event) during NREM sleep may blur the phenomenologic distinction between sleep and wakefulness. That is, one cue for knowing that one is asleep is the lack of awareness for events occurring during sleep. Enhanced information processing may therefore account for the tendency in Insomnia to judge polysomnogram (PSG) sleep as wakefulness.

Finally, enhanced long-term memory (detection of, and discrimination between, stimuli and recollection of a stimulating event hours after its occurrence) around sleep onset and during NREM sleep may interfere with the subjective experience of sleep initiation and duration. Normally, individuals cannot recall information from periods immediately prior to sleep, during sleep, or during brief arousals from sleep. An enhanced ability to encode and retrieve information in Insomnia would be expected to influence judgments about sleep latency, wakefulness after sleep onset, and sleep duration.

HOMEOSTATIC AND CIRCADIAN INFLUENCES

The two-process model of sleep regulation (Borbely, 1982) proposes that sleep and wake are dependent on a homeostatic process and a sleep-wake independent circadian process (Borbely & Achermann, 2005). Sleep homeostasis influences sleep propensity—that is, sleep homeostasis results in an increased tendency to sleep when a person has been sleep-deprived, and a decreased tendency to sleep after having had a substantial amount of sleep. The circadian rhythm is an internal biological clock that is responsible for oscillations of melatonin, cortisol, temperature, and other biological functions with one complete oscillation of about 24 hours (Lack & Bootzin, 2003).

Some, but not all, studies have found impaired sleep homeostasis in persons with Insomnia (Besset, Villemin, Tafti, & Billiard, 1998; Stepanski, Zorick, Roehrs, & Roth, 2000). There is a similar lack of consensus in the research about whether circadian rhythm abnormalities play a role in Insomnia. Environmentally-induced phase shifts—such as those occurring as a result of shift work or jet lag—can cause acute Insomnia, which in some cases can lead to chronic Insomnia per the Spielman model (Perlis, Smith, & Pigeon, 2005). There is also evidence that hyperarousal may not be a 24-hour issue for some but rather may fluctuate according to circadian influences (Perlis et al., 2005).

HYBRID MODELS

At least three models have been proposed that incorporate a range of levels of explanation (e.g., behavioral, physiological) and across various points of the disorder (e.g., precipitating factors, perpetuating factors). These will now be described.

Morin's (1993) cognitive-behavioral model of Insomnia incorporates cognitive, temporal, and environmental variables as both precipitating and perpetuating factors. Morin places hyperarousal as the key precipitating factor of Insomnia. The hyperarousal can be cognitive-affective, behavioral, or physiological. Stimulus conditioning can then exacerbate this arousal. For example, a person may associate temporal (e.g., bedtime routines) and environmental (e.g., bedroom) stimuli with fear of being unable to sleep. Worry and rumination may then result. Additional perpetuating factors may ensue, including—as in the cognitive model—daytime fatigue, worry and emotional distress about sleep loss, and maladaptive habits (e.g., excessive time in bed). Thus, hyperarousal may serve as a trigger but a multitude of factors perpetuate the negative cycle. However, the consequences of sleeplessness can also serve as a trigger for the cycle.

Lundh's (1998) cognitive-behavioral model of Insomnia also considers cognitive and physiological arousal, as well as stressful life events, as factors. However, Lundh's model proposes sleep interpreting processes as additional factors. Sleep interpreting processes are thoughts about sleep, including perceptions about sleep onset latency, total sleep time, and sleep quality; thoughts about sleep quantity requirements and the consequences of not meeting these requirements; how variations in sleep quality are explained; and the degree to which negative aspects of daily functioning are attributed to poor sleep. Thus, a central tenet of this model is that individual's cognitions and perceptions about their poor sleep and their consequent daytime functioning play key roles in maintaining Insomnia.

Espie's (2002) psychobiological inhibition model posits that Insomnia is a disorder of the automaticity of homeostatic and circadian processes. That is, in good sleepers these two processes naturally default to good sleep and can adjust to some variability, but in persons with Insomnia the central problem is with inhibition of de-arousal processes critical to good sleep. The attention-intention-effort pathway (Espie, Broomfield, MacMahan, Macphee, & Taylor, in press) extends this model by providing an explanation for how Insomnia develops and what critical factors maintain it. More specifically, this pathway suggests that sleep-wake automaticity is inhibited by selectively attending to sleep, by explicitly intending to sleep, and by introducing effort into the sleep engagement process.

THE ROLE OF EMOTION

Though there is currently minimal empirical research on the role of emotion in Insomnia, it is intuitive that an individual's emotion regulation ability is likely to play a role in whether or not he or she can sufficiently cognitively and physiologically down-regulate in order to sleep. One study that is consistent with this hypothesis has been reported by Morin, Rodrigue, and Ivers (2003) who found that persons with Insomnia rate the impact of daily minor stressors and the intensity of major negative life events higher than good sleepers. Also, persons with Insomnia were found to use more emotion-oriented coping strategies and have greater presleep arousal than good sleepers. A path model showed that emotion-focused coping indirectly negatively impacted sleep by increasing both the stress impact and the cognitive presleep arousal. Hence, this study suggests a detrimental impact of emotional arousal on sleep.

It seems likely, based on preliminary evidence, that emotion regulation ability and sleep exist in a bidirectional relationship (Dahl, 2002). The previous paragraph made the case that emotion regulation difficulty makes it difficult to get to sleep, and there is evidence that sleep impacts emotion and mood the next day. For example, in a meta-analysis of 19 studies of sleep deprivation (Pilcher & Huffcutt, 1996), mood was more negatively affected than either cognitive performance or motor performance. In another study, Dinges et al. (1997) restricted the sleep of healthy participants to five hours per night for one week and found that mood disturbance progressively increased throughout the week. Future research is needed to test the possibility that Insomnia adversely affects mood and emotion the subsequent day.

Clearly the role of emotion in Insomnia—as a predisposer, precipitator, and perpetuator—is an important area in which more research is needed. Such research should focus on testing the bi-directionality of association between sleep and mood/emotion via prospective research (e.g., ecological momentary assessment) and/or experimental manipulations of sleep and mood and emotion.

ENVIRONMENTAL FACTORS

The impact of the environment on Insomnia is yet another understudied area. It is certainly tempting to speculate that one aspect of the environment—the interpersonal context of sleep—is an important contributor to Insomnia: bed partners can interfere with each others' sleep, whether by snoring sounds, movement, or out of sync bedtimes; noisy or otherwise uncomfortable environments could also create sleep disturbance; and unsafe bedroom environments likely result in hypervigilance.

Also, increased technology and busier schedules may also have an effect on Insomnia. These effects may be particularly profound in adolescence. A recent study of sleep habits in 7th through 12th graders found that 45% of adolescents report getting insufficient sleep on school nights and 28% complain they often feel "irritable and cranky" as a result of getting too little sleep (Carskadon, Mindell, & Drake, 2006). Technology options (i.e., TV, movies, video-games, internet, music, cell phone, and text-messaging) and busier schedules (i.e., increased homework, part-time employment, and increased time spent on sports and other extracurricular activities) contribute to delays in bedtimes in adolescents, yet it is known that there is an increased sleep need during the adolescent years (Dahl & Lewin, 2002).

Assessment of Disorder

The assessment of Insomnia varies depending on whether it is being done in a clinical or research context. As the latter has already been articulated (Buysse, Ancoli-Israel, Edinger, Lichstein, & Morin, 2006), this next section will focus on the assessment of Insomnia for clinical purposes.

ASSESSMENT OF SUBJECTIVELY PERCEIVED SLEEP

As evident from the *DSM-IV-TR* criteria, Insomnia is defined subjectively. As such, three levels of self-reported sleep data are collected from patients during an assessment for Insomnia. First, a clinical sleep history is taken to assess for the diagnostic criteria and the presence of comorbid problems. Information gathered includes the duration, frequency, and severity of nighttime sleep disturbance including estimates of the key sleep parameters: sleep onset latency (SOL), number of awakenings after sleep onset

(NWAKE), total amount of time awake after sleep onset (WASO), total sleep time (TST), and an estimate of sleep quality (SQ). Information about the onset and duration of the Insomnia and type of symptoms (i.e., sleep onset, sleep maintenance, early morning awaking problem, or combinations of these) is collected. A description of the daytime correlates and consequences of Insomnia is key. In addition, obtaining information about medications (prescription and over the counter) and a screen for the presence of comorbid psychiatric disorders and medical problems (including other sleep disorders) are also important.

Second, one or more validated questionnaire measures can be used to index the presence and severity of sleep disturbance (e.g., Pittsburgh Sleep Quality Index) (Buysse, Reynolds, Monk, Berman, & Kupfer, 1989), Insomnia (e.g., Insomnia Severity Index) (Bastien, Vallieres, & Morin, 2001), and daytime sleepiness (e.g., Stanford Sleepiness Scale) (Hoddes, Zarcone, Smythe, Phillips, & Dement, 1973). Third, asking the patient to complete a sleep diary each morning as soon as possible after waking for two weeks provide prospective estimates of sleep. A sleep diary provides a wealth of information including night-to-night variability in sleeping difficulty and sleep-wake patterns, and can be used to determine the presence of circadian rhythm problems, such as a delayed sleep phase or an advance sleep phase. Also, sleep diaries reduce several problems associated with the methods just discussed that rely on retrospective report; such as answering on the basis of saliency (i.e., the worst night) or recency (i.e., last night) (Smith, Nowakowski, Soeffing, Orff, & Perlis, 2003). Interestingly, the "enhanced awareness" of sleep patterns facilitated by diary keeping can reduce anxiety over sleep loss and thus contribute to better sleep (Morin, 1993, p. 71).

OBJECTIVE ESTIMATES

The gold standard measure of sleep is polysomnography (PSG). Polysomnography is used to classify sleep into the aforementioned stages. It involves placing surface electrodes on the scalp and face to measure electrical brain activity (electroencephalogram), eye movement (electro-oculogram), and muscle tone (electromyogram). The data obtained are used to classify each epoch of data by sleep stage and in terms of sleep cycles (NREM and REM). Disadvantages associated with PSG include its expense, discomfort for participants, and labor-intensive nature. Although PSG is not needed for the routine assessment of Insomnia, it is important if the patient is suspected of having a comorbid sleep disorder such as sleep apnea or periodic limb movement disorder (Chesson et al., 2000).

Actigraphy is an alternative means of providing an objective estimate of sleep. Actigraphs are small, wrist-worn devices within which are located a sensor, a processor, and memory storage. The sensor samples physical motion and the processor translates it into numerical digital data, summarizing the frequency of motions into epochs of specified time duration and storing the summary in memory. These data are then downloaded to a computer and analyzed to generate various sleep parameters (but cannot differentiate stages of sleep). Because the body becomes more quiescent during sleep, actigraphy can be used to differentiate between periods of wakefulness and periods of sleep. In fact, the correlation between actigraphy- and polysomnography-defined estimates of total sleep time is quite strong, ranging from 0.88 to 0.97 in adult nonpatients (Jean-Louis et al., 1997). The accuracy of actigraphy in identifying sleep and wakefulness is 82% in adult nonpatients (Blood, Sack, Percy, & Pen, 1997), with accuracy referring to the proportion of polysomnography epochs (sleep and wake) correctly identified by actigraphy. Although actigraphy is not required for the assessment of Insomnia, it provides an overview of the sleep wake cycle in a way that is minimally intrusive.

Interventions

A number of treatments are available to address Insomnia in adults. However, most of the research to date has focused on cognitive-behavioral therapy for Insomnia (CBT-I) and psychopharmacologic interventions, each of which is described below.

PSYCHOLOGICAL INTERVENTIONS: CBT-I

The primary goal of CBT-I is to address the cognitive and behavioral maintaining mechanisms involved in perpetuating sleep disturbance. A second important goal is to teach coping techniques that patients can use in instances of residual sleep difficulty. CBT-I is currently considered the treatment of choice for Insomnia. It is a multicomponent treatment that is typically comprised of one or more of the following components: stimulus control, sleep restriction, sleep hygiene, paradoxical intention, relaxation therapy, imagery training, and cognitive restructuring for unhelpful beliefs about sleep.

Stimulus Control

The rationale for stimulus control therapy lies in the notion that Insomnia is a result of conditioning that occurs when the bed becomes associated with inability to sleep. As described by Bootzin, Epstein, and Wood (1991), stimulus control requires patients to: (a) set a regular sleep schedule with a consistent waking time and no daytime naps; (b) only go to bed and stay in bed when sleepy and when sleep is imminent—this requires the individual to leave the bed if they are not falling asleep and to return to bed only when they are feeling very sleepy; and (c) eliminate all sleep-incompatible activities (like upsetting conversations, problem-solving, and watching TV) from the bedroom.

Sleep Restriction

Sleep restriction therapy, developed by Spielman and colleagues (1987), rests on the general premise that time in bed should be limited to maximize the sleep drive and so that the association between the bed and sleeping is strengthened. This behavioral treatment begins with a reduction of time spent in bed so that time in bed is equivalent to the time the patient estimates he or she spends sleeping. Thus, for instance, if an individual thinks he or she gets approximately 6 hours of sleep per night, but usually spends about 2 additional hours trying to get to sleep, the sleep restriction therapy would begin by limiting his or her time spent in bed to 6 hours. This initial reduction in time spent in bed is intended to heighten a person's homeostatic sleep drive (Perlis & Lichstein, 2003). Following this restriction, sleep gradually becomes more efficient, at which point time spent in bed is gradually increased to reach optimal sleep efficiency. Sleep efficiency is defined as total sleep time divided by time in bed multiplied by 100. The goal is to increase sleep efficiency to more than 85 to 90%.

Sleep Hygiene

Information about sleep and sleep incompatible behaviors and the daytime consequences of sleep disturbance is often given to inform patients of the basic steps that they can take to improve their sleep. Interventions targeting sleep hygiene are behavioral in nature and target sleep-incompatible routines. Factors that are typically addressed in sleep hygiene interventions include alcohol, tobacco, and caffeine use; diet; exercise; and the bedroom environment (Morin & Espie, 2003). Although sleep hygiene education is typically included as one component of CBT-I, its use as the sole intervention in treating Insomnia has not been empirically supported (Morin et al., in press).

Paradoxical Intention

In paradoxical intention, patients are instructed to stay awake for as long as possible. The aim is to reduce performance anxiety related to sleep (Espie & Lindsay, 1985). Paradoxical intention aims to replace the tendency to actively try to get to sleep that is often employed by individuals struggling with Insomnia. Because employing an active focus and strategy to induce sleep is actually generally sleep-incompatible (Espie, 2002), paradoxical intention places patients in the role of passive observer thereby decreasing anxiety and increasing the likelihood of sleep onset.

Relaxation Therapy

Patients are taught to implement a variety of exercises while in the therapy session. They are then encouraged to practice these exercises as much as they can between sessions, but the emphasis is on practice during the day (as opposed to using them only at night is an effort to get to sleep). Practice is essential and is often aided by making a tape of the relaxation instructions that the patient can use at home. Morin and Espie (2003) make a number of recommendations to maximize the effectiveness of relaxation therapy. Specifically, among the available relaxation techniques they suggest a focus on imagery, breathing exercises, and the release of muscle tension. Additionally, Morin and Espie (2003) note that while patients are generally receptive to relaxation therapy it is important for them to understand that relaxation serves to set a context in which sleep is more likely to occur as opposed to functioning as a sleeping medication.

Cognitive Restructuring and Therapy

The formal cognitive therapy component of CBT-I, often administered in one session, involves altering faulty beliefs about sleep by education and discussion about sleep requirements, the biological clock, and the effects of sleep loss on sleep-wake functions (Edinger, Wohlgemuth, Radtke, Marsh, & Quillian, 2001). This approach is distinct to the intervention we referred to earlier in which the entire treatment is focused on reversing cognitive maintaining processes (Harvey, 2005). An empirical question that remains to be answered is whether combining CBT-I and the cognitive therapy intervention will improve overall outcome.

EVIDENCE FOR CBT-I COMPONENTS

A number of randomized controlled trials have compared one or more components of CBT-I to each other or to placebo or both. In a recent review of CBT-I, the Standards of Practice Committee of the American Academy of Sleep Medicine found CBT-I to be highly effective and to have sustainable gains over long-term follow-up up to 24 months in adult and older adult samples (Morin et al., 2006). This review used the American Psychological Association (APA) criteria for well-supported empirically-based treatments (Chambless & Hollon, 1998) and concluded that these criteria are met by stimulus control, paradoxical intention, relaxation, sleep restriction approaches, and the administration of multiple components in the form of CBT-I. The sleep hygiene intervention alone has not been found to be effective as a treatment for Insomnia. Cognitive therapy for Insomnia is a promising new approach, but randomized controlled trials are still needed in order for it to meet APA criteria for an empirically supported treatment.

IMPLEMENTATION

Four to ten weekly sessions of CBT-I are typically needed to administer the components chosen from those described above. These sessions have been conducted in individual therapy, in group therapy, and with the addition of self-help interventions.

TREATMENT OF COMORBID INSOMNIA

Until recently, it had often been assumed Insomnia that is comorbid with another psychiatric or medical disorder could not be successfully treated if the primary condition with which they were associated was not treated first. While it is certainly true that cases of comorbid Insomnia present additional challenges, recent evidence suggests that Insomnia does respond to treatment when it is treated with CBT-I—even if the psychiatric or medical disorder is not under control. For example, in an randomized controlled trial comparing CBT-I to an active control condition (in this case, stress management) in a sample of older adults suffering from a range of chronic illnesses (such as osteoarthritis and pulmonary disease), CBT-I was associated with a significant improvement in 8 out of 10 sleep measures compared to the control condition (Rybarczyk, Lopez, Schelble, & Stepanski, 2005). Morin et al. (in press) and Smith et al. (2005) present similar examples across a range of psychiatric and medical conditions. Notably, Smith et al. (2005) concluded that treatment effects are generally moderate to large for participants with medical and psychiatric illnesses, and are comparable to treatment effects in primary Insomnia.

Pharmacological Interventions

Several different classes of medications may be used to treat Insomnia, including antihistamines and antidepressants. The term hypnotics is used to refer to medications whose primary purpose is to induce sleep. Among the hypnotics, benzodiazepine receptor agonists (BzRAs) are the only class of medication that are currently indicated as a first line treatment for sleep difficulties (Walsh, Roehrs, & Roth, 2005). In instances where Insomnia is comorbid or secondary to an anxiety disorder, BzRAs are also the most popular pharmacological choices (Nutt, 2005). Although not all BzRAs have a chemical structure that is similar to benzodiazepines, the primary action mechanism involves the inhibition of gamma-aminobutyric acid (GABA) through the occupation of benzodiazepine receptors.

All benzodiazepines have been shown to improve sleep in controlled clinical trials (Holbrook, Crowther, Lotter, Cheng, & King, 2000; Kupfer & Reynolds, 1997). Additionally all BzRAs lead to a decrease in sleep onset latency and an increase in total sleep time—with the exception of zaleplon (Nowell et al., 1997; Walsh et al., 2005). While the bulk of these studies were conducted over a short period of time (typically, no longer than 35 days), two recent trials raise the possibility that longer term treatment may also be effective for some individuals with Insomnia (Krystal et al., 2003; Perlis, McCall, Krystal, & Walsh, 2004). However, neither of these studies included a follow-up to evaluate whether the benefits to sleep were sustained after treatment ceased.

Additionally, it is important to note that although there is little risk of overdose or severe adverse effects, pharmacological interventions for Insomnia do carry some risk of daytime residual effects (such as memory disturbance or anterograde amnesia), as well as risks of tolerance and dependence. When used on a regular and prolonged basis, rebound Insomnia is a common problem associated with discontinuation. Even short term use can result in several days of rebound Insomnia following discontinuation (Roehrs, Vogel, & Roth, 1990). However, discontinuation from the newer hypnotic medications (e.g., zolpidem and eszopiclone) is associated with fewer withdrawal symptoms (Morin & Espie, 2003).

Although there is no official indication for the use of nonhypnotics as an Insomnia treatment, it is not uncommon for sedating antidepressants to be used as such. A review conducted by Compton-McBride, Schweitzer, and Walsh (2004), concluded that there is very little data to support the notion that antidepressants can improve sleep in non-depressed patients with Insomnia (i.e., that they are effective in primary Insomnia). Additionally, while the mechanisms of action for hypnotics are known, it is unclear how antidepressants affect sleep. In sum, while hypnotic medications have been shown to be effective and safe for the treatment of sleep difficulties, the literature does not support the use of sedating antidepressants over BzRAs based on the safety profiles and efficacy trials for the two classes of medications (Walsh et al., 2005).

PSYCHOLOGICAL VERSUS PHARMACOLOGICAL INTERVENTIONS

It is important to conduct a thorough efficacy and cost-benefits analysis for the different available treatment options in order to determine the best course of action in addressing Insomnia. Primarily, a choice between CBT-I, pharmacology, or a combination of the two must be made. There is an accruing evidence base to support this choice.

A meta-analysis of 21 randomized control trials of CBT-I (primarily stimulus control and sleep restriction therapies) and pharmacological (BzRA) treatments for primary Insomnia concluded that treatment effects for the two treatment modalities were comparable in the short-term, but CBT-I is more effective in decreasing sleep onset latency (Smith et al., 2002). As longer term post-treatment follow-ups are often not included in studies of pharmacological interventions, questions of comparable efficacy several months after treatment has ceased cannot yet be answered. More recently, a study by Sivertsen et al. (2006) compared CBT-I, zopiclone, and placebo. The results clearly favored CBT-I, which resulted in improved short- and long-term functioning relative to zopiclone on 3 out of the 4 outcome measures. Moreover, for most outcomes zopiclone was no better than placebo.

Addressing the issue of whether a combined pharmacological plus CBT-I approach is indicated, Morin, Hauri, et al. (1999) compared pharmacological treatment alone (temazepam, with an initial dosage of 7.5 mg and a maximum dosage of 30 mg per night), CBT-I alone (delivered in 8 weekly sessions), temazepam plus CBT-I (combination treatment), and placebo medication as treatments for Insomnia in older adults. All three active treatments were associated with short-term clinical gains, while placebo was not. However, only individuals who received CBT-I were found to sustain treatment gains over time (up to the 24-month follow-up). The combination treatment was associated with some sustained gains but more attrition in efficacy over follow-up than in the CBT-I-alone group. Additionally, study participants, their significant others, and their treating clinicians rated the CBT-I to be more effective and preferable than pharmacotherapy alone (Morin, Hauri, et al., 1999).

Brief Overview of Other Sleep Disorders

Although a full description of other sleep disorders and their treatment is beyond the scope of this chapter, we provide a very brief description of each of the other major sleep disorders here. The presence of one of these disorders is exclusionary criteria for an Insomnia diagnosis (American Psychiatric Association, 2000). As such, their presence should be assessed in all Insomnia cases. Each of these disorders is relatively common and can have serious consequences for the health and daytime functioning of the sufferer. Kryger, Roth, and Dement (2005) offer further information on the following disorders.

SLEEP APNEA

Transient closure of the upper airway during sleep is associated with disruption to sleep. The nighttime symptoms can include snoring, pauses in breathing during sleep, shortness of breath during sleep, choking during sleep, headaches on waking, difficulty getting breath, or breathlessness on waking. The adverse outcomes include daytime sleepiness and cardiovascular problems.

RESTLESS LEGS SYNDROME

The symptoms of Restless Legs Syndrome are a sensation of an urge to move the limbs (usually legs) and a feeling of restlessness because of sensations in the limbs (usually legs). The sensations start or get worse when resting, relaxing, or first going to bed. A clear circadian pattern must be present.

PERIODIC LIMB MOVEMENT DISORDER

The hallmark feature of Periodic Limb Movement Disorder is repetitive episodes of limb movements during sleep, usually the legs. The movements are associated with a partial or full awakening.

CIRCADIAN RHYTHM DISORDERS

There are two main circadian rhythm disorders: advance phase (common among older adults) that involves falling asleep early and waking up early, and delayed sleep phase (common among adolescents) that involves not being able to fall asleep until the early hours in the morning and sleeping well into the next day.

NARCOLEPSY

This is a disorder characterized by excessive sleepiness. Episodes of short uncontrollable naps during the day are typical. Often the nap is associated with cataplexy (loss of muscle tone triggered by strong emotion), sleep paralysis, or hypnogogic hallucinations.

Summary and Future Directions

In this chapter we have focused on the most common sleep disorder: chronic Insomnia. We have provided a description of the disorder and an overview of the various theories of the factors that predispose an individual to developing Insomnia, that precipitate Insomnia, and that perpetuate Insomnia. In addition, an overview of the assessment and treatment of Insomnia and a brief introduction to other sleep disorders has been presented. Although we spend approximately one third of our lives sleeping, sleep is a relatively new topic of scientific study. As such, there are a myriad of mysteries and questions about the function of sleep and sleep disorders that are yet to be answered. The results that have emerged clearly place sleep as critical for the health and wellbeing of humans throughout the age range. As such, it is a domain that holds a large number of exciting opportunities for future research. Before closing, three of the many interesting questions that remain to be answered relating to chronic Insomnia and the role of sleep in other psychiatric and medical disorders need to be described.

SLEEP ACROSS DEVELOPMENT

As evident, there is evidence for the efficacy and effectiveness of CBT-I for both adults and older adults. What about adolescents? What about children? What about toddlers and infants? Researchers know that sleep varies substantially across the age range. In newborns, average total sleep time is approximately 16–18 hours, organized into 3- to 4-hour sleep periods across the 24-hour cycle. The average amount of sleep obtained by a five year old is 11.1 hours and in a 9-year-old 10.2 hours (Hoban, 2004). In adolescence, nighttime sleep reduces from an average of 9 hours at age 13 to 7.9 hours in 16-year-olds (Hoban, 2004). In young adults, average nighttime sleep varies between 7 and 9 hours and in the middle adult years between 6 and 8 hours. There are also alterations in sleep architecture over the course of development. Newborn infants are thought to start sleep with REM and then move into NREM, with each REM-NREM cycle lasting about 50 minutes (Carskadon & Dement, 2005). In newborns REM and NREM phases are called active and quiet sleep, respectively, because of the difficulty in differentiating sleep stages at this age. Whereas at birth approximately 50% of sleep is spent in active sleep, once a child is 2 years of age this percentage has reduced to 20–30% of total sleep time. Between the ages of 6 and 11, the amount of Stages 3 and 4 sleep reduces, and Stage 2 sleep increases (Hoban, 2004). Across the adolescent years, the adult sleep cycle length becomes established, with Stages 3 and 4 further decreasing in length, accompanied by increases in Stage 2 sleep (Carskadon & Dement, 2005). During the adolescent years there is a delay in circadian phase and a corresponding delay in sleep onset, often shifting past midnight to the early morning hours (Carskadon, 2002; Tate, Richardson, & Carskadon, 2002). This has been attributable to a number of influences, which include a tendency toward increasing autonomy in deciding what time to go to bed, which coincides with both a natural biological delay in the circadian cycle plus irregularity in the sleep schedule associated with psychosocial stress and social activities (Carskadon, 2002; Hoban, 2004). There is a small evidence base reporting on the effectiveness of some interventions just described with children and adolescents who suffer from sleep disturbance (Owens, France, & Wiggs, 1999; Sadeh, 2005). However, this is domain has not been adequately investigated given the scope of the problem (Dahl, 2002).

IMPROVING TREATMENTS

There is no doubt that CBT-I is an effective treatment—as indicated by two meta-analyses (Morin, Culbert, & Schwartz, 1994; Murtagh & Greenwood, 1995) and a review conducted by the Standards of Practice Committee of the American Academy of Sleep Medicine (Chesson et al., 1999; Morin, Hauri, et al., 1999; Morin et al., 2006). However, the field is not as yet at a point where patients can be offered a maximally effective psychological treatment as indicated by: (a) the significant subset of patients who do not improve following CBT-I (19–26%), (b) the average overall improvement being in the range of 50 to 60% (Morin et al., 1994; Murtagh & Greenwood, 1995), and (c) the fact that only a minority of patients reach a high end state (i.e., become good sleepers; Harvey & Tang, 2003). Furthermore, the widely held assumption that a treatment that addresses sleep will also effectively address the daytime consequences of Insomnia, has not yet been supported (Means, Lichstein, Epperson, & Johnson, 2000). In fact, there is some evidence that aspects of the daytime impairment suffered by patients with Insomnia are independent of nighttime sleep (Neitzert Semler & Harvey, 2005). Hence, treatment development efforts that improve outcome and target daytime symptoms are an important direction for the future.

COMORBIDITY

Morin and colleagues (2006) as well as Smith and colleagues (2005) have concluded that the outcome data suggest that improvement in sleep following CBT-I treatment has great potential to facilitate improvement in medical and psychological symptoms of the primary psychiatric or medical disorder. This is an exciting direction for future exploration. Theoretically this links back to issues covered earlier in this chapter that sleep likely has a mood and emotion regulatory role as well as a role in bodily repair and immune system functioning. Hence, sleep disturbance is likely to contribute to the exacerbation of symptoms in psychiatric and medical disorders and the treatment of sleep disturbance may be critical for full recovery.

References

American Academy of Sleep Medicine. (2005). *International classification of sleep disorders (ICSD): Diagnostic and coding manual* (2nd Ed.). Westchester, IL: Author.

American Psychiatric Association. (2000). *Diagnostic and statistical manual of mental disorders* (Text Rev.). Washington, DC: Author.

Ancoli-Israel, S., & Roth, T. (1999). Characteristics of Insomnia in the United States: Results of the 1991 National Sleep Foundation Survey. *I. Sleep, 22*(Suppl 2), S347–353.

Bastien, C. H., Vallieres, A., & Morin, C. M. (2001). Validation of the Insomnia Severity Index as an outcome measure for Insomnia research. *Sleep Medicine, 2*, 297–307.

Besset, A., Villemin, E., Tafti, M., & Billiard, M. (1998). Homeostatic process and sleep spindles in patients with sleep-maintenance Insomnia: Effect of partial (21 h) sleep deprivation. *Electroencephalogr Clin Neurophysiol, 107*(2), 122–132.

Blood, M. L., Sack, R. L., Percy, D. C., & Pen, J. C. (1997). A comparison of sleep detection by wrist actigraphy, behavioral response and polysomnography. *Sleep, 20*, 388–395.

Bonnet, M. H., & Arand, D. L. (1992). Caffeine use as a model of acute and chronic Insomnia. *Sleep, 15*, 526–536.

Bootzin, R. R. (1972). Stimulus control treatment for Insomnia. *Proceedings of the American Psychological Association, 7*, 395–396.

Bootzin, R. R. (1979). Effects of self-control procedures for Insomnia. *American Journal of Clinical Biofeedback, 2*, 70–77.

Bootzin, R. R., Epstein, D., & Wood, J. M. (1991). Stimulus control instructions. In P. J. Hauri (Ed.), *Case studies in Insomnia* (pp. 19–28). New York: Plenum.

Borbely, A. A. (1982). A two process model of sleep regulation. *Human Neurobiology, 1*, 195–204.

Borbely, A. A., & Achermann, P. (2005). Sleep homeostasis and models of sleep regulation. In M. H. Kryger, T. Roth, & W. C. Dement (Eds.), *Principles and practice of sleep medicine* (4th Ed.) Philadelphia: Elsevier.

Bonnet, M. H., & Arand, D. L. (1995). 24-hour metabolic rate in insomniacs and matched normal sleepers. *Sleep, 18*, 581–588.

Buysse, D. J., Ancoli-Israel, S., Edinger, J. D., Lichstein, K. L., Morin, C. M. (2006). Recommendations for a standard research assessment of Insomnia. *Sleep, 29*, 1155–1173.

Buysse, D. J., Reynolds, C. F., Monk, T. H., Berman, S. R., & Kupfer, D. J. (1989). The Pittsburgh Sleep Quality Index: A new instrument for psychiatric practice and research. *Psychiatry Research, 28*, 193–213.

Carskadon, M. A. (2002). Factors influencing sleep patterns of adolescents. In *Adolescent sleep patterns: Biological, social, and psychological influences* (pp. 4–26). New York: Cambridge University Press.

Carskadon, M. A., & Dement, W. C. (2005). Normal human sleep: An overview. In M. H. Kryger, T. Roth, & W. C. Dement (Eds.), *Principles and practice of sleep medicine* (4th Ed.) Philadelphia: Elsevier.

Carskadon, M. A., Mindell, J. A., & Drake, C. (2006). Sleep in America Poll. Washington, DC: The National Sleep Foundation.

Chambless, D. L., & Hollon, S. D. (1998). Defining empirically supported theories. *Journal of Consulting and Clinical Psychology, 1*, 7–18.

Chesson, A., Jr., Hartse, K., Anderson, W. M., Davila, D., Johnson, S., Littner, M., et al. (2000). Practice parameters for the evaluation of chronic Insomnia. An American Academy of Sleep Medicine report. Standards of Practice Committee of the American Academy of Sleep Medicine. *Sleep, 23*, 237–241.

Chesson, A. L., Jr., Anderson, W. M., Littner, M., Davila, D., Hartse, K., Johnson, S., et al. (1999). Practice parameters for the nonpharmacologic treatment of chronic Insomnia. An American Academy of Sleep Medicine report. Standards of Practice Committee of the American Academy of Sleep Medicine. *Sleep, 22*, 1128–1133.

Compton-McBride, S., Schweitzer, P., & Walsh, J. (2004, June). Most commonly used drugs to treat insomnia in 2002. Associated Professional Sleep Societies 18th Annual meeting, Philadelphia, PA.

Crick, F., & Mitchison, G. (1983). The function of dream sleep. *Nature, 304*, 111–114.

Dahl, R. E. (1992). Child and adolescent sleep disorders. In D. M. Kaufman (Ed.), *Child and adolescent neurology for the psychiatrist* (pp. 169–194). Baltimore, MD: Williams & Wilkins.

Dahl, R. E. (2002). The regulation of sleep-arousal, affect, and attention in adolescence: Some questions and speculations. In M. A. Carskadon (Ed.), *Adolescent sleep patterns: Biological, social and psychological influences* (pp. 269–284). Cambridge: Cambridge University Press.

Dahl, R. E., & Lewin, D. S. (2002). Pathways to adolescent health sleep regulation and behavior. *Journal of Adolescent Health, 31,* 175–184.

Dinges, D. F., Pack, F., Williams, K., Gillen, K. A., Powell, J. W., Ott, G. E., et al. (1997). Cumulative sleepiness, mood disturbance, and psychomotor vigilance performance decrements during a week of sleep restricted to 4–5 hours per night. *Sleep, 20,* 267–267.

Dinges, D. F., Rogers, N. L., & Baynard, M. D. (2005). Chronic sleep deprivation. In M. H. Kryger, T. Roth & W. C. Dement (Eds.), *Principles and practice of sleep medicine* (4th Ed. pp. 67–76). Philadelphia: Elsevier Saunders.

Edinger, J. D., Bonnet, M. H., Bootzin, R. R., Doghramji, K., Dorsey, C. M., Espie, C. A., et al. (2004). Derivation of research diagnostic criteria for Insomnia: Report of an American Academy of Sleep Medicine Work Group. *Sleep, 27,* 1567–1596.

Edinger, J. D., Wohlgemuth, W. K., Radtke, R. A., Marsh, G. R., & Quillian, R. E. (2001). Cognitive behavioral therapy for treatment of chronic primary Insomnia: A randomized controlled trial. *Journal of the American Medical Association, 285,* 1856–1864.

Espie, C. A. (2002). Insomnia: Conceptual issues in the development, persistence, and treatment of sleep disorder in adults. *Annual Review of Psychology, 53,* 215–243.

Espie, C. A., Broomfield, N. M., MacMahan, K. M., Macphee, L. M., & Taylor, L. M. (2006). The attention-intention-effort pathway in the development of psychophysiologic insomnia: A theoretical review. Sleep Medicine Reviews, *10,* 215–45.

Espie, C. A., & Lindsay, W. R. (1985). Paradoxical intention in the treatment of chronic Insomnia: Six case studies illustrating variability in therapeutic response. *Behaviour Research and Therapy, 23,* 703–709.

Ford, D. E., & Kamerow, D. B. (1989). Epidemiologic study of sleep disturbances and psychiatric disorders. An opportunity for prevention? *Journal of the American Medical Association, 262,* 1479–1484.

Harvey, A. G. (2001). Insomnia: Symptom or diagnosis? *Clinical Psychology Review, 21,* 1037–1059.

Harvey, A. G. (2002). A cognitive model of Insomnia. *Behaviour Research and Therapy, 40,* 869–894.

Harvey, A. G. (2005). A cognitive theory of and therapy for chronic Insomnia. *Journal of Cognitive Psychotherapy: An International Quarterly, 19,* 41–60.

Harvey, A. G. (in press). Sleep and Emotion. In D. Sander & K. Scherer (Eds.), *Oxford Companion of Affective Sciences.* Oxford: Oxford University Press.

Harvey, A. G., Mullin, B. C., & Hinshaw, S. P. (2006). Sleep and circadian rhythms in children and adolescents with bipolar disorder. *Development and Psychopathology, 18,* 1147–1168.

Harvey, A. G., Sharpley, A., Ree, M. J., Stinson, K., & Clark, D. M. (2007). An open trial of cognitive therapy for chronic Insomnia. *Behavior Research and Therapy, 45,* 2491–2501.

Harvey, A. G., & Tang, N. K. J. (2003). Cognitive behavior therapy for Insomnia: Can we rest yet? *Sleep Medicine Reviews, 7,* 237–262.

Hoban, T. F. (2004). Sleep and its disorders in children. *Seminars in Neurology, 24,* 327–340.

Hoddes, E., Zarcone, V., Smythe, H., Phillips, R., & Dement, W. C. (1973). Quantification of sleepiness: A new approach. *Psychophysiology, 10,* 431–436.

Hohagen, F., Rink, K., Kappler, C., Schramm, E., Riemann, D., Weyerer, S., et al. (1993). Prevalence and treatment of Insomnia in general practice: A longitudinal study. *European Archives of Psychiatry and Clinical Neuroscience, 242,* 329–336.

Holbrook, A. M., Crowther, R., Lotter, A., Cheng, C., & King, D. (2000). The diagnosis and management of Insomnia in clinical practice: A practical evidence-based approach. *Canadian Medical Association Journal, 162,* 216–220.

Jacobson, E. (1934). *Progressive Relaxation.* Chicago: University of Chicago Press.

Jean-Louis, G., von Gizycki, H., Zizi, F., Spielman, A., Hauri, P., & Taub, H. (1997). The actigraph data analysis software: II. A novel approach to scoring and interpreting sleep-wake activity. *Perceptual and Motor Skills, 85,* 219–226.

Karni, A., Tanne, D., Rubenstien, B. S., Askenasy, J. J. M., & Sagi, D. (1994). Dependence on REM sleep of overnight improvement of a perceptual skill. *Science, 265*(5172), 679–682.

Kryger, M. H., Roth, T., & Dement, W. C. (2005). *Principles and Practice of Sleep Medicine* (4th Ed.) Philadelphia: WB Saunders.

Krystal, A. D., Walsh, J. K., Laska, E., Caron, J., Amato, D. A., Wessel, T., et al. (2003). Sustained efficacy of eszopiclone over 6 nights of nightly treatment: Results of a randomized, double-blind, placebo-controlled study in adults with chronic Insomnia. *Sleep*, *26*, 793–799.

Kupfer, D. J., & Reynolds, C. F., 3rd. (1997). Management of Insomnia. *New England Journal of Medicine*, *336*, 341–346.

Lack, L. C., & Bootzin, R. B. (2003). Circadian rhythm factors in Insomnia and their treatment. In M. Perlis & K. Lichstein (Eds.), *Treatment of sleep Disorders: Principles and Practice of behavioral sleep medicine*. New York: Wiley.

Lichstein, K. (2000). Secondary Insomnia. In K. Lichstein & C. Morin (Eds.), *Treatment of late-life Insomnia* (pp. 297–319). Thousand Oaks, CA: Sage.

Lichstein, K. L., Durrence, H. H., Taylor, D. J., Bush, A. J., & Riedel, B. W. (2003). Quantitative criteria for Insomnia. *Behaviour Research and Therapy*, *41*, 427–445.

Lundh, L. G. (1998). Cognitive-behavioural analysis and treatment of Insomnia. *Scandinavian Journal of Behaviour Therapy*, *27*, 10–29.

Martin, S. A., Aikens, J. E., & Chervin, R. D. (2004). Toward cost-effectiveness analysis in the diagnosis and treatment of Insomnia. *Sleep Medicine Reviews*, *8*, 63–72.

Means, M. K., Lichstein, K. L., Epperson, M. T., & Johnson, C. T. (2000). Relaxation therapy for Insomnia: Nighttime and daytime effects. *Behaviour Research and Therapy*, *38*, 665–678.

Monroe, L. J. (1967). Psychological and physiological differences between good and poor sleepers. *Journal of Abnormal Psychology*, *72*, 255–264.

Morin, C. M. (1993). *Insomnia: Psychological assessment and management*. New York: Guilford Press.

Morin, C. M., Bootzin, R. R., Buysse, D. J., Edinger, J., Espie, D. C. A., & Lichstein, K. L. (2006). Psychological and behavioral treatment of Insomnia: An update of recent evidence (1998–2004). *Sleep*, *29*, 1398–1414.

Morin, C. M., Culbert, J. P., & Schwartz, S. M. (1994). Nonpharmacological Interventions for Insomnia: A meta-analysis of treatment efficacy. *American Journal of Psychiatry*, *151*, 1172–1180.

Morin, C. M., & Espie, C. A. (2003). *Insomnia: A clinical guide to assessment and treatment*. New York: Kluwer Academic/Plenum Publishers.

Morin, C. M., Hauri, P. J., Espie, C. A., Spielman, A. J., Buysse, D. J., & Bootzin, R. R. (1999). Nonpharmacologic treatment of chronic Insomnia: An American Academy of Sleep Medicine review. *Sleep*, *22*, 1134–1156.

Morin, C. M., LeBlanc, M., Daley, M., Gregoire, J. P., & Merette, C. (2006). Epidemiology of Insomnia: Prevalence, self-help treatments, consultations, and determinants of help-seeking behaviors. *Sleep Med*, *7*(2), 123–130.

Morin, C. M., Rodrigue, S., & Ivers, H. (2003). Role of stress, arousal, and coping skills in primary Insomnia. *Psychosomatic Medicine*, *65*, 259–267.

Murtagh, D. R., & Greenwood, K. M. (1995). Identifying effective psychological treatments for Insomnia: A meta-analysis. *Journal of Consulting and Clinical Psychology*, *63*, 79–89.

Neitzert Semler, C., & Harvey, A. G. (2005). Misperception of sleep can adversely affect daytime functioning in Insomnia. *Behaviour Research and Therapy*, *43*, 843–856.

National Institute of Health. (2005). National Institutes of Health State-of-the-Science Conference Statement: Manifestations and management of chronic Insomnia in adults. June 13–15, 2005. *Sleep*, *28*, 1049–1057.

Nowell, P. D., Mazumdar, S., Buysse, D. J., Dew, M. A., Reynolds, C. F., III, & Kupfer, D. J. (1997). Benzodiazepines and zolpidem for chronic Insomnia: A meta-analysis of treatment efficacy. *Journal of the American Medical Association*, *278*, 2170–2177.

Nutt, D. J. (2005). Overview of diagnosis and drug treatments of anxiety disorders. *CNS Spectr*, *10*, 49–56.

Ohayon, M. M. (2002). Epidemiology of Insomnia: What we know and what we still need to learn. *Sleep Medicine Reviews*, *6*, 97–111.

Ohayon, M. M., Caulet, M., Philip, P., Guilleminault, C., & Priest, R. G. (1997). How sleep and mental disorders are related to complaints of daytime sleepiness. *Archives of Internal Medicine*, *157*, 2645–2652.

Owens, J. L., France, K. G., & Wiggs, L. (1999). Behavioural and cognitive-behavioural interventions for sleep disorders in infants and children: A review. *Sleep Medicine Reviews*, *3*, 281–302.

Perlis, M., & Lichstein, K.,(Eds.). (2003). *Treating sleep disorders: Principles and practice of behavioral sleep medicine*. New York: Wiley.

Perlis, M. L., Giles, D. E., Mendelson, W. B., Bootzin, R. R., & Wyatt, J. K. (1997). Psychophysiological Insomnia: The behavioural model and a neurocognitive perspective. *Journal of Sleep Research*, *6*, 179–188.

Perlis, M. L., McCall, W. V., Krystal, A. D., & Walsh, J. K. (2004). Long-term, non-nightly administration of zolpidem in the treatment of patients with primary Insomnia. *Journal of Clinical Psychiatry*, *65*, 1128–1137.

Perlis, M. L., Merica, H., Smith, M. T., & Giles, D. E. (2001). Beta EEG activity and Insomnia. *Sleep Medicine Reviews, 5,* 363–374.

Perlis, M. L., Smith, M. T., & Pigeon, W. R. (2005). Etiology and pathophysiology of Insomnia. In M. H. Kryger, T. Roth, & W. C. Dement (Eds.), *Principles and practice of sleep medicine* (4th Ed. pp. 714–725). Philadelphia: Elsevier Saunders.

Pilcher, J. J., & Huffcutt, A. I. (1996). Effects of sleep deprivation on performance: A meta-analysis. *Sleep, 19,* 318–326.

Roehrs, T., Vogel, G., & Roth, T. (1990). Rebound Insomnia: Its determinants and significance. *Am J Med, 88* (3A), 39S–42S.

Roth, T., & Ancoli-Israel, S. (1999). Daytime consequences and correlates of Insomnia in the United States: Results of the 1991 National Sleep Foundation Survey. II. *Sleep, 22,* S354–S358.

Rybarczyk, B., Lopez, M., Schelble, K., & Stepanski, E. (2005). Home-based video CBT for comorbid geriatric Insomnia: A pilot study using secondary data analyses. *Behavioral Sleep Medicine, 3,* 158–175.

Sadeh, A. (2005). Cognitive-behavioral treatment for childhood sleep disorders. *Clinical Psychology Review, 25,* 612–628.

Shneerson, J. M. (2000). *Handbook of sleep medicine.* Oxford: Blackwell Science.

Sivertsen, B., Omvik, S., Pallesen, S., Bjorvatn, B., Havik, O. E., Kvale, G., et al. (2006). Cognitive behavioral therapy vs zopiclone for treatment of chronic primary Insomnia in older adults: A randomized controlled trial. *Journal of the American Medical Association, 295,* 2851–2858.

Smith, L. J., Nowakowski, S., Soeffing, J. P., Orff, H. J., & Perlis, M. L. (2003). The measurement of sleep. In M. L., Perlis & K. L., Lichstein (Eds.), *Treating sleep disorders: Principles and practice of behavioral sleep medicine* (pp. 29–73). New York: Wiley.

Smith, M. T., Huang, M. I., & Manber, R. (2005). Cognitive behavior therapy for chronic Insomnia occurring within the context of medical and psychiatric disorders. *Clinical Psychology Review, 25,* 559–592.

Smith, M. T., Perlis, M. L., Park, A., Smith, M. S., Pennington, J., Giles, D. E., et al. (2002). Comparative meta-analysis of pharmacotherapy and behavior therapy for persistent Insomnia. *American Journal of Psychiatry, 159,* 5–11.

Spielman, A. J., Saskin, P., & Thorpy, M. J. (1987). Treatment of chronic Insomnia by restriction of time in bed. *Sleep, 10,* 45–56.

Stepanski, E. J., Zorick, F., Roehrs, T., & Roth, T. (2000). Effects of sleep deprivation on daytime sleepiness in primary Insomnia. *Sleep, 23,* 215–219.

Tate, B. A., Richardson, G. S., & Carskadon, M. A. (2002). Maturational changes in sleep-wake timing: Longitudinal studies of the circadian activity rhythm of a diurnal rodent. In Carskadon, Mary A. (Ed.), *Adolescent sleep patterns: Biological, social, and psychological influences* (pp. 40–49). New York: Cambridge University Press.

Walker, M. P., & Stickgold, R. (2006). Sleep, memory, and plasticity. *Annual Review of Psychology, 57,* 139–166.

Walsh, J. K., Roehrs, T., & Roth, T. (2005). Pharmacological treatment of primary Insomnia. In M. H. Kryger, T. Roth, & W. C. Dement (Eds.), *Principles and practice of sleep medicine* (4th Ed. pp. 749–760). Philadelphia: Elsevier Saunders.

Zee, P. C., & Turek, F. W. (2006). Sleep and health: Everywhere and in both directions. *Archives of Internal Medicine, 166,* 1686–1688.

Chapter 16

Sexual Dysfunction

CINDY M. MESTON AND ALESSANDRA RELLINI

Sexual problems are broadly defined as the inability to participate in a sexual relationship as one wishes. In order for the problem to be diagnosed as a sexual dysfunction in the *Diagnostic and Statistical Manual of Mental Disorders* (*DSM-IV-TR*) (American Psychiatric Association, 2000), the individual needs to report distress and should identify the problem as persistent and recurrent. While people may complain of a variety of sexual concerns, the *DSM-IV-TR* recognizes only four major categories of sexual dysfunction: Sexual Desire, Sexual Arousal, Orgasm, and Sexual Pain Disorders. This chapter provides an overview of the definition, prevalence, etiology, assessment, and treatment of each of the sexual disorders described by the *DSM-IV-TR* that fall within these categories.

Sexual Desire Disorders

HYPOACTIVE SEXUAL DESIRE DISORDER (HSDD)

Definition, Diagnosis, and Prevalence

The *DSM-IV-TR* refers to clinically low levels of sexual desire as Hypoactive Sexual Desire Disorder (HSDD). In order to meet the diagnostic criteria for HSDD the person must experience a persistent or recurrent deficiency or absence of sexual fantasies and desire for sexual activity that causes marked distress or interpersonal difficulty. Whether a person is distressed by his or her level of desire is necessarily impacted by whether his or her partner has similar sexual needs. For example, a couple in which both partners prefer sexual activity only once a month or less would, by most standards, be exhibiting levels of desire below normal. However, because they are well matched in their sexual needs, it is unlikely they would be distressed by their low levels and, therefore, would not meet the *DSM-IV-TR* diagnostic criteria.

544

The *DSM-IV-TR* criteria for HSDD is based on early models of sexual response outlined by Masters and Johnson (1966) and Kaplan (1979) in which desire is assumed to precede arousal and orgasm in a linear, sequential manner. Clinical experience indicates, however, that oftentimes arousal precedes desire in women. For example, a woman may not necessarily feel a desire to engage in sexual activity but, if approached, she may be receptive to sexual activity and, once engaged, she may then experience a desire for further sexual activity. A consensus panel of 19 experts in female sexual dysfunction selected from five countries was recently assembled to readdress the classification of women's sexual problems (Basson et al., 2003). The panel suggested that a lack of responsive desire (i.e., unwilling or uninterested in engaging in sexual activity when approached) be added to the *DSM-IV-TR* diagnostic criteria. Under this new classification, women who may not have sexual thoughts, fantasies, or seek out sexual interactions but are open to engaging in sexual activity when approached by their partner would not necessarily have HSDD.

In a random probability sample of 1,410 U.S. men and 1,749 U.S. women, Laumann, Gagnon, Michael, and Michaels (1994) reported 32% of women between the ages of 18 and 29 experienced a lack of sexual interest compared to 14% of men in the same age group. Though these estimates for women are somewhat higher than estimated levels of clinically diagnosed HSDD, they are consistent with the notion that desire problems are the number one sexual complaint reported by women. Findings from the Laumann et al. study also revealed a number of interesting gender differences in sexual drive mechanisms. For example, women did not show a change in rates of inhibited desire according to age, whereas men were significantly more likely to report lack of sexual interest as they aged—particularly after age 50. Women did not differ in rates of inhibited desire based on marital status; whereas, married men were significantly less likely to report inhibited desire compared to divorced or never married men. Women—but not men—who had less than a high school level of education reported significantly higher rates of inhibited desire compared to women with more education. Possibly, more educated women are more open to improving sexual communication and sexual knowledge that, in turn, may allow them to better fulfill their sexual needs. African American women reported significantly higher rates of inhibited desire compared to Caucasian or Hispanic women, whereas (among men) there were no ethnic differences in sexual desire (Laumann, Paik, & Rosen, 1999).

Same-sex couples show different patterns of sexual desire compared to heterosexual couples. For example, men in relationships with men are more likely to report low sexual desire when they view their sexual orientation more negatively. The lesbian "deathbed," referring to a complete lack of sexual desire from both partners in lesbian relationships, has recently received much attention from the literature. Women-focused studies have revealed that although lesbian couples may not express interest in more traditional sexual activities including vaginal penetration, they do maintain an active sexual life rich in foreplay and other forms of sexual stimulation (Nichols, 2004).

Factors Associated with HSDD

Cases of low desire in men are often related to medical conditions or pharmacological treatments that affect hormone levels, particularly testosterone. Men receiving testosterone replacement therapy because of a deficient secretion of gonadal hormones show a significant drop in sexual interest when treatment is stopped, and a return of sexual interest when hormone treatment is reinstated. This indicates that very low testosterone levels may impair sexual desire in men. However, once testosterone levels reach a certain threshold, additional testosterone does not further enhance sexual desire. In other words, testosterone administration to men with normal testosterone levels will not increase sexual desire even if they are experiencing low sexual desire. In adolescent males, higher testosterone levels are associated with increased frequency of sexual fantasies and sexual activity but this relationship does not hold true in adult men. Possibly, during and around puberty internal factors including hormones trigger sexual appetite, while in adulthood external cues such as relationship factors play a more key role in facilitating desire. Some evidence suggests that estrogen and progesterone administration reduces sexual desire in men with excessive or inappropriate desire, although few studies have been published on this topic (Meston & Frohlich, 2000).

In pre-menopausal women, androgens are secreted from both the adrenal glands and the ovaries. Unusually low testosterone levels that result from removal of the adrenal glands (adrenalectomy), removal of the ovaries (oophorectomy), or as a consequence of menopause, impair sexual desire in women. In the case of surgery-related declines in desire, it is often difficult to discriminate between the effects of reduced hormones on sexual desire and the negative psychological factors surrounding the circumstances that led to the surgery (e.g., cancer, polycystic ovaries). There has been recent interest in whether decreases in testosterone resulting from estrogenic oral contraceptive use negatively impacts desire mechanisms in women. Indeed, a number of studies have reported complaints of impaired desire among women on oral contraceptives, and it is well known that oral contraceptives produce substantial increases in sex hormone-binding globulin, which can lower testosterone levels.

Evidence for the role of testosterone in women's sexual desire is also provided by studies showing that testosterone effectively restores sexual desire in women with abnormally low testosterone levels. The enhancing effects of testosterone could be via direct hormonal mechanisms or indirectly by positively impacting mood and overall well-being (Traish & Kim, 2006). As is the case with men, administering testosterone to women with normal testosterone levels does not enhance sexual desire in women and—in the case of women—may lead to a number of undesirable side effects (e.g., acne, facial hair).

It is well known that many psychoactive medications affect sexual drive. Selective serotonin reuptake inhibitors (SSRIs)—used most commonly for treating depression—increase serotonin levels and produce a variety of sexual side effects in both men and women, including decreased desire. Sexual dysfunction secondary to SSRI use is believed to result, in part, from activation of the serotonin$_2$ receptor. Newer generations of antidepressants that act as antagonists (blockers) at the serotonin$_2$ receptor (e.g., nafazodone) are associated with fewer sexual side effects. Drugs that facilitate dopamine activity—such as the antiparkinsonian medication levodopa—tend to increase sexual desire in men but the role of dopamine activity in female sexual desire is not known.

HSDD has also been linked with a number of psychosocial factors in both men and women (Kaplan, 1979). Daily hassles such as worrying about children, paying the bills, and high stress jobs are offenders for suppressing sexual desire—as are a multitude of relationship or partner-related issues. In regard to the latter, couples reporting sexual difficulties—compared to nonclinical control couples—have been characterized as having less overall satisfaction within their relationships, an increased number of disagreements, more communication and conflict resolution problems, and more sexual communication problems including discomfort discussing sexual activities. They also tend to display less playfulness and spontaneity within their relationships, less closeness, intimacy, and feelings of mutual love, and more aversive feelings and thoughts within their sexual interactions. Warmth, caring, and affection within the relationship are undoubtedly linked to feelings of sexual desire.

In a recent study, McCall and Meston (2006) reported four distinct factors that describe triggers or cues for sexual desire in women. These include, emotional bonding cues (e.g, feeling a sense of love with your partner, feeling a sense of commitment from your partner), erotic/explicit cues (e.g., watching an erotic movie, asking for or anticipating sexual activity), visual/proximity cues (e.g., seeing/talking with someone famous, seeing a well toned body), and romantic/implicit cues (e.g., having a romantic dinner with your partner, laughing with a romantic partner). Not surprisingly, women diagnosed with HSDD scored significantly lower than sexually healthy women on each of these domains.

Psychological conditions most commonly associated with a lack of sexual desire include Social Phobia, Obsessive-Compulsive Disorder, Panic Disorder, and Mood Disorders—depression in particular. It is feasible that sexuality becomes of secondary importance when an individual is experiencing substantial distress in other areas of his or her life. With regards to depression, it is feasible that rumination of negative events, a common cognitive aspect of depression, may contribute to the decrease in desire noted in depressed persons by causing an exclusive focus on aspects of sexuality that are unpleasant. Also, it is well known that people with depression are prone to interpret negative events as caused by stable, global causes (Hankin, Fraley, & Abela, 2005) and this cognitive style could certainly negatively affect one's perception of sexuality.

A history of unwanted sexual experiences can also negatively affect sexual desire. Many, but not all, women with a history of childhood sexual abuse fear sexual intimacy, are likely to avoid sexual interactions with a partner, and are less receptive to sexual approaches from their partners (Rellini, 2006). A high proportion of women with a history of childhood sexual abuse also engage in risky sexual behaviors—such as engaging in sex with strangers while intoxicated (Bensley, Eenwyk, & Simmons, 2000). It is unknown whether this behavior is a reflection of high levels of sexual desire, a lack of ability to maintain or enforce physical boundaries, a compulsive act, or some combination of the three.

Assessment and Treatment of HSDD

Diagnosing HSDD is difficult because of the subjective nature of what constitutes sexual desire. Clinicians and researchers have often used frequency of sexual thoughts and fantasies as a measure of desire. Research suggests that this may accurately reflect desire mechanisms in men but not women. Engaging in sexual fantasy seems to be characteristic of women in new relationships, but research strongly suggests that the majority of sexually healthy women in longer-term relationships do not frequently engage in sexual fantasies. Measuring sexual desire according to frequency of sexual interactions is also problematic since this is dependent on partner availability. Also, people engage in sexual activities for a multitude of reasons other than desire (e.g., attempts to please a partner), and often there is a great discrepancy between the amount of sexual desire and the frequency of sexual activities. Comparing a client's sexual desire to the norms derived from the population does not provide an accurate assessment because it ignores important relational variables and also the diagnostic criteria of distress. Diagnosis of HSDD needs to be carefully considered within the context of the dyadic relationship and must take into consideration factors known to affect sexual functioning—such as the person's age, religion, culture, the length of the relationship, the partner's sexual function, and the context of the person's life.

Assessment of HSDD should comprise a complete sexual, medical, and psychosocial history, which can be obtained through standardized interviews and validated self-administered questionnaires. The clinician should explore the onset of the sexual problem keeping in mind dates of surgeries, medication changes, and diagnoses of medical conditions. Laboratory testing may be warranted, especially for men given the close relationship between androgens and sexual desire. A complete psychosocial history should include: situational problems, relationship history, sexual problems of the partner, mood, sexual satisfaction, and psychological disorders.

Testosterone treatment is effective for restoring desire in men and women with abnormally low levels of testosterone. Psychological treatments for HSDD include education about factors that affect sexual desire, couples exercises (e.g., scheduling times for physical and emotional intimacy), communication training (e.g., opening up about sexual issues and needs), cognitive restructuring of dysfunctional beliefs (e.g., a good sexual experience does not always end with an orgasm), sexual fantasy training (e.g., training people to develop and explore mental imagery), and *sensate focus*. Sensate focus, introduced by Masters and Johnson in the 1970s, is a behavioral technique in which couples learn to focus on the pleasurable sensations that are brought about by touching, while decreasing attention on goal directed sex (e.g., orgasm).

For persons in satisfying relationships, treatment may include identifying potential distracting, negative thoughts and helping them let go of these thoughts during sexual activity. Leiblum and Wiegel (2002) described four such types of distracting thoughts in women: myths and misconceptions (e.g., women are not supposed to enjoy sex), negative emotions, performance anxiety, and body image concerns (e.g., focusing on unattractive aspects of one's body). Behavioral techniques designed to help men and women explore their sexual likes and dislikes—alone or with their partners—can be used to help them associate sexual behaviors with positive affect and experiences. For individuals who are distracted by feelings of shame or embarrassment about their bodies, cognitive restructuring might involve helping them to identify their fears (e.g., a fear of rejection) and dysfunctional beliefs (e.g., "My partner thinks my body isn't sexy") and then test the accuracy of these beliefs through a series of strategically designed behavioral experiments. The experiments aim at reducing avoidance behavior and provide corrective experiences to counteract dysfunctional beliefs. For example, a woman who keeps her clothing on during sex because she feels that her partner would reject her if he saw her naked would be encouraged to incrementally remove pieces of clothing and test the reaction of her partner.

SEXUAL AVERSION

Sexual aversion is conceptualized as a phobic reaction to sexual contact and, in many ways, is more similar to an Anxiety Disorder than to a Sexual Disorder. In the *DSM-IV-TR*, it is defined as the recurrent or persistent extreme avoidance of (or aversion to) all or nearly all genital sexual contact with a sexual partner. It can be so severe that an individual may avoid any type of physical contact including holding hands for fear that such contact may lead to sexual interaction. There is a paucity of information on the prevalence of Aversion Disorder, but it is generally not thought to be a rare disorder.

Little is known about the etiology of Sexual Aversion Disorder other than people with sexual aversion report high levels of anxiety in anticipation of potential sexual contact. The aversion is not always towards intercourse, but may be towards specific sexual elements such as semen, which, over time, may or may not become more generalized. Clinical reports have found that many women reporting sexual aversion symptoms are survivors of child sexual abuse (Van Berlo & Ensinck, 2000).

Sexual Aversion Disorder is commonly treated with anxiety-reduction techniques such as systematic desensitization, which involves creating a hierarchy of sexual activities that provoke increasing levels of anxiety and then exposing the person to the anxiety-producing stimuli while he or she engages in relaxation exercises. After several sessions of pairing the fear-arousing stimuli with a state of relaxation, the person is usually able to imagine the scenario without becoming intensely anxious and can then proceed to the next scenario on the hierarchy. Once the person is able to imagine all of the scenarios on the hierarchy without experiencing substantial distress, the same technique is applied to experiencing the scenarios in real life either alone or with a partner.

Sexual Arousal Disorders

ERECTILE DYSFUNCTION (ED)

Definition, Diagnosis, and Prevalence

ED is defined in the *DSM-IV-TR* as the inability to reach or maintain adequate erection of the penis to engage in intercourse. Patients are diagnosed with ED when their erectile difficulties are exclusively psychogenic in nature or are caused by a combination of psychological and medical factors. Men of all ages occasionally have difficulty obtaining or maintaining an erection but true Erectile Disorder is more common after age 50. Laumann et al. (1999) reported approximately 7% of men aged 18–29 years have erectile problems compared to 18% of men aged 50–59 years. Level of education and ethnicity are not associated with erectile difficulties, but married men are less likely to report erectile problems compared to never married or divorced men (Laumann et al., 1999). It has been estimated that approximately 60 to 80% of ED cases are of organic etiology. However, anxiety, self-confidence, and relationship factors can contribute to the maintenance or exacerbation of the condition even when the etiology is organic.

Factors Associated with Erection and Erectile Dysfunction

Erections are caused by increased blood pressure in the corpora cavernosa (the sinusoid of the erectile tissue) via increased blood inflow and decreased blood outflow. The increment of blood inflow is regulated by the relaxation of the smooth muscles surrounding the arterioles—a phenomenon that allows the arteriole to dilate. Smooth muscle relaxation has been attributed to an increase in parasympathetic activity that causes a release of the neurotransmitters acetylcholine, vasoactive intestinal polypeptide, and nitric oxide. Nitric oxide causes a greater amount of cyclic guanosine monophosphate (cGMP) to be available in the smooth muscles and this causes the smooth muscles to relax. Normally, cGMP is broken down by enzymes known as phosphodiesterases (PDEs). However, this may be circumvented by inhibiting the activity of these enzymes. Viagra (sildenafil) and other drugs used to treat ED inhibit PDE type 5. In doing so, these drugs enhance the concentration of cGMP, allowing for greater smooth muscle relaxation and therefore improved erection. Detumescence (i.e., loss of erection) occurs with the release of catecholamines during orgasm and ejaculation.

Surgery, metabolic disorders such as diabetes mellitus, alcoholism, hypothyroidism, infectious diseases such as HIV and other viral infections, and pelvic pathologies such as systemic lupus, and vascular problems associated with atherosclerosis and hypertension, are all potential causes of ED. Drugs that decrease dopamine or reduce testosterone production are also implicated in ED. These include antihypertensive medications, antipsychotic drugs, anxiolitics, antiandrogens, anticholesterol agents, and drugs used to regulate heart rate. Antiparkinsonian medications increase dopamine and facilitate erection.

The major psychological contributors to ED as identified by Barlow's (1986) model of sexual dysfunction are anxiety, negative expectations, and spectatoring. Men who are anxious about not being able to have an erection tend to focus on themselves and how they are performing more than on what gives them pleasure. This *spectatoring* increases anxiety that (physiologically) inhibits the relaxation of the smooth muscles necessary for erection and (psychologically) leads to a negative mood state and a focus on negative expectancies. Since the result is impaired erectile response, the man's fears of not being able to perform are confirmed and they are likely to repeat the process in subsequent sexual situations. By contrast, men with normal erectile responding approach sexual situations with positive expectancies and a focus on erotic cues. Consequently, they become aroused and are able to obtain and sustain an erection, which creates a positive feedback loop for future sexual encounters.

Assessment and Treatment of Erectile Dysfunction

The assessment of ED includes identifying the situation(s) surrounding the onset of ED and the potential beliefs that were formed at that time. Beliefs may be specific to the relationship (i.e., a feeling of inadequacy with one specific partner) or generalize to all situations. In cases where ED is the result of a vascular problem, laboratory assessments that measure genital blood inflow and outflow during sexual stimulation may be helpful. Blood outflow can be measured by injecting agents such as papaverine into the penile corpora cavernosa. The substance relaxes the smooth muscles at the base of the penis, which—in presence of normal blood outflow—produces penile erection even without sexual stimulation. When the drug fails to provide the expected erection, it is considered evidence for impairment in vascular mechanisms. Measurement of nocturnal penile erections—which are expected to increase during the REM sleep cycle in sexually healthy men—is another commonly used technique for assessing potential vascular causes of ED. Assays of free and bioavailable serum testosterone are used to rule out abnormal hormone levels.

Treatments for ED include vacuum devices and constriction rings, intracavernosal injections, intraurethral pharmacotherapy, topical pharmacotherapy, oral pharmacotherapy, and penile implants. Vacuum constriction devices are the most safe and least expensive ED treatment. These consist of a tube that is placed over the penis, and a vacuum pump that draws blood into the penile arteries. A constriction ring is placed at the base of the penis to prevent blood outflow so that the erection is maintained until completion of the sexual act. Intracavernosal injections refer to medications such as papaverine, phentolamine, and prostaglandin E_1 that are injected into the corpus cavernosum of the penis to induce erection. These all act to dilate penile capillaries, allowing blood to flow into the penis. Although intracavernosal injections are effective in approximately 70 to 90% of patients, a large percentage of users discontinue treatment due to the inconvenience, cost, and/or invasiveness of treatment.

The most popular and effective pharmacological treatments for ED are phosphodiesterase type 5 (PDE_5) inhibitors such as sildenafil (Viagra), verdanafil (Levitra), and tadalafil (Cialis). In fact, since Viagra was introduced to the market in 1998, many of these other rather cumbersome and involved treatments have become less popular. Viagra has been estimated to successfully treat two-thirds of men with ED, is well tolerated by a variety of patients, and is an effective treatment for both organic and psychogenic ED. However, despite these drugs' success with facilitating erection, one study reported between 40 and 80% of men with ED who began treatment with Viagra stopped taking the medication (Leiblum, 2002). Some men discontinue Viagra use because, although it enhances their ability to have an erection, this is not always enough to restore overall sexual desire and satisfaction—which may be more closely intertwined with psychological and relational factors. In a recent study, Melnik and Abdo (2005) compared the effects of six months treatment with Viagra to psychotherapy or Viagra plus psychotherapy, and psychotherapy alone outperformed Viagra in terms of decreasing erectile problems. The psychotherapy aimed at developing realistic and positive expectations for the sexual relationship, and also encouraged patients to explore the emotional components linked to ED.

Penile implants are generally considered a last resort treatment technique when tissue damage or deterioration is severe or when other treatments have failed. This may be the case in men with severe diabetes mellitus or who have had radical prostatectomy. Implants can be hydraulic, semirigid, or soft silicone, and consist of two or three cylinders placed in the space normally occupied by the spongy tissue in the penis. The patient's ability to ejaculate after the implant surgery remains in tact; however, the implant does not restore sensitivity or sexual drive that may have been present prior to the onset of ED. Implant surgeries usually result in decreased penis size, which may dissuade some men from undergoing surgery.

FEMALE SEXUAL AROUSAL DISORDER (FSAD)

Definition, Diagnosis, and Prevalence

The *DSM-IV-TR* defines Female Sexual Arousal Disorder (FSAD) exclusively in physiological terms as a persistent or recurrent inability to attain or maintain an adequate lubrication, swelling response until completion of sexual activity. It has been suggested by a committee of experts in the field of women's sexuality that three subtypes of FSAD would more accurately reflect women's experiences with sexual arousal problems (Basson et al., 2003). These are: Subjective Sexual Arousal Disorder, which refers to the absence of feelings of sexual arousal (sexual excitement and sexual pleasure) but vaginal lubrication or other signs of physical response still occur; Genital Sexual Arousal Disorder, which refers to absent or impaired genital sexual arousal (e.g., minimal vaginal lubrication from any type of sexual stimulation and reduced sexual sensations from caressing genitalia) but psychological sexual excitement still occurs; and Combined Genital and Subjective Arousal Disorder. Most women who complain of arousal problems would meet criteria for the combined category. Though no prevalence data are available on the FSAD subtypes, the estimated lifetime prevalence of problems with general FSAD is 20% (Laumann et al., 1999).

Factors Associated with Women's Sexual Arousal and FSAD

Estrogen is critical for the maintenance of vaginal tissue function and structure, and estrogen deficiency has been linked with various vaginal problems including reduced or delayed lubrication, reduced vaginal blood flow, and increased likelihood of pain during sex. The majority of research on the effects of estrogen on sexual function has been conducted in postmenopausal women and women who have undergone surgery to remove their ovaries (oophorectomy). In post-menopausal women, the reduction in estrogen levels that occurs when the menstrual cycle ends is associated with increased pH levels in the vagina, a reduction or delayed onset of lubrication in response to sexual stimulation, and structural changes to the vagina and vulva such as thinning and reduction of elasticity of the vaginal wall, changes to the vaginal epithelium, and loss of collagen in the vulva (Bachmann, Ebert, & Burd, 1999). All of these changes can lead to arousal difficulties due to a reduction in tissue sensitivity and vaginal lubrication.

As noted earlier, in premenopausal women androgens secreted from the adrenal glands and the ovaries have been linked to desire mechanisms in women. Some speculate that androgens are also involved in female sexual arousal. One study found a positive correlation between testosterone (a form of androgen) and genital arousal in healthy, premenopausal women when levels of testosterone and arousal were compared across the menstrual cycle (Schreiner-Engel, Schiavi, Smith, & White, 1981). A more recent study found that administering testosterone to premenopausal women increased their genital arousal (Tuiten et al., 2002). Nitric oxide—the neurotransmitter involved in male erection—is produced in clitoral tissue and may also be important for women's sexual arousal.

Sympathetic and parasympathetic nervous system arousal (SNS and PNS) both play a role in genital arousal in women but the relationship between the two systems is not well understood. Norepinephrine (NE) is the primary neurotransmitter involved in SNS communication, and when measured after exposure to a sexually arousing film, blood levels of NE are higher than prefilm levels (Exton et al., 2000). Women with spinal cord injuries between areas T10 and T12 in the spinal cord show a lack of lubrication during psychological sexual arousal (Berard, 1989). This is the area of the spinal cord where sympathetic nerves project to the genital region. A number of laboratory studies have also provided evidence for the role of SNS involvement in women's sexual arousal. For example, Hoon, Wincze, and Hoon (1977) demonstrated that when women were shown an anxiety-evoking film prior to an erotic film, they experienced higher levels of vaginal blood volume (a measure of genital engorgement) than when they were shown a neutral (i.e., travel) film prior to an erotic film. Anxiety-evoking films are likely to increase SNS activation. Recent research has shown a curvilinear relationship between acute anxiety and vaginal engorgement, with the optimal arousal response occurring at moderate levels of anxiety (Bradford & Meston, 2006). Meston and colleagues have completed several studies on the effects of exercise (Meston & Gorzalka, 1996) and ephedrine (Meston & Heiman,

1998) on sexual arousal, two manipulation techniques designed to increase SNS activity. These studies also support the notion that there is an optimal level of SNS arousal that is necessary for adequate genital arousal in women. Mechanisms that interfere with normal SNS activity—such as stress—can negatively impact a woman's ability to become aroused.

Given the high coexistence of sexual desire and arousal problems in women, it is not surprising that the myriad of factors affecting women's sexual desire noted earlier also affect women's sexual arousal. According to the Dual-Control Model proposed by Bancroft and colleagues (Bancroft & Janssen, 2000), sexual arousal is the combination of both excitatory and inhibitory forces. Five main themes have been described as potential inhibitors or enhancers of sexual arousal for women ages 18 to 84 years: feelings about one's body, negative consequences of sexual activity (e.g., bad reputation, pregnancy), feeling desired and accepted by a sexual partner, feeling used by a sexual partner, and negative mood (Graham, Sanders, Milhausen, & McBride, 2004).

Assessment and Treatment of FSAD

The assessment of FSAD is similar to that of HSDD in women and should include a comprehensive sexual, medical, and psychosocial history. Levels of physiological sexual arousal can be assessed indirectly using a vaginal photoplethysmograph to assess vaginal blood engorgement, sonograms (pictures of internal organs derived by sound waves bouncing off organs and other tissues) and fMRI (imaging techniques that track changes in blood concentration in inner organs) to assess blood engorgement in the genitals. These techniques are more commonly used for research purposes than as diagnostic tools.

Many of the psychological treatments described earlier to treat HSDD are used to treat psychological feelings of impaired sexual arousal. Physiological aspects of FSAD are most commonly treated with topical lubricants that help mask impairments in vaginal lubrication. They do not, however, enhance genital/clitoral blood flow or genital sensations that are often decreased with FSAD, and they do not directly impact psychological sexual arousal.

Currently, there are no Food and Drug Administration (FDA) approved pharmacological treatments for FSAD. However, since the enormous success of using PDE5 inhibitors (e.g., sildenafil, levitra, cialis) for treating Male Arousal Disorder (ED), a number of pharmaceutical companies have examined whether these and similar vasodilator drugs may also be effective for treating FSAD. Evidence from limited placebo-controlled studies indicates Viagra increases genital engorgement in healthy, premenopausal women (Laan et al., 2002) and in postmenopausal women with severe levels of genital arousal concerns (Basson & Brotto, 2003). Despite reports of increased physiological sexual arousal, studies in general have not found that these drugs positively impact a woman's psychological experience of sexual arousal. This suggests that—for women—psychological factors such as relationship satisfaction, mood state, and sexual scenarios may play a more important role in assessing feelings of sexual desire and arousal than do physiological genital cues. The EROS clitoral therapy device is an FDA-approved treatment for women's sexual concerns. This small hand held device increases vasocongestion in the clitoral and labial region via a suction mechanism and has been reported to increase vaginal lubrication and sensation (Billups et al., 2001).

Orgasm

MALE ORGASMIC DISORDER

Delayed or Inhibited Ejaculation

Delayed or inhibited ejaculation following normal sexual arousal and adequate sexual stimulation is a rare condition, affecting up to only 3% of the male population (Laumann et al., 1994). Impairments in orgasm and ejaculation have often been noted as a side effect of SSRI antidepressant use and has led some researchers to speculate that serotonin may play a role in the etiology of this disorder. In most cases, however, delayed or inhibited ejaculation tends to be psychological rather than physiological, and performance anxiety seems to play a major role. Also, rigid views about sexuality—such as the belief that orgasm is the only way to experience sexual satisfaction—can direct the focus of attention during sexual activity to reaching an orgasm and this may distract a man from experiencing sexual pleasure, which can cause impaired ejaculation and orgasm. Lack of communication about sexual likes and dislikes between partners, and feeling uncomfortable with one's partner are typical relational factors that may prevent a man from enjoying sexual interactions with his partner and impair ejaculatory ability. Treatment for delayed or inhibited ejaculation generally includes helping the couple to break their focus on orgasm and refocus their attention to sexual pleasure and intimacy.

Premature Ejaculation

Definition, Diagnosis, and Prevalence. The *DSM-IV-TR* defines premature ejaculation (PE) as ejaculation that occurs with limited stimulation before, or shortly after, penetration and sooner than the man desires. An important criterion for this condition is the feeling that the man does not have control over ejaculation and this causes him distress. The time from penetration to ejaculation (ejaculation latency) varies greatly between men, with 10 minutes being the average for men with no sexual problems. An individual with PE tends to ejaculate within the first minute of intercourse, with the majority of men reporting an average of 15 seconds or 15 thrusts of intercourse before ejaculation. At times, a man may report distress because he is unable to prevent ejaculation for 20 or 30 minutes. In this instance, the diagnosis of PE is not warranted even if the individual reports high levels of distress.

PE is the most commonly reported Sexual Disorder in men, with approximately 30% of men in the United States reporting PE in the previous year (Laumann et al., 1994). Unlike ED, this condition has been estimated to affect younger men more than older men. As many as 40% of men under 40 years of age and only 10% of men over age 70 have been estimated to experience PE (Corona et al., 2004). The cause of PE is usually assumed to be psychological rather than physiological, although both medical and psychotherapy techniques have been developed to treat this problem.

Factors Associated with Ejaculation and PE. During the first stage of ejaculation (sperm emission), sperm is emitted from the epididymus into the vas deferens. This process is controlled by the contraction of smooth muscles, which is generated by the sympathetic branch of the autonomic nervous system. After sperm emission, the individual has the subjective experience that ejaculation is inevitable—known as the "point of inevitable ejaculation" or, more commonly, "the point of no return." The striate muscles surrounding the spongious tissue, the cavernous tissue, and in the pelvic floor, contract rhythmically causing ejaculation to occur. Usually, the subjective experience of orgasm is associated with the contractions of the striate muscles and—in most men— emission, ejaculation, and orgasm are interconnected. For a small portion of men, however, these phenomena are independent. For example, some men train themselves to have the subjective experience of orgasm without ejaculation and some men with PE experience emission without ejaculation.

The precise cause of PE is not known, but it can arise from a deficiency in any of the afferent or efferent circuits involved in the ejaculatory process. For what concerns the sensory (afferent) circuits, researchers have postulated that men with PE have a lower sensitivity threshold such that less stimulation is needed to attain ejaculation. This explanation cannot account for all cases of PE, however, as studies show that PE exists in men with both high and low sensitivity thresholds. It has also been proposed that men with PE may respond with a higher level of arousal to sexual stimuli (hyperarousability). Again, this explanation cannot account for all cases of PE. One psychophysiological study (Rowland & Slob, 1997) that measured penile rigidity in the laboratory showed that men with PE had a weaker genital response to visual stimuli compared to men with no sexual dysfunction, but had a comparable genital response to men with no sexual dysfunction during tactile plus visual stimuli.

Anxiety has most frequently been hypothesized to be the primary cause and maintaining factor for PE. Anxiety increases sympathetic nervous system activity, which is involved in semen emission, and, thus, high levels of anxiety could feasibly accelerate ejaculation. Laboratory studies have generally not shown significant differences in levels of anxiety reported by men with and without PE. One psychological variable that has shown significant differences between men with and without PE is perceived control over ejaculation. During exposure to visual and tactile stimuli, men with and without PE showed comparable degrees of genital sexual arousal (measured in penile circumference), but men with PE reported significantly less control over their ejaculation. A greater understanding of the meaning men attribute to ejaculatory control may provide important insight into the psychological factors involved in this disorder.

Assessment and Treatment of PE.   A thorough assessment of PE includes measuring three factors: length of time from penetration to ejaculation (ejaculation latency), subjective feelings of control over ejaculation, and personal and relational distress caused by the condition. Usually these dimensions of PE are assessed with retrospective self-reports provided by the patient. Sometimes the patient is asked to use a chronometer to measure the time from insertion to ejaculation or to have their partner provide an estimate of the man's ejaculatory latency in order to help increase measurement reliability.

The most commonly used psychotherapy techniques for increasing ejaculatory latency are the squeeze technique developed by Masters and Johnson (1970) and the pause technique (Kaplan, 1989). The squeeze technique consists of engaging in sexual stimulation alone or with a partner for as long as possible before ejaculation. Before reaching the point of inevitable ejaculation the man is instructed to stop the activity and apply tactile pressure to the penile glands to decrease the urge to ejaculate but not to the point that he completely loses his erection. When the urge has subsided, the man resumes masturbation or intercourse stopping as many times as needed in order to delay ejaculation. The pause technique is similar to the squeeze technique with the exception that no pressure is applied to the penis. At times, clinicians may suggest using a PDE_5

inhibitor (e.g., Viagra) along with these techniques so that the man can practice delaying ejaculation without worrying about maintaining an erection.

Medical treatments include the use of topical anesthetics to diminish sensitivity used in combination with condoms (to prevent to the partner's genitals from being anesthetized). SSRIs such as sertaline, fluoxetine, and paroxetine have been used because of their known side effects of delaying or inhibiting orgasm. In men with PE, there is some evidence these drugs increase ejaculation latency and sexual pleasure and satisfaction.

FEMALE ORGASMIC DISORDER (FOD)

Definition, Diagnosis, and Prevalence

Female Orgasmic Disorder (FOD) is diagnosed when the woman experiences persistent or recurrent delay in—or absence of—orgasm following a normal sexual excitement phase. In order to meet *DSM-IV-TR* diagnostic criteria, the woman's orgasmic capacity must be less than what would be reasonable for her age, sexual experience, and adequacy of sexual stimulation she receives (APA, 2000). Clinical consensus is that women who can achieve orgasm through masturbation or through manual stimulation with a partner, but not from intercourse alone, would not meet diagnostic criteria for FOD.

Orgasm difficulties are the second most frequently reported sexual problems for women in the United States, with between 22 to 28% of women ages 18 to 59 years reporting they are unable to attain orgasm (Laumann et al., 1994). Young women (18 to 24 years) show rates of orgasm lower than older women for both orgasm with a partner and orgasm during masturbation (Laumann et al., 1994). This is likely due to age differences in sexual experience.

Factors Associated with Women's Orgasm and FOD

In most cases, FOD is thought to stem from psychological causes and there are no specific physiological factors linked to orgasmic dysfunction in women. Impairments in endocrine, nervous system, or brain mechanisms involved in female orgasm, however, may cause orgasmic dysfunction in women. Studies examining blood plasma levels of neuromodulators before, during, and after orgasm suggest that epinephrine and norepinephrine levels peak during orgasm in normally functioning women (Exton et al., 2000). Among orgasmic women, oxytocin levels are positively correlated with subjective intensity of orgasm and prolactin levels are elevated for up to 60 minutes following orgasm (Meston & Frohlich, 2000). Studies in humans suggest that the paraventricular nucleus of the hypothalamus—an area of the brain that produces oxytocin—is involved in the orgasmic response (McKenna, 1999). Impairments in any of these systems could feasibly lead to FOD.

Medical conditions that affect women's orgasmic ability include: damage to the sacral/pelvic nerves, multiple sclerosis, Parkinson's disease, epilepsy, hysterectomy complications, vulvodynia, diabetes mellitus, hypothalamus-pituitary disorders, and sickle cell anemia. A number of psychotherapeutic drugs have also been noted to affect the ability of women to attain orgasm. The SSRIs frequently affect orgasmic functioning, leading to delayed orgasm or a complete inability to reach orgasm. There is variability, however, in that some antidepressants have been associated with impaired orgasm more often than others. This seems to be related to which specific serotonin receptor subtype is being activated. As noted earlier, drugs that inhibit serotonin activity at the serotonin$_2$ receptor (e.g., nefazodone, cyproheptadine) cause fewer sexual side effects in women (Meston, Hull, Levin, & Sipski, 2004).

The psychological factors associated with FOD include sexual guilt, anxiety related to sex, childhood loss or separation from the father, and relationship issues (Meston et al., 2004). Sexual guilt can affect orgasmic abilities by increasing anxiety and discomfort during sex, and also by distracting a woman from what gives her pleasure. Women who strictly abide to the values of western religions sometimes view sexual pleasure as a sin. Sins are later connected with a sense of shame and guilt, which could produce negative affect and cause distracting thoughts during sexual activities. Indeed, a reduction in sexual guilt has been associated with improvements in orgasmic abilities (Shotly et al., 1984). Women who initiate and are more active participants during sexual activities report more frequent orgasms, most likely because being active allows women to assume positions that can provide a greater sense of sexual pleasure. More frequent masturbation and sexual activities are associated with more frequent orgasms. It is likely that women who engage in more sexual activities have a greater understanding of what gives them sexual pleasure and this can help them reach orgasm more easily. Culturally, women who live in societies that value female orgasm tend to have more orgasms than women living in societies that discourage the concept of sexual pleasure for women (Meston et al. (2004). Examples of societies that foster sexual pleasure for women and expect them to enjoy intercourse include the Mundugumor and the Mangaia. Mangaian women are taught to have orgasms, hopefully two or three to each one of her male partner's, and to try to attain mutual orgasm. Mangaian males who are not able to give their partners multiple orgasms are not held in high esteem. At the opposite end of the spectrum are societies that assume women will have no pleasure from coitus and that the female orgasm does not exist. The Arapesh are such a society. In fact, they do not even have a word in their language for the female orgasm. It is feasible that women in societies that promote women's sexual pleasure are more likely to experiment and, therefore, learn about what facilitates their ability to have an orgasm. It may also be that in societies where sexual pleasure is discouraged it may be shameful to admit to having an orgasm.

Assessment and Treatment of FOD

Assessment of FOD involves a comprehensive sexual, medical, and psychosocial history similar to that used for assessing HSDD and FSAD. It is important for the clinician to determine whether the woman is unable to attain orgasm in all situations or just with a certain partner or during certain intercourse positions or sexual techniques because this information may determine the type of therapy she receives. In general, sex therapy for FOD focuses on promoting healthy changes in attitudes and sexually relevant thoughts, decreasing anxiety, and increasing orgasmic ability and satisfaction. Sensate focus and systematic desensitization (described earlier) are used to treat FOD when anxiety seems to play a role. Sex education and communication skills training are often included as adjuncts to treatment. Kegel exercises (Kegel, 1952), which involve tightening and relaxing the pubococcygeous muscle, are also sometimes included as part of a treatment regime. Feasibly, they could help facilitate orgasm by increasing blood flow to the genitals, or by helping the woman become more aware of and comfortable with her genitals.

To date, the most efficacious treatment for FOD is directed masturbation (DM). The first step of DM involves having the woman visually examine her nude body with the help of a mirror and diagrams of female genital anatomy. She is then instructed to explore her genitals using touch with an emphasis on locating sensitive areas that produce feelings of pleasure. Once pleasure-producing areas are located, the woman is instructed to concentrate on manual stimulation of these areas and to increase the intensity and duration until "something happens." The use of topical lubricants, vibrators, and erotic videotapes are often incorporated into the exercises. Next, once the woman is able to attain orgasm alone, her partner is usually included in the sessions in order to desensitize her to displaying arousal and orgasm in his presence, and to educate the partner on how to provide her with effective stimulation. DM has been shown to effectively treat FOD, with some studies reporting a 100% success rate (Meston et al., 2004). Given masturbation can be performed alone, any anxiety that may be associated with partner evaluation is necessarily eliminated.

For women who have orgasm difficulties resulting from hysterectomy and oophorectomy, combined estrogen and testosterone therapy has been shown to enhance orgasmic ability (Shifren et al., 2000). A number of psychotherapeutic drugs have been used to try to eliminate orgasm problems that are secondary to antidepressant drug treatments. Results from placebo-controlled studies, to date, suggest none of the drugs enhance orgasmic ability better than placebo.

Sexual Pain Disorders

DEFINITION, DIAGNOSIS, AND PREVALENCE

Sexual pain can affect men as well as women—albeit much less frequently—and very little is known about sexual pain in men. In this chapter we discuss sexual pain only as it pertains to women. The *DSM-IV-TR* Sexual Pain Disorders include Dyspareunia and Vaginismus. Dyspareunia is defined as persistent and recurrent genital pain during sexual activity. The pain may also occur in situations other than sexual encounters, such as gynecological examinations. Dyspareunia is usually described by women as a sharp, dull, burning, or shooting pain, and can be either localized or generalized. Most often, the pain is considered a superficial pain in that it is associated with the vulva or entrance to the vagina. It may, however, also be experienced as a deeper pain in the abdomen or internal organs. Laumann et al. (1999) reported that approximately 16% of American women reported persistent or recurrent sexual pain in the past year. Sexual pain was noted to be three times more likely among women in the 18–29 age range than those in the 50–59 age range. Poor health, lower education, low family income, high stress, more frequent emotional problems, and the presence of urinary tract symptoms are more common among women with sexual pain.

Vaginismus is defined by the *DSM-IV-TR* as a repeated and persistent involuntary spasm of the vaginal muscles that interferes with intercourse. Although it is clear that contraction of the pelvic floor musculature can prevent vaginal penetration in women, recent empirical work has demonstrated that vaginal spasms can also occur in women who do not report difficulty with vaginal penetration, and not all women who have difficulty with vaginal penetration experience vaginal spasms (Reissing, Binik, Khalife, Cohen, & Amsel, 2004). Also of note is the fact that, although Vaginismus is classified as a

Pain Disorder and appears to be associated with genital pain in most cases (Ter Kuile, Van Lankveld, Vlieland, Willekes, & Weigenborg, 2005), the presence of pain is not required to make a diagnosis of Vaginismus. Epidemiological studies generally exclude questions about Vaginismus; thus, the prevalence of the disorder is not well established. However, it has been estimated to be between 1% and 6% (Lewis et al., 2004).

FACTORS ASSOCIATED WITH DYSPAREUNIA AND VAGINISMUS

Dyspareunia may result from a variety of medical conditions and anatomical complications that should be ruled out by medical examination. Superficial pain may be a symptom of dermatological disorders affecting the external genitalia, vaginal atrophy, anatomical variations, urinary tract infections, injury, and other diseases and infections of the vulva. The majority of women who experience superficial sexual pain show a reliable symptom pattern that includes sensitivity to touch and pressure of the vulvar vestibule, a region bounded by the inner labia minora, the frenulum of the clitoris, and the lower portion of the vaginal opening. Touch or pressure to these areas evokes a sharp, burning pain (Pukall, Payne, Kao, Khalife, & Binik, 2005). This disorder is known as Vulvar Vestibulitis Syndrome, and it is considered separate from other pain syndromes of the vulva. The etiology of Vulvar Vestibulitis Syndrome is uncertain, but women with the disorder often have a history of yeast infections and may have had significant hormonal events in adolescence, including early onset of menstruation and early use of oral contraceptives (Pukall et al., 2005).

Deep sexual pain may result from uterine fibroids, endometriosis, urinary disease, and ovarian disease, among other conditions. Sensitization of the neurons in the spinal cord and in parts of the brain has been postulated as one of the most likely causes of Dyspareunia. According to this theory, intense stimulation of peripheral tissue that occurs because of a trauma or because repetitive abrasive stimulation can sensitize the neurons that bring the pain information to the brain. Consequently, the sensitized neurons require less stimulation to be activated, or they may even be activated without the presence of stimulation. Thus, the individual may feel pain after only a slight touch or even in the presence of no touch. Low pain threshold has been identified as a potential correlate of women with Dyspareunia (Pukal, Reissing, Binik, Khalife, & Abbott, 2000). The low pain thresholds in women with Dyspareunia is not specific to the genital area but, rather, it includes the overall body which supports some theorists views that Dyspareunia should be classified as a Pain Disorder rather than a Sexual Disorder (Binik, Meana, Berkley, & Kalippe, 1999). Indeed, sexual pain shares many etiological similarities with chronic low back pain and other chronic pain syndromes.

The fear of pain and anxiety has been postulated as both a psychological symptom and cause of Dyspareunia. Empirical studies have indeed found a strong association between the presence of sexual pain and anxiety, although the degree of anxiety is not correlated with the intensity of pain, and not all women who experience sexual anxiety experience sexual pain. Women with Dyspareunia tend to fear sexual interactions and show more phobic anxiety than do women with no sexual pain. Payne, Binik, Amsel, and Khalife (2005) found that women with Vulvar Vestibulitis Syndrome reported hypervigilance for sexual pain, and displayed an attentional bias toward pain-related stimuli on an emotional Stroop task when compared to matched control women without Vulvar Vestibulitis Syndrome.

Depression has also been frequently associated with Dyspareunia; however, longitudinal studies have failed to find a direct relationship between depression and sexual pain. It is likely that women who are more depressed are more likely to report pain in general and sexual pain specifically, but there is no evidence at this point that depression *causes* sexual pain or vice versa. Negative cognitions such as: "My partner will leave me," "I am a failure as a woman," and "I must be tearing inside," are commonly reported by women with sexual pain. From a relational point of view, women with dyspareunia report more pain when their relational distress increases, an indication that sexual pain may be partially associated with negative feelings between partners.

The precise factors associated with Vaginismus are unknown. Experts have proposed that Vaginismus may be a physiological response to an intense pain. That is, the hypothesized vaginal spasm in Vaginismus could be an automatic reaction of the body to protect itself from an expected pain. Indeed, the comorbidity between Vaginismus and Dyspareunia is relatively high (Basson & Riley, 1994). Sexual trauma has been linked to Vaginismus in the empirical literature, but the data to support this association are inconsistent.

ASSESSMENT AND TREATMENT OF DYSPAREUNIA AND VAGINISMUS

The assessment of Dyspareunia should include an accurate description of the location, intensity, quality, duration, and time course of the pain, the degree of interference it has with sexuality, a summary of what elicits the pain (both sexual and nonsexual behaviors), and the meaning attributed to the pain. Assessment usually requires a gynecological examination to help identify the specific area(s) of the pain. Vaginismus is diagnosed if (a) the woman reports she has never been able to have intercourse after at least 10 attempts, and (b) she has showed active avoidance. Active avoidance is either less than one attempt at intercourse every two months, the inability to have a complete pelvic exam or the inability to use tampons.

Treatments for Dyspareunia include cognitive-behavioral therapy, electromyographic feedback, and vestibulectomy. Topical anesthetics and other medications are also sometimes used to alleviate genital pain, but well controlled studies examining their long-term effectiveness are currently lacking. Cognitive-behavioral therapy generally includes educating the woman about sexual pain, the effect it has on sexual desire, arousal, and orgasm, and the factors that maintain the pain. Often cognitive restructuring exercises are used to help the women identify faulty cognitions (e.g., "If I have sex my vagina may tear apart") and to replace them with more accurate beliefs (e.g., "My vagina is made of stretchable muscles that stretch out during intercourse"). Bergeron et al. (2001) found that eight sessions of group cognitive behavior therapy for Vulvar Vestibulitis Syndrome significantly reduced genital pain from pre- to post-treatment, with 39% of women endorsing great improvement or complete pain relief at the six-month follow-up interval.

Electromyographic biofeedback consists of providing information to the woman about the tension in her pelvic floor muscles with the goal of helping her to maintain a relaxed pelvic musculature state during sexual activity. This technique was developed by Glazer, Rodke, Swencionis, Hertz, and Young (1995), who observed a relationship between Vulvar Vestibulitis Syndrome and abnormal responding of the pelvic floor musculature. Evidence suggests that the pelvic floor training approach significantly reduces Vulvar Vestibulitis Syndrome pain and may occasionally eliminate it altogether (e.g., Bergeron et al., 2001). Vestibulectomy, an outpatient procedure that involves removal of vulvar vestibular tissue, has also been shown to significantly reduce or completely alleviate genital pain among the majority of recipients (Goldstein & Goldstein, 2006).

Treatment for Vaginismus includes many of the same elements as those employed for Dyspareunia. In addition, relaxation exercises and vaginal dilation exercises, which involve having the women insert progressively larger dilation cones into her vagina, are used to teach the woman to pair thoughts of vaginal penetration with positive affect and muscular relaxation.

Summary and Future Directions

In summary, this chapter provided an overview of the four major categories of sexual concerns in men and women as outlined by the *DSM-IV-TR*. It is apparent that biological, psychological, and social factors all play a prominent role in the etiology of sexual dysfunctions in men and women and must be carefully considered both in assessment and treatment. To date, efficacious treatments exist for Orgasm Disorders in men (Premature Ejaculation Disorder) and women (Female Orgasmic Disorder), for Arousal Disorders in men (Erectile Disorder) and—to a more limited extent—for Pain Disorders (Vaginismus, Dyspareunia) in women. Sexual Desire Disorders remain the most challenging of sexual disorders to treat perhaps due to the subjective nature of what constitutes desire, and the vastly individual nature of what leads a person to desire sexual activity.

References

American Psychiatric Association. (2000). *Diagnostic and statistical manual of mental disorders* (4th ed., Text Rev.). Washington, DC: Author.

Bachmann, G. A., Ebert, G. A., & Burd, I. D. (1999). Vulvovaginal complaints. In R. A. Lobo (Ed.), *Treatment of the postmenopausal woman: Basic and clinical aspects* (pp. 195–201). Philadelphia: Lippincott, Williams and Wilkins.

Bancroft, J., & Janssen, E. (2000). The dual control model of male sexual response: A theoretical approach to centrally mediated erectile dysfunction. *Neuroscience and Biobehavioral Review, 24,* 571–579.

Barlow, D. H. (1986). Causes of sexual dysfunction: The role of anxiety and cognitive interference. *Journal of Consulting and Clinical Psychology, 54,* 140–148.

Basson, R., & Brotto, L. A. (2003). Sexual psychophysiology and effects of sildenafil citrate in oestrogenised women with acquired genital arousal disorder and impaired orgasm: A randomized controlled trial. *British Journal of Obstetrics and Gynaecology, 110,* 1014–1024.

Basson, R., Leiblum, S., Brotto, L., Derogatis, L., Fourcroy, J., Fugl-Meyer, K., et al. (2003). Definitions of women's sexual dysfunction reconsidered: Advocating expansion and revision. *Journal of Psychosomatic Obstetrics and Gynecology, 24,* 221–229.

Basson, R., & Riley, A. J. (1994). Vulvar vestibulitis syndrome: A common condition which may present as vaginismus. *Sexual and Marital Therapy, 9,* 221–224.

Bensley, L. S., Eenwyk, J. V., & Simmons, K. W. (2000). Self-reported childhood sexual and physical abuse and adult HIV-risk behavior and heavy drinking. *American Journal of Preventive Medicine, 18,* 151–158.

Berard, E. J. J. (1989). The sexuality of spinal cord injured women: Physiology and pathophysiology. A review. *Paraplegia, 27,* 99–112.

Bergeron, S., Binik, Y. M., Khalifé, S., Pagidas, K., Glazer, H. I., Meana, M., et al. (2001). A randomized comparison of group cognitive-behavioral therapy, surface electromyographic feedback, and vestibulectomy in the treatment of dyspareunia resulting from vulvar vestibulitis. *Pain, 91,* 297–306.

Billups, K. L., Berman, L., Berman, J., Metz, M. E., Glennon, M. E., & Goldstein, I. (2001). A new non-pharmacological vacuum therapy for female sexual dysfunction. *Journal of Sex and Marital Therapy, 27,* 435–441.

Binik, Y. M., Meana, M., Berkley, K. & S Kalippe, S. (1999). The sexual pain disorder: Is the pain sexual or is the sex painful? *Annual Review of Sex Research, 10,* 210–235.

Bradford, A., & Meston, C. M. (2006). The impact of anxiety on sexual arousal in women. *Behavior Research and Therapy, 44,* 1067–1077.

Corona, G., Petrone, L., Mannucci, E., Jannini, E. A., Mansani, R., Magini, A., et al. (2004). Psychobiological correlates of rapid ejaculation in patients attending to an Andrologic Unit for Sexual Dysfunctions. *European Urology, 46,* 615–622.

Exton, N. G., Truong, T. C., Exton, M. S., Wingenfeld, S. A., Leygraf, N., Saller, B., et al. (2000). Neuroendocrine response to film-induced sexual arousal in men and women. *Psychoneuroendocrinology, 25,* 187–199.

Glazer, H. I., Rodke, G., Swencionis, C., Hertz, B., & Young, A. W. (1995). Treatment of vulvar vestibulitis syndrome with electromyographic biofeedback of pelvic floor musculature. *Journal of Reproductive Medicine, 40,* 283–290.

Goldstein, A. T., & Goldstein, I. (2006). Sexual pain disorders within the vulvar vestibule: Current techniques. In I. Goldstein, C. M. Meston, S. R. Davis & A. M. Traish, (Eds.), *Women's sexual function and dysfunction: Study, diagnosis, and treatment* (pp. 98–101). New York: Taylor and Francis.

Graham, C. A., Sanders, S. A., Milhausen, R. R., & McBride, K. R. (2004). Turning on and turning off: A focus group study of the factors that affect women's sexual arousal. *Archives of Sexual Behavior, 33,* 527–538.

Hankin, B. L., Fraley, R. C., & Abela, J. R. Z. (2005). Daily depression and cognition about stress: Evidence for a traitlike depressogenic cognitive style and the prediction of depressive symptoms in a prospective daily dairy study. *Journal of Personality and Social Psychology, 88,* 673–685.

Hoon P. W., Wincze J. P., & Hoon E. F. (1977). A test of reciprocal inhibition: Are anxiety and sexual arousal in women mutually inhibitory? *Journal of Abnormal Psychology, 86,* 65–74.

Kaplan, H. S. (1979). *Disorders of sexual desire.* New York: Brunner/Mazel.

Kaplan, H. S. (1989). *Premature ejaculation: Overcoming premature ejaculation.* New York: Brunner/Mazel.

Kegel, A. H. (1952). Sexual functions of the pubococcygeus muscle. *Western Journal of Surgical Obstetrics & Gynecology, 60,* 521–524.

Laan, E., van Lunsen, R. H., Everaerd, W., Riley, A., Scott, E., & Boolell, M. (2002). The enhancement of vaginal vasocongestion by sildenafil in healthy premenopausal women. *Journal of Women's Health and Gender-Based Medicine, 11,* 357–365.

Laumann, E. O., Gagnon, J. H., Michael, R. T., & Michaels, S. (1994). *The social organization of sexuality: Sexual practices in the United States.* Chicago: University of Chicago Press.

Laumann, E. O., Paik, A., & Rosen, R. C. (1999). Sexual dysfunction in the United States: Prevalence and predictors. *Journal of the American Medical Association, 281,* 537–544.

Leiblum, S. (2002) After sildenafil: Bridging the gap between pharmacology treatment and satisfying relationships. *Journal of Clinical Psychiatry, 63,* 17–22.

Leiblum, S. R., & Wiegel, M. (2002). Psychotherapeutic interventions for treating female sexual dysfunction. *World Journal of Urology, 20,* 127–136.

Lewis, R. W., Fugl-Meyer, K. S., Bosch, R., Fugl-Meyer, A. R., Laumann, O., Lizza, E., et al. (2004). Definitions, classification, and epidemiology of sexual dysfunction. In T. F. Lue, R. Basson, R. Rosen, F. Giuliano, S. Khoury, & F. Montorsi (Eds.), *Sexual medicine: Sexual dysfunctions in men and women* (pp. 39–72) Paris: Health Publications.

Masters, W. H., & Johnson, V. E. (1966). *Human Sexual Response.* Boston: Little, Brown.

Masters, W., & Johnson, V. E. (1970). *Human sexual inadequacy.* Boston: Little, Brown.

McCall, K. M., & Meston, C. M. (2006). Cues resulting in desire for sexual activity in women. *Journal of Sexual Medicine, 3,* 838–852.

McKenna, K. (1999). The brain is the master organ in sexual function: Central nervous system control of male and female sexual function. *International Journal of Impotence Research, 11,* S48–S55.

Melnik, T., & Abdo, C. H. (2005.) Psychogenic erectile dysfunction: Comparative study of three therapeutic approaches. *Journal of Sex & Marital Therapy, 31,* 243–255.

Meston, C. M., & Frohlich, P. F. (2000). The neurobiology of sexual function. *Archives of General Psychiatry, 57,* 1012–1030.

Meston, C. M., & Gorzalka, B. B. (1996). The effects of immediate, delayed, and residual sympathetic activation on sexual arousal in women. *Behaviour Research and Therapy, 34,* 143–148.

Meston C. M., & Heiman, J. R. (1998). Ephedrine-activated physiological sexual arousal in women. *Archives of General Psychiatry, 55,* 652–656.

Meston, C. M., Hull, E., Levin, R. J., & Sipski, M. (2004). Women's orgasm. In T. F. Lue, R. Basson, R. Rosen, F. Giuliano, S. Khoury, & F. Montorsi (Eds.), *Sexual medicine: Sexual dysfunctions in men and women* (pp. 783–850). Paris: Health Publications.

Nichols, M. (2004). Lesbian sexuality/female sexuality: Rethinking 'lesbian bed death.' *Sexual and Relationship Therapy, 19,* 363–371.

Payne, K., Binik, Y., Amsel, R., & Khalifé, S. (2005). When sex hurts, anxiety and fear orient attention towards pain. *European Journal of Pain, 9*(4), 427–436.

Pukall, C. F., Reissing, E. D., Binik, Y. M., Khalife, S., & Abbott, F. V. (2000). New clinical and research perspectives on the sexual pain disorders. *Journal of Sex Education and Therapy, 25,* 36–44.

Pukall, C. F., Payne, K. A., Kao, A., Khalife, S., & Binik, Y. M. (2005). Dyspareunia. In R. Balon & R. T. Segraves (Eds.), *Handbook of Sexual Dysfunction* (pp. 249–272). New York: Taylor and Francis.

Reissing, E. D., Binik, Y. M., Khalife, S., Cohen, D., & Amsel, R. (2004). Vaginal spasm, pain, and behavior: An empirical investigation of the diagnosis of vaginismus. *Archives of Sexual Behavior, 33,* 5–17.

Rellini, A. H. (2006). Sexual abuse. In I. Goldstein, C. M. Meston, S. R. Davis, & A. M. Traish (Eds.), *Women's sexual function and dysfunction: Study, diagnosis, and treatment* (pp. 98–101). New York: Taylor and Francis.

Rowland, D. L., & Slob, A. K. (1997). Premature ejaculation: Psychophysiological considerations in theory, research, and treatment. *Annual Review of Sex Research, 8,* 224–253.

Schreiner-Engel, P., Schiavi, R. C., Smith, H., & White, D. (1981). Sexual arousability and the menstrual cycle. *Psychosomatic Medicine, 43,* 199–214.

Shifren, J. L., Braunstein, G. D., Simon, J. A., Casson, P. R., Buster, J. E., Redmond, G. P., et al. (2000). Transdermal testosterone treatment in women with impaired sexual function after oophorectomy. *New England Journal of Medicine, 343,* 682–688.

Shotly, M. J., Ephross, P. H., Plaut, S. M., Fischman, S. H., Charnas, J. F., & Cody, C. A. (1984). Female orgasmic experience: A subjective study. *Archives of Sexual Behavior, 13,* 155–164.

Ter Kuile, M. M., Van Lankveld, J. J., Vlieland, C. V., Willekes, C., & Weijenborg, P. T. (2005). Vulvar vestibulitis syndrome: An important factor in the evaluation of lifelong vaginismus? *Journal of Psychosomatic Obstetrics and Gynecology, 26,* 24–249.

Tuiten, A., van Honk, J., Verbaten, R., Laan, E., Everaerd, W., & Stam, H. (2002). Can sublingual testosterone increase subjective and physiological measures of laboratory-induced sexual arousal *Archives of General Psychiatry, 59,* 465–466.

Traish, A. M., & Kim, N. N. (2006). Modulation of female genital sexual arousal by sex steroid hormones. In I. Goldstein, C. M. Meston, S. R. Davis, & A. M. Traish (Eds.), *Women's sexual function and dysfunction: Study, diagnosis and treatment* (pp. 181–193). New York: Taylor and Francis.

Van Berlo, W., & Ensinck, B. (2000). Problems with sexuality after sexual assault. *Annual Review of Sex Research, 11,* 235–258.

Chapter 17

Psychopathy as Psychopathology: Key Developments in Etiology, Assessment, and Treatment

Jennifer E. Vitale and Joseph P. Newman

"We know them, if we know them at all, by their acts"
(Simon, 1996, p. 26)

Introduction

Psychopathy has been referred to as "the elusive category" (Lewis, 1974), a clinical syndrome only recently distinguished clearly from general criminal behavior, from sociopathy, and from Antisocial Personality Disorder. The personality style we now know as psychopathy appears throughout psychiatric history, under different labels and as different subtypes of other disorders. For example, today's psychopath would have been classified as one of Kraepelin's "morbid personalities", individuals who were impulsive and antisocial as well as predisposed to deception; as Schneider's "affectionless" personalities, who lacked compassion and acted in a callous manner towards other individuals; or as Millon's (1981) "aggressive" personalities, with "faith only in themselves and . . . secure only when they are independent of those whom they fear may undo, harm, or humiliate them" (p. 181).

Historically, individuals in the field typically trace the evolution of the concept of psychopathy to Pinel's *manie sans delire*, which was a syndrome characterized by an individual's repeated engagement in impulsive, destructive actions, in spite of intact reasoning (Pinel, 1806). This early, relatively objective conceptualization would later give way to conceptualizations of the syndrome that placed greater emphasis on moral considerations—hence Rush's "innate, preternatural moral depravity" (1812, p. 112)

TABLE 17.1   Cleckley's (1941, 1988) Criteria for Psychopathy

Superficial charm and good intelligence

Absence of delusions and other signs of irrational thinking

Absence of "nervousness" or psychoneurotic manifestations

Unreliability

Untruthfulness and insincerity

Lack of remorse or shame

Inadequately motivated antisocial behavior

Poor judgment and failure to learn by experience

Pathological egocentricity and incapacity for love

General poverty in major affective reactions

Specific loss of insight

Unresponsiveness in general interpersonal relations

Fantastic and uninviting behavior with drink and sometimes without

Suicide rarely carried out

Sex life impersonal, trivial, and poorly integrated

Failure to follow any life plan

and Prichard's (1835) "moral insanity." Although the labels have varied, what has been constant is nosologists' desire to classify this syndrome in such a way that it could be distinguished from other forms of mental illness and from general criminality.

It was such a desire that motivated Cleckley's (1941, 1988) work *The Mask of Sanity*, which is now viewed as the seminal clinical description of the psychopathy syndrome. *The Mask of Sanity* provided detailed case histories and a set of specific criteria meant to distinguish the syndrome from the number of other disorders that had come to be included under the psychopathy label. Thus, through this work, Cleckley (1988) provided a means for distinguishing the psychopath from the psychotic, the psychoneurotic, the mental defective, the criminal, and the alcoholic.

The Mask of Sanity provided case descriptions of fifteen psychopathic individuals and outlined the 16 core traits of psychopathy that Cleckley formulated on the basis of these cases (see Table 17.1). Although later conceptualizations of the syndrome have, to different extents, attempted to encapsulate each of the criteria, the following six have most strongly influenced modern conceptualizations of the syndrome.

First, Cleckley (1988) described the psychopath as exhibiting "superficial charm and good intelligence" (p. 337). In his words, "the typical psychopath will seem particularly agreeable and make a distinctly positive impression when he is first encountered . . . there is nothing at all odd or queer about him and in every respect he tends to embody the concept of a well adjusted, happy person . . . signs of affectation or excessive affability are not characteristic. He looks like the real thing" (p. 338).

Second, the psychopath is "lacking in remorse or shame" (p. 337). The psychopath does not express genuine contrition for the antisocial acts he or she commits, and often cannot even see the purpose in feeling such remorse. When remorse is expressed it is often hollow and rings false. As Cleckley writes: "Usually he denies emphatically all responsibility and directly accuses others as responsible, but often he will go through an idle ritual of saying that much of his trouble is his own fault. . . . More detailed questioning about just what he blames himself for and why may show that a serious attitude is not only absent but altogether inconceivable to him" (p. 343).

Third, the psychopath engages in "inadequately motivated antisocial behavior" (p. 337). Among the behaviors Cleckley included in this category were minor infractions such as lies, cheating, brawling, as well as more serious offenses like theft, fraud, and forgery. According to Cleckley, however, the crucial factor was not necessarily the type or severity of the behavior itself, but the psychopath's tendency to "commit such deeds in the absence of any apparent goal at all" (p. 343).

Fourth, the psychopath shows "poor judgment and failure to learn by experience" (p. 337). Despite the fact that these individuals are characterized by average intelligence, they nevertheless repeatedly make poor choices and evidence poor judgment in their attempts at goal attainment. Further, although the psychopath may be able to explain what went wrong in a particular situation (i.e., what he did that may have lead to the poor outcome), he seems incapable of using this knowledge in future situations, thereby exhibiting an inability to use prior experience to guide future behavior.

Fifth, the psychopath is characterized by "incapacity for love" (p. 337). Although he or she may be "capable of fondness, of likes, of dislikes . . . these affective reactions are, however, always strictly limited in degree" (p. 348). This apparent inability to experience deep emotion or to connect emotionally with others is an important criteria for distinguishing the psychopath from other antisocial individuals (Cooke, Michie, Hart, 2006).

The sixth characteristic is related to the fifth, and is the tendency for the psychopath to exhibit "general poverty in major affective reactions." Although the psychopath may express himself in ways that suggest that he is experiencing affective reactions (e.g., a short-temper, a declaration of affection), these expressions do not convey a sense of long-lasting, deep emotional experience. There is no "mature, wholehearted anger, true or consistent indignation, honest, solid grief, sustaining pride, deep joy, and genuine despair" (p. 348).

Like Cleckley, McCord and McCord (1964) provided rich descriptions of the psychopathic individual. Harkening back to figures such as Billy the Kid as early examples of a prototypical psychopath, McCord and McCord placed great emphasis on defining characteristics such as aggression, impulsivity, excitement seeking, guiltlessness, and "warped capacity for love." This last characteristic, also a core component of the syndrome described by Cleckley, receives particular emphasis. Psychopaths, as Maslow (1951) writes, "have no love identifications with other human beings and can therefore hurt them or even kill them casually, without hate, and without pleasure" (p. 173).

Early versions of the *Diagnostic and Statistical Manual of the American Psychiatric Association* (*DSM*) (American Psychiatric Association, 1952, 1968) criteria for Sociopathy and Antisocial Personality Disorder included characteristics such as selfishness, guiltlessness, callousness, and impulsivity—which overlapped in many ways with the Cleckley criteria. However, although there was some overlap, the *DSM* criteria were not meant to reflect the psychopathy syndrome described by Cleckley and developed separate from the psychopathy literature. Thus, although psychopathy has often been used synonymously with Sociopathy and Antisocial Personality Disorder, this is a mistake. This is particularly relevant given recent editions of the *DSM*—including the *DSM-IV* (APA, 1994)—which have limited the criteria for ASPD to more specific behavioral criteria (e.g., Conduct Disorder present before age 15, repeatedly performing acts that are grounds for arrest), thereby excluding many of the individuals who would be considered psychopathic using Cleckley's criteria but who would not meet the specific behavioral criteria for ASPD (Hare, 1996).

Because much of the research on psychopathy has been conducted in institutional settings, our understanding of the rates of the disorder in these samples is more advanced. For example, among North American male offenders, the rates of psychopathy range from 15% (Ogloff, 2006; Salekin, Rogers, Ustad, & Sewell, 1998) to 49% (Herve, Mitchell, & Cooper, 2004).

Rates tend to be lower in female samples and European populations, with rates among incarcerated females as low as 11%–16% (Louks, 1995; Neary, 1990; Salekin, Rogers, & Sewell, 1997). Lower base-rates also appear to be the norm in European samples. For example, Cooke and Michie (1999) found that using a standard diagnostic cut-score yielded 29% psychopaths in North American offenders, whereas an even lower criterion score in Scotland yielded only 8%.

In summary, the psychopath is an individual characterized by limited affective experiences, known to act impulsively and often antisocially, but who nevertheless seems calm and at ease in the presence of others. The psychopath represents a significant proportion of most incarcerated offender populations, but less is known about the prevalence of the syndrome outside of institutional settings. Although clinically intriguing figures in their own right, the psychopaths overrepresentation in criminal samples provides strong, pragmatic motivation for understanding the factors that underlie the syndrome. In the next section, we consider the most prominent etiological models of psychopathy.

Etiology of Psychopathy

GENETICS

There are over 100 studies examining the relative contributions of genetic and environmental factors to antisocial behavior. Generally, evidence supports a moderate contribution of each factor. For example, in their recent meta-analysis Waldman and Rhee (2006) found moderate additive genetic ($a^2 = 0.32$), nonadditive genetic ($c^2 = 0.09$), shared environmental ($d^2 = 0.16$), and nonshared environmental ($e^2 = 0.43$) influences on antisocial behavior and the best fitting model included each of these four components ($\chi^2 = 1394.46$, df = 146, $p < .001$; AIC = 1102.46). Importantly, the studies included in this analysis focused primarily on antisocial behavior, and used diagnoses of ASPD or Conduct Disorder, criminal activity, and delinquency, or self-reports of aggression as outcome variables. Although antisocial behavior is a component of psychopathy, the psychopathy syndrome is distinct from general criminality or antisociality (Cleckley, 1988; Hare, 1996; Lykken, 1995). As a result, the meta-analysis only indirectly addresses the genetic basis of psychopathy. Fortunately, there is an emerging literature focused on examining the relative contribution of genetics to traits more specifically associated with the psychopathy syndrome.

In a recent study of adolescent monozygotic and dizygotic twin pairs, Larsson, Andershed, and Lichtenstein (2006) used the Youth Psychopathic Traits Inventory (YPI) (Andershed, Kerr, Stattin, & Levander, 2002) to assess the affective, interpersonal, and behavioral components of the psychopathy syndrome. Their results indicated that for each of the three components of psychopathy (i.e., interpersonal, affective, and behavioral) assessed by the YPI, genetic[1], and nonshared environmental factors accounted

---

[1] In their analysis, the authors do not separately analyze additive and nonadditive genetic factors. Thus, their "genetic" contributions would include both components.

for the majority of variance, with little or no influence of shared environmental factors. Further, because their sample included both males and females the authors were able to test for gender differences in the relative influences of the factors. None were found, suggesting that there may not be significant differences in the heritability of psychopathic traits across gender (Larsson et al., 2006).

The data from Larsson et al. (2006) are consistent with Blonigen, Hicks, Kreuger, Patrick, and Iacono's (2006) analysis of 626 twin pairs from the Minnesota twin family study. In this study, psychopathy was represented by the fearless dominance (representing a combination of the interpersonal/affective components of psychopathy) and impulsive antisociality (representing the behavioral component of psychopathy) subscales of the Multidimensional Personality Questionnaire (MPQ) (Tellegen, 2000). As in Larsson et al. (2006), a model including additive genetic and nonshared environmental factors provided the best fit to the data and there appeared to be no significant differences in the model fit across gender (Blonigen et al., 2006).

Using the detachment and antisocial subscales from the Minnesota Temperament Inventory to assess the affective and behavioral components of psychopathy, Taylor, Loney, Bobadilla, Iacono, and McGue (2003) examined the influence of genetic and shared/nonshared environmental factors in two samples of adolescent male twins (ages 16–18). As both Larsson et al. (2006) and Blonigen et al. (2006) found, the best-fitting model for both the affective and behavioral dimensions included additive genetic factors and nonshared environmental factors; there was little contribution from shared environmental factors (Taylor et al., 2003).

Each of the preceding studies supports the importance of both genetic and nonshared environmental factors and the negligible influence of shared environmental factors. In this light, the distinction between shared and nonshared environmental influences becomes crucial for later investigation of the factors associated with psychopathy. Nonshared environmental factors are represented by the divergence of monozygotic twins, whose shared environments are identical. One potentially potent nonshared environmental factor is peer relationships (Manke, McGuire, Reiss, Hetherington, & Plomin, 1995), which play an important role in adolescent development (Savin-Williams & Berndt, 1990). Their importance to psychopathic personality, in particular, is highlighted by the finding that the level of psychopathic traits exhibited by an individual adolescent appears to be correlated with the levels of psychopathic traits exhibited by members of his or her peer friendship group (Andershed, Kerr, Stattin, & Engels as cited in Larsson et al., 2006).

The key role of genetic and nonshared environmental factors is further emphasized by a second meta-analysis of psychopathy-related studies conducted by Waldman and Rhee (2006). Only using studies that included self-report measures of the interpersonal and affective traits associated with the psychopathy syndrome—for example, the pychopathic deviate (Pd) subscale of the MMPI and MMPI-2 (Butcher, 1979; Butcher et al., 2001), socialization (So) subscale of the California Personality Inventory (Gough & Bradley, 1996), the Minnesota Temperament Inventory (Taylor et al., 2003), and the Psychopathic Personality Inventory (Lilienfeld & Andrews, 1996)—the authors found that a model including only additive genetic and nonshared environmental influences represented the best data fit ($\chi^2 = 45.77$, df = 20, $p < .001$; AIC = 5.77), with each component acting as a moderate influence ($a^2 = 0.49$, $e^2 = 0.51$).

Taken together, these data provide good evidence for the roles of genetic and nonshared environmental factors in the development of the psychopathy syndrome. Further, these new studies have also provided a means for examining the independence of the genetic contribution to each component of the syndrome. For example, Larsson et al. (2006) found that in their sample additive genetic and nonshared environmental factors were more important to the affective and impulsivity components than to the interpersonal component. Specifically, genetic factors accounted for 22% of the variance in the affective and impulsivity components of psychopathy, but only 1% of the variance in the interpersonal component. Similarly, non-shared environmental factors accounted for a greater proportion of the variance in the affective (45%) and impulsivity (28%) components compared to the interpersonal component (17%).

In their study using the MPQ subscales fearless dominance (FD) and impulsive antisociality (IA), Blonigen et al. (2006) examined the relative contributions of environmental and genetic factors to the separate development of these dimensions. To this end, the authors used data from two time points (ages 17 and 24). The authors partitioned the variance at age 24 into the variance contributed from the first time point (age 17) and the variance unique to this second time point. Thus, they were able to differentiate the influences of genetic and environmental factors on the stable proportion of variance and the genetic and environmental factors influencing the variance associated with change. Consistent with expectation, for both dimensions the stable proportion of variance in the traits was due primarily to additive genetic (FD $a^2 = 0.25$; IA $a^2 = 0.23$) rather than nonshared environmental factors (FD $e^2 = 0.12$; IA $e^2 = 0.07$); whereas, the proportion of variance associated with change was influenced by nonshared environmental factors (FD $e^2 = 0.45$; AI $e^2 = 0.44$) more than by additive genetic factors (FD $a^2 = 0.17$ IA $a^2 = 0.26$).

In summary, there is considerable evidence that psychopathy—as it has been assessed in the preceding studies—includes an additive genetic component. These data have opened a new area of investigation characterized by hypotheses surrounding the precise nature of this influence. Some lines of investigation appear promising—for example, dopamine genes theorized to underlie ADHD (Waldman & Gizer, 2006), serotonergic genes associated with aggression and violence (Berman, Kavoussi, & Coccaro, 1997), and the MAOA gene that is implicated in antisocial behavior associated with childhood abuse (Kim-Cohen, Caspi, & Taylor, 2006). Yet, it is still too early to know which of these avenues—if any—will provide the best explanation for the psychopathy syndrome. In the meanwhile, alternative theories of psychopathy continue to flourish.

Prefrontal Cortex

It was the pseudopsychopathy of Phineas Gage that first drew psychopathy researchers' attention to the prefrontal cortex (Raine & Yang, 2006). Gage, who had suffered damage to the ventromedial region of the prefrontal cortex, subsequently developed a range of problem behaviors akin to those observed among psychopaths, including sexual promiscuity, recklessness, and irresponsibility. Research examining the associations between frontal dysfunction and antisocial behavior has been equivocal, however. Although there is support for an association between frontal lobe dysfunction and antisocial behavior (e.g., Moffitt, 1993; Raine, 1997), research attempting to demonstrate damage or impairment of the prefrontal cortex of psychopaths has yielded mixed findings (e.g., Gorenstein, 1982; Hare, 1984).

Even when abnormalities have been detected, they are primarily evidenced only on the context of particular stimuli or test paradigms. For example, Hare (1984) examined the performance of 46 incarcerated males who were assessed for psychopathy using an early form of the Psychopathy Checklist. They were also assessed on several neuropsychological tasks, including the Wisconsin Card Sort, the Necker Cube, and a sequential matching memory task. When controlling for age, IQ, education, and substance abuse history, no differences were detected between the performances of the psychopathic versus nonpsychopathic participants (Hare, 1984). Similarly, when Schmitt, Brinkley, and Newman (1999) utilized a gambling task that has reliably differentiated controls from patients with ventromedial frontal lesions (Bechara, Damasio, Damasio, & Anderson, 1994; Damasio, 1994), they found no differences between the performances of incarcerated psychopaths assessed using the Psychopathy Checklist–Revised (Hare, 1991) and incarcerated nonpsychopathic controls.

In a meta-analysis of studies examining the association between tasks of Executive Functioning (EF; including the Porteus Mazes, the Wisconsin Card Sorting Test, and the Trail Making Test, parts A and B) and measures of antisocial behavior (including criminality, Conduct Disorder, ASPD diagnoses, and psychopathy), Morgan and Lilienfeld (2000) calculated an average mean effect size of 0.62 across studies comparing individuals exhibiting high- versus low-levels of antisocial behavior. Because this analysis collapsed across several forms of antisocial behavior, however, this effect size does not specifically represent the psychopathy studies. When these studies were examined separately, the mean effect size was in the small to medium range ($d = 0.25$) (Morgan & Lilienfeld, 2000). Thus, although there is some evidence for deficits among psychopaths on measures of EF, these deficits may be far less pronounced than those evinced by nonpsychopathic individuals engaging in general criminality.

Although behavioral evidence for frontal dysfunction is mixed, examinations of gray matter volume in the prefrontal cortex have consistently demonstrated volume reductions in psychopaths relative to controls (Raine, Lencz, Bihrle, LaCasse, & Coletti, 2000; Yang, Raine, Lencz, LaCasse, & Colletti, 2005; Laakso et al., 2002). For example, Raine et al. (2000) found an 11% volume reduction among psychopaths relative to comparison control groups (including substance abusers). Further, Yang et al. (2005) observed a 22.3% reduction in prefrontal gray matter volume in psychopaths relative to controls. However, this difference was specific to incarcerated psychopaths (i.e., "unsuccessful psychopaths"), and no volume reduction was observed among psychopaths living in the community (i.e., "successful psychopaths"), thereby suggesting that the abnormality may not characterize many psychopathic individuals.

More recent research has fruitfully shifted focus from global deficits in the frontal lobes of psychopaths to examinations of specific regions, including the dorsolateral prefrontal cortex (DLPFC) (e.g., Kandel & Freed, 1989; LaPierre, Braun, Hodgins, 1995; Mitchell, Colledge, Leonard, & Blair, 2002), the orbitofrontal cortex (OFC) (e.g., LaPierre et al., 1995; Roussy & Toupin, 2000; Michell et al., 2002) and the medial frontal/anterior cingulate cortex (ACC) (Veit et al., 2002; Kiehl et al., 2001).

This work has provided some evidence for reliable deficits on tasks requiring OFC (e.g., Porteus Maze Test, motor go/no go tasks) and ACC (e.g., Stroop tasks) functioning, but normal performance on tasks involving the DLPFC (e.g., Wisconsin Card Sorting Task, the Controlled Oral Word Association Task). In a recent study, Blair and colleagues (2006) compared 25 psychopaths assessed using the PCL-R with 30 controls on measures of DLPFC, OFC, and ACC functioning. Results showed that, as expected, psychopaths did not exhibit deficits on the task primarily involving DLPFC functioning, but did show deficits in performance on the task involving the OFC, and (to a lesser degree) the ACC. Specifically, psychopaths performed abnormally relative to controls on an object alternation task designed to preferentially involve the OFC and the number-Stroop reading task—which recruits ACC functioning—but not on a second measure involving ACC functioning (i.e., a number-Stroop counting task). Taken together, these data support the presence of abnormalities in frontal regions of psychopaths, but also suggest that there is not a global deficit in frontal lobe functioning. Further, as this research continues to develop, it will be important to integrate it with existing research on the behavioral deficits associated with psychopathy. Historically, it has been these deficits—including poor passive avoidance learning, poor aversive conditioning, and abnormal startle responses—that have been the primary focus of many of the most influential theories of psychopathy.

Theories of Psychopathy

Several theoretical formulations have emphasized fearlessness or insensitivity to punishment as underlying causes of the psychopathy syndrome (e.g., Fowles, 1980; Lykken, 1995). Early theories of psychopathy embraced Gray's (1987) model of BIS/BAS functioning, which proposed three systems that served to regulate behavior: the fight/flight system (FFS), which responds to unconditioned or innately aversive stimuli; the behavioral activation system (BAS), which was described as sensitive to reward stimuli and likely to activate responses in the face of cues or conditioned stimuli signaling reward; and the behavioral inhibition system (BIS), described as sensitive to punishment stimuli and likely to inhibit ongoing responses in response to cues or conditioned stimuli signaling punishment or frustrative nonreward. Importantly, recent formulations of the model have de-emphasized the idea that the BIS generalized sensitivity to threat, and instead has suggested that the BIS is activated specifically under conditions of goal conflict (Gray & McNaughten, 2000).

Working from Gray's original model, Fowles (1980) proposed that the psychopathy syndrome characterized by impulsivity, callousness, and an absence of neurosis was associated with deficits in the BIS. According to this formulation, a hyporeactive BIS—in conjunction with a normal BAS response—could result in the types of symptoms observed among psychopaths. Specifically, these individuals would show the poor punishment learning and weak behavioral inhibition characteristic of the psychopath (Fowles, 1980). Self-report data have supported this proposition, with those psychopaths characterized by low levels of neuroticism showing significantly lower scores on self-report measures of BIS functioning and punishment sensitivity (Book & Quinsey, 2004; Newman, MacCoon, Vaughn, & Sadeh, 2005). Conversely, it was found that those individuals whose psychopathy symptoms were combined with high levels of trait anxiety or neuroticism (so called "secondary psychopaths") were characterized not by deficits in the BIS, but in hyper-responsivity of the BAS (Newman et al., 2005).

Early and current experimental data support the weak BIS formulation. For example, passive avoidance tasks that require the individual to inhibit responses to previously punished stimuli, have reliably differentiated psychopaths from controls with psychopaths committing significantly more passive avoidance errors (e.g. Lykken, 1957; Newman & Kosson, 1986; Newman & Schmitt, 1998; Thornquist & Zuckerman, 1995). Similarly, on a card-playing task that requires the ability to modulate responses in the context of increasing punishment contingencies, psychopaths play significantly more cards and lose significantly more money than controls (e.g., Newman, Patterson, & Kosson, 1987).

Physiological data also supports the BIS hypothesis. For example, psychopaths show decreased electrodermal responsivity in anticipation of an aversive event (Arnette, Howland, Smith, & Newman, 1993; Hare, 1978) and show abnormalities in eye-blink startle responses (Flor, Birbaumer, Hermann, Ziegler, & Patrick, 2002; Levenston, Patrick, Bradley, & Lang, 2000; Patrick, Cuthbert, & Lang, 1993; Patrick, Bradley, & Lang, 1993). Specifically, research has demonstrated that exposure to aversive or unpleasant stimuli will potentiate an eye-blink startle response in controls. Psychopaths, however, show significantly reduced startle potentiation in response to these stimuli, although their startle response to pleasant stimuli does not differ from that of controls.

Taken together, these self-report and laboratory data provide some evidence for deficient BIS functioning. However, other theorists have focused less on BIS functioning than on fearlessness as a trait. For example, although Lykken's (1957, 1995) low-fear hypothesis dovetails well with Fowles' (1980) emphasis on deficient BIS functioning, Lykken places less emphasis on the particulars of Gray's model. Rather, Lykken (1995) proposed that the psychopath is characterized by fearlessness, which impedes normal socialization and results in the cluster of symptoms characteristic of the syndrome (e.g., failure to learn from experience, lack of empathy, irresponsibility, manipulativeness). This proposal is based, in part, upon the results of his highly influential 1957 study of conditioning in psychopaths. The results of this seminal study showed that the psychopaths (designated on the basis of their similarity to Cleckley's prototype) had lower scores on a self-report measure of fearfulness (i.e., the Activity Preference Questionnaire), showed poor electrodermal conditioning relative to controls in a paradigm wherein electric shock served as the unconditional stimulus (UCS), and also exhibited deficient passive avoidance performance (Lykken, 1957). Taken together, these data suggested deficient fear conditioning among psychopaths, and served as the basis for Lykken's "low-fear" hypothesis.

Although there are data to support the weak-BIS and low-fear theories, Blair (2006) has criticized these traditional low-fear formulations on the basis of increasing specificity in the neurocognitive literature. Specifically, as Blair (2006) has noted, our understanding of the structures and areas involved in specific types of punishment learning have become more refined and this greater refinement necessitates increased specificity among low-fear theories of psychopathy.

In contrast to Lykken or Fowles, Blair (2006) has emphasized the role of the amygdala in psychopathy and has focused primarily on punishment-based learning associated with this structure. Specifically, Blair (2006) has argued that psychopaths should show abnormalities only on those tasks that involve the formation of associations between a conditioned stimulus and an unconditioned response (CS-UR; e.g., a galvanic skin response to a stimulus previously associated with a shock), between a conditioned stimulus and an affect representation, and between a conditioned stimulus and the valenced sensory properties of the unconditioned stimulus associations (e.g., the visual appearance or smell of the unconditioned stimulus).

Consistent with Blair's proposal, psychopaths have demonstrated deficits on tasks that preferentially involve these types of learning. For example, psychopaths show impairment on aversive conditioning tasks, which involve amygdala-specific learning—that is, CS-UR and CS-affect representation associations (Flor et al., 2002; Hare, 1970;

Lykken, 1957). Further, there is evidence that, relative to controls, psychopaths show reduced amygdala activation during such aversive conditioning tasks (e.g., Veit et al., 2002). Paradigms using the fear-potentiated startle response to differentiate psychopaths and controls also provide support for Blair's hypothesis. Modulation of the startle response on such tasks is controlled by the amygdala (e.g., Davis, 2000), and so psychopaths' deficient performance on such tasks implicates the amygdala, providing further support that amygdala functioning is associated with the psychopathy syndrome.

Blair (2006) is also able to explain why psychopaths show performance deficits on some tasks but not on others. For example, the low-fear and punishment insensitivity models for psychopathy have been criticized on the basis of psychopaths' normal performance on punishment-only versions of the passive avoidance task. On this version of the task, participants are punished for responding to some stimuli and punished for not responding to other stimuli. Psychopaths' normal performance on such tasks suggests that—contrary to the punishment and fear based theories—psychopaths do demonstrate adequate passive avoidance of punishment-related stimuli under certain conditions.

To explain this discrepancy, Blair (2006) incorporates into his model the theoretical formulations of Baxter and Murray (2002) that distinguish instrumental tasks that involve the amygdala (e.g., passive avoidance learning) and those instrumental-learning tasks that do not (e.g., conditional learning and object discrimination). Specifically, according to Blair (2006) the psychopaths are not affected on the punishment only task because this task requires the formation of stimulus-response associations rather than CS-affect representation associations. In other words, because the punishment-only version of the passive avoidance task does not involve learning that requires the amygdala, psychopaths are able to perform normally.

Although there is much evidence to support the low-fear and punishment-learning theories of psychopathy, they are overly focused on tasks involving valenced stimuli (e.g., the positive and negative visual stimuli presented as part of the acoustic startle paradigm, the punishment and reward stimuli used in the passive avoidance tasks). In an alternative line of investigation, Newman and colleagues (e.g. Newman, Schmitt, & Voss, 1990; Hiatt, Schmitt, &Newman, 2004; Vitale, Hiatt, Brinkley, & Newman, in press) have utilized affectively and motivationally neutral tasks designed to examine attention processing among psychopaths. On such tasks, psychopaths have reliably exhibited abnormalities in attention processing, particularly when stimuli are secondary or peripheral to their primary focus of selective attention (e.g., Hare & Jutai, 1988; Hiatt et al., 2004; Kiehl, Newman, Schmitt, & Voss, 1997; Vitale et al., in press).

The response modulation hypothesis (RMH; Gorenstein & Newman, 1980; Newman & Lorenz, 2003; Patterson & Newman, 1993) proposes that the abnormalities in psychopathic individuals' attention processing are associated with an underlying information processing deficit involving the relatively automatic shift of attention from the effortful organization and implementation of goal directed behavior to the evaluation of that behavior. According to the model, a deficit in response modulation interferes with the psychopathic individual's ability to modify a dominant response set (i.e., the top-down focus of selective attention) in response to nondominant, secondary, or contextual (i.e., unexpected bottom-up) information that may contraindicate an anticipated response (see MacCoon, Wallace, & Newman, 2003; Newman, MacCoon, et al., in press). This focus on attention processing distinguishes the RMH from the low-fear and punishment-learning based models of psychopathy (e.g., Blair, 2006; Fowles, 1980; Lykken, 1995). Specifically, although the RMH predicts a situation-specific deficit in processing threat and other emotion cues (see Newman, 1998; Newman & Lorenz, 2003), the RMH also predicts that the abnormalities evidenced among psychopathic individuals should also be exhibited in emotionally neutral contexts (Patterson & Newman, 1993).

To test the proposal of the RMH, Newman et al. (1997) used a computerized picture-word task. On this task, participants are presented with two consecutive pictures or words, and they are instructed to indicate whether or not the two pictures (or words) are conceptually related. On word trials, the first word is presented with a superimposed picture. On picture trials, the first picture is presented with a superimposed word. In each case, participants are instructed to ignore this secondary (i.e., the superimposed) stimulus. However, on half of the trials when the consecutively presented stimuli are conceptually unrelated, the superimposed picture (or word) presented over the first stimulus is conceptually related to the second stimulus. In these trials, the correct response is "unrelated," but the response indicated by the secondary stimulus is incongruent with this response (e.g., the word sweep superimposed over a picture of a hat, followed by a picture of a broom). Among healthy participants, responses on these incongruent trials are slower than responses to congruent trials (see Gernsbacher & Faust, 1991). Consistent with the performance of healthy participants, nonpsychopathic male offenders responded significantly more slowly on incongruent versus congruent trials (i.e., they showed interference). However, this effect was significantly smaller in psychopathic male offenders, thus, demonstrating significantly less sensitivity to the secondary stimulus among this group (Newman et al., 1997). This effect was subsequently replicated by Hiatt et al. (2004) and Vitale et al. (in press), suggesting that there is a reliable difference in the performance of psychopathic and nonpsychopathic participants on these Stroop-like tasks. Importantly, this finding was the result of differences in the performance of low-anxious psychopathic participants versus low-anxious controls, suggesting that the attention abnormalities associated with psychopathy and predicted by the response modulation hypothesis may be relatively specific to a subgroup of psychopathic individuals characterized by good intelligence, low anxiety, and relatively high levels of psychopathy. As a result, this subgroup has been the focus of subsequent tests of the RMH and theoretical conceptualizations of the model (e.g., Brinkley, Newman, & Widiger, 2004; Hiatt et al., 2004; Lorenz & Newman, 2002; Newman & Lorenz, 2003; Vitale, Newman, Bates, Goodnight, Dodge, & Pettit, 2005). This specific focus on a subgroup of psychopathic individuals further differentiates the RMH from other theories of psychopathy, and it is important to bear in mind that not all individuals assessed as psychopathic using the Psychopathy Checklist-Revised will fall into this group.

The evidence from the Stroop-like tasks supports the RMH specification that states psychopathic individuals will demonstrate performance abnormalities in response to emotionally neutral stimuli. A second specification of the RMH holds that psychopathic individuals will show performance abnormalities when a situation requires them to process information that is secondary or peripheral to the dominant task (Patterson & Newman, 1993). Recent re-statements of the RMH (e.g., MacCoon, et al., 2003; Newman & Wallace, 2003) have conceptualized this process as a deficit in the integration of bottom-up information with a top-down selective attention focus.

According to Hiatt et al. (2004), the relative insensitivity to secondary cues demonstrated by psychopathic individuals in the PW and PW Stroop tasks is consistent with this specification. Specifically, the authors propose that the response interference experienced by the nonpsychopathic participants on the PW Stroop task results from the relatively automatic integration of bottom-up information (i.e., the incongruent, super-imposed word) with the top-down mediated focus of selective attention (i.e., attending to the line drawing to be named). However, as a result of their response modulation deficits, the top-down mediated focus of selective attention adopted by psychopathic participants is relatively immune to the bottom-up information. Thus, no interference is experienced (Hiatt et al., 2004).

Evidence for this second specification of the model also comes from the passive avoidance literature. According to Newman and colleagues, deficient performance of psychopaths on these tasks should be relatively specific to circumstances that require participants to alter the top-down focus of selective attention to process bottom-up (i.e., punishment) cues (Newman & Kosson, 1986; Newman, Patterson, Howland, & Nichols, 1990; Newman & Schmitt, 1998). However, when this dependence is obviated by the use of a punishment-only condition (Newman & Kosson, 1986) or by the use of a reward-punishment task that forces participants to attend to both the reward and punishment contingencies from the outset (Newman et al., 1990), psychopathic participants show adequate response inhibition. Thus, like Blair et al. (2006), Newman and colleagues are able to reconcile the discrepant passive-avoidance literature, although with an emphasis on the attentional demands of the task, rather than the associations that must be formed.

SOCIAL COGNITION

Clearly, understanding the biopsychological processes underlying the psychopathy syndrome is a priority among psychopathy researchers. However, some psychopathy researchers have turned their attention to explaining the antisocial and impulsive behaviors associated with the syndrome using models of social cognition. Such investigations are initiated on the basis of the argument that understanding the content of psychopathic thought, in addition to the process, will provide new alternatives for treatment (e.g., Serin & Kuriychuk, 1994), as well as new ways for understanding how the biopsychological processes may interact with the individual's social and familial environments (e.g., Vitale, Serin, Bolt, & Newman, 2005).

Serin (1991) examined the association between aggression and psychopathy within a group of adult male offenders in the context of a social cognitive model of aggression proposed by Crick and Dodge (1994); their model highlights the role of causal attributions in the development of aggression. Tests of this model have resulted in an extensive literature examining causal attributions of hostility made by children and adolescents with conduct problems and the ways that these attributions contribute to aggressive behavior (see Crick & Dodge, 1994; Pettit, Polaha, & Mize, 2001 for reviews).

One of the most robust findings in this area is the tendency for aggressive individuals to exhibit a hostile attribution bias (HAB). When they are confronted by another person's provocative yet ambiguous behaviors, these aggressive children are more likely than others to attribute those behaviors to hostile intent (Crick & Dodge, 1994). Research with children has shown that the HAB is present in both boys and girls (Burks, Laird, Dodge, Pettit, & Bates, 1999; Dodge, Lochman, Harnish, Bates, & Pettit, 1997) and can be elicited through the use of hypothetical as well as real-life situations (Orobio de Castro, Veerman, Koops, Bosch, & Monshouwer, 2002; Steinberg & Dodge, 1983). HABs also appear to be specific to reactive aggression and are unrelated to nonviolent crime and socialized aggression (Dodge, Price, Bachorowski, & Newman, 1990; Dodge et al., 1997). Finally, children's hostile attributional biases have been linked to their aggressive behaviors. Children who exhibit attributional biases display high rates of reactive aggression when interacting with their peers (Dodge & Coie, 1987; Dodge & Frame, 1982; Van Oostrum & Horvath, 1997) and commit greater numbers of violent crimes (Dodge et al., 1990).

Serin (1991) tested for the presence of HABs in psychopathic adults using a series of six hypothetical, provocative vignettes. Participants were 87 adult male offenders who were classified as psychopathic or nonpsychopathic using a cutting score of 28 on the PCL-R. Although studies of hostile attributional style have primarily focused on adolescents with conduct problems, the potential importance of HABs in the behavior of psychopathic adults is apparent from the theoretical and descriptive literature on this syndrome. For example, researchers and clinicians have conceptualized the psychopathic individual as one who views the world as a hostile, unpredictable place (Cleckley, 1988; Hare, 1991; Millon, 1981; Newman & Wallace, 1993). This extreme hostility is often indexed by callous and antisocial beliefs such as: "The victims got what they deserved" and "This world is about survival—you have to look out for number one" (Hare, 1991). Further, such hostile distortions have been invoked as a contributory factor to psychopathic individuals' antisocial behaviors (e.g., Newman & Wallace, 1993; Serin & Kuriychuk, 1994), and they have also been described as the psychopathic individual's attempt to rationalize his behavior after the fact (e.g., Millon, 1981). Consistent with these proposals, the results of Serin's (1991) study showed that—in situations that they rated as particularly provocative—psychopathic individuals were more likely than nonpsychopathic individuals to make attributions of hostile intent. Specifically, they were more likely to say that the provocateur was behaving deliberately, out of disrespect, and because the provocateurs believed that they were right (Serin, 1991). Thus, in situations where they placed themselves in the role of the victim, the psychopathic individuals were more likely than the nonpsychopathic individuals to perceive others as behaving in an intentionally harmful way towards them. In an attempt to replicate Serin's (1991) finding, Vitale et al. (2005) used the six vignettes from his study as well as three additional ambiguous, provocative scenarios to assess hostile attributions in a group of Caucasian and African American adult offenders. The results of this study supported the presence of an association between PCL-R scores and an increased tendency to make hostile attributions in both races (Vitale et al., 2005).

Taken together, these studies (Serin, 1991; Vitale et al., 2005) support the possibility that—like conduct disordered children—psychopathic individuals are characterized by a tendency to view the behaviors of other people as hostile and provoking. However, a study by Doninger and Kosson (2001) does not support this position. In this study of adult offenders, the authors used the Role Construct Repertory Test (RCRT) to examine how psychopathic individuals would describe a series of interpersonal interactions. On this task, participants are presented with a series of interpersonal scenarios. After each scenario, participants are presented with ten bipolar constructs (e.g., nice-rude, aggressive-nonaggressive) they can use to describe the interaction. The constructs lie along a dimension from -3 to $+3$ with one attribute (e.g., rude) at the negative pole and the other attribute (e.g., nice) at the positive pole. Participants use an integer in this range to designate which attribute applies most strongly to the situation. A response of zero indicates that neither attribute applies to the situation. The authors proposed that psychopathic individuals would be more likely than nonpsychopathic individuals to use negative attributes to describe the interactions (Doninger & Kosson, 2001). Although psychopathic individuals were more likely than nonpsychopathic individuals to utilize the dimension of aggressive-nonaggressive to characterize interactions, they were not more likely to utilize the negative poles (Doninger & Kosson, 2001). Thus, it remains unclear if psychopathic individuals are characterized by a hostile attribution bias and if this bias contributes directly to their violent behavior. Nevertheless, the data do suggest that psychopaths may be sensitive to environmental cues involving hostility or aggression, which could potentially exacerbate any underlying deficits in information processing or behavioral inhibition.

Assessment of Psychopathy

THE PSYCHOPATHY CHECKLIST

Like many psychological disorders, the assessment of psychopathy has a complicated history. Although there has long been consensus regarding the core features of the syndrome, there has been less agreement regarding the best methods for assessing these features. Early on, the detailed, case-based conceptualizations of Cleckley (1988) and McCord and McCord (1964) enabled researchers and clinicians to assess psychopathy according to an individual's similarity to the prototypes described in the clinical literature (e.g., Hare, Frazell, & Cox, 1978), but such assessments can be unreliable. Alternative assessments have included the *DSM* criteria for Antisocial Personality Disorder, but as previously discussed, those who view psychopathy as a syndrome distinct from ASPD are not satisfied with such a classification system. In fact, Hare (1998) and others (Rogers, Salekin, Sewell, & Cruise, 2000) have argued that the inclusion of psychopathy as a synonym for ASPD in the current version of the *DSM* does "a considerable disservice to diagnostic clarity" (Rogers et al., 2000, pp. 236–237).

As a result of the field's decision to forgo ASPD criteria in favor of more psychopathy-specific assessments, measures believed to capture the personality traits associated with the syndrome became popular alternatives. Among these are relevant subscales from measures of normal personality including the socialization (So) subscale of the California Personality Inventory and the psychopathic deviate (Pd) scale of the MMPI. Although such measures are conceptually related to some of the characteristics associated with the psychopathy syndrome, this method is also fraught with limitations. For example, the use of these measures prevented uniformity in the field, as psychopathy findings based on the So scale were not necessarily generalizable to psychopaths assessed using the Pd scale.

This point was highlighted by Hare's (1985) examination of the inter-correlations between these traditional measures of psychopathy. Among others, Hare generated correlations between the Pd scale, the So scale, the *DSM-III* criteria for ASPD, and ratings based on the Cleckley prototype. The results showed that the intercorrelations among these measures ranged from weak to moderate. For example, the Pd scale was not highly correlated with the So scale (-0.34), with *DSM-III* ASPD (0.29), or with the Cleckley ratings (0.21). The So scale did not fare much better, correlating only -0.37 with the *DSM-III* ASPD and -0.29 with the Cleckley ratings. Taken together, these data emphasized the limits of psychopathy assessment, making it clear that measures once viewed as interchangeable assessments of a similar construct were far from being such.

TABLE 17.2   PCL-R Items (Hare, 1991)

Glibness/superficial charm

Grandiose sense of self-worth

Need for stimulation/proneness to boredom

Pathological lying

Conning/manipulative

Lack of remorse or guilt

Shallow affect

Callous/lack of empathy

Parasitic lifestyle

Poor behavioral controls

Promiscuous sexual behavior

Early behavior problems

Lack of realistic, long term goals

Impulsivity

Irresponsibility

Failure to accept responsibility

Many short-term marital relationships

Juvenile delinquency

Revocation of conditional release

Criminal versatility

It was in this context that Hare (1980) developed the Research Scale for the Assessment of Psychopathy (Psychopathy Checklist). Designed to capture the prototypical psychopath as conceptualized by Cleckley, the measure transformed Cleckley's 16 criteria into 22 items that could be scored using a semistructured interview and institutional file review. In 1991, a revised version of the checklist that deleted two items from the original scale was published (see Table 17.2). This Psychopathy Checklist-Revised (PCL-R) (Hare, 1991), quickly moved to the forefront of psychopathy assessment and it has been called the "state-of-the-art measure of psychopathy" (Fulero, 1995) for clinical and research purposes. Each item on the 20-item checklist can be scored using interview and file review as zero "not applicable to the individual," one "applicable only to a certain extent," or two "applicable to the individual." Scores range from 0–40 and a diagnostic cut-off of 30 has become the accepted standard in North American, male samples.

The development of the PCL-R provided a reliable method for assessing the psychopathy syndrome and—by providing a common metric for researchers and clinicians—it also facilitated much of the psychopathy research conducted in the late twentieth century. In fact, over the course of the past twenty years, researchers and clinicians would be more likely to be called upon to justify not using the PCL-R as their primary measure of psychopathy than vice versa. This is not to say, however, that the instrument is without controversy. Several key issues are currently being debated in the literature with direct relevance to the PCL-R, including its inclusion of items measuring criminality (e.g., Cooke et al., 2006; Cooke, Michie, Hart, & Clark, 2004; Lilienfeld, 1994;

Lilienfeld & Andrews, 1996), its factor structure (e.g., Cooke et al., 2006; Cooke & Michie, 2001), and the generalizability of the instrument to alternative samples (e.g., Cooke & Michie, 1999; Kosson, Smith, & Newman, 1990; Vitale & Newman, 2001a).

One of the PCL-R's clinical strengths is its power in predicting future dangerousness. High PCL-R scorers commit more violent criminal offenses than individuals with low scores, and are more likely to violently recidivate than low scorers (Hare & Hart, 1993; Hemphill, Hare, & Wong, 1998; Hemphill, Templeman, Wong, & Hare, 1998; Salekin, Rogers, & Sewell, 1996). In fact, on the basis of its associations with criminal recidivism and behavior, Hare (1998a) has argued that PCL-R assessed psychopathy is "the single most important clinical construct in the criminal justice system," citing its usefulness in both risk assessments and treatment placements. This statement is not without controversy. For example, Freedman (2001) has noted that the PCL-R is associated with high false positive rates when predicting dangerousness and should not be used in forensic decision-making.

Also controversial is the strong association between PCL-R assessed psychopathy and violent criminal behavior, which inspires some of the most passionate criticism of the measure. This is especially true given that the crucial role that the PCL-R plays in the criminal justice system highlights the ways in which PCL-R psychopathy departs from the construct first described by Cleckley (1988). For example, although Cleckley (1988) included inadequately motivated antisocial behavior among his 16 criteria, criminal behavior (and specifically violent criminal behavior) was not viewed as a necessary component of the syndrome. Rather, Cleckley (1988) argued that "many persons showing the characteristics of those described here do commit major crimes and sometimes crimes of maximal violence. There are so many, however, who do not, that such tendencies should be regarded as the exception rather than as the rule (p. 262)."

Thus, one of the most potentially divisive arguments in the field today is the PCL-R's emphasis on antisocial behaviors and its inclusion of items assessing specific forms of criminal behavior (e.g., juvenile delinquency, criminal versatility, revocation of conditional release). Critics of the measure have argued that such items are unnecessary for diagnosing the syndrome originally conceptualized by Cleckley (Cooke & Michie, 2001; Cooke et al., 2006), and they believe that the reliance on specific criminal behaviors overemphasizes this aspect of the syndrome at the expense of the personality traits theorized to lie at its core (Lilienfeld, 1994). In some cases, it has been argued that these behaviors are best conceptualized as a consequence of psychopathy, rather than as core diagnostic features (Cooke et al., 2006).

It is important to note that although the PCL-R is a powerful lightning rod for such controversy, the debate surrounding the association between psychopathy and violence is not new. In 1974, Lewis wrote, regarding the assessment of the psychopathy syndrome:

These reveal a preoccupation with the nosological status of the concept . . . its forensic implications, its subdivisions, limits, [and] the propriety of identifying psychopathic personality with antisocial behavior. The effect of reading solid blocks of literature is disheartening; there is so much fine-spun theorizing, repetitive argument, and therapeutic gloom. (pp. 137–138)

Similarly, in 1981, Millon wrote, "50 years ago the same issues were in the forefront, notably whether the psychopathic personality was or was not synonymous with overt antisocial behavior" (p. 184).

Twenty-six years later, the debate continues and researchers look for ways to address the concerns raised by the overly antisocial items. For example, researchers will conduct analyses to examine separately the contributions only those items associated with the interpersonal and affective components of the syndrome when investigating the deficits underlying the syndrome (e.g., Patrick et al., 1993). Despite this trend, however, there are those who argue there is not good evidence to suggest that any one component of psychopathy is a consequence of any other component (e.g., Hare, 2003; Neumann, Hare, & Newman, in press) and that psychopathy is best conceptualized as a unidimensional construct. Essentially, this argument holds that the PCL-R as a whole best captures the syndrome originally described by Cleckley (1988), and that this "'whole' may be greater than the sum of the 'parts'" (Neumann et al., in press). Thus, although psychopathy may have several components, it is best conceptualized as a "super-factor" (Neumann et al., in press).

The second related controversy surrounding the PCL-R involves analysis and interpretation of the measure's factor structure. Initial exploratory factor analysis of the PCL-R revealed two correlated (0.50) factors (Hare, 1991; Harpur, Hakstian, & Hare, 1988; Harpur, Hare, & Hakstian, 1989). The first, Factor 1, was dubbed the affective/interpersonal factor as it included those items representing many of the deficient emotional and interpersonally manipulative characteristics of the syndrome (e.g., glib/superficial charm, manipulative, callous, shallow affect). The second, Factor 2, became known as the social deviance or impulsive/antisocial lifestyle factor on the basis of its inclusion of those items measuring the psychopath's antisocial and criminal behavior (e.g., poor behavioral controls, impulsivity, early behavior problems).

Recently, the traditional two-factor structure has been called into question. Cooke et al. (2006) have argued that analyses suggest that the two factor solution represents a poor fit to the data and have campaigned for a reconceptualization of the measure as comprising three factors: Factor 1 (interpersonal), Factor 2 (affective), and Factor 3 (lifestyle). The first two factors essentially divide the original Factor 1 into two component parts, interpersonal and affective. Importantly, this three factor solution—although a significantly better fit to existing data than the traditional two-factor model (Cooke & Michie, 2001; Cooke et al., 2004)—also excludes seven PCL-R items. Cooke et al. have argued that this exclusion is necessary to purge the instrument of the specifically criminal behavior items that they believe are not core features of the syndrome, but rather consequences of the syndrome (Cooke et al., 2006), an argument strongly refuted by Hare and others (Hare, 2003; Neumann et al., in press). Partly in response to the Cooke model, Hare has introduced a revised two-factor model comprising four facets. These first three facets are the same as Cooke's three factors (i.e., interpersonal, affective, lifestyle). The fourth facet reflects the items deleted from Cooke's analysis and it is referred to as the antisocial facet (Hare, 2003; Hare & Neumann, 2006).

The factor debate reflects the larger debate regarding the nature of psychopathy and questions regarding the core features of the syndrome and the best ways to assess those features. Some might argue that a tally of the number of short-term relationships (e.g., item #17: "Many short-term marital relationships") is no more valid an indicator of the syndrome than a tally of the number of crimes committed as a juvenile (e.g., item #18: "Juvenile Delinquency"), because both serve as indicators of the psychopath's impulsive, unreliable nature. Others prefer to separate serious criminal behaviors, worried that these items foment a definition of psychopathy that will exclude individuals with many of the same features who have not committed an explicitly criminal act (Lilienfeld & Andrews, 1996). Such individuals may actually be "commended and reinforced in a competitive society where tough hard-headed realism is admired as an attribute necessary for survival" and who may live on "the rugged side of the business, military, or political world" (Millon, 1981, p. 181–182).

It is a key debate, because understanding the core features of the disorder is crucial, not only for improving our understanding of the etiology of the syndrome, but also for understanding how the syndrome may be expressed across populations. This debate is directly relevant to the third controversy, which involves the generalizability of psychopathy assessment, and the PCL-R especially, across groups.

Much of the PCL-R psychopathy research has been limited by a reliance on samples of institutionalized, Caucasian, North American, adult males. Although there is an emerging literature examining the expression and correlates of psychopathy in other groups, particularly female offenders (e.g., Bolt, Hare, Vitale, & Newman, 2004; Cale & Lilienfeld, 2002; Rutherford, Cacciola, Alterman, & McKay, 1996; Salekin et al., 1997; Weiler & Widom, 1996; Vitale, Smith, Brinkley, & Newman, 2002), the results have not always been clear-cut. For example, although evidence supports the reliability of psychopathy assessments among female populations (e.g., Cale & Lilienfeld, 2002; Vitale et al., 2002; Verona & Vitale, 2005), the evidence for the generalizability of laboratory-based, etiological-relevant correlates of psychopathy across gender is more limited.

In a study of incarcerated females that tested the generalizability of deficits in response inhibition on a card-playing task (CPT), Vitale and Newman (2001a) failed to find significant differences in the performance of psychopathic and nonpsychopathic women. Similarly, psychopathic females do not display the behavioral disinhibition on passive-avoidance tasks or deficient emotion facilitation on lexical decision tasks that characterize psychopathic males (Vitale et al., 2005; Lorenz & Newman, 2002). Conversely, like psychopathic men, psychopathic women do show anomalous startle modulation in a picture viewing paradigm (Sutton, Vitale, & Newman, 2002) and abnormal performance on the Picture-Word Stroop (Vitale et al., in press). Reconciling these discrepancies will rely, in part, on the continued development of our conceptualization of the syndrome. As we become clearer on what processes and traits lie at the core of psychopathy, we will be better able to determine if psychopathy translates across populations, with variations only in its expression, or if the syndrome itself is limited to particular groups (Vitale et al., in press).

ALTERNATIVE MEASURES OF PSYCHOPATHY

Although the PCL-R is the most commonly used assessment of psychopathy, other measures—some designed specifically to address limitations in the use of the PCL-R—have been developed over the past two decades. Some of these measures, such as the PCL-Screening Version (PCL-SV) (Forth, Brown, Hart, & Hare, 1996), PCL-Youth Version (PCL-YV) (Forth, Kosson, & Hare, 2003), and the Self-Report Psychopathy scale (SRP-II) (e.g., Williams & Paulhus, 2004) are direct descendants of the PCL-R, designed to be used with specialized groups or in noninstitutional contexts.

For example, the PCL-SV was created as a way to assess psychopathy using less information and without formal criminal records, which increases its utility in psychiatric and noninstitutional settings (Forth et al., 1996). The scale has only 12 items—all based on existing PCL-R items—designed to be rated on the basis of less detailed information than is required for the PCL-R. To this end, many of the PCL-R items were combined together to form the PCL-SV. For example, the PCL-SV item "lacks empathy" assesses many of the behaviors and attitudes used to score the separate PCL-R items "callous/ lack of empathy" and "shallow affect" (Forth et al., 1996). Generally, research suggests that the PCL-SV captures a syndrome similar to the PCL-R. The two measures are highly correlated (with an average correlation of 0.8; Cooke, Michie, Hart, & Hare, 1999), the PCL-SV exhibits a factor structure and item functioning similar to the PCL-R (Hill, Neumann, & Rogers, 2004), and the PCL-SV is a good predictor of violent behavior (Hill, Rogers, & Bickford, 1996; Douglas, Ogloff, Nicholls, & Grant, 1999; Skeem & Mulvey, 2001).

Whereas the PCL-SV is predicated on the belief that psychopathy can be assessed using less detailed information, the PCL-YV is based on the assumption that the psychopathy syndrome observed among adults can be extended back into adolescence. Thus, although the items in the PCL-YV are closely based on the adult PCL-R, they have been modified to capture the syndrome as it might appear in adolescents ages 12– 18 (Forth et al., 2003). The assumption that psychopathy may be apparent at these early ages is reasonable, given the design of the PCL-R itself that includes items focused specifically on problem behaviors that occur in childhood and adolescence (i.e., "early behavior problems," "juvenile delinquency"), as well as on research that demonstrates an association between adult PCL-R scores and childhood behavior problems (Harris, Rice, & Quinsey, 1994).

Research using the PCL-YV has demonstrated that the measure relates to criterion variables in ways that would be predicted based on PCL-R research with adults. For example, relative to adolescents with low scores, adolescents with high scores on the instrument commit more and more violent crimes (Kosson, Cyterski, Steuerwald, Neumann, & Walker-Matthews, 2002). PCL-YV scores are also significantly, inversely associated with familial attachment (Kosson et al., 2002).

Because the PCL-YV, like the PCL-R, requires a lengthy interview procedure, alternative measures of psychopathy for youth have been developed. For example, the Antisocial Process Screening Device (APSD) (Frick & Hare, 2001) is a 20-item rating scale that can be used as a self-report measure or as a teacher and parent report measure. Items on the APSD tap the interpersonal (e.g., superficial charm, lack of empathy), emotional (e.g., shallow affect), and behavioral (e.g., reckless antisocial behaviors, impulsivity) characteristics of psychopathy. Research has shown that the APSD is associated with many of the personality traits and laboratory deficits exhibited by psychopathic adults. For example, high scores on the APSD delineate a group of individuals who exhibit higher rates of conduct problems and police contacts, and stronger family histories of antisocial behavior than groups characterized by lower scores (Christian, Frick, Hill, Tyler, & Frazer, 1997). Higher scores on the APSD are also associated with decreased empathy, perspective taking, and fearfulness (Blair, 1999; Blair, Monson, & Frederickson, 2001). Finally, laboratory studies have demonstrated that adolescents characterized by the callous, unemotional traits assessed by the APSD exhibit perseverative responding on a task requiring them to modify an initial reward-oriented response strategy in light of increasing rates of punishment (e.g., O'Brien & Frick, 1996), as well as deficits in passive avoidance on a go-no-go task and significantly reduced interference on a Picture-Word Stroop (Vitale et al., 2005).

It is interesting to note that, consistent with the mixed picture emerging from studies of the PCL-R among adult females, the PCL-YV and APSD also exhibit inconsistencies across gender. For example, Schmidt, McKinnon, Chattha, and Brownlee (2006) examined the associations between PCL-YV scores and violent and nonviolent recidivism among youths over a three-year period and found that—although the PCL-YV was significantly associated with violent recidivism among males—there were no significant associations between PCL-YV scores and any measure of recidivism among the females. Further, Vitale et al. (2005) showed that although females assessed using the APSD demonstrated similar abnormalities on the Picture-Word Stroop task as males assessed with the measure, they failed to show expected deficits in passive-avoidance learning on a go-no-go task.

Although there appears to be good evidence—especially among males—that measures such as the PCL-YV and the APSD can assess a syndrome in adolescents similar to the psychopathy syndrome assessed in adults, there is considerable controversy regarding the assessment of psychopathy in youth. A psychopathy label has become synonymous in some arenas with increased dangerousness and poor treatment response (Edens, 2006; Lykken, 1995). Because the psychopathy-like syndrome assessed among children and adolescents may reflect transient developmental processes, some have argued that it is inappropriate to use such a label in this group (e.g., Edens, Skeem, Cruise, & Cauffman, 2001; Skeem & Cauffman, 2003).

As noted above, however, there is emerging evidence that many of the behaviors and performance abnormalities associated with adult psychopathy are apparent in youth. Further, those who use measures such as the PCL-YV and APSD with youth note that ratings of items are based on the frequency, duration, and intensity of the attitudes and behaviors exhibited by the individual (Gretton, Hare, & Catchpole, 2004; Lynam, 1996), thereby decreasing the likelihood that scores will represent normal, transitory developmental processes. Consistent with this assertion, in community samples the mean PCL-YV scores low (i.e., a score of 5 out of a possible 40) (Forth et al., 2003). On this basis, the counter-argument is made that by neglecting to examine psychopathy in adolescents, researchers and clinicians may be giving up an important opportunity for examining the development of the syndrome across time and for designing interventions that might prevent the adolescent with psychopathic traits from becoming the adult psychopath (Lynam, 1996; Frick, 1998; Vitale et al., 2005).

Just as we have sought new, more efficient ways to assess the psychopathy syndrome among adolescents, we have developed more efficient alternative measures of the syndrome in adults. Thus, in addition to the PCL-SV and PCL-YV, Hare and colleagues have developed the Self-Report Psychopathy scale (SRP and SRP-II) as a self-report measure of the syndrome in adult samples. The SRP—and its current revision the SRP-II—were developed on the basis of PCL and PCL-R items. Like the PCL-R, the measure has two factors: one that indexes the interpersonal/affective component of the syndrome and a second that indexes the impulsive/antisocial lifestyle component. The SRP-II is reliable (Hare, 1985) and relates in expected ways with correlates of the psychopathy syndrome, including correlating with scores on the PCL (Hare, 1985). Zagon and Jackson (1994) showed that SRP-II scores correlated positively with measures of narcissism and negatively associated with measures of empathy. Similarly, Paulhus and Williams (2002) showed positive associations with Machiavellianism and negative associations with agreeableness and conscientiousness.

One of the great advantages of the PCL-R and its progeny has been the unification of the field. Although some have cautioned that this unification may have come at the expense of the development of alternative measures, the benefit to clinical work and laboratory research of having a shared conceptualization of the syndrome should not be underestimated (Hare, 1996). Further, the PCL-R has not entirely inhibited the development of alternative, non-PCL based measures. For example, a number of self-report measures, including the Primary and Secondary Psychopathy Scales (SRPS) (Levenson, Kiehl, & Fitzpatrick, 1995) and the Psychopathic Personality Inventory (PPI) (Lilienfeld & Andrews, 1996), were developed relatively independently in order to provide a means of assessing psychopathy in noninstitutionalized samples. These measures emphasize the traits associated with the syndrome, rather than emphasizing the numbers of disinherited behaviors or criminal acts.

The SRPS is a 26-item self-report measure developed by Levenson et al. (1995). The scale has two components: the primary scale that is positively correlated with disinhibition and boredom susceptibility and negatively correlated with harm avoidance on the Multidimensional Personality Questionnaire, and the secondary scale that is associated with stress reactions and is considered a measure of trait anxiety. In a test of the validity of the SRPS, Brinkley, Schmitt, Smith, & Newman (2001) compared scores on the measure to PCL-R scores in an institutional sample. Results showed that the PCL-R was associated with the SRPS and, more importantly, that the SRPS related in predictable ways to substance abuse, criminal versatility, and passive avoidance task performance. Similarly, Lynam, Whiteside, and Jones (1999) examined the validity of the scale in a university sample and found that SRPS scores related in expected ways with self-reported delinquency, with personality traits such as low agreeableness, and with performance on a go-no-go passive avoidance task.

Like the SRPS, the PPI was developed to emphasize the traits associated with psychopathy (Lilienfeld & Andrews, 1996). The PPI is a 187 item self-report measure with eight subscales, including Machiavellian egocentricity, coldheartedness, social potency, carefree nonplanfulness, fearlessness, impulsive nonconformity, blame externalization, and stress immunity. Research shows that the PPI correlates with PCL-R total scores (Poythress, Edens, & Lilienfeld, 1998), as well as Factor 1 and 2 scores. In addition, the PPI correlates with adult and childhood antisocial behavior (Benning, Patrick, Hicks, Blonigen, & Krueger, 2003), measures of emotional empathy (Sandoval, Hancock, Poythress, Edens, & Lilienfeld, 2000), and self-report aggression and dominance (Edens, Poythress, & Watkins, 2001).

Although some have argued these measures that are designed specifically to assess psychopathy are preferable over personality measures that may simply assess generalized behavioral deviance (Lilienfeld, 2006), others have argued that traditional personality measures are entirely appropriate in the assessment of psychopathy. For example, Lynam and Derefinko (2006) have argued that psychopathy is best conceptualized according to the traditional Five-Factor Model (FFM) of personality, and that psychopathy is easily captured by the traits and facets of personality measures like the NEO-PI-R.

According to the proponents of this approach, conceptualizing psychopathy in accordance with existing personality traits places the syndrome within the context of well-validated personality theory that is already strongly connected to research in diverse areas including genetics, development, and neurobiology (Lynam & Derefinko, 2006). According to this argument, understanding psychopathy as a constellation of traits from the FFM allows researchers to use what we already know about the FFM to better understand psychopathy.

Widiger and Lynam (1998) have suggested that facets within the FFM can easily represent each item of the PCL-R. For example, according to the authors: "glibness/ superficial charm" is represented by low self-consciousness; "parasitic lifestyle" by low straightforwardness, low altruism, low modesty, low tender-mindedness, low achievement striving, and low self-discipline; and "shallow affect" as low warmth, low positive emotionality, low altruism, and low tender-mindedness. In order to test the validity of this profile, Miller, Lynam, Widiger, and Leukefeld (2001) asked psychopathy experts to generate a FFM profile of the prototypical psychopath on the basis of their understanding and knowledge of the syndrome. Importantly, the profile generated by these experts was similar to that generated by the theorists.

Further, in later research Lynam and colleagues (Lynam & Widiger, 2001; Miller & Lynam, 2003) have been able to calculate the Psychopathy Resemblance Index (PRI), which is a measure of the extent to which an individual resembles the FFM prototype. The PRI can then be studied as it relates to correlates of psychopathy. Research supports the argument that scores on the PRI do capture many of the qualities associated with psychopathy, as these scores are associated with an earlier age of onset of delinquency, greater criminal versatility, earlier drug use, and low internalizing problems (Miller, Lynam, Widiger, and Leukefeld, 2001). Among college students, PRI scores were associated with higher rates of substance abuse, riskier sex, criminal versatility, and more aggression (Miller & Lynam, 2003). Importantly, PRI scores also related to performance on three laboratory tasks: individuals with higher PRI scores were more aggressive on a laboratory measure of aggression, were more likely to prefer aggressive responses on a social-information task, and were less willing to delay gratification on a time-discounting task (Miller & Lynam, 2003). Although these results provide preliminary support for the utility of the PRI as a measure of psychopathy, it is important to note that the majority of evidence appears to relate to the impulsive, antisocial behavior of these individuals. Further research examining other laboratory correlates of psychopathy (e.g., PW Stroop performance, startle-response abnormalities) is needed.

Treatment of Psychopathy

Historically, the prognosis for psychopathy has been poor and most individuals in the field considered the syndrome to be relatively untreatable (e.g., Lykken, 1995; Hare, 1993). Although a considerable amount of data supports this view, there is still some possibility for future development in this area as we increase our knowledge of the etiological factors that underlie the syndrome. However, the current treatment literature in psychopathy might best be conceptualized as a demonstration of what does *not* work.

Ogloff, Wong, and Greenwood (1990) conducted one of the most important treatment studies in the area. Ogloff and colleagues assessed psychopaths' performance in a therapeutic community setting and they found that psychopaths were more likely to experience early discharge from the program, were less motivated, and showed less overall improvement (Ogloff et al., 1990). This study is particularly important because the authors used the early version of the Psychopathy Checklist to classify participants as psychopathic. As a result, in addition to ensuring a more homogenous psychopathic group for comparison purposes, the study is also directly relevant to current practice in the field, where the PCL-R is the clinical standard for assessment.

In a similar study, Rice, Harris, and Cormier (1992) examined psychopaths' performance in an intensive therapeutic community contained within a maximum-security prison. The treatment program was geared towards increasing empathy and responsibility for peers and was primarily peer-operated. In a follow-up comparison, the authors compared 146 treated offenders with a matched comparison group of 146 untreated offenders on measures of recidivism. The results were consistent with those of Ogloff et al. (1990), in that psychopaths did not appear to benefit from the therapeutic community program. In fact, although treatment was associated with lower recidivism among nonpsychopathic participants, the reverse was true for the psychopaths; psychopaths in the treatment group were actually more likely to violently recidivate (Rice et al., 1992), a finding that has been attributed to the possibility that the new social skills developed in the treatment setting merely improved the psychopaths' ability to manipulate and control others (Harris & Rice, 2006).

Consistently, research suggests that psychopaths are resistant to treatment. Compared to nonpsychopaths, psychopaths in treatment demonstrate poor program adjustment (e.g., Ogloff et al., 1990; Rice et al., 1992; Hobson, Shine, & Roberts, 2000; Richards, Casey, & Lucente, 2003) and lower levels of therapeutic gain (Hughes, Hogue, Hollin, & Champion, 1997). Further, treatment appears to be associated with heightened recidivism rates for psychopaths (e.g. Harris et al., 1994; Hare, Clark, Grann, & Thornton, 2000; Rice et al., 1992).

The negative outcomes associated with treatment of psychopaths may not always be apparent to the individuals administering the programs, which is another source of concern. For example, Rice et al. (1992) found that although the psychopathic participants in the therapeutic community program showed more problem behaviors while in the program, they were no less likely than nonpsychopaths to be given positions of trust within the program or to receive early recommendations for release. Similarly, Seto and Barbaree (1999) examined a cognitive-behavioral and relapse prevention program and found that it was the highly psychopathic participants who were also rated by their therapists as showing the greatest improvement (on the basis of motivation to change, quality of homework, conduct during sessions) who were most likely to violently re-offend.

The Seto and Barbaree finding is particularly crucial when considering a meta-analysis of psychopathy treatment studies conducted by Salekin (2002). Overall, the results of the meta-analysis suggested that there was more reason for optimism than previously expected. In this analysis, when the proportion of treatment participants who would have been expected to improve without treatment was subtracted from the proportion of treatment participants who were judged to have improved, the mean rate of successful intervention was 0.62 across 42 treatment studies. However, this conclusion has some important limitations. First, the PCL-R was used to assess psychopathy in only four of the studies, with the remaining studies using everything from diagnoses of "constitutional psychopathic inferiors" (e.g., Korey, 1944) to the So scale (e.g., Maas, 1966). Several of the studies were also conducted in juvenile samples, which is problematic given our limited understanding of the assessment and development of psychopathy in this group. In addition, only a minority of the studies included aggressive or criminal behavior as one of the outcome variables. Relatedly, in the majority of the studies, the primary outcome evaluation was therapist impressions. Given the results of Seto and Barbaree (1999), there is reason to be cautious regarding how well these therapists' impressions correctly predicted improvement in the psychopaths' behaviors.

In light of these findings, there are several alternatives. One is to de-emphasize treatments for psychopaths that are geared towards building social skills or empathy, and instead to create behavior modification programs with the goal of reducing harm (i.e., criminal recidivism) caused by psychopaths (Harris & Rice, 2006). A second alternative is to turn to research on the etiology of psychopathy in order to devise treatment strategies better suited to the particular deficits demonstrated by this group (Serin & Kuriychuk, 1994; Wallace, Schmitt, Vitale, & Newman, 2000).

For example, Newman and colleagues (Newman, 1998; Newman et al., 2003) have proposed that psychopaths are characterized by a deficit in response modulation. Specifically, psychopaths are proposed to be deficient in their ability to automatically redirect attention from the primary focus of their goal directed behavior to the evaluation of secondary stimuli. Wallace et al. (2000) have argued that—on the basis of such a deficit—it would be unlikely that simply changing the content of psychopathic thought (e.g., teaching social skills and anger management, traditional cognitive therapy) would result in significant improvement in these individuals' behavior. This is because the psychopath would be unable to benefit from changes in their thinking that they could not subsequently access automatically in key situations as a result of their response modulation deficit. Instead, the primary emphasis should be on developing and teaching strategies for compensating for the basic information-processing deficit that makes accessing these cognitions so challenging (Wallace et al., 2000). For example, in experimental paradigms where psychopaths are forced to pause before engaging in a response, their performance deficits disappear and they are able to perform as well as controls (Arnette et al., 1993; Newman et al., 1997). Although only in their infancy, such propositions highlight the importance of considering etiological factors when designing and implementing treatments for this group.

Summary and Future Directions

Societies throughout history have recognized the existence of the psychopathic personality. These individuals were distinguished by their fleeting, shallow interpersonal ties, their casual antisociality, and their sometimes explosive violence. Although a reliable assessment classification was a long-time coming, the understanding that these individuals needed to be identified in order to prevent or at least limit their effects on society, has been longstanding. Today is little different. The individual we know as the psychopath is a drain on society's financial and emotional resources, since psychopaths commit a disproportionate number of crimes and represent a significant proportion of our inmate populations.

Clinical descriptions of psychopathy have resulted in the development of reliable and valid measures of the syndrome across different populations. Early, disparate assessments gave way in the 1990s to more unified assessment relying on the PCL-R (Hare, 1991) and conceptually related measures (e.g., the PCL-YV and PCL-SV). More recently, the field has again seen the emergence of greater diversity in psychopathy assessments as self-report measures such as the PPI (Lilienfeld & Andrews, 1996) and SRPS (Levenson et al., 1995) have been increasingly utilized.

Greater unification in the assessment of psychopathy has allowed research on the etiology of the syndrome to flourish, and we know more than ever about the factors associated with this syndrome. Research has reliably demonstrated that there is a genetic component to the psychopathic personality (e.g., Waldman & Rhee, 2006). Research has also indicated that these individuals exhibit performance deficits that could be explained in terms of dispositional "fearlessness" (e.g., Lykken, 1995), poor behavioral inhibition (e.g., Fowles, 2006), or in terms of abnormalities in the functioning of the amygdala and associated structures (e.g., Blair, 2006). Still, other lines of investigation have examined the attention-processing of psychopathic individuals and shown that psychopaths appear deficient in their ability to initiate the relatively automatic shift in attention from the ongoing enactment of goal directed behavior to the contextual cues that would indicate that the behavior required modulation (e.g., Hiatt & Newman, 2006).

Understanding the causal factors that underlie psychopathy may prove invaluable to the prevention and treatment of the syndrome. Currently, little empirical data exist to suggest that psychopaths will benefit from treatment (e.g., Harris & Rice, 2006). However, this conclusion may be challenged in the future as proposed etiological processes begin to inform our interventions (e.g., Wallace et al., 2000), and we are able better to address the specific deficits associated with the psychopathy syndrome.

As we move forward in the field, research focused on the existing controversies and currently popular etiological theories will likely continue to dominate. We will learn more about the factor structure of the PCL-R, and we will better understand how the psychobiological processes associated with the syndrome develop into the full-blown psychopathy syndrome. However, several new areas are also emerging and they are likely to become increasingly important with the passage of time.

First, on the assessment front, researchers will be trying to determine whether it is best to conceptualize psychopathy as a discrete taxon or as a dimensional construct. Currently, there are competing claims regarding the best way to conceptualize the construct (e.g., Brinkley, Newman, & Widiger, 2004; Edens, Marcus, & Lilienfeld, 2006; Harris, et al., 1994; Vasey, Kotov, & Frick, 2006). In practice, this distinction may be made on the basis of anything from practical concerns to theoretical considerations. For example, when the PCL-R is used in clinical risk assessment the designation psychopathic versus nonpsychopathic may be required, whereas in a study of the genetic contributions to psychopathy, the syndrome may be conceptualized in dimensional, trait-like manner. The answer to the question of whether psychopathy is best conceptualized as a discrete category or as an extreme variation on normal personality may depend on whether we are focused on the behaviors, the traits, or the underlying psychobiological mechanisms associated with the syndrome (Brinkley et al., 2004).

Second, as we attempt to resolve the category-dimension question, we will likely see the emergence of subtypes of psychopathy. This would not be an altogether new development. Individuals have long differentiated the "primary" from the "secondary" or "neurotic" psychopath (e.g., Cleckley, 1941; Karpman, 1941; Lykken 1957)—the latter being characterized by relatively higher levels of neuroticism or anxiety. Further, researchers have already moved forward by proposing and beginning to test the ways in which psychopathy might be usefully divided on the basis of symptom profile, etiological mechanism, or the presence of criminal behavior (e.g., Brinkley et al., 2004; Poythress & Skeem, 2006). Such a development is consistent with what has been the practice among other clinical disorders (for example, schizophrenia) where subtypes representing different symptom profiles, different prognoses, and potentially different underlying psychobiological mechanisms have been differentiated from each other for clinical and research purposes. Although such a development may help to resolve many of the controversies currently existing in the field, it will inevitably lead us to the question of whether each subtype can reasonably be considered psychopathy. Such a fragmented future is still in the distance, but it is likely that it is one we will have to eventually confront.

References

American Psychiatric Association. (1951). *Diagnostic and statistical manual of mental disorders*. Washington, DC: Author.

American Psychiatric Association. (1968). *Diagnostic and statistical manual of mental disorders*. Washington, DC: Author.

American Psychiatric Association. (1994). *Diagnostic and statistical manual of mental disorders*. Washington, DC: Author.

Andershed, H., Kerr, M., Stattin, H., & Levander, S. (2002). Psychopathic traits in non-referred youths: A new assessment tool. In E. Blaauw & L. Sheridan (Eds.), *Psychopaths: Current international perspectives* (pp. 131–158) The Hague, the Netherlands: Elsevier.

Arnett, P. A., Howland, E. W., Smith, S. S., & Newman, J. P. (1993). Autonomic responsivity during passive avoidance in incarcerated psychopaths. *Personality and Individual Differences, 14*, 173–184.

Baxter, M. G., & Murray, E. A. (2002). The amygdala and reward. *Nature Reviews Neuroscience, 3*, 563–573.

Blair, K. S., Newman, C., Mitchell, D. G. V., Richell, R. A., Leonard, A., Morton, J., & Blair, R. J. R. (2006). Differentiating among prefrontal substrates in psychopathy: Neuropsychological findings. *Neuropsychology, 20*, 153–165.

Bechara, A., Damasio, A. R., Damasio, H., & Anderson, S. W. (1994). Insensitivity to future consequences following damage to human prefrontal cortex. *Cognition, 50*, 7–15.

Benning, S. D., Patrick, C. J., Hicks, B. M., Blonigen, D. M., & Krueger, R. F. (2003). Factor structure of the Psychopathic Personality Inventory: Validity and implications for clinical assessment. *Psychological Assessment, 15*, 340–350.

Berman, M. E., Kavoussi, R. J., & Coccaro, E. F. (1997). Neurotransmitter correlates of human aggression. In D. M. Stoff, J. Breiling, & J. D. Masur (Eds.), *Handbook of Antisocial Behavior* (pp. 305–313). New York: Wiley.

Blair, R. J. R. (1999). Responsiveness to distress cues in the child with psychopathic tendencies. *Personality and Individual Differences, 27*, 135–145.

Blair, R. J. R. (2006). Subcortical brain systems in psychopathy: The amygdala and associated structures. In C. Patrick (Ed.), *Handbook of Psychopathy* (pp. 296–312). New York: Guilford.

Blair, R. J. R., Monson, J., & Frederickson, N. (2001). Moral reasoning and conduct problems in children with emotional and behavioural difficulties. *Personality and Individual Differences, 31*, 799–811.

Blonigen, D. M., Hicks, B. M., Krueger, R. F., Patrick, C. J., & Iacono, W. G. (2006). Continuity and change in psychopathic traits as measured via normal-range personality: A longitudinal-biometric study. *Journal of Abnormal Psychology, 115*, 85–95.

Bolt, D. M., Hare, R. D., Vitale, J. E., & Newman, J. P. (2004). A multigroup item response theory analysis of the Psychopathy Checklist-Revised. *Psychological Assessment, 16* (2), 155–168.

Book, A. S., & Quinsey, V. L. (2004). Psychopaths: Cheaters or warrior-hawks? *Personality and Individual Differences. 36*, 33–45.

Brinkley, C. A., Newman, J. P., & Widiger, T. A. (2004). Two approaches to parsing the heterogeneity of psychopathy. *Clinical Psychology: Science and Practice, 11*, 69–94.

Brinkley, C. A., Schmitt, W. A., Smith, S. S., & Newman, J. P. (2001). Construct-validation of a self report psychopathy scale: Does Levenson's SRPS measure the same construct as Hare's PCL-R? *Personality and Individual Differences, 31*, 1021–1038.

Burks, V. S., Laird, R. D., Dodge, K. A., Pettit, G. S., & Bates, J. E. (1999). Knowledge structures, social information processing, and children's aggressive behavior. *Social Development, 8*, 220–236.

Butcher, J. N. (Ed.). (1979). *New developments in the use of the MMPI*. Minneapolis: University of Minnesota Press.

Butcher, J. N., Graham, J. R., Ben-Porath, Y. S., Tellegen, A., Dahlstrom, W. G., & Kaemmer, B. (2001). *MMPI-2: Manual for administration, scoring, and interpretation* (Rev. ed.). Minneapolis: University of Minnesota Press.

Cale, E. M. & Lilienfeld, S. O. (2002). Sex differences in psychopathy and antisocial personality disorder. A review and integration. *Clinical Psychology Review, 22*, 1179–1207.

Christian, R. E., Frick, P. J., Hill, N. L., Tyler, A. L., & Frazer, D. (1997). Psychopathy and conduct problems in children: II. Implications for subtyping children with conduct problems. *Journal of the American Academy of Child & Adolescent Psychiatry, 36*, 233–241.

Cleckley, H. (1976). *The Mask of Sanity.* St. Louis: Mosby.

Cooke, D. & Michie, C. (1999). Psychopathy across cultures: North America and Scotland compared. *Journal of Abnormal Psychology, 108*, 58–68.

Cooke, D. J., & Michie, C. (2001). Refining the construct of psychopathy: Towards a hierarchical model. *Psychological Assessment, 13*, 171–188.

Cooke, D. J., Michie, C., & Hart, S. D. (2006). Facets of clinical psychopathy: Towards clearer measurement. In C. Patrick (Ed.), *Handbook of Psychopathy* (pp. 91–106). New York: Guilford.

Cooke, D. J., Michie, C., Hart, S. D., & Clark, D. (2004). Reconstructing psychopathy: Clarifying the significance of antisocial and socially deviant behavior in the diagnosis of psychopathic personality disorder. *Journal of Personality Disorder, 18*, 337–357.

Cooke, D. J., Michie, C., Hart, S. D., & Hare, R. D. (1999). Evaluating the Screening Version of the Hare Psychopathy Checklist-Revised: An item response theory analysis. *Psychological Assessment, 11*, 3–13.

Crick, N. R., & Dodge, K. A. (1994). A review and reformulation of social information-processing mechanisms in children's social adjustment. *Psychological Bulletin, 115*, 74–101.

Damasio, A. R. (1994). *Descartes' error: Emotion, reason, and the human brain.* New York: Putnam.

Davis, M. (2000). The role of the amygdala in conditioned and unconditioned fear and anxiety. In J. P. Aggleton (Ed.), *The amygdala: A functional analysis* (pp. 289–310). Oxford, UK: Oxford University Press.

Dodge, K. A., & Coie, J. D. (1987). Social information processing factors in reactive and proactive aggression in children's peer groups. *Journal of Personality and Social Psychology, 53*, 1146–1158.

Dodge, K. A., & Frame, C. M. (1982). Social cognitive biases and deficits in aggressive boys. *Child Development, 53*, 620–635.

Dodge, K. A., Lochman, J. E., Harnish, J. D., Bates, J. E., & Pettit, G. S. (1997). Reactive and proactive aggression in school children and psychiatrically impaired chronically assaultive youth. *Journal of Abnormal Psychology, 106*, 37–51.

Dodge, K. A., Price, J. M., Bachorowski, J., & Newman, J. P. (1990). Hostile attributional biases in severely aggressive adolescents. *Journal of Abnormal Psychology, 99*, 385–392.

Doninger, N. A., & Kosson, D. S. (2001). Interpersonal construct systems among psychopaths. *Personality and Individual Differences, 30*, 1263–1281.

Douglas, K. S., Ogloff, J. R. P., Nicholls, T. L. & Grant, I. (1999). Assessing risk for violence among psychiatric patients: The HCR-20 violence risk assessment scheme and the Psychopathy Checklist: Screening Version. *Journal of Consulting and Clinical Psychology, 67*, 917–930.

Edens, J. F. (2006). Unresolved controversies concerning psychopathy: Implications for clinical and forensic decision making. *Professional Psychology: Research and Practice, 37*, 59–65.

Edens, J. F., Marcus, D. K., & Lilienfeld, S. O. (2006) Psychopathic, not psychopath: Taxometric evidence for the dimensional structure of psychopathy. *Journal of Abnormal Psychology, 115*, 131–144.

Edens, J. F., Poythress, N. G., & Watkins, M. M. (2001). Further validation of the Psychopathic Personality Inventory among offenders: Personality and behavioral correlates. *Journal of Personality Disorders, 15*, 403–415.

Edens, J. F., Skeem, J. L., Cruise, K. R., & Cauffman, E. (2001). Assessment of "juvenile psychopathy" and its association with violence: A critical review. *Behavioral Sciences and the Law, 19*, 53–80.

Flor, H., Birbaumer, N., Hermann, C., Ziegler, S., & Patrick, C. J. (2002). Aversive Pavolvian conditioning in psychopaths: Peripheral and central correlates. *Psychophysiology, 39*, 505–518.

Forth, A. E., Brown, S. L., Hart, S. D., & Hare, R. D. (1996). The assessment of psychopathy in male and female noncriminals: Reliability and validity. *Personality and Individual Differences, 20*, 531–543.

Forth, A. E., Kosson, D. S., & Hare, R. D. (2003). *The Psychopathy Checklist: Youth Version.* Toronto, Canada: Multi-Health Systems.

Fowles, D. C. (1980). The three-arousal model: Implications of Gray's two-factor learning theory for heart rate, electrodermal activity, and psychopathy. *Psychophysiology, 17*, 87–104.

Freedman, D. (2001). False prediction of future dangerousness: Error rates and Psychopathy Checklist-Revised. *Journal of American Academy of Psychiatry and the Law, 29*, 89–95.

Frick, P. J. (1998). Callous-unemotional traits and conduct problems: Applying the two-factor model of psychopathy to children. In D. J. Cooke, A. E. Forth, and R. D. Hare (Eds.), *Psychopathy: Theory, research and implications for society* (pp. 161–187). Boston: Kluwer.

Frick, P. J. & Hare, R. D. (2001). *The Antisocial Process Screening Device.* Toronto, Canada: Multi-Health Systems.

Fulero, S. M. (1995). Review of the Hare Psychopathy Checklist-Revised. In J. C. Conoley & J. C. Impara (Eds.), *Twelfth mental measurements yearbook* (pp. 453–454). Lincoln, NE: Buros Institute.

Gernsbacher, M. A., & Faust, M. E. (1991). The mechanism of suppression: A component of general comprehension skill. *Journal of Experimental Psychology: Learning, Memory, and Cognition, 17,* 245–262.

Gorenstein, E. E. (1982). Frontal lobe functions in psychopaths. *Journal of Abnormal Psychology, 91,* 368–379.

Gorenstein, E. E., & Newman, J. P. (1980). Disinhibitory psychopathology: A new perspective and a model for research. *Psychological Review, 87,* 301–315.

Gough, H. G., & Bradley, P. (1996). *CPI manual* (3rd ed.) Palo Alto, CA: Consulting Psychologists Press.

Gray, J. A. (1987). *The psychology of fear and stress* (2nd ed.). New York: Cambridge University Press.

Gray, J. A. & McNaughton, N. (2000). *The Neuropsychology of Anxiety* (2nd Ed.). Oxford, UK: Oxford University Press.

Gretton, H. M., Hare, R. D., & Catchpole, R. E. H. (2004). Psychopathy and offending from adolescence to adulthood: A 10-year follow-up. *Journal of Consulting and Clinical Psychology, 72,* 636–645.

Hare, R. D. (1970). *Psychopathy: Theory and research.* Oxford, UK: John Wiley.

Hare, R. D. (1978). Psychopathy and electrodermal responses to nonsignal stimulation. *Biological Psychology, 6,* 237–246.

Hare, R. D. (1980). A research scale for the assessment of psychopathy in criminal populations. *Personality and Individual Differences, 1,* 111–119.

Hare, R. D. (1984). Performance of psychopaths on cognitive tasks related to frontal lobe function. *Journal of Abnormal Psychology, 93,* 133–140.

Hare, R. D. (1985). Comparison of procedures for the assessment of psychopathy. *Journal of Consulting and Clinical Psychology, 53,* 7–16.

Hare, R. D. (1991). *Manual for the Hare Psychopathy Checklist-Revised.* Toronto, Ontario, Canada: Multi-Health Systems.

Hare, R. D. (1993). *Without conscience: The disturbing world of the psychopaths among us.* New York: Guilford Press.

Hare, R. D. (1996). Psychopathy: A clinical construct whose time has come. *Criminal Justice and Behavior, 23,* 25–54.

Hare, R. D. (1998a). Psychopaths and their nature: Implications for the mental health and criminal justice systems. In T. Millon & E. Sorenson (Eds.), *Psychopathy: Antisocial, criminal, and violent behavior* (pp. 188–212). New York: Guilford.

Hare, R. D. (1998b). Psychopathy, Affect and Behavior. In D. J. Cooke, R. D. Hare, & A. Forth (Eds.), *Psychopathy: Theory, research and implications for society* (pp. 81–104). The Netherlands: Kluwer Academic Publishers.

Hare, R. D. (2003). *Manual for the Hare Psychopathy Checklist-Revised* (2nd ed.). Toronto, Canada: Multi-Health Systems.

Hare, R. D., Clark, D., Grann, M., & Thornton, D. (2000). Psychopathy and the predictive validity of the PCL-R: An international perspective. *Behavioral Sciences and the Law, 18,* 623–645.

Hare, R. D., Frazelle, J., & Cox, D. N. (1978). Psychopathy and physiological responses to threat of an aversive stimulus. *Psychophysiology, 15,* 165–172.

Hare, R. D., & Hart, S. D. (1993). Psychopathy, mental disorder, and crime. In S. Hodgins (Ed.), *Mental disorder and crime* (pp. 104–115). London: Sage.

Hare, R. D., Hemphill, J. F., & Paulhus, D. (2002). The self-report psychopathy scale-II.

Hare, R. D., & Jutai, J. W. (1988). Psychopathy and cerebral asymmetry in semantic processing. *Personality and Individual Differences, 9,* 329–337.

Hare, R. D., & Neumann, C. S. (2006). The PCL-R assessment of psychopathy: Development, structural properties, and new directions. In C. Patrick (Ed.), *Handbook of Psychopathy* (pp. 58–90) New York: Guilford.

Harpur, T. J., Hakstian, A. R., & Hare, R. D. (1988). Factor structure of the Psychopathy Checklist. *Journal of Consulting and Clinical Psychology, 56,* 741–747.

Harpur, T. J., Hare, R. D., & Hakstian, A. R. (1989). Two-factor conceptualization of psychopathy: Construct validity and assessment implications. *Psychological Assessment, 1,* 6–17.

Harris, G. T., & Rice, M. E. (2006). Treatment of psychopathy: A review of empirical findings. In C. Patrick (Ed.), *Handbook of Psychopathy* (pp. 555–572). New York: Guilford.

Harris, G. T., Rice, M. E., & Quinsey, V. L. (1994). Psychopathy as a taxon: Evidence that psychopaths are a discrete class. *Journal of Consulting and Clinical Psychology, 62,* 387–397.

Hemphill, J. F., Hare, R. D., & Wong, S. (1998). Psychopathy and recidivism: A review. *Legal and Criminological Psychology*, *3*, 139–170.

Hemphill, J. F., Templeman, R., Wong, S., & Hare, R. D. (1998). Psychopathy and crime: Recidivism and criminal careers. In D. J. Cooke, R. D. Hare, & A. Forth (Eds.), *Psychopathy: Theory, research and implications for society* (pp. 375–399). Dordrecht: Kluwer Academic Publishers.

Herve, H., Mitchell, D., Cooper, B. S. (2004) Psychopathy and unlawful confinement: An examination of perpetrator and event characteristics. *Canadian Journal of Behavioural Science*, *36*, 137–145.

Hiatt, D. D., Schmitt, W. A., & Newman, J. P. (2004). Stroop tasks reveal abnormal selective attention among psychopathic offenders. *Neuropsychology*, *18*, 50–59.

Hill, C. D., Neumann, C. S., & Rogers, R. (2004). Confirmatory factor analysis of the Psychopathy Checklist: Screening Version in offenders with Axis I disorders. *Psychological Assessment*, *16*, 90–95.

Hill, C. D., Rogers, R., & Bickford, M. E. (1996). Predicting aggressive and socially disruptive behavior in a maximum security forensic psychiatric hospital. *Journal of Forensic Sciences*, *41*, 56–59.

Hobson, J., Shine, J., & Roberts, R. (2000). How do psychopaths behave in a prison therapeutic community? *Psychology, Crime and Law*, *6*, 139–154.

Hughes, G., Hogue, T., Hollin, C., & Champion, H. (1997). First stage evaluation of a treatment programme for personality disordered offenders. *Journal of Forensic Psychiatry*, *8*, 515–527.

Kandel, E., & Freed, D. (1989). Frontal lobe dysfunction and antisocial behavior: A review. *Journal of Clinical Psychology*, *45*, 404–413.

Karpman, B. (1941). On the need of separating psychopathy into two distinct clinical types: The symptomatic and the idiopathic. *Journal of Criminal Psychopathology*, *3*, 112–137.

Kosson, D. S., Cyterski, T. D., Steuerwald, B. L., Neumann, C. S., & Walker-Matthews, S. (2002). The reliability and validity of the Psychopathy Checklist: Youth Version (PCL-YV) in nonincarcerated adolescent males. *Psychological Assessment*, *14*, 97–109.

Kiehl, K. A., Smith, A. M., Hare, R. D., Mendrek, A., Forster, B. B., Brink, J., et al. (2001). Limbic abnormalities in affective processing by criminal psychopaths as revealed by functional magnetic resonance imaging. *Biological Psychiatry*, *50*, 677–684.

Kim-Cohen, J., Caspi, A., & Taylor, A. (2006). MAOA, maltreatment, and gene-environment interaction predicting children's mental health: New evidence and a meta-analysis. *Molecular Psychiatry*, *11*, 903–913.

Korey, S. R. (1944). The effects of Benzedine sulfate on the behavior of psychopathic and neurotic juvenile delinquents. *Psychiatric Quarterly*, *18*, 127–137.

Kosson, D. S., Smith, S. S., & Newman, J. P. (1990). Evaluating the construct validity of psychopathy in black and white male inmates: Three preliminary studies. *Journal of Abnormal Psychology*, *99*, 250–259.

Laakso, M. P., Gunning-Dixon, F., Vaurio, O., Repo-Tihonen, E., Soininen, H., & Tihoenen, J. (2002). Prefrontal volumes in habitually violent subjects with antisocial personality disorder and type 2 alcoholism. *Psychiatry Research: Neuroimaging*, *114*, 95–102.

LaPierre, D., Braun, C. M. J., & Hodgins, S. (1995). Ventral frontal deficits in psychopathy: Neuropsychological test findings. *Neuropsychologia*, *33*, 139–151.

Larsson, H., Andershed, H., & Lichtenstein, P. (2006). A genetic factor explains most of the variation in psychopathic personality. *Journal of Abnormal Psychology*, *115*, 221–230.

Levenson, M. R., Kiehl, K. A., & Fitzpatrick, C. M. (1995). Assessing psychopathic attributes in a noninstitutionalized population. *Journal of Personality and Social Psychology*, *68*, 151–158.

Levenston, G. K., Patrick, C. J., Bradley, M. M., & Lang, P. J. (2000). The psychopath as observer: Emotion and attention in picture processing. *Journal of Abnormal Psychology*, *109*, 373–389.

Lewis, A. (1974). Psychopathic Personality: A most elusive category. *Psychological Medicine*, *4*, 133–140.

Lilienfeld, S. O. (1994). Conceptual problems in the assessment of psychopathy. *Clinical Psychology Review*, *14*, 17–38.

Lilienfeld, S. O. (1998). Recent methodological advances and developments in the assessment of psychopathy. *Behavior Research and Therapy*, *36*, 99–125.

Lilienfeld, S. O. (2006). The self-report assessment of psychopathy. In C. Patrick (Ed.), *Handbook of Psychopathy* (pp. 107–132). New York: Guilford.

Lilienfeld, S. O. & Andrews, B. P. (1996). Development and preliminary validation of a self-report measure of psychopathic personality traits in noncriminal populations. *Journal of Personality Assessment*, *66*, 488–524.

Lorenz, A. R., & Newman, J. P. (2002). Utilization of emotion cues in male and female offenders with antisocial personality disorder: Results from a lexical decision task. *Journal of Abnormal Psychology*, *111*, 513–516.

Louks, A. D. (1995). *Criminal behavior, violent behavior, and prison maladjustment in federal female offenders.* Unpublished doctoral dissertation, Queen's University, Kingston, Ontario.

Lykken, D. T. (1957). A study of anxiety in the sociopathic personality. *Journal of Abnormal Psychology*, *55*, 6–10.

Lykken, D. T. (1995). *The Antisocial Personalities.* Hillsdale, NJ: Lawrence Erlbaum.

Lynam, D. R. (1996). Early identification of chronic offenders: Who is the fledgling psychopath? *Psychological Bulletin*, *120*, 209–234.

Lynam D. R., & Derefinko, K. J. (2006). Psychopathy and personality. In C. Patrick (Ed.), *Handbook of Psychopathy* (pp. 133–155). New York: Guilford.

Lynam, D. R., Whiteside, S., & Jones, S. (1999). Self-reported psychopathy: A validation study. *Journal of Personality Assessment*, *73*, 110–132.

Lynam, D. R., & Widiger, T. A. (2001). Using the Five Factor Model to represent the *DSM-IV* personality disorders: An expert consensus approach. *Journal of Abnormal Psychology*, *110*, 401–412.

Maas, J. (1966). The use of actional procedures in group psychotherapy with sociopathic women. *International Journal of Group Psychotherapy*, *16*, 190–197.

MacCoon, D., Wallace, J. F., & Newman, J. P. (2003) Self-regulation: The context-appropriate allocation of attentional capacity to dominant and nondominant cues. Manuscript submitted for publication.

Manke, B., McGuire, S., Reiss, D., Hetherington, E. M., & Plomin, R. (1995). Genetic contributions to adolescents' extrafamilial social interactions: Teachers, best friends, and peers. *Social Development*, *4*, 238–256.

Maslow, A. H. (1951). *Principles of abnormal psychology: The dynamics of psychic illness.* Oxford, UK: Harper.

McCord, W., & McCord, J. (1964). *The psychopath: An essay on the criminal mind.* Oxford, UK: D. Van Nostrand.

Miller, J. D., & Lynam, D. R. (2003). Psychopathy and the Five Factor Model of personality: A replication and extension. *Journal of Personality Assessment*, *81*, 168–178.

Miller, J. D., Lynam, D. R., Widiger, T. A., & Leukefeld, C. (2001). Personality disorders as extreme variants of common personality dimensions: Can the Five Factor Model adequately represent psychopathy? *Journal of Personality*, *69*, 253–276.

Millon, T. (1981). *Disorders of personality: DSM-III: Axis II.* New York: Wiley.

Mitchell, D. G. V., Colledge, E., Leonard, A., & Blair, R. J. R. (2002). Risky decisions and response reversal: Is there evidence of orbito-frontal cortex dysfunction in psychopathic individuals. *Neuropsychologia*, *40*, 2013–2022.

Moffitt, T. E. (1993). The neuropsychology of conduct disorder. *Development and Psychopathology*, *5*, 135–151.

Morgan, A. B., & Lilienfeld, S. O. (2000). A meta-analytic review of the relation between antisocial behavior and neuropsychological measures of executive function. *Clinical Psychology Review*, *20*, 113–136.

Neary, A. (1990). *DSM-III and psychopathy checklist assessment of Antisocial Personality Disorder in black and white female felons.* Unpublished doctoral dissertation, University of Missouri, St. Louis.

Neumann, C. S., Hare, R. D., & Newman, J. P. (In press). The super-ordinate nature of psychopathy. *Journal of Personality Disorders.*

Newman, J. P. (1998). Psychopathic behavior: An information processing perspective. In D. J. Cooke, A. E. Forth, & R. D. Hare (Eds.), *Psychopathy: Theory, research and implications for society* (pp. 81–104). Boston: Kluwer Academic Publishers.

Newman, J. P., & Kosson, D. S. (1986). Passive avoidance learning in psychopathic and nonpsychopathic offenders. *Journal of Abnormal Psychology*, *96*, 257–263.

Newman, J. P., & Lorenz, A. R. (2003). Response modulation and emotion processing: Implications for psychopathy and other dysregulatory psychopathology. In R. J. Davidson, K. Scherer, & H. H. Goldsmith (Eds.), *Handbook of Affective Sciences* (pp. 1043–1067). Oxford, UK: Oxford University Press.

Newman, J. P., MacCoon, D. G., Buckholtz, J. W., Bertsch, J. D., Hiatt, K. D., & Vaughn, L. J. (2007). Deficient integration of top-down and bottom-up influences on attention in psychopaths: Potential contribution of the septo-hippocampal system. In D. Barch (Ed.), *Cognitive and affective neuroscience of psychopathology.* New York: Oxford University Press.

Newman, J. P., MacCoon, D. G., Vaughn, L. J., & Sadeh, N. (2005). Validating a distinction between primary and secondary psychopathy with measures of Gray's BIS and BAS constructs. *Journal of Abnormal Psychology*, *114*, 319–323.

Newman, J. P., Patterson, C. M., & Kosson, D. S. (1987). Response perseveration in psychopaths. *Journal of Abnormal Psychology*, *96*, 145–148.

Newman, J. P., Patterson, C. M., Howland, E. W., & Nichols, S. L. (1990). Passive avoidance in psychopaths: The effects of reward. *Personality and Individual Differences*, *11*, 1101–1114.

Newman, J. P. & Schmitt, W. A. (1998). Passive avoidance in psychopathic offenders: A replication and extension. *Journal of Abnormal Psychology*, *107*, 527–532.

Newman, J. P., Schmitt, W. A., & Voss, W. (1997). Processing of contextual cues in psychopathic and nonpsychopathic offenders. *Journal of Abnormal Psychology*, *106*, 563–575.

Newman, J. P., & Wallace, J. F. (1993). Diverse pathways to deficient self-regulation: implications for disinhibitory psychopathology in children. *Clinical Psychology Review*, 13.

O'Brien, B. S., & Frick, P. J. (1996). Reward dominance: Associations with anxiety, conduct problems, and psychopathy in children. *Journal of Abnormal Child Psychology*, *24*, 223–240.

Ogloff, J. R. P. (2006). Psychopathy/antisocial personality disorder conundrum. *Australian and New Zealand Journal of Psychiatry*, *40*, 519–528.

Ogloff, J. R., Wong, S., & Greenwood, A. (1990). Treating criminal psychopaths in a therapeutic community program. *Behavioral Sciences and the Law*, *8*, 181–190.

Orobio de Castro, B., Veerman, J. W., Koops, W., Bosch, J. D., & Monshouwer, H. J. (2002). Hostile attributions of intent and aggressive behavior: A meta-analysis. *Child Development*, *73*, 916–934.

Patrick, C. J., Bradley, M. M., & Lang, P. J. (1993). Emotion in the criminal psychopath: Startle reflex modulation. *Journal of Abnormal Psychology*, *102*, 82–92.

Patrick, C. J., Cuthbert, B. N., & Lang, P. J. (1994). Emotion in the criminal psychopath: Fear image processing. *Journal of Abnormal Psychology*, *103*, 523–534.

Patterson, C. M., & Newman, J. P. (1993). Reflectivity and learning from aversive events: Toward a psychological mechanism for the syndromes of disinhibition. *Psychological Review*, *100*, 716–736.

Paulhus, D. L., & Williams, K. M. (2002). The dark triad of personality: Narcissism, Machiavellianism, and psychopathy. *Journal of Research in Personality*, *36*, 556–563.

Pettit, G. S., Polaha, J. A., & Mize, J. (2001). Perceptual and attributional processes in aggression and conduct problems. In J. Hill & B. Maughan (Eds.), *Conduct disorders in childhood and adolescence* (pp. 292–319). New York: Cambridge University Press.

Pinel, P. (1806). *A treatise on insanity* (D. Davis, Trans.). New York: Hafner.

Prichard, J. C. (1835). *A treatise on insanity*. London: Sherwood, Gilbert, & Piper.

Poythress, N. G., Edens, J. F., & Lilienfeld, S. O. (1998). Criterion-related validity of the Psychopathic Personality Inventory in a prison sample. *Psychological Assessment*, *10*, 426–430.

Poythress, N. G., & Skeem, J. L. (2006). Disaggregating psychopathy: Where and how to look for subtypes. In C. Patrick (Ed.), *Handbook of Psychopathy* (pp. 172–192). New York: Guilford.

Raine, A. (1997). Antisocial behavior and psychophysiology: A biosocial perspective and a prefrontal dysfunction hypothesis. In D. M. Stoff, J. Breiling, & J. D. Maser (Eds.), *The handbook of antisocial behavior* (pp. 289–304). New York: Wiley.

Raine, A., Lenca, T., Bihrle, S., LaCasse, L., & Coletti, P. (2000). Reduced prefrontal gray matter volume and reduced autonomic activity in antisocial personality disorder. *Archives of General Psychiatry*, *57*, 119–127.

Raine, A. & Yang, Y. (2006). The neuroanatomical bases of psychopathy: A review of brain imaging findings. In C. Patrick (Ed.), *Handbook of Psychopathy* (pp. 278–295). New York: Guilford.

Richards, H. J., Casey, J. O., & Lucente, S. W. (2003). Psychopathy and treatment response in incarcerated female substance abusers. *Criminal Justice and Behavior*, *30*, 251–276.

Rice, M. E., Harris, G. T., & Cormier, C. (1992). A follow-up of rapists assessed in a maximum security psychiatric facility. *Journal of Interpersonal Violence*, *5*, 435–448.

Rogers, R., Salekin, R., Sewell, K. W., & Cruise, K. R. (2000). Prototypical analysis of antisocial personality disorder: A study of inmate samples. *Criminal Justice and Behavior*, *27*, 234–255.

Roussy, S., & Toupin, J. (2000). Behavioral inhibition deficits in juvenile psychopaths. *Aggressive Behavior*, *26*, 413–424.

Rush, B. (1812). *Medical inquiries and observations upon the diseases of the mind*. Philadelphia: Kimber & Richardson.

Rutherford, M. J., Cacciola, J. S., Alterman, A. I., & McKay, J. R. (1996). Reliability and validity of the

Revised Psychopathy Checklist in women methadone patients. *Assessment, 3,* 145–156.

Salekin, R. T. (2002). Psychopathy and therapeutic pessimisms: Clinical lore or clinical reality? *Clinical Psychology Review, 22,* 79–112.

Salekin, R. T., Rogers, R., & Sewell, K. W. (1996). Review and meta-analysis of the Psychopathy Checklist and Psychopathy Checklist-Revised: Predictive validity of dangerousness. *Clinical Psychology: Science and Practice, 3,* 203–215.

Salekin, R. T., Rogers, R., & Sewell, K. W. (1997). Construct validity of psychopathy in a female offender sample: A multitrait-multimethod evaluation. *Journal of Abnormal Psychology, 106,* 576–585.

Salekin, R. T., Rogers, R., Ustad, K. L., & Sewell, K. W. (1998). Psychopathy and recidivism among female inmates. *Law and Human Behavior, 22,* 109–128.

Sandoval, A. R., Hancock, D., Poythress, N., Edens, J., & Lilienfeld, S. (2000). Construct validity of the Psychopathic Personality Inventory in a correctional sample. *Journal of Personality Assessment, 74,* 262–281.

Savin-Williams, R. C., & Berndt, T. J. (1990). Friendship and peer relations. In S. S. Feldman & G. R. Elliott (Eds.), *At the threshold: The developing adolescent* (pp. 277–307). Cambridge, MA: Harvard University Press.

Schmidt, F., McKinnon, L., Chattha, H. K., & Brownlee, K. (2006). Concurrent and predictive validity of the Psychopathy Checklist: Youth Version across gender and ethnicity. *Psychological Assessment, 18,* 393–401.

Schmitt, W. A., Brinkley, C. A., & Newman, J. P. (1999). Testing Damasio's somatic marker hypothesis with psychopathic individuals: Risk takers or risk averse? *Journal of Abnormal Psychology, 108,* 538–543.

Serin, R. C. (1991). Psychopathy and violence in criminals. *Journal of Interpersonal Violence, 6,* 423–431.

Serin, R. C., & Kuriychuk, M. (1994). Social and cognitive processing deficits in violent offenders: Implications for treatment. *International Journal of Law and Psychiatry, 17,* 431–441.

Seto, M. C., & Barbaree, H. (1999). Psychopathy, treatment behavior, and sex offender recidivism. *Journal of Interpersonal Violence, 14,* 1235–1248.

Simon, R. I. (1996). *Bad men do what good men dream.* Washington, DC: American Psychiatric Press.

Skeem, J. L., & Mulvey, E. P. (2001). Psychopathy and community violence among civil psychiatric patients: Results from the MacArthur Violence Risk Assessment Study. *Journal of Consulting and Clinical Psychology, 69,* 358–374.

Skeem, J. L., & Cauffman, E. (2003). Views of the downward extension: Comparing the youth version of the Psychopathy Checklist with the Youth Psychopathic Traits Inventory. *Behavioural Sciences and the Law, 21,* 737–770.

Steinberg, M. S., & Dodge, K. A. (1983). Attributional bias in aggressive adolescent boys and girls. *Journal of Social and Clinical Psychology, 1,* 312–321.

Sutton, S. K., Vitale, J. E., & Newman, J. P. (2002). Emotion among females with psychopathy during picture presentation. *Journal of Abnormal Psychology, 111,* 610–619.

Taylor, J., Loney, B. R., Bobadilla, L. Iacono, W. G., & McGue, M. (2003). Genetic and environmental influences on psychopathy trait dimensions in a community sample of male twins. *Journal of Abnormal Child Psychology, 31,* 633–645.

Tellegen, A. (2000). *Manual for the Multidimensional Personality Questionnaire.* Minneapolis: University of Minnesota Press.

Thornquist, M. H., & Zuckerman, M. (1995). Psychopathy, passive avoidance learning, and basic dimensions of personality. *Personality and Individual Differences, 19,* 525–534.

Vasey, M. W., Kotoc, R., & Frick, P. J. (2005). The latent structure of psychopathy in youth: A taxometric investigation. *Journal of Abnormal Child Psychology, 33,* 411–429.

Veit, R., Flor, H., Erb, M., Hermann, C., Lotze, M., Grodd, W., et al. (2002). Brain circuits involved in emotional learning in antisocial behavior and social phobia in humans. *Neuroscience Letters, 328,* 233–236.

Van Oostrum, N., & Horvath, P. (1997). Effects of hostile attributions on adolescent aggressive responses to social situations. *Canadian Journal of School Psychology, 13,* 48–59.

Verona, E., & Vitale, J. E. (2005). Psychopathy in women: Assessment, manifestations, and etiology. In C. Patrick (Ed.), *Handbook of Psychopathy* (pp. 415–436). New York: Guilford.

Vitacco, M. J., Neumann, C. S., & Jackson, R. (2005). Testing a four-factor model of psychopathy and its association with ethnicity, gender, intelligence, and violence. *Journal of Consulting and Clinical Psychology, 73,* 466–76.

Vitale, J. E., Hiatt, K. D., Brinkley, C. A., & Newman, J. P. (in press). Abnormal selective attention in psychopathic female offenders. *Neuropsychology.*

Vitale, J. E., & Newman, J. P. (2001a). Response perseveration in psychopathic women. *Journal of Abnormal Psychology, 110*, 644–647.

Vitale, J. E., & Newman, J. P. (2001b). Using the Psychopathy Checklist-Revised with female samples: Reliability, validity, and implications for clinical utility. *Clinical Psychology: Science and Practice, 8*, 117–132.

Vitale, J. E., Newman, J. P., Bates, J. E., Goodnight, J., Dodge, K. A., & Petit, G. S. (2005). Deficient behavioral inhibition and anomalous selective attention in a community sample of adolescents with psychopathic and low-anxiety traits. *Journal of Abnormal Child Psychology, 33*, 461–470.

Vitale, J. E., Serin, R., Bolt, D., & Newman, J. P. (2005). Hostile attributions in incarcerated adult male offenders: An exploration of two pathways. *Aggressive Behavior, 31*, 99–115.

Vitale, J. E., Smith, S. S., Brinkley, C. A., & Newman, J. P. (2002). The reliability and validity of the Psychopathy Checklist-Revised in a sample of female offenders. *Criminal Justice and Behavior, 29*, 202–231.

Waldman, I. D., & Gizer, I. R. (2006). The genetics of attention deficit hyperactivity disorder. *Clinical Psychology Review, 26*, 396–432.

Waldman, I. D., & Rhee, S. H. (2006). Genetic and environmental influences on psychopathy and anti-social behavior. In C. Patrick (Ed.), *Handbook of Psychopathy* (pp. 205–228). New York: Guilford.

Wallace, J. F., Schmitt, W. A., Vitale, J. E., & Newman, J. P. (2000). Experimental investigations of information processing deficiencies and psychopathy: Implications for diagnosis and treatment. In C. Gacono (Ed.), *Clinical and Forensic Assessment of Psychopathy* (pp. 87–110). Hillsdale, NJ: Lawrence Erlbaum.

Weiler, B. L., & Widom, C. S. (1996). Psychopathy and violent behavior in abused and neglected young adults. *Criminal Behavior and Mental Health, 6*, 253–271.

Widiger, T. A., & Lynam, D. (1998). Psychopathy and the five-factor model of personality. In T. Millon, E. Simonsen, M. Birket-Smith, & R. Davis (Eds.), *Psychopathy: Antisocial, criminal, and violent behavior* (pp. 171–187). New York: Guilford.

Williams, K. M., & Paulhus, D. L. (2004). Factor structure of the Self-Report Psychopathy scale (SRP-II) in non-forensic samples. *Personality and Individual Differences, 37*, 765–778.

Yang, Y., Raine, A., Lenca, T., Lacasse, L., & Colletti, P. (2005). Volume reduction in prefrontal gray matter in unsuccessful criminal psychopaths. *Biological Psychiatry, 57*, 1109–1116.

Zagon, I., & Jackson, H. (1994). Construct validity of a psychopathy measure. *Personality and Individual Differences, 17*, 125–135.

Chapter 18

Borderline Personality Disorder

JILL M. HOOLEY AND SARAH ST. GERMAIN

Borderline Personality Disorder (BPD) is a complex and challenging clinical problem. It is among the most severe forms of personality disorder that mental health professionals treat. Moreover, because BPD is typically a chronic form of psychopathology that involves a high suicide rate and a high level of suffering on the part of patients, it is a disorder that warrants a great deal of attention from clinicians and researchers.

Unfortunately, many in the mental health professions often regard the diagnosis of BPD in a pejorative way. Yet few other groups of patients are in as much need of high quality, thoughtful, and caring clinical care as those diagnosed with BPD. In this chapter, we try to illustrate some of the complexities of this disorder and some of the confusions that still surround it. We begin with a consideration of the clinical features of BPD and the symptoms that are at the heart of the *DSM* diagnosis.

The Clinical Symptoms of BPD

The suffering experienced by people with BPD is not easily captured in the list of *DSM-IV* criteria (APA, 2000) shown in Table 18.1. BPD is a disorder that is characterized by profound emotional pain. As Zanarini and Frankenburg (1999) have noted, this pain is often perceived and described as being "the worst pain anyone has felt since the history of the world began." Other hallmarks of the disorder are instability and impulsivity. There is instability in mood reflected in inappropriate, intense anger or in periods of rapidly changing negative emotions—often in response to interpersonal stress. There is also instability in self-image, with patients having difficulty maintaining a sense of who they are, what they want from their lives, or what their goals and values are. In addition

598

TABLE 18.1 *DSM-IV* Criteria for Borderline PD[1]

1. Frantic efforts to avoid real or imagined abandonment.

2. A pattern of unstable and intense interpersonal relationships characterized by alternating between extremes of idealization and devaluation.

3. Identity disturbance: Markedly and persistently unstable self-image or sense of self.

4. Impulsivity in at least two areas that are potentially self-damaging (e.g., spending, sex, substance abuse, reckless driving, binge eating). Does not include suicidal or self-mutilating behavior covered in Criterion 5.

5. Recurrent suicidal behavior, gestures, or threats, or self-mutilating behavior

6. Affective instability due to a marked reactivity of mood (e.g., intense episodic dysphoria, irritability, or anxiety usually lasting a few hours and only rarely more than a few days).

7. Chronic feelings of emptiness.

8. Inappropriate, intense anger or difficulty controlling anger (e.g., frequent displays of temper, constant anger, recurrent physical fights).

9. Transient, stress-related paranoid ideation or severe dissociative symptoms.

[1]From APA (2000)

to difficulties in these areas, people with BPD also have highly unstable interpersonal relationships. The person they idolize in the morning may be the person they despise as the day draws to a close.

Impulsivity further characterizes the BPD sufferer. This is not carefree spontaneity. Rather, it is the kind of impulsivity that is potentially self-damaging and likely to create trouble. People with BPD frequently abuse alcohol or drugs, drive recklessly, or spend money that they do not have. They may engage in risky sexual behavior, gamble, or go on eating binges. Unstable and strong emotions—together with profound feelings of emptiness—also place people with BPD at high risk of engaging in other more direct forms of self harming behavior such as cutting themselves with razor blades or burning themselves with cigarettes. Suicidal thoughts and behaviors are also not uncommon, especially in response to fears of being abandoned. Indeed, around 10% of patients with BPD will eventually take their own lives (Oldham et al., 2006). Simply put, the emotional pain that people with BPD experience is intense; managing their affective reactions presents borderline patients, as well as their families, with serious challenges. In some cases, suicidal and self-injurious behaviors are used as strategies to regulate strong negative emotions, as in the following case example.

CASE EXAMPLE

CB is a 22-year-old single Hispanic woman who engages in nonsuicidal self-injury to manage feelings of anger, anxiety, and guilt. When she is angry at her boyfriend or another significant person in her life, she feels guilty for feeling angry and this leads to feelings of deep self-hatred, which she believes she cannot tolerate and she begins to pinch her skin in order to feel physical pain that will distract her from these feelings. Sometimes the pinching leads to intense scratching until she draws blood. This provides a sense of relief from her emotions. The relief is experienced as being back in control. CB describes two low-lethality suicide attempts that she distinguishes from the nonsuicidal self-injury. On two separate occasions, both on the anniversary of the death of her father, she became extremely angry with her boyfriend for not acknowledging the difficulty of the day for her. She became hopeless, feeling her boyfriend would never be able to understand her, and that she would always be unbearably sad about losing her father and would be unable to get the help she needed to deal with it. She also felt that there was something wrong with her for feeling this way. These thoughts led to a decision to take an overdose of her medication in order to kill herself. On both occasions, as soon as she took about 10 pills (not enough to cause lethal harm), she felt a sense of relief that at least she had done something to take control of her situation and she no longer wished to die. She then fell asleep and had no other medical consequences from the overdose, and she woke up feeling much better (from Stanley & Brodsky, 2005, p. 54).

In addition to the clinical hallmarks of affective disturbances and impulsivity, people with BPD also show significant cognitive symptoms. We have already noted presence of a disorganized and unstable self-image in BPD. In addition, in *DSM-IV* a ninth symptom ("brief paranoid ideas or severe dissociative symptoms related to stress") was added to the diagnostic criteria. This change was made after research showed that approximately 75% of patients with BPD also had paranoid ideas and/or dissociative episodes (Skodol et al., 2002; Lieb et al., 2004).

It is important to understand that the cognitive symptoms of BPD differ significantly from the symptoms of patients with psychotic disorders or schizophrenia. For instance, patients with BPD may have hallucinations; however, because they have more insight than most psychotic patients, they tend to realize that these experiences are misperceptions. Moreover, when BPD patients have paranoid ideas these typically are not so firmly held that they reach delusional levels. Finally, the episodes of dissociation that are experienced by BPD patients are relatively brief and stress-related, often being experienced as a general feeling of estrangement.

History of the Borderline Diagnosis

Borderline Personality Disorder formally entered the diagnostic nomenclature in 1980 with the publication of *DSM-III*. However, the origins of the concept date back to the 1930s when the psychoanalyst Adolf Stern (1938) first described *borderline* patients. Stern's use of the term *borderline* was meant to reflect his view that the disorder did not fit well within the existing classification system, which was principally oriented around differentiating between neurosis and psychosis. Many of the characteristics of the borderline patient that Stern described—including hypersensitivity, difficulties in reality testing, and negative reactions in therapy—are recognizable to those familiar with the disorder, even today.

Knight (1953) subsequently described a group of patients with severely impaired ego functions and primary process thinking, which is a type of thinking that reflects unconscious wishes and urges. Although others (e.g., Hoch & Polantin, 1949) had referred to such patients as suffering from pseudo-neurotic schizophrenia, Knight used Stern's term borderline. However, Knight considered the disorder to be on the border, not just of neurosis but also of both neurosis and psychosis. Knight also observed that this group of patients had special needs in treatment settings and that failure to meet these needs could create tensions among staff members working with these patients in hospital settings. Subsequently, borderline came to be used to describe atypical patients who were neither neurotic, nor psychotic, but who were problematic to deal with when they were in the hospital (Gunderson, 2001).

Nonetheless, the borderline diagnosis remained relatively ignored until the late 1960s. After the psychoanalyst Otto Kernberg began to offer clinically rich and theoretically insightful perspectives on the disorder (Kernberg, 1967) interest began to increase. Around the same time, Grinker and his colleagues also published the first empirical study of the borderline syndrome (Grinker, Werble, & Drye, 1968). A third key event was the highly influential literature review of Gunderson and Singer (1975). This integrated the earlier descriptive efforts and attempted to provide diagnostic criteria for BPD. By 1980, the construct of Borderline Personality Disorder was considered to be sufficiently well developed and valid enough for it to be included in the most important revision of the diagnostic nomenclature—the *DSM-III* (Spitzer, 1979; APA, 1980). It has since become the most researched of all the personality disorders.

One other historical note warrants mention. Just before BPD was added to the *DSM-III*, American psychiatrists were polled about whether an alternative name for the disorder should be considered. More specifically, Spitzer and his colleagues (1979) had proposed that the term unstable personality disorder be used instead. However, a majority of clinicians felt inclined to retain the familiar term borderline personality, and so it was this that entered the diagnostic nomenclature.

As Paris (1999) has noted, however, this decision may have been a mistake. The term borderline is strongly linked to the psychoanalytic tradition. This may have led to the disorder being less accepted by clinicians from other perspectives. The term borderline is also inherently confusing because it is not immediately clear what border is being referred to. Indeed, Akiskal and his colleagues (Akiskal, Chen, & Davies, 1985) have described borderline as "an adjective in search of a noun." These factors may have created resistance to accepting the disorder—resistance that, until relatively recently, has been especially strong in Europe (e.g., Tyrer, 1988). Although BPD is now included in the International Classification of Diseases, 10th revision (ICD-10), the more descriptive term of Emotionally Unstable Disorder is used. Not only is this term without psychoanalytic legacy or theoretical baggage, but from a clinical perspective it also comes much closer to capturing some of the key elements of the disorder.

Epidemiology and Clinical Aspects

With an estimated prevalence in the general population of 1–2% (Lenzenweger, Lane, Loranger, & Kessler, 2007) and a prevalence in outpatient samples of 10 to 15% (Hyman, 2002), BPD is far from a rare disorder. As we noted earlier, BPD is also associated with a high level of mortality from suicide. These factors, combined with the high propensity for patients with BPD to both utilize treatment resources (Bender et al., 2001; Zanarini, Frankenburg, Khera, & Bleichmar, 2001) and terminate treatment prematurely (Percudani, Belloni, Conti, & Barbui, 2002), makes BPD a significant problem—both for those who suffer from it and for society in general.

It has long been accepted that BPD is more commonly found in women than in men, with women accounting for approximately 75% of cases (APA, 2000). However, this may be an artifact caused by sampling in clinical settings (Skodol & Bender, 2003). If women are more likely to seek treatment, prevalence estimates from clinical settings will naturally be biased in the direction of finding more females than males with the disorder.

Consistent with this idea, two representative, population-based studies, one conducted in Norway (Torgersen, Kringlen, & Kramer, 2001) and one conducted in the United States, (Lenzenweger et al., 2007) have reported no gender differences in the prevalence of BPD. Further findings from community samples in Great Britain have even indicated that, in the United Kingdom, BPD is more prevalent in men (Coid, Yang, Tyrer, Roberts, & Ullrich, 2006). In light of these data, we believe that there is now no evidence to support the once commonly-held assumption that there is a 3:1 female to male gender ratio in BPD.

HETEROGENEITY AND COMORBIDITY

BPD is a clinically heterogeneous disorder. The *DSM* lists nine different symptoms, with five symptoms being necessary for the diagnosis. Because no one specific symptom is required, there are 256 different ways that these symptoms can be combined to yield the same diagnostic outcome. This means that the BPD phenotype varies widely across those diagnosed with the disorder. The heterogeneity in BPD has prompted research into the core aspects of the disorder and led to debate about its most important features.

Linehan (1993) considers affective instability to be at the core of BPD. According to this view, it is the rapid mood changes, extreme reactivity to the environment, and dysthymic baseline mood that best characterize the disorder (Linehan, 1993). Bateman and Fonagy (2003) have suggested that emotional instability is a secondary phenomenon that results from instability in the self-structure. Gunderson (1996) takes a more interpersonal perspective and highlights the importance of fear and intolerance of aloneness as being central to the disorder. According to this perspective, the extreme fear of abandonment and the accompanying frantic efforts to avoid it are at the core of BDP. Still others, working from a more neurobiologic framework, have asserted that disinhibition and general negative affectivity underlie borderline pathology (Siever & Davis, 1991; Trull, 2001). Finally, Zanarini, Frankenburg, Hennen, and Silk (2003) have noted that, even when other symptoms of the disorder remit, high levels of negative affectivity tend to remain in people with BPD. This suggests that a core aspect of the personality structure of those inclined to BPD may be an enduring dysphoria (Westen, Bradley, & Shedler, 2005). In short, although BPD is the most common personality disorder found in clinical settings worldwide (Loranger et al., 1994; Torgersen, Kringlen, & Cramer, 2001; Widiger & Frances, 1989) it is far from being clearly conceptualized.

Another important problem concerns comorbidity. Patients with BPD are much more likely to be diagnosed with other disorders than are psychiatric patients who do not have BPD (Gunderson, 2001; Zanarini et al., 1998). In a representative study, Zimmerman and Mattia (1999a) conducted clinical interviews with 409 psychiatric outpatients and compared the Axis I diagnosis of the 59 patients who had BPD to the Axis I diagnosis of the 305 patients who did not have BPD. A diagnosis of BPD was associated with high rates of concurrent Major Depression (61%), Dysthymia (12%), Bipolar Disorder (20%), Eating Disorders (17%), PTSD (36%), and substance abuse problems (14%). Indeed, the large overlap between BPD and mood disorders has led some to speculate that BPD is more appropriately regarded as a variant of depression (Akiskal, Chen, & Davis, 1985; Akiskal, 2002). However, this view is not widely endorsed (Gunderson & Phillips, 1991; Paris, 2004).

Current Theoretical Perspectives

It is important to state from the outset that the etiology of Borderline Personality Disorder is still unknown. However, most prominent theorists, regardless of their orientation, highlight the role of both biological vulnerabilities and environmental factors.

PSYCHODYNAMIC APPROACHES

Working within the psychodynamic tradition, Kernberg (1975) presented one of the earliest theories of the pathogenesis of BPD. Within this perspective, a high level of constitutional aggression in the child is regarded as being a predisposing factor. This temperamental factor interferes with normal developmental processes such as the integration of different (positive and negative) perspectives of the self and others. Accordingly, memories of experiences with significant others are stored separately from each other as either good or bad (that is, by affective valence) rather than being integrated (good and bad). In the face of environmental frustrations or failures in caretaking, good representations are threatened by strong negative feelings such as rage or hostile impulses. Borderline personality organization (Kernberg's conceptualization encompasses more than just the pathology that is represented in the *DSM* diagnosis of BPD) is characterized by an unstable sense of self, together with the use of primitive (immature) defense mechanisms designed to protect these split representations of the self and others. At times, temporary problems in reality testing are apparent as the person experiences difficulty in determining what is real and what is imagined.

Another theorist whose ideas have been influential is Heinz Kohut (1971, 1977). As represented by Kohut, the tradition of self-psychology psychoanalytic theory emphasizes the importance of the caretaker's attunement to the needs of the child. This is not to say that caretakers have to be perfect. Rather, what is needed is what Winnicot (1953) referred to as "good enough mothering." Key components here are empathic responses that mirror the child's strengths and efforts to explore the world and that validate the child's sense of mastery. When caretakers are able to meet the child's needs in this way, the child is able to develop a stable sense of self and an ability to regulate self esteem by drawing on an internal representation of the caretaker as a source of emotional comfort and soothing. In an unresponsive family environment, however, the child's angry emotions disrupt the development of a positive sense of self. In an application of this to BPD, Adler and Buie (Adler & Buie, 1979; Buie & Adler, 1982) have theorized that borderline patients lack the ability to call upon memories of good objects (internal representations or images of nurturing and empathic caretakers) to provide self-soothing in times of distress. The absence of these images for the borderline patient thus becomes an important factor in their inability to regulate their own emotions.

BEHAVIORAL APPROACHES

The most influential example of the cognitive behavioral approach to understanding BPD is provided by the work of Marsha Linehan. According to Linehan's biosocial theory, BPD results when biological or temperamental vulnerabilities interact with failures in the child's social environment to either create or further exacerbate preexisting problems with emotions and emotion regulation (Linehan, 1993). More specifically, problems such as a high level of sensitivity to negative emotions, high emotional reactivity, and a slow return to baseline after becoming emotionally aroused are thought to be precursors of the chronic problems with emotional regulation that are so characteristic of BPD. If the emotionally vulnerable person is able to manage these vulnerabilities successfully, all may be well. However, if the family environment does not provide the emotionally vulnerable child with the skills necessary to contain strong emotions, more severe emotional dysregulation (and a diagnosis of BPD) may be the result.

Within Linehan's model, the key environmental factor is an invalidating family environment. This is a concept that, although deeply rooted in the behavioral tradition, may have some overlap with the parental failures identified by Kohut and described in the psychoanalytic literature. What this means is that the child's communications of his or her actual internal experiences are met by responses on the part of the parents that are inappropriate, erratic, or otherwise out of touch with what is truly happening to the child (Fruzetti, Shenk, & Hoffman, 2005). For example, if the child sees something desirable to eat and says "I'm hungry," an invalidating response from the parent might be to say, "No you aren't. You don't want to eat that." In other words, the child's experience of seeing the treat and wanting to eat it is dismissed and denied. In contrast, a validating response might involve the parent saying, "Yes, I know you want to eat that. But we will be having dinner very soon so I don't want you to spoil your appetite by eating that now." Notice that in neither instance does the child receive the treat—validation is not the same thing as gratification. However, in the second (validated) example, the child's internal experience of feeling hungry and wanting the treat is not ignored or rendered illegitimate.

There are many problems that are thought to stem from pervasive invalidation. These range from heightened emotional arousal immediately after being invalidated, to a failure to learn how to accurately label one's own emotions. These difficulties, in turn, may create problems managing emotions and also lead towards a tendency to self-invalidate (not trust one's own emotional responses). As we shall later see, some of the most important psychological treatments for BPD are designed to help patients learn some of the key skills that they failed to develop with regard to the appraisal and management of the emotional events that they experience.

Factors Involved in the Pathogenesis and Maintenance of BPD

BPD is perhaps best regarded as reflecting the final end product of the continued interplay between biological vulnerabilities and environmental factors. This is important to keep in mind because new developments in research are making it increasingly clear that biological processes and psychosocial events can be separated only in the abstract. For example, it is fast becoming apparent that different genotypes are associated with differential sensitivities to environmental stressors such as life events, child abuse, or maternal neglect (Caspi et al., 2002; Gabbard, 2005). Other studies also support the conclusion that both nature and nurture play critical roles in such behaviors as impulsive aggression (Higley, Suomi, & Linnoila, 1991; Bennet et al., 2002) and responsiveness to stress (Fish et al., 2004; Francis & Meaney, 1999). In the sections below, we encourage readers to keep in mind that genes create differential sensitivities to environmental factors, that experiences turn some genes on while shutting other genes off, and that psychosocial events can lead to changes in the neurobiology and neurochemistry of the brain (Kandel, 1998; Gabbard, 2005).

GENETICS

There is some evidence to suggest that Borderline Personality Disorder runs in families. Studies of the biological relatives of patients with BPD suggest that they have an increased prevalence of the disorder that is somewhere between 4 and 20 times that found in the general population (White, Gunderson, Zanarini, & Hudson, 2003). It should be kept in mind, however, that it not uncommon in family studies of BPD to use the patients themselves as the sole source of information. In other words, the relatives might not be assessed directly. Studies that employ indirect assessment methods run the risk that people with BPD might exaggerate the extent to which their relatives show elements of the disorder themselves.

In support of this notion, Links, Steiner, and Huxley (1988) reported a prevalence rate for BPD of 3.4% when the relatives were assessed in person. This stands in sharp contrast to the prevalence rate of 15.1% that was obtained when patients' reports of their relatives were used. Until a large-scale study using direct assessments of the relatives themselves is conducted, the familiarity of BPD cannot be considered fully established.

We must also remember that just because a disorder runs in families, this does not necessarily mean that is genetic. Many problems in children could arise as a consequence of being raised by a psychiatrically disturbed parent or from living in the chaotic family environment that might result from having a mentally ill sibling. To fully disentangle genetic from rearing effects, adoption studies are necessary. To date, no such studies have been conducted on adopted offspring of women with BPD. However, using a twin sample Torgersen et al. (2000) have reported a concordance rate for BPD of 35% in monozygotic (MZ) twins compared with a concordance rate of 7% for dizygotic (DZ) twins. This suggests that BPD has a heritable component.

But exactly what might be being inherited? It is noteworthy that the family pedigrees of people with BPD also show increased prevalence rates of Antisocial Personality Disorder as well as increased rates of major depression (White et al., 2003). It is also the case that the elements of BPD are more commonly found in the relatives of those with the disorder than is the diagnosis itself (Zanarini et al., 2004). This suggests that what may be being inherited are traits that are linked to the neurobehavioral dimensions that might underlie a diagnosis of BPD (Depue & Lenzenweger, 2005). Heritability has been demonstrated for such traits such as neuroticism, cognitive dysregulation, anxiety, and affective lability (Livesley, Jang, Jackson, & Vernon, 1993; Jang, Livesley, Vernon, & Jackson, 1996). Impulsivity also appears to have a genetic component (Goodman, New, & Siever, 2004). Rather than inheriting a *DSM* disorder, it is much more likely that individuals inherit genetic propensities to exhibit traits that might underlie the behavioral manifestations of BPD.

For example, evidence is beginning to accumulate linking the serotonin transporter gene (5-HTT) with suicide and impulsivity, as well as with emotional lability (Bondy, Erfurth, deJonge, Kruger, & Meyer, 2000; Frankle et al., 2005; Hoefgen et al., 2005). Because these are characteristics of BPD, the serotonin transporter gene is now being investigated as a possible candidate gene for this disorder. Preliminary findings indicate an association between certain aspects of the 5-HTT gene and BPD (Ni et al., 2006).

Another candidate gene currently attracting the attention of researchers is an allele of the dopamine transporter gene (DAT1). Dopamine is involved in the reward pathways of the brain. Cloninger (2000) has suggested that the trait of high novelty seeking, which is associated with BPD, may be related to altered dopaminergic function in the brain. The link between dopamine and BPD is supported by the high levels of comorbidity between substance abuse disorders and BPD (Ebstein, Benjamin, & Belmaker, 2000). Using a sample of depressed patients, Joyce et al. (2006) have now replicated their earlier finding that the 9-repeat allele of the DAT1 gene is more likely to be found in depressed patients with BPD than in depressed patients who do not have BPD. The findings of Joyce et al. (2006) suggest that this polymorphism may be a risk factor for BPD and further support the possible role of abnormalities in the dopamine system of the disorder. It is also intriguing to note that dopamine is an important neurotransmitter in psychotic disorders and that, when under stress, people with BPD sometimes experience transient psychotic episodes (APA, 2000).

NEUROBIOLOGY

The high level of comorbidity between BPD and other Axis I and II disorders makes it difficult to evaluate the extent to which BPD has specific neurobiological correlates. It is also rather unlikely that the disorder itself has a distinct and specific neurobiologic signature. More likely is that it is the various dimensions of BPD (e.g., impulsivity or anger and aggressiveness) that are important and associated with underlying neurochemical or neuroanatomical differences.

NEUROCHEMISTRY

Neurotransmitters

There are several reasons to believe that disturbances in the neurotransmitter serotonin might be implicated in BPD. Both animal and human studies have linked low levels of 5-hydroxyindolacetic acid (5-HIAA), which is a major metabolite of serotonin, to higher levels of impulsive aggression (Coccaro, Siever, Klar, & Maurer, 1989; Goodman et al., 2004). A large body of literature has also linked low 5-HIAA in the cerebrospinal fluid (CSF) to suicide, especially violent forms of suicide (Asberg, 1997). Moreover, rhesus monkeys with low levels of CSF 5-HIAA are also more inclined to consume alcohol when it is made available in experimental settings (Suomi, 2003). Because all of these behaviors are associated with BPD, it seems reasonable to expect that patients with the disorder might have disturbances in serotonergic function.

To test this hypothesis, Rinne, Westenberg, den Boer, and van den Brink (2000) administered a neuroendocrine challenge test to 12 women with BPD and 9 healthy control subjects. The neuroendocrine challenge involved the oral ingestion of meta-Chlorophenylpiperazine (m-CPP), a serotonin agonist that acts on serotonin receptors to trigger the release of prolactin and cortisol. After receiving the m-CPP challenge, patients with BPD showed significantly lower levels of prolactin and cortisol in their blood than did the healthy controls. In particular, a history of physical and sexual abuse was highly negatively correlated with the overall prolactin response. The results suggest that traumatic stress in childhood—which is reported by 20 to 75% of patients (Herman, Perry, & van der Kolk, 1989; Ogata et al., 1990; Salzmann et al., 1993)—may in some way alter aspects of the serotonin system, perhaps at the level of the serotonin receptors.

Noradrenergic function may also be disturbed in BPD, possibly due to the link between norepinephrine function and aggression. Coccaro, Lee, and McClosky (2003) measured plasma levels of the major metabolite of norepinephrine (3-methoxy

-4-hydroxyphenylglycol or MHPG) in 30 males with personality disorders. Levels of MHPG were lower in the men who had BPD than those who had other disorders. However, the strongest association was between MHPG levels and the life history of aggression that was reported by the subjects, with higher levels of aggressive behavior being correlated with lower levels of MHPG. These findings suggest that norepinephrine may play an important role in modulating aggressive behaviors.

Simeon, Knutelska, Smith, Baker, & Hollander (2007) have also reported a positive correlation between levels of urinary norepinephrine and severity of dissociation in a small sample of subjects ($n = 11$) with BPD. However, no differences were found between the BPD subjects and the controls, with respect to baseline levels of urinary norepinephrine. To the extent that aggression and dissociation form part of the clinical picture of BPD, norepinephrine (therefore) remains a neurotransmitter of interest to BPD researchers. However, trying to understand the role of norepinephrine in BPD is complicated by the high level of comorbidity between BPD and depression, and the link between noradrenergic dysregulation and mood disorders (Thase, Jindal, & Howland, 2002).

Finally, we wish to draw attention to the possibility of dopamine dysfunction in BPD. As we have already mentioned, an allele of the dopamine transporter gene is currently being explored as a possible candidate gene for BPD. Friedel (2004) has also noted that antipsychotic medications, which act primarily through the blockade of dopamine receptors, often provide clinical benefits for BPD patients. Human and animal studies have further illustrated the importance of dopamine in emotion, impulsivity, and cognition (Friedel, 2004)—all of which are domains that are highly relevant to borderline pathology. Although dopamine dysfunction in BPD has not received a great deal of attention from researchers to date, we anticipate that it will become more of a focus of empirical interest in the years to come.

Hypothalamic-pituitary-adrenal (HPA) Axis

Other biological disturbances in BPD involve the hypothalamic-pituitary-adrenal (HPA) axis. The HPA axis, which is involved in stress regulation, has been widely studied in depression through the use of the dexamethasone suppression test (DST). This test involves administering an oral dose of dexamethasone, a synthetic glucocorticoid that acts via a feedback mechanism to suppress cortisol production. The normal response to the DST is a reduction in cortisol.

In a naturalistic study, Lieb and colleagues (2004) collected a total of 32 saliva samples from 23 women with BPD who were not taking any medications and 24 matched healthy controls. Using the saliva samples, they then measured cortisol levels in the two groups of women. Although far from conclusive, the data were suggestive of heightened adrenal activity in the BPD patients. When assessments from the first two days of the study were combined, total cortisol levels obtained in the first hour after awakening from sleep were significantly higher in the women with BPD than they were in the control women. Moreover, after receiving a dose of dexamethasone, women with BPD still had a higher total daily level of cortisol compared to the healthy control women.

One problem with the Lieb et al. (2004) study, as well as with many other studies of HPA axis function in patients with BPD, is that the investigators did not assess comorbid PTSD. This is important, because 20 to 40% of patients with BPD also suffer from PTSD (see Gunderson & Sabo, 1993) and because PTSD is often associated with abnormalities in HPA axis function (Rinne, van den Brink, Wouters, & van Dyck, 2002). In a related vein, controlling for the possible effects of concurrent major depression is also necessary—again because Major Depressive Disorder is highly comorbid with BPD (Corruble, Ginestet, & Guelfi, 1996) and because abnormal responses to a challenge with dexamethasone are often found in patients who are depressed. These problems make it difficult to interpret the existing data.

A large-scale study of HPA axis function in BPD using a carefully diagnosed sample with full attention given to issues of comorbidity as well as exposure to trauma is much needed. In fact, trauma may even be more important with regard to hyperesponsiveness of the HPA axis than either BPD, Major Depressive Disorder (MDD), or even PTSD. When Rinne, de Kloet, et al. (2002) gave a combined dexamethasone/CRH challenge to a sample of 39 patients with BPD, those who had experienced childhood abuse (n = 24) showed higher levels of cortisol and ACTH after the challenge than did those (n = 15) who experienced little or no abuse in their childhoods. Importantly, these elevated responses were independent of BPD pathology and unrelated to the presence of comorbid diagnosis of PTSD or major depression (although patients with comorbid PTSD tended to have an attenuated ACTH response to the challenge regardless of whether or not they had a history of childhood abuse). Overall, Rinne, de Kloet, et al.'s (2002) data support the idea that sustained abuse early in life may lead to a hyperresponsiveness of ACTH release. This is consistent with other research in women with histories of early childhood trauma (Heim et al., 2000). To the extent that many people with BPD report early traumatic life experiences, we might therefore expect to find evidence of hyperreactivity of the HPA axis in unselected samples of BPD patients.

Neuroimaging Studies of BPD

Although neuroimaging studies of BPD are still in their infancy, there is reason to believe that patients with this disorder may have some abnormalities in limbic and prefrontal brain areas when compared to nonpatient controls (Putnam & Silk, 2005). Such findings are of interest because prefrontal and limbic circuits are thought to be involved in emotion and emotion regulation (LeDoux, 1996; Davidson, 2002).

STRUCTURAL APPROACHES

Structural imaging studies have shown a 13–21% reduction in the volume of the hippocampus and an 8–25% reduction in the volume of the amygdala in patients with BPD compared to controls (Driessen et al., 2000; Schmahl, Elzinga, et al., 2003; Tebartz van Elst, et al., 2003). However, the finding of reduced amygdala volume in BPD should be treated with caution in light of some recent failures to replicate (New et al., 2007). In addition, some regions of prefrontal cortex (PFC) also have been found to be reduced in volume. Tebarts, van Elst, et al. (2003) reported a 24% reduction in left orbitofrontal cortex (OFC) and a 26% reduction in right anterior cingulate cortex (ACC) in eight unmedicated female patients with BPD when compared to eight matched healthy controls. Hazlett et al. (2005) also reported a reduced volume of grey matter in anterior cingulate in patients with BPD compared to controls. This study is noteworthy because of its unusually large sample size of 50 BPD patients and 50 healthy controls.

It is important to mention that decreased hippocampal volume is not a structural brain abnormality that is specific to BPD. Volume loss in the hippocampus has also been reported in other disorders, including unipolar and bipolar depression, schizophrenia, and PTSD (Putnam & Silk, 2005). Researchers have also observed a decrease in the volume of the orbitofrontal cortex in people with depression (Bremner, 2002) and Obsessive-Compulsive Disorder (Szezko et al., 1999). Although it is possible that reliable abnormalities in specific brain areas might eventually be linked to BPD, the data is currently more suggestive than conclusive. Most likely is that the overall pattern of findings will prove to be more important than any particular abnormality in a given brain region.

Functional Imaging

Positron emission tomography (PET) approaches can be used to examine differences in resting brain activation in people with BPD compared to healthy controls or people with other forms of psychopathology. Several research groups have now reported that BPD is associated with lower metabolic activity in the OFC relative to comparison subjects (Putnam & Silk, 2005). This is interesting because the OFC is a brain area that is thought to play a role in the regulation of emotion and responses to stress. It is also involved in impulse control (Berlin, Rolls, & Iversen, 2005) and may facilitate the inhibition of responses to external stimuli (Davidson, Putnam, & Larson, 2000).

Particularly interesting is the finding that when people with BPD are treated with fluoxetine—a selective serotonin reuptake inhibitor (SSRI) that is helpful in the treatment of depression and BPD—there is a significant increase in OFC metabolism at 12 weeks post-treatment (New et al., 2004). Treatment with fluoxetine (Prozac) also led BPD patients to report reduced levels of aggressive feelings and irritability. We have already noted the role of serotonin with respect to impulsivity, aggression, and suicidality (Oquendo & Mann, 2000). Taken together, these findings suggest that reduced serotonergic activity in brain areas such as the OFC may help us understand why high levels of impulsiveness and aggression may be commonly found in those who suffer from BPD.

Finally, we note that investigations that have used imaging methods to study the brain at work (i.e., PET and functional magnetic resonance imaging [fMRI] studies), have also implicated some of the same brain regions that have been identified in structural and resting brain investigations. For example, when people with BPD are exposed to aversive and neutral pictures they show increased activation in the amygdala compared to healthy controls (Herpertz et al., 2001). They also show increased amygdala activation relative to controls when they view pictures of fearful, sad, or neutral faces (Donegan et al., 2003). Other studies suggest differences in activation in such areas as the dorsolateral prefrontal cortex (DLPFC) and anterior cingulate cortex (ACC) in patients with BPD relative to controls when exposed to personalized abandonment scripts (Schmahl, Elzinga, et al. 2003) or during personal memories of abandonment (Schmahl, Vermetten, Elzinga, & Bremner, 2003). Overall, although results of individual studies are often inconsistent (possibly reflecting sample differences or differences in the task employed), they tend to support the idea that abnormalities in frontolimbic circuitry may underlie many of the key clinical features of BPD (Brendel, Stern, & Silbersweig, 2005; Schmahl & Bremner, 2006). More specifically, a major problem in BPD may be that there is a disconnection between activity in prefrontal cortex and activity in amygdala. Although metabolic activity in these areas appears to be tightly coupled in healthy controls, the same degree of metabolic linkage is not found in people with BPD (New et al., 2007). This lack of functional connectivity may be one reason why emotion regulation is such a problem for those who suffer from this disorder.

Psychosocial Aspects

CHILDHOOD MALTREATMENT

High levels of trauma and adversity often characterize the early lives of people with BPD. Several studies have now demonstrated that, compared to patients with other Axis I and Axis II disorders, patients with BPD are significantly more likely to report experiencing physical abuse, sexual abuse, or neglect during childhood (Weaver & Clum, 1993; Zanarini et al., 2000; Ogata et al., 1990). Indeed, in a sample of 69 outpatients with BPD, only 4 (6.1%) reported that they had not experienced traumatic events in their childhoods, although this was true for the majority (61.5%) of the 109 psychiatrically healthy controls (Bandelow et al., 2005). Compared to the healthy controls, the early lives of the BPD sufferers involved significantly more maternal and paternal absences (i.e., mother in the hospital; father in jail), more discord between the parents, more experiences of being raised by other relatives or in a foster home, more physical violence in the family, and more sexual abuse during childhood.

One problem with almost all of the studies on the early life experiences of BPD patients, however, is that they rely on retrospective reporting. This renders them vulnerable to the criticism that such data may be unreliable due to problems with recall or reporting biases. However, in an important longitudinal study Johnson, Cohen, Brown, Smailes, and Bernstein (1999) used records from the State of New York to collect data on documented cases of abuse or neglect in the lives of children in a representative sample of 639 families. Consistent with the findings of other studies, childhood maltreatment was significantly associated with increased levels of BPD symptoms later in life. More specifically, those who experienced early abuse or neglect were 7.73 times more likely to be diagnosed with BPD at a follow up assessment than those who did not experience such maltreatment. With its longitudinal design and its focus on verified cases of abuse, the Johnson et al. study provides strong support for the link between traumatic or abusive experiences in early life and the subsequent development of BPD.

ATTACHMENT

Relationships are extremely problematic for people with BPD. Not only do they have problems in their relationships with others but they also have problems in their relationships with themselves. BPD is characterized by high levels of interpersonal impairment and extreme concern about abandonment. Also prominent are chronic feelings of emptiness, a lack of a sense of identity, self-harming behaviors, and an inability to self-soothe appropriately during times of distress.

Recent years have witnessed a growing interest in the concept of attachment with regard to BPD, no doubt because attachment theory provides a useful approach for conceptualizing this disorder (Levy, 2005). Bowlby (1973) proposed that through the relationships and transactions that they have with their caregivers, infants develop mental representations of themselves and others and develop "internal working models" about interpersonal relationships. These are, essentially, sets of expectations about relationships that function to both organize personality development and shape the nature of relationships that are developed in the future (Levy, 2005). If an attentive and nurturing caretaker reliably meets an infant's needs he or she will come to regard others as reliable, responsive, and trustworthy. If an abusive, neglectful, or emotionally disengaged caretaker raises an infant, however, the working model of relationships that he or she develops is likely to be very different, and may involve expectations of lack of care, unreliability, and unresponsiveness.

In young children, secure attachment is characterized by using the mother as a secure base from which to explore the world and return to in times of stress. Attachment style is thought to have some continuity from childhood to adulthood, with securely attached children being more likely to create and maintain securely attached relationships in later life. According to Bowlby (1977, p. 206), childhood attachment influences the "later capacity to make affectional bonds as well as a whole range of adult dysfunctions." These dysfunctions would include marital problems, difficulties with parenting, as well as personality disorders.

Given our prior discussion of the link between early life adversity and BPD, it should come as no surprise that people with this disorder show low rates of secure attachment when this is measured in adulthood. The vast majority of people with BPD are assessed (using interview-based or self-report methods) as insecurely attached, with only a minority (approximately 6–8%) being rated as having secure attachment patterns (Levy, 2005). Although there is no specific style of insecure attachment that appears particularly linked to BPD in empirical studies, problems with attachment may underlie many of the fundamental aspects of BPD. It should be noted that real or misperceived interpersonal events often serve as triggers for the emotional outbursts, impulsivity, and self-damaging behaviors that are so central to the BPD syndrome (Gurvits, Koenigsberg, & Siever, 2000; Yeomans & Levy, 2002). Bateman and Fonagy (2003) consider an inability to mentalize (that is, to understand and interpret one's own mental states as well as those of others) to be fundamental to BPD and to be linked to failures in early attachment relationships. Finally, even when they are in therapy, patients with BPD find it much harder than other patients to sustain a mental representation of the therapist as helpful and the treatment relationship as caring and supportive (Bender et al., 2003). Simply stated, problems in early attachment relationship may set the stage for a broad range of relationship problems in later life.

Cognitive Aspects of Borderline Personality Disorder

Trying to summarize the results of different studies of neurocognitive function in patients with Borderline Personality Disorder is far from easy. Because of the polythetic nature of *DSM-IV*, patients with the same diagnosis can show quite different clinical presentations. Issues of comorbidity further complicate the interpretation of the findings. As we have noted earlier, many patients with BPD have a concurrent diagnosis of Major Depressive Disorder (Zimmerman & Mattia, 1999a). The extent to which the empirical findings are linked to BPD or simply reflect cognitive processing deficits associated with depression is therefore a source of concern. A third difficulty is that, in the typical research study, the majority of participants are taking medications. Although researchers usually try to control for this by noting the presence or absence of medications in a particular participant, it is rare that more detailed information about the class of medication, number of different medications, dosages, and duration of medication usage are provided (Fertuck, Lenzenweger, Clarkin, Hoermann, & Stanley, 2006). Finally, the majority of research studies have involved only females, or else included very few males in their samples. We therefore know very little about cognition in men with BPD.

There are many reasons to suspect that basic executive cognition and memory processes might be disrupted in BPD. The disorder itself involves unstable and dysregulated inhibitory control. This is readily apparent in the behavior, emotions, and cognitions of the BPD patient. Also, as we have already discussed, the results of neuroimaging studies have implicated abnormalities in fronto-limbic neurocircuitry in patients with the disorder. A thorough review of executive neurocognitive functioning, memory, and BPD can be found in Fertuck et al. (2006). In the sections below we highlight some of the most important findings.

EXECUTIVE NEUROCOGNITION

Executive neurocognition involves being able to delay or terminate a given response (cognitive or motor) for the purpose of achieving another goal or reward that is less immediate. There are several types of execution neurocognition. For example, when we make a conscious and deliberate effort to control our attention or motor behavior we are engaging what is referred to *interference control* (Nigg, 2000). This method of control uses a neural system that relies on the connection between cortical (dorsolateral and orbitofrontal cortex) and subcortical (anterior cingulate) structures (Fertuck et al., 2006). The Stroop Task (Stroop, 1935) is an example of a test that taps this aspect of neuroexecutive function. It requires a person to name the color of the ink used to print a color word (e.g., saying the word red when the word blue is printed in red ink), and to suppress the tendency to simply read the word as printed.

Another form of executive neurocognition is *cognitive inhibition*. This is the ability to suppress information from working memory. An example of a task that requires effortful suppression is the directed forgetting task. In this task, subjects are presented with a list of words. After each word is presented, subjects see either an F (for forget) or an R (for remember). Subjects are instructed to remember words followed by an R and forget words followed by an F. However, at the end of the task, subjects are asked to recall all the words that were presented to them. Problems in cognitive inhibition can also be measured using implicit (unconscious) approaches using negative priming tasks.

A third type of executive neurocognition requires the person to inhibit an expected motor behavior or cognitive response in order to follow a different direction. This is termed *behavioral inhibition*. For example, in the Go-No-Go Task (Casey et al., 1997) the subject is required to press a button when a particular (and frequent) stimulus such as an X appears. This is the go response. However, when another, less frequent stimulus is shown (e.g., the letter Y), the subject must refrain from pressing the button.

The final form of executive neurocognition is *motivational or affective inhibition*. This requires the purposeful interruption of a tendency or a behavior that results from a particular motivational-emotional state. For example, some forms of the Stroop task involve the use of emotional words (e.g., angry). In the Emotional Stroop Test, subjects typically take longer to name the ink color of emotional words than they do to name to color of ink used to print nonemotional words such as table. The Emotional Stroop Test is therefore thought to provide a measure of how well the subject can engage in affective inhibition. An example of a task that requires motivational inhibition is the passive avoidance task (Newman & Kosson, 1986). Here, subjects have to learn by trial and error whether responding to stimuli will lead to gaining or losing money. If the subject responds to a losing stimulus, this is considered to reflect a passive avoidance error (i.e., doing something that leads to a negative outcome). Failures to respond to a winning stimulus are considered to be errors of omission, where the subject misses out on a good outcome.

Inhibitory deficits are involved in inattention, impulsivity, and problems with affect regulation. The clinical presentation of BPD, therefore, makes it reasonable to expect that people with this disorder would show impairments on neurocognitive tasks requiring inhibition. In keeping with this, research is beginning to show that patients with BPD do indeed show impairments on tasks that challenge inhibitory processes.

Posner et al. (2002) compared 39 BPD patients without Comorbid Mood Disorder to 30 healthy controls on the Attention Network Task (ANT) (Fan, McCandliss, Sommer, Raz, & Posner, 2002). This cognitive task, which measures interference control, taps three different aspects of attention. The first (alerting) is the ability to sustain an alert cognitive state, the second (orienting) is the ability to focus attention and select stimuli, and the third (conflict) is the capacity to decide among competing responses based on a predetermined organizing principle. Although the subjects with BPD performed similarly to the controls on the alerting and orienting components of the task, they showed impairments— relative to the controls—on the conflict task.

Impairments have also been found on tasks that require cognitive inhibition. Korfine and Hooley (2000) administered a directed forgetting task to healthy controls and people diagnosed with BPD. Some of the BPD participants were hospital outpatients; others were drawn from a community sample. Participants were then exposed to borderline words (e.g., abandon, enraged, alone, suicidal) as well as positive and neutral words. Even when they were specifically instructed to forget them, the BPD participants remembered more of the borderline words than the controls did, suggesting that they were unable to inhibit material that was emotionally salient to them. In a subsequent replication of this general finding, Domes et al. (2006) reported that, compared to healthy controls, unmedicated patients with BPD showed poorer inhibition of negative material on the directed forgetting task. This was true even though the negative words that they were exposed to were not borderline specific. These findings suggest one problem people with BPD have is that it is hard for them to suppress aversive material—even when they wish to do so.

BPD patients are also impaired on measures of behavioral inhibition. As noted earlier, behavioral inhibition involves inhibiting a cognitive expectancy or motor behavior in order to follow a different directive or goal. Lenzenweger, Clarkin, Fertuck, and Kernberg (2004) have reported that BPD patients (without concurrent mood disorders) exhibit deficits in cognitive planning and set-shifting on the Wisconsin Card Sort Task (WCST) (Heaton, 1981). Problems in motivational inhibition (poorer performance on a decision making task) have also been found in BPD subjects when compared to healthy controls (Bazanis et al., 2002). People with BPD also show deficits on the Go-No-Go Task, showing that they have difficulty learning when to respond (or not respond) to a stimulus (Leyton et al., 2001). Impairments on the passive avoidance task (described above) have also been reported (Hochhausen, Lorenz, & Newman, 2002).

Finally, some (but not all) researchers have reported differences between healthy controls and participants with BPD on the Emotional Stroop Test (Arntz, Appels, & Sieswerda, 2000; Domes et al., 2006). These findings suggest that people with BPD may sometimes be less able than controls to inhibit interference from emotional words. Taken together, the pattern of results across domains is highly consistent with the idea that BPD is associated with deficits in executive cognition. More specifically, people with BPD often perform relatively poorly when they are engaged in tasks that make demands on inhibitory processes (Fertuck et al., 2006). The more symptomatic patients are (e.g., more severe symptoms, more *DSM* criteria met) the less well they tend to do on these tasks (Fertuck, Lenzenweger, & Clarkin, 2005).

MEMORY SYSTEMS

People with BPD appear to have some difficulties on conventional tests of memory. A recent meta-analysis of six studies has shown that BPD patients perform worse than controls on measures of both verbal and nonverbal memory (Ruocco, 2005).

The topic of autobiographical memory has been a focus of interest. The Autobiographical Memory Test (AMT) (Williams & Broadbent, 1986) requires subjects to generate precise and specific memories to prompted words (e.g., birthday). A memory is considered to be specific if it references an occasion or an event and involves a time or a place (e.g., "for my birthday last year my friend and I went to dinner at Mario's"). Overgeneralized memories, which are characteristic of depressed patients, are hypothesized to occur as a way of avoiding the emotional turmoil that could result from more specific recall of negatively valanced emotional memories (Renneberg, Theobald, Nobs, & Weisbrod, 2005)

Jones et al. (1999) initially reported that patients with BPD recalled more overgeneral (i.e., fewer specific) memories compared to controls. However, other investigators have failed to replicate this finding (Arntz, Meeren, & Wessell, 2002; Renneberg et al., 2005). Worthy of comment though, is that the BPD patients in the Renneberg et al. study retrieved more negative memories when prompted by the cue words than the controls did. This was also true of the depressed participants who were studied. Unlike the depressed participants, however, the BPD patients retrieved these more negative memories with a speed and a level of specificity that was comparable to that of the healthy controls. In other words, the BPD patients were rapidly able to access memories that were both specific and negative. Although the implications of this finding remain unclear, it is interesting to speculate whether such a retrieval style could play a role in the emotional turmoil that is so characteristic of BPD.

Contemporary Issues in the Diagnosis and Assessment of BPD

The *DSM* definition of BDP combines theoretical perspectives that are often quite different. There are also no required symptoms that must be present for the diagnosis to be made. This means that all nine symptoms are assumed to be of equal importance in the diagnosis of BPD. This clearly does not reflect the current debate about the core features of BPD.

Beyond this, however, many clinicians and researchers have reservations about whether personality disorders (including BPD) can even be classified in a categorical (e.g., *DSM*-like) fashion. Most personality researchers favor a dimensional (rather than categorical) view of personality disorders. Within this perspective, disorders of personality are theorized to occur along a continuum that envelops normal personality functioning.

Some empirical evidence is consistent with this view. Using taxometric statistical procedures to analyze data from a clinical sample, Rothschild, Cleland, Haslam, and Zimmerman (2003) failed to find evidence of a distinct borderline taxon or categorical entity. Instead, the data suggested that BPD is better considered as a dimensional concept. To the extent that this is true, differences between people with and without the BPD diagnosis might therefore be more quantitative than qualitative, with people with BPD simply exhibiting more extreme forms of normal personality traits.

Not surprisingly, these issues have led to the development of a variety of different methods and techniques used to assess and diagnose BPD. The clinical approach assumes that there is a reliable set of symptoms that define the disorder, and that the task of the researcher or clinician is to answer the question, "does this person have the disorder?" Most often, clinical assessment approaches use semistructured interviews and require skilled ratings of the presence or absence of the agreed-upon criteria for the disorder.

An alternative approach to assessment, however, involves the use of psychometric methods. Here, there are no concrete criteria that are assumed to make up a disorder— in fact the assessment is designed to yield information about how best to define the disorder in question. In this way, psychometric methods address a quite different question from that implicit in the clinical approach, specifically, "what makes up (the concept of) Borderline PD?" In the sections that follow, we consider some of the most widely used instruments from both assessment traditions.

CLINICAL APPROACHES TO ASSESSING BORDERLINE PERSONALITY DISORDER

Diagnostic Interviews

Clinical approaches to assessment are based on the fundamental assumption that there is a known and accepted concept that exists to be assessed in the first place. Because of this, their form directly reflects the current definitions of the disorders that they assess. For BPD, the two most widely-used clinical interviews are the Structured Clinical Interview for *DSM-IV* Personality Disorders (SCID-II) (First, Gibbon, Spitzer, Williams, & Benjamin, 1997) and the Diagnostic Interview for Borderlines-Revised (DIB-R) (Zanarini, Gunderson, Frankenburg, & Chauncey, 1989).

The SCID-II is an interview based on the current *DSM* criteria. Designed to be used by a trained interviewer, it can be used to assess all 11 different personality disorders included in the *DSM*. The SCID-II has good sensitivity, specificity, validity, and inter-rater reliability (Jacobsberg, Perry, & Frances, 1995). Although the SCID-II does assess for the presence of all personality disorders, the subset of questions specific to BPD is often used on its own.

Unlike the SCID-II, the DIB-R (and its predecessor, the DIB) is focused solely on BPD. The original Diagnostic Interview for Borderlines (Gunderson, Kolb, & Austin, 1981) was developed to distinguish BPD from Schizophrenia and Major Depressive Disorder. Accordingly, the questions covered such domains as social adaptation, impulse action patterns, affects, psychosis, and interpersonal relations. The goal of the revision of the instrument was to improve its power to discriminate BPD from other personality disorders. To this end, questions about such symptoms as anxiety, odd thinking, quasi-psychotic thought, and concerns of abandonment were included. The authors also adopted a standard duration of 2 years for all symptoms and established a predetermined scoring algorithm.

One measure of the success of this approach is that the DIB-R is now considered the best assessment instrument for distinguishing BPD from other personality disorders (Skodol et al., 2002). This semistructured interview produces scores on each of four scales: affect, cognition, impulsivity, and interpersonal relationships. The presence of BPD is then determined by a score of 8 or more on a 10-point scale. The DIB-R subscales map well onto the major behavioral patterns associated with BPD, including abandonment fears, demandingness and entitlement, treatment regressions, and the ability to arouse inappropriately close or hostile relationships during treatment. Perhaps the most important difference between the DIB-R and any of the measures based solely on *DSM* criteria is that the DIB-R—far from overidentifying cases of BPD—seems to identify a more homogenous and severe subset of patients (Zanarini, Frankenburg, & Vujanovic, 2002).

There are several other interviews that, like the SCID-II, assess BPD according to the *DSM* diagnostic criteria. The Structured Interview for *DSM-IV* Personality Disorders (SIDP-IV) (Pfohl, Blum, & Zimmerman, 1997) is popular because it incorporates both the *DSM-IV*-TR criteria and the ICD-10 criteria for personality disorders. This is also true of the International Personality Disorder Examination (IPDE) (Loranger, 1999). However, one disadvantage of the IPDE is that it is the longest of all the semistructured interviews.

Finally, there are two other assessment interviews that are reliable, based on the *DSM* criteria, and can be used to provide a BPD diagnosis. The Personality Disorder Interview (PDI-IV) (Widiger, Mangine, Corbitt, Ellis, & Thomas, 1995) and the Diagnostic Interview for Personality Disorders (DIPD-IV) (Zanarini, Frankenburg, Chauncey, & Gunderson, 1987) both have good empirical support. However, they tend not to be used as often as the SCID-II, SIDP-IV, or IPDE.

Self-Report Questionnaires

The Personality Disorders Questionnaire (PDQ-4) (Hurt, Hyler, Frances, Clarkin, & Brent, 1984) is a 99-item self-report instrument that is based on the *DSM-IV* criteria. It contains items to assess each *DSM-IV* Personality Disorder. Because it is brief, it is commonly used. However, the PDQ does have some psychometric weakness.

Measuring Change in BPD

Before we move on, one last clinician-administered interview warrants brief mention. The Zanarini Rating Scale for Borderline Personality Disorder (Zanarini et al., 2003) is the only presently available measure that can be used to assess severity and change in borderline pathology. The items for this rating scale were adapted from the BPD module of the DIPD-IV, and converted so that each criterion was rated on a 0–4 scale and covered a one-week time period. The rating points (0–4) in the scale were designed and anchored to consider both the severity and frequency of symptoms. The ZAN-BPD culminates in four sector scores that reflect the primary areas of dysfunction in BPD: affective (anger/emptiness/mood stability), cognitive (stress-related dissociation or paranoia, identity disturbance), impulsive (self-mutilation, suicide attempts, and other forms of impulsivity), and interpersonal (abandonment, unstable relationships). This clinician rating scale has achieved good convergent validity (for example, scores correlate with the DIB-R), discriminant validity (the ZAN-BPD accurately discriminates BPD from Axis I disorders), and inter-rater reliability.

PSYCHOMETRIC APPROACHES TO BORDERLINE PERSONALITY DISORDER

A different approach to assessing borderline symptomatology is reflected in symptom and personality inventories that inquire about a broad range of possible pathology. Such measures can be utilized to help determine what actually makes up the borderline construct. When people with BPD complete such measures, researchers can gain insight into the basic aspects of the disorder.

One such inventory is the Personality Assessment Inventory (PAI) (Morey, 1991). This 344-question inventory, which is based on an interpersonal model of psychopathology, covers all *DSM* personality disorders. There are four BPD feature subscales included in the measure; these probe affective instability, identity problems, negative relationships, and self-harming behavior. The PAI has shown good reliability and validity. It can also be used for diagnosing BPD because the BPD subscale incorporates all of the *DSM* criteria.

Another broad personality inventory that can be used to assess personality and symptoms of distress is the Minnesota Multiphasic Personality Inventory (MMPI-2) (Colligan, Morey, & Offord, 1994; Hathaway et al., 1989). This well-known measure is made up of over 500 statements that are rated by the patient as being either true or false. The clinical scales of the MMPI-2 assess to what degree the answers that a person gives are similar to the answers given by the prototypical patient who has a particular diagnosis. Because there is so much clinical heterogeneity in Borderline Personality Disorder, it is difficult to detail what the personality profile of a typical patient with BPD might look like. However, as a whole, patients with BPD do tend to score high on the neurotic (scales 1–4) and psychotic (scales 6–8) subscales of the MMPI-2. However, a unique pattern has yet to be found that can adequately distinguish a patient with BPD from a patient with another cluster B personality disorder.

The Schedule for Nonadaptive and Adaptive Personality (SNAP) (Clark, 1993) is a 275-item self-report measure that is based on a dimensional model of personality disorders. Within this perspective, personality disorders are characterized as extreme forms of otherwise normal personality functioning. The SNAP has diagnostic subscales for all of the *DSM* personality disorders, as well as various trait and temperament scales that measure common factors (e.g., self-harm vulnerability, negative temperament, impulsivity) that have obvious relevance for researchers interested in BPD.

Like the SNAP, the Revised NEO Personality Inventory (NEO PI-R) (Costa & McCrae, 1992) is also based on a dimensional view of personality disorders, although in the case of the NEO the underlying basis is five factor theory. Rather than being solely concerned with the abnormal traits characteristic of personality disorders, the NEO is designed to cover both normal and abnormal traits. Although the validity of the recent *DSM-IV* personality disorder subscales in the NEO is still under scrutiny, the NEO does have excellent empirical support, especially in relation to traits that may impact treatment (Clarkin, Hull, Cantor & Sanderson, 1993).

Finally, it is appropriate to mention one psychometric measure that is specific to BPD. The Borderline Personality Inventory (BPI; Leichsenring, 1999) is based on Kernberg's psychodynamic formulation of the borderline diagnosis. Accordingly, the measure probes patient functioning in four discrete areas: identity diffusion, primitive defense mechanisms, reality testing, and fear of closeness. The BPI combines both categorical and dimensional aspects of personality, in that although it is dimensionally based, it is compatible with *DSM-IV* criteria for a BPD diagnosis. The construction of the scales in the BPI is rooted in factor analysis, and cut-off scores are proposed based on previous research.

PROBLEMS IN THE ASSESSMENT OF **BPD**

A major problem in the assessment of BPD is the large number of measures that exist. This creates serious obstacles with respect to interpreting research findings. When different measures are used, different results are likely to be obtained. For this reason, some researchers (Pilknois, 1997; Regier et al., 1998; Shea, 1997) have advocated for the adoption of a common clinical interview. Additionally, it has been suggested that a uniform assessment battery be adopted to measure treatment outcome. Although such an approach would make it easier to compare findings across studies, it is still unclear which of the current instruments might be most valuable to include.

Treatment

Treating patients who suffer from BPD is not easy. Patients often enact their interpersonal issues in the therapeutic relationship, leading to complicated impasses and emotional storms. Self-harming behaviors are common (60 to 80% of cases; Bateman & Fonagy, 2003) and the mean number of lifetime suicide attempts in patients with BPD is 3.4 (Soloff, Lis, Kelly, Cornelius, & Ulrich, 1994). Moreover, as we have already noted, the 10% rate of completed suicide in BPD is alarmingly high (Oldham 2006). When considered with the tendency of BPD patients to drop out of treatment (Percudani et al., 2002) it is easy to see why the treatment of BPD patients is among the most challenging tasks that clinicians face.

However, the situation is less bleak than it might appear at first glance. Despite the profound emotional pain that characterizes BPD sufferers and the turbulent nature of the treatment process, the long-term outcome of the disorder may be more benign than was previously assumed. Zanarini, Frankenburg, Hennen, Reich, and Silk (2006) conducted a 10-year follow-up study of a carefully diagnosed group of 290 patients with BPD who had initially received inpatient treatment. The researchers interviewed the patients every two years and collected data on their symptoms and levels of functioning. Drop out rates were remarkably low, with 249 participants from the original sample still remaining at the time of the 10-year follow-up assessment. Importantly, the results showed that over the 10-year follow-up the vast majority (88%) of the patients with BPD showed significant reductions in their symptoms and entered remission. What this means is that they no longer met criteria for a diagnosis of BPD. Moreover, in many cases clinical remission was achieved quite rapidly, with 39.3% of the patients experiencing remission by the time of the 2-year follow up. For another 22.4% of the patients, remission had occurred by the time of the 4-year-follow up and by 6 years, another 21.9% of the original sample no longer met diagnostic criteria for BPD. Predictors of a more rapid time to clinical remission included being younger, not having a history of childhood sexual abuse, and not having a family history of substance abuse disorders. Having a good recent work history, as well a having an agreeable temperament, scoring low on measures of neuroticism, and not having an anxious personality were also associated with patients getting better more rapidly.

Time clearly plays a major role in helping to heal the emotional wounds of the patient with BPD. However, time alone is not a sufficient treatment. Clinical interventions are thought to speed up the process of natural recovery (Paris, 2005). In the sections below, we briefly consider the major clinical interventions that are currently used to help patients with this disorder. These include pharmacological treatments as well as various kinds of psychotherapy.

PHARMACOLOGICAL APPROACHES

Medications are routinely used in the treatment of BPD. Yet, despite their widespread use there is a surprising paucity of randomized controlled trials attesting to their efficacy. This is not to say that medications do not help patients. However, their benefits may be more modest than would be expected, particularly in light of how often they are prescribed.

Selective serotonin reuptake inhibitors (SSRIs) are commonly used to treat BPD. One rationale for using these medications is that many people with BPD are also depressed and these medications have demonstrated efficacy for depression. SSRIs also make sense when considering the data linking aggression and suicide to low levels of serotonin (Asberg, 1997). Open trial studies with small samples of patients have suggested that SSRIs may be helpful for patients with BPD (e.g., Cornelius, Soloff, Perel, & Ulrich, 1991). However, in efficacy studies, their effects are often quite modest.

In a double blind study, Rinne et al. (2002) randomly assigned 38 women with BPD to either 6 weeks of SSRI treatment (fluvoxamine) or 6 weeks of treatment with placebo. At the end of the 6-week trial, half of the patients who had been given placebo were switched to fluvoxamine (Luvox). All patients (who were still blind to the type of treatment they were receiving) were then followed for a further 6 weeks. All of the patients showed some clinical improvements after they entered the study. At the end of the 6-week period, patients in both the SSRI and the placebo condition showed improvements in anger and impulsivity and there were no significant differences between the groups. However, patients who had been treated with fluvoxamine showed a more significant improvement in mood stability than the patients who had received placebo. These results suggest that treatment with an SSRI may help BPD patients experience fewer rapid mood shifts. However, what is also important to note is that even when they received the placebo, the patients with BPD still experienced clinical improvement.

Other medications in widespread use in the treatment of BPD include atypical antipsychotics such as olanzapine, clozapine, and risperidone. Again, most of these have been studied in the context of open trials and more placebo-controlled studies are needed (Markovitz, 2004). However, as a class, antipsychotic medications have been shown to have a beneficial effect on impulsivity and aggression (Nose, Cipriani, Biancosino, Grassi, & Barbui, 2006). Moreover, in a double blind placebo controlled trial of olanzapine (Zyprexa), Zanarini and Frankenburg (2001) reported that the 19 female patients who were randomly assigned to receive olanzapine reported decreases in their levels of anxiety, paranoia, interpersonal sensitivity, as well as anger/hostility compared to the nine women who received placebo. A recent placebo controlled trial of a new antipsychotic agent, aripiprazole, has also yielded promising preliminary results (Nickel et al., 2006).

Finally we note that anti-epileptic drugs are also now being used in the treatment of BPD. Mood stabilizers such as divalproex sodium have been shown to have beneficial effects on anger and mood instability in randomized controlled trials (Nose et al., 2006). However, they do not appear to help alleviate such problems as impulsivity and aggression, or suicidality. Lithium has also been used in one small randomized clinical trial, although it was not associated with any improvements in mood or impulsivity (Links, Steiner, Boiago, & Irwin, 1990).

Considered together, it is clear that medications do offer some benefits for patients. However, there is no medication that can be considered to be an adequate treatment for

BPD. Some medications help with some symptoms, other medications help with other problems. Recognizing this, we now turn our attention to some of the psychological approaches that are important in the treatment of this disorder.

PSYCHOLOGICAL APPROACHES

Perhaps the best-known treatment for BPD is Dialectical Behavior Therapy. Developed by Marsha Linehan, this cognitive behavioral approach involves weekly psychotherapy sessions as well as weekly skills training administered in a group format. Patients are also permitted to call their therapists for telephone consultations. Finally, the therapists themselves attend weekly team consultation meeting to help them stay motivated and provide them with additional treatment skills (Linehan et al., 2006).

DBT was specifically designed to treat patients with BPD, and research to date supports its efficacy for this disorder (Linehan, Armstrong, Suarez, & Heard, 1991; Linehan et al., 2006). In the most recent controlled trial, Linehan et al. (2006) randomly assigned patients either to DBT or to treatment with experts who had been nominated by community health leaders as being particularly skilled in the treatment of difficult patients. Patients in both groups received one full year of treatment and were then followed for another year. Both groups of patients showed significant improvements in suicidal ideation and motivation to live. Both treatments were also successful in reducing patients' self-injurious behaviors. However, at the end of the two years the rate of suicide attempts in the patients who received DBT were significantly lower than the rate of suicide attempts in the patients who received treatment by the expert therapists (23.1% versus 46.0%). Patients assigned to DBT were also less likely to drop out of treatment and less likely to require hospitalization than were the patients who did not receive DBT. These findings support the value of DBT and highlight its particular benefits with regard to reducing suicide attempts.

Although DBT is an extremely popular treatment, it is no longer the only empirically validated psychological approach. In recent years, several other treatment approaches have been developed, all of which are showing great promise. Working from a psychodynamic perspective, Bateman and Fonagy (2003, 2004) have developed a new therapeutic approach called *mentalization*. Based on attachment theory, mentalization uses the therapeutic relationship to help patients develop the skills they need to accurately understand their own feelings and emotions, as well as the feeling and emotions of others. The first randomized controlled trial of mentalization-based therapy for BPD (Bateman & Fonagy, 1999, 2001) has shown it to be an efficacious treatment for BPD with benefits that endure through an 18-month follow-up.

Another psychodymanically oriented therapy that is also showing a great deal of promise is Transference-Focussed Psychotherapy or TFP. Developed by Kernberg and his colleagues, this treatment approach uses the therapeutic relationship to help the patient understand and correct the distortions that occur in his or her perception of other people. Clarification, confrontation, and interpretation are key techniques here with the transference relationship between the patient and the therapist being a central focus of interest (Clarkin, Levy, Lenzenweger, & Kernberg, 2004).

In a recent clinical trial, 90 patients with BPD were randomly assigned to receive either TFP, DBT, or supportive psychotherapy (Clarkin, Levy, Lenzenweger, & Kernberg, 2007). After one year of treatment, patients in all three groups showed significant clinical improvements in their levels of depression, anxiety, social adjustment, and overall functioning. Patients who received TFP and DBT also showed decreases in suicidality. One additional advantage of TFP relative to the other forms of treatment, however, was that it was also associated with a reduction in anger.

Other studies, while also supporting the clinical benefits of TFP, are further showing that schema-focused therapy (SFT) may be a valuable treatment for patients with BPD. Schema-focused cognitive therapy uses cognitive, behavioral and also experiential techniques to explore and modify 4 schema modes (organized sets of schemas or constellations of underlying beliefs) that are thought to occur in BPD. These are the detached protector, punitive parent, abandoned/abused child, and angry/impulsive child modes. Patient and therapist work together in an effort to stop these dysfunctional schemas from controlling the patient's life.

In a randomized trial, Giesen-Bloo et al. (2006) compared the effectiveness of both TFP and SFT for 88 patients in community mental health centers. After three years of therapy, patients in both groups showed clinical improvement. More specifically, both treatments were associated with reductions in BPD symptoms, improvements in quality of life, and decreases in dysfunctional behaviors. In many cases, clinical improvements began to be apparent after one year of treatment. Of note, however, is that patients who received SFT showed significantly more clinical improvements on all measures (including borderline symptomatology, personality pathology, quality of life) than did patients who received TFP. They were also significantly less likely to drop out of treatment and significantly more likely to recover.

Within this climate of optimism, however, we wish to remind readers that not all therapeutic approaches provide significant benefits to patients. Davidson et al. (2006) randomly assigned 106 patients with BPD to either treatment as usual (TAU) or TAU plus cognitive behavior therapy. In CBT, patients were helped to develop new and more adaptive beliefs about themselves as well as behavioral strategies that would improve their social and emotional well-being. Major targets of clinical intervention were patients' core beliefs as well as typical behaviors that got in the way of adaptive functioning. At the end of the 12-month treatment period (during which patients attended an average of 16 sessions), patients who had received CBT in addition to TAU did not look significantly better than patients who had received TAU on a broad range of outcomes measures. These included the presence or absence of suicide attempts, self-harming behaviors, depressed mood, and interpersonal and social functioning. Overall, the findings from this rigorously conducted trial are disappointing. They attest to the difficulties inherent in getting patients to engage in treatment and suggest that long-term intensive treatment may need to be provided in order for any real clinical gains to occur.

Summary and Future Directions

Despite being the most researched Axis II disorder, BPD still remains something of a mystery. Although we can reliable diagnose it, its core features are still the subject of debate. We also know little about its etiology although it is almost certainly the result of the interaction of multiple factors. Finally, although medications and psychological treatments offer a great deal of help for BPD sufferers, we still have much to learn.

BPD is characterized by disturbances in a broad range of systems. This makes a full understanding of its nature both difficult and elusive. Genetic factors are likely to play an important role in the etiology of the disorder and early life experiences of abuse and trauma are also implicated. Yet many people who suffer from BPD do not have childhood histories of maltreatment. In some cases, it may simply be that genetic factors render them especially sensitive to other less malevolent (and common) forms of parental failure such as invalidation or lack of empathic attunement. It is also possible that there is a pathway to BPD that is primarily based on genetic vulnerability and in which environmental factors play an even more limited role.

Because biological and environmental factors are so inextricably linked, however, the clinical heterogeneity of BPD may actually be illustrating the range of outcomes that can result when temperamentally vulnerable individuals sustain damage from the psychosocial environment. Animal research is making it apparent that adverse circumstances occurring during early development may have a permanent effect on the HPA axis, neurotransmitter systems, and cognitive functioning, as well as on attachment relationships and social adjustment (Fish et al., 2004; Fish & Meaney, 1999; Oital, Workel, Fluttert, Frosch, & De Kloet, 2000). We need to learn more about the consequences of trauma and other forms of psychosocial damage on the developing brain. We also need to use genomic methods to further identify which genetic polymorphisms might be associated with differential reactivity to aversive early environments.

We believe that even the most complicated of clinical pictures can be assessed and connected back to basic psychological systems and processes (Lenzenweger & Hooley, 2003). Studying endophenotypes may be especially valuable in this endeavor. An endophenotype is something that can be measured or indexed and that is thought to lay along the pathway between the genotype and the disease (Gottesman & Gould, 2003; Lenzenweger & Cicchetti, 2005). This could be something neurobiological, endocrinolological, neuroanatomical, neuropsychological, or cognitive. The rationale for studying endophenotypes (e.g., people who show problems with inhibitory processes on neuropsychological tests, people who have chronic high negative affect, etc.) rather than people with the disorder itself is that the endophenotype (because it is a more simple clue) may help lead researchers closer to the genetic underpinnings of the disorder. Quite commonly used in schizophrenia research, the endophenotype concept, as Lenzenweger and Cicchetti (2005) note, may have much to offer those who wish to understand BPD.

Finally, we would like to end by making a call for more research in two key areas. The fact that we know so little about men with BPD is a major source of concern. Going forward, much more attention must be devoted to learning about the influence of gender on the disorder. Future research efforts also need to explore BPD in its earliest stages and identify the prodromal signs of the disorder. In all probability, the events that set the stage for the development of BPD happen early. If we can study these events and their biological and psychological sequelae closer in time to when they occur we may gain much leverage in the research process. In so doing, we may also be better placed to reduce the years of suffering that people with BPD have to endure.

References

Adler, G., & Buie, D. H., Jr., (1979). Aloneness and borderline psychopathology: The possible relevance of child development issues. *International Journal of Psychoanalysis*, *60*, 83–96.

Akiskal, H. S. (2002). The bipolar spectrum—the shaping of a new paradigm in psychiatry. *Current Psychiatry Reports*, *4*, 1–3.

Akiskal, H. S., Chen, S. E., & Davis, G. C. (1985). Borderline: An adjective in search of a noun. *Journal of Clinical Psychiatry*, *46*, 41–48.

American Psychiatric Association. (1980). *Diagnostic and statistical manual of mental disorders* (3rd ed.) Washington, DC: Author.

American Psychiatric Association. (2000). *Diagnostic and statistical manual of mental disorders (Text Rev)*. Washington, DC: Author.

Arntz, A., Appels, C., & Sieswerda, S. (2000). Hypervigilance in borderline personality disorder: A test with the emotional Stroop paradigm. *Journal of Personality Disorders*, *14*(4), 366–373.

Arntz, A., Meeren, M., & Wessel, I. (2002). No evidence for over general memories in borderline personality disorder. *Behaviour Research and Therapy*, *40*(9), 1063–1068.

Asberg, M. (1997). Neurotransmitters and suicidal behavior: The evidence from cerebrospinal fluid studies. *Annals of the New York Academy of Sciences*, *836*, 158–181.

Bandelow, B., Broocks, A., Hajak, G., Krause, J., Wedekind, D., & Rüther, E. (2005). Early traumatic life events, parental attitudes, family history, and birth risk factors in patients with borderline personality disorder and healthy controls. *Psychiatry Res*, *134*(2), 169–179.

Bateman, A. W., & Fonagy, P. (1999). Effectiveness of partial hospitalization in the treatment of borderline personality disorder: A randomized controlled trial. *American Journal of Psychiatry*, *156*, 1563–1569.

Bateman, A. W., & Fonagy, P. (2001). Treatment of borderline personality disorder with psychoanalytically oriented partial hospitalization: An 18-month follow-up. *American Journal of Psychiatry*, *158*, 36–42.

Bateman, A.W., & Fonagy, P. (2003). The development of an attachment-based treatment program for borderline personality disorder. *Bulletin of the Menninger Clinic*, *67*, 187–211.

Bateman, A. W., & Fonagy, P. (2004). Mentalization-based treatment of BPD. *Journal of Personality Disorders*, *18*, 36–51.

Bazanis, E., Rogers, R. D., Dowson, J. H., Taylor, P., Meux, C., Staley, C., et al. (2002). Neurocognitive deficits in decision-making and planning of patients with *DSM-III-R* borderline personality disorder. *Psychological Medicine*, *32*, 1395–1405.

Bender, D. S., Dolan, R. T., Skodol, A. E., Sanislow, C. A., Dyck, I. R., McGlashan, T. H., et al. (2001). Treatment utilization by patients with personality disorders. *American Journal of Psychiatry*, *158*, 295–302.

Bender, D. S., Farber, B. A., Sanislow, C. A., Dyck, I. R., Geller, J. D., & Skodol, A. E. (2003). Representations of therapists by patients with personality disorders. *American Journal of Psychotherapy*, *57*, 219–236.

Bennett, A. J., Lesch, K. P., Heils, A., Long, J. C., Lorenz, J. G., Shoaf, S. E., et al. (2002). Early experience and serotonin transporter gene variation interact to influence primate CNS function. *Molecular Psychiatry*, *7*, 118–122.

Berlin, H. A., Rolls, E. T., & Iversen, S. D. (2005). Borderline personality disorder: Impulsivity and the orbitofrontal cortex. *American Journal of Psychiatry*, *162*, 2360–2373.

Bondy, B., Erfurth, A., deJonge, S., Kruger, M., & Meyer, H. (2000). Possible association of the short allele of the serotonin transporter promoter gene polymorphism (5-HTTLPR) with violent suicide. *Molecular Psychiatry*, *5*, 193–195.

Bowlby, J. (1973). *Attachment and loss: Separation* (*Vol. 2*) New York: Basic Books.

Bowlby, J. (1977). The making and breaking of affectional bonds: I Aetiology and psyhopathology in the light of attachment theory. *British Journal of Psychiatry*, *130*, 210–210.

Bremner, J. D. (2002). Structural changes in the brain in depression and relationship to symptom recurrence. *CNS Spectrums*, *7*, 129–130, 135-139

Brendel, G. R., Stern, E., & Silbersweig, D. A. (2005). Defining the neurocircuitry of borderline personality disorder: Functional neuroimaging approaches. *Developmental Psychopathology*, *17*, 1197–1206.

Buie, D. H., & Adler, G. (1982). Definitive treatment of the borderline personality. *International Journal of Psychoanalytic Psychotherapy*, *9*, 51–87.

Casey, B. J., Castellanos, F. X., Giedd, J. N., Marsh, W. L., Hamburger, S. D., Schubert, et al. (1997). Implication of right frontostriatal circuitry in response inhibition and attention-deficit/hyperactivity disorder. *Journal of the American Academy of Child and Adolescent Psychiatry*, *36*, 374–383.

Caspi, A., McClay, J., Moffitt, T. E., Mill, J., Martin, J., Craig, I. W., et al. (2002). Role of genotype in the cycle of violence in maltreated children. *Science*, *297*, 851–854.

Clark, L. A. (1993). *Manual for the schedule for nonadaptive and adaptive personality*. Minneapolis: University of Minnesota Press.

Clarkin, J. F., Levy, K. N., Lenzenweger, M. F., & Kernberg, O. F. (2004). The personality disorders institute/borderline personality disorder research foundation randomized control trial for borderline personality disorder: Rationale, methods, and patient characteristics. *Journal of Personality Disorders*, *18*, 52–72.

Clarkin, J. F., Levy, K. N., Lenzenweger, M. F., & Kernberg, O. F. (2007). Evaluating three treatments for borderline personality disorder: A multiwave study. *American Journal of Psychiatry*, *164*, 922–928.

Cloninger, C.R. (2000). Biology of personality dimensions. *Current Opinion in Psychiatry*, *13*, 611–616.

Coccaro, E.F., Lee, R., & McClosky, M. (2003). Norepinephrine function in personality disorder: Plasma free MHPG correlates inversely with a life history of aggression. *CNS Spectrum*, *8*, 731–736.

Coccaro, E. F., Siever, L. J., Klar, H. M., & Maurer, G. (1989). Serotonergic studies in patients with affective and personality disorders: Correlates with suicidal and impulsive aggressive behavior. *Archives of General Psychiatry*, *46*587–599.

Coid, J., Yang, M., Tyrer, P. T., Roberts, A., & Ullrich, S. (2006). Prevalence and correlates of personality disorder in Great Britain. *British Journal of Psychiatry*, *188*, 423–431.

Colligan, R.C., Morey, L.C., & Offord, K.P. (1994). MMPI/MMPI-2 personality disorder scales: Contemporary norms for adults and adolescents. *Journal of Clinical Psychology*, *50*, 168–200.

Cornelius, J. R., Soloff, P. H., Perel, J. M., & Ulrich, R. F. (1991). A preliminary trial of fluoxetine in refractory borderline patients. *Journal of Clinical Psychopharmacology*, *11*(2), 116–120.

Corruble, E., Ginestet, D., & Guelfi, J. D. (1996). Comorbidity of personality disorders and unipolar major depression: A review. *Journal of Affective Disorders*, *37*, 157–170.

Costa, P. T., & McCrae, R. R. (1992). *Revised NEO personality inventory (NEO PI-R) and NEO five-factor inventory (NEO-FFI) professional manual*. Odessa, FL: Psychological Assessment Resources.

Davidson, K., Norrie, J., Tyrer, P., Gumley, A., Tata, P., Murray, H., et al. (2006). The effectiveness of cognitive behavior therapy for borderline personality disorder: Results from the borderline personality disorder study of cognitive therapy. *Journal of Personality Disorders*, *20*, 450–465.

Davidson, R. J. (2002). Anxiety and affective style: Role of prefrontal cortex and amygdala. *Biological Psychiatry*, *51*, 68–80.

Davidson, R. J., Putnam, K. M., & Larson, C. L. (2000). Dysfunction in the neural circuitry of emotion regulation—a possible prelude to violence. *Science*, *289*, 591–594.

Depue, R. A., & Lenzenweger, M. F. (2005). A neurobehavioral model of personality disturbance. In J. F. Clarkin and M. F. Lenzenweger (Eds.), *Major theories of personality disorder* (2nd ed. pp. 391–453). New York: Guilford.

Domes, G., Winter, B., Schnell, K., Vohs, K., Fast, K., & Herpertz, S. C. (2006). The influence of emotions on inhibitory functioning in borderline personality disorder. *Psychological Medicine*, *36*, 1163–1172.

Donegan, N. H., Sanislow, C. A., Blumberg, H. P., Fulbright, R. K., Lacadie, C., Skudlarski, P., et al. (2003). Amygdala hyperreactivity in borderline personality disorder: Implications for emotional dysregulation. *Biological Psychiatry*, *54*, 1284–1293.

Driessen, M., Herrmann, J., Stahl, K., Zwaan, M., Meier, S., Hill, A., et al. (2000). Magnetic resonance imaging volume of the hippocampus and the amygdala in women with borderline personality disorder and early traumatization. *Archives of General Psychiatry*, *57*, 1115–1122.

Ebstein, R.P., Benjamin, J., & Belmaker, R.H. (2000). Personality and polymorphisms of genes involved in aminergic neurotransmission. *European Journal of Pharmacology*, *410*, 205–214.

Fan, J., McCandliss, B. D., Sommer, T., Raz, M., & Posner, M. I. (2002). Testing the efficiency and independence of attentional networks. *Journal of Cognitive Neuroscience*, *3*(14), 340–347.

Fertuck, E., Lenzenweger, M., & Clarkin, J. (2005) The association between attentional and executive controls in the expression of borderline personality disorder features: A preliminary study. *Psychopathology*, *38*(2), 75–81.

Fertuck, E. A., Lenzenweger, M. F., Clarkin, J. F., Hoermann, S., & Stanley, B. (2006). Executive neurocognition, memory systems, and borderline personality disorder. *Clinical Psychology Review, 26*, 346–375.

First, M., Gibbon, M., Spitzer, R. L., Williams, J. B. W., & Benjamin, L. S. (1997). *User's guide for the structured clinical interview for DSM-IV Axis II personality disorders*. Washington, DC: American Psychiatric Press.

Fish, E. W., Shahrokh, D., Bagot, R., Caldji, C., Bredy, T., Szyf, M., et al. (2004). Epigenetic programming of stress responses through variations in maternal care. *Annals of the New York Academy of Sciences, 1036*, 167–180.

Francis, D. D., & Meaney, M. J. (1999). Maternal care and the development of stress responses. *Current Opinion in Neurobiology, 9*, 128–134.

Frankle, W. G., Lombardo, I., New, A. S., Goodman, M., Talbot, P. S., Huang, Y., et al. (2005). Brain serotonin transporter distribution in subjects with impulsive aggressivity: A positron emission study with [11C]McN 5652. *American Journal of Psychiatry, 162*, 915–923.

Friedel, R. O. (2004). Dopamine dysfunction in borderline personality disorder: A hypothesis. *Neuropsychopharmacology, 29*, 1029–1039.

Fruzzetti, A. E., Shenk, C., & Hoffman, P.D. (2005). Family interaction and the development of borderline personality disorder: A transitional model. *Development Psychopathology, 17*, 1007–1030.

Gabbard, G.O. (2005). Mind, brain, and personality disorders. *American Journal of Psychiatry, 162*, 648–655.

Giesen-Bloo, J., van Dyck, R., Spinhoven, P., van Tilberg, W., Dirksen, C., van Asselt, T., et al. (2006). Outpatient psychotherapy for borderline personality disorder: Randomized trial of schema-focused therapy vs. transference focused psychotherapy. *Archives of General Psychiatry, 63*, 649–658.

Goodman, M., New, A., & Siever, L. (2004). Trauma, genes, and the neurobiology of personality disorders. *Annals of the New York Academy of Sciences, 1032*, 104–116.

Gottesman, I. I., & Gould, T. D. (2003). The endophenotype concept in psychiatry: Etymology and strategic intentions. *American Journal of Psychiatry, 160*, 636–645.

Grinker, R., Werble, B., & Drye, R. (1968). *The borderline syndrome: A behavioral study of ego functions*. New York: Basic Books.

Gunderson, J. G. (1996). The borderline patient's intolerance of aloneness: Insecure attachments and therapist availability. *American Journal of Psychiatry, 153*(6), 752.

Gunderson J. G. (2001). *Borderline personality disorder: A clinical guide*. Washington, DC: American Psychiatric Publishing.

Gunderson, J. G., Kolb, J. E., & Austin, V. (1981). The diagnostic interview for borderline patients. *American Journal of Psychiatry, 138*, 896–903.

Gunderson, J. G., & Phillips, K. A. (1991). A current view of the interface between borderline personality disorder and depression. *American Journal of Psychiatry, 48*, 967–975.

Gunderson, J. G., & Sabo, A. N. (1993). The phenomenological and conceptual interface between borderline personality and PTSD. *American Journal of Psychiatry, 150*, 19–27.

Gunderson, J. G., & Singer, M. (1975). Defining borderline patients: An overview. *American Journal of Psychiatry, 132*, 1–10.

Gurvits, I. G., Koenigsberg, H. W., & Siever, L. J. (2000). Neurotransmitter dysfunction in patients with borderline personality disorder. *Psychiatric Clinics of North America, 23*(1), 27–40.

Hathaway, S. R., McKindley, J. C., Butcher, J. N., Dahlstrom, W. G., Graham, J. R., & Tellegen, A. (1989). *Minnesota multiphasic personality inventory test booklet*. Minneapolis: Regents of the University of Minnesota.

Hazlett, E. A., New, A. S., Newmark, R., Haznedar, M. M., Lo, J. N., Speiser, L. J., et al. (2005). Reduced anterior and posterior cingulated gray matter in borderline personality disorder. *Biological Psychiatry, 58*, 614–623.

Heaton, R. K. (1981). *Wisconsin card sorting test manual*. Odessa, FL: Psychological Assessment Resources.

Heim, C., Newport, C. J., Heit, S., Graham, Y. P., Wilcox, M., Bonsall, R., et al. (2000). Pituitary, adrenal and autonomic responses to stress in women after sexual and physical abuse in childhood. *JAMA, 284*, 592–597.

Herman, J., Perry, J., & van der Kolk, B. (1989). Childhood trauma in borderline personality disorder. *American Journal of Psychiatry, 146*, 490–495.

Herpertz, S. C., Dietrich, T. M., Wenning, B., Krings, T., Erberich, S. G., Willmes, K., et al. (2001). Evidence of abnormal amygdala functioning in borderline personality disorder: A functional MRI study. *Biological Psychiatry, 50*, 292–298.

Higley, J. D., Suomi, S. J., & Linnoila, M. (1991). CSF monoamine metabolite concentrations vary according to age, rearing, and sex, and are influenced by the stressor of social separation in rhesus monkeys. *Psychopharmacology, 103*, 551–556.

Hoch, P. & Polantin, P. (1949). Pseudo neurotic forms of schizophrenia. *Psychiatric Quarterly, 23*, 248–276.

Hochhausen, N., Lorenz, A., & Newman, J. (2002). Specifying the impulsivity of female inmates with borderline personality disorder. *Journal of Abnormal Psychology, 111*(3), 495–501.

Hoefgen, B., Schulze, T.G., Ohlraun, S., vonWiddern, O., Hofels, S., Gross, M., et al. (2005). The power of sample size and homogenous sampling: Association between the 5-HTTLPR serotonin transporter polymorphism and major depressive disorder. *Biological Psychiatry, 57*, 247–251.

Hurt, S. W., Hyler, S. E., Frances, A., Clarkin, J. F., & Brent, R. (1984). Assessing borderline personality-disorder with self-report, clinical interview, or semi-structured interview. *American Journal of Psychiatry, 141*(10), 1228–1231.

Hyman, S. E. (2002). A new beginning for research on borderline personality disorder. *Biological Psychiatry, 51*, 933–935.

Jacobsberg, L., Perry, S., & Frances, A. (1995). Diagnostic agreement between the SCID-II screening questionnaire and the personality disorder examination. *Journal of personality assessment, 65*(3), 428–433.

Jang, K. L., Livesley, W. J., Vernon, P. A., & Jackson, D. N. (1996). Heritability of personality disorder traits: A twin study. *Acta Psychiatrica Scandinavica, 94*, 438–444.

Johnson, J. G., Cohen, P., Brown, J., Smailes, E. M., & Bernstein, D. P. (1999). Childhood maltreatment increases risk for personality disorders during early adulthood. *Archives of General Psychiatry 56*, 600–606.

Jones, B., Heard, H., Startup, M., Swales, M., Williams, J., & Jones, R. (1999). Autobiographical memory and dissociation in borderline personality disorder. *Psychological Medicine, 29*(6), 1397–1404.

Joyce, P. R., McHugh, P. C., McKenzie, J. M., Sullivan, P. F., Mulder, R. T., Luty, S. E., et al. (2006). A dopamine transporter polymorphism is a risk factor for borderline personality disorder in depressed patients. *Psychological Medicine, 36*(6), 807–813.

Kandel, E. R. (1998). A new intellectual framework for psychiatry. *American Journal of Psychiatry, 155*, 457–469.

Kernberg, O. (1967). Borderline personality organization. *Journal of the American Psychoanalytic Association, 15*, 641–675.

Kernberg, O. (1975). *Borderline conditions and pathological narcissism.* New York: J. Aronson.

Knight, R. (1953). Borderline states. *Bulletin of the Menninger Clinic, 17*, 1–12.

Kohut, H. (1971). *The analysis of the self: A systematic approach to the treatment of narcissistic personality disorders.* New York: International Universities Press.

Kohut, H. (1977). *The restoration of the self.* New York: International Universities Press.

Korfine, L., & Hooley, J. (2000) Directed forgetting of emotional stimuli in borderline personality disorder. *Journal of Abnormal Psychology, 109*(2), 214–221.

LeDoux, J. (1996). *The emotional brain: The mysterious underpinnings of emotional life.* New York: Touchstone.

Leichsenring, F. (1999). Development and first results of the borderline personality inventory: A self-report instrument for assessing borderline personality organization. *Journal of Personality Assessment, 73*, 45–63.

Lenzenweger, M. F., & Cicchetti, D. (2005). Toward a developmental psychopathology approach to borderline personality disorder. *Development and Psychopathology, 17*, 893–898.

Lenzenweger, M. F., Clarkin, J. F., Fertuck, E. A., & Kernberg, O. F. (2004). Executive neurocognitive functioning and neurobehavioral systems indicators in borderline personality disorder: A preliminary study. *Journal of Personality Disorders, 18*(5), 421–438.

Lenzenweger, M. F., & Hooley, J. M. (Eds.). (2003). *Principles of experimental psychopathology: Essays in honor of Brendan A. Maher.* Washington DC: American Psychological Association.

Lenzenweger, M. F., Lane, M. C., Loranger, A. W., & Kessler, R. C. (2007). *DSM-IV* personality disorders in the national comorbidity survey replication. *Biological Psychiatry, 62*(6), 553–564.

Lenzenweger, M. F., Loranger, A. W., Korfine, L., & Neff, C. (1979). Detecting personality disorders in a nonclinical population: Application of a 2-stage for case identification. *Archives of General Psychiatry, 54*, 345–351.

Levy, K. N. (2005). The implications of attachment theory and research for understanding borderline personality disorder. *Development and Psychopathology, 17*, 959–986.

Leyton, M., Okazawa, H., Diksic, D., Paris, J., Rosa, P., Mzengeza, S., et al. (2001). Brain regional α-[^{11}C]methyl-L-tryptophan trapping in impulsive subjects with borderline personality disorder. *The American Journal of Psychiatry, 158*, 775–782.

Lieb, K., Rexhausen, J. E., Kahl, K. G., Schweiger, U., Philipsen, A., Hellhammer, D. M., et al. (2004). Increased diurnal salivary cortisol in women with borderline personality disorder. *Journal of Psychiatric Research*, 38, 559–565.

Linehan, M. M. (1993). *Cognitive-behavioral treatment of borderline personality disorder: The dialectics of effective treatment*. New York: Guilford.

Linehan, M. M., Armstrong, H. E., Suarez, A. D. A., & Heard, H. L. (1991). Cognitive-behavioral treatment of chronically parasuicidal borderline patients. *Archives of General Psychiatry*, 48, 1060–1064.

Linehan, M. M., Comtois, C. A., Murray, A. M., Brown, M. Z., Gallop, R. J., Heard, H. L., et al. (2006). Two-year randomized controlled trial and follow-up of dialectical behavior therapy vs therapy by experts for suicidal behaviors and borderline personality disorder. *Archives of General Psychiatry*, 63, 757–766.

Links, P., Steiner, M., Boiago, I., & Irwin, D. (1990). Lithium therapy for borderline patients: Preliminary findings. *Journal of Personality disorders*, 2, 14–20.

Links, P. S., Steiner, M., & Huxley, G. (1988). The occurrence of borderline personality disorder in the families of borderline patients. *Journal of Personality Disorders*, 2, 14–20.

Livesley, W. J., Jang, K. L., Jackson, D. N., & Vernon, P. A. (1993). Genetic and environmental contributions to dimensions of personality disorder. *American Journal of Psychiatry*, 150, 1826–1831.

Loranger, A. W. (1999). *International Personality Disorder Examination (IPDE)*. Odessa, FL: Psychological Assessment Resources.

Loranger, A. W., Sartorius, N., Andreoli, A., Berger, P., Buckheim, P., & Channabasavanna, S. (1994). The International Personality Disorders Examination: The World Health Organization/alcohol, drug abuse, and mental health administration international pilot study of personality disorders. *Archives of General Psychiatry*, 51, 215–224.

Markovitz, P. J. (2004). Recent trends in the pharmacotherapy of personality disorders. *Journal of Personality Disorders*, 18, 90–101.

Morey, L. C. (1991). *The Personality Assessment Inventory professional manual*. Odessa, FL: Psychological Assessment Resources.

New, A. S., Buchsbaum, M. S., Hazlett, E. A., Goodman, M., Koenigsberg, H. W., Lo, J., et al. (2004). Fluoxetine increases metabolic rate in prefrontal cortex in impulsive aggression. *Psychopharmacology*, 176, 451–458.

New, A. S., Hazlett, E. A., Buchsbaum, M. S., Goodman, M., Mitelman, S. A., Newmark, R., et al. (2007). Amygdala-prefrontal disconnection in borderline personality disorder. *Neuropsychopharmacology*, 32, 1629–1640.

Newman, J. P., & Kosson, D. S. (1986). Passive avoidance learning in psychopathic and nonpsychopathic offenders. *Journal of Abnormal Psychology*, 95, 257–263.

Ni, X., Chan, K., Bulgin, N., Sicad, T., Bismil, R., McMain, S., et al. (2006). Association between serotonin transporter gene and borderline personality disorder. *Journal of Psychiatric Research*, 40, 448–453.

Nickel, M. K., Muehlbacher, M., Nickel, C., Kettler, C., Pedrosa Gil, F., Bachler, E., et al. (2006). Ariprprazole in the treatment of patients with borderline personality disorder: A double-blind, placebo-controlled study. *American Journal of Psychiatry*, 163, 833–838.

Nigg, J. T. (2000). On inhibition/disinhibition in developmental psychopathology: Views from cognitive and personality psychology and a working inhibition taxonomy. *Psychological Bulletin*, 126, 220–246.

Nose, M., Cipriani, A., Biancosino, B., Grassi, L., & Barbui, C. (2006). Efficacy of pharmacotherapy against core traits of borderline personality disorder: Meta-analysis of randomized controlled trials. *International Clinical Psychopharmacology*, 21(6), 345–353.

Ogata, S. N., Silk, K. R., Goodrich, S., Lohr, N. E., Westen, D., & Hill, E. M. (1990). Childhood sexual and physical abuse in adults patients with borderline personality disorder. *American Journal of Psychiatry*, 147, 1008–1013.

Oital, M. S., Workel, J. O. Fluttert, M., Frosch, F., & De Kloet, E. R. (2000). Maternal deprivation affects behavior from youth to senescence: Amplification of individual differences in spatial learning and memory in senescent brown Norway rats. *European Journal of Neuroscience*, 12, 3771–3780.

Oldham, J. M. (2006). Borderline personality disorder and suicidality. *American Journal of Psychiatry*, 163, 20–26.

Oquendo, M. A., & Mann, J. J. (2000). The biology of impulsivity and suicidality. *Psychiatric Clinics of North America*, 23, 11–25.

Paris, J. (1999). Borderline personality disorder. In T. Millon, P. H. Blaney, and R. G. Davis (Eds.), *Oxford textbook of psychopathology*. New York: Oxford University Press.

Paris, J. (2004). Borderline or bipolar? Distinguishing borderline personality disorder from bipolar spectrum disorders. *Harvard Review of Psychiatry, 12,* 140–145.

Paris, J. (2005). Recent advances in the treatment of borderline personality disorder. *Canadian Journal of Psychiatry, 50,* 435–441.

Percudani, M., Belloni, G., Conti, A., & Barbui, C. (2002). Monitoring community psychiatric services in Italy: Differences between patients who leave care and those who stay in treatment. *British Journal of Psychiatry, 180,* 254–259.

Pfohl, B., Blum, N., & Zimmerman, M. (1997). *Structured interview for* DSM-IV *personality.* Washington, DC: American Psychiatric Press.

Pilknois, P. A. (1997). Measurement issues relevant to personality disorders. In H. H. Strupp, M. J. Lambert & L. M. Horowitz (Eds.), *Measuring patient change in mood, anxiety, and personality disorders: Toward a core battery* (pp. 371–388). Washington, DC: American Psychological Association.

Posner, M. I., Rothbart, M. K., Vizueta, N., Levy, K., Evans, D. E., Thomas, K. M., et al. (2002). Mechanisms of borderline personality disorder. *Proceedings of the National Academy of Sciences of the United States of America, 99,* 16366–16370.

Putnam, K. M., & Silk, K. R. (2005). Emotion dysregulation and the development of borderline personality disorder. *Developmental Psychopathology, 17,* 899–925.

Regier, D. A., Kaelber, C. T., Rae, D. S., Farmer, M. E., Knauper, B., Kessler, R. C., et al. (1998). Limitations of diagnostic criteria and assessment instruments for mental disorders: Implications for research and policy. *Archives of General Psychiatry, 55,* 109–115.

Renneberg, B. Theobald, E., Nobs, M., & Weisbrod, M. (2005). Autobiographical memory in borderline personality disorder and depression. *Cognitive Therapy and Research, 29,* 343–358.

Rinne, T., de Kloet, R., Wouters, L., Goekoop, J. G., DeRijk, R. H., & van den Brink, W. (2002). Hyperresponsiveness of hypothalamic-pituitary-adrenal axis to combined dexamethasone/corticotrophinreleasing hormone challenge in female borderline personality disorder subjects with a history of sustained childhood abuse. *Biological Psychiatry, 52,* 1102–1112.

Rinne, T., Westenberg, H. G. M., den Boer, J. A., & van den Brink, W. (2000). Serotonergic blunting to meta-Chlorophenylpiperazine (m-CPP) highly correlates with sustained childhood abuse in impulsive and autoaggressive female borderline patients. *Biological Psychiatry, 47,* 548–556.

Rinne, T., van den Brink, W., Wouters, L., & van Dyck, R. (2002). SSRI treatment of borderline personality disorder: A randomized, placebo-controlled clinical trial for female patients with borderline personality disorder. *American Journal of Psychiatry, 159,* 2048–2054.

Rothschild, L., Cleland, C., Haslam, N., & Zimmerman, M. (2003). A taxometric study of borderline personality disorder. *Journal of Abnormal Psychology, 112,* 657–666.

Ruocco, A. C. (2005). The neuropsychology of borderline personality disorder: A meta-analysis and review. *Psychiatry Research, 137,* 191–202.

Salzman, J., Salzman, C., Wolfson, A., Albanese, A., Looper, J., Ostacher, M., et al. (1993). Association between borderline personality structure and history of childhood abuse in adult volunteers. *Comprehensive Psychiatry, 34,* 254–257.

Schmahl, C., & Bremner, J. D. (2006). Neuroimaging in borderline personality disorder. *Journal of Psychiatric Research, 40,* 419–427.

Schmahl, C. G., Elzinga, B. M., Vermetten, E., Sanislow, C., McGlashan, T. H., & Bremner, J. D. (2003). Neural correlates of memories of abandonment in women with and without borderline personality disorder. *Biological Psychiatry, 54,* 142–151.

Schmahl, C. G., Vermetten, E., Elzinga, B. M., & Bremner, J. D. (2003). Magnetic resonance imaging of hippocampal and amygdala volume in women with childhood abuse and borderline personality disorder. *Psychiatry Research, 122,* 193–198.

Shea, M. T. (1997). Core battery conference: Assessment of change in personality disorders. In H. H. Strupp, L. M. Horowitz & M. J. Lambert (Eds.), *Measuring patient changes in mood, anxiety, and personality disorders: Toward a core battery* (pp. 389–400). Washington, DC: American Psychological Association.

Siever, L. J., & Davis, K. L. (1991). A psychobiological perspective on the personality disorders. *American Journal of Psychiatry, 148,* 1647–1658.

Simeon, D., Knutelska, M., Smith, L., Baker, B. R., & Hollander, E. (2007). A preliminary study of cortisol and norephinephrine reactivity to psychosocial stress in borderline personality disorder with high and low dissociation. *Psychiatry Research, 149,* 177–184.

Skodol, A. E., & Bender, D. S. (2003). Why are women diagnosed borderline more than men? *Psychiatric Quarterly, 74,* 349–360.

Skodol, A. E., Skodol, A. E., Gunderson, J. G., Pfohl, B., Widiger, T. A., Livesley, W. J., et al. (2002). The borderline diagnosis I: Psychopathology, co-morbidity, and personality structure. *Biological Psychiatry, 51(12),* 936.

Soloff, P. H., Lis, J. A., Kelly, T., Cornelius, J., & Ulrich, R. (1994). Risk factors for suicidal behavior in borderline personality disorder. *American Journal of Psychiatry, 151,* 1316–1323.

Spitzer, R. L., Endicott, J., & Gibbon, M. (1979). Crossing the border into borderline personality and borderline schizophrenia: The development of criteria. *Archives of General Psychiatry, 36,* 17–34.

Spitzer, R. L., Forman, J. B. W., & Nee, J. (1979). *DSM-III* field trials: I. Initial inter-rater diagnostic reliability. *American Journal of Psychiatry, 136,* 815–817.

Stanley, B., and Brodsky, B. (2005). Suicidal and self-injurious behavior in borderline personality disorder: A self-regulation model. In J. G. Gunderson and P. D. Hoffman (Eds.), *Understanding and treating borderline personality disorder: A guide for professionals and families* (pp. 43–63). Washington, DC: American Psychiatric Publishing.

Startup, M., Heard, H., Swales, M., Jones, B., Williams, J., & Jones, R. (2001) Autobiographical memory and para suicide in borderline personality disorder. *British Journal of Clinical Psychology, 40*(2), 113–120.

Stern, A. (1938). Psychoanalytic investigation of and therapy in the borderline group of neuroses. *Psychoanalytical Quarterly, 7,* 467–489.

Stroop, J. R. (1935). Studies of interference in serial verbal reactions. *Journal of Experimental Psychology, 18,* 643–662.

Suomi, S. J. (2003). Social and biological mechanisms underlying impulsive aggressiveness in Rhesus monkeys. In B. B. Lahey, T. Moffitt & A. Caspi (Eds), *The causes of conduct disorder and severe juvenile delinquency* (pp. 345–362). New York: Guildford.

Szeszko, P. R., Robinson, D., Alvir, J. M., Bilder, R. M., Lencz, T., Ashtari, M., et al. (1999). Orbitofrontal and amygdala volume reductions in obsessive-compulsive disorder. *Archives of General Psychiatry, 56,* 913–919.

Tebartz van Elst, L., Hesslinger, B., Thiel, T., Geiger, E., Haegele, K., Lemieux, L., et al. (2003). Fronto-limbic brain abnormalities in patients with borderline personality disorder: A volumetric magnetic resonance imaging study. *Biological Psychiatry, 54,* 163–171.

Thase, M. E., Jindal, R., & Howland, R. H. (2002). Biological aspects of depression. In I. H. Gotlib and C. L. Hammen (Eds.), *Handbook of depression* (pp. 192–218). New York: Guildford.

Torgersen, S., Kringlen, E., & Cramer, V. (2001). The prevalence of personality disorders in a community sample. *Archives of General Psychiatry, 58,* 590–596.

Torgersen, S., Lygren, S., Oien, P. A., Skre, I., Onstad, S., Edvardsen, J., et al. (2000). A twin study of personality disorders. *Comprehensive Psychiatry, 41,* 416–425.

Trull, T. J. (2001). Structural relations between borderline personality disorder features and putative etiological correlates. *Journal of Abnormal Psychology, 110,* 471–481.

Tyrer, P. (1988). *Personality disorders: Diagnosis, management, and course.* Boston: Wright.

Weaver, T. L., & Clum, G. A. (1993). Early family environments and traumatic experiences associated with borderline personality disorder. *Journal of Consulting and Clinical Psychology, 61,* 1068–1075.

Westen D, Bradley, R., & Shedler, J. (2005). *Refining the borderline construct: Diagnostic criteria and endophenotypes.* Unpublished manuscript.

White, C. N., Gunderson, J. G., Zanarini, M. C., & Hudson, J. I. (2003). Family studies of borderline personality disorder: A review. *Harvard Review of Psychiatry, 11,* 8–19.

Widiger, T. A., & Frances, A. (1989). Epidemiology, diagnosis, and co-morbidity of borderline personality disorder. *American Psychiatric Press Review of Psychiatry* (Vol. 8, pp. 8–24). Washington, DC: American Psychiatric Press.

Widiger, T. A., Mangine, S., Corbitt, E., Ellis, C., & Thomas, G. (1995). *Personality disorder interview - IV: A semi-structured interview for the assessment of personality disorders. Professional manual.* Odessa, FL: Psychological Assessment Resources.

Williams, J. M. G., & Broadbent, K. (1986). Autobiographical memory in suicide attempters. *Journal of Abnormal Psychology, 95,* 144–149.

Winnicott, D. W. (1953). Transitional objects and transitional phenomena: A study of the first not-me possession. *International Journal of Psychoanalysis, 34,* 89–97.

Yeomans, F. E., & Levy, K. N. (2002). An object relations perspective on borderline personality. *Acta Neuropsychiatrica 14,* 76–80.

Zanarini, M. C., & Frankenburg, F. R. (1999). Pathways to the development of borderline personality disorder. *Journal of Personality Disorders, 11,* 93–104.

Zanarini, M. C., & Frankenburg, F. R. (2001). Olanzapine treatment of female borderline personality disorder patients: A double-blind, placebo-controlled pilot study. *Journal of Clinical Psychiatry*, *62*, 849–854.

Zanarini, M. C., Frankenburg, F. R., Chauncey, D. L., & Gunderson, J. G. (1987). The Diagnostic Interview for Personality Disorders: Inter-rater and test-retest reliability. *Comprehensive Psychiatry*, *28*, 467–480.

Zanarini, M. C., Frankenburg, F. R., Dubo, E. D., Sickel, A. E., Trikha, A., Levin, A., et al. (1998). Axis I co-morbidity of borderline personality disorder. *American Journal of Psychiatry*, *155*, 1733–1739.

Zanarini, M. C., Frankenburg, F. R., Hennen, J., & Silk, K. R. (2003). The longitudinal course of borderline psychopathology: 6-year prospective follow-up of the phenomenology of borderline personality disorders. *American Journal of Psychiatry*, *160*, 274–283.

Zanarini, M. C., Frankenburg, F. R., Hennen, J., Reich, D. B., & Silk, K. S. (2006). Prediction of the 10-year course of borderline personality disorder. *American Journal of Psychiatry*, *163*, 827–832.

Zanarini, M. C., Frankenburg, F. R., Khera, G. S., & Bleichmar, J. (2001). Treatment histories of borderline inpatients. *Comprehensive Psychiatry*, *42*, 144–150.

Zanarini, M. C., Frankenburg, F. R., Reich, D. B., Marino, M. F., Lewis, R. E., Williams, A. A., et al. (2000). Biparental failure in the childhood experiences of borderline patients. *Journal of Personality Disorders*, *14*, 264–273.

Zanarini, M. C., Frankenburg, F. R., Yong, L., Raviola, G., Bradford Reich, D., Hennen, J., et al. (2004). Borderline psychopathology in the first-degree relatives of borderline and axis II comparison probands. *Journal of Personality Disorders*, *18*, 439–447.

Zanarini, M. C., Gunderson, J. G., Frankenburg, F. R., & Chauncey, D. L. (1989). The revised Diagnostic Interview for Borderlines: Discriminating BPD from other Axis II disorders. *Journal of Personality Disorders*, *3*, 10–18.

Zimmerman, M., & Mattia, J. I. (1999a). Axis I diagnostic co-morbidity and borderline personality disorder. *Comprehensive Psychiatry*, *40*, 245–251.

Zimmerman, M., & Mattia, J. I. (1999b). Differences between clinical and research practices in diagnosing borderline personality disorder. *American Journal of Psychiatry*, *156*(10), 1570–1574.

Author Index

Farmer, R., 514
Farrell, J., 87
Fast, K., 613
Fatemi, S. H., 367
Faucher, B., 371
Faust, D., 5
Faust, M. E., 575
Fava, G. A., 139, 140
Fava, J. L., 42
Fava, M., 298, 304, 312, 335, 351
Favaro, A., 436, 445, 447, 448
Favrod, J., 425
Fawcett, J., 370
Fayyad, R., 102
Fazaa, N., 504
Fazekas, I., 336, 339, 341
Feeny, N. C., 261
Feighner, J., 16
Feighner, J. P., 406, 499
Feinberg, M., 341
Feinn, R., 512
Feinstein, A. R., 20
Feistel, H., 374, 379
Feldman, M. E., 250, 253, 259
Feldman, P. D., 382
Feldman-Koffler, F., 336
Fennell, M., 219, 222
Fenton, T., 259
Fergusson, D. M., 118, 131, 282
Fernandez-Corres, B., 382
Ferrara, S., 436, 445
Ferrari, P., 381
Ferri, S., 172
Ferrier, I. N., 341, 356
Ferriter, M., 262
Ferro, T., 335, 348
Ferster, C. B., 284, 286
Fertig, J., 514
Fertuck, E., 614
Fertuck, E. A., 611, 612, 613, 614
Feske, U., 246, 260, 371
Feuer, C. A., 247, 250, 261, 262
Fichter, M., 475, 477
Fichter, M. M., 445, 447
Fichtner, C., 242
Fichtner, C. G., 242
Fidell, L. S., 46, 47
Field, N. P., 246
Finch, C. E., 304
Findling, R. L., 42, 52, 56, 60, 351, 369, 370, 380, 381, 382, 383
Fine, S., 63
Fingeret, M. C., 458, 459
Fingerhut, R., 377

Fink, M., 302, 311
Finkelstein, S. N., 143, 280
Finn, C. T., 372, 373
Finn, P. R., 505
Finn, S. E., 35
Finney, J. W., 512
Fins, A. I., 259
First, M., 615
First, M. B., 16, 17, 18, 19, 96, 97, 135, 180, 215, 255, 307, 308, 350, 380
Fischer, H., 203, 217
Fischman, S. H., 557
Fish, E. W., 622
Fisher, A. C., 458
Fisher, M., 476
Fisher, P. L., 100
Fitzgerald, K. D., 169
Fitzpatrick, C. M., 585, 588
Fitzsimmons, L., 311
Flaherty, J. F., 379
Flament, M., 475
Flament, M. E., 348
Flament, M. F., 446
Flanagan, D. J., 35
Flannery, B. A., 514
Flaschka, G., 472
Fleck, M. P. A., 330, 336
Fleischmann, R. L., 180
Fletcher, J. M., 41
Fletcher, K., 142
Fletcher, K. E., 142
Flint, E. P., 346
Flor, H., 513, 571, 573, 574
Flores, A. T., 445, 469, 476
Florin, I., 127, 172
Florio, L., 333, 334
Flugge, G., 304
Flum, H., 252
Fluttert, M., 622
Flynn, C., 380, 478
Foa, E., 172, 189, 263
Foa, E. B., 160, 164, 176, 177, 182, 183, 187, 188, 189, 201, 206, 207, 218, 222, 234, 238, 240, 243, 244, 245, 246, , 247, 248, 249, 250, 255, 256, 257, 260, 261, 262, 263
Fogler, J., 251
Follette, V. M., 125, 126
Folstein, S. E., 380
Fonagy, P., 310, 311, 602, 611, 618, 620
Fong, G. W., 375
Fontaine, M., 242
Fontana, A., 250
Fooskas, S., 132
Forbes, D., 252, 256

Subject Index

Absolute risk reduction (ARR), 56, 57, 59
Abusus non tollit usum, 7
Acceptance and Commitment Therapy (ACT), 142, 287
Actigraphy, 532–533
Adrenocorticotrophic hormone (ACTH), 301, 302
Agoraphobia Cognitions Questionnaires, 135
Albany Panic and Phobia Questionnaire, 135–136
Alcoholics Anonymous (AA), 497
Alcohol use disorders:
  biological factors of, 506–508
  cross-cultural differences in, 500–502
  diagnosis of, 508–511
  history of, 497–500
  overview, 495–497, 516
  pharmacological treatments for, 514–516
  psychological theories of, 502–506
  psychosocial treatments for, 512–514
  and twin studies, 507–508
Allostatic model of substance dependence, 507
Allotetrahydrodeoxycorticosterone/
    allopregnanolone, 241–242
Amotivation, and MDD, 285–286
Anhedonia, and MDD, 285–286
Anorexia hysterica, 470. *See also* Anorexia
    Nervosa (AN)
Anorexia hystérique, 470. *See also* Anorexia
    Nervosa (AN)
Anorexia Nervosa (AN):
  assessment of, 478–479
  and behavioral dysfunction, 473–474
  case example of, 470
  and cognitive dysfunction, 474–475
  criteria for, 467–470
  and emotional dysfunction, 475
  and environmental factors, 475–477
  epidemiology of, 471
  history of, 470–471
  interventions
    cognitive-behavioral therapy, 483
    family therapy, 482
    individual therapies, 482–483
    inpatient, 483–484
    outpatient, 479–481
    psychopharmacologic, 484
    recommendations for, 484
  neurobiology of, 471–473
  overview, 487
  subtypes of, 469–470

symptoms of, 467–470
  See also Binge Eating Disorder (BED); Bulimia
    Nervosa (BN); Eating Disorder Not
    Otherwise Specified (EDNOS)
Anosognosia, 12
Antiadrenergics, 259
Antisocial Personality Disorder, 2, 572–578
Antisocial Process Screening Device (APSD), 583–584
Anxiety Disorder Interview Schedule for *DSM-IV*
    (ADIS-IV):
  and Generalized Anxiety Disorder, 96, 97
  and Obsessive Compulsive Disorder, 180
  and Panic Disorder, 135
  and Social Anxiety Disorder, 215
Anxiety Sensitivity Index, 135
Area under the curve (AUC), 52–53
Assertive Community Treatment (ACT), 425
Assessment in developmental psychopathology:
  background, 35–36
  current, 36–38
  improving, 65–70
  prediction
    concurrent criterion validity, 39
    future of, 48
    prognosis, 46–48
    statistical methods, 39–46
  prescription
    assessment as aid in diagnosis, 52–56
    assessment as aid in treatment, 56–57
    categorical classification, 51
    thresholds, 48–51
  process
    mediators, 62–63
    moderators, 63–65
    outcome assessment, 58–62
  See also individual disorders
Assessment threshold, 49
Attention-Deficit Hyperactivity Disorder (ADHD):
  and Bipolar Disorder, 371
Attention Network Task (ANT), 613
Autobiography Memory Test (AMT), 614
Autonomic instability, 132
Avoidance, 163–164, 184–185, 286–287
Avoidant Personality Disorder, 201–202
Axis I–Axis II distinction, 17, 22–23

Base rate, 8. *See also* Diagnosis of mental illness,
    and reliability
Basic tendencies, 24–25